AMERICA

AMERICA

A NARRATIVE HISTORY

Seventh Edition

GEORGE BROWN TINDALL

DAVID EMORY SHI

W · W · NORTON & COMPANY · NEW YORK · LONDON

FOR BRUCE AND SUSAN
AND FOR BLAIR

FOR
JASON AND JESSICA

Copyright © 2007, 2004, 1999, 1996, 1992, 1988, 1984 by W. W. Norton & Company, Inc.

Printed in the United States of America

Composition by TechBooks
Manufacturing by Quebecor, Taunton
Book design by Antonina Krass
Editor: Karl Bakeman
Manuscript editor: Abigail Winograd
Project editor: Lory A. Frenkel
Director of Manufacturing, College: Roy Tedoff
Editorial assistant: Rebecca Arata
Cartographer: CARTO-GRAPHICS/Alice Thiede and William Thiede

Acknowledgments and copyrights continue on page A104,
which serves as a continuation of the copyright page.

Library of Congress Cataloging-in-Publication Data

Tindall, George Brown.
    America : a narrative history / George Brown Tindall,
David E. Shi.—7th ed.
        p.   cm.
    Includes bibliographical references and index.
    ISBN 13: 978-0-393-92820-4
    ISBN 10: 0-393-92820-9
    1. United States—History.   I. Shi, David E. II.   Title.

E178.1 .T55 2006   2006047300
973—dc22

W. W. Norton & Company, Inc., 500 Fifth Avenue, New York, NY 10110
www.wwnorton.com

W. W. Norton & Company Ltd., Castle House, 75/76 Wells Street, London W1T 3QT

2 3 4 5 6 7 8 9 0

*W. W. Norton & Company has been independent since its founding in 1923,
when William Warder Norton and Mary D. Herter Norton first published
lectures delivered at the People's Institute, the adult education division of
New York City's Cooper Union. The Nortons soon expanded their program
beyond the Institute, publishing books by celebrated academics from America
and abroad. By mid-century, the two major pillars of Norton's publishing
program—trade books and college texts—were firmly established. In the 1950s,
the Norton family transferred control of the company to its employees, and
today—with a staff of four hundred and a comparable number of trade, college, and professional titles published each year—W. W. Norton & Company
stands as the largest and oldest publishing house owned wholly by its employees.*

CONTENTS

List of Maps • *xv*
Preface • *xix*

Part One / A N E W W O R L D

1 | THE COLLISION OF CULTURES   5

PRE-COLUMBIAN INDIAN CIVILIZATIONS   7   •   EUROPEAN VISIONS OF
AMERICA   12   •   THE EXPANSION OF EUROPE   13   •   THE VOYAGES OF
COLUMBUS   15   •   THE GREAT BIOLOGICAL EXCHANGE   18
•   PROFESSIONAL EXPLORERS   22   •   THE SPANISH EMPIRE   23   •
THE PROTESTANT REFORMATION   35   •   CHALLENGES TO THE SPANISH EMPIRE   38
•   FURTHER READING   43

2 | BRITAIN AND ITS COLONIES   45

THE ENGLISH BACKGROUND   46   •   SETTLING THE CHESAPEAKE   50
•   SETTLING NEW ENGLAND   61   •   INDIANS IN NEW ENGLAND   72
•   THE ENGLISH CIVIL WAR IN AMERICA   76   •   SETTLING THE
CAROLINAS   77   •   SETTLING THE MIDDLE COLONIES AND GEORGIA   83
•   THRIVING COLONIES   94   •   FURTHER READING   96

3 | COLONIAL WAYS OF LIFE   98

THE SHAPE OF EARLY AMERICA   99   •   SOCIETY AND ECONOMY IN THE
SOUTHERN COLONIES   107   •   SOCIETY AND ECONOMY IN NEW
ENGLAND   118   •   SOCIETY AND ECONOMY IN THE MIDDLE COLONIES   131
•   COLONIAL CITIES   134   •   THE ENLIGHTENMENT   138   •   THE GREAT
AWAKENING   141   •   FURTHER READING   145

4 | THE IMPERIAL PERSPECTIVE   147

ENGLISH ADMINISTRATION OF THE COLONIES   148   •   THE HABIT OF SELF-
GOVERNMENT   153   •   TROUBLED NEIGHBORS   157   •   THE COLONIAL
WARS   162   •   FURTHER READING   173

5 | FROM EMPIRE TO INDEPENDENCE   174

THE HERITAGE OF WAR   175   •   BRITISH POLITICS   176   •   WESTERN LANDS   177
•   GRENVILLE AND THE STAMP ACT   177   •   FANNING THE FLAMES   184
•   DISCONTENT ON THE FRONTIER   188   •   A WORSENING CRISIS   189
•   SHIFTING AUTHORITY   195   •   INDEPENDENCE   202
•   FURTHER READING   206

Part Two / BUILDING A NATION

6 | THE AMERICAN REVOLUTION   213

1776: WASHINGTON'S NARROW ESCAPE   214   •   AMERICAN SOCIETY AT
WAR   218   •   1777: SETBACKS FOR THE BRITISH   221   •   1778: BOTH SIDES
REGROUP   225   •   THE WAR IN THE SOUTH   229   •   NEGOTIATIONS   234
•   THE POLITICAL REVOLUTION   235   •   THE SOCIAL REVOLUTION   239
•   THE EMERGENCE OF AN AMERICAN CULTURE   246   •   FURTHER READING   248

7 | SHAPING A FEDERAL UNION 249

THE CONFEDERATION 250 • ADOPTING THE CONSTITUTION 263
• FURTHER READING 277

8 | THE FEDERALIST ERA 279

A NEW NATION 280 • HAMILTON'S VISION 285 • THE REPUBLICAN
ALTERNATIVE 293 • CRISES FOREIGN AND DOMESTIC 295 • SETTLEMENT OF
NEW LAND 303 • TRANSFER OF POWER 307 • THE ADAMS YEARS 308
• FURTHER READING 319

9 | THE EARLY REPUBLIC 320

JEFFERSONIAN SIMPLICITY 322 • JEFFERSON IN OFFICE 324
• DIVISIONS IN THE REPUBLICAN PARTY 333 • WAR IN EUROPE 334
• THE WAR OF 1812 339 • FURTHER READING 351

Part Three / A N E X P A N S I V E N A T I O N

10 | NATIONALISM AND SECTIONALISM 357

ECONOMIC NATIONALISM 358 • "GOOD FEELINGS" 362 • CRISES
AND COMPROMISES 367 • JUDICIAL NATIONALISM 371 • NATIONALIST
DIPLOMACY 374 • ONE-PARTY POLITICS 376 • FURTHER READING 384

11 | THE JACKSONIAN IMPULSE 385

SETTING THE STAGE 387 • NULLIFICATION 389 • JACKSON'S INDIAN
POLICY 396 • THE BANK CONTROVERSY 400 • VAN BUREN AND THE NEW
PARTY SYSTEM 406 • ASSESSING THE JACKSON YEARS 412 • FURTHER
READING 414

12 | THE DYNAMICS OF GROWTH   416

AGRICULTURE AND THE NATIONAL ECONOMY   417   ·   TRANSPORTATION
AND THE NATIONAL ECONOMY   421   ·   A COMMUNICATIONS REVOLUTION   430
·   THE INDUSTRIAL REVOLUTION   432   ·   THE POPULAR CULTURE   439
·   IMMIGRATION   443   ·   ORGANIZED LABOR   449   ·   THE RISE OF THE
PROFESSIONS   452   ·   JACKSONIAN INEQUALITY   455
·   FURTHER READING   456

13 | AN AMERICAN RENAISSANCE: RELIGION, ROMANTICISM, AND REFORM   458

RATIONAL RELIGION   459   ·   THE SECOND GREAT AWAKENING   460
·   ROMANTICISM IN AMERICA   466   ·   THE FLOWERING OF AMERICAN
LITERATURE   470   ·   EDUCATION   475   ·   ANTEBELLUM REFORM   479
·   FURTHER READING   487

14 | MANIFEST DESTINY   489

THE TYLER YEARS   490   ·   THE WESTERN FRONTIER   492   ·   MOVING
WEST   501   ·   ANNEXING TEXAS   507   ·   POLK'S PRESIDENCY   511
·   THE MEXICAN WAR   515   ·   FURTHER READING   524

Part Four / A HOUSE DIVIDED

15 | THE OLD SOUTH   531

THE DISTINCTIVENESS OF THE OLD SOUTH   532   ·   WHITE SOCIETY IN THE SOUTH
538   ·   BLACK SOCIETY IN THE SOUTH   543   ·   THE CULTURE OF THE
SOUTHERN FRONTIER   554   ·   ANTI-SLAVERY MOVEMENTS   556
·   FURTHER READING   563

16 | THE CRISIS OF UNION   565

SLAVERY IN THE TERRITORIES   566   ·   THE COMPROMISE OF 1850   572
·   FOREIGN ADVENTURES   580   ·   THE KANSAS-NEBRASKA CRISIS   581

• THE DEEPENING SECTIONAL CRISIS   591   •   THE CENTER COMES
APART   599   •   FURTHER READING   606

17 | THE WAR OF THE UNION   607

THE END OF THE WAITING GAME   608   •   THE BALANCE OF FORCE   612
• THE WAR'S EARLY COURSE   614   •   EMANCIPATION   629
• REACTIONS TO EMANCIPATION   630   •   BLACKS IN THE MILITARY   632
• WOMEN AND THE WAR   634   •   GOVERNMENT DURING THE WAR   635
• THE FALTERING CONFEDERACY   640   •   THE CONFEDERACY'S DEFEAT   645
• A MODERN WAR   655   •   FURTHER READING   657

18 | RECONSTRUCTION: NORTH AND SOUTH   659

THE WAR'S AFTERMATH   659   •   THE BATTLE OVER RECONSTRUCTION   664
• RECONSTRUCTING THE SOUTH   673   •   THE RECONSTRUCTED SOUTH   679
• THE GRANT YEARS   686   •   FURTHER READING   698

Part Five / GROWING PAINS

19 | THE SOUTH AND THE WEST TRANSFORMED   705
THE NEW SOUTH   706   •   THE NEW WEST   721   •   FURTHER READING   742

20 | BIG BUSINESS AND ORGANIZED LABOR   743
THE RISE OF BIG BUSINESS   743   •   ENTREPRENEURS   753   •   LABOR
CONDITIONS AND ORGANIZATION   760   •   FURTHER READING   777

21 | THE EMERGENCE OF URBAN AMERICA   779
AMERICA'S MOVE TO TOWN   780   •   THE NEW IMMIGRATION   786
• POPULAR CULTURE   793   •   EDUCATION AND THE PROFESSIONS   801
• THEORIES OF SOCIAL CHANGE   804   •   THE SOCIAL GOSPEL   810
• EARLY EFFORTS AT URBAN REFORM   812   •   FURTHER READING   818

22 | GILDED AGE POLITICS AND AGRARIAN REVOLT 819

PARADOXICAL POLITICS 820 • CORRUPTION AND REFORM 822 • THE FARM
PROBLEM AND AGRARIAN PROTEST MOVEMENTS 838 • THE ECONOMY
AND THE SILVER SOLUTION 846 • FURTHER READING 853

Part Six | M O D E R N A M E R I C A

23 | AN AMERICAN EMPIRE 859

TOWARD THE NEW IMPERIALISM 860 • EXPANSION IN THE PACIFIC 862
• THE SPANISH-AMERICAN WAR 865 • IMPERIAL RIVALRIES IN EAST ASIA 878
• BIG-STICK DIPLOMACY 880 • FURTHER READING 889

24 | THE PROGRESSIVE ERA 890

ELEMENTS OF REFORM 891 • FEATURES OF PROGRESSIVISM 893
• ROOSEVELT'S PROGRESSIVISM 898 • ROOSEVELT'S SECOND TERM 902
• FROM ROOSEVELT TO TAFT 910 • WILSON'S PROGRESSIVISM 916
• LIMITS OF PROGRESSIVISM 927 • FURTHER READING 928

25 | AMERICA AND THE GREAT WAR 930

WILSON AND FOREIGN AFFAIRS 931 • AN UNEASY NEUTRALITY 934
• AMERICA'S ENTRY INTO THE WAR 944 • "THE DECISIVE POWER" 950
• THE FIGHT FOR THE PEACE 955 • LURCHING FROM WAR TO PEACE 962
• FURTHER READING 967

26 | THE MODERN TEMPER 968

REACTION IN THE TWENTIES 969 • THE ROARING TWENTIES 975
• THE CULTURE OF MODERNISM 984 • FURTHER READING 990

27 | REPUBLICAN RESURGENCE AND DECLINE 991

"NORMALCY" 992 • THE NEW ERA 1000 • PRESIDENT HOOVER,
THE ENGINEER 1010 • FURTHER READING 1021

28 | NEW DEAL AMERICA   1022
FROM HOOVERISM TO THE NEW DEAL   1023   • RECOVERY THROUGH
REGULATION   1032   • THE HUMAN COST OF THE DEPRESSION   1038
• CULTURE IN THE THIRTIES   1043   • THE SECOND NEW DEAL   1046
• ROOSEVELT'S SECOND TERM   1052   • THE LEGACY OF THE NEW DEAL   1059
• FURTHER READING   1062

29 | FROM ISOLATION TO GLOBAL WAR   1063
POSTWAR ISOLATIONISM   1063   • WAR CLOUDS   1069   • THE STORM IN
EUROPE   1078   • THE STORM IN THE PACIFIC   1084
• FURTHER READING   1090

30 | THE SECOND WORLD WAR   1091
AMERICA'S EARLY BATTLES   1092   • MOBILIZATION AT HOME   1094
• SOCIAL EFFECTS OF THE WAR   1096   • THE ALLIED DRIVE TOWARD BERLIN   1102
• LEAPFROGGING TO TOKYO   1114   • A NEW AGE IS BORN   1118
• THE FINAL LEDGER   1129   • FURTHER READING   1130

Part Seven / T H E   A M E R I C A N   A G E

31 | THE FAIR DEAL AND CONTAINMENT   1137
DEMOBILIZATION UNDER TRUMAN   1138   • THE COLD WAR   1143   • CIVIL
RIGHTS DURING THE 1940s   1152   • THE COLD WAR HEATS UP   1160
• FURTHER READING   1170

**32 | THROUGH THE PICTURE WINDOW: SOCIETY AND CULTURE,
    1945–1960   1171**
PEOPLE OF PLENTY   1172   • A CONFORMING CULTURE   1179   • CRACKS IN THE
PICTURE WINDOW   1184   • ALIENATION AND LIBERATION   1187
• A PARADOXICAL ERA   1193   • FURTHER READING   1194

33 | CONFLICT AND DEADLOCK: THE EISENHOWER YEARS   1195
"TIME FOR A CHANGE"   1196   • EISENHOWER'S HIDDEN-HAND PRESIDENCY   1198
• FOREIGN INTERVENTION   1203   • REELECTION AND FOREIGN CRISES   1209

• FESTERING PROBLEMS ABROAD   1215   • THE EARLY YEARS OF THE CIVIL RIGHTS
MOVEMENT   1218   • ASSESSING THE EISENHOWER YEARS   1223
• FURTHER READING   1225

34 | NEW FRONTIERS: POLITICS AND SOCIAL CHANGE
IN THE 1960S   1226

THE NEW FRONTIER   1227   • EXPANSION OF THE CIVIL RIGHTS MOVEMENT   1232
• FOREIGN FRONTIERS   1238   • LYNDON JOHNSON AND THE GREAT SOCIETY   1244
• FROM CIVIL RIGHTS TO BLACK POWER   1251   • THE TRAGEDY OF VIETNAM   1254
• SIXTIES CRESCENDO   1260   • FURTHER READING   1264

35 | REBELLION AND REACTION IN THE 1960S AND 1970S   1266

THE ROOTS OF REBELLION   1267   • NIXON AND VIETNAM   1283   • NIXON AND
MIDDLE AMERICA   1290   • NIXON TRIUMPHANT   1295   • WATERGATE   1299   •
AN UNELECTED PRESIDENT   1303   • THE CARTER INTERREGNUM   1306
• FURTHER READING   1311

36 | A CONSERVATIVE INSURGENCY   1313

THE REAGAN REVOLUTION   1314   • REAGAN'S FIRST TERM   1319
• REAGAN'S SECOND TERM   1324   • THE BUSH ADMINISTRATION   1334
• FURTHER READING   1341

37 | TRIUMPH AND TRAGEDY:
AMERICA AT THE TURN OF THE CENTURY   1342

AMERICA'S CHANGING MOSAIC   1343   • CULTURAL CONSERVATISM   1347
• BUSH TO CLINTON   1349   • DOMESTIC POLICY IN CLINTON'S FIRST TERM   1353
• REPUBLICAN INSURGENCY   1356   • ECONOMIC AND SOCIAL TRENDS OF
THE 1990S   1360   • FOREIGN-POLICY CHALLENGES   1365   • THE ELECTION
OF 2000   1369   • COMPASSIONATE CONSERVATISM   1372   • GLOBAL TERRORISM
1374   • A STALLED PRESIDENCY   1389   • FURTHER READING   1390

GLOSSARY   A1

APPENDIX   A43

THE DECLARATION OF INDEPENDENCE   A45   •   ARTICLES OF
CONFEDERATION   A50   •   THE CONSTITUTION OF THE UNITED STATES   A58
•   PRESIDENTIAL ELECTIONS   A80   •   ADMISSION OF STATES   A88
•   POPULATION OF THE UNITED STATES   A89   •   IMMIGRATION TO THE UNITED
STATES, FISCAL YEARS 1820–2005   A90   •   IMMIGRATION BY REGION AND
SELECTED COUNTRY OF LAST RESIDENCE, FISCAL YEARS 1820–2004   A92
•   PRESIDENTS, VICE-PRESIDENTS, AND SECRETARIES OF STATE   A99

CREDITS   A104

INDEX   A112

MAPS

The First Migration 6

Pre-Columbian Civilizations in Middle
  and South America 8

Pre-Columbian Civilizations in North America 10

Norse Discoveries 12

Columbus's Voyages 17

Spanish and Portuguese Explorations 23

Spanish Explorations of the Mainland 30

English, French, and Dutch Explorations 39

Land Grants to the Virginia Company 53

Early Virginia and Maryland 61

Early New England Settlements 64

The West Indies, 1600–1800 67

Early Settlements in the South 79

The Middle Colonies 88

European Settlements and Indian Tribes in Early America 92–93

The African Slave Trade, 1500–1800 113

Atlantic Trade Routes 124

Major Immigrant Groups in Colonial America 133

The French in North America 160

Major Campaigns of the French and Indian War 164

North America, 1713 170

North America, 1763 171

Lexington and Concord, April 19, 1775 196

Major Campaigns in New York and New Jersey, 1776–1777 216

Major Campaigns in New York and Pennsylvania, 1777 — 222
Western Campaigns, 1776–1779 — 227
Major Campaigns in the South, 1778–1781 — 231
Yorktown, 1781 — 231
North America, 1783 — 236
Western Land Cessions, 1781–1802 — 253
The Old Northwest, 1785 — 254
The Vote on the Constitution, 1787–1790 — 275
Treaty of Greenville, 1795 — 300
Pinckney's Treaty, 1795 — 303
The Election of 1800 — 317
Explorations of the Louisiana Purchase, 1804–1807 — 330
Major Northern Campaigns of the War of 1812 — 343
Major Southern Campaigns of the War of 1812 — 345
The National Road, 1811–1838 — 361
Boundary Treaties, 1818–1819 — 364
The Missouri Compromise, 1820 — 369
The Election of 1828 — 383
Indian Removal, 1820–1840 — 398
The Election of 1840 — 412
Population Density, 1820 — 420
Population Density, 1860 — 421
Transportation West, about 1840 — 422–423
The Growth of Railroads, 1850 — 428
The Growth of Railroads, 1860 — 429
The Growth of Industry in the 1840s — 437
The Growth of Cities, 1820 — 440
The Growth of Cities, 1860 — 441
The Mormon Trek, 1830–1851 — 466
The Webster-Ashburton Treaty, 1842 — 492
Wagon Trails West — 503
The Election of 1844 — 512
The Oregon Dispute, 1818–1846 — 516
Major Campaigns of the Mexican War — 521
Cotton Production, 1821 — 534
Population Growth and Cotton Production, 1821–1859 — 535
The Slave Population, 1820 — 546
The Slave Population, 1860 — 547

The Compromise of 1850 576

The Gadsden Purchase, 1853 582

The Kansas-Nebraska Act, 1854 584

The Election of 1856 590

The Election of 1860 603

Secession, 1860–1861 610

The First Battle of Bull Run, July 21, 1861 615

Campaigns in the West, February–April 1862 621

The Peninsular Campaign, 1862 625

Campaigns in Virginia and Maryland, 1862 626

The Vicksburg Campaign, 1863 642

Campaigns in the East, 1863 643

Grant in Virginia, 1864–1865 649

Sherman's Campaigns, 1864–1865 652

Reconstruction, 1865–1877 685

The Election of 1876 696

Sharecropping and Tenancy, 1880–1900 709

The New West 726–727

Indian Wars, 1864–1890 731

Transcontinental Railroad Lines, 1880s 749

The Emergence of Cities, 1880 781

The Emergence of Cities, 1920 782

Women's Suffrage, 1869–1914 815

The Election of 1896 851

The Spanish-American War in the Pacific, 1898 870

The Spanish-American War in the Caribbean, 1898 872

U.S. Interests in the Pacific 875

U.S. Interests in the Caribbean 885

The Election of 1912 920

World War I in Europe, 1914 937

World War I, the Western Front, 1918 952

Europe after the Treaty of Versailles, 1918 960

The Election of 1932 1026

The Tennessee Valley Authority 1037

Aggression in Europe, 1935–1939 1074

Japanese Expansion before Pearl Harbor 1086

World War II Military Alliances, 1942 1104

World War II in Europe and Africa, 1942–1945 1106–1107

World War II in the Pacific, 1942–1945 1116–1117
The Occupation of Germany and Austria 1151
The Election of 1948 1159
The Korean War, 1950 1163
The Korean War, 1950–1953 1163
The Election of 1952 1197
Postwar Alliances: The Far East 1208
Postwar Alliances: Europe, North Africa, the Middle East 1211
The Election of 1960 1230
Vietnam, 1966 1256
The Election of 1968 1262
The Election of 1980 1318
The Election of 1988 1333
The Election of 2000 1370
The Election of 2004 1385

PREFACE

Just as history is never complete, neither is a historical textbook. We have learned much from the responses of readers and instructors to the first six editions of *America: A Narrative History*. Perhaps the most important and reassuring lesson is that our original intention has proved valid: to provide a compelling narrative history of the American experience, a narrative animated by human characters, informed by analysis and social texture, and guided by the unfolding of events. Readers have also endorsed the book's distinctive size and format. *America* is designed to be read and to carry a moderate price. While the book retains its classic look, *America* sports a new color design for the Seventh Edition. We have added new eye-catching maps and included new art in full color. Despite these changes, we have not raised the price between the Sixth and the Seventh Editions.

As in previous revisions of *America,* we have adopted an overarching theme that informs many of the new sections we introduce throughout the Seventh Edition. In previous editions we have traced such broad-ranging themes as immigration, the frontier and the West, popular culture, and work. In each case we blend our discussions of the selected theme into the narrative, where they reside through succeeding editions.

The Seventh Edition of *America* highlights environmental history, a relatively new field that examines how people have shaped—and been shaped by—the natural world. Geographic features, weather, plants, animals, and diseases are important elements of environmental history. Environmental historians study how environments have changed as a result of natural processes such as volcanic eruptions, earthquakes, hurricanes, wildfires, droughts, floods, and climatic changes. They also study how societies have used and abused their natural environment through economic activities such as hunting, farming, logging and mining, manufacturing, building dams, and irrigation. Equally interesting is how different societies over time have perceived nature, as reflected in their religion, art, literature, and popular culture, and how they have reshaped nature according to those perceptions through the creation of parks, preserves, and designed landscapes. Finally, another major area of inquiry among environmental historians centers on the development of laws and regulations to govern the use of nature and maintain the quality of the natural environment.

Some of the new additions to the Seventh Edition related to environmental history are listed below.

- Chapter 1 includes discussions of the transmission of deadly infectious diseases from Europe to the New World and the ecological and social impact of the arrival of horses on the Great Plains.
- Chapter 3 examines the ways in which European livestock reshaped the New World environment and complicated relations with Native Americans.
- Chapters 5 and 6 describe the effects of smallpox on the American armies during the Revolution.
- Chapter 12 details the impact of early industrialization on the environment.
- Chapter 17 describes the impact of the Civil War on the southern landscape.
- Chapter 19 includes new material related to the environmental impact of the sharecrop-tenant farm system in the South after the Civil War, industrial mining in the Far West, and the demise of the buffalo on the Great Plains.
- Chapter 21 describes the dramatic rise of large cities after the Civil War and the distinctive aspects of the urban environment.
- Chapter 24 surveys the key role played by sportsmen in the emergence of the conservation movement during the late nineteenth century and details Theodore Roosevelt's efforts to preserve the nation's natural resources.
- Chapter 28 surveys the environmental and human effects of the "dust bowl" during the Great Depression.
- Chapter 37 discusses President George W. Bush's controversial environmental policies and describes the devastation in Mississippi and Louisiana wrought by Hurricane Katrina.

Beyond these explorations of environmental history we have introduced other new material throughout the Seventh Edition. Fresh insights from important new scholarly works have been incorporated, and we feel confident that the book provides students with an excellent introduction to the American experience.

To enhance the pedagogical features of the text, we have added Focus Questions at the beginning of each chapter. Students can use these review tools to remind themselves of the key themes and central issues in the chapters. These questions are also available online as quizzes, the results of which students can e-mail to their instructors. In addition, the maps feature new Enhanced Captions designed to encourage students to think analytically about the relationship between geography and American history.

We have also revised the outstanding ancillary package that supplements the text. *For the Record: A Documentary History of America,* Third Edition, by David E. Shi and Holly A. Mayer (Duquesne University), is a rich resource with over 300 primary source readings from diaries, journals, newspaper articles, speeches, government documents, and novels. The *Study Guide,* by Charles Eagles (University of Mississippi), is another valuable resource. This edition contains chapter outlines, learning objectives, timelines, expanded vocabulary exercises, and many new short-answer and essay questions. *America: A Narrative History* Study Space is an online collection of tools for review and research. It includes chapter summaries, review questions and quizzes, interactive map exercises, timelines, and research modules, many new to this edition. *Norton Media Library* is a CD-ROM slide and text resource that includes images from the text, four-color maps, additional images from the Library of Congress archives, and audio files of significant historical speeches. Finally, the *Instructor's Manual and Test Bank,* by Mark Goldman (Tallahassee Community College) and Stephen Davis (Kingwood College) includes a test bank of short-answer and essay questions, as well as detailed chapter outlines, lecture suggestions, and bibliographies.

In preparing the Seventh Edition, we have benefited from the insights and suggestions of many people. Some of these insights have come from student readers of the text and we encourage such feedback. Among the scholars and survey instructors who offered us their comments and suggestions are: James Lindgren (SUNY Plattsburgh), Joe Kudless (Raritan Valley Community College), Anthony Quiroz (Texas A&M University – Corpus Christi), Steve Davis (Kingwood College), Mark Fiege (Colorado State University), David Head (John Tyler Community College), Hutch Johnson (Gordon College), Charles

Eagles (University of Mississippi), Christina White and Eddie Weller at the South campus of San Jacinto College, Blanche Brick, Cathy Lively, Stephen Kirkpatrick, Patrick Johnson, Thomas Stephens, and others at the Bryan Campus of Blinn College, Evelyn Mangie (University of South Florida), Michael McConnell (University of Alabama – Birmingham), Alan Lessoff (Illinois State University), Joseph Cullon (Dartmouth University), Keith Bohannon (University of West Georgia), Tim Heinrichs (Bellevue Community College), Mary Ann Heiss (Kent State University), Edmund Wehrle (Eastern Illinois University), Adam Howard (University of Florida), David Parker (Kennesaw State University), Barrett Esworthy (Jamestown Community College), Samantha Barbas (Chapman University), Jason Newman (Cosumnes River College), Paul Cimbala (Fordham University), Dean Fafoutis (Salisbury University), Thomas Schilz (Miramar Community College), Richard Frucht (Northwest Missouri State University), James Vlasich (Southern Utah University), Michael Egan (Washington State University), Robert Goldberg (University of Utah), Jason Lantzer (Indiana University), and Beth Kreydatus (College of William & Mary). Our special thanks go Tom Pearcy (Slippery Rock University) for all of his work on the timelines. Once again, we thank our friends at W. W. Norton, especially Steve Forman, Steve Hoge, Karl Bakeman, Neil Hoos, Lory Frenkel, Roy Tedoff, Dan Jost, Rebecca Arata, and Matt Arnold, for their care and attention along the way.

—George B. Tindall
—David E. Shi

Part One

A NEW WORLD

History is filled with ironies. Luck and accident often shape human affairs. Long before Christopher Columbus accidentally discovered the New World in his effort to find a passage to Asia, the tribal peoples he mislabeled Indians had occupied and shaped the lands of the Western Hemisphere. The first people to settle the New World were nomadic hunters and gatherers who had migrated from northeastern Asia during the last glacial advance of the Ice Age, nearly 20,000 years ago. By the end of the fifteenth century, when Columbus began his voyage west, there were millions of Native Americans living in the Western Hemisphere. Over the centuries they had developed diverse and often highly sophisticated societies, some rooted in agriculture, others in trade or imperial conquest.

The Native American cultures were, of course, profoundly affected by the arrival of peoples from Europe and Africa. Indians were exploited, enslaved, displaced, and exterminated. Yet this conventional tale of conquest oversimplifies the complex process by which Indians, Europeans, and Africans interacted. The Indians were more than passive victims; they were also trading partners and rivals of the transatlantic newcomers. They became enemies and allies, neighbors and advisers, converts and spouses. As such they fully participated in the creation of the new society known as America.

The Europeans who risked their lives to settle in the New World were themselves quite varied. Young and old, men and women, they came from Spain, Portugal, France, Great Britain, the Netherlands, Italy, and the various German states. A variety of motives inspired them to undertake the often harrowing transatlantic voyage. Some were adventurers and fortune seekers eager to find gold and spices. Others were fervent Christians determined to create kingdoms of God in the New World. Still others were convicts, debtors, indentured servants, or political or religious exiles. Many were simply seeking a piece of land, higher wages, and greater economic opportunity. A settler in Pennsylvania noted that "poor people (both men and women) of all kinds can here get three times the wages for their labour than they can in England or Wales."

Yet such enticements were not sufficient to attract enough workers to keep up with the rapidly expanding colonial economies. So the Europeans began to force Indians to work for them. But there were never enough laborers to meet the unceasing demand. Moreover, captive Indians often escaped or were so rebellious that several colonies banned their use. The Massachusetts legislature did so because it claimed that Indians were of such "a malicious, surly and revengeful spirit; rude and insolent in their behavior, and very ungovernable."

Beginning early in the seventeenth century more and more colonists turned to the African slave trade for their labor needs. In 1619 white traders began transporting captured Africans to the English colonies. This development would transform American society in ways that no one at the time envisioned. Few Europeans during the colonial era saw the contradiction between the New World's promise of individual freedom and the expanding institution of race-based slavery. Nor did they reckon with the problems associated with introducing into the new society people they considered alien and unassimilable.

The intermingling of peoples, cultures, and ecosystems from the continents of Africa, Europe, and North America gave colonial American society its distinctive vitality and variety. In turn, the diversity of the environment and the climate led to the creation of quite different economies and patterns of living in the various regions of North America. As the original settlements grew into prosperous and populous colonies, the transplanted Europeans had to fashion social institutions and political systems to manage growth and control tensions.

At the same time, imperial rivalries among the Spanish, French, English, and Dutch produced numerous intrigues and costly wars. The monarchs of Europe struggled to manage and exploit this fluid and often volatile colonial society. Many of the colonists, they discovered, had brought with them to the New World a feisty independence that led them to resent government interference in their affairs. A British official in North Carolina reported that the residents of the Piedmont region were "without any Law or Order. Impudence is so very high [among them], as to be past bearing." As long as the reins of imperial control were loosely applied, the two parties maintained an uneasy partnership. But as the British authorities tightened their control during the mid–eighteenth century, they met resistance, which became revolt and culminated in revolution.

1

THE COLLISION
OF CULTURES

FOCUS QUESTIONS

· What civilizations existed in pre-Columbian America? What were their origins?

· What were the goals of the European voyages of discovery and of the explorers who probed the shorelines of America?

· What were the consequences of the exchanges and clashes that accompanied European contact with the plants, animals, and people of the New World?

The "New World" discovered by Christopher Columbus was in fact home to civilizations thousands of years old. Until recently archaeologists had long assumed that the first humans in the Western Hemisphere were Siberians who some 12,000 to 15,000 years ago had crossed the Bering Strait on a land bridge to Alaska made accessible by receding waters during the last Ice Age. These nomadic hunters and their descendants had then drifted south in pursuit of grazing herds of large mammals: mammoths, musk oxen, bison, and woolly rhinoceroses. Over the next 500 years these people had fanned out in small bands across the entire hemisphere, from the Arctic Circle to the tip of South America. Recent archaeological discoveries in Pennsylvania, Virginia, and Chile, however, suggest that ancient humans may have arrived by sea much earlier (perhaps 18,000 to 40,000 years ago) from various parts of Asia—and some may even have crossed the Atlantic Ocean from southwestern Europe.

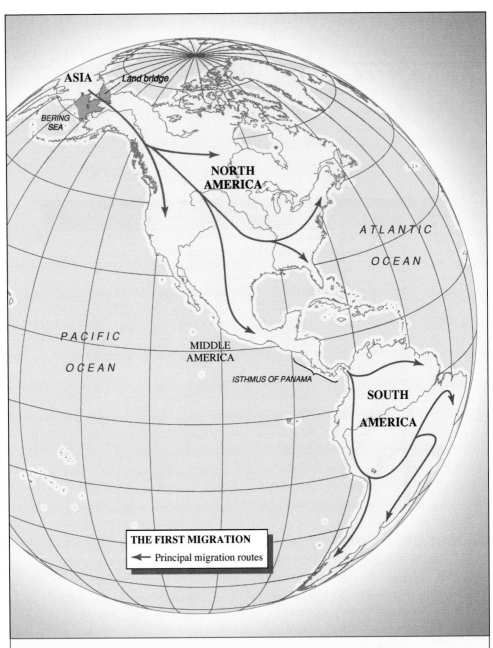

When did people first cross the Bering Sea? What evidence have archaeologists and anthropologists found from the lives of the first people in America? Why did they travel to North America?

PRE-COLUMBIAN INDIAN CIVILIZATIONS

The first humans in North America discovered an immense continent with extraordinary climatic and environmental diversity. Coastal plains, broad grasslands, harsh deserts, and soaring mountain ranges generated distinct environments, social structures, and cultural patterns. By the time Columbus happened upon the New World, the native peoples of North America had developed a diverse array of communities in which more than 400 languages were spoken. Yet despite the distances and dialects separating them, the Indian societies created extensive trading networks that helped spread ideas and innovations. Contrary to the romantic myth of early Indian civilizations living in perfect harmony with nature and one another, the native societies exerted great pressure on their environment and engaged in frequent warfare with one another.

EARLY CULTURES   After centuries of nomadic life, the ancient Indians settled in more permanent villages. Thousands of years after people first appeared in North America, climatic changes and extensive hunting had killed off the largest mammals. Global warming diminished grasslands and stimulated forest growth, which provided plants and small animals for human consumption. The ancient Indians adapted to the new environments by inventing fiber snares, basketry, and mills for grinding nuts, and they domesticated the dog and the turkey. A new cultural stage arrived with the introduction of farming, fishing, and pottery making. Hunting now focused on faster and more elusive mammals: deer, antelope, elk, moose, and caribou. Already by about 5000 B.C., Indians of the Mexican highlands were consuming plant foods that became the staples of the New World: chiefly maize (corn), beans, and squash but also chili peppers, avocados, and pumpkins.

THE MAYAS, AZTECS, CHIBCHAS, AND INCAS   Between about 2000 and 1500 B.C., permanent farming towns appeared in Mexico. The more settled life in turn provided time for the cultivation of religion, crafts, art, science, administration—and warfare. From about A.D. 300 to 900, Middle America (Mesoamerica) developed great city centers complete with gigantic pyramids, temples, and palaces, all supported by the surrounding peasant villages. Moreover, the Mayas developed enough mathematics and astronomy to devise a calendar more accurate than the one the Europeans were using at the time of Columbus.

In about A.D. 900 the complex Mayan culture collapsed. The Mayas had overexploited the rain forest upon whose fragile ecosystem they depended.

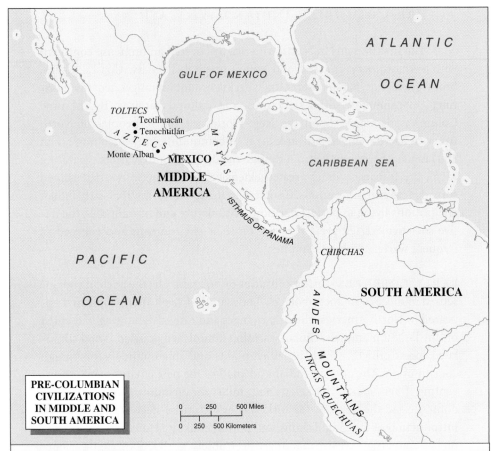

GULF OF MEXICO

ATLANTIC

OCEAN

TOLTECS
Teotihuacán
Tenochtitlán
AZTECS
Monte Albán
MEXICO
MIDDLE
AMERICA

MAYAS

ISTHMUS OF PANAMA

CARIBBEAN SEA

CHIBCHAS

SOUTH AMERICA

PACIFIC

OCEAN

ANDES
MOUNTAINS
INCAS (QUECHUAS)

PRE-COLUMBIAN
CIVILIZATIONS
IN MIDDLE AND
SOUTH AMERICA

0   250   500 Miles

0   250   500 Kilometers

What were the major pre-Columbian civilizations? What factors caused the demise of the Mayan civilization? When did the Aztecs build Tenochtitlán?

As an archaeologist has explained, "Too many farmers grew too many crops on too much of the landscape." Deforestation led to hillside erosion and a catastrophic loss of farmland. Overpopulation added to the strain on Mayan society. Unrelenting civil wars erupted among the Mayas. Mayan war parties destroyed one another's cities and took prisoners, who were then sacrificed to the gods in theatrical rituals. Whatever the reasons for the weakening of Mayan society, it succumbed to the Toltecs, a warlike people who conquered most of the region in the tenth century. But around A.D. 1200 the Toltecs mysteriously withdrew.

Mayan Society

A fresco depicting the social divisions of Mayan society. A Mayan lord, at the center, receives offerings.

The Aztecs arrived from the northwest to fill the vacuum, founded the city of Tenochtitlán (twenty-five miles north of what is now Mexico City) in 1325, and gradually expanded their control over central Mexico. When the Spanish invaded in 1519, the Aztec Empire under Montezuma II ruled over perhaps 5 million people—though estimates range as high as 20 million.

Farther south, in what is now Colombia, the Chibchas built a similar empire on a smaller scale. Still farther south the Quechuas (better known as the Incas, from the name for their ruler) controlled an empire that by the fifteenth century stretched 1,000 miles along the Andes Mountains from Ecuador to Chile. It was crisscrossed by an elaborate system of roads and organized under an autocratic government.

INDIAN CULTURES OF NORTH AMERICA The Indians of the present-day United States developed three identifiable civilizations: the Adena-Hopewell culture of the Northeast (800 B.C.–A.D. 600), the Mississippian culture of the Southeast (A.D. 600–1500), and the Pueblo-Hohokam culture of the Southwest (400 B.C.–present). None of these developed as fully as the civilizations of the Mayas, Aztecs, and Incas to the south.

What were the three dominant pre-Columbian civilizations in North America? Where was the Adena-Hopewell culture centered? How was the Mississippian civilization similar to that of the Mayans or Aztecs? What made the Anasazi culture different from the other North American cultures?

The Adena-Hopewell culture, centered in the Ohio River valley, left behind enormous earthworks and burial mounds—some of them elaborately shaped like great snakes, birds, or other animals. Evidence from the mounds suggests a complex social structure and a specialized division of labor. Moreover, the Hopewell Indians developed an elaborate trade network that spanned the continent.

The Mississippian culture, centered in the Mississippi River valley, resembled the Mayan and Aztec societies in its intensive agriculture, substantial towns built around central plazas, temple mounds (vaguely resembling pyramids), and death cults, which involved human torture and sacrifice. The Mississippians developed a specialized labor force, an effective government, and an extensive trading network. They worshipped the sun. The Mississippian culture peaked in the fourteenth and fifteenth centuries and finally succumbed to diseases transmitted from Europe.

The arid Southwest hosted irrigation-based cultures, elements of which persist today and heirs of which (the Hopis, Zunis, and others) still live in the adobe pueblos erected by their ancestors. The most widespread and best known of the cultures, the Anasazi ("enemy's ancestors" in the Navajo language), developed in the "four corners," where the states of Arizona, New Mexico, Colorado, and Utah meet.

Mississippian Artifacts

Mississippian people produced finely made pottery, such as this deer-effigy jar.

The Anasazis lived in baked-mud adobe structures built four or five stories high. In contrast to the Mesoamerican and Mississippian cultures,

Cliff Dwellings

Ruins of Anasazi cliff dwellings in Mesa Verde National Park, Colorado.

Anasazi society lacked a rigid class structure. The religious leaders and warriors labored much as the rest of the people did. In fact, they engaged in warfare only as a means of self-defense (*Hopi* means "Peaceful People"), and there is little evidence of human sacrifice or human trophies. Environmental factors shaped Anasazi culture and eventually caused its demise. Toward the end of the thirteenth century, a lengthy drought and the pressure of new arrivals from the north began to restrict the territory of the Anasazis. Into their peaceful world came the aggressive Navajos and Apaches, followed two centuries later by Spaniards marching up from the south.

EUROPEAN VISIONS OF AMERICA

The European discovery of America was fueled by curiosity. People had long imagined what lay beyond the western horizon. Norse expeditions to the New World during the tenth and eleventh centuries are the earliest

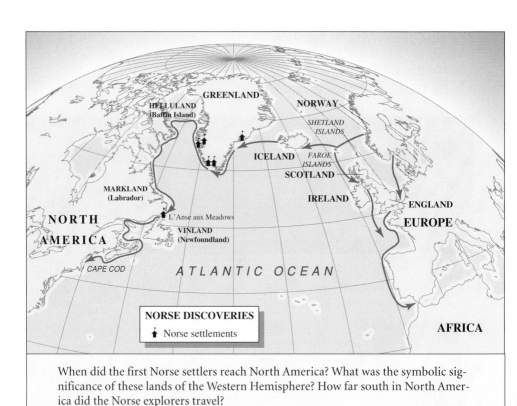

When did the first Norse settlers reach North America? What was the symbolic significance of these lands of the Western Hemisphere? How far south in North America did the Norse explorers travel?

that can be verified, and even they have dissolved into legend. Around A.D. 985 an Icelander named Erik the Red—the New World's first real-estate booster—colonized the west coast of a rocky, fogbound island he deceptively called Greenland, and about a year later a trader missed Greenland and sighted land beyond. Knowing of this, Leif Eriksson, son of Erik the Red, sailed out from Greenland about A.D. 1001 and sighted the coasts of Hellu-land (Baffin Island), Markland (Labrador), and Vinland (Newfoundland), where he settled for the winter. The Norse settlers withdrew from North America in the face of hostile natives, and the Greenland colonies vanished mysteriously in the fifteenth century. Nowhere in Europe had the forces yet developed that would inspire adventurers to subdue the New World.

THE EXPANSION OF EUROPE

During the late fifteenth century, Europeans developed the maritime technology to venture around the world and the imperial ambitions to search for riches, colonies, and pagans to convert. This age of discovery coin-cided with the rise of an inquiring spirit; the growth of trade, towns, and modern corporations; the decline of feudalism and the formation of na-tional states; the Protestant and Catholic Reformations; and the resurgence of some old sins—greed, conquest, exploitation, oppression, racism, and slavery—that quickly defiled the fancied innocence of the New World.

RENAISSANCE GEOGRAPHY For more than two centuries before Columbus, the mind of Europe quickened with the so-called Renaissance—the rediscovery of ancient texts, the rebirth of secular learning, the spirit of inquiry, all of which spread more rapidly after Johannes Gutenberg's inven-tion of a printing press with movable type around 1440. Learned Europeans of the fifteenth century held in almost reverential awe the authority of an-cient learning. The age of discovery was especially influenced by ancient con-cepts of geography. As early as the sixth century B.C., the Pythagoreans had taught the sphericity of the earth, and in the third century B.C. the earth's size was computed very nearly correctly. All this was accepted in Renaissance universities on the word of Aristotle, and the myth that Columbus was try-ing to prove this theory is one of those falsehoods that will not disappear even in the face of evidence. No informed person at that time thought the earth was flat.

Progress in the art of navigation accompanied the revival of learning. In the fifteenth century, mariners employed new instruments to sight stars and find the latitude. Steering across the open sea, however, remained a matter of dead reckoning. A ship's captain set his course along a given latitude and calculated it from the angle of the North Star or, with less certainty, the sun, estimating speed by the eye. Longitude remained a matter of guesswork since accurate timepieces were needed to determine it. Ship's clocks remained too inaccurate until the development of more precise chronometers in the eighteenth century.

THE GROWTH OF TRADE, TOWNS, AND NATION-STATES   The forces that would invade and reshape the New World found their focus in Europe's rising towns, the centers of a growing trade that slowly broadened the narrow horizons of feudal culture. In its farthest reaches this commerce moved either overland or through the eastern Mediterranean all the way to east Asia, where Europeans acquired medicine, silks, precious stones, dyewoods, perfumes, and rugs. There they also purchased the spices—pepper, nutmeg, clove—so essential to the preserving of food and for enhancing its flavor. The trade gave rise to a merchant class and to the idea of corporations through which stockholders would share risks and profits.

The foreign trade was chancy and costly. Goods commonly passed from hand to hand, from ships to pack trains and back to ships along the way, subject to tax levies by all sorts of princes and potentates. The Muslim world, from Spain across North Africa into central Asia, straddled the important trade routes, adding to the hazards. Muslims tenaciously opposed efforts to "Christianize" their lands. Little wonder, then, that Europeans should dream of an all-water route to the coveted spices of east Asia and the Indies.

Another spur to exploration was the rise of national states, ruled by kings and queens who had the power and the money to sponsor the search for foreign riches. The growth of the merchant class went hand in hand with the growth of centralized political power. Merchants wanted uniform currencies, trade laws, and the elimination of trade barriers. They thus became natural allies of the monarchs who could meet their needs. In turn, merchants and university-trained professionals supplied the monarchs with money, lawyers, and government officials. The Crusades to capture the Holy Land (1095–1270) had also advanced the process of international trade and exploration. They had brought Europe into contact with the Middle East and had decimated the ranks of the feudal lords. And new means of warfare—the use of gunpowder and standing armies—further weakened the independence of the nobility relative to royal power.

By 1492 the map of western Europe showed several united kingdoms: France, where in 1453 Charles VII had emerged from the Hundred Years'

War as head of a unified state; England, where in 1485 Henry VII had emerged victorious after thirty years of civil strife known as the Wars of the Roses; Portugal, where John I had fought off the Castilians to ensure national independence; and Spain, where in 1469 Ferdinand of Aragon and Isabella of Castile had ended an era of chronic civil war when they united two great kingdoms in marriage. The Spanish king and queen were crusading expansionists. On January 1, 1492, after nearly eight centuries of religious warfare between Spanish Christians and Moorish Muslims on the Iberian peninsula, Ferdinand and Isabella declared victory at Granada, the last Muslim stronghold. They gave the defeated Muslims a desperate choice: convert to Christianity or leave Spain. Soon thereafter the Christian monarchs gave Sephardi, Jews from Spain or Portugal, the same awful ultimatum: baptism or exile.

These factors—urbanization, world trade, the rise of centralized national states, and advances in knowledge, technology, and firepower—combined with natural human curiosity, greed, and religious zeal to create an outburst of energy, spurring the discovery and conquest of the New World. Beginning in the late fifteenth century, Europeans set in motion the events that, as one historian has observed, bound together "four continents, three races, and a great diversity of regional parts."

THE VOYAGES OF COLUMBUS

It was in Portugal, with the guidance of King John's son Prince Henry the Navigator, that exploration and discovery began in earnest. In 1422 Prince Henry dispatched his first naval expedition to map the African coast. Driven partly by the hope of outflanking the Islamic world and partly by the hope of trade, the Portuguese by 1446 had reached Cape Verde and then the equator and, by 1482, the Congo River. In 1488 Bartholomeu Dias rounded the Cape of Good Hope at Africa's southern tip.

Christopher Columbus, meanwhile, was learning his trade in the school of Portuguese seamanship. Born in 1451, the son of an Italian weaver, Columbus took to the sea at an early age, making up for his lack of formal education by teaching himself geography, navigation, and Latin. By the 1480s, Columbus, a tall, white-haired, pious man, was an experienced mariner and a skilled navigator. Dazzled by the prospect of Asian riches, he developed an outrageous plan to reach the Indies (India, China, the East Indies, or Japan) by sailing west across the Atlantic. Columbus won the support of Ferdinand and Isabella, the Spanish monarchs. They awarded him a tenth share of any pearls; gold, silver,

Christopher Columbus

A portrait by Sebastiano del Piombo, ca. 1519.

or other precious metals; and valuable spices he found in any new territories. The legend that the queen had to hock the crown jewels is as spurious as the fable that Columbus set out to prove the earth was round.

Columbus chartered one seventy-five-foot ship, the *Santa María,* and the Spanish city of Palos supplied two smaller caravels, the *Pinta* and the *Niña.* From Palos this little squadron, with eighty-seven officers and men, set sail westward for what Columbus thought was Asia. The expedition stopped at the Canary Islands, the westernmost Spanish possessions, off the west coast of Africa. Early on October 12, 1492, a lookout on the *Santa María* yelled, "*Tierra! Tierra!*" (Land! Land!) It was an island in the Bahamas east of Florida that Columbus named San Salvador (Blessed Savior). Columbus decided they were near the Indies, so he called the island people *los Indios.* He described the "Indians" as naked people, "very well made, of very handsome bodies and very good faces." He added that "with fifty men they could all be subjugated and compelled to do anything one wishes." The natives, Columbus wrote, were "to be ruled and set to work, to cultivate the land and to do all else that may be necessary... and to adopt our customs."

Columbus continued to search for a passage to the fabled Indies through the Bahamian Cays, down to Cuba (a place-name that suggested Marco Polo's Cipangu [associated with modern-day Japan]), and then eastward to the island he named Española (or Hispaniola, now the site of Haiti and the Dominican Republic), where he first found significant amounts of gold jewelry. Columbus learned of, but did not encounter until his second voyage, the fierce Caribs of the Lesser Antilles. The Caribbean Sea was named after them, and because of their alleged bad habits the word *cannibal* was derived from a Spanish version of their name (Caníbal).

On the night before Christmas 1492, the *Santa María* ran aground off Hispaniola. Columbus, still believing he had reached Asia, decided to return home. He left about forty men behind and seized a dozen natives to present as gifts to Spain's royal couple. When Columbus reached Palos, he received a hero's welcome. The news of his discovery spread rapidly across Europe

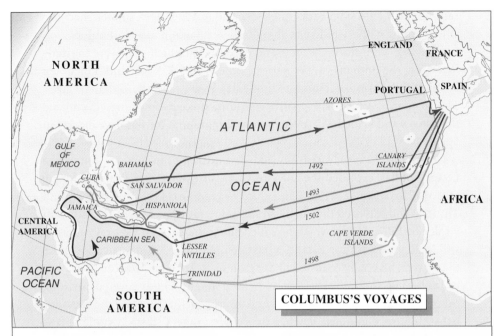

COLUMBUS'S VOYAGES

How many voyages did Columbus make to the Americas? What is the origin of the name for the Caribbean Sea? What happened to the colony that Columbus left on Hispaniola in 1493?

thanks to the improved communications brought about by Gutenberg's printing press. In Italy, Pope Alexander VI, himself a Spaniard, was so convinced that God favored the conquest of the New World that he awarded Spain the right to control the entire hemisphere so that its pagan natives could be brought to Christ. Buoyed by such support and by the same burning religious zeal to battle heathens that had forced the Moors into exile or conversion, Ferdinand and Isabella instructed Columbus to prepare for a second voyage. The Spanish monarchs also set about shoring up their legal claim against Portugal's pretensions to the newly discovered lands. Spain and Portugal reached a compromise agreement, called the Treaty of Tordesillas (1494), which drew an imaginary line west of the Cape Verde Islands and stipulated that the area west of it would be a Spanish sphere of exploration and settlement.

Columbus returned across the Atlantic in 1493 with seventeen ships, livestock, and over 1,000 men, as well as royal instructions to "treat the Indians very well." Back in the New World, Admiral Columbus discovered that the camp he had left behind was in chaos. The unsupervised soldiers had run amok, raping native women, robbing Indian villages, and as Columbus's son later added, "committing a thousand excesses for which they were mortally hated by the Indians." The natives finally struck back and killed ten Spaniards. A furious Columbus immediately attacked the Indian villages. The Spaniards, armed with crossbows, guns, and ferocious dogs, decimated the natives and loaded 550 of them onto ships bound for the slave market in Spain.

Columbus then ventured out across the Caribbean Sea. He found the Lesser Antilles, explored the coast of Cuba, discovered Jamaica, and finally returned to Spain in 1496. On a third voyage, in 1498, Columbus found Trinidad and explored the northern coast of South America. He led a fourth voyage in 1502, during which he sailed along the coast of Central America, still looking in vain for Asia. Having been marooned on Jamaica for more than a year, he finally returned to Spain in 1504. He died two years later.

To the end, Columbus refused to believe that he had discovered anything other than outlying parts of Asia. Full awareness that a great land mass lay between Europe and Asia dawned on Europeans very slowly. By one of history's greatest ironies, this led the New World to be named not for its discoverer but for another Italian explorer, Amerigo Vespucci, who sailed to the New World in 1499. Vespucci landed on the coast of South America and reported that it was so large it must be a new continent. European mapmakers thereafter began to label the New World using a variant of Vespucci's first name: America.

THE GREAT BIOLOGICAL EXCHANGE

The first European contacts with the New World began an unprecedented worldwide biological exchange. It was in fact more than a diffusion of cultures: it was a diffusion of distinctive social and ecological elements that ultimately worked in favor of the Europeans at the expense of the natives. Indians, Europeans, and eventually Africans intersected to create new religious beliefs and languages, adopt new tastes in food, and develop new modes of dress.

If anything, the plants and animals of the two worlds were more different than the people and their ways of life. Europeans had never seen such creatures as the fearsome (if harmless) iguana, the flying squirrel, fish with whiskers like those of a cat, or the rattlesnake, nor had they seen anything quite like several other species: bison, cougars, armadillos, opossums, sloths, tapirs, anacondas, American eels, toucans, condors, and humming-birds. Among the few domesticated animals they could recognize the dog and the duck, but turkeys, guinea pigs, llamas, and alpacas were all new. Nor did the Native Americans know of horses, cattle, pigs, sheep, goats, and (maybe) chickens, which soon arrived from Europe in abundance. Yet within a half century whole islands of the Caribbean would be overrun by pigs.

A land Sort to the Savages esteeme above all other Torts

Unfamiliar Wildlife

A box tortoise drawn by John White, one of the earliest English settlers in America.

The exchange of plant life between Old and New Worlds worked a revolution in the diets of both hemispheres. Before Columbus's voyage three staples of the modern diet were unknown in Europe: maize (corn), potatoes (sweet and white), and many kinds of beans (snap, kidney, lima, and others). The white potato, although commonly called Irish, actually migrated from South America to Europe and reached North America only with the Scotch-Irish immigrants of the early eighteenth century. Other New World food plants include peanuts, squash, peppers, tomatoes, pumpkins, pineapples, sassafras, papayas, guavas, avocados, cacao (the source of chocolate), and chicle (for chewing gum). Europeans in turn soon introduced rice, wheat, barley, oats, wine grapes, melons, coffee, olives, bananas, "Kentucky" bluegrass, daisies, and dandelions to the New World.

The beauty of the exchange was that the food plants were more complementary than competitive. Corn, it turned out, could flourish almost anywhere—in highland or low, in hot climates or cold, in wet land or dry. It spread quickly throughout the world. Before the end of the 1500s, American maize and sweet potatoes were staple crops in China. The nutritious food crops exported from the Americas thus helped nourish a worldwide population explosion probably greater than any since the invention of agriculture. The dramatic increase in the European populations fueled by the new foods in turn helped provide the surplus of people that colonized the New World.

Europeans, moreover, adopted many Native American devices: canoes, snowshoes, moccasins, hammocks, kayaks, ponchos, dogsleds, and tobog-gans. The rubber ball and the game of lacrosse have Indian origins. New words entered European languages: *wigwam, tepee, papoose, tomahawk, succotash, hominy, moose, skunk, raccoon, opossum, woodchuck, chipmunk, hickory, pecan,* and hundreds of others. And new terms appeared in translation: *warpath, war paint, paleface, medicine man, firewater.* The natives also left the map dotted with place-names of Indian origin long after they were gone, from Miami to Yakima, from Penobscot to Yuma. There were still other New World contributions: tobacco and a number of other drugs, including coca (for cocaine), curare (a muscle relaxant), and cinchona bark (for quinine).

By far, however, the most significant aspect of the biological exchange was the transmission of infectious diseases from Europe and Africa to the New World. European colonists and enslaved Africans brought with them deadly pathogens that Native Americans had never experienced: smallpox, typhus, diphtheria, bubonic plague, malaria, yellow fever, and cholera. In dealing with such diseases over the centuries, people in the Old World had developed antibodies that enabled most of them to survive infection. Disease-toughened

Smallpox

Aztec victims of the 1538 smallpox epidemic are covered in shrouds (center) as two others lie dying (at right).

adventurers, colonists, and slaves invading the New World thus carried viruses and bacteria that consumed Indians, who lacked the immunologic resistance that forms from experience with the diseases.

The results were catastrophic. Epidemics are one of the most powerful forces shaping history, and disease played a profound role in decimating the indigenous peoples of the Western Hemisphere. Far more Indians died of contagions than from combat. Major diseases such as typhus and smallpox produced pandemics in the New World on a scale never witnessed in history. The social chaos caused by the European invaders contributed to the devastation of native communities. In the face of such terrible and mysterious diseases, panic-stricken and often malnourished Indians fled to neighboring villages, unwittingly spreading the diseases in the process. Unable to explain or cure the contagions, Indian chiefs and religious leaders often lost their stature. Consequently, tribal cohesion and cultural life disintegrated, and

Impact of European Diseases

This 1592 engraving shows a shaman in a Tupinamba village in Brazil (at left) using his rattle to attract benevolent spirits to heal the diseases brought by Europeans.

efforts to resist European assaults collapsed. Over time, Native Americans adapted to the presence of the diseases and better managed their effects. They began to quarantine victims and infected villages to confine the spread of germs, and they developed elaborate rituals to sanctify such practices.

Smallpox was an especially ghastly and highly contagious disease in the New World. Santo Domingo boasted almost 4 million inhabitants in 1496; by 1570 the number of natives had plummeted to 125. In central Mexico alone, some 8 million people, perhaps one third of the entire Indian population, died of smallpox within a decade of the arrival of the Spanish. Smallpox brought horrific suffering. The virus passes through the air on moisture droplets or dust particles that enter the lungs of its victims. After incubating for twelve days, the virus causes headaches, backache, fever, and nausea. Victims then develop sores in the mouth, nose, and throat. Within a few days gruesome skin eruptions cover the body. Death usually results from massive internal bleeding.

In colonial America, as Indians died by the thousands, disease became the most powerful weapon of the European invaders. A Spanish explorer noted that "half the natives" died from smallpox and "blamed us." Many Europeans, however, interpreted such epidemics as diseases sent by God to punish Indians who resisted conversion to Christianity.

PROFESSIONAL EXPLORERS

Undeterred by new diseases and encouraged by Columbus's discoveries, professional explorers, mostly Italians, hired themselves out to look for the elusive western passage to Asia. They probed the shorelines of America during the early sixteenth century in the vain search for an opening and thus increased by leaps and bounds European knowledge of the New World.

The first to sight the North American continent was John Cabot, a Venetian sponsored by Henry VII of England. Cabot sailed across the North Atlantic in 1497. His landfall at what the king called "the new founde lande" gave England the basis for a later claim to all of North America. During the early sixteenth century, however, the English grew so preoccupied with internal divisions and conflicts with France that they failed to capitalize on Cabot's discoveries. Only fishermen exploited the teeming waters of the Grand Banks. In 1513 the Spaniard Vasco Núñez de Balboa became the first European to sight the Pacific Ocean, having crossed the Isthmus of Panama on foot.

The Spanish were eager to find a nautical passage from the Atlantic to the Pacific. To that end, in 1519 Ferdinand Magellan, a haughty Portuguese

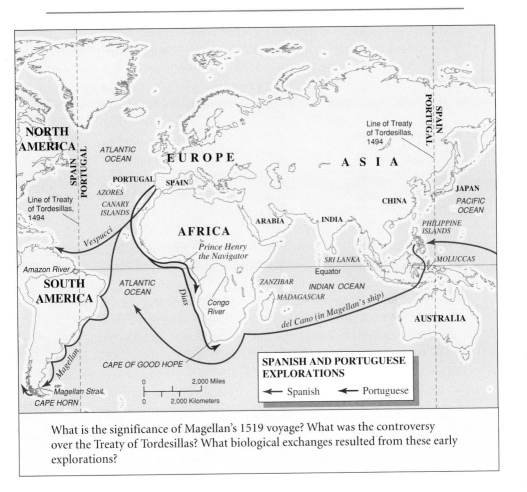

What is the significance of Magellan's 1519 voyage? What was the controversy over the Treaty of Tordesillas? What biological exchanges resulted from these early explorations?

seaman hired by the Spanish, discovered the strait that now bears his name at the southern tip of South America. Magellan kept sailing north and west across the Pacific Ocean, discovering Guam and eventually the Philippines, where he was killed by natives. Surviving crew members made their way back to Spain, arriving in 1522, having been at sea for three years. Their accounts of the global voyage quickened Spanish interest in exploration.

THE SPANISH EMPIRE

During the sixteenth century, Spain created the most powerful empire in the world by conquering and colonizing the Americas. The Caribbean Sea served as the funnel through which Spanish power entered the New World. After establishing colonies on Hispaniola, including Santo Domingo, which became the capital of the West Indies, the Spanish proceeded eastward to Puerto Rico (1508) and westward to Cuba (1511–1514). Their motives were explicit. Said one soldier, "We came here to serve God and the king, and also to get rich." Like the French and the British after them, the Spanish who explored and conquered new worlds in the Western Hemisphere were willing to risk everything in pursuit of wealth, power, glory, or divine approval. The first adventurers were often larger-than-life figures. They displayed ambition and courage, ruthlessness and duplicity, resilience and creativity, as well as crusading religiosity and imperial arrogance.

The European colonization of the New World was difficult and deadly. Most of those in the first wave of settlement died of malnutrition or disease. But the natives suffered even more casualties. A Spaniard on Hispaniola reported in 1494 that over 50,000 Indians had died from infectious diseases carried by the Europeans, and more were "falling each day, with every step, like cattle in an infected herd." Even the most developed Indian societies of the sixteenth century were ill equipped to resist the European cultures invading their world. Disunity everywhere—civil disorder and rebellion plagued the Aztecs, Mayas, and Incas—left the native peoples of the New World vulnerable to division and foreign conquest. The onslaught of men and microbes from Europe perplexed and overwhelmed the Indians. Prejudices and misunderstandings had tragic consequences. Europeans presumed that their civilization was superior to those they discovered in the New World. And such presumed superiority justified in their minds the conquest and enslavement of Indians, the destruction of their way of life, and the seizure of their land and resources.

A CLASH OF CULTURES   The violent encounter between Spaniards and Indians in North America involved more than a clash between different peoples. It also involved contrasting forms of technological development. The Indians of Mexico had copper and bronze but no iron. They had domesticated dogs and llamas but no horses. Whereas Indians used dugout canoes for transport, Europeans sailed heavily armed oceangoing vessels. The Spanish ships not only carried human cargo; they also brought steel swords, firearms, explosives, and armor. These advanced military tools struck fear into many Indians. A Spanish priest in Florida observed that gunpowder "frightens the most valiant and courageous Indian and renders him slave to the white man's command." Such weaponry helps explain why the Europeans were able to defeat far superior numbers of Indians. Arrows and tomahawks were seldom a match for guns and cannon.

The Europeans enjoyed other cultural advantages. For example, the only domestic four-legged animals in North America were dogs and llamas. The Spaniards, on the other hand, brought with them horses, pigs, and cattle, all of which served as sources of food and leather. Horses provided greater speed in battle and introduced a decided psychological advantage. "The most essential thing in new lands is horses," reported one Spanish soldier. "They instill the greatest fear in the enemy and make the Indians respect the leaders of the army." Even more feared among the Indians were the greyhound dogs that the Spaniards used to guard their camps.

CORTÉS'S CONQUEST   The first European conquest of a major Indian civilization on the North American mainland began on February 18, 1519, when Hernando Cortés, driven by dreams of gold and glory, set sail from Cuba with nearly 600 soldiers and sailors. Also on board were 200 Cuban natives, sixteen horses, and several cannons. When the invaders landed at Vera Cruz, on the Mexican Gulf coast, they were assaulted by thousands of Indian warriors. After defeating the native force, Cortés invited the warriors to join his advance on the Aztecs. He then burned all but one of the Spanish ships. There would be no turning back.

Cortés in Mexico

Page from the Tlaxcala Lienzo, a historical narrative from the sixteenth century. The scene, in which Cortés is shown seated on a throne, depicts the arrival of the Spaniards in Tlaxcala.

Cortés's expedition was unauthorized. His soldiers, called conquistadores, received no pay; they were military entrepreneurs willing to risk their lives for a share in the expected plunder and slaves. The ruthless Cortés had participated in the Spanish occupation of Cuba and had acquired his own plantations and gold mines. But he yearned for even more wealth and glory. Against the wishes of the Spanish governor in Cuba, who wanted the Aztec Empire for himself, Cortés launched the daring invasion of Mexico. The 200-mile march from Vera Cruz through difficult mountain passes to the magnificent Aztec capital of Tenochtitlán (north of present-day Mexico City) and the subjugation of the Aztecs, who thought themselves "masters of the world," constituted one of the most remarkable feats in history.

Tenochtitlán, with some 200,000 inhabitants, was the largest city in the Americas and was much larger than Seville, the most populous city in Spain. Graced by wide canals and verdant gardens and boasting beautiful stone pyramids and other buildings, the fabled capital seemed impregnable. But Cortés made the most of his assets. His invasion force had landed in a coastal region where the local Indians were still fighting off the spread of Aztec power and were ready to embrace new allies, especially those possessing strange animals (horses) and powerful weapons. By a combination of threats and deceptions, Cortés entered Tenochtitlán peacefully and made the emperor, Montezuma II, his puppet. Cortés explained to Montezuma why the invasion was necessary: "We Spaniards have a disease of the heart that only gold can cure." Montezuma mistook Cortés for a returning god.

After taking all the Aztec gold, the Spanish forced Montezuma to provide Indian laborers to mine more. This state of affairs lasted until the spring of 1520, when disgruntled Aztecs, regarding Montezuma as a traitor, rebelled, stoned him to death, and attacked Cortés's forces. The Spaniards lost about one third of their men as they retreated. Their 20,000 Indian allies remained loyal, however, and Cortés gradually regrouped his men. In 1521, having been reinforced with troops from Cuba and thousands of Indians eager to defeat the Aztecs, he besieged the imperial city for eighty-five days, cutting off its access to water and food and allowing a smallpox epidemic to decimate the inhabitants. An African slave infected with the virus spawned the contagion. As a Spaniard observed, the smallpox "spread over the people as great destruction. Some it covered on all parts—their faces, their heads, their breasts, and so on. There was great havoc. Very many died of it.... They could not move; they could not stir." The ravages of smallpox help explain how such a small force of determined Spaniards lusting for gold and silver was able to vanquish a proud nation of nearly 1 million people. Montezuma's nephew led the final fierce assault by the desperate Aztecs. Some 15,000 died in the battle. After the Aztecs surrendered, a merciless Cortés ordered the leaders hanged and the priests devoured by dogs. He and his officers replaced them as rulers over the Aztec Empire. In two years the brilliant Cortés and his disciplined army had conquered a fabled empire that had taken thirty centuries to develop.

Cortés and his army set the style for plundering conquistadores to follow, who within twenty years had established a sprawling Spanish Empire in the New World. Between 1522 and 1528 various lieutenants of Cortés's conquered the remnants of Indian culture in the Yucatán Peninsula and Guatemala. In 1531 Francisco Pizarro led a band of soldiers down the Pacific coast from Panama toward Peru, where they brutally subdued the Inca Empire. From Peru, conquistadores had extended Spanish authority south through Chile by about 1553 and north, to present-day Colombia, by 1536 to 1538.

SPANISH AMERICA   The Spaniards sought to displace the "pagan" civilizations of the Americas with their Catholic-based culture. Believing that God was on their side in this cultural exchange, the Spaniards carried with them a fervent sense of mission that bred both intolerance and zeal. The conquistadores transferred to America a system known as the *encomienda*, whereby favored officers became privileged landowners who controlled Indian villages or groups of villages. As *encomenderos*, they were called upon to protect and care for the villages and support missionary priests. In turn they could require Indians to provide them with goods and labor. Spanish America therefore developed from the start a society of extremes: wealthy conquistadores and *encomenderos* at one end of the spectrum and native peoples held in poverty at the other end.

What was left of them, that is. By the mid-1500s native Indians were nearly extinct in the West Indies, reduced more by European diseases than by Spanish brutality. To take their place, as early as 1503 the colonizers began to transport Africans to work as slaves, the first in a wretched traffic that eventually would carry over 9 million people across the Atlantic. In all of Spain's New World empire, by one informed estimate, the Indian population dropped from about 50 million at the outset to 4 million in the seventeenth century and slowly rose again to 7.5 million by the end of the eighteenth century. Whites, who totaled no more than 100,000 in the mid–sixteenth century, numbered over 3 million by the end of the colonial period.

The Indians, however, did not always lack advocates. In many cases Catholic missionaries offered a sharp contrast to the conquistadores. Setting an example of self-denial, they ventured into remote areas, usually without weapons or protection, to spread the gospel—and often suffered martyrdom for their efforts. Among them rose defenders of the Indians, the most noted of whom was Bartolomé de Las Casas, a priest in Hispaniola and later a bishop in Mexico, author of *A Brief Relation of the Destruction of the Indies* (1552).

From such violently contrasting forces, Spanish America gradually developed into a settled society. The independent conquistadores were replaced by a second generation of bureaucrats, and the *encomienda* was succeeded by the hacienda (a great farm or ranch) as the claim to land became a more important source of wealth than the Spanish claim to labor. From the outset, in sharp contrast to the later English experience, the Spanish government regulated every detail of colonial administration. After 1524 the Council of the Indies, directly under the crown, issued laws for America, served as the appellate court for civil cases arising in the colonies, and administered the bureaucracy.

The culture of Spanish America would be fundamentally unlike the English-speaking culture that would arise to the north. In fact, a difference already existed among the pre-Columbian Indians with largely nomadic tribes to the north and the more complex civilizations inhabiting Mesoamerica. On the latter world the Spaniards imposed an overlay of their own peculiar ways, but without uprooting the deeply planted cultures they found. Catholicism, which for centuries had absorbed pagan gods and transformed pagan feasts into such holy days as Christmas and Easter, in turn adapted Indian beliefs and rituals to its own purposes. The Mexican Virgin of Guadalupe Hidalgo, for instance, evoked memories of feminine divinities in native cults. Thus Spanish America, in the words of the modern-day Mexican writer Octavio Paz, became a land of superimposed pasts: "Mexico City was built on the ruins of Tenochtitlán, the Aztec city that was built in the likeness of Tula, the Toltec city that was built in the likeness of Teotihuacán, the first great city on the American continent. Every Mexican bears within him this continuity, which goes back two thousand years."

SPANISH EXPLORATIONS Throughout the sixteenth century no European power other than Spain had more than a brief foothold in the New World. Spain had the advantage not only of having sponsored the discovery but also of having stumbled onto those parts of America that would bring the quickest profits. While France and England struggled with domestic quarrels and religious conflict, Spain had forged an intense national unity. Under Charles V, heir to the throne of Austria and the Netherlands and Holy Roman emperor to boot, Spain dominated Europe as well as the

New World. The treasures of the Aztecs and the Incas added to its power, but the easy reliance on American gold and silver also undermined the basic economy of Spain and tempted the government to live beyond its means. The influx of gold from the New World also caused inflation throughout Europe.

For most of the colonial period, much of what is now the United States belonged to Spain, and Spanish culture has left a lasting imprint upon American ways of life. Spain's colonial presence lasted more than three centuries, much longer than either England's or France's. New Spain was centered in Mexico, but its frontiers extended from the Florida Keys to Alaska and included areas not currently thought of as formerly Spanish, such as the Deep South and the lower Midwest. Hispanic place-names—San Francisco, Santa Barbara, Los Angeles, San Diego, Tucson, Santa Fe, San Antonio, Pensacola, and St. Augustine—survive to this day, as do Hispanic influences in art, architecture, literature, music, law, and cuisine.

The Spanish encounter with Native American populations and their diverse cultures produced a two-way exchange by which the two societies blended, coexisted, and interacted. Even when locked in mortal conflict and riven by hostility and mutual suspicion, the two cultures necessarily affected each other. The imperative of survival forced both natives and conquerors to devise creative adaptations. In other words, the frontier world, while permeated with violence, coercion, and intolerance, also produced a mutual accommodation that enabled two living traditions to persist side by side. For example, the Pueblo Indians of the Southwest practiced two religious traditions simultaneously, adopting Spanish Catholicism while retaining the essence of their inherited animistic faith.

The "Spanish borderlands" of the southern United States preserve many reminders of the Spanish presence. The earliest known exploration of Florida was made in 1513 by Juan Ponce de León, then governor of Puerto Rico. Meanwhile, Spanish explorers skirted the Gulf coast from Florida to Vera Cruz, scouted the Atlantic coast from Key West to Newfoundland, and established a short-lived colony on the Carolina coast.

Sixteenth-century knowledge of the North American interior came mostly from would-be conquistadores who sought to plunder the hinterlands. The first, Pánfilo de Narváez, landed in 1528 at Tampa Bay, marched northward to Apalachee, an Indian village in present-day Alabama, and then returned to the coast near present-day St. Marks, Florida, where his party contrived crude vessels in the hope of reaching Mexico. Wrecked on the coast of Texas, a few survivors under Álvar Núñez Cabeza de Vaca worked their way painfully overland and after eight years stumbled into a Spanish outpost in western Mexico.

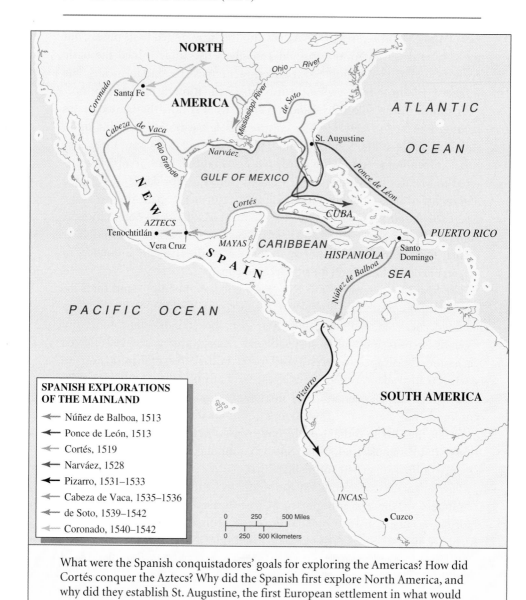

SPANISH EXPLORATIONS OF THE MAINLAND

← Núñez de Balboa, 1513
← Ponce de León, 1513
← Cortés, 1519
← Narváez, 1528
← Pizarro, 1531–1533
← Cabeza de Vaca, 1535–1536
← de Soto, 1539–1542
← Coronado, 1540–1542

What were the Spanish conquistadores' goals for exploring the Americas? How did Cortés conquer the Aztecs? Why did the Spanish first explore North America, and why did they establish St. Augustine, the first European settlement in what would become the United States?

Hernando de Soto followed their example. With 600 men, as well as horses, and war dogs, he landed on Florida's west coast in 1539, hiked up as far as western North Carolina and then moved westward beyond the Mississippi River and up the Arkansas River, looting and destroying Indian villages along the way. In the spring of 1542, de Soto died near Natchez; the next year the survivors among his party floated down the Mississippi, and 311 of the original adventurers found their way to Mexico. In 1540 Francisco Vásquez de Coronado, inspired by rumors of gold, traveled northward into New Mexico and northeast across Texas and Oklahoma as far as Kansas. He returned in 1542 without gold but with a more realistic view of what lay in those arid lands.

The Spanish established provinces in North America not so much as commercial enterprises but as defensive buffers protecting their more lucrative trading empire in Mexico and South America. They were concerned about French traders infiltrating from Louisiana, English settlers crossing into Florida, and Russian seal hunters wandering down the California coast.

Yet the Spanish settlements in what is today the United States never flourished. Preoccupied with a lust for gold, the Spanish never understood the significance of developing a viable market economy. England and France eventually surpassed Spain in America because Spain mistakenly assumed that developing a thriving trade in goods with the Native Americans was less important than the conversion of "heathens" and the relentless search for gold and silver.

The first Spanish outpost in the present United States emerged in response to French encroachments on Spanish claims. In the 1560s French Huguenots (Protestants) established short-lived colonies in what became South Carolina and Florida. In 1565 a Spanish outpost, St. Augustine, became the first European town in the present-day United States and is now its oldest urban center, except for the pueblos of New Mexico. Spain's colony at St. Augustine included fort, church, hospital, fish market, and over 100 shops and houses—all built decades before the first English settlements at Jamestown and Plymouth. While other outposts failed, St. Augustine survived as a defensive base perched on the edge of a continent.

THE SPANISH SOUTHWEST   The Spanish eventually established other permanent settlements in what is now New Mexico, Texas, and California. Eager to pacify rather than fight the far more numerous Indians of the region, the Spanish used religion as an effective instrument of colonial control. Missionaries, particularly Franciscans and Jesuits, established isolated Catholic missions where they taught Christianity to the Indians. After about ten years a mission would be secularized: its lands would be divided among the converted Indians, the mission chapel would become a parish church, and the inhabitants would be given full Spanish citizenship—including the privilege of paying taxes. The soldiers who were sent to protect the missions were housed in presidios, or forts; their families and the merchants accompanying them lived in adjacent villages.

The land that would later be called New Mexico was the first center of mission activity in the American Southwest. In 1598 Juan de Oñate, the wealthy son of a Spanish mining family in Mexico, received a patent for the territory north of Mexico above the Rio Grande. With an expeditionary military force made up mostly of Mexican Indians and mestizos (sons of Spanish fathers and native mothers), he took possession of New Mexico, established a capital north of present-day Santa Fe at San Gabriel, and sent out expeditions to search for evidence of gold and silver deposits. He promised the Pueblo Indian leaders that Spanish dominion would bring them peace, justice, prosperity, and protection. Conversion to Catholicism offered even greater benefits: "an eternal life of great bliss" instead of "cruel and everlasting torment."

Some Indians welcomed the missionaries as "powerful witches" capable of easing their burdens. Others tried to use the invaders as allies against rival tribes. Still others saw no alternative but to submit. The Indians living in Spanish New Mexico were required to pay tribute to their *encomenderos* and perform personal tasks for them, including sexual favors. Disobedient Indians were flogged, by soldiers and priests.

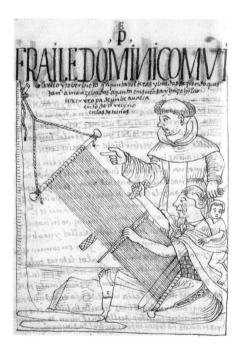

Cultural Conflict

This 1616 Peruvian illustration, from a manuscript by Felipe Guamán Poma de Ayala, shows a Dominican friar forcing a native woman to weave.

Before the end of the province's first year, the Indians revolted, killing several soldiers and incurring Oñate's wrath. During three days of relentless fighting, the army killed 500 Pueblo men and 300 women and children. Survivors were enslaved. Pueblo males over the age of twenty-five had one foot severed in a public ritual intended to strike fear in the hearts of the Indians and keep them from escaping or resisting. Children were taken from their parents and placed under the care of a Franciscan mission, where, Oñate remarked, "they may attain the knowledge of God and the salvation of their souls."

During the first three quarters of the seventeenth century, Spanish New Mexico expanded very slowly. The hoped-for deposits of gold and silver were never found, and a sparse food supply blunted the interest of potential colonists. The Spanish king prepared to abandon the colony only to realize that Franciscan missionaries had baptized so many Pueblo Indians that they could not be deserted. In 1608 the government decided to turn New Mexico into a royal province. The following year it dispatched a royal governor, and in 1610, as English settlers were struggling to survive at Jamestown, in Virginia, the Spanish moved the capital of New Mexico to Santa Fe, the first permanent seat of government in the present-day United States. By 1630 there were fifty Catholic churches and friaries in New Mexico and some 3,000 Spaniards.

The leader of the Franciscan missionaries claimed that 86,000 Pueblo Indians had been converted to Christianity. In fact, however, resentment among the Indians increased with time. In 1680 a charismatic Indian leader named Popé organized a massive rebellion that spread across hundreds of miles. Within a few weeks the Spaniards had been driven from New Mexico. The outraged Indians burned churches; tortured, mutilated, and executed priests; and destroyed all relics of Christianity. The Pueblo revolt of 1680 was the greatest setback that the natives ever inflicted on European efforts to conquer and colonize the New World. It took fourteen years and four military assaults for the Spaniards to reestablish control over New Mexico. Thereafter, except for sporadic raids by Apaches and Navajos, the Spanish pacified the region. Spanish outposts on the Florida and Texas Gulf coasts and in California did not appear until the eighteenth century.

HORSES AND THE GREAT PLAINS   Another major consequence of the Pueblo Revolt was the opportunity it afforded Indian rebels to acquire hundreds of coveted Spanish horses (Spanish authorities had made it illegal for Indians to own horses). The Pueblos in turn established a thriving horse trade with Navajos, Apaches, and other tribes. By 1690 horses were evident in Texas, and they soon spread across the Great Plains, the vast rolling grasslands extending from the Missouri River valley in the east to the base of the Rocky Mountains in the west.

Horses were a disruptive ecological force in North America; they provided the pedestrian Plains Indians with a transforming source of mobility and power. Prior to the arrival of horses, Indians hunted on foot and used dogs as their beasts of burden, hauling their supplies on travois, devices made from two long poles connected by leather straps. But dogs are carnivores, and it was often difficult to find enough meat to feed them. Horses changed everything. They are grazing animals, and the endless grasslands of the Great Plains offered plenty of forage. Horses could also haul up to seven times as much weight as dogs, and their speed and endurance made the Indians much more effective hunters and warriors. In addition, horses enabled Indians to travel farther to trade and fight.

The ready availability of large numbers of horses thus worked a revolution in the economy and ecology of the Great Plains. Such tribes as the Arapaho, Cheyenne, Comanche, Kiowa, and Sioux reinvented themselves as equestrian societies. They left their traditional woodland villages on the fringes of the plains and became nomadic bison (buffalo) hunters. Using horses, they could haul larger tepees and more meat and hides with them, building temporary camps as they migrated year-round with the immense bison herds, wintering in sheltered glades along rivers. The once-deserted plains soon were a crossroads of activity. Indians used virtually every part of the bison they killed: meat for food; hides for clothing, shoes, bedding, and shelter; muscles and tendons for thread and bowstrings; intestines for containers; bones for tools; horns for eating utensils; hair for headdresses; and dung for fuel. One scholar has referred to the bison as the "tribal department store." The Plains Indians supplemented bison meat with roots and berries they gathered along the way. In the fall the nomadic tribes would travel

Plains Indians

The horse-stealing raid depicted in this hide painting demonstrates the essential role horses played in Plains life.

south to exchange hides and robes for food or to raid Indian farming villages.

In the short run the horse brought prosperity and mobility to the Plains Indians. Horses became the center and symbol of Indian life on the plains. Yet the noble animal also brought insecurity, instability, and conflict. Indians began to kill more bison than the herds could replace. In addition, the herds of horses competed with the bison for food, often depleting the grass and compacting the soil in the river valleys during the winter. As tribes traveled greater distances and encountered more people, infectious diseases spread more widely.

Horses became so valuable that they provoked thievery and intensified intertribal competition and warfare. Within tribes a family's status was determined by the number of horses it possessed. Horses eased some of the physical burdens on women but imposed new demands. Women and girls were assigned the responsibility of tending to the horses. They also had to butcher and dry the buffalo meat and tan the hides. As the value of the hides grew, male hunters began to indulge in polygamy: more wives could process more buffalo. The rising economic value of wives eventually led Plains Indians to raid farming tribes in search of captive brides as well as horses. The introduction of horses into the Great Plains, then, was a decidedly mixed blessing. By 1800 a plains trader could observe that "this is a delightful country, and were it not for perpetual wars, the natives might be the happiest people on earth."

THE PROTESTANT REFORMATION

While Spain was building her empire in the Americas, a new movement was growing in Europe: the Protestant Reformation. It would intensify national rivalries and, by encouraging serious challenges to Catholic Spain's power, profoundly affect the course of early American history. When Columbus sailed in 1492, all of western Europe acknowledged the supremacy of the Catholic Church and its pope in Rome. The unity of Christendom began to crack in 1517, however, when Martin Luther, a German theologian and monk, posted his ninety-five theses in protest against abuses in the church. He especially criticized the sale of indulgences, whereby priests would forgive sins in exchange for money or goods. Sinners, Luther argued, could win salvation neither by good works nor through the mediation of the church but only by faith in the redemptive power of Christ and through a direct relationship with God—the "priesthood of all believers."

Lutheranism spread rapidly among the people and their rulers—some of them with an eye to seizing church property. When the pope expelled Luther from the church in 1521, reconciliation became impossible. The German states erupted in conflict over religious differences; a settlement did not come until 1555, when they agreed to let each prince determine the religion of his subjects. Most of northern Germany, along with Scandinavia, became Lutheran. The principle of close association between church and state thus carried over into Protestant lands, but Luther had unleashed volatile ideas that ran beyond his control.

Other Protestants pursued Luther's doctrine to its logical end and preached religious liberty for all. Further divisions on doctrinal matters led to the appearance of various sects, such as the Anabaptists, who rejected infant baptism and favored the separation of church and state. Other offshoots— including the Mennonites, Amish, Bretheren (Dunkers), Familists, and Schwenkfelders—appeared first in Europe and later in America, but the more numerous like-minded groups would be the Baptists and the Quakers, whose origins were English.

CALVINISM   Soon after Martin Luther began his revolt, Swiss Protestants also challenged the authority of Rome. In Geneva the reform movement looked to John Calvin, a French scholar who had fled to that city and brought it under the sway of his beliefs. In his great theological work, *The Institutes of the Christian Religion* (1536), Calvin set forth a stern doctrine. All people, he taught, were damned by Adam's original sin, but the sacrifice of Christ made possible their redemption. The experience of grace, however, was open only to those whom God had elected and thus had predestined to salvation from the beginning of time. Predestination was an uncompromising doctrine, but the infinite wisdom of God was beyond human understanding.

Calvin insisted upon strict morality and hard work, values that especially suited the rising middle class. Moreover, he taught that people serve God through any legitimate labor, and he permitted lay members a share in the governance of the church through a body of elders and ministers called the presbytery. Calvin's doctrines became the basis for the beliefs of the German Reformed Church, the Dutch Reformed Church, the Presbyterians in Scotland, some of the Puritans in England, and the Huguenots in France. Through these and other groups, Calvin exerted a greater effect upon religious belief and practice in the English colonies than did any other single leader of the Reformation.

THE REFORMATION IN ENGLAND   In England the Reformation followed a unique course. The Church of England, or the Anglican Church, took form through a gradual process of integrating Calvinism with English

Catholicism. In early modern England, church and state were united and mutually supportive. The government required citizens to attend religious services and to pay taxes to support the Church of England. The English monarchs also supervised the hierarchy of church officials: two archbishops, twenty-six bishops, and thousands of parish clergy. The royal rulers often instructed the religious leaders to preach sermons in support of particular government policies. As one English king explained, "People are governed by the pulpit more than the sword in time of peace."

Purely political reasons initially led to the rejection of papal authority in England. Henry VIII (r. 1509–1547), the second monarch of the Tudor dynasty, had in fact won from the pope the title of Defender of the Faith for refuting Martin Luther's ideas. But Henry's marriage to Catherine of Aragon had produced no male heir, and to marry again he required an annulment. In the past, popes had found ways to accommodate such requests, but Catherine was the aunt of Charles V, king of Spain and ruler of the Holy Roman Empire, whose support was vital to the church's cause on the Continent. So the pope refused to grant an annulment. Unwilling to accept the rebuff, Henry severed England's connection with Rome, named a new archbishop of Canterbury, who granted the annulment, and married his mistress, the lively Anne Boleyn.

In one of history's greatest ironies, Anne Boleyn gave birth not to the male heir that Henry demanded but to a daughter, named Elizabeth. The disappointed king later accused his wife of adultery, ordered her beheaded, and declared the infant Elizabeth a bastard. Yet Elizabeth received a first-rate education and grew up to be quick-witted and nimble, cunning and courageous. After the bloody reigns of her Protestant half brother, Edward VI, and her Catholic half sister, Mary I, she ascended the throne in 1558 and over the next forty-five years proved to be the most remarkable female ruler in history. Her long reign over the troubled island kingdom was punctuated by political turmoil, religious tension, economic crises, and foreign wars. Yet Queen Elizabeth came to rule over England's golden age.

Queen Elizabeth I

Shown here in her coronation robes, ca. 1590.

Born into a man's world and given a man's role, Elizabeth could not be a Catholic, for in the Catholic view she was illegitimate. During her reign, therefore, the Church of England became Protestant, but in its own way. The organizational structure, centered on bishops and archbishops, remained much the same, but the doctrine and practice changed: the Latin liturgy became, with some changes, the English *Book of Common Prayer*, the cult of saints was dropped, and the clergy were permitted to marry. For the sake of unity, the "Elizabethan settlement" allowed some latitude in theology and other matters, but this did not satisfy all. Some Britons tried to enforce the letter of the law, stressing traditional Catholic practices. Many others, however, especially those under Calvinist influence, wished to "purify" the church of all its Catholic remnants. Some of these Puritans would leave England to build their own churches in America. Those who broke altogether with the Church of England were called Separatists. Thus, the religious controversies associated with the English Reformation so dominated the nation's political life that interest in colonizing the New World was forced to the periphery of concern.

CHALLENGES TO THE SPANISH EMPIRE

The Spanish monopoly on New World colonies remained intact throughout the sixteenth century, but not without challenge from national rivals spurred by the emotion unleashed by the Protestant Reformation. The French were the first to pose a serious threat. Spanish treasure ships from the New World were tempting targets for French privateers. In 1524 the French king sent the Italian Giovanni da Verrazano in search of a passage to Asia. Sighting land (probably at Cape Fear, North Carolina), Verrazano ranged along the coast as far north as Maine. On a second voyage, in 1528, his life met an abrupt end in the West Indies at the hands of the Caribs.

Unlike the Verrazano voyages, those of Jacques Cartier, beginning in the next decade, led to the first French effort at colonization. On three voyages, Cartier explored the Gulf of St. Lawrence and ventured up the St. Lawrence River. Twice he got as far as present-day Montreal and twice wintered at or near the site of Quebec, near which a short-lived French colony appeared in 1541–1542. From that time forward, however, French kings lost interest in Canada. France after midcentury plunged into religious civil wars, and the colonization of Canada had to await the coming of Samuel de Champlain, "the Father of New France," after 1600.

From the mid-1500s, greater threats to Spanish power arose from the growing strength of the Dutch and the English. The provinces of the Netherlands,

ENGLISH, FRENCH, AND DUTCH EXPLORATIONS

← English
← French
← Dutch

Who were the first European explorers to rival Spanish dominance in the New World, and why did they cross the Atlantic? Why was the defeat of the Spanish Armada important to the history of English exploration? What was the significance of the voyages of Gilbert and Raleigh?

which had passed by inheritance to the Spanish king and had become largely Protestant, rebelled against Spanish rule in 1567. A bloody struggle for independence ensued. Spain did not accept the independence of the Dutch republic until 1648.

Almost from the beginning of the Dutch revolt against Spain, the Dutch "Sea Beggars," privateers working out of English and Dutch ports, plundered Spanish ships in the Atlantic and carried on illegal trade with Spain's colonies. The Sea Beggars soon had their counterpart in the English "sea dogges": John Hawkins, Francis Drake, and others. While Queen Elizabeth steered a tortuous course to avoid open war with Catholic Spain, she encouraged both Dutch and English captains to engage in smuggling and piracy. In 1577 Drake embarked on his famous adventure around South America, raiding Spanish towns along the Pacific and surprising a treasure ship from Peru. Continuing in a vain search for a passage back to the Atlantic, he spent seven weeks at Drake's Bay in New Albion, as he called California. Eventually he found his way westward around the world and arrived home in 1580. Elizabeth knighted him upon his return.

THE ARMADA'S DEFEAT   The plundering of Spanish shipping by English privateers continued for some twenty years before open war erupted. In 1568 Queen Elizabeth's cousin Mary, Queen of Scots, ousted by Scottish Presbyterians in favor of her infant son, fled to England. Mary, who was Catholic, had a claim to the English throne by virtue of her descent from Henry VII and soon became the focus of Spanish-Catholic intrigues to overthrow the Protestant Elizabeth. In 1587, after the discovery of a plot to kill her and elevate Mary to the throne, Elizabeth yielded to the demands of her ministers and had Mary beheaded.

Seeking revenge for Mary's execution, Spain's king, Philip II, decided to crush Protestant England and so began to gather his ill-fated Armada, whereupon Admiral Francis Drake's warships destroyed part of the Spanish fleet before it was ready to sail. Drake's foray postponed for a year the departure of the "Invincible Armada," which set out to invade England in 1588. As the two fleets positioned themselves for the great naval battle, Elizabeth donned a silver breastplate and told the English forces, "I know I have the body of a weak and feeble woman, but I have the heart and stomach of a king, and a King of England too." As the battle unfolded, the heavy Spanish galleons could not compete with the smaller, faster English vessels. Drake's fleet harried the Spanish ships through the English Channel on their way to the Netherlands, where the Armada was to pick up an invasion force. But caught up in a powerful "Protestant wind" from the south, the storm-tossed

The "Invincible Armada"

The fleet of the Spanish Armada in a contemporary English oil painting.

Spanish fleet was swept into the North Sea instead. What was left of it finally found its way home around the British Isles, scattering wreckage on the shores of Scotland and Ireland.

Defeat of the Spanish Armada marked the beginning of English naval supremacy and cleared the way for English colonization of America. The naval victory was the climactic event of Queen Elizabeth's reign. England at the end of the sixteenth century was in the springtime of its power, filled with a youthful zest for new worlds and new wonders.

ENGLISH EXPLORATION   The history of the English efforts to colonize America begins with Sir Humphrey Gilbert and his half brother, Sir Walter Raleigh. In 1578 Gilbert, who had long been a favorite of the queen's, secured a royal patent to possess "heathen and barbarous landes countries and territories not actually possessed of any Christian prince or people." Significantly, the patent guaranteed to settlers and their descendants in such a colony the rights and privileges of Englishmen "in suche like ample manner and fourme as if they were borne and personally residaunte within our sed Realme of England." Their laws had to be "agreable to the forme of the lawes and pollicies of England."

Gilbert, after two false starts, set out with a colonial expedition in 1583, intending to settle near Narragansett Bay (in present-day Rhode Island). He instead landed in Newfoundland and took possession of the land for Elizabeth. With winter approaching and his largest vessels lost, Gilbert resolved to return home. While in transit, however, his ship vanished, and he was never seen again.

RALEIGH'S LOST COLONY   The next year, Sir Walter Raleigh persuaded the queen to renew Gilbert's colonizing mission in his own name. Sailing by way of the West Indies, the flotilla came to the Outer Banks of North Carolina and discovered Roanoke Island, where the soil seemed fruitful and the natives friendly. After several false starts, Raleigh in 1587 sponsored an expedition of about 100 colonists, including women and children,

The Arrival of the English in Virginia

The 1585 arrival of English explorers on the Outer Banks, with Roanoke Island at left.

under Governor John White. White spent a month in Roanoke and then returned to England for supplies, leaving behind his daughter Elinor and his granddaughter Virginia Dare, the first English child born in the New World. White's return was delayed because of the war with Spain. When he finally landed, in 1590, he found Roanoke abandoned and pillaged.

No trace of the "lost colonists" was ever found. Hostile Indians may have destroyed the colony, or hostile Spaniards—who had certainly planned to attack—may have done the job. The most recent evidence indicates that the "Lost Colony" fell prey to the region's worst drought in eight centuries. Tree-ring samples reveal that the colonists arrived during the driest seven-year period in 770 years. While some may have gone south, the main body of colonists appears to have gone north, to the southern shores of Chesapeake Bay, as they had talked of doing, and lived there for some years until they were killed by local Indians. Unless some remnant of the Roanoke settlement did survive in the woods, there was not a single English colonist in North America when Queen Elizabeth died in 1603.

MAKING CONNECTIONS

- The funding of the voyages of discovery by various European nations had implications for the settlement and control of the New World, as will be discussed in later chapters.

- The settlement pattern of the Spanish in the New World and the wealth they plundered will be contrasted in the next chapter with the patterns of English settlement and the English sources of wealth in the New World.

- The next chapter describes how the Reformation and religious controversies in Europe led various groups to found their own settlements in the New World, where they did not face religious discrimination and persecution.

FURTHER READING

A fascinating study of pre-Columbian migration is Brian M. Fagan's *The Great Journey: The Peopling of Ancient America*, rev. ed. (2004). Alice B. Kehoe's

North American Indians: A Comprehensive Account, 2nd ed. (1992) provides an encyclopedic treatment of Native Americans.

The conflict between Native Americans and Europeans is treated well in James Axtell's *The Invasion Within: The Contest of Cultures in Colonial North America* (1986) and *Beyond 1492: Encounters in Colonial North America* (1992). Colin G. Calloway's *New Worlds for All: Indians, Europeans, and the Remaking of Early America* (1997) explores the ecological effects of European settlement.

The most comprehensive overviews of European exploration are two volumes by Samuel Eliot Morison, *The European Discovery of America: The Northern Voyages, A.D. 500–1600* (1971) and *The Southern Voyages A.D. 1492–1616* (1974).

The voyages of Columbus are surveyed in William D. Phillips Jr. and Carla Rahn Phillips's *The Worlds of Christopher Columbus* (1992). For sweeping overviews of Spain's creation of a global empire, see Henry Kamen's *Empire: How Spain Became a World Power, 1492–1763* (2003) and Hugh Thomas's *Rivers of Gold: The Rise of the Spanish Empire, from Columbus to Magellan* (2004). David J. Weber examines Spanish colonization in *The Spanish Frontier in North America* (1992). For the French experience, see William J. Eccles's *France in America*, rev. ed. (1990).

2

BRITAIN AND
ITS COLONIES

FOCUS QUESTION

· What were the reasons for the founding of the different colonies in North America?

· How did the British colonists and the Native Americans adapt to each other's presence?

· What factors made England successful in North America?

The England that Queen Elizabeth bequeathed to the Scottish King James I in 1603, like the colonies it would plant, was a unique blend of elements. The language and the people themselves mixed Germanic and Latin ingredients. The Anglican Church mixed Protestant theology and Catholic rituals. And the growth of royal power paradoxically had been linked to the rise of English liberties, in which even Tudor monarchs took pride. In the course of their history, the English people have displayed a genius for "muddling through," a gift for the pragmatic compromise that defies logic but in the light of experience somehow works.

The English Background

Dominated by England, the British Isles included the distinct kingdoms of Wales, Ireland, and Scotland. England, set off from continental Europe by the English Channel, had safe frontiers after the union of the English and Scottish crowns in 1603. Such comparative isolation enabled the nation to develop institutions quite different from those on the Continent. Unlike the absolute monarchs of France and Spain, the British rulers had to share power with the aristocracy and a lesser aristocracy, known as the gentry, whose representatives formed the bicameral legislature known as Parliament.

By 1600 the decline of feudal practices was far advanced. The great nobles, decimated by the Wars of the Roses, had been brought to heel by Tudor monarchs and their ranks filled with men loyal to the crown. In fact the only nobles left, strictly speaking, were those who sat in the House of Lords. All others were commoners, and among their ranks the aristocratic pecking order ran through a great class of landholding squires, distinguished mainly by their wealth and bearing the simple titles of "esquire" and "gentleman," as did many well-to-do townsmen. They in turn mingled freely, and often intermarried, with the classes of yeomen (small freehold farmers) and merchants.

ENGLISH LIBERTIES   It was to these middle classes that the Tudors looked for support and, for want of bureaucrats or a standing army, local government. Chief reliance in the English counties was on the country gentlemen, who usually served as officials without pay. Government, therefore, allowed a large measure of local initiative. Self-rule in the counties and towns became a habit—one that, along with the offices of justice of the peace and sheriff, English colonists took along to the New World as part of their cultural baggage.

In the making of laws, the monarch's subjects consented through representatives in the House of Commons. Subjects could be taxed only with the consent of Parliament. By its control of the purse strings, Parliament drew other strands of power into its hands. This structure of powers served as an unwritten constitution. The Magna Carta (Great Charter) of 1215 was a statement of privileges wrested by certain nobles from the king, but it became part of a broader assumption that the people as a whole had rights that even the monarch could not violate.

A further safeguard of English liberty was the tradition of common law, which had developed since the twelfth century in royal courts established to check the arbitrary power of local nobles. Without laws to cover every detail, judges had to exercise their own ideas of fairness in settling disputes. Decisions once made became precedents for subsequent decisions, and over the years a body of judge-made law developed, the outgrowth more of practical experience than of abstract logic. The courts evolved the principle that people could be arrested or their goods seized only upon a warrant issued by a court and that individuals were entitled to a trial by a jury of their peers (their equals) in accordance with established rules of evidence.

ENGLISH ENTERPRISE   English liberties inspired a sense of personal initiative and enterprise that spawned prosperity and empire. The ranks of entrepreneurs and adventurers were constantly replenished by the younger sons of the squirearchy, cut off from the estate that the oldest son inherited according to the law of primogeniture (or firstborn). At the same time the formation of joint-stock companies spurred commercial expansion. These entrepreneurial companies were the ancestors of the modern corporation, in which stockholders, not the government, shared the risks and profits, sometimes for a single venture but more and more on a permanent basis. In the late sixteenth century some of the larger companies managed to get royal charters that entitled them to monopolies in certain areas and even government powers in their outposts. Such companies would become the first instruments of colonization.

For all the vaunted glories of English liberty and enterprise, it was not the best of times for the common people. During the late sixteenth century the "lower sort" in Britain experienced a population explosion that outstripped the ability of the economy to support so many workers. An additional strain on the population was the "enclosure" of farmlands where peasants had lived and worked. For more than two centuries, serfdom had been on the way to extinction as the feudal duties of serfs were transformed into rents and the serfs themselves into tenants. But while tenancy gave people a degree of independence, it also allowed landlords to increase demands and, as the trade in woolen products grew, to "enclose" farmlands and evict the human tenants in favor of sheep. The enclosure movement of the sixteenth century, coupled with the rising population, gave rise to the great number of beggars and rogues who peopled the literature of Elizabethan times and gained immortality in Mother Goose: "Hark, hark, the dogs do bark. The beggars have come to town." The needs of this displaced peasant population, on the move throughout Great Britain, became another powerful argument for colonial expansion. The displaced poor migrated from farms to crowded towns and cities. London became a powerful magnet for vagabonds. By the seventeenth century the English capital was notorious for its filth, poverty, crime, and class tensions—all of which helped persuade the ruling elite to send idle and larcenous commoners abroad to settle new colonies.

PARLIAMENT AND THE STUARTS   With the death of Elizabeth, who never married and did not give birth to an heir, the Tudor family line ran out and the throne fell to the first of the Stuarts, whose dynasty would span most of the seventeenth century, a turbulent time during which the English planted their overseas empire. In 1603 James VI of Scotland, son of the ill-fated Mary, Queen of Scots, and great-great-grandson of Henry VII, became James I of England—as Elizabeth had planned. A man of ponderous learning, James fully earned his reputation as the "wisest fool in Christendom." Tall and broad-shouldered, he was bisexual, conceited, profligate, and lazy and possessed an undiplomatic tongue. He lectured the people on every topic but remained blind to English traditions and sensibilities. Whereas the Tudors had wielded absolute power through constitutional forms, James promoted the theory of divine right, by which monarchs answered only to God. Whereas the Puritans hoped to find a Presbyterian ally in their opposition to Anglican trappings, they found instead a testy autocrat who

Stuart Kings

(Left) James I, the successor to Queen Elizabeth and the first of England's Stuart kings. (Right) Charles I in a portrait by Gerrit van Honthorst.

promised to banish them. He even offended Anglicans, by deciding to end his cousin Elizabeth's war with Catholic Spain.

Charles I, who succeeded his father James, in 1625, proved even more stubborn about royal power. He disbanded Parliament from 1629 to 1640 and levied taxes by decree. In the religious arena the archbishop of Canterbury, William Laud, directed a systematic persecution of Puritans but finally overreached himself when he tried to impose Anglican worship on Presbyterian Scots. In 1638 Scotland rose in revolt, and in 1640 Charles called Parliament to raise money for the defense of his kingdom. The "Long Parliament" impeached Laud instead and condemned to death the king's chief minister. In 1642, when the king tried to arrest five members of Parliament, civil war erupted between the "Roundheads," who backed Parliament, and the "Cavaliers," who supported the king.

In 1646 Royalist resistance collapsed, and parliamentary forces captured the king. Parliament, however, could not agree on a permanent settlement. A dispute arose between Presbyterians and Independents (who preferred a congregational church government), and in 1648 the Independents purged the Presbyterians, leaving a "Rump Parliament" that then instigated the trial and execution of King Charles I on charges of treason.

Oliver Cromwell, the tenacious commander of the army, operated like a military dictator, ruling first through a council chosen by Parliament (the Commonwealth) and, after forcible dissolution of Parliament, as lord protector (the Protectorate). Cromwell extended religious toleration to all Britons except Catholics and Anglicans, but his arbitrary governance and his stern moralistic codes provoked growing public resentment. When, after his death in 1658, his son proved too weak to carry on, the army once again took control, permitted new elections for Parliament, and in 1660 supported the Restoration of the monarchy under Charles II, son of the martyred king.

Charles II accepted as terms of the Restoration settlement the principle that he must rule jointly with Parliament. By tact or shrewd maneuvering, he managed to hold his throne. His younger brother, the duke of York (who became James II upon succeeding to the throne in 1685), was less flexible. He openly avowed Catholicism and assumed the same unyielding stance as the first two Stuarts. The people could bear it so long as they expected one of his Protestant daughters, Mary or Anne, to succeed him. In 1688, however, the birth of a son who would be reared a Catholic finally brought matters to a crisis. Leaders of Parliament invited Mary and her husband, William of Orange, a Dutch prince, to assume the throne jointly, and James fled the country.

By this "Glorious Revolution," Parliament finally established its freedom from royal control. Under the Bill of Rights, in 1689, William and Mary gave up the royal prerogatives of suspending laws, erecting special courts, keeping a standing army, or levying taxes except by Parliament's consent. They further agreed to hold frequent legislative sessions and allow freedom of speech in Parliament, freedom of petition to the crown, and restrictions against excessive bail and cruel and unusual punishments. The Act of Toleration of 1689 extended a degree of freedom of worship to all Christians except Catholics and Unitarians, although dissenters from the established church still had few political rights. In 1701 the Act of Settlement ensured Protestant succession through Queen Anne (r. 1702–1714). And by the Act of Union in 1707, England and Scotland became the United Kingdom of Great Britain.

SETTLING THE CHESAPEAKE

During these eventful years all but one of Britain's thirteen North American colonies had their start. They began as corporations rather than new countries. In 1606 King James I chartered a joint-stock enterprise called the Virginia Company, with two divisions, the First Colony of London and the Second Colony of Plymouth. The London group of investors could plant a settlement between the 34th and 38th parallels, the Plymouth group between the 41st and 45th parallels, and either between the 38th and 41st parallels, provided they kept 100 miles apart. The stockholders expected a potential return from gold and other minerals; products—such as wine, citrus fruits, and olive oil—that would free England from dependence on Spain; trade with the Indians; pitch, tar, potash, and other forest products needed for naval use; and perhaps a passage to east Asia. Some investors saw colonization as an opportunity to transplant the growing number of jobless vagrants from Britain to the New World. Others dreamed of finding another Aztec or Inca Empire. Few if any foresaw what the first English colony would actually become: a place to grow tobacco.

From the outset the pattern of English colonization diverged significantly from the Spanish pattern, which involved conquering highly sophisticated peoples and regulating all aspects of colonial life. While interest in America was growing, the English were already involved in planting settlements, or "plantations," in Ireland, which the English had conquered by military force under Queen Elizabeth. Within their own pale (or limit) of settlement in Ireland, the English set about transplanting their familiar way of life insofar as possible.

The English would apply the same pattern as they settled North America, subjugating (and converting) the Indians there as they had the Irish in Ireland. Yet in America the English settled along the Atlantic seaboard, where the native populations were relatively sparse. There was no Aztec or Inca Empire to conquer. The colonists thus had to establish their own communities in a largely wilderness setting. Describing the "settlement" of the Atlantic seaboard is somewhat misleading, however, for the British colonists who arrived in the seventeenth century rarely *settled* in one place for long. They were migrants more than settlers, people who had been on the move in Britain and continued to pursue new opportunities in different places once they arrived in America.

VIRGINIA   The London group of the Virginia Company planted the first permanent colony in Virginia, named after Elizabeth I, "the Virgin Queen." On May 6, 1607, three tiny ships carrying 105 men reached Chesapeake Bay

"Ould Virginia"

A 1624 map of Virginia by John Smith, showing Chief Powhatan in the upper left.

after four storm-tossed months at sea. They chose a river with a northwest bend—in the hope of finding a passage to Asia—and settled about forty miles inland, to hide from marauding Spaniards.

The river they called the James and the colony, Jamestown. The seaweary colonists began building a fort, thatched huts, a storehouse, and a church. They then set to planting, but most were either townsmen unfamiliar with farming or "gentleman" adventurers who scorned manual labor. They had come expecting to find gold, friendly natives, and easy living. Instead they found disease, starvation, dissension, and death. Ignorant of woodlore, they did not know how to exploit the area's abundant game and fish. Supplies from England were undependable, and only some effective leadership and trade with the Indians, who taught the colonists to grow maize, enabled them to survive.

The Indians of the region were loosely organized. Powhatan was the powerful, charismatic chief of numerous Algonquian-speaking towns in eastern Virginia, representing over 10,000 Indians. The Indians making up the so-called Powhatan Confederacy were largely an agricultural people focused on raising corn. They lived along rivers in fortified towns and resided in wood houses sheathed with bark. Chief Powhatan collected tribute from the tribes he had conquered—fully 80 percent of the corn that they grew was handed over. Despite occasional clashes with the colonists, the Indians initially adopted a stance of nervous assistance and watchful waiting. Powhatan developed a lucrative trade with the colonists, exchanging corn and hides for hatchets, swords, and muskets; he realized too late that the newcomers intended to expropriate his lands and subjugate his people.

The colonists, as it happened, had more than a match for Powhatan in Captain John Smith, a stocky twenty-seven-year-old soldier of fortune with rare powers of leadership and self-promotion. The Virginia Company, impressed by Smith's exploits in foreign wars, had appointed him a member of the council to manage the new colony in America. It was a wise decision. Of the original 105 settlers, only 38 survived the first nine months. With the colonists on the verge of starvation, Smith imposed strict discipline and forced all to labor, declaring that "he that will not work shall not eat." In dealing with mutinies, skirmishes, and ambushes, he imprisoned, whipped, and forced colonists to labor. Smith also bargained with the Indians and explored and mapped the Chesapeake region. Through his efforts, Jamestown survived, but Smith's dictatorial acts did not endear him to many of the colonists.

In 1609 the Virginia Company moved to reinforce Jamestown. More colonists were dispatched, including several women. A new charter replaced

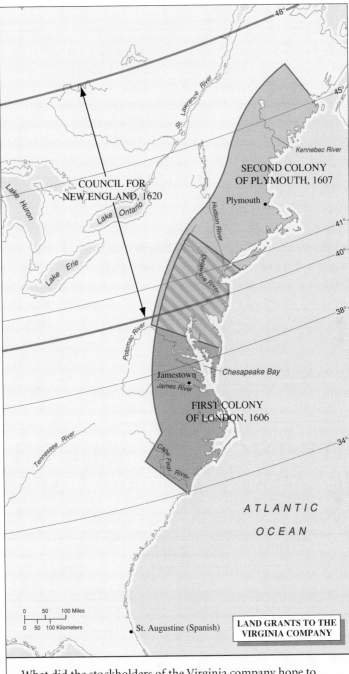

COUNCIL FOR
NEW ENGLAND, 1620

SECOND COLONY
OF PLYMOUTH, 1607

Plymouth

Lake Huron

Lake Ontario

Lake Erie

St. Lawrence River

Kennebec River

Hudson River

Delaware River

Potomac River

Jamestown

James River

Chesapeake Bay

FIRST COLONY
OF LONDON, 1606

Tennessee River

Cape Fear River

ATLANTIC

OCEAN

48°

45°

41°

40°

38°

34°

0   50   100 Miles
0   50   100 Kilometers

St. Augustine (Spanish)

**LAND GRANTS TO THE
VIRGINIA COMPANY**

What did the stockholders of the Virginia company hope to
gain from the first two English colonies in North America? How
were the first English settlements different from the Spanish
settlements in North America? What were the major differences
between the first colony of London and the second colony of
Plymouth?

the largely ineffective council with an all-powerful governor whose council was only advisory. The company then lured new investors and attracted new settlers with the promise of free land after seven years of labor. The company in effect had given up hope of prospering except through the sale of land, which would rise in value as the colony grew. The governor, the noble Lord De La Warr (Delaware), sent as interim governor Sir Thomas Gates. In 1609 Gates set out with a fleet of nine vessels and about 500 passengers and crew. On the way he was shipwrecked on Bermuda, where he and the other survivors wintered in comparative ease, subsisting on fish, fowl, and wild pigs. (Their story was transformed by William Shakespeare into his play *The Tempest*.)

Most of the fleet did reach Jamestown, however. Some 400 settlers overwhelmed the remnant of about 80. All chance that John Smith might control things was lost when he suffered a gunpowder burn and sailed back to England. The consequence was anarchy and the "starving time" of the winter of 1609–1610, during which most of the colonists, weakened by hunger, died of disease or starvation. A prolonged drought had hindered efforts to grow

Colonial Necessities

A list of provisions recommended to new settlers by the Virginia Company in 1622.

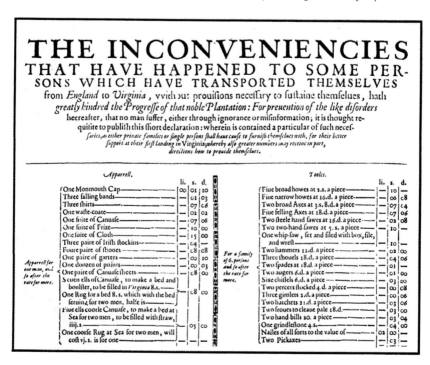

food. By May 1610, when Gates and his companions made their way to Jamestown on two small ships built in Bermuda, only about 60 settlers remained alive. During the winter of 1610, as starvation grew pervasive, desperate colonists consumed their horses, cats, and dogs, then rats and mice. A few even ate the leather from their shoes and boots. Some fled to nearby Indian villages, only to be welcomed with arrows. One man was executed for killing his pregnant wife and feasting on her remains.

In June 1610, as the colonists made their way down the river toward the sea, the new governor, Lord Delaware, providentially arrived with three ships and 150 men. The colonists returned to Jamestown and created new settlements upstream at Henrico (Richmond) and two more downstream, near the mouth of the river. It was a critical turning point for the colony, whose survival required a combination of stern measures and not a little luck. When Lord Delaware returned to England in 1611, Gates took charge of the colony and established a strict system of laws. Severe even by the standards of a ruthless age, the new code enforced a militaristic discipline needed for survival. When one laborer was caught stealing oatmeal, the authorities had a long needle thrust through his tongue, chained him to a tree, and let him starve to death as a grisly example to the community. Desperate colonists who fled to join the Indians were caught and hanged or burned at the stake. The new colonial regime also assaulted the local Indians. English colonists attacked Indian villages and destroyed their crops. One commander reported that they marched a captured Indian queen and her children to the river, where they "put the Children to death . . . by throwing them overboard and shooting out their brains in the water."

Over the next seven years the Jamestown colony limped along until it gradually found a reason for being: tobacco. The plant had been grown in the West Indies for years, and smoking had become a popular habit in Europe. In 1612 John Rolfe had begun to experiment with the harsh Virginia tobacco. Eventually he got hold of some seed from the more savory Spanish varieties, and by 1616 the weed had become a profitable export staple. Even though King James dismissed smoking as "loathsome to the eye, hateful to the nose, harmful to the brain, and dangerous to the lungs," he swallowed his objections to the "noxious weed" when he realized how much revenue it provided the monarchy. Virginia's tobacco production soared during the seventeenth century. Tobacco was such a profitable crop for Virginia planters that they could afford to purchase more indentured servants, thus increasing the flow of immigrants to the colony.

Meanwhile John Rolfe had made another contribution to stability by marrying Pocahontas, the daughter of Chief Powhatan. Pocahontas (a nickname

Pocahontas

Shown here in European dress, by 1616 Pocahontas was known as "Lady Rebecca."

usually translated as "Frisky"; her given name was Matoaka) had been a familiar figure in Jamestown almost from the beginning. In 1607, then only eleven, she figured in perhaps the best-known story of the settlement, her plea for the life of John Smith. Smith had gotten into trouble when he led a small group up the James River in search of a northwest passage. When the Englishmen trespassed on Powhatan's territory, the Indians attacked. Smith was wounded and captured. Others in his scouting party were tortured and disemboweled. Smith was marched to Powhatan's village, interrogated, and readied for execution. At that point, according to Smith, Pocahontas made a dramatic appeal for his life, and Powhatan eventually agreed to release the foreigner in exchange for muskets, hatchets, beads, and trinkets.

Schoolchildren still learn the dramatic story of Pocahontas intervening to save Smith. Such dramatic events are magical; they inspire movies, excite our imagination, animate history—and confuse it. Pocahontas and John Smith were never in love. Moreover, the young Indian princess saved the swashbuckling Smith on more than one occasion. Then she herself was captured. In 1614 the Jamestown settlers kidnapped Pocahontas in an effort to blackmail Powhatan. As the weeks passed, however, she surprised her captors by choosing to join them. She embraced Christianity, was renamed Rebecca, and fell in love with John Rolfe. They married and in 1616 moved with their infant son, Thomas, to London. There the young princess drew excited attention from the royal family and curious Londoners. But only a few months after arriving, Rebecca, aged twenty, contracted a lung disease and died.

In 1618 Sir Edwin Sandys, a prominent member of Parliament, became head of the Virginia Company and instituted a series of reforms. First of all he inaugurated a new "headright" policy: anyone who bought a share in the company and could get to Virginia could have fifty acres, and fifty more for any servants. The following year the company relaxed the colony's military regime and promised that the settlers would have the "rights of Englishmen," including a representative assembly.

A new governor arrived with instructions to put the new order into effect, and on July 30, 1619, the first General Assembly of Virginia, including the governor, six councilors, and twenty-two burgesses, met in the church at Jamestown and deliberated for five days, "sweating & stewing, and battling flies and mosquitoes." It was an eventful year in two other respects. The promoters also saw a need to send out more wives for the men. During 1619 a ship arrived with ninety young women, who were to be sold to likely husbands of their own choice for the cost of transportation (about 125 pounds of tobacco). And a Dutch ship stopped by and dropped off "20 Negars," the first Africans known to have reached English America.

The profitable tobacco trade intensified the settlers' lust for land. They especially coveted Indian fields because they had already been cleared and were ready to be planted. In 1622 the Indians, led by Opechancanough, Powhatan's brother and successor, tried to repel the land-grabbing English. They killed one fourth of the settlers, some 350 colonists, including John Rolfe (who had returned from England). In England, John Smith denounced the Indian assault as a "massacre" and dismissed the "savages" as "cruel beasts" whose "brutishness" exceeded that of wild animals. Whatever moral doubts had earlier plagued English settlers were now swept away. The English thereafter sought to wipe out the Indian presence along their frontier.

Some 14,000 men, women, and children had migrated to Jamestown since 1607, but most of them had died; the population in 1624 stood at a precarious 1,132. Despite the initial achievements of the company, after about 1617 a handful of insiders appropriated large estates and began to monopolize the indentured workers. Some made fortunes from the tobacco boom, but most of the thousands sent out died before they could prove themselves. In 1624 an English court dissolved the struggling Virginia Company, and Virginia became a royal colony.

The king did not renew instructions for a legislative assembly, but his governors found it impossible to rule the troublesome Virginians without one. Annual assemblies met after 1629, although they were not recognized by the crown for another ten years. After 1622 relations with the Indians continued in a state of what the governor's council called "perpetual enmity." The combination of warfare and disease decimated the Indians in Virginia. The 24,000 Algonquians who inhabited the colony in 1607 were reduced to 2,000 by 1669.

Sir William Berkeley, who arrived as Virginia's governor in 1642, presided over the colony's growth for most of the next thirty-five years. The turmoil of Virginia's early days gave way to a more stable period. Tobacco prices peaked, and the large planters began to consolidate their economic gains through political action. They assumed key civic roles as justices of the peace and sheriffs, helped initiate internal improvements such as roads and bridges, supervised elections, and collected taxes. They also formed the able-bodied men into local militias. Despite the presence of a royal governor, the elected Virginia assembly continued to assert its sovereignty, making laws for the colony and resisting the governor's encroachments.

Virginia at midcentury continued to serve as a magnet for new settlers. As the sharp rise in tobacco profits leveled off, planters began to grow corn and raise cattle. The increase in the food supply helped lower mortality rates and fuel a rapid rise in population. By 1650 there were 15,000 white residents of Virginia. Many former servants became planters in their own right. Women typically improved their status through marriage. If they outlived their husbands—and many did—they inherited the property and often increased their wealth through second and even third marriages.

The relentless stream of new settlers into Virginia exerted constant pressure on Indian lands and produced unwanted economic effects. The increase in the number of planters spurred a dramatic rise in agricultural production. That in turn caused the cost of land to soar and the price of tobacco to plummet. To sustain their competitive advantage, the largest planters bought up the most fertile land along the coast, thereby forcing freed servants to become tenants or claim less fertile land inland. In either case the tenants found themselves at a disadvantage. They grew dependent on planters for land and credit, and small farmers along the frontier became more vulnerable to Indian attacks.

The plight of the common folk worsened after 1660, when a restored monarchy under Charles II instituted new trade regulations for the colonies. By 1676 one fourth of the free white men in Virginia were landless. Vagabonds roamed the roads, squatting on private property, working at odd jobs, or poaching game or engaging in other petty crimes in order to survive. Alarmed by the growing social unrest, the large planters who controlled the assembly—generally ruthless and callous men—lengthened terms of indenture, passed more stringent vagrancy laws, stiffened punishments, and stripped the landless of their political rights. Such efforts only increased social friction.

BACON'S REBELLION   A variety of simmering tensions—caused by depressed tobacco prices, rising taxes, roaming livestock, and crowds of freed servants greedily eyeing Indian lands—contributed to the tangled events that have come to be labeled Bacon's Rebellion. The roots of the revolt grew out of a festering hatred for the domineering colonial governor,

William Berkeley. He had limited his circle of friends to the wealthiest planters, and he had granted them most of the frontier land and public offices. He despised commoners. The large planters who dominated the assembly levied high taxes to finance Berkeley's regime, which in turn supported their interests at the expense of the small farmers and servants. With little nearby land available, newly freed indentured servants were forced to migrate westward in their quest for farms. Their lust for land led them to displace the Indians. When Governor Berkeley failed to support the aspiring farmers, they rebelled. The tyrannical governor expected as much. Just before the outbreak of rebellion, Berkeley had remarked in a letter: "How miserable that man is that Governes a People where six parts of seaven at least are Poore, Endebted, Discontented and Armed."

The discontent turned to violence in 1675 when a petty squabble between a frontier planter and the Doeg Indians on the Potomac River led to the murder of the planter's herdsman and, in turn, to retaliation by frontier militiamen, who killed ten or more Doegs and, by mistake, fourteen Susquehannocks. Soon a force of Virginia and Maryland militiamen attacked the Susquehannocks and murdered five chieftains who had come out to negotiate. The enraged survivors took their revenge on frontier settlements. Scattered attacks continued on down to the James River, where Nathaniel Bacon's overseer was killed.

By then, their revenge accomplished, the Susquehannocks had pulled back. What followed had less to do with a state of war than with a state of hysteria. Governor Berkeley proposed that the assembly erect a series of forts along the frontier. But that would not slake the English thirst for revenge— nor would it open new lands to settlement. Besides, it would be expensive. Some thought Berkeley was out to preserve a profitable fur trade for himself.

In 1676 Nathaniel Bacon defied Governor Berkeley's authority by assuming command of a group of frontier vigilantes. The tall, slender twenty-nine-year-old Bacon, a graduate of Cambridge University, had been in Virginia only two years, but he had been well set up by an English father relieved to get his vain, ambitious, hot-tempered son out of the country. Later historians would praise Bacon as the "Torchbearer of the Revolution" and leader of the first struggle of common folk versus aristocrats. In part that was true. The rebellion he led was largely a battle of servants, small farmers, and even slaves against Virginia's wealthiest planters and political leaders. But Bacon was also a rich squire's spoiled son with a talent for trouble. It was his ruthless assaults against peaceful Indians and his desire for power and land rather than any commitment to democratic principles that sparked his conflict with the governing authorities.

Bacon despised the Indians and resolved to kill them all. Berkeley opposed Bacon's genocidal plan not because he liked Indians but because he wanted to protect his lucrative monopoly over the deerskin trade with the Indians. Bacon ordered the governor arrested. Berkeley's forces resisted—but only feebly—and Bacon's men burned Jamestown. Bacon, however, could not savor the victory long; he fell ill and died of dysentery a month later.

Governor Berkeley quickly regained control; he hanged twenty-three rebels and confiscated several estates. When his men captured one of Bacon's closest lieutenants, Berkeley gleefully exclaimed: "I am more glad to see you than any man in Virginia. Mr. Drummond, you shall be hanged in half an hour." For such severity the king denounced Berkeley as a "fool" and recalled him to England, where he died within a year. A royal commission made peace treaties with the remaining Indians, about 1,500 of whose descendants still live in Virginia on tiny reservations guaranteed them in 1677. The end result of Bacon's Rebellion was that new lands were opened to the colonists, and the wealthy planters became more cooperative with the small farmers.

MARYLAND   In 1634, ten years after Virginia became a royal colony, a neighboring settlement appeared on the northern shores of Chesapeake Bay. Named Maryland in honor of Queen Henrietta Maria, it was granted to Lord Baltimore by King Charles I and became the first proprietary colony— that is, it was owned by an individual, not a joint-stock company. Sir George Calvert, the first Lord Baltimore, had announced in 1625 his conversion to Catholicism and sought the colony as a refuge for English Catholics, who were subjected to discrimination at home. His son, Cecilius Calvert, the second Lord Baltimore, actually founded the colony.

In 1634 Calvert planted the first settlement in Maryland at St. Marys, on a small stream near the mouth of the Potomac River. Calvert brought Catholic gentlemen as landholders, but a majority of the servants were Protestants. The charter gave Calvert power to make laws with the consent of the freemen (all property holders). The first legislative assembly met in 1635 and divided into two houses in 1650, with governor and council sitting separately. This action was instigated by the predominantly Protestant freemen— largely servants who had become landholders and immigrants from Virginia. The charter also empowered the proprietor to grant huge manorial estates, and Maryland had some sixty before 1676, but the Lords Baltimore soon found that to draw settlers they had to offer them small farms. The colony was meant to rely upon mixed farming, but its fortunes, like those of Virginia, soon came to depend upon tobacco.

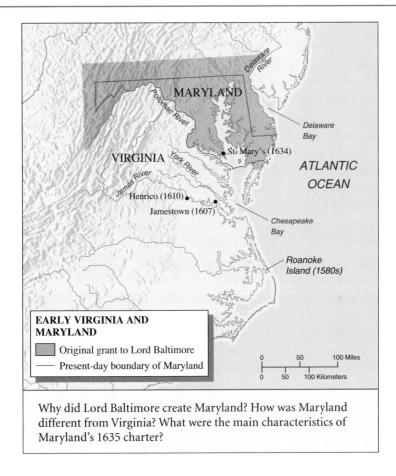

EARLY VIRGINIA AND
MARYLAND

▨ Original grant to Lord Baltimore

--- Present-day boundary of Maryland

Why did Lord Baltimore create Maryland? How was Maryland
different from Virginia? What were the main characteristics of
Maryland's 1635 charter?

SETTLING NEW ENGLAND

Far to the north of the Chesapeake Bay colonies, quite different settlements were emerging. The New England colonists were generally made up of
middle-class families who could pay their own way across the Atlantic. In the
Northeast there were relatively few indentured servants, and there was no
planter elite. Most male settlers were small farmers, merchants, seamen, or
fishermen. New England also became home to more women than did the
southern colonies. Although its soil was not as fertile as that of the Chesapeake and its farmers not as wealthy as the southern planters, New England
was a much healthier place to settle. Because of its colder climate, the region
did not foster the infectious diseases that ravaged the southern colonies. Life
expectancy was much longer. During the seventeenth century only 21,000

colonists arrived in New England, compared with the 120,000 who went to the Chesapeake. But by 1700 New England's white population exceeded that of Maryland and Virginia.

Most early New Englanders were devout Puritans, who embraced a much more rigorous faith than the Anglicans of Virginia and Maryland. In 1650, for example, Massachusetts boasted one minister for every 415 persons, compared with one minister per 3,239 persons in Virginia. The Puritans who arrived in America believed themselves to be on a divine mission to create a model society committed to the proper worship of God. In their efforts to separate themselves from a sinful England and its authoritarian Anglican bishops, New England's zealous Puritans sought to create "holy commonwealths" that would help inspire a spiritual transformation in their homeland. In the New World these self-described "saints" could purify their churches of all Catholic and Anglican rituals, supervise one another in practicing a communal faith, and enact a code of laws and a government structure based on biblical principles. Such a holy settlement, they hoped, would provide a beacon of righteousness for a wicked England to emulate.

PLYMOUTH   In 1620 a band of English settlers headed for Virginia strayed off course and made landfall at Cape Cod, off the coast of Massachusetts. There they decided to establish a colony, naming it Plymouth after the English port from which they had embarked. The "Pilgrims" who established the Plymouth Plantation belonged to the most uncompromising sect of Puritans, the Separatists, who had severed all ties with the Church of England. Many Separatists had fled to Holland in 1607 to escape persecution. After ten years in the Dutch city of Leiden, they longed for English ways and the English flag. If they could not have them at home, perhaps they might transplant them to the New World.

The Leiden Separatists secured a land patent from the Virginia Company and set up a joint-stock company. In 1620, 102 men, women, and children, led by William Bradford, crammed aboard the three-masted *Mayflower*. Their ranks included both "saints" (people recognized as having been elected by God for salvation) and "strangers" (those yet to receive the gift of grace). The latter group included John Alden, a cooper (barrel maker), and Myles Standish, a soldier hired to organize their defenses. The stormy voyage had led them to Cape Cod. "Being thus arrived at safe harbor, and brought safe to land," William Bradford wrote, "they fell upon their knees and blessed the God of Heaven who had brought them over the vast and furious ocean." Since they were outside the jurisdiction of any organized government, forty-one of the Pilgrim leaders entered into a formal agreement

New World Navigation

Sailors on a sixteenth-century oceangoing vessel navigating by the stars.

to abide by the laws made by leaders of their own choosing—the Mayflower Compact.

On December 26 the *Mayflower* reached the harbor of the place they named Plymouth and stayed there until April to give shelter and support while the Pilgrims built dwellings on the site of an abandoned Indian village. Nearly half the colonists died of exposure and disease, but friendly relations with the neighboring Wampanoag Indians proved their salvation. In the spring of 1621, the colonists met Squanto, an Indian who spoke English and showed them how to grow maize. By autumn the Pilgrims had a bumper crop of corn, a flourishing fur trade, and a supply of lumber for shipment. To celebrate, they held a harvest feast in the company of Chief Massasoit and the Wampanoags. That event provided the inspiration for what has become Thanksgiving.

In 1623 Plymouth gave up its original communal economy and stipulated that now each male settler was to provide for his family from his own land. Throughout its separate existence, until absorbed into Massachusetts in 1691, the Plymouth colony remained in the anomalous position of holding a

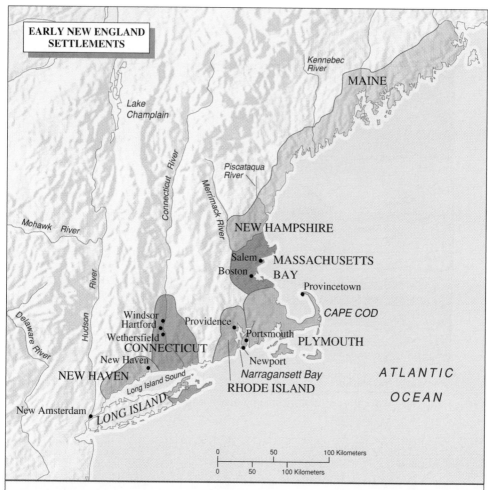

EARLY NEW ENGLAND SETTLEMENTS

Kennebec River

MAINE

Lake Champlain

Connecticut River

Merrimack River

Piscataqua River

Mohawk River

NEW HAMPSHIRE

Salem

Boston

MASSACHUSETTS BAY

Provincetown

CAPE COD

Hudson River

Windsor

Hartford

Providence

Wethersfield

CONNECTICUT

Portsmouth

PLYMOUTH

Delaware River

New Haven

Newport

NEW HAVEN

Narragansett Bay

ATLANTIC

Long Island Sound

RHODE ISLAND

OCEAN

New Amsterdam

LONG ISLAND

| 0 | | 50 | | 100 Kilometers |
| 0 | 50 | | 100 Kilometers | |

Why did European settlers first populate the Plymouth colony? How were the settlers of the Massachusetts Bay Colony different from those of Plymouth? What was the origin of the Rhode Island colony?

land grant but no charter of government from any English authority. The government grew instead out of the Mayflower Compact, which was neither exactly a constitution nor a precedent for later constitutions. Rather, it was the obvious recourse of a group that had made a covenant (or agreement) to form a church and believed God had made a covenant with them to provide a way to salvation. Thus the civil government grew naturally out of the church government, and the members of each were identical at the start. The signers of the compact at first met as the General Court, which chose the governor and his assistants (or council). Later others were admitted as members, or "freemen," but only church members were eligible. Eventually, as the colony grew, the General Court became a body of representatives from the various towns.

MASSACHUSETTS BAY   The Plymouth colony's population never rose above 7,000, and after ten years it was overshadowed by its larger neighbor, the Massachusetts Bay Colony. It, too, was originally intended to be a holy commonwealth made up of religious folk bound together in the harmonious worship of God and the pursuit of their "callings." Like the Pilgrims, most of the Puritans who colonized Massachusetts Bay were Congregationalists, who formed self-governing churches with membership limited to "visible saints"—those who could demonstrate receipt of the gift of God's grace. But unlike the Plymouth Separatists, the Puritans (who referred to themselves as the "godly") still hoped to reform the Church of England, and therefore they were called Nonseparating Congregationalists.

In 1629 King Charles I issued a charter for the Massachusetts Bay Company to a group of English Puritans led by John Winthrop, a lawyer from East Anglia animated by profound religious convictions. Winthrop, tall and strong with a long face, resolved to use the colony as a refuge for persecuted Puritans and as an instrument for building a "wilderness Zion" in America.

Winthrop shrewdly took advantage of a fateful omission in the royal charter for the Massachusetts Bay Company: the usual proviso that the company maintain its home office in England. Winthrop's group took its charter with them, thereby transferring government authority to Massachusetts Bay, where they hoped to ensure Puritan control. So unlike the Virginia Company, which ruled Jamestown from London, the Massachusetts Bay Company was self-governing.

In 1630 the *Arbella*, with John Winthrop and the charter aboard,

John Winthrop

The first governor of Massachusetts Bay Colony, in whose vision the colony would be as "a city upon a hill."

embarked with six other ships for Massachusetts. In "A Modell of Christian Charity," a lay sermon delivered on board, Winthrop told his fellow Puritans that "we must consider that we shall be a city upon a hill"—a shining example of what a godly community could be. They landed in Massachusetts, and by the end of the year seventeen ships bearing 1,000 more colonists had arrived. As settlers—both Puritan and non-Puritan—poured into the region, Boston became the new colony's chief city and capital.

The *Arbella* migrants proved to be the vanguard of a massive movement, the Great Migration, that carried some 80,000 Britons to new settlements around the world over the next decade. Fleeing religious persecution and economic depression at home, they gravitated to Ireland, the Netherlands, and the Rhineland. But the majority traveled to the New World. They went not only to New England and the Chesapeake but also to new English settlements in the Caribbean.

The transfer of the Massachusetts charter, whereby an English trading company evolved into a provincial government, was a unique venture in colonization. Under the royal charter, power in the company rested with the Massachusetts General Court, which elected the governor and the assistants. The General Court consisted of shareholders, called freemen (those who had the "freedom of the company"), but only a few besides Winthrop and his assistants had such status. That suited Winthrop and his friends, but then over 100 settlers asked to be admitted as freemen. Rather than risk trouble, the ruling group finally admitted 118 in 1631, stipulating that only church members could become freemen.

At first the freemen had no power except to choose "assistants," who in turn chose the governor and deputy governor. The procedure violated provisions of the charter, but Winthrop kept the document hidden and few knew of the exact provisions. Controversy simmered until 1634, when each town sent two delegates to Boston to confer on matters coming before the General Court. There they demanded to see the charter, which Winthrop reluctantly produced, and they read that the power to pass laws and levy taxes rested in the General Court. Winthrop argued that the body of freemen had grown too large, but when it met, the General Court responded by turning itself into a representative body with two or three deputies to represent each town. The freemen also chose a new governor, and Winthrop did not resume the office until three years later.

A final stage in the evolution of the government, a two-house legislature, came in 1644, when, according to Winthrop, "there fell out a great business upon a very small occasion." The "small occasion" pitted a poor widow against a well-to-do merchant over ownership of a stray sow. The General Court, being the supreme judicial as well as legislative body, was the final authority in the case. Popular sympathy and the deputies favored the widow,

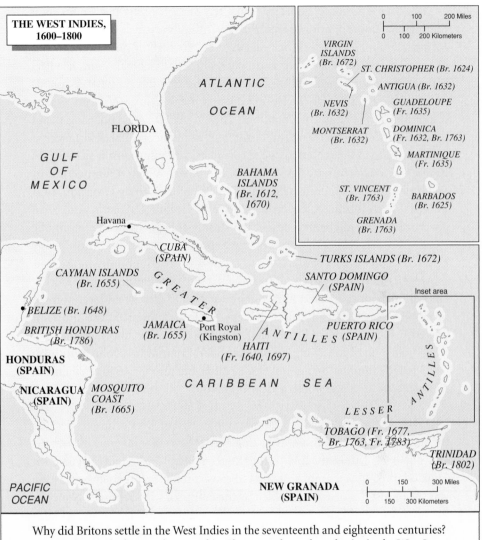

THE WEST INDIES, 1600–1800

0   100   200 Miles

0   100   200 Kilometers

ATLANTIC

OCEAN

FLORIDA

GULF
OF
MEXICO

Havana

CUBA
(SPAIN)

BAHAMA
ISLANDS
(Br. 1612,
1670)

VIRGIN
ISLANDS
(Br. 1672)

ST. CHRISTOPHER (Br. 1624)

ANTIGUA (Br. 1632)

NEVIS
(Br. 1632)

GUADELOUPE
(Fr. 1635)

MONTSERRAT
(Br. 1632)

DOMINICA
(Fr. 1632, Br. 1763)

MARTINIQUE
(Fr. 1635)

ST. VINCENT
(Br. 1763)

BARBADOS
(Br. 1625)

GRENADA
(Br. 1763)

TURKS ISLANDS (Br. 1672)

CAYMAN ISLANDS
(Br. 1655)

SANTO DOMINGO
(SPAIN)

Inset area

BELIZE (Br. 1648)

BRITISH HONDURAS
(Br. 1786)

JAMAICA
(Br. 1655)

Port Royal
(Kingston)

GREATER ANTILLES

PUERTO RICO
(SPAIN)

HAITI
(Fr. 1640, 1697)

HONDURAS
(SPAIN)

NICARAGUA
(SPAIN)

MOSQUITO
COAST
(Br. 1665)

CARIBBEAN   SEA

LESSER

ANTILLES

PACIFIC
OCEAN

NEW GRANADA
(SPAIN)

TOBAGO (Fr. 1677,
Br. 1763, Fr. 1783)

TRINIDAD
(Br. 1802)

0   150   300 Miles

0   150   300 Kilometers

Why did Britons settle in the West Indies in the seventeenth and eighteenth centuries? Keeping in mind what you have read in Chapter 1 about the colonies in the West Indies, what products would you expect those colonies to produce? Why would those colonies have had strategic importance to the British?

but the assistants disagreed. The case was finally settled out of court, but the assistants feared being outvoted on some greater occasion. They therefore secured a separation into two houses, and Massachusetts thenceforth had a bicameral assembly, the deputies and assistants sitting apart, with all decisions requiring a majority in each house.

Thus over a period of fourteen years, the Massachusetts Bay Company, a trading corporation, evolved into the governing body of a commonwealth. Membership in a Puritan church replaced the purchase of stock as the means of becoming a freeman, which was to say a voter. The General Court, like Parliament, became a representative body of two houses: the House of Assistants corresponding roughly to the House of Lords and the House of Deputies corresponding to the House of Commons. The charter remained unchanged, but practice under the charter was quite different from the original expectation.

It is hard to exaggerate the crucial role played by John Winthrop in establishing the Massachusetts Bay Colony. He had been a man of limited means and little stature who nonetheless, as the new colony's godly governor, summoned up extraordinary leadership abilities. A devout pragmatist who often governed as an enlightened despot, he steadfastly sought to steer a middle course between clerical absolutists and Separatist zealots. Winthrop firmly believed that God had chosen him to create a godly community in the New World. His stern charisma and his indefatigable faith in the ideal of Christian republicanism enabled him to fend off Indian attacks and antinomian insurgencies as well as political challenges. He also thwarted the efforts of powerful foes in England who challenged the infant colony's legality. An iron-souled man governing a God-saturated community, John Winthrop provided the foundation not only for a colony but also for major elements in America's cultural and political development.

RHODE ISLAND   More by accident than design, Massachusetts became the staging area for the rest of New England as new colonies grew out of religious quarrels within the fold. Young Roger Williams, who had arrived from England in 1631, was among the first to cause problems, precisely because he was the purest of Puritans, troubled by the failure of Massachusetts Nonconformists to repudiate the Church of England entirely. Whereas John Winthrop cherished authority, Roger Williams championed liberty. Unlike the Puritans and the Pilgrims, who asserted that God created a covenant with each congregation, Williams came to believe that the true covenant was between God and the individual. He was one of a small but growing number of Puritans who began to question the seeming contradiction at the heart of Calvinism: if one's salvation depends solely upon God's grace and one can do nothing to affect it, why bother to have churches at all? Why not endow individuals with the authority to exercise their free will in worshipping God?

Williams held a brief pastorate in Salem, then moved to Separatist Plymouth. Governor Bradford found Williams to be gentle and kind in his personal relations as well as a charismatic speaker. But he charged that

The Anabaptiſt   The Brownift

The Familiſt   The Papiſt

The Church of England

Religious quarrels within the Puritan fold led to the founding of new colonies. In this seventeenth-century cartoon, four Englishmen, each representing a party in opposition to the established church, are shown fighting over the Bible.

Williams "began to fall into strange opinions," specifically, questioning the king's right to confiscate Indian lands. Williams then returned to Salem. Williams's belief that a true church must include only those who had received God's gift of grace led him eventually to the conclusion that no true church was possible, unless perhaps consisting of his wife and himself.

In Williams's view the purity of the church required complete separation of church and state and freedom from coercion in matters of faith. "Forced worship," he declared, "stinks in God's nostrils." Williams therefore questioned the authority of government to impose an oath of allegiance and rejected laws imposing religious conformity. Such views were too radical even for the progressive church of Salem, which finally removed him, whereupon Williams retorted so hotly against "ulcered and gangrened" churches that the General Court in 1635 banished him to England. Governor Winthrop, however, permitted Williams to slip away with his family and a few followers and seek shelter among the Narragansett Indians, whom he had befriended. In 1636 Williams established the town of Providence at the head of Narragansett Bay, the first permanent settlement in Rhode Island and the first in America to legislate freedom of religion. There he welcomed all who fled religious persecution in Massachusetts Bay. For their part, Boston officials came to view Rhode Island as a refuge for rogues.

Anne Hutchinson quarreled with the Puritan leaders for different reasons. The articulate, strong-willed, intelligent wife of a prominent merchant, she raised thirteen children, served as a healer and midwife, and hosted meetings in her Boston home to discuss sermons. Soon, however, the discussions turned into large forums for Hutchinson's commentaries on religious matters. She claimed to have experienced direct revelations from the Holy Spirit that convinced her that only two or three Puritan ministers actually preached the appropriate "covenant of grace." The others, she claimed, were godless hypocrites, deluded and incompetent; the "covenant of works" they promoted led people to believe that good conduct would ensure salvation. Eventually Hutchinson claimed to know which of her neighbors had been saved and which were damned.

Hutchinson's beliefs were provocative for several reasons. Puritan theology was grounded in the Calvinist doctrine that people could be saved only by God's grace rather than through their own willful actions. But Puritanism in practice also insisted that ministers were necessary to interpret God's will for the people so as to "prepare" them for the possibility of their being selected for salvation. In challenging the very legitimacy of the ministerial community as well as the hard-earned assurances of salvation enjoyed by current church members, Hutchinson was undermining the stability of an already fragile social system. Moreover, her critics likened her claim of direct revelations from the Holy Spirit to the antinomian heresy, a subversive belief that one is freed from obeying the moral law by one's own faith and by God's grace. Unlike Roger Williams, Hutchinson did not advocate religious individualism. Instead, she sought to eradicate the concept of "grace by good works" infecting Puritan orthodoxy. She did not represent a forerunner of modern feminism or freedom of conscience. Instead, she was a proponent of a theocratic extremism that threatened the solidarity of the commonwealth.

What made the situation worse in the male-dominated society of seventeenth-century New England was that a *woman* was making such charges and assertions. Mrs. Hutchinson had both offended authority and sanctioned a disruptive self-righteousness.

A pregnant Hutchinson was hauled before the General Court in 1637, and for two days she sparred on equal terms with the presiding magistrates and testifying ministers. Her skillful deflections of the charges and her ability to cite chapter-and-verse biblical defenses of her actions led an exasperated Governor Winthrop at one point to explode, "We do not mean to discourse with those of your sex." He found Hutchinson to be "a woman of haughty and fierce carriage, of a nimble wit and active spirit, and a very voluble tongue." As the trial continued, an overwrought Hutchinson was eventually lured into convicting herself by claiming direct divine inspiration—blasphemy in the eyes of orthodox Puritans.

Banished in 1638 as a leper not fit for "our society," Hutchinson settled with her family and a few followers on an island south of Providence, near what is now Portsmouth, Rhode Island. But the arduous journey had taken its toll. Hutchinson grew sick, and her baby was stillborn, leading her critics in Massachusetts to assert that the "monstrous birth" was God's way of punishing her for her sins. Hutchinson's spirits never recovered. After her husband's death, in 1642, she moved to New York City, then under Dutch jurisdiction, and the following year she and five of her children were massacred and scalped during an Indian attack. Her fate, wrote a vindictive Winthrop, was "a special manifestation of divine justice."

Thus the colony of Rhode Island and Providence Plantations, the smallest in America, grew up in Narragansett Bay as a refuge for dissenters who agreed that the state had no right to coerce religious belief. In 1640 they formed a confederation and in 1643 secured their first charter of incorporation as Providence Plantations. Roger Williams lived until 1683, an active and beloved citizen of the commonwealth he founded, in a society that, during his lifetime at least, lived up to his principles of religious freedom and a government based on the consent of the people.

CONNECTICUT   Connecticut had a more orthodox beginning than Rhode Island. In 1633 a group from Plymouth settled in the Connecticut River valley. Three years later Thomas Hooker led three entire church congregations from Massachusetts Bay to the Connecticut River towns of Wethersfield, Windsor, and Hartford.

For a year the settlers in the river towns were governed under a commission from the Massachusetts General Court, but the inhabitants organized the self-governing colony of Connecticut in 1637. Two years later the Connecticut General Court adopted the Fundamental Orders, a series of laws that provided for a government like that of Massachusetts, except that voting was not limited to church members. New Haven had by then emerged as a major settlement within Connecticut. A group of English Puritans, led by their minister and a wealthy merchant, had migrated first to Massachusetts and then, seeking a place to establish themselves in commerce, to New Haven, on Long Island Sound, in 1638. The New Haven colony became the most rigorously Puritan of all. Like all the other offshoots of Massachusetts, it lacked a charter and for a time maintained a self-governing independence. In 1662 it was absorbed into Connecticut under the terms of that colony's first royal charter.

NEW HAMPSHIRE AND MAINE   To the north of Massachusetts, most of what are now the states of New Hampshire and Maine was granted in 1622 by the Council for New England to Sir Ferdinando Gorges and Captain John Mason and their associates. In 1629 Mason and Gorges divided their territory at the Piscataqua River, Mason taking the southern part, which he named New Hampshire, and Gorges taking the northern part, which became the province of Maine. In the 1630s Puritan immigrants began filtering in, and in 1638 the Reverend John Wheelwright, one of Anne Hutchinson's group, founded Exeter, New Hampshire. Maine at that time consisted of a few scattered settlements, mostly fishing stations.

An ambiguity in the Massachusetts charter brought the proprietorships into doubt, however. The charter set the boundary three miles north of the Merrimack River, and the Bay Colony took that to mean north of the river's northernmost reach, which gave it a claim to nearly the entire Gorges-Mason grant. During the English civil strife in the early 1640s, Massachusetts took over New Hampshire and in the 1650s extended its authority to the scattered settlements in Maine. This led to lawsuits with the heirs of the proprietors, and in 1678 English judges and the Privy Council decided against Massachusetts in both cases. In 1679 New Hampshire became a royal colony, but Massachusetts bought out the Gorges heirs and continued to control Maine as its proprietor. A new Massachusetts charter in 1691 finally incorporated Maine into Massachusetts.

INDIANS IN NEW ENGLAND

The English settlers who poured into New England found not a "virgin land" of uninhabited wilderness but a developed region populated by over 100,000 Indians of diverse tribes. The white colonists considered the natives wild pagans incapable of fully exploiting nature's bounty. In their view, God meant for the Puritans to take over Indian lands as a reward for their piety and hard work. The town meeting of Milford, Connecticut, for example, voted in 1640 that the land was God's "and that the earth is given to the Saints; voted, we are the Saints."

Indians coped with the newcomers in different ways. Many resisted, others sought accommodation, and still others grew dependent on European culture. In some areas, Indians survived and even flourished in concert with European settlers over long periods of time and with varying degrees of advantage. In other areas, land-hungry whites quickly displaced or decimated the native populations. The interactions of the two cultures involved misunderstandings, the mutual need for trade and adaptation, and sporadic outbreaks of epidemics and warfare.

In general, the English colonists adopted a strategy for dealing with the Native American quite different from that of the French and the Dutch. Merchants from France and the Netherlands were preoccupied with exploiting the fur trade. To do so, they built permanent trading outposts and established amicable relations with the far more numerous Indians in the region. In contrast, the English colonists were more interested in pursuing their "God-given" right to fish and farm. They were quite willing to manipulate and exploit Indians rather than deal with them on an equal footing. Their goal was subordination rather than reciprocity.

THE NEW ENGLAND INDIANS In Maine the Abenakis were primarily hunters and gatherers dependent upon the natural offerings of the land and waters. The men did the hunting and fishing; the women retrieved the dead game and prepared it for eating. Women were also responsible for setting up and breaking camp, gathering fruits and berries, and raising the children. The Algonquian tribes of southern New England—the Massachusetts, Nausets, Narragansets, Pequots, and Wampanoags—were more horticultural. Their highly developed agricultural system centered on three primary crops: corn, beans, and pumpkins.

The Indians' dependence on nature for their survival shaped their religious beliefs. They believed in a Creator who provided them with the land and its bountiful resources. Many rituals, ceremonies, and taboos acknowledged their dependence upon the gods. Rain dances, harvest festivals, and sacrificial offerings bespoke a culture whose fate was dependent upon supernatural powers.

Initially the coastal Indians helped the white settlers develop a subsistence economy. They taught the Europeans how to plant corn and use fish for fertilizer. They also developed a flourishing trade with the newcomers, exchanging furs for manufactured goods and "trinkets." The various Indian tribes of New England often fought among themselves, usually over disputed land. Had they been able to forge a solid alliance, they would have been better able to resist the encroachments of white settlers. As it was, they were not only fragmented but also vulnerable to the infectious diseases carried on board the ships transporting European settlers to the New World. Epidemics of smallpox soon devastated the Indian population, leaving the coastal areas "a widowed land." Between 1610 and 1675 the Abenakis declined from 12,000 to 3,000 and the southern New England tribes from 65,000 to 10,000. Governor William Bradford of Plymouth reported that the Indians "fell sick of the smallpox, and died most miserably." By the hundreds they died "like rotten sheep."

THE PEQUOT WAR   Indians who survived the epidemics and refused to yield their lands were often dislodged by force. In 1636 settlers in Massachusetts accused a Pequot of murdering a colonist. Joined by Connecticut colonists, they exacted their revenge by setting fire to a Pequot village on the Mystic River. As the Indians fled their burning huts, the Puritans shot and killed them—men, women, and children. In less than an hour, all but seven escapees were dead.

Sassacus, the Pequot chief, organized the survivors among his followers and attacked the whites. During the Pequot War of 1637, the colonists and their Narragansett allies indiscriminately killed hundreds of Pequots in their village near West Mystic, in the Connecticut River valley. The magisterial Puritan minister Cotton Mather later described the slaughter as a "sweet sacrifice" and "gave the praise thereof to God."

Only a few colonists regretted the massacre. Roger Williams warned that the lust for land would become "as great a God with us English as God Gold was with the Spanish." With poignant clarity, Pequot survivors recognized the motives of the English settlers: "We see plainly that their chiefest desire is to deprive us of the privilege of our land, and drive us to our utter ruin." Indeed, the colonists captured most of the surviving Pequots and sold them into slavery in Bermuda. Under the terms of the Treaty of Hartford (1638), the Pequot Nation was declared dissolved.

KING PHILIP'S WAR   After the Pequot War the prosperous fur trade contributed to peaceful relations between whites and the remaining Indians, but the relentless growth of the New England colonies and the decline of the beaver population began to reduce the eastern tribes to relative poverty. The colonial government repeatedly encroached upon Indian settlements, forcing them to acknowledge English laws and customs. At the same time that colonial leaders expropriated Indian lands, Puritan missionaries sought to

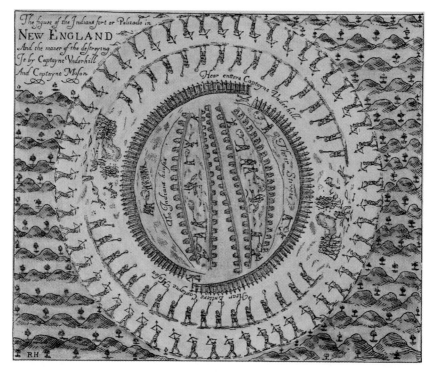

Pequot Fort

The Puritans and their Indian allies, the Narragansetts, mount a ferocious attack on the Pequots at Mystic, Connecticut (1637).

convert the tribes to Christianity. Hundreds of converts settled in special "praying Indian" towns. By 1675 the natives and settlers had come to know each other well—and fear each other deeply.

The era of fairly peaceful coexistence that began with the Treaty of Hartford came to an end during the last quarter of the seventeenth century. In 1675 Philip (Metacom), chief of the Wampanoags and the son of Massasoit, who had helped the original Pilgrims, forged an alliance among the remaining tribes of southern New England. The spark that set New England ablaze was the murder of John Sassamon, a "praying Indian" who had attended Harvard and served as a British spy. He had warned the colonists that Metacom was planning to attack them. The officials of the Plymouth colony tried and executed three Wampanoags for the murder of Sassamon. In retaliation the Indians attacked and burned colonial settlements throughout Massachusetts.

Both sides suffered incredible losses in what came to be called King Philip's War or Metacomet's War. The fighting killed more people and caused more destruction in New England in proportion to the population than any American conflict since. Bands of Indian warriors assaulted thirty towns. Within a year the Indians were threatening Boston itself. Finally, however, depleted supplies and staggering casualties wore down Indian resistance. Philip's wife and son were captured and sold into slavery. Some of the tribes surrendered, a few succumbed to disease, while others fled to the west. Those who remained were forced to resettle in villages supervised by white settlers. Philip initially escaped, only to be hunted down and killed in 1676. The victorious colonists marched Philip's severed head on a pike to Plymouth, where it sat atop a pole for twenty years, a gruesome reminder of the British determination to assert control over the Indians. King Philip's War devastated the Native American culture in New England. Combat deaths, deportations, and flight cut the region's Indian population in half. Military victory also enabled the Puritan authorities to increase their political, economic, legal, and religious control over the 9,000 Indians who remained.

THE ENGLISH CIVIL WAR IN AMERICA

By 1640 English settlers in New England and around Chesapeake Bay had established two great beachheads on the Atlantic coast, with the Dutch colony of New Netherland in between. After 1640, however, the struggle between king and Parliament distracted attention from colonization, and migration dwindled to a trickle for more than twenty years. During the English Civil War and Oliver Cromwell's Puritan dictatorship, the struggling colonies were left pretty much to their own devices, especially in New England, where English Puritans saw little need to intervene.

In 1643 four of the New England colonies—Massachusetts Bay, Plymouth, Connecticut, and New Haven—formed the New England Confederation to provide joint defense against the Dutch, French, and Indians. Two commissioners from each colony met annually to transact business. In some ways the confederation behaved like a sovereign power. It made treaties, and in 1653 it declared war against the Dutch, who were supposedly inciting the Indians to attack Connecticut. Massachusetts, far from the scene of trouble, failed to cooperate, greatly weakening the confederation. But the commissioners continued to meet annually until 1684, when Massachusetts lost its charter.

Virginia and Maryland remained almost as independent as New England. At the behest of Governor William Berkeley, the Virginia burgesses in 1649 denounced the execution of King Charles and recognized his son, Charles II, as the lawful king. In 1652, however, the assembly yielded to parliamentary commissioners and overruled the governor. In return for the surrender, the commissioners let the assembly choose its own council and governor, and the colony grew rapidly in population during its years of independent government, some of the growth coming from the arrival of Royalists, who found a friendly haven in Virginia, despite its capitulation to the English Puritans.

The parliamentary commissioners who won the submission of Virginia proceeded to Maryland where the proprietary governor faced particular difficulties with his Protestant majority, largely Puritan but including some earlier refugees from Anglican Virginia. At the governor's suggestion the assembly had passed, and the proprietor had accepted, the Maryland Toleration Act of 1649, an assurance that Puritans would not be molested in the practice of their religion. In 1654 the commissioners revoked the Toleration Act and deprived Lord Baltimore of his government rights, though not of his lands and revenues. Still, the more extreme Puritan elements were dissatisfied, and a brief clash in 1654 brought civil war to Maryland and led to the deposing of the governor. But Oliver Cromwell took the side of Lord Baltimore and restored his full rights in 1657, whereupon the Toleration Act was reinstated. The act deservedly stands as a landmark to human liberty, albeit enacted more out of expediency than conviction.

Cromwell let the colonies go their own way, but he was not indifferent to Britain's North American empire. He fought trade wars with the Dutch, and his navy harassed England's traditional enemy, Catholic Spain, in the Caribbean. In 1655 a British force wrested Jamaica from the Spaniards, thereby improving the odds for English privateers and pirates who pillaged Spanish ships.

The Restoration of King Charles II in 1660 led to an equally painless restoration of previous governments in the colonies. The process involved scarcely any change since little had changed under Cromwell. Immigration rapidly expanded the populations in Virginia and Maryland. Fears of reprisals against Puritan New England proved unfounded, at least for the time being. Agents hastily dispatched by the colonies won reconfirmation of the Massachusetts charter in 1662 and the very first royal charters for Connecticut and Rhode Island in 1662 and 1663. All three retained their status as self-governing corporations. Plymouth still had no charter, but it went unmolested. New Haven, however, disappeared as a separate entity, absorbed into the colony of Connecticut.

SETTLING THE CAROLINAS

The Restoration of Charles II in 1660 revived interest in colonial expansion. Within twelve years the English would conquer New Netherland, settle Carolina, and very nearly fill out the shape of the colonies. In the middle region formerly claimed by the Dutch, four new colonies sprang into being: New York, New Jersey, Pennsylvania, and Delaware. Without exception the new colonies were proprietary, awarded by the king to men who had remained loyal or had brought about his restoration or, in one case, to whom he was indebted. In 1663, for example, he granted Carolina to eight prominent allies, who became lords proprietors of the region.

NORTH CAROLINA   Carolina was from the start made up of two widely separated areas of settlement, which finally became separate colonies. The northernmost part, long called Albemarle, had been settled in the 1650s by stragglers who had drifted southward from Virginia. For half a century, Albemarle remained a remote scattering of settlers along the shores of Albemarle Sound, isolated from Virginia by the Dismal Swamp and lacking easy access for oceangoing vessels. Albemarle had no governor until 1664, no assembly until 1665, and not even a town until a group of French Huguenots founded the village of Bath in 1704.

SOUTH CAROLINA   The eight lords proprietors (owners) to whom the king had given Carolina neglected Albemarle from the outset and focused on more promising sites to the south. They recruited seasoned British planters from Barbados to replicate in South Carolina the West Indian sugar-plantation system based on African slave labor. The first British colonists arrived in South Carolina in 1669 at Charles Town (later named Charleston). Over the next twenty years, half the British colonists came from Barbados.

The government of South Carolina rested upon one of the most curious documents of colonial history, the Fundamental Constitutions of Carolina, drawn up by one of the proprietors, Lord Anthony Ashley Cooper, with the help of his secretary, the philosopher John Locke. Its cumbersome frame of government and its provisions for an elaborate nobility had little effect in the colony except to encourage a practice of large land grants. From the beginning, however, smaller headrights were given to every immigrant who could afford the cost of transit. The most enticing provision was a grant of religious toleration, designed to encourage immigration, which gave South Carolina a greater degree of indulgence (extending even to Jews and "heathens") than England or any other colony except Rhode Island and, once it was established, Pennsylvania. South Carolina became a separate royal colony in 1719. North Carolina remained under the proprietors' rule for ten more years, until they transferred their governing rights to the British crown.

EARLY
SETTLEMENTS
IN THE SOUTH

VIRGINIA

James River

Roanoke River

Albemarle
Sound

*Occaneechi
Trading
Path* Bath

Roanoke
Island

APPALACHIAN MOUNTAINS

PIEDMONT

Cape Fear River

NORTH
CAROLINA

SOUTH
CAROLINA

Savannah River

Oconee R.

Ashley
River

Cooper River

Charles Town

GEORGIA

Altamaha River

Savannah

ATLANTIC
OCEAN

Added to Georgia,
1763

St. Mary's River

FLORIDA
(Spanish)

St. Augustine
(Spanish)

GULF
OF
MEXICO

0   100   200 Miles

0   100   200 Kilometers

How were the Carolina colonies created? What were the impedi-
ments to settling North Carolina? How did the lord proprietors
settle South Carolina? What were the major items traded by settlers in South Carolina?

THE SOUTHERN INDIAN TRADE The English proprietors of
South Carolina wanted the colony to focus on producing commercial crops
(staples). Such production took time to develop, however. Land had to be
cleared and grubbed, crops planted and harvested. These activities required
laborers. Some Carolina planters brought enslaved Africans and indentured
servants with them. But many more workers were needed, yet slaves and
servants were expensive. The quickest way to raise capital in the early years
of South Carolina's development was through trade with the Indians.

In the late seventeenth century, English merchants—mostly illiterate adventurers—began traveling southward from Virginia into the Piedmont region of Carolina, where they developed a prosperous exchange with the
Catawba Indians. By 1690 traders from Charles Town, South Carolina, had
made their way up the Savannah River to arrange deals with the Cherokees,

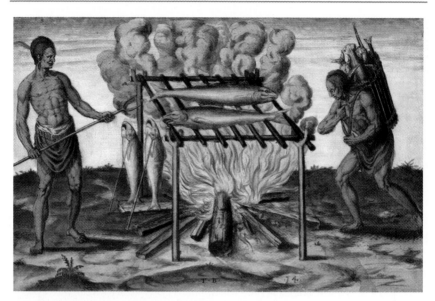

The Broiling of Their Fish Over the Flame

In this drawing by John White, reproduced in an engraving by Theodor de Bry, Algonquian men in North Carolina broil fish, a dietary staple of coastal societies.

Creeks, and Chickasaws. Thus between 1699 and 1715 Carolina exported an average of 54,000 deerskins per year. Europeans transformed the valuable hides into bookbindings, gloves, belts, hats, and work aprons. The voracious demand for the soft skins almost exterminated the deer population.

The growing trade with the English exposed the Indians to contagious diseases that decimated the population. Commercial activity also entwined the Indians in a dependent relationship that would prove disastrous to their traditional way of life. Eager to receive more finished goods, weapons, and ammunition, the Indians became pliable trading partners, easily manipulated by wily English entrepreneurs and government officials. The English traders began providing the Indians with firearms and rum as incentives to persuade them to capture rivals to be sold as slaves.

While colonists themselves captured and enslaved Indians, the Westos, Creeks, and most other tribes willingly captured other Indians and drove them to the coast to be exchanged for British trade goods, guns, and rum. Colonists, in turn, put some of the Indian captives to work on their plantations. But because Indian captives often ran away, the traders preferred to ship the enslaved Indians to New York, Boston, and the West Indies and import enslaved Africans to work in the Carolinas.

Cherokee Chiefs

A contemporary print depicting seven chiefs of the Cherokee Indians who had been taken from Carolina to England in 1730.

The complex profitability of Indian captives prompted a frenzy of slaving activity. Slave traders turned Indian tribes against one another in order to ensure a continuous supply of captives. As many as 50,000 Indians, most of them women and children, were sold as slaves in Charles Town between 1670 and 1715. More Indians were exported during that period than Africans were imported. Thousands more captured Indians circulated through such New England ports as Boston and Salem. Although the South Carolina proprietors in England expressly prohibited the enslavement of Indians, the traders paid no attention. The burgeoning trade in Indian slaves triggered bitter struggles between tribes, gave rise to unprecedented colonial warfare, and spawned massive internal migrations across the southern colonies.

During the last quarter of the seventeenth century, the trade in Indian slaves spread across the entire Southeast. Slave raiding became the region's single most important economic activity and a powerful weapon in Britain's global conflict with France and Spain. During the early eighteenth century, Indians equipped with British weapons and led by English soldiers crossed into Spanish territory in south Georgia and north Florida. They destroyed thirteen Spanish missions, killed several hundred Indians and Spaniards, and enslaved over 300 Indian men, women, and children. By 1710 the Florida tribes were on the verge of extinction. In 1708, when the total population of

A War Dance

The Westo Indians of Georgia, pictured here doing a war dance, were among the first Native Americans to obtain firearms and used this advantage to enslave Indians throughout Georgia, Florida, and the Carolinas.

South Carolina was 9,580, including 2,900 Africans, there were 1,400 enslaved Indians.

The continuing Indian trade led to escalating troubles. Fears of slave raids disrupted the planting cycle in Indian villages. Some tribes fled the South altogether. In 1712 the Tuscaroras of North Carolina attacked German and English colonists who had encroached upon their land. North Carolina authorities appealed to South Carolina for aid, and the colony, eager for more slaves, dispatched two expeditions made up mostly of Indian allies—Yamasees, Cherokees, Creeks, and Catawbas— led by whites. In 1713 they destroyed a Tuscarora town, executed 162 male warriors, and took 392 women and children captive for sale in Charles Town. The surviving Tuscaroras fled north, where they joined the Iroquois Confederacy.

The Tuscarora War led to more conflict. The Yamasees felt betrayed when white traders paid them less for their Tuscarora captives than they wanted. What made this shortfall so acute was that the Yamasees owed debts to traders totaling 100,000 deerskins—almost five years worth of hunting. To recover their debts, white traders cheated Yamasees, confiscated their lands, and began enslaving their women and children. In April 1715 the enraged Yamasees attacked coastal plantations and killed over 100 whites. Their vengeful assaults continued for months, aided by Creeks. Most of the white traders were killed, including one who had pine splinters shoved under his skin and then lit. Whites throughout the low country of South Carolina panicked; hundreds fled to Charles Town. The governor mobilized all white and black males to defend the colony. Other colonies supplied weapons. But it was not until the governor persuaded the Cherokees (with the inducement of many gifts) to join them against the Yamasees and Creeks that the Yamasee War ended—in the spring of 1716. The defeated Yamasees fled to Spanish-controlled Florida. By then some 400 whites had been killed and dozens of plantations destroyed and abandoned. To prevent another tragic conflict, the colonial government outlawed all private trading with Indians. Commerce between whites and Indians could now occur only through a colonial agency created to end abuses and shift activity from slaving to deerskins.

The end of the Yamasee War did not stop infighting among the Indians, however. For the next ten years or so the Creeks and Cherokees engaged in a costly blood feud, much to the delight of the English. One Carolinian explained that their challenge was to figure "how to hold both [tribes] as our friends, for some time, and assist them in cutting one another's throats without offending either. This is the game we intend to play if possible." The French played the same brutal game, doing their best to excite hatred between the Choctaws and the Chickasaws. Between 1700 and 1730 the Indian population in the Carolinas dwindled from 15,000 to just 4,000.

SETTLING THE MIDDLE COLONIES AND GEORGIA

NEW NETHERLAND BECOMES NEW YORK   King Charles II resolved early to pluck out that old thorn in the side of the English colonies: New Netherland. The Dutch colony was older than New England, having been planted when the two Protestant powers allied in opposition to Catholic Spain. The Dutch East India Company (organized in 1602) had hired an English captain, Henry Hudson, to seek the elusive passage to China. Sailing along the upper coast of North America in 1609, Hudson had discovered Delaware Bay and explored the river named for him, venturing 160 miles to a point probably beyond what is now Albany, where he and a group of Mohawks began a lasting trade relationship between the Dutch and the Iroquois Nations. In 1610 the Dutch established fur-trading posts on Manhattan Island and upriver at Fort Orange (later Albany). In 1626 Governor Peter Minuit purchased Manhattan from the resident Indians, and a Dutch fort appeared at the lower end of the island. The village of New Amsterdam, which grew up around the fort, became the capital of New Netherland and developed into the rollicking commercial New World powerhouse. Unlike their Puritan counterparts in Massachusetts Bay, the Dutch in New Amsterdam were preoccupied more with profits and freedoms than with piety and restrictions. They embraced free enterprise and ethnic and religious diversity.

Dutch settlements gradually dispersed in every direction in which furs might be found. In 1638 a Swedish trading company established Fort

Christina at the site of present-day Wilmington, Delaware, and scattered a few hundred settlers up and down the Delaware River. The Dutch, at the time allied with the Swedes in the Thirty Years' War, made no move to challenge the claim until 1655, when a force outnumbering the entire Swedish colony subjected them without bloodshed to the rule of New Netherland. The chief contribution of the short-lived New Sweden to American culture was the idea of the log cabin, which the Swedes and a few Finnish settlers had brought from the woods of Scandinavia.

Like the French, the Dutch were interested mainly in the fur trade rather than agricultural settlements. In 1629, however, the Dutch West India Company (organized in 1623) decided that it needed a mass of settlers to help protect the colony's "front door" at the mouth of the Hudson River. It provided that any stockholder might obtain a large estate (a patroonship) if he peopled it with fifty adults within four years. The "patroon" was obligated to supply cattle, tools, and buildings. His tenants, in turn, paid him rent, used his gristmill, gave him first option to purchase surplus crops, and submitted to a court he established. It amounted to transplanting the feudal manor to the New World, and it met with as little luck as similar efforts in Maryland and South Carolina. Volunteers for serfdom were hard to find when there was land to be had elsewhere; most settlers took advantage of the company's provision that one could have as farms (*bouweries*) all the lands one could improve.

The colony's government was under the almost absolute control of a governor sent out by the Dutch West India Company. The governors were mostly stubborn autocrats, either corrupt or inept, and especially clumsy at Indian relations. They depended on a small army garrison for defense, and the inhabitants (including a number of English on Long Island), were hardly devoted to the Dutch government. New Amsterdam was by far the most diverse of the American colonies. Its residents included Swedes, Norwegians, Spaniards, Sephardic Jews, free blacks, English, Germans, and Finns—as well as Dutch. The polyglot colonists prized their liberties and lived in a smoldering state of near mutiny against the colony's governors. In fact, in 1664 they showed almost total indifference when Governor Peter Stuyvesant called them to arms against a threatening British fleet. Almost defenseless, old soldier Stuyvesant blustered and stomped about on his wooden leg but finally surrendered without firing a shot and stayed on quietly at his farm in what became the colony of New York.

The plan of conquest had been hatched by the king's brother, the duke of York, later King James II. As lord high admiral and an investor in the African trade, he had already harassed Dutch shipping and forts in Africa. When he

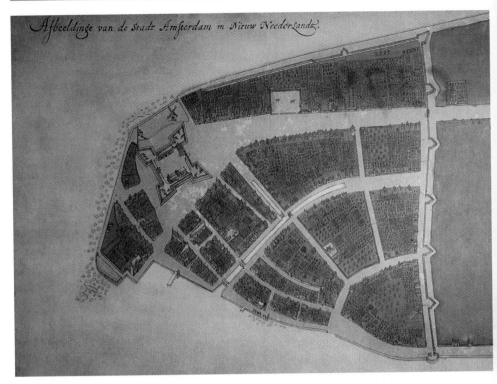

Afbeeldinge van de Stadt Amsterdam in Nieuw Nederlandt.

Castello Plan of New Amsterdam

A map of New Amsterdam in 1660, shortly before the English took the colony from the Dutch and christened it New York.

and his advisers counseled that New Netherland could easily be conquered, Charles II simply granted the region to his brother as proprietor and permitted the hasty gathering of an invasion force, and the English thus transformed New Amsterdam into New York and Fort Orange into Albany. The Dutch, however, left a permanent imprint on the land and the language: the Dutch vernacular faded, but place-names such as Block Island, Wall Street (the original wall being for protection against Indians), and Broadway (Breede Wegh) remained, along with family names like Rensselaer, Roosevelt, and Van Buren. The Dutch presence lingered, too, in the Dutch Reformed Church; in words like *boss, cookie, crib, snoop, stoop, spook,* and *kill* (for "creek"); and in the legendary Santa Claus and in Washington Irving's Rip van Winkle.

Even more important to the development of the American colonies was New Netherland's political principles, as embodied in the formal document transferring governance of the colony from the Dutch to the British. Called the Articles of Capitulation, the document provided a guarantee of individual rights unparalleled in the colonies. The articles, which endorsed free trade, religious liberty, and local political representation, were incorporated into the New York City Charter of 1686 and thereafter served as a benchmark for disputes with Britain over colonial rights.

THE IROQUOIS LEAGUE   One of the most significant effects of European settlement in North America during the seventeenth century was the intensification of warfare among Indian peoples. The same combination of forces that decimated the Indian populations of New England and the Carolinas affected the tribes around New York City and the lower Hudson Valley. Dissension among the Indians and susceptibility to infectious disease left them vulnerable to exploitation by whites and other Indians.

In the interior of New York, however, a different situation arose. There the tribes of the Iroquois (an Algonquian term signifying "Snake" or "Terrifying Man") forged an alliance so strong that the outnumbered Dutch and, later, English traders were forced to work with the Indians in exploiting the lucrative fur trade. By the early 1600s some fifty sachems (chiefs) governed the 12,000 members of the Iroquois League, or Iroquois Confederacy. The sachems made decisions for all the villages and mediated tribal rivalries and dissension within the confederacy.

Wampum Belt

The diamond shapes at the center of this "covenant chain" belt indicate community alliances. Wampum belts such as this one were often used to certify treaties or record transactions.

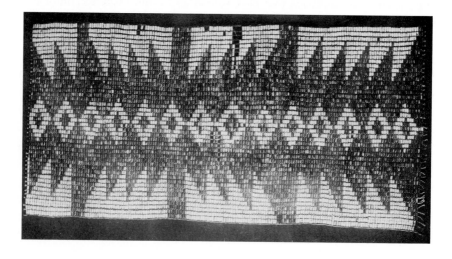

When the Iroquois began to deplete the local game during the 1640s, they used firearms supplied by their Dutch trading partners to seize the Canadian hunting grounds of the neighboring Hurons and Eries. During the so-called Beaver Wars the Iroquois defeated the western tribes and thereafter hunted the beaver in the region to extinction.

Iroquois men were proud, ruthless warriors. Participation in a war party served as the crucial rite of passage for young men. They fought opponents to gain status or ease the grief caused by the deaths of friends and relatives. Their skill and courage in battle determined their social status. A warrior's success was measured not only by his fighting prowess but also by his ability to take prisoners and bring them back alive for adoption or ritualistic execution.

During the second half of the seventeenth century, the relentless search for furs and captives led Iroquois war parties to range far across what is today eastern North America. They gained control over a huge area from the St. Lawrence River to Tennessee and from Maine to Michigan. The Iroquois's wars helped reorient the political relationships in the whole eastern half of the continent, especially in the area from the Ohio River valley northward across the Great Lakes basin. Besieged by the Iroquois League, the western tribes forged defensive alliances with the French.

For over twenty years, warfare raged across the Great Lakes region. In the 1690s the French and their Indian allies gained the advantage over the Iroquois. They destroyed Iroquois crops and villages, infected them with smallpox, and reduced the male population by more than one third. Facing extermination, the Iroquois made peace with the French in 1701. During the first half of the eighteenth century, they maintained a shrewd neutrality in the struggle between the two rival European powers, which enabled them to play the British off against the French while creating a thriving fur trade for themselves.

NEW JERSEY   Shortly after the conquest of New Netherland, the duke of York granted his lands between the Hudson and Delaware rivers to Sir George Carteret and Lord John Berkeley (brother of Virginia's governor) and named the territory for Carteret's native Jersey, an island in the English Channel. In 1676, by mutual agreement, the colony was divided by a diagonal line into East and West Jersey, with Carteret taking the east. Finally, in 1682, Carteret sold out to a group of twelve, including William Penn, who in turn brought into the partnership twelve more proprietors, for a total of twenty-four. In East Jersey, peopled at first by perhaps 200 Dutch who had crossed the Hudson River, new settlements gradually arose: some disaffected Puritans from New Haven founded Newark, Carteret's brother brought a

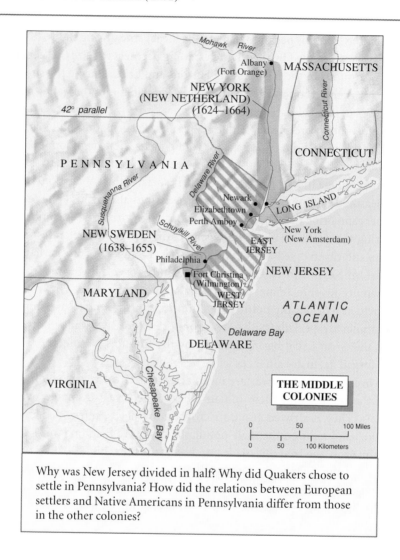

Why was New Jersey divided in half? Why did Quakers chose to settle in Pennsylvania? How did the relations between European settlers and Native Americans in Pennsylvania differ from those in the other colonies?

group to found Elizabethtown (Elizabeth), and a group of Scots founded Perth Amboy. In the west, facing the Delaware River, a scattering of Swedes, Finns, and Dutch remained, soon to be overwhelmed by swarms of English Quakers. In 1702 East and West Jersey were united as the single royal colony of New Jersey.

PENNSYLVANIA AND DELAWARE   The Quaker sect, as the Society of Friends was called in ridicule (because they were supposed to "tremble at the word of the Lord"), became the most influential of many radical

The Quakers Meeting

A Quaker meeting, at which the presence of women is evidence of Quaker views on the equality of the sexes.

groups that sprang from the turbulence of the English Civil War. Founded by George Fox in about 1647, the Quakers carried further than any other group the doctrine of individual inspiration and interpretation—the "inner light," they called it. They discarded all formal sacraments and formal ministry, refused deference to persons of rank, used the familiar *thee* and *thou* in addressing everyone, refused to take oaths, claiming they were contrary to Scripture, and embraced pacifism. Quakers were subjected to intense persecution—often in their zeal they seemed to invite it—but never inflicted it on others. Their tolerance extended to complete religious freedom for everyone, whatever one's belief or disbelief, and to the equality of the sexes, including the full participation of women in religious affairs.

The settling of Quakers in West Jersey encouraged other Friends to migrate, especially to the Delaware River side of the colony. And soon across the river arose William Penn's Quaker commonwealth, the colony of Pennsylvania.

Penn was the son of Admiral Sir William Penn, who had supported Parliament in the civil war. Young William was reared as a proper gentleman, but as a student at Oxford he had become a Quaker. Upon his father's death, Penn inherited a substantial estate, including proprietary rights to a huge tract in America. The land was named, at the king's insistence, for Penn's father: Pennsylvania (literally, "Penn's Woods").

When Penn assumed control of the area, there was already a scattering of Dutch, Swedish, and English settlers on the west bank of the Delaware. But Penn soon made vigorous efforts to bring more settlers. He published glowing descriptions of the colony, which were translated into German, Dutch, and French. By the end of 1681, about 1,000 settlers were living in his province. By that time a town was growing up at the junction of the Schuylkill and Delaware rivers. Penn called it Philadelphia (City of Brotherly Love). Because of the generous terms on which Penn offered land—because indeed he offered aid to immigrants—the colony grew rapidly.

The relations between the Indians and the Quakers were cordial from the beginning, because of the Quakers' friendliness and because of Penn's careful policy of purchasing land titles from the Indians. Penn even took the trouble to learn an Indian language, something few colonists ever tried. For some fifty years the settlers and the natives lived side by side in peace, in relationships of such trust that Quaker farmers sometimes left their children in the care of Indians when they were away from home.

The colony's government, which rested on three Frames of Government promulgated by Penn, resembled that of other proprietary colonies except that the freemen (taxpayers and property owners) elected the councilors as well as the assembly. The governor had no veto—although Penn, as proprietor, did. Penn hoped to show that a government could operate in accordance with Quaker principles, that it could maintain peace and order without oaths or wars, and that religion could flourish without an established church and with absolute freedom of conscience. Because of its tolerance, Pennsylvania became a refuge not only for Quakers but also for a variety of dissenters—as well as Anglicans—and early reflected the ethnic mixture of Scotch-Irish and Germans that became common to the middle colonies and the southern backcountry. Penn himself stayed only four years in the colony.

In 1682 the duke of York also granted Penn the area of Delaware, another part of the former Dutch territory. At first, Delaware became part of Pennsylvania, but after 1704 it was granted the right to choose its own assembly. From then until the American Revolution, it had a separate assembly but shared Pennsylvania's governor.

GEORGIA Georgia was the last of the British continental colonies to be established—half a century after Pennsylvania. During the seventeenth century, English settlers pushed southward into the borderlands between the Carolinas and Florida. They brought with them their African slaves and a desire to win the Indian trade from the Spanish. Each side used guns, goods, and rum to influence the Indians, and the Indians in turn played off the English against the Spanish in order to gain the most favorable terms.

In 1732 King George II gave the land between the Savannah and Altamaha rivers to the twenty-one trustees of Georgia. In two respects, Georgia was unique among the colonies: it was set up as a philanthropic

Savannah, Georgia

The earliest known view of Savannah, Georgia (1734). The town's layout was carefully planned.

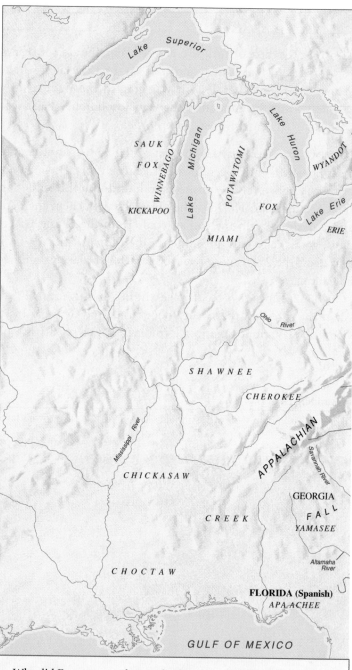

Why did European settlement lead to the expansion of hostilities among Indian peoples? What were the consequences of the trade and commerce between the English settlers and the southern Indian tribes? How were the relationships between the settlers and the members of the Iroquois League different from those between settlers and tribes in other regions?

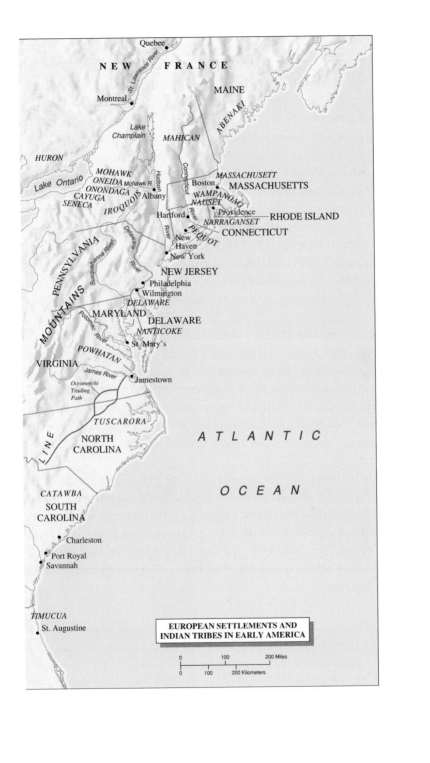

EUROPEAN SETTLEMENTS AND
INDIAN TRIBES IN EARLY AMERICA

0		100		200 Miles

0	100	200 Kilometers

experiment and as a military buffer against Spanish Florida. General James E. Oglethorpe, who accompanied the first colonists as resident trustee, represented both concerns: he served as a soldier who organized the defenses and as a philanthropist who championed prison reform and sought a colonial refuge for the poor and religiously persecuted.

In 1733 a band of about 120 colonists founded Savannah on the coast near the mouth of the Savannah River. Carefully laid out by Oglethorpe, the old town, with its geometric pattern and numerous little parks, remains a monument to the city planning of a bygone day. A group of Protestant refugees from Austria began to arrive in 1734, followed by Germans and German-speaking Moravians and Swiss, who made the colony for a time more German than English. The addition of Welsh, Highland Scots, Sephardic Jews, and others gave the early colony a cosmopolitan character much like that of Charleston.

As a buffer against Florida, the colony succeeded, but as a philanthropic experiment it failed. Efforts to develop silk and wine production foundered. Landholdings were limited to 500 acres, rum was prohibited, and the importation of slaves was forbidden, partly to leave room for servants brought on charity, partly to ensure security. But the utopian rules soon collapsed. The regulations against rum and slavery were widely disregarded and finally abandoned. By 1759 all restrictions on landholding had been removed.

In 1754 the trustees' charter expired, and the province reverted to the crown. As a royal colony, Georgia acquired an effective government for the first time. The province developed slowly over the next decade but grew rapidly in population and wealth after 1763. Instead of wine and silk, as was Oglethorpe's plan, Georgians exported rice, indigo, lumber, beef, and pork and carried on a lively trade with the West Indies. The colony had become a commercial success.

THRIVING COLONIES

By the early eighteenth century the English had outstripped both the French and the Spanish in the New World. British America had become the most populous, prosperous, and powerful region on the continent. By the mid–seventeenth century, American colonists on average were better fed, clothed, and housed than their counterparts in Europe, where a majority of the people lived in destitution. But the English colonization of North America included many failures as well as successes. Lots of settlers found only hard labor and an early death in the New World. Others flourished only because they exploited Indians, indentured servants, or Africans.

The British succeeded in creating a lasting American empire because of crucial advantages they had over their European rivals. The centralized control imposed by the monarchs of Spain and France got them off the mark more quickly but eventually hobbled innovation and responsiveness to new circumstances. The enterprising British acted by private investment and with a minimum of royal control. Not a single colony was begun at the direct initiative of the crown. In the English colonies poor immigrants had a much greater chance of getting at least a small parcel of land. The English, unlike their rivals, welcomed people from a variety of nationalities and dissenting sects who came in search of a new life or a safe harbor. And a greater degree of self-government made the English colonies more responsive to new circumstances—though they were sometimes hobbled by controversy.

The compact pattern of English settlement contrasted sharply with the pattern of Spain's far-flung conquests and France's far-reaching trade routes to the interior by way of the St. Lawrence and Mississippi rivers (discussed in Chapter 4). Geography reinforced England's bent for the concentrated occupation and settlement of its colonies. The rivers and bays that indent the Atlantic seaboard served as communication arteries along which colonies first sprang up, but no great river offered a highway to the far interior. About 100 miles inland in Georgia and the Carolinas, and nearer the coast to the north, the fall line of the rivers presented rocky rapids that marked the limit of navigation and the end of the coastal plain. About 100 miles beyond that, and farther back in Pennsylvania, stretched the rolling expanse of the Piedmont, literally, "Foothills." And the final backdrop of English America was the Appalachian Mountain range, some 200 miles from the coast in the South and reaching the coast at points in New England, with only one significant break—up the Hudson and Mohawk valleys of New York. For 150 years the farthest outreach of British settlement stopped at the slopes of those mountains. To the east lay the wide expanse of ocean, which served not only as a highway for the transport of ideas and ways of life from Europe to America but also as a barrier that separated old ideas from new, allowing the new to evolve in the new environment.

MAKING CONNECTIONS

- What we now know about the early settlements sets the stage for the regional differences in social patterns discussed in the next chapter.

- This chapter contained the observation that in founding its American colonies, "the British acted by private investment and with a minimum of royal control." As we will see in Chapter 4, that situation changed as England began to take control of the American colonies.

- Later relations between colonists and Native Americans, described in Chapter 4, had their roots in the history of these early settlements.

FURTHER READING

Bernard Bailyn's *Voyagers to the West: A Passage in the Peopling of America on the Eve of the Revolution* (1986) provides a comprehensive view of migration to the New World. Jack P. Greene offers a brilliant synthesis of British colonization in *Pursuits of Happiness: The Social Development of Early Modern British Colonies and the Formation of American Culture* (1988). The best overview of the colonization of North America is Alan Taylor's *American Colonies: The Settling of North America* (2001). On the interactions among Indian, European, and African cultures, see Gary B. Nash's *Red, White, and Black: The Peoples of Early America*, 4th ed. (1999). See Daniel K. Richter's *The Ordeal of the Longhouse: The Peoples of the Iroquois League in the Era of European Colonization* (1992) for a history of the Iroquois Confederacy.

Andrew Delbanco's *The Puritan Ordeal* (1989) is a powerful study of the tensions inherent in the Puritan outlook. For information regarding the Puritan settlement of New England, see Virginia DeJohn Anderson's *New England's Generation: The Great Migration and the Formation of Society and Culture in the Seventeenth Century* (1991). The best biography of John Winthrop is Francis J. Bremer's *John Winthrop: America's Forgotten Founding Father* (2003).

The pattern of settlement in the middle colonies is illuminated in Barry Levy's *Quakers and the American Family: British Settlement in the Delaware*

Valley (1988). On the early history of New York, see Russell Shorto's *The Island at the Center of the World* (2004). Settlement of the areas along the Atlantic in the South is traced in James Horn's *Adapting to a New World: English Society in the Seventeenth-Century Chesapeake* (1994). For a study of race and the settlement of South Carolina, see Peter H. Wood's *Black Majority: Negroes in Colonial South Carolina from 1670 through the Stono Rebellion* (1974). A brilliant book on relations between the Catawba Indians and their black and white neighbors is James H. Merrell's *The Indians' New World: Catawbas and Their Neighbors from European Contact through the Era of Removal* (1989). On the flourishing trade in captive Indians, see Alan Gallay's *The Indian Slave Trade: The Rise of the English Empire in the American South, 1670–1717* (2002).

3

COLONIAL WAYS OF LIFE

FOCUS QUESTIONS

· What were the social and economic differences among the southern, middle, and New England colonies?

· How did people of different genders, races, and classes fit into colonial society?

· What was the impact of the Enlightenment and the Great Awakening on the American colonies?

The process of carving a new civilization out of an abundant yet violent frontier involved a clash of European, African, and Indian cultures. War, duplicity, displacement, and enslavement were the tragic results. Yet on another level the process of transforming the "New World" was largely the story of thousands of diverse folk engaged in the everyday tasks of building homes, planting crops, trading goods, raising families, enforcing laws, and worshipping their God. Those who colonized America during the seventeenth and eighteenth centuries were part of a massive social migration occurring throughout Europe and Africa. Everywhere, it seemed, people were moving from farms to villages, from villages to cities, and from homelands to colonies. They moved for different reasons. Most were responding to powerful social and economic forces as rapid population growth and the rise of commercial agriculture squeezed people off the land. Many traveled in search of political security or religious freedom. An exception was the Africans, who were captured and transported to new lands against their will.

America's settlers were mostly young (over half were under twenty-five), male, and poor. Almost half were indentured servants or slaves, and during the eighteenth century England would transport some 50,000 convicts to the North American colonies. Only about one third of the settlers came with their families. Once in America, many kept moving, trying to take advantage of new opportunities. Whatever their status or ambition, this extraordinary mosaic of ordinary yet adventurous people created America's enduring institutions and values.

THE SHAPE OF EARLY AMERICA

BRITISH FOLKWAYS   The vast majority of early European settlers came from the British Isles in four mass migrations over the seventeenth and eighteenth centuries. The first involved some 20,000 Puritans who settled Massachusetts between 1630 and 1641 and for the most part hailed from the East Anglian counties east of London. A generation later a smaller group of wealthy Royalist Cavaliers and their indentured servants migrated from southern England to Virginia. These English aristocrats, mostly Anglicans, had few qualms about the introduction of African slavery. The third wave brought some 23,000 Quakers from the north Midlands of England to the Delaware Valley colonies of West Jersey, Pennsylvania, and Delaware. They brought with them a sense of spiritual equality, a suspicion of class distinctions and powerful elites, and a commitment to plain living and high thinking. The fourth and largest surge of colonization occurred between 1717 and 1775 and included hundreds of thousands of Celtic Britons and Scotch-Irish from northern Ireland; these were mostly coarse, feisty, clannish folk who settled in the rugged backcountry along the Appalachian Mountains. Generally poorer than their English counterparts, the Scots and Scotch-Irish had more to gain by moving to the New World.

It was long assumed that the strenuous demands of the American frontier served as a great "melting pot" that stripped such immigrants of their native identities and melded them into homogeneous Americans. Yet for all of the transforming effects of the New World, British ways of life have persisted to this day. Although most British settlers spoke a common language and shared the Protestant faith, they carried with them—and retained—sharply different cultural attitudes and customs. They spoke distinct dialects, cooked different foods, named and raised their children differently, adopted different philosophies of education and attitudes toward time, preferred different architectural styles, and organized their societies differently.

In gender relations, religious practices, criminal propensities, and dozens of other ways, many American customs today reflect age-old British customs. Of course, such cultural continuity is not unique to British Americans. Enduring folkways are also evident among the descendants of settlers from Africa, continental Europe, Latin America, the Middle East, and Asia. Americans thus constitute a mosaic rather than a homogeneous mass, and they share a quite varied social and cultural heritage.

SEABOARD ECOLOGY   One of the cherished legends of American history has it that those settling the New World arrived to find an unspoiled wilderness little touched by human activity. But that was not the case. For thousands of years, Indian hunting practices had produced what one scholar has called the "greatest known loss of wild species" in the continent's history. The Indians had regularly burned forests and dense undergrowth in order to provide cropland, ease travel through hardwood forests, and make way for grasses, berries, and other forage for the animals they hunted. Indians worked the cleared lands for six to eight years, until the nutrients in the soil were depleted, and then they moved on to new areas. This migratory "slash-and-burn" agriculture increased the rate at which plant nutrients were recycled and allowed more sunlight to reach the forest floor. These conditions in turn created rich soil and ideal grazing grounds for elk, deer, turkeys, bears, moose, and beavers. Nutrients from the topsoil also fertilized the streams and helped produce teeming schools of sturgeons, smelts, and small herrings called alewives. Indian farming practices also halted the normal forest succession and, especially in the Southeast, created large stands of longleaf pine, still the most common source of timber in the region.

Colonial Farm

This plan of a newly cleared American farm shows how trees were cut down and the stumps left to rot.

Equally important in shaping the ecosystem of America was the European attitude toward the environment. Whereas the Native Americans tended to be migratory, considering land and animals as communal resources to be shared and consumed only as necessary, many European colonizers viewed natural resources as privately owned commodities to be sold for profit. Settlers thus quickly set about evicting Indians; clearing, fencing, improving, and selling land; cutting timber for masts; growing surplus crops and trapping game for commercial use. These practices transformed the seaboard environment. In many places—Plymouth, for instance, and St. Marys, Maryland—settlers occupied the sites of former Indian towns, and corn, beans, and squash quickly became colonial staples, along with new crops brought from Europe.

British ships brought to America domesticated animals—such as cattle, oxen, sheep, goats, horses, and pigs—that were unknown in the New World. By 1650 English farm animals outnumbered the colonists. Rapidly multiplying livestock reshaped the American environment and affected Indian life in unexpected ways. British settlers discovered that they did not have time to feed and care for livestock in pens, as they had in the Old World. Chesapeake farmers, for example, were too busy tending profitable tobacco plants to devote time to animal husbandry. So from late spring to harvest time in New England and year-round in Maryland and Virginia, hard-pressed farmers allowed their cows, horses, and pigs to roam freely through the woods, clipping their ears to identify them. Such free-range husbandry made sense in the short run, since the labor shortage made it too expensive to pen the animals in barnyards or fence them in pastures. In the longer term, however, the failure to constrain farm animals denied the planted fields dung for use as a valuable fertilizer. The fertility of the soil declined with each passing year. The Virginia planter Robert Beverley chastised his neighbors for engaging in such "exceeding ill-husbandry" and for making their hogs "find their own support in the woods."

Hogs especially thrived in the New World. The animals eat virtually anything and breed frequently. In a few years a dozen transplanted English pigs had spawned thousands of hogs throughout the colonies. A sow can give birth three times a year to as many as sixteen piglets at a time. In 1700 a visitor to Virginia observed that the pigs "swarm like vermin upon the earth. . . . The hogs run where they want and find their own support in the woods without any care of the owners."

Many of the farm animals turned wild (feral), ran amok in Indian cornfields, and devastated native flora and fauna. In New England, rooting pigs devoured the shellfish that local Indians depended upon for subsistence. Colonists often had trouble finding their wandering herds. One Marylander spent three days hunting for stray hogs. Others hired Indians to track them down. As livestock herds grew, settlers felt the need to acquire more land, which often meant seizing Indian land. A single cow needed five acres of woodland to subsist. Trespassing livestock and expanding colonial settlements caused friction with the Indians, which in turn helped ignite such violent confrontations as King Philip's War and Bacon's Rebellion. One historian, in fact, has referred to roaming English livestock as four-legged "agents of empire" invading Indian land. As a frustrated Maryland Indian charged in 1666, "Your hogs & cattle injure us. You come too near us to live & drive us from place to place. We can fly no farther. Let us know where to live & how to be secured for the future from the hogs & cattle."

Roaming livestock exacerbated other environmental problems. European ships brought weeds as well as animals. Native weeds, such as ragweed, goldenrod, and milkweed, were not nearly as tenacious as the weeds that arrived from Europe: dandelion, thistle, plantain, and sedge. Their seeds were transported in the hay and grain brought from abroad. As pigs, cattle, and horses ate the hay, the weed seeds passed through their digestive tracts and were deposited in manure wherever the animals roamed. In 1672 a British naturalist reported that he had identified twenty-two English weeds that were flourishing in America. The Indians nicknamed plantain Englishman's foot because it seemed to sprout wherever the colonists walked. Today biologists estimate that half the weeds in the United States originated in Europe or Africa.

In time a more dense population of humans and their domestic animals created a new landscape of fields, meadows, fences, barns, and houses. Such innovations further altered the ecology of the New World. Foraging cattle, sheep, horses, and pigs gradually changed the distribution of trees, shrubs, and grasses. Because cleared and grazed land is warmer, drier, and more compacted, it floods and erodes more easily. The transformed landscape made such regions as New England sunnier, windier, and colder than they had been before colonization. And many Indians, far from being passive observers in this frenzy of environmental change, contributed to the process by trading furs for metal or glass trinkets. The increased hunting ravaged the populations of large mammals and rodents that had earlier been central to Indian culture—and to the ecological balance. Between 1600 and 1800 the physical environment of the eastern seaboard changed markedly.

POPULATION GROWTH   England's first footholds in America were bought at a fearsome price: many settlers died in the first years. But once the brutal seasoning was past and the colonies were on their feet, Virginia and its successors grew rapidly. By 1750 the number of colonists had passed 1 million; by 1775 it stood at about 2.5 million. In 1700 the English at home outnumbered the colonists by about twenty to one; by 1775, on the eve of the

American Revolution, the ratio had fallen to three to one. The prodigious increase of the colonial population did not go unnoticed. Benjamin Franklin, a keen observer of many things, published in 1751 his *Observations Concerning the Increase of Mankind,* in which he pointed out two facts of life that distinguished the colonies from Europe: land was plentiful and cheap, and labor was scarce and expensive. The opposite conditions prevailed in the Old World. From this reversal of conditions flowed many of the changes that European culture underwent in the New World—not the least being that good fortune beckoned the enterprising immigrant and induced the settlers to replenish the earth with large families. Where labor was scarce, children could lend a hand and, once grown, find new land for themselves if need be. Colonists tended, as a result, to marry and start families at an earlier age than did their Old World counterparts.

BIRTHRATES AND DEATH RATES   Given the better economic prospects in the colonies, a greater proportion of American women married, and the birthrate remained much higher than it did in Europe. Whereas in England the average age at marriage for women was twenty-five or twenty-six, in America it dropped to twenty or twenty-one. Men also married younger in the colonies than in the Old World. The birthrate rose accordingly, since women who married earlier had time for about two additional pregnancies during the childbearing years.

John Freake, and Mrs. Elizabeth Freake and Baby Mary

Elizabeth married John at age nineteen; Mary, born when Elizabeth was thirty-two, was the Freakes' eighth and last child.

Equally responsible for the burgeoning population in the colonies was a much lower death rate than that in Europe. After the difficult first years of settlement, infants generally had a better chance of reaching maturity, and adults had a better chance of reaching old age. In seventeenth-century New England, apart from childhood mortality, men could expect to reach seventy and women nearly that age.

This longevity resulted from several factors. Since the land was bountiful, famine seldom occurred after the first year, and although the winters were more severe than those in England, firewood was plentiful. Being younger on the whole—the average age in the new nation in 1790 was sixteen!—Americans were less susceptible to disease than were Europeans. That they were more scattered than in the Old World meant they were also less exposed to disease. That began to change, of course, as population centers grew and trade and travel increased. By the mid–eighteenth century the colonies were beginning to have levels of contagion much like those in Europe.

The greatest variations in these patterns occurred in the earliest years of the southern colonies. From the first century after the Jamestown settlement until about 1700, a high rate of mortality and a chronic shortage of women meant that the population increase there could be sustained only by immigration. In the humid southern climate, English settlers contracted malaria, dysentery, and a host of other diseases. The mosquito-infested rice paddies of the Carolina Tidewater were notoriously unhealthy. And ships that docked at the Chesapeake tobacco plantations brought with their payloads unseen cargoes of smallpox, diphtheria, and other infections. Given the higher mortality rate, families were often broken by the early death of parents.

SEX RATIOS AND THE FAMILY   Whole communities of religious or ethnic groups migrated more often to the northern colonies than to the southern, bringing more women in their company. There was no mention of any women among the first arrivals at Jamestown. Males were most needed in the early years of new colonies. In fact, as a pamphlet promoting opportunities in America stressed, the infant colonies needed "lusty labouring men . . . capable of hard labour, and that can bear and undergo heat and cold," men adept with the "axe and the hoe." Virginia's seventeenth-century sex ratio of two or three white males to each female meant that many men never married, although nearly every adult woman did. Counting only the unmarried, the ratio was about eight men for every woman.

A population made up largely of bachelors without strong ties to family and the larger community made for instability of a high order in the first years. And the high mortality rates of the early years further loosened family ties. A majority of the women who arrived in the Chesapeake colonies during the seventeenth century were unmarried indentured servants, most of whom died before the age of fifty. Whereas the first generations in New England proved to be long-lived and many more children there knew their grandparents than in the motherland, young people in the seventeenth-century South were apt never to see their grandparents and in fact to lose one or both parents before reaching maturity. But after a time of seasoning, immunities built up. Eventually the southern colonies reverted to a more even sex ratio, and family sizes approached those of New England.

WOMEN IN THE COLONIES   Most colonists brought to America deeply rooted convictions about the inferiority of women. As one preacher stressed, "The woman is a weak creature not endowed with like strength and constancy of mind." The prescribed role of women in life was clear: to obey and serve their husbands, nurture their children, and endure the taxing labor required to maintain their households. John Winthrop insisted that a "true wife" would find contentment only "in subjection to her husband's authority." Even high-spirited women such as Virginia's Lucy Parke Byrd submitted to their husbands' absolute authority. The imperious patrician William Byrd II of Westover managed his wife's estate without consulting her, kept a tenacious grip on his property—even to the point of forbidding his wife to borrow a book from his library without explicit permission—and saw fit to interfere in her own field of domestic management. In his secret diary he recorded their stormy relationship:

> [April 7] I reproached my wife with ordering the old beef to be kept and the fresh beef to be used first, contrary to good management, on which she was pleased to be very angry . . . then my wife came and begged my pardon and we were friends again. . . .
> [April 8] My wife and I had another foolish quarrel about my saying she listened at the top of the stairs . . . she came soon after and begged my pardon.
> [April 9] My wife and I had another scold about mending my shoes, but it was soon over by her submission.

Both social custom and legal codes ensured that most women, like Lucy Byrd, remained deferential. In most colonies they could not vote, preach, hold office, attend public schools or colleges, bring lawsuits, make contracts, or own property.

WOMEN'S WORK   In the eighteenth century, "women's work" typically involved activities in the house, garden, and yard. Farm women usually rose at four in the morning and prepared breakfast by five-thirty. They then fed and watered the livestock, wakened the children, churned butter, tended the garden, prepared lunch, played with the children, worked the garden again, cooked dinner, milked the cows, got the children ready for bed, and cleaned the kitchen before retiring, at about nine. Women also combed, spun, spooled, wove, and bleached wool for clothing, knit linen and cotton, hemmed sheets, pieced quilts, made candles and soap, chopped wood, hauled water, mopped floors, and washed clothes. Female indentured servants in the southern colonies commonly worked as field hands, weeding, hoeing, and harvesting.

Despite the conventions that limited the sphere of women, the scarcity of labor opened opportunities. Quite a few women went into gainful occupations by necessity or choice. In her role as a paid midwife, for example, Martha Ballard, a farm woman in Maine, delivered almost 800 babies. In the towns, women commonly served as tavern hostesses and shopkeepers and

The First, Second, and Last Scene of Mortality

Prudence Punderson's needlework (ca. 1776) shows the domestic path, from cradle to coffin, followed by most colonial women.

occasionally also worked as doctors, printers, upholsterers, glaziers, painters, silversmiths, tanners, and shipwrights—often, but not always, they were widows carrying on their husbands' trades. Some managed plantations, again usually carrying on in the absence of husbands.

The New World environment did generate slight improvements in the status of women. The acute shortage of women in the early years made them more highly valued than in Europe, and the Puritan emphasis on well-ordered family life led to laws protecting wives from physical abuse and allowing for divorce. In addition, colonial laws allowed wives greater control over property that they had contributed to a marriage or that was left after a husband's death. But the traditional notion of female subordination and domesticity remained firmly entrenched in the New World. As a Massachusetts boy maintained in 1662, the superior aspect of life was "masculine and eternal; the feminine inferior and mortal."

Society and Economy in the Southern Colonies

CROPS   The southern colonies had one unique advantage: the climate. The warm climate and plentiful rainfall enabled the colonies to grow exotic staples (market crops) prized by the mother country. Virginia, as Charles I put it, was "founded upon smoke." By 1619 tobacco production had reached 20,000 pounds, and in the year of the Glorious Revolution, 1688, it was up to 18 million pounds. "In Virginia and Maryland," wrote Governor Leonard Calvert in 1629, "Tobacco as our Staple is our All, and indeed leaves no room for anything else."

After 1690 rice was as much the staple in South Carolina as tobacco was in Virginia. The rise and fall of tidewater rivers made the region ideally suited to a crop that required the alternate flooding and draining of fields. Annual rice exports soared from 400,000 pounds in 1700 to 43 million pounds in 1740.

In the 1740s another exotic staple appeared: indigo, the blue dyestuff that found an eager market in the British clothing industry. Southern pine trees provided harvests of lumber and key items for the maritime industry. The resin from pine trees could be boiled to make tar, which was in great demand for waterproofing ropes and caulking wooden ships. From their early leadership in the production of pine tar, North Carolinians would earn the nickname of Tar Heels. In the interior a fur trade flourished, and in the Carolinas a cattle industry presaged life on the Great Plains—with cowboys, roundups, brandings, and long drives to the market.

English customs records showed that for the years 1698 to 1717 South Carolina and the Chesapeake colonies enjoyed a favorable balance of trade with England. But the surplus revenues earned on American goods sold to England were more than offset by "invisible" charges: freight payments to shippers; commissions, storage charges, and interest payments to English merchants; insurance premiums; inspection and customs duties; and outlays to purchase indentured servants and slaves. Thus began a pattern that would plague the southern staple-crop system into the twentieth century. Planters' investments went into land and slaves while the profitable enterprises of shipping, trade, investment, and manufacture fell under the sway of outsiders.

LAND   The economy of the southern colonies centered on the fundamental fact of colonial life that Benjamin Franklin highlighted: land was plentiful, and laborers were scarce. The low cost of land lured most colonists. Under colonial law, land titles rested ultimately upon grants from the crown, and in

Virginia Plantation

Southern colonial plantations were constructed with easy access for oceangoing vessels, as shown on this 1730 tobacco label.

colonial practice the evolution of land policy in the first colony set patterns that were followed everywhere save in New England. In 1618 the Virginia Company, lacking any assets other than land, sold each investor a fifty-acre "share-right" and gave each settler a "headright" for paying his own way or bringing in others.

If one distinctive feature of the South's agrarian economy was a ready market in England, another was a trend toward large-scale production. Those who planted tobacco discovered that it quickly exhausted the soil, thereby giving an advantage to the planter who had extra fields in which to plant beans and corn or to leave fallow. With the increase of the tobacco crop, moreover, a fall in prices meant that economies of scale might come into play—the large planter with the lower cost per unit might still make a profit. Gradually he would extend his holdings along the riverfronts and thereby secure the advantage of direct access to the oceangoing vessels that plied the waterways of the Chesapeake, discharging goods from London and taking on hogsheads of tobacco. So easy was the access, in fact, that the Chesapeake colonies never required a city of any size as a center of commerce, and the larger planters functioned as merchants and harbormasters for their neighbors.

LABOR   Voluntary indentured servitude accounted for probably half the white settlers (mostly from England, Ireland, or Germany) in all the colonies outside New England. The name derived from the indenture, or contract, by which a penniless person promised to work for a fixed number of years in return for transportation to the New World. Poverty and disease in British cities prompted many rootless vagabonds and petty criminals to board ship for America. Not all the servants went voluntarily. The London underworld developed a flourishing trade in "kids" and "spirits," who were "kidnapped" or "spirited" into servitude. After 1717, by act of Parliament, convicts guilty of certain crimes could escape the hangman by relocating to the colonies.

Once in the colonies, servants contracted with masters. Their rights were limited. They could own property but not engage in trade. Marriage required the master's permission. Runaway servants were hunted down and punished just as runaway slaves were. Masters could whip servants and extend their indentures for bad behavior. Many servants died from disease or the exhaustion of cultivating tobacco in the broiling sun and intense humidity. In due course, however, usually after four to seven years, the indenture ended, and the servant claimed the "freedom dues" set by custom and law: money, tools, clothing, food, and occasionally small tracts of land. Some former servants did very well for themselves. In 1629 seven members of the

JUST ARRIVED,
THE SEARSDALE, Capt. REED,
with one hundred thirty-nine healthy
SERVANTS,
Men, women, and boys,
Among which are many tradefmen, viz.
SMITHS, bricklayers, plaifterers,
fhoemakers, houfe-carpenters and joiners, weavers,
barbers and perukemakers, a cletk, a hatter, a rope-
maker, a plumber, a glazier, a taylor, a printer, a
bookbinder, a painter, a matuamaker, feveral femp-
ftreffes, and others ; there are alfo farmers, waggoners,
and other country labourers. The fale will commence
on *Wednefday* the 10th of *Oftober*, at *Leeds* town, on
Rappahannock. A reafonable credit will be allowed,
giving bond with approved fecurity, to
THOMAS HODGE.

Indentured Servants

An advertisement from the *Virginia Gazette*, October 4,
1779, for indentured servants. The people whose services
are being offered secured a life in America, but at a steep
price. Servants endured years of labor before their contracts expired and they were granted their freedom.

Virginia legislature were former indentured servants. Others, including
Benjamin Franklin's maternal grandmother, married the men who had originally bought their services. Many servants died before completing their
indenture, however, and recent evidence suggests that most of those who
served their term remained relatively poor thereafter.

SLAVERY   Colonial America was a land of white opportunity and black
slavery. Most immigrants to America were not British or European, and they
did not come willingly. During the eighteenth century there were more than
three times as many slaves as free immigrants in the British colonies. Black
slavery evolved in the Chesapeake after 1619, when a Dutch vessel dropped off
twenty Africans in Jamestown. Some of the first Africans were treated as indentured servants, with a limited term. Those few African servants who
worked out their term of indenture gained freedom and a fifty-acre parcel of
land. They themselves sometimes acquired slaves and white indentured servants. Gradually, however, with rationalizations based on color difference or
"heathenism," the practice of hereditary life service for blacks became the

custom of the land. By the 1660s colonial assemblies recognized slavery through laws that were later expanded into elaborate and restrictive slave codes.

The sugar islands of the French and British West Indies and the cane fields of Portuguese Brazil had the most voracious appetite for enslaved Africans, using them up in the tropical heat on average within seven years. By 1675 the English West Indies had over 100,000 slaves while the colonies in North America had only about 5,000. But as staple crops became established on the American continent and as economic growth in England slowed the number of white laborers traveling to the New World, the demand for slaves grew. As readily available lands diminished, Virginians were less eager to bring in indentured servants, who would lay claim to them at the end of their service. Though British North America took less than 5 percent of the total slaves imported to the Western Hemisphere during more than three centuries of that squalid traffic, it offered better chances for survival, if few for human fulfillment. The natural increase of blacks in America approximated that of whites by the end of the colonial period. By that time every fifth American was either an African or a descendant of one. Slavery was recognized in the laws of all the colonies but flourished in the Tidewater South; one colony, South Carolina, had a black majority through most of the eighteenth century.

AFRICAN ROOTS Enslaved Africans are so often lumped together as a social group that their great ethnic diversity is overlooked. They came from lands as remote from each other as Angola and Senegal, and they spoke

Slavery

A newspaper advertisement placed by Ignatius Davis of Fredericktown, Maryland, in 1741, offering a reward for the capture of a runaway slave.

TEN DOLLARS

REWARD.

R AN away, on the 23d inſt. a handſome active *Mulatto* ſlave, named A R C H, about 21 years of age, is ſlender built and of middle ſtature, talks ſenſible and artful, but if cloſly examined is apt to tremble, has a ridge or ſcar on

Mandingo, Ibo, Kongo, and other languages. Still, the many peoples of Africa did share similar kinship and political systems. Not unlike the Native American cultures, the African societies were often matrilineal: property and political status descended through the mother rather than the father. When a couple married, the wife did not leave her family; the husband left his family to join that of his bride.

West African tribes were organized hierarchically. Priests and the nobility lorded over the masses of farmers and craftspeople. Below the masses were the slaves, typically war captives, criminals, or debtors. Slaves in Africa, however, did have certain rights. They could marry, receive an education, and have children. Their servitude was not permanent, nor were children automatically slaves by virtue of their parentage, as would be the case in North America.

The West African economy centered on hunting, fishing, planting, and animal husbandry. Men and women typically worked alongside each other in the fields. Religious belief served as the spine of West African life. All tribal groups believed in a supreme Creator and an array of lesser gods tied to specific natural forces, such as rain, fertility, and animal life. West Africans were pantheistic in that they believed that spirits resided in trees, rocks, and streams. People who died were also subjects of reverence, because they served as mediators between the living and the gods.

Africans preyed upon Africans. For centuries rival tribes had conquered and enslaved one another, and during the seventeenth and eighteenth centuries African middlemen brought captives to the coast to sell to European slave traders. Once selected and purchased, the slaves were branded with a company mark and packed tightly in slave ships, where they endured a four- to six-week Atlantic passage so brutal that one in seven captives died en route. Once in America, they were thrown indiscriminately together and treated like animals. Some slaves rebelled against their new masters, resisting work orders, sabotaging crops and tools, or running away to the frontier. In a few cases they organized rebellions, which were ruthlessly suppressed. "You would be surprised at their perseverance," noted one white planter. "They often die before they can be conquered." Captured slaves faced ghastly retribution; many were burned at the stake. After rounding up slaves who participated in the Stono Uprising in South Carolina in 1739, enraged planters "cutt off their heads and set them up at every Mile Post."

SLAVE CULTURE   Slavery in British North America differed greatly from region to region. Africans were a small minority in New England

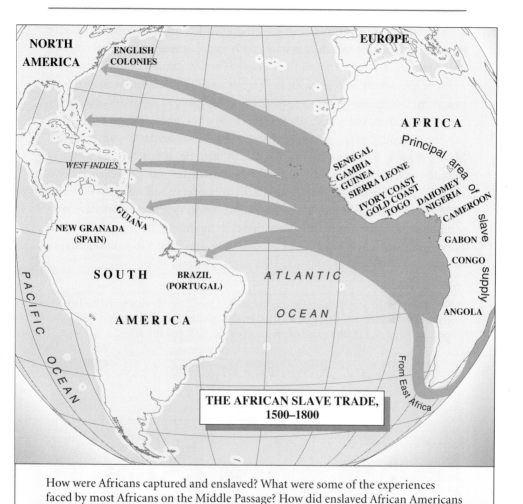

NORTH AMERICA

ENGLISH COLONIES

EUROPE

AFRICA

WEST INDIES

Principal area of slave supply

SENEGAL
GAMBIA
GUINEA
SIERRA LEONE
IVORY COAST
GOLD COAST
TOGO DAHOMEY
NIGERIA
CAMEROON
GABON
CONGO
ANGOLA

GUIANA

NEW GRANADA (SPAIN)

SOUTH

BRAZIL (PORTUGAL)

ATLANTIC

OCEAN

AMERICA

PACIFIC OCEAN

From East Africa

THE AFRICAN SLAVE TRADE, 1500–1800

How were Africans captured and enslaved? What were some of the experiences faced by most Africans on the Middle Passage? How did enslaved African Americans create a new culture?

(about 2 percent) and in the middle colonies (about 8 percent). Most northern slaves lived in cities. In the South, slaves were far more numerous, and most of them worked on farms and plantations. In 1750 the vast majority of slaves in British America resided in Virginia and Maryland, about 150,000 compared with 60,000 in South Carolina and Georgia and only 33,000 in all of the northern colonies.

In the process of being forced into lives of bondage, diverse blacks from diverse homelands forged a new identity as African Americans while leaving entwined in the fabric of American culture more strands of African heritage than historians and anthropologists can ever disentangle. Among them were new words that entered the language, such as *tabby, tote, cooter, goober, yam,* and *banana,* and the names of the Coosaw, Pee Dee, and Wando rivers.

More important were African influences in music, folklore, and religious practices. On one level, slaves used such cultural activities to distract themselves from their servitude; on another level they used songs, stories, and sermons as coded messages expressing their distaste for masters or overseers. Slave religion, a unique blend of African and Christian beliefs, was frequently practiced in secret. Its fundamental theme was deliverance: God would eventually free African Americans from slavery and open up the gates to heaven's promised land. The planters, however, sought to strip slave religion of its liberationist hopes. They insisted that being "born again" had no effect upon their workers' status as slaves. In 1667 the Virginia legislature

African Heritage

The survival of African culture among enslaved Americans is evident in this late-eighteenth-century painting of a South Carolina plantation. The musical instruments, pottery, and clothing are of African (probably Yoruban) origin.

declared that "the conferring of baptism does not alter the condition of the person as to his bondage or freedom."

Africans brought to America powerful kinship ties. Even though most colonies outlawed slave marriages, many masters realized that slaves would work harder and be more stable if allowed to form families. Though many families were broken up when members were sold, slave culture retained its powerful domestic ties. It also developed gender roles distinct from those of white society. Most enslaved women were by necessity field workers as well as wives and mothers responsible for household affairs. Since they worked in proximity to enslaved men, they were treated more equally than were most of their white counterparts.

Most, but not all, slaves were fated to become field hands. Many from the lowlands of Africa used their talent as boatmen in the coastal waterways. Some had linguistic skills that made them useful interpreters. Others tended cattle and swine or hacked away at the forests and operated sawmills. In a society forced to construct itself, slaves became skilled artisans: blacksmiths, carpenters, coopers, bricklayers, and the like. Some worked as cooks or maids.

Slavery and the growth of a biracial South had economic, political, and cultural effects far into the future and set America on a course that would lead to tragic conflicts. Questions about the beginnings of slavery still have a bearing on the present. Did a deep-rooted color prejudice lead to slavery, for instance, or did the existence of slavery produce the prejudice? Clearly slavery evolved because of a demand for labor, and the English adopted a trade established by the Portuguese and Spanish more than a century before—the very word *negro* is Spanish for "black." English settlers often enslaved Indian captives, but they did not enslave captured Europeans. Color was the crucial difference, or at least the crucial rationalization.

The English associated the color black with darkness and evil; they stamped the different appearance, behavior, and customs of Africans as "savagery." At the very least such perceptions could soothe the conscience of people who traded in human flesh. On the other hand, most of the qualities that colonial Virginians imputed to blacks to justify slavery were the same qualities that the English assigned to their own poor to explain *their* status: their alleged bent for laziness, improvidence, treachery, and stupidity, among other shortcomings. Similar traits, moreover, were imputed by ancient Jews to the Canaanites and by the Mediterranean peoples of a later date to the Slavic captives sold among them. The names Canaanite and Slav both became synonymous with slavery—the latter lingers in our very word for it. Such expressions would seem to be the product of power relationships and not the other way around. Dominant peoples repeatedly assign ugly traits to those they bring into subjugation.

THE GENTRY   By the early eighteenth century, Virginia and South Carolina were moving into the golden age of the Tidewater gentry, leaving the more isolated and rustic colony of North Carolina as "a valley of humiliation between two mountains of conceit." The first rude huts of Jamestown had given way to frame and brick houses, but it was only as the seventeenth century yielded to the eighteenth that the stately countryseats in the Georgian, or "colonial," style began to emerge along the banks of the great rivers. In South Carolina the mansions along the Ashley, Cooper, and Wando rivers boasted spacious gardens and avenues of moss-draped live oaks.

The great houses of the new colonial aristocracy became centers of sumptuous living and legendary hospitality. In their zest for the good life, the planters purchased products that reflected the latest refinements of London style and fashion, living precariously on credit extended for future crops. Dependence on outside capital remained a chronic southern problem far beyond the colonial period.

In season the carriages of the Chesapeake Bay elite rolled to the villages of Annapolis and Williamsburg, and the city of Charleston in South Carolina became the center of political life and high fashion. Throughout much of the year, the outdoors beckoned planters to the pleasures of hunting, fishing, and riding. Gambling on horse races, cards, and dice became consuming passions for men and women alike. But a few cultivated high culture. Virginia's William Byrd of Westover pursued learning with a passion. He built a library of some 3,600 volumes and often rose early to keep up his Latin, Greek, and Hebrew. The wealthy families commonly sent their sons—and often

Colonial Aristocracy

This painting from about 1710 portrays Henry Darnall III, a youth from one of Maryland's richest families, flanked by a slave. In the background are buildings and gardens that attest to the southern preoccupation with the trappings of English nobility.

their daughters—abroad for an education, usually to England, sometimes to France.

RELIGION   After 1642 Virginia governor William Berkeley decided that his colony was to be Anglican, and he passed laws requiring "all nonconformists . . . to depart the colony with all conveniency." Puritans and Quakers were hounded out. By the end of the seventeenth century, Anglicanism predominated in the Chesapeake region, and it proved especially popular among the large landholders. In the early eighteenth century it became the established (official) church in all the South—and some counties of New York and New Jersey, despite the presence of many dissenters. In the new American environment, however, the Anglican Church evolved into something quite unlike the state church of England. The scattered population and the absence of bishops made centralized control difficult.

It has often been said that Americans during the seventeenth century took religion more seriously than they have at any time since. That may have been true, but it is important to remember how many early Americans were not active communicants. One estimate holds that fewer than one in fifteen residents of the southern colonies was a church member. There the tone of

Anglicanism in the South

The exterior of St. James Episcopal Church, built in the 1700s in an Anglican parish in Maryland.

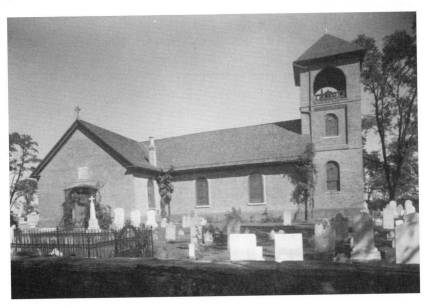

religious belief and practice was different from that in Puritan New England or Quaker Pennsylvania. As in England, colonial Anglicans tended to be more conservative, rational, and formal in their forms of worship than their Puritan, Quaker, or Baptist counterparts. Anglicans tended to stress collective rituals over personal religious experience.

SOCIETY AND ECONOMY IN NEW ENGLAND

TOWNSHIPS   In contrast to the seaboard planters, who transformed the English manor into the southern plantation, the Puritans transformed the English village into the New England town, although there were several varieties. Land policy in New England had a stronger social and religious purpose than elsewhere. Towns shaped by English precedent and Puritan policy also fitted the environment of a rockbound land, confined by sea and mountains and unfit for large-scale agriculture.

Unlike the pattern of settlement in the southern colonies or in Dutch New York, few New England colonists received huge tracts of land. The standard system was one of township grants to organized groups. A group of settlers, often gathered already into a church, would petition the general court for a town (what elsewhere was commonly called a township) and then divide it according to a rough principle of equity—those who invested more or had larger families or greater status might receive more land—retaining some pasture and woodland in common and holding some for later arrivals. In some early cases the towns arranged each settler's land in separate strips after the medieval practice, but with time land was commonly divided into separate farms to which landholders would move, away from the close-knit village. Still later, by the early eighteenth century, the colonies used their remaining land as a source of revenue, selling townships to proprietors whose purpose, more often than not, was speculation and resale.

DWELLINGS AND DAILY LIFE   The first colonists in New England initially lived in caves, tents, or "English wigwams," but they soon built simple small frame houses clad with hand-split clapboards. The roofs were steeply pitched to reduce the buildup of snow and were covered with thatched grasses or reeds. By the end of the seventeenth century, most New England homes were plain but sturdy dwellings centered on a fireplace. Some had glass windows brought from England. The interior walls were often plastered and whitewashed, but the exterior boards were rarely painted. It was not until the eighteenth century that most houses were painted, and

Housing in New England

This frame house, built in the 1670s, belonged to Rebecca Nurse, one of the women hanged as a witch in Salem Village in 1692.

they were usually a dark "Indian red." New England homes were not commonly painted white until the nineteenth century. The interiors were dark, illuminated only by candles or oil lamps, both of which were expensive; most people usually went to sleep soon after sunset.

Family life revolved around the main room on the ground floor, called the hall, where meals would be cooked in a large fireplace. Pots would be suspended on an iron rod over the fire, and food would be served at a table of rough-hewn planks, called the board. The father was sometimes referred to as the chair man because he sat in the only chair (hence the origin of the term *chairman of the board*). The rest of the family usually stood to eat or sat on stools or benches. People in colonial times ate with their hands and wooden spoons. Forks were not introduced until the eighteenth century. The fare was usually corn, boiled meat, and vegetables washed down with beer, cider, rum, or milk. Corn bread was a daily staple, as was cornmeal mush, known as hasty pudding. Colonists also relished succotash, an Indian meal of corn and kidney beans cooked in bear grease.

ENTERPRISE   New England farmers faced strenuous challenges. Simply clearing rocks from the glacier-scoured soil might require sixty days of hard

Profitable Fisheries

Fishing for, curing, and drying codfish in Newfoundland
in the early 1700s. For centuries the rich fishing grounds of
the North Atlantic provided New Englanders with a prosperous industry.

labor per acre. The growing season was short, and no profitable crops grew
in that harsh climate. The crops and livestock were those familiar to the English countryside: wheat, barley, oats, some cattle, swine, and sheep.

With rich fishing grounds that stretched northward to Newfoundland, it is
little wonder that New Englanders turned to the sea for their livelihood. The
Chesapeake Bay region afforded a rich harvest of oysters, but New England, by
its proximity to waters frequented by cod, mackerel, halibut, and other varieties
of fish, became the more important maritime center. Whales, too, abounded in
New England waters and supplied oil for lighting and lubrication, as well as
ambergris, a waxy substance used in the manufacture of perfumes.

The fisheries, unlike the farms, supplied profitable exports to Europe,
while lesser grades of fish went to the West Indies as food for slaves. Fisheries
encouraged the development of shipbuilding, and experience at seafaring
spurred commerce. This in turn encouraged wider contacts in the Atlantic
world and a degree of materialism and cosmopolitanism that clashed with
the Puritan credo of plain living and high thinking. In 1714 a worried Puritan deplored the "great extravagance that people are fallen into, far beyond
their circumstances, in their purchases, buildings, families, expenses, ap-
parel, generally in the whole way of living."

NEW ENGLAND SHIPBUILDING   The abundant forests of New England represented a source of enormous wealth. Old-growth trees were especially prized by the British government for maritime use as masts and spars. Early on, the British government claimed the tallest and straightest American trees, mostly white pines and oaks, for use by the Royal Navy. At the same time, British officials encouraged the colonists to develop their own shipbuilding industry. The New England economy was utterly dependent on fishing and maritime commerce, and this placed a premium on the availability of boats and ships—and shipbuilders. In 1641 the Massachusetts General Court declared that shipbuilding "is a business of great importance to the common good" and therefore care must be taken to ensure that boatbuilding was "well performed." American seaports recruited British shipwrights to emigrate. In 1637, for example, the town of Salem lured William Stevens, a skilled London shipwright, by granting him free land "for the building of Ships, provided that it shall be employed for that end." American-built ships quickly became prized by British and European traders for their quality and price. It was much less expensive to purchase American-built ships than to transport American timber to Britain for ship construction, especially since a large ship might require the timber from as many as 2,000 trees.

Nearly one third of all British ships were made in the colonies. Shipbuilding was one of colonial America's first big industries, and it in turn helped nurture many businesses: timber, sawmills, iron foundries, sail lofts, fisheries, and taverns. The availability of "all manner of materials for ship building very cheap" allowed New Englanders to keep freight charges low compared with those of other trading nations, thus winning the entire West Indian and North American trade with the exception of products only the English could produce.

Constructing a large ship required as many as thirty skilled trades and 200 workers. The vessel's hull was laid out by master shipwrights, talented maritime carpenters who used axes and adzes to cut and fit together the pieces to form the keel, or spine of the hull. They then fashioned U-shaped ribs for the hull before enclosing the frame with planking and decking boards that had been prepared by sawyers. Carpenters carefully secured the boards with treenails (pronounced—and sometimes spelled—"trunnels"), strong wooden pegs pounded into bored holes. Caulkers made the ship watertight by stuffing the seams with oakum, a loose hemp fiber that was sealed with hot tar.

As the new ship took shape, rope makers created the ship's extensive rigging. Rope was made by hand. Workers walked backward, away from a spinning wheel, twisting handfuls of hemp into a long coil. The workers were called rope walkers, and the wooden shed where they worked, often 1,000 feet long, was called a ropewalk. After the coils of rope were spun, they were dipped in heated tar to preserve them from saltwater rot. Sailmakers, meanwhile, fashioned sails out of canvas, laying them out in large lofts.

Other craftsmen produced the dozens of other items needed for a sailing vessel: blacksmiths forged iron anchors, chains, hinges, bolts, rudder braces, and circular straps that secured sections of a mast to each other. Block makers created the dozens of metal-strapped wooden pulleys needed to hoist sails. Joiners built hatches, ladders, lockers, and furnishings. Painters finished the trim and interiors. Ship chandlers provided lamps, oil, and candles. Instrument makers fashioned compasses, chronometers, and sextants for navigation.

Such skilled workers were trained in the apprentice-journeyman system then common in England. A master craftsman taught an apprentice the skills of his trade in exchange for wages. After the apprenticeship period, lasting from four to seven years, a young worker would receive a new suit of clothes from the master craftsman and then become a journeyman, literally moving from shop to shop, working for wages as he honed his skills. Over time, journeymen joined local guilds and became master craftsmen, who themselves took on apprentices. In the colonies the acute demand for skilled laborers and the absence of guilds to regulate work standards and wages by limiting competition resulted in a more flexible labor system. With wages high and land cheap or free, journeymen could often start their own shipyards with a small amount of capital. The workday in a colonial shipyard lasted from dawn to dusk. Laborers were given breaks, at eleven in the morning and four in the afternoon, for grog, a heated mixture of rum and water.

It took four to six months to build a major sailing ship. The ship christenings and launchings were festive occasions that attracted large crowds and dignitaries. Shops and schools would often close to enable workers and students to attend. All of the workers joined the celebration. The ceremony would begin with a clergyman blessing the new vessel. Then the ship's owner or a senior member of the crew would "christen" the ship before ropes were cut and blocks removed to allow the hull to slide into the water.

TRADE   By the end of the seventeenth century, the colonies had become part of a great North Atlantic commercial connection, trading not only with the British Isles and the British West Indies but also—and often illegally—with Spain, France, Portugal, Holland, and their colonies from America to the shores of Africa. Out of necessity the colonists imported manufactured goods from Europe: hardware, machinery, paint, instruments for navigation, and various household items. The colonies thus served as an important market for goods from the mother country. The central problem for the colonies was to find the means to pay for the imports—the eternal problem of the balance of trade and the shortage of currency.

The mechanism of trade in New England and the middle colonies differed from that in the South in two respects: the lack of staples to exchange for English goods was a relative disadvantage, but the abundance of their own shipping and mercantile enterprise worked in their favor. After 1660, in order to protect England's agriculture and fisheries, the English government placed prohibitive duties on certain major colonial exports—fish, flour, wheat, and meat—while leaving the door open to timber, furs, and whale oil, products in great demand in the home country. New York and New England between 1698 and 1717 bought more from England than they sold there, incurring an unfavorable trade balance.

The northern colonies solved the problem partly by using their own ships and merchants, thus avoiding the "invisible" charges for trade and transport, and by finding other markets for the staples excluded from England, thus acquiring goods or bullion to pay for imports from the mother country. American lumber and fish therefore went to southern Europe, Madeira, and the Azores for money or in exchange for wine; lumber, rum, and provisions went to Newfoundland; and all of these and more went to the West Indies, which became the most important outlet of all. American merchants could sell fish, bread, flour, corn, pork, bacon, beef, and horses to West Indian planters, who specialized in sugarcane. In return they got money, sugar, molasses, rum, indigo, dyewoods, and other products, many of which went eventually to England.

These circumstances gave rise to the famous "triangular trade" (more a descriptive convenience than a rigid pattern), in which New Englanders shipped rum to the west coast of Africa, where they bartered for slaves; took the slaves to the West Indies; and returned home with various commodities, including molasses, from which they manufactured rum. In another version they shipped provisions to the West Indies, carried sugar and molasses to England, and returned with goods manufactured in Europe.

The colonies suffered from a chronic shortage of hard currency, which drifted away to pay for imports and shipping charges. Various expedients met the shortage of currency: the use of wampum or commodities, the monetary value of which colonial governments tried vainly to set by law. Promissory notes of individuals or colonial treasurers often passed as a crude sort of paper money. Most of the colonies at one time or another issued bills of credit, on promise of payment later (hence the dollar "bill"), and most set up land banks that issued paper money for loans to farmers on the security of their land, which was mortgaged to the banks. Colonial

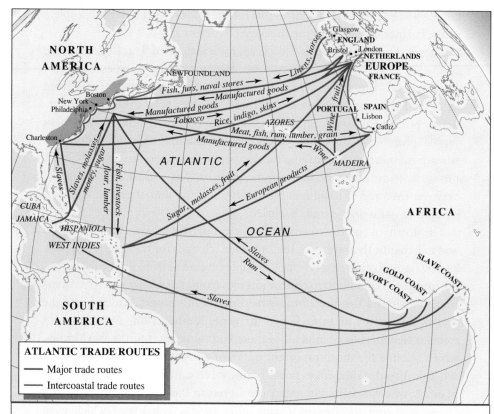

How was overseas trade in the South different from that in New England and the middle Atlantic colonies? What was the "triangular trade"? What were North America's most important exports?

farmers began to recognize that an inflation of paper money led to an inflation of crop prices and therefore asked for more and more paper money. Thus began in colonial politics what was to become a recurrent issue in later times, the question of currency inflation. Whenever the issue arose, debtors commonly favored growth in the money supply, which would make it easier for them to settle accounts, whereas creditors favored a limited money supply, which would increase the value of their capital. Parliament outlawed legal-tender paper money in New England in 1751 and throughout the colonies in 1764.

RELIGION   New England was settled by religious fundamentalists. The Puritans were colonists for God who looked to the Bible for authority and inspiration. They read the Bible daily and memorized its passages and stories. They read it silently alone and aloud as families and in church services, which lasted from eight until noon on Sunday mornings. The Christian faith was a living source of daily inspiration and obligation for most New Englanders.

The Puritans had come to America to create pious and prosperous communities, not to tolerate sinfulness in their new Zion. Yet the picture of the dour Puritan, hostile to anything that gave pleasure, is false. Puritans, especially those of the upper class, wore colorful clothing, enjoyed secular music, and imbibed prodigious quantities of rum. "Drink is in itself a good creature of God," said the Reverend Increase Mather, "but the abuse of drink is from Satan." If found incapacitated by reason of strong drink, a person was subject to arrest. A Salem man, for example, was tried for staggering into a house where he "eased his stomak in the Chimney." Repeat offenders were forced to wear the letter *D* in public.

Moderation in all things except piety was the Puritan guideline, and it applied to sexual activity as well. Contrary to prevailing images of Puritan prudery, Puritans quite openly acknowledged natural human desires. Of course, sexual activity outside the bounds of marriage was strictly forbidden, but like most social prohibitions it provoked transgression. New England court records are filled with cases of adultery and fornication. A man found guilty of coitus with an unwed woman could be jailed, whipped, fined, disenfranchised, and forced to marry the woman. Female offenders were also jailed and whipped, and in some cases adulterers were forced to wear the letter *A* in public. In part the abundance of sex offenses is explained by the disproportionate number of men in the colonies. Many were unable to find a wife and were therefore tempted to satisfy their sexual desires outside marriage.

The Puritans who settled Massachusetts, unlike the Separatists of Plymouth, proposed only to form a purified version of the Anglican Church. They believed that they could remain loyal to the Church of England, the unity of church and state, and the principle of compulsory uniformity. But their remoteness from England led them to adopt a congregational form of church government identical with that of the Pilgrim Separatists and for that matter little different from the practice of Anglicans in the southern colonies.

In the Puritan version of John Calvin's theology, God had voluntarily entered into a covenant, or contract, with worshippers through which they could secure salvation. By analogy, therefore, an assembly of true Christians could enter into a church covenant, a voluntary union for the common worship of God. From this it was a fairly short step to the idea of a voluntary union for the purpose of government. The history of New England affords examples of several such limited steps toward constitutional government: the Mayflower Compact, the Cambridge Agreement of John Winthrop and his followers, the Fundamental Orders of Connecticut, and the informal arrangements whereby the Rhode Island settlers governed themselves until they secured a charter in 1663.

The covenant theory contained certain kernels of democracy in both church and state, but democracy was no part of Puritan political thought, which like so much else in Puritan belief began with original sin. Humanity's innate depravity made government necessary. The Puritan was dedicated to seeking not the will of the people but the will of God, and the ultimate source of authority was the Bible. But the Bible had to be explained. Hence, most Puritans deferred to an intellectual elite for a true knowledge of God's will. By law every town had to support a church through taxes levied on every household. And every community member was required to attend midweek and Sunday religious services. The average New Englander heard 7,000 sermons in a lifetime.

The church exercised a pervasive influence over the life of the New England town, but unlike the Church of England it technically had no political power. Thus although Puritan New England has often been called a theocracy, the church was entirely separate from the state—except that the residents were taxed for its support. And if not all inhabitants were church members, all were nonetheless required to attend church services.

New England Puritans were assailed by doubts, by a fear of falling away from godly living, by the haunting fear that despite their best outward efforts they might not be among God's elect. Add such concerns to the long winters that kept the family cooped up during the dark, cold months, and one has a formula for seething resentments and recriminations that, for the sake of peace in the family, had to be projected outward, toward neighbors. The New Englanders of those peaceable kingdoms therefore built a reputation as the most litigious people on the face of God's earth, continually quarreling over property disputes, business dealings, and other issues and building in the process a flourishing legal profession.

DIVERSITY AND SOCIAL STRAINS Despite long-enduring myths, New England towns were not always pious, harmonious, and self-sufficient utopias populated by praying Puritans. Many communities were founded not as religious refuges but as secular centers of fishing, trade, or commercial agriculture, and the animating concerns of residents in such towns tended to be more entrepreneurial than spiritual. After a Puritan minister delivered his

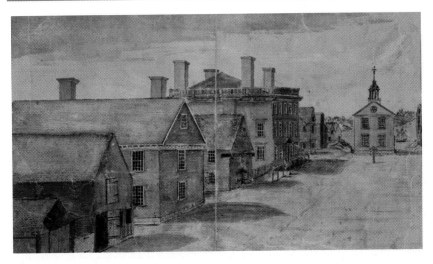

School Street, Salem, in about 1765

The mansion of a wealthy merchant dominates this street scene, typical of a prosperous port town.

first sermon to a congregation in the fishing port of Marblehead, a crusty fisherman admonished him: "You think you are preaching to the people of the Bay. Our main end was to catch fish."

In many of the godly backwoods communities, social strains increased as time passed, a consequence primarily of population pressure on the land and increasing disparities of wealth. "Love your neighbor," said Benjamin Franklin's Poor Richard, "but don't pull down your fence." Initially among the first settlers, fathers exercised strong authority over sons through their control of the land. They kept the sons and their families in the town, not letting them set up their own households or get title to their farmland until they reached middle age. In New England, as elsewhere, fathers tended to subdivide their land among all the male children. But by the eighteenth century, with land scarcer, the younger sons were either getting control of the property early or moving on. Often they were forced out, with family help and blessings, to seek land elsewhere or new kinds of work in the commercial cities along the coast or inland rivers. With the growing pressure on land in the settled regions, poverty and social tension increased in what had once seemed a country of unlimited opportunity.

The emphasis on a direct accountability to God, which lies at the base of all Protestant theology, itself caused a persistent tension and led believers to challenge authority in the name of private conscience. Massachusetts repressed such heresy in the 1630s, but it resurfaced during the 1650s among

Quakers and Baptists, and in 1659–1660 the colony hanged four Quakers who persisted in returning after they had been expelled. These acts caused such revulsion—and an investigation by the crown—that they were not repeated, although heretics continued to face harassment and persecution.

More damaging to the Puritan utopia was the growing materialism of New England, which placed strains on church discipline. More and more children of the "visible saints" found themselves unable to give the required testimony of regeneration. In 1662 an assembly of ministers at Boston accepted the "Half-Way Covenant," whereby baptized children of church members could be admitted to a "halfway" membership and secure baptism for their own children in turn. Such members, however, could neither vote in church nor take communion. A further blow to Puritan control came with the Massachusetts royal charter of 1691, which required toleration of dissenters and based the right to vote in public elections on property rather than church membership.

THE DEVIL IN NEW ENGLAND The strains accompanying Massachusetts's transition from Puritan utopia to royal colony reached an unhappy climax in the witchcraft hysteria at Salem Village (now the town of Danvers) in 1692. Belief in witchcraft was widespread throughout Europe and New England in the seventeenth century. Prior to the dramatic episode in Salem, almost 300 New Englanders (mostly middle-aged women) had been accused of being witches, and more than 30 had been hanged. New England was, in the words of Cotton Mather, "a country . . . extraordinarily alarum'd by the wrath of the Devil."

Still, the outbreak in Salem was distinctive in its scope and intensity. Salem Village was about eight miles from the larger Salem Town, a thriving port. A contentious community made up of independent farm families and people who depended upon the commercial activity of the port, the village struggled to free itself from the influence and taxes of Salem proper. The tensions that arose apparently made the residents especially susceptible to the idea that the devil was at work in the village.

During the winter of 1691–1692, several adolescent girls began meeting in the kitchen of the town minister, the Reverend Samuel Parris. There they gave rapt attention to the African tales told by Tituba, Parris's West Indian slave. As the days passed, the entranced girls began to behave oddly—shouting, barking, groveling, and twitching for no apparent reason. A doctor concluded that the girls were bewitched. When asked who was tormenting them, the girls replied that three women—Tituba, Sarah Good, and Sarah Osborne—were Satan's servants.

Authorities thereupon arrested the three women. At a special hearing before the magistrates, the "afflicted" girls rolled on the floor in convulsive fits as the accused women were questioned. In the midst of the hearing, Tituba shocked listeners by not only confessing to the charge but also divulging the names of many others in the community who she claimed were also performing the devil's work. Soon thereafter, dozens more girls and young women began to experience the same violent contortions. The accusations spread throughout the community. Within a few months the Salem Village jail was filled with townspeople—men, women, and children—accused of practicing witchcraft.

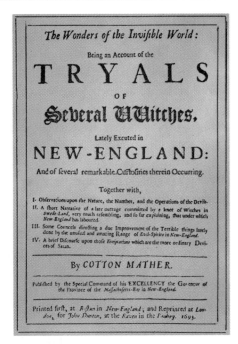

The Wonders of the Invisible World

Title page of the 1693 London edition of Cotton Mather's account of the Salem witchcraft cases. Mather, a Boston minister, advocated the admission of "spectral" evidence in witchcraft trials and warned his congregation that the devil's legions had been set upon New England.

At the end of May, the authorities arrested Martha Carrier. A farmer had testified that several of his cattle suffered "strange deaths" soon after he and Carrier had had an argument. Little Phoebe Chandler added that she had been stricken with terrible stomach pains soon after she heard Carrier's voice telling her she was going to be poisoned. Even Carrier's own children testified against her: they reported that their mother had recruited them to be witches. But the most damning testimony was provided by several young girls. When they were brought into the hearing room, they began writhing in agony at the sight of Carrier. They claimed that they could see the devil whispering in her ear. Carrier declared that it was "a shameful thing that you should mind these folks that are out of their wits. I am wronged." A few days later she was hanged. Rebecca Nurse, a pious seventy-one-year-old matriarch of a large family, went to the gallows in July. George Jacobs, an old man whose servant girl accused him of witchcraft, dismissed the whole chorus of accusers as "bitch witches." He was hanged in August.

But as the net of accusation spread wider, extending far beyond the confines of Salem, leaders of the Massachusetts Bay Colony began to worry that the witch hunts were out of control. The governor intervened when his own wife was accused of serving the devil. He disbanded the special court in Salem and ordered the remaining suspects released. A year after it had begun, the fratricidal event was finally over. Nineteen people (including some men married to women who had been convicted) had been hanged, one man—the stubborn Giles Corey— was pressed to death by heavy stones, and more than 100 others were jailed. Nearly everybody responsible for the Salem executions later recanted, and nothing quite like it happened in the colonies again.

What explains the witchcraft hysteria at Salem? Some have argued that it may have represented nothing more than a contagious exercise in adolescent imagination intended to enliven the dreary routine of everyday life. Yet adults pressed the formal charges against the accused and provided most of the testimony. This fact has led some scholars to speculate that long-festering local feuds and property disputes may have triggered the prosecutions.

More recently historians have focused on the most salient fact about the accused witches: almost all of them were women. Many of the supposed witches, it turns out, had in some way defied the traditional roles assigned to females. Some had engaged in business transactions outside the home; others did not attend church; some were curmudgeons. Most of them were middle-aged or older and without sons or brothers. They thus stood to inherit property and live as independent women. The notion of autonomous spinsters flew in the face of prevailing social conventions.

Still another interpretation stresses the hysteria caused in the late seventeenth century by frequent Indian attacks occurring just north of Salem, along New England's northern frontier. The outbreak of King William's War in 1689 had revived fighting with the northern Indians, and some of the participants in the witch trials were orphan girls from Maine who had witnessed the violence firsthand. Their proximity to such horrific events and the terrifying specter of new Indian attacks exacerbated anxieties and may help explain why witchcraft hysteria developed so rapidly and extensively. "Are you guilty or not?" the Salem magistrate John Hathorne demanded of fourteen-year-old Abigail Hobbs in 1692. "I have seen sights and been scared," she answered.

Whatever the precise cause, there is little doubt that the witchcraft controversy reflected the peculiar social dynamics of the Salem community. Late in 1692, as the hysteria in Salem subsided, several of the afflicted girls were traveling through nearby Ipswich when they encountered an old woman resting on a bridge. "A witch!" they shouted and began writhing as if possessed. But the people of Ipswich were unimpressed. Passersby showed no interest in the theatrics. Unable to generate either sympathy or curiosity, the girls picked themselves up and continued on their way.

SOCIETY AND ECONOMY IN THE MIDDLE COLONIES

AN ECONOMIC MIX   Both geographically and culturally the middle colonies stood between New England and the South, blending their own influences with elements derived from the older regions on either side. In so doing, they more completely reflected the diversity of colonial life and more fully foreshadowed the pluralism of the American nation than the other regions did. Their crops were those of New England but more bountiful, owing to better land and a longer growing season, and they developed surpluses of foodstuffs for export to the plantations of the South and the West Indies: wheat, barley, oats, and other cereals, flour, and livestock. Three great rivers—the Hudson, the Delaware, and the Susquehanna—and their tributaries gave the middle colonies ready access to the backcountry and to the fur trade of the interior, where New York and Pennsylvania long enjoyed friendly relations with the Iroquois, the Delaware, and other tribes. As a consequence the region's commerce rivaled that of New England, and indeed Philadelphia in time supplanted Boston as the largest city in the colonies.

Land policies in the middle colonies followed the headright system of the South. In New York the early royal governors carried forward, in practice if not in name, the Dutch device of the patroonship, granting influential favorites vast estates on Long Island and up the Hudson and Mohawk River valleys. These realms most nearly approached the medieval manor. They were self-contained domains farmed by tenants who paid fees to use the landlords' mills, warehouses, smokehouses, and wharves. But with free land available elsewhere, New York's population languished, and the new waves of immigrants sought the promised land of Pennsylvania.

AN ETHNIC MIX   In the makeup of their population, the middle colonies stood apart from both the mostly English Puritan settlements and the biracial plantation colonies to the south. In New York and New Jersey, for instance, Dutch culture and language lingered, along with the Dutch Reformed Church. Along the Delaware River the few Swedes and Finns, the first settlers, were overwhelmed by the influx of English and Welsh Quakers, followed in turn by Germans and Scotch-Irish.

The Germans came mainly from the Rhineland, a region devastated by incessant war. (Until German unification in 1871, ethnic Germans—those Europeans speaking German as their native language—lived in a variety of areas and principalities in central Europe.) William Penn's brochures encouraging settlement in Pennsylvania circulated throughout central Europe in German translation, and his promise of religious freedom appealed to persecuted sects, especially the Mennonites, German Baptists whose beliefs resembled those of the Quakers.

In 1683 a group of Mennonites founded Germantown, near Philadelphia. They were the vanguard of a swelling migration in the eighteenth century that included Lutherans, Reformed Calvinists, Moravians, and others, a large proportion of whom paid their way as indentured servants, or "redemptioners," as they were commonly called. West of Philadelphia they created a belt of settlement in which the "Pennsylvania Dutch" (a corruption of *Deutsch*, meaning "German") predominated, as well as a channel for the dispersion of German populations throughout the colonies.

The feisty Scotch-Irish began to arrive later and moved still farther out into the backcountry throughout the eighteenth century. (*Scotch-Irish* is an enduring misnomer for Ulster Scots, Presbyterians transplanted from Scotland to confiscated lands in northern Ireland to give that country a more Protestant tone.) The Scotch-Irish, mostly Presbyterians, fled both Anglican persecution and economic disaster caused by English taxes. Between 1717 and 1775 over 250,000 Scots and Scotch-Irish left northern England, southern Scotland, and northern Ireland for America. They settled in Pennsylvania and the fertile valleys stretching southwestward into Virginia and Carolina.

The Germans and Scotch-Irish became the largest non-English elements in the colonies, but other groups enriched the population in New York and the Quaker colonies: Huguenots (Calvinists whose religious freedom had been revoked in France in 1685), Irish, Welsh, Swiss, Jews, and others. New York had inherited from the Dutch a tradition of tolerance that had given the colony a diverse population before the English conquest: French-speaking Walloons and French, Germans, Danes, Portuguese, Spaniards, Italians, Bohemians, Poles, and others, including some New England Puritans. The Protestant Netherlands had given haven to the Sephardic Jews expelled from Spain and Portugal, and enough of them found their way into New Netherland to found a synagogue there.

What could be said of Pennsylvania as a refuge for the persecuted might be said as well of Rhode Island and South Carolina, which practiced a similar religious toleration. Newport and Charleston, like New York and Philadelphia, became centers of minuscule Jewish populations. Huguenots

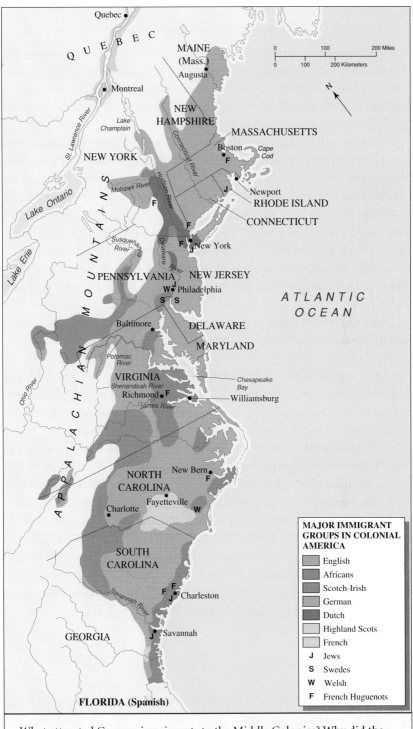

Quebec

QUEBEC

Montreal

Lake
Champlain

MAINE
(Mass.)

Augusta

NEW
HAMPSHIRE

MASSACHUSETTS

Boston
F

Cape
Cod

NEW YORK

Lake Ontario

St. Lawrence River

Mohawk River

Connecticut River

Hudson River

J

Newport

RHODE ISLAND

CONNECTICUT

Lake Erie

Susquehanna
River

F

Delaware River

F
New York

A
P
P
A
L
A
C
H
I
A
N
M
O
U
N
T
A
I
N
S

PENNSYLVANIA

NEW JERSEY

J
W
S S
Philadelphia

ATLANTIC
OCEAN

Baltimore

DELAWARE

MARYLAND

Ohio River

Potomac
River

VIRGINIA

Shenandoah River
F
Richmond
James River

Chesapeake
Bay

Williamsburg

NORTH
CAROLINA

New Bern
F

Charlotte

Fayetteville
W

SOUTH
CAROLINA

Savannah River

F F
J
Charleston

GEORGIA

J
Savannah

FLORIDA (Spanish)

**MAJOR IMMIGRANT
GROUPS IN COLONIAL
AMERICA**

- English
- Africans
- Scotch-Irish
- German
- Dutch
- Highland Scots
- French
- **J** Jews
- **S** Swedes
- **W** Welsh
- **F** French Huguenots

What attracted German immigrants to the Middle Colonies? Why did the
Scotch-Irish spread across the Appalachian backcountry? What major population changes were reflected in the 1790 census?

made their greatest mark on South Carolina, more by their enterprise than by their numbers. A number of Highland Scots came directly from their homeland rather than by way of Ulster, especially after the suppression of a rebellion in 1745 on behalf of the Stuart pretender to the throne, Bonnie Prince Charlie.

The eighteenth century was the period of great expansion and population growth in British North America, and during those years a large increase in the non-English stock took place. A rough estimate of the national origins of the white population as of 1790 found it to be 61 percent English, 14 percent Scottish and Scotch-Irish, 9 percent German, 5 percent Dutch, French, and Swedish, 4 percent Irish, and 7 percent miscellaneous or unassigned. If one adds to the 3,172,444 whites in the 1790 census the 756,770 nonwhites, not even considering uncounted Indians, it seems likely that only about half the populace, and perhaps fewer, could trace their origins to England. Of the black slaves, about 75 percent had been transported from the bend of the African coastline between the Senegal and Niger rivers; most of the rest came from the Congo-Angola region.

THE BACKCOUNTRY Pennsylvania in the eighteenth century became the great distribution point for the different ethnic groups of European origin, just as the Chesapeake Bay region and Charleston became the distribution points for African peoples. Before the mid–eighteenth century, settlers in the Pennsylvania backcountry had reached the Appalachian Mountain range. Rather than crossing the steep ridges, the Scotch-Irish and Germans filtered southward along what came to be called the Great Philadelphia Road, the primary internal migration route during the colonial period. It headed west from the port city, traversing Chester and Lancaster counties, and turned southwest at Harris' Ferry (now Harrisburg), where it crossed the Susquehanna River. Continuing south across western Maryland, it headed down the Shenandoah Valley of Virginia and on into the Carolina and Georgia backcountry. Germans were the first white settlers in the upper Shenandoah Valley, and Scotch-Irish filled the lower valley.

COLONIAL CITIES

During the seventeenth century the American colonies remained in comparative isolation from one another, evolving distinctive folkways and unfolding separate histories. Boston and New York and Philadelphia and Charleston were more likely to keep in close touch with London than with each other. The Carolina up-country had more in common with the Pennsylvania backcountry than either had with the urban cultures of Charleston or Philadelphia. Since commerce was their chief reason for being, colonial cities hugged the coastline or, like Philadelphia, sprang up on rivers where oceangoing vessels could reach them. Never holding more than 10 percent of the colonial population, the large cities exerted a disproportionate influence in commerce, politics, and culture. By the end of the colonial period, Philadelphia, with some 30,000 people, was the largest city in the colonies and second only to London in the British Empire. New York, with about 25,000, ranked second; Boston numbered 16,000; Charleston, 12,000; and Newport, 11,000.

THE SOCIAL AND POLITICAL ORDER   The urban social elite was dominated by the merchants who bartered the products of American farms and forests for the molasses and rum of the West Indies, the manufactured goods of Europe, and the slaves of Africa. After the merchants, who constituted the chief urban aristocracy, came a middle class of retailers, innkeepers, and artisans. Almost two thirds of the urban adult male workers were artisans, people who made their living at handicrafts. They included carpenters and coopers (barrel makers), shoemakers and tailors, silversmiths and blacksmiths, sailmakers, stonemasons, weavers, and potters. At the bottom of the pecking order were sailors and unskilled workers.

Class stratification in the cities became more pronounced as time passed. One study of Boston found that in 1687 the richest 15 percent of the population held 52 percent of the taxable wealth; by 1771 the top 15 percent held about 67 percent and the top 5 percent held some 44 percent. In Philadelphia the concentration of wealth was even more pronounced.

Colonial cities were busy, crowded, and dangerous. They

The Rapalje Children

John Durand (ca. 1768). These children of a wealthy Brooklyn merchant wear clothing typical of upper-crust urban society.

required not only paved roads and streetlights but regulations to protect children and animals from reckless riders. Regulations restrained citizens from tossing their garbage into the street. Fires that on occasion swept through closely packed buildings led to preventive standards in building codes, restrictions on burning rubbish, and the organization of fire companies. Rising crime and violence required more police protection. And in cities the poor became more visible than they were in the countryside.

Colonists brought with them the English principle of public responsibility for the indigent. The number of Boston's poor receiving public assistance rose from 500 in 1700 to 4,000 in 1736; in New York the number rose from 250 in 1698 to 5,000 in the 1770s. Most of such public assistance went to "outdoor" relief in the form of money, food, clothing, and fuel. Almshouses appeared to house the destitute.

THE URBAN WEB Transit within and between cities was initially difficult. The first roads were Indian trails, which themselves often followed the tracks of bison through the forests. Those trails widened with travel, then were made into roads by order of provincial and local authorities. Land travel was initially by horse or by foot. The first public stagecoach line opened in 1732. From the main ports good roads might reach thirty or forty miles inland, but all were dirt roads subject to washouts and mud holes. Aside from city streets there was not a single hard-surfaced road constructed during the entire colonial period.

Taverns were an important aspect of colonial travel, since movement by night was too risky to undertake. By the end of the seventeenth century, there were more taverns in America than any other business. Indeed, they became the most important social institution in the colonies—and the most democratic. By 1690 there were fifty-four taverns in Boston alone, half of them operated by women. Colonial taverns and inns were places to drink, relax, read the newspaper, play cards or billiards, gossip about people or politics, learn news from travelers, or conduct business. Local ordinances regulated them, setting prices and usually prohibiting them from serving liquor to African Americans, Indians, servants, or apprentices.

In 1726 a concerned Bostonian wrote a letter to the community, declaring that "the abuse of strong Drink is becoming Epidemical among us, and it is very justly Supposed . . . that the Multiplication of Taverns has contributed not a little to this Excess of Riot and Debauchery." Despite the objections by some that crowded taverns engendered disease and unruly behavior, colonial taverns and inns continued to proliferate, and by the mid–eighteenth century they would become the gathering place for protests against British rule.

Taverns

A tobacconist's business card from 1770 captures the atmosphere of late-eighteenth-century taverns. Here men in a Philadelphia tavern share conversation while they drink ale and smoke pipes.

Taverns served as a collective form of communication; long-distance communication, however, was more complicated. Postal service in the seventeenth century was almost nonexistent—people entrusted letters to travelers or sea captains. Under a parliamentary law of 1710, the postmaster of London named a deputy in charge of the colonies, and a postal system eventually extended the length of the Atlantic seaboard. Benjamin Franklin, who served as deputy postmaster for the colonies from 1753 to 1774, sped up the service with shorter routes and night-traveling post riders, and he increased the volume by inaugurating lower rates.

More reliable mail delivery gave rise to newspapers in the eighteenth century. Before 1745 twenty-two newspapers had been started: seven in New England, ten in the middle colonies, and five in the South. An important landmark in the progress of freedom of the press was John Peter Zenger's trial for seditious libel, for publishing criticisms of New York's governor in his newspaper, the *New York Weekly Journal*. Zenger was imprisoned for ten months and brought to trial in 1735. English common law held that one might be punished for criticism that fostered "an ill opinion of the government." The jury's function was only to determine whether the defendant had published the opinion. Zenger's lawyer startled the court with his claim that the editor had published the truth—which the judge ruled an unacceptable defense. The jury, however, agreed with the assertion and held the editor not guilty. The libel law remained standing as before, but editors thereafter were emboldened to criticize officials more freely.

THE ENLIGHTENMENT

DISCOVERING THE LAWS OF NATURE   Through their commercial contacts, newspapers, and other channels, colonial cities became centers for the dissemination of fashion and ideas. In the world of ideas, a new fashion was abroad: the Enlightenment. During the seventeenth century, Europe experienced a scientific revolution in which the ancient view of an earth-centered universe was overthrown by the heliocentric (sun-centered) system of the sixteenth-century Polish astronomer Nicolaus Copernicus. A climax to the scientific revolution came with Sir Isaac Newton's *Principia* (*Mathematical Principles of Natural Philosophy*, 1687), which set forth his theory of gravitation. Newton depicted a mechanistic universe moving in accordance with natural laws that could be grasped by human reason and explained by mathematics. He implied that natural laws govern all things—the orbits of the planets and the orbits of human relations: politics, economics, and society. Reason could make people aware, for instance, that the natural law of supply and demand governs economics or that the natural rights to life, liberty, and property determine the limits and functions of government.

Much of enlightened thought could be reconciled with established beliefs: the idea of natural law existed in Christian theology, and religious people could reason that the rational universe of Copernicus and Newton simply demonstrated the glory of God. Yet when people carried Newton's outlook to its ultimate logic, as the Deists did, the idea of natural law reduced God to a remote Creator—as the French philosophe Voltaire put it, the master clockmaker who planned the universe and set it in motion. Evil in the world, in this view, results not from original sin and innate depravity so much as from ignorance, an imperfect understanding of the laws of nature. Humanity, the English philosopher John Locke argued in his *Essay Concerning Human Understanding* (1690), is largely the product of the environment, the mind being a blank tablet on which experience is written. The way to improve both society and human nature was by the application and improvement of Reason—which was the highest Virtue (Enlightenment thinkers often capitalized both words).

THE ENLIGHTENMENT IN AMERICA   However interpreted, such ideas profoundly affected the climate of thought in the eighteenth century.

The premises of Newtonian science and the Enlightenment, moreover, fitted the American experience, which placed a premium on observation, experiment, and the need to think anew. America was therefore especially receptive to the new science.

John Winthrop Jr.(1606–1676), three times governor of Connecticut, wanted to establish industries and mining in America. Those interests led to his work in chemistry and to his membership in the Royal Society of London. He owned probably the first telescope brought to the colonies. His relative, John Winthrop (1714–1779), was a professional scientist and Harvard professor who introduced to the colonies the study of calculus and ranged over the fields of astronomy, geology, chemistry, and electricity. David Rittenhouse of Philadelphia, a clock maker, became a self-taught scientist who was probably the first to build a telescope in America. John Bartram, also of Philadelphia, spent a lifetime traveling and studying American plant life and developed an extensive botanical garden.

FRANKLIN'S INFLUENCE   Benjamin Franklin epitomized the Enlightenment in the eyes of both Americans and Europeans. Born in Boston in 1706, he was the son of a maker of candles and soap. Apprenticed to his older brother, a printer, Franklin left home at the age of seventeen, bound for Philadelphia. There, before he was twenty-four, he owned a print shop, where he edited and published the *Pennsylvania Gazette*. When he was twenty-six, he brought out *Poor Richard's Almanack*, a collection of homely maxims on success and happiness. Before he retired from business, at the age of forty-two, Franklin, among other achievements, had founded a library, set up a fire company, helped start the academy that became the University of Pennsylvania, and organized a debating club that grew into the American Philosophical Society.

Science was Franklin's passion. His *Experiments and Observations on Electricity* (1751) went through many editions in several languages and established his reputation as a leading thinker and experimenter. His

Benjamin Franklin

Shown here as a young man in a portrait by Robert Feke.

speculations extended widely, to the fields of medicine, meteorology, geology, astronomy, physics, and other areas of science. He invented the Franklin stove, the lightning rod, and a glass harmonica, for which Mozart and Beethoven wrote works. The triumph of this untutored genius confirmed the Enlightenment trust in the powers of Nature and Reason.

EDUCATION IN THE COLONIES   For the colonists at large, education in the traditional ideas and manners of society—even literacy itself—remained primarily the responsibility of family and church. The modern conception of free public education was slow in coming and failed to win universal acceptance until the twentieth century. Yet colonists were concerned from the beginning that steps needed to be taken lest the children of settlers grow up untutored.

Conditions in New England proved most favorable for the establishment of schools. The Puritan emphasis on Scripture reading, which all Protestants shared to some degree, implied an obligation to ensure literacy. And the compact towns of that region made schools more feasible than they were among the scattered settlers of the southern colonies. In 1647 the Massachusetts Bay Colony enacted the famous "ye olde deluder Satan" act (designed to thwart the evil one), which required every town of fifty or more families to set up a grammar school (a "Latin school" that could prepare a student for college). Although the act was widely evaded, it did signify a serious attempt to promote education.

Colonial Education

A page from the rhymed alphabet of *The New England Primer,* a popular American textbook first published in the 1680s.

The Dutch in New Netherland were as interested in education as the New England Puritans. In Pennsylvania the Quakers never heeded William Penn's instructions to establish public schools, but they did finance a number of private schools, where practical as well as academic subjects were taught. In the southern colonies efforts to establish schools were hampered by the more scattered population and in parts of the backcountry by indifference and neglect. Some of the wealthiest planters and merchants of the Tidewater sent their children to England or hired tutors. In some places wealthy patrons or the people collectively managed to raise some kind of support for "old field" schools (primitive one-room buildings usually made of logs) and academies at the secondary level.

THE GREAT AWAKENING

STIRRINGS   During the early eighteenth century the currents of rationalism stimulated by the Enlightenment aroused concerns among orthodox believers in Calvinism. Many people seemed to be drifting away from the moorings of piety. Despite the belief that the Lord had allowed great Puritan and Quaker merchants of Boston and Philadelphia to prosper, there remained a haunting fear that the devil had lured them into the vain pursuit of worldly gain, Deism, and skepticism. And out along the fringes of settlement, many of the colonists were unchurched. On the frontier, people had no minister to preach or administer sacraments or perform marriages. According to some ministers, these pioneers had lapsed into a primitive and sinful life, little different from that of the "heathen" Indians. By the 1730s the sense of religious decline provoked a widespread revival of faith, known as the Great Awakening.

In 1734–1735 a remarkable spiritual revival occurred in the congregation of Jonathan Edwards, a Congregationalist minister in Northampton, in western Massachusetts. One of America's most brilliant philosophers and theologians, Edwards had entered Yale in 1716, at age thirteen, and graduated as valedictorian four years later. In 1727 Edwards was called to serve the Congregational church in Northampton. There he found the town's spirituality at a low ebb. More people frequented taverns than churches, and Christians, he believed, had become preoccupied with making and spending money. Religion had also become too intellectual, thereby losing its emotional force. "Our people," he said, "do not so much need to have their heads stored [with new knowledge] as to have their hearts touched." His own vivid descriptions of the torments of hell and the delights of heaven helped rekindle spiritual fervor among his congregants. By 1735 Edwards could report that "the town seemed to be full of the presence of God; it never was so full of love, nor of joy." To judge the power of the Awakening, he thought, one need only observe that "it was no longer the Tavern" that drew local crowds, "but the Minister's House."

George Whitefield

The English minister's dramatic eloquence roused American congregants, inspiring many to experience a religious rebirth.

About the same time, William Tennent, an Irish-born Presbyterian revivalist, set up a "Log College" in Neshaminy, Pennsylvania, for the education of ministers to serve the Scotch-Irish Presbyterians living around Philadelphia. The true catalyst of the Great Awakening, however, was a young English minister, George Whitefield, whose reputation as a spellbinding evangelist preceded him to the colonies. Congregations were lifeless, he claimed, "because dead men preach to them." Too many ministers were "slothful shepherds and dumb dogs." His objective was to restore the fires of religious fervor to American congregations. In the autumn of 1739, Whitefield, then twenty-five, arrived in Philadelphia and began preaching to huge crowds. After visiting Georgia, he made a triumphal procession northward to New England, drawing great crowds and releasing "Gales of Heavenly Wind" that blew gusts throughout the colonies.

Possessed of a golden voice, Whitefield enthralled audiences with his unparalleled eloquence. Even the skeptical Benjamin Franklin, who went to see Whitefield preach in Philadelphia, found himself so carried away that he emptied his pockets into the collection plate. Whitefield urged his listeners to experience a "new birth"—a sudden, emotional moment of conversion and salvation. By the end of his sermon, one listener reported, the entire congregation was "in utmost Confusion, some crying out, some laughing, and Bliss still roaring to them to come to Christ, as they answered, *I will, I will, I'm coming, I'm coming.*"

Jonathan Edwards took advantage of the commotion stirred up by Whitefield to spread his own revival gospel throughout New England. The Awakening reached its peak in 1741 when Edwards delivered his most famous sermon at Enfield, Massachusetts (in present-day Connecticut). Titled "Sinners in the Hands of an Angry God," it represented a devout appeal to repentance. Edwards reminded the congregation that hell is real and that God's vision is omnipotent, his judgment certain. He noted that God "holds you over the pit of hell, much as one holds a spider, or some loathsome insect, over the fire, abhors you, and is dreadfully provoked . . . he looks upon you

as worthy of nothing else, but to be cast into the fire." When Edwards finished, he had to wait several minutes for the congregants to quiet down before leading them in a closing hymn.

Edwards and Whitefield inspired many imitators, some of whom carried
evangelism to extremes. Once unleashed, spiritual enthusiasm is hard to
control. In many ways the Awakening backfired on those who had intended
it to bolster church discipline and social order. Some of the revivalists began
to court those at the bottom of society—laborers, seamen, servants, and
farm folk. The Reverend James Davenport, for instance, a fiery New England
Congregationalist, set about shouting, raging, and stomping on the devil,
beseeching his listeners to renounce the established clergy and become the
agents of their own salvation. The churched and unchurched flocked to his
theatrical sermons. Seized by terror and ecstasy, they groveled on the floor or
lay unconscious on the benches, to the chagrin of more decorous churchgo-
ers. One never knew, the more traditional clergymen warned, whence came
these enthusiasms—perhaps they were devilish delusions intended to discredit the true faith.

PIETY AND REASON   Everywhere the fragmenting force of the Awaken-
ing induced splits, especially in the more Calvinistic churches. Presbyterians
divided into the "Old Side" and "New Side," Congregationalists into "Old
Lights" and "New Lights." New England religious life would never be the same.
The more traditional clergy were undermined as church members chose sides
and either dismissed their ministers or deserted them. Many of the "New
Lights" went over to the Baptists, and others flocked to Presbyterian or, later,
Methodist groups, which in turn divided and subdivided into new sects.

New England Puritanism disintegrated amid the ecstatic revivals of the
Great Awakening. The precarious balance in which the founders had held the
elements of emotionalism and reason collapsed. Thereafter, New England
attracted more and more Baptists, Presbyterians, Anglicans, and other denominations while the revival frenzy scored its most lasting victories along
the frontiers of the middle and southern colonies. In the more sedate
churches of Boston, moreover, the principle of rational religion gained the
upper hand in a reaction against the excesses of revival emotion. Boston
ministers such as Charles Chauncey and Jonathan Mayhew reexamined
Calvinist theology and found too forbidding and irrational the concept that
people could be forever damned by predestination.

In reaction to taunts that the "born-again" revivalist ministers lacked
learning, the Awakening gave rise to the denominational colleges that
became characteristic of American higher education. The three colleges already in existence had their origins in religious motives: Harvard College,

founded in 1636 because the Puritans dreaded "to leave an illiterate ministry to the church when our present ministers shall lie in the dust"; the College of William and Mary, created in 1693 to strengthen the Anglican ministry; and Yale College, set up in 1701 to educate the Puritans of Connecticut, who believed that Harvard was drifting from the strictest orthodoxy. The College of New Jersey, later Princeton University, was founded by Presbyterians in 1746. In close succession came King's College (1754) in New York, later renamed Columbia University, an Anglican institution; the College of Rhode Island (1764), later called Brown University, which was Baptist; Queens College (1766), later known as Rutgers, which was Dutch Reformed; and Dartmouth College (1769), which was Congregationalist and the outgrowth of an earlier school for Indians. Among the colonial colleges, only the University of Pennsylvania, founded as the Academy of Philadelphia in 1751, arose from a secular impulse.

The Great Awakening, like the Enlightenment, set in motion powerful currents that still flow in American life. It implanted in American culture the evangelical crusade and the emotional appeal of revivalism. The movement weakened the status of the old-fashioned clergy, encouraged believers to exercise their own judgment, and thereby weakened habits of deference generally. By encouraging the proliferation of denominations, it heightened the need for toleration of dissent. But in some respects the counterpoint between the Awakening and the Enlightenment, between the principles of spirit and reason, led by different roads to similar ends. Both movements emphasized the power and right of individual decision making, and both aroused millennial hopes that America would become the promised land in which people might attain the perfection of piety or reason, if not both.

MAKING CONNECTIONS

- This chapter reveals tensions in colonial Virginia society; such tensions would periodically come to a head, as in Bacon's Rebellion, discussed in Chapter 2.

- During the imperial crisis of the 1760s and 1770s, the ideas of the Great Awakening and especially the Enlightenment helped shape the American response to British actions and thereby contributed to a revolutionary mentality.

FURTHER READING

The diversity of colonial societies may be seen in David Hackett Fischer's *Albion's Seed: Four British Folkways in America* (1989). On the economic development of New England, see Christine Leigh Heyrman's *Commerce and Culture: The Maritime Communities of Colonial Massachusetts, 1690–1750* (1984) and Stephen Innes's *Creating the Commonwealth: The Economic Culture of Puritan New England* (1995). John Frederick Martin's *Profits in the Wilderness: Entrepreneurship and the Founding of New England Towns in the Seventeenth Century* (1991) indicates that economic concerns rather than spiritual motives were driving forces in many New England towns. For a fascinating account of the impact of livestock on colonial history, see Virginia DeJohn Anderson's *Creatures of Empire: How Domestic Animals Transformed Early America* (2004).

Paul Boyer and Stephen Nissenbaum's *Salem Possessed: The Social Origins of Witchcraft* (1974) connects the notorious witch trials to changes in community structure. Bernard Rosenthal challenges many myths concerning the Salem witch trials in *Salem Story: Reading the Witch Trials of 1692* (1993). Mary Beth Norton's *In the Devil's Snare: The Salem Witchcraft Crisis of 1692* (2002) emphasizes the role of Indian violence.

Discussions of women in the New England colonies can be found in Laurel Thatcher Ulrich's *Good Wives: Image and Reality in the Lives of Women in Northern New England, 1650–1750* (1980), Joy Day Buel and Richard Buel Jr.'s *The Way of Duty: A Woman and Her Family in Revolutionary America* (1984), and Carol F. Karlsen's *The Devil in the Shape of a Woman: Witchcraft in Colonial New England* (1987). John Demos describes family life in *A Little Commonwealth: Family Life in Plymouth Colony*, new ed. (2000).

On New England Indians, see Kathleen J. Bragdon's *Native People of Southern New England, 1500–1650* (1996). For analyses of Indian wars, see Alfred A. Cave's *The Pequot War* (1996) and Jill Lepore's *The Name of War: King Philip's War and the Origins of American Identity* (1998). The story of the Iroquois is told well in Daniel K. Richter's *The Ordeal of the Longhouse: The Peoples of the Iroquois League in the Era of European Colonization* (1992). Indians in the southern colonies are the focus of James Axtell's *The Indians' New South: Cultural Change in the Colonial Southeast* (1997).

For the social history of the southern colonies, see Allan Kulikoff's *Tobacco and Slaves: The Development of Southern Cultures in the Chesapeake, 1680–1800* (1986) and Kathleen M. Brown's *Good Wives, Nasty Wenches, and Anxious Patriarchs: Gender, Race, and Power in Colonial Virginia* (1996).

Family life along the Chesapeake Bay is described in Gloria L. Main's *Tobacco Colony: Life in Early Maryland, 1650–1720* (1982) and Daniel Blake Smith's *Inside the Great House: Planter Family Life in Eighteenth-Century Chesapeake Society* (1980).

Edmund S. Morgan's *American Slavery, American Freedom: The Ordeal of Colonial Virginia* (1975) examines Virginia's social structure, environment, and labor patterns in a biracial context. On the interaction of the cultures of blacks and whites, see Mechal Sobel's *The World They Made Together: Black and White Values in Eighteenth-Century Virginia* (1987). African-American viewpoints are presented in Timothy H. Breen and Stephen Innes's *"Myne Owne Ground": Race and Freedom on Virginia's Eastern Shore, 1640–1676*, new ed. (2004). David W. Galenson's *White Servitude in Colonial America: An Economic Analysis* (1981) looks at the indentured labor force.

Henry F. May's *The Enlightenment in America* (1976) examines intellectual trends in eighteenth-century America. Lawrence A. Cremin's *American Education: The Colonial Experience, 1607–1783* (1970) surveys educational developments.

On the Great Awakening, see Patricia U. Bonomi's *Under the Cope of Heaven: Religion, Society, and Politics in Colonial America* (1986) and Frank Lambert's *Inventing the "Great Awakening"* (1999). For evangelism in the South, see Christine Leigh Heyrman's *Southern Cross: The Beginnings of the Bible Belt* (1997).

4

THE IMPERIAL PERSPECTIVE

FOCUS QUESTIONS

· How did England's policies change the political and economic administration of the colonies?

· How were colonial governments structured?

· What were relations like between the English colonists and their neighbors in North America: the French, the Spanish, and the Indians?

The English differed from the Spanish and the French in the degree of freedom they initially allowed their American colonies. Unlike New France and New Spain, New England was in effect a self-governing community. There was much less control by the mother country, in part because the English were unwilling to incur the expenses of a vast colonial bureaucracy. The constant struggle between Parliament and the Stuart kings prevented England from perfecting either a systematic colonial policy or effective agencies of imperial control. After the Restoration of Charles II and the Stuart monarchy in 1660, a more comprehensive plan of colonial administration slowly emerged, but even so it lacked coherence and efficiency.

As a result of inefficient—and often lax—colonial administration by the mother country, Americans grew accustomed to loose and often paradoxical imperial policies. For instance, the English government granted home rule to the settlements along the Atlantic coast and then sought to keep them from exercising it. It regarded the English colonists as citizens but refused to grant them the privileges of citizenship. It insisted that the settlers contribute to the expense of maintaining the colonies but refused to allow them a voice in the shaping of administrative policies. Such inconsistencies spawned tensions. By the mid–eighteenth century, when Britain tried to tighten control of its American colonies, it was too late. British Americans had developed a far more powerful sense of their rights than any other colonial people, and they resolved to assert and defend those rights.

English Administration of the Colonies

Throughout the colonial period the king was the source of legal authority in America, and land titles derived ultimately from royal grants to individuals and groups. All the colonies except Georgia received charters from the king before the Glorious Revolution of 1688, when the crown lost supremacy to Parliament. The colonies therefore continued to stand as "dependencies of the crown," and the important colonial officials held office at its pleasure. The English Civil War, which lasted from 1642 to 1649, led to Oliver Cromwell's Puritan Commonwealth and Protectorate, and both developments gave the colonies a respite from efforts at royal control.

THE MERCANTILE SYSTEM   Oliver Cromwell showed little passion for regulating daily life in the American colonies, but he had a lively concern for colonial trade, which had fallen largely to Dutch shipping during the civil war. Therefore, in 1651 Parliament adopted the Navigation Act, requiring that all goods imported to England or the colonies be carried only on English ships and that the majority of each crew be English.

On economic policy if nothing else, Restoration England under Charles II followed the lead of Cromwell and all the other major European powers of the seventeenth and eighteenth centuries. The new Parliament adopted the mercantile system, or mercantilism, a nationalistic program that assumed that the total of the world's gold and silver remained essentially fixed, with only a nation's share in that wealth subject to change. Thus one nation could gain wealth only at the expense of another—by seizing its gold and silver and dominating its trade. To acquire gold and silver, a government had to control all economic activities, limiting foreign imports and preserving a favorable balance of trade. This required a mercantilist government to encourage manufacturers, through subsidies and monopolies if need be. Mercantilism also required a nation to develop and protect its own shipping and to exploit colonies as sources of raw materials and markets for its finished goods.

The Navigation Act of 1660 gave Cromwell's act of 1651 a new twist: ships' crews had to be three-quarters, not just a majority, English, and specified goods were to be shipped only to England or other English colonies. The list of "enumerated" goods initially included tobacco, cotton, indigo, ginger, dyewoods, and sugar. Rice, hemp, masts, copper ore, and furs, among other items, were added later. Not only did England (and its colonies) become the sole outlet for those "enumerated" colonial exports, but the Navigation Act of 1663 required that *all* colonial imports from Europe to America stop first in England, be offloaded, and have duty paid on them before reshipment to the colonies. The Navigation Acts, also called the British Act of Trade, gave England a monopoly over the tobacco and sugar produced in the Chesapeake and the West Indies. The acts also increased customs revenues collected in England, channeled all colonial commerce through English merchants, and enriched English shipbuilders. Over time, these regulations meant that the commercial activities of the American colonies became ever more important to the strength of the British Empire.

ENFORCING THE NAVIGATION ACTS The Navigation Acts supplied a convenient rationale for a colonial system: to serve the economic needs of the mother country. Yet enforcement was spotty. During the reign of Charles I, a bureaucracy of colonial administrators began to emerge, but it took shape slowly and incompletely. In 1675 Charles II introduced some order into the chaos when he designated the Lords of Trade to make the colonies abide by the mercantile system and seek out ways to make them more profitable to England and the crown. To these ends the lords served as the clearinghouse for all colonial affairs, building up a bureaucracy of colonial experts. The Lords of Trade named governors, wrote or reviewed the governors' instructions, and handled all reports and correspondence dealing with colonial affairs.

During the 1670s collectors of customs duties appeared in all the colonies, and a surveyor general of customs in the American colonies was named. The most notorious of these, insofar as resentful colonists were concerned, was Edward Randolph, the first man to make a career in the colonial service and the nemesis of insubordinate colonials for a quarter century. Randolph arrived

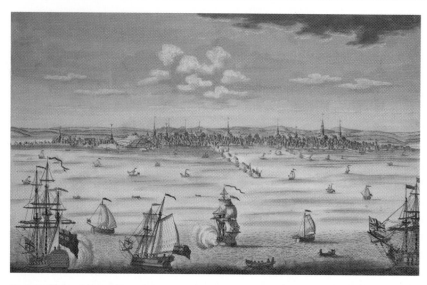

Boston from the Southeast

This view of eighteenth-century Boston shows the importance of shipping and its regulation in the colonies, especially in Massachusetts Bay.

at Boston in 1676 and soon demanded that Massachusetts abide by the Navigation Acts. He set up shop as the king's collector of customs in Boston, and within months his efforts to tighten control over commercial activity excited massive resentment. In 1678 a defiant Massachusetts legislature declared that the Navigation Acts had no legal standing in the colony. Eventually, in 1684, the Lords of Trade won a court decision that annulled the charter of Massachusetts. The Puritan utopia was fast becoming a lost cause.

THE DOMINION OF NEW ENGLAND   Temporarily the government of Massachusetts Bay was placed in the hands of a special royal commission. Then, in 1685, Charles II died, to be succeeded by his brother the duke of York, as James II, the first Catholic sovereign since the death of Queen Mary in 1558. James II asserted power more forcefully than his brother had. The new king readily approved a proposal to create a Dominion of New England that included all the colonies south through New Jersey.

The dominion was to have a government named by royal authority; a governor and council would rule without any assembly. The royal governor, Sir Edmund Andros, appeared in Boston in 1686 to establish his rule, which he soon extended over Connecticut and Rhode Island and, in 1688, over New York and East and West Jersey. Andros was a soldier, accustomed to taking—and giving—orders. He seems to have been honest, efficient, and loyal to the crown but tactless in circumstances that called for the utmost diplomacy—the uprooting of long-established institutions in the face of popular hostility.

A rising resentment greeted Andros's measures, especially in Massachusetts. Taxation was now levied without the consent of the General Court, and when residents of one seaboard town protested taxation without representation, several of them were imprisoned or fined. Andros suppressed

King James II

English monarch from 1685 to 1688.

town governments, enforced the trade laws, and punished smugglers. Most ominous of all, Andros and his lieutenants took over a Puritan church in Boston for Anglican worship. Puritan leaders believed, with good reason, that he was conspiring to break their power and authority.

But the Dominion of New England was scarcely established before the Glorious Revolution of 1688 erupted in England. King James II, like Andros in New England, had aroused resentment by instituting arbitrary measures—and by openly parading his Catholic faith. The birth of a son, sure to be reared a Catholic, put the opposition on notice that James's system would survive him. The Catholic son, rather than the Protestant daughters, Mary and Anne, would be next in line for the throne. Parliamentary leaders, their patience exhausted, invited Protestant Mary Stuart and her husband, the Dutch leader William III of Orange, to assume the throne as joint monarchs. James, seeing his support dwindling, fled to France.

THE GLORIOUS REVOLUTION IN AMERICA When news reached Boston that William had landed in England, the city staged its own Glorious Revolution. Andros and his councilors were arrested, and Massachusetts reverted to its former government. In rapid sequence the other colonies that had been absorbed into the dominion followed suit. All were permitted to retain their former status except Massachusetts Bay and Plymouth which after some delay were united under a new charter in 1691 as the royal colony of Massachusetts Bay.

In New York, however, events took a different course. There Andros's lieutenant governor was deposed by a German immigrant, Jacob Leisler, who assumed the office of governor pending approval from England. For two years he kept the province under his control with the support of the militia. Finally, in 1691, the king appointed a new governor. When Leisler hesitated to turn over authority, he was charged with treason, and he and his son-in-law were hanged on May 16, 1691. Four years too late, in 1695, Parliament exonerated them of all charges. Leisler and anti-Leisler factions would poison the political atmosphere of New York for years to come.

The new British monarchs, William and Mary, made no effort to restore the Dominion of New England, but they brought more colonies under royal control through the appointment of governors in Massachusetts, New York, and Maryland. Maryland, however, reverted to proprietary status in 1715, after the fourth Lord Baltimore became Anglican. Pennsylvania had an even briefer career as a royal colony, from 1692 to 1694, before reverting to William Penn's proprietorship. New Jersey became a royal province in 1702, South Carolina in 1719, North Carolina in 1729, and Georgia in 1752.

The Glorious Revolution had significant long-term effects on American history in that the Bill of Rights and the Act of Toleration, passed in England in 1689, influenced attitudes and the course of events in the colonies. Even more significant, the overthrow of James II set a precedent for revolution against the monarch. In defense of that action, the English philosopher John Locke published his *Two Treatises on Government* (1690), which had an enormous impact on political thought in the colonies. The first treatise refuted theories of the divine right of kings. The more important second treatise set forth Locke's contract theory of government, which claimed that people were endowed with certain natural rights to life, liberty, and property. The need to protect such rights led people to establish governments. Kings were parties to such agreements and obligated to protect the property and lives of their subjects. When they failed to do so, the people had the right—in extreme cases— to overthrow the monarch and change their government.

The idea that governments emerged by contract out of a primitive state of nature is of course hypothetical, not an account of actual events. But in the American experience, governments had actually grown out of contractual arrangements such as those Locke described: the Mayflower Compact, the Cambridge Agreement, the Fundamental Orders of Connecticut. The royal charters themselves constituted a sort of contract between the crown and the settlers. John Locke's writings understandably appealed to colonial readers, and his philosophy probably had more influence in America than in England.

AN EMERGING COLONIAL SYSTEM   The accession of William and Mary to the English throne led to a refinement of the existing Navigation

Acts. In 1696 two developments created at last the semblance and, to some degree, the reality of a coherent administrative system for the colonies. First, the Act to Prevent Frauds and Abuses of 1696 required colonial governors to enforce the trade laws, allowed customs officials to use "writs of assistance" (general search warrants that did not have to specify the place to be searched), and ordered that accused violators be tried in admiralty courts (because colonial juries habitually refused to convict their peers). Admiralty cases were decided by judges whom the royal governors appointed.

Second, also in 1696, William III created the Lords Commissioners of Trade and Plantations (the Board of Trade) to investigate the enforcement of the Navigation Acts and recommend ways to limit colonial manufactures and encourage the production of raw materials. At the board's behest, Parliament enacted a bounty for the production of ship timber, masts, hemp, rice, indigo, and other commodities. The board examined all colonial laws and made recommendations for their disallowance by the crown. In all, 8,563 colonial laws were eventually examined, and 469 were eliminated.

SALUTARY NEGLECT   From 1696 to 1725, the Board of Trade worked vigorously to subject the colonies to a more efficient royal control. After the death of Queen Anne, in 1714, however, its energies waned. The throne went in turn to the Hanoverian monarchs, George I (r. 1714–1727) and George II (r. 1727–1760), German princes who were next in the Protestant line of succession by virtue of descent from James I. Under these monarchs the cabinet (a kind of executive committee in the Privy Council) emerged as the central agency of administration. Robert Walpole, as first minister (1721–1742), deliberately followed a policy toward the colonies that the philosopher Edmund Burke later called "a wise and salutary neglect." Walpole's relaxed policy toward the colonies not only gave them greater freedom to pursue their economic interests; it unwittingly also enabled the Americans to pursue greater political independence.

THE HABIT OF SELF-GOVERNMENT

Government within the American colonies, like colonial policy, evolved without plan. In broad outline the governor, council, and assembly in each colony corresponded to the king, lords, and commons of the mother country. At the outset all the colonies except Georgia had begun as projects of trading companies or feudal proprietors holding charters from the crown, but eight colonies eventually relinquished or forfeited their charters and became royal provinces. In these the crown named the governor. In Maryland, Pennsylvania, and Delaware the governor remained the choice of a proprietor, although each had an interim period of royal government. Connecticut and Rhode Island were the last of the corporate colonies; they elected their own governors to the end of the colonial period. In the corporate and proprietary colonies and in Massachusetts, the charter served as a rough equivalent to a written constitution. Over the years certain anomalies appeared as colonial governments diverged from that of England. On the one hand, the governors retained powers and prerogatives that the king had lost in the course of the seventeenth century. On the other hand, the assemblies acquired powers, particularly with respect to government appointments, that Parliament had yet to gain.

POWERS OF THE GOVERNORS   The crown never vetoed acts of Parliament after 1707, but the colonial governors, most of whom were mediocre or incompetent, still held an absolute veto, and the crown could disallow (in effect, veto) colonial legislation on advice of the Board of Trade. With respect to the assembly, the governor still had the power to determine when and where it would meet, prorogue (adjourn or recess) legislative sessions, and dissolve the assembly for new elections or postpone elections indefinitely at his pleasure. The crown, however, had to summon Parliament every three years and call elections at least every seven and could not prorogue sessions. The royal or proprietary governor, moreover, nominated for life appointment the members of his council (except in Massachusetts, where they were chosen by the lower house), and the council functioned as both the upper house of the legislature and the highest court of appeal within the colony. With respect to the judiciary, in all but the charter colonies the governor held the prerogative of creating courts and naming and dismissing judges, powers explicitly denied the king in England. Over time, however, the colonial assemblies generally made good their claim that courts should be created only by legislative authority, although the crown repeatedly disallowed acts to grant judges life tenure in order to make them more independent.

As chief executive the governor could appoint and remove officials, command the militia and naval forces, and grant pardons. In these respects his authority resembled the crown's, for the king still exercised executive authority and had the power to name administrative officials. For the king those powers often strengthened an effective royal influence in Parliament, since the king could appoint members or their friends to lucrative offices. While the arrangement might seem a breeding ground for corruption or

The Boston Statehouse

Built in 1713.

tyranny, it was often viewed in the eighteenth century as a stabilizing influence, especially by the king's friends. But it was an influence less and less available to the governors. On the one hand, colonial assemblies nibbled away at their power of appointment; on the other hand, the authorities in England more and more drew the control of colonial patronage into their own hands.

POWERS OF THE ASSEMBLIES   Unlike the governor and members of the council, who were appointed by an outside authority, either king or proprietor, the colonial assembly was elected. Whether called the House of Burgesses (Virginia), Delegates (Maryland), or Representatives (Massachusetts) or simply the assembly, the lower houses were chosen by popular vote in counties, towns, or, in South Carolina, parishes. Although the English Toleration Act of 1689 did not apply to the colonies, religious tests for voting tended to be abandoned thereafter (the Massachusetts charter of 1691 so specified), and the chief restriction remaining was a property qualification, based upon the notion that only men who held a "stake in society" could vote responsibly. Yet the property qualifications generally set low hurdles in the way of potential voters. Property holding was widespread, and a greater proportion of the population could vote in the colonies than anywhere else in the world of the eighteenth century.

Women, children, Indians, and African Americans were excluded from the political process—as a matter of course—and continued to be excluded for the most part into the twentieth century, but the qualifications excluded few free white adult males. Virginia, which at one time permitted all freemen to vote, in the eighteenth century required the ownership of only 25 acres of improved land or 100 acres of wild land, the ownership of a "house" and part of a lot in town, or service in a five-year apprenticeship in Williamsburg or Norfolk. Qualifications for membership in the assembly ran somewhat higher, and officeholders tended to come from the more well to do—a phenomenon not unknown today—but there were exceptions. One unsympathetic colonist observed in 1744 that the New Jersey Assembly "was chiefly composed of mechanicks and ignorant wretches; obstinate to the last degree."

Colonial politics of the eighteenth century mirrored English politics of the seventeenth. In one case there had been a tug-of-war between king and Parliament, ending with the supremacy of Parliament and confirmed by the Glorious Revolution. In the other case, colonial governors were still trying to wield powers that the king had lost. The assemblies knew this; they also knew the arguments for the "rights" and "liberties" of the people and their legislative bodies and against the dangers of despotic power.

By the early eighteenth century the colonial assemblies, like Parliament, held two important strands of power—and they were perfectly aware of the parallel. First, they held the power of the purse strings in their right to vote on taxes and expenditures. Second, they held the power to initiate legislation and not merely, as in the early history of some colonies, the right to act on proposals from the governor and the council. Assemblies, because they controlled finance, demanded and often got the right to name tax collectors and treasurers. Then they stretched the claim to cover public printers, Indian agents, supervisors of public works and services, and other officers of the government.

All through the eighteenth century the assemblies expanded their power and influence, sometimes in conflict with the governors, sometimes in harmony with them, and often in the course of routine business, passing laws and setting precedents, the collective significance of which neither they nor the imperial authorities fully recognized. Once established, however, these laws and practices became fixed principles, part of the "constitution" of the colonies. Self-government became first a habit, then a "right."

TROUBLED NEIGHBORS

SPANISH AMERICA IN DECLINE   By the start of the eighteenth century, the Spanish were ruling over a huge colonial empire spanning North America. Yet their settlements in the borderlands north of Mexico were a colossal failure when compared with the colonies of the other European powers. In 1821, when Mexico declared its independence from Spain without firing a shot and the Spanish withdrew from North America, the most populated Hispanic settlement, Santa Fe, had only 6,000 residents. The next largest, San Antonio and St. Augustine, had only 1,500 each.

The Spanish failed to create thriving colonies in the American Southwest for several reasons. Perhaps the most obvious was that the region lacked the gold and silver, as well as the large native populations, that attracted Spanish priorities to Mexico and Peru. In addition, the Spanish were distracted by their need to control the perennial unrest in Mexico among the natives and the mestizos (people of mixed Indian and European ancestry). Moreover, those Spaniards who led the colonization effort in the borderlands were so preoccupied with military and religious exploitation that they neglected the factors necessary for producing viable settlements with self-sustaining economies. They never understood that the main factor in creating a successful community was a thriving market economy. Instead, they concentrated on building missions and forts and looking—in vain—for gold. Whereas the French and the English based their Indian policies on trade (that included providing Indians with firearms), Spain emphasized conversion to Catholicism, forbade manufacturing within the colonies, and strictly limited trade with the natives.

NEW FRANCE   Permanent French settlements in the New World differed considerably from both the Spanish and the English models. The French settlers were predominantly male but much smaller in number than the English and Spanish settlers. About 40,000 French colonists came to the New World during the seventeenth and eighteenth centuries. The relatively small French population proved to be an advantage in forcing the French to develop cooperative relationships with the Indians. Unlike the English settlers the French established trading outposts rather than farms, mostly along the St. Lawrence River, on lands not claimed by Indians. They thus did not have to confront initial hostility. In addition, the French served as effective mediators between rival Great Lakes tribes. This diplomatic role gave them much more local authority and influence than their English counterparts, who disdained such mediation.

The heavily outnumbered and disproportionately male French settlers sought to integrate themselves with Indian culture rather than displace it. Many French traders married Indians, exchanging languages and customs in the process of raising families. The French also encouraged the Indians to embrace Catholicism and hate the English. This more fraternal bond between the French and the Indians proved to be a source of strength in the wars with the English, enabling New France to survive until 1760 despite the lopsided disparity in numbers between the two colonial powers.

French exploration began when the enterprising Samuel de Champlain landed on the shores of the St. Lawrence River in 1603 and, two years later, at Port Royal, Acadia (later Nova Scotia). Champlain led another expedition in 1608, during which he founded Quebec, a year after the Jamestown landing. While Acadia remained a remote outpost, New France expanded well beyond Quebec, from which Champlain pushed his explorations up the great river and into the Great Lakes as far as Lake Huron, and southward to the lake that still bears his name. There, in 1609, he joined a band of Huron and Algonquian allies in a fateful encounter, fired his musket into the ranks of their Iroquois foes, and kindled a hatred that pursued New France to the end. The Iroquois stood as a buffer against French designs to move toward the English of the middle colonies and as a constant menace on the flank of the French waterways to the interior. In fact, for over a century Indians determined the military balance

Champlain in New France

Samuel de Champlain firing at a group of Iroquois, killing two chiefs (1609).

of power within North America. In 1711 the governor general of New France declared that "the Iroquois are more to be feared than the English colonies."

Until his death, in 1635, Champlain governed New France under a trading company whose charter imposed a fatal weakness. The company won a profitable monopoly of the huge fur trade but had to limit the population to French Catholics. Neither the enterprising, seafaring Huguenots of coastal France nor foreigners of any faith were allowed to populate the country. Great land grants went to persons who promised to bring settlers to work the land under feudal tenure. The colony therefore remained a scattered patchwork of dependent peasants, Jesuit missionaries, priests, soldiers, officials, and *coureurs de bois* (literally, "runners of the woods"), who roamed the interior in quest of furs.

In 1663 King Louis XIV and his chief minister, Jean-Baptiste Colbert, changed New France into a royal colony and pursued a plan of consolidation and stabilization. Colbert dispatched new settlers, including shiploads of young women to lure disbanded soldiers and traders into settled matrimony. He sent out tools and animals for farmers and nets for fishermen and tried to make New France self-sufficient in foodstuffs. The population grew from about 4,000 in 1665 to about 15,000 in 1690.

FRENCH LOUISIANA   From the Great Lakes, French explorers moved southward. In 1673 Louis Jolliet and Père Jacques Marquette, a Jesuit priest, ventured onto Lake Michigan, up the Fox River from Green Bay, then down the Wisconsin River to the Mississippi and on as far as the Arkansas River. Satisfied that the great Mississippi River flowed to the Gulf of Mexico, they turned back for fear of meeting with Spaniards. Nine years later René-Robert Cavelier, sieur de La Salle, went all the way to the Gulf of Mexico and named the country he explored Louisiana, after King Louis XIV of France.

Settlement of the Louisiana country finally began in 1699, when Pierre Le Moyne, sieur d'Iberville, established a colony near Biloxi, Mississippi. The main settlement then moved to Mobile Bay and, in 1710, to the present site of Mobile, Alabama. For nearly half a century the driving force in Louisiana was Jean-Baptiste Le Moyne, sieur de Bienville, a younger brother of Iberville. Bienville arrived with settlers in 1699, when he was only nineteen, and left the colony for the last time in 1743, when he was sixty-three. Sometimes called the Father of Louisiana, he served periodically as governor and always as adviser during those years. In 1718 he founded New Orleans, which shortly thereafter became the capital. Louisiana, first a royal colony, then a proprietary colony, and then a corporate colony, again became a royal province in 1731.

In contrast to the English colonies, French Louisiana grew haltingly in the first half of the eighteenth century. Its population in 1732 was only 2,000

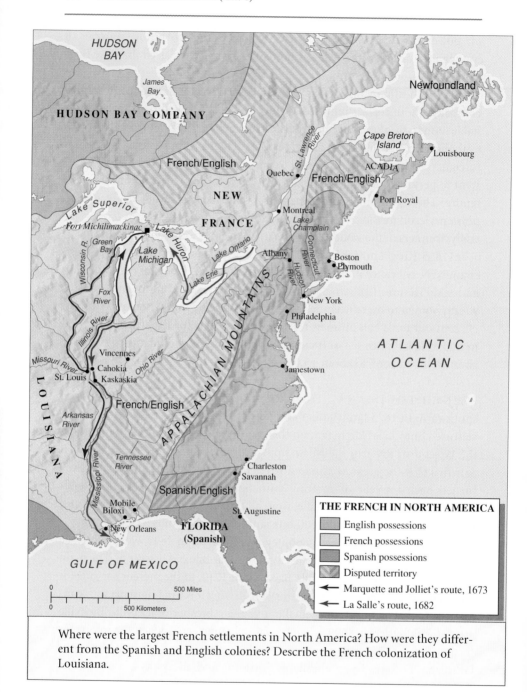

THE FRENCH IN NORTH AMERICA

- English possessions
- French possessions
- Spanish possessions
- Disputed territory
- ← Marquette and Jolliet's route, 1673
- ← La Salle's route, 1682

Where were the largest French settlements in North America? How were they different from the Spanish and English colonies? Describe the French colonization of Louisiana.

whites and about 3,800 slaves. The sweltering climate and mosquito-infested environment enticed few settlers. Poorly administered, dependent on imports for its sustenance, and expensive to defend, it continued throughout the century to be a financial liability to the French government. It never became the thriving trade center with the Spanish that its founders had envisioned.

"France in America had two heads," the historian Francis Parkman wrote, "one amid the snows of Canada, the other amid the canebrakes of Louisiana." The French thus had one enormous advantage: access to the great inland water routes that led to the heartland of the continent. In the Illinois region scattered settlers began farming the fertile soil, and courageous priests established missions at places such as Terre Haute (High Land) and Des Moines (Some Monks). Because of geography as well as deliberate policy, however, French America remained largely a vast wilderness traversed by a mobile population of traders, trappers, missionaries—and, mainly, Indians. In 1750, when the English colonials numbered about 1.5 million, the total French population was no more than 80,000.

Yet in some ways the French had the edge on the British. They offered European goods to Indians in return for furs, encroached far less upon Indian lands, and so won Indian allies against the English who came to possess the

Cities in New France

Quebec in the 1740s, the skyline marked by the spires of cathedrals and seminaries.

land. French governors could mobilize for action without any worry about quarreling assemblies or ethnic and religious diversity. The British may have had the greater population, but their separate colonies often worked at cross purposes. The middle colonies, for instance, protected by the Iroquois buffer, could afford to ignore the French threat—for a long time at least. Whenever conflict threatened, colonial assemblies extracted new concessions from their governors. Colonial merchants, who built up a trade supplying foodstuffs to the French, persisted in smuggling supplies even in wartime.

THE COLONIAL WARS

For most of the seventeenth century, the French and British empires in America developed in relative isolation from each other, and for most of that century the homelands remained at peace with each other. After the Restoration of 1660, Charles II and James II pursued a policy of friendship with the French king, Louis XIV. The Glorious Revolution of 1688, however, worked an abrupt reversal in English diplomacy. William III, the new king, as leader of the Dutch republic, had engaged in a running conflict against the ambitions of Louis XIV. His ascent to the throne brought England almost immediately into a Grand Alliance against Louis in the War of the League of Augsburg, sometimes called the War of the Palatinate or the War of the Grand Alliance and known in the American colonies simply as King William's War (1689–1697).

From Laroque's *Encyclopedia des Voyages*

An Iroquois warrior in an eighteenth-century French engraving.

This was the first of four great European and intercolonial wars that would be fought over the next seventy-four years, the others being the War of the Spanish Succession (Queen Anne's War, 1702–1713), the War of the Austrian Succession (King George's War, 1744–1748), and the Seven

Years' War (the French and Indian War, which lasted nine years in America, from 1754 to 1763). In all except the last, the battles in America were but a sideshow accompanying greater battles in Europe, where British policy pivoted on keeping a balance of power with the French. The alliances shifted from one fight to the next, but Britain and France were pitted against each other every time.

Thus for much of the eighteenth century, the colonies were embroiled in global wars and rumors of wars. The effect on much of the population was devastating. New England, especially Massachusetts, suffered probably more than the rest, for it was closest to the centers of French population. It is estimated that 900 Boston men (about 2.5 percent of the men eligible for service) died in the fighting. This meant that the city was faced with assisting a large population of widows and orphans. Even more important, these prolonged conflicts had profound consequences for Britain that later would reshape the contours of its relationship with America. The wars with France led the English government to incur an enormous debt, establish a huge navy and a standing army, and excite a militant sense of nationalism. During the early eighteenth century the changes in British financial policy and political culture led critics in Parliament to charge that traditional liberties were being usurped by a tyrannical central government. After the French and Indian War, American colonists began making the same point.

THE FRENCH AND INDIAN WAR   Of the four major wars involving the European powers and their New World colonies, the climactic conflict between Britain and France in North America was the French and Indian War. It began in 1754, after enterprising Virginians during the early 1750s had crossed the Allegheny Mountains into the Ohio River valley in order to trade with Indians and survey some 200,000 acres granted them by the king. The incursion by the Virginians infuriated the French, and they established forts in what is now western Pennsylvania to defend their interests. When news of these developments reached Williamsburg, the Virginia governor sent out an emissary to warn off the French. An ambitious young Virginia militia officer, Major George Washington, whose older brothers owned part of the Ohio Company, a business venture to develop settlement and trade in western Pennsylvania, volunteered for the mission. With a few companions, Washington made his way to Fort Le Boeuf in late 1753 and returned with a polite but firm French refusal. The Virginia governor then sent a small force to erect a fort at the strategic fork where the Allegheny and Monongahela rivers meet to form the great Ohio. No sooner had the English started building than a larger French force appeared and ousted them.

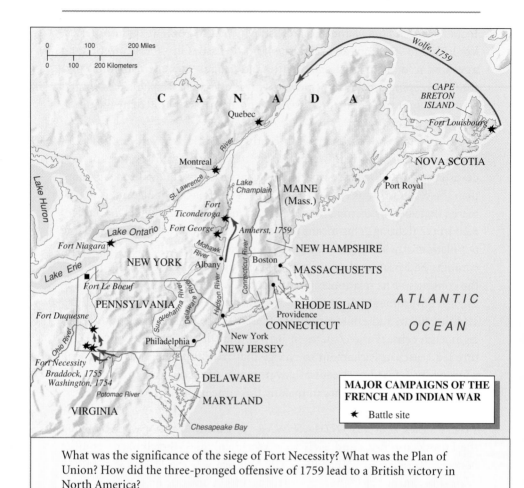

What was the significance of the siege of Fort Necessity? What was the Plan of Union? How did the three-pronged offensive of 1759 lead to a British victory in North America?

Meanwhile, the twenty-two-year-old Washington, hungry for combat and yearing for military glory, had been organizing a regiment of Virginians. In the spring of 1754, the tall, muscular surveyor-turned-soldier led his 150 volunteers and Iroquois allies across the Alleghenies. Their mission was to build a fort at the convergence of the Allegheny, Monongahela, and Ohio rivers (where the city of Pittsburgh later developed). Along the way, Washington learned that French soldiers had beaten them to the strategic site and erected Fort Duquesne, named for the French governor of Canada. Washington decided to make camp about forty miles from the fort and await reinforcements. The next day the Virginians ambushed a French detachment. Ten French soldiers were killed, one escaped, and twenty-one were captured. The

Indians then scalped several of the wounded soldiers as a stunned Major Washington looked on. Washington was unaware that the French had been on a peaceful mission to discuss the disputed fort. The mutilated soldiers were the first fatalities in what would become the French and Indian War.

Washington and his troops retreated and hastily constructed a crude stockade at Great Meadows, dubbed Fort Necessity, which a large force of vengeful French soldiers attacked a month later, on July 3, 1754. After a day-long battle, George Washington surrendered, having seen all his horses and cattle killed and one third of his 300 men killed or wounded. The French permitted his surviving troops to withdraw after stripping them of their weapons. After the Virginia regiment limped home, Washington decided to resign rather than accept a demotion. His blundering expedition triggered a series of events that would ignite a protracted world war. As a prominent British politician exclaimed, "The volley fired by a young Virginian in the backwoods of America set the world on fire."

Back in London the Board of Trade already had taken notice of the growing conflict in the backwoods of North America and had called commissioners from all the colonies as far south as Maryland to a meeting in Albany, New York, to confer on precautions. The Albany Congress (June 19–July 10, 1754), which was meeting when the first shots sounded at Great Meadows, ended with little having been accomplished. The delegates conferred with Iroquois chieftains and sent them away loaded with gifts in return for some

The First American Political Cartoon

Benjamin Franklin's exhortation to the colonies to unite against the French in 1754 would become popular again twenty years later, when the colonies faced a different threat.

half-hearted promises of support. The congress is remembered mainly for the Plan of Union, worked out by a committee under Benjamin Franklin and adopted by a unanimous vote of the commissioners. The plan called for a chief executive, a kind of supreme governor, to be called the president general of the United Colonies, appointed and supported by the crown, and a supreme assembly, called the Grand Council, with forty-eight members chosen by the colonial assemblies. This federal body would oversee matters of defense, Indian relations, and trade and settlement in the West and would levy taxes to support its programs.

It must have been a good plan, Franklin reasoned, since the assemblies thought it gave too much power to the crown and the crown thought it gave too much to the colonies. At any rate the assemblies either rejected or ignored it. Only two substantive results came out of the congress. Its idea of a supreme commander of British forces in America was adopted, as was its advice that a New Yorker who was a friend of the Iroquois be made British superintendent of the northern Indians.

In London the government decided to force a showdown in America. In 1755 the British fleet captured Nova Scotia and expelled most of its French population. Some 5,000 to 7,000 Acadians who refused to take an oath of allegiance to the British crown were scattered through the colonies, from Maine to Georgia. Impoverished and homeless, many of them desperately found their way to French Louisiana, where they became the Cajuns (a corruption of *Acadians*), whose descendants still preserve elements of the French language along the remote bayous and in many urban centers.

The backwoods, however, became the scene of one British disaster after another over the next three years. In 1755 a new British commander in chief, General Edward Braddock, arrived in Virginia with two regiments of army regulars. Braddock was a seasoned, confident officer, but neither he nor his red-clad British troops had any experience fighting in the wilderness. Braddock viewed Indians with contempt, and his cocksure ignorance would prove fatal.

With the addition of some colonial troops, including a still-headstrong George Washington as a volunteer staff officer, Braddock hacked a 125-mile road through the mountain wilderness from the upper Potomac River in Maryland to the vicinity of Fort Duquesne. Hauling heavy artillery to surround the French fort, along with a lumbering wagon train of supplies, Braddock's force achieved a great feat of military logistics and was on the verge of success when, six miles from Fort Duquesne, the surrounding woods suddenly came alive with Ojibwa and French soldiers in Indian costume. Beset on three sides by concealed enemies, the British troops panicked and retreated in disarray, abandoning most of their artillery and supplies. Brave General Braddock had several horses shot out from under him before he was mortally wounded. George Washington, his own coat riddled by bullets, helped other officers contain the rout and lead a hasty retreat. More than 900 British and Virginia soldiers were killed or wounded in one of the worst British defeats of the eighteenth century. Braddock died four days later. The overconfident general's last words were prophetic: "We shall know better how to deal with them another time." Twelve of the surviving British soldiers left behind on the battlefield were stripped, bound, and burned at the stake by Indians. A devastated George Washington wrote his brother that they had "been scandalously beaten by a trifling body of men." The vaunted redcoats "broke & run as sheep before Hounds," but the Virginians "behaved like Men and died like Soldiers." The French victory demonstrated that backwoods warfare depended on Indian allies and frontier tactics for success.

A WORLD WAR   For two years, war raged along the American frontier without becoming a cause of war in Europe. In 1756, however, the colonial war became the Seven Years' War in Europe. In the final alignment of European powers, France, Austria, Russia, Saxony, Sweden, and Spain fought against Britain, Prussia, and Hanover. The onset of world war brought into office a new British government, with the eloquent William Pitt as head of the ministry. Pitt's ability and assurance ("I know that I can save England and no one else can") instilled confidence at home and abroad.

A brilliant visionary and a superb administrator, charismatic and supremely self-confident, Pitt decided that America should be the primary theater of conflict with France, and he sought to bludgeon the French with overwhelming force, on land and at sea. He eventually mobilized some 45,000 troops in North America, half of whom were British regulars and the other half American colonists. Pitt was able to garner such substantial colonial participation by reversing Britain's administrative policies. His predecessors had demanded that the colonial legislatures help fund the defense effort. Pitt decided to treat the colonies as allies rather than subordinate possessions, offering them subsidies for their participation in the war effort. The colonists readily embraced this invitation to become partners in an imperial crusade, and they contributed key resources and large numbers of men to the war effort.

Pitt's America-first policy had long-term consequences. The massive frontier war with the French and their Indian allies fostered a sense of nationalism among the colonists that would culminate in a war for independence from Britain. Pitt used the powerful British navy to cut off French reinforcements and supplies to the New World—and the goods with which they bought

Indian allies. Pitt improved the British forces, gave command to younger men of ability, and carried the battle to the enemy. In 1758 the tides began to turn when the English captured Fort Louisbourg in Canada. The Iroquois, sensing the turn of fortunes, pressed their dependents, the Delawares, to call off the frontier attacks on English settlements.

In 1759 the war reached its climax with a series of resounding British victories on land and at sea. Pitt ordered a three-pronged offensive against the French in Canada, along what had become the classic invasion routes: the Niagara River, Lake Champlain, and the St. Lawrence River. On the Niagara expedition the British were joined by a group of Iroquois, and they captured Fort Niagara, virtually cutting the French lifeline to the interior. On Lake Champlain, General Jeffrey Amherst took Forts George and Ticonderoga, then paused to await reinforcements for an advance northward.

Meanwhile, the most decisive battle was shaping up at Quebec, the gateway to Canada. There, British forces led by General James Wolfe waited out the advance of General Louis-Joseph de Montcalm and his French infantry until they were within close range, then loosed volleys that devastated the French ranks—and ended French power in North America for all time. News of the British victory reached London along with similar reports from India, where English forces had reduced French outposts one by one and established the base for expanded British control of India.

The war in North America dragged on until 1763, but the rest was a process of mopping up. In the South, where little significant action had occurred, belated hostility flared up between the settlers and the Cherokee Nation. A force of British regulars and colonial militia broke Cherokee resistance in 1761.

In 1760 King George II died, and the twenty-two-year-old grandson he despised ascended the throne as George III. The new king resolved to seek peace and forced William Pitt out of office. Pitt had wanted to declare war on Spain before the French could bring that other Bourbon monarchy into the conflict. He was forestalled, but Spain belatedly entered the war, in 1761, and during the next year met the same fate as the French: in 1762 British forces took Manila in the Philippines and Havana in Cuba. By 1763 the French and the Spanish were ready to negotiate a surrender. Britain ruled the world.

THE PEACE OF PARIS   The Treaty of Paris of 1763 brought an end to the world war and to French power in North America. Victorious Britain took all French North American possessions east of the Mississippi River (except New Orleans) and all of Spanish Florida. The English invited the Spanish settlers to remain and practice their Catholic religion, but few

End of the War

With Quebec in the background, France kneels before a victorious Britain (1763).

accepted the offer. The Spanish king ordered them to evacuate the colony and provided free transportation to Spanish possessions in the Caribbean. Within a year most of the Spaniards sold their property at bargain prices to English speculators and began an exodus to Cuba and Mexico.

When the Indian tribes that had been allied with the French learned of the 1763 peace settlement, they were despondent. Their lands were being given over to the British without any consultation. The Shawnees, for instance, demanded to know "by what right the French could pretend" to transfer Indian territory to the British. The Indians also worried that a victorious Britain had "grown too powerful & seemed as if they would be too strong for God itself." The Indians had hoped that the departure of the French from the Ohio Valley would mean that the area would revert to their control. Instead, the British cut off the trade and giftgiving practices that had bound the Indians to the French. General Jeffrey Amherst, the British military governor for the western region, demanded that the Indians learn to live without "charity." British forces also moved into the French frontier forts. In a desperate effort to recover their autonomy, tribes struck back, in the spring of 1763, capturing most of the British forts around the Great Lakes and in the Ohio Valley. They also raided colonial settlements in Pennsylvania, Maryland, and Virginia, destroying hundreds of homesteads and killing several thousand people. In the midst of the Indian

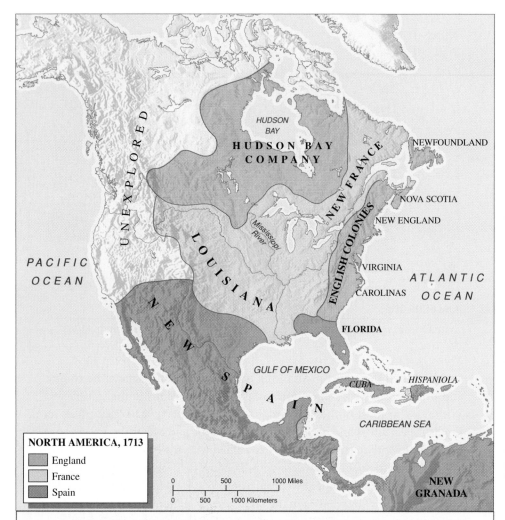

NORTH AMERICA, 1713

- England
- France
- Spain

0 — 500 — 1000 Miles
0 — 500 — 1000 Kilometers

What events led to the first clashes between the French and the British in the late seventeenth century? Why did New England suffer more than other regions of North America during the wars of the eighteenth century? What were the long-term financial, military, and political consequences of the wars between France and Britain?

attack on Fort Pitt (formerly Fort Duquesne), General Amherst approved the distribution of smallpox-infested blankets and handkerchiefs from the fort's hospital to the Indians besieging the garrison. His efforts at germ warfare were intended to "extirpate this Execrable race" of Indians.

Called Pontiac's Rebellion because of the prominent role played by the Ottawa chief, the far-flung Indian attacks on the frontier forts convinced most American colonists that all Indians must be removed. The British government,

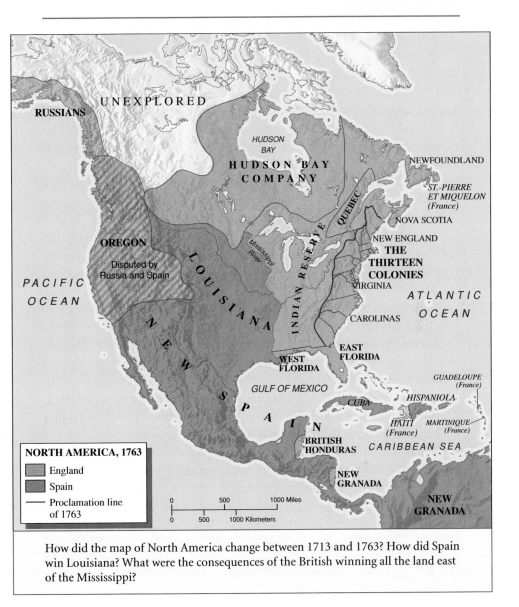

NORTH AMERICA, 1763

- England
- Spain
- Proclamation line of 1763

How did the map of North America change between 1713 and 1763? How did Spain win Louisiana? What were the consequences of the British winning all the land east of the Mississippi?

meanwhile, negotiated an agreement with the Indians that allowed redcoats to reoccupy the frontier forts in exchange for a renewal of trade and gift giving. Still, as Pontiac stressed, the Indians asserted their independence and denied the legitimacy of the British claim to their territory under the terms of the Treaty of Paris. He told a British official that the "French never conquered us, neither did they purchase a foot of our Country, nor have they a right to give it to you." The British may have won a global empire as a result of the Seven Years' War, but their grip on the American colonies grew ever weaker.

In compensation for the loss of Florida, Spain received Louisiana (New Orleans and all French land west of the Mississippi River) from France. Unlike the Spanish in Florida, however, few of the French settlers left Louisiana after 1763. The French government encouraged them to work with their new Spanish governors to create a bulwark against further English expansion. Spain would hold title to Louisiana for nearly four decades but would never succeed in erasing the territory's French roots. The French-born settlers always outnumbered the Spanish. The loss of Louisiana left France with no territory on the continent of North America. In the West Indies, France gave up Tobago, Dominica, Grenada, and St. Vincent. British power reigned supreme over North America east of the Mississippi River.

But a fatal irony would pursue the British victory. In gaining Canada, the British government put in motion a train of events that would end twenty years later with the loss of the rest of British North America. Britain's success against France threatened the Indian tribes of the interior because they had long depended upon playing off one European power against the other. Now, with the British dominant on the continent, American settlers were emboldened to encroach even more upon Indian land. In addition, victory on the battlefields encouraged the British to tighten their imperial control over the American colonists and demand more financial contributions to pay for military defense. Meanwhile, a humiliated France thirsted for revenge. In London, Benjamin Franklin, agent for the colony of Pennsylvania (1764–1775), found the French minister inordinately curious about America and suspected him of wanting to ignite the coals of controversy. Less than three years after Franklin left London and only fifteen years after the conquest of New France, he would be in Paris arranging an alliance on behalf of Britain's rebellious colonists.

MAKING CONNECTIONS

- Although the British victory in the French and Indian War brought the colonies and England closer together in some ways, it was also an important factor in the approach of the American Revolution, as demonstrated in Chapter 5.

- One of the great struggles of the Revolution would be transforming the dependent British colonies, as described in this chapter, into independent American states, as described in Chapter 6.

FURTHER READING

The economics motivating colonial policies is covered in John J. McCusker and Russell R. Menard's *The Economy of British America, 1607–1789*, rev. ed. (1991). The problems of colonial customs administration are explored in Michael Kammen's *Empire and Interest: The American Colonies and the Politics of Mercantilism* (1970).

The Andros crisis and related topics are treated in Jack M. Sosin's *English America and the Revolution of 1688: Royal Administration and the Structure of Provincial Government* (1982). Stephen Saunders Webb's *The Governors-General: The English Army and the Definition of the Empire, 1569–1681* (1979) argues that the crown was more concerned with military administration than with commercial regulation, and Webb's *1676: The End of American Independence* (1984) shows how the Indian wars undermined the autonomy of the colonial governments.

The early Indian wars are treated in Jill Lepore's *The Name of War: King Philip's War and the Origins of American Identity* (1998) and in Francis Jennings's *The Invasion of America: Indians, Colonialism, and the Cant of Conquest* (1975). See also Richard Aquila's *The Iroquois Restoration: Iroquois Diplomacy on the Colonial Frontier, 1701–1754* (1983). Gregory Evans Dowd describes the unification efforts of Indians east of the Mississippi in *A Spirited Resistance: The North American Indian Struggle for Unity, 1745–1815* (1992). See also James H. Merrell's *Into the American Woods: Negotiations on the Pennsylvania Frontier* (1999).

A good introduction to the imperial phase of the colonial conflicts is Howard H. Peckham's *The Colonial Wars, 1689–1762* (1964). More analytical is Douglas Edward Leach's *Arms for Empire: A Military History of the British Colonies in North America, 1607–1763* (1973). Fred Anderson's *Crucible of War: The Seven Years' War and the Fate of Empire in British North America, 1754–1766* (2000) is the best history of the Seven Years' War. On the French colonies in North America, see Allan Greer's *The People of New France* (1997).

5

FROM EMPIRE
TO INDEPENDENCE

FOCUS QUESTIONS

- How did British colonial policy change after 1763?
- How did the Whig ideology shape the colonial response to changes in British policy?
- What was the role of Revolutionary leaders, including Samuel Adams, John Dickinson, Thomas Paine, and Thomas Jefferson?

Seldom if ever since the days of Queen Elizabeth had England thrilled with such pride as it did in the closing years of the Seven Years' War. In 1760 young George III, headstrong and obstinate, had ascended the throne. Three years later the Treaty of Paris confirmed a vast new British Empire spanning the globe. Most important, the Treaty of Paris effectively ended the French imperial domain in North America. This in turn influenced the development of the region between the Appalachian Mountains and the Mississippi River, from the Gulf of Mexico to Hudson Bay in Canada. The maturing mainland colonies began to experience a dynamic agricultural and commercial growth that enormously increased their importance to the British economy. Yet the colonies remained both extraordinarily diverse in composition and outlook and peculiarly averse to cooperative efforts. That they would manage to unify themselves and declare independence in 1775 was indeed surprising—even to them.

The Heritage of War

The triumph in what England called the Great War saw Americans celebrating as joyously as Londoners in 1763. Colonists were proud of their partnership in British liberty, a supportive Parliament, an ancient and revered constitution, and a prosperity fostered by wartime spending. Most Americans, as Benjamin Franklin explained, "submitted willingly to the government of the Crown." He himself proudly proclaimed, "I am a BRITON." But victory celebrations masked festering resentments and new problems that would be the heritage of the war. Underneath the pride in the British Empire, an American nationalism was maturing. Colonials were beginning to think and speak of themselves more as Americans than as English or British. With the French out of the way and vast new lands to exploit, they looked to the future with confidence.

Many Americans had a new sense of importance after fighting a major war with such success. Some harbored resentment, justified or not, at the haughty air of the British soldiers, and many in the early stages of the war had lost their awe of British troops, who were so inept at frontier fighting. At least one third of military-age New England men fought in the Seven Years' War. For them army life was both a revelation and an opportunity. Although they admired the courage and discipline of British redcoats under fire, many New Englanders abhorred the carefree cursing, whoring, and Sabbath breaking they observed among the British troops. But most upsetting were the daily "shrieks and cries" resulting from the brutal punishments imposed by British officers on their wayward men. Minor offenses might earn hundreds of lashes. One American soldier recorded in his diary in 1759 that "there was a man whipped to death belonging to the Light Infantry. They say he had twenty-five lashes after he was dead." The brutalities of British army life thus heightened the New Englanders' sense of their separate identity and of their greater worthiness to be God's chosen people. It also emboldened Americans to defy British rule, because the colonists no longer needed military protection from the French.

British forces nevertheless had borne the brunt of the war and had won it for the American colonists, who had supplied men and materials, sometimes reluctantly, and who persisted in trading with the enemy. Molasses in the French West Indies, for instance, continued to draw New England ships like flies. The trade was too important for the colonists to give up but was more than British authorities could tolerate. Along with naval patrols, one important means of disrupting this illegal trade was the use of writs of assistance, general search warrants that allowed officers to enter any place during daylight hours to seek evidence of illegal trade.

In 1760 Boston merchants hired the attorney James Otis to fight the writs in the courts. Otis lost the case but in the process advanced the provocative argument that any act of Parliament that authorized such "instruments of slavery" violated the British constitution and was therefore void. This was a radical idea for its time. Otis sought to overturn a major tenet of the English legal system, namely, that acts of Parliament were by their very nature constitutional.

The peace that secured an empire in 1763 also laid upon the British government new burdens. How should the British manage the defense and governance of their new global possessions? What should they do about the American lands inhabited by Indians but coveted by whites? How was the British government to pay for an unprecedented debt built up during the war and bear the new expenses of expanded colonial administration and defense? And—the thorniest problem of all, as it turned out—what role should the colonies play in all this? The problems were of a magnitude and complexity to challenge men of the greatest statemanship and vision, but those qualities were rare among the ministers of George III.

BRITISH POLITICS

In the English government during the late eighteenth century, nearly every politician was a Whig. *Whig* was the name given to those who had opposed James II, led the Glorious Revolution of 1688, and secured the Protestant Hanoverian succession in 1714. The Whigs were the champions of individual liberty and parliamentary supremacy, but with the passage of time Whiggism had drifted into complacency. The dominant group of landholding Whig families was concerned mostly with the pursuit of personal gain and local questions rather than great issues of statecraft. George III, a tall young man with full lips, bulging eyes, and an obstinate disposition, sought at first to eliminate the Whig influence on the monarchy. Whig politicians had dominated his grandfather, and the new king was determined

George III

At age thirty-three, the young king of a victorious empire.

to rule in his own right. Thus he ousted the powerful William Pitt as prime minister and established his own inner circle of obedient advisers, known as the "king's friends." They exercised influence by controlling appointments to government offices; they retained their influential positions only by ensuring that they did not contradict the cocksure king.

Throughout the 1760s the king turned first to one and then to another mediocre leader, ineffective ministries came and went, and the government fell into instability just as the new problems of empire required creative solutions. Ministries rose and fell usually because somebody offended the king or somebody's friend failed to get a government post. Colonial policy remained marginal to the chief concerns of British politics. The result was inconsistency and vacillation followed by stubborn inflexibility.

WESTERN LANDS

In America no sooner was peace formally arranged in 1763 than the problem of the western lands erupted in the form of Pontiac's Rebellion. To keep the peace on the frontier and to keep earlier promises to the Delawares and Shawnees, officials in London postponed further colonial settlement along the frontier. The king also issued the Royal Proclamation of 1763. That order drew an imaginary line along the crest of the Appalachians, beyond which settlers were forbidden to go and colonial governors were forbidden to authorize surveys or issue land grants. It also established the new British colonies of Quebec and East and West Florida. Yet the proclamation line was ineffective. Hardy settlers defined the prohibitions against intrusions into Indian land and pushed across the Appalachian ridges.

GRENVILLE AND THE STAMP ACT

GRENVILLE'S COLONIAL POLICY   Just as the Royal Proclamation of 1763 was being drafted, a new British ministry had begun to grapple with the problems of imperial finances. The new prime minister and first lord of the Treasury, George Grenville, was much like the king: industrious, honest, and hardheaded. He was a strong-willed accountant whose humorless self-assurance verged on pomposity. George III came to despise him, but the inexperienced king needed the dull but dogged prime minister because they agreed on basic policies: cutting government expenses, reducing the national debt, and generating more revenue from the colonies to pay for their defense. As a colleague said of Grenville, he had "a rage for regulation and restriction."

In developing new policies regulating the American colonies, Grenville took for granted the need for redcoats to defend the American frontier, although the colonies had been left mostly to their own devices before 1754. He also wanted to keep a large army (10,000 men) in America to avoid a rapid demobilization, which would retire a large number of influential officers, thereby provoking political criticism at home. But he faced sharply rising costs for American frontier defense, on top of an already staggering government debt. During the mid-1760s the interest payments on the government's debts consumed 60 percent of the annual budget.

Because there was a large tax burden at home and a much lighter one in the colonies, Grenville reasoned that the prosperous Americans should share the cost of their own defense. He also learned that the royal customs service in America was grossly inefficient. Evasion by American merchants and corruption among customs officers were rampant. Grenville issued stern orders to colonial officials to tighten enforcement and ordered the British navy to patrol the coast for smugglers. He also set up a new maritime, or vice-admiralty,

The Great Financier, or British Economy for the Years 1763, 1764, 1765

This cartoon, critical of Grenville's tax policies, shows America, depicted as an Indian (at left), groaning under the burden of new taxes.

court in Halifax (replacing the ineffectual admiralty courts established in 1696), granting it jurisdiction over all the colonies and ensuring that there would be no juries of colonists sympathetic to smugglers. Under Grenville the period of "salutary neglect" in the enforcement of the Navigation Acts was coming to an end, causing American shippers great annoyance.

Strict enforcement of the Molasses Act of 1733 posed a serious threat to New England's prosperity. The tax on molasses had been set prohibitively high, not for the purpose of raising revenue but to prevent illegal trade with the French sugar islands. Yet the rum distilleries consumed more molasses than the British West Indies provided. Grenville recognized that the molasses tax, if enforced, would be ruinous to a major colonial enterprise. So he put through the Revenue Act of 1764, commonly known as the Sugar Act, which cut the duty in half. This, he believed, would reduce the temptation to smuggle or to bribe customs officers. In addition, the Sugar Act levied new duties on imports of foreign textiles, wine, coffee, indigo, and sugar. The Sugar Act, Grenville estimated, would help defray "the necessary expenses of defending, protecting, and securing, the said colonies and plantations." For the first time, Parliament had adopted duties (taxes on imports or exports) frankly designed to raise revenues in the colonies and not merely intended to regulate trade.

Another of Grenville's regulatory measures had an important impact on the colonies: the Currency Act of 1764. The colonies faced a chronic shortage of money, which kept going out to pay debts in England. To meet the shortage, they issued their own paper money. British creditors feared payment in such a depreciated currency, however. To alleviate their fears, Grenville prohibited the colonies from printing money. The result was a decline in the value of existing paper money, since nobody was obligated to accept it in payment of debts, even in the colonies. The deflationary impact of the Currency Act, combined with new duties on commodities and stricter enforcement, jolted a colonial economy already suffering a postwar decline.

THE STAMP ACT   George Grenville had a knack for doing the wrong thing—repeatedly. The Sugar Act, for example, did not produce additional revenue. Its administrative costs were four times greater than the revenue it generated. Yet he compounded the problem by pushing through still another measure to raise money in America, a stamp tax. On February 13, 1765, Parliament created revenue stamps and required that they be purchased and fixed to printed matter and legal documents of all kinds: newspapers, pamphlets, broadsides, almanacs, bonds, leases, deeds, licenses, insurance policies, ship clearances, college diplomas, even playing cards. The requirement was to go into effect on November 1.

That same year, Grenville completed his new system of colonial regulations when he put through the Quartering Act. In effect it was yet another tax. The Quartering Act required the colonies to supply British troops with provisions and provide them with barracks or submit to their use of inns and vacant buildings. It applied to all colonies but affected mainly New York, headquarters of the British forces.

THE IDEOLOGICAL RESPONSE The cumulative effect of Grenville's measures raised colonial suspicions to a fever. Unwittingly this plodding minister of a plodding king stirred up a storm of protest and set in motion a profound exploration of English traditions and imperial relations. The radical ideas of the minority "Real Whigs" slowly began to take hold in the colonies. These ideas derived from various sources but above all from John Locke's justification of the Glorious Revolution, his *Two Treatises on Government*. Locke and other Real Whigs viewed English history as a struggle by Parliament to preserve life, liberty, and property against royal tyranny.

In 1764 and 1765 the colonists felt that Grenville and Parliament had loosed upon them the very engines of tyranny from which Parliament had rescued England in the seventeenth century. A standing army was the historic ally of despots, and now with the French gone and Chief Pontiac subdued, thousands of British soldiers remained in the colonies. For what purpose—to protect the colonists or to subdue them? It was beginning to seem clear that it was the latter. Among the fundamental rights of English people were trial by jury and the presumption of innocence, but the new vice-admiralty courts excluded juries and put the burden of proof on the defendant. Most important, English citizens had the right to be taxed only by their elected representatives. Parliament claimed that privilege in England, and the colonial assemblies had long exercised it as their most cherished principle in America. Now, however, Parliament was usurping the assemblies' power of the purse strings. This could only lead to tyranny and enslavement. Sir Francis Bernard, the royal governor of Massachusetts, correctly predicted that the new stamp tax "would cause a great Alarm & meet much Opposition" in the colonies. Indeed, the seed of American independence was planted by the debates over the stamp tax.

PROTEST IN THE COLONIES In a flood of colonial pamphlets, speeches, and resolutions, critics of the Stamp Act repeated a slogan familiar to all Americans: "No taxation without representation." The Stamp Act became the chief target of colonial outrage at British greed and arrogance. Unlike the Sugar Act, which affected mainly New England, the Stamp Act burdened all colonists who did any kind of business. And it affected most of all the articulate elements in the community: merchants, planters, lawyers, printer-editors—all strategically placed to influence public opinion. Through the spring and summer of 1765, colonial resentment boiled over in meetings, parades, bonfires, and other demonstrations. The militants began to call themselves Sons of Liberty. They met underneath "liberty trees"—in Boston a great elm on Hanover Square, in Charleston a live oak.

One day in mid-August 1765, nearly three months before the effective date of the Stamp Act, an effigy of Boston's stamp agent swung from the city's liberty tree. In the evening a mob carried it through the streets, destroyed the stamp office, and used the wood to burn the effigy. Somewhat later another mob sacked the homes of Lieutenant Governor Thomas Hutchinson and the local customs officer. Thoroughly shaken, the Boston stamp agent resigned his commission, and stamp agents throughout the colonies were hounded out of office. Loyalists, those colonists supportive of British policies, deplored the riotous violence, arguing that the American rebels were behaving more tyrannically than the British.

By November 1, its effective date, the Stamp Act was a dead letter. Business went on without the stamps. Newspapers appeared with a skull and crossbones where the stamp belonged. After passage of the Sugar Act, a movement had begun to boycott British goods rather than pay the import duties. Now colonists adopted nonimportation agreements to exert pressure on British merchants. Americans knew that they had become a major market for British products. By shutting off imports, they could exercise real leverage. Homegrown sage and sassafras took the place of British tea. Homespun garments became the fashion as a symbol of colonial defiance.

The widespread protests involved women as well as men, and the boycotts of British goods encouraged colonial unity as Americans discovered that they had more in common with each other than with London. The Virginia House of Burgesses struck the first blow against the Stamp Act with the Virginia Resolves, a series of resolutions inspired by the fiery young Patrick Henry. Virginians, the burgesses declared, were entitled to the rights of Englishmen, and Englishmen could be taxed only by their own representatives. Virginians, moreover, had always been governed by laws passed with their own consent. Newspapers spread the Virginia Resolves throughout the colonies, and other assemblies hastened to copy Virginia's example.

In 1765 the Massachusetts House of Representatives issued a circular letter inviting the various assemblies to send delegates to confer in New York on appeals for relief from the king and Parliament. Nine responded, and from October 7 to 25, 1765, the Stamp Act Congress, with twenty-seven

Opposition to the Stamp Act

In protest of the Stamp Act, which was to take effect the next day, the *Pennsylvania Journal* printed a skull and crossbones on its masthead.

delegates, issued expressions of colonial sentiment: a Declaration of the Rights and Grievances of the Colonies, a petition to the king for relief, and a petition to Parliament for repeal of the Stamp Act. The delegates acknowledged that the colonies owed a "due subordination" to Parliament and recognized its right to regulate colonial trade, but they questioned Parliament's right to levy taxes, which were a free gift granted by the people through their representatives. "The boldness of the minister [Grenville] amazes our people," wrote a New Yorker. "This single stroke has lost Great Britain the affection of all of her Colonies." Grenville responded by denouncing the colonists as "ungrateful."

REPEAL OF THE ACT   The storm had scarcely broken before Grenville's ministry was out of office, dismissed not because of the colonial turmoil but because Grenville had fallen out with the king over the appointment of government officials. The king installed a new minister, the marquis of Rockingham, Charles Watson-Wentworth, leader of the "Rockingham Whigs," the "Old Whig" faction, which included Britons who sympathized with the colonies. Pressure from British merchants who feared the economic consequences of the

The Repeal, or the Funeral Procession of Miss America-Stamp

This 1766 cartoon shows Grenville carrying the dead Stamp Act in its coffin. In the background, trade with America starts up again.

nonimportation movement bolstered Rockingham's resolve to repeal the act. When Parliament assembled early in 1766, William Pitt demanded that the Stamp Act be repealed "absolutely, totally, and immediately" but urged that Britain's authority over the colonies "be asserted in as strong terms as possible," except on the point of taxation.

In 1766 Parliament repealed the Stamp Tax but at the same time passed the Declaratory Act, which asserted the full power of Parliament to make laws binding the colonies "in all cases whatsoever." It was a cunning evasion that made no concession with regard to taxes but made no mention of them either. It reinforced a distinction between "external" taxes on trade and "internal" taxes within the colonies, a distinction that would have fateful consequences. For the moment, however, the Declaratory Act was a face-saving gesture. News of the repeal of the Stamp Act set off excited demonstrations throughout the colonies. In mid-May 1766 Boston church bells signaled the news of Parliament's favorable vote. Grateful New Yorkers commissioned statues to honor George III and William Pitt. Amid the rejoicing and relief on both sides of the Atlantic, few expected that the quarrel between Britain and its American colonies would be reopened within a year. To be sure, the Sugar Act remained on the books, but Rockingham reduced the molasses tax from threepence a gallon to a penny.

FANNING THE FLAMES

Meanwhile, the king continued to play musical chairs with his ministers. Rockingham soon lost the confidence of the king. William Pitt then formed a ministry that included the major factions of Parliament. The ill-matched combination would have been hard to manage even if Pitt had remained in charge, but the old warlord began to slip over the fine line between genius and madness. For a time in 1767, the guiding force in the ministry was the witty and reckless Charles Townshend, chancellor of the Exchequer (Treasury), whose "abilities were superior to those of all men," according to Horace Walpole, "and his judgement below that of any man." Like George Grenville before him, Townshend held the "factious and turbulent" Americans in contempt and was determined to force their obedience. The erratic Townshend took advantage of Pitt's mental confusion to reopen the question of colonial taxation. He asserted that "external" taxes were tolerable to the colonies—not that he believed it for a moment.

THE TOWNSHEND ACTS   In 1767 Townshend put his ill-fated revenue plan through the House of Commons, and a few months later he died, at age forty-two, leaving behind a bitter legacy: the Townshend Acts. With this legislation, Townshend had sought first to bring the New York assembly to its senses. That body had defied the Quartering Act and refused to provide beds or supplies for the king's troops. Parliament, at Townshend's behest, had suspended all acts of New York's colonial assembly until it would yield. New York protested but finally caved in, inadvertently confirming the British suspicion that too much indulgence had encouraged colonial bad manners. Townshend had followed up with the Revenue Act of 1767, which levied duties ("external taxes") on colonial imports of glass, lead, paint, paper, and tea. Third, he had set up a Board of Customs Commissioners at Boston, the colonial headquarters of smuggling. Finally, he had reorganized the vice-admiralty courts, providing four in the continental colonies: at Halifax, Boston, Philadelphia, and Charleston.

The Townshend duties increased government revenues, but the intangible costs were greater. The duties taxed goods exported from England, indirectly hurting British manufacturers, and had to be collected in colonial ports, increasing collection costs. But the highest cost was a new drift into evergreater conflict with the colonists. The Revenue Act of 1767 posed a more severe threat to colonial assemblies than Grenville's taxes had, for Townshend proposed to apply these revenues to pay governors and other officers and thereby release them from financial dependence on the colonial assemblies.

DICKINSON'S "LETTERS"   The Townshend Acts surprised the colonists, but this time the storm gathered more slowly than it had two years before. Once again citizens resolved to resist, to boycott British goods, to develop their own manufactures. Once again the colonial press spewed out expressions of protest, most notably the essays of John Dickinson. The son of a Maryland planter, Dickinson was a prosperous Philadelphia lawyer who hoped to resolve the latest dispute by persuasion. Late in 1767 his twelve "Letters from a Farmer in Pennsylvania" (as he chose to style himself) began to appear in the *Pennsylvania Chronicle*, from which they were copied in other papers and in pamphlet form. His argument repeated in greater detail and more elegance what the Stamp Act Congress had already said. The colonists held that Parliament might regulate commerce and collect duties incidental to that purpose, but it had no right to levy taxes for *revenue*, whether they were internal or external. Dickinson used moderate language. "The cause of Liberty is a cause of too much dignity to be sullied by turbulence and tumult," he argued. "Anger produces anger," he warned. The colonial complaints should "speak at the same time the language of affliction and veneration" so as to avoid "an incurable rage."

SAMUEL ADAMS AND THE SONS OF LIBERTY   But the outraged affliction grew, and the veneration waned. British officials could neither conciliate moderates like Dickinson nor cope with firebrands like Samuel Adams of Boston, who was emerging as the supreme genius of revolutionary agitation. Born in 1722, Adams graduated from Harvard and soon thereafter inherited the family brewery, which he quickly ran into bankruptcy. Politics, not profit, was his abiding passion, and he spent most of his time debating political issues with sailors, roustabouts, and stevedores at local taverns. Adams insisted that Parliament had no right to legislate at all for the colonies, that Massachusetts must return to the spirit of its Puritan founders and defend itself from a new conspiracy against its liberties.

While other men tended their private affairs, Sam Adams was whipping up the Sons of Liberty and organizing protests at the Boston town meeting and in the provincial assembly. Early in 1768 he and James Otis formulated a

Samuel Adams

Adams was an organizer of the Sons of Liberty.

Massachusetts circular letter, which the assembly dispatched to the other colonies. The letter's tone was polite and logical: it restated the illegality of taxation by Parliament without colonial representation in Parliament and invited the support of other colonies. In London the earl of Hillsborough, just appointed to the new office of secretary of state for the colonies, only made matters worse. He ordered the Massachusetts assembly to withdraw the Adams-Otis letter. The assembly refused and was dissolved.

In 1769 the Virginia assembly reasserted its exclusive right to tax Virginians and called upon the colonies to unite in the cause. Virginia's royal governor promptly dissolved the assembly, but the members met independently, dubbed themselves a convention after Boston's example, and adopted a new set of nonimportation agreements.

In London, events across the Atlantic still aroused only marginal interest. The king's long effort to reorder British politics to his liking was coming to fulfillment, and that was the big news. In 1769 new elections for Parliament finally produced a majority of the "King's Friends." And George III found a minister to his taste in Frederick, Lord North, who had replaced Townshend as chancellor of the Exchequer. In 1770 the king installed a cabinet of the King's Friends, with North as first minister. North, who venerated the traditions of Parliament, was no stooge for the king, but the two worked in harmony.

THE BOSTON MASSACRE   By 1770 the nonimportation agreements in the American colonies were strangling British trade and causing unemployment in England. The impact of colonial boycotts on English commerce had persuaded Lord North to modify the Townshend Acts—just in time to halt a perilous escalation of tensions. The presence of British soldiers in Boston had been a constant provocation. Crowds heckled and ridiculed the red-coated soldiers, many of whom earned the abuse by harassing and intimidating colonists.

On March 5, 1770, in the square before the custom house, a group of rowdies began taunting and hurling icicles at the British sentry on duty. His call

The Bloody Massacre

Paul Revere's partisan engraving of the Boston Massacre.

for help brought reinforcements. Then somebody rang the town fire bell, drawing a larger crowd to the scene. At their head, or so the story goes, was Crispus Attucks, a runaway mulatto slave who had worked for some years on ships out of Boston. Attucks and others continued to bait the British troops. Finally a soldier was knocked down, rose to his feet, and fired into the crowd. When the smoke cleared, five people lay on the ground dead or dying, and eight more were wounded. The cause of colonial resistance now had its first martyrs, and the first to die was Crispus Attucks. Those involved in the "massacre" were indicted for murder, but they were defended by John Adams, Sam's cousin, who thought they were the victims of circumstance, provoked, he said, by a "motley rabble of saucy boys, negroes and mulattoes, Irish teagues and outlandish Jack tars." All of the British soldiers were acquitted except two, who were convicted of manslaughter and branded on their thumbs.

The so-called Boston Massacre sent shock waves through the colonies—and to London. Late in April 1770 Parliament repealed all the Townshend duties save one. The cabinet, by a fateful vote of five to four, had advised keeping the tea tax as a token of parliamentary authority. Colonial die-hards insisted that pressure should be kept on British merchants until Parliament gave in altogether, but the nonimportation movement soon faded. Parliament, after all, had given up the substance of the taxes, with one exception, and much of the colonists' tea was smuggled in from Holland anyway.

For two years thereafter colonial discontent simmered down. The Stamp Act was gone, as were all the Townshend duties except that on tea. But most of the Grenville-Townshend innovations remained in effect: the Sugar Act, the Currency Act, the Quartering Act, the vice-admiralty courts, the Board of Customs Commissioners. The redcoats had left Boston, but they remained nearby, and the British navy still patrolled the coast. Each remained a source of irritation and the cause of occasional incidents. There was still tinder awaiting a spark, and the most rebellious among the colonists were eager to provide the flame. As Sam Adams stressed, "Where there is a spark of patriotick fire, we will enkindle it."

DISCONTENT ON THE FRONTIER

Many American colonists had no interest in the disputes over British regulatory policy raging along the seaboard. Parts of the backcountry stirred with quarrels that had nothing to do with the Stamp and Townshend Acts. Rival land claims to the east of Lake Champlain pitted New York against New Hampshire and the Green Mountain Boys, led by Ethan Allen, against both. Eventually the denizens of the area would set up shop on their own as the state of Vermont, created in 1777 although not recognized as a member of the Union until 1791. In Pennsylvania sporadic quarrels broke out among land claimants who held grants from Virginia and Connecticut, whose boundaries under their charters overlapped those granted to William Penn, or so they believed.

A more dangerous division in Pennsylvania had arisen in 1763 when a group of frontier ruffians took the law into their own hands. Outraged at the lack of frontier protection during Pontiac's Rebellion, a consequence of pacifist Quaker influence in the Pennsylvania assembly, a group from Paxton, near Harrisburg, called the Paxton Boys, took revenge by massacring peaceful Susquehannock Indians in Lancaster County; then they threatened the so-called Moravian Indians, a group of Christian converts near Bethlehem. When the Indians took refuge in Philadelphia, some 1,500 angry Paxton Boys marched on the capital, where Benjamin Franklin talked the vengeful frontiersmen into returning home by enabling them to present their demands to the governor and the assembly.

Farther south frontier folk of South Carolina also had complaints about the lack of protection—from horse thieves, cattle rustlers, and Indians. Backcountry residents organized societies, called Regulators, to administer vigilante justice in the region and refused to pay taxes until they gained effective government. In 1769 the assembly finally set up six new circuit courts in the region but still did not respond to the backcountry's demand for representation.

In North Carolina the protest was less over the lack of government than over the abuses and extortion by appointees from the eastern part of the colony. Farmers felt especially oppressed by the government's refusal to either issue paper money or accept produce in payment of taxes, and in 1766 they organized to resist. Efforts of these Regulators to stop seizures of property and other court proceedings led to more disorders and the enactment of a bill that made the rioters guilty of treason. In the spring of 1771, Governor William Tryon led 1,200 militiamen into the Piedmont center of Regulator activity. There his forces defeated some 2,000 ill-organized Regulators in the Battle of Alamance, in which eight were killed on each side. Tryon's men then ranged through the backcountry, forcing some 6,500 Piedmont settlers to sign an oath of allegiance to the king.

These disputes and revolts within the colonies illustrate the fractious diversity of opinion and outlook evident among Americans on the eve of the Revolution. Colonists were of many minds about many things, including British rule. The disputatious frontier in colonial America also helped convince British authorities that the colonies were inherently unstable and that they required firmer oversight, including the use of military force to ensure civil stability.

A WORSENING CRISIS

Two events in 1772 further eroded the colonies' fragile relationship with the mother country. Near Providence, Rhode Island, a British schooner, the *Gaspee,* patrolling for smugglers, accidentally ran aground, and its crew proceeded to comandeer local sheep, hogs, and poultry. An angry crowd from the town boarded the ship, removed the crew, and set fire to the vessel. A commission of inquiry was formed with authority to hold suspects, but no witnesses could be found. Three days after the burning, on June 13, 1772, Governor Thomas Hutchinson told the Massachusetts assembly that his salary thenceforth would come out of customs revenues. Then word came that judges of the Massachusetts Superior Court would be paid from the same source and would no longer be dependent on the assembly for their income. The assembly expressed a fear that this portended "a despotic administration of government."

The existence of the *Gaspee* investigative commission, which bypassed the courts of Rhode Island, and the independent salaries for royal officials in Massachusetts suggested to the residents of other colonies that similar events might be in store for them. The discussion of colonial rights and parliamentary encroachments regained momentum. Ever the agitator, Sam Adams convinced the Boston town meeting to form the Committee of Correspondence, which issued a statement of rights and grievances and invited other towns to do the same. Committees of Correspondence sprang up across Massachusetts and in other colonies. In 1773 the Virginia assembly proposed the formation of such committees on an intercolonial basis, and a network of them spread across the colonies, mobilizing public opinion and keeping colonial resentments at a simmer. In unwitting tribute to their effectiveness, a Massachusetts Loyalist called the committees "the foulest, subtlest, and most venomous serpent ever issued from the egg of sedition."

THE BOSTON TEA PARTY   Lord North soon provided the colonists with the occasion to bring resentment from a simmer to a boil. In 1773 he undertook to help some friends bail out the East India Company, which had

The Able Doctor, or America Swallowing the Bitter Draught

This 1774 engraving shows Lord North, the Boston Port Act in his pocket, pouring tea down America's throat and America spitting it back.

in its British warehouses some 17 million pounds of tea. Under the Tea Act of 1773, the government would allow the grossly mismanaged company to send its south Asian tea directly to America without paying any duties. British tea merchants could thereby undercut their colonial competitors, most of whom were smugglers who bought tea from the Dutch. At the same time, Lord North ordered British authorities in New England to clamp down on American smuggling.

The Committees of Correspondence, backed by colonial merchants, alerted colonists to the new danger. The British government, they said, was trying to purchase colonial acquiescence with cheap tea. Before the end of the year, large shipments of tea had gone out to major colonial ports. In Boston several thousand irate colonists decided that their passion for liberty outweighed their love for tea. On December 16, 1773, a group of sixteen men, disguised as Mohawk Indians, boarded three ships and threw the 342 chests of East India Company tea overboard—cheered on by a crowd along the shore. Like those who had burned the *Gaspee*, they remained parties unknown—except to hundreds of Bostonians. John Adams relished the vigilante action. The destruction of the disputed tea, he said, was "so bold, so daring, so firm, intrepid and inflexible" that it would have "important consequences."

Yet given a more tactful response from London, the Boston Tea Party might easily have undermined the radicals' credibility. Many Americans, especially merchants, were aghast at the wanton destruction of property. Benjamin Franklin, an American agent in London trying to improve relations with Britain, declared that the destruction of the tea was a violent injustice. He urged his native city of Boston to reimburse the shipowners for their ruined cargo. Sam Adams dismissed Franklin's reservations. "Franklin may be a good philosopher," Adams said, "but he is a bungling politician."

The Boston Tea Party had pushed British officials to the breaking point. They were now convinced that the very existence of the empire was at stake. The rebels in Boston had instigated what could become a widespread effort to evade royal authority and imperial regulations. A firm response was required. "The colonists must either submit or triumph," a furious George III wrote to Lord North, and North strove to make an example of Boston. In the end, however, he helped make a revolution.

THE COERCIVE ACTS In 1774 Parliament enacted four harsh measures designed by Lord North to discipline Boston. The Boston Port Act closed the harbor from June 1, 1774, until the city had paid for the lost tea. An Act for the Impartial Administration of Justice let the governor transfer to England the trial of any official accused of committing an offense in the line of duty—no more redcoats would be tried on technicalities. A new Quartering Act directed local authorities to provide lodging for British soldiers, in private homes if necessary. Finally, the Massachusetts Government Act made the colony's council and law-enforcement officers all appointive rather than elective, declared that sheriffs would select jurors, and stipulated that no town meeting could be held without the governor's consent, except for the annual election of town officers. In May, General Thomas Gage replaced Hutchinson as governor and assumed command of the 4,000 British soldiers in Boston. Massachusetts now had a military governor.

These Coercive Acts were designed to isolate Boston and make an example of the colony. Instead, they galvanized colonial resistance. At last, it seemed to the colonists, their worst fears were being confirmed. If these "Intolerable Acts," as the colonists labeled the Coercive Acts, were not resisted, they would eventually be applied to the other colonies.

Further confirmation of British "tyranny" came with news of the Quebec Act, passed in June. That act provided that the government in Canada would

The State Blacksmiths Forging Fetters for the Americans

A British cartoon attacking Parliament's anti-colonial measures of 1775 and 1776.

not have a representative assembly and would instead be led by an appointed governor and council. It also gave a privileged position to the Catholic Church. The measure seemed merely another indicator of British authoritarianism. In addition, colonists pointed out that they had lost many lives in an effort to liberate the trans-Appalachian West from the control of French Catholics. Now the British seemed to be protecting papists at the expense of their own colonists. What was more, the act placed within the boundaries of Quebec the western lands north of the Ohio River, lands that Pennsylvania, Virginia, and Connecticut claimed.

Meanwhile, colonists rallied to the cause of besieged Boston, raising money, sending provisions, and boycotting, as well as burning, tea. In Williamsburg, when the Virginia assembly met in May, a young member of the Committee of Correspondence, Thomas Jefferson, proposed to set aside June 1, the effective date of the Boston Port Act, as a day of fasting and prayer in Virginia. The governor immediately dissolved the assembly, whose members then retired to the Raleigh Tavern and resolved to form a Continental Congress to represent all the colonies. Similar calls were coming from Providence, New York, Philadelphia, and elsewhere, and in June the Massachusetts assembly suggested a meeting in Philadelphia in September. Shortly before George Washington left to represent Virginia at the gathering, he wrote to a friend, "The crisis is arrived when we must assert our rights." Otherwise, he warned, British tyranny "shall make us as tame and abject slaves, as the blacks we rule over with such arbitrary sway."

THE CONTINENTAL CONGRESS   On September 5, 1774, the First Continental Congress assembled in Philadelphia. There were fifty-five members representing twelve continental colonies, all but Georgia, Quebec, Nova Scotia, and the Floridas. Peyton Randolph of Virginia was elected president, and Charles Thomson, "the Sam Adams of Philadelphia," became secretary. The Congress agreed to vote by colonies, although Patrick Henry urged the members to vote as individuals on the grounds that they were not Virginians or New Yorkers or whatever but Americans.

The Congress endorsed the Suffolk Resolves, which declared the Intolerable Acts null and void, urged Massachusetts to arm for defense, and called for economic sanctions against British commerce. The Congress then adopted a Declaration of American Rights, which conceded only Parliament's right to regulate commerce and those matters that were strictly imperial affairs. It proclaimed once again the rights of Americans as English citizens, denied Parliament's authority with respect to internal colonial affairs, and proclaimed the right of each colonial assembly to determine the need for British troops within its own province.

Finally the Continental Congress adopted the Continental Association of 1774, which recommended that every county, town, and city form committees to enforce a boycott of all British goods. These elected committees of virtuous citizens would monitor the economic activities of their neighbors to ensure compliance with the boycott. The local committees became in effect the organizational and communications network for the Revolutionary movement, connecting every locality to the leadership and enforcing public behavior. The Continental Association also included provisions for the non-importation of British goods (implemented in 1774) and the nonexportation of American goods to Britain (to be implemented in 1775 unless colonial grievances were addressed).

Seven thousand men across the colonies served on the committees of the Continental Association. They developed an effective form of political protest using an economic weapon available to all colonists: refusal to purchase British products and sell American goods to Britain. Such economic leverage, it was hoped, would pressure the British government to repeal its hated taxes on Americans. The committees often required colonists to sign an oath to join the boycotts. Those who refused to sign and to abide by the agreements were ostracized and intimidated; some were tarred and feathered.

Such efforts to gain economic self-sufficiency helped bind the diverse colonies by ropes of resistance. In this sense the emerging colonial desire for greater political independence involved concrete economic objectives. Gaining economic independence from Britain required not only decreasing imports but also increasing American production. Many colonial artisans, mechanics, and manufacturers recognized the benefits of the boycott movement. By cutting off British imports, they could earn greater freedom and long-term prosperity and security. As David Ramsay, a South Carolina physician, remembered, colonists rebelled against Britain's efforts to make Americans captive consumers in the hope of *"increasing the sale of her manufactures*, and of *perpetuating our subordination."*

Thousands of ordinary men and women participated in the boycott of British goods, and their sacrifices on behalf of colonial liberties provided the momentum leading to revolution. As the *Boston Gazette* observed, "However meanly some people may think about the populace or mob of a country, it is certain that the power or strength of every FREE country depends entirely on the populace." It was common folk who implemented and enforced the boycott, volunteered in local militia units, attended town meetings, and increasingly exerted pressure on royal officials in the colonies. In 1774 over 4,600 militiamen from Massachusetts lined the streets of Worcester and forced royal officials, hats in hands, to walk a gauntlet while recanting their support for imperial policies. The Founding Fathers could not have led the Revolutionary movement without such widespread popular support. As the people of Pittsfield, Massachusetts, declared in a petition, "We have always believed that the people are the fountain of power."

In London the king fumed. He wrote his prime minister that the "New England colonies are in a state of rebellion," and "blows must decide whether they are to be subject to this country or independent." British critics of the American actions reminded the colonists that Parliament had absolute sovereignty. Power could not be shared. Parliament could not abandon its claim to authority in part without abandoning it altogether. King and Parliament insisted that there would be no negotiation with the rebellious colonies. Force was the only option.

Parliament declared Massachusetts in rebellion and prohibited the New England colonies from trading with any nation outside the empire. Lord North's Conciliatory Resolution, adopted on February 27, 1775, was as far as the British would go. Under its terms, Parliament would refrain from using any measures but taxes to regulate trade and would grant to each colony the duties collected within its boundaries, provided the colonies would contribute voluntarily to a quota for defense of the empire. It was a formula, said one English skeptic, not for peace but for new quarrels. In Virginia in March 1775, the colony's leaders met to discuss what had occurred at the Continental Congress in Philadelphia. While most of the participants believed that Britain would relent in the face of united colonial resistance, Patrick Henry was convinced that war was imminent. He urged that the militia begin preparing for combat. Henry claimed that the colonies "have done everything that could be done to avert the storm which is now coming on. We have petitioned; we have remonstrated; we have supplicated; we have prostrated ourselves before the throne," yet such efforts had been met only by "violence and insult." By this point, Henry had whipped himself into a fury. Freedom, he shouted, could be bought only with blood. While staring at his reluctant comrades, he refused to predict what they might do for the cause of liberty. "But as for me," he declared through clenched teeth, "give me liberty—" He paused dramatically, clenched his fist as if it held a dagger, then plunged it as if into his heart— "or give me death."

SHIFTING AUTHORITY

As Patrick Henry had predicted, events moved beyond conciliation. The king and Parliament had lost control of their colonies; they could neither persuade nor coerce them to accept new regulations and revenue measures. Colonial resistance had become open rebellion. All through late 1774 and early 1775 the defenders of American rights were seizing the initiative. The unorganized Loyalists, if they did not submit to nonimportation agreements, found themselves confronted with persuasive committees of "Whigs," with tar and feathers at the ready. The Continental Congress urged each colony to mobilize its militia units. The militia, as much a social as a military organization in the past, now began serious training in formations, tactics, and marksmanship. Royal and proprietary officials were losing control as provincial congresses assumed authority and colonial militias organized, raided military stores, and gathered arms and gunpowder. But British military officials remained smugly confident. Major John Pitcairn wrote home from Boston in 1775, "I am satisfied that one active campaign, a smart action, and burning two or three of their towns, will set everything to rights."

LEXINGTON AND CONCORD   Pitcairn soon had his chance to suppress the rebellion. On April 14, 1775, the besieged military commander and new royal governor of Massachusetts, General Thomas Gage, received secret orders to stop the "open rebellion" in Massachusetts. He decided to capture and arrest leaders of the Provincial Congress and seize the militia's supply depot at Concord, about twenty miles outside Boston. On the night of April 18, Lieutenant Colonel Francis Smith and Major Pitcairn gathered 700 redcoats on Boston Common and set out by way of Lexington. When local Patriots got wind of the plan, Boston's Committee of Safety sent Paul Revere and William Dawes by separate routes on their famous ride to spread the alarm. Revere reached Lexington about midnight and alerted John Hancock and Sam Adams, who were hiding there. Joined by Dawes and Samuel Prescott, Revere rode on toward Concord. A British patrol intercepted the trio, but Prescott slipped through and delivered the warning.

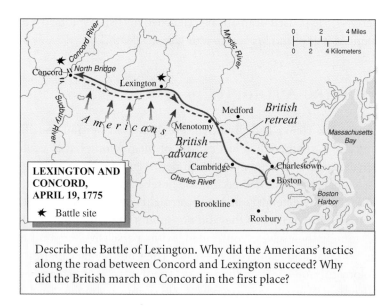

Describe the Battle of Lexington. Why did the Americans' tactics along the road between Concord and Lexington succeed? Why did the British march on Concord in the first place?

At dawn on April 19, the British advance guard of 238 redcoats found Captain John Parker and about seventy "Minutemen"—mostly dairy farmers and artisans—lined up on the dewy Lexington green. Parker apparently intended only a silent protest, but Major Pitcairn rode onto the green, swung his sword, and yelled, "Disperse, you damned rebels! You dogs, run!" The Americans had already begun quietly backing away when someone fired a shot, whereupon the British soldiers loosed a volley into the Minutemen, then charged them with bayonets, leaving eight dead and ten wounded.

The British officers hastily brought their men under control and led them to Concord. There the Americans had already carried off most of their munitions, but the British destroyed what they could. At Concord's North Bridge the growing American militia inflicted fourteen casualties on a British platoon, and by about noon the British had begun marching back to Boston. By then, however, the narrow road back to Boston had turned into a gauntlet of death as rebels from "every Middlesex village and farm" sniped from behind stone walls, trees, barns, houses—all the way back to the Charlestown peninsula. Among the Americans were Captain Parker and the reassembled Lexington militia. By nightfall the redcoat survivors were safe under the protection of the fleet and army at Boston, having suffered three times as many casualties as the Americans. A British general reported to London that the Americans had earned his respect: "Whoever looks upon them as an irregular

The Battle of Lexington

Amos Doolittle's impression of the Battle of Lexington as combat begins.

mob will find himself much mistaken." During the fighting along the road leading to Lexington from Concord, a British soldier was searching a house for rebel snipers when he ran into James Hayward of the Acton militia. The redcoat pointed his musket at the American and said, "You're a dead man." Hayward raised his weapon and answered, "So are you." They fired simultaneously.

THE SPREADING CONFLICT The Revolutionary War had begun. When the Second Continental Congress convened at Philadelphia on May 10, 1775, British-held Boston was under siege by Massachusetts militia units. On the very day that Congress met, Fort Ticonderoga, in northern New York, fell to a force of Green Mountain Boys under the hotheaded Ethan Allen of Vermont and Massachusetts volunteers under Benedict Arnold of Connecticut. Two days later the colonial force took Crown Point, north of Ticonderoga.

The Continental Congress, with no legal authority and no resources, met amid reports of spreading warfare. On June 15 it named George Washington commander in chief of a Continental army. Washington accepted on the condition that he receive no pay. The Congress fastened on the charismatic Washington because his service in the French and Indian War had made him one of the most experienced officers in America. The fact that he was from influential Virginia, the wealthiest and most populous province, added to his attractiveness. And as many people commented then and later, Washington looked like a leader. He was tall and strong, a superb horseman, and a fearless fighter. As a Philadelphian explained, Washington "had so much martial dignity in his deportment that you would distinguish him as a general and a soldier from among ten thousand people."

On June 17, the very day that George Washington was commissioned, the colonials and British forces engaged in their first major fight, the Battle of Bunker Hill. While the Continental Congress deliberated, American and British forces in and around Boston had increased. Militiamen from Rhode Island, Connecticut, and New Hampshire joined in the siege, as did several freed slaves. British reinforcements included three major generals: William Howe, Sir Henry Clinton, and John Burgoyne. On the day before the battle, American forces fortified the high ground overlooking Boston. Breed's Hill was the battle location, nearer to Boston than Bunker Hill, the site first chosen (and the source of the battle's erroneous name).

The rebels were spoiling for a fight. As Joseph Warren, a dapper Boston physician, put it, "The British say we won't fight; by heavens, I hope I shall die up to my knees in blood!" He soon got his wish. With civilians looking on from rooftops and church steeples, the British attacked in the blistering heat,

BOSTON

View of the Attack on Bunker's Hill

The Battle of Bunker Hill and the burning of Charlestown peninsula.

with 2,400 troops moving in tight formation through tall grass. The Americans, pounded by naval guns, watched from behind their earthworks as the waves of British troops in their beautiful but impractical uniforms advanced up the hill. The militiamen waited until the attackers had come within fifteen to twenty paces, then loosed a shattering volley. The Americans cheered as they watched the greatest soldiers in the world retreating in panic.

The British re-formed their lines and attacked again. Another sheet of flames and lead greeted them, and the vaunted redcoats retreated a second time. Still, the proud British generals, led by William Howe, were determined not to let the ragtag rustics humiliate them. On the third attempt, when the colonials began to run out of gunpowder and were forced to throw stones, a bayonet charge ousted them. The British took the high ground, but at the cost of 1,054 casualties. Colonial losses were about 400. Every one of General Howe's aides had been killed or wounded. "A dear bought victory," recorded General Clinton, "another such would have ruined us."

The Battle of Bunker Hill had two profound effects. First, the high number of British casualties made the English generals more cautious in subsequent encounters with the Continental army. Second, Congress recommended that all able-bodied men enlist in a militia. This tended to divide the male population into Patriot and Loyalist camps. A middle ground was no longer tenable.

In early March 1776 American forces occupied Dorchester Heights, to the south of Boston, and brought the city under threat of bombardment with cannons and mortars. General Howe retreated by water to Halifax. The last British forces, along with fearful American Loyalists, embarked on March 17, 1776. By that time the British forces were facing not the suppression of a rebellion but the reconquest of a continent.

While American forces held Boston under siege, the Continental Congress pursued the dimming hope of a compromise settlement. On July 5 and 6, 1775, the delegates issued two major documents: an appeal to the king known as the Olive Branch Petition and a Declaration of the Causes and Necessity of Taking Up Arms. The Olive Branch Petition, written by Pennsylvanian John Dickinson, professed continued loyalty to George III and begged the king to restrain further hostilities pending a reconciliation. The declaration, also largely Dickinson's work, traced the history of the controversy, denounced the British for the unprovoked assault at Lexington, and rejected independence but affirmed the colonists' purpose to fight for their rights rather than submit to slavery. When the Olive Branch Petition reached London, George III refused even to look at it. On August 22 he declared the American colonists "open and avowed enemies." The next day he issued a proclamation of rebellion.

Before the end of July 1775, the Congress had authorized an ill-fated attack on British troops in the walled city of Quebec, in the vain hope of rallying support from the French inhabitants of Canada. One force, under Richard Montgomery, advanced toward Quebec by way of Lake Champlain; another, under Benedict Arnold, struggled through the Maine woods. The American units arrived outside Quebec in September, exhausted and hungry. Then they were ambushed by a silent killer: smallpox. "The small pox [is] very much among us," wrote one soldier. As the deadly virus raced through the American camp, General Montgomery faced a brutal dilemma. Most of his soldiers had signed up for short tours of duty, many of which were scheduled to expire at the end of the year. He could not afford to wait until spring for the smallpox to subside. Seeing little choice but to fight, Montgomery ordered a desperate attack on the British forces at Quebec during a blizzard, on December 31, 1775. The assault was a disaster. Montgomery was killed early in the battle and Benedict Arnold wounded. Over 400 Americans were taken prisoner. The rest of the Patriot force retreated to its camp outside the walled city and appealed to the Continental Congress for reinforcements.

The smallpox virus continued attacking both the Americans in the camp and their comrades taken captive by the British. As fresh troops arrived, they, too, fell victim to the deadly virus. Benedict Arnold warned George Washington in February 1776 that the runaway disease would soon lead to "the entire ruin of the Army." By May there were only 1,900 American soldiers left outside Quebec, and 900 of them were infected with smallpox. Sensing the weakness of the American force, the British attacked and sent the ragtag Patriots on a frantic retreat up the St. Lawrence River to the American-held city of Montreal and eventually back to New York and New England. The sick were left behind, but the smallpox virus traveled with the fleeing soldiers. Major General Horatio Gates later remarked that "every thing about this Army is infected with the Pestilence; The Clothes, The Blankets, the Air & the Ground they Walk on."

Quebec was the first military setback for the Revolutionaries. It would not be the last. And smallpox would continue to bedevil the American war effort. The veterans of the failed Canadian campaign brought home both smallpox and demoralizing stories about the disease, thus spreading the epidemic to civilians and making the recruitment of new soldiers more difficult. Men who might risk British gunfire balked at the more terrifying thought of contracting smallpox in a military camp.

In the South, Virginia's royal governor raised a Loyalist force, including slaves recruited with the promise of freedom, but met defeat in December 1775. In North Carolina, Loyalist Highland Scots, joined by some former Regulators, lost a battle with a Patriot force at Moores Creek Bridge. The Loyalists had set out for Wilmington to join a British expeditionary force under Lord Cornwallis and Sir Henry Clinton. That plan frustrated, the British commanders decided to attack Charleston instead. The Patriot militia there had partially finished a palmetto-log fort on Sullivans Island (later named in honor of its commander, Colonel William Moultrie), and when the British fleet attacked, on June 28, 1776, the spongy palmetto logs absorbed the naval fire, and Fort Moultrie's cannon returned it with devastating effect. The fleet, with over 200 casualties and every ship damaged, was forced to retire. South Carolina would honor the palmetto tree by putting it on its state flag.

As the fighting spread north into Canada and south into Virginia and the Carolinas, the Continental Congress appointed commissioners to negotiate treaties of peace with Indian tribes, organized a Post Office Department, with Benjamin Franklin as postmaster general, and authorized the formation of a navy and a marine corps.

The delegates continued to hold back from declaring independence. Yet through late 1775 and early 1776 word came of one British action after another that proclaimed rebellion and war. In December 1775 a Prohibitory Act declared the colonies closed to all commerce. The king and cabinet also recruited mercenaries in Europe. Eventually almost 30,000 Germans served, about 17,000 of them from the principality of Hesse-Cassel—thus *Hessian* became the name applied to all of them. Parliament remained deaf to members who warned that the reconquest of America would not only be costly in itself but also might lead to another great war with France and Spain.

COMMON SENSE In 1776 Thomas Paine's pamphlet *Common Sense* was published anonymously in Philadelphia. Paine had arrived there from England thirteen months before. Coming from a humble Quaker background, Paine had distinguished himself chiefly as a drifter, a failure in marriage and business. At age thirty-seven he had set sail for America with a letter of introduction from Benjamin Franklin and the purpose of setting up a school for young ladies. When the school did not work out, he moved into the political controversy as a freelance writer and with *Common Sense* proved himself the consummate Revolutionary rhetorician. Until his pamphlet appeared, the squabble had been mainly with Parliament; few colonists considered independence an option. Paine, however, directly attacked allegiance to the monarchy, which had remained the last frayed connection to Britain, and he refocused the hostility previously vented on Parliament. The common sense of the matter, it seemed, was that King George III bore the responsibility for the malevolence toward the colonies. Americans should consult their own interests, abandon George III, and declare their independence: "The blood of the slain, the weeping voice of nature cries, 'TIS TIME TO PART."

Independence

Within three months more than 150,000 copies of Thomas Paine's pamphlet were in circulation, an enormous number for the time. "*Common Sense* is working a powerful change in the minds of men," George Washington said. A visitor to North Carolina's Provincial Congress could "hear nothing praised but *Common Sense* and independence." One by one the provincial governments authorized their delegates in the Continental Congress to take the final step. On June 7 Richard Henry Lee of Virginia moved "that these United Colonies are, and of right ought to be, free and independent states." Lee's resolution passed on July 2, a date that

The Coming Revolution

The Continental Congress votes for independence, July 2, 1776.

"will be the most memorable epoch in the history of America," John Adams wrote to his wife, Abigail. The memorable date, however, became July 4, 1776, when the Congress adopted the Declaration of Independence, a statement of political philosophy that still retains its dynamic force.

JEFFERSON'S DECLARATION   Although Thomas Jefferson is often called the author of the Declaration of Independence, he is more accurately termed its draftsman. In June 1776 the Continental Congress appointed a committee of five men—Jefferson, Benjamin Franklin, John Adams, Robert Livingston of New York, and Roger Sherman of Connecticut—to develop a public explanation of the reasons for colonial discontent and to provide a rationale for independence. John Adams convened the committee on June 11. The group asked Adams and Jefferson to produce a first draft, whereupon Adams deferred to Jefferson because of the thirty-three-year-old Virginian's reputation as an eloquent writer.

During two days in mid-June 1776, in his rented lodgings in Philadelphia, Jefferson wrote the first statement of American grievances and principles. He later explained that his purpose was "not to find out new principles, or new arguments, never before thought of, not merely to say things which had never been said before; but to place before mankind the common sense of the subject, in terms so plain and firm as to command their assent." He intended his words to serve as "an expression of the American mind, and to give to that expression the proper tone and spirit called for by the occasion."

Jefferson drew primarily upon two sources: his own draft preamble to the Virginia Constitution, written a few weeks earlier, and George Mason's draft of Virginia's Declaration of Rights, which had appeared in Philadelphia newspapers in mid-June. It was Mason's text that stimulated many of Jefferson's most famous phrases. Mason, for example, had written that "all men are born equally free and independent, and have certain inherent natural Rights, . . . among which are the Enjoyment of Life and Liberty, with the Means of acquiring and possessing Property, and pursuing and obtaining Happiness and Safety."

Jefferson shared his draft with the committee members, and they made several minor revisions before submitting the document to the Congress. The legislators made eighty-six changes in Jefferson's declaration, including the insertion of two references to God and deleting a section blaming the English monarch for imposing African slavery on the colonies (delegates from Georgia and South Carolina had protested that it smacked of abolitionism).

The resulting Declaration of Independence constitutes a compelling restatement of John Locke's contract theory of government—the theory, in Jefferson's words, that governments derived "their just Powers from the consent of the people," who were entitled to "alter or abolish" those that denied their "unalienable rights" to "life, Liberty, and the pursuit of Happiness." The appeal was no longer simply to "the rights of Englishmen" but to the broader "laws of Nature and Nature's God." Parliament, which had no proper authority over the colonies, was never mentioned by name. The enemy was a king who had tried to establish "an absolute Tyranny over these States." The "Representatives of the United States of America," therefore, declared the thirteen "United Colonies" to be "Free and Independent States." General George Washington ordered the Declaration read to every brigade in the Continental army in New York. He prayed that the muscular statement of colonial principles would "serve as a fresh incentive to every officer, and soldier, to act with Fidelity and Courage." An equally excited but sober John Adams recognized that "the Toil and Blood and Treasure, that it will cost Us to maintain this Declaration" would be immense. Benjamin Franklin acknowledged how high the stakes were: "Well, Gentlemen," he told the Congress, "we must now hang together, or we shall most assuredly hang separately."

"WE ALWAYS HAD GOVERNED OURSELVES" So it had come to this, thirteen years after Britain acquired domination of North America with the Treaty of Paris. In explaining the causes of the Revolution, historians have advanced many theories and explanations: the excessive regulation of trade, the restrictions on settling western lands, the tax burden, the mounting debts to British merchants, the growth of a national consciousness, the lack of representation in Parliament, ideologies of Whiggery and the Enlightenment, the abrupt shift from a mercantile to an "imperial" policy after 1763, class conflict, and revolutionary conspiracy.

Each factor contributed something to the collective grievances that rose to a climax in a gigantic failure of British statesmanship. A conflict between British sovereignty and American rights had come to a point of confrontation that adroit statesmanship might have avoided, sidestepped, or outflanked. Irresolution and vacillation in the British ministry finally gave way to the stubborn determination to force an issue long permitted to drift. The colonists, conditioned by the Whig interpretation of history, saw these developments as the conspiracy of a corrupted oligarchy—and finally, they decided, of a despotic king—to impose an "absolute Tyranny."

The individual motives of the Revolutionaries varied considerably. The most frequent explanation for rebelling against British authority was the necessity of preserving rights and freedoms. George Washington, for example, saw in British policies a conspiracy to "fix the Shackles of Slavery upon us." Yet colonists sought liberty from British tyranny for many reasons, not all of which were selfless or noble. The Boston merchant John Hancock, for example, embraced the Patriot cause in part because he was the region's foremost smuggler. Paying British taxes would have cost him a fortune. Likewise, South Carolina's Henry Laurens and Virginia's Landon Carter, wealthy planters, were concerned about the future of slavery under British control. The seeming contradiction between American slaveholders demanding liberty from British oppression was not lost on observers at the time. John Fletcher, a leading Methodist in Britain, wrote in 1776 that the Americans were "hypocritical friends of liberty who buy and sell and whip their fellow men as if they were brutes, and absurdly complain that they are enslaved." Even George Washington was not devoid of self-interest in his opposition to British policies. He owned 60,000 acres of land west of the Appalachians and very much resented British efforts to restrict white settlement on the frontier.

Perhaps the last word on the complex causes of the Revolution should belong to an obscure participant, Levi Preston, a Minuteman from Danvers, Massachusetts. Asked sixty-seven years after Lexington and Concord about British oppressions, the ninety-one-year-old veteran responded, as his young interviewer reported later:

"What were they? Oppressions? I didn't feel them." "What, were you not oppressed by the Stamp Act?" "I never saw one of those stamps. . . . I am certain I never paid a penny for one of them." "Well, what then about the tea-tax?" "Tea-tax! I never drank a drop of the stuff; the boys threw it all overboard." "Well, then, what was the matter? and what did you mean in going to the fight?" "Young man, what we meant in going for those redcoats was this: we always had governed ourselves, and we always meant to. They didn't mean we should."

MAKING CONNECTIONS

· Revolutionary rhetoric was important not only for fighting the American Revolution; it also provided the framework for the creation of state and national governments after independence was won. This framework will be discussed in the next two chapters.

· The section titled "Discontent on the Frontier" showed the tension between colonists in the more urban eastern areas of several states and those on the western frontier. These tensions will reappear in several chapters—for example, in the Federalist–anti-Federalist debate over ratification of the Constitution (in Chapter 7).

FURTHER READING

For a narrative survey of the events leading to the Revolution, see Edward Countryman's *The American Revolution*, rev. ed. (2003). For Great Britain's perspective on the imperial conflict, see Ian R. Christie's *Crisis of Empire* (1966).

The intellectual foundations of revolt are traced in Bernard Bailyn's *The Ideological Origins of the American Revolution*, enlarged ed. (1992). To understand how these views were connected to organized protest, see Pauline Maier's *From Resistance to Revolution: Colonial Radicals and the Development of American Opposition to Britain, 1765–1776* (1972) and Jon Butler's *Becoming America: The Revolution before 1776* (2000).

Several books deal with specific events in the crisis. Oliver M. Dickerson's *The Navigation Acts and the American Revolution* (1951) stresses the change from trade regulation to taxation in 1764. Edmund S. Morgan and Helen M.

Morgan's *The Stamp Act Crisis: Prologue to Revolution,* rev. ed. (1962) gives the colonial perspective on that crucial event. Also valuable are Hiller B. Zobel's *The Boston Massacre* (1970), Benjamin Woods Labaree's *The Boston Tea Party, 1773: Catalyst for Revolution* (1964), and David Ammerman's *In the Common Cause: American Response to the Coercive Acts of 1774* (1974). On the efforts of colonists to boycott the purchase of British goods, see T. H. Breen's *The Marketplace of Revolution: How Consumer Politics Shaped American Independence* (2004). An excellent overview of the political turmoil leading to war is John Ferling's *A Leap in the Dark: The Struggle to Create the American Republic* (2003). A fascinating analysis of the smallpox epidemic during the Revolutionary War is Elizabeth A. Fenn's *Pox Americana: The Great Smallpox Epidemic of 1775–82* (2001).

Pauline Maier's *American Scripture: Making the Declaration of Independence* (1997) is the best analysis of the framing of that document. For accounts of how the imperial controversy affected individual colonies, see Edward Countryman's *A People in Revolution: The American Revolution and Political Society in New York, 1760–1790* (1981), Richard L. Bushman's *King and People in Provincial Massachusetts* (1985), James H. Hutson's *Pennsylvania Politics, 1746–1770: The Movement for Royal Government and Its Consequences* (1972), Rhys Isaac's *The Transformation of Virginia, 1740–1790* (1982), and A. Roger Ekirch's *"Poor Carolina": Politics and Society in Colonial North Carolina, 1729–1776* (1981).

Events west of the Appalachians are chronicled concisely by Jack M. Sosin in *The Revolutionary Frontier, 1763–1783* (1967). Military affairs in the early phases of the war are handled in John W. Shy's *Toward Lexington: The Role of the British Army in the Coming of the American Revolution* (1965) and in works listed in Chapter 6.

Part Two

BUILDING

A

NATION

he signing of the Declaration of Independence generated great excitement among the rebellious colonists. Yet while it was one thing for Patriot leaders to declare American independence from British authority, it was quite another to win it on the battlefield. The odds favored the British: barely one third of the colonists actively supported the Revolution, the political stability of the new nation was uncertain, and George Washington found himself in command of a poorly supplied, inexperienced army.

Yet the Revolutionary movement would persevere and prevail. The skill and fortitude of Washington and his lieutenants enabled the American forces to exploit their geographic advantages. Equally important was the intervention of the French on behalf of the Revolutionary cause. The Franco-American alliance proved decisive. In 1783, after eight years of sporadic fighting and heavy human and financial losses, the British gave up the fight and their American colonies.

Amid the Revolutionary turmoil the Patriots faced the daunting task of forming new governments for themselves. Their deeply engrained resentment of British imperial rule led them to decentralize political power and grant substantial sovereignty to the individual states. As Thomas Jefferson declared, "Virginia, Sir, is my country." Such powerful local ties help explain why the colonists focused their attention on creating new state constitutions rather than a national government. The Articles of Confederation, ratified in 1781, provided only the semblance of national authority. Final power to make and execute laws remained with the states.

After the end of the Revolutionary War, the flimsy political bonds authorized by the Articles of Confederation proved inadequate to the needs of the new—and expanding—nation. This realization led to the Constitutional Convention in 1787. The process of drafting and ratifying the new constitution prompted a debate on the relative significance of national power, local control, and individual freedom that has provided the central theme of American political thought ever since.

The Revolution involved much more than the apportionment of political power, however. It also unleashed social forces and posed social questions that would help reshape the very fabric of American culture. What would be the role of women, African Americans, and Native Americans in the new republic? How would the quite different economies of the various regions of the new United States be developed? Who would control and facilitate access to the vast territories to the west of the original thirteen states? How would the new republic relate to the other nations of the world?

These controversial questions helped foster the first national political parties in the United States. During the 1790s Federalists, led by Alexander Hamilton, and Republicans, led by Thomas Jefferson and James Madison, furiously debated the political and economic future of the new nation. With Jefferson's election as president in 1800, the Republicans gained the upper hand in national politics for the next quarter century. In the process they presided over a maturing society that aggressively expanded westward at the expense of the Native Americans, ambivalently embraced industrial development, fitfully engaged in a second war with Great Britain, and ominously witnessed a growing sectional controversy over slavery.

6

THE AMERICAN
REVOLUTION

FOCUS QUESTIONS

- What were the American and British military strategies and the Revolutionary War's major turning points?
- How did the war affect the home front?
- How was the American Revolution a "social revolution" in matters of social equality, slavery, the rights of women, and religious freedom?
- What factors led to the emergence of a distinctive American culture?

To answer these questions and access additional review material, please visit www.wwnorton.com/studyspace.

Few foreign observers thought that the upstart Revolutionaries could win a war against the world's greatest empire—and the Americans did lose most of the battles of the Revolution. But they eventually forced the British to sue for peace and grant their independence, a stunning result that reflects the tenacity of the Patriots as well as the peculiar difficulties facing the British as they tried to conduct a far-flung campaign thousands of miles from home. The British Empire dispatched two thirds of its entire army and one half of its formidable navy to suppress the American revolt. The costly military commitments the British maintained elsewhere around the globe further complicated their war effort.

Fighting in the New World was not an easy task for either side, however. The Americans had to create a military force capable of opposing the foremost army in the world. Recruiting, supplying, equipping, training, and paying soldiers were monumental challenges, especially for a fledgling nation in the midst of forming its first governments. The Patriot army encircling Boston in 1775 was little more than a rustic militia made up of volunteers who had enlisted for six months. The citizen-soldiers lacked training and discipline. They came and went as they pleased, did not salute officers, gambled frequently, and drank liquor freely. General George Washington recognized immediately that the foremost needs of the new army were capable officers, intensive training, strict discipline, and longer enlistment contracts. He soon began whipping his army into shape. Recruits who violated army rules were placed in the stockade, flogged, or sent packing. Yet the tenacity of Washington and the Revolutionaries bore fruit as war-weariness and political dissension in London hampered British efforts to suppress the rebel forces.

Like all major military events the Revolution had unexpected consequences affecting political, economic, and social life. It not only secured American independence, generated a new sense of nationalism, and created a unique system of self-governance; it also began a process of societal definition and change that has yet to run its course. The turmoil of revolution upset traditional class and social relationships and helped transform the lives of people who had long been relegated to the periphery of historical concern—African Americans, women, and Indians. In important ways, then, the Revolution was much more than simply a war for independence. It was an engine for political experimentation and social change.

1776: WASHINGTON'S NARROW ESCAPE

On July 2, 1776, the day that Congress voted for independence, British redcoats landed on undefended Staten Island, across New York Harbor from Manhattan. They were the vanguard of a gigantic effort to reconquer America and the first elements of an enormous force that gathered around New York Harbor over the next month. By mid-August, Major General William Howe, with the support of a fleet under his older brother, Admiral Richard, Lord Howe, had some 32,000 men at his disposal, the largest single force mustered by the British in the eighteenth century. George Washington transferred most of his troops to New York from Boston, but he could gather only about 19,000 poorly trained militiamen and members of the Continental army—much too small a force to defend New York, but Congress wanted it held. This meant Washington had to expose his men to entrapments from which they escaped more by luck and Howe's caution than by any strategic genius of the American commander. Although a veteran of frontier fighting, Washington had never commanded a unit larger than a regiment. In 1776 he was still learning the art of generalship, and the New York campaign afforded some expensive lessons.

FIGHTING IN NEW YORK AND NEW JERSEY By invading and occupying New York, the British hoped to sever New England from the rest of the rebellious colonies. They enjoyed complete naval superiority as well as overwhelming advantages in men and weaponry. In late August 1776 the massive British armada of 427 battleships and transports began landing troops on Long Island. Although short of munitions, greatly outnumbered, and leading a force in which one quarter of the men were affected by an epidemic of smallpox, Washington was determined to defend New York. It was a colossal mistake. The new American army suffered a humiliating defeat at the Battle of Long Island. British invaders caught Washington's forces by surprise. The American commander knew early on that his defenses could not hold. "Good God!" he exclaimed. "What brave fellows I must lose this day!" Only a timely rainstorm with strong winds, high tides, and fog enabled the retreating Americans to cross the harbor from Brooklyn to Manhattan under cover of darkness.

Had Howe moved quickly, he could have trapped Washington's army in lower Manhattan. The main American force, however, withdrew northward to the mainland of New York, crossed the Hudson River, and retreated slowly across New Jersey and over the Delaware River into Pennsylvania. As the ragged remnants of the American army fled across New Jersey, the British buglers giving chase mocked them by trumpeting fox-hunting calls.

At the end of August 1776, General Washington had more than 28,000 men under his command. By December he had only 3,000. The supreme commander was disconsolate; the American war effort was in desperate straits. Thousands of militiamen had simply gone home. Unless a new army could be raised quickly, Washington warned, "I think the game is pretty near up." But it wasn't. In the August retreat marched a British volunteer, Thomas Paine. Having opened an eventful year with his inspiring pamphlet *Common Sense*, Paine now composed *The American Crisis*, in which he penned this immortal line:

These are the times that try men's souls: The summer soldier and the sunshine patriot will, in this crisis, shrink from the service of his country; but he that stands it NOW deserves the love and thanks of man and woman. Tyranny, like Hell, is not easily conquered. Yet we have this consolation with us, that the harder the conflict, the more glorious the triumph.

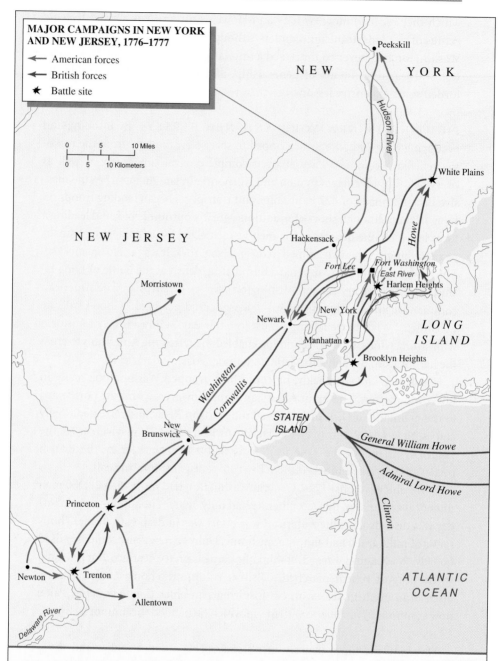

MAJOR CAMPAIGNS IN NEW YORK AND NEW JERSEY, 1776–1777

← American forces
← British forces
★ Battle site

Why did Washington lead his army from Brooklyn Heights to Manhattan and from there to New Jersey? How could General Howe have ended the rebellion in New York? What is the significance of the battle at Trenton?

The pamphlet, ordered read in the American army camps, bolstered the shaken morale of the Patriots—as events would soon do more decisively.

General Howe, firmly—and luxuriously—based in New York (which the British held throughout the war), settled down with his mistress to wait out the winter. Washington, however, was not yet ready to hibernate. He knew that the morale of his men and the hopes of a new nation required "some stroke" of good news in the face of their devastating losses in New York. So he seized the initiative with a desperate gamble to achieve a victory before more of his soldiers returned home once their enlistment contracts expired. On Christmas night 1776 he led some 2,400 men across the icy

George Washington at Princeton

By Charles Willson Peale.

Delaware River. Near dawn at Trenton, New Jersey, the Americans surprised a garrison of 1,500 sleeping Hessians (German mercenaries). It was a total rout, from which only 500 Hessians escaped death or capture. Only six of Washington's men were wounded, one of whom was Lieutenant James Monroe, the future president. A week later, at nearby Princeton, the Americans repelled three regiments of British redcoats before taking refuge in winter quarters at Morristown, in the hills of northern New Jersey. The campaigns of 1776 had ended, after repeated defeats, with two minor victories that bolstered the Patriot cause. The unexpected victories at Princeton and Trenton may well have saved the cause of independence. Having learned of the American triumphs in New Jersey, a Virginia Tory glumly reported that a few days before, the Revolutionaries "had given up the cause for lost. Their late successes have turned the scale and now they are all liberty mad again." General Howe had missed his great chance—indeed, several chances—to bring the rebellion to a speedy end. Grumbled one British officer, the Americans had "become a formidable enemy" even though they had yet to win a full-scale conventional battle.

In fact, George Washington had come to realize that the only way to defeat the British was to wear them down in a long war of attrition and exhaustion. As the combat in New York had shown, he could not best the British army in a conventional battle. The only hope of winning the war was not to lose it.

Time became his greatest weapon. Over the next eight years he and his troops would outlast the invaders.

AMERICAN SOCIETY AT WAR

CHOOSING SIDES The American Revolution was as much a civil war as it was a struggle against a foreign nation. The act of choosing sides divided families and friends, towns and cities. Benjamin Franklin's illegitimate son William, for example, was the royal governor of New Jersey. He sided with Great Britain during the Revolution, and his father later removed him from his will. The passions unleashed by the Revolution erupted in brutalities on both sides. Mobs of Patriots executed Tories (or Loyalists, as the British sympathizers were sometimes known), and state governments confiscated their homes and property. One Loyalist, John Stevens, testified that he "was dragged by a rope fixed about his neck" across the Susquehanna River because he refused to sign an oath supporting the rebellion. In Virginia the planter Charles Lynch set up vigilante courts to punish Tories by "lynching" them—which in this case meant having them whipped.

Opinion among the colonists concerning the war divided in three ways: Patriots, or Whigs (as the Revolutionaries called themselves); Tories; and an indifferent middle group swayed mostly by the better organized and more energetic radicals. That the Loyalists were numerous is evident from the departure, during and after the war, of roughly 100,000 of them, more than 3 percent of the total population. But the Patriots were probably the largest of the three groups. There was a like division in British opinion. The aversion of so many English to the war was one reason for the government's hiring German mercenaries to fight with the British army.

Estimating how many Americans remained loyal to Britain was a central concern of English military planners, for they based many of their decisions on such figures. Through most of the war, the British sought to align themselves with an elusive Tory majority that the Loyalists kept telling them was waiting only for British regulars to show the flag. Often they miscalculated. Generally Tories were concentrated in the seaport cities, but they came from all walks of life. Governors, judges, and other royal officials were almost all Loyalists; most Anglican ministers also preferred the mother country; colonial merchants might be tugged one way or the other, depending upon how much they had benefited or suffered from mercantilist regulation; the wealthy southern planters were swayed one way by dependence upon British bounties, another by their debts to British merchants. In the backcountry of New York and the Carolinas, many humble folk rallied to the crown. Where planter aristocrats tended to be Whig, as in North Carolina, backcountry farmers (many of them recently Regulators) leaned to the Tories.

In few places, however, were there enough Tories to assume control without the presence of British troops, and nowhere for very long. Repeatedly the British forces were frustrated by both the failure of Loyalists to materialize in strength and the collapse of Loyalist militia units once regular detachments pulled out. Even more disheartening was what one British officer called "the licentiousness of the [Loyalist] troops, who committed every species of rapine and plunder," and thereby converted potential friends to enemies. British and Hessian regulars, brought up in a hard school of warfare, tended to treat all civilians as hostile.

The inability of the British to use Loyalists effectively as pacification troops led them to abandon areas once they had conquered them. Because Patriot militias quickly returned whenever the British left an area, any Loyalists in the region faced a difficult choice: either accompany the British and leave behind their property or stay and face the wrath of the Patriots. In addition, the British policy of offering slaves their freedom in exchange for their loyalty and service alienated large numbers of neutral or even Tory planters.

The Patriot militia sprang to life whenever redcoats appeared nearby, and all adult white males, with few exceptions, were obligated under state law to serve when called. With time even the most apathetic would be pressed to a commitment, if only to turn out for drill. And sooner or later nearly every colonial county experienced military action that called for armed resistance. The war itself, then, whether through British and Loyalist behavior or the call of the militia, mobilized the apathetic to make at least an appearance of support for the American cause. Once made, this commitment was seldom reversed.

MILITIA AND ARMY   American militiamen served two purposes: they constituted a home guard, defending their communities, and they helped augment the Continental army. Dressed in hunting shirts and armed with muskets, they preferred to ambush their opponents or engage them in hand-to-hand combat rather than fight in traditional formations. They also tended to kill unnecessarily and to torture prisoners. To repel an attack, the militia somehow materialized; the danger past, it evaporated, for there were chores to do at home. They "come in, you cannot tell how," George Washington said in exasperation, "go, you cannot tell when, and act you cannot tell where, consume your provisions, exhaust your stores, and leave you at last at a critical moment."

The Continental army, by contrast, was on the whole well trained. Unlike the professional soldiers in the British army, Washington's troops were citizen-

American Militia

This sketch of the militiamen by a French soldier at Yorktown shows "one of those ubiquitous American frontiersman-turned-soldiers" (second from right).

soldiers, mostly poor native-born Americans or immigrants who had been indentured servants or convicts. Many found camp life debilitating and combat horrifying. As General Nathanael Greene, Washington's ablest commander, pointed out, few of the Patriots had ever engaged in mortal combat, and they were hard pressed to "stand the shocking scenes of war, to march over dead men, to hear without concern the groans of the wounded." Desertions grew as the war dragged on. At times, General Washington could put only 2,000 to 3,000 men in the field. Regiments were organized state by state, and the states were supposed to keep them filled with volunteers or with conscripts if need be, but Washington could never be sure that his requisitions would be met.

PROBLEMS OF FINANCE AND SUPPLY Congress found it difficult to supply the army. None of the states provided more than a part of its share, and Congress reluctantly let army agents take supplies directly from farmers in return for certificates promising future payment. Many of the states found a ready source of revenue in the sale of abandoned Loyalist estates. Nevertheless, Congress and the states fell short of funding the war's cost and resorted to printing paper money.

Congress did better at providing munitions than at providing other supplies. In 1777 it established a government arsenal at Springfield, Massachusetts, and during the war, states offered bounties for the manufacture of guns and powder. Still, most munitions were supplied either by wartime captures or by importation from France, whose government was all too glad to help the rebels fight its archenemy.

During the harsh winter at Morristown (1776–1777), George Washington's army nearly disintegrated as enlistments expired and deserters fled the hardships of brutally cold weather, inadequate food, and widespread disease. Smallpox continued to wreak havoc among the American armies. "The small Pox! The small Pox!" John Adams wrote to his wife, Abigail. "What shall We do with it?" By 1777 George Washington had come to view the virus with greater dread than "the Sword of the Enemy." On any given day, one fourth of the American troops were deemed unfit for duty, usually because of smallpox. Some Americans suspected that the British were practicing biological warfare by sending infected civilians and clothing behind the American lines.

The threat of smallpox to the war effort was so great that in early 1777 Washington ordered a mass inoculation, which he managed to keep secret from the British. Inoculating an entire army was an enormous and risky undertaking. Each soldier had to be interviewed to determine whether he had ever had smallpox. Then those who believed they had never been infected were inoculated. The virus was implanted in an incision, usually on the arm or hand. For unknown reasons the resulting smallpox produced less severe symptoms than natural infections—fewer pustules, less scarring, and far fewer deaths. Inoculated soldiers had to be quarantined while the virus ran its course, but the infected soldiers were thereafter immune to the disease. Washington's daring gamble paid off. One of the 400 Connecticut soldiers who was inoculated in the summer of 1777 reported its success: "We lost none. I had the smallpox favorably as did the rest." The successful inoculation of the American army marks one of Washington's greatest strategic accomplishments of the war.

Only about 1,000 Continentals and a few militiamen stuck out the Morristown winter. With the spring thaw, however, recruits began arriving to claim the bounty of $20 and 100 acres of land offered by Congress to those who would enlist for three years or for the duration of the conflict, if less. With some 9,000 regulars, Washington began sparring and feinting with Howe in northern New Jersey. Howe had been making other plans, however, and so had other British officers.

1777: SETBACKS FOR THE BRITISH

Divided counsels, overconfidence, poor communications, and indecision plagued British military planning in the campaigns of 1777. After the

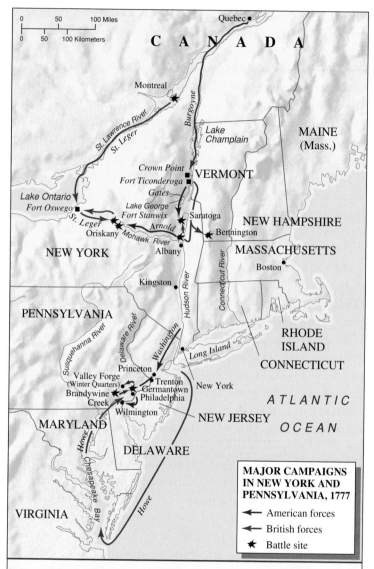

What were the consequences of Burgoyne's strategy of dividing the colonies with two British forces? How did life in Washington's camp at Valley Forge transform the American army? Why was Saratoga a turning point in the American Revolution?

removal of General Gage during the siege of Boston, "Gentleman Johnny" Burgoyne took command of the northern British armies. He proposed to bisect the colonies. His men would advance southward from Canada to the Hudson River while another force moved eastward from Oswego, in western New York, down the Mohawk River valley. General Howe, meanwhile, would lead a third force up the Hudson from New York City. Howe in fact had proposed a similar plan, combined with an attack on New England. Had he stuck to it, he might have cut the colonies in two and delivered them a disheartening blow. But he changed his mind and decided to move against the Patriot capital, Philadelphia, expecting that the Pennsylvania Tories would rally to the crown and secure the colony.

Washington, sensing Howe's purpose, withdrew most of his men from New Jersey to meet the new threat. At Brandywine Creek, south of Philadelphia, Howe outmaneuvered and routed Washington's forces on September 11, and fifteen days later the British occupied Philadelphia. Washington counterattacked in a dense fog at Germantown on October 4, but British reinforcements from Philadelphia under General Charles Cornwallis arrived in time to repulse the Americans. Washington retired with his army to winter quarters at Valley Forge, Pennsylvania, while Howe and his men remained for the winter in the relative comfort of Philadelphia, twenty miles away. Howe's plan had suc-

ceeded, up to a point. He had taken Philadelphia—or as Benjamin Franklin put it, Philadelphia had taken him. But the Tories there proved fewer than Howe had expected, and his decision to move on Philadelphia from the south, by way of Chesapeake Bay, put his forces even farther from Burgoyne's army. Meanwhile, Burgoyne was stumbling into disaster in the north.

SARATOGA General Burgoyne moved south from Canada toward Lake Champlain in 1777 with about 7,000 men, his mistress, and a baggage train that included some thirty carts carrying his personal belongings and a large supply of champagne. Such heavily laden forces struggled to cross the wooded and marshy terrain. Burgoyne

General John Burgoyne

Commander of England's northern forces. Burgoyne and most of his British troops surrendered to the Americans at Saratoga on October 17, 1777.

sent part of his forces down the St. Lawrence River with Lieutenant Colonel Barry St. Leger, and at Oswego they were joined by a force of Iroquois allies. The combined force headed east toward Albany.

The American army in the north had dwindled during the winter. When Burgoyne brought his cannon to bear on Fort Ticonderoga, the Continentals prudently abandoned the fort, with a substantial loss of gunpowder and supplies. An angry Congress thereupon fired the American commander and replaced him with Horatio Gates, a favorite of the New Englanders. Fortunately for the American forces, Burgoyne delayed at Ticonderoga, enabling American reinforcements to arrive from the south and New England.

The more mobile Patriots inflicted two serious reversals on the British forces. At Oriskany, New York, on August 6, 1777, a band of militiamen repulsed an ambush by Tories and Indians under St. Leger and gained time for General Benedict Arnold to bring 1,000 Continentals to the relief of Fort Stanwix. Convinced they faced an even greater force than they actually did, the Indians deserted, and the Mohawk Valley was secured for the Patriot forces. To the east, at Bennington, Vermont, on August 16, New England militiamen, led by Colonel John Stark, decimated a British foraging party. Stark had pledged that morning, "We'll beat them before night, or Molly Stark will be a widow." As American reinforcements continued to gather and after two other defeats by the Americans, Burgoyne pulled back to Saratoga, where General Horatio Gates's forces surrounded him.

On October 17, 1777, Burgoyne, resplendent in his scarlet, gold, and white uniform, surrendered to the plain, blue-coated Gates, and most of his 5,700 soldiers were imprisoned in Virginia. Gates allowed Burgoyne himself to go home, where he received an icy reception. Gates was ecstatic. He wrote his wife, "If old England is not by this lesson taught humility, then she is an obstinate old slut, bent upon her ruin."

ALLIANCE WITH FRANCE   In early December 1777 news of the surprising American triumph at Saratoga reached Paris, where it was celebrated almost as if it were a French victory. In 1776 the French had taken their first step toward aiding the colonists, sending fourteen ships with crucial military supplies to America; most of the Continental army's gunpowder in the first years of the war came from that source. The Spanish government added a donation and soon established its own supply company.

Word of the American victory at Saratoga led in early 1778 to the signing of two treaties: the Treaty of Amity and Commerce, in which France recognized the new United States and offered trade concessions, including important privileges to American shipping, and the Treaty of Alliance. Under the latter both parties agreed, first, that if France entered the war, both countries would fight until American independence was won; second, that neither would conclude a "truce or peace" without "the formal consent of the other first obtained"; and third, that each guaranteed the other's possessions in America "from the present time and forever against all other powers." France further bound itself to seek neither Canada nor other British possessions on the mainland of North America.

By June 1778 British vessels had fired on French ships, and the two nations were at war. In 1779, after extracting French promises to help it regain territories taken by the British in previous wars, Spain entered the war as an ally of France but not of the United States. In 1780 Britain declared war on the Dutch, who persisted in a profitable trade with the French and the Americans. The rebellious farmers at Lexington and Concord had indeed fired a shot "heard round the world." Like Washington's encounter with the French in 1754, it was the start of another world war, and the fighting now spread to the Mediterranean, Africa, India, the West Indies, and the high seas.

1778: BOTH SIDES REGROUP

After the British defeat at Saratoga, Lord North knew that the war was unwinnable, but the king refused to let him either resign or make peace. On March 16, 1778, the House of Commons in effect granted all the American demands prior to independence. Parliament repealed the Townshend tea duty, the Massachusetts Government Act, and the Prohibitory Act, which had closed the colonies to commerce, and sent peace commissioners to Philadelphia to negotiate an end to hostilities. But Congress refused to begin any negotiations until Britain recognized American independence or withdrew its forces.

Unbeknownst to the British peace commissioners, the crown had already authorized the evacuation of British troops from Philadelphia, a withdrawal that further weakened what little bargaining power they had. After Saratoga, General Howe had resigned his command, and Sir Henry Clinton had replaced him, with orders to pull out of Philadelphia and, if necessary, New York but to keep Newport, Rhode Island. He was to supply troops for an expedition in the South, where the government believed a latent Tory sentiment in the backcountry needed only a British presence for its release. The ministry was right, up to a point, but the Loyalist sentiment turned out once again, as in other theaters of war, to be weaker than it had seemed.

For Washington's army at Valley Forge, the winter of 1777–1778 was a season of intense suffering. The American force, encamped near Philadelphia, endured unrelenting cold, hunger, and disease. Some troops lacked shoes and blankets. Their makeshift log-and-mud huts offered little protection from the howling winds and bitter cold. Most of the army's horses died of exposure or starvation. By February 7,000 troops were too ill for duty. More than 2,500 soldiers died at Valley Forge; another 1,000 deserted. Fifty officers resigned on one December day. Several hundred more left before winter's end.

Desperate for relief, Washington sent troops on foraging expeditions into New Jersey, Delaware, and the Eastern Shore of Maryland, confiscating horses, cattle, and hogs in exchange for "receipts" to be honored by the Continental Congress. By March 1778 the once-gaunt troops at Valley Forge saw their strength restored. Their improved health enabled Washington to begin a rigorous training program designed to bring unity to his motley array of forces. Because few of the regimental commanders had any formal military training, their troops lacked leadership, discipline, and skill. To remedy this defect, Washington turned to an energetic Prussian soldier of fortune, Friedrich Wilhelm, baron von Steuben. Steuben used an interpreter and frequent profanity to instruct the troops, teaching them the fundamentals of close-order drill: how to march in formation and how to handle their weapons. By the end of the winter, the ragtag soldiers were beginning to resemble a professional army. The army's morale stiffened when Congress promised extra pay and bonuses after the war. The good news from France about the formal military alliance helped as well.

As General Clinton's British forces withdrew eastward toward New York, Washington pursued them across New Jersey. On June 28 he engaged the British in an indecisive battle at Monmouth Court House. But the battle was significant for revealing Washington's temper and leadership qualities. In the midst of the fighting, he discovered that his potbellied subordinate, General Charles Lee, was retreating rather than attacking. Infuriated, Washington swore at Lee "till the leaves shook the trees." Then Washington rallied the troops just in time to stave off defeat. Clinton slipped away to New York while Washington took up a position at White Plains, north of the city. From that time on, the northern theater, scene of the major campaigns and battles in the first years of the war, settled into a long stalemate, interrupted by minor and mostly inconclusive engagements.

ACTIONS ON THE FRONTIER   The one major American success of 1778 occurred far from the New Jersey battlefields. Out to the west the British, under Colonel William Hamilton at Forts Niagara and Detroit, had incited frontier Tories and Indians to raid western settlements and offered to pay bounties for American scalps. To end the attacks, young George Rogers Clark took 175 frontiersmen on flatboats down the Ohio River early in 1778, marched

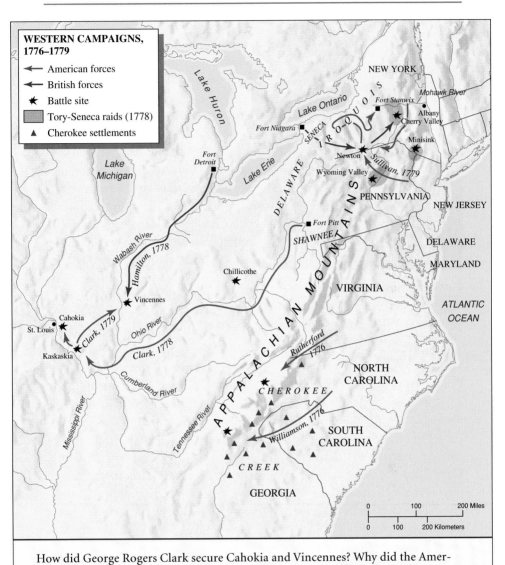

WESTERN CAMPAIGNS, 1776–1779

- ← American forces
- ← British forces
- ✶ Battle site
- ▨ Tory-Seneca raids (1778)
- ▲ Cherokee settlements

How did George Rogers Clark secure Cahokia and Vincennes? Why did the American army destroy Iroquois villages in 1779? Why were the skirmishes between settlers and Indian tribes significant for the future of the trans-Appalachian frontier?

through the woods, and on the evening of July 4 took Kaskaskia (in present-day Illinois) by surprise. The French inhabitants, terrified at first, "fell into transports of joy" at news of the French alliance with the Americans. Then, without bloodshed, Clark took Cahokia (opposite St. Louis) and Vincennes (in present-day Indiana). After the British retook Vincennes, Clark marched

Thayendanegea (Joseph Brant)
This 1786 portrait by Gilbert Stuart features the Mohawk leader who fought against the Americans in the Revolution.

his men (almost half of them French volunteers) through icy rivers and flooded prairies, sometimes in water neck deep, and laid siege to the astonished British garrison. Clark, the hardened woodsman, tomahawked Indian captives in sight of the fort to show that the British afforded them no protection. He spared the British captives when they surrendered, however.

While Clark's captives traveled eastward, a much larger American expedition moved through western Pennsylvania to attack Iroquois strongholds in western New York. There the Tories and Indians had terrorized frontier settlements throughout the summer of 1778. Led by the charismatic Mohawk Joseph Brant, the Iroquois had killed hundreds of militiamen along the Pennsylvania frontier. In response, Washington dispatched an expedition of 4,000 men under General John Sullivan. At Newton (near Elmira), New York, on August 29, 1779, Sullivan defeated the only serious opposition and proceeded to carry out Washington's instruction that the Iroquois country be not "merely overrun but destroyed." The American force burned about forty Seneca and Cayuga villages, together with their orchards and food supplies, leaving many of the Indians homeless and without enough provisions to survive. The action broke the power of the Iroquois federation for all time, but it did not completely pacify the frontier. Sporadic encounters with various tribes continued to the end of the war.

In the Kentucky territory, Daniel Boone and his small band of settlers risked constant attack from the Shawnees and their British and Tory allies. During the Revolution they survived frequent ambushes, at least seven skirmishes, and three pitched battles. In 1778 Boone and some thirty men, aided by their wives and children, held off an assault by more than 400 Indians at Boonesborough (now Boonesboro). Thereafter, Boone himself was twice shot and twice captured. Indians killed two of his sons, a brother, and two brothers-in-law. His daughter was captured, and another brother was wounded four times. Despite such ferocious fighting and dangerous circumstances, the white settlers refused to leave Kentucky.

In early 1776 a delegation of northern Indians—Shawnees, Delawares, and Mohawks—had talked the Cherokees into striking at frontier settlements in Virginia and the Carolinas. Swift retaliation had followed as Carolina forces burned Cherokee towns and destroyed corn. By weakening the major Indian tribes along the frontier, the American Revolution cleared the way for rapid settlement of the trans-Appalachian West after the war.

THE WAR IN THE SOUTH

At the end of 1778, the focus of the British military efforts shifted suddenly to the South. The whole region from Virginia southward had been free from major action since 1776. Now the British would test King George's belief that a sleeping Tory power in the South needed only the presence of a few redcoats to be awakened. General Clinton decided to take Savannah, on the Georgia coast, and roll northeast, gathering momentum from the Loyalist countryside. For a while the idea seemed to work, but it ran afoul of two developments: first, the Loyalist strength was less than estimated, and second, the British forces behaved so harshly that they drove even Loyalists into rebellion.

SAVANNAH AND CHARLESTON In November 1778 a British force attacked Savannah. The invaders quickly overwhelmed the Patriots, took the town, and hurried toward Charleston, plundering plantation houses along the way. The seesaw campaign took a major turn when General Clinton, accompanied by General Charles Cornwallis, brought new naval and land forces southward to join a massive amphibious attack that bottled up an American force led by General Benjamin Lincoln on the Charleston peninsula. On May 12, 1780, Lincoln surrendered the city and its 5,500 defenders, the greatest single American loss of the war. At that point, Congress, against Washington's advice, turned to the victor of Saratoga, Horatio Gates, to take command and sent him south. General Cornwallis, in charge of the British troops in the South, subdued the Carolina interior and surprised Gates's force at Camden, South Carolina, routing his new army, which retreated all the way to Hillsborough, North Carolina, 160 miles away.

THE CAROLINAS From the point of view of British imperial goals, the southern colonies were ultimately more important than the northern ones because they produced valuable staple crops such as tobacco, indigo, and naval stores (tar, pitch, and turpentine). Eventually the war in the Carolinas not only involved opposing British and American armies but also degenerated into brutal guerrilla-style civil conflicts between local Loyalists and local Patriots.

Cornwallis had South Carolina just about under control, but two subordinates, Sir Banastre Tarleton and Patrick Ferguson, who mobilized Tory militiamen, overreached themselves in their effort to subdue the Whigs. "Tarleton's quarter" became an epithet for savagery because "Bloody Tarleton" gave little quarter to vanquished foes. Ferguson sealed his own doom when he threatened to march over the mountains and hang the backcountry leaders. Instead, the feisty "overmountain men" went after Ferguson. They caught him and his Tories on Kings Mountain, just inside South Carolina. There, on October 7, 1780, they routed his force. By then feelings were so strong that American militiamen continued firing on Tories trying to surrender and later indiscriminately slaughtered Tory prisoners. Kings Mountain was the turning point of the war in the South. By proving that the British were not invincible, it emboldened small farmers to join guerrilla bands under such partisan leaders as Francis Marion, "the Swamp Fox," and Thomas Sumter, "the Carolina Gamecock."

While the overmountain men were closing in on Ferguson, Congress chose a new commander for the southern theater, General Nathanael Greene, "the fighting Quaker" of Rhode Island. A man of infinite patience, skilled at managing men and saving supplies, careful to avoid needless risks, he was suited to a war of attrition against the British forces. From Charlotte, North Carolina, where he arrived in December 1780, Greene moved his army eastward and sent General Daniel Morgan with about 700 men on a sweep to the west of Cornwallis's headquarters at Winnsboro, South Carolina.

Taking a position near Cowpens, a cow-grazing area in northern South Carolina, Morgan's force engaged Tarleton's army on January 17, 1781. Once the battle was joined, Tarleton mistook a readjustment in the American line for a militia panic and rushed his men forward, only to be ambushed by Morgan's cavalry. Tarleton escaped, but more than 100 of his men were killed and more than 700 were taken prisoner.

Morgan then fell back into North Carolina and linked up with General Greene's main force at Guilford Courthouse (near what became Greensboro). Greene lured Cornwallis's army north, stretching the British supply lines to the breaking point. The Americans attacked the redcoats at Guilford Courthouse on March 15, 1781, inflicted heavy losses, and then withdrew. Cornwallis marched off toward Wilmington, on the North Carolina coast, to lick his wounds and take on supplies. Greene then resolved to go back into

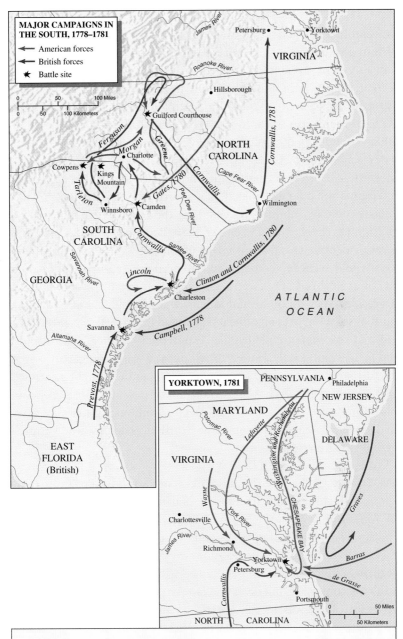

←— American forces
←— British forces
★ Battle site

0   50   100 Miles
0   50   100 Kilometers

VIRGINIA

James River

Roanoke River

Petersburg ●   ● Yorktown

Hillsborough ●

★ Guilford Courthouse

Ferguson

Morgan

Greene

● Charlotte

NORTH
CAROLINA

Cornwallis, 1781

Cape Fear River

Cowpens ★

Kings
Mountain ★

Tarleton

Gates, 1780

Cornwallis

Winnsboro ★ Camden

Pee Dee River

● Wilmington

SOUTH
CAROLINA

Cornwallis

Santee River

GEORGIA

Savannah River

Lincoln

★ Charleston

Clinton and Cornwallis, 1780

ATLANTIC
OCEAN

Savannah ●★

Campbell, 1778

Altamaha River

Prevost, 1778

EAST
FLORIDA
(British)

YORKTOWN, 1781

PENNSYLVANIA ●

● Philadelphia

NEW JERSEY

MARYLAND

Potomac River

Lafayette

Washington and Rochambeau

DELAWARE

VIRGINIA

Wayne

York River

CHESAPEAKE BAY

Graves

Charlottesville ●

James River

Richmond ●

● Yorktown ★

● Petersburg

Barras

Cornwallis

de Grasse

● Portsmouth

0   50 Miles
0   50 Kilometers

NORTH   CAROLINA

Why did the British suddenly shift their campaign to the south? Why
were the battles at Savannah and Charleston major victories for the
British? How did Nathaniel Greene undermine British control of the
Deep South? Why did Cornwallis march to Virginia and camp at
Yorktown? How was the French navy crucial to the American victory?
Why was Cornwallis forced to surrender?

South Carolina in the hope of drawing Cornwallis after him or forcing the British to give up the state. There he joined forces with the local guerrillas and in a series of brilliant actions kept losing battles while winning the war. "We fight, get beat, rise, and fight again," he said. By September 1781 he had narrowed British control in the Deep South to Charleston and Savannah, although for more than a year longer Whigs and Tories slashed at each other "with savage fury" in the backcountry, where there was "nothing but murder and devastation in every quarter," Greene said.

Meanwhile, Cornwallis had headed north, away from Greene, reasoning that Virginia must be eliminated as a source of reinforcement before the Carolinas could be subdued. In May 1781 the British force marched north into Virginia. There, since December 1780, Benedict Arnold, now a *British* general, had been engaged in a war of maneuver against the American forces. Arnold, until September 1780, had been the American commander at West Point, New York. Overweening in ambition, lacking in moral scruples, and a reckless spender on his fashionable wife, Arnold had nursed a grudge against Washington over an official reprimand for his extravagances as commander of reoccupied Philadelphia. Traitors have a price, and Arnold had found his: he had crassly plotted to sell out the American garrison at West Point to the British, and he even suggested how they might seize George Washington himself. Only the fortuitous capture of the British go-between, Major John André, had ended Arnold's plot. Forewarned that his plan had been discovered, Arnold had joined the British in New York while André was hanged by the Americans as a spy.

YORKTOWN   When Cornwallis linked up with Arnold at Petersburg, Virginia, their combined British forces totaled 7,200 men, far more than the small American army in the South. The arrival of American reinforcements led Cornwallis to pick Yorktown, Virginia, on Chesapeake Bay, as a defensible site. There appeared to be little reason to worry about a siege, since Washington's main land force seemed preoccupied with attacking New York, and the British navy controlled American waters.

To be sure, there was a small American navy, but it was no match for the British fleet. Yet American privateers distracted and wounded the British fleet. Most celebrated were the exploits of Captain John Paul Jones. Off England's coast on September 23, 1779, Jones and his crew won a desperate battle with a British frigate, which the Americans captured and occupied before their own ship sank. This was the occasion for Jones's stirring and oft-repeated response to a British demand for surrender: "I have not yet begun to fight."

Still, such heroics were little more than nuisances to the British. But at a critical point, thanks to the French navy, the British lost control of Chesapeake Bay. Indeed, it is impossible to imagine an American victory in the Revolution without the assistance of the French. As long as the British navy maintained supremacy at sea, the Americans could not hope to force a settlement to their advantage. For three years, Washington had waited to get some strategic military benefit from the French alliance. In July 1780 the French had finally landed a force of about 6,000 at Newport, Rhode Island, which the British had given up to concentrate on the South, but the French force had sat there for a year, blockaded by the British fleet.

Then, in 1781, the elements for a combined action suddenly fell into place. In May, as Cornwallis moved into Virginia, George Washington persuaded the commander of the French army to join forces for an attack on New York. The two armies linked up in July, but before they could strike at New York, word came from the West Indies that Admiral de Grasse was bound for the Chesapeake with his entire French fleet and some 3,000 soldiers. Washington immediately began moving his army south toward Yorktown. Meanwhile, French ships slipped out of the British blockade at Newport and also headed toward Chesapeake Bay.

On August 30 de Grasse's fleet reached Yorktown, and the admiral landed his French troops to join the American force already watching Cornwallis. On September 6, the day after a British fleet appeared, de Grasse gave battle and forced the British to give up the effort to relieve Cornwallis, whose fate was quickly sealed. De Grasse then sent ships up the Chesapeake to ferry down the allied armies, bringing the total American and French forces to more than 16,000, or better than double the size of Cornwallis's army.

The siege of Yorktown began on September 28. On October 14 two major redoubts guarding the left of the British line fell to French and American attackers, the latter led by Washington's aide, Alexander Hamilton. A British counterattack failed to retake them. Later that day a squall forced Cornwallis to abandon a desperate plan to escape across the York River. On October 17, 1781, four years to the day after Saratoga, Cornwallis sued for peace, and on October 19, their colors cased (that is, their flag lowered, a sign of surrender), the British force of more than 7,000 marched out as its band played somber tunes along with the English nursery rhyme "The World Turned Upside Down." Cornwallis himself claimed to be too "ill" to appear. His dispatch to his superior was telling: "I have the mortification to inform your Excellency that I have been forced to . . . surrender the troops under my command."

Surrender of Lord Cornwallis

By John Trumbull. The artist completed his painting of the pivotal British surrender at Yorktown in 1794.

NEGOTIATIONS

Whatever lingering hopes of victory the British may have harbored vanished at Yorktown. "Oh God, it's all over," Lord North groaned at news of the surrender. On February 27, 1782, the House of Commons voted against continuing the war and on March 20 Lord North resigned. The Continental Congress named a five-man commission to negotiate a peace treaty. Only three of its members were active, however: John Adams, who was on state business in the Netherlands; John Jay, minister to Spain; and Benjamin Franklin, already in Paris. Franklin and Jay did most of the work.

The French commitment to Spain complicated matters. Spain and the United States were allied with France but not with each other. America was bound by its alliance to fight on until the French made peace, and the French were bound to help the Spanish recover Gibraltar from England. Unable to deliver Gibraltar, or so the tough-minded Jay reasoned, the French might try to bargain off American land west of the Appalachians in its place. Fearful that the French were angling for a separate peace with the British, Jay persuaded Franklin to play the same game. Ignoring their instructions to consult fully with the French, they agreed to further talks with the British. On November 30, 1782, the talks produced a preliminary treaty with Great Britain. If it violated the spirit of the alliance with France, it did not violate the strict letter of the treaty, for the French minister was notified the day before it was signed, and final agreement still depended on a Franco-British settlement.

THE TREATY OF PARIS   Early in 1783 France and Spain gave up on Gibraltar and reached an armistice with Britain. The final signing of the Treaty of Paris came on September 3, 1783. In accord with the bargain already struck, Great Britain recognized the independence of the United States and agreed to a Mississippi River boundary to the west. Both the northern and the southern borders left ambiguities that would require further definition. Florida, as it turned out, passed back to Spain. The British further granted the Americans the "liberty" of fishing off Newfoundland and in the Gulf of St. Lawrence and the right to dry their catch on the unsettled Atlantic coast of Canada. On the matter of prewar debts, the best the British could get was a promise that their merchants should "meet with no legal impediment" in seeking to collect money owed them by Americans. And on the tender point of Loyalists whose estates had been confiscated, the negotiators agreed that Congress would "earnestly recommend" to the states the restoration of confiscated property. Each of the last two points was little more than a face-saving gesture to the British.

American Commissioners of the Preliminary Peace Negotiations with Great Britain

An unfinished painting from 1782 by Benjamin West. From left, John Jay, John Adams, Benjamin Franklin, Henry Laurens, and Franklin's grandson William Temple Franklin.

THE POLITICAL REVOLUTION

REPUBLICAN IDEOLOGY   The Americans had won their War of Independence. Had they undergone a political revolution as well? Years later

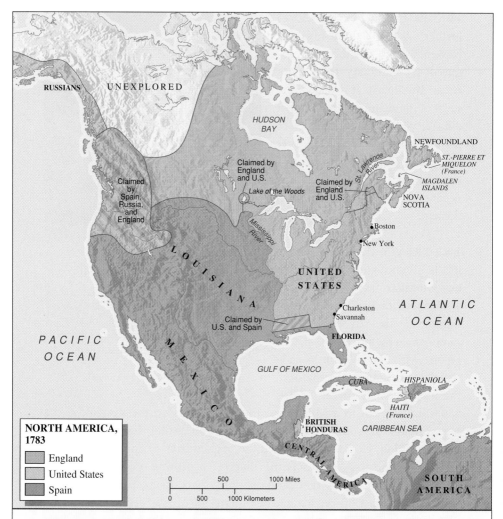

NORTH AMERICA, 1783

- England
- United States
- Spain

How did France's treaties with Spain complicate the peace-treaty negotiations with the British? What were the terms of the Treaty of Paris? Why might the ambiguities in the treaty have led to conflicts among the Americans, the Spanish, and the English?

John Adams offered an answer: "The Revolution was effected before the war commenced. The Revolution was in the minds and hearts of the people. . . . This radical change in the principles, opinions, sentiments, and affections of the people, was the real American Revolution." Yet Adams's observation ignores the fact that the Revolutionary War itself served as the catalyst for a prolonged internal debate about what new forms of government would best serve an independent republic. The conventional British model of mixed government sought to balance monarchy, aristocracy, and the common people and thereby protect individual liberty. Because of the more democratic nature of their society, however, Americans knew that they must devise new political assumptions and institutions. They had no monarchy or aristocracy. Yet how could sovereignty reside in the common people? How could Americans ensure the survival of a republican form of government, long assumed to be the most fragile? The war thus provoked a spate of state constitution making that remains unique in history.

A struggle for the rights of English citizens in the colonies became a fight for independence in which those rights found expression in governments that were new yet deeply rooted in the colonial experience and the prevailing viewpoints of Whiggery and the Enlightenment. With the Loyalists displaced or dispersed, such ideas as the contract theory of government, the sovereignty of the people, the separation of powers, and natural rights found their way into the new state government constitutions that were devised while the fight went on—amid other urgent business.

The very idea of republican government was a radical departure in that day. A republic, it was presumed, would endure only as long as the majority of the people were virtuous and willingly placed the good of society above the self-interest of individuals. Herein lay the hope and the danger of the new American experiment in popular government: even as leaders enthusiastically fashioned new state constitutions, they feared that their experiments in republicanism would fail because of a lack of civic virtue among the people.

STATE CONSTITUTIONS Most of the political experimentation between 1776 and 1787 occurred at the state level in the form of written constitutions in which the people were sovereign and delegated limited authority to the government. In addition, the states initiated bills of rights guaranteeing particular individual freedoms and fashioned procedures for constitutional conventions that have also remained an essential part of the American political system. In sum, the innovations at the state level during the Revolution created a reservoir of ideas and experience that formed the basis for the creation of the federal constitution in 1787.

The first state constitutions varied mainly in detail. They formed governments much like the colonial governments, but with elected governors and senates instead of appointed governors and councils. Generally they embodied a separation of powers (legislative, executive, and judicial) as a safeguard against abuses. Most of them also included a bill of rights that protected the time-honored rights of petition, freedom of speech, trial by jury, freedom from self-incrimination, and the like. Most tended to limit the powers of governors and increase the powers of the legislatures, which had led the people in their quarrels with the colonial governors.

THE ARTICLES OF CONFEDERATION The central American government, the Continental Congress, exercised government powers without any constitutional sanction before March 1781. Plans for a permanent frame of government emerged very early, however. Richard Henry Lee's motion for independence included a call for a plan of confederation. As early as July 1776, a committee headed by John Dickinson had produced a draft constitution, the Articles of Confederation and Perpetual Union. For more than a year, Congress had debated the articles in between more urgent matters and had finally adopted them in November 1777. All states ratified them promptly except Maryland, which insisted that the seven states claiming western lands should cede them to the authority of Congress. Maryland did not relent until early 1781, when Virginia gave up its claims, under the old colonial charter, to the vast region north of the Ohio River. New York had already relinquished a dubious claim based upon its "jurisdiction" over the Iroquois, and the other states eventually abandoned their charter claims as well.

When the Articles of Confederation became effective, in March 1781, they did little more than legalize the status quo. "The United States of America in Congress Assembled" had a multitude of responsibilities but little authority to carry them out. Congress was intended not as a legislature, nor as a sovereign entity unto itself, but as a collective substitute for the monarch. In essence it was to be a plural executive rather than a parliamentary body. It had full power over foreign affairs and questions of war and peace; it could decide disputes between the states; it had authority over coinage, the postal service, and Indian affairs and responsibility for the government of the western territories. But it had no courts and no power to enforce its resolutions and ordinances at either the state or individual level. It also had no power to levy taxes and had to rely on requisitions, which state legislatures could ignore.

The states, after their battles with Parliament, were in no mood for a strong central government. Congress in fact had less power than the colonists had once accepted in Parliament, since it could not regulate interstate and foreign commerce. For certain important acts, moreover, a "special majority" was required. Nine states had to approve measures dealing with war, treaties, coinage, finances, and the army and navy. Unanimous approval of the states was needed to levy tariffs (often called duties) on imports. Amendments to the Articles also required unanimous ratification by all the states. The Confederation had neither an executive nor a judicial branch; there was no administrative head of government (only the president of Congress, chosen annually) and no federal courts.

For all its weaknesses, however, the Confederation government represented the most pragmatic structure for the new nation. After all, the Revolution on the battlefields had yet to be won, and America's statesmen could not risk the prolonged and divisive debates over the distribution of power that other forms of government would have provoked.

THE SOCIAL REVOLUTION

Political revolutions and the chaos of war often spawn social revolutions. The turmoil of the American Revolution allowed long-pent-up frustrations among the lower ranks to find expression. What did the Revolution mean to those workers, servants, farmers, and freed slaves who participated in the Stamp Act demonstrations, supported the boycotts, idolized Tom Paine, and fought with Washington and Greene? Many laboring folk hoped that the Revolution would remove, not reinforce, the elite's traditional political and social advantages. The more conservative Patriots would have been content to replace royal officials with the rich, the well born, and the able and let it go at that. But more radical revolutionaries raised the question not only of home rule but also of who should rule at home.

EQUALITY AND ITS LIMITS   This spirit of equality found outlet in several directions, one of which was simply a weakening of old habits of deference. A Virginia gentleman remembered being in a tavern when a group of farmers came in, spitting and pulling off their muddy boots without regard for the sensibilities of the gentlemen present: "The spirit of independence was converted into equality," he wrote, "and every one who bore arms, esteems himself upon a footing with his neighbors. . . . No doubt each of these men considers himself, in every respect, my equal." No doubt each did.

Participation in the army or militia excited men who had taken little interest in politics before. The new political opportunities afforded by the creation of state governments led more ordinary citizens to participate than ever before. The social base of the new legislatures was thus much broader than that of the old assemblies. Men fighting for their liberty found it difficult to justify denying other white men the rights of suffrage and representation.

Social Democracy

In this watercolor by Benjamin Latrobe, a gentleman plays billiards with artisans, suggesting that "the spirit of independence was converted into equality."

The property qualifications for voting, which already admitted an overwhelming majority of white men, were lowered still further. In Pennsylvania, Delaware, North Carolina, and Georgia, any male taxpayer could vote, although officeholders usually had to meet more stringent property requirements. Men who had argued against taxation without representation now questioned the denial of proportional representation for the backcountry, which generally enlarged its presence in the legislatures. More often than not, the political newcomers were men with less property and little formal education. All states concentrated power in a legislature chosen by a wide suffrage, but not even Pennsylvania, which adopted the most radical of the state constitutions, went quite so far as to grant universal male suffrage.

New developments in land tenure that grew out of the Revolution extended the democratic trends of suffrage requirements. All state legislatures seized Tory estates. These properties were of small consequence, however, in contrast to the unsettled areas formerly at the disposal of the crown and proprietors but now in the hands of popular assemblies. Much of that land was now used for bonuses to veterans of the war. Moreover, western lands, formerly closed by the Royal Proclamation of 1763 and the Quebec Act of 1774, were soon thrown open to settlers.

THE PARADOX OF SLAVERY   The Revolutionary generation of leaders was the first to confront slavery and consider abolishing it. The principles of liberty and equality invoked in debates over British policies had clear implications for enslaved blacks. Before the Revolution only Rhode Island, Connecticut, and Pennsylvania had halted the importation of slaves. After independence all the states except Georgia stopped the traffic, although South Carolina later reopened it.

African-American soldiers or sailors were present at most major battles from Lexington to Yorktown, most on the Loyalist side. When the Revolution began, the British had promised freedom to slaves, as well as to indentured servants, who would bear arms for the Loyalist cause. In December 1775 Lord Dunmore, the royal governor of Virginia, issued such an offer and within a month had attracted 300 former servants and slaves to the British army. Within a year the number had grown to almost 1,000. One of the deserters was a white servant of George Washington. The overseer of Mount Vernon reported to General Washington that the rest of his slaves and servants would also leave if they got the chance. "Liberty is sweet," he explained. Dunmore's effort to recruit slaves and servants infuriated Washington and other Virginia planters. Washington predicted that if Dunmore were "not crushed" soon, the number of slaves joining him would "increase as a Snow ball by Rolling."

In December 1775 a Patriot militia defeated Lord Dunmore and the Ethiopian Regiment and forced the British units to flee Norfolk, Virginia, and board ships in the Chesapeake Bay. No sooner had the former slaves crowded onto the British ships than they contracted smallpox. The epidemic raced through the fleet, eventually forcing the Loyalist forces to disembark on an offshore island. During the winter and spring of 1776, disease devastated the primitive camp. "Dozens died daily from Small Pox and rotten Fevers by which diseases they are infected," wrote a visitor. Before the Loyalists fled the island in the summer of 1776, over half of the troops, most of them former slaves, had died.

In response to the British recruitment of American slaves, General Washington, at the end of 1775, reversed the policy of excluding blacks from the American forces—except the few already in militia companies—and Congress quickly approved the new policy. Only two states, South Carolina and Georgia, refused to allow blacks to serve in the military. No more than about 5,000 African Americans were admitted to the total American forces of about 300,000, and most were free blacks from northern states. They served mainly in white units, although Massachusetts did organize two all-black companies, and Rhode Island organized one.

Slaves who served in the cause of independence won their freedom and, in some cases, land bounties. But the British army, which liberated tens of thousands of slaves during the war, was a greater instrument of emancipation than

Elizabeth Freeman

Also known as Mum Bett, Freeman was born around 1742 and sold as a slave to a Massachusetts family. She won her freedom by claiming in court that the Bill of Rights and the new state constitution gave liberty to all, and her case contributed to the eventual abolition of slavery in Massachusetts. One of Freeman's great-grandchildren was scholar and civil rights leader W.E.B. Du Bois.

the American forces. Most of the newly freed blacks found their way to Canada or to British colonies in the Caribbean. American Whigs showed no mercy to blacks caught aiding or abetting the British cause. A Charleston mob hanged and then burned Thomas Jeremiah, a free black who was convicted of telling slaves that the British "were come to help the poor Negroes." White Loyalists who were caught encouraging slave militancy were tarred and feathered.

In the northern states, which had fewer slaves than the southern states, the doctrines of liberty led swiftly to emancipation for all, either during the fighting or shortly afterward. The Vermont Constitution of 1777 specifically forbade slavery. The Massachusetts Constitution of 1780 proclaimed the "inherent liberty" of all. In 1780 Pennsylvania declared that all children born thereafter to slave mothers would become free at age twenty-eight, after enabling their owners to recover their initial cost. In 1784 Rhode Island provided freedom to all children of slaves born thereafter, at age twenty-one for males, eighteen for females. New York lagged until 1799 in granting freedom to mature slaves born after enactment of its constitution, but an act of 1817 set July 4, 1827, as the date for emancipation of all remaining slaves.

In the states south of Pennsylvania, emancipation was less popular. Yet even there, slaveholders expressed moral qualms. Thomas Jefferson wrote in his *Notes on the State of Virginia* (1785): "Indeed I tremble for my country when I reflect that God is just; that his justice cannot sleep forever." But he, like many other white southerners, could not bring himself to free his slaves. In the southern states anti-slavery sentiment went no further than a relaxation of the manumission laws, under which owners might free their slaves through individual acts. Some 10,000 enslaved Virginians were manumitted during the 1780s. A much smaller number would be shipped back to Africa during the early nineteenth century. By the outbreak of the Civil War, in 1861, approximately half the blacks living in Maryland were free.

Manumission freed slaves by the action of a white owner. But slaves, especially in the upper South, also earned freedom through their own actions during the Revolutionary era, frequently by running away. They often gravitated to the growing number of African-American communities in the North. Because of emancipation laws in the northern states, and with the formation of free black neighborhoods in the North and in several southern cities, runaways found refuge and the opportunities for new lives. It is estimated that 55,000 slaves fled to freedom during the Revolution.

THE STATUS OF WOMEN   The logic of liberty spawned by the Revolution applied to the status of women as much as to that of African Americans. Women in the colonies had remained essentially confined to the domestic sphere during the eighteenth century. They could not vote or preach or hold office. Few had access to formal education. Although women could usually own property and execute contracts, in several colonies married women could not legally own property—even their own clothes—and they had no legal rights over their children. Divorces were extremely difficult to obtain.

Yet the Revolution offered women new opportunities and engendered in many a new outlook. The war drew women at least temporarily into new pursuits. Women supported the armies in various roles—by handling supplies, serving as couriers, and working as camp followers—cooking, cleaning, and nursing the soldiers. Wives often followed their husbands to camp and on occasion took their place in the line, as Margaret Corbin did at Fort Washington when her husband fell at his artillery post and as Mary Ludwig Hays (better known as Molly Pitcher) did when her husband collapsed of heat exhaustion. An exceptional case was Deborah Sampson, who joined a Massachusetts regiment as Robert Shurtleff and served from 1781 to 1783 by the "artful concealment" of her sex.

To be sure, most women retained the domestic outlook that had long been imposed on them by society. But a few free-spirited reformers demanded equal treatment. In an essay titled "On the Equality of the Sexes," written in 1779 and published in 1790, Judith Sargent Murray of Gloucester, Massachusetts, stressed that women were perfectly capable of excelling outside the domestic sphere.

Early in the Revolutionary struggle, Abigail Adams, one of the most learned, spirited, and independent women of the time, wrote to her husband, John: "In the new Code of Laws which I suppose it will be necessary

Frontispiece from *Lady's Magazine* (1792)

"The Genius of the Ladies Magazine, accompanied by the Genius of Emulation, who carries in her hand a laurel crown, approaches Liberty, and kneeling, presents her with a copy of *The Rights of Woman.*" The *Lady's Magazine* reprinted extensive extracts from Mary Wollstonecraft's *A Vindication of the Rights of Woman* (1792).

for you to make I desire you would remember the Ladies. . . . Do not put such unlimited power into the hands of the Husbands." Since men were "Naturally Tyrannical," she wrote, "why then, not put it out of the power of the vicious and the Lawless to use us with cruelty and indignity with impunity." Otherwise, "if particular care and attention is not paid to the Ladies we are determined to foment a Rebellion, and will not hold ourselves bound by any Laws in which we have no voice, or Representation." Husband John expressed surprise that women might be discontented, but he clearly knew the privileges enjoyed by males and was determined to retain them: "Depend upon it, we know better than to repeal our Masculine systems." Thomas Jefferson was of one mind with Adams on the matter. When asked about women's voting rights, he replied that "the tender breasts of ladies were not formed for political convulsion."

The legal status of women did not improve dramatically as a result of the Revolutionary ferment. Married women in most states still forfeited control of their own property to their husbands, and women gained no permanent political rights. Under the 1776 New Jersey Constitution, which neglected to specify an exclusively male franchise because the delegates apparently took the distinction for granted, women who met the property qualifications for voting exercised the right until they were denied access early in the nineteenth century.

FREEDOM OF RELIGION   The Revolution also set in motion a transition from the toleration of religious dissent to a complete freedom of religion in the separation of church and state. The Anglican Church, established as the official religion in five colonies and parts of two others, was especially vulnerable because of its association with the crown and because dissenters outnumbered Anglicans in all states except Virginia. And all but Virginia eliminated tax support for the church before the fighting was over. In 1776 the Virginia Declaration of Rights guaranteed the free exercise of religion, and in 1786 the Virginia Statute of Religious Freedom (written by Thomas Jefferson) declared that "no man shall be compelled to frequent or support any religious worship, place or ministry whatsoever" and "that all men shall be free to profess, and by argument to maintain, their opinions in matters of religion." These statutes and the Revolutionary ideology that justified them helped shape the course that religion would take in the new United States: pluralistic and voluntary rather than state supported and monolithic.

In churches as in government, the Revolution set off a period of constitution making as some of the first national church bodies emerged. In 1784 the Methodists, who at first were an offshoot of the Anglicans, came together in a general conference at Baltimore under Bishop Francis Asbury. The Anglican Church, rechristened Episcopal, gathered in a series of meetings that by 1789 had united the various dioceses in a federal union; in 1789 the

Religious Development

The Congregational Church developed a national presence in the early nineteenth century, and Lemuel Haynes, depicted here, was its first African-American preacher.

Presbyterians also held their first general assembly, in Philadelphia. That same year the Catholic Church got its first higher official in the United States when John Carroll was named bishop of Baltimore.

THE EMERGENCE OF AN AMERICAN CULTURE

The Revolution helped generate among some Americans a sense of common nationality. One of the first ways in which to forge a national consciousness was through the annual celebration of the new nation's independence from Great Britain. On July 2, 1776, when the Second Continental Congress had resolved "that these United Colonies are, and of right ought to be, free and independent states," John Adams had written his wife, Abigail, that future generations would remember that date as their "day of deliverance." People, he predicted, would celebrate the occasion with "solemn acts of devotion to God Almighty" and with "pomp and parade, with shows, games, sports, guns, bells, bonfires and illuminations [fireworks] from one end of this continent to the other, from this time forward, forever more."

Adams got everything right but the date. Americans fastened not upon July 2 but upon July 4 as their Independence Day. To be sure, it was on the Fourth that Congress formally adopted the Declaration of Independence and ordered it to be printed and distributed throughout the states, but America by then had been officially independent for two days. As luck would have it, July 4 became Independence Day by accident. In 1777 Congress forgot about any acknowledgment of the first anniversary of independence until July 3, when it was too late to honor July 2. As a consequence, the Fourth won by default.

Independence Day quickly became the most popular and most important public ritual in the United States. Huge numbers of people from all walks of life suspended their normal routine in order to devote a day to parades, formal orations, and fireworks displays. In the process the infant republic began to create its own myth of national identity that transcended local or regional concerns. "What a day!" exclaimed the editor of the *Southern Patriot* in 1815. "What happiness, what emotion, what virtuous triumph must fill the bosoms of Americans!"

AMERICA'S "DESTINY" American nationalism embodied a stirring idea. This first new nation, unlike the Old World nations of Europe, was not rooted in antiquity. Its people, except for the Indians, had not inhabited it over the centuries, nor was there any notion of a common ethnic descent. "The American national consciousness," one observer wrote, "is not a voice crying out of the depth of the dark past, but is proudly a product of the enlightened present, setting its face resolutely toward the future."

Many people, at least since the time of the Pilgrims, had thought of America as singled out for a special identity, a special mission. Jonathan Edwards said God had chosen America as "the glorious renovator of the world," and later John Adams proclaimed the opening of America "a grand scheme and design in Providence for the illumination and the emancipation of the slavish part of mankind all over the earth." This sense of mission was neither limited to New England nor rooted solely in Calvinism. From the democratic rhetoric of Thomas Jefferson to the pragmatism of George Washington to heady toasts bellowed in South Carolina taverns, patriots everywhere articulated a special role for American leadership in history. The mission was now a call to lead the world toward greater liberty and equality. Meanwhile, however, Americans had to address more immediate problems created by their new nationhood. The Philadelphia doctor and scientist Benjamin Rush issued a prophetic statement in 1787: "The American war is over: but this is far from being the case with the American Revolution. On the contrary, but the first act of the great drama is closed."

MAKING CONNECTIONS

- The American Revolution was the starting point for the foreign policy of the United States. Many of the specific foreign concerns that will be discussed in Chapters 8 and 9 sprang from issues directly relating to the Revolution.

- Much of what became Jacksonian democracy (introduced in Chapter 10) can be traced to social and political movements associated with the American Revolution.

- The Articles of Confederation, the document that established the first national government for the United States, saw the new nation through the Revolution, but within a few years the Articles were discarded in favor of a new government, set forth in the Constitution.

FURTHER READING

The Revolutionary War is the subject of Colin Bonwick's *The American Revolution* (1991), Gordon S. Wood's *The Radicalism of the American Revolution* (1991), and Jeremy Black's *War for America: The Fight for Independence, 1775–1783* (1991). John Ferling's *Setting the World Ablaze: Washington, Adams, Jefferson, and the American Revolution* (2000) highlights the role played by key leaders.

On the social history of the Revolutionary War, see John W. Shy's *A People Numerous and Armed: Reflections on the Military Struggle for American Independence*, rev. ed. (1990), Charles Royster's *A Revolutionary People at War: The Continental Army and American Character, 1775–1783* (1979), and E. Wayne Carp's *To Starve the Army at Pleasure: Continental Army Administration and American Political Culture, 1775–1783* (1984). Colin G. Calloway tells the neglected story of the Indian experiences in the Revolution in *The American Revolution in Indian Country: Crisis and Diversity in Native American Communities* (1995). The imperial, aristocratic, and racist aspects of the Revolution are detailed in Francis Jennings's *The Creation of America: Through Revolution to Empire* (2000).

Why some Americans remained loyal to the crown is the subject of Robert M. Calhoon's *The Loyalists in Revolutionary America, 1760–1781* (1973) and Mary Beth Norton's *The British-Americans: The Loyalist Exiles in England, 1774–1789* (1972).

The definitive study of African Americans during the Revolutionary era remains Benjamin Quarles's *The Negro in the American Revolution* (1961). Mary Beth Norton's *Liberty's Daughters: The Revolutionary Experience of American Women, 1750–1800,* new ed. (1996) and Linda K. Kerber's *Women of the Republic: Intellect and Ideology in Revolutionary America* (1980) document the role women played in securing independence. Joy Day Buel and Richard Buel Jr.'s *The Way of Duty: A Woman and Her Family in Revolutionary America* (1984) shows the impact of the Revolution on one New England family.

The standard introduction to the diplomacy of the Revolutionary era is Jonathan R. Dull's *A Diplomatic History of the American Revolution* (1985).

7

SHAPING
A FEDERAL UNION

FOCUS QUESTIONS

· What were the achievements and weaknesses of the
  Confederation government?

· What were the issues involved in writing the Constitution?

· What issues framed the debate over ratifying the Constitution?

To answer these questions and access additional review material, please visit
www.wwnorton.com/studyspace.

In an address to fellow graduates at the Harvard commencement
ceremony in 1787, young John Quincy Adams lamented "this
critical period" when the country was "groaning under the intolerable burden of . . . accumulated evils." The same phrase, "critical period,"
has often been used to label the history of the United States under the Articles of Confederation. Fear of a central government dominated the period,
and the result was fragmentation and stagnation. Yet while there were weaknesses of the Confederation, there were also major achievements. Moreover,
lessons learned under the Confederation would serve well in the formulation of a new constitution and in the balancing of central and local authority
under that constitution.

THE CONFEDERATION

The Congress of the Confederation had little government authority. "It could ask for money but not compel payment," as one historian wrote; "it could enter into treaties but not enforce their stipulations; it could provide for raising of armies but not fill the ranks; it could borrow money but take no proper measures for repayment; it could advise and recommend but not command." Congress was virtually helpless to cope with foreign relations and a postwar economic depression that would have challenged the resources of a much stronger government. It was not easy to find men of stature to serve in such a body, and it was often hard to gather a quorum of those who did. Yet in spite of its handicaps, the Confederation Congress somehow managed to survive and to lay important foundations. It concluded the Treaty of Paris in 1783. It created the first executive departments. And it formulated principles of land distribution and territorial government that guided westward expansion all the way to the Pacific coast.

Throughout most of the War of Independence, Congress distrusted and limited executive power. It assigned administrative duties to its committees and thereby imposed a painful burden on conscientious members. John Adams, for instance, served on some eighty committees at one time or another. In 1781, however, Congress began to set up three departments: Foreign Affairs, Finance, and War, each with a single head responsible to Congress.

FINANCE   The closest thing to an executive head of the Confederation was Robert Morris, who as superintendent of finance in the final years of the war became the most influential figure in the government. Morris wanted to make both himself and the Confederation government more powerful. He envisioned a coherent program of taxation and debt management to make the government financially stable; "a public debt supported by public revenue will prove the strongest cement to keep our confederacy together," he confided to a friend. It would wed to the support of the federal government the powerful influence of the public creditors who had provided wartime supplies. Morris therefore welcomed the chance to enlarge the debt by issuing new government bonds that would help pay off wartime debts. Because of the government's precarious finances, these bonds brought only 10¢ to 15¢ on the dollar, but with a sounder Treasury—certainly one with the power to raise taxes—the bonds could be expected to rise in value, creating new capital with which to finance banks and economic development.

In 1781, as part of his plan, Morris secured a congressional charter for the Bank of North America, which would hold government cash, lend money to the government, and issue currency. Though a national bank, it was in part privately owned and was expected to turn a profit for Morris and other shareholders, in addition to performing a crucial public service. But Morris's program depended ultimately upon a secure income for the government, and it foundered on the requirement of unanimous state approval for amendments to the Articles of Confederation. Local interests and the fear of a central authority—a fear strengthened by the recent quarrels with king and Parliament—hobbled action.

To carry their point, Morris and his nationalist friends in 1783 risked a dangerous gamble. George Washington's army, encamped at Newburgh, New York, on the Hudson River, had grown restless in the final winter of the war. The soldiers' pay was late as usual, and experience had given them reason to fear that promised land bounties and life pensions for officers might never be honored once their service was no longer needed. A delegation of concerned officers traveled to Philadelphia with a petition for redress. Soon they found themselves drawn into a scheme to line up the army and public creditors with nationalists in Congress and confront the states with the threat of a coup d'état unless they yielded more power to Congress. Alexander Hamilton, congressman from New York and former aide-de-camp to General Washington, sought to bring his old commander into the plan.

Washington sympathized with the general purpose of Hamilton's scheme. If congressional powers were not enlarged, he had told a friend, "the band which at present holds us together, by a very feeble thread, will soon be broken, when anarchy and confusion must ensue." But Washington was just as deeply convinced that a military coup would be both dishonorable and dangerous. In March 1783, when he learned that some of the plotters had planned an unauthorized meeting of officers, he confronted the conspirators. He told them that any effort by officers to intimidate the government by threatening a mutinous coup violated the very purposes for which the war was being fought and directly challenged his own integrity. While agreeing that the officers had been poorly treated by the government and deserved their long-overdue back pay and future pensions, he expressed his "horror and detestation" of any effort by the military to assume dictatorial powers. A military revolt would open "the flood-gates of civil discord" and "deluge our rising empire in blood." Before closing his remarks, Washington paused dramatically as he produced a pair of eyeglasses. "Gentlemen," he apologized, "you will permit me to put on my spectacles, for I have not only grown gray but blind in the service of my country." He then read a letter from a congressman that explained the nation's financial plight. It was a virtuoso performance. When he had finished, his officers, many of them fighting back tears, unanimously adopted resolutions denouncing the recent "infamous proposi-tions," and the so-called Newburgh Conspiracy came to a sudden end.

The Confederation never did put its finances in order. The Continental currency had long since become a byword for worthlessness. It was never re-deemed. The debt, domestic and foreign, grew from $11 million to $28 mil-lion as Congress paid off citizens' and soldiers' claims. Each year, Congress ran a deficit in its operating expenses.

LAND POLICY   Congress might ultimately have hoped to draw an inde-pendent income from the sale of western lands. Thinly populated by Indians, French settlers, and a growing number of American squatters, the region north of the Ohio River and west of the Appalachian Mountains had long been the site of overlapping claims by colonies and speculators. Under the Articles of Confederation, land not included within the boundaries of the thirteen original states became public domain, owned and administered by the national government.

As early as 1779, Congress had declared that it would not treat the western lands as colonies. The delegates resolved instead that western lands "shall be . . . formed into distinct Republican states," equal in all respects to other states. Between 1784 and 1787 policies for the development of the West emerged in three major ordinances of the Confederation Congress. These documents, which rank among its greatest achievements—and among the most important in American history—set precedents that the United States would follow in its expansion all the way to the Pacific. Thomas Jefferson in fact was prepared to grant self-government to western states at an early stage, allowing settlers to meet and choose their own officials. Under the land ordinance that Jefferson wrote in 1784, when the population equaled that of the smallest existing state, the territory would achieve full statehood.

In the Land Ordinance of 1785, the delegates outlined a plan of land sur-veys and sales that would eventually stamp a rectangular pattern on much of the nation's surface, a rectilinear grid pattern that is visible from the air in many parts of the country today because of the layout of roads and fields. Wherever Indian titles had been extinguished, the Northwest was to be sur-veyed and six-mile-square townships established along east-west and north-south lines. Each township was in turn divided into thirty-six lots (or sections) one mile square (or 640 acres). The 640-acre sections were to be sold at auc-tion for no less than $1 per acre, or $640 total. Such terms favored land spec-ulators, of course, since few common folk had that much money or were able to work that much land. In later years new land laws would make smaller plots available at lower prices, but in 1785 Congress was faced with

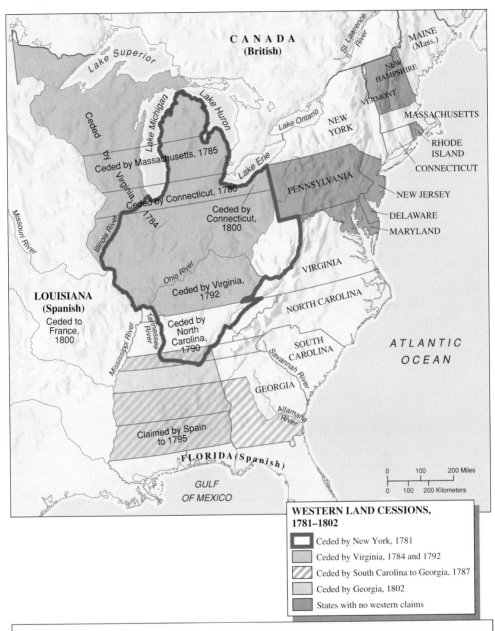

**WESTERN LAND CESSIONS,
1781–1802**

Ceded by New York, 1781

Ceded by Virginia, 1784 and 1792

Ceded by South Carolina to Georgia, 1787

Ceded by Georgia, 1802

States with no western claims

Why were there so many overlapping claims to the western lands? What were the terms of the Land Ordinance of 1785? How did it arrange for future states to enter the Union?

an empty Treasury, and delegates believed this system would raise the needed funds most effectively. In each township, however, Congress did reserve the income from the sixteenth section for the support of schools—a significant departure at a time when public schools were rare.

THE NORTHWEST ORDINANCE   Spurred by the plans for land sales and settlement, Congress drafted a more specific frame of territorial government to replace Jefferson's ordinance of 1784. The new plan backed off from Jefferson's recommendation of early self-government. Because of the trouble that might be expected from squatters who were clamoring for free land, the

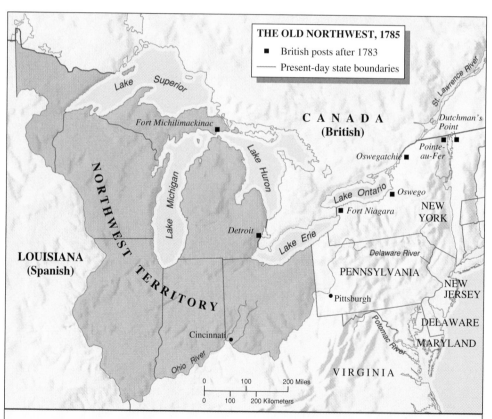

THE OLD NORTHWEST, 1785

■ British posts after 1783
── Present-day state boundaries

How did the Northwest Ordinance of 1787 revise Jefferson's plan for territorial government? How were settlement patterns in the Northwest territories different from those on the frontier in the South? How did the United States treat Indian claims to territory in the West?

Northwest Ordinance of 1787 required a period of colonial tutelage. At first the territory fell subject to a governor, a secretary, and three judges, all chosen by Congress. Eventually there would be three to five territories in the region, and when any one had a population of 5,000 free male adults, it could choose an assembly. Congress then would name a council of five from ten names proposed by the assembly. The governor would have a veto over actions by the territorial assembly, and so would Congress.

The resemblance to the old royal colonies is clear, but there were two significant differences. For one, the ordinance anticipated statehood when any territory's population reached a population of 60,000 "free inhabitants." At that point a convention could be called to draft a state constitution and apply to Congress for statehood. For another, it included a bill of rights that guaranteed religious freedom, legislative representation in proportion to the population, trial by jury, habeas corpus, and the application of common law. Finally, the ordinance excluded slavery permanently from the Northwest—a proviso Jefferson had failed to get accepted in his ordinance of 1784. This proved a fateful decision. As the progress of emancipation in the existing states gradually freed all slaves above the Mason-Dixon line, the Ohio River boundary of the Old Northwest extended the line between freedom and slavery all the way to the Mississippi River, encompassing what would become the states of Ohio, Indiana, Illinois, Michigan, and Wisconsin.

The Northwest Ordinance had a larger importance, beyond establishing a formal procedure for transforming territories into states. It represented a sharp break with the imperialistic assumption behind European expansion into the Western Hemisphere. The new states were to be admitted to the American republic as equals.

In seven mountain ranges to the west of the Ohio River, an area in which recent treaties had voided Indian titles, surveying began in the mid-1780s. But before any land sales occurred, a group of speculators from New England presented cash-poor Congress with a seductive offer. Organized in Boston, the group of former army officers took the name of the Ohio Company of Associates and sent the Reverend Manasseh Cutler to present its plan. Cutler, a former chaplain in the Continental army and a co-author of the Northwest Ordinance, proved a persuasive lobbyist, and in 1787 Congress voted a grant of 1.5 million acres for about $1 million in certificates of indebtedness to Revolutionary War veterans. The arrangement had the dual merit, Cutler argued, of reducing the debt and encouraging new settlement and sales of federal land.

The lands south of the Ohio River followed a different line of development. Title to the western lands remained with Georgia, North Carolina, and Virginia for the time being, but settlement proceeded at a far more rapid pace during and after the Revolution, despite the Indians' fierce resentment of encroachments upon their hunting grounds. Substantial centers of population grew up around Harrodsburg and Boonesborough in Kentucky and along the Watauga, Holston, and Cumberland Rivers as far west as Nashborough (Nashville). In the Old Southwest active movements for statehood arose early. North Carolina tentatively ceded its western claims in 1784, whereupon the Holston settlers formed the short-lived state of Franklin, which became little more than a bone of contention among rival speculators until North Carolina reasserted control in 1789, shortly before the cession of its western lands became final.

Indian land claims, too, were being extinguished. The Iroquois and Cherokees, badly battered during the Revolution, were in no position to resist encroachments by American settlers. By the Treaty of Fort Stanwix (1784), the Iroquois were forced to cede land in western New York and Pennsylvania. With the Treaty of Hopewell (1785), the Cherokees gave up all claims in South Carolina, much of western North Carolina, and large portions of present-day Kentucky and Tennessee. Also in 1785 the major Ohio tribes dropped their claim to most of Ohio, except for a chunk bordering the western part of Lake Erie. The Creeks, pressed by the state of Georgia to cede portions of their lands in 1784–1785, went to war in the summer of 1786 with covert aid from Spanish Florida. When Spanish aid diminished, however, the Creek chief traveled to New York and in 1791 finally struck a bargain that gave the Creeks favorable trade arrangements with the United States but did not restore the lost land.

TRADE AND THE ECONOMY   In its economic life, as in planning westward expansion, the young nation dealt vigorously with difficult problems. Congress had little to do with achievements in the economy, but neither could it bear the blame for an acute economic contraction that occurred between 1770 and 1790, the result primarily of the war and separation from the British Empire. Although farmers enmeshed in local markets maintained their livelihood during the Revolutionary era, commercial agriculture dependent upon trade with foreign markets suffered a severe downturn. The Tidewater region saw many enslaved people carried off by the British. Chesapeake planters also lost their lucrative foreign markets. Tobacco was especially hard hit. The British decision to close its West Indian colonies to American trade devastated what had been a thriving commerce in timber, wheat, and other foodstuffs.

Merchants suffered even more wrenching adjustments than the farmers. Cut out of the British mercantile system, they had to find new outlets.

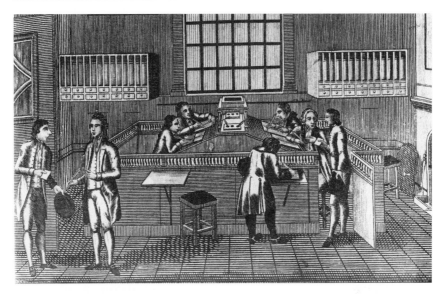

Merchants' Counting House

Americans involved in overseas trade, such as the merchants depicted here, had been sharply affected by the dislocations of war.

Circumstances that impoverished some enriched those who financed privateers, supplied the armies on both sides, and hoarded precious goods while demand and prices soared. By the end of the war, a strong sentiment for free trade had developed in both Britain and America. In the memorable year 1776 the Scottish economist Adam Smith published *Inquiry into the Nature and Causes of the Wealth of Nations,* a classic manifesto against mercantilism. Some British statesmen embraced the new gospel of free trade, but the public and Parliament would cling to the conventions of mercantilism for many years to come.

After the war British trade with America did resume, and American ships were allowed to deliver American products and return to the United States with British goods. American ships could not carry British goods anywhere else, however. The pent-up demand for familiar goods created a vigorous market in postwar exports to America, fueled by British credit and the hard money that had come into America with foreign aid, the expenditures of foreign armies, and wartime trade and privateering. The result was a quick cycle of postwar boom and bust, a buying spree followed by a money shortage and economic troubles that lasted several years.

In colonial days the chronic trade deficit with Britain had been offset by the influx of coins from trade with the West Indies. Now American ships found themselves excluded altogether from the British West Indies. The islands, however, still demanded wheat, fish, lumber, and other products from the mainland, and American shippers had not lost their talent for smuggling. Already American shippers had begun exploring new outlets, and by 1787 their seaports were flourishing more than ever. Freed from colonial restraints, American merchants now had the run of the seas. Trade treaties opened new markets with the Dutch (1782), the Swedes (1783), the Prussians (1785), and the Moroccans (1787), and American shippers found new outlets on their own in Europe, Africa, and Asia. The most spectacular new development, if not the largest, was trade with China. It began in 1784–1785, when the *Empress of China* sailed from New York to Canton (present-day Guangzhou) and back, around the tip of South America. Profits from its cargo of silks and tea encouraged the outfitting of other ships, which carried ginseng root and other American goods to exchange for the luxury goods of east Asia.

By 1790 the dollar value of American commerce and exports had far outrun the trade of the colonies. Merchants had more ships than they had had before the war. Farm exports were twice what they had been. Although most of the exports were the products of forests, fields, and fisheries, during and after the war more Americans had turned to small-scale manufacturing, mainly for domestic markets.

DIPLOMACY   The shortcomings and failures of the Articles of Confederation prompted a growing chorus of complaints. In diplomacy there remained the nagging problems of relations with Great Britain and Spain, both of which still kept military posts on American soil and conspired with Indians and white settlers in the West. The British, despite the peace treaty of 1783, held on to a string of forts along the Canadian border. From these they kept a hand in the lucrative fur trade and a degree of influence with the Indian tribes, whom they were suspected of stirring up to make sporadic attacks on American settlements along the frontier. They gave as a reason for their continued occupation the failure of Americans to pay their prewar debts to British creditors. According to one Virginian, a common question in his state was "If we are now to pay the debts due to British merchants, what have we been fighting for all this while?"

Another major irritant to U.S.-British relations was the American confiscation of Loyalist property. The Treaty of Paris had encouraged Congress to stop confiscations of Tory property, to guarantee immunity to Loyalists for twelve months, during which they could return and wind up their affairs, and to recommend that the states give back confiscated property. Persecutions, even lynchings, of Loyalists occurred even after the end of the war. Some Loyalists who had fled to Canada or Britain returned unmolested, however, and resumed their lives in their former homes. By the end of 1787, moreover, at the request of Congress, all the states had rescinded the laws that were in conflict with the peace treaty.

With Spain the chief issues were the southern boundary of the United States and the right to navigate the Mississippi River. According to the preliminary treaty with Britain, the United States claimed a line as far south as the 31st parallel; Spain held out for the line running eastward from the mouth of the Yazoo River (at 32°28′N), which it claimed as the traditional boundary. The Treaty of Paris had also given the Americans the right to navigate the Mississippi River to its mouth. Still, the international boundary ran down the middle of the river for most of its length, and the Mississippi was entirely within Spanish Louisiana in its lower reaches. The right to navigation was crucial to the growing American settlements in Kentucky and Tennessee, but in 1784 Louisiana's Spanish governor closed the river to American commerce and began to intrigue with Indians against the American settlers and with settlers against the United States.

THE CONFEDERATION'S PROBLEMS   The problems of trans-Appalachian settlers with the British and the Spanish seemed remote from the everyday concerns of most Americans, however. What touched most Americans more were economic troubles and the acute currency shortage after the war. Merchants who found themselves excluded from old channels of imperial trade began to agitate for reprisals. State governments, in response, laid special tonnage duties on British vessels and special tariffs on the goods they brought to the United States. State action alone, however, failed to work because of a lack of uniformity among the states. British ships could be diverted to states whose duties were less restrictive. The other states tried to meet this problem by taxing British goods that flowed across state lines, creating the impression that states were involved in commercial war with each other. Although these duties seldom affected American goods, there was a clear need—it seemed to commercial interests—for a central power to regulate trade.

Mechanics (skilled workers who made, used, or repaired tools and machines) and artisans (skilled workers who made products) were developing an infant industry. Their products ranged from crude iron nails to the fine silver bowls of such smiths as Paul Revere. These skilled workers wanted reprisals against British goods as well as British ships. They sought, and to various degrees obtained from the states, tariffs (taxes) on foreign goods that

Domestic Industry

American craftsmen, such as this cabinet-maker, favored tariffs against foreign goods that competed with theirs.

competed with theirs. The country would be on its way to economic independence, they argued, if only the money that flowed into the country were invested in domestic manufactures instead of being paid out for foreign goods. Nearly all the states gave some preference to American goods, but again the lack of uniformity in their laws put them at cross-purposes, and so urban mechanics along with merchants were drawn into the movement calling for a stronger central government in the interest of uniform regulation.

The shortage of cash and other economic difficulties gave rise to more immediate demands for paper currency as legal tender, for postponement of tax and debt payments, and for laws to "stay" the foreclosure of mortgages. Farmers who had profited during the war found themselves squeezed afterward by depressed crop prices and mounting debts while merchants opened up new trade routes. Creditors demanded hard money, but it was in short supply—and paper money was almost nonexistent after the depreciation of the Continental currency. The result was an outcry for relief, and around 1785 the demand for new paper money became the most divisive issue in state politics. Debtors demanded the addition of paper money as a means of easing repayment, and farmers saw paper money as an inflationary way to raise commodity prices.

In 1785–1786 seven states (Pennsylvania, New York, New Jersey, South Carolina, Rhode Island, Georgia, and North Carolina) began issuing paper money. It served in five of those states—Pennsylvania, New York, New Jersey, South Carolina, and Rhode Island—as a means of extending credit to hard-pressed farmers through state loans on farm mortgages. It was variously used to fund state debts and to pay off the claims of veterans. In spite of the cries of calamity at the time, the money never seriously depreciated in Pennsylvania, New York, and South Carolina. In Rhode Island, however, the debtor party ran wild. In 1786 the Rhode Island legislature issued more paper money than any other state in proportion to its population and declared it legal tender in payment of all debts. Creditors fled the state to avoid being paid in worthless paper.

SHAYS'S REBELLION   Newspapers throughout the country followed the chaotic developments in Rhode Island. The little commonwealth, stubbornly independent since the days of Roger Williams, became the prime example of democracy run riot—until its riotous neighbor, Massachusetts, provided the final proof (some said) that the new country was poised on the brink of anarchy: Shays's Rebellion. There the trouble was not too much paper money but too little, as well as too much taxation.

After 1780 Massachusetts had remained in the grip of a rigidly conservative regime, which levied ever-higher poll and land taxes to pay off a heavy war debt, held mainly by wealthy creditors in Boston. The taxes fell most heavily upon beleaguered farmers and the poor in general. When the Massachusetts legislature adjourned in 1786 without providing either paper money or any other relief from taxes and debts, three western counties erupted in revolt.

Armed bands closed the courts and prevented foreclosures. A ragtag "army" of some 1,200 disgruntled farmers led by Daniel Shays, a destitute war veteran, advanced upon the federal arsenal at Springfield in 1787. Shays and his followers sought a more flexible monetary policy, laws allowing them to use corn and wheat as money, and the right to postpone paying taxes until the depression lifted.

The state responded by sending 4,400 militiamen armed with cannon. The soldiers scattered the debtor army with a single volley that left four farmers dead. The rebel farmers nevertheless had a victory of sorts. The new state legislature included members sympathetic to the agricultural crisis. The legislature omitted direct taxes the following year, lowered court fees, and exempted clothing, household goods, and tools from the debt process. But a more important consequence was the impetus the rebellion gave to conservatism and nationalism.

Rumors, at times deliberately inflated, greatly exaggerated the extent of this pathetic rebellion of desperate men. The Shaysites were linked to the conniving British and accused of seeking to pillage the wealthy. Panic set in among the republic's elite. "Good God!" George Washington exclaimed when he heard of the incident. Although the rebellion had been suppressed, he worried that it might tempt other disgruntled groups around the country to adopt similar measures. In a letter to Thomas Jefferson, Abigail Adams tarred the Shaysites as "ignorant, restless desperadoes, without conscience or principles, . . . mobbish insurgents [who] are for sapping the foundation" of the struggling young government. Jefferson disagreed. If Abigail Adams and others were overly critical of Shays's Rebellion, Jefferson was, if anything, too complacent. From his post in Paris, he wrote to a friend back home, "The tree of liberty must be refreshed from time to time with the blood of patriots and tyrants." Abigail Adams was so infuriated by Jefferson's position that she would not correspond with him for months.

CALLS FOR A STRONGER GOVERNMENT   Well before the outbreaks in New England, the advocates of a stronger central authority had been calling for a convention to revise the Articles of Confederation. Self-interest led bankers, merchants, and mechanics to promote a stronger central government as the only alternative to anarchy. Gradually Americans were losing the fear of a strong central government as they saw evidence that tyranny might come from other quarters, including the common people themselves.

Such developments led many of the Revolutionary leaders to revise their assessment of the American character. "We have, probably," concluded George Washington in 1786, "had too good an opinion of human nature in forming our confederation." Washington and others decided that at any given time only a distinct minority of citizens could be relied upon to set aside their private interests in favor of the common good. Madison and other so-called Federalists concluded that the new republic must now depend for its success upon the constant virtue of the few rather than the public-spiritedness of the many.

In 1785 commissioners from Virginia and Maryland had met at Mount Vernon, at George Washington's invitation, to promote commerce and economic development and to settle outstanding questions about the navigation of the Potomac River and the Chesapeake Bay. Washington had a personal interest in the river flowing by his door: it was a potential route to the West, with its upper reaches close to the upper reaches of the Ohio, where his military career had begun thirty years before and where he owned substantial property. The delegates agreed on interstate cooperation, and Maryland suggested a further pact with Pennsylvania and Delaware to encourage water transportation between the Chesapeake Bay and the Ohio River; the Virginia legislature agreed and, at Madison's suggestion, invited all thirteen states to a general discussion of commercial problems. Nine states named representatives, but those from only five appeared at the Annapolis Convention in 1786—neither the New England states nor the Carolinas and Georgia were represented. Apparent failure soon turned into success, however, when the alert Alexander Hamilton, representing New York, presented a resolution for still another convention, in Philadelphia, to consider all measures necessary "to render the constitution of the Federal Government adequate to the exigencies of the Union."

ADOPTING THE CONSTITUTION

THE CONSTITUTIONAL CONVENTION   After stalling for several months, Congress fell in line in 1787 with a resolution endorsing a convention "for the sole and express purpose of revising the Articles of Confederation." By then five states had already named delegates; before the meeting, called to begin on May 14, 1787, six more states had acted. New Hampshire delayed until June, and its delegates arrived in July. Fearful of consolidated power, tiny Rhode Island kept aloof throughout. (Critics labeled the fractious little state Rogue Island.) Virginia's Patrick Henry, an implacable foe of centralized government, claimed to "smell a rat" and refused to represent his state. Twenty-nine delegates from nine states began work on May 25. Altogether, the state legislatures had elected seventy-three men. Fifty-five attended at one time or another, and after four months of deliberations in stifling summer heat, thirty-nine signed the constitution they drafted.

The durability and flexibility of that document testify to the remarkable quality of the men who made it. The delegates were surprisingly young:

Drafting the Constitution

George Washington presides over a session of the Constitutional Convention.

forty-two was the average age. They were farmers, merchants, lawyers, and bankers, many of them widely read in history, law, and political philosophy, yet they were also practical men of experience, tested in the fires of the Revolution. Twenty-one had served in the conflict, seven had been state governors, most had been members of the Continental Congress, and eight had signed the Declaration of Independence.

The magisterial George Washington served as presiding officer but participated little in the debates. Eighty-one-year-old Benjamin Franklin, the oldest delegate, also said little from the floor but provided a wealth of experience, wit, and common sense behind the scenes. More active in the debates were James Madison, the ablest political philosopher in the group; Massachusetts's dapper Elbridge Gerry, a Harvard graduate who earned the nickname Old Grumbletonian because, as John Adams once said, he "opposed everything he did not propose"; George Mason, the irritable author of the Virginia Declaration of Rights and a slaveholding planter with a deep-rooted suspicion of all government; the eloquent, arrogant New York aristocrat Gouverneur Morris, who harbored a venomous contempt for the masses; Scottish-born James Wilson of Pennsylvania, one of the ablest lawyers in the new nation and next in importance at the convention only to Washington and Madison; and Roger Sherman of Connecticut, a self-trained lawyer adept at negotiating compromises. John Adams, like Jefferson, was serving abroad on diplomatic missions. Also conspicuously absent during most of the convention was Alexander Hamilton, the staunch nationalist who regretfully went home when the other two New York delegates walked out to protest what they saw as the loss of states' rights.

James Madison

Madison was only thirty-six when he assumed a major role in the drafting of the Constitution. This miniature (ca. 1783) is by Charles Willson Peale.

Madison emerged as the central figure at the convention. Small of stature—barely over five feet tall—and frail in health, the thirty-six-year-old bookish bachelor was descended from wealthy slaveholding Virginia planters. He suffered from chronic headaches and was painfully shy. Crowds made him nervous, and he hated to use his high-pitched voice in public, much less in open debate. But the Princeton graduate possessed a keen, agile mind and had a voracious appetite for learning, and the convincing eloquence of his arguments proved decisive. "Every person seems to acknowledge his greatness," wrote one delegate. Another said that Madison "blends together the profound politician with the scholar . . . [and] always comes forward as the best informed man of any point in the debate." Madison had arrived in Philadelphia with trunks full of books and a head full of ideas. He had been preparing for the convention for months and probably knew more about historic forms of government than any other delegate.

For the most part the delegates' differences on political philosophy fell within a narrow range. On certain fundamentals they generally agreed: that government derived its just powers from the consent of the people but that society must be protected from the tyranny of the majority; that the people at large must have a voice in their government but that any one group must be kept from abusing power; that a stronger central authority was essential but that all power was subject to abuse. They assumed with Madison that even the best people were naturally selfish, and government, therefore, could not be founded altogether upon a trust in goodwill and virtue. Yet by a careful arrangement of checks and balances, by checking power with countervailing power, the Founding Fathers hoped to devise institutions that could constrain individual sinfulness and channel self-interest to benefit the public good.

THE VIRGINIA AND NEW JERSEY PLANS   At the outset the delegates unanimously elected George Washington president of the convention. One of the first decisions was to meet behind closed doors in order to discourage outside pressures and theatrical speeches to the galleries. The secrecy of the proceedings was remarkably well kept, and knowledge of the debates comes mainly from Madison's extensive notes.

It was Madison, too, who drafted the proposals that set the framework of the discussions. These proposals, which came to be called the Virginia Plan, embodied a revolutionary idea: that the delegates scrap their instructions to revise the Articles of Confederation and submit an entirely new document to the states. The plan proposed separate legislative, executive, and judicial branches and a truly national government to make laws binding upon individual citizens as well as states. Congress would be divided into two houses: a lower house chosen by popular vote and an upper house of senators elected by the state legislatures. Congress could disallow state laws under the plan and would itself define the extent of its and the states' authority.

On June 15 delegates submitted the "New Jersey Plan," which proposed to keep the existing structure of equal representation of the states in a unicameral Congress but to give Congress the power to levy taxes and regulate commerce and the authority to name a plural executive (with no veto) and a supreme court.

The plans presented the convention with two major issues: whether to amend the Articles of Confederation or draft a new document and whether to determine congressional representation by state or by population. On the first point the convention voted to work toward establishing a national government as envisioned by the Virginians. Regarding the powers of this government, there was little disagreement except in the details. Experience with the Articles had persuaded the delegates that an effective central government, as distinguished from a confederation, needed the power to levy taxes, regulate commerce, raise an army and navy, and make laws binding upon individual citizens. The lessons of the 1780s suggested to them, moreover, that in the interest of order and uniformity the states must be denied certain powers: to issue money, abrogate contracts, make treaties, wage war, and levy tariffs.

But furious disagreements arose. The first clash in the convention involved the issue of congressional representation, and it was resolved by the Great Compromise (sometimes called the Connecticut Compromise, as it was proposed by Roger Sherman), which gave both groups their way. The more populous states won apportionment by population in the House of Representatives; the states that sought to protect states' power won equality in the Senate, with the vote by individuals, not by states.

An equally contentious struggle ensued between northern and southern delegates over slavery and the regulation of trade, an omen of sectional controversies to come. A South Carolinian stressed that his delegation and the Georgians would oppose any constitution that failed to protect slavery. Few if any of the framers of the Constitution even considered the notion of abolition, and they carefully avoided using the term *slavery* in the final document. In this they reflected the prevailing attitudes among white Americans. Most agreed with South Carolina's John Rutledge when he asserted, "Religion and humanity [have] nothing to do with this [slavery] question. Interest alone is the governing principle of nations."

The "interest" of southern delegates, with enslaved African Americans so numerous in their states, dictated that slaves be counted as part of the population in determining the number of a state's congressional representatives. Northerners were willing to count slaves when deciding each state's share of direct taxes but not for purposes of representation. On this issue the Congress of the Confederation had supplied a handy precedent when it sought an amendment to make population rather than land values the standard for

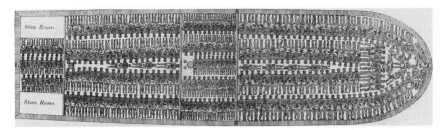

Slave Trade

This cross-sectional view of the British slave ship *Brookes* shows the crowded conditions that enslaved Africans endured in the international slave trade.

fiscal requisitions. The proposed amendment to the Articles of Confederation would have counted three fifths of the slaves for this purpose. The delegates, with little dissent, agreed to incorporate the same three-fifths ratio into the new constitution as a basis for apportioning both representatives and direct taxes.

A more sensitive issue involved an effort to prevent the central government from stopping the transatlantic slave trade. Virginia's George Mason, himself a slaveholder, condemned the "infernal traffic," which his state had already outlawed. He argued that the issue concerned "not the importing states alone but the whole union." People in the western territories were "already calling out for slaves for their new lands." He feared that they would "fill the country" with enslaved people. Such a development would bring forth "the judgment of Heaven" on the country. Southern delegates were quick to challenge Mason's reasoning. They argued that the continued importation of slaves was vital to their states' economies.

To resolve the question, the delegates established a time limit: Congress could not forbid the foreign slave trade before 1808, but it could levy a tax of $10 a head on all imported slaves. In both provisions a sense of delicacy— and hypocrisy—dictated the use of euphemisms. The Constitution spoke of "free Persons" and "all other persons," of "such persons as any of the States Now existing shall think proper to admit," and of persons "held to Service of Labor." The odious word *slavery* did not appear in the Constitution until the Thirteenth Amendment (1865) abolished the practice.

If the delegates found the slavery issue distracting, they considered irrelevant any discussion of the legal or political role of women under the new constitution. The Revolutionary rhetoric of liberty prompted some women to demand political equality. "The men say we have no business [with politics]," Eliza Wilkinson of South Carolina observed as the Constitution was being framed, "but I won't have it thought that because we are the weaker sex as to bodily strength we are capable of nothing more than domestic concerns." Her complaint, however, fell on deaf ears. There was never any formal discussion of women's rights at the convention. The new nationalism still defined politics and government as outside the realm of female endeavor.

The Constitution also said little about the processes of immigration and naturalization, and most of what it said was negative. In Article II, Section 1, it prohibits any future immigrant from becoming president, limiting that office to a "natural born Citizen." In Article I, Sections 2 and 3, respectively, it stipulates that no person can serve in the House of Representatives who has not "been seven Years a Citizen of the United States" or in the Senate who has not "been nine Years a Citizen." On the matter of defining citizenship, the Constitution gives Congress the authority "to establish an uniform Rule of Naturalization," but offers no further guidance on the matter. As a result, naturalization policy has changed significantly over the years in response to fluctuating social attitudes and political moods. In 1790 the first Congress passed a naturalization law that allowed "free white persons" who had been in the country for as few as two years to be made naturalized citizens in any court. This meant that persons of African descent were denied citizenship by the federal government; it was left to individual states to determine whether free blacks were citizens. And because Indians were not "free white persons," they were also treated as aliens rather than citizens. Not until 1924 would American Indians be granted citizenship—by an act of Congress rather than a constitutional amendment.

THE SEPARATION OF POWERS The details of the government structure embedded in the Constitution aroused less debate than the basic issues pitting the large states against the small and the northern states against the southern. Existing state constitutions, several of which already separated powers among legislative, executive, and judicial branches, set an example that reinforced the convention's resolve to disperse power with checks and balances. Although the Founding Fathers hated royal tyranny, most of them also feared rule by the people and favored various mechanisms to check public passions. Some delegates displayed a thumping disdain for any democratizing of the political system. Elbridge Gerry asserted that most of the nation's problems "flow from an excess of democracy." Alexander Hamilton once called the people "a great beast."

Those elitist views were accommodated by the Constitution's mixed legislative system. The lower house was designed to be closest to the voters, who elected its delegates every two years. It would be, according to Virginia's

George Mason, "the grand repository of the democratic principle of the Government." House members should "sympathize with their constituents, should think as they think, & feel as they feel; and for these purposes should even be residents among them." The upper house, or Senate, its members elected by the state legislatures, was intended to be more detached from the voters. Staggered six-year terms prevent the choice of a majority in any given year and thereby further isolate senators from the passing fancies of public passion.

The decision that a single person be made the chief executive caused the delegates "considerable pause," according to James Madison. George Mason protested that this would create a "fetus of monarchy." Indeed, several of the chief executive's powers actually exceeded those of the British monarch. This was the sharpest departure from the recent experience in state government, where the office of governor had commonly been diluted because of the recent memory of struggles with royal governors. The president had a veto over acts of Congress, subject to being overridden by a two-thirds vote in each house, whereas the royal veto had long since fallen into complete disuse. The president was commander in chief of the armed forces and responsible for the execution of the laws. The chief executive could make treaties with the advice and consent of two thirds of the Senate and had the power to appoint diplomats, judges, and other officers with the consent of a majority of the Senate. The president was instructed to report annually on the state of the nation and was authorized to recommend legislation, a provision that presidents eventually would take as a mandate to promote extensive programs.

But the president's powers were limited in certain key areas. The chief executive could neither declare war nor make peace; those powers were reserved for Congress. Unlike the British monarch, moreover, the president could be removed from office. The House could impeach (indict) the chief executive—and other civil officers—on charges of treason, bribery, or "other high crimes and misdemeanors," and upon conviction the Senate could remove an impeached president by a two-thirds vote. The presiding officer at the trial of a president would be the chief justice, since the usual presiding officer of the Senate (the vice president) would have a personal stake in the outcome.

The leading nationalists—men like James Madison, James Wilson, and Alexander Hamilton—wanted to strengthen the independence of the executive by entrusting the choice to popular election. But an elected executive was still too far beyond the American experience. Besides, a national election would have created enormous problems of organization and voter qualification. Wilson suggested instead that the people of each state choose presidential electors equal to the number of their senators and representatives. Others proposed that the legislators make the choice. Finally, the convention voted to let the legislature decide the method in each state. Before long nearly all the states were choosing the electors by popular vote, and the electors were acting as agents of the party will, casting their votes as they had pledged them before the election. This method diverged from the original expectation that the electors would deliberate and make their own choices.

On the third branch of government, the judiciary, there was surprisingly little debate. Both the Virginia and the New Jersey Plans had called for a supreme court, which the Constitution established, providing specifically for a chief justice of the United States and leaving up to Congress the number of other justices. Although the Constitution nowhere authorizes the courts to declare laws void when they conflict with the Constitution, the power of judicial review is implied and was soon exercised in cases involving both state and federal laws. Article VI declares the federal constitution, federal laws, and treaties "to be the supreme Law of the Land," state laws or constitutions "to the Contrary notwithstanding." The advocates of states' rights thought this a victory, since it eliminated the proviso in the Virginia Plan for Congress to settle all conflicts between the federal government and individual states. As it

Signing the Constitution, September 17, 1787

Thomas Pritchard Rossiter's painting shows George Washington presiding over what Thomas Jefferson called an assembly of demigods.

turned out, however, the clause became the basis for an important expansion of judicial review of legislative actions.

Although the Constitution extended vast new powers to the national government, the delegates' mistrust of unchecked power is apparent in repeated examples of countervailing forces: the separation of the three branches of government, the president's veto, the congressional power of impeachment and removal, the Senate's power to approve or reject treaties and appointments, the courts' implied right of judicial review. In addition, the new frame of government specifically forbade Congress to pass bills of attainder (criminal condemnation by a legislative act) or ex post facto laws (laws adopted after an event to criminalize deeds that have already been committed). It also reserved to the states large areas of sovereignty—a reservation soon made explicit by the Tenth Amendment. By dividing sovereignty between the people and the government, the framers of the Constitution provided a distinctive contribution to political theory. That is, by vesting ultimate authority in the people, they divided sovereignty *within* the government. This constituted a dramatic break with the colonial tradition. The British had always insisted that the sovereignty of the king-in-Parliament was indivisible.

The most glaring defect of the Articles of Confederation, the rule of state unanimity that defeated every effort to amend them, led the delegates to provide a less forbidding though still difficult method of amending the new constitution. Amendments can be proposed either by a two-thirds vote of each house or by a convention specially called, upon application of two thirds of the legislatures. Amendments can be ratified by approval of three fourths of the states acting through their legislatures or in special conventions. The national convention has never been used, however, and state conventions have been called only once—to ratify the repeal of the Eighteenth Amendment, which had prohibited "the manufacture, sale, or transportation of" alcoholic beverages.

THE FIGHT FOR RATIFICATION   The final article of the Constitution provided that it would become effective upon ratification by nine states (not quite the three-fourths majority required for amendment). After fighting off efforts to censure the convention for exceeding its authority, the Confederation Congress submitted its work to the states on September 28, 1787.

In the ensuing political debate, advocates of the Constitution, who might properly have been called Nationalists because they preferred a strong central government, assumed the more reassuring name of Federalists. Opponents, who favored a more decentralized federal system, became anti-Federalists. The initiative that the Federalists took in assuming their name was characteristic of the whole campaign. They got the jump on their critics. Their leaders had been members of the convention and were already familiar with the document and the arguments on each point. They were not only better prepared but also better organized and, on the whole, made up of the more able leaders in the political community.

Historians have hotly debated the motivation of the advocates of the Constitution. For more than a century the tendency prevailed to idolize the Founding Fathers. In 1913, however, Charles A. Beard's book *An Economic Interpretation of the Constitution* advanced the shocking thesis that the Philadelphia convention was made up of men who had a selfish economic interest in the outcome. Beard argued that the delegates represented an economic elite of speculators in western lands, holders of depreciated government securities, and creditors whose wealth was mostly in "paper": mortgages, stocks, bonds, and the like. The holders of western lands and government bonds would benefit from a stronger government. Creditors generally stood to gain from the prohibitions against state currency issues and the impairment of contract, provisions clearly aimed at the paper-money issues and the stay laws that were then effective in many states. Stay laws prevented people to whom money was due from enforcing their contractual rights to foreclose on debtors.

Beard's thesis provided a useful antidote to unquestioning hero worship and still contains a germ of truth, but he exaggerated. Most of the delegates, according to evidence unavailable to Beard, had no compelling stake in paper wealth, and most were far more involved in landholding. Many prominent nationalists, including "the Father of the Constitution," James Madison, had no western lands, bonds, or much other personal property. Some opponents of the Constitution, on the other hand, held large blocks of land and securities. Economic interests certainly figured in the process, but they functioned in a complex interplay of state, sectional, group, and individual interests that turned largely on how well people had fared under the Confederation.

The most notable aspect of the new American republic was not selfishness but cooperation. The American Revolution had led not to general chaos and terror but to "an outbreak of constitution-making." From the 1760s through the 1780s, there occurred a prolonged debate over the fundamental issues of government, which in its scope and depth—and in the durability of its outcome—is without parallel.

THE FEDERALIST   Among the supreme legacies of the debate over the Constitution is *The Federalist,* a collection of essays originally published in the New York press between 1787 and 1788. Instigated by Alexander

Hamilton, the eighty-five articles published under the name Publius include about fifty by Hamilton, thirty by James Madison, and five by John Jay. The authorship of some selections remains in doubt. Written in support of ratification, the essays defended the principle of a supreme national authority, but sought to reassure doubters that the people and the states had little reason to fear usurpations and tyranny by the new government.

In perhaps the most famous essay, Number 10, Madison argued that the very size and diversity of the country would make it impossible for any single faction to form a majority that could dominate the government. This contradicted the conventional wisdom of the time, which insisted that republics could survive only in small, homogeneous countries like Switzerland and the Netherlands. Large republics, on the other hand, would fragment, dissolving into anarchy and tyranny through the influence of factions. Quite the contrary, Madison insisted. Given a balanced federal polity, a republic could work in large and diverse countries probably better than in smaller nations. "Extend the sphere," he wrote, "and you take in a greater variety of parties and interests; you make it less probable that a majority of the whole will have a common motive to invade the rights of other citizens."

The Federalists insisted that the new union would contribute to prosperity. The anti-Federalists, however, talked more of the dangers of power in terms that had become familiar during the long struggles with Parliament and the crown. They noted the absence of a bill of rights to protect the rights of individuals and states. They found the process of ratification highly irregular, as it was—indeed, it was illegal under the Articles of Confederation. Not only did Patrick Henry refuse to attend the Constitutional Convention, but he later demanded (unsuccessfully) that it be investigated as a conspiracy. The anti-Federalist leaders—George Mason, Patrick Henry, and Richard Henry Lee of Virginia, George Clinton of New York, Samuel Adams and Elbridge Gerry of Massachusetts, Luther Martin of Maryland—were often men whose careers and reputations had been established well before the Revolution. The Federalist leaders were more likely to be younger men whose careers had begun in the Revolution—men such as Hamilton, Madison, and John Jay.

The disagreement between the two groups was more over means than ends, however. Both sides, for the most part, agreed that a stronger national authority was needed and that it required an independent income to function properly. Both were convinced that the people must erect safeguards against tyranny, even the tyranny of the majority. Few of the Constitution's supporters liked it in its entirety, but most believed that it was the best document obtainable; few of its opponents found it unacceptable in its entirety. Once the new government had become an accomplished fact, few wanted to undo the work of the Philadelphia convention.

THE DECISION OF THE STATES   Ratification gained momentum before the end of 1787, and several of the smaller states were among the first to act, apparently satisfied that they had gained all the safeguards they could hope for in equality of representation in the Senate. Delaware, New Jersey, and Georgia voted unanimously in favor. Massachusetts, still sharply divided in the aftermath of Shays's Rebellion, was the first state in which the outcome was close. There the Federalists carried the day by winning over two hesitant leaders of the popular party. They dangled before John Hancock the possibility of his becoming vice president and won the acquiescence of Samuel Adams when they agreed to recommend amendments designed to protect human rights, including one that would specifically reserve to the states all powers not granted to the new government. Massachusetts approved the Constitution by 187 to 168 on February 6, 1788.

New Hampshire was the ninth state to ratify the Constitution, allowing it to be put into effect, but the Union could hardly succeed without the approval of Virginia, the most populous state, or New York, which had the third highest population and occupied a key position geographically. Both states harbored strong opposition groups. In Virginia, Patrick Henry became the chief spokesman for backcountry farmers who feared the powers of the new government, but wavering delegates were won over by the same strategem as in Massachusetts. When it was proposed that the convention

RATIFICATION OF THE CONSTITUTION

Order of Ratification	State	Date of Ratification
1	Delaware	December 7, 1787
2	Pennsylvania	December 12, 1787
3	New Jersey	December 18, 1787
4	Georgia	January 2, 1788
5	Connecticut	January 9, 1788
6	Massachusetts	February 6, 1788
7	Maryland	April 28, 1788
8	South Carolina	May 23, 1788
9	New Hampshire	June 21, 1788
10	Virginia	June 25, 1788
11	New York	July 26, 1788
12	North Carolina	November 21, 1789
13	Rhode Island	May 29, 1790

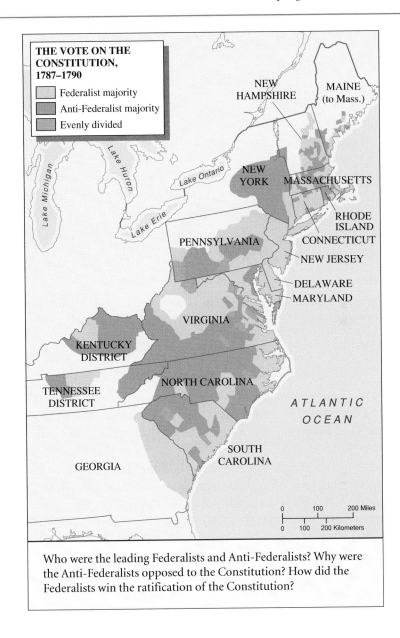

THE VOTE ON THE CONSTITUTION, 1787–1790

☐ Federalist majority
☐ Anti-Federalist majority
☐ Evenly divided

Who were the leading Federalists and Anti-Federalists? Why were the Anti-Federalists opposed to the Constitution? How did the Federalists win the ratification of the Constitution?

should recommend a bill of rights, Edmund Randolph, who had refused to sign the finished document, announced his conversion to the cause.

Upon notification that New Hampshire had become the ninth state to ratify the Constitution, the Confederation Congress began to draft plans for an orderly transfer of power. On September 13, 1788, it selected New York City as

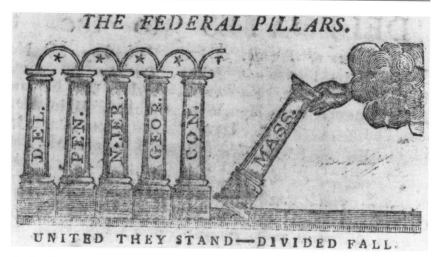

THE FEDERAL PILLARS.

UNITED THEY STAND—DIVIDED FALL.

Sixth Pillar

An engraving published in 1788 in the American newspaper *The Centinel* after Massachusetts became the sixth state to ratify the new Constitution. By the end of 1788, five more states would ratify and the Constitution would go into effect. The last two states to ratify were North Carolina in 1789 and Rhode Island in 1790.

the seat of the new government and fixed the date for elections. Each state would set the date for electing the first members of Congress. On October 10, 1788, the Confederation Congress transacted its last business and passed into history.

"Our constitution is in actual operation," the elderly Benjamin Franklin wrote to a friend; "everything appears to promise that it will last; but in this world nothing is certain but death and taxes." George Washington was even more uncertain about the future under the new plan of government. He had told a fellow delegate as the convention adjourned, "I do not expect the Constitution to last for more than twenty years."

The Constitution has lasted much longer, of course, and in the process it has provided a model of resilient republican government whose features have been repeatedly borrowed by other nations through the years. Yet what makes the U.S. Constitution so distinctive is not its specific provisions but its remarkable harmony with the particular "genius of the people" it governs. The Constitution has been neither a static abstraction nor a "machine that would go of itself," as the poet James Russell Lowell would later assert. Instead, it has provided a flexible system of government that presidents, legislators, judges, and the people have adjusted to changing social, economic, and political circumstances. In this sense the Founding Fathers not only created "a more perfect Union" in 1787; they also engineered a frame of government whose resilience has enabled later generations to continue to perfect their republican experiment. But the framers of the Constitution failed in one significant respect: in skirting the issue of slavery so as to cement the Union, they unknowingly allowed tensions over the "peculiar institution" to reach the point where there would be no political solution—only civil war.

MAKING CONNECTIONS

- The debate over the nature of the national government and its relationship to the people and the states will reemerge in the Kentucky and Virginia Resolutions (Chapter 8), the Hartford Convention (Chapter 9), and the nullification crisis (Chapter 11).

- Slavery, viewed by the delegates to the Constitutional Convention as little more than a "distracting question," would soon become a major political problem, especially after the Missouri Compromise (Chapter 10).

FURTHER READING

A good overview of the Confederation period is Richard B. Morris's *The Forging of the Union, 1781–1789* (1987). Another useful analysis of this period is Richard Buel Jr.'s *Securing the Revolution: Ideology in American Politics, 1789–1815* (1972).

David P. Szatmary's *Shays's Rebellion: The Making of an Agrarian Insurrection* (1980) covers that fateful incident. For a fine account of cultural change during the period, see Joseph J. Ellis's *After the Revolution: Profiles of Early American Culture* (1979).

Excellent treatments of the post-Revolutionary era include Edmund S. Morgan's *Inventing the People: The Rise of Popular Sovereignty in England and America* (1988), Michael Kammen's *Sovereignty and Liberty: Constitutional Discourse in American Culture* (1988), and Joyce Appleby's *Inheriting the Revolution: The First Generation of Americans* (2000). Among the better collections of essays on the Constitution are *Toward a More Perfect Union: Six*

Essays on the Constitution (1988), edited by Neil L. York, and *The Framing and Ratification of the Constitution* (1987), edited by Leonard W. Levy and Dennis J. Mahoney.

Bruce Ackerman's *We the People,* vol. 1, *Foundations* (1991) examines Federalist political principles. For the Bill of Rights that emerged from the ratification struggles, see Robert A. Rutland's *The Birth of the Bill of Rights, 1776–1791* (1955).

8

THE FEDERALIST ERA

FOCUS QUESTIONS

- How did the new national government operate?
- What was Alexander Hamilton's Federalist program?
- How did the first party system begin?
- What were the elements of the Federalists' foreign policy?

To answer these questions and access additional review material, please visit www.wwnorton.com/studyspace.

The federal Constitution, ratified in 1788, was a bundle of deft compromises intended to create a more powerful central government better capable of managing a sprawling—and rapidly growing—new republic. Although the U.S. Constitution has become the world's most enduring national charter, skeptics in the late eighteenth century doubted that it would survive more than a few years. A Massachusetts anti-Federalist said that governing such an "extensive empire . . . upon republican principles" was impossible. It was one thing to draft a dramatic new constitution but quite another to exercise such expanded powers. The Constitution's ideals were profound, but its premises and theories were untested. Creating a "more perfect union" would prove to be a long, complicated, and painful process. During the 1790s the new federal government would confront civil rebellions, threats of secession, international intrigues, and foreign wars. In 1789 Americans wildly celebrated the inauguration of George Washington as the nation's first president. But amid the excitement was a powerful undercurrent of uncertainty, suspicion, and anxiety. The Constitution provided a framework but not a blueprint; it left unanswered many questions about the actual structure and conduct of the new government. As James Madison had acknowledged, "We are in a wilderness without a single footstep to guide us."

A NEW NATION

In 1789 the United States and the western territories reached from the Atlantic Ocean to the Mississippi River and hosted almost 4 million people. This vast new nation, much larger than any in Europe, harbored distinct regional differences. A southerner noted the clashing regional outlooks when he said that "men who come from New England are different from us." Although still characterized by small farms and bustling seaports, New England was on the verge of developing a manufacturing sector. The middle Atlantic states boasted the most well-balanced economy, the largest cities, and the most diverse collection of ethnic and religious groups. The South was an

A New Society

An engraving from the title page of *The Universal Asylum and Columbian Magazine,* (published in Philadelphia in 1790). America is represented as a woman laying down her shield to engage in education, art, commerce, and agriculture.

agricultural region more ethnically homogeneous and increasingly dependent upon slave labor. By 1790 the southern states were exporting as much tobacco as they had been before the Revolution. Most important, however, was the surge in cotton production. Between 1790 and 1815 the annual production of cotton rose from less than 3 million pounds to 93 million pounds.

Overall, the United States in 1790 was predominantly a rural society. Eighty percent of households were involved in agricultural production. Only a few cities had more than 5,000 residents. The first national census, taken in 1790, counted 750,000 African Americans, almost one fifth of the population. Most of them lived in the five southernmost states; less than 10 percent lived outside the South. Most African Americans, of course, were enslaved, but there were many free blacks as a result of the Revolution. In fact, the proportion of free to enslaved blacks was never higher than in 1790.

The 1790 census did not even count the many Indians still living east of the Mississippi River. Most Americans viewed the Native Americans as those people whom the Declaration of Independence had dismissed as "merciless Indian Savages." It is estimated that there were over eighty tribes totaling perhaps as many as 150,000 persons in 1790. In the Old Northwest along the Great Lakes, the British continued to arm the Indians and encouraged them to resist American encroachments. Between 1784 and 1790 Indians killed or captured some 1,500 settlers in Kentucky alone. Such bloodshed generated a ferocious reaction. "The people of Kentucky," observed an official frustrated by his inability to negotiate a treaty between whites and Indians, "will carry on private expeditions against the Indians and kill them whenever they meet them, and I do not believe there is a jury in all Kentucky that will punish a man for it." In the South the five most powerful tribes—the Cherokees, Chickasaws, Choctaws, Creeks, and Seminoles—numbered between 50,000 and 100,000. They steadfastly refused to recognize U.S. authority and used Spanish-supplied weapons to thwart white settlement.

Only about 125,000 whites and blacks lived west of the Appalachian Mountains in 1790. But that was soon to change. The great theme of nineteenth-century American history would be the ceaseless stream of migrants flowing westward from the Atlantic seaboard. By foot, horse, boat, and wagon, pioneers and adventurers headed west. Kentucky, still part of Virginia but destined for statehood in 1792, harbored 75,000 settlers in 1790. In 1776 there had been only 150 pioneers there. Rapid population growth, cheap land, and new economic opportunities fueled the western migration. The average white woman gave birth to eight children, and the white population doubled approximately every twenty-two years. This made for a very young population on average. In 1790 almost half of all white Americans were under the age of sixteen.

A NEW GOVERNMENT   The men who drafted the Constitution knew that many questions were left unanswered, and they feared that putting the new frame of government into practice would pose unexpected challenges. On the appointed date, March 4, 1789, the new Congress of the United States, meeting in New York City, could muster only eight senators and thirteen representatives. A month passed before both chambers gathered a quorum. Only then could the temporary presiding officer of the Senate count the ballots and certify the foregone conclusion that George Washington, with sixty-nine votes, was the unanimous choice of the Electoral College for president. John Adams, with thirty-four votes, the second-highest number, became vice president.

Washington was a reluctant president. He greeted the news of his election with "a heart filled with distress" because he imagined "the ten thousand embarrassments, perplexities and troubles to which I must again be exposed." He told a friend as he prepared to assume office in New York that he felt like a "culprit who is going to the place of his execution." Yet Washington felt compelled to serve because he had been "summoned by my country." A self-made man with little formal education, he brought to his new office a remarkable capacity for moderation and mediation that helped keep the infant republic from disintegrating. In his inaugural address, Washington appealed for national unity, pleading with the new Congress to abandon "local prejudices" and "party animosities" in order to create the "national" outlook necessary for the fledgling republic to thrive. Within a few months the new president would see his hopes dashed. Personal rivalries, sectional tensions, and partisan conflict characterized political life in the 1790s.

THE GOVERNMENT'S STRUCTURE   President Washington had a larger staff at his Mount Vernon estate than he did as president. During the summer of 1789, Congress created executive departments corresponding to those formed under the Confederation. To head the Department of State, Washington named Thomas Jefferson, recently back from his diplomatic duties in France. To head the Department of the Treasury, Washington picked his devoted wartime aide, Alexander Hamilton, now a prominent lawyer in New York. The new position of attorney general was occupied by Edmund Randolph, former governor of Virginia.

Almost from the beginning, Washington routinely called these men to sit as a group to discuss matters of policy. This was the origin of the president's cabinet, an advisory body for which the Constitution made no formal provision. The office of vice president also took on what would become its typical character. "The Vice-Presidency," John Adams wrote his wife, Abigail, is the most "insignificant office . . . ever . . . contrived."

The structure of the court system, like that of the executive departments, was left to Congress, except for a chief justice and the Supreme Court. Congress determined to set the membership of the highest court at six—the chief justice and five associates—and it created thirteen federal district courts. From these, appeals might go to one of three circuit courts, composed of two Supreme Court justices and the district judge, who met twice a year in each district. Members of the Supreme Court, therefore, became itinerant judges riding the circuit during a good part of the year. All federal cases originated in a district court and, if appealed on issues of procedure or legal interpretation, went to the circuit courts and from there to the Supreme Court.

Washington named John Jay as the first chief justice of the Supreme Court, and he served until 1795. Born in New York City in 1745, Jay graduated from King's College (now Columbia University). His distinction as a lawyer led New York to send him as its representative to the First and Second Continental Congresses. After serving as president of the Continental Congress in 1778–1779, Jay became the American minister in Spain. While in Europe he helped John Adams and Benjamin Franklin negotiate the Treaty of Paris in 1783. After the Revolution, Jay served as secretary of foreign affairs. He joined Madison and Hamilton as co-author of the *The Federalist* and became one of the most effective champions of the Constitution.

John Jay

Chief justice of the Supreme Court (painted in 1794). Jay favored a strong union and emphatically supported the Constitution.

THE BILL OF RIGHTS In the new House of Representatives, James Madison made a bill of rights a top priority. The lack of provisions guaranteeing individuals' and states' rights had been one of the anti-Federalists' major objections to the Constitution. Madison viewed a bill of rights as "the most dramatic single gesture of conciliation that could be offered the remaining opponents of the government." Those "opponents" included prominent statesmen as well as artisans, small traders, and backcountry farmers who doubted that even the "best men" were capable of subordinating self-interest to the good of the republic. They believed that all people are prone to corruption; that no one can be trusted. Therefore, a bill of rights must be added to the Constitution protect the liberties of all against the encroachments of a few.

The first eight Amendments to the Constitution were modeled after the Virginia Declaration of Rights that George Mason had written in 1776. They provided safeguards for specified rights of individuals: freedom of religion, press, speech, and assembly; the right to keep and bear firearms; the right to refuse to house soldiers in private homes; protection against unreasonable searches and seizures; the right to refuse to testify against oneself; the right to a speedy public trial, with legal counsel present, before an impartial jury; and protection against cruel and unusual punishment.

The Ninth and Tenth Amendments addressed the demand for specific statements that the enumeration of rights in the Constitution "shall not be construed to deny or disparage others retained by the people" and that "powers not delegated to the United States by the Constitution, nor prohibited by it to the States, are reserved to the States respectively, or to the people." The first ten amendments, which constitute the Bill of Rights, became effective on December 15, 1791. The Bill of Rights provided no rights or legal protection to African Americans or Indians.

RAISING REVENUE   Revenue was the new federal government's most critical need. When George Washington took office, the nation's finances were in shambles. There was an acute shortage of capital. To raise funds, Madison proposed a modest tariff (a tax on imports) for revenue only, but the demands of manufacturers in the northern states for tariffs high enough to protect them from foreign competition forced a compromise that imposed higher tariffs on specified items. Madison linked the tariff to a proposal for a mercantile system that would levy extra tonnage duties on foreign ships, and an especially heavy duty on countries that had no commercial treaty with the United States.

Madison's goal was to wage economic war against Great Britain, which had no such treaty but more foreign trade with the new nation than any other country. Northern businessmen, however, fearing any disruption in the economy, were in no mood for a renewal of economic pressures. Hamilton, as secretary of the Treasury, agreed with them. In the end the only discrimination built into the Tonnage Act of 1789 was between U.S. and all foreign ships: U.S. ships paid a duty of 6¢ per ton; American-built foreign-owned ships paid 30¢; and ships that were foreign built and owned paid 50¢ per ton.

The disagreements created by the trade measures were portents of quarrels yet to come. Should economic policy favor Britain or France? The more persistent question was whether tariff and tonnage duties should penalize farmers in the interest of northern manufacturers and shipowners. By imposing a tax on imports, tariffs and tonnage duties resulted in higher prices on goods bought by Americans, most of whom were tied to the farm economy. This raised a basic and perennial question: should rural consumers be forced to subsidize the nation's infant manufacturing sector? This issue became a sectional question of South versus North.

Hamilton's Vision

The tariff and tonnage duties, linked as they were to other issues, marked but the beginning of the effort to get the country on sound fiscal footing. In 1789, thirty-four-year-old Alexander Hamilton seized the initiative. The first secretary of the Treasury was a protégé of the president. Born out of wedlock on a Caribbean island and deserted by his ne'er-do-well Scottish father, Hamilton was left an orphan at thirteen by the death of his mother and soon became a clerk in a trading house. With the help of friends and relatives, he found his way, at seventeen, to New York, attended King's College, and entered the Continental army, where he became a favorite aide of George Washington's. After the war he studied law, passed the bar examination, established a thriving legal practice in New York City, and became a self-made aristocrat, serving as a collector of revenues and as a member of the Confederation Congress. An early convert to nationalism, Hamilton had a major role in promoting the Constitutional Convention. Shrewd, energetic, determined and combative, the red-haired, blue-eyed attorney was consumed with social and political ambition. As he recognized at age fourteen, "To confess my weakness, my ambition is prevalent." The same could be said of most of the Founding Fathers.

During the Revolutionary War, Colonel Hamilton had witnessed the near-fatal weaknesses of the Confederation Congress. Its lack of authority and money almost lost the war. Now, as the nation's first secretary of the Treasury, he was determined to transform an economically weak and fractious nation. To flourish in a warring world, Hamilton believed, the United States needed to unleash the energy and ambition of its citizens so as to create a vibrant economy driven by the engines of capitalism. He wanted to nurture the

Alexander Hamilton

Secretary of the Treasury from 1789 to 1795.

hustling, bustling, aspiring spirit that he believed distinguished Americans from others. Just as he had risen from poverty and shame to become immensely successful, he wanted to ensure that Americans would always have such opportunities. To do so, he envisioned a limited but assertive government that encouraged new fields of enterprise and fostered investment and entrepreneurship. Thriving markets and new industries would best ensure the fate of the republic, and a secure federal debt would give investors a stake in the success of the new national government. The young Hamilton was supremely confident in his ability to shape fiscal policies that would provide economic opportunity and ensure government stability. His success in minting a budget, a funded debt, a federal tax system, a national bank, a customs service, and a coast guard provided the foundations for American capitalism and American government.

In a series of brilliant reports submitted to Congress in the two years from January 1790 to December 1791, Hamilton outlined his far-sighted program for government finances and the economic development of the United States. The reports were soon adopted, with some alterations in detail but little in substance. The last of the series, the "Report on Manufactures," outlined a program of protective tariffs and other government supports of business, which would eventually become government policy, despite much brave talk of free enterprise and free trade.

ESTABLISHING THE PUBLIC CREDIT Hamilton submitted the first and most important of his reports to the House of Representatives in 1790. This first of two "Reports on Public Credit," as the work has since been called, dealt with the vexing issue of war-generated debt. Both the federal government and the individual states had emerged from the Revolution with substantial debts. France, Spain, and Holland had lent the United States money and matériel to fight the war, and Congress had incurred more debt by printing paper money and selling government bonds. State governments had also accumulated huge obligations. After the war some states had set about paying off their debts, but the efforts were uneven. Only the federal government could wipe the slate clean. Hamilton insisted that the debts from the Revolution were a *national* responsibility because all Americans had benefited from independence. He also knew that federal assumption of state debts would enhance a sense of nationalism by helping the people see the benefits of a strong central government. Finally, the Treasury secretary was determined to shore up the federal government's finances because he believed that preserving individual freedom and the sanctity of property went hand in hand.

Hamilton's controversial report on public credit made two key recommendations: first, it called for funding the federal debt at face value, which meant that citizens holding deflated war bonds could exchange them for new interest-bearing bonds, and second, it declared that the federal government should assume state debts from the Revolution. Holders of state bonds would exchange them for new national bonds.

The funding scheme was controversial because many farmers and farmer soldiers in immediate need of money had sold their securities for a fraction of their value to speculators who were eager to buy them up after reading Hamilton's first report. These common folk argued that they should be reimbursed for their losses; otherwise, the speculators would gain a windfall from the new government's funding of bonds at face value. Hamilton sternly resisted their pleas. The speculators, he argued, had "paid what the commodity was worth in the market, and took the risks." Therefore, they should reap the benefits. In fact, Hamilton insisted, the government should favor the financial community because it represented the bedrock of a successful nation.

The report sparked lengthy debates before its substance was adopted. Then, in short order, Hamilton authored three more reports: the second of the "Reports on Public Credit," which included a proposal for an excise tax on liquor to aid in raising revenue to cover the nation's debts, a report recommending the establishment of a national bank and a national mint, which were set up in 1791–1792; and the "Report on Manufactures," which proposed an extensive program of government aid and other encouragement to stimulate the development of manufacturing enterprises.

Hamilton's economic program was substantially the one that Robert Morris had urged upon the Confederation a decade before and Hamilton had strongly endorsed at the time. "A national debt," he had written Morris in 1781, "if it is not excessive, will be to us a national blessing; it will be a powerful cement of our union. It will also create a necessity for keeping up taxation to a degree which without being oppressive, will be a spur to industry."

Payment of the national debt, in short, would be not only a point of national honor and sound finance, ensuring the country's credit for the future; it would also be an occasion to assert the federal power of taxation and thus instill respect for the authority of the national government. Not least, the plan would win the new government the support of wealthy, influential creditors who would now have a direct financial stake in the survival of the government.

THE EMERGENCE OF SECTIONAL DIFFERENCES The Virginian James Madison, who had been Hamilton's close ally in promoting ratification of the Constitution, broke with him over the matter of a national debt. Madison did not question whether the debt should be paid; he was troubled, however, that speculators and stockjobbers would become the chief beneficiaries. That the far greater portion of the debt was owed to northerners than to southerners further troubled him. Madison, whom Hamilton had expected to champion his program in the House, advanced an alternative plan, one that gave a larger share to the first owners of government bonds than to the later speculators. Madison's opposition to Hamilton's plan touched off a vigorous debate, but Hamilton carried his point by a margin of three to one when the House brought it to a vote.

Madison's opposition to the assumption of state debts got more support, however, and more clearly set up a political division along sectional lines. The southern states, with the exception of South Carolina, had whittled down their debts. New England, with the largest unpaid debts, stood to be the greatest beneficiary of the assumption plan. Rather than see Virginia victimized, Madison held out another alternative. Why not, he suggested, have the government assume state debts as they stood in 1783, at the conclusion of the peace treaty? Debates on this point deadlocked the whole question of debt funding and assumption, and Hamilton grew so frustrated with the legislative stalemate that he considered resigning.

The gridlock finally ended in the summer of 1790, when Jefferson, Hamilton, and Madison agreed to a compromise. In return for northern votes in favor of locating the permanent national capital on the Potomac River, Madison pledged to seek enough southern votes to pass the assumption, with the further arrangement that those states with smaller debts would get in effect outright grants from the federal government to equalize the difference. With these arrangements enough votes were secured to carry Hamilton's funding and assumption schemes. The national capital would be moved from New York City to Philadelphia for ten years, after which it would be settled at a federal city on the Potomac, the site to be chosen by the president. Jefferson later claimed to have been "duped" by Hamilton into agreeing to the "Compromise of 1790" because he did not fully understand the implications of the debt-assumption plan. It is more likely that Jefferson had been outsmarted. He only later realized how relatively insignificant the location of the national capital was when compared with the far-reaching effects of Hamilton's economic program.

A NATIONAL BANK   By this vast new financial program, Hamilton had called up from nowhere, as if by magic, a great sum of capital for the federal government. Having established the public credit, the relentless Hamilton moved on to a related measure essential to his vision of national greatness: a national bank, which by issuance of bank notes (paper money) might provide a uniform currency that would address the chronic shortage of gold and silver. Government bonds held by the bank would back up the value of its new bank notes. The national bank, chartered by Congress, would remain under government control, but private investors would supply four fifths of the $10 million capital and name twenty of the twenty-five directors; the government would provide the other one fifth of the capital and name five directors. Government bonds would be received in payment for three

The Bank of the United States

Proposed by Alexander Hamilton, the bank opened in Philadelphia in 1791.

fourths of the stock in the bank, and the other fourth would be payable in gold and silver.

The bank, Hamilton explained, would serve many purposes. Like the national banks of Europe, it would provide a stable and flexible national currency and a source of capital for loans to fund the development of business and commercial development. Bonds, which might otherwise be stowed away in safes, would become the basis for a productive capital by backing up bank notes available for loan at low rates of interest, the "natural effect" of which would be "to increase trade and industry." What is more, the existence of the bank would serve certain housekeeping needs of the government: a safe place to keep its funds, a source of "pecuniary aids" in sudden emergencies, and the ready transfer of funds to and from branch offices through bookkeeping entries rather than the shipment of metals.

Once again James Madison rose to lead the opposition, arguing that he could find no basis in the Constitution for a national bank. That was enough to raise in President Washington's mind serious doubts as to the constitutionality of the measure, which Congress passed fairly quickly over Madison's objections. The vote in Congress revealed the growing sectional division in the young United States. Representatives from the northern states voted thirty-three to one in favor of the national bank; southern congressmen opposed the bank nineteen to six.

Before signing the bill into law, President Washington sought the advice of his cabinet, where he found an equal division of opinion. The result was the first great debate on constitutional interpretation. Should there be a strict or a broad construction of the document? Were the powers of Congress only those explicitly stated, or were others implied? The argument turned chiefly on Article I, Section 8, which authorizes Congress to "make all Laws which shall be necessary and proper for carrying into Execution the foregoing Powers."

Such language left room for disagreement and led to a confrontation between Jefferson and Hamilton. Secretary of State Jefferson pointed to the Tenth Amendment, which reserves to the states and the people powers not delegated to Congress. "To take a single step beyond the boundaries thus specially drawn around the powers of Congress," he wrote, "is to take possession of a boundless field of power, no longer susceptible of any definition." A bank might be a convenient aid to Congress in collecting taxes and regulating the currency, but it was not, as Article I, Section 8, specified, *necessary.*

In a lengthy report to the president, Hamilton countered that the power to charter corporations was included in the sovereignty of any government, whether or not expressly stated. And in a classic summary he expressed his criterion on constitutionality:

> This criterion is the *end,* to which the measure relates as a *mean.* If the *end* be clearly comprehended within any of the specified powers, collecting taxes and regulating the currency, and if the measure have an obvious relation to that *end,* and is not forbidden by any particular provision of the Constitution, it may safely be deemed to come within the compass of the national authority.

Hamilton's sophisticated analysis convinced Washington to sign the controversial bank bill. In doing so, the president had indeed, in Jefferson's words, opened up "a boundless field of power," which in the coming years would lead to a further broadening of implied powers with the approval of the Supreme Court. Under the leadership of Chief Justice John Marshall the Court would eventually adopt Hamilton's words almost verbatim. On July 4, 1791, stock in the new Bank of the United States was put up for sale, and it sold out within an hour.

ENCOURAGING MANUFACTURES Alexander Hamilton's fertile imagination and his audacious ambitions for the new country were not yet exhausted. In the last of his great reports, the "Report on Manufactures," he set in place the capstone of his design for a modern national economy: the active encouragement of manufacturing to provide productive uses for the new capital created by his funding, assumption (of state debts), and banking schemes. Hamilton believed that several advantages would flow from the aggressive development of manufactures: the diversification of labor in a country given over too much to farming; improved productivity through greater use of machinery; paid work for those not ordinarily employed outside the home, such as women and children; the promotion of immigration; a greater scope for the diversity of talents in business; more ample and various opportunities for entrepreneurial activity; and a better domestic market for agricultural products.

To secure his ends, Hamilton proposed to use the means to which other countries had resorted: tariffs (taxes) on foreign goods, or in Hamilton's words, "protecting duties," which in some cases might be put so high as to deter imports altogether; restraints on the export of raw materials; government-paid bounties and premiums to encourage certain industries; tariff exemptions for imported raw materials needed for American manufacturing; the encouragement of inventions and discoveries; regulations for the

Certificate of the New York Mechanick Society

An illustration of the growing diversification of labor, by Abraham Godwin (ca. 1785).

inspection of commodities; and finally, the financing of improvements in transportation, including the development of roads, canals, and rivers.

Some of Hamilton's tariff proposals were enacted in 1792. Otherwise the program was filed away—but not forgotten. It became an arsenal of arguments for the advocates of manufactures in years to come. Hamilton denied that there was any necessary economic conflict between the northern and southern regions of the Union. If, as seemed likely, the northern and middle Atlantic states should become the chief scenes of manufacturing, they would create robust markets for agricultural products, some of which the southern states were peculiarly qualified to produce. Both North and South would benefit, he argued, as more commerce moved between those regions than across the Atlantic, thus strengthening the Union.

HAMILTON'S ACHIEVEMENT   Largely owing to the skillful Hamilton, the Treasury Department began to retire the Revolutionary War debt during the early 1790s, and foreign capital began to flow in once again. Economic growth, so elusive in the 1780s, was widespread by the end of the century. A Bostonian reported in late 1790 that the United States had never "had a brighter sunshine of prosperity. . . . Our agricultural interest smiles, our commerce is blessed, our manufactures flourish." But Hamilton's policies had done much more than revive the economy. Against fierce opposition, Hamilton had established the foundations for a capitalist republic that has since demonstrated its resilience and durability. In the process he helped Americans see beyond their local interests. Hamilton was a consummate nationalist. As an immigrant he never developed the intense loyalty to a state felt by most Americans. And during the Revolutionary War he had seen how shortsighted and selfish states could be in refusing to provide adequate support of the Continental army. He dreamed of the United States' becoming a commercial and industrial empire, a world power remarkable for its ability to balance individual freedom with government power. As he recognized, "Liberty may be endangered by the abuses of liberty as well as by the abuses of power."

Yet however profound Hamilton's economic insights were and however beneficial his policies were to the nation's long-term economic development, they initially provoked fierce opposition. Hamilton admired the British system of government and professed a cynical view of human nature. People, he believed, were naturally selfish and greedy. The role of government, therefore, was to channel the public's "ambition and avarice" into activities that would strengthen the nation. Like Adam Smith, the Scotsman who wrote *The Wealth of Nations,* Hamilton believed that private vices could be turned into public virtues through the natural operations of the capitalist marketplace. What he did not acknowledge was that the rich do not always choose the national interest over their own. He persistently displayed a naïve faith in merchants and capitalists. By championing industry and commerce as well as the expansion of federal authority at the expense of the states, Hamilton infuriated a growing number of people, especially in the South. Competition between Jefferson and Hamilton boiled over into a nasty feud between the government's two most talented men. The concerted opposition to Hamilton's politics and policies soon fractured George Washington's cabinet and spawned the nation's first political parties.

THE REPUBLICAN ALTERNATIVE

Hamilton's ideas became the foundation of the party known as the Federalists; Madison and Jefferson led those who took the name Republicans (also called the Democratic Republicans) and thereby implied that the Federalists aimed at a monarchy. Neither side in the disagreement over national policy deliberately set out to create a party system. But there were growing differences of both philosophy and self-interest that would not subside. At the outset, Madison assumed leadership of Hamilton's opponents in Congress. Madison, like Thomas Jefferson, was rooted in Virginia, where opposition to Hamilton's economic policies flourished. Patrick Henry, for example, proclaimed that Hamilton's policies were "dangerous to the rights and subversive of the interests of the people."

After the Compromise of 1790, which assured the federal assumption of state debts, Madison and Jefferson ever more resolutely opposed Hamilton's policies: his effort to place an excise tax on whiskey, which laid a burden especially on the trans-Appalachian farmers, whose livelihood depended upon the production and sale of the beverage; his proposal for the national bank; and his "Report on Manufactures." As the differences built, hostility between Jefferson and Hamilton festered within the cabinet, much to the distress of President Washington.

Thomas Jefferson, twelve years Hamilton's senior, was in most respects his opposite. Jefferson was an agrarian aristocrat, his father a successful surveyor and land speculator, his mother a Randolph, from one of the first families of Virginia. Jefferson was brilliant. He developed a breadth of cultivated interests that ranged widely in science, the arts, and the humanities. He read or spoke seven languages. He was an architect of distinction (Monticello, the Virginia state capitol, and the University of Virginia are monuments to his talent), a courtly gentleman who understood mathematics and engineering, an inventor, and an agronomist. He knew music and practiced the violin, although one wit remarked that only Patrick Henry played it worse.

Thomas Jefferson

A portrait by Charles Willson Peale (1791).

Hamilton and Jefferson represented opposite visions of the character of the Union and defined certain contrasting philosophical and political issues that still echo more than two centuries later. Hamilton was a hardheaded realist who foresaw a diversified capitalist economy, with agriculture balanced by commerce and industry, and was thus the better prophet. Jefferson was an agrarian idealist who feared that the growth of crowded cities would divide society into a capitalist aristocracy on the one hand and a deprived proletariat on the other. Hamilton feared anarchy and loved order; Jefferson feared tyranny and loved liberty.

Hamilton championed a strong central government actively engaged in encouraging capitalist enterprise. Jefferson wanted a decentralized republic made up primarily of small farmers. "Those who labor in the earth," he wrote, "are the chosen people of God, if ever he had a chosen people, whose breasts He has made His peculiar deposit for genuine and substantial virtue." Jefferson did not oppose all forms of manufacturing; he feared that the unlimited expansion of commerce and industry would produce a growing class of wage laborers who were dependent upon others for their livelihood and therefore subject to political manipulation and economic exploitation.

In their quarrel, Hamilton isolated Jefferson as the leader of the opposition to his policies. In the summer of 1791, Jefferson and Madison set out on a "botanizing" excursion up the Hudson River in New York and into New England. The supposed vacation trip was actually a cover for consultations with New York political figures who personally and politically opposed Hamilton. Although the significance of that single trip was blown out of proportion, there did ultimately arise an informal alliance of Jeffersonian Republicans in the South and New York that would become a constant if sometimes divisive feature of the new party and its successor, the Democratic party. By mid-1792 Hamilton and Jefferson could no longer disguise their disdain for each other. Jefferson told a friend that the two rivals "daily pitted in the cabinet like two cocks."

Still, amid the rising political tensions, there was little opposition to George Washington, who longed to end his exile from his beloved Mount Vernon and even began drafting a farewell address but was urged by both Hamilton and Jefferson to continue in public life. In the fragile infancy of the new nation, Washington was the only man who could transcend party differences and hold things together with his unmatched prestige. In 1792 Washington was unanimously reelected.

CRISES FOREIGN AND DOMESTIC

During George Washington's second term the problems of foreign relations surged to center stage, delivered by the consequences of the French Revolution, which had begun in 1789, during the first months of his presidency.

Americans followed the tumultuous events in France with almost universal sympathy, up to a point. By the spring of 1792, the French experiment in liberty, equality, and fraternity had transformed itself into a monster. France plunged into war with Austria and Prussia. The French Revolution began devouring its own children, along with its enemies, during the Terror of 1793–1794. Thousands of political prisoners were executed, and barbarism ruled the streets of Paris.

After the execution of King Louis XVI, early in 1793, Great Britain and Spain entered into the coalition of monarchies at war with the chaotic French republic. For the next twenty-two years, Britain and France were at war, with only a brief respite, until the final defeat of the French forces under Napoléon in 1815. The European war presented George Washington, just beginning his second term, with an awkward decision. By the 1778 Treaty of Alliance, the United States was a perpetual ally of France, obligated to defend her possessions in the West Indies.

But Americans wanted no part of the European war. They were determined to maintain their lucrative trade with both sides in the conflict. And besides, the Americans had no navy with which to wage a war on the high seas. Neutrality was the only sensible policy. For their part, Hamilton and Jefferson found in the neutrality policy one issue on which they could agree. Where they differed was in how best to implement it. Hamilton had a simple and direct answer: declare the French alliance invalid because it was made with a French government that no longer existed. Jefferson preferred to delay and use the alliance as a bargaining point with the British. In the end, however, Washington followed the advice of neither. Taking a middle course, the president issued a neutrality proclamation on April 22, 1793, that declared the United States "friendly and impartial toward the belligerent powers" and warned U.S. citizens that "aiding or abetting hostilities" or other nonneutral acts might be prosecuted. Instead of settling matters in his cabinet, however, Washington's proclamation brought to a boil the feud between Hamilton and Jefferson. Jefferson dashed off an angry letter to James Madison, urging his ally to "take up your pen" and cut Hamilton "to pieces" in the newspapers.

CITIZEN GENET   At the same time, Washington accepted Jefferson's argument that the United States should recognize the new French republican government (becoming the first country to do so) and receive its new ambassador, the headstrong and indiscreet Edmond-Charles-Édouard Genet. Early in 1793, Citizen Genet landed at Charleston, to a hero's welcome. Along the route to Philadelphia, the enthusiasm of his American sympathizers gave the swaggering Genet an inflated notion of his influence. In Charleston he had engaged privateers to capture British ships, and in Philadelphia he continued the process. He also intrigued with frontiersmen and land speculators with an eye to an attack on Spanish Florida and Louisiana.

In the American capital, Genet quickly became an embarrassment even to his Republican friends. Among other missteps he denounced President Washington's neutrality policy. Jefferson decided that the French minister had overreached himself when he violated a promise not to outfit a captured British ship as a French privateer—the action could have provoked a British declaration of war against the United States. When Genet threatened to appeal his cause directly to the American people over the head of their president, the cabinet unanimously agreed that the French troublemaker had to go; in August 1793 Washington demanded his recall. Meanwhile, a new party of radicals had gained power in France and sent its own minister with a warrant for Genet's arrest. Instead of returning to Paris and risk the guillotine, Genet sought asylum in the United States.

Genet's foolishness and the growing excesses of the French radicals were fast cooling U.S. support for their wayward revolution. To Hamilton's followers what was occurring in France began to resemble their worst nightmares of democratic anarchy. The French made it hard even for American Republicans to retain sympathy, but they swallowed hard and made excuses. "The liberty of the whole earth was depending on the issue of the contest," the genteel Jefferson wrote, "and . . . rather than it should have failed, I would have seen half the earth devastated." Nor did the British make it easy for Federalists to rally to their side. Near the end of 1793, they informed the U.S. government that they intended to occupy their Great Lakes forts indefinitely and began to seize the cargoes of American ships trading with the French islands in the West Indies.

The French and British causes deeply divided American opinion. In the contest, it seemed, one had to either be a Republican and support liberty, reason, and France or become a Federalist and support order, religious faith, and Britain. The division gave rise to curious loyalties: slaveholding planters joined the cheers for radical revolutionaries who dispossessed aristocrats in France, and they supported the protest against British seizures of New England ships; Massachusetts shippers still profited from the British trade and kept quiet. Boston, once a hotbed of revolution, became a bastion of Federalism. Thomas Jefferson was so disgusted by George Washington's refusal to support the French Revolution and by his own ideological warfare with Alexander Hamilton that he resigned as secretary of state at the end of 1793.

JAY'S TREATY   By 1794 a prolonged foreign-policy crisis between the United States and Great Britain threatened to renew warfare between the two old enemies. Early in 1794 the Republican leaders in Congress were gaining support for commercial retaliation to end British trade abuses when the British gave President Washington a timely opening for a settlement. They stopped seizing American ships, and on April 16, 1794, Washington named Chief Justice John Jay as a special envoy to Great Britain. Jay left with instructions to settle all major issues: to get the British out of the northwestern forts and to secure reparations for the losses of American shippers, compensation for Southern slaves carried away in 1783, and a commercial treaty that would legalize American commerce with the British West Indies.

To win his objectives, Jay accepted the British definition of neutral rights—that exports of tar, pitch, and other products needed for naval ships were contraband and that provisions could not go in neutral ships to enemy ports—and the "rule of 1756" prevailed, meaning that trade that was prohibited in peacetime because of mercantilist restrictions could not be opened in wartime. Britain also gained most-favored-nation treatment in American commerce and a promise that French privateers would not be outfitted in American ports. Finally, Jay conceded that the British need not compensate U.S. citizens for the enslaved people who escaped during the war and that the pre-Revolutionary American debts to British merchants would be paid by the U.S. government. In return for these concessions, he won three important points: British evacuation of the northwestern forts by 1796, reparations for the seizures of American ships and cargo in 1793–1794, and legalization of trade with the British West Indies. But the last of these (Article XII) was so hedged with restrictions that the Senate eventually struck it from the treaty.

Trade Limitations

A 1794 watercolor of Fort Detroit, a major center of Indian trade that the British agreed to evacuate under the terms of Jay's Treaty.

Public outrage greeted the terms of Jay's Treaty. The debate was so intense that some Americans feared civil war might erupt. Even Federalist shippers, ready for a settlement with the British on almost any terms, were disappointed by the limitations on their trading privileges in the British West Indies. But much of the outcry was simply an expression of disappointment by Republican partisans who had sought an escalation of the conflict with the hated Great Britain. Some of it, too, was the outrage of Virginia planters at the concession on old debts to British merchants and the failure to get reparations for slaves liberated by British forces during the Revolution. George Washington himself wrestled with doubts over the treaty and delayed making it available to the public. He worried that his opponents were prepared to separate "the Union into Northern & Southern." Once he endorsed it, there were even calls for his impeachment. Yet the president, while acknowledging that the proposed agreement was imperfect, concluded that adopting it was the only way to avoid war with Britain. Still, the Senate debated the treaty in secret, and without a single vote to spare, Jay's Treaty got the necessary two-thirds majority on June 24, 1795, with Article XII (the provision regarding the West Indies) expunged. The major votes in Congress were again aligned by region; 80 percent of the votes for the treaty came from New England or the middle Atlantic states; 74 percent of those voting against the treaty were cast by southerners.

President Washington still hesitated but finally signed the flawed treaty, concluding that it was the best he was likely to get. In the House, opponents, spurred on by James Madison, went so far as to demand that the president produce all papers relevant to the treaty, but the president refused on the grounds that approval of treaties was solely the business of the Senate. He thereby set an important precedent of executive privilege (a term not used at the time), and the House finally relented, supplying by a close vote the money required to carry out the terms of the treaty. The desperate effort to thwart Jay's Treaty cost James Madison his friendship with George Washington.

THE FRONTIER   Other events also had an important bearing on Jay's Treaty, adding force to the importance of its settlement of the Canadian frontier and strengthening Spain's conviction that it, too, needed to settle long-festering problems along America's southwestern frontier. While John Jay was haggling in London, frontier conflict with Indians escalated, with U.S. troops twice crushed by northwestern Indians. At last, Washington named General Wayne, known as Mad Anthony, to head an expedition into the Northwest Territory. In the fall of 1793, Wayne marched into Indian country

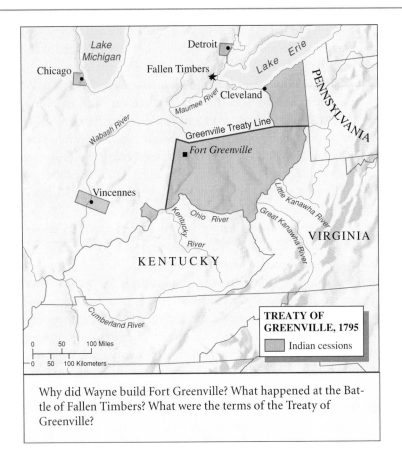

Why did Wayne build Fort Greenville? What happened at the Battle of Fallen Timbers? What were the terms of the Treaty of Greenville?

with some 2,600 men, built Fort Greenville, and with reinforcements from Kentucky went on the offensive in 1794.

In August some 2,000 Shawnee, Ottawa, Chippewa, and Potawatomi warriors, reinforced by Canadian militias, attacked Wayne's troops at the Battle of Fallen Timbers, south of Detroit. The Americans repulsed them. The Indians' heavy losses were exacerbated when American soldiers destroyed their fields and villages. The Indians finally agreed to the Treaty of Greenville, signed in August 1795. According to the terms of the treaty, the United States bought from twelve tribes, at the cost of a $10,000 annuity, the rights to the southeastern quarter of the Northwest Territory (now Ohio and Indiana) and enclaves at the sites of Detroit, Chicago, and Vincennes, Indiana.

THE WHISKEY REBELLION   General Wayne's forces were still mopping up after the Battle of Fallen Timbers when the administration resolved on another show of strength in the backcountry, against the so-called Whiskey Rebellion. Alexander Hamilton's excise tax on liquor, levied in 1791, had outraged frontier farmers because it taxed their most profitable commodity. During the eighteenth and early nineteenth centuries nearly all Americans regularly drank alcoholic beverages: beer, hard cider, ale, wine, rum, brandy, or whiskey. In the areas west of the Appalachian Mountains, the primary cash commodity was liquor distilled from grain or fruit. Such emphasis on distilling reflected a practical problem. Many farmers could not afford to transport bulky crops of corn and rye across the mountains or down the Mississippi River to the seaboard markets. Instead, it was much more profitable to distill liquor from corn and rye or apples and peaches. Unlike grain crops, distilled spirits could be easily stored, shipped, or sold— and at higher profits. A bushel of corn worth 25¢ could yield two and a half gallons of liquor, worth ten times as much.

Western farmers were also suspicious of the new federal government in Philadelphia. The frontiersmen considered the whiskey tax another part of Hamilton's scheme to pick the pockets of the poor to enrich the pockets of urban speculators. All through the backcountry, from Georgia to Pennsylvania and beyond, the tax provoked resistance and evasion.

In the summer of 1794, discontent over the federal tax on whiskey exploded into open rebellion in western Pennsylvania. Vigilantes began terrorizing revenue officers and taxpayers. They blew up the stills of those who paid the tax, robbed the mails, stopped court proceedings, and threatened an assault on Pittsburgh. On August 7, 1794, President Washington issued a proclamation ordering the insurgents home and calling out 12,900 militiamen from Virginia, Maryland, Pennsylvania, and New Jersey. Getting no response from the "Whiskey boys," he ordered the army to suppress the rebellion.

Under the command of General Henry Lee, the army marched out from Harrisburg across the Alleghenies with Alexander Hamilton in its midst, itching to smite the insurgents. But the rebels vanished into the hills, and the troops met with little opposition. They finally rounded up twenty barefoot, ragged prisoners, whom they paraded down Market Street in Philadelphia and clapped into prison. Eventually two of them were found guilty of treason, but they were pardoned by Washington on the grounds that one was a "simpleton" and the other "insane." Although Washington had overreacted, the government had made its point and gained "reputation and strength," according to Hamilton, by suppressing a rebellion that, according to Jefferson, "could never be found." The use of such excessive force, however, led many who sympathized with the frontiersmen to become Republicans, and Jefferson's party scored heavily in the next Pennsylvania elections.

Whiskey Rebellion

George Washington as commander in chief reviews the troops mobilized to quell the Whiskey Rebellion in 1794.

Nor was it the end of the whiskey rebellions, which continued in an unending war of wits between moonshiners and revenue officers.

PINCKNEY'S TREATY   While these stirring events were transpiring in Pennsylvania, Spanish intrigues among the Creeks, Choctaws, Chickasaws, and Cherokees in the Southwest were keeping up the same sort of turmoil that the British had fomented along the Ohio. In Tennessee, settlers reacted by burning and leveling Indian villages. The defeat of their Indian allies, combined with Britain's concessions in the north and worries about possible American intervention in Louisiana, led the Spanish to enter into treaty negotiations with the Americans. U.S. negotiator Thomas Pinckney pulled off a diplomatic triumph in 1795 when he won acceptance of a boundary at the

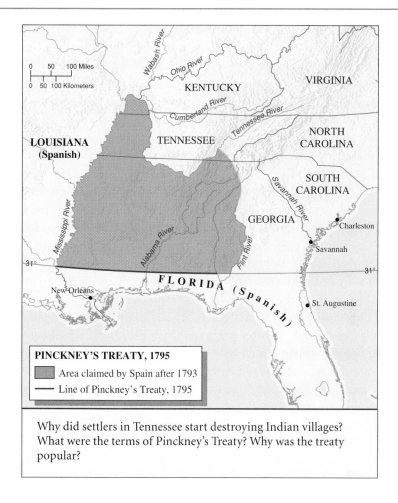

PINCKNEY'S TREATY, 1795

Area claimed by Spain after 1793
Line of Pinckney's Treaty, 1795

Why did settlers in Tennessee start destroying Indian villages? What were the terms of Pinckney's Treaty? Why was the treaty popular?

31st parallel, free navigation of the Mississippi River, the right to deposit goods at New Orleans for three years with a promise of renewal, a commission to settle American claims against Spain, and a promise on each side to refrain from inciting Indian attacks on the other. Ratification of Pinckney's Treaty ran into no opposition. In fact, it was immensely popular, especially among westerners eager to use the Mississippi River to transport their crops to market.

SETTLEMENT OF NEW LAND

Now that Jay and Pinckney had settled matters with Britain and Spain and the army in the Northwest and the Tennessee settlers in the South had subdued the Indians, the West was open for a renewed surge of settlers. New lands, ceded by the Indians in the Treaty of Greenville, revealed a Congress once again divided on the issue of federal land policy. There were two basic viewpoints on the matter: that the public domain should serve mainly as a source of revenue and that it was more important to get the new country settled, an endeavor that required low land prices. In the long run the evolution of policy would be from the first to the second viewpoint, but for the time being the federal government's need for revenue took priority.

LAND POLICY   Opinions on land policy, like opinions on other issues, separated Federalists from Republicans. Federalists involved in speculation might prefer lower land prices, but the more influential Federalists, like Hamilton and Jay, preferred to build the population of the eastern states first, lest the East lose political influence and a labor force important to the growth of manufactures. Men of their persuasion favored high land prices to enrich the Treasury, the sale of relatively large parcels of land to speculators rather than small parcels to settlers, and the development of compact settlements. Jefferson and Madison were reluctantly prepared to go along for the sake of reducing the national debt, but Jefferson expressed the hope for a plan by which the lands could be more readily settled. In any case, he suggested, frontiersmen would do as they had done before: "They will settle the lands in spite of everybody."

For the time being, however, Federalist policy prevailed. With the Land Act of 1796, Congress resolved to extend the rectangular surveys ordained in 1785 but doubled the price to $2 per acre, with only one year in which to complete payment. Half the townships would be sold in 640-acre sections, making the minimum cost $1,280, and alternate townships would be sold in blocks of eight sections, or 5,120 acres, making the minimum cost $10,240. Either price was well beyond the means of ordinary settlers and a bit much even for speculators, who could still pick up state lands at lower prices. By 1800 federal land offices had sold fewer than 50,000 acres under the act. Continuing criticism in the West led to the Land Act of 1800, which reduced the minimum unit to 320 acres and spread payments over four years. Thus, with a down payment of $160, one could buy a farm. All land went for the minimum price if it did not sell at auction within three weeks. Under the Land Act of 1804, the minimum unit was reduced to 160 acres, which became the traditional homestead, and the price per acre went down to $1.64.

THE WILDERNESS ROAD   The lure of western lands led thousands of settlers to follow Daniel Boone into the territory known as Kentucky or

The Emergence of Agriculture

This painting by Edward Hicks shows the residence of David Twining, a Pennsylvania farmer, as it appeared in 1785.

Kaintuck, from the Cherokee name Ken-Ta-Ke (Great Meadow). In the late eighteenth century, Kentucky was a farmer's fantasy and a hunter's paradise, with its fertile soil and abundant forests teeming with buffalo, deer, and wild turkeys.

Boone himself was the product of a pioneer background. Born on a small farm in 1734 in central Pennsylvania, he was a deadeye marksman by the age of twelve and would soon become an experienced farmer and an accomplished woodsman. In 1750 the Boone family moved to western North Carolina. There Daniel emerged as the region's greatest hunter, trading animal skins for salt and other household needs. After hearing numerous reports about the territory over the mountains, Boone set out alone in 1769 to find a trail into Kentucky. Armed with a long rifle, tomahawk, and hunting knife and dressed in a hunting shirt, deerskin leggings, and moccasins, he found what was called the

The Wilderness Trail

Daniel Boone Escorting Settlers through the Cumberland Gap by George Caleb Bingham.

Warriors' Path, a narrow foot trail that buffalo, deer, and Indians had worn along the steep ridges. It took him through the Cumberland Gap in southwestern Virginia. For two years thereafter, Boone explored the region, living off the plentiful game. He returned to North Carolina with exciting stories about the riches of Kentucky.

In 1773 Boone led the first group of settlers through the Appalachian Mountains at the Cumberland Gap. Two years later Boone and thirty woodsmen used axes to widen the Warriors' Path into what became known as the Wilderness Road, a passage that more than 300,000 settlers would use over the next twenty-five years. At a point where a branch of the Wilderness Road intersected with the Kentucky River, near what is now Lexington, Boone built a settlement known as Boonesborough in an area called Transylvania.

A steady stream of settlers, mostly Scotch-Irish from Pennsylvania, Virginia, and North Carolina, poured into Kentucky during the last quarter of the eighteenth century. The backcountry settlers came on foot or horseback, often leading a mule or a cow that carried their few tools and other possessions. On a good day they might cover fifteen miles. Near a creek or spring they would buy a parcel or stake out a claim and mark its boundaries by chopping notches into "witness trees." They would then build a lean-to for temporary shelter and clear the land for planting. The larger trees could not be felled with an ax. Instead, they were girdled: a cut would be made around the trunk, and the tree would be left to die. Because the process often took years, a farmer had to hoe and plant a field filled with stumps and trees. The pioneers grew melons, beans, turnips, and other vegetables, but corn was the preferred crop because it kept well and had so many uses. Ears were roasted and eaten on the cob, and kernels were ground into meal for making mush, hominy grits, and hoecakes, or johnnycakes (dry flourcakes suitable for travelers that were originally called journeycakes). Pigs provided pork, and cows supplied milk, butter, and cheese. Many frontier families also built crude stills to manufacture a potent whiskey they called corn likker.

TRANSFER OF POWER

By 1796 President Washington had decided that two terms in office were enough. Weary of increasingly bitter political quarrels and the venom of the partisan press, he was ready to retire at last to Mount Vernon. He would leave behind a formidable record of achievement: the organization of a national government with demonstrated power, a secure national credit, the recovery of territory from Britain and Spain, a stable northwestern frontier, and the admission of three new states: Vermont (1791), Kentucky (1792), and Tennessee (1796).

WASHINGTON'S FAREWELL   With the considerable help of Alexander Hamilton, Washington drafted a valedictory speech to the nation. His farewell address, dated September 17, 1796, called for unity among the people in backing their new government. Washington decried the rising spirit of sectionalism; he feared the emergence of regional political parties promoting local interests. In foreign relations, Washington said, the United States should show "good faith and justice toward all nations" and avoid either "an habitual hatred or an habitual fondness" for other countries. Europe, he noted, "has a set of primary interests which to us have none or a very remote relation. Hence she must be engaged in frequent controversies, the causes of

Mount Vernon

George Washington and the marquis de Lafayette at Mount Vernon in 1784. Washington enlarged the estate, which overlooks the Potomac River, to nearly 8,000 acres, dividing it among five farms.

which are essentially foreign to our concerns." The United States should keep clear of those quarrels. It was, moreover, "our true policy to steer clear of permanent alliances with any portion of the foreign world." A key word here is *permanent*. Washington opposed permanent arrangements like the one with France, still technically in effect. He specifically advised that "we may safely trust to temporary alliances for extraordinary emergencies." Washington's warning against permanent foreign entanglements served as a fundamental principle in U.S. foreign policy until the early twentieth century.

THE ELECTION OF 1796   With George Washington out of the race, the United States had its first partisan election for president. The logical choice of the Federalists would have been Washington's protégé, Alexander Hamilton, the chief architect of their programs. But Hamilton's policies had left scars and made enemies. Nor did he suffer fools gladly, a common affliction of Federalist leaders, including the man on whom the choice fell. In Philadelphia a caucus of Federalist congressmen chose John Adams as their heir apparent, with Thomas Pinckney of South Carolina, fresh from his triumph in Spain, as the nominee for vice president. As expected, the Republicans drafted Thomas Jefferson and added geographic balance to the ticket with Aaron Burr of New York.

The increasing strength of the Republicans, fueled by the smoldering resentment of Jay's Treaty, very nearly swept Jefferson into office and perhaps would have but for the public appeals of the French ambassador for his election—an action that backfired. Then, despite a Federalist majority among the electors, Alexander Hamilton hatched an impulsive scheme that very nearly threw the election away after all. Thomas Pinckney, Hamilton thought, would be subject to more influence than the strong-minded Adams. He therefore sought to have the South Carolina Federalists withhold a few votes for Adams and bring Pinckney in first. The Carolinians more than cooperated—they divided their vote between Pinckney and Jefferson—but the New Englanders got wind of the scheme and dropped Pinckney. The upshot of Hamilton's failed scheme was to cut Pinckney out of both the presidency and the vice presidency and elect Jefferson vice president with sixty-eight electoral votes, to Adams's seventy-one.

THE ADAMS YEARS

Vain and cantankerous, short and paunchy, John Adams had crafted a distinguished career as a Massachusetts lawyer; a leader in the Revolutionary movement; the hardest-working member of the Continental Congress; a diplomat in France, Holland, and Britain; and George Washington's vice president. His political philosophy fell somewhere between Jefferson's and Hamilton's. He shared neither the one's faith in the common people nor the other's fondness for a financial aristocracy of "paper wealth." Adams feared the concept of democracy and considered equality a fanciful notion. He favored the classic mixture of aristocratic, democratic, and monarchical elements, though his use of *monarchical* interchangeably with *executive* exposed him to the attacks of Republicans who saw a monarchist in every Federalist. Adams was always haunted by a feeling that

John Adams

Political philosopher and politician. Adams was the first president to take up residence in the White House, in 1801.

he was never properly appreciated—and he may have been right. Yet on the overriding issue of his administration, war and peace, he kept his head when others about him were losing theirs—probably at the cost of his reelection.

WAR WITH FRANCE   John Adams faced the daunting task of succeeding the most popular man in America. He also inherited an undeclared naval war with France, a byproduct of Jay's Treaty. When John Jay had accepted the British position that food supplies and naval stores—as well as war matériel— were contraband subject to seizure, the French reasoned that American cargo headed for British ports was subject to the same interpretation and loosed their corsairs in the British West Indies, with an even more devastating effect than the British had had in 1793–1794. By the time of Adams's inauguration, in 1797, the French had plundered some 300 American ships and broken diplomatic relations with the United States. As ambassador to Paris, James Monroe had become so pro-French and so hostile to Jay's Treaty that George Washington had removed him for his indiscretions. France, grown haughty and contemptuous with Napoléon's military conquests, had then refused to accept Monroe's replacement, Charles Cotesworth Pinckney (brother of Thomas Pinckney), and ordered him out of the country.

John Adams immediately acted to restore relations with France in the face of an outcry for war from the "high Federalists," including Secretary of State Timothy Pickering. Alexander Hamilton agreed with Adams on this point and approved his last-ditch effort for a diplomatic settlement. In 1797 Pinckney returned to Paris with John Marshall (a Virginia Federalist) and Elbridge Gerry (a Massachusetts Republican) for further negotiations. After nagging delays the three commissioners were accosted by three French counterparts (whom Adams labeled X, Y, and Z in his report to Congress), agents of France's unscrupulous foreign minister, Charles-Maurice de Talleyrand, a past master of the diplomatic shakedown. The French diplomats delicately let it be known that negotiations could begin only if the Americans paid a bribe of $250,000.

Such bribes were common eighteenth-century diplomatic practice, but Talleyrand's price was high for a mere promise to negotiate. The answer from the American side, according to the commissioners' report, was "no, no, not a sixpence." When the XYZ affair was reported in Congress and the

Conflict with France

A cartoon indicating the anti-French sentiment generated by the XYZ affair. The three American ministers (at left) reject the "Paris Monster's" demand for money.

public press, the response was translated into the more stirring slogan "Millions for defense but not one cent for tribute." Thereafter, the expressions of hostility toward France rose in a crescendo and even the most partisan Republicans—with the exception of Thomas Jefferson—were hard put to make any more excuses for the French, and many of them joined the cry for war. Yet President Adams resisted a formal declaration of war; the French would have to bear the onus for that. Congress, however, authorized the capture of armed French ships, suspended commerce with France, and renounced the 1778 Treaty of Alliance, which was already a dead letter.

In 1798 George Logan, a Pennsylvania Quaker and Republican sympathizer, visited Paris at his own expense, hoping to head off war. He did secure the release of some American seamen and won assurances that a new U.S. minister to France (ambassador) would be welcomed. The fruit of his mission, otherwise, was passage of the Logan Act (1799), which still forbids private citizens to negotiate with foreign governments without official authorization.

Amid a nation churning with patriotism and war fever, Adams strengthened American defenses. Militias marched and mobilized, and a navy began to emerge. An American navy had ceased to exist at the end of the Revolution. No armed ships were available when Algerian brigands began to prey on American commerce in 1794. As a result, Congress had authorized the arming of six ships. These were incomplete in 1796, when Washington bought peace with the Algerians, but Congress allowed work on three of them to continue: the *Constitution,* the *United States,* and the *Constellation,* all completed in 1797. In 1798 Congress authorized a Department of the Navy and by the end of the year an undeclared naval war had begun in the West Indies with the French capture of an American schooner.

While the naval war was being fought, Congress, in 1798, authorized a force of 10,000 men to serve three years. Adams called George Washington from retirement to be its commander, and Washington agreed only on condition that Alexander Hamilton be his second in command. Adams relented but resented the slight to his authority as commander in chief. The rift among the Federalists thus widened further.

Peace overtures began to come from the French by the autumn of 1798, before the naval war was fully under way. Adams took it upon himself, without consulting his cabinet, to name the U.S. minister to the Netherlands, William Vans Murray, as special envoy to Paris. The Hamiltonians, infected with a virulent case of war fever, fought the nomination but finally compromised, in the face of Adams's threat to resign, on a commission of three envoys. After a long delay the men left late in 1799 and arrived in France to find themselves confronting a new government under First Consul Napoléon

Bonaparte. By the Convention of 1800, they won the best terms they could from the triumphant Napoléon. In return for giving up all claims of indemnity for American losses, they got official suspension of the 1778 perpetual alliance with France and an end to the quasi war. The Senate ratified the agreement, contingent upon outright abrogation of the alliance, and it became effective on December 21, 1801.

THE WAR AT HOME   The simmering naval conflict with France mirrored a ferocious ideological war at home between Federalists and Republicans. Already-heated partisan politics had begun boiling over during the latter years of Washington's administration. The rhetoric grew so personal and tempers grew so short that opponents commonly resorted to duels. Federalists and Republicans saw each other as traitors to the principles of the American Revolution. Jefferson, for example, decided that Alexander Hamilton, George Washington, John Adams, and other Federalists were suppressing individual liberty in order to promote selfish interests. He adamantly opposed Jay's Treaty because it was pro-British and anti-French, and he was disgusted by the army's suppression of the Whiskey Rebellion.

Such volatile issues forced Americans to take sides, and the Revolutionary generation of leaders, a group that John Adams had called the band of brothers, began to fragment into die-hard factions. Long-standing political friendships disintegrated amid the partisan attacks, and sectional divisions between North and South grew more fractious. Jefferson observed that a "wall of separation" had come to divide the nation's political leaders. "Politics and party hatreds," he told his daughter, "destroy the happiness of every being here."

Jefferson's combative tactics contributed directly to the partisan tensions. He frequently planted rumors about his opponents in the press, wrote anonymous newspaper attacks himself, and asked others to disparage his opponents. As vice president under Adams, he displayed a gracious deviousness. He led the Republican faction opposed to Adams and actively schemed to embarrass him. In 1797 Jefferson secretly hired a rogue journalist, James Callender, to produce a scurrilous pamphlet that described President Adams as a deranged monarchist intent upon naming himself king. By the end of the century, Jefferson had become an ardent advocate of polarized party politics: "I hold it as immoral to pursue a middle line, as between parties of Honest men and Rogues, into which every country has divided."

For his part John Adams refused to align himself completely with the Federalists, preferring instead to mimic George Washington and retain his independence as chief executive. He was too principled and too prickly to toe a party line. Soon after his election he invited Jefferson to join with him in creating a bipartisan administration. After all, they had worked well together in the Continental Congress and in France, and they harbored great respect for each other. After consulting with James Madison, however, Jefferson refused to accept the new president's offer. Within a year he and Adams were at each other's throats. Adams expressed regret at losing Jefferson as a friend but "felt obliged to look upon him as a man whose mind is warped by prejudice." He had become "a child and the dupe" of the Republican faction in Congress, which was led by James Madison.

The conflict with France only deepened the partisan divide emerging in the young United States. The real purpose of the French crisis all along, the more ardent Republicans suspected, was to provide Federalists with an excuse to put down the domestic opposition. The infamous Alien and Sedition Acts of 1798 lent credence to their suspicions. These and two other acts, passed in the wave of patriotic war fever, limited freedom of speech and the press and the liberty of aliens. Proposed by extreme Federalists in Congress, the acts did not originate with John Adams but had his blessing. Goaded by his wife, Abigail, his primary counselor, Adams signed the controversial statutes and in doing so made the greatest mistake of his presidency. Timothy Pickering, his disloyal secretary of state, claimed that Adams acted without consulting "any member of the government and for a reason truly remarkable—because he knew we should all be opposed to the measure." By succumbing to the partisan hysteria and enacting the vindictive acts, Adams seemed to bear out what Benjamin Franklin had said about him years before: he "means well for his country, is always an honest man, often a wise one, but sometimes and in some things, [is] absolutely out of his senses."

Three of the four repressive acts reflected hostility to foreigners, especially the French and the Irish, a large number of whom had become active Republicans and were suspected of revolutionary intent. The Naturalization Act lengthened from five to fourteen years the residency requirement for citizenship. The Alien Act empowered the president to deport "dangerous" aliens on pain of imprisonment. The Alien Enemies Act authorized the president in time of declared war to expel or imprison enemy aliens at will. Finally, the Sedition Act defined as a high misdemeanor any conspiracy against legal measures of the government, including interference with federal officers and insurrection or rioting. What is more, the law forbade writing, publishing, or speaking anything of "a false, scandalous and malicious" nature against the government or any of its officers.

The Sedition Act was designed to punish Republicans, whom Federalists could scarcely distinguish from French revolutionary radicals and traitors.

To be sure, partisan Republican journalists were resorting to scandalous lies and misrepresentations, but so were Federalists; it was a time when both sides seemed afflicted with paranoia. But the fifteen indictments brought under the act, with ten convictions, were all directed at Republicans.

In the very first case one inebriated Republican was fined $100 for wishing out loud that the wad of a salute cannon might hit President Adams in his rear. The most conspicuous targets of prosecution were Republican editors and a Republican congressman, Matthew Lyon of Vermont, a rough-and-tumble Irishman who castigated Adams's "continual grasp for power" and "un-bounded thirst for ridiculous pomp, foolish adulation, and selfish avarice." Lyon was imprisoned for four months and fined $1,000, but from his cell he continued to write articles and letters for the Republican papers. The few convictions under the act only created martyrs to the cause of freedom of speech and the press and exposed the vindictiveness of Federalist judges.

Lyon and the others based their defense on the unconstitutionality of the Sedition Act, but Federalist judges dismissed the notion. It ran against the Republican grain, anyway, to have federal courts assume the authority to declare

Dispute in the House

Republican representative Matthew Lyon and Connecticut Federalist Roger Griswold attack each other on the floor of the House (1798). Lyon soon became a target of the Sedition Act.

laws unconstitutional. To offset the "reign of witches" unleashed by the Alien and Sedition Acts, therefore, Jefferson and Madison drafted what came to be known as the Kentucky and Virginia Resolutions. These passed the legislatures of their respective states in 1798, and further Kentucky Resolutions, adopted in 1799, responded to counterresolutions from northern states. These resolutions, much alike in their arguments, denounced the Alien and Sedition Acts as "alarming infractions" of constitutional rights. Since the Constitution arose as a compact among the states, the resolutions argued, the states should decide when Congress had exceeded its powers. The Virginia Resolutions, drafted by Madison, declared that states "have the right and are in duty bound to interpose for arresting the progress of the evil." The second set of Kentucky Resolutions, in restating the states' right to judge violations of the Constitution, added, "That a nullification of those sovereignties, of all unauthorized acts done under color of that instrument, is the rightful remedy."

These doctrines of interposition and nullification, reworked and edited by later theorists, were destined to be used for causes unforeseen by their authors. (Years later Madison would disclaim the doctrine of nullification as developed by John C. Calhoun, but his own doctrine of interposition would resurface as late as the 1950s as a device to oppose racial integration.) At the time, it seems, both men intended the resolutions to serve chiefly as propaganda, the opening guns in the political campaign of 1800. Neither Kentucky nor Virginia took steps to nullify or interpose its authority in the enforcement of the Alien and Sedition Acts. Instead, both called upon the other states to help them win a repeal. In Virginia, citizens talked of armed resistance to the federal government. Jefferson counseled against any thought of violence: it was "not the kind of opposition the American people will permit." He assured a fellow Virginian that the Federalist "reign of witches" would soon end, that it would be discredited by the arrival of the tax collector more than anything else.

REPUBLICAN VICTORY   As the presidential election of 1800 approached, civil unrest boiled over. Grievances were mounting against Federalist policies: taxation to support an unneeded army; the Alien and Sedition Acts, which cast the Federalists as anti-liberty; the lingering fears of "monarchism"; the hostilities aroused by Alexander Hamilton's economic programs; the suppression of the Whiskey Rebellion; and Jay's Treaty. When Adams opted for peace with France in 1800, he probably doomed his one chance for reelection—a wave of patriotic war fever with a united party behind him. His decision gained him much goodwill among Americans at large but left the Hamiltonians angry and his party divided. In 1800 the

Federalists summoned enough unity to name as their candidates Adams and Charles Cotesworth Pinckney; they agreed to cast all their electoral votes for both. But the Hamiltonian Federalists continued to snipe at Adams and his policies, and soon after his renomination Adams removed two of them from his cabinet. A furious Hamilton struck back with a pamphlet questioning Adams's fitness to be president, citing his "disgusting egotism." Intended for private distribution among Federalist leaders, the pamphlet reached the hands of New York Republican Aaron Burr, who put it in general circulation.

Jefferson and Burr, as the Republican presidential candidates, once again represented the alliance of Virginia and New York. Jefferson, perhaps even more than Adams, was attacked by Federalists as a supporter of the radical French revolutionaries and an atheist. His election, Americans were warned, would bring civil war—"dwellings in flames, hoary hairs bathed in blood, female chastity violated . . . children writhing on the pike and halberd." Jefferson kept quiet, refused to answer the attacks, and directed the campaign by mail from his home at Monticello. His supporters portrayed him as the farmers' friend, the champion of states' rights, frugal government, liberty, and peace.

Adams proved more popular than his party, whose candidates generally fared worse than the president, but the Republicans edged him out by seventy-three electoral votes to sixty-five. The decisive states were New York and South Carolina, either of which might have given the victory to Adams. But in New York former senator Aaron Burr's organization won control of the legislature, which cast the electoral votes. In South Carolina, Charles Pinckney (cousin of the Federalist Pinckneys) won over the legislature by well-placed promises of Republican patronage. Still, the result was not final, for Jefferson and Burr had tied with seventy-three votes each, and the choice of the president was thrown into the House of Representatives, where Federalist diehards tried vainly to give the election to Burr. This was too much for Hamilton, who opposed Jefferson but held a much lower opinion of Burr. The stalemate in the House continued for thirty-five ballots. The deadlock was broken only when a confidant of Jefferson's assured a Delaware congressman that Jefferson would refrain from the wholesale removal of Federalists appointed to federal offices and would uphold Hamilton's financial policies. The representative resolved to vote for Jefferson, and several other Federalists agreed simply to cast blank ballots, permitting Jefferson to win without any of them having to vote for him.

Before the Federalists relinquished power to the Jeffersonian Republicans on March 4, 1801, their lame-duck Congress passed the Judiciary Act of 1801. Intended to ensure Federalist control of the judicial system, this act provided that the next vacancy on the Supreme Court would not be filled, created sixteen

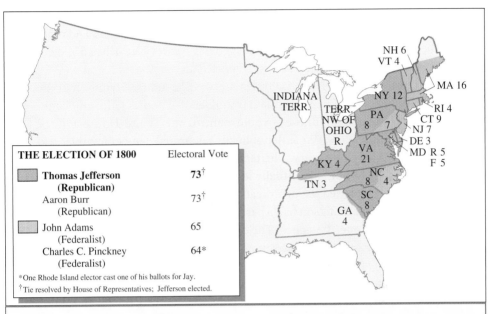

THE ELECTION OF 1800	Electoral Vote
Thomas Jefferson (Republican)	**73**[†]
Aaron Burr (Republican)	73[†]
John Adams (Federalist)	65
Charles C. Pinckney (Federalist)	64*

*One Rhode Island elector cast one of his ballots for Jay.
[†]Tie resolved by House of Representatives; Jefferson elected.

Why was the election of 1800 a key moment in American history? How did the Republicans win New York and South Carolina? How did Congress break the tie between Jefferson and Burr?

circuit courts with a new judge for each, and increased the number of attorneys, clerks, and marshals. Before he left office, Adams named John Marshall to the vacant office of chief justice and appointed Federalists to all the new positions, including forty-two justices of the peace for the new District of Columbia. The Federalists, defeated and destined never to regain national power, had in the words of Jefferson "retired into the judiciary as a stronghold."

The election of 1800 marked a major turning point in American political history. It was the first time that one political party, however ungracefully, relinquished power to the opposition party. Jefferson's victory signaled the emergence of a new, more democratic political system, dominated by parties, partisanship, and wider public participation—at least among white men. Before and immediately after independence, politics was popular but not democratic: people took a keen interest in public affairs, but socially prominent families, the "rich, the able, and the wellborn," dominated political life. However, the fierce political battles of the late 1790s, culminating in 1800 with Jefferson's election as the nation's third president, wrested control of politics from the governing elite and established the right of more people to play an active role in

governing the young republic. With the gradual elimination of property qualifications for voting and the proliferation of newspapers, pamphlets, and other
publications, the "public sphere" in which political issues were debated and decided expanded enormously in the early nineteenth century.

The Republican victory in 1800 also marked the political triumph of the
slaveholding South. Three Virginia slaveholders—Thomas Jefferson, James
Madison, and James Monroe—would control the White House for the
next twenty-four years. While Republicans celebrated democracy, they also
prospered because of slavery. The tensions between republican ideals and
plantation slavery would eventually lead to civil war.

John Adams regretted the democratization of politics and the rise of fractious partisanship. "Jefferson had a party, Hamilton had a party, but the commonwealth had none," he sighed. The defeated president was so distraught at
the turn of events that he decided not to participate in Jefferson's inauguration in Washington, D.C. Instead, he boarded a stagecoach for the 500-mile
trip to his home in Quincy, Massachusetts. He and Jefferson would not communicate for the next twelve years. As Adams returned to work on his Massachusetts farm, he reported that he had exchanged "honors and virtue for manure."
He told his son John Quincy, who would become president himself, that the
American president "has a hard, laborious, and unhappy life."

MAKING CONNECTIONS

- Thomas Jefferson's Republican philosophy offered a strong
  alternative to Alexander Hamilton's Federalism. As the next
  chapter shows, however, once the Republicans got into power,
  they adopted several Federalist principles and positions.

- The Bank of the United States and the protective tariff
  continued to be controversial. The bank's charter was renewed
  for another twenty years in 1816, the same year in which the
  first truly protective tariff was passed (Chapter 10), but in the
  1830s the bank was eliminated, and the tariff became a major
  source of sectional conflict (Chapter 11).

- The foreign-policy crises with England and France described
  in this chapter will lead to the War of 1812, discussed in
  Chapter 9.

FURTHER READING

The best introduction to the early Federalists remains John C. Miller's *The Federalist Era, 1789–1801* (1960). Other works analyze the ideological debates among the nation's first leaders. Richard Buel Jr.'s *Securing the Revolution: Ideology in American Politics, 1789–1815* (1972), Joyce Appleby's *Capitalism and a New Social Order: The Republican Vision of the 1790s* (1984), Drew R. McCoy's *The Last of the Fathers: James Madison and the Republican Legacy* (1989), and Stanley Elkins and Eric McKitrick's *The Age of Federalism: The Early American Republic, 1788–1800* (1993) trace the persistence and transformation of ideas first fostered during the Revolutionary crisis.

The 1790s may also be understood through the views and behavior of national leaders. Joseph J. Ellis's *Founding Brothers: The Revolutionary Generation* (2000) is a superb group study. See also the following biographies: Richard Brookhiser's *Founding Father: Rediscovering George Washington* (1996) and *Alexander Hamilton, American* (1999) and Joseph J. Ellis's *Passionate Sage: The Character and Legacy of John Adams* (1993). For a female perspective, see Phyllis Lee Levin's *Abigail Adams: A Biography* (1987). The Republican viewpoint is the subject of Lance Banning's *The Jeffersonian Persuasion: Evolution of a Party Ideology* (1978).

Federalist foreign policy is explored in Jerald A. Comb's *The Jay Treaty: Political Battleground of the Founding Fathers* (1970) and William Stinchcombe's *The XYZ Affair* (1980). For specific domestic issues, see Thomas P. Slaughter's *The Whiskey Rebellion: Frontier Epilogue to the American Revolution* (1986) and Harry Ammon's *The Genet Mission* (1973). The treatment of Indians in the Old Northwest is explored in Richard H. Kohn's *Eagle and Sword: The Federalists and the Creation of the Military Establishment in America, 1783–1802* (1975). For the Alien and Sedition Acts, consult James Morton Smith's *Freedom's Fetters: The Alien and Sedition Laws and American Civil Liberties* (1966).

Several books focus on social issues of the post-Revolutionary period, including *Keepers of the Revolution: New Yorkers at Work in the Early Republic* (1992), edited by Paul A. Gilje and Howard B. Rock; Ronald Schultz's *The Republic of Labor: Philadelphia Artisans and the Politics of Class, 1720–1830* (1993); and Peter Way's *Common Labour: Workers and the Digging of North American Canals, 1780–1860* (1993).

The African-American experience in the Revolutionary era is detailed in Mechal Sobel's *The World They Made Together: Black and White Values in Eighteenth-Century Virginia* (1987) and Gary B. Nash's *Forging Freedom: The Formation of Philadelphia's Black Community, 1720–1840* (1988).

9

THE EARLY REPUBLIC

FOCUS QUESTIONS

· What were the domestic policies of the Republicans once they were in power?

· How did politics divide the early republic?

· What were the causes and effects of the War of 1812?

To answer these questions and access additional review material, please visit www.wwnorton.com/studyspace.

The early years of the new republic laid the foundation for the nation's development as the first society in the world organized by the principle of democratic capitalism and its promise of equal opportunity for all—except slaves, Indians, and women. White American men in the fifty years after independence were on the move and on the make. Their prospects seemed unlimited, their optimism unrestrained. As John Adams observed, "There is no people on earth so ambitious as the people of America . . . because the lowest can aspire as freely as the highest."

Land sales west of the Appalachian Mountains soared in the early nineteenth century as aspiring farmers shoved Indians aside in order to establish homesteads of their own. Enterprising, mobile, and increasingly diverse in religion and national origin, tens of thousands of ordinary folk uprooted themselves from settled communities and went in search of personal advancement, occupying more territory in a single generation than had been settled in the 150 years of colonial history. "Never again," as the historian Joyce Appleby wrote, "would so large a portion of the nation live in new settlements." Between 1800 and 1820 the trans-Appalachian population soared from 300,000 to 2 million. By 1840, over 40 percent of Americans lived west of the mountains in eight new states.

The migrants flowed westward in three streams between 1780 and 1830. One ran from the Old South—Virginia, Maryland, and the Carolinas—through Georgia into the newer states of Alabama and Mississippi. Another wave traversed the Blue Ridge Mountains from Maryland and Virginia, crossing into Kentucky and Tennessee. The third route was in the North, taking New Englanders westward across the Berkshires into New York, Pennsylvania, Ohio, and Michigan. Many of the pioneers stayed only a few years before continuing westward in search of cheaper and more fertile land.

The spirit of opportunistic independence affected free African Americans as well as whites, Indians as well as immigrants. Free blacks were the fastest growing segment of the population during the early nineteenth century. Many enslaved Americans had gained their freedom during the Revolutionary War by escaping, by joining the British forces, or by serving in American units. Every state except South Carolina promised freedom to slaves who fought the British. Afterward, state after state in the North outlawed slavery, and anti-slavery societies blossomed, exerting increasing pressure on the South to end the degrading practice. The westward migration of whites brought incessant conflict with Native Americans. Indians fiercely resisted but ultimately succumbed to a federal government and a federal army determined to displace them.

Most white Americans, however, were less concerned about Indians and slavery than they were about seizing their own opportunities. Politicians sought to suppress the volatile issue of slavery rather than confront it; their priorities were elsewhere. Westward expansion, economic growth, urban development, and the democratization of politics fostered a pervasive entrepreneurial spirit among the generation of Americans born after 1776—especially outside the South. In 1790 nine out of ten Americans lived on the land and engaged in what is called household production; their sphere of activity was local. But with each passing year, farmers increasingly focused on producing surplus crops and livestock to be sold in regional markets. Cotton prices soared, and in the process the Deep South grew ever more committed to a plantation economy dependent upon slave labor, New England merchants, and world markets. The burgeoning market economy produced boom-and-bust cycles, but overall the years from 1790 to 1830 were quite prosperous, with young Americans experiencing a "widening scope of opportunity."

The colonial economy had been organized according to what Great Britain wanted from its New World possessions. This dependency brought the hated imperial restrictions on manufacturing, commerce, and shipping. With independence, however, Americans could create new industries, pursue new careers, and exploit new markets. It was not simply Alexander Hamilton's financial initiatives and the actions of wealthy investors and speculators that sparked America's dramatic commercial growth in these years. It was also the efforts of ordinary men and women who were willing to take risks, uproot families, use unstable paper money issued by unregulated local banks, purchase factory-made goods, and tinker with new machines and tools. Free enterprise was the keynote of the era.

While most Americans continued to work as farmers, a growing number of young adults found employment in new or greatly expanded enterprises: textiles, banking, transportation, publishing, retailing, teaching, preaching, medicine, law, construction, and engineering. Technological innovations (steam power, power tools, and new modes of transportation) and their social applications (mass communication, turnpikes, the postal service, banks, and corporations) fostered an array of new industries and businesses. The emergence of a factory system transformed the nature of work for many Americans. Proud apprentices, journeymen, and master craftsmen, who controlled their labor and invested their work with an emphasis on quality rather than quantity, resented the proliferation of mills and factories populated by "half-trained" workers dependent upon an hourly wage and subject to the sharp fluctuations of the larger economy.

The decentralized agrarian republic of 1776, nestled along the Atlantic seaboard, had become by 1830 a sprawling commercial nation connected by networks of roads and canals and cemented by economic relationships—all animated by a restless spirit of enterprise, experimentation, and expansion.

JEFFERSONIAN SIMPLICITY

On March 4, 1801, the fifty-seven-year-old Thomas Jefferson, tall and thin, with red hair and a ruddy complexion, became the first president to be inaugurated in the new federal city, Washington, District of Columbia. The city was still a motley array of buildings around two centers, Capitol Hill and the executive mansion. Congress, having met in eight towns and cities since 1774, had at last found a permanent home but enjoyed few amenities. There were only two places of amusement, one a racetrack, the other a theater thick with "tobacco smoke, whiskey breaths, and other stenches."

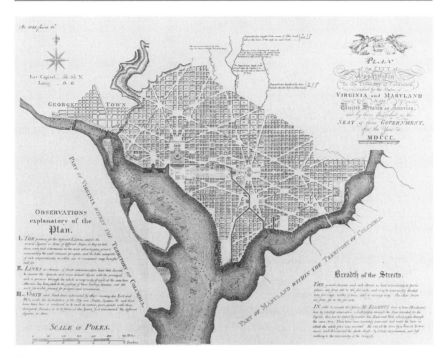

The New Federal City

Plan of Washington, D.C., from 1792.

Jefferson's informal inauguration befitted the primitive surroundings. The new president left his lodgings and walked down a stump-strewn Pennsylvania Avenue to the unfinished Capitol. He entered the Senate chamber, took the oath administered by Chief Justice John Marshall, read his inaugural address in a barely audible voice, and returned to his boardinghouse for dinner. A tone of simplicity and conciliation ran through his inaugural speech. The campaign between Federalists and Republicans had been so fierce that some had predicted civil war. Jefferson appealed for unity. "We are all Republicans—we are all Federalists. If there be any among us who would wish to dissolve this Union or to change its republican form, let them stand undisturbed as monuments of the safety with which error of opinion may be tolerated where reason is left free to combat it." Jefferson concluded with a summary of the "essential principles" that would guide his administration: "Equal and exact justice to all men . . . ; peace, commerce, and honest friendship with all nations, entangling alliances with none . . . ; freedom of religion; freedom of the press; and freedom of person, under the protection of the habeas corpus; and trial by juries impartially selected. . . . The wisdom of our sages and the blood of our heroes have been devoted to their attainment."

JEFFERSON IN OFFICE

The deliberate display of republican simplicity at Jefferson's inauguration set the style of his administration. Although a man of expensive personal tastes, he took pains to avoid the occasions of pomp and circumstance that had characterized the Federalist administrations and to his mind suggested the trappings of monarchy. Presidential messages went to Congress in writing lest they resemble the parliamentary speech from the throne. The practice also allowed Jefferson, a notoriously bad public speaker, to exploit his skill as a superb writer.

Jefferson liked to think of his election as the "revolution of 1800," but the electoral margin had been razor thin, and the policies that he followed were more conciliatory than revolutionary. His overwhelming reelection in 1804 attests to the popularity of his philosophy. Jefferson placed in policy-making positions men of his own party, and he was the first president to pursue the role of party leader, cultivating congressional support at his dinner parties and elsewhere. In the cabinet the leading figures were Secretary of State James Madison, a longtime neighbor and political ally, and Secretary of the Treasury Albert Gallatin, a Swiss-born Pennsylvania Republican whose

The Executive Mansion

A watercolor of the president's house during Jefferson's term in office. Jefferson called it "big enough for two emperors, one pope, and the grand lama in the bargain."

financial skills had won him the respect of the Federalists. In an effort to cultivate Federalist New England, Jefferson chose men from that region for the positions of attorney general, secretary of war, and postmaster general.

In lesser offices, however, Jefferson often succumbed to pressure from the Republicans to remove Federalists. In one area he removed the offices rather than the appointees. In 1802 Congress repealed the Judiciary Act of 1801 and so abolished the circuit judgeships and other offices to which John Adams had made his "midnight appointments." A new judiciary act restored to six the number of Supreme Court justices and set up six circuit courts, each headed by a justice.

MARBURY V. MADISON The "midnight appointments" that John Adams made just before leaving office sparked the pathbreaking case of *Marbury v. Madison* (1803), the first in which the Supreme Court declared a federal law unconstitutional. The case involved the appointment of the Maryland Federalist William Marbury as justice of the peace in the District of Columbia. Marbury's letter of appointment, or commission, signed by President Adams two days before he left office, was still undelivered when Madison took office as secretary of state, and Jefferson directed him to withhold it. Marbury then sued for a court order (a writ of mandamus) directing Madison to deliver his commission.

The Court's unanimous opinion, written by Chief Justice John Marshall, a brilliant Virginian, held that Marbury deserved his commission but then denied that the Court had jurisdiction in the case. Section 13 of the Federal Judiciary Act of 1789, which gave the Court original jurisdiction in mandamus proceedings, was unconstitutional, the Court ruled, because the Constitution specified that the Court should have original jurisdiction only in cases involving ambassadors or states. The Court, therefore, could issue no order in the case. With one bold stroke the Federalist Marshall had chastised the Jeffersonians while avoiding an awkward confrontation with an administration that might have defied his order. At the same time he established the stunning precedent of the Court's declaring a federal law invalid on the grounds that it violated provisions of the Constitution. Marshall stressed that it "is emphatically the province and duty of the judicial department to say what the law is." In other words, the Supreme Court was assuming the right of judicial review, meaning that it would decide whether acts of Congress were constitutional. So even though Marbury never gained his judgeship, Marshall established the Supreme Court as the final judge of constitutional interpretation. Since the Marbury decision the Court has struck down over 150 acts of Congress and over 1,100 acts of state legislatures.

The Court's decision, about which Jefferson could do nothing, confirmed his fear of the judges' partisanship, and he resolved to counter the Federalist influence. In 1804 Republicans used the impeachment power against two of the most partisan Federalist judges and succeeded in ousting one of them, District Judge John Pickering of New Hampshire. Pickering was clearly insane, which was not a "high crime or misdemeanor," but he was also given to profane and drunken harangues from the bench, which the Senate quickly decided was an impeachable offense.

DOMESTIC REFORMS Jefferson's first term was a succession of triumphs in both domestic and foreign affairs. The president did not set out to dismantle Alexander Hamilton's economic program. Under the tutelage of Treasury Secretary Gallatin, he learned to accept the national bank as an essential convenience, and he did not endorse the bank's repeal, which more dogmatic Republicans promoted. It was too late, of course, to undo Hamilton's funding and debt-assumption operations but none too soon, in the opinion of both Jefferson and Gallatin, to begin retiring the resultant federal debt. Jefferson detested Hamilton's belief that a regulated federal debt was a national "blessing" because it gave the bankers and investors who lent money to the U.S. government a direct stake in the success of the new republic. Jefferson believed that a large federal debt would bring only high taxes and government corruption, so he set about reducing government expenses and paying down the debt. At the same time he won the repeal of the whiskey tax and other Federalist excises, much to the relief of backwoods distillers, drinkers, and grain farmers.

Without income from the excise taxes, frugality was all the more necessary to a federal government dependent chiefly upon tariffs and the sale of western lands for its revenue. Happily for the Treasury, both sources of income flourished. The European war continually increased American shipping traffic, and thus tariff revenues padded the federal Treasury. At the same time, settlers flocked to western land they purchased from the government. Ohio's admission to the Union in 1803 increased to seventeen the number of states.

By the "wise and frugal government" the president promised in his inaugural address, Jefferson and Gallatin reasoned, the United States could live within its income, like a prudent farmer. The basic formula was simple: cut back military expenses. A standing army menaced a free society anyway, Jefferson believed. It therefore should be kept to a minimum and the national defense left, in Jefferson's words, to "a well-disciplined militia, our best reliance in peace, and for the first moments of war, till regulars may relieve them." The navy, which the Federalists had already reduced, ought to be

Cincinnati in 1800

Though its population was only about 750, its inhabitants were already promoting Cincinnati as "the metropolis of the NorthWestern Territory."

reduced further. Coastal defense, Jefferson argued, should rely upon land-based fortifications and a "mosquito fleet" of small gunboats.

In 1807 Jeffersonian reforms culminated in an act that outlawed the foreign slave trade as of January 1, 1808, the earliest date possible under the Constitution. At the time, South Carolina was the only state that still permitted the trade, having reopened it in 1803. But for years to come, an illegal traffic would continue. By one informal estimate perhaps 300,000 enslaved blacks were smuggled into the United States between 1808 and 1861.

THE BARBARY PIRATES Issues of foreign relations intruded upon Jefferson early in his term, when events in the Mediterranean gave him second thoughts about the need for a navy. On the Barbary Coast of North Africa, the rulers of Morocco, Algiers, Tunis, and Tripoli had for years practiced piracy and extortion. After the Revolution, American shipping in the Mediterranean became fair game, no longer protected by British payments of tribute. The new U.S. government yielded up protection money too, first to Morocco in 1786, then to the others in the 1790s. In 1801, however, the pasha of Tripoli upped his demands and declared war on the United States by the symbolic gesture of chopping down the flagpole at the U.S. consulate. Jefferson sent warships to blockade Tripoli.

A wearisome war dragged on until 1805, punctuated in 1804 by the notable exploit of Lieutenant Stephen Decatur, who slipped in to Tripoli harbor by night and set fire to the frigate *Philadelphia,* which had been captured (along with its crew) after it ran aground. The pasha finally settled for a $60,000 ransom and released the *Philadelphia*'s crew, whom he had held hostage for more than a year. It was still tribute, but less than the $300,000 the pasha had demanded at first and much less than the cost of war.

THE LOUISIANA PURCHASE While the conflict with the Barbary pirates continued, events elsewhere led to the greatest single achievement of the Jefferson administration. The Louisiana Purchase of 1803 more than doubled the territory of the United States. It included the entire Mississippi River valley west of the river itself. Louisiana, settled by the French, had been ceded to Spain by victorious Great Britain in 1763 in exchange for West Florida. Since that time the dream of retaking Louisiana had stirred the French. In 1800 Napoléon had secured its return to France. When word of the deal between Spain and France reached Washington in 1801, Jefferson hastened the New Yorker Robert R. Livingston, the new U.S. minister to France, on his way to Paris. Spain in control of the Mississippi River outlet was bad enough, but Napoléon in control could only mean serious trouble. "The day that France takes possession of New Orleans," Jefferson wrote Livingston, "we must marry ourselves to the British fleet and nation," an unhappy prospect for the French-loving Jefferson.

Negotiations with the French dragged into 1803 while Spanish forces remained in control in Louisiana, awaiting the arrival of the French. Early that year, Jefferson sent his trusted Virginia friend James Monroe to assist Livingston in Paris. But no sooner had Monroe arrived than Napoléon's foreign minister, Talleyrand, surprised Livingston by asking if the United States would like to buy the whole of the Louisiana Territory. Livingston, once he regained his composure, snapped up the offer.

Disease again played an important role in shaping history. Napoléon was willing to sell the territory because his French army in Haiti had been decimated not only by a slave revolt but also by yellow fever. Concerned about financing another round of warfare in Europe, Napoléon decided to cut French losses in the New World by selling the North American property.

By the treaty of cession, dated April 30, 1803, the United States obtained the Louisiana Territory for about $15 million. The treaty was vague in defining the precise boundaries of the territory stretching from the Mississippi River to the Rocky Mountains. When Livingston asked about the boundaries, Talleyrand responded: "I can give you no direction. You have made a noble bargain for yourselves, and I suppose you will make the most of it."

The surprising turn of events had presented Jefferson with a "noble bargain," a great new "empire of liberty," but also with a constitutional dilemma.

Nowhere did the Constitution mention the purchase of territory. Jefferson at first suggested a constitutional amendment, but his advisers argued against delay lest Napoléon change his mind. The power to purchase territory, they reasoned, resided in the power to make treaties. Jefferson relented, trusting, he said, "that the good sense of our country will correct the evil of loose construction when it shall produce ill effects." New England Federalists boggled at the prospect of new western states that would probably strengthen the Jeffersonian party. They aimed their fire at a proviso in the treaty that the inhabitants be "incorporated in the Union" as citizens. In a reversal that anticipated many more reversals on constitutional issues, Federalists found themselves arguing for strict construction of the Constitution while Republicans brushed aside their scruples in favor of implied power. Gaining over 800,000 square miles trumped any legal reservations.

The Senate ratified the treaty by an overwhelming vote of twenty-six to six, and on December 20, 1803, U.S. officials took formal possession of the sprawling Louisiana Territory. For the time being the Spanish kept West Florida, but within a decade that area would be ripe for the plucking. In 1808 Napoléon put his brother on the throne of Spain. With the Spanish colonial administration in disarray, American settlers in 1810 staged a rebellion in Baton Rouge and proclaimed the republic of West Florida, which was quickly annexed and occupied by the United States as far east as the Pearl River. In 1812, upon becoming the Union's eighteenth state, Louisiana absorbed the region, still known as the Florida parishes. In 1813, with Spain itself a battlefield for French and British forces, Americans took over the rest of West Florida, the Gulf coast of the future states of Mississippi and Alabama. Legally, the U.S. government has claimed ever since, all these areas were included in the Louisiana Purchase.

LEWIS AND CLARK   As an amateur scientist long before he became president, Thomas Jefferson wished to nourish his curiosity about the vast region west of the Mississippi River, its geography, its flora and fauna, and its prospects for trade and agriculture. Thus in 1803 he asked Congress to finance a mapping and scientific expedition to the far Northwest, beyond the Mississippi River, in what was still foreign territory. Congress approved, and Jefferson assigned as commanders the twenty-nine-year-old Meriwether Lewis, his former private secretary, and another Virginian, a former army officer, William Clark.

In 1804 the "Corps of Discovery," numbering nearly fifty, set out from the small village of St. Louis to ascend the muddy Missouri River. Forced to live off the land, they quickly adapted to the new environment. Local Indians

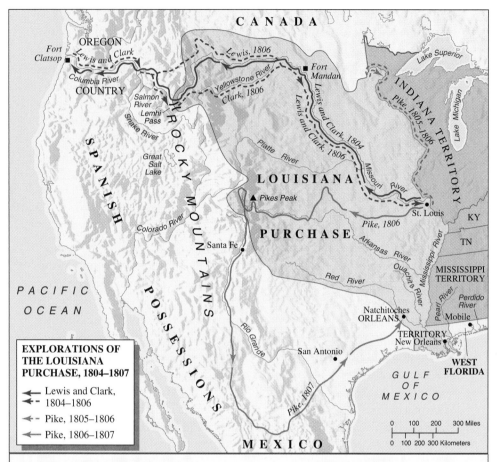

EXPLORATIONS OF
THE LOUISIANA
PURCHASE, 1804–1807

←--- Lewis and Clark,
1804–1806
←--- Pike, 1805–1806
←— Pike, 1806–1807

How did the United States acquire the Louisiana Purchase? What was the mission of
Lewis and Clark's expedition? What were the consequences of Lewis and Clark's reports about the Western territory?

introduced them to clothes made from deer hides and taught them hunting
techniques. Lewis and Clark kept detailed journals of their travels and drew
maps of the unexplored regions. As they moved up the Missouri, the landscape changed from forest to prairie grass. They saw huge herds of bison and
other animals, which had become more abundant after a smallpox epidemic
had wiped out most of the Indian villages in the area. They passed trappers
and traders headed south with rafts and boats laden with furs. Six months after leaving St. Louis, near the Mandan Sioux villages in what would become
North Dakota, they built Fort Mandan and wintered in relative comfort,

sending downriver a barge loaded with maps, soil samples, and live specimens such as the prairie dog and the magpie, previously unknown in America.

In the spring, Lewis and Clark added to their main party a remarkable Shoshone woman named Sacagawea, who proved an enormous help as an interpreter of Indian languages, and the group set out westward into uncharted territory. At the head of the Missouri River, they took the north fork, which they named the Jefferson River, crossed the Rocky Mountains at Lemhi Pass, and in dugout canoes descended the Snake and Columbia rivers to the Pacific. Near the future site of Astoria, Oregon, at the mouth of the Columbia, they built Fort Clatsop, in which they spent the winter. The following spring they split into two parties, with Lewis heading back by almost the same route and Clark going by way of the Yellowstone River. They rejoined at the juncture of the Missouri and Yellowstone rivers, returning together to St. Louis in 1806, having been gone nearly two and a half years. Along the way they had been chased by grizzly bears, attacked and aided by Indians, buffeted by blizzards and illness, and forced by starvation to eat their own horses. "I have been wet and as cold in every part as I ever was in my life," William Clark wrote in his journal. "Indeed I was at one time fearful my feet would freeze in the thin moccasins which I wore." But the intrepid discoverers had, in their own words, "proceeded on" day after day against the odds.

Exploring the Far Northwest

Captain Clark and his men shooting bears, from a book of engravings of the Lewis and Clark expedition (ca. 1810).

No longer was the far West unknown country. It would be nearly a century before a good edition of the *Journals of the Lewis and Clark Expedition* appeared in print; many of the explorers' findings came out piecemeal, however, including an influential map in 1814. Their reports of friendly Indians and abundant beaver pelts quickly attracted traders and trappers to the region and gave the United States a claim to the Oregon Country by right of discovery and exploration.

POLITICAL SCHEMES Jefferson's policies, including the Louisiana Purchase, brought him solid support in the South and the West. Even New Englanders were moving to his side. By 1809 John Quincy Adams, the son of the second president, would become a Republican! Federalists read the handwriting on the wall. The acquisition of a vast new empire in the West would reduce New England and the Federalist party to insignificance in political affairs. Under the leadership of Thomas Pickering, secretary of state under Washington and Adams and now a U.S. senator, a group of ardent Massachusetts Federalists called the Essex Junto considered seceding from the Union, an idea that would simmer in New England circles for another decade.

Federalists also hatched a scheme to link New York with New England and consequently contacted Vice President Aaron Burr, who had been on the outs with the Jeffersonians. Their plan, which depended upon Burr's election as governor of New York, could not win the support of even the extreme Federalists: Alexander Hamilton bitterly opposed it on the grounds that Burr was "a dangerous man, and one who ought not to be trusted with the reins of government."

Those remarks led to Hamilton's famous duel with Burr, in July 1804 at Weehawken, New Jersey. Hamilton personally opposed dueling, but his romantic streak and sense of honor compelled him to meet the vice president's challenge and demonstrate his courage—he was determined not to fire at his opponent. Burr had no such scruples. On a grassy ledge about the Hudson River, he shot Hamilton through the heart. Hamilton went to his death, as his son had gone to his in a similar affair, also settled in Weehawken, the previous year. Hamilton's death ended both Pickering's scheme and Burr's political career—but not Burr's intrigues.

Burr would lose the gubernatorial election. In the meantime the presidential campaign of 1804 began when a congressional caucus of Republicans renominated Jefferson and chose the New Yorker George Clinton for vice president. (By then, to avoid the problems associated with parties running multiple candidates for the presidency, Congress had passed, and the states would soon ratify, the Twelfth Amendment, providing that electors use separate ballots to vote for the president and vice president.) Opposed by the Federalists Charles C. Pinckney and Rufus King, Jefferson and Clinton won 162 of the 176 electoral votes. It was the first landslide election in American history. Jefferson's policy of conciliation had made him a national rather than a sectional candidate.

Divisions in the Republican Party

JOHN RANDOLPH AND THE OLD REPUBLICANS Freed from a strong opposition—Federalists made up only one quarter of the new Congress—the Republican majority began to fragment. The Virginian John Randolph—known as John Randolph of Roanoke—initially a loyal Jeffersonian, became the most conspicuous of the dissidents. He was a powerful combination of principle, eccentricity, and rancor. Famous for his venomous assaults delivered in a shrill soprano, the colorful congressman strutted about the House floor with a whip in his hand, a symbol of his relish for contrarian positions. Few colleagues had the stomach for his tongue-lashings.

Randolph became the crusty spokesman for a shifting group of "old Republicans," whose adherence to party principles had rendered them more Jeffersonian than Jefferson himself. The Old Republicans were mostly southerners who defended states' rights and strict construction of the Constitution. They opposed any compromise with the Federalists and promoted an agrarian way of life. The Jeffersonian, or moderate, Republicans tended to be more pragmatic and nationalist in their orientation. As Thomas Jefferson himself demonstrated, they were willing to go along with tariffs and national banks.

THE BURR CONSPIRACY Sheer brilliance and opportunism had carried Aaron Burr to the vice presidency in 1800. He might easily have become Jefferson's heir apparent, but a taste for intrigue was the tragic flaw in his character. Caught up in the dubious schemes of Federalist diehards in 1800 and again in 1804, he ended his political career for good when he killed Alexander Hamilton. Indicted for murder and heavily in debt, the vice president fled to Spanish-held Florida. Once the furor subsided, he boldly returned to Washington to preside over the Senate. As long as he stayed out of New York and New Jersey, he was safe.

But Burr focused his attention less on the Senate than on a cockeyed scheme to carve out a personal empire for himself in the West. What came to be known as the Burr conspiracy was hatched when Burr met with General James Wilkinson. Just what Wilkinson and Burr were up to may never be known. The most likely explanation is that they conspired to get the Louisiana Territory

Aaron Burr

Burr graduated from what is now Princeton University, where he changed his course of study from theology to law.

to secede and set up an independent republic. Earlier Burr had solicited British support for his scheme to separate "the western part of the United States in its whole extent."

Whatever the goal, Burr learned in early 1807 that Jefferson had ordered his arrest. He tried to flee to Florida but was caught and taken to Richmond, Virginia. Charged with treason, Burr was brought for trial before Chief Justice John Marshall. The case revealed both Marshall and Jefferson at their partisan worst, and it established two major constitutional precedents. First, Jefferson ignored a subpoena requiring him to appear in court with certain papers in his possession. He refused, as had George Washington, to submit papers to Congress on the grounds that the independence of the executive branch would be compromised if the president were subject to a court writ. The second major precedent was Marshall's rigid definition of treason. Treason under the Constitution, Marshall wrote, consists of "levying war against the United States or adhering to their enemies" and requires "two witnesses to the same overt act" for conviction. Since the prosecution failed to produce two witnesses to an overt act of treason by Burr, the jury found him not guilty.

Whether or not Burr escaped his just deserts, Marshall's strict construction of the Constitution protected the United States, as its framers clearly intended, from the capricious judgments of "treason" that governments through the centuries have used to terrorize dissenters. As for Burr, with further charges pending, he skipped bail and took refuge in France but returned unmolested in 1812 to practice law in New York. He survived to a virile old age. At age seventy-eight, shortly before his death in 1836, he was divorced on grounds of adultery.

WAR IN EUROPE

Oppositionists of whatever stripe were more an annoyance than a threat to Jefferson. The more intractable problems of his second term involved the renewal of the European war in 1803, which helped resolve the problem of Louisiana but put more strains on Jefferson's desire to avoid "entangling alliances" and the quarrels of Europe. In 1805 Napoléon's crushing defeat of Russian and Austrian forces at Austerlitz left him in control of western Europe. The same year, Britain's defeat of the French and Spanish fleets in the Battle of Trafalgar secured control of the seas. The war devolved into a battle of elephant and whale, Napoléon dominant on land, the British dominant on the water, neither able to strike a decisive blow at the other, and neither restrained by concerns over neutral rights or international law.

HARASSMENT BY BRITAIN AND FRANCE   For two years after the renewal of European warfare, American shippers reaped the benefits, taking over trade with the French and Spanish West Indies. But in the case of the *Essex* (1805), a British court ruled that the practice of shipping French and Spanish goods through U.S. ports on their way elsewhere did not neutralize enemy goods. The practice violated the British rule of 1756, under which trade closed in time of peace remained closed in time of war. Goods shipped in violation of the rule, the British held, were liable to seizure at any point under the doctrine of continuous voyage. In 1807 the commercial provisions of Jay's Treaty expired, and James Monroe, the U.S. minister to Great Britain, failed to get a renewal satisfactory to Jefferson. After that the British interference with American shipping increased, not just to keep supplies from Napoléon's continent but also to hobble competition with British merchant ships.

In a series of orders in council adopted in 1806 and 1807, the British government set up a "paper blockade" of Europe that barred all trade between England and continental Europe. Moreover, vessels headed for European ports were required to get British licenses and were subject to British inspection. It was a paper blockade because even the powerful British navy was not large enough to monitor every European port. Napoléon retaliated with his "Continental System," proclaimed in the Berlin Decree of 1806 and the Milan Decree of 1807. In the Berlin Decree he declared his own paper blockade of the British Isles and barred British ships from ports under French control. In the Milan Decree he ruled that neutral ships that complied with British regulations were subject to seizure when they reached Continental ports. The situation presented American shippers with a dilemma: if they complied with the demands of one side, they were subject to seizure by the other.

The risks were daunting, but the prospects for profits were so great that American shippers ran the risk. For seamen the danger was heightened by a renewal of the practice of impressment. The use of press-gangs to kidnap men in British (and colonial) ports was a long-standing method of recruitment used by the British navy. The seizure of British subjects from American vessels became a new source of recruits, justified on the principle that British citizens remained British subjects for life: "Once an Englishman, always an Englishman." Mistakes might be made, of course, since it was sometimes hard to distinguish British subjects from Americans; indeed, a flourishing trade in fake citizenship papers arose in American ports. Impressment was mostly confined to merchant vessels, but on at least two occasions before 1807 vessels of the U.S. Navy had been stopped on the high seas and seamen removed.

Preparation for War to Defend Commerce

In 1806 and 1807 American shipping was caught in the crossfire of the war between Britain and France.

In the summer of 1807, the British frigate *Leopard* accosted a U.S. naval vessel, the frigate *Chesapeake,* just outside territorial waters off Norfolk, Virginia. After the *Chesapeake*'s captain refused to be searched, the *Leopard* opened fire, killing three Americans and wounding eighteen. The *Chesapeake,* unready for battle, was forced to strike its colors. A British search party seized four men, one of whom was later hanged for desertion from the British navy. Soon after the *Chesapeake* limped back into Norfolk, the *Washington Federalist* editorialized: "We have never, on any occasion, witnessed . . . such a thirst for revenge." Public wrath was so aroused that Jefferson could have had a war on the spot. Had Congress been in session, he might have been forced into one. But Jefferson, like John Adams before him, resisted war fever—and suffered politically as a result. One Federalist called him a "dish of skim milk curdling at the head of our nation."

THE EMBARGO   Jefferson resolved to use public indignation at the British to promote "peaceable coercion." In 1807, in response to his request, Congress passed the Embargo Act, which stopped all exports of American goods and prohibited American ships from leaving for foreign ports. The constitutional basis of the embargo was the power to regulate commerce, which in this case Republicans interpreted broadly as the power to prohibit commerce.

Jefferson's embargo failed from the beginning, however, because few Americans were willing to make the necessary sacrifices. The idealistic spirit that had made economic pressures effective in the pre-Revolutionary crises was lacking. Illegal trade with Britain and France remained profitable despite the risks, and violation of Jefferson's embargo was almost laughably easy. While American ships sat idle in ports, their crews laid off and unpaid, smugglers flourished and the British enjoyed a near monopoly of legitimate trade. As it turned out, France was little hurt by the embargo. The lack of American cotton hurt some British manufacturers and workers, but they carried little weight with the government, and British shippers benefited. With American ports closed, they found a new trade in Latin American ports thrown open by the colonial authorities when Napoléon occupied the mother countries of Spain and Portugal.

American resistance to the embargo revived the Federalist party in New England, which renewed the charge that Jefferson was in league with the French. At the same time, farmers in the South and West suffered for want of foreign outlets for their grain, cotton, and tobacco. After fifteen months of

The Election of 1808

This 1807 Federalist cartoon compares Washington and Jefferson. Washington (left) is flanked by the British lion and the American eagle, while Jefferson (right) is flanked by a snake and a lizard. Below Jefferson are volumes by French philosophers.

ineffectiveness, Jefferson accepted failure and repealed the embargo in 1809, shortly before he relinquished the "splendid misery" of the presidency.

In the election of 1808 the presidential succession passed to another Virginian, Secretary of State James Madison. George Clinton was again the candidate for vice president. The Federalists, backing Charles C. Pinckney of South Carolina and Rufus King of New York, revived enough as a result of the embargo to win 47 electoral votes to Madison's 122.

THE DRIFT TO WAR   From the beginning, James Madison's presidency was entangled in foreign affairs. Still insisting on neutral rights and freedom of the seas, Madison pursued Jefferson's policy of "peaceable coercion" by different but no more effective means. In place of the embargo, Congress had substituted the Nonintercourse Act, which reopened trade with all countries except France and Great Britain and authorized the president to reopen trade with whichever of these gave up its restrictions. The British minister in Washington, David Erskine, assured Madison's secretary of state that Britain would revoke its restrictions in 1809. With that assurance, Madison reopened trade with Britain, but Erskine had acted on his own, and the foreign secretary, repudiating his action, recalled him. Nonintercourse resumed, but it proved as ineffective as the embargo. In the vain search for an alternative, Congress in 1810 reversed itself and adopted a measure introduced by Nathaniel Macon of North Carolina, Macon's bill number 2, which reopened trade with the warring powers but provided that if either dropped its restrictions, nonintercourse would be restored with the other.

This time, Napoléon took a turn at trying to bamboozle Madison. Napoléon's foreign minister, the duke de Cadore, informed the U.S. minister in Paris that he had withdrawn the Berlin and Milan Decrees, but the carefully worded Cadore letter had strings attached: revocation of the decrees depended upon withdrawal of the British orders in council. The strings were plain to see, but Madison either misunderstood or, more likely, went along in the hope of putting pressure on the British. The British initially refused to give in, and on June 1, 1812, Madison reluctantly asked Congress to declare war. On June 16, 1812, however, the British foreign minister, facing economic crisis, announced revocation of the orders in council. Britain preferred not to risk war with the United States on top of its war with Napoléon. But on June 18, 1812, not having heard of the British actions, Congress concurred with Madison's request. With more time, with more patience, or with a transatlantic cable, Madison's policy would have been vindicated without resort to war.

THE WAR OF 1812

CAUSES   The main cause of the war—the demand for neutral shipping rights—seems clear enough. Neutral rights dominated Madison's war message and provided the salient reason for a mounting hostility toward the British. Yet the geographic distribution of the congressional vote for war raises a troubling question. The preponderance of the vote came from members of Congress representing the farm regions from Pennsylvania southward and westward. The maritime states of New York and New England, the region that bore the brunt of British attacks on U.S. trade, voted against the declaration of war. One explanation for this seeming anomaly is simple enough. The farming regions suffered damage to their markets for grain, cotton, and tobacco while New England shippers made profits from smuggling in spite of the British restrictions.

Other plausible explanations for the sectional vote, however, include frontier Indian attacks that were blamed on the British, western land hunger, and the desire for new land in Canada and the Floridas. Indian troubles were endemic to a rapidly expanding West. Land-hungry settlers and speculators kept moving out ahead of government surveys and sales in search of fertile acres. The constant pressure to open new lands repeatedly forced or persuaded Indians to sign treaties they did not always understand, causing stronger resentment among tribes that were losing more and more of their land. It was an old story, dating from the Jamestown settlement, but one that took a new turn with the rise of two Shawnee leaders, Tecumseh and his twin brother, Tenskwatawa, "the Prophet."

Tecumseh saw with blazing clarity the consequences of Indian disunity. From his base on the Tippecanoe River in northern Indiana, he traveled from Canada to the Gulf of Mexico in an effort to form a confederation of tribes to defend Indian hunting grounds,

Tecumseh

The Shawnee leader who tried to unite Indian tribes in defense of their land. He was killed in 1813 at the Battle of the Thames.

insisting that no land cession was valid without the consent of all tribes, since they held the land in common. His brother supplied the inspiration of a religious revival, calling upon Indians to worship the "Master of Life," resist the white man's liquor, and lead a simple life within their means. By 1811 Tecumseh had matured his plans and headed south to win the Creeks, Cherokees, Choctaws, and Chickasaws to his cause.

William Henry Harrison, the governor of the Indiana Territory, learned of Tecumseh's plans, met with him twice, and pronounced him "one of those uncommon geniuses who spring up occasionally to produce revolutions and overturn the established order of things." In the fall of 1811, Harrison decided that Tecumseh must be stopped. He gathered 1,000 troops and advanced on Tecumseh's capital, Prophetstown, on the Tippecanoe River, while the leader was away. Tecumseh's followers attacked Harrison's encampment on the Tippecanoe River, although Tecumseh had warned against any fighting in his absence. The Shawnees lost a bloody engagement that left about one quarter of Harrison's men dead or wounded. Only later did Harrison realize that he had inflicted a defeat on the Indians, who had become so demoralized that many fled to Canada. Harrison burned the town and destroyed its supplies. Tecumseh's dreams of an Indian confederacy went up in smoke, and Tecumseh himself fled to British protection in Canada.

The Battle of Tippecanoe reinforced suspicions that the British were inciting the Indians. Actually the incident was mainly Harrison's doing. With little hope of help from war-torn Europe, British officials in Canada had steered a careful course, discouraging warfare but seeking to keep the Indians' friendship and fur trade. To eliminate the Indian menace, frontiersmen reasoned, they needed to remove its foreign support, and they saw the province of Ontario as a pistol pointing at the United States. Conquest of Canada would accomplish a twofold purpose: it would eliminate British influence among the Indians and open a new empire for land-hungry Americans. It was also one place where the British, in case of war, were vulnerable to an American attack. Madison and others acted on the mistaken assumption that the Canadians were eager to be liberated from British control. Thomas Jefferson had told Madison that the American "acquisition of Canada" was "[a] matter of marchin [north with a military force]." To the far south the British were also vulnerable. East Florida, still under Spanish control, posed a similar threat to the Americans. Spain was too weak or simply unwilling to prevent sporadic Indian attacks across the frontier. In addition, the British were suspected of smuggling goods through Florida and intriguing with the Indians on the southwestern border.

Such concerns helped generate war fever. In the Congress that assembled in late 1811, new members from southern and western districts clamored for war in defense of "national honor." Among them were Henry Clay and Richard Mentor Johnson of Kentucky, Felix Grundy of Tennessee, and John C. Calhoun of South Carolina. John Randolph of Roanoke christened these "new boys" the war hawks. After they entered the House, Randolph said, "We have heard but one word—like the whip-poor-will, but one eternal monotonous tone—Canada! Canada! Canada!" The young senator Henry Clay, a tall, rawboned westerner known for his combative temperament and propensity for dueling, yearned for war. "I am for resistance by the *sword*," he vowed. He promised that the Kentucky militia stood ready to march on Canada and acquire its lucrative fur trade.

PREPARATIONS   As it turned out, the war hawks would get neither Canada nor Florida, for James Madison had carried into war a nation that was ill prepared both financially and militarily. The Republican program of small federal budgets and military cutbacks was not an effective way to win a war. And Madison, a studious, soft-spoken man, lacked anything resembling martial qualities. He was no George Washington.

In 1811, despite earnest pleas from Treasury Secretary Gallatin, Congress had let the twenty-year charter of the Bank of the United States expire. A combination of strict-constructionist Republicans and Anglophobes, who feared the large British interest in the bank, had done it in. In addition, many state banks were being mismanaged, resulting in deposits lost through bankruptcy. Trade had dried up, and tariff revenues had declined. Loans were now needed to cover about two thirds of the war costs, and northeastern opponents of the war were reluctant to lend money.

The military situation was almost as bad. War had been likely for nearly a decade, but Republican defense cutbacks had prevented preparations. When the War of 1812 began, the army numbered only 6,700 men, ill trained, poorly equipped, and led by aging officers. Most of the senior officers were veterans of the Revolution. A young Virginia officer named Winfield Scott, destined for military distinction, commented that most of the veteran commanders "had very generally slunk into either sloth, ignorance, or habits of intemperate drinking."

The navy, on the other hand, was in comparatively good shape, with able officers and trained men whose seamanship had been tested in the fighting against France and Tripoli. Its ships were well outfitted and seaworthy—all sixteen of them. In the first year of the war, it was the navy that produced the only U.S. victories, in isolated duels with British vessels, but their effect was

The American Navy

John Bull (the personification of England) stung to agony by the *Wasp* and *Hornet*, two American ships that won early victories in the War of 1812.

mainly an occasional boost to morale. Within a year the British had blockaded the U.S. coast, except for New England, where they hoped to cultivate anti-war feeling, and most of the little American fleet was bottled up in port.

THE WAR IN THE NORTH   The only place where the United States could effectively strike at the British was Canada. Madison's best hope was a quick attack on Quebec or Montreal to cut Canada's lifeline, the St. Lawrence River, but inadequate preparations, poor leadership, untrained troops, and faulty coordination stymied the American forces—and led to disaster.

The Madison administration opted for a three-pronged drive against Canada: along the Lake Champlain route toward Montreal, with General Henry Dearborn in command; along the Niagara River, with forces under General Stephen Van Rensselaer; and into Upper Canada (north of Lake Erie) from Detroit, with General William Hull and some 2,000 men. In 1812 Hull marched his men across the Detroit River but was pushed back by the British. Sickly and senile, Hull procrastinated in Detroit while his position

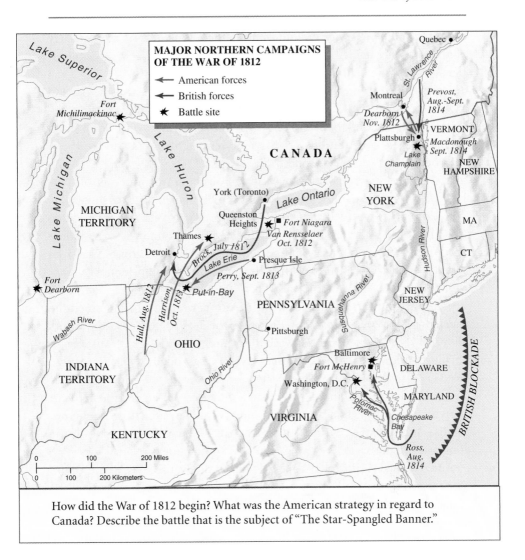

MAJOR NORTHERN CAMPAIGNS
OF THE WAR OF 1812

← American forces

← British forces

★ Battle site

How did the War of 1812 begin? What was the American strategy in regard to
Canada? Describe the battle that is the subject of "The Star-Spangled Banner."

worsened. The British commander cleverly played upon Hull's worst fears.
Gathering what redcoats he could to parade in view of Detroit's defenders,
he announced, that thousands of Indian allies were at the rear and that once
fighting began, he would be unable to control them. Fearing a massacre,
Hull surrendered his entire force.

Along the Niagara River front, General Van Rensselaer was more aggressive. An advance party of 600 Americans crossed the river and worked their
way up the bluffs on the Canadian side. The stage was set for a major victory,
but the New York militia refused to reinforce Van Rensselaer's men, claiming

that their military service did not obligate them to leave the country. They complacently remained on the New York side and watched their outnumbered countrymen fall to a superior force across the river.

On the third front, the old invasion route via Lake Champlain, General Dearborn led his army north from Plattsburgh, New York, toward Montreal. He marched them up to the border, where the state militia once again stood on its alleged constitutional rights and refused to cross, so Dearborn marched them back to Plattsburgh.

Madison's navy secretary now pushed vigorously for American control of inland waters. At Presque Isle (near Erie), Pennsylvania, in 1813, twenty-eight-year-old Oliver Hazard Perry, already a fourteen-year veteran, was building ships from the wilderness lumber. By the end of the summer, Commodore Perry had superior numbers and set out in search of the British, whom he found at Lake Erie's Put-in-Bay on September 10. After completing the preparations for battle, Perry told an aide, "This is the most important day of my life."

Two British warships used their superior weapons to pummel the *Lawrence*, Perry's flagship. Blood flowed on the deck so freely that the sailors slipped and fell as they wrestled with the cannon. After four hours of intense shelling, none of the *Lawrence*'s guns was working, and most of the crew was dead or wounded. The British expected the Americans to flee, but Perry refused to quit. He had himself rowed to another vessel, carried the battle to the enemy, and finally accepted surrender of the entire British squadron. Hatless and bloodied, Perry sent to General William Henry Harrison the long-awaited message: "We have met the enemy and they are ours."

American naval control of Lake Erie forced the British to evacuate Upper Canada. They gave up Detroit, and when they took a defensive stand at the Battle of the Thames on October 5, General Harrison inflicted a defeat that eliminated British power in Upper Canada. In the course of the battle, Tecumseh fell, his dream of Indian unity dying with him.

THE WAR IN THE SOUTH   In the South, too, the war flared up in 1813. On August 30 Creeks allied with the British attacked Fort Mims, on the Alabama River above Mobile, killing 553 people and scalping half of them. The news found Andrew Jackson at home in Tennessee, recovering from a street brawl with Thomas Hart Benton, later a senator from Missouri. As major general of the Tennessee militia, Jackson summoned about 2,000 volunteers and set out on a vengeful campaign that crushed the Creek resistance. The decisive battle occurred on March 27, 1814, at Horseshoe Bend, on the Tallapoosa River, in the heart of the Upper Creek country in east-central Alabama. With the Treaty of Fort Jackson, the Creeks ceded two thirds of their land to the

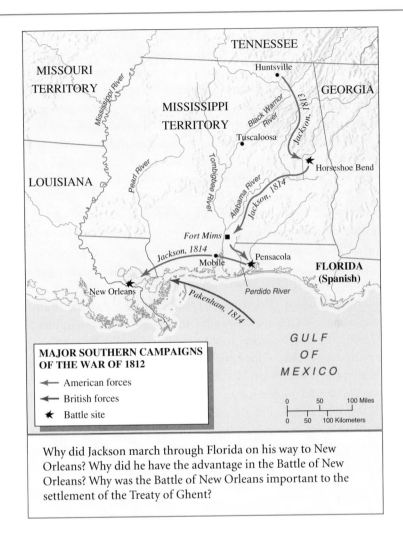

MAJOR SOUTHERN CAMPAIGNS
OF THE WAR OF 1812

← American forces

← British forces

★ Battle site

Why did Jackson march through Florida on his way to New
Orleans? Why did he have the advantage in the Battle of New
Orleans? Why was the Battle of New Orleans important to the
settlement of the Treaty of Ghent?

United States, including part of Georgia and most of Alabama. Red Eagle, the
chief of the Creeks, told Jackson: "I am in your power. . . . My people are all
gone. I can do no more but weep over the misfortunes of my nation."

Four days after the Battle of Horseshoe Bend, Napoléon's empire collapsed.
Now free to deal solely with the United States, the British developed a three-
fold plan of operations for 1814: they would launch a two-pronged invasion of
America from Canada via Fort Niagara and Lake Champlain to increase the
clamor for peace in the Northeast; extend the naval blockade to New England, subjecting coastal towns to raids; and seize New Orleans to cut the Mississippi River, lifeline of the West.

MACDONOUGH'S VICTORY   The main British effort focused on a massive invasion via Lake Champlain. From the north, General George Prevost, governor general of Canada, advanced with the finest army yet assembled on American soil: fifteen regiments of regulars and Canadian militia, a total of about 15,000. The front was saved only by Prevost's vacillation and the superb ability of Commodore Thomas Macdonough, commander of the U.S. naval squadron on Lake Champlain. England's army bogged down while its flotilla engaged Macdonough in a deadly battle that ended with the entire British fleet either destroyed or captured.

FIGHTING IN THE CHESAPEAKE   Meanwhile, however, U.S. forces suffered the most humiliating experience of the war as the British captured and burned Washington, D.C. With attention focused on the Canadian front, the Chesapeake Bay offered the British several inviting targets, including Baltimore, now the fourth-largest city in America. In 1814 a British force landed without opposition at Benedict, Maryland, and headed for Washington, thirty miles away. To defend the capital, the Americans had a militia force of about 7,000, which melted away in the face of the smaller British force.

The redcoats marched unopposed into Washington, where British officers ate a meal in the White House that had been prepared for President and Mrs. Madison, who had joined other refugees in Virginia. The British then burned the White House, the Capitol, and most other government buildings. A tornado the next day compounded the damage, but a violent thunderstorm dampened both the fires and the enthusiasm of the British forces, who left to prepare a new assault on Baltimore in September.

The British attack on Baltimore was a different story. About 1,000 men held Fort McHenry, on an island in the harbor. The British fleet bombarded the fort to no avail, and the invaders abandoned the attack. Francis Scott Key, a Washington lawyer, watched the siege from a vessel in the harbor. The sight of the flag still in place at dawn inspired him to draft the verses of what came to be called "The Star-Spangled Banner." Later revised and set to the tune of an English drinking song, it eventually became America's national anthem.

THE BATTLE OF NEW ORLEANS   The British failure at Baltimore followed by three days their failure on Lake Champlain; their offensive against New Orleans, however, had yet to run its course. Along the Gulf coast, General Andrew Jackson had been busy shoring up the defenses of Mobile and New Orleans. Without authorization he invaded Spanish Florida and took Pensacola, putting an end to British intrigues there. Back in Louisiana he began to erect defenses on the approaches to New Orleans as the British

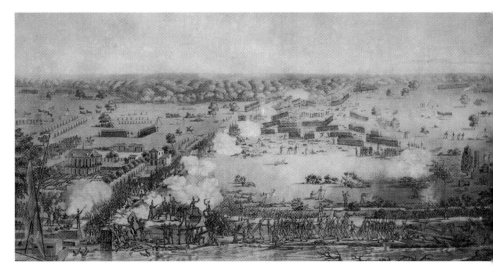

Jackson's Army Defends New Orleans

Andrew Jackson's defeat of the British at New Orleans, January 1815.

fleet, with some 8,000 European veterans under General Sir Edward Paken-ham, took up positions on a level plain on the banks of the Mississippi just south of New Orleans.

Pakenham's painfully careful approach—he waited until all his artillery was available—gave Jackson time to build earthworks bolstered by cotton bales. It was an almost invulnerable position, but Pakenham, contemptuous of Jack-son's force of frontier militiamen, Creole aristocrats, free blacks, and pirates, rashly ordered his veterans forward in a frontal assault at dawn on January 8, 1815. His redcoats ran into a murderous hail of artillery shells and rifle fire. Before the British withdrew, about 2,000 had been wounded or killed, includ-ing Pakenham himself. A British officer, after watching his battered and re-treating troops, wrote that there "never was a more complete failure."

The slow pace of transatlantic communications during the early nine-teenth century meant that the Battle of New Orleans occurred after a peace treaty had been signed in Europe. But this is not to say that it was an anticli-max or that it had no effect on the outcome of the war, for the treaty was yet to be ratified, and the British might have exploited the possession of New Orleans had they won it. The battle did ensure ratification of the treaty as it stood, and both governments acted quickly.

THE TREATY OF GHENT   Peace efforts had begun in 1812, even be-fore hostilities got under way. The British, after all, had repealed their orders in council two days before the declaration of war and confidently expected at least an armistice. Secretary of State James Monroe, however, had told the British that they would have to give up the outrage of impressment as well. Meanwhile, Czar Alexander of Russia had offered to mediate the dispute, hoping to relieve the pressure on Great Britain, his ally against France. Madison had sent Albert Gallatin and James Bayard to join John Quincy Adams, the U.S. minister to Russia, in St. Petersburg. They arrived in 1813, but the czar was at the war front, and they waited impatiently for six months. At that point the British refused Russia's mediation and instead offered to negotiate directly. Madison then appointed Henry Clay and Jonathan Russell to join the other three commissioners in talks that finally got under way in 1814 in the Flemish city of Ghent in August.

In contrast to the array of talent gathered in the American contingent, the British diplomats were nonentities. The Americans had more leeway to use their own judgment, and sharp disagreements developed that were patched up by Albert Gallatin. The sober John Quincy Adams and the hard-drinking, poker-playing Henry Clay, especially, rubbed each other the wrong way. The American delegates at first were instructed to demand that the British abandon impressment and paper blockades and to get payment for the seizure of American ships. The British opened the discussions with demands for territory in New York and Maine, removal of U.S. warships from the Great Lakes, an autonomous Indian buffer state in the Northwest, access to the Mississippi River, and abandonment of U.S. fishing rights off Labrador and Newfoundland. If the British insisted on such a position, the Americans informed them, the negotiations would be at an end.

But the British were stalling, awaiting news of victories to strengthen their hand. The news of the U.S. victory on Lake Champlain arrived in October and weakened the British resolve. The British will to fight was further eroded by a continuing power struggle with France, by the eagerness of British merchants to renew trade with America, and by the war-weariness of a tax-burdened public. The British finally decided that the American war was not worth the cost. One by one, demands were dropped on both sides, until the envoys agreed to end the war, return the prisoners, restore the previous boundaries, and settle nothing else. The questions of fisheries and disputed boundaries were referred to commissions for future settlement. The Treaty of Ghent was signed on Christmas Eve of 1814.

THE HARTFORD CONVENTION While the diplomats converged on a peace settlement in Europe, an entirely different kind of meeting was taking place in Hartford, Connecticut. An ill-fated affair, the Hartford Convention represented the climax of New England's disaffection with "Mr. Madison's war." New England had managed to keep aloof from the war and extract a profit from illegal trading and privateering. Both Massachusetts and Connecticut had refused to contribute militias to the war effort; merchants had continued to sell supplies to British troops in Canada. After the fall of Napoléon, however, the British extended their blockade to New England, occupied Maine, and conducted several raids along the coast. Even Boston seemed threatened. Instead of rallying to the American flag, however, Federalists in the Massachusetts legislature voted in October 1814 for a convention of New England states to plan independent action.

On December 15 the Hartford Convention assembled with delegates chosen by the legislatures of Massachusetts, Rhode Island, and Connecticut as well as two delegates from Vermont and one from New Hampshire—twenty-two in all. The convention proposed seven constitutional amendments designed to limit Republican (and southern) influence: abolishing the counting of slaves in apportioning state representation in Congress, requiring a two-thirds vote to declare war or admit new states, prohibiting embargoes lasting more than sixty days, excluding foreign-born individuals from holding federal offices, limiting the president to one term, and forbidding successive presidents from the same state.

Their call for a later convention in Boston carried the unmistakable threat of secession if the demands were ignored. Yet the threat quickly evaporated. In February 1815, when messengers from Hartford reached Washington, D.C., they found the battered capital celebrating the good news from Ghent and New Orleans. "Their position," according to a French diplomat, was "awkward, embarrassing, and lent itself to cruel ridicule," and they swiftly withdrew their recommendations. The consequence was a fatal blow to the Federalist party, which never recovered from the stigma of disloyalty stamped on it by the Hartford Convention.

THE AFTERMATH   For all the fumbling ineptitude with which the War of 1812 was fought, it generated an intense patriotism. Despite the standoff with which it ended at Ghent, the public nourished a sense of victory, courtesy of Andrew Jackson and his men at New Orleans as well as the heroic exploits of American frigates in their duels with British ships. Under Republican leadership the nation had survived a "second war of independence" against the greatest power on earth and emerged with new symbols of nationhood and a new gallery of heroes. The war also launched the United States toward economic independence, as the interruption of trade with Europe had encouraged the growth of American manufactures. After forty

We Owe Allegiance to No Crown

The War of 1812 generated a renewed spirit of nationalism.

years of independence, it dawned on the world that the new American republic might be emerging as a world power.

As if to underline the point, Congress authorized a quick, decisive blow at the pirates of the Barbary Coast. During the War of 1812, North Africans had again set about plundering American ships. On March 3, 1815, little more than two weeks after the Senate ratified the Treaty of Ghent, Congress sent Captain Stephen Decatur with ten vessels to the Mediterranean. Decatur seized two Algerian ships and then sailed boldly into the harbor of Algiers. On June 30, 1815, the dey of Algiers agreed to cease molesting American ships and to give up all U.S. prisoners. Decatur's show of force induced similar treaties from Tunis and Tripoli. This time there was no tribute; this time, for a change, the Barbary pirates paid for the damage they had done. This time, victory put an end to the piracy and extortion in that quarter permanently.

One of the strangest results of the War of 1812 and its aftermath was a reversal of roles by the Republicans and the Federalists. Out of the wartime experience the Republicans had learned some lessons in nationalism. Certain needs and inadequacies revealed by the war had "Federalized" Madison or "re-Federalized" this Father of the Constitution. Perhaps, he reasoned, a peacetime army and navy were necessary. The lack of a national bank had added to the problems of financing the war. Now Madison wanted it back. The rise of new industries during the war led to a clamor for increased tariffs on imports to protect the infant companies from foreign competition. Madison went along. The problems of overland transportation in the West had revealed the need for internal improvements. Madison agreed, but on that point kept his constitutional scruples. He wanted a constitutional amendment. So while Madison embraced nationalism and broad construction of the Constitution, the Federalists took up the Jeffersonians' position of states' rights and strict construction. It was the first great reversal of roles in constitutional interpretation. It would not be the last.

MAKING CONNECTIONS

- Jefferson's embargo and the War of 1812 encouraged the beginnings of manufacturing in the United States, an important subject, to be discussed in Chapter 12.

- The Federalist party collapsed because of its opposition to the War of 1812. But as the next chapter shows, Republicans did not prosper as much as might have been expected in the absence of political opposition.

- The American success in the War of 1812 (a moral victory at best) led to a tremendous sense of national pride and unity, a spirit analyzed in the next chapter.

FURTHER READING

Marshall Smelser's *The Democratic Republic, 1801–1815* (1968) presents an overview of the Republican administrations. The standard biography of Jefferson is Joseph J. Ellis's *American Sphinx: The Character of Thomas Jefferson* (1996). On the life of Jefferson's friend and successor, see Drew R. McCoy's *The Last of the Fathers: James Madison and the Republican Legacy* (1989). Joyce Appleby's *Capitalism and a New Social Order: The Republican Vision of the 1790s* (1984) minimizes the impact of republican ideology.

Linda K. Kerber's *Federalists in Dissent: Imagery and Ideology in Jeffersonian America* (1970) explores the Federalists while out of power. The concept of judicial review and the courts can be studied in Richard E. Ellis's *The Jeffersonian Crisis: Courts and Politics in the Young Republic* (1971). On John Marshall, see G. Edward White's *The Marshall Court and Cultural Change, 1815–1835* (1988). Milton Lomask's two-volume *Aaron Burr: The Years from Princeton to Vice President, 1756–1805* (1979) and *The Conspiracy and the Years of Exile, 1805–1836* (1982) trace the career of that remarkable American.

For the Louisiana Purchase, consult Alexander De Conde's *This Affair of Louisiana* (1976). For a captivating account of the Lewis and Clark expedition, see Stephen Ambrose's *Undaunted Courage: Meriwether Lewis, Thomas Jefferson, and the Opening of the American West* (1996). Bernard W. Sheehan's *Seeds of Extinction: Jeffersonian Philanthropy and the American Indian* (1973) is more analytical in its treatment of the Jeffersonians' Indian policy and the opening of the West.

Burton Spivak's *Jefferson's English Crisis: Commerce, Embargo, and the Republican Revolution* (1979) discusses Anglo-American relations during Jefferson's administration; Clifford L. Egan's *Neither Peace Nor War: Franco-American Relations, 1803–1812* (1983) covers Franco-American relations. An excellent revisionist treatment of the events that brought on war in 1812 is J.C.A. Stagg's *Mr. Madison's War: Politics, Diplomacy, and Warfare in the Early American Republic, 1783–1830* (1983). The war itself is the focus of Donald R. Hickey's *The War of 1812: A Forgotten Conflict* (1989). See also David Curtis Skaggs and Gerard T. Altoff's *A Signal Victory: The Lake Erie Campaign, 1812–1813* (1997).

Part Three

AN
EXPANSIVE
NATION

mericans during the early nineteenth century formed a relentless migratory stream that spilled over the Appalachian Mountains, spanned the Mississippi River, and in the 1840s reached the Pacific Ocean. Wagons, canals, flatboats, steamboats, and eventually railroads helped transport them. The feverish expansion of the United States into new western territories brought Americans into conflict with Native Americans, Mexicans, the British, and the Spanish. Only a few people, however, expressed moral reservations about displacing others. Most Americans believed it was the "manifest destiny" of the United States to spread across the entire continent—at whatever cost and at whomever's expense. Americans generally believed that they enjoyed the blessing of Providence in their efforts to consolidate the entire continent under their control.

While most Americans continued to earn their living from the soil, textile mills and manufacturing plants began to dot the landscape and transform the nature of work and the pace of life. By midcentury the United States was emerging as one of the world's major industrial powers. In addition, the lure of cheap land and plentiful jobs, as well as the promise of political equality and religious freedom, attracted hundreds of thousands of immigrants from Europe. The newcomers, mostly from Germany and Ireland, faced ethnic prejudices, religious persecution, and language barriers that made assimilation into American culture difficult.

These developments gave American life in the second quarter of the nineteenth century a dynamic and fluid quality. The United States, said the philosopher-poet Ralph Waldo Emerson, was "a country of beginnings, of projects, of designs, of expectations." A restless optimism characterized the period. People of a lowly social status who heretofore had accepted their lot in life now strove to climb the social ladder and enter the political arena. The patrician republic espoused by Jefferson and Madison gave way to the frontier democracy promoted by the Jacksonians. Americans were no longer content to be governed by a small, benevolent aristocracy of talent and wealth. They began to demand—and obtain—government of, by, and for the people.

The fertile economic environment during the antebellum era helped foster the egalitarian idea that individuals (except African Americans, Native Americans, and women) should have an equal opportunity to better themselves and should be granted political rights and privileges.

In America, observed a journalist in 1844, "one has as good a chance as another according to his talents, prudence, and personal exertions."

The exuberant individualism embodied in such mythic expressions of economic equality and political democracy spilled over into the cultural arena during the first half of the century. The so-called Romantic movement applied democratic ideals to philosophy, religion, literature, and the fine arts. In New England, Ralph Waldo Emerson and Henry David Thoreau joined other transcendentalists in espousing a radical individualism. Other reformers were motivated more by a sense of spiritual mission than by democratic individualism. Reformers sought to promote public-supported schools, abolish slavery, promote temperance, and improve the lot of the disabled, the insane, and the imprisoned. Their efforts ameliorated some of the problems created by the frenetic economic growth and territorial expansion. But the reformers made little headway against slavery. It would take a brutal civil war to dislodge America's "peculiar institution."

10

NATIONALISM AND SECTIONALISM

FOCUS QUESTIONS

· What were the elements of the "Era of Good Feelings"?

· How did economic policies, diplomacy, and judicial decisions reflect the nationalism of those years?

· What were the various issues that promoted sectionalism?

· What was the fate of the Republican party after the collapse of the Federalists?

To answer these questions and access additional review material, please visit www.wwnorton.com/studyspace.

Amid the jubilation that followed the War of 1812, Americans began to transform their young nation. Hundreds of thousands of people streamed westward at the same time that the largely local economy was being transformed into a national market. The spread of plantation slavery and the cotton culture into the Old Southwest—Georgia, Alabama, Mississippi, Louisiana, and Texas—disrupted family ties and transformed social life. In the North and the West, meanwhile, a dynamic urban middle class began to emerge and grow in towns and cities. Such dramatic changes prompted vigorous political debates over economic policies, transportation improvements, and the extension of slavery into the new territories. In the process the nation began to divide into three powerful regional blocs—North, South, and West—whose shifting alliances would shape the political landscape until the Civil War.

ECONOMIC NATIONALISM

Immediately after the War of 1812, Americans experienced a new surge of nationalism. The young United States was growing from a loose confederation of territories into a fully functioning nation-state that spanned almost an entire continent. An abnormal economic prosperity after the war fed a feeling of well-being and enhanced the prestige of the national government. Thomas Jefferson's embargo ironically had spawned the factories that he abhorred. The idea spread that the country needed a more balanced economy of farming, commerce, and manufacturing. After a generation of war, shortages of farm products in Europe forced up the prices of American products and stimulated agricultural expansion—indeed, it induced a wild speculation in farmland. Southern cotton, tobacco, and rice came to account for about two thirds of American exports. At the same time the postwar market was flooded with cheap English goods that planters and farmers could buy. The new manufacturers would seek protection from this foreign competition.

President James Madison, in his first annual message to Congress after the war, recommended several steps to strengthen the government: improved fortifications, a permanent army and a strong navy, a new national bank, effective protection of new industries, a system of canals and roads for commercial and military use, and to top it off, a great national university. "The

The Union Manufactories of Maryland in Patapsco Falls, Baltimore County (ca. 1815)

A textile mill established during the embargo of 1807. The Union Manufactories would employ over 600 people.

Republicans have out-Federalized Federalism," one New Englander remarked. Congress responded by authorizing a standing army of 10,000 and strengthening the navy as well.

THE BANK OF THE UNITED STATES   The trinity of economic nationalism—proposals for a second national bank, a protective tariff, and internal improvements—inspired the greatest controversies. After the first national bank expired in 1811, the country had fallen into a financial muddle. State-chartered banks mushroomed with little or no control, and their bank notes (paper money) flooded the channels of commerce with currency of uncertain value. Because hard money had been so short during the war, many state banks had suspended specie (gold or silver) payments when redeeming their paper notes, thereby depressing their value. The absence of a central bank had been a source of financial embarrassment to the government, which had neither a ready means of floating loans nor a way of transferring funds across the country.

Madison and most younger Republicans salved their constitutional scruples about a national bank with a dash of pragmatism. The issue of a central bank, Madison said, had been decided "by repeated recognitions . . . of the validity of such an institution in acts of the legislative, executive, and judicial branches of the Government, accompanied by . . . a concurrence of the general will of the nation." In 1816 Congress adopted, over the protest of Old Republicans, a provision for a new Bank of the United States, which would be located in Philadelphia. Once again the charter ran for twenty years, and the federal government owned one fifth of the stock and named five of the twenty-five directors, with the Bank of the United States serving as the government depository for federal funds. Its bank notes were accepted in payments to the government. In return for its privileges, the bank had to take care of the government's funds without charge, lend the government up to $5 million upon demand, and pay the government a cash bonus of $1.5 million.

The bitter debate over the bank, then and later, helped to set the pattern of regional alignment for most other economic issues. Missouri senator Thomas Hart Benton predicted that the currency-short western towns would be at the mercy of a centralized eastern bank. "They may be devoured by it any moment! They are in the jaws of the monster! A lump of butter in the mouth of a dog! One gulp, one swallow, and all is gone!"

The debate over the Bank of the United States was also noteworthy because of the leading roles played by the era's greatest statesmen: John C. Calhoun of South Carolina, Henry Clay of Kentucky, and Daniel Webster of New Hampshire. Calhoun, still in his youthful phase as a war-hawk nationalist, introduced the banking bill and pushed it through, justifying its constitutionality by citing the congressional power to regulate the currency. Clay, who had long opposed a national bank, now asserted that circumstances had made one indispensable. Webster, on the other hand, led the opposition of the New England Federalists, who did not want the banking center moved from Boston to Philadelphia. Later, after he had moved from New Hampshire to Massachusetts, Webster would return to Congress as the champion of a much stronger national power, whereas events would steer Calhoun toward a defiant embrace of states' rights.

A PROTECTIVE TARIFF   The shift of capital from commerce to manufactures, begun during the embargo of 1807, had speeded up during the war. Peace in 1815 brought a sudden renewal of cheap British imports and generated pleas for tariffs (taxes on imports) to protect infant American industries from foreign competition. The self-interest of the manufacturers, who as yet had little political influence, was reinforced by a patriotic desire for economic independence from Britain. New England shippers and southern farmers opposed tariffs, but in both sections sizable minorities believed that the promotion of industry by means of tariffs enhanced both sectional and national welfare.

The tariff of 1816, the first intended more to protect industry against foreign competition than to raise revenue, easily passed in Congress. Both the South and New England split their votes, with New England supporting the tariff and the South opposing it, and the middle Atlantic states and the Old Northwest cast only five negative votes altogether. Nathaniel Macon of North Carolina opposed the tariff and defended the Old Republican doctrine of strict construction. The power to protect industry, Macon said, like the power to establish a bank, rested on the idea that there were implied powers embedded in the Constitution; Macon worried that such implied powers might one day be used to abolish slavery. The minority of southerners who voted for the tariff, led by John Calhoun, did so because they hoped that the South might itself become a manufacturing center. South Carolina was then developing a few textile mills. According to the census of 1810, the southern states had approximately as many manufacturers as New England. Within a few years, however, New England would move well ahead of the South, and Calhoun would accept Macon's views on protection. The tariff would then become a sectional issue, with manufacturers, wool processors, and food, sugar, and hemp growers favoring higher tariffs while cotton planters and shipping interests favored lower duties.

INTERNAL IMPROVEMENTS   The third major issue of the time involved government support for internal improvements: the building of

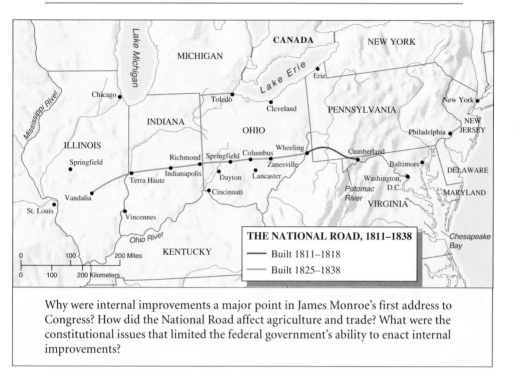

THE NATIONAL ROAD, 1811–1838

—— Built 1811–1818

—— Built 1825–1838

Why were internal improvements a major point in James Monroe's first address to Congress? How did the National Road affect agriculture and trade? What were the constitutional issues that limited the federal government's ability to enact internal improvements?

roads and the development of water transportation. The war had high-lighted the shortcomings of existing facilities. Troop movements through the western wilderness proved very difficult, and settlers found that unless they located themselves near navigable waters, they were cut off from trade and limited to a frontier subsistence.

The federal government had entered the field of internal improvements under Thomas Jefferson. He and both of his successors recommended a constitutional amendment to give the federal government undisputed power in the field. Lacking that, the constitutional grounds for federal action rested mainly on the provision of national defense and the expansion of the postal system. In 1803, when Ohio became a state, Congress decreed that 5 percent of the proceeds from land sales in the state would go to building a National Road from the Atlantic coast into Ohio and beyond as the territory developed. Construction of the National Road began in 1815.

Originally called the Cumberland Road, it was the first federally financed interstate roadway. By 1818 it was open from Cumberland, Maryland, to Wheeling, Virginia (now West Virginia), on the Ohio River. By 1838 the road extended all the way to Vandalia, Illinois. By reducing transportation costs and opening up new markets, the National Road and other privately financed turnpikes helped accelerate the commercialization of agriculture.

In 1817 John C. Calhoun put through the House a bill to place in a fund for internal improvements the $1.5 million bonus that the Bank of the United States had paid for its charter, as well as all future dividends on the government's bank stock. Opposition to federal spending on transportation projects centered in New England and the South, which expected to gain the least from western development, and support came largely from the West, which badly needed good roads. On his last day in office, President Madison vetoed the bill. While sympathetic to its purpose, he could not overcome his "insuperable difficulty . . . in reconciling the bill with the Constitution" and suggested instead a constitutional amendment. Internal improvements remained for another hundred years, with few exceptions, the responsibility of states and private enterprise. The federal government did not enter the field on a large scale until passage of the Federal Highways Act of 1916.

"GOOD FEELINGS"

JAMES MONROE   As James Madison approached the end of a turbulent presidency, he, like Jefferson, turned to a fellow Virginian, another secretary of state, to be his successor. For Madison that man would be James Monroe.

James Monroe

Portrayed as he entered the presidency in 1817.

In the Republican caucus, Monroe won the nomination. In the 1816 election he overwhelmed his Federalist opponent, Rufus King of New York, with 183 to 34 votes in the Electoral College. The "Virginia dynasty" continued. Like three of the four presidents before him, Monroe was a Virginia planter, but with a difference: his plantation holdings were much smaller. At the outbreak of the Revolution, he was just beginning his studies at the College of William and Mary. He joined the army at the age of sixteen, fought with Washington during the Revolution, and later studied law with Jefferson.

Monroe had served in the Virginia assembly, as governor of the state, in the Confederation Congress and in the U.S. Senate, and as U.S. minister in Paris, London, and Madrid. Under Madison he was secretary of state and doubled as secretary of war. Monroe, with his powdered wig, cocked hat, and knee breeches, was the last of the Revolutionary generation to serve in the White House and the last president to dress in the old style.

Firmly grounded in Republican principles, Monroe failed to keep up with the onrush of the new nationalism. He accepted as an accomplished fact the Bank of the United States and the protective tariff, but during his tenure there was no further extension of economic nationalism. Indeed, there was a minor setback: he permitted the National Road to be carried forward, but in his veto of the Cumberland Road bill (1822), he denied the authority of Congress to collect tolls to pay for its repair and maintenance. Like Jefferson and Madison he urged a constitutional amendment to remove all doubt about federal authority in the field of internal improvements.

Monroe surrounded himself with some of the ablest young Republican leaders. John Quincy Adams became secretary of state. William H. Crawford of Georgia continued as secretary of the Treasury. John C. Calhoun headed the War Department after Henry Clay refused the job in order to stay on as Speaker of the House. The new administration found the country in a state of well-being: America was at peace, and the economy was flourishing. Soon after his 1817 inauguration, Monroe embarked on a goodwill tour of New England. In Boston, lately a hotbed of wartime dissent, a Federalist paper commented on the president's visit under the heading "Era of Good Feelings." The label became a popular catchphrase for Monroe's administration, one that historians would later seize upon. Yet the Era of Good Feelings was very brief. A resurgence of factionalism and sectionalism erupted just as the postwar prosperity collapsed in the panic of 1819.

In 1820 the president was reelected without opposition. The Federalists were too weak to put up a candidate. Monroe won all the electoral votes except for three abstentions and one vote from New Hampshire for John Quincy Adams. The Republican party was dominant—for the moment. In fact, it was about to follow the Federalists into oblivion. Amid the general political contentment of the era, the first party system was fading away, but rivals for the succession soon commenced the process of forming new parties.

RELATIONS WITH BRITAIN   Fueling the contentment after the War of 1812 was a growing trade with Britain (and India). The Treaty of Ghent had left unsettled a number of minor disputes, but subsequently two important compacts—the Rush-Bagot Agreement of 1817 and the Convention of

1818—removed several potential causes of irritation. In the first, resulting from an exchange of notes between Acting Secretary of State Richard Rush and the British minister Charles Bagot, the threat of naval competition on the Great Lakes vanished with an arrangement to limit forces there to several federal ships collecting customs duties. Although the exchange made no reference to the land boundary between the United States and Canada, its spirit gave rise to the tradition of an unfortified border, the longest in the world.

The Convention of 1818 covered three major points. The northern limit of the Louisiana Purchase was settled by extending the national boundary along the 49th parallel west from Lake of the Woods in what would become Minnesota to the crest of the Rocky Mountains. West of that point the Oregon Country would be open to joint occupation by the British and the Americans, but the boundary remained unsettled. The right of Americans to fish off Newfoundland and Labrador, granted in 1783, was acknowledged once again.

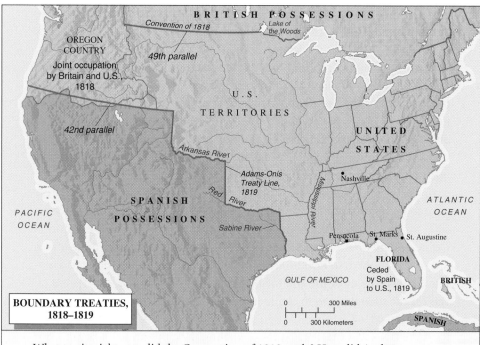

BOUNDARY TREATIES, 1818–1819

What territorial terms did the Convention of 1818 settle? How did Andrew Jackson's actions in Florida help John Q. Adams claim the territory from Spain? What were the terms of the treaty with Spain?

The chief remaining problem was Britain's exclusion of American ships from the West Indies in order to reserve that lucrative trade for the British. This remained a chronic irritant, and the United States retaliated with several measures. Under the Navigation Act of 1817, importation of West Indian produce was restricted to American vessels or vessels belonging to West Indian merchants. In 1818 U.S. ports were closed to all British vessels arriving from a colony that was legally closed to vessels of the United States. In 1820 Monroe approved an act of Congress that specified total nonintercourse—with British vessels, with all British colonies in the Americas, and even in goods taken to England and reexported. The rapprochement with Britain therefore fell short of perfection.

THE EXTENSION OF BOUNDARIES   The year 1819 was one of the more fateful years in American history. Controversial efforts to expand U.S. territory, an intense financial panic, a tense debate over the extension of slavery, and several landmark Supreme Court cases combined to bring an unsettling end to the Era of Good Feelings. The new nationalism reached a climax with the acquisition of Florida and the extension of America's southwestern boundary to the Pacific, but nationalism quickly began to run afoul of domestic crosscurrents that would submerge the country in sectional squabbles.

In the calculations of global power, it had perhaps long since been reckoned that Florida would someday pass to the United States. Spanish sovereignty was more a technicality than an actuality and extended little beyond St. Augustine on the east coast and Pensacola and St. Marks on the Gulf. The province had been a thorn in the side of the United States during the recent war, when it had served as a center of British intrigue; a haven for Creek refugees, who were beginning to take the name Seminole (Runaway or Separatist); and a harbor for runaway slaves and criminals.

Spain, once dominant in the Americas, was now a declining power unable to enforce its obligations, under Pinckney's Treaty of 1795, to pacify the frontier. In 1816 U.S. forces clashed with a group of escaped slaves who had taken over a British fort on the Appalachicola River. Seminoles were soon fighting

Unrest in Florida

Portrait of an escaped slave who lived with the Seminoles in Florida.

white settlers in the area, and in 1817 Americans burned a Seminole border settlement, killed five of its inhabitants, and dispersed the rest across the border into Florida.

At that point, Secretary of War Calhoun authorized a campaign against the Seminoles, and he summoned General Andrew Jackson from Nashville to take command. Jackson's orders allowed him to pursue the offenders into Spanish territory but not to attack any Spanish post. A frustrated Jackson pledged to President Monroe that if the United States wanted Florida, he could wind up the whole controversy in sixty days.

When it came to Spaniards or Indians, few white Tennesseans—and certainly not Andrew Jackson—were likely to bother with technicalities. Jackson pushed eastward through Florida, reinforced by Tennessee volunteers and friendly Creeks, taking a Spanish post, skirmishing with the Seminoles, and destroying their settlements. He hanged two of their leaders. He then turned west, seized Pensacola, and returned home to Nashville. The whole episode had taken about four months; the Florida Panhandle was in American hands by 1818.

The news of Jackson's exploits aroused anger in Madrid and concern in Washington. Spain demanded the return of its territory and the punishment of Jackson, but Spain's impotence was plain for all to see. Monroe's cabinet was at first prepared to disavow Jackson's actions, especially his direct attack on Spanish posts. Calhoun, as secretary of war, was inclined, at least officially, to discipline Jackson for disregard of orders—a stand that would later cause bad blood between the two men—but privately confessed a certain pleasure at the outcome. In any case a man as popular as Jackson was almost invulnerable. And he had one important friend, Secretary of State John Quincy Adams, who realized that Jackson had strengthened his own hand in negotiations already under way with the Spanish minister. U.S. forces withdrew from Florida, but negotiations resumed with the knowledge that the United States could retake Florida at any time.

With the fate of Florida a foregone conclusion, John Quincy Adams turned

Andrew Jackson

Victor at the Battle of New Orleans, Indian fighter, and future president.

his eye to a larger purpose, a definition of the ambiguous western boundary of the Louisiana Purchase and—his boldest stroke—extension of its boundary to the Pacific coast. In lengthy negotiations, Adams gradually gave ground on claims to Texas but stuck to his demand for a transcontinental line. Agreement came early in 1819. Spain ceded all of Florida in return for the U.S. government's assumption of private American claims against Spain up to $5 million. The western boundary of the Louisiana Purchase would run along the Sabine River and then, in stair-step fashion, up to the Red River, along the Red, and up to the Arkansas River. From the source of the Arkansas, it would go north to the 42nd parallel and thence west to the Pacific coast. A dispute over land claims held up ratification for another two years, but those claims were revoked and final ratifications were exchanged in 1821. Florida became a U.S. territory, and its first governor, albeit briefly, was Andrew Jackson. In 1845 Florida achieved statehood.

CRISES AND COMPROMISES

THE PANIC OF 1819   John Quincy Adams's Transcontinental Treaty of 1819 was a diplomatic triumph and the climactic event of the postwar nationalism. Even before it was signed, however, two thunderclaps signaled the end of the brief Era of Good Feelings and gave warning of stormy weather ahead: the financial panic of 1819 and the controversy over Missouri statehood. The occasion for the panic was the sudden collapse of cotton prices. At one point in 1818, cotton had soared to 32.5¢ per pound. The high prices prompted British textile mills to turn from American sources to cheaper East Indian cotton, and by 1819 cotton was averaging only 14.3¢ per pound in New Orleans. The price collapse set off a decline in the demand for other American goods and suddenly revealed the fragility of the prosperity that had begun after the War of 1812.

Since 1815 a speculative bubble had grown, with expectations that economic expansion would go on forever. But American industry struggled to find markets for its goods. Even the tariff of 1816 had not been a strong enough force to eliminate British competition. What was more, businessmen, farmers, and land speculators had inflated the bubble with a volatile expansion of credit. The sources of this credit were both government and the banks. Under the Land Act of 1800, the government had extended four years' credit to those who bought western land. After 1804 one could buy as little as 160 acres at a minimum price of $1.64 per acre (although in auctions the best land went for more). In many cases, speculators took up large tracts, paying only one fourth down, and then sold them to settlers with the understanding that the settlers would pay the remaining installments. With the collapse of crop prices and, subsequently, land values, both speculators and settlers saw their income plummet.

The reckless practices of the state banks compounded the inflation of credit. To enlarge their loans, they issued more bank notes than they could redeem. Even the second Bank of the United States, which was supposed to introduce some order to the financial arena, got caught up in the mania. Its first president yielded to the contagion of the get-rich-quick fever that was sweeping the country. The proliferation of branches, combined with little supervision by Philadelphia, carried the bank into the same reckless extension of loans that state banks had pursued. In 1819, just as alert businessmen began to take alarm, a case of extensive fraud and embezzlement in the Baltimore branch of the Bank of United States came to light. The disclosure prompted the appointment of Langdon Cheves, a former congressman from South Carolina, as the bank's president.

Cheves reduced salaries and other costs, postponed the payment of dividends, restrained the extension of credit, and presented for redemption the state bank notes that came in, thereby forcing the state-chartered banks to keep specie reserves. Cheves rescued the bank from near ruin, but only by putting heavy pressure on the state banks. State banks in turn put pressure on their debtors, who found it harder to renew old loans or get new ones. In 1822, considering his task completed, Cheves retired and was succeeded the following year by Nicholas Biddle of Philadelphia. The Cheves policies were the result rather than the cause of the panic, but they pinched debtors. Hard times lasted about three years, and the bank took much of the blame in the popular mind. The panic passed, but resentment of the bank lingered in the South and the West.

THE MISSOURI COMPROMISE   Just as the financial panic spread over the country, another cloud appeared on the horizon: the onset of a fierce sectional controversy over slavery. By 1819 the country had an equal number of slave and free states—eleven of each. The line between them was defined by the southern and western boundaries of Pennsylvania and the Ohio River. Although slavery lingered in some places north of the line, it was on the way to extinction there. Beyond the Mississippi River, however, no move had been made to extend the dividing line across the Louisiana Territory, where slavery had existed since the days when France and Spain had colonized the area. At the time the Missouri Territory embraced all of the Louisiana Purchase except the state of Louisiana (1812) and the Arkansas

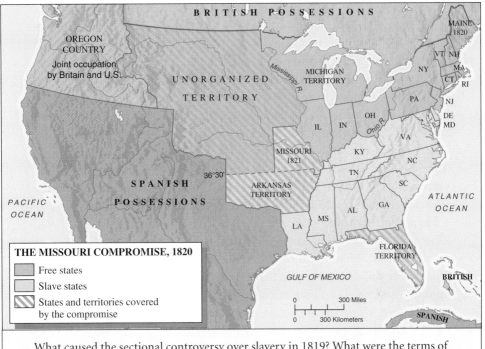

THE MISSOURI COMPROMISE, 1820

- Free states
- Slave states
- States and territories covered by the compromise

What caused the sectional controversy over slavery in 1819? What were the terms of the Missouri Compromise? What was Henry Clay's solution to the Missouri constitution's ban on free blacks in that state?

Territory (1819). The old French town of St. Louis became the funnel through which settlers rushed westward beyond the Mississippi. They were largely from the South—and they brought their slaves with them.

In 1819 the House of Representatives was asked to approve legislation enabling Missouri to draft a state constitution, its population having passed the minimum of 60,000. At that point, Representative James Tallmadge Jr., a New York congressman, proposed a resolution prohibiting the further introduction of slaves into Missouri, which already had some 10,000, and providing freedom at age twenty-five to those born after the territory's admission as a state. After brief but fiery exchanges, the House passed the amendment on an almost strictly sectional vote. The Senate rejected it by a similar tally, but with several northerners joining in the opposition. With population at the time growing faster in the North, a balance between the two sections could be held only in the Senate. In the House, slave states had 81 votes while free states had 105; a balance was unlikely ever to be restored there.

Maine's application for statehood made it easier to arrive at an agreement. Since colonial times, Maine had been the northern province of Massachusetts. The Senate linked its request for separate statehood with Missouri's and voted to admit Maine as a free state and Missouri as a slave state, thus maintaining the balance between free and slave states in the Senate. An Illinois senator further extended the compromise by an amendment to exclude slavery from the rest of the Louisiana Purchase north of 36°30′, Missouri's southern border. Slavery thus would continue in the Arkansas Territory and in the state of Missouri but would be excluded from the remainder of the area. People at that time presumed that what remained was the Great American Desert, unlikely ever to be settled. Thus the arrangement seemed to be a victory for the slave states. By a very close vote it passed the House on March 2, 1820.

Then another problem arose. The pro-slavery elements that dominated Missouri's constitutional convention inserted in the proposed new state constitution a proviso excluding free blacks and mulattoes from the state. This clearly violated the requirement of Article IV, Section 2, of the Constitution: "The Citizens of each State shall be entitled to all Privileges and Immunities of Citizens in the several States." Free blacks were citizens of many states, including the slave states of North Carolina and Tennessee, where until the mid-1830s they also voted.

Henry Clay

Clay entered the Senate at age twenty-eight despite the requirement that senators be at least thirty years old.

The renewed controversy threatened final approval of Missouri's admission until Henry Clay formulated a "second" Missouri Compromise: admission of Missouri as a state would depend upon assurance from the Missouri legislature that it would never construe the offending clause in such a way as to sanction the denial of privileges that citizens held under the Constitution. It was one of the more artless dodges in American history, for it required the legislature to affirm that the state constitution did not mean what it clearly said, but the compromise worked. The Missouri legislature duly adopted the pledge while denying that the legislature had any power to bind the people of the state to it. On August 10, 1821, President Monroe proclaimed the admission of Missouri as the twenty-fourth state. For the moment the controversy subsided. "But this momentous question," the aging Thomas Jefferson wrote to a friend after the first compromise, "like a firebell in the night awakened and filled me with terror. I considered it at once as the knell of the Union."

JUDICIAL NATIONALISM

JOHN MARSHALL, CHIEF JUSTICE   Meanwhile, nationalism still flourished in the Supreme Court, where Chief Justice John Marshall preserved Hamiltonian Federalism for yet another generation. Marshall, a survivor of the Revolution and a distant cousin of Thomas Jefferson's, established the power of the Supreme Court by his force of mind and crystalline logic.

During Marshall's early years on the Court (he served thirty-four years altogether), he affirmed the principle of judicial review. In *Marbury v. Madison* (1803) and *Fletcher v. Peck* (1810) the Court struck down first a federal law and then a state law as unconstitutional. In the cases of *Martin v. Hunter's Lessee* (1816) and *Cohens v. Virginia* (1821), the Court assumed the right to take appeals from state courts on the grounds that the Constitution, the laws, and the treaties of the United States could be kept uniformly the supreme law of the land only if the Court could review decisions of state courts. In the first case the Court overruled Virginia's confiscation of Loyalist property after the Revolution, because it violated treaties with Great Britain; in the second the Court upheld Virginia's right to forbid the sale of lottery tickets.

PROTECTING CONTRACT RIGHTS   In the fateful year of 1819, John Marshall and the Court made two more decisions of major importance in checking the states and building the power of the central government. One of them, *Dartmouth College v. Woodward*, involved an attempt by the New Hampshire legislature to alter

John Marshall

Chief Justice and pillar of judicial nationalism.

a provision in Dartmouth's charter, under which the college's trustees became a self-perpetuating board. In 1816 the state's Republican legislature, offended by this relic of monarchy and even more by the Federalist majority on the board, placed Dartmouth under a new board named by the governor. The original trustees sued, lost in the state courts, but with Daniel Webster as counsel won on appeal to the Supreme Court. The charter, Marshall said, was a valid contract that the legislature had impaired, an act forbidden by the Constitution. This decision implied a new and enlarged definition of *contract* that seemed to put private corporations beyond the reach of the states that chartered them. Thereafter states commonly wrote into charters and general laws of incorporation provisions making them subject to modification. Such provisions were then part of the "contract."

STRENGTHENING THE FEDERAL GOVERNMENT The second major Supreme Court case of 1819 was John Marshall's single most important interpretation of the constitutional system: *McCulloch v. Maryland.* James McCulloch, a clerk in the Baltimore branch of the Bank of the United States, had failed to affix state revenue stamps to bank notes as required by a Maryland law taxing the notes. Indicted by the state, McCulloch, acting for the bank, appealed to the Supreme Court, which handed down a unanimous judgment upholding the power of Congress to charter the bank and denying any right of the state to tax it. In a lengthy opinion, Marshall rejected Maryland's argument that the federal government was the creature of sovereign states. Instead, he argued, it arose directly from the people acting through the conventions that had ratified the Constitution. Whereas sovereignty was divided between the states and the national government, the latter, "though limited in its powers, is supreme within its sphere of action."

Marshall went on to endorse the doctrine of the federal government's having implied constitutional powers. The "necessary and proper" clause, he argued, did not mean "absolutely indispensable." The test of constitutionality was, in his view, a practical one: "Let the end be legitimate, let it be within the scope of the Constitution, and all means which are appropriate, which are plainly adapted to that end, which are not prohibited, but consistent with the letter and spirit of the Constitution, are constitutional."

Maryland's effort to tax the national bank conflicted with the supreme law of the land. One great principle that "entirely pervades the Constitution," Marshall wrote, was "that the Constitution and the laws made in pursuance thereof are supreme: that they control the Constitution and laws of the respective states, and cannot be controlled by them." The effort by a state to tax a federal bank therefore was unconstitutional, for the "power to tax involves the power to destroy"—which was precisely what the legislatures of Maryland and several other states had in mind with respect to the bank.

REGULATING INTERSTATE COMMERCE   John Marshall's last great decision, *Gibbons v. Ogden* (1824), established national supremacy in regulating interstate commerce. In 1808 Robert Fulton and Robert R. Livingston (Jefferson's minister to France in 1801), who pioneered commercial use of the steamboat, won from the New York legislature the exclusive right to operate steamboats on the state's waters. From them in turn Aaron Ogden received the exclusive right to navigate the Hudson River between New York and New Jersey. Thomas Gibbons, however, operated a coastal trade under a federal license and came into competition with Ogden. On behalf of a unanimous Court, Marshall ruled that the monopoly granted by the state conflicted with the federal Coasting Act, under which Gibbons operated. Congressional power to regulate commerce, the Court said, "like all others vested in

Deck Life on the Paragon, 1811–1812

The *Paragon*, "a whole floating town," was the third steamboat operated on the Hudson by Robert Fulton and Robert R. Livingston.

Congress, is complete in itself, may be exercised to its utmost extent, and acknowledges no limitations other than are prescribed in the Constitution."

The opinion stopped just short of stating an exclusive federal power over commerce, and later cases would clarify the point that states had a concurrent jurisdiction so long as it did not come into conflict with federal action. For many years there was in fact little federal regulation of commerce, so that in striking down the monopoly created by the state, Marshall had opened the way to extensive development of steamboat navigation and, soon afterward, railroads. Economic expansion often depended upon judicial nationalism.

NATIONALIST DIPLOMACY

THE NORTHWEST   In foreign affairs, too, nationalism continued to be an effective force. Within two years of final approval of John Quincy Adams's Transcontinental Treaty, the secretary of state was able to draw another important transcontinental line. In 1819 Spain had abandoned its claim to the Oregon Country above the 42nd parallel, but in 1821 the Russian czar claimed the Pacific coast as far south as the fifty-first parallel, which in the American view lay within the Oregon Country.

In 1823 Secretary of State Adams contested "the right of Russia to any territorial establishment on this continent." The U.S. government, he informed the Russian minister, assumed the principle "that the American continents are no longer subjects for any new European colonial establishments." His protest resulted in a treaty signed in 1824, whereby Russia, which had more pressing concerns in Europe, accepted the line of 54°40' as the southern boundary of its claim. In 1825 a similar agreement between Russia and Britain gave the Oregon Country clearly defined boundaries, although it was still subject to joint occupation by the United States and Great Britain under their agreement of 1818. In 1827 both countries agreed to extend indefinitely the provision for joint occupation, subject to termination by either power.

THE MONROE DOCTRINE   Secretary of State Adams's disapproval of further hemispheric colonization had clear implications for Latin America as well. One consequence of the Napoleonic Wars and the French occupation of Spain and Portugal was a series of wars of liberation in Latin America. Within little more than a decade after the flag of rebellion was first raised in 1811, Spain had lost almost its entire empire in the Americas. All that was left were the islands of Cuba and Puerto Rico and the colony of Santo

Domingo on the island of Hispaniola. The only other European possessions in the Americas, 330 years after Columbus's first voyage, were Russian Alaska, British Canada, British Honduras, and the Dutch, French, and British Guianas.

In 1823 rumors began to circulate that France wanted to restore the Spanish king's power over Spain's American empire. President Monroe and Secretary of War Calhoun were alarmed at the possibility, although John Quincy Adams took the more realistic view that any such action was unlikely. The British foreign minister, George Canning, told the American minister to London that the two countries should jointly oppose any incursions by France or Spain in the Western Hemisphere.

Monroe at first agreed, with the support of his sage advisers Jefferson and Madison. Adams, however, urged upon Monroe and the cabinet the independent course of proclaiming a unilateral policy against the restoration of Spain's colonies. "It would be more candid," Adams said, "as well as more dignified, to avow our principles explicitly to Russia and France, than to come in as a cockboat in the wake of the British man-of-war." Adams knew that the British navy would stop any action by the Quintuple Alliance (Austria, France, Great Britain, Prussia, and Russia) in Latin America, and he suspected that the alliance had no intention to intervene anyway. The British, moreover, wanted the United States to agree not to acquire any more Spanish territory, including Cuba, Texas, and California, but Adams preferred to avoid such a commitment.

Monroe incorporated the substance of Adams's views into his annual message to Congress in 1823. The Monroe Doctrine, as it was later called, comprised four major points: (1) that "the American continents . . . are henceforth not to be considered as subjects for future colonization by any European powers"; (2) that the political system of European powers was different from that of the United States, which would "consider any attempt on their part to extend their system to any portion of this hemisphere as dangerous to our peace and safety"; (3) that the United States would not interfere with existing European colonies; and (4) that the United States would keep out of the internal affairs of European nations and their wars.

At the time the statement drew little attention either in the United States or abroad. The Monroe Doctrine, not even so called until 1852, became one of the cherished principles of American foreign policy, but for the time being it slipped into obscurity for want of any occasion to invoke it. In spite of Adams's affirmation, the United States came in as a cockboat in the wake of the British man-of-war after all, for the effectiveness of the doctrine depended upon British naval supremacy. The doctrine had no standing in international law. It was merely a statement of intent by an American president to Congress and did not even draw enough interest at the time for European powers to acknowledge it.

ONE-PARTY POLITICS

Almost from the start of James Monroe's second term, in 1821, the jockeying for the presidential succession began. Three members of Monroe's cabinet were active candidates: Secretary of War John Calhoun, Secretary of the Treasury William H. Crawford, and Secretary of State John Quincy Adams. Henry Clay, longtime Speaker of the House, also hungered for the office. And on the fringes of the Washington scene, a new force appeared in the person of Andrew Jackson, the scourge of the British, Spanish, Creeks, and Seminoles, the epitome of what every frontiersman admired, who became a senator from Tennessee in 1823. All were Republicans, for again no Federalist stood a chance, but they were competing in a new political world, complicated by the crosscurrents of nationalism and sectionalism. With only one party there was in effect no party, for there existed no generally accepted method for choosing a "regular" candidate.

PRESIDENTIAL NOMINATIONS   Selection of presidential candidates by congressional caucus, already under attack in 1816, had disappeared in the wave of unanimity that reelected Monroe in 1820 without the formality of a nomination. The friends of William Crawford sought in vain to breathe life back into "King Caucus," but only a minority of congressmen appeared in answer to the call. They duly named Crawford for president, but the endorsement was so weak as to be more a handicap than an advantage. Crawford was in fact the logical successor to the Virginia dynasty, a native of the state though a resident of Georgia. He had flirted with nationalism but swung back to states' rights and strict construction and assumed leadership of a faction, called the Radicals, that included Old Republicans and those who distrusted the nationalism of John Quincy Adams and John Calhoun. Crawford's candidacy foundered from the beginning, for the candidate had been stricken in 1823 by some unknown disease that left him half-paralyzed and half-blind. His friends protested that he would soon be well, but he never did fully recover.

Long before the Crawford caucus met in early 1824, indeed for two years before, the country had broken out in a rash of presidential endorsements by state legislatures and public meetings. In 1822 the Tennessee legislature named Andrew Jackson as their choice to succeed Monroe. In 1824 a mass meeting of Pennsylvanians added their endorsement. Jackson, who had previously kept silent, responded that while the presidency should not be sought, it should not be declined. The same meeting named Calhoun for vice president, and Calhoun accepted. The youngest of the candidates, he was content to take second place and bide his time. Meanwhile, the Kentucky legislature had named its favorite son, Henry Clay, in 1822. The Massachusetts legislature named John Quincy Adams in 1824.

Of the four candidates, only two had clearly defined programs, and the outcome was an early lesson in the danger of committing oneself on the issues too soon. Crawford's friends emphasized his devotion to states' rights and strict construction. Clay, on the other hand, took his stand for the "American system": he favored the national bank, the protective tariff, and a national program of internal improvements to bind the country together and strengthen its economy. Adams was close to Clay, openly dedicated to internal improvements but less strongly committed to the tariff. Jackson, where issues were concerned, carefully avoided commitment so as to capitalize on his popularity as the hero of the Battle of New Orleans at the end of the War of 1812.

THE "CORRUPT BARGAIN" The 1824 election turned on personalities and sectional allegiance more than issues. Adams, the only northern candidate, carried New England, the former bastion of Federalism, and most of New York's electoral votes. Clay took Kentucky, Ohio, and Missouri. Crawford carried Virginia, Georgia, and Delaware. Jackson swept the Southeast plus Illinois and Indiana and, with Calhoun's support, the Carolinas, Pennsylvania, Maryland, and New Jersey. All candidates got scattered votes elsewhere. In New York, where Clay was strong, his supporters were outmaneuvered by the Adams forces in the legislature, which still chose the presidential electors.

The result was inconclusive in both the electoral vote and the popular vote wherever the state legislature permitted the choice of electors by the people. In the Electoral College, Jackson had 99 votes, Adams 84, Crawford 41, Clay 37. In the popular vote the trend ran about the same: Jackson 154,000, Adams 109,000, Crawford 47,000, and Clay 47,000. Whatever else might have been said about the outcome, one thing seemed apparent—it was a defeat for Clay's program of national economic development: New England and New York opposed him on internal improvements, the South and the Southwest on the protective tariff. Sectionalism had defeated the national economic program.

Yet the advocate of economic nationalism now assumed the role of president maker, as the election was thrown into the House of Representatives,

The Presidential "Race" of 1824

John Adams, William Crawford, and Andrew Jackson stride to the finish line (on the left) and Henry Clay lags behind (far right).

where the Speaker's influence was decisive. Clay had little trouble choosing, since he regarded Jackson as unfit for the office. "I cannot believe," he muttered, "that killing 2,500 Englishmen at New Orleans qualifies for the various, difficult and complicated duties of the Chief Magistracy." He eventually threw his support to Adams. The final vote in the House, which was by state, carried Adams to victory with thirteen votes to Jackson's seven and Crawford's four.

It was a costly victory, for the result united Adams's foes and crippled his administration before it got under way. There is no evidence that Adams entered into any bargain with Clay to win his support. Still, the charge was widely believed after Adams made Clay his secretary of state and thus put him in the office from which three successive presidents had risen. Adams's Puritan conscience could never quite overcome a sense of guilt at the maneuverings that were necessary to gain his election, and his opponents decried the "corrupt bargain" between Adams and Clay. A campaign to elect Jackson in 1828 was launched almost immediately after the 1824 decision. The Crawford people, including Martin Van Buren, "the Little Magician" of New York politics, soon moved into the Jackson camp. So, too, did the new vice president, John Calhoun of South Carolina, who had run on the ticket with both Adams and Jackson but favored the general from Tennessee.

JOHN Q. ADAMS John Quincy Adams was one of the ablest men, one of the hardest workers, and one of the finest intellects ever to enter the White House. Yet he lacked the common touch and the politician's gift for maneuver. A stubborn man who saw two brothers and two sons die from alcoholism, he suffered from chronic bouts of depression that aroused in him a grim self-righteousness and self-pity, qualities that did not endear him to fellow politicians. His idealism also irritated the party faithful. He refused to play the game of patronage, arguing that it would be dishonorable to dismiss "able and faithful political opponents to provide for my own partisans." In four years he removed only twelve officeholders. His first annual message to Congress included a grandiose blueprint for national development, set forth in such a blunt way that it became a disaster of political ineptitude.

John Quincy Adams

A brilliant man but an ineffective leader.

In the boldness and magnitude of its conception, the Adams plan outdid the plans of both Hamilton and Clay. The central government, the president proposed, should promote internal improvements, set up a national university, finance scientific explorations, build astronomical observatories, and create a department of the interior. To refrain from using broad federal powers, Adams insisted, "would be treachery to the most sacred of trusts."

Whatever grandeur of conception the message to Congress had, it was obscured by an unhappy choice of language. For the son of John Adams to cite the example "of the nations of Europe and of their rulers" was downright suicidal. At one fell swoop he had revived all the Republican suspicions of the Adamses as closet monarchists and served to define a new party system. The minority who cast their lot with Adams and Clay were turning into National Republicans; the opposition, the growing party of Jacksonians, were the Democratic Republicans, who would eventually drop the name Republican and become Democrats.

Adams's headstrong plunge into nationalism and his refusal to play the game of politics condemned his administration to utter frustration. Congress ignored his domestic proposals, and in foreign affairs the triumphs that he had scored as secretary of state had no sequels. The climactic effort to discredit Adams came on the tariff issue. The panic of 1819 had provoked calls for a higher tariff in 1820, but the effort failed by one vote in the Senate. In 1824 the advocates of protection renewed the effort, with greater success. The tariff of 1824 favored the middle Atlantic and New England manufacturers with higher duties on woolens, cotton, iron, and other finished goods. Clay's Kentucky won a tariff on hemp, and a tariff on raw wool brought the wool-growing interests to the support of the measure. Additional revenues were provided by duties on sugar, molasses, coffee, and salt. The tariff on raw wool was in obvious conflict with that on manufactured woolens, but the two groups got together and reached an agreement.

At this point, Jackson's supporters saw a chance to advance their candidate through an awkward scheme hatched by John Calhoun. The plan was to present a bill with such outrageously high tariffs on raw materials that the manufacturers of the East would join the commercial interests there and, with the votes of the agricultural South and Southwest, defeat the measure. In the process, Jackson supporters in the Northeast could take credit for supporting the tariff, and wherever it fit their interests, other Jacksonians elsewhere could take credit for opposing it—while Jackson himself remained in the background. John Randolph of Roanoke saw through the ruse. The bill, he asserted, "referred to manufactures of no sort or kind, but the manufacture of a President of the United States."

The complicated scheme helped elect Jackson, but in the process Calhoun became a victim of his own machinations. The high tariffs ended up becoming law. Calhoun had calculated upon neither the defection of Van Buren, who supported a crucial amendment to satisfy the woolens manufacturers, nor the growing strength of manufacturing interests in New England. Daniel Webster, now a senator from Massachusetts, explained that he was ready to deny all he had said against the tariff because New England had built up its manufactures on the understanding that the protective tariff was a settled policy.

When the tariff bill passed, in May 1828, it was Calhoun's turn to explain his newfound opposition to the gospel of protection, and nothing so well illustrates the flexibility of constitutional principles as the switch in positions by Webster and Calhoun. Back in South Carolina, Calhoun prepared the *South Carolina Exposition and Protest* (1828), which was issued anonymously along with a series of resolutions by the South Carolina legislature. In that document, Calhoun declared that a state could nullify an act of Congress that it found unconstitutional.

THE ELECTION OF JACKSON   Thus far the stage was set for the election of 1828, which might more truly than that of 1800 be called a revolution.

The Bloody Deeds of General Andrew Jackson

This anti-Jackson handbill, published during the 1828 campaign, depicts Jackson as a merciless frontier ruffian.

But if the issues of the day had anything to do with the election, they were hardly visible in the campaign, in which politicians on both sides reached depths of scurrilousness that had not been plumbed since 1800. Those campaigning for Adams denounced Jackson as a hot-tempered and ignorant barbarian, a participant in repeated duels and frontier brawls, a man whose fame rested upon his reputation as a killer. In addition, his enemies dredged up the story that Jackson had lived in adultery with his wife, Rachel, before they had been legally married; in fact they had lived together for two years in the mistaken belief that her divorce from her former husband was final. As soon as the official divorce had come through, Andrew and Rachel had been remarried.

The Jacksonians, however, got in their licks against Adams, condemning him as a man who had lived his adult life on the public treasury, who had been corrupted by foreigners in the courts of Europe, and who had allegedly delivered up an American girl to serve the lust of Czar Alexander I while serving as minister to Russia. They called him a gambler and a spendthrift for having bought a billiard table and a chess set for the White House and a puritanical hypocrite for despising the common people and warning Congress to ignore the will of its constituents. He had finally reached the presidency, the Jacksonians claimed, by a "corrupt bargain" with Henry Clay.

In the campaign of 1828, Jackson held most of the advantages. As a military victor he projected patriotism. As a son of the West and a fabled Indian fighter, he was a hero in the frontier states. As a farmer, lawyer, and slaveholder he had the trust of southern planters. Debtors and local bankers who hated the national bank also turned to Jackson. In addition, his vagueness on the issues protected him from attack by interest groups. Not least of all, Jackson benefited from a spirit of democracy in which the common folk were no longer satisfied to look to their betters for leadership, as they had

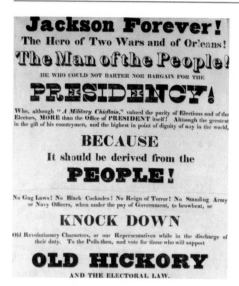

Jackson Forever!

The Hero of Two Wars and of Orleans!

The Man of the People!

HE WHO COULD NOT BARTER NOR BARGAIN FOR THE

PRESIDENCY,

Who, although "*A Military Chieftain*," valued the purity of Elections and of the Electors, MORE than the Office of PRESIDENT itself! Although the greatest in the gift of his countrymen, and the highest in point of dignity of any in the world,

BECAUSE

It should be derived from the

PEOPLE!

No Gag Laws! No Black Cockades! No Reign of Terror! No Standing Army or Navy Officers, when under the pay of Government, to browbeat, or

KNOCK DOWN

Old Revolutionary Characters, or our Representatives while in the discharge of their duty. To the Polls then, and vote for those who will support

OLD HICKORY

AND THE ELECTORAL LAW.

The Man of the People

This 1828 handbill identifies Andrew Jackson with the democratic impulse of the time.

done in the eighteenth century. It had become politically fatal to be labeled an aristocrat.

Since the Revolution and especially since 1800, white male suffrage had been gaining ground. The traditional story is that a surge of Jacksonian democracy came out of the West like a great wave, supported mainly by small farmers, leading the way for the East. But in the older states there were other forces working toward a wider franchise: the Revolutionary doctrine of equality and the feeling on the part of the workers, artisans, and small merchants of the towns, as well as small farmers and landed gentry, that a democratic ballot provided a means to combat the rising commercial and manufacturing interests. From the beginning, Pennsylvania had opened the ballot box to all adult males who paid taxes; by 1790 Georgia and New Hampshire had similar arrangements. Vermont, in 1791, became the first state with universal manhood suffrage, having first adopted it in 1777. Kentucky, admitted to the Union in 1792, became the second. Tennessee, admitted in 1796, had only a light taxpaying qualification. New Jersey in 1807 and Maryland and South Carolina in 1810 abolished property and taxpaying requirements, and after 1815 the new states of the West came in with either white manhood suffrage or a low taxpaying requirement. Connecticut in 1818, Massachusetts in 1821, and New York in 1821 abolished their property requirements.

Along with the broadening of the suffrage went a liberalization of other features of government. Representation was reapportioned more nearly in line with the population. An increasing number of officials, even judges, were chosen by popular vote. Final disestablishment of the Congregational Church in New England came in Vermont in 1807, New Hampshire in 1817, Connecticut in 1818, Maine in 1820, and Massachusetts in 1834. In 1824 six state legislatures still chose presidential electors. By 1828 the popular vote prevailed in all but South Carolina and Delaware and by 1832 in all but South Carolina.

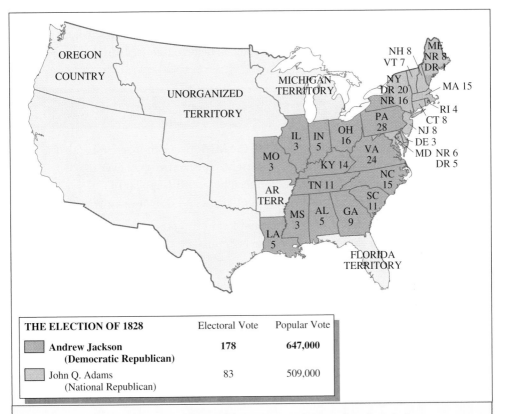

THE ELECTION OF 1828	Electoral Vote	Popular Vote
Andrew Jackson (Democratic Republican)	178	647,000
John Q. Adams (National Republican)	83	509,000

How did the two presidential candidates, John Q. Adams and Andrew Jackson, portray each other? Why did Jackson seem to have the advantage in the election of 1828? How did the broadening of suffrage affect the presidential campaign?

The spread of the suffrage brought a new type of politician to the fore: the man who had special appeal to the masses or knew how to organize the people for political purposes and who became a vocal advocate of the people's right to rule. Jackson fit the ideal of this new political world, a leader sprung from the people rather than a member of the aristocracy, a frontiersman of humble origin who had scrambled up the political ladder by will and tenacity. "Adams can write," went one of the campaign slogans, "Jackson can fight." He could write, too, but he once said that he had no respect for a man who could think of only one way to spell a word.

When the 1828 returns came in, Jackson won by a comfortable margin. The electoral vote was 178 to 83, and the popular vote was about 647,000 to

509,000 (the figures vary). Adams had won all of New England (except one of Maine's nine electoral votes), sixteen of the thirty-six from New York, and six of the eleven from Maryland. All the rest belonged to Jackson.

MAKING CONNECTIONS

- Thomas Jefferson referred to the Missouri Compromise as "a firebell in the night." He was right. The controversy over the expansion of slavery, introduced here, will reappear in Chapter 14, in the discussion of Texas and the Mexican War.

- John Quincy Adams's National Republicans, who could trace some of their ideology to the Federalists, will be at the core of the Whig coalition that opposes Jackson in Chapter 11.

- Several of the issues on which the nation united during the Era of Good Feelings—the bank and the protective tariff, for example—will become much more divisive, as discussed in the next chapter.

FURTHER READING

The standard overview of the Era of Good Feelings remains George Dangerfield's *The Awakening of American Nationalism, 1815–1828* (1965). A classic summary of the economic trends of the period is Douglass C. North's *The Economic Growth of the United States, 1790–1860* (1961). An excellent synthesis of the era is Charles Sellers's *The Market Revolution: Jacksonian America, 1815–1846* (1991).

On diplomatic relations during James Monroe's presidency, see Williams Earl Weeks's *John Quincy Adams and American Global Empire* (1992). For relations after 1812, see Ernest R. May's *The Making of the Monroe Doctrine* (1975).

Background on Andrew Jackson can be obtained from works cited in Chapter 11. The campaign that brought Jackson to the White House is analyzed in Robert Vincent Remini's *The Election of Andrew Jackson* (1963).

11

THE JACKSONIAN IMPULSE

FOCUS QUESTIONS

· What was the social and political context of the Jackson and Van Buren administrations?

· What were Andrew Jackson's attitudes and actions concerning the tariff (and nullification), Indian policy, and the Bank of the United States?

· Why did a new party system of Democrats and Whigs emerge?

To answer these questions and access additional review material, please visit www.wwnorton.com/studyspace.

The election of Andrew Jackson initiated a new era in American politics and social development. Jackson was the first president not to come from a prominent colonial family. As a self-made soldier, politician, and land speculator from the backcountry, he symbolized the changing social scene. The nation he prepared to govern was vastly different from that led by George Washington and Thomas Jefferson. In 1828 the United States boasted twenty-four states and nearly 13 million people, many of them recent arrivals from Germany and Ireland. The national population was growing at a phenomenal rate, doubling every twenty-three years. An extraordinary surge in foreign demand for cotton and other goods, along with British investment in American enterprises, helped fuel an economic boom and a transportation revolution. Textile mills sprouted like mushrooms across the New England countryside, their ravenous

All Creation Going to the White House

The scene following Jackson's inauguration as president, according to the satirist Robert Cruikshank.

spinning looms fed by cotton grown in the newly cultivated lands of Alabama and Mississippi. This fluid new economic environment fostered a mad scramble for material gain and political advantage. People of all backgrounds engaged in a frenzied effort to acquire wealth and thereby gain social status and prestige.

The Jacksonians sought to democratize economic opportunity and political participation. Yet to call the Jacksonian era the age of the common man, as many historians have, is misleading. While political participation increased during the Jacksonian era, most of the common folk remained *common* folk. The period never produced true economic and social equality. Power and privilege, for the most part, remained in the hands of an "uncommon" elite of powerful men. Jacksonians in power proved to be as opportunistic and manipulative as the patricians they displaced. And they never embraced the principle of economic equality. "Distinctions in society will always exist under every just government," Andrew Jackson observed. "Equality of talents, or education, or of wealth cannot be produced by human institutions." He and other Jacksonians wanted every American to have an equal chance to compete in the marketplace and in the political arena, but they never sanctioned equality of results. "True republicanism," one commentator declared, "requires that every man shall have an equal chance— that every man shall be free to become as unequal as he can." But in the afterglow of Jackson's electoral victory, few observers troubled with such distinctions. It was time to celebrate the commoner's ascension to the presidency.

SETTING THE STAGE

Andrew Jackson's father had died before Andrew was born, and his mother had scratched out a meager living as a housekeeper before dying of cholera when her son was fifteen. Jackson grew to be proud, gritty, and short-tempered, and he became a good hater. During the Revolution, when he was a young boy, two of his brothers were killed by redcoats, and the young Jackson was scarred by a British officer's saber. He also carried with him the conviction that it was not enough for a man to be right; he had to be tough as well, a quality that inspired his soldiers to nickname him Old Hickory. During a duel with a man reputed to be the best shot in Tennessee, Jackson nevertheless let his opponent fire first. For his gallantry the future president received a bullet wedged next to his heart. But he straightened himself, patiently took aim, and killed his foe. "I should have hit him," Jackson claimed, "if he had shot me through the brain."

APPOINTMENTS AND RIVALRIES   Jackson believed that a man should serve a term in government, then return to the status of private citizen, for officials who stayed in office too long grew corrupt. During his first year in office, however, Jackson replaced only about 9 percent of the appointed officials in the federal government and during his entire term replaced fewer than 20 percent.

Jackson's administration was from the outset divided between the partisans of Secretary of State Martin Van Buren and those of Vice President John C. Calhoun. Much of the political history of the next few years would turn upon the rivalry of the two statesmen as each jockeyed for position as Jackson's successor. Van Buren held most of the advantages, foremost among them his skill at timing and tactics. Jackson, new to political administration, leaned heavily upon him for advice and for help in soothing the ruffled feathers of rejected office seekers. Van Buren had perhaps more skill at maneuvering than Calhoun and certainly more freedom to maneuver because his home base of New York was more secure politically than Calhoun's base in South Carolina. But Calhoun, a man of towering intellect, humorless outlook, and apostolic zeal, could not be taken lightly. A visitor remarked after a three-hour discussion with the bushy-browed Calhoun, "I hate a man who makes me think so much . . . and I hate a man who makes me feel my own inferiority." As vice president, Calhoun was determined to defend southern interests against the worrisome advance of northern industrialism and abolitionism.

THE EATON AFFAIR   In his battle with Calhoun over political power, Van Buren had luck on his side. Fate handed him a trump card: the succulent scandal known as the Peggy Eaton affair. The daughter of an Irish tavern owner, Margaret Eaton was a vivacious widow whose husband had supposedly committed suicide upon learning of her affair with the Tennessee senator John Eaton. Her marriage to Eaton, three months before he became Jackson's secretary of war, had scarcely made a virtuous woman of her in the eyes of the proper ladies of Washington. Floride Calhoun, the vice president's wife, especially objected to Peggy Eaton's lowly origins and unsavory past. She pointedly snubbed her, and the cabinet wives followed suit.

Peggy's plight reminded Jackson of the gossip that had pursued his own wife Rachel, and he pronounced Peggy "chaste as a virgin." To a friend he wrote: "I did not come here to make a Cabinet for the Ladies of this place, but for the Nation." His cabinet members, however, were unable to cure their wives of what Van Buren dubbed "the Eaton Malaria." Van Buren, though, was a widower and therefore free to lavish on poor Peggy all the attention that Jackson thought was her due. Mrs. Eaton herself finally gave in to the chill and withdrew from society. The outraged Jackson came to link Calhoun with what he called a conspiracy against her and drew even closer to Van Buren.

INTERNAL IMPROVEMENTS   While Washington social life weathered the winter of 1829–1830, Van Buren delivered some additional blows to Calhoun. It was easy to bring Jackson into opposition to federal financing of transportation improvements, programs with which Calhoun had long been identified. Jackson did not oppose road building per se, but he had the same constitutional scruples as Madison and Monroe about using federal aid to fund local projects. In 1830 the Maysville Road bill, passed by Congress, offered Jackson a happy chance for a dual thrust at rivals John Calhoun and Henry Clay. The bill authorized the government to buy stock in a road from Maysville to Clay's hometown of Lexington. The road lay entirely within the state of Kentucky, and though part of a larger scheme to link up with the National Road via Cincinnati, it could be viewed as a purely local undertaking. On that ground, Jackson vetoed the bill, calling it unconstitutional, to widespread popular acclaim.

Yet while Jackson continued to oppose federal aid to local projects, he supported interstate projects such as the National Road, as well as road building in the territories and river and harbor bills, the "pork barrels" from which every congressman tried to pluck a morsel for his district. Even so, Jackson's attitude toward the Maysville Road set an important precedent, on the eve of the railroad age, for limiting federal support of internal improvements. Railroads would be built altogether by state and private capital at least until 1850.

King Andrew the First

Opponents considered Jackson's veto of the Maysville Road bill an abuse of power. This cartoon shows "King Andrew" trampling on the Constitution, internal improvements, and the Bank of the United States.

NULLIFICATION

CALHOUN'S THEORY   There is a fine irony to John Calhoun's plight in the Jackson administration, for the South Carolinian was now midway between his early phase as a war-hawk nationalist and his later phase as a states' rights sectionalist. Conditions in his home state had brought on the change. Suffering from agricultural depression, South Carolina lost almost 70,000 residents to emigration during the 1820s and was fated to lose nearly twice that number in the 1830s. Most South Carolinians blamed the protective tariff for raising the price of manufactured goods. Insofar as tariffs discouraged the sale of foreign goods in the United States, they reduced the ability of British and French traders to buy southern cotton. This situation worsened already existing problems of low cotton prices

John C. Calhoun

During the Civil War the Confederate government printed, but never issued, a one-cent postage stamp bearing Calhoun's likeness.

and exhausted lands. Compounding the South Carolinians' malaise was growing anger over the North's criticism of slavery. Hardly had the country emerged from the Missouri controversy when Charleston, South Carolina, was thrown into panic by the Denmark Vesey slave insurrection of 1822, though the Vesey plot was quickly put down.

The unexpected passage of the tariff of 1828 (called the tariff of abominations by its critics) left Calhoun no choice but to join those in opposition or give up his home base. Calhoun's *South Carolina Exposition and Protest,* written in opposition to the new tariff, had actually been an effort to check the most extreme states' rights advocates with finespun theory, in which nullification stopped short of secession from the Union. The unsigned statement accompanied resolutions of the South Carolina legislature protesting the tariff and urging its repeal. Calhoun, it was clear, had not entirely abandoned his earlier nationalism. He wanted to preserve the Union by protecting the minority rights that the agricultural and slaveholding South claimed. The fine balance he struck between states' rights and central authority was actually not as far removed from Jackson's own philosophy as it might seem, but growing tensions between the two men would complicate the issue. The flinty Jackson, in addition, was determined to draw the line at any defiance of federal law.

Nor would Calhoun's theory permit any state to take up such defiance lightly. His concept of nullification, or interposition, whereby a state could interpose state authority and in effect repeal a federal law, followed that by which the original thirteen states had ratified the Constitution. A special state convention, like the ratifying conventions, which embody the sovereign power of the people, could declare a federal law null and void within the state's borders because it violated the Constitution, the original compact among the states. One of two outcomes would then be possible: the federal government would have to abandon the law, or it would have to propose a constitutional amendment removing all doubt as to its validity. The immediate issue was the constitutionality of a tariff designed mainly to protect American industries from foreign competition. The South Carolinians argued that the Constitution authorized tariffs for revenue only.

THE WEBSTER-HAYNE DEBATE   South Carolina's leaders hated the tariff, but they had postponed any action against its enforcement, awaiting with hope the election of 1828, in which anti-tariff Calhoun was the Jacksonian candidate for vice president. Yet after Jackson assumed the presidency in early 1829, neither he nor Congress saw fit to reduce the tariff duties. There the issue stood until 1830, when the great Webster-Hayne debate sharpened the lines between states' rights and the Union.

The immediate occasion for the debate, however, was the question of public land. The federal government owned immense tracts of unsettled land, and what to do with them set off an intense sectional debate. Late in 1829 Senator Samuel A. Foot of Connecticut proposed that the federal government restrict land sales in the West. When the Foot Resolution came before the Senate in 1830, Thomas Hart Benton of Missouri denounced it as a northern effort to hamstring the settlement of the West so that the East might maintain its supply of cheap factory labor. Senator Robert Y. Hayne of South Carolina took Benton's side. Hayne saw in the issue a chance to strengthen the alliance of South and West reflected in the vote for Jackson. Perhaps by supporting a policy of cheap land in the West, southerners could gain western support for lower tariffs. The government, said Hayne, endangered the Union by imposing any policy that would cause a hardship on one section of the nation to the benefit of another. The sale of public land as a source of revenue for the central government would create "a fund for corruption—fatal to the sovereignty and independence of the states."

Daniel Webster of Massachusetts rose to defend the East. Possessed of a thunderous voice and a theatrical flair, Webster was widely recognized as the nation's foremost orator and lawyer. With the gallery hushed, he denied that the East had ever shown a restrictive policy toward the West. He then rebuked those southerners who disparaged the Union. Webster had adroitly lured Hayne into defending states' rights and upholding the doctrine of nullification instead of pursuing a coalition with the West.

Hayne took the bait. He defended the *South Carolina Exposition,* appealed to the example of the Virginia and Kentucky Resolutions of 1798, and called attention to the Hartford Convention, in which New Englanders had taken much the same position against majority measures as South Carolina now did. The Union constituted a compact of the states, Hayne argued, and the

Daniel Webster

The eloquent Massachusetts senator stands to rebut the argument for nullification in the Webster-Hayne debate.

federal government, which was their "agent," could not be the judge of its own powers, else its powers would be unlimited. Rather, the states remained free to judge when their agent had overstepped the bounds of its constitutional authority. The right of state interposition was "as full and complete as it was before the Constitution was formed."

In rebutting the idea that a state could thwart a federal law, Webster defined a nationalistic view of the Constitution. From the beginning, he asserted, the American Revolution had been a crusade of a united nation rather than one of separate colonies. True sovereignty resided in the people as a whole, for whom both federal and state governments acted as agents in their respective spheres. If a single state could nullify a law of the national government, then the Union would be a "rope of sand," a practical absurdity. A state could neither nullify a federal law nor secede from the Union. The practical outcome of nullification would be a confrontation leading to civil war.

Hayne may have had the better argument historically in advancing the states' compact theory, but the Senate galleries and much of the country at large thrilled to the eloquence of "the God-like Daniel." Webster's closing statement became an American classic, reprinted in school texts and committed to memory by young orators: "Liberty and Union, now and forever, one and inseparable." In the practical world of coalition politics, Webster had the better argument, for the Union and majority rule meant more to westerners, including Jackson, than the abstractions of state sovereignty and nullification. As for the public lands, the Foot Resolution was soon defeated anyway. And whatever one might argue about the origins of the Union, its evolution would more and more validate Webster's position: the states could not act separately from the national government.

THE RIFT WITH CALHOUN   As yet, however, Jackson had not spoken out on the issue. Like Calhoun he was a slaveholder, albeit a westerner, and might be expected to sympathize with South Carolina, his native state. Soon all doubt was removed, at least on the point of nullification. On April 13, 1830, the Jefferson Day dinner was held in Washington to honor the birthday of the former president. Jackson and Van Buren agreed that Jackson should present a toast proclaiming his opposition to nullification. When his turn came, after twenty-four toasts, many of them extolling states' rights, Jackson raised his glass, pointedly stared at Calhoun, and announced: "Our Union— It must be preserved!" Calhoun, who followed, tried quickly to retrieve the situation with a toast to "The Union, next to our liberty most dear! May we all remember that it can only be preserved by respecting the rights of the States and distributing equally the benefit and the burden of the Union!" But Jackson had set off a bombshell that exploded the plans of the states' righters.

Nearly a month afterward a final nail was driven into the coffin of Calhoun's presidential ambitions. On May 12, 1830, Jackson first saw a letter confirming reports of Calhoun's stand in 1818, when as secretary of war he had proposed disciplining General Jackson for his invasion of Florida. A tense correspondence between Jackson and Calhoun followed, ending with a curt note from Jackson cutting it off. "Understanding you now," Jackson wrote two weeks later, "no further communication with you on this subject is necessary."

The acidic rift between the two proud men prompted Jackson to remove all Calhoun partisans from the cabinet. Before the end of the summer of 1831, the president had a new cabinet, one entirely loyal to him. He named Martin Van Buren, who had resigned from the cabinet, minister to Great Britain, and Van Buren departed for London. Van Buren's friends now urged Jackson to repudiate his previous intention of serving only one term. It might be hard, they believed, to win the 1832 nomination for the New Yorker, who had been charged with intrigues against Calhoun, and the still-popular Carolinian might yet gain the presidency.

The Rats Leaving a Falling House

During his first term, Jackson was beset by dissension within his administration. Here "public confidence in the stability and harmony of this administration" is toppling.

Jackson relented and in the fall of 1831 announced his readiness for one more term, with the idea of returning Van Buren from London in time to win the presidency in 1836. But in 1832, when the Senate reconvened, Van Buren's enemies opposed his appointment as minister to England, and gave Calhoun, as vice president, a chance to reject the nomination with a tie-breaking vote. "It will kill him, sir, kill him dead," Calhoun told Senator Thomas Hart Benton. Benton disagreed: "You have broken a minister, and elected a Vice President." So, it turned out, he had. Calhoun's vote against Van Buren evoked popular sympathy for the New Yorker, who returned from London and would soon be nominated to succeed Calhoun as vice president.

Now that his presidential hopes were blasted, Calhoun assumed public leadership of the South Carolina nullificationists. They thought that despite Jackson's gestures, tariff rates remained too high and represented an unconstitutional tax designed to enrich the industrial North at the expense of the agricultural South. Jackson accepted the principle of using tariffs to protect new American industries from foreign competition. Nevertheless, he had called upon Congress in 1829 to reduce tariffs on goods "which cannot come in competition with our own products." Late in the spring of 1830, Congress lowered duties on such consumer products as tea, coffee, salt, and molasses. That and the Maysville veto, coming at about the same time, mollified a few South Carolinians, but nullifiers regarded the two actions as "nothing but sugar plums to pacify children." By the end of 1831, Jackson was calling for further reductions to take the wind out of the nullificationists' sails, and the tariff of 1832, pushed through by John Quincy Adams (back in Washington as a congressman), cut rates again. But tariffs on cloth and iron remained high.

THE SOUTH CAROLINA ORDINANCE   South Carolinians, living in the only state where slaves were a majority of the population, feared that the federal authority to impose tariffs might eventually be used to end slavery. In the state elections of 1832, attention centered on the nullification issue. The nullificationists took the initiative in organization and agitation, and the newly formed Unionist party was left with distinguished leaders but little support. A special session of the legislature called for the election of a state convention, which overwhelmingly adopted an ordinance of nullification that repudiated the federal tariff acts of 1828 and 1832 and forbade collection of the duties in the state after February 1, 1833. The reassembled legislature then provided that any citizen whose property was seized by federal authorities for failure to pay the duty could get a state court order to recover twice its value. The legislature chose Robert Hayne as governor and elected Calhoun to succeed him as senator. Calhoun promptly resigned as vice president in order to defend nullification on the Senate floor.

JACKSON'S FIRM RESPONSE   In the crisis, South Carolina found itself standing alone: other states expressed sympathy, but none endorsed nullification. Jackson's response was measured but not rash—at least not in public. In private he threatened to hang Calhoun and all other traitors—and later expressed regret that he had failed to hang at least Calhoun. In his annual message on December 4, 1832, Jackson announced his firm intention to enforce the tariff but once again urged Congress to lower the rates. On December 10, Jackson followed up with his nullification proclamation, which characterized the doctrine of nullification as an "impractical absurdity." He appealed to the people of his native state not to follow false leaders: "The laws of the United States must be executed. . . . Those who told you that you might peaceably prevent their execution, deceived you; they could not have been deceived themselves. . . . Their object is disunion. But be not deceived by names. Disunion by armed force is treason."

CLAY'S COMPROMISE   Jackson then sent federal soldiers and ships to South Carolina. The nullifiers mobilized the state militia while Unionists in the state organized a volunteer force. In 1833 the president requested from Congress a "force bill" specifically authorizing him to use the army to compel compliance with federal law in South Carolina. Under existing legislation he already had such authority, but this affirmation would strengthen his hand. At the same time he supported a bill in Congress that would have lowered tariff duties substantially within two years.

The nullifiers postponed enforcement of their ordinances in anticipation of a compromise. Passage of the compromise bill depended upon the support of the Kentucky senator Henry Clay, who finally yielded to those urging him to save the day. On February 12, 1833, he circulated a plan to reduce the tariff gradually until 1842. It was less than South Carolina preferred, but it got the nullifiers out of the corner into which they had painted themselves.

On March 1, 1833, Congress passed the compromise tariff and the force bill, and the next day Jackson signed both. The South Carolina convention then met and rescinded its nullification of the tariff acts. In a face-saving gesture, it nullified the force bill, for which Jackson no longer had any need. Both sides were able to claim victory. Jackson had upheld the supremacy of the Union, and South Carolina had secured a reduction of the tariff. Calhoun, worn out by the controversy, returned to his plantation. "The struggle, so far from being over," he ominously wrote, "is not more than fairly commenced."

JACKSON'S INDIAN POLICY

During the 1820s and 1830s the United States was fast becoming a multicultural nation of peoples from many countries. Most whites, however, were openly racist in their treatment of blacks and Indians. As economic growth reinforced the institution of slavery and accelerated westward expansion, policy makers struggled to preserve white racial homogeneity and hegemony. "Next to the case of the black race within our bosom," declared former president James Madison, "that of the red [race] on our borders is the problem most baffling to the policy of our country."

Andrew Jackson, however, saw nothing baffling about Indian policy. His attitude toward Indians was the typically western one: Native Americans were barbarians and better off out of the way. At the Battle of Horseshoe Bend in Alabama in 1814, General Jackson's federal troops had massacred nearly 900 Creeks. Jackson and most Americans on the frontier despised and feared Indians—and vice versa. Jackson believed that a "just, humane, liberal policy toward Indians" dictated moving all of them onto the plains west of the Mississippi River, to the Great American Desert, which white settlers would never covet, since it was believed to be fit mainly for horned toads and rattlesnakes.

INDIAN REMOVAL   In response to a request by Jackson, Congress in 1830 approved the Indian Removal Act. It authorized the president to give

Indians federal land west of the Mississippi River in exchange for the land they occupied in the East and the South. By 1835 Jackson was able to announce that the policy had been carried out or was in the process of completion for all but a handful of Indians. Some 46,000 people were relocated at government expense. The policy was effected with remarkable speed, but even that was too slow for state authorities in the South and Southwest. Unlike the Ohio River valley and the Great Lakes region, where the flow of white settlement had constantly pushed the Indians westward before it, in the Old Southwest settlement moved across Kentucky and Tennessee and down the Mississippi, surrounding the Creeks, Choctaws, Chickasaws, Seminoles, and Cherokees. These tribes had over the years taken on many of the features of white society. The Cherokees even had such products of white "civilization" as a constitution, a written language, and African-American slaves.

Most of the northern tribes were too weak to resist the offers of commissioners who, if necessary, used bribery and alcohol to woo the chiefs. On the whole, there was remarkably little resistance. In Illinois and the Wisconsin Territory an armed clash erupted in 1832, which came to be known as the Black Hawk War. Under Chief Black Hawk the Sauk and Fox sought to reoccupy some lands they had abandoned in the previous year. Facing famine and hostile Sioux west of the Mississippi, they were simply seeking a place to raise a crop of corn. The Illinois militia mobilized to expel them, chased them into the Wisconsin Territory, and massacred women and children as they tried to escape across the Mississippi. The Black Hawk War came to be remembered, however, less because of the atrocities inflicted on the Indians than because among the participants were two native Kentuckians later pitted against each other: Lieutenant Jefferson Davis of the regular army and Captain Abraham Lincoln of the Illinois volunteers.

In the South two nations, the Seminoles and the Cherokees, put up a stubborn resistance to the federal removal policy. The Seminoles of Florida fought a protracted guerrilla war in the Everglades from 1835 to 1842. But their resistance waned after 1837, when their leader, Osceola, was seized by treachery under a flag of truce, imprisoned, and left to die at Fort Moultrie near Charleston harbor. After 1842 only a few hundred Seminoles remained, hiding out in the swamps. Most of the rest had been banished to the West.

THE TRAIL OF TEARS   The Cherokees had, by the end of the eighteenth century, fallen back into the mountains of northern Georgia and western North Carolina, onto land guaranteed to them in 1791 by treaty

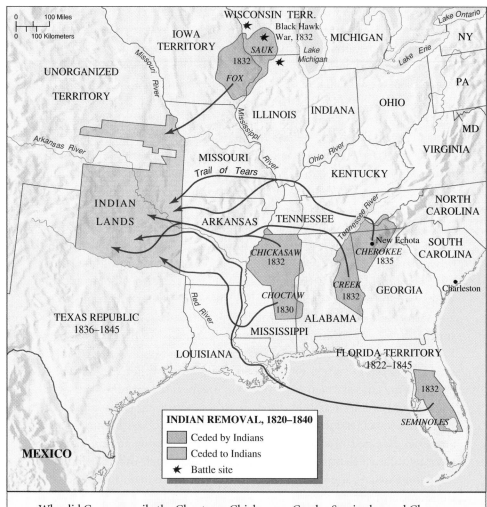

Why did Congress exile the Choctaws, Chickasaws, Creeks, Seminoles, and Cherokees to the territory west of Arkansas and Missouri? How far did the tribes have to travel, and what were the conditions on the trip? Why were the Indians not forced to move earlier than the 1830s?

with the United States. But when Georgia ceded its western lands in 1802, it did so on the ambiguous condition that the United States extinguish all Indian titles within the state "as early as the same can be obtained on reasonable terms." In 1827 the Cherokees, relying on their treaty rights, adopted a constitution in which they declared pointedly that they were not subject to any other state or nation. In 1828 Georgia responded by declaring that after

June 1, 1830, the authority of state law would extend over the Cherokees living within the boundaries of the state.

The discovery of gold in 1829 whetted the whites' appetite for Cherokee land and brought bands of rough prospectors into the country. The Cherokees sought relief in the Supreme Court, but in *Cherokee Nation v. Georgia* (1831) John Marshall ruled that the Court lacked jurisdiction because the Cherokees were a "domestic dependent nation" rather than a foreign state in the meaning of the Constitution. Marshall added, however, that the Cherokees had "an unquestionable right" to their lands "until title should be extinguished by voluntary cession to the United States." In 1830 a Geor-

The Trail of Tears

Elias Boudinot (Gallegina Watie), editor of the *Cherokee Phoenix*, signed the Indian removal treaty in 1835 and was subsequently murdered.

gia law had required whites in the territory to obtain licenses authorizing their residence there and to take an oath of allegiance to the state. Two New England missionaries among the Indians refused to abide by the law and were sentenced to four years at hard labor. On appeal their case reached the Supreme Court as *Worcester v. Georgia* (1832), and the Court held that the Cherokee Nation was "a distinct political community" within which Georgia law had no force. The Georgia law was therefore unconstitutional.

Six years earlier Georgia had faced down President John Quincy Adams when he tried to protect the rights of the Creeks. Now Georgia faced down the Supreme Court with the tacit consent of another president. Andrew Jackson did nothing to enforce the Court's decision. Under the circumstances there was nothing for the Cherokees to do but give in and sign a treaty, which they did in 1835. They gave up their land in the Southeast in exchange for tracts in the Indian Territory west of Arkansas, $5 million from the federal government, and expenses for transportation.

By 1838 some 17,000 Cherokees had departed westward on the "Trail of Tears," following other tribes on an 800-mile journey marked by the cruelty and neglect of soldiers and private contractors and scorn and pilferage by whites along the way. A few held out in the mountains and acquired title to federal land in North Carolina; thenceforth they were the "Eastern Band" of the Cherokees. Some Seminoles were able to hide out in the Everglades in south Florida, and a few of the others remained scattered in the Southeast, especially mixed-blood Creeks who could pass for white. Only 8,000 of the exiles survived the forced march to Oklahoma.

THE BANK CONTROVERSY

THE BANK'S OPPONENTS   The overriding national issue in the campaign of 1832 was neither Jackson's Indian policy nor South Carolina's obsession with the tariff. It was the question of rechartering the Bank of the United States. On the bank issue, as on others, Jackson had made no public commitment, but his personal opposition to the bank was already formed. Jackson had absorbed the western attitude of hostility toward the bank after the panic of 1819. He was convinced that the central bank was unconstitutional no matter what Chief Justice John Marshall had said in *McCulloch v. Maryland*.

Under the management of Nicholas Biddle, the Bank of the United States had prospered and grown. It had facilitated business expansion and supplied a stable currency by forcing the 464 state banks to keep a specie (gold or silver) reserve on hand to back their paper currency. The bank also acted as the collecting and disbursing agent for the federal government, which held one fifth of the bank's $35 million capital stock. From the start this combination of private and public functions caused problems for the Bank of the United States. As the government's revenues soared, the bank became the most powerful lending institution in the country, a central bank, in effect, whose huge size enabled it to determine the amount of available credit for the nation.

Arrayed against the bank were powerful enemies: some of the state and local banks that had been forced to reduce their volume of paper money, groups of debtors who suffered from the reduction, and businessmen and speculators "on the make," who wanted easier credit. States' rights groups questioned the bank's constitutionality, though Calhoun, who had sponsored the original charter and valued the bank's function of regulating the currency, was not among them. Financiers on New York's Wall Street resented the supremacy of the bank, which was located on Philadelphia's Chestnut Street.

Like Jackson, many westerners and workingmen felt in their bones that the bank was, in Thomas Hart Benton's word, a "Monster," a monopoly controlled by a wealthy few with power that was irreconcilable with a democracy. "I think it right to be perfectly frank with you," Jackson told Biddle in 1829.

"I do not dislike your Bank any more than [I dislike] all banks." Jackson was perhaps right in his instinct that the bank lodged too much power in private hands, but he was mistaken in his understanding of the bank's policies. By issuing paper money of its own, the bank provided a stable and uniform currency for the expanding economy as well as a mechanism to control the pace of growth.

Biddle at first tried to conciliate Jackson by appointing a number of Jackson men to branch offices. In 1829, however, in his first annual message, the president questioned the bank's constitutionality and asserted (whatever the evidence to the contrary) that it had failed to maintain a sound and uniform currency. Jackson talked of a compromise, perhaps a bank completely owned by the government with its operations confined chiefly to government deposits, its profits payable to the government, and its authority to set up branches in any state dependent upon the state's wishes. But Jackson would never commit himself on the precise terms of compromise. The defense of the bank was left up to Biddle.

THE RECHARTER EFFORT   The bank's twenty-year charter would run through 1836, but Biddle could not afford the uncertainty of waiting until then for a renewal. He pondered whether to force the issue of recharter before the election of 1832 or after. On this point, leaders of the National Republicans, especially Henry Clay and Daniel Webster (who was legal counsel to the bank as well as a senator), argued that the time to move was before the election. Clay, already the presidential candidate of the National Republicans, proposed making the bank the central election issue. Friends of the bank held a majority in Congress, and Jackson would risk loss of support in the election if he vetoed a renewal. But they failed to grasp the depth of public suspicion of the bank and succeeded mainly in handing Jackson a popular issue on the eve of the election. "The Bank," Jackson told Martin Van Buren in May 1832, "is trying to kill me. But I will kill it."

Both houses passed the recharter by a comfortable margin but without the two-thirds majority needed to override a veto. On July 10, 1832, Jackson vetoed the bill, sending it back to Congress with a ringing denunciation of monopoly and special privilege. Jackson argued that the bank was unconstitutional no matter what the Court and Congress said: "The opinion of the judges has no more authority over Congress than the opinion of Congress had over the judges, and on that point the President is independent of both." Besides, there were substantive objections apart from the question of constitutionality. Foreign stockholders in the bank had an undue influence. The bank, Jackson added, had shown favors to members of Congress and

Rechartering the Bank

Jackson battling the Hydra-headed Bank of the United States.

exercised an improper power over state banks. An effort to overrule the veto failed in the Senate, thus setting the stage for a nationwide financial crisis.

CAMPAIGN INNOVATIONS   The year 1832 witnessed another presidential election. For the first time a third party entered the field. The Anti-Masonic party grew out of popular hostility toward the Masonic order, members of which were suspected of having kidnapped and murdered a New Yorker for revealing the "secrets" of his lodge. Opposition to a fraternal order was hardly the foundation on which to build a lasting political party, but the Anti-Masonic party had three important firsts to its credit: in addition to being the first third party, it was the first party to hold a national nominating convention and the first to announce a platform, both of which it accomplished in 1831 when it nominated William Wirt of Maryland for president.

The major parties followed its example by holding national conventions of their own. In December 1831 the delegates of the National Republican party assembled in Baltimore to nominate Henry Clay. Jackson endorsed the idea of a nominating convention for the Democratic party (the name Republican was

Verdict of the People

George Caleb Bingham's painting depicts the increasingly democratic politics of the mid–nineteenth century.

now formally dropped) to demonstrate popular support for its candidates. To that purpose the convention, also meeting at Baltimore, first adopted the two-thirds rule for nomination (which prevailed until 1936, when it became a simple majority) and then named Martin Van Buren as Jackson's running mate. The Democrats, unlike the other two parties, adopted no formal platform at their first convention and relied to a substantial degree upon hoopla and the personal popularity of the president to carry their cause.

The outcome was an overwhelming endorsement of Jackson in the Electoral College, by 219 votes to 49 for Clay, and a less overwhelming but solid victory in the popular vote, 688,000 to 530,000. William Wirt carried only Vermont, winning several electoral votes. South Carolina, preparing for nullification and unable to stomach either Jackson or Clay, delivered its eleven votes to Governor John Floyd of Virginia.

THE REMOVAL OF GOVERNMENT DEPOSITS   Andrew Jackson interpreted his election as a mandate to further weaken the Bank of the United States. He asked Congress to investigate the safety of government deposits in the bank, since a rumor told of empty vaults, carefully concealed. After a committee had checked on the bank's operations, the Calhoun and

Clay forces in the House of Representatives passed a resolution affirming that government deposits were safe and could be continued. The resolution passed on March 2, 1833, by chance the same day that Jackson signed the compromise tariff and the force bill. With the nullification issue out of the way, however, Jackson was free to wage his unrelenting war on the bank, that "hydra of corruption," which still had nearly four years to run on its charter. Despite the House study and resolution, Jackson now resolved to remove all government deposits from the bank.

When Secretary of the Treasury Louis McLane opposed removal of the government deposits and suggested a new and modified version of the bank, Jackson again shook up his cabinet. In the reshuffling, Attorney General Roger Taney moved to the Treasury Department, where he gladly complied with the presidential wishes, which corresponded to his own views, against the bank.

Taney continued to draw on government accounts with Biddle's bank but deposited all new federal receipts in state banks. By the end of 1833, twenty-three state banks—"pet banks," as they came to be called—had the benefit of federal deposits. Transferring the government's deposits was a highly questionable action under the law, and the Senate voted to censure Jackson for it. Biddle refused to surrender. "This worthy President," he declared, "thinks that because he has scalped Indians and imprisoned Judges he is to have his way with the Bank. He is mistaken." Biddle ordered that the bank curtail loans throughout the nation and demand the redemption of state bank notes in gold or silver as quickly as possible. He sought to bring the economy to a halt, create a sharp depression, and reveal to the nation the importance of maintaining the bank. By 1834 the tightness of credit was creating distress in the business community. Most likely both sides were exaggerating for political effect: Biddle to show the evil consequences of the withdrawal of deposits, the Jacksonians to show how Biddle abused his power.

Biddle's contraction policy, however, unwittingly unleashed a speculative binge encouraged by the deposit of government funds in the pet banks. With the restraint of Biddle's bank removed, the state banks gave full rein to their wildcat tendencies. New banks mushroomed, printing bank notes with abandon for the purpose of lending money to speculators. Sales of public lands rose from 4 million acres in 1834 to 15 million in 1835 and 20 million in 1836. At the same time the states plunged heavily into debt to finance the building of roads and canals, inspired by the success of New York's Erie Canal. By 1837 total state indebtedness had soared to $170 million, a very large sum for the time. The supreme irony of Jackson's war on the bank was that it sparked the speculative mania that he most feared.

FISCAL MEASURES   The surge of cheap money reached its peak in 1836, when events combined suddenly to deflate it. Most important among these were the Distribution Act and the Specie Circular. Distribution of the government's surplus funds to the states had long been a pet project of Henry Clay's. One of its purposes was to eliminate the federal surplus, thus removing one argument for cutting the tariff. Much of the surplus, however, resulted from the "land-office business" in western property sales and was therefore in the form of bank notes that had been issued to speculators. Many westerners thought that the solution to the surplus was simply to lower the price of land; southerners preferred to lower the tariff—but such action would now upset the compromise achieved with the tariff of 1833. For a time the annual surpluses could be applied to paying off the government debt, but the debt, reduced to $7 million by 1832, was entirely paid off by 1835.

Still, the federal surplus continued to mount. Clay again proposed distribution of the dollars to the states, but Jackson had constitutional scruples about the process. Finally a compromise was worked out whereby the government would distribute most of the surplus as loans to the states. To satisfy Jackson's concerns, the funds were technically deposits, but in reality they were never demanded. Distribution of the surplus was to be in proportion to each state's representation in the two houses of Congress and was to be paid out in quarterly installments beginning in 1837.

The Specie Circular, issued by the secretary of the Treasury at Jackson's order, applied the president's hard-money conviction to the sale of public lands. According to his order, the government would accept only gold or silver coins in payment for land. The purposes declared in the circular were to "repress frauds," to withhold support "from the monopoly of the public lands in the hands of speculators and capitalists," and to discourage the "ruinous extension" of bank notes and credit.

Irony dogged Jackson to the end on this matter. Since few settlers could get their hands on gold or silver, they were now left all the more at the mercy of speculators for land purchases. Both the Distribution Act and the Specie Circular put many state banks in a plight. The distribution of the surplus to the state governments resulted in federal funds' being withdrawn from the state banks. In turn the state banks had to require many borrowers to pay back their loans immediately in order to be able to transfer the federal funds to the state governments. This situation caused greater disarray in the already chaotic state banking community. At the same time the new requirement that only hard money be accepted for federal land purchases put an added strain on the supplies of gold and silver.

BOOM AND BUST   But the boom-and-bust cycle of the 1830s had causes larger even than Andrew Jackson, causes that were beyond his control. The inflation of the mid-1830s was rooted not so much in a prodigal expansion of bank notes, as it seemed at the time, but in an increase of gold and silver payments from England and France and, especially, Mexico, for investment and for the purchase of American cotton and other products. At the same time, British credits enabled Americans to buy British goods without having to export gold or silver. Meanwhile, the flow of hard cash to China, where silver had been much prized, decreased. Now the Chinese took in payment for their goods British credits, which they could in turn use to cover rapidly increasing imports of opium from British India.

Contrary to appearances, therefore, the reserves of gold and silver in U.S. banks kept pace with the increase of bank notes, despite reckless behavior on the part of some banks. But by 1836 a tighter British economy caused a decline in both British investments and British demand for American cotton just when the new western lands were creating a rapid increase in the cotton supply. Fortunately for Jackson the financial panic of 1837 did not erupt until he was out of the White House. His successor would serve as the scapegoat.

In May 1837 New York banks suspended gold and silver payments on their bank notes, and fears of bankruptcy set off runs on banks around the country, many of which were soon overextended. A brief recovery followed in 1838, stimulated in part by a bad wheat harvest in England, which forced the British to buy American wheat. But by 1839 that stimulus had passed. The same year a bumper cotton crop overloaded the market, and a collapse of cotton prices set off a depression from which the economy did not fully recover until the mid-1840s.

VAN BUREN AND THE NEW PARTY SYSTEM

THE WHIG COALITION   Before the depression set in, however, the Jacksonian Democrats reaped a political bonanza. Jackson had slain the dual monsters of nullification and the bank, and the people loved him for it. The hard times following the contraction of the economy turned Americans against Biddle and the Bank of the United States but not against Jackson, the professed friend of "the people" and foe of the "selfish" interests of financiers and speculators. But in 1834 his opponents began to pull together a new coalition of diverse elements, united chiefly by their hostility to him. The imperious demeanor of the feisty champion of democracy had given rise to the name King Andrew I. Jackson's followers therefore were Tories, supporters of the king, and his opponents became Whigs, a name that linked them to the Patriots of the American Revolution.

The diverse coalition making up the Whigs clustered around the National Republican party of John Quincy Adams, Henry Clay, and Daniel Webster. Into the combination came remnants of the Anti-Masonic and Democratic parties, who for one reason or another were alienated by Jackson's stand on the bank or states' rights. Of the forty-one Democrats in Congress who had voted to recharter the bank, twenty-eight had joined the Whigs by 1836.

Whiggery always had about it an atmosphere of social conservatism and superiority. The core Whigs were the supporters of the charismatic Henry Clay and his economic nationalism. In the South the Whigs enjoyed the support of the urban banking and commercial interests, as well as their planter associates, owners of most of the slaves in the region. In the West, farmers who valued internal improvements joined the Whig ranks. Most states' rights supporters eventually dropped away, and by the early 1840s the Whigs were becoming more clearly the party of Henry Clay's nationalism, even in the South. Unlike the Democrats, who attracted Catholics from Germany and Ireland, Whigs tended to be native-born or British-American evangelical Protestants—Presbyterians, Baptists, and Congregationalists—who were active in promoting social reforms such as abolition and temperance.

THE ELECTION OF 1836   By the presidential election of 1836, a new two-party system was emerging from the Jackson and anti-Jackson forces, a system that would remain in fairly even balance for twenty years. In 1835, eighteen months before the election, the Democrats held their second national convention, nominating Jackson's hand picked successor, Vice President Martin Van Buren. The Whig coalition, united chiefly in its opposition to Jackson, held no convention but adopted a strategy of multiple candidacies, hoping to throw the election into the House of Representatives.

The result was a free-for-all reminiscent of 1824, except that this time one candidate stood apart from the rest. It was Van Buren against the field. The Whigs put up three favorite sons: Daniel Webster, named by the Massachusetts legislature; Hugh Lawson White, chosen by anti-Jackson Democrats in the Tennessee legislature; and William Henry Harrison of Indiana, nominated by a predominantly Anti-Masonic convention in Harrisburg, Pennsylvania. In the South the Whigs made heavy inroads on the Democratic vote by arguing that Van Buren would be soft on anti-slavery advocates and that the South could trust only a southerner—that is, Hugh White—as president. In the popular vote, Van Buren outdistanced the entire Whig field, with 765,000

Martin Van Buren

"The Little Magician."

votes to 740,000 for the Whigs, most of which were cast for Harrison. Van Buren had 170 electoral votes, Harrison 73, White 26, and Webster 14.

Martin Van Buren, the eighth president, was the first of Dutch ancestry. The son of a tavern keeper in Kinderhook, New York, he had attended a local academy, studied law, and entered politics. Although he kept up a limited legal practice, he had been for most of his adult life a professional politician, so skilled in the arts of organization and manipulation that he came to be known as the Little Magician. In 1824 he supported Crawford, then switched his allegiance to Jackson in 1828 but continued to look to the Old Republicans of Virginia as the southern anchor of his support. Elected governor of New York, he quickly resigned to join Jackson's cabinet and because of the president's favor became vice president.

THE PANIC OF 1837 Van Buren inherited a financial panic. An already precarious economy was tipped over by a depression in England, which resulted in a drop in the price of American cotton and caused English banks and investors to cut back their commitments in the New World and refuse extensions of loans. This was a particularly hard blow because much of America's economic expansion depended upon European—and mainly English—investment capital. On top of everything else, in 1836 there had been a failure of the wheat crop, the export of which in good years helped offset the drain of payments abroad. As creditors hastened to foreclose, the inflationary spiral went into reverse. States curtailed ambitious plans for roads and canals and in many cases felt impelled to repudiate their debts. In the crunch many of the wildcat state banks succumbed, and the federal government itself lost some $9 million it had deposited in pet banks.

The working class, as always, was particularly hard hit during the economic slump and largely had to fend for itself. By the fall of 1837, one third of the workforce was jobless, and those still fortunate enough to have jobs saw their wages cut by 30 to 50 percent within two years. At the same time, prices for food and clothing soared. As the winter of 1837 approached, a journalist reported that in New York City 200,000 people were "in utter and hopeless distress with no means of surviving the winter but those provided

Jacksonian Treasury Note

A parody of the often-worthless fractional currencies, or shinplasters, issued by banks and businesses in lieu of coins. These fractional notes proliferated during the panic of 1837, with the emergency suspension of gold and silver payments. In the main scene, Van Buren, a monster on a wagon driven by Calhoun, is about to pass through an arch labeled "Wall Street" and "Safety Fund Banks."

by charity." There was no government aid; churches and voluntary societies were the major sources of support for the indigent.

Van Buren's advisers and supporters were inclined to blame the depression on speculators and bankers, at the same time expecting the evildoers would get what they deserved in a healthy shakeout that would restabilize the economy. Van Buren did not believe that he or the government had any responsibility to rescue hard-pressed farmers or businessmen or to provide public relief. He did feel obliged to keep the government itself in a healthy financial situation, however. To that end he called a special session of Congress in 1837, which quickly voted to postpone indefinitely the distribution of the surplus because of a probable upcoming deficit and approved an issue of Treasury notes to cover immediate expenses.

AN INDEPENDENT TREASURY   Van Buren believed that the government should cease risking its deposits in shaky state banks and set up an independent Treasury. Under this plan the government would keep its funds in its own vaults and do business entirely in hard money. The Independent Treasury Act elicited opposition from a combination of Whigs and conservative Democrats who feared deflation. It had taken Van Buren several years of maneuvering to get what he wanted. Calhoun signaled a return to the Democratic fold, after several years of flirting with the Whigs, when he came out for the treasury act. Van Buren gained western support by backing a more liberal policy regarding federal land sales. Congress finally passed the Independent Treasury Act on July 4, 1840. Although it lasted little more than a year (the Whigs repealed it in 1841), it would be restored in 1846.

The drawn-out struggle over the Treasury was only one of several squabbles that kept Washington preoccupied through the Van Buren years. A flood of petitions for Congress to abolish slavery and the slave trade in the District of Columbia brought on tumultuous debate, especially in the House of Representatives. Border incidents growing out of a Canadian insurrection in 1837 and a dispute over the Maine boundary kept British-American animosity at a simmer, but General Winfield Scott, the president's ace troubleshooter, managed to keep the hotheads in check along the border. The spreading malaise of the time was rooted in the depressed condition of the economy, which lasted through Van Buren's term. Fairly or not, the administration became the target of growing discontent. The president won renomination easily enough but could not get the Democratic convention to agree on his vice-presidential choice, which was left up to the Democratic electors.

THE "LOG CABIN AND HARD CIDER" CAMPAIGN   The Whigs got an early start on their campaign when they met at Harrisburg, Pennsylvania, on December 4, 1839, to choose a candidate. Henry Clay expected 1840 to be his year and had soft-pedaled talk of his economic nationalism in the interest of building broader support. Although Clay led on the first ballot, the convention sought a Whiggish Jackson, as it were, a military hero who could enter the race with few known political convictions or enemies, and the delegates finally turned to William Henry Harrison. His credentials were impressive: victor at the Battle of Tippecanoe against the Shawnees in 1811, former governor of the Indiana Territory, briefly congressman and senator from Ohio, more briefly minister to Colombia. Another advantage of Harrison's was that the Anti-Masons liked him. To rally their states' rights wing, the Whigs chose for vice president John Tyler of Virginia, a close friend of Clay's.

The Whigs had no platform. A platform would have risked dividing a coalition united chiefly by opposition to the Democrats. But they had a catchy slogan, "Tippecanoe and Tyler too." And they soon had a rousing campaign theme, which a Democratic newspaper unwittingly supplied: the *Baltimore Republican* declared sardonically "that upon condition of his receiving a pension of $2,000 and a barrel of cider, General Harrison would no doubt consent to withdraw his pretensions, and spend his days in a log cabin on the banks of the Ohio." The Whigs seized upon the cider and log-cabin symbols to depict Harrison as a simple man sprung from the people. Actually, he sprang from one of the first families of Virginia and lived in a large farmhouse.

The Whig "Log Cabin and Hard Cider" campaign featured portable log cabins rolling through the streets along with barrels of cider. All the devices of hoopla were mobilized: placards, emblems, campaign buttons, floats, effigies, great rallies, and a campaign newspaper, the *Log Cabin*. Building on the example of the Jacksonians' campaign to discredit John Quincy Adams, the Whigs pictured Van Buren, who unlike Harrison really did have humble origins, as an aristocrat living in luxury at "the Palace."

"We have taught them to conquer us!" the *Democratic Review* lamented. The Whig party had not only learned its lessons well, but it had also improved upon its teachers in the art of campaigning. "Van! Van! Is a Used-Up Man!" went one campaign refrain, and down he went by the thumping

Uncle Sam's Pet Pups

A woodcut showing William Henry Harrison luring "Mother Bank," Jackson, and Van Buren into a barrel of hard cider. While Jackson and Van Buren sought to destroy the Bank of the United States, Harrison promised to reestablish it, hence his providing "Mother Bank" a refuge in this scene.

UNCLE SAM'S PET PUPS!
Or, Mother BANK'S last refuge.

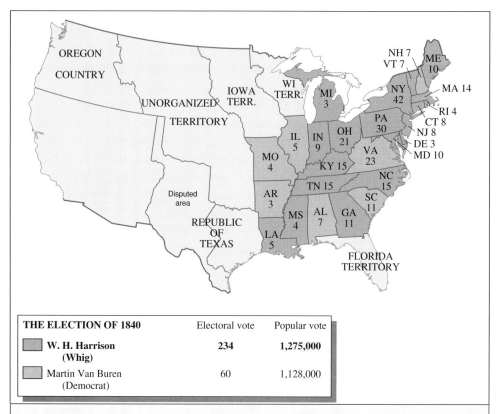

THE ELECTION OF 1840	Electoral vote	Popular vote
W. H. Harrison (Whig)	234	1,275,000
Martin Van Buren (Democrat)	60	1,128,000

Why did Van Buren carry several western states but few others? How did the Whigs achieve a decisive electoral victory over the Democrats? How was their strategy in 1840 different from their campaign in 1836?

margin of 234 votes to 60 in the Electoral College. In the popular vote it was closer: 1,275,000 for Harrison, 1,128,000 for Van Buren.

ASSESSING THE JACKSON YEARS

The Whigs may have won in 1840, but the Jacksonian impulse had permanently altered American politics. By 1840 both parties were organized down to the precinct level, and the proportion of adult white males who voted in the presidential election had tripled, from 26 percent in 1824 to 78 percent in 1840. That much is beyond dispute, but the phenomenon of Jackson, the heroic symbol for an age, continues to spark historical debate.

The earliest historians of the Jackson era belonged largely to an eastern elite nurtured in a "Whiggish" culture, men who could never quite forgive Jackson for the spoils system, which in their view excluded the fittest from office. A later school of "progressive" historians depicted Jackson as the leader of a vast democratic movement that welled up in the West and mobilized a farmer-labor alliance to sweep the "monster" national bank into the dustbin of history. Some historians have recently focused on local power struggles, in which the great national debates of the time often seemed empty rhetoric or at most snares to catch the voters. One view of Jackson makes him out to be essentially a frontier opportunist for whom democracy "was good talk with which to win the favor of the people."

Most recently scholars have highlighted the fact that Jacksonian "democracy" was for white males only; it did not apply to African Americans, Indians, or women. These revisionist historians have also stressed the finding that greater participation in politics was much more a northern development than a southern development. As late as 1857, for example, North Carolina's fifty-acre property requirement for voting disenfranchised almost half the state's voters.

Yet there seems little question that whatever else Jackson and his supporters had in mind, they followed an ideal of republican virtue, of returning to the Jeffersonian vision of the old republic, in which government would play as limited a role as possible. In the Jacksonian view the alliance of government and business was always an invitation to special favors and an eternal source of corruption. The national bank was the epitome of such evil. The right policy for government, at the national level in particular, was to refrain from granting special privileges and to let free competition in the marketplace regulate the economy.

In the bustling world of the nineteenth century, however, the idea of a return to agrarian simplicity was a futile exercise in nostalgia. Instead, free-enterprise policies opened the way for a host of aspiring entrepreneurs eager to replace the established economic elite with a new order of free-enterprise capitalism. And in fact there was no great conflict in the Jacksonian mentality between the farmer or planter who delved in the soil and the independent speculator and entrepreneur who grew wealthy by other means. Jackson himself was both. What the Jacksonian mentality did not foresee was the degree to which, in a growing country, unrestrained enterprise could lead to new centers of economic power largely independent of government regulation. But history is forever marked by unintended consequences. Here the ultimate irony would be that the laissez-faire rationale for republican simplicity eventually became the justification for the growth of unregulated corporate powers far greater than any ever wielded by Biddle's bank.

> ## MAKING CONNECTIONS
>
> · This chapter analyzed the political side of "Jacksonian Democracy." Chapter 12 concludes with an assessment of the accuracy of that term from social and economic perspectives.
>
> · John C. Calhoun, Henry Clay, and Daniel Webster, three of the statesmen considered in this chapter, continued for many years to be the major spokesmen for their positions. Their last great debate, over the Compromise of 1850, is discussed in Chapter 16.

FURTHER READING

An excellent survey of events covered in this chapter is Daniel Feller's *The Jacksonian Promise: America, 1815–1840* (1995). A more political focus can be found in Harry L. Watson's *Liberty and Power: The Politics of Jacksonian America* (1990).

A still-valuable standard introduction to the development of the political parties of the 1830s is Richard Patrick McCormick's *The Second Party System: Party Formation in the Jacksonian Era* (1966). For an outstanding analysis of women in New York City during the Jacksonian period, see Christine Stansell's *City of Women: Sex and Class in New York, 1789–1860* (1986). In *Chants Democratic: New York City and the Rise of the American Working Class, 1788–1850* (1984), Sean Wilentz analyzes the social basis of working-class politics. More recently, Wilentz has traced the democratization of politics in *The Rise of American Democracy: Jefferson to Lincoln* (2005).

The best biography of Jackson remains Robert Vincent Remini's three-volume work: *Andrew Jackson: The Course of American Empire, 1767–1821* (1977), *Andrew Jackson: The Course of American Freedom, 1822–1832* (1981), and *Andrew Jackson: The Course of American Democracy, 1833–1845* (1984). On Jackson's successor, consult John Niven's *Martin Van Buren: The Romantic Age of American Politics* (1983). Studies of other major figures of the period include John Niven's *John C. Calhoun and the*

Price of Union: A Biography (1988), Merrill D. Peterson's *The Great Triumvirate: Webster, Clay, and Calhoun* (1987), and Robert Vincent Remini's *Henry Clay: Statesman for the Union* (1991) and *Daniel Webster: The Man and His Time* (1997).

The political philosophies of Jackson's opponents are treated in Michael F. Holt's *The Rise and Fall of the American Whig Party: Jacksonian Politics and the Onset of the Civil War* (1999) and Harry L. Watson's *Andrew Jackson vs. Henry Clay: Democracy and Development in Antebellum America* (1998).

Two studies of the impact of the bank controversy are William G. Shade's *Banks or No Banks: The Money Issue in Western Politics, 1832–1865* (1972) and James Roger Sharp's *The Jacksonians versus the Banks: Politics in the States after the Panic of 1837* (1970).

The outstanding book on the nullification issue remains William W. Freehling's *Prelude to Civil War: The Nullification Controversy in South Carolina, 1816–1836* (1965). John M. Belohlavek's *"Let the Eagle Soar!": The Foreign Policy of Andrew Jackson* (1985) is a thorough study of Jacksonian diplomacy. Ronald N. Satz's *American Indian Policy in the Jacksonian Era* (1974) surveys the controversial relocation policy.

12

THE DYNAMICS
OF GROWTH

FOCUS QUESTIONS

· What caused the expansion of agriculture, industry, and
  transportation?

· How did patterns of immigration change by the middle of the
  nineteenth century?

· What was the status of labor unions?

To answer these questions and access additional review material, please visit
www.wwnorton.com/studyspace.

The Jacksonian-era political debate between democratic
ideals and elitist traditions was rooted in a profound transformation of American social and economic life. Between
1815 and 1850 the United States expanded all the way to the Pacific coast.
An industrial revolution in the Northeast began to reshape the region's
economy and propel an unrelenting process of urbanization. In the West an
agricultural empire began to emerge, based upon the foundation of corn,
wheat, and cattle. In the South, cotton became king, and its reign came to
depend upon the expanding institution of slavery. At the same time, innovations in transportation—larger horse-drawn wagons, called Conestogas;
canals; steamboats; and railroads—knit together a national market for
goods and services. An eighteenth-century economy based primarily upon
small-scale farming and local commerce matured into a far-flung capitalist
marketplace entwined with world markets. These economic developments

in turn generated changes in every other area of life, from politics to the legal system, from the family to social values, from work to recreation.

AGRICULTURE AND THE NATIONAL ECONOMY

The first stage of industrialization brought with it an expansive commercial and urban outlook that by the end of the century would supplant the agrarian philosophy espoused by Thomas Jefferson and many others. "We are greatly, I was about to say fearfully, growing," South Carolina's John C. Calhoun told his congressional colleagues in 1816, and many other statesmen shared his ambivalent outlook. Would the republic retain its virtue and cohesion amid the turmoil of chaotic commercial development? In the brief period of good feelings after the War of 1812, such a troublesome question was easily brushed aside. Economic opportunities seemed abundant, and nowhere more than in Calhoun's native South Carolina. The reason was cotton, the new staple crop of the South, which spread rapidly from South Carolina and Georgia into the fertile new lands of Mississippi, Alabama, Louisiana, and Arkansas.

COTTON Cotton had been used from ancient times, but the Industrial Revolution and its spread of textile mills created a rapidly growing market for the fluffy fiber. It had remained for many years rare and expensive because of the need for hand labor to separate the lint from tenacious seeds. One person working all day could manage to separate barely one pound by hand. Cotton could not be king until a better way was found to separate the seeds from the fiber.

The rising cotton kingdom of the lower South was born at a plantation called Mulberry Grove in coastal Georgia, the home of Catharine Greene, widow of the

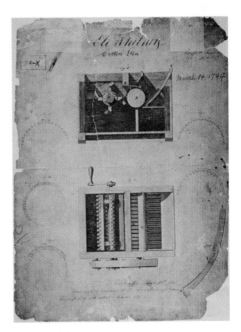

Whitney's Cotton Gin

Eli Whitney's drawing, which accompanied his 1794 federal patent application, shows the side and the top of the machine and the saw teeth that separated the seeds from the fiber.

Revolutionary War hero Nathanael Greene. At Mulberry Hill, discussion often focused on the problem of separating cotton seeds from the cotton fiber. In 1792 young Eli Whitney, recently graduated from Yale, visited fellow graduate Phineas Miller, who was overseer at Mulberry Hill. Catharine Greene noticed her visitor's mechanical aptitude and suggested that young Whitney devise a mechanism for removing the seeds from upland cotton. He mulled over the problem and solved it in ten days. In the spring of 1793, Whitney had a working model of a cotton "gin" (short for *engine*). With it one person could separate fifty times as much cotton as a worker could separate by hand.

Whitney had unwittingly begun a revolution. Green-seed cotton first engulfed the up-country hills of South Carolina and Georgia and after the War of 1812 migrated into the former Creek, Choctaw, and Chickasaw lands to the west. Cotton production soared, and in the process planters found a new and profitable use for slavery. Planters migrated westward with their gangs of workers in tow, and a lucrative trade began to develop in the sale of slaves from the coastal South to the Southwest. The cotton culture became a way of life that tied the Old Southwest to the coastal Southeast in a common interest.

Not the least of the cotton gin's revolutionary consequences, although less apparent at first, was that cotton became almost immediately a major export commodity. Cotton exports averaged about $9 million annually from 1803 to 1807, about 22 percent of the value of all exports; from 1815 to 1819, they averaged over $23 million, or 39 percent of the total; and from the mid-1830s to 1860, they accounted for more than half the value of all exports in the nation. The South supplied the North with both raw materials and markets for manufactures. Income from the North's role in handling the cotton trade then provided surpluses for capital investment. Cotton thereby became a crucial element of the national economy.

FARMING THE WEST   The westward flow of planters and their slaves to Alabama and Mississippi during these flush times mirrored another migration through the Ohio Valley and the Great Lakes region, where the Indians had been steadily pushed westward. By 1860 more than half the nation's population resided in trans-Appalachia, and the restless movement had long since spilled across the Mississippi River and touched the shores of the Pacific.

North of the expanding cotton belt, in the Gulf states, the fertile woodland soil, riverside bottomlands, and black loam of the prairies drew farmers from the rocky lands of New England and the exhausted soils of the Southeast. A new land law of 1820, passed after the panic of 1819, reduced the price of federal land. A settler could get a farm for as little as $100, and over the years the proliferation of state banks made it possible to continue buying on credit. Even that was not enough for westerners, however, who began a long—and eventually victorious—agitation for further relaxation of the land laws. They favored "preemption," the right of squatters to purchase land at the minimum price, and graduation, the progressive reduction of the price on lands that did not sell.

Congress eventually responded with two bills. Under the Preemption Act of 1830, squatters could stake out claims ahead of the land surveys and later get 160 acres at the minimum price of $1.25 per acre. In effect the law recognized a practice enforced more often than not by frontier vigilantes. Under the Graduation Act of 1854, prices of unsold lands were to go down in stages until the lands could sell for 12.5¢ per acre after thirty years.

The process of settling new lands followed the old pattern of clearing trees, grubbing out the stumps and underbrush, and settling down at first to a crude subsistence. The development of effective iron plows greatly eased the backbreaking job of tilling the soil. In 1819 Jethro Wood of New York developed an improved iron plow with separate replaceable parts. The iron plow was a godsend to those farmers who first ventured onto the sticky black loam of the treeless midwestern prairies. Further improvements would follow, including John Deere's steel plow (1837) and the chilled-iron and steel plow of John Oliver (1855).

By the 1840s new mechanical seeders had replaced the process of sowing seed by hand. Even more important, twenty-two-year-old Cyrus Hall

McCormick's Reaping Machine

This illustration appeared in the catalogue of the Great Exhibition, held at the Crystal Palace in London in 1851. The plow eased the transformation of rough plains into fertile farmland, and the reaping machine accelerated farm production.

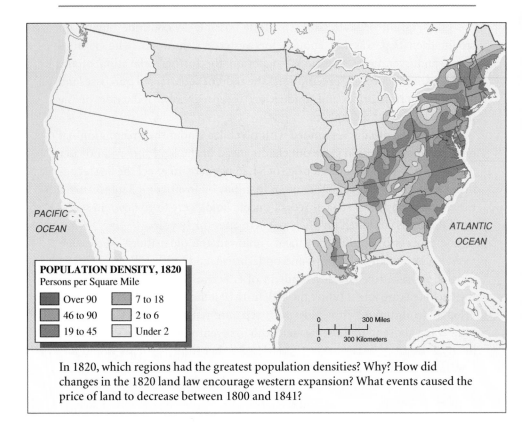

PACIFIC
OCEAN

ATLANTIC
OCEAN

POPULATION DENSITY, 1820
Persons per Square Mile

- Over 90
- 46 to 90
- 19 to 45
- 7 to 18
- 2 to 6
- Under 2

0   300 Miles
0   300 Kilometers

In 1820, which regions had the greatest population densities? Why? How did changes in the 1820 land law encourage western expansion? What events caused the price of land to decrease between 1800 and 1841?

McCormick of Virginia invented a primitive grain reaper in 1831, a development as significant to the agricultural economy of the Old Northwest as the cotton gin was to the South. After tinkering with his strange-looking horse-drawn machine for almost a decade, McCormick began selling it so fast that in 1847 he moved to Chicago and built a manufacturing plant for his reapers and mowers. Within a few years he had sold thousands of new machines, transforming the scale of agriculture. Using a hand-held sickle, a farmer could harvest half an acre of wheat a day; with a McCormick reaper two people could work twelve acres a day.

McCormick's success inspired other manufacturers and inventors, and soon there were mechanical threshers to separate the grains of wheat from the straw. Farming remained, as it still is, a precarious vocation, subject to the whims of climate, assaults by insects, and the fluctuations of foreign markets, but by the 1850s it had become a major commercial activity. As the volume of agricultural products soared, prices dropped, income rose, and for many farm families in the Old Northwest the standard of living improved.

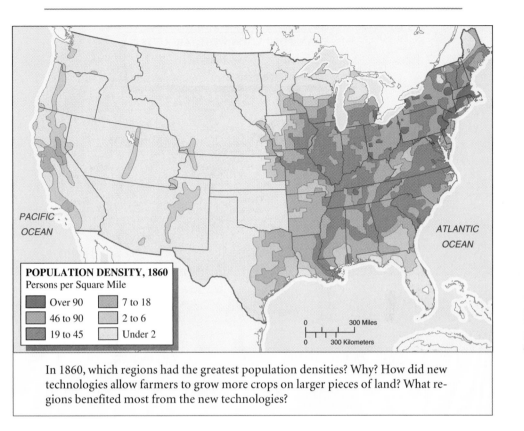

POPULATION DENSITY, 1860
Persons per Square Mile

- Over 90
- 46 to 90
- 19 to 45
- 7 to 18
- 2 to 6
- Under 2

In 1860, which regions had the greatest population densities? Why? How did new technologies allow farmers to grow more crops on larger pieces of land? What regions benefited most from the new technologies?

TRANSPORTATION AND THE NATIONAL ECONOMY

NEW ROADS   Transportation improvements helped spur the development of a national market. As settlers moved west, people demanded better roads. In 1795 the Wilderness Road, along the trail blazed by Daniel Boone twenty years before, was opened to wagon and stagecoach traffic, thereby easing the route through the Cumberland Gap into Kentucky and along the Walton roads, completed the same year, into Tennessee. Even so, travel was difficult at best. Stagecoaches crammed with as many as a dozen people crept along at four miles per hour. South of these roads there were no such major highways. South Carolinians and Georgians pushed westward on whatever trails or rutted roads had appeared.

To the northeast a movement for graded and paved roads (macadamized with crushed stones packed down) gathered momentum after completion of

TRANSPORTATION WEST, ABOUT 1840

Why were towns like Terre Haute, Albany, and Pittsburgh important commercial centers? What was the impact of the steamboat and the flatboat on travel in the West? How did the Erie Canal transform the economy of New York and the Great Lakes region?

the Philadelphia-Lancaster Turnpike in 1794 (the term *turnpike* derives from a pole, or pike, at the tollgate, which was turned to admit the traffic). By 1821 some 4,000 miles of turnpikes had been completed, mainly connecting eastern cities. Western traffic moved along the Frederick Turnpike to Cumberland and thence along the National Road to Wheeling, Virginia, on the Ohio River (opened in 1818), then to Columbus in the Northwest Territory and (by about mid century) on to Vandalia, Illinois.

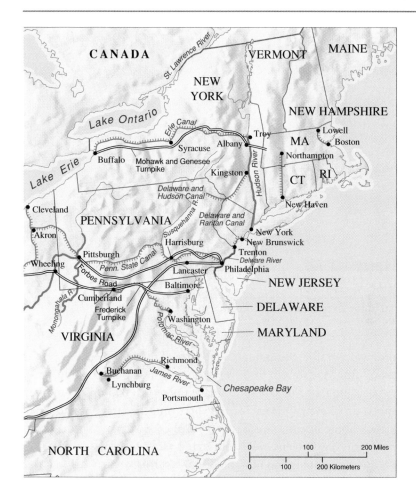

WATER TRANSPORTATION   Once turnpike travelers had reached the Ohio River, they could float westward on flatboats in comparative comfort. In the early 1820s an estimated 3,000 flatboats went down the Ohio every year, and for many years after that the flatboat remained the chief conveyance for heavy traffic downstream.

By the early 1820s the turnpike boom was giving way to new developments in water transportation: the river steamboat and the canal barge, which carried people and commodities far more cheaply than did wagons on the National Road. The first commercially successful steamboat appeared when Robert Fulton and Robert R. Livingston sent the *Clermont* up the Hudson River to Albany in 1807. Thereafter the use of steamboats spread rapidly to other eastern rivers and to the Ohio and Mississippi, opening nearly half a

Traveling the Western Waters

Steamboats at the levee at St. Paul, Minnesota in 1859.

continent to water traffic. Steamboats transformed inland water transportation. To travel from Pittsburgh to New Orleans on a flatboat took up to six weeks. And because flatboats could not make the return trip upstream, they were chopped up in New Orleans for firewood, and the crews had to make their way back home by other means. In 1815 the first steamboat made the trip upriver from New Orleans to Pittsburgh in twenty-five days.

By 1836, 361 steamboats had navigated the western waters, reaching ever farther up the tributaries that fed into the Mississippi River. The durable flatboat, however, still carried to market most of the western wheat, corn, flour, meal, bacon, ham, pork, whiskey, soap and candles (byproducts of slaughterhouses), lead from Missouri, copper from Michigan, wood from the Rockies, and ironwork from Pittsburgh. But the steamboat, by bringing two-way traffic to the Mississippi River valley, created a continental market and an agricultural empire that became the nation's new breadbasket. Farming became even more a commercial activity, producing surpluses for the livestock and commodities markets. Along with the new farmers came promoters, speculators, and boomers. Villages at strategic trading points along the streams evolved into centers of commerce and urban life. The port of New Orleans grew in the 1830s and 1840s to lead all others in exports.

But by then the Erie Canal in New York was drawing eastward much of the trade that once went down to the Gulf, and this development would have major economic and political consequences, tying together the West and the East while further isolating the Deep South. In 1817 the New York legislature endorsed Governor DeWitt Clinton's dream of connecting the Hudson River with Lake Erie. Eight years later, in 1825, the canal, forty feet wide and four feet deep, was open for the entire 363 miles from Albany to Buffalo; branches soon put most of the state within its reach. The Erie Canal brought a "river of gold" to New York City.

The Erie Canal was an engineering marvel. The longest canal in the world, it traversed rivers and valleys, forests and marshes. It reduced travel time from New York City to Buffalo from twenty days to six, and the cost of moving a ton of freight plummeted from $100 to $5. After 1828 the Delaware and Hudson Canal linked New York to the coalfields of northeastern Pennsylvania. The speedy success of the New York system inspired a mania for canals in other states that lasted more than a decade and resulted in the completion of about 3,000 miles of waterways by 1837. But no canal ever matched the spectacular success of the Erie, which rendered the entire Great Lakes region an economic tributary to the port of New York. With the further development

The Erie Canal

Junction of the Northern and Western Canals (1825), an aquatint by John Hill.

of canals spanning Ohio and Indiana from north to south, much of the upper Ohio River valley also came within the economic sphere of New York.

RAILROADS   The panic of 1837 and the subsequent depression cooled the canal fever. Meanwhile, a new and more versatile form of transportation was gaining on the canal: the railroad. As early as 1814, the first practical steam locomotive was built in England. In 1825, the year the Erie Canal was completed, the world's first commercial steam railway began operation in England. By the 1820s the port cities of Baltimore, Charleston, and Boston were alive with schemes to connect the hinterlands by rail. Over the next forty years, railroads grew nearly tenfold to cover 30,626 miles; more than two thirds of that total was built in the 1850s.

Travel on the early railroads was a risky venture. Iron straps on top of wooden rails tended to work loose and curl up into "snakesheads" that sometimes pierced the railway coaches. Wood was used for fuel, and sparks often caused fires or damaged passengers' clothing. Land travel, whether by stagecoach or train, was a jerky, bumpy, wearying ordeal.

Water travel, where available, offered far more comfort, but the railroad gained supremacy over other forms of transportation because of its economy, speed, and reliability. Trains averaged ten miles per hour, more than twice the speed of stagecoaches and four times that of boats. By 1859 railroads had greatly reduced the cost of transportation. Railroads also provided indirect benefits, by encouraging new settlement and the expansion of farming. During the antebellum period the reduced freight costs resulting from the growth of railroads aided the expansion of farming more than manufacturing, since manufacturers in the Northeast, especially New England, had better access to water transportation. The railroads' demand for iron and equipment of various kinds did provide an enormous market for the industries that made these capital goods, however. And the ability of railroads to operate year round in most kinds of weather gave them an advantage in carrying finished goods, too.

OCEAN TRANSPORTATION   For oceangoing traffic the start of regularly scheduled passenger service was the most important change of the early 1800s. In the first week of 1818, ships of the Black Ball Line inaugurated weekly transatlantic service between New York and Liverpool, England. Beginning with four ships in all, the Black Ball Line thereafter had one ship leaving each port monthly at an announced time. By 1845 some fifty-two transatlantic shipping lines were based in New York City, with three regular sailings per week. Many others ran in the coastwise trade, to Charleston, Savannah, New Orleans, and elsewhere.

The same year, 1845, witnessed a great innovation with the launching of the first clipper ship, the *Rainbow*. Built for speed, the sleek clippers were the nineteenth-century equivalent of the supersonic jetliner. They doubled the speed of the older merchant vessels. Long and lean, with taller masts and many sails, they cut dashing figures during their brief but colorful career, which lasted less than two decades. What prompted the clipper boom was the lure of Chinese tea, a drink long coveted in America but in scarce supply. Tea leaves were a perishable commodity that had to reach the market quickly, and the new clipper ships made this possible. Even more important, the discovery of California gold in 1848 lured thousands of prospectors and entrepreneurs from the Atlantic seaboard. The new settlers generated an urgent demand for goods, and the clippers met it. In 1854 the *Flying Cloud* took eighty-nine days and eight hours to travel from New York to San Francisco. But clippers, while fast, lacked ample cargo space, and after the Civil War they would give way to the steamship.

THE ROLE OF GOVERNMENT   The dramatic transportation improvements of the antebellum era were the product of initiatives by both state governments and private ventures, undertaken sometimes jointly and sometimes separately. After the panic of 1837, however, the states left railroad development mainly to private corporations. Still, several southern and

New Oceangoing Vessels

Clipper ship in New York Harbor in the 1840s.

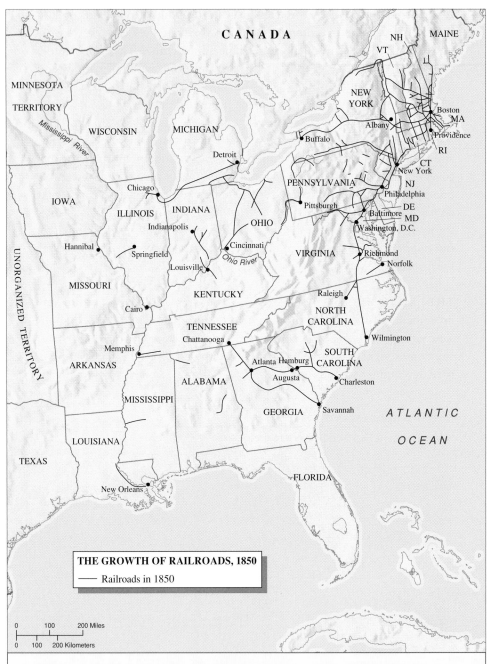

THE GROWTH OF RAILROADS, 1850

—— Railroads in 1850

Where was the first railroad built? Where did the railroads that had been built by 1850 in the United States begin and end? Why? Describe some of the experiences of travel on the first railroads.

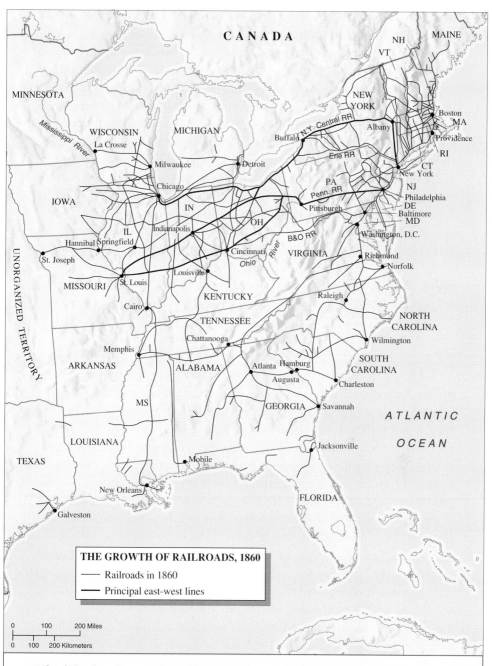

THE GROWTH OF RAILROADS, 1860

— Railroads in 1860

— Principal east-west lines

0   100   200 Miles

0   100   200 Kilometers

Why did railroads expand rapidly in the 1850s? What were the principal east-west lines? Why did many lines terminate in places like St. Louis and Chicago?

western states built their own lines, and most states granted generous tax concessions to railroad companies.

The federal government helped too, despite the belief of some politicians that direct involvement in internal improvements was unconstitutional. The national government bought stock in turnpike and canal companies and after the success of the Erie Canal extended land grants to several western states for the support of canal projects. Congress provided for railroad surveys by government engineers and reduced the tariff duties on iron used in railroad construction. In 1850 Senator Stephen A. Douglas of Illinois and others prevailed upon Congress to extend a major land grant to support a north-south line connecting Chicago and Mobile, Alabama. Grants of three square miles for each mile of railroad subsidized the building of the Illinois Central and the Mobile and Ohio Railroads. Regarded at the time as a special case, the 1850 grant set a precedent for other bounties that totaled about 20 million acres by 1860—a small amount compared with the land grants for transcontinental lines during the Civil War decade.

A COMMUNICATIONS REVOLUTION

During the first half of the nineteenth century, the transportation revolution helped spark dramatic improvements in communications. At the beginning of the century, it took days—often weeks—for news to travel along the Atlantic seaboard. For example, after George Washington died, in 1799 at his estate at Mount Vernon in Virginia, the news of his death did not appear in New York City newspapers until a week later. Naturally news took even longer to travel to and from Europe. It took forty-nine days for news of the peace treaty ending the War of 1812 to reach New York from Europe.

The speed of communications accelerated greatly as the nineteenth century unfolded. The construction of turnpikes, canals, and railroads and the development of steamships and the telegraph generated a communications revolution. By 1829 it was possible to "convey" Andrew Jackson's inaugural address from Washington, D.C., to New York City in sixteen hours. It took six days to reach New Orleans. Mail began to be delivered by "express," a system in which riders could mount fresh horses at a series of relay stations. Still, even with such advances the states and territories west of the Appalachian Mountains struggled to get timely deliveries and news.

AMERICAN TECHNOLOGY Americans became famous for their "practical" inventiveness. One of the most striking examples of the connection between pure research and innovation was in the work of Joseph Henry, a Princeton physicist. His research in electromagnetism provided the basis for Samuel F. B. Morse's invention of the telegraph and for the invention of electrical motors. In 1846 Henry became head of the new Smithsonian Institution, founded with a bequest from the Englishman James Smithson "for the increase and diffusion of knowledge." Two years later, in 1848, the American Association for the Advancement of Science was founded to "advance science and serve society."

Technological advances helped improve living conditions: houses could be larger, better heated, and better illuminated. Although working-class residences had few creature comforts, the affluent were able to afford indoor plumbing, central heating, gas lighting, bathtubs, iceboxes, and sewing machines. Even the lower classes were able to afford new coal-burning cast-iron cooking stoves, which facilitated the preparation of more varied meals and improved heating. The first sewer systems helped cities begin to rid their streets of human and animal waste, while underground water lines enabled fire companies to use hydrants rather than bucket brigades. Machine-made clothes fit better and were cheaper than those sewed by hand from homespun cloth; newspapers and magazines were more abundant and affordable, as were clocks and watches.

A spate of inventions in the 1840s generated dramatic changes. In 1844 Charles Goodyear patented a process for vulcanizing rubber, which made the product stronger and more elastic. In 1846 Elias Howe patented his design of the sewing machine, soon improved upon by Isaac Merrit Singer. The sewing machine, incidentally, actually slowed the progress of the factory. Since it was adapted to use in the home, it gave the "putting-out" system a new life in the clothing industry.

In 1844 the first intercity telegraph message was transmitted, from Baltimore to Washington, D.C., on the device Samuel Morse had invented back in 1832. The telegraph may have triggered more social changes than any other invention. Until it appeared, communications were conveyed by boat, train, or horseback or delivered by hand. With the telegraph, people could learn of events and exchange messages instantaneously. The invention was slow to catch on, but by the mid-1850s the North American Telegraph Company and the Western Union Telegraph Company had consolidated national networks. In 1861, seventeen years after the first demonstration, connections to San Francisco were completed, and an entire continent had been wired for instant communication.

Taken together, the communications and transportation improvements of the first half of the nineteenth century reshaped the contours of economic, social, and political life. Steamboats, canals, and railroads helped unite the western portion of the country with the East, boost trade, and open up the West for settlement. Between 1800 and 1860 an undeveloped land dotted with scattered farms, primitive roads, and modest local markets was transformed into an engine of capitalist expansion, audacious investment, and global reach.

THE INDUSTRIAL REVOLUTION

While the South and the West developed the agricultural basis for a national economy, the Northeast was engineering an industrial revolution. Technology in the form of the cotton gin and the mechanical harvester and improvements in transportation had quickened agricultural development and to some extent decided its direction. But technology altered the economic landscape even more profoundly, by giving rise to the factory system.

EARLY TEXTILE MANUFACTURES At the end of the colonial period, manufacturing remained at the household, or handicraft, stage of development or, at most, at the "putting-out" stage, in which a merchant capitalist would distribute raw materials (say, leather patterns for shoes) to be worked up at home, collected, and sold. Farm families had to produce much of what they needed in the way of crude implements, shoes, and clothing, and in their simple workshops inventive genius was sometimes nurtured. The transition from home production to the factory was slow, but one for which a base had been laid before 1815.

In the eighteenth century, Great Britain had gotten a long head start in industrial production. The foundations of Britain's advantage were the invention of the steam engine in 1705, its improvement by James Watt in 1765, and a series of inventions that mechanized the production of textiles. Britain carefully guarded its hard-won secrets, forbidding the export of machines or even publication of descriptions of them, even restricting the emigration of informed mechanics. But the secrets could not be kept. In 1789 Samuel Slater arrived in America from England with the plan of a water-powered spinning machine in his head. He contracted with an enterprising merchant-manufacturer in Rhode Island to build a mill in Pawtucket, and in that little mill, completed in 1790, nine children turned out a satisfactory cotton yarn, which was then worked up by the putting-out system.

The progress of textile production was slow and faltering until Thomas Jefferson's embargo in 1807 stimulated domestic production. Policies adopted during the War of 1812 restricted imports and encouraged the

New England Factory Village (1830)

Mills and factories gradually transformed the New England landscape in the early nineteenth century.

merchant capitalists of New England to transfer their resources to manufacturing. New England, it happened, had the distinct advantage of many rivers, which provided power and transportation. By 1815 textile mills numbered in the hundreds. A flood of British imports after the War of 1812 dealt a temporary setback to the infant industry, but the foundations of textile manufacture were laid, and they spurred the growth of garment trades and a machine-tool industry that built and serviced the mills.

THE LOWELL SYSTEM   The factory system sprang full-blown upon the American scene at Waltham, Massachusetts, in 1813, in the plant of the Boston Manufacturing Company, formed by the Boston Associates, one of whom was Francis Cabot Lowell. Their plant was the first factory in which the processes of spinning and weaving by power machinery were brought together under one roof, with every process mechanized, from the production of the raw material to that of finished cloth. In 1822 the Boston Associates developed a new water-powered center at a village along the Merrimack River.

At the village, which they renamed Lowell, the founders of the enterprise sought to establish an industrial center compatible with the republican values of plain living and high thinking. They insisted that they could design model factory communities that would strengthen rather than corrupt the social fabric. To avoid the drab, crowded, and wretched life of the English mill villages, they located their mill in the countryside and established an ambitious program of paternal supervision of the workers.

The Lowell factory workers were mostly young women from New England farm families. Employers preferred to hire women because of their dexterity in operating machines and their willingness to work for wages lower than those paid to men. Moreover, by the 1820s there was a surplus of women in the region because so many men had migrated westward in search of cheap land and new economic opportunities. As many of the household goods produced by families' daughters gave way to the "store-bought" goods of a market economy, young farm women faced diminishing prospects for employment as well as marriage. The chance to escape the routine of farm life, earn cash, and thus help their families or improve their own circumstances also drew many women to the Lowell mills. In the early 1820s a steady stream of single women began flocking toward Lowell. To reassure worried parents, the mill owners promised to provide the "Lowell girls" with tolerable work, prepared meals, secure and comfortable boardinghouses, moral discipline, and a variety of educational and cultural opportunities.

Initially the "Lowell idea" worked pretty much according to plan. Visitors commented on the well-designed red-brick mills with their lecture halls and libraries. The laborers appeared "healthy and happy." The female workers lived in dormitories staffed by matronly supervisors who enforced mandatory church attendance and curfews. Despite thirteen-hour days and six-day workweeks spent tending the knitting looms, some of the women found the time and energy to form study groups, publish a literary magazine, and attend lectures. But Lowell soon lost its innocence as it experienced mushrooming growth. By 1840 there were thirty-two mills and factories in operation, and the blissful rural town had become an industrial city—bustling, grimy, and bleak.

Other factory centers sprouted up across New England, displacing forests and farms and engulfing villages, filling the air with smoke, noise, and stench. Between 1820 and 1840 the number of Americans engaged in manufacturing increased eightfold, and the number of city dwellers more than doubled. Booming growth transformed the Lowell experiment in industrial republicanism. By 1846 a concerned worker told young farm women thinking about taking a job in a factory that "it will be better for you to stay at home on your fathers' farms than to run the risk of being ruined in a manufacturing village."

During the 1830s, as textile prices and mill wages dropped, relations between workers and managers deteriorated. A new generation of owners and foremen began stressing efficiency and profit margins over community

Merrimack Mills and Boarding Houses (1848)

One of the milling companies in Lowell, Massachusetts.

values. They worked employees and machines at a faster pace. The women organized strikes to protest deteriorating conditions. In 1834, for instance, they unsuccessfully "turned out" (went on strike) against the mills after learning of a proposed sharp cut in their wages.

The "Lowell girls" drew attention less because they were typical than because they were special. An increasingly common pattern in industrial New England was the family system, sometimes called the Rhode Island system or the Fall River system, which prevailed in textile companies outside northern New England. The Rhode Island factories, which relied on waterpower, were often built in unpopulated areas, and the complexes included tenements or mill villages. Whole families might be hired, the men for heavy labor, the women and children for lighter work. Like the Lowell model, the Rhode Island system promoted paternalism. Employers dominated the life of the mill villages. Employees worked from sunup to sunset and longer in winter—a sixty-eight- to seventy-two-hour week. Such hours were common on the farms of the time, but in textile mills the work was more intense and offered no seasonal letup.

Mill Girls

Massachusetts mill workers of the mid–nineteenth century, photographed holding shuttles. Although mill work initially provided women with an opportunity for independence and education, conditions soon deteriorated as profits took precedence.

INDUSTRIALIZATION AND THE ENVIRONMENT Between 1820 and 1850 some forty textile and flour mills were built along the Merrimack River, which runs from New Hampshire through northeastern Massachusetts. In pre-industrial England and America the common-law tradition required that water be permitted to flow as it had always flowed; the right to use it was reserved to those who owned land adjoining streams and rivers. In other words, running water, by nature, could not be converted into private property. People living along rivers could divert water for domestic use or to water livestock but could not use natural flowing water to irrigate land or drive machinery.

The rise of the water-powered textile industry challenged those long-standing assumptions. Entrepreneurs acquired water rights by purchasing land adjoining rivers and buying the acquiescence of nearby landowners; then, in the 1820s, they began renting the water that flowed to the textile mills. Water suddenly became a commodity independent of the land. It was then fully incorporated into the industrial process. Canals, locks, and dams were built to facilitate the needs of the proliferating mills. Flowing water was transformed from a societal resource to a private commodity.

The changing uses of water transformed the region's ecology. Rivers shape regions far beyond their banks, and the changing patterns of streams now affected marshlands, meadows, vegetation, and the game and wildlife that depended upon those habitats. The dams built to harness water to turn the mill wheels that ground corn and wheat flooded pastures and decimated fish populations, spawned urban growth that in turn polluted the river, and aroused intense local resentment, particularly among the New Hampshire residents far upstream of the big Massachusetts textile factories. In 1859

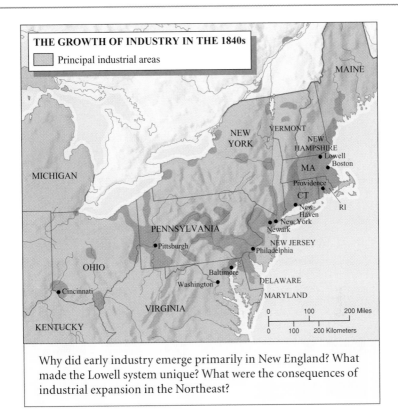

THE GROWTH OF INDUSTRY IN THE 1840s

Principal industrial areas

MAINE

NEW YORK

VERMONT

NEW HAMPSHIRE
•Lowell
•Boston

MA
Providence•

MICHIGAN

CT

New Haven•

RI

PENNSYLVANIA

•New York
Newark•

•Pittsburgh

NEW JERSEY
•Philadelphia

OHIO

Baltimore•
Washington•

DELAWARE

MARYLAND

•Cincinnati

VIRGINIA

0   100   200 Miles

KENTUCKY

0   100   200 Kilometers

Why did early industry emerge primarily in New England? What made the Lowell system unique? What were the consequences of industrial expansion in the Northeast?

angry farmers, loggers, and fishermen tried to destroy a massive dam in Lake Village, New Hampshire. But their axes and crow bars caused little damage. By then the Industrial Revolution could not be stopped. It was not only transforming lives and property; it was reshaping nature as well.

INDUSTRY AND CITIES   The rapid growth of commerce and industry spurred the growth of cities. In terms of the census definition of *urban* as a place with 8,000 inhabitants or more, the proportion of urban to rural populations grew from 3 percent in 1790 to 16 percent in 1860. Because of their strategic locations, the four great Atlantic seaports of New York, Philadelphia, Baltimore, and Boston remained the largest cities. New Orleans became the nation's fifth-largest city from the time of the Louisiana Purchase. Its focus on cotton exports to the neglect of imports eventually caused it to lag behind its northeastern competitors, however. New York outpaced all its competitors and the nation as a whole in its population growth. By 1860 it

Milling and the Environment

A mill dam on the Appomattox River near Petersburg, Virginia, in 1865.

was the first city to reach a population of more than 1 million, largely because of its superior harbor and its unique access to commerce.

Pittsburgh, at the head of the Ohio River, was already a center of iron production by 1800, and Cincinnati, at the mouth of the Little Miami River, soon surpassed all other meatpacking centers. Louisville, because it stood at the falls of the Ohio River, became an important trading center. On the Great Lakes the leading cities—Buffalo, Cleveland, Detroit, Chicago, and Milwaukee—also stood at important breaking points in water transportation. Chicago was well located to become a hub of both water and rail transportation, connecting the Northeast, the South, and the trans-Mississippi West. During the 1830s St. Louis tripled in size mainly because most of the trans-Mississippi fur trade was funneled down the Missouri River. By 1860 St. Louis and Chicago were positioned to challenge Baltimore and Boston for third and fourth places.

Before 1840 commerce dominated the activities of major cities, but early industry often created new concentrations of population at places convenient to waterpower or raw materials. During the 1840s and 1850s, however, the

Broadway and Canal Street, New York City (1836)

New York's economy and industry, like those of many other cities, grew rapidly in the early nineteenth century.

stationary steam engine and declining transportation costs offset the advantages of such locations and enhanced the attractions of older cities: pools of experienced labor, capital, warehousing and trading services, access to information, the savings in bulk purchasing and handling, and the many amenities of city life. Urbanization thus was both a consequence of economic growth and a positive force in its promotion.

THE POPULAR CULTURE

During the colonial era, Americans had little time for play or amusement. Their priority was sheer survival, and most adults worked from dawn to dusk six days a week. In rural areas free time was often spent in communal activities, such as barn raisings and corn-husking parties, shooting matches and footraces, while residents of the seacoast sailed and fished. In colonial cities, people attended balls, went on sleigh rides and picnics, and played "parlor games" at home—billiards, cards, and chess.

By the early nineteenth century, however, a more urban society could indulge in more diverse forms of recreation. As more people moved to cities in the first half of the nineteenth century, they began to create a distinctive urban

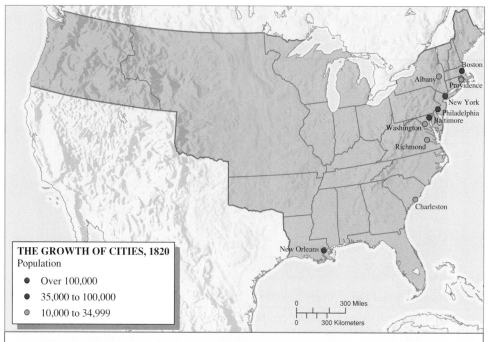

THE GROWTH OF CITIES, 1820
Population

- Over 100,000
- 35,000 to 100,000
- 10,000 to 34,999

What were the largest cities in the United States in 1820? Why did those cities have the densest populations? Why did New Orleans grow rapidly yet eventually lag behind its northeastern counterparts?

culture. Laborers and shopkeepers sought new forms of leisure and entertainment as pleasant diversions from their long workdays.

URBAN RECREATION   Social drinking was pervasive during the first half of the nineteenth century. In 1829 the secretary of war estimated that three quarters of the nation's laborers drank at least four ounces of "hard liquor" daily. The drinking of distilled spirits accompanied virtually every social event or public occasion. Barn raisings, corn huskings, quilting parties, militia musters, church socials, court sessions, holidays, and political gatherings—all featured liquor, cider, or beer.

This drinking culture cut across all regions, races, and classes. Taverns and social or sporting clubs in the burgeoning cities served as the nexus of recreation and leisure. So-called blood sports were also a popular form of amusement. Cockfighting and dogfighting at saloons attracted excited crowds and frenzied betting. Prizefighting, also known as boxing, eventually displaced

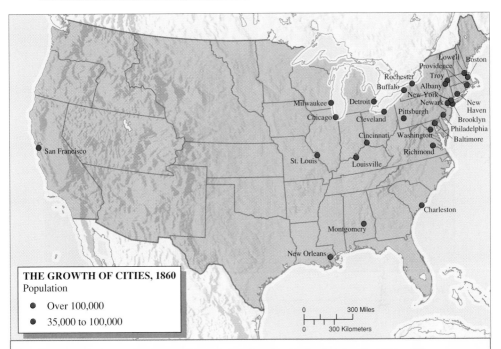

THE GROWTH OF CITIES, 1860
Population

● Over 100,000

● 35,000 to 100,000

What is the connection between industrialization and urbanization? Why did Chicago, Pittsburgh, Cincinnati, and St. Louis become major urban centers in the mid–nineteenth century? How did new technologies make cities more appealing for commerce?

the animal contests. Imported from Britain, boxing proved popular with all social classes. The early contestants tended to be Irish or English immigrants, often sponsored by a neighborhood fire company, fraternal association, or street gang. In the antebellum era, boxers fought with bare knuckles, and the results were brutal. A match ended only when a contestant could not continue. A bout in 1842 lasted 119 rounds and ended when one fighter died in his corner. Such deaths prompted clergymen to condemn prizefighting, and several cities outlawed the practice, only to see it reappear as an underground activity.

THE PERFORMING ARTS   Theaters were the most popular form of indoor entertainment during the first half of the nineteenth century. People of all classes flocked to opera houses and theaters to watch a wide spectrum of performances: Shakespeare's tragedies, "blood and thunder" melodramas,

Bare Knuckles

Blood sports emerged as popular urban entertainment for men of all social classes.

comedies, minstrel shows, operas, magic shows, performances by acrobatic troupes, and local pageants. Audiences were predominantly young and middle-aged men. "Respectable" women rarely attended because women were dissuaded from entering any boisterous establishment, and the prevailing "cult of domesticity" kept women in the home. Behavior in antebellum theaters was raucous and at times disorderly. Audiences cheered the heroes and heroines and hissed at the villains. If an actor did not meet expectations, audiences hurled curses, nuts, eggs, fruit, shoes, or chairs.

The 1830s witnessed the emergence of the first uniquely American form of mass entertainment: the blackface minstrel show. Rooted in a tradition of folk theatricals, minstrel shows featured white performers made up as blacks. "Minstrelsy" drew upon African-American subjects and reinforced prevailing racial stereotypes. It featured banjo and fiddle music, "shuffle" dances, and lowbrow humor. Between the 1830s and the 1870s minstrel shows were immensely popular throughout the nation, especially among northern working-class ethnic groups and southern whites.

The most popular minstrel songs were written by a young white composer named Stephen Foster. Born near Pittsburgh on July 4, 1826, Foster was a self-taught musician who could pick up any tune by ear. In 1846 he composed "Oh! Susanna," which immediately became a national favorite. Its popularity catapulted Foster into the national limelight, and equally popular tunes followed, such as "Old Folks at Home" (popularly known as "Way Down upon the Swanee River"), "Massa's in de Cold, Cold Ground," "My Old Kentucky Home," and "Old Black Joe," all of which perpetuated the sentimental myth of contented slaves, and none of which used actual African-American melodies.

IMMIGRATION

Throughout the nineteenth century, land in America remained plentiful and relatively cheap, while labor was scarce and relatively dear. The United States thus remained a strong magnet for immigrants, offer-

The Crow Quadrilles

This sheet-music cover, printed in 1837, shows eight vignettes caricaturing African Americans. Minstrel shows enjoyed nationwide popularity while reinforcing racial stereotypes.

ing them chances to take up farming or urban employment. Glowing reports from early arrivals who made good reinforced romantic views of American opportunity and freedom. "Tell Miriam," one immigrant wrote, "there is no sending children to bed without supper, or husbands to work without dinner in their bags." A German immigrant in Missouri applauded America's "absence of overbearing soldiers, haughty clergymen, and inquisitive tax collectors." In 1834 an English immigrant reported that America is ideal "for a poor man that is industrious, for he has to want for nothing."

During the forty years from the outbreak of the Revolution to the end of the War of 1812, immigration had slowed to a trickle. The French Revolution and the Napoleonic Wars restricted travel from Europe until 1815. Thereafter, however, the number of new arrivals rose steadily. After 1845 the tempo picked up rapidly. The years from 1845 to 1854 saw the greatest proportional influx of immigrants in U.S. history, 2.4 million, or about 14.5 percent of the total population in 1845. In 1860 America's population was 31 million, with more than one of every eight residents foreign born. The largest groups were the Irish (1.6 million), the Germans (1.2 million), and the British—mostly English (588,000).

THE IRISH What caused so many Irish to flee their homeland in the nineteenth century was the onset of a prolonged depression that brought immense social hardship. The most densely populated country in Europe, Ireland was so ravaged by its economic collapse that in rural areas the average age at death declined to nineteen. After an epidemic of potato rot in 1845 brought to rural Ireland a famine that killed more than 1 million peasants, the flow of Irish immigrants to Canada and the United States became a flood. Buoyed by the promise of a better life in America, immigrants braved the Atlantic crossing under crowded, unsanitary conditions. Thousands died of dysentery, typhus, and malnutrition during the six-week ocean crossing on what came to be called coffin ships. In 1847 alone 40,000 Irish perished at sea.

By 1850 the Irish constituted 43 percent of the foreign-born population of the United States. Unlike the German immigrants, who were predominantly male, the Irish newcomers were more evenly apportioned by sex; in fact a slight majority of them were women, most of whom were single young adults. Most of the Irish arrivals had been tenant farmers, but their rural sufferings left them with little taste for farmwork and little money with which to buy land in America. Great numbers of the men hired on with the construction gangs building canals and railways. Others worked in iron foundries, steel mills, warehouses, and shipyards. Many Irish women found jobs as domestic servants, laundresses, or workers in textile mills in New England. In 1845 the Irish constituted only 8 percent of the workforce in the Lowell mills; by 1860 they made up 50 percent. Relatively few immigrants during the Jacksonian era found their way to the South, where land was expensive and industries scarce. The widespread use of slavery also left few opportunities in the region for free manual laborers.

Irish Immigration

In 1847 nearly 214,000 Irish immigrated to the United States and Canada aboard ships of the White Star Line and other companies. Despite promises of spacious, well-lit, well-ventilated, and heated accommodations in steerage, 20 percent of these immigrants died on board.

Too poor to move inland, most of the destitute Irish congregated in the eastern cities, in or near their port of entry. By the 1850s the Irish made up over half the population of Boston and New York City and were almost as prominent in Philadelphia. Irish newcomers crowded into filthy, poorly ventilated tenements, plagued by high rates of crime, infectious disease, prostitution, alcoholism, and infant mortality. The archbishop of New York at midcentury described the Irish as "the poorest and most wretched population that can be found in the world."

But many enterprising Irish immigrants forged remarkable careers. Twenty years after arriving in New York, Alexander T. Stewart became the owner of the nation's largest department store and thereafter accumulated vast real-estate holdings in Manhattan. Michael Cudahy, who began work in a Milwaukee meatpacking business at age fourteen, became head of the Cudahy Packing Company and developed a process for the curing of meats under refrigeration. Dublin-born Victor Herbert emerged as one of America's most revered composers, and Irish dancers and playwrights came to dominate the stage. Irishmen were equally successful in the boxing arena and on the baseball diamond.

These accomplishments did little to quell the anti-Irish sentiments prevalent in nineteenth-century America. Irish immigrants confronted demeaning stereotypes and intense anti-Catholic prejudices. The Irish were characterized as ignorant, filthy, clannish folk incapable of assimilation. Many employers posted "No Irish Need Apply" signs. But Irish Americans could be equally contemptuous of other groups, such as free African Americans, who competed with them for low-status jobs. In 1850 the *New York Tribune* expressed concern that the Irish, having themselves escaped from "a galling, degrading bondage" in their homeland, typically voted against any proposal for equal rights for the Negro and frequently arrived at the polls shouting, "Down with the Nagurs! Let them go back to Africa, where they belong." For their part, many African Americans viewed the Irish with equal disdain. In 1850 a slave expressed a common sentiment: "My Master is a great tyrant, he treats me badly as if I were a common Irishman."

After becoming citizens, the Irish formed powerful voting blocs. Drawn mainly to the party of Andrew Jackson, they set a crucial example of identification with the Democrats, one that other ethnic groups by and large followed. In Jackson the Irish immigrants found a hero. Himself the son of Irish colonists, he was also popular for having defeated the hated British at New Orleans. In addition, the Irish immigrants' loathing of aristocracy, which they associated with British rule, attracted them to a politician and a party claiming to represent "the common man." Although property requirements initially kept most Irish Americans from voting, a New York State law extended the franchise in 1821, and five years later the state removed the property qualification altogether. In the 1828 election, masses of Irish voters made the difference in the race between Jackson and John Quincy Adams. One newspaper expressed alarm at this new force in politics: "It was emphatically an Irish triumph. The foreigners have carried the day." With African Americans, women, and Native Americans still years from enfranchisement, Irish men became perhaps the first "minority group" to exert a remarkable political influence.

Perhaps the greatest collective achievement of the Irish immigrants was their stimulating the growth of the Catholic Church in the United States. Years of persecution had instilled in Irish Catholics a fierce loyalty to the doctrines of the church as "the supreme authority over all the affairs of the world." Such passionate attachment to Catholicism generated both community cohesion among Irish Americans and fears of Roman Catholicism among American Protestants. By 1860 Catholics had become the largest denomination in the United States.

THE GERMANS   A new wave of German migration peaked in 1854, just a few years after the crest of Irish arrivals, when 215,000 Germans disembarked in U.S. ports. These immigrants included a large number of learned, cultured professional people—doctors, lawyers, teachers, engineers—some of them refugees from the failed German revolution of 1848. In addition to an array of political opinions ranging from laissez faire conservatism to Marxism, the Germans brought with them a variety of religious preferences. One third of the new arrivals were Catholics, most were Protestants (usually Lutherans), and a significant number were Jews or freethinking atheists or agnostics. By the end of the century, some 250,000 German Jews had emigrated to the United States.

Unlike the Irish more Germans settled in rural areas than in cities, and the influx included many independent farmers, skilled workers, and shopkeepers who arrived with the means to get themselves established in skilled jobs or on the land. More so than the Irish, they migrated in families and groups rather than individually, and this clannish quality helped them better sustain elements of their language and culture in the New World. More of them also tended to return to their native country. About 14 percent of the Germans eventually went back to their homeland, compared with 9 percent of the Irish.

Among the German immigrants who prospered in the New World were Ferdinand Schumacher, who began peddling flaked oatmeal in Ohio and whose company eventually became part of the Quaker Oats Company;

German Beer Garden, New York (1825)

German immigrants established their own communities, where they maintained the traditions of their homeland.

Heinrich Steinweg, a piano maker from the Harz Mountains, who in America changed his name to Steinway and became famous for the quality of his instruments; and Levi Strauss, a Jewish tailor who followed the gold rushers to California and began making durable work pants that were later dubbed blue jeans, or Levi's. Major centers of German settlement developed in southwestern Illinois and Missouri (around St. Louis), Texas (near San Antonio), Ohio, and Wisconsin (especially around Milwaukee). The larger German communities developed traditions of bounteous food, beer, and music, along with German turnvereins (gymnastic societies), sharpshooter clubs, fire-engine companies, and kindergartens.

THE BRITISH, SCANDINAVIANS, AND CHINESE   British immigrants continued to arrive in the United States in large numbers during the first half of the nineteenth century. They included a great many professionals, independent farmers, and skilled workers. Some British workers, such as Samuel Slater, helped transport the technology of British factories to the United States. Two other groups that began to arrive in noticeable numbers during the 1840s and 1850s served as the vanguard for greater numbers of their compatriots. Annual arrivals from Scandinavia did not exceed 1,000 until 1843, but by 1860, 72,600 Scandinavians lived in the United States. The Norwegians and Swedes gravitated to Wisconsin and Minnesota, where the climate and woodlands reminded them of home. By the 1850s the rapid development of California was attracting Chinese, who, like the Irish in the

East, did the heavy work of construction. Infinitesimal in number until 1854, the Chinese in America numbered 35,500 by 1860.

NATIVISM Not all Americans welcomed the flood of immigrants. Many "natives" resented the newcomers, with their alien languages and mysterious customs. The flood of Irish and German Catholics aroused Protestant hostility to "popery." A militant Protestantism growing out of the evangelical revivals of the early nineteenth century fueled the anti-Catholic hysteria. There were also fears that German communities were fomenting political radicalism and that the Irish were forming voting blocs, but above all hovered the menace of unfamiliar religious practices. Catholic authoritarianism was widely perceived as a threat to hard-won liberties, religious and political.

In 1834 a series of anti-Catholic sermons by Lyman Beecher, a popular Congregationalist minister who served as president of Lane Theological Seminary in Cincinnati, incited a mob to attack and burn the Ursuline Convent in Charlestown, Massachusetts. In 1844 armed clashes between Protestants and Catholics in Philadelphia ended with about 20 killed and 100 injured. Sporadically the nativist spirit took organized form in groups that claimed to prove their patriotism by hating foreigners and Catholics.

As early as 1837, a Native American Association was formed in Washington D.C., but the most significant such group was the Order of the Star-Spangled Banner, founded in New York City in 1849. Within a few years this group had grown into a formidable third party known as the American party, which had the trappings of a secret fraternal order. Members pledged never to vote for any foreign-born or Catholic candidate. When asked about the organization, they were to say "I know nothing." In popular parlance the American party became the Know-Nothing party. For a season it appeared to be on the brink of achieving major-party status. In state and local campaigns during 1854, the Know-Nothings carried one election after another. They swept the Massachusetts legislature, winning all but two seats in the lower house. That fall they elected more than forty congressmen. For a while the Know-Nothings threatened to control New England, New York, and Maryland and showed strength elsewhere, but the anti-Catholic movement subsided when slavery became the focal issue of the 1850s.

The Know-Nothings demanded the exclusion of immigrants and Catholics from public office and the extension of the period for naturalization (citizenship) from five to twenty-one years, but the party never gathered the political strength to effect such legislation. Nor did Congress act during the period to restrict immigration in any way. The first federal law on immigration, passed

A Know-Nothing Cartoon

The Catholic Church supposedly attempts to control American religious and political life through Irish immigration.

in 1819, enacted only safety and health regulations regarding supplies and the number of passengers on immigrant ships. That and subsequent acts designed to protect immigrants from overcrowding and unsanitary conditions were, however, poorly enforced.

ORGANIZED LABOR

Skilled workers in American cities before and after the Revolution were called artisans, craftsmen, or mechanics. They made or repaired shoes, hats, saddles, ironware, silverware, jewelry, glass, ropes, furniture, tools, weapons, and an array of wooden products, and printers published books, pamphlets, and newspapers. These skilled workers operated within a guild system, a centuries-old economic and social structure developed in medieval Europe.

Workers in several of the skilled trades, especially shoemaking and printing, formed their own professional associations. Like medieval guilds, which were organized by particular trades, these trade associations were local societies intended to promote the interests of the members. The trade groups pressured politicians for tariffs to protect them from foreign imports, provided insurance benefits, and drafted regulations to improve working conditions, ensure quality control, and provide equitable treatment of apprentices and journeymen. In addition, they sought to control the total number of tradesmen in their profession so as to maintain wage levels. The New York shoemakers, for instance, complained about employers taking on too many apprentices, insisting that "two was as many as one man can do justice by."

The use of slaves as skilled workers also caused controversy among tradesmen. White journeymen in the South objected to competing with enslaved laborers. Other artisans refused to take advantage of slave labor. The Baltimore Carpenters' Society, for example, admitted as members only those employers who refused to use forced labor.

During the 1820s and 1830s artisans who emphasized quality and craftsmanship for a custom trade found it hard to meet the low prices made possible by the new factories and mass-production workshops. At the time few workers belonged to unions, but a growing fear that they were losing status led artisans in the major cities to become involved in labor politics and unions.

The Shoemaker, from The Book of Trades (1807)

When Philadelphia boot makers and shoemakers went on strike in 1806, a court found them guilty of a "conspiracy to raise their wages."

EARLY UNIONS Early labor unions faced serious legal obstacles—they were prosecuted as unlawful conspiracies. In 1806, for instance, Philadelphia shoemakers were found guilty of a "combination to raise their wages." The court's decision broke the union. Such precedents were used for many years to hamstring labor organizations until the Massachusetts Supreme Judicial Court made a landmark ruling in the case of *Commonwealth v. Hunt* (1842). In this case the court ruled that forming a trade union was not in itself illegal, nor was a demand that employers hire only members of the union. The court also declared that workers could strike if an employer hired nonunion laborers.

Until the 1820s labor organizations took the form of local trade unions, confined to one city and one craft. From 1827 to 1837, however, organization on a larger scale began to take hold. In 1834 the National Trades' Union was set up to federate the city societies. At the same time, national craft unions were established by the shoemakers, printers, combmakers, carpenters, and handloom weavers, but all the national groups and most of the local ones vanished in the economic collapse of 1837.

LABOR POLITICS   With the widespread removal of property qualifications for voting, labor politics flourished briefly during the Jacksonian era, especially in Philadelphia. A Workingmen's party, formed there in 1828, gained the balance of power in the city council that fall. This success inspired other Workingmen's parties in about fifteen states. The Workingmen's parties were broad reformist groups devoted to the interests of labor, but they faded quickly. The inexperience of labor politicians left the parties prey to manipulation by political professionals. In addition, some of their issues were co-opted by the major parties. Labor parties also proved vulnerable to charges of extreme radicalism.

Once the labor parties had faded, many of their supporters found their way into a radical wing of the Jacksonian Democrats. This faction acquired the name Locofocos in 1835, when their opponents in New York City's regular Democratic organization, Tammany Hall, turned off the gaslights at one of their meetings and they produced candles, lighting them with the new friction matches known as locofocos. The Locofocos soon faded as a separate group but endured as a radical faction within the Democratic party.

While the labor parties elected few candidates, they did succeed in drawing notice to their demands, many of which attracted the support of middle-class reformers. Above all they promoted free public education for all children and the abolition of imprisonment for debt, causes that won widespread popular support. The labor parties and unions actively promoted the ten-hour workday to prevent employers from abusing workers. In 1836 President Jackson established the ten-hour workday at the Naval Shipyard in Philadelphia in response to a strike, and in 1840 President Van Buren extended the limit to all government offices and projects. In private jobs the ten-hour workday became increasingly common, although by no means universal, before 1860. Other reforms put forward by the Workingmen's parties included mechanics' lien laws to protect workers from nonpayment of wages; limits on the militia system, which allowed the rich to escape military service with fines but forced poor resisters to face jail terms; the abolition of "licensed monopolies," especially banks; measures to ensure payment in hard money and to protect workers from inflated bank-note currency; measures to restrict competition from prison labor; and the abolition of child labor.

THE REVIVAL OF UNIONS After the financial panic of 1837, the nascent labor movement went into decline, and unions did not begin to revive until business conditions improved in the early 1840s. Even then unions remained local and weak. Often they came and went with a single strike. The greatest single labor dispute before the Civil War occurred on February 22, 1860, when shoemakers at Lynn and Natick, Massachusetts, walked out after their requests for higher wages were denied. Before the strike ended, it had spread through New England, involving perhaps twenty-five towns and 20,000 workers. The strike stood out not just for its size but also because the workers won. Most of the employers agreed to wage increases, and some also agreed to recognize the union as a bargaining agent.

By the mid–nineteenth century the labor-union movement was maturing. Workers began to emphasize the importance of union recognition and regular collective-bargaining agreements. They also shared a growing sense of solidarity. In 1852 the National Typographical Union revived the effort to organize skilled crafts on a national scale. Others followed, and by 1860 about twenty such organizations had appeared, although none was strong enough as yet to do much more than hold national conventions and pass resolutions.

The Rise of the Professions

The dramatic social changes of the first half of the nineteenth century opened up an array of new professions for Americans to pursue. Bustling new towns required new services—retail stores, printing shops, post offices, newspapers, schools, banks, law firms, doctors' offices, and others—that created more high-status jobs than had ever existed before. By definition professional workers are those who have specialized knowledge and skills that ordinary people lack. To be a professional in Jacksonian America, to be a self-governing individual exercising trained judgment in an open society, was the epitome of the democratic ideal, an ideal that rewarded hard work, ambition, and merit.

The workforce was broadened and diversified by the rapid expansion of new communities, public schools, and institutions of higher learning; the emergence of a national market economy; and the growing sophistication of American life and society, which was fostered by new technologies. In the process, expertise garnered special prestige. In 1849 Henry Day delivered a lecture titled "The Professions" at the Western Reserve School of Medicine. He declared that the most important social functions in modern life were the professional skills. In fact, Day claimed, American society had become utterly dependent upon "professional services."

TEACHING   Teaching was one of the fastest growing vocations in the antebellum period. Public schools initially preferred men over women as teachers, usually hiring them at age seventeen or eighteen. The pay was so low that few stayed in the profession their entire career, but for many educated, restless young adults, teaching was a convenient first job that offered independence and stature, as well as an alternative to the rural isolation of farming. The New Englander Bronson Alcott remembered being attracted to teaching by "a curiosity to see beyond the limits of my paternal home and become acquainted with the great world." Church groups and civic leaders started private academies or seminaries for girls. Initially viewed as finishing schools for young women, these institutions soon added courses in the liberal arts: philosophy, literature, Latin, and Greek.

LAW, MEDICINE, AND ENGINEERING   Teaching was a common stepping-stone for men who became lawyers. In the decades after the Revolution, young men, often hastily or superficially trained, swelled the ranks of the legal profession. They typically would teach for a year or two before clerking for a veteran attorney, who would train them in the law in exchange for their labors. The absence of formal standards for legal training and the scarcity of law schools help explain why there were so many attorneys in the antebellum period. In 1820 eleven of the twenty-three states required no specific length or type of study for aspiring lawyers.

Like attorneys, physicians in the early nineteenth century often had little formal academic training. Healers of every stripe and motivation assumed the title of *doctor* and established a medical practice without regulation. Most of them were self-taught or had learned their profession by assisting a doctor for several years, occasionally supplementing such internships with a few classes at the handful of new medical schools, which in 1817 graduated a total of only 225 students. That same year there were almost 10,000 physicians in the nation. By 1860 there were 60,000 self-styled physicians, and quackery was abundant. As a result, the medical profession lost its social stature and the public's confidence. Yet despite their relative lack of a first-rate medical education, physicians were responsible for many breakthroughs in the treatment of a variety of illnesses.

The physical and industrial expansion of the United States during the first half of the nineteenth century gave rise to the profession of engineering, a field that has since become the single largest professional occupation for men in the United States. Specialized expertise was required for the building of canals and railroads, the development of machine tools and steam engines, and the construction of roads and bridges. Beginning in the 1820s, Americans gained access to technical knowledge in mechanics' institutes, scientific libraries, and special schools that sprouted up across the young nation. Rensselaer Polytechnic Institute was founded in Troy, New York, in 1824 to teach the "applications of science to the common purposes of life." The already existing Franklin Institute of Philadelphia shifted its emphasis in the 1830s to mechanical engineering. By the outbreak of the Civil War, engineering had become one of the largest professions in the nation.

WOMEN'S WORK Women during the first half of the nineteenth century still worked primarily in the home. The prevailing assumption was that women by nature were most suited to marriage, motherhood, and the accompanying domestic duties. The only professions readily available to women were nursing (often midwifery, the delivery of babies) and teaching, both of which were extensions of the domestic roles of health care and child care. Teaching and nursing commanded relatively lower status and pay than did the male-dominated professions.

Many middle-class and affluent women spent their time outside the home engaged in religious and benevolent work. They were unstinting volunteers in churches and reform societies. A very few women, however, courageously pursued careers in male-dominated professions. Harriet Hunt of Boston was a teacher who, after nursing her sister through a serious illness, set up shop in 1835 as a self-taught physician and persisted in medical practice although she was twice rejected for admission by the Harvard Medical School. Elizabeth Blackwell of Ohio managed to gain admission to the Geneva Medical College of Western New York, despite the disapproval of the faculty. When she walked in to her first class, "a hush fell upon the class as if each member had been struck with paralysis." Blackwell had the last laugh when she finished at the head of her class in 1849, but thereafter the medical school refused to admit any more women. Blackwell went on to found the New York Infirmary for Women and Children and later had a long career as a professor of gynecology at the London School of Medicine for Women.

JACKSONIAN INEQUALITY

During the years before the Civil War, the American legend of rags to riches, the image of the self-made man, was a durable myth. Speaking to the Senate in 1832, Kentucky's Henry Clay claimed that almost all the successful factory owners he knew were "enterprising self-made men, who have whatever wealth they possess by patient and diligent labor." The legend had just enough basis in fact to gain credence. John Jacob Astor, the wealthiest man in America (worth more than $20 million at his death in 1848), came of humble if not exactly destitute origins. The son of a minor official in Germany, he arrived in the United States in 1784 with little or nothing and made a fortune on the western fur trade, which he then parlayed into a much larger fortune in New York real estate. But his and similar cases were more exceptional than common.

Social historians' research on the wealthy in major eastern cities shows that while men of moderate means could sometimes turn an inheritance into a fortune by good management and prudent speculation, those who started out poor and uneducated seldom made it to the top. In 1828 the top 1 percent of New York's families (worth $34,000 or more) held 40 percent of the wealth, and the top 4 percent held 76 percent. Similar circumstances prevailed in Philadelphia, Boston, and other cities.

A supreme irony of the times was that the age of the common man, the age of Jacksonian democracy, seems actually to have been an age of growing economic and social inequality. Why that happened is difficult to say, except that the boundless wealth of the untapped frontier narrowed as the land was taken up and claims on various entrepreneurial opportunities were staked out. Such developments took place in New England towns even before the end of the seventeenth century. But despite growing social distinctions, it seems likely that the white population of America, at least, was better off than the general run of Europeans. New frontiers, both geographic and technological, raised the level of material well-being for all. And religious as well as political freedoms continued to attract people eager for liberty in a new land.

MAKING CONNECTIONS

- Eli Whitney's invention of the cotton gin had a profound effect on southern economic and social development. Chapter 15 describes the economy and society of the Old South in greater detail.

- The westward migration traced in this chapter increased tremendously in the 1840s, a trend discussed in Chapter 14.

- As this chapter demonstrated, the birth and expansion of railroads in the first half of the nineteenth century were an important part of "the dynamics of growth." Chapter 16 shows how a proposal for the first transcontinental railroad had an unexpected side effect: it intensified the debate over the spread of slavery westward.

FURTHER READING

On economic development in the nation's early decades, see Stuart Bruchey's *Enterprise: The Dynamic Economy of a Free People* (1990). The classic study of transportation and economic growth is George Rogers Taylor's *The Transportation Revolution, 1815–1860* (1951). A fresh view is provided in Sarah H. Gordon's *Passage to Union: How the Railroads Transformed American Life, 1829–1929* (1996). On the Erie Canal, see Carol Sheriff's *The Artificial River: The Erie Canal and the Paradox of Progress, 1817–1862* (1996).

The impact of technology is traced in David J. Jeremy's *Transatlantic Industrial Revolution: The Diffusion of Textile Technologies between Britain and America, 1790–1830s* (1981). On the invention of the telegraph, see Kenneth Silverman's *Lightning Man: The Accursed Life of Samuel F. B. Morse* (2003). For the story of steamboats, see Andrea Sutcliffe's *Steam: The Untold Story of America's First Great Invention* (2004). The best treatment of public works such as the Erie Canal in the development of nineteenth-century America is John Lauritz Larson's *Internal Improvement: National Public Works and the Promise of Popular Government in the United States* (2001).

Paul E. Johnson's *A Shopkeeper's Millennium: Society and Revivals in Rochester, New York, 1815–1837* (1978) studies the role religion played in the emerging industrial order. The attitude of the worker during this time of transition is surveyed in Edward E. Pessen's *Most Uncommon Jacksonians: The Radical Leaders of the Early Labor Movement* (1967). Detailed case studies of working communities include Anthony F. C. Wallace's *Rockdale: The Growth of an American Village in the Early Industrial Revolution* (1978), Thomas Dublin's *Women at Work: The Transformation of Work and Community in Lowell, Massachusetts, 1826–1860* (1979), and Sean Wilentz's *Chants Democratic: New York and the Rise of the American Working Class, 1788–1850* (1984). Walter Licht's *Working for the Railroad: The Organization of Work in the Nineteenth Century* (1983) is rich in detail.

For a fine treatment of urbanization, see Charles N. Glaab and A. Theodore Brown's *A History of Urban America* (1967). On immigration, see *The Irish in America,* edited by Michael Coffey with text by Terry Golway, (1997).

13

AN AMERICAN RENAISSANCE: RELIGION, ROMANTICISM, AND REFORM

FOCUS QUESTIONS

· Why did new religious movements emerge in the early nineteenth century?

· How did a distinctive American literary culture develop?

· What were the goals of the different social-reform movements?

To answer these questions and access additional review material, please visit www.wwnorton.com/studyspace.

The American novelist Nathaniel Hawthorne once lamented the difficulty of writing "about a country where there is no shadow, no antiquity, no mystery, no picturesque and gloomy wrong." Unlike nations of the Old World, which have long been steeped in history and romance, the United States in the nineteenth century was an infant republic swaddled in the rational ideas of the Enlightenment. Those ideas, most vividly set forth in Thomas Jefferson's Declaration of Independence, had in turn a universal application that would influence religion, literature, and various social-reform movements.

RATIONAL RELIGION

After the Revolution many Americans assumed that the United States had a mission to stand before the world as an example of republican virtue, much as Puritan New England had once stood before erring humanity as an example of an ideal Christian community. The concept of America's having a special mission in fact still carried strong spiritual overtones, for the religious fervor that quickened in the Great Awakening had reinforced the idea of the nation's fulfilling a providential purpose. This idea infused the national character with an element of perfectionism—and an element of impatience when reality fell short of expectations. The combination of widespread religious belief and fervent social idealism brought major reforms and advances in human rights during the first half of the nineteenth century. It also brought disappointments that at times festered and became cynicism and alienation.

DEISM   The currents of the Enlightenment and the Great Awakening, now mingling, now parting, flowed on into the nineteenth century and in different ways eroded the remnants of Calvinist orthodoxy. As time passed, the image of a just but stern God promising predestined hellfire and damnation gave way to a more optimistic religious outlook. Enlightenment rationalism increasingly stressed humankind's inherent goodness rather than its depravity and encouraged a belief in social progress and the promise of individual perfectibility.

Many leaders of the Revolutionary War era, such as Thomas Jefferson and Benjamin Franklin, became Deists, even while nominally attached to existent churches. Deism, which arose in eighteenth-century Europe, carried to its logical conclusion Sir Isaac Newton's image of the world as a smoothly operating machine. The God of the Deist planned the universe, built it, set it in motion, and then left it to its own fate. By the use of reason, people might grasp the natural laws governing the universe. Deists rejected the belief that every statement in the Bible was literally true. They were skeptical of miracles and questioned the divinity of Jesus. Deists also defended free speech and freedom from religious coercion of all sorts.

Orthodox Christians could hardly distinguish such doctrine from atheism, but Enlightenment rationalism soon began to make deep inroads into American Protestantism. The old Puritan churches around Boston proved most vulnerable to the logic of Enlightenment rationalism. Boston's progress—or, some would say, its degeneration—from Puritanism to prosperity had persuaded many affluent families that they were anything but sinners in the hands of an angry God. Drawn to more consoling and less strenuous religious doctrines, some went back to the traditional rites of the Episcopal Church. More of them simply dropped or qualified their adherence to Calvinism while remaining in the Congregational churches.

UNITARIANISM AND UNIVERSALISM   By the end of the eighteenth century, many well-educated New Englanders were drifting into Unitarianism, a belief that emphasized the oneness and benevolence of God, the inherent goodness of humankind, and the primacy of reason and conscience over established creeds and confessions. People were not inherently depraved, Unitarians stressed; they were capable of doing tremendous good, and *all* were eligible for salvation. Boston was very much the center of the movement, and it flourished chiefly within Congregational churches. During the early nineteenth century more and more liberal churches adopted the name *Unitarian*.

William Ellery Channing of Boston's Federal Street Congregational Church emerged as the most inspiring Unitarian leader. "I am surer that my rational nature is from God," he said, "than that any book is an expression of his will." The American Unitarian Association in 1826 had 125 churches (all but a handful of them in Massachusetts). That same year, when the Presbyterian minister Lyman Beecher moved to Boston, he deplored the inroads that had been made by the new rationalist faith: "All the literary men of Massachusetts were Unitarian; all the trustees and professors of Harvard College were Unitarian; all the elite of wealth and fashion crowded Unitarian churches."

A parallel anti-Calvinist movement, Universalism, attracted a different social group: working-class people of a humbler status. In 1779 John Murray founded the first Universalist church at Gloucester, Massachusetts. Universalism stressed the salvation of all men and women, not just a predestined few. God, it taught, was too merciful to condemn anyone to eternal punishment. "Thus, the Unitarians and Universalists were in fundamental agreement," wrote one historian of religion, "the Universalists holding that God was too good to damn man; the Unitarians insisting that man was too good to be damned." Although both sects remained relatively small, they exercised a powerful influence over intellectual life, especially in New England.

The Second Great Awakening

By the end of the eighteenth century, Enlightenment secularism had made deep inroads into American thought. Yet for all the impact of rationalism,

Americans remained a profoundly religious people—as they have been ever since. There was, the perceptive French visitor Alexis de Tocqueville observed, "no country in the world where the Christian religion retains a greater influence over the souls of men than in America."

Around 1800, however, fears that secularism was taking root sparked an intense revival that soon grew into the Second Great Awakening, sometimes called the Great Revival. An early revivalist leader, Timothy Dwight, became president of Yale College in 1795 and struggled to purify a place that, in Lyman Beecher's words, had turned into "a hotbed of infidelity." Like his grandfather Jonathan Edwards, Dwight helped launch a series of revivals that captivated Yale students and spread to all of New England.

FRONTIER REVIVALS   In its frontier phase the Second Great Awakening, like the first, generated great excitement and dramatic manifestations. It gave birth, moreover, to a new institution, the camp meeting, in which the fires of faith were repeatedly rekindled. Evangelists found ready audiences among lonely frontier folk hungry for spiritual intensity and a sense of community. Women especially flocked to the rural revivals and sustained religious life on the frontier. In the backwoods and in small rural hamlets, the traveling revival was as welcome an event as the traveling circus.

Among the established sects the Presbyterians were entrenched among the Scotch-Irish from Pennsylvania to Georgia. They gained further from the Plan of Union, worked out in 1801 with the Congregationalists of Connecticut and later with Congregationalists of other states. Since the Presbyterians and Congregationalists agreed on doctrine and differed mainly on the form of church government they adopted, they were able to form unified congregations and call a minister from either church. The result through much of the Old Northwest was that New Englanders became Presbyterians by way of the "Presbygational" churches.

The Baptists embraced a simplicity of doctrine and organization that appealed especially to the common people of the frontier. Their theology was grounded in the infallibility of the Bible and the recognition of humankind's innate depravity. But they replaced the Calvinist notion of predestination with the concepts of free will and universal redemption and highlighted the ritual of adult baptism. They also stressed the equality of all before God, regardless of wealth, social standing, or education. Since each congregation was its own highest authority, a frontier church needed to appeal to no hierarchy before setting up shop and calling a Baptist minister or naming one of its own. Sometimes whole congregations moved across the mountains as a body.

The Methodists, who shared with the Baptists an emphasis on salvation by free will, established a much more centralized church structure. They also developed the most effective evangelical method of all: the minister on horseback, who sought out people in the most remote areas with the message of salvation as a gift free for the taking. The "circuit rider" system began with Francis Asbury, a tireless British-born revivalist who scoured the trans-Appalachian frontier for lost souls, traversing fifteen states and preaching thousands of sermons while defying hostile Indians and suffering through harsh winters. Asbury established a mobile evangelism perfectly suited to the frontier environment and the new democratic age. After Asbury, Peter Cartwright emerged as the most successful circuit rider and grew justly famous for his highly charged sermons. Cartwright roamed across Kentucky, Tennessee, Ohio, and Indiana, preaching a sermon a day for over twenty years. His message was simple: salvation is free for all to embrace. By the 1840s the Methodists had grown into the largest Protestant church in the country.

During the early nineteenth century, the Great Revival spread through the West and into more settled regions back East. Camp meetings were typically held in late summer or fall, when farmwork slackened. People came from far and wide, camping in wagons, tents, or crude shacks. African Americans, whether enslaved or free, were allowed to set up their own adjacent camp revivals. The largest camp meetings tended to be ecumenical affairs, with Baptist, Methodist, and Presbyterian ministers working as a team. The crowds often numbered in the thousands, and the unrestrained atmosphere made for chaos. If a particular hymn or sermon excited someone, he or she would cry, shout, dance, or repeat the phrase. One visitor to a Kentucky camp revival noted that no fewer than seven ministers at one time were scattered among the thousands of faithful, all preaching at the top of their lungs. Mass excitement swept up even the most skeptical onlookers, and infusions of the spirit moved participants to strange manifestations. Some went into trances; others contracted the "jerks," laughed the "holy laugh," babbled in unknown tongues, or got down on all fours and barked like dogs to "tree the devil," as a hound might tree a raccoon.

But to dwell on the bizarre aspects of the camp meetings would be to distort an activity that offered a redemptive social outlet to isolated rural folk. This was especially true for women, for whom the camp meetings provided an alternative to the rigors and loneliness of frontier domesticity. Camp meetings also brought a more settled community life through the churches they spawned and helped spread a more democratic faith among people living on the frontier.

Religious Revival

An aquatint of a backwoods Methodist camp meeting in 1819.

THE BURNED-OVER DISTRICT   Regions swept by revival fevers might be compared to forests devastated by fire. Western New York, in fact, experienced such intense levels of evangelical activity that it was labeled the burned-over district. The most successful evangelist in the burned-over district was a lawyer named Charles Grandison Finney. In the winter of 1830–1831, he preached for six months in upstate New York and helped generate 100,000 conversions. Finney wrestled with a question that had plagued Protestantism for centuries: What role can the individual play in earning salvation? Orthodox Calvinists had long argued that people could neither earn nor choose salvation of their own accord. Grace was a gift of God, a predetermined decision incapable of human understanding or control. In contrast, Finney insisted that the only thing preventing conversion was the individual. And what most often discouraged individual conversion was the terrifying loneliness of the decision. So Finney transformed revivals into collective conversion experiences in which spectacular public events displaced private communion. At his marathon revivals, Finney would call people forward to the "anxious bench," a front pew where they struggled to confess their sins and seek conversion and forgiveness, assisted by friends and neighbors helping to "pray them through" the intense experience.

Finney compared his methods with those of politicians who used advertising and showmanship to attract attention. He carried the methods of the frontier revival to the cities of the East and as far as Great Britain. His gospel combined faith and good works: one led to the other. "All sin consists in selfishness," he said, "and all holiness or virtue, in disinterested benevolence." In 1835 Finney took the professorship of theology in the newly established Oberlin College, founded by pious New Englanders in northern Ohio's Western Reserve. Later he served as its president. From the start, Oberlin College radiated a spirit of reform predicated on faith; it was the first college in America to admit women and blacks, and it was a hotbed of anti-slavery agitation.

THE MORMONS   The burned-over district gave rise to several new religious movements, of which the most important was the Church of Jesus Christ of Latter-day Saints, or the Mormons. The founder, Joseph Smith, was born in Vermont, the child of wandering parents who finally settled in the village of Palmyra, in western New York. In 1820 the fourteen-year-old Smith was praying in the woods when he had a vision of God and his Son. They cautioned the boy that all existing religious denominations were false. About three years later, Smith claimed, an angel led him to a hill near his father's farm, where he claimed to have found the *Book of Mormon* engraved on golden tablets in a language he called "reformed Egyptian." Four years later the barely literate Smith rendered into English what he described as a lost section of the Bible, which tells the story of ancient Hebrews who inhabited the New World and to whom Jesus had made an appearance. The *Book of Mormon* links the native Indians to the lost tribes of Israel and predicts the Second Coming of Christ.

On the basis of this revelation, the charismatic Smith began forming his own church in 1830. Within a few years he had gathered converts by the thousands, most of them New England farmers who had migrated to western New York. They found in Mormonism the promise of a pure kingdom of Christ in America and an alternative to the era's social turmoil and degrading materialism. But their orthodox Christian neighbors found in Mormonism a threat to their faith. Like the Puritans in sixteenth-century England, Mormons were subjected to abuse and disdain. In their search for a refuge from persecution, the Mormons moved from New York to Kirtland, Ohio, where Smith was tarred and feathered, then to several places in Missouri, and finally, in 1839, to Commerce, Illinois, along the Mississippi River, which they renamed Nauvoo. There they settled and grew rapidly for some five years. Smith was a compelling preacher and an organizational genius. He named himself mayor of Nauvoo and general of the community's 5,000 militiamen. He also owned the hotel and the general store. In 1844 a crisis arose when dissidents attacked Smith for practicing polygamy. Non-Mormons in the neighboring counties attacked Nauvoo, and Smith and his brother Hyrum were arrested. On June 27, 1844, an anti-Mormon mob of masked men stormed the jail and shot to death both Joseph and Hyrum Smith.

In Brigham Young, the remarkable successor to Joseph Smith, the Mormons found a new leader of uncommon qualities: strong-minded, intelligent, and decisive but also stern and authoritarian. After the murder of Smith, Young patched up an unsure peace with the neighbors by promising an early exodus from Nauvoo. Before the year was out, Young had chosen a new land near the Great Salt Lake in Utah, then part of Mexico, guarded by mountains to the east and north, deserts to the west and south, yet fed by mountain streams. Despite its isolation, it was close enough to the Oregon Trail for the Mormon "saints" to prosper by trade with passing "gentiles."

A New Christianity

The Mormon Temple in Nauvoo, Illinois, ca. 1840.

The Mormon trek to Utah was better organized and less burdensome than most of the overland migrations of the time. Early in 1846 a small band of courageous believers crossed the frozen Mississippi River into Iowa to set up the Camp of Israel, the first in a string of way stations along the route. By the fall of 1846, in wagons and on foot, all 15,000 of the migrants had reached the prepared winter quarters on the Missouri River, where they paused until the first bands set out the next spring for "the Promised Land."

The first arrivals at Salt Lake in 1847 found only "a broad and barren plain hemmed in by mountains . . . the paradise of the lizard, the cricket and the rattlesnake." Young tapped the ground with his cane and announced that their new holy city would be built upon the spot, "laid out perfectly square, north and south, east and west." By the end of 1848, the Mormons had developed an efficient irrigation system, and over the next decade they brought about the greening of the desert. The Mormons had scarcely arrived when their land became part of the United States. At first they organized their own state, Deseret (meaning "Land of the Honey Bee," according to Young), with ambitious boundaries that reached the Pacific in southern California. But

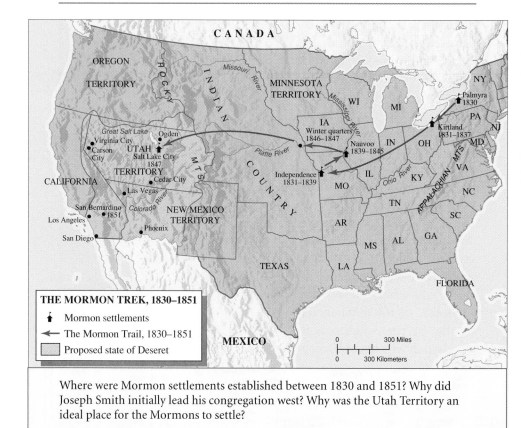

THE MORMON TREK, 1830–1851

- 🛉 Mormon settlements
- ← The Mormon Trail, 1830–1851
- ▢ Proposed state of Deseret

Where were Mormon settlements established between 1830 and 1851? Why did Joseph Smith initially lead his congregation west? Why was the Utah Territory an ideal place for the Mormons to settle?

the Utah Territory, which Congress created, afforded the Mormons almost the same control, with Governor Young the chief political and theocratic authority. By 1869 some 80,000 Mormons had settled in Utah.

ROMANTICISM IN AMERICA

The revival of emotional piety during the early 1800s represented a widespread tendency throughout the United States and Europe to accentuate the stirrings of the spirit rather than the dry logic of reason and the allure of material gain. Another great victory of heart over head was the Romantic movement in thought, literature, and the arts. By the 1780s a revolt was brewing in Europe against the well-ordered world of scientific rationalism. Were there not, after all, more things in this world than reason and logic could box up and explain: moods, impressions, and feelings; mysterious, unknown, and half-seen things? Americans also took readily to the Romantics' emphasis on individualism, idealizing now the virtues of common people, now the idea of original or creative genius in the artist, the author, or the great personality.

The German philosopher Immanuel Kant gave the transatlantic Romantic movement a summary definition in the title of his *Critique of Pure Reason* (1781), an influential book that emphasized the limits of science and reason in explaining the universe. People have innate conceptions of conscience and beauty, the Romantics believed, and religious impulses too strong to be dismissed as illusions. In areas in which science could neither prove nor disprove concepts, people were justified in having faith. The impact of such ideas elevated intuitive knowledge at the expense of rational knowledge.

TRANSCENDENTALISM   The most intense expression of such Romantic ideals was the transcendentalist movement of New England, which drew its name from its emphasis on those things that transcended (or rose above) the limits of reason. Transcendentalism, said one of its apostles, meant an interest in areas "a little beyond" the scope of reason. If transcendentalism drew much

Kaaterskill Falls, 1825

Thomas Cole's painting captures the romantic ideals that swept America in the wake of the Enlightenment.

of its inspiration from Kant, it was also rooted in New England Puritanism, to which it owed a pervasive moralism and profound spirituality. It also had a close affinity with the Quaker doctrine of the inner light. The inner light, a gift from God's grace, was transformed by Romantics into intuition, a faculty of the mind. Transcendentalism during the 1830s became the most energetic and influential intellectual and spiritual force in American culture.

An element of mysticism had always lurked in Puritanism, even if viewed as a heresy—Anne Hutchinson, for instance, had been banished from the Massachusetts Bay Colony for claiming direct revelations from God. The re-assertion of mysticism had something in common, too, with the meditative religions of Asia, a continent with which New England now had a flourishing trade. Transcendentalists steeped themselves in the teachings of the Buddha, the Sufis of Islam, the Upanishads, and the Bhagavad Gita.

In 1836 an informal discussion group known as the Transcendental Club began to meet in Boston and Concord, Massachusetts. It was a loose association of diverse individualists. The club included liberal clergymen such as Theodore Parker, George Ripley, and James Freeman Clarke; writers such as Henry David Thoreau, Bronson Alcott, Nathaniel Hawthorne, and Orestes Brownson; and learned women such as Elizabeth and Sophia Peabody (who married Hawthorne in 1842) and Margaret Fuller. Fuller edited the group's quarterly review, the *Dial* (1840–1844), for two years before the duty fell to Ralph Waldo Emerson, soon to become the acknowledged high priest of transcendentalism.

Ralph Waldo Emerson
Transcendental poet and essayist.

RALPH WALDO EMERSON More than any other person, Emerson spread the transcendentalist gospel. Sprung from a line of New England ministers, he set out to be a Unitarian parson but quit the "cold and cheerless" denomination before he was thirty. After travel to Europe, where he met England's greatest writers, Emerson settled in Concord to take up the life of an essayist, poet, and popular speaker on the lecture circuit, preaching the good news of optimism, self-reliance, and the individual's unlimited potential. Having found pure reason "cold as a cucumber," he was determined to *transcend* the limitations of inherited conventions and rationalism in order to penetrate the inner recesses of the self.

Emerson's lectures and writings expressed the core of the transcendentalist worldview. His notable address "The American Scholar," delivered at Harvard in 1837, urged young Americans to put aside their awe of European culture and explore their own new world. It was "our intellectual Declaration of Independence," said one observer.

Emerson's essay on "Self-Reliance" (1841) has a timeless appeal to youth with its message of individualism and independence. Like most of Emerson's writings, it is crammed with pungent quotations:

> Whoso would be a man, must be a nonconformist. . . . Nothing is at last sacred but the integrity of your own mind. . . . It is easy in the world to live after the world's opinion; it is easy in solitude to live after our own; but the great man is he who in the midst of a crowd keeps with perfect sweetness the independence of solitude. . . . A foolish consistency is the hobgoblin of little minds, adored by little statesmen and philosophers and divines. . . . Speak what you think now in hard words and tomorrow speak what tomorrow thinks in hard words again, though it contradict everything you said today. . . . To be great is to be misunderstood.

HENRY DAVID THOREAU Emerson's young friend and Concord neighbor Henry David Thoreau practiced the reflective self-reliance that Emerson preached. "I like people who can do things," Emerson stressed, and Thoreau, fourteen years his junior, could do many things well: carpentry, masonry, painting, surveying, sailing, gardening. The philosophical son of a father who was a pencil-maker and a mother who was a domineering abolitionist, Thoreau displayed a sense of uncompromising integrity, outdoor vigor, and tart individuality that Emerson found captivating. "If a man does not keep pace with his companions," Thoreau wrote, "perhaps it is because he hears a different drummer."

Thoreau himself marched to a different drummer all his life. After Harvard, where he exhausted the resources of the library in gargantuan bouts of reading, and after a brief stint as a teacher, in which he got in trouble for refusing to cane his students, Thoreau settled down to eke out a living by making pencils with his father. But he made frequent escapes to drink in the beauties of nature. He showed no interest in the contemporary scramble for wealth. It too often corrupted the pursuit of happiness. "The mass of men," he wrote, "lead lives of quiet desperation."

Determined to practice plain living and high thinking, Thoreau boarded with the Emersons for a time and then embarked on an experiment in

Henry David Thoreau

Author of the American classics *Walden* and "Civil Disobedience."

self-reliance. On July 4, 1845, he took to the woods to live in a cabin he had built on Emerson's land beside Walden Pond, about a mile outside Concord. Thoreau wanted to see to what degree he could free himself from the complexities and hypocrisies of conventional life so as to devote his time to observation, reflection, and writing. His purpose was not to lead a hermit's life. He frequently walked the mile or so to town to dine with his friends and often welcomed guests at his cabin. "I went to the woods because I wished to live deliberately," he wrote in *Walden, or Life in the Woods* (1854), "and not, when I came to die, discover that I had not lived."

While Thoreau was at Walden Pond, the Mexican War erupted. He saw it as an unjust war to advance the cause of slavery, so he refused to pay his poll tax as a gesture of opposition, for which he was put in jail (for only one night; an aunt paid the tax). The incident was so trivial as to be almost comic, but out of it grew the classic essay "Civil Disobedience" (1849), which would influence the passive-resistance movements of Mahatma Gandhi in India and Martin Luther King Jr. in the South. "If the law is of such a nature that it requires you to be an agent of injustice to another," Thoreau wrote, "then, I say, break the law."

The broadening ripples of influence more than a century after Thoreau's death show the impact a contemplative person can have on the world of action. Thoreau and the transcendentalists taught a powerful lesson: people must follow their conscience. Though these thinkers attracted only a small following in their own time, they inspired reform movements and were the quickening force for a generation of writers that produced the first great age of American literature.

The Flowering of American Literature

The half decade of 1850–1855 witnessed an outpouring of great literature. It saw the publication of *Representative Men* by Emerson, *Walden* by

Thoreau, *The Scarlet Letter* and *The House of the Seven Gables* by Nathaniel Hawthorne, *Moby-Dick* by Herman Melville, and *Leaves of Grass* by Walt Whitman. As a noted literary critic wrote, "You might search all the rest of American literature without being able to collect a group of books equal to these in imaginative quality." The flowering of New England literature featured, too, a foursome of poets who shaped the American imagination in a day when poetry was popular among the public: Henry Wadsworth Longfellow, John Greenleaf Whittier, Oliver Wendell Holmes Sr., and James Russell Lowell.

LITERARY GIANTS   Nathaniel Hawthorne, the supreme writer of the New England group, never shared the sunny optimism of his neighbors or their perfectionist belief in reform. A sometime resident of Concord, Massachusetts, but a native and longtime inhabitant of Salem, he was haunted by the knowledge of evil bequeathed to him by his Puritan forebears—one of whom (John Hathorne) had been a judge at the Salem witchcraft trials. After college he worked in obscurity in Salem, gradually began to sell a few stories, and finally earned a degree of fame with his collection of *Twice-Told Tales* (1837). In these, as in most of his later work, he presented powerful moral allegories. His central themes examined sin and its consequences: pride and selfishness, secret guilt, and the impossibility of rooting sin out of the human soul.

Emily Dickinson, the most original and powerful of the New England poets, remained a white-gowned recluse in her second-story bedroom in Amherst, Massachusetts. As she once prophetically wrote, "Success is counted sweetest / By those who ne'er succeed." Only a few of her almost 1,800 poems were published (anonymously) before her death, in 1886, and the full corpus of her work remained unknown for years thereafter. Born in Amherst in 1830, the child of a stern father and a gentle mother, she received a first-rate secondary education and attended the new Mount Holyoke Female Seminary. Neither she nor her sister married, and they both lived out their lives in their parents' home. Perhaps it was Emily's severe eye trouble during the 1860s

Emily Dickinson

Dickinson offered a fresh, female voice to the world of New England literature.

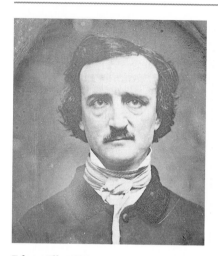

Edgar Allan Poe

Perhaps the most inventive American writer of the period.

that induced her solitary withdrawal from the larger society; perhaps it was the aching despair generated by her unrequited love for a married minister. Whatever the reason, her intense isolation led her to focus her writings on her own shifting psychological state. Her themes were elemental: life, death, fear, loneliness, nature, and above all, God, a "Force illegible," a "distant, stately lover."

Edgar Allan Poe, born in Boston but reared in Virginia, was a master of gothic horror and the inventor of the detective story. He judged prose by its ability to provoke emotional tension, and since he considered fear to be the most powerful emotion, he focused his efforts on making the grotesque and supernatural seem disturbingly real to his readers. Anyone who has read "The Tell-Tale Heart" or "The Pit and the Pendulum" can testify to his success.

Herman Melville was a New Yorker who went to sea as a youth. After eighteen months aboard a whaler, he arrived in the Marquesas Islands, in the South Seas, and jumped ship with a companion. He spent several weeks with a friendly tribe in "the valley of the Typees" before signing on with an Australian whaler. He joined a mutiny in Tahiti and finally returned home as a seaman aboard a U.S. Navy frigate. An embroidered account of his exotic adventures, *Typee* (1846), became an instant popular success, which he repeated in *Omoo* (1847), based on his stay in Tahiti.

In 1851 Melville produced one of the world's greatest novels. In *Moby-Dick*, the story of Captain Ahab's obsessive quest for the white whale that had devoured his leg, Melville explored the darker recesses of the soul. The book was aimed at two audiences. On one level it was a ripping good yarn of adventure on the high seas. But on another level it explored profound philosophical and psychological realms: Ahab's single-minded mission to slay the evildoer turned the captain into a monster of destruction who sacrificed his ship, his crew, and himself to his folly, leaving as the one survivor the narrator of the story. Yet neither the public nor the critics at the time accepted the novel on either level. Melville's career wound down into futility. He supported himself for years with a job in the New York Customhouse and

The Perilous Situation of Whalemen (ca. 1861)

A harpooned whale breaks the surface of the water, as described by Herman Melville in *Moby-Dick*.

turned to poetry, much of which, especially the Civil War *Battle-Pieces* (1866), won acclaim in later years.

WALT WHITMAN   The most provocative writer during the antebellum period was Walt Whitman, a vibrant personality who disdained inherited conventions and artistic traditions. There was something elemental in Whitman's character, something bountiful and generous and compelling— even his faults and inconsistencies were ample. Born on a Long Island farm, he moved with his family to Brooklyn and from the age of twelve worked mainly as a handyman and journalist, frequently taking the ferry across the harbor to booming, bustling Manhattan. The city fascinated him, and he gorged himself on the urban spectacle: shipyards, crowds, factories, shop windows. From such material he drew his editorial opinions and poetic inspiration, but he remained relatively obscure until the first edition of *Leaves of Grass* (1855) caught the eye and aroused the ire of readers. Emerson found it "the most extraordinary piece of wit and wisdom that America has yet contributed," but more conventional critics shuddered at Whitman's explicit sexual references and groused at his indifference to rhyme and meter as well as his buoyant egotism. The jaunty Whitman was a startling figure, with his frank sexual references and homoerotic overtones. He also stood out from the pack of fellow writers in rejecting the idea that a woman's proper sphere was in a supportive and dependent role. Thoreau described Whitman as "the greatest democrat the world has seen."

THE POPULAR PRESS   The flowering of American literature during the first half of the nineteenth century coincided with a massive expansion in the popular press. Technology sparked a reading revolution. The steam-driven Napier press, introduced from England in 1825, could print 4,000 sheets of newsprint in an hour. Richard Hoe of New York improved on it, inventing in 1847 the rotary press, which printed 20,000 sheets an hour. Like many advances in technology, this one was a mixed blessing. The high cost of the press made it harder for a person of small means to break into publishing. On the other hand, it expedited production of inexpensive newspapers, magazines, and books.

The availability of daily newspapers costing only a penny each transformed daily reading into a form of popular entertainment. Newspaper circulation skyrocketed. The "penny dailies," explained one editor, "are to be found in every street, lane, and alley; in every hotel, tavern, countinghouse, [and] shop." The United States had more newspapers than any nation in the world. It needed them to forge a network of communications across the expanding republic. As readership soared, the content of the newspapers expanded beyond political news and commentary to include society gossip, sports, and reports of sensational crimes and accidents. The number of newspapers around the country grew from about 1,200 in 1833 to some 3,000 in 1860. The proliferation of newspapers was largely a northern and western

Politics in an Oyster House (1848) by Richard Caton Woodville

A newspaper reader engages in eager discussion.

phenomenon. Literacy rates in the South lagged behind those of the rest of the country. Before any state had even been formed in the Northwest Territory, for example, the region boasted thirteen newspapers while North Carolina had only four.

Magazines found a growing market, too. *Niles' Weekly Register* (1811–1849) of Baltimore and Washington, founded by the printer Hezekiah Niles, featured accurate and unbiased coverage of public events—all of which make it a basic source for historians. Boston's *North American Review* (1815–1940) was a favorite among scholarly readers. Its editor adorned the journal with materials on American history and biography. It also covered European literature. *Harper's Magazine* (1850–present), originally the organ of the publishers Harper and Brothers, pirated the output of popular English writers in the absence of an international copyright agreement. Gradually, however, *Harper's* began paying for fresh contributions and published original material by American authors. In New York, *Frank Leslie's Illustrated Newspaper* (1855–1922) used striking pictures to illustrate its material. *Leslie's* and a vigorous competitor of somewhat higher quality, *Harper's Illustrated Weekly* (1857–1916), appeared in time to provide a thoroughgoing pictorial record of the Civil War.

EDUCATION

A literate and well-informed citizenry, equipped with knowledge not only for obtaining a vocation but also for promoting self-government and self-culture, was one of the animating ideals of the Founding Fathers. Literacy in Jacksonian America was surprisingly widespread, given the condition of public education. By 1840, according to census data, some 78 percent of the total population and 91 percent of the white population could read and write. Ever since the colonial period, in fact, Americans had had the highest literacy rate in the Western world. Most children learned to read in church or in private "dame" schools, from formal tutors, or from their families. By 1830 no state had a school system in the modern sense, although for nearly two centuries Massachusetts had required towns to maintain schools.

EARLY PUBLIC SCHOOLS   In the 1830s the demand for public schools peaked. Workers wanted free schools to give their children an equal chance to pursue the American dream. In 1830 the Workingmen's party of Philadelphia called for "a system of education that shall embrace equally all the children of the state, of every rank and condition." Education, it was argued, would improve manners and at the same time lessen crime and poverty.

Horace Mann of Massachusetts led the early drive for statewide school systems. Trained as a lawyer, he sponsored the creation of a state board of education, then served as its secretary. Mann went on to sponsor many reforms in Massachusetts, including the first state-supported "normal school" for the training of teachers, a state association of teachers, and a minimum school year of six months. He repeatedly promoted the public-school system as the way to achieve social stability and equal opportunity.

In the South, North Carolina led the way in state-supported education. By 1860 North Carolina had enrolled more than two thirds of its white school-age population for an average term of four months, kept so low because of the rural state's need for children to do farmwork. But the educational pattern in the South continued to reflect the aristocratic pretensions of the region: the South had a higher percentage of college students than any other region but a lower percentage of public-school students. And the South had some 500,000 white illiterates, more than half the total number in the young nation.

Greek Class at the Western Reserve Eclectic Institute at Hiram, Ohio (1853)

At front right are the young James A. Garfield and his future wife, Lucretia Randolph.

For all the effort to establish state-supported schools, conditions for public education were seldom ideal. Funds were insufficient for buildings, books, and equipment; teachers were poorly paid and often poorly prepared. Most students going beyond the elementary grades went to private academies, often subsidized by church and public funds. Such schools, begun in colonial days, multiplied until in 1850 there were more than 6,000 of them. In 1821 the Boston English High School opened as the first free public secondary school, set up mainly for students not going on to college. By a law of 1827, Massachusetts required a high school in every town of 500; in towns of 4,000 or more, the school had to offer Latin, Greek, rhetoric, and other college-preparatory courses. Public high schools became well established only after the Civil War. In 1860 there were barely 300 in the whole country.

HIGHER EDUCATION   The post-Revolutionary proliferation of colleges continued after 1800 with the spread of small church-supported schools and state universities. Nine colleges had been founded in the colonial period, all of which survived; but not many of the fifty that sprang up between 1776 and 1800 lasted. Of the seventy-eight colleges and universities in 1840, fully thirty-five had been founded after 1830, almost all affiliated with a religious denomination. A post-Revolutionary movement for state-supported universities flourished in those southern states that had had no colonial university. Federal policy abetted the spread of universities into the West. When Congress granted statehood to Ohio in 1803, it set aside two townships for the support of a state university and kept up that policy in other new states.

The coexistence of state and religious colleges led to conflicts over funding and curriculum, however. Beset by the need for funds, as colleges usually were, denominational schools often competed with tax-supported schools. Regarding curricula, many of the denominational colleges emphasized theology at the expense of science and the humanities. On the other hand, America's development required broader access to education and programs geared to vocations. The University of Virginia, "Mr. Jefferson's University," founded in 1819, introduced a curriculum modeled on Jefferson's view that education ought to combine pure knowledge with "all the branches of science useful *to us*, and *at this day*." The model influenced the other new state universities of the South and those of the West.

Technical education grew slowly. The U.S. Military Academy at West Point, founded in 1802, and the U.S. Naval Academy at Annapolis, opened in 1845, trained a limited number of engineers. More young men learned technical skills through practical experience with railroad and canal companies and by apprenticeship to experienced technologists. The president of Brown

University remarked that there were no colleges to provide "the agricultural-ist, the manufacturer, the mechanic, and the merchant with any kind of pro-fessional preparation."

Elementary education for girls met with general acceptance, but training beyond that level did not. Most people viewed higher education as unsuited to a woman's destiny in life. Some did argue that education would produce better wives and mothers, but few were ready to demand equality on princi-ple. Progress began with the academies, some of which taught boys and girls alike. Good "female seminaries," like those founded by Emma Willard at Troy, New York (1821), and by Mary Lyon at South Hadley, Massachusetts (1837), grew into colleges. The curricula in female seminaries usually dif-fered from the courses in men's schools, giving more attention to the social amenities and such "embellishments" as music and art. Vassar, opened at Poughkeepsie, New York, in 1861, is usually credited with being the first women's college to give priority to academic standards. In general the West gave the greatest impetus to coeducation, with state universities in the lead. But once admitted, female students remained in a subordinate status. At

The George Barrell Emerson School, Boston (ca. 1850)

Although higher education for women initially met with some resistance, semi-naries like this one, started in the 1820s and 1830s, taught women mathematics, physics, and history, as well as music, art, and the social graces.

Oberlin College in Ohio, for instance, they were expected to clean male students' rooms and were not allowed to speak in class or recite at graduation exercises. Coeducation did not mean equality.

ANTEBELLUM REFORM

The United States in the antebellum period was awash in reform movements. The urge to eradicate evil had its roots in the widespread sense of spiritual zeal and moral mission, which in turn drew upon rising faith in human perfectibility. Reformers tackled such issues as observance of the Sabbath, dueling, crime and punishment, the hours and conditions of work, poverty, vice, care of the disabled, pacifism, foreign missions, temperance, women's rights, and the abolition of slavery. Some crusaders challenged a host of evils; others focused on pet causes. One Massachusetts reformer, for example, insisted that "a vegetable diet lies at the basis of all reforms."

TEMPERANCE   The temperance crusade was perhaps the most widespread of all. The census of 1810 reported some 14,000 distilleries producing 25 million gallons of alcoholic spirits each year. William Cobbett, an English reformer who traveled in the United States, noted in 1819 that one could "go into hardly any man's house without being asked to drink wine or spirits, even *in the morning.*"

The temperance movement rested on a number of arguments. Foremost was the religious concern that "soldiers of the cross" should lead blameless lives. The bad effects of distilled beverages on body and mind were noted by the respected physician Benjamin Rush as early as 1784. The dynamic new economy, with factories and railroads moving on strict schedules, made tippling by the labor force a far more dangerous problem than it had been in a simpler time. Humanitarians also emphasized the relations between drinking and poverty. Much of the movement's propaganda focused on the sufferings of innocent mothers and children. "Drink," said a pamphlet from the Sons of Temperance, "is the prolific source (directly or indirectly) of nearly all the ills that afflict the human family."

In 1826 a group of ministers in Boston organized the American Society for the Promotion of Temperance. The society worked through lecturers, press campaigns, essay contests, and the formation of local and state societies. A favorite device was to ask each person who took the pledge to put by his or her signature a *T* for "total abstinence." With that a new word entered the language: *teetotaler.*

The Temperance Crusade

A temperance banner, ca. 1850, depicts a young man being tempted by a woman who is offering him a glass of wine.

In 1833 the society called a national convention in Philadelphia, where the American Temperance Union was formed. The convention revealed internal tensions, however: was the goal moderation or total abstinence, and if the latter, abstinence merely from liquor or also from wine, cider, and beer? Should activists work by persuasion or by legislation? Like nearly every reform movement of the day, temperance had a wing of absolutists. They would brook no compromise with Demon Rum and carried the day with a resolution that liquor traffic was morally wrong and ought to be prohibited by law. The temperance union, at its spring convention in 1836, called for abstinence from all alcoholic beverages—a costly victory that caused moderates to abstain from the temperance movement instead.

The demand for the prohibition of alcoholic beverages led in the 1830s and thereafter to experiments with more stringent regulations and local option laws. In 1838 Massachusetts forbade the sale of spirits in lots of less than fifteen gallons, thereby cutting off sales in taverns and to the poor—who could not handle it as well as their "betters," or so their betters thought. By 1855 thirteen states had such laws. Rum-soaked New England had gone legally dry, along with New York and parts of the Midwest. But most of the laws were poorly drafted and vulnerable to court challenge. Within a few years they survived only in northern New England. Still, between 1830 and 1860 the temperance agitation drastically reduced per capita consumption of alcohol.

PRISONS AND ASYLUMS   The Romantic era's liberal belief that people were innately good and capable of improvement brought about major changes in the treatment of prisoners, the disabled, and dependent children. Public institutions arose that were dedicated to the treatment and cure of social ills.

Earlier these had been "places of last resort," historian David Rothman has written. Now they "became places of first resort, the preferred solution to the problems of poverty, crime, delinquency, and insanity." Removed from society, the theory went, the needy and the deviant could be made whole again. Unhappily, however, the asylums had a way of turning into breeding grounds for brutality and neglect.

In the colonial period, prisons were usually places for brief confinement before punishment, which was either death or some kind of pain or humiliation: whipping, mutilation, confinement in stocks, branding, and the like. A new attitude began to emerge after the Revolution, as reformers argued against the harshness of the penal code and asserted that the certainty of punishment was more important than its severity. Society, moreover, would benefit more from the prevention than the punishment of crime.

Gradually the idea of the penitentiary developed. It would be a place where the guilty experienced penitence and underwent rehabilitation, not just punishment. An early model of the new system, widely copied, was the Auburn Penitentiary, which opened in New York in 1816. The prisoners at Auburn had separate cells and gathered for meals and group labor. Discipline was severe. The men were marched out in lockstep and never put face-to-face or allowed to talk. But prisoners were at least reasonably secure from abuse by other prisoners. The system, its advocates argued, had a beneficial effect on the prisoners and saved money since the workshops supplied prison needs and produced goods for sale at a profit. By 1840 there were twelve prisons of the Auburn type scattered across the nation.

It was still more common, and the persistent curse of prisons, however, for inmates to be thrown together willy-nilly. In an earlier day of corporal punishment, jails housed mainly debtors. But as practices changed, debtors found themselves housed with convicts. The absurdity of the system was so obvious that the tardiness of reform seems strange. New York in 1817 made a debt of $25 the minimum for which one could be imprisoned, but no state eliminated the practice altogether until Kentucky acted in 1821. Other states gradually fell in line, but it was still more than three decades before debtors' prisons became a thing of the past.

The reform impulse also found outlet in the care of the insane. The Pennsylvania Hospital (1751), one of the first in the country, had a provision in its charter that it should care for "lunaticks," but before 1800 few hospitals provided care for the mentally ill. The insane were usually confined at home with hired keepers or in jails and almshouses. In the years after 1815, however, asylums that separated the disturbed from criminals began to appear.

The most important figure in arousing the public conscience about the plight of the mentally ill was Dorothea Lynde Dix. A pious Boston schoolteacher, she was called upon to instruct a Sunday-school class at the East Cambridge House of Correction in 1841. There she found a roomful of insane persons completely neglected and left without heat on a cold March day. Dix was so disturbed by the scene that she commenced a two-year investigation of jails and almshouses in Massachusetts. In a report to the state legislature in 1843, she revealed that insane persons were confined "in *cages, closets, cellars, stalls, pens! Chained, naked, beaten with rods, and lashed into obedience!*" Keepers of the institutions dismissed her charges as "slanderous lies," but she won the support of leading reformers. From Massachusetts she carried her campaign throughout the country and abroad. By 1860 she had persuaded twenty states to heed her advice, thereby helping to transform social attitudes toward mental illness.

WOMEN'S RIGHTS Whereas Dorothea Dix stood out as an example of the opportunity that reform gave middle-class women to enter public life, Catharine Beecher, a leader in the education movement and founder of women's schools in Connecticut and Ohio, published a guide prescribing the domestic sphere for women. *A Treatise on Domestic Economy* (1841) became the leading handbook of what historians have labeled the cult of domesticity. While Beecher upheld high standards in women's education, she also accepted the prevailing view that the "woman's sphere" was the home and argued that young women should be trained in the domestic arts.

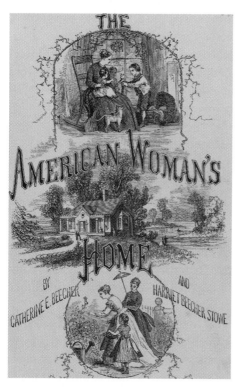

The American Woman's Home (1869)

An illustrated page from Catharine Beecher's book.

The social custom of assigning the sexes different roles was not new, of course. In earlier agrarian societies gender-based functions were closely tied to the household and often overlapped. As the more complex economy of the nineteenth century matured, economic production came to be increasingly separated from the home, and the home in turn became a refuge from the outside world, with separate and distinctive functions for men and women. Some have argued that the home became a trap for women, a prison that hindered fulfillment. But others have noted that it often gave women a sphere of independence in which they might exercise a degree of initiative and leadership. The so-called cult of domesticity idealized a woman's moral role in civilizing husband and family.

The official status of women during this period remained much as it had been in the colonial era. Women were barred from the ministry and most other professions. Higher education was hardly an option. Women could not serve on juries, nor could they vote. A wife had no control of her property or even of her children. A wife could not make a will, sign a contract, or bring suit in court without her husband's permission. Her legal status was like that of a minor, a slave, or a free black.

Gradually, however, women began to protest their status, and men began to listen. The organized movement for women's rights had its origins in 1840, when the anti-slavery movement split over the question of women's right to participate. Women decided then that they needed to organize on behalf of their own emancipation, too.

In 1848 two prominent moral reformers and advocates of women's rights, Lucretia Mott, a Philadelphia Quaker, and Elizabeth Cady Stanton, a graduate of Troy Female Seminary who refused to be merely "a household drudge," called a convention to discuss "the social, civil, and religious condition and rights of women." The hastily organized Seneca Falls Convention, the first of its kind, issued on July 19, 1848, a clever paraphrase of Jefferson's Declaration of Independence. Called the Declaration of Sentiments, it proclaimed the self-evident truth that "all men and women are created equal," and the attendant resolutions said that all laws that placed women "in a position inferior to that of men, are contrary to the great precept of nature, and therefore of no

Elizabeth Cady Stanton and Susan B. Anthony

Stanton (left) "forged the thunderbolts and Miss Anthony hurled them."

force or authority." Such language was too strong for most of the 1,000 delegates, and only about one third of them signed it. Yet the Seneca Falls gathering represented an important first step in the evolving campaign for women's rights.

From 1850 until the Civil War, the women's rights leaders held annual conventions and carried on a program of organizing, lecturing, and petitioning. The movement struggled in the face of meager funds and anti-feminist women and men. Its success resulted from the work of a few undaunted women who refused to be cowed by the odds against them. Susan B. Anthony, already active in temperance and anti-slavery groups, joined the crusade in the 1850s. Unlike Stanton and Mott she was unmarried and therefore able to devote most of her attention to the women's crusade. As one observer put it, Stanton "forged the thunderbolts and Miss Anthony hurled them." Both were young when the movement started, and both lived into the twentieth century, focusing after the Civil War on demands for women's suffrage. Many of the feminists, like Elizabeth Stanton and Lucretia Mott, had supportive husbands, and the movement won prominent male champions, such as Ralph Waldo Emerson, Walt Whitman, William Ellery Channing, and William Lloyd Garrison.

The fruits of the women's rights movement ripened slowly. Women did not gain the vote but did make some legal gains. In 1839 Mississippi became the first state to grant married women control over their property; by the 1860s eleven more states had such laws. Still, the only jobs open to educated women in any number were nursing and teaching, both of which extended the domestic roles of health care and nurture to the outside world. Both brought relatively lower status and pay than "man's work" despite the skills, training, and responsibility involved.

UTOPIAN COMMUNITIES Amid the pervasive climate of reform during the Jacksonian era, the quest for utopia flourished. Plans for ideal communities had long been an American passion, at least since the Puritans set out to build a wilderness Zion. More than 100 utopian communities sprang up between 1800 and 1900. Those founded by the Shakers, officially the United Society of Believers in Christ's Second Appearing, proved to be long lasting. Ann Lee (Mother Ann Lee) arrived in New York from England with eight followers in 1774. Believing religious fervor to be a sign of inspiration from the Holy Ghost, Mother Ann and her followers had strange fits in which they saw visions and prophesied. These manifestations later evolved into a ritual dance—hence the name Shakers. Shaker doctrine held God to be a dual personality: in Christ the masculine side was manifested; in

The Shakers

Officially the United Society of Believers in Christ's Second Appearing, the Shakers participate in a ritual dance.

Mother Ann, the feminine element. Mother Ann preached celibacy to prepare Shakers for the perfection that was promised them in Heaven.

Mother Ann died in 1784, but the group found new leaders. From the first community, at New Lebanon, New York, the movement spread into New England, Ohio, and Kentucky. By 1830 about twenty groups were flourishing. In these Shaker communities all property was held in common. Governance of the colonies was concentrated in the hands of select groups chosen by the ministry, or "Head of Influence" at Mount Lebanon. To outsiders this might seem almost despotic, but the Shakers emphasized equality of labor and reward, and members were free to leave at will. The Shakers' farms were among the nation's leading sources of garden seed and medicinal herbs, and many of their manufactures, including clothing, household items, and especially furniture, were prized for their simple beauty. By the mid–twentieth century, however, few members remained alive; Shakers had reached the peak of activity between 1830 and 1860.

John Humphrey Noyes, founder of the Oneida Community, had a quite different model of the ideal community. The son of a Vermont congressman, educated at Dartmouth and Yale Divinity School, Noyes was converted at one of Charles G. Finney's revivals and entered the ministry. He was forced out, however, when he declared that with true conversion came perfection and a complete release from sin. In 1836 he gathered a group of "Perfectionists" around his home in Putney, Vermont. Ten years later Noyes announced a new doctrine of "complex marriage," which meant that every man in the community was married to every woman and vice versa. "In a holy community," he claimed, "there is no more reason why sexual intercourse should be restrained by law, than why eating and drinking should be." Authorities thought otherwise, and Noyes was arrested for practicing his "free love" theology. He fled to New York State and in 1848 established the Oneida Community, which numbered more than 200 by 1851.

The communal group eked out a living with farming and logging until the mid-1850s, when the inventor of a new steel animal trap joined the community. Oneida traps were soon known as the best in the country. The community then branched out into sewing silk, canning fruit, and making silver spoons. The spoons were so popular that, with the addition of knives and forks, tableware became the Oneida specialty. In 1879, however, the community faced a crisis when Noyes fled to Canada to avoid prosecution for adultery. The members then abandoned universal marriage and in 1881 decided to convert the community to a joint-stock company, the Oneida Community, Ltd., which today remains a successful flatware company.

In contrast to these religious-based communities, Robert Owen's New Harmony was based upon a secular principle. A British capitalist who worried about the degrading social effects of the factory system, Owen built a model factory town, supported labor legislation, and set forth a scheme for a model community in his pamphlet *A New View of Society* (1813). Later he bought the town of Harmonie, Indiana, promptly christening it New Harmony. In 1825 a varied group of about 900 colonists gathered in New Harmony for a period of transition from Owen's ownership to the new system of cooperation. After a trial period of only nine months, Owen turned over management of the colony to a town meeting of all residents and a council of town officers. The high proportion of learned participants generated a certain intellectual electricity about the place. For a time it looked like a brilliant success, but New Harmony soon fell into discord. Every idealist wanted his or her own patented plan put into practice. In 1827 Owen returned from a visit to England to find New Harmony insolvent. The following year he dissolved the project and sold or leased the land on good terms, in many cases to the settlers. All that remained he turned over to his sons, who stayed and became U.S. citizens.

Brook Farm in Massachusetts was surely the most celebrated of all the utopian communities because it had the support of Ralph Waldo Emerson and other well-known literary figures of New England. Nathaniel Hawthorne, a member, later memorialized its failure in his novel *The Blithedale Romance* (1852). George Ripley, a Unitarian minister and transcendentalist, conceived of Brook Farm as a kind of early-day think tank, combining high thinking and plain living. The place survived, however, mainly because of an excellent community school that drew tuition-paying students from outside. In 1846 Brook Farm's main building burned down, and the community spirit expired in the embers.

Utopian communities, with few exceptions, quickly ran out of steam. The experiments, performed in relative isolation, had little effect on the outside world, where reformers wrestled with the sins of the multitudes. Among all the targets of the reformers' wrath, one great evil would finally take precedence over the others: human bondage. The paradox of American slavery coupled with American freedom, of "the world's fairest hope linked with man's foulest crime," in the novelist Herman Melville's words, would inspire the climactic crusade of the age, abolitionism, one that would ultimately move to the center of the political stage and sweep the nation into an epic civil war.

MAKING CONNECTIONS

· The anti-slavery campaign, especially its abolitionist aspect, was related to the reform movements discussed in this chapter. It is discussed again in Chapter 15, following the section on slavery.

· Chapter 17 will show how the Civil War had a significant impact on the status of women in American society, a continuation of a theme discussed here.

FURTHER READING

Russel Blaine Nye's *Society and Culture in America, 1830–1860* (1974) provides a wide-ranging survey of the Romantic movement. On the reform impulse, consult Ronald G. Walter's *American Reformers, 1815–1860* (1997). Revivalist religion is treated in Nathan O. Hatch's *The Democratization of American Christianity* (1989) and Christine Leigh Heyrman's *Southern Cross: The Beginnings of the Bible Belt* (1997). On the Mormons, see Leonard Arrington's *Brigham Young: American Moses* (1985).

The best introduction to transcendentalist thought is Paul F. Boller's *American Transcendentalism, 1830–1860: An Intellectual Inquiry* (1974). Several good works describe various aspects of the antebellum reform movement. For temperance, see W. J. Rorabaugh's *The Alcoholic Republic: An American Tradition* (1979) and Barbara Leslie Epstein's *The Politics of Domesticity: Women, Evangelism, and Temperance in Nineteenth-Century America* (1981). Stephen Nissenbaum's *Sex, Diet, and Debility in Jacksonian America: Sylvester Graham and Health Reform* (1980) looks at a pioneering reformer concerned with diet and lifestyle. On prison reform and other humanitarian projects, see David J. Rothman's *The Discovery of the Asylum: Social Order and Disorder in the New Republic* (2002) and Thomas J. Brown's biography *Dorothea Dix: New England Reformer* (1998). Lawrence A. Cremin's *American Education: The National Experience, 1783–1876* (1980) traces early school reform.

On women during the antebellum period, see Nancy F. Cott's *The Bonds of Womanhood: "Woman's Sphere" in New England, 1780–1835* (1997) and Ellen C. DuBois's *Feminism and Suffrage: The Emergence of an Independent Women's Movement in America, 1848–1869* (1978). Michael Fellman's *The Unbounded Frame: Freedom and Community in Nineteenth-Century American Utopianism* (1973) surveys the utopian movements.

14

MANIFEST DESTINY

FOCUS QUESTIONS

- What were the main issues in national politics in the 1840s?
- Why did settlers migrate west, and what conditions did they face?
- What were the causes and consequences of the Mexican War?

To answer these questions and access additional review material, please visit www.wwnorton.com/studyspace.

During the 1840s and after, Americans moved west in droves, seeking a better chance and more space. "If hell lay to the west," one pioneer declared, "Americans would cross heaven to get there." Millions of Americans crossed the Mississippi River and experienced unrelenting hardships in order to fulfill their "providential destiny" to subdue the entire continent. By 1860 some 4.3 million people had settled in the trans-Mississippi West.

Most of these settlers and adventurers sought to exploit the many economic opportunities afforded by the new land. Trappers and farmers, miners and merchants, hunters, ranchers, teachers, domestics, and prostitutes, among others, headed west seeking their fortune. Others sought religious freedom or new converts to Christianity. Whatever the reason, the pioneers formed an unceasing migratory stream flowing across the Great Plains and the Rocky Mountains. The Indian and Mexican inhabitants of the region soon found themselves swept aside by successive waves of American settlement.

THE TYLER YEARS

When William Henry Harrison took office in 1841, elected, like Andrew Jackson, mainly on the strength of his military record and his lack of a public stand on key issues, the Whig leaders expected him to be a figurehead, a tool in the hands of the era's most prominent—and most cunning—statesmen, Daniel Webster and Henry Clay. Webster became secretary of state. Clay, who preferred to stay in the Senate, tried to fill the cabinet with his friends. Within a few days of the inauguration, signs of strain appeared between Harrison and Clay, whose disappointment at missing the nomination had made him peevish. At one point an exasperated Harrison exploded: "Mr. Clay, you forget that I am the President." But the quarrel never had a chance to develop, for Harrison served the shortest term of any president. At the inauguration, held on a chilly, rainy day, he caught cold after delivering a two-hour speech. On April 4, 1841, exactly one month after the inauguration, he died of pneumonia at age sixty-eight.

Thus John Tyler of Virginia, the first vice president to succeed on the death of a president, served practically all of Harrison's term. And if there was ambiguity about where Harrison stood, there was none about Tyler's convictions. At age fifty-one, the Virginian was the youngest president to date, but he already had a long career behind him as legislator, governor, congressman, and senator, and his opinions on all the important issues had been forcefully stated and were widely known. Although officially a Whig, at an earlier time he might have been called an Old Republican: he was stubbornly opposed to everything associated with Henry Clay's program of economic nationalism—protective tariffs, a national bank, and internal improvements at national expense—and in favor of states' rights and strict construction of the Constitution.

When asked about the concept of nationalism, Tyler replied that he had "no such word in my political vocabulary." Originally a Democrat, he had broken with the party over Andrew Jackson's denial of South Carolina's attempt to nullify federal laws and Jackson's heavyhanded use of executive authority. In 1840 Tyler had been chosen to "balance" the Whig ticket, with no expectation that he would wield power. Acid-tongued John Quincy Adams said that Tyler was "a political sectarian of the slave-driving, Virginian, Jeffersonian school, principled against all improvement, with all the interests and passions and vices of slavery rooted in his moral and political constitution."

DOMESTIC AFFAIRS   Given more finesse on Henry Clay's part, he might have bridged the divisions among the Whigs over financial issues.

But for once, driven by an unrelenting quest to be president, the Great Compromiser lost his instinct for compromise. When Congress met in a special session in 1841, Clay introduced a series of resolutions designed to supply the platform that the party had evaded in the previous election. The chief points were repeal of the Independent Treasury Act, establishment of a third Bank of the United States, distribution to the states of money from federal land sales, and higher tariffs. The "haughty and imperious" Clay then set out to push his program through Congress. "Tyler dares not resist. I will drive him before me," he said.

Tyler, it turned out, was not easily driven. Although he agreed to allow the repeal of the Independent Treasury Act and signed a higher tariff bill in 1842, Tyler vetoed Clay's bill for a new national bank. Clay was furious. The domineering leader of the Senate developed a ferocious hatred for Tyler, calling him a traitor who had abandoned his party. Tyler's veto also prompted his entire cabinet to resign, with the exception of Secretary of State Daniel Webster. Tyler replaced the defectors with anti-Jackson Democrats who, like him, had become Whigs. Irate congressional Whigs expelled Tyler from the party, and Democrats viewed him as an untrustworthy renegade. By 1842 Clay's legislative program was in ruins. Yet by opposing Clay and the Whigs, Tyler had become a president without a party, shunned by both Whigs and Democrats.

FOREIGN AFFAIRS   In foreign relations, tensions with Great Britain captured Tyler's attention. In 1841 British ships patrolling off the coast of Africa threatened to board and search vessels flying the American flag to see if they carried slaves. The U.S. government refused to accept such enforcement. Relations were further strained late in 1841 when slaves on the *Creole*, bound from Hampton Roads, Virginia, to New Orleans, mutinied and sailed into Nassau, in the Bahamas, where the British set them free. Secretary of State Daniel Webster demanded that the slaves be returned as American property, but the British refused.

At this point a new British ministry decided to accept Webster's overtures for negotiations and sent Lord Ashburton to Washington, D.C. The disputed Maine boundary was settled in what Webster later called "the battle of the maps." Webster settled for about seven twelfths of the contested land along the Maine boundary, and except for Oregon, which remained under joint occupation, he settled the other border disputes with Great Britain by accepting the existing line between the Connecticut and St. Lawrence rivers and compromising on the line between Lake Superior and Lake of the Woods. The Webster-Ashburton Treaty (1842) also provided for joint naval patrols off Africa to suppress the slave trade.

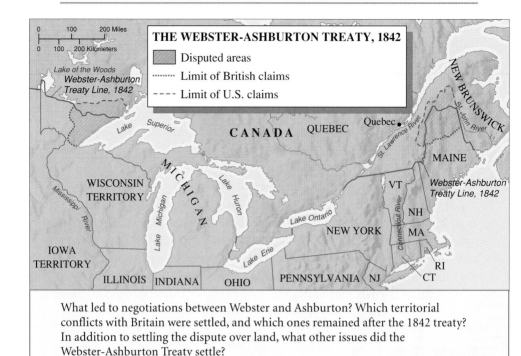

THE WEBSTER-ASHBURTON TREATY, 1842

Disputed areas

·········· Limit of British claims

- - - - Limit of U.S. claims

What led to negotiations between Webster and Ashburton? Which territorial conflicts with Britain were settled, and which ones remained after the 1842 treaty? In addition to settling the dispute over land, what other issues did the Webster-Ashburton Treaty settle?

THE WESTERN FRONTIER

In the early 1840s most Americans were no more stirred by the quarrels of John Tyler and Henry Clay over such issues as the banking system and the tariff policy than students of history would be at a later date. What aroused public interest was the mounting evidence that the "empire of freedom" was hurdling the barriers of the Great American Desert and the Rocky Mountains, reaching out toward the Pacific coast. In 1845 a New York newspaper editor and Democratic-party propagandist named John L. O'Sullivan gave a name to this aggressive spirit of expansion. "Our manifest destiny," he wrote, "is to overspread the continent allotted by Providence for the free development of our yearly multiplying millions." God, in other words, felt that the United States should extend itself from the Atlantic to the Pacific—and beyond. At its best this much-trumpeted notion of Manifest Destiny offered a moral justification for expansion, a prescription for what an enlarged United States could and should be. At its worst it was a cluster of flimsy rationalizations for naked greed and imperial ambition. Whatever the case, settlers began streaming into the Far West in the aftermath of the panic of 1837 and the prolonged economic depression.

WESTERN INDIANS   The sprawling territory across the Mississippi River was a new environment as well as a new culture. The Great Plains and the Far West were already occupied by Indians and Mexicans, who had lived in the region for centuries and had established their own distinctive customs and ways of life. Historians estimate that over 325,000 Indians inhabited the Southwest, the Great Plains, California, and the Pacific Northwest in 1840, when the great migration of white settlers began to pour into the region. The Native Americans often competed with and warred against each other. They were divided into more than 200 tribes, each with its own language, religion, economic base, kinship practices, and system of governance. Some were primarily farmers; others were nomadic hunters who preyed upon game animals as well as other Indians.

Some twenty-three tribes resided on the Great Plains, a vast grassland stretching from the Mississippi River west to the Rocky Mountains and from Canada south to Mexico. This region had been virtually devoid of a human presence until the Spaniards introduced the horse and the gun in the late sixteenth century. Horses dramatically increased the mobility of the Plains Indians, enabling them to leave their villages and follow the

Buffalo Hunt, Chasing Back (1860s)

This painting by George Catlin shows a hunter outrunning a buffalo.

migrating buffalo herds. They used buffalo meat for food and transformed the skins into clothing, bedding, and tepee coverings. The bones and horns served as tools and utensils. Buffalo manure could be dried and burned for heat.

Plains Indians such as the Arapaho, Blackfoot, Cheyenne, Kiowa, and Sioux were horse-borne nomads; they migrated across the grasslands, carrying their tepees with them. Quite different Indian tribes lived to the south and west of them. In the arid region including what is today Arizona, New Mexico, and southern Utah were the peaceful Pueblo tribes: Acoma, Hopi, Laguna, Taos, Zia, Zuni. They were sophisticated farmers who lived in adobe villages along rivers that irrigated their crops of corn, beans, and squash. Their rivals were the Apache and the Navajo, warlike hunters who roamed the countryside in small bands and preyed upon the Pueblos. They, in turn, were periodically harassed by their powerful enemies, the Comanches.

To the north, in the Great Basin between the Rocky Mountains and the Sierra Nevadas, Paiutes and Gosiutes struggled to survive in the harsh, arid region of what is today Nevada, Utah, and eastern California. They traveled in family groups and subsisted on berries, pine nuts, insects, and rodents. West of the mountains, along the California coast, Indians lived in small villages. They gathered wild plants and acorns and were adept at fishing in the rivers and bays.

The Indian tribes living in the Northwest—the Nisqually, Spokane, Yakama, Chinook, Klamath, and Nez Perce (Pierced Nose)—enjoyed the most abundant natural resources and the most temperate climate. The ocean and rivers provided bountiful supplies of seafood: whales, seals, salmon, crabs. The lush inland forests harbored game, berries, and nuts. And the majestic stands of fir, redwood, and cedar offered wood for cooking and shelter.

All these Indian tribes eventually felt the unrelenting pressure of white expansion and conquest. Because Indian life on the plains depended upon the buffalo, the influx of white settlers posed a direct threat to the Indians' cultural survival. When federal officials could not coerce, cajole, or confuse Indian leaders into selling the title to their tribal lands, fighting ensued. And after the discovery of gold in California in 1848, the tidal wave of white expansion flowed all the way to the west coast.

In 1851 U.S. officials invited the Indian tribes from the northern plains to a conference in the grassy valley along the North Platte River, near Fort Laramie in what is now southeastern Wyoming. Almost 10,000 Indians—men, women, and children—attended the treaty council. What made the huge gathering even more remarkable is that so many of the tribes were at war with one another. After nearly three weeks of heated discussions during which the chiefs were presented with a mountain of gifts, federal negotiators and tribal leaders agreed to what became known as the Fort Laramie Treaty. The government promised to provide an annual cash payment to the Indians as compensation for the damage caused by wagon trains traversing their hunting grounds. In exchange the Indians agreed to stop harassing white caravans, to allow federal forts to be built, and to confine themselves to a specified area "of limited extent and well-defined boundaries."

Several tribes, however, refused to accept the provisions. The most powerful, the Lakota Sioux, reluctantly signed the agreement but thereafter failed to abide by its restrictions. "You have split my lands and I don't like it," declared Black Hawk, a Sioux chief at Fort Laramie. "These lands once belonged to the Kiowas and the Crows, but we whipped these nations out of them, and in this we did what the white men do when they want the lands of the Indians." Despite the dissension the agreement was significant. As the first comprehensive treaty with the Plains Indians, it foreshadowed the "reservation" concept of Indian management.

THE SPANISH WEST AND MEXICAN INDEPENDENCE   As settlers moved westward, they also encountered Spanish-speaking peoples. Many whites were as contemptuous of Latinos as they were of Indians. Senator Lewis Cass, the expansionist from Michigan, expressed the sentiment of many Americans during a debate over the annexation of New Mexico. "We do not want the people of Mexico," he declared, "either as citizens or as subjects. All we want is a portion of territory." The vast majority of the Spanish-speaking people in what is today the American Southwest resided in New Mexico. Most of them were of mixed Indian and Spanish blood and were ranch hands or small farmers and herders.

The Spanish efforts at colonization had been less successful in Arizona and Texas than in New Mexico and Florida. The Yuma and Apache Indians in Arizona and the Comanches and Apaches in Texas thwarted their efforts to establish Catholic missions. After years of fruitless missionary efforts among the Pueblo Indians, one Spaniard complained that "most [of them] have never forsaken idolatry, and they appear to be Christians more by force than to be Indians who are reduced to the Holy Faith." By 1790 the Latino population in Texas numbered only 2,510, while in New Mexico it exceeded 20,000.

In 1807 French forces had occupied Spain and imprisoned the king, creating consternation and confusion throughout Spain's colonial possessions, including Mexico. Miguel Hidalgo y Costilla, a creole priest (born in the New World but of European ancestry), took advantage of the fluid situation

¡Viva El Cura Hidalgo!

This patriotic broadside celebrating Mexican independence shows Father Miguel Hidalgo in an oval medallion.

to organize a revolt of Indians and mestizos against Spanish rule in Mexico. But the poorly organized uprising failed miserably. In 1811 Spanish troops captured Hidalgo and executed him. Other Mexicans, however, continued to yearn for independence. In 1820 Mexican creoles again tried to liberate themselves from Spanish authority. By then the Spanish forces in Mexico had lost much of their cohesion and dedication. Facing a growing revolt, the last Spanish officials withdrew in 1821, and Mexico became an independent nation.

Mexican independence from Spain unleashed tremors throughout the Southwest. American fur traders streamed into New Mexico and Arizona and developed a lucrative commerce in beaver pelts. Wagon trains carrying American settlers began to make their way from St. Louis along the Santa Fe Trail. American entrepreneurs flooded into the western Mexican province of California and soon became a powerful force for change; by 1848 Americans made up half of the non-Indian population. In Texas, American adventurers decided to promote their own independence from a newly independent— and chaotic—Mexican government. Suddenly, it seemed, the Southwest was a ripe new frontier for American exploitation and settlement.

THE ROCKY MOUNTAINS AND OREGON COUNTRY During the early nineteenth century the far Northwest consisted of the Nebraska, Washington, and Oregon territories. Fur traders especially were drawn to the Missouri River, with its many tributaries. By the mid-1820s the "rendezvous system" had developed, in which trappers, traders, and Indians from all over the Rocky Mountain country gathered annually at some designated place, usually in or near the Grand Tetons, to trade pelts and hides. But by 1840 the great days of the western fur trade were over. The streams no longer teemed with beavers.

Fur Traders Descending the Missouri (**1845**)
By George Caleb Bingham.

During the 1820s and 1830s the fur trade had inspired a uniquely reckless breed of "mountain men" who deserted civilization for the pursuit of the beaver and reverted to a primitive existence in the wilderness. The rugged trappers lived sometimes in splendid isolation, sometimes in the shelter of primitive forts, and sometimes among Indians. They were the first whites to find their way around the Rocky Mountains, and they pioneered the trails that settlers by the 1840s were beginning to travel as they flooded the Oregon Country and trickled across the border into California.

Beyond the mountains the Oregon Country stretched from the 42nd parallel north to 54°40′, a region in which Spain and Russia had given up their rights, leaving Great Britain and the United States as the only claimants. By the Convention of 1818, the two countries had agreed to "joint occupation" of the region. Until the 1830s, however, joint occupation had been a legal technicality, because the only American presence was the occasional mountain man who wandered across the Sierra Nevadas or the infrequent trading vessel from Boston or New York.

Word of Oregon's fertile soil, plentiful rainfall, and magnificent forests gradually spread eastward. By the late 1830s, during the economic hard times after the panic of 1837, a trickle of emigrants was flowing along the Oregon Trail. Soon, however, "Oregon fever" swept the nation. In 1841 and 1842 the first sizable wagon trains made the trip, and in 1843 the movement became a mass migration. "The Oregon fever has broke out," wrote a settler in 1843, "and is now raging like any other contagion." By 1845 there were about 5,000 settlers in Oregon's Willamette Valley.

THE SETTLEMENT OF CALIFORNIA   California was also an allur-
ing attraction for new settlers and entrepreneurs. It first felt the influence of
European culture in 1769, when Spain grew concerned about Russian seal
traders moving south along the Pacific coast from their base in Alaska. To
thwart Russian intentions, Spain sent a naval expedition to settle the region. The Spanish discovered San Francisco Bay and constructed presidios
(military garrisons) at San Diego and Monterey. Even more important,
Franciscan friars, led by Junípero Serra, established a Catholic mission at
San Diego.

Over the next fifty years, Franciscans built twenty more missions, spaced
a day's journey apart along the coast from San Diego northward to San
Francisco. The mission-centered culture created by the Hispanic settlers
who migrated to California from Mexico was quite different from the patterns of conquest and settlement in Texas and New Mexico. In those more
settled regions the original missions were converted into secular parishes,
and the property was divided among the Indians. In California the missions
were much larger, more influential, and longer lasting.

Franciscan missionaries, aided by Spanish soldiers, gathered most of
the coastal Indian population in California under their control. They
viewed the Indians as ignorant and indolent heathens living in a "free and
undisciplined" society. The friars were determined to convert them to
Catholicism and make them useful members of the Spanish Empire.
Viewing the missions as crucial outposts of their empire, the Spanish government provided military support, annual cash grants, and supplies
from Mexico. The Franciscan friars enticed the local Indians into the
adobe-walled, tile-roofed missions by offering them gifts or impressing
them with their "magical" religious rituals. Once inside the missions, the
Indians were baptized Catholics, taught the Spanish language, and
stripped of their native heritage. Soldiers living in the mission enforced
the will of the friars.

LABOR IN THE MISSIONS   The California mission served multiple
roles. It was church, fortress, home, town, farm, and imperial agent. The
missions were economic as well as religious and cultural institutions: they
quickly became substantial agricultural enterprises. Missions produced
crops, livestock, clothing, and household goods, both for profit and to supply the neighboring presidios. Indians provided the labor. The Franciscans
viewed regimented Indian labor as more than a practical necessity: they saw
it as a morally enriching responsibility essential to transforming unproduc-
tive Indians into industrious Christians.

Sketch of the Order of San Francisco in the Former Mission of Santa Barbara

From Edward Vischer's collection of reminiscences of California under Spain and Mexico.

The daily routine began at dawn with the ringing of a bell, which summoned the mission community to prayer. Work began an hour later and did not end until an hour before sunset. Indians worked at the missions six days a week; they did not work on Sundays and religious holidays. Children and the elderly were expected to work as well. Most Indian men performed manual labor in the fields. Some were trained in special skills, such as masonry, carpentry, or leatherwork. Women handled domestic chores, such as cooking, sewing, cleaning, and shucking corn. During harvest season everyone was expected to help in the fields. Instead of wages the Indians received clothing, food, housing, and religious instruction.

The Franciscans used overwhelming force to maintain the captive labor system in the missions. Rebellious Indians were whipped or imprisoned. Soldiers hunted down runaways. Mission Indians died at an alarming rate. One Franciscan friar reported that "of every four Indian children born, three die in their first or second year, while those who survive do not reach the age of twenty-five." Infectious disease was the primary threat, but the grueling labor regimen took a high toll as well. The Indian population along the California coast declined from 72,000 in 1769 to 18,000 by 1821. Saving souls cost many lives.

EARLY DEVELOPMENT IN CALIFORNIA   For all of its rich natural resources, California remained thinly populated by Indians and mission friars well into the nineteenth century. It was a simple, almost feudal agrarian society without schools, industry, or defenses. In 1821, when Mexico wrested its independence from Spain, Californians took comfort in the fact that

Mexico City was so far away that it would exercise little effective control over its farthest state. During the next two decades, Californians, including many recent American arrivals, staged ten revolts against the Mexican governors dispatched to lord over them.

Yet Mexican rule did produce a dramatic change in California history. In 1824 Mexico passed a colonization act that granted hundreds of huge "rancho" estates to Mexican settlers. With free labor extracted from Indians, who were treated like slaves, the rancheros lived a life of self-indulgent luxury and ease, roaming their lands, gambling, horse racing, bull baiting, and dancing. The freebooting rancheros soon cast covetous eyes on the vast estates controlled by the Franciscan missions. In 1833–1834 they persuaded the Mexican government to confiscate the California missions, exile the Franciscan friars, release the Indians from church control, and make the mission lands available to new settlement. Within a few years some 700 huge new rancho grants of 4,500 to 50,000 acres were issued along the California coast. Organized like feudal estates, these ranches resembled southern plantations—but the death rate among Indian workers was twice as high as that of enslaved blacks in the Deep South.

Few accounts of life in California took note of the brutalities inflicted upon the Indians, however. Instead, they portrayed the region as a proverbial land of milk and honey, ripe for development. Such a natural paradise could not long remain a secret. By the late 1820s American trappers had wandered in from time to time, and American ships had begun to enter the "hide and tallow" trade: the ranchos of California produced cowhide and beef tallow in large quantities, and both products enjoyed a brisk demand, cowhides mainly for shoes and tallow chiefly for candles.

By the mid-1830s shippers had begun setting up representatives in California to buy the hides and store them until a company ship arrived. One of these agents, Thomas O. Larkin at Monterey, would play a leading role in the acquisition of California by the United States. Larkin stuck pretty much to his trade, operating a retail business on the side, while others branched out and struck it rich in ranching. The most noteworthy of the traders, however, was not American but Swiss. John A. Sutter had abandoned his family in Europe in order to avoid arrest for bankruptcy. He found his way to California and persuaded the Mexican governor to give him land on which to plant a colony of Swiss émigrés.

At the juncture of the Sacramento and American rivers (later the site of Sacramento), Sutter built an enormous enclosure that guarded an entire village of settlers and shops. At New Helvetia (Americans called it Sutter's Fort), completed in 1843, no Swiss colony materialized, but the baronial

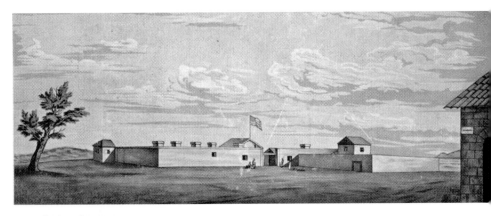

Sutter's Fort in 1847

Renamed Fort Sacramento during the Mexican War.

estate, worked by local Indians, became the mecca for Americans bent on settling the Sacramento country. It stood at the end of what became the most traveled route through the Sierra Nevadas, the California Trail, which forked off the Oregon Trail and led through the mountains near Lake Tahoe. By the start of 1846, there were perhaps 800 Americans in California, along with some 8,000 to 12,000 Californios (settlers of Spanish descent).

MOVING WEST

Most of the western pioneers during the second quarter of the nineteenth century were American-born whites from the upper South and the Midwest. Only a few African Americans joined in the migration. Although some emigrants traveled by sea to California, most went overland. Between 1841 and 1867 some 350,000 men, women, and children made the arduous trek to California or Oregon, while hundreds of thousands of others settled along the way in Colorado, Texas, Arkansas, and other areas.

THE SANTA FE TRAIL   After gaining its independence in 1821, the new government of Mexico was much more interested in trade with the United States than Spain had been. In Spanish-controlled Santa Fe, in fact, all commerce with the United States had been banned. After 1821, however, trade flourished. Hundreds of entrepreneurs made the 1,000-mile trek from St. Louis to Santa Fe, forging a route that became known as the Santa Fe Trail. These traders braved deserts, mountains, and possible Indian attacks.

Soon Mexican traders began leading caravans east to Missouri. By the 1830s there was so much commercial activity between Mexico and St. Louis that the Mexican silver peso had become the primary medium of exchange in Missouri.

Thousands of Americans risked their lives along the Santa Fe Trail to exploit the commercial opportunities afforded by trade with the Mexicans. On a good day their wagons might travel twelve to fourteen miles through rough terrain. Water was scarce, as was forage for their livestock. Indians occasionally raided the wagon trains. In 1847 almost fifty pioneers were killed, 330 wagons destroyed, and 6,500 animals stolen by hostile Indians. The traders who survived pioneered more than a new trail. They showed that heavy wagons could cross the plains and the mountains, and they developed the technique of organized caravans for common protection.

THE OVERLAND TRAIL   Like those on the Santa Fe Trail, people bound for Oregon and California traveled in wagon caravans. But on the Overland Trails to the West Coast (also known as the Oregon Trail), most of the pioneers were settlers rather than traders. They traveled mostly in family groups and came from all over the United States. The wagon trains headed for Oregon followed the trail west from Independence, Missouri, along the North Platte River into what is now Wyoming, through South Pass down to Fort Bridger (abode of a celebrated mountain man, Jim Bridger), then down the Snake River to the Columbia River and along the Columbia to their goal in Oregon's fertile Willamette Valley. They usually left Missouri in late spring, completing the grueling 2,000-mile trek in six months. Traveling in ox-drawn canvas-covered wagons nicknamed prairie schooners, they jostled their way across the dusty or muddy trails and rugged mountains. By 1845 some 5,000 people were making the arduous journey annually. The discovery of gold in California in 1848 brought some 30,000 pioneers along the Oregon Trail in 1849. By 1850, the peak year of travel along the trail, the annual count had risen to 55,000.

Contrary to popular myth, Indians rarely attacked wagon trains. Less than 4 percent of the fatalities associated with the Overland Trail experience were the result of Indian attacks. More often the Indians either allowed the settlers to pass through their tribal lands unmolested or demanded payment. Many wagon trains never encountered a single Indian, and others received generous aid from Indians who served as guides, advisers, or traders. The Indians, one woman pioneer noted, "proved better than represented." To be sure, as the number of pioneers increased dramatically during the 1850s, disputes between pioneers and Indians over land and water increased, but never to the degree portrayed in Western novels and films.

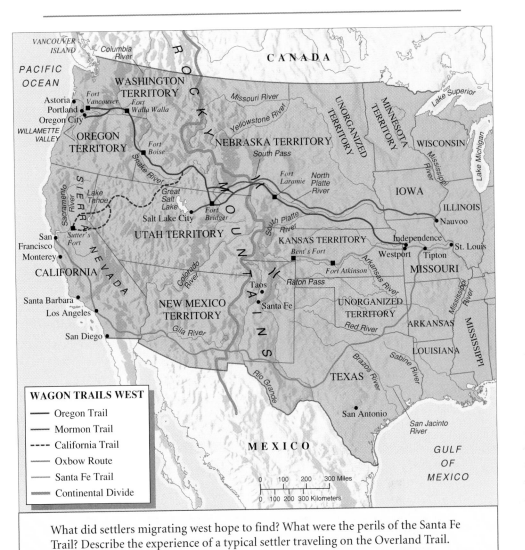

What did settlers migrating west hope to find? What were the perils of the Santa Fe Trail? Describe the experience of a typical settler traveling on the Overland Trail.

Still, the journey west was extraordinarily difficult. The diary of Amelia Knight, who set out for Oregon in 1853 with her husband and their seven children, reveals the mortal threats along the trail: "Chatfield quite sick with scarlet fever. A calf took sick and died before breakfast. Lost one of our oxen; he dropped dead in the yoke. I could hardly help shedding tears. Yesterday my eighth child was born." Cholera claimed many lives. On average there was one grave every eighty yards along the trail between the Missouri River and the Willamette Valley.

Initially the pioneers along the Overland Trail adopted the same division of labor used back East. Women cooked, washed, sewed, and monitored the children while men drove the wagons, tended the horses and cattle, and handled the heavy labor. But the unique demands of the trail soon dissolved such neat distinctions and posed new tasks. Women found themselves gathering buffalo dung for fuel, pitching in to help dislodge a wagon mired in mud, helping to construct a makeshift bridge, or participating in a variety of other "unladylike" activities.

The hard labor of the trail understandably provoked tensions within families and powerful yearnings for home. Many a tired pioneer could identify with the following comment in a girl's journal: "Poor Ma said only this morning, 'Oh, I wish we had never started.' She looks so sorrowful and dejected." Another woman wondered "what had possessed my husband, anyway, that he should have thought of bringing us away out through this God forsaken country." Some turned back, but most continued on. And once in Oregon or California they set about establishing stable communities. Noted one settler: "Friday, October 27.—Arrived at Oregon City at the falls of the Willamette. Saturday, October 28.—Went to work."

Gathering Buffalo Chips

Women on the Overland Trail not only cooked and washed and took care of their children but also gathered dried buffalo dung to use as fuel as their wagons crossed the treeless plains.

GREAT PLAINS ECOLOGY
The massive migrations along the
Santa Fe and Overland Trails
wreaked havoc on the environment of the Great Plains. Hundreds of thousands of settlers and
traders brought with them millions of animals—horses, cattle,
oxen, and sheep—all of which
consumed huge amounts of
prairie grass. The wagons and
herds trampled vegetation and
gouged ruts in the landscape that
survive to this day. With the onset of the California gold rush in

Wagon-wheel Ruts near Guernsey, Wyoming

The wheels of thousands of wagon's traveling to Oregon cut into solid rock as oxen
strained up hillsides, leaving indentations
that are still visible today.

1849, Plains Indians, led by Cheyennes, seized the opportunity to supply buffalo meat and skins to the white pioneers. Tracking and killing buffalo required a great many horses, and the four-legged creatures added to the strain
on the prairie grasslands and river bottoms. A major climatic change coincided with the mass migrations sparked by the discovery of gold in California.
In 1849 a prolonged drought struck the region west of the Mississippi River
and produced widespread suffering. Starving Indians demanded or begged
for food from passing wagon trains. Tensions between Native Americans and
white travelers brought additional federal cavalry units to the plains, exacerbating the shortage of forage grasses.

THE DONNER PARTY   The most tragic story of the Overland Trail involved the party led by George Donner, a prosperous sixty-two-year-old
farmer from Illinois, who led his family and a train of other settlers along the
Oregon Trail in 1846. They made every mistake possible: they started too
late in the year, overloaded their wagons, and took a foolish shortcut to
California across the Wasatch Mountains in the Utah Territory. In the
Wasatch they were joined by a group of thirteen other pioneers, bringing the
total to eighty-seven. Finding themselves lost on their "shortcut," they backtracked before finally finding their way across the Wasatch and into the
desert leading to the Great Salt Lake. Crossing the desert exacted a terrible
toll. They lost over 100 oxen and were forced to abandon several wagons and
their precious supplies. Tempers flared as the tired and hungry travelers
trudged on. One leader of the party killed a young teamster and was expelled, leaving his wife and children to proceed without him.

By the time the Donner party reached Truckee Pass, the last mountain barrier before the Sacramento Valley, the group had grown surly. They knew that they must cross the pass before a major snowfall hemmed them in, but they were too late. A two-week-long snowfall trapped them in two separate camps. By December eighty-one settlers, half of them children, were marooned with only enough meat to last through the end of the month. Seventeen of the strongest members decided to cross the pass on their own, only to be trapped by more snow on the western slope. Two of them died of exposure and starvation. Just before he died, Billy Graves urged his daughters to eat his body. The daughters were appalled by the prospect of cannibalism but a day later saw no other choice. The group struggled on, and when two more died, they, too, were consumed. Only seven lived to reach the Sacramento Valley.

Four search parties were dispatched to save the rest of the Donner party. Back at the main camps, at Alder Creek and Truckee Lake, the survivors had slaughtered and eaten the last of the livestock, then proceeded to boil hides and bones. When the rescue party finally reached them, they discovered a grisly scene. Thirteen people had died, and cannibalism had become commonplace; one pioneer had noted casually in his diary, "Mrs. Murphy said here yesterday that she thought she would commence on Milt and eat him." As the rescuers led the forty-seven survivors over the pass, George Donner, so weakened that he was unable to walk, stayed behind to die. His wife chose to remain with him.

THE PATHFINDER: JOHN FRÉMONT   Despite the hardships and dangers of the overland crossing, the Far West proved an irresistible attraction. The most enthusiastic champion of American settlement of Mexican California and the Far West was John Charles Frémont, "the Pathfinder"—who mainly "found" paths that the mountain men showed him. Born in Savannah and raised in the South, he had a robust love of the outdoors and an exuberant, self-promoting personality. Frémont studied at the College of Charleston before being commissioned a second lieutenant in the U.S. Topographical Corps in 1838. In the early 1840s his new father-in-law, Missouri senator Thomas Hart Benton, arranged the explorations

"The Pathfinder"

John Charles Frémont.

that made Frémont famous. In 1842 Frémont mapped the Oregon Trail—
and met Christopher "Kit" Carson, one of the most knowledgeable of the
mountain men, who became his frequent associate. In 1843–1844 Frémont,
typically clad in a deerskin shirt, blue army trousers, and moccasins, went on
to Oregon, then swept down the eastern slopes of the Sierra Nevadas, headed
southward through the central valley of California, bypassed the mountains
in the south, and returned via the Great Salt Lake. His excited reports on
both expeditions, published together in 1845, gained a wide circulation and
helped arouse the interest of easterners.

CALIFORNIA IN TURMOIL   American presidents beginning with
Andrew Jackson had tried to purchase at least northern California, down to
San Francisco Bay, from Mexico. Jackson reasoned that as a free state,
California would balance the future admission of Texas as a slave state.
But Jackson's agent had to be recalled after a clumsy effort to bribe Mexi-
can officials. Rumors flourished that the British and the French were scheming
to grab California, though neither government actually had such intentions.
Political conditions in Mexico left the remote territory in near anarchy much
of the time as governors came and went in rapid succession. Amid the chaos
many Californios reasoned that they would be better off if they cut ties to
Mexico altogether. Some favored an independent state, perhaps under
French or British protection. A larger group wanted to join the United
States. By the time the Americans were ready to fire the spark of rebellion in
California, there was little will in Mexico to resist.

ANNEXING TEXAS

AMERICAN SETTLEMENTS   The lust for new land focused on the
most accessible of all the Mexican borderlands, Texas. By the 1830s Texas
was rapidly turning into a province of the United States, for Mexico initially
welcomed American settlers as a means of stabilizing the border.

Foremost among the promoters of American settlement in Texas was
Stephen F. Austin, a Missouri resident who gained from Mexico a huge land
grant originally given to his father by Spanish authorities. Before Mexican
independence from Spain was fully won, Austin had started a colony on the
lower Brazos River, in central Texas, late in 1821, and by 1824 more than
2,000 hardy souls had settled on his land. In 1825, under a national colonization law, the Mexican state of Coahuila-Texas offered large tracts to *em-
presarios* (ranchers) who promised to sponsor immigrants from the United

States and elsewhere. Most of the newcomers were southern farmers drawn to rich new cotton lands selling for only a few cents an acre. By 1830 the coastal region of Texas had about 20,000 white settlers and 1,000 black slaves brought in to work the cotton.

The Mexican government, opposed to slavery, grew alarmed at the flood of strangers engulfing the province and in 1830 forbade further immigration. But illegal immigrants from the United States moved across the long border as easily as illegal Mexican immigrants would later cross in the opposite direction. By 1835 the American population in Texas had grown to around 30,000, about ten times the Mexican population there. Friction mounted in 1832 and 1833 as Americans organized conventions to demand a state of their own. Instead of granting the request, General Antonio López de Santa Anna, who had seized power in Mexico, dissolved the national congress late in 1834, abolished the federal system, and became dictator of a centralized state. White American Texans feared that the Mexicans intended to free "our slaves and to make slaves of us." In the fall of 1835 Texans rebelled against Santa Anna's "despotism." Delegates from all the towns and settlements met in November and drafted a Declaration of Causes explaining the rebellion. It forcefully expressed their grievances against the Mexican government but stopped short of declaring independence. A furious Santa Anna ordered all Americans expelled, all Texans disarmed, and all rebels arrested. As fighting erupted, volunteers from southern states rushed to assist the 30,000 Texans in their revolution against a Mexican nation of 7 million people.

TEXAS INDEPENDENCE   At San Antonio the Mexican army assaulted a small garrison of Texans and Southern allies holed up behind the adobe walls of an abandoned mission, the Alamo. Led by Colonel William B. Travis, a hot-tempered young Mississippi lawyer, the troops included not only Tejanos (Texas settlers of Mexican or Spanish descent) but also American volunteers, the most celebrated of whom was Davy Crockett, the Tennessee frontiersman who had fought Indians under Andrew Jackson and served as a congressman. Full of bounce and brag, Crockett was thoroughly expert at killing. As he once told his men, "Pierce the heart of the enemy as you would a feller that spit in your face, knocked down your wife, burnt up your houses, and called your dog a skunk! Cram his pesky carcass full of thunder and lightning like a stuffed sassidge . . . and bite his nose off into the bargain."

On February 23, 1836, Santa Anna had demanded that the 189 defenders of the Alamo surrender. They answered with a cannon shot. The Mexicans then launched a series of frontal assaults against the outnumbered defenders. For twelve days the Mexicans were repulsed, suffering fearful losses. Then, on March 6, the defenders of the Alamo were awakened by the sound of Mexican bugles playing the dreaded "Deguello" ("No mercy to the defenders"). Soon thereafter Santa Anna's men attacked from every side. They were twice repulsed, but on the third try the Mexicans broke through the battered north wall and swarmed through the breach. Colonel Travis was killed by a bullet to the forehead. The frontiersmen used their muskets as clubs, but soon they were all killed or wounded. The notorious slave smuggler, Indian fighter, and inventor of the Bowie knife, James Bowie, his pistols emptied, his famous knife bloodied, and his body riddled with Mexican bullets, lay dead on his cot.

Santa Anna ordered the wounded Americans put to death and their bodies burned with the rest. The only survivors were sixteen women, children, and servants. It was a complete victory for the Mexicans, but a costly one. The defenders of the Alamo gave their lives at the price of 1,544 Mexicans, and their heroic stand inspired the rest of the Americans in Texas to stage a fanatical resistance. While Santa Anna dictated a glorious victory declaration, his aide wrote in his diary, "One more such 'glorious victory' and we are finished."

On March 2, 1836, while the siege of the Alamo continued, delegates from all fifty-nine Texas towns met at the village of Washington-on-the-Brazos and signed a declaration of independence. Over the next seventeen days the delegates drafted a constitution for the Republic of Texas and established an interim government. The delegates then hastily adjourned as Santa Anna's troops, fresh from their victory at the Alamo, bore down upon them.

The commander in chief of the Texas forces was Sam Houston, a Tennessee frontiersman who had learned war under the tutelage of Andrew Jackson, had later represented the Nashville district in Congress, and had moved to Texas only three years before. After learning of the Texan defeat at the Alamo, Houston beat a strategic retreat eastward from Gonzales, gathering reinforcements as he went, including volunteer recruits from the United States. Just west of the San Jacinto River he paused near the site of the city that later bore his

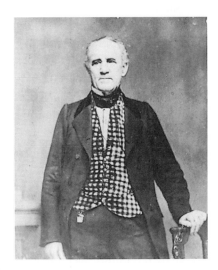

Sam Houston

Commander-in-chief of the Texas forces.

name and on April 21, 1836, surprised a Mexican encampment there. The Texans charged, yelling "Remember the Alamo," and overwhelmed the panic-stricken Mexican force. Santa Anna was captured trying to escape. The Mexican dictator bought his freedom by signing a treaty recognizing the independence of Texas, with the Rio Grande as the boundary. The Mexican congress repudiated the treaty and never officially recognized the loss of its northern province, but the war was at an end.

NEGOTIATIONS FOR ANNEXATION   The Lone Star Republic drafted a constitution that legalized slavery and banned free blacks, made Sam Houston its first president, and voted for annexation to the United States. The American president then was Houston's old friend Andrew Jackson, who desperately wanted Texas to join the Union, but even Old Hickory could be discreet when delicacy demanded it. The addition of Texas as a new slave state in 1836 threatened a serious sectional quarrel that might endanger the election of Martin Van Buren, his handpicked successor. Worse than that, it raised the specter of war with Mexico. Jackson delayed official recognition of the Republic of Texas until his last day in office, and Van Buren shied away from the issue of annexation during his term as president.

Rebuffed in Washington, Texans began to talk of expanding their nation to the Pacific, thus rivaling the United States. France and Britain extended formal recognition to the republic and began to develop trade relations. Meanwhile, thousands more Americans poured into Texas. The population grew from 40,000 in 1836 to 150,000 in 1845. Many settlers were attracted by the low land prices. And most brought with them a desire to join the United States.

Most Texans never abandoned their hope of annexation, although reports of growing British influence in Texas created anxieties in the U.S. government and among southern slaveholders, who became the chief advocates of annexation. Secret negotiations with Texas began in 1843, and that April, John C. Calhoun, then President Tyler's secretary of state, completed an annexation treaty that went to the Senate for ratification.

Calhoun chose this moment to send the British minister to the United States a letter instructing him on the blessings of slavery and stating that the annexation of Texas was needed to foil the British abolitionists. Publication of the note fostered the claim that annexation was planned less in the national interest than to promote the expansion of slavery. It was so worded, one observer wrote Andrew Jackson, as to "drive off every northern man from the support of the measure." Sectional division, plus fear of a war with Mexico, contributed to the Senate's overwhelming rejection of the Texas annexation treaty. Solid Whig opposition was the most important factor behind its defeat.

POLK'S PRESIDENCY

THE ELECTION OF 1844   Although adding Texas to the Union was an enormously popular idea among the citizenry, prudent leaders in both political parties had hoped to keep the divisive issue out of the 1844 presidential campaign. Whig Henry Clay and Democrat Martin Van Buren, the leading candidates, had reached the same conclusion about pro-slavery Texas: when the annexation treaty was submitted to the Senate, they both wrote letters opposing it for fear that it might spark civil war. The two letters, dated three days apart, appeared in separate Washington newspapers on April 27, 1844. Clay's "Raleigh letter" (written while he was on a southern tour) stated that annexation was "dangerous to the integrity of the Union . . . and not called for by any general expression of public opinion." Clay feared that the furor over Texas would distract the nation from more important issues. Clay worried that John Calhoun and other southern Democrats were using the Texas issue in a deliberate attempt to outflank the Whig party and divide the nation along sectional lines. The outcome of the Whig convention, held in Baltimore, seemed to bear out his view. Party leaders showed no qualms about Clay's stance. The convention nominated him unanimously, and the Whig platform omitted any reference to Texas.

The Democratic convention was a different story. Martin Van Buren's southern supporters, including Andrew Jackson, abandoned him because of his opposition to Texas annexation. Jackson wrote his former vice president a brutally frank letter, conveying his intense disappointment with Van Buren's anti-Texas stance. He told the New Yorker that he now had as much chance of being elected as there was to reverse "the current of the Mississippi River." The future president James Buchanan, the head of the Pennsylvania Democrats, declared that Van Buren's principled stance against annexing Texas would cost him the party's nomination. Van Buren was like a "dead cock in the pit." With the convention deadlocked, expansionists, including Andrew Jackson, brought forward James Knox Polk, former Speaker of the House and governor of Tennessee, an ardent expansionist. On the ninth ballot he became the first "dark horse" candidate to win a major-party nomination. The party platform embraced territorial expansion, and to win support in the North and the West as well as in the South, it called for the annexation of both Oregon and Texas. Missouri senator Thomas Hart Benton, a Van Buren supporter, lamented what had taken place at the convention. The single-minded preoccupation with Texas among the southern delegates foreshadowed national disaster. "Under the pretext of getting Texas into the Union," he observed, "the scheme is to get the South out of it."

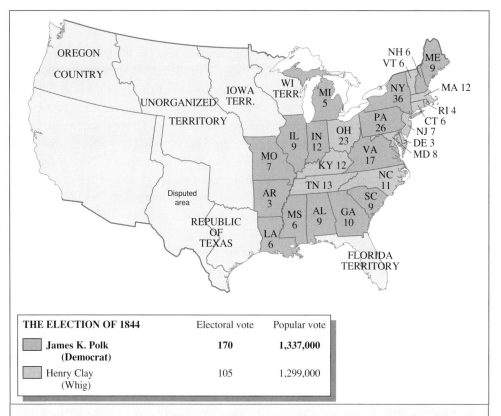

THE ELECTION OF 1844	Electoral vote	Popular vote
James K. Polk (Democrat)	170	1,337,000
Henry Clay (Whig)	105	1,299,000

Why was the annexation of Texas a divisive issue? Why was Polk's platform appealing to Americans in the South and the West? How did Polk win the election in New York, and why was winning that state important?

The Democratic combination of southern and western expansionism offered a winning strategy, one so popular it forced the Whig Henry Clay to alter his position on Texas; now he claimed that he had "no personal objection to the annexation" if it could be achieved "without dishonor, without war, with the common consent of the Union, and upon just and fair terms." His explanation seemed clear enough, but prudence was no match for spread-eagle oratory and the emotional pull of Manifest Destiny. The net result of Clay's stand was to turn more anti-slavery votes to the new Liberty party, which increased its count from about 7,000 in 1840 (the year it was founded) to more than 62,000 in 1844. In the western counties of New York, the Liberty party drew enough votes away from the Whigs to give the state to Polk and the Democrats. Had he carried New York, the overconfident Clay would have won the election by seven electoral votes. Instead, Polk won a narrow plurality of 38,000 popular votes (the first president since John Quincy Adams to win without a majority) but a clear majority of the Electoral College, 170 to 105. Clay had lost his third and last effort to win the presidency he had long coveted. His rival, Daniel Webster, blamed the savagely ambitious Clay for the Whig defeat, declaring that he had behaved as if he were willing to say or do anything to gain the White House, and "his temper was bad—resentful, violent & unforgiving." Clay never understood why so many people did not trust him.

The humiliated Clay could not understand how a statesman of his stature could have lost to James K. Polk, a "third-rate" politician. Yet Polk had been surprising people his whole career. Born near Charlotte, North Carolina, trained in mathematics and the classics at the University of North Carolina Polk had moved to Tennessee as a young man. A successful lawyer and planter, he had entered politics early, served fourteen years in Congress (four as Speaker of the House) and two as governor of Tennessee. Young Hickory, as his partisans liked to call him, was a short, slender man with a shock of grizzled hair and a seemingly permanent grimace. Humorless and dogmatic, he had none of Andrew Jackson's charisma but shared Jackson's opposition to a national bank and other Whig economic policies. Although America's youngest president up to that time, he worked so hard during his four years in the White House that his health deteriorated, and he died at age fifty-four just three months after leaving office.

POLK'S PROGRAM   In domestic affairs, "Young Hickory" Polk hewed to the principle of the older hero, but the new Jacksonians subtly reflected the growing influence of the slaveholding South on the Democratic party. Abolitionism, Polk warned, could destroy the Union. Anti-slavery northerners had already begun to drift away from the Democratic party, which they complained was coming to represent the slaveholding interests. Raised in a family that held slaves, Polk himself had slaves on his Tennessee and Mississippi plantations. Like Andrew Jackson and most Americans of the time, Polk was a racist who sought to avoid any public discussion of slavery.

Polk's major objectives were tariff reduction, reestablishment of Van Buren's independent Treasury, settlement of the Oregon boundary dispute with Britain, and acquisition of California from Mexico. He gained them all. The Walker Tariff of 1846, in keeping with Democratic tradition, reduced the tariff rates. In the same year, Polk persuaded Congress to restore the independent Treasury, which the Whigs had eliminated. Twice Polk vetoed internal-improvement bills. In each case his blows to the economic nationalism of Henry Clay's Whigs satisfied the urges of the slaveholding South, but at the cost of annoying northerners who wanted higher tariffs and westerners who longed for internal improvements in the form of roads and harbors.

THE STATE OF TEXAS   Polk's chief concern was geographic expansion. He privately vowed to acquire California and New Mexico as well, preferably by purchase. The acquisition of slaveholding Texas was already under way when Polk took office. In his final months in office, President John Tyler, taking Polk's election as a mandate to act, asked Congress to accomplish annexation by joint resolution, which required only a simple majority in each house and avoided the two-thirds Senate vote needed to ratify a treaty. Congress had read the election returns, too, and after a bitter debate over slavery, the resolution passed by votes of 27 to 25 in the Senate and 120 to 98 in the House. The Whig leader Daniel Webster was aghast. He felt "sick at heart" to see Congress take a step toward civil strife because of "greediness for more slave Territory and for the greater increase of Slavery!" Tyler signed the resolution on March 1, 1845, offering to admit Texas to the Union. A Texas convention accepted the offer, and the voters of Texas ratified the action. The new state formally entered the Union on December 29, 1845. Mexico was furious and dispatched troops to the Rio Grande border.

OREGON   Meanwhile, the Oregon boundary issue heated up as expansionists insisted that the newly elected president abandon previous offers to settle with Britain on the 49th parallel and stand by the Democrats' platform pledge ("54°40′ or Fight") to take all of Oregon. The expansionists were prepared to risk war with Britain while relations with Mexico were moving toward the breaking point. "All of Oregon or none," the expansionists cried. In his inaugural address, Polk had claimed that the American title to Oregon was "clear and unquestionable," but privately he favored a prudent compromise. War with Mexico was brewing; the territory up to 54°40′ seemed of less importance than the Puget Sound or the ports of California, on which the British were also thought to have designs.

Fortunately for Polk the British government had no enthusiasm for war over a remote wilderness territory at the cost of profitable trade relations with the United States. From the British viewpoint the only land in dispute all along had been between the 49th parallel and the Columbia River. But now the region's fur trade was a dying industry. In 1846 the British government submitted a draft treaty that extended the border along the 49th

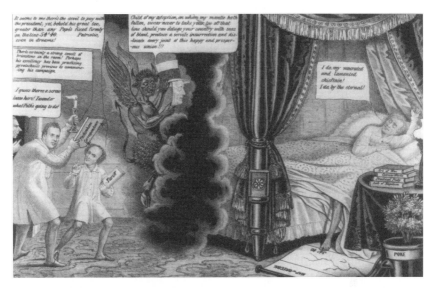

Polk's Dream (1846)

The devil advises Polk to pursue 54° 40′ even if "you deluge your country with seas of blood, produce a servile insurrection, and dislocate every joint of this happy and prosperous union."

parallel and through the main channel south of Vancouver Island and kept the right to navigate all of the Columbia River. On June 15 James Buchanan, now Polk's secretary of state, signed it, and three days later it was ratified in the Senate. The only opposition came from a group of expansionists who wanted more. Most of the country was satisfied. Southerners cared less about Oregon than about Texas, and northern business interests valued British trade more than they valued Oregon. Besides, the country by then was at war with Mexico.

THE MEXICAN WAR

THE OUTBREAK OF WAR   On March 6, 1845, two days after James Polk took office, the Mexican government broke off relations with the United States to protest the American annexation of Texas. When an effort at negotiation failed, the hard-driving Polk focused his efforts on fostering American intrigues meant to subvert Mexican authority in California. He wrote Consul Thomas O. Larkin in Monterey that he would make no effort to induce the admission of California to the Union, but "if the people should desire to unite their destiny with ours, they would be received as brethren."

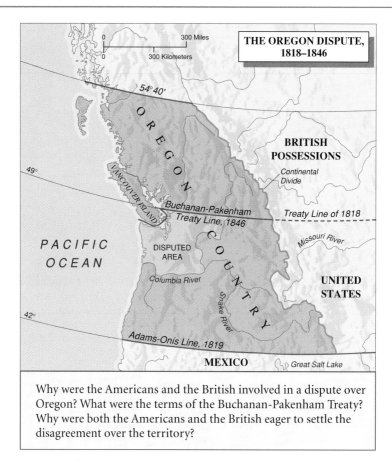

THE OREGON DISPUTE, 1818–1846

Why were the Americans and the British involved in a dispute over Oregon? What were the terms of the Buchanan-Pakenham Treaty? Why were both the Americans and the British eager to settle the disagreement over the territory?

Larkin, who could take a hint, began to line up Americans and sympathetic Californios. Meanwhile, Polk ordered U.S. troops under General Zachary Taylor to take up positions around Corpus Christi, near the Rio Grande in Texas. These positions lay in territory that was doubly disputed: Mexico recognized neither the American annexation of Texas nor the Rio Grande boundary.

The last hope for peace died when John Slidell, sent to Mexico City to negotiate a settlement, gave up on his mission in March 1846. Polk then resolved that he could achieve his purposes only by force. He won cabinet approval of a war message to Congress. That very evening, May 9, the news arrived that Mexicans had attacked U.S. soldiers north of the Rio Grande. Eleven Americans were killed, five wounded, and the remainder taken prisoner. Polk's provocative scheme had worked.

In his war message, Polk claimed that his call to arms was a response to Mexican aggression, a recognition that war had been forced upon the United States. Mexico, he reported, "has invaded our territory, and shed American blood upon the American soil." Congress quickly passed the war resolution, and Polk signed the declaration of war on May 13, 1846. But support for the war was guarded. The House authorized a call for 50,000 volunteers and a war appropriation of $10 million, but sixty-seven Whigs voted against the measure, a sign of rising opposition, especially in the North, where people assumed that the southerner Polk wanted a war in order to acquire more slave territory.

OPPOSITION TO THE WAR   In the Mississippi Valley, where expansion fever ran high, the war with Mexico was immensely popular. In New England, however, there was less enthusiasm for "Mr. Polk's war." Whig opinion ranged from lukewarm to hostile. Congressman John Quincy Adams, who voted against participation, called it "a most unrighteous war." An obscure congressman from Illinois named Abraham Lincoln, upon taking his seat in 1847, began introducing "spot resolutions," calling on President Polk to name the spot where American blood had been shed on American soil, implying that U.S. troops may, in fact, have been in Mexico when fired upon. The Whig leader Daniel Webster was convinced that the outbreak of war with Mexico was driven by the desire to add more slave states to the Union. The Massachusetts senator worried that an "expensive and bloody war" would end up fragmenting the Union. He was "quite alarmed for the state of the Country." Many New Englanders denounced the war as the work of pro-slavery southerners seeking new territories. But before the war ended, some anti-slavery leaders had a change of heart. Mexican territory seemed so unsuited to slave-based agriculture that they endorsed expansion in the hope of enlarging the area of free soil. The lure of more land and the idea of "manifest destiny" exerted a potent influence even upon those who opposed the war.

PREPARING FOR BATTLE   Both the United States and Mexico approached the war ill prepared. American policy had been incredibly reckless, risking war with both Britain and Mexico while doing nothing to strengthen the armed forces until war came. At the outset of the war, the regular army numbered barely over 7,000, in contrast to the Mexican force of 32,000. Before the war ended, the U.S. military had grown to 78,718 troops, of whom about 31,000 were regular army troops and marines. Most of the new soldiers were six- and twelve-month state volunteers from the West. The volunteer militia companies, often filled with frontier toughs, lacked uniforms, standard equipment, and discipline. Repeatedly, despite the best efforts of the commanding generals, these undisciplined forces engaged in plunder, rape, and murder.

The motley American troops outmatched larger Mexican forces, which had their own problems with training, discipline, morale, and munitions. Many of the Mexicans were pressed into service or recruited from prisons, and they made less than enthusiastic fighters. Mexican artillery pieces were generally obsolete, and the powder was so faulty that American soldiers could often dodge cannonballs that fell short and bounced ineffectively along the ground.

The United States entered the war without even a tentative plan of action, and politics complicated matters. Polk sought to manage every detail of the conflict. What Polk wanted, Thomas Hart Benton wrote later, was "a small war, just large enough to require a treaty of peace, and not large enough to make military reputations, dangerous for the presidency." Winfield Scott, general in chief of the army, was a politically ambitious Whig. Nevertheless, Polk at first named him to take charge of the Rio Grande front. When Scott quarreled with Polk's secretary of war, however, the exasperated president withdrew the appointment.

There now seemed a better choice for commander. General Zachary Taylor's men had scored two victories over Mexican forces north of the Rio Grande, at Palo Alto (May 8) and Resaca de la Palma (May 9). On May 18 Taylor crossed the river and occupied Matamoros, which a demoralized and bloodied Mexican army had abandoned. These quick victories brought Taylor instant popularity, and the president responded willingly to the demand that he be made commander for the conquest of Mexico. "Old Rough-and-Ready" Taylor impressed Polk as less of a political threat than Scott. Without a major battle he had achieved Polk's main objective, the conquest of Mexico's northern provinces.

THE ANNEXATION OF CALIFORNIA Along the Pacific coast, conquest was under way before definitive news of the Mexican War erupting arrived. Near the end of 1845, John C. Frémont brought out a band of sixty frontiersmen, ostensibly on another exploration of California and Oregon. When the Mexican commanding officer at Monterey ordered him out of the Salinas Valley, Frémont at first dug in his heels and refused to go, but he soon changed his mind and headed for Oregon. In 1846 he and his men again moved south, this time into the Sacramento Valley. Americans in the area fell upon Sonoma on June 14, proclaimed the Republic of California, and hoisted

The Battle of the Plains of Mesa

This sketch was made at the battle, which took place just before U.S. forces entered Los Angeles.

the hastily designed flag: a grizzly bear and star painted on white cloth, a version of which would become the state flag.

But the Bear Flag Republic lasted only a month. In July, John D. Sloat, commodore of the Pacific Fleet, having heard of the outbreak of hostilities with Mexico, sent a party ashore to raise the American flag and proclaim California part of the United States. Most Californians of whatever origin welcomed a change that promised order in preference to the confusion of the Bear Flag Republic.

Before the end of July, a new commodore, Robert F. Stockton, began preparations to move against Mexican forces in southern California. Stockton's forces occupied Santa Barbara and Los Angeles. By mid-August, Mexican resistance had dissipated. On August 17 Stockton declared himself governor, with Frémont as military commander in the north. At the same time another expedition was closing on Santa Fe. On August 18 Colonel Stephen Kearny and 1,600 men entered Santa Fe. After naming a civilian governor, Kearny divided his force, leading 300 men west toward California.

In southern California, where most of the poorer Mexicans and Mexicanized Indians resented American rule, a rebellion broke out. By the end of October, the rebels had ousted the token American force. Kearny walked right in to this rebel zone when he arrived. At San Diego he met up with Stockton and joined him in the reconquest of southern California, which they achieved after two brief clashes, entering Los Angeles on January 10, 1847. Rebel forces capitulated three days later.

TAYLOR'S BATTLES Both California and New Mexico had been taken before General Zachary Taylor fought his first major battle in northern Mexico. Having waited for more men and munitions, he finally moved out of his Matamoros base in September 1846 and assaulted the fortified city of Monterrey, which he took after a five-day siege. President Polk, however, was none too happy with the easy terms of surrender to which Taylor agreed, or with Taylor's growing popularity. The whole episode merely confirmed the president's impression that Taylor was too passive to be trusted further with the major campaign. Besides, his victories, if flawed, were leading to talk of General Taylor as the next Whig candidate for president.

Yet Polk's grand strategy was itself flawed. Having never seen the Mexican desert, he wrongly assumed that Taylor's men could live off the country and need not depend upon resupply. Polk therefore misunderstood the general's reluctance to strike out across several hundred miles of barren land just north of Mexico City. On another point the president was simply duped. The old dictator General Antonio López de Santa Anna, forced out of power in 1845, got word to Polk from his exile in Cuba that in return for the right considerations he would bring about a settlement of the war. Polk in turn assured the Mexican leader that the U.S. government would pay well for any territory taken through a settlement. In August 1846, Santa Anna was permitted to pass through the American blockade into Vera Cruz. Soon he was again in command of the Mexican army and was named president once more. Polk's intrigue unintentionally put perhaps the ablest Mexican general back in command of the enemy army, where he busily organized his forces to strike at Taylor.

By then another American front had been opened, and Taylor was ordered to wait in place. In October 1846 Polk and his cabinet decided to move against Mexico City by way of Vera Cruz. Polk named General Winfield Scott to the field command. Taylor, miffed at his reduction to a minor role, disobeyed orders and attacked Mexican forces near the hacienda of Buena Vista. Santa Anna met Taylor's untested volunteers with a large but ill-trained and tired army. The Mexican general invited the outnumbered Americans to surrender. "Tell him to go to hell," Taylor replied. In the hard-fought Battle of Buena Vista (February 22–23, 1847), Taylor's son-in-law, Colonel Jefferson Davis, the future president of the Confederacy, led a regiment that broke up a Mexican cavalry charge. Neither side could claim victory. It was the last major action on the northern front, and Taylor was granted leave to return home. Taylor's growing popularity forced Polk to promote him, despite the president's concerns about the general's political aspirations. In a self-serving moment, Polk recorded in his diary that Taylor was a "hard fighter" but had "none of the other qualities of a great general."

Why did John C. Frémont initially settle in the Salinas Valley before marching north, only to march south to San Francisco? How did Polk's fear of Zachary Taylor's popularity undermine the Americans' military strategy? What was the significance of Winfield Scott's assault on Mexico City?

SCOTT'S TRIUMPH Meanwhile, the long-planned assault on Mexico City had begun on March 9, 1847, when Winfield Scott's army landed on the beaches south of Vera Cruz. It was the first major amphibious operation by U.S. military forces and was carried out without loss. Vera Cruz surrendered on March 27 after a weeklong siege. Scott then set out on the route taken by

Cortés more than 300 years before. Santa Anna tried to set a trap for him at the mountain pass of Cerro Gordo, but Scott's men took more than 3,000 Mexican prisoners.

On May 15 Scott's army entered Puebla, the second-largest Mexican city. There Scott lost about one third of his army because men whose twelve-month enlistments had expired felt free to go home, leaving Scott with about 7,000 troops in all. There was nothing to do but hang on until reinforcements and supplies came up from the coast. Finally, after three months, with his numbers almost doubled, Scott set out on August 7 through the mountain passes into the valley of Mexico, cutting his supply line to the coast.

Scott directed a brilliant flanking operation around the lakes and marshes that guard the eastern approaches to Mexico City. After a series of battles in which they overwhelmed Mexican defenses, U.S. forces entered Mexico City on September 13, 1847. At the national palace a battalion of marines raised the American flag and occupied the "halls of Montezuma." News of the victory led some expansionists to new heights of land lust. The editor John O'Sullivan, who had coined the term *manifest destiny,* shouted, "More, More, More! Why not take all of Mexico?"

THE TREATY OF GUADALUPE HIDALGO   After the fall of the capital, Santa Anna resigned and a month later left the country. Meanwhile, Polk had appointed as chief peace negotiator Nicholas P. Trist, chief clerk of the State Department and a Virginia Democrat of impeccably partisan credentials. Formal talks got under way on January 2, 1848, at the village of Guadalupe Hidalgo, just outside the capital, and dragged on through the month. By the Treaty of Guadalupe Hidalgo, signed on February 2, 1848, Mexico gave up all claims to Texas above the Rio Grande and ceded California and New Mexico to the United States. In return the United States agreed to pay Mexico $15 million and assume the claims of U.S. citizens against Mexico up to a total of $3.25 million.

Polk submitted the treaty to the Senate. A growing movement to annex all of Mexico briefly excited the president, but as Polk confided in his diary, rejecting the treaty would be too risky. If he should reject a treaty made in accord with his own original terms in order to gain more territory, "the probability is that Congress would not grant either men or money to prosecute the war." In that case he might eventually have to withdraw the army and lose everything. The treaty went to the Senate, which ratified it on March 10, 1848. By the end of July, the last remaining American soldiers had left Mexico.

THE WAR'S LEGACIES   The seventeen-month-long Mexican War cost the United States 1,733 killed in battle, 4,152 wounded, and far more—11,550—dead of disease, mostly dysentery and chronic diarrhea ("Montezuma's revenge"). It remains the deadliest war in American history in terms of the percentage of combatants killed. Out of every 1,000 soldiers in Mexico, some 110 died. The next highest death rate would be in the Civil War, with 65 dead out of every 1,000 participants.

As a result of the Mexican War, the United States acquired more than 500,000 square miles of territory (almost 1 million, counting Texas), including the great Pacific harbors of San Diego, Monterey, and San Francisco. Except for a small addition made by the Gadsden Purchase of 1853, these annexations rounded out the continental United States.

Several important firsts are associated with the Mexican War: the first successful offensive American war, the first occupation of an enemy capital, the first war in which martial law was declared on foreign soil, the first in which West Point graduates played a major role, and the first reported by modern war correspondents. It was also the first significant combat experience for a group of junior officers who would later serve as leading generals during the Civil War: Robert E. Lee, Ulysses S. Grant, Thomas "Stonewall" Jackson, George B. McClellan, George Meade, and others.

Initially the victory in Mexico unleashed a surge of national pride, but as the years passed, the Mexican War was increasingly seen as a war of conquest directed by a president bent on expansion. For a brief season the glory of conquest added luster to the names of Zachary Taylor and Winfield Scott. Despite Polk's best efforts, he had manufactured the next, and last, two Whig candidates for president. One of them, Taylor, would replace him in the White House, with the storm of sectional conflict already on the horizon.

The acquisition of Oregon, Texas, California, and the new Southwest made the United States a transcontinental nation. Extending authority over this vast new land greatly expanded the scope of the federal government. In 1849, for example, Congress created the Department of the Interior to supervise the distribution of land, the creation of new territories and states, and the "protection" of the Indians and their land. President Polk naively assumed that the dramatic expansion of American territory to the Pacific would strengthen "the bonds of Union." He was wrong. No sooner was Texas annexed than a violent debate erupted over the extension of slavery into the new territories. That debate would culminate in a civil war that would nearly destroy the Union.

MAKING CONNECTIONS

- This chapter opened with an account of the brief administration of William Henry Harrison, the first Whig president. The collapse of the Whig party is detailed in Chapter 16.

- The West developed quickly after the expansionist policies of the 1840s. Chapter 19 takes the story to the 1890s.

- This chapter ended by noting how expansionism fueled a "debate [that] would culminate in a civil war that would nearly destroy the Union." Chapter 16's discussion of "The Crisis of Union" traces the relationship between the Mexican War and the Civil War more explicitly.

FURTHER READING

For background on Whig programs and ideas, see Michael F. Holt's *The Rise and Fall of the American Whig Party: Jacksonian Politics and the Onset of the Civil War* (1999). Several works help interpret the expansionist impulse. Frederick Merk's *Manifest Destiny and Mission in American History* (1963) remains a classic. A more recent treatment of expansionist ideology is Thomas R. Hietala's *Manifest Design: Anxious Aggrandizement in Late Jacksonian America* (1985).

The best survey of western expansion is Richard White's *"It's Your Misfortune and None of My Own": A New History of the American West* (1991). Robert M. Utley's *A Life Wild and Perilous: Mountain Men and the Paths to the Pacific* (1997) tells the dramatic story of the rugged pathfinders who discovered corridors over the Rocky Mountains. The movement of settlers to the West is ably documented in John Mack Faragher's *Women and Men on the Overland Trail* (2001) and David Dary's *The Santa Fe Trail: Its History, Legends, and Lore* (2000). The best account of the California gold rush is Malcolm J. Rohrbough's *Days of Gold: The California Gold Rush and the American Nation* (1997).

Gene M. Brack's *Mexico Views Manifest Destiny, 1821–1846: An Essay on the Origins of the Mexican War* (1975) takes Mexico's viewpoint on U.S. designs on the West. On the siege of the Alamo, see William C. Davis's *Three Roads to the Alamo: The Lives and Fortunes of David Crockett, James Bowie, and William Barret Travis* (1998). An excellent biography related to the emergence of Texas is Gregg Cantrell's *Stephen F. Austin: Empresario of Texas* (1999). On James K. Polk, see John H. Schroeder's *Mr. Polk's War: American Opposition and Dissent, 1846–1848* (1973). The best survey of the military conflict is John S. D. Eisenhower's *So Far from God: The U.S. War with Mexico, 1846–1848* (1989). On the diplomatic aspects of Mexican-American relations see David M. Pletcher's *The Diplomacy of Annexation: Texas, Oregon, and the Mexican War* (1973).

Part Four

A
HOUSE
DIVIDED

O f all the regions of the United States during the first half of the nineteenth century, the South was the most distinctive. Southern society remained fundamentally rural and agricultural long after the rest of the nation embraced the Industrial Revolution. Likewise, the southern elite's tenacious desire to preserve and expand the institution of slavery muted social-reform impulses in the South and ignited a prolonged political controversy that would end in civil war.

The rapid settlement of the western territories set in motion a ferocious competition between North and South for political influence in the burgeoning West. Would the new states in the West be "slave" or "free"? The issue of allowing slavery into the new territories involved more than humanitarian concern for the plight of enslaved blacks. By the 1840s North and South had developed quite different economic interests. The North wanted high tariffs on imported manufactures to "protect" its infant industries from foreign competition. Southerners, on the other hand, favored free trade because they wanted to import British goods in exchange for the cotton they provided British textile mills.

A series of political compromises glossed over the fundamental differences between the regions during the first half of the nineteenth century. But abolitionists refused to give up their crusade against slavery. Moreover, a new generation of politicians emerged in the 1850s, leaders from both the North and the South who were less willing to seek political compromises. The continuing debate over allowing slavery into the new western territories kept sectional tensions at a fever pitch. By the time Abraham Lincoln was elected president in 1860, many Americans had decided that the nation could not survive half-slave and half-free; something had to give.

In a last-ditch effort to preserve the institution of slavery, eleven southern states seceded from the Union and created a separate confederate nation. That, in turn, prompted northerners such as Lincoln to support a civil war to preserve the Union. No one realized in 1861 how prolonged and costly the War between the States would become. Over 630,000 soldiers and sailors died of wounds or disease. The colossal carnage caused even the most seasoned observers to blanch in disbelief. As President Lincoln confessed in his second inaugural address, no one expected the war to become so "fundamental and astonishing."

Nor did anyone envision how sweeping the war's effects would be on the future of the country. The northern victory in 1865 restored the Union and in the process helped accelerate America's transformation into a modern nation-state. National power and a national consciousness began to displace the sectional emphases of the antebellum era. A Republican-led Congress pushed through federal legislation to foster industrial and commercial development and western expansion. In the process the United States began to leave behind the Jeffersonian dream of a decentralized agrarian republic.

The Civil War also ended slavery, yet the actual status of the freed blacks remained precarious. How would they fare in a society built upon a slavery maintained by racism? In 1865 the daughter of a Georgia planter expressed her concern about such issues when she wrote in her diary that "there are sad changes in store for both races. I wonder the Yankees do not shudder to behold their work" in trying to "reconstruct" the defeated South.

Former slaves found themselves legally free, but most were without property, homes, education, or training. Although the Fourteenth Amendment (1868) set forth guarantees for the civil rights of African Americans and the Fifteenth Amendment (1870) provided that black men could vote, local authorities found ingenious—and often violent— ways to avoid the spirit and the letter of the new laws.

The restoration of the former Confederate states to the Union did not come easily. Much bitterness and resistance remained among the vanquished. Although Confederate leaders were initially disenfranchised, they continued to exercise considerable authority in political and economic matters. Indeed, in 1877 the last federal troops were removed from the occupied South, and former Confederates declared themselves "redeemed" from the stain of occupation. By the end of the nineteenth century, most states of the former Confederacy had devised a system of legal discrimination that re-created many aspects of slavery.

15

THE OLD SOUTH

FOCUS QUESTIONS

- What were the dominant industries and forms of agriculture in the Old South?
- How did the dependence upon agriculture and slavery shape southern society?
- How did the anti-slavery movement emerge, and what were the South's reactions to it?

To answer these questions and access additional review material, please visit www.wwnorton.com/studyspace.

Southerners, a North Carolina editor once wrote, are "a mythological people, created half out of dream and half out of slander, who live in a still legendary land." Most Americans, including southerners themselves, harbor a cluster of myths and stereotypes about the South. Perhaps the most enduring myths come from such classic movies as *Gone with the Wind* (1939). The South portrayed in romanticized Hollywood productions is a stable agrarian society led by paternalistic white planters and their families, who live in white-columned mansions and represent a "natural" aristocracy of virtue and talent within their communities. In these accounts, southerners are kind to their slaves and devoted to the rural values of independence and chivalric honor, values celebrated by Thomas Jefferson.

By contrast, a much darker myth about the Old South emerged from abolitionist pamphlets and Harriet Beecher Stowe's best-selling novel, *Uncle Tom's Cabin* (1852). Those exposés of southern culture portrayed the planters as arrogant aristocrats who raped enslaved women, brutalized enslaved workers, and lorded over their communities with haughty disdain for the rights and needs of others. They bred slaves like cattle, broke up slave families, and sold slaves "down the river" to certain death in the Louisiana sugar mills and rice plantations.

Such contrasting myths die hard, in large part because each one is rooted in reality. Nonetheless, efforts to get at what really set the Old South apart from the rest of the nation generally pivot on two lines of thought: the impact of the environment (climate and geography) and the effects of human decisions and actions. The South's warm, humid climate was ideal for the cultivation of commercial crops such as tobacco, cotton, rice, and sugarcane. The growth of those lucrative cash crops helped foster the plantation system and slavery. In the end those developments brought about the sectional conflict over the extension of slavery and the civil war that shook the foundations of the Old South.

THE DISTINCTIVENESS OF THE OLD SOUTH

While geography was and is a key determinant of the South's economy and culture, much of southern distinctiveness resulted from the institution of slavery. The resolve of slaveholders to retain control of their socioeconomic order created a sense of racial unity that bridged class divisions among whites. Yet the biracial character of the population exercised an even greater influence over southern culture. In shaping patterns of speech and folklore, music, religion, literature, and recreation, black southerners immeasurably influenced and enriched the region's development.

The South differed from other sections of the country, too, in its high proportion of native-born Americans in its population, both whites and blacks. Despite a great diversity of origins in the colonial population, the South drew few overseas immigrants after the Revolution. One reason was that the main shipping lines went from Europe to northern ports; another, that the prospect of competing with slave labor deterred immigrants. After the Missouri controversy of 1819–1821, the South increasingly became a consciously minority region, its population growth lagging behind that of other sections of the country, its "peculiar institution" of slavery more and more an isolated and odious phenomenon in Western civilization. Attitudes of defensiveness strongly affected its churches. The religious culture of the white South retreated from the liberalism of the Revolutionary War era into a brittle orthodoxy, which provided one line of defense against new doctrines of any kind, while black southerners found in their own version of Christianity a refuge from their hardships, a promise of release on some future day of Jubilee.

Slavery in the South

Slave quarters on a South Carolina plantation.

The South also differed from the rest of the nation in its architecture; its penchant for fighting, guns, and the military; and its attachment to an agrarian ideal. The preponderance of farming remained a distinctive regional characteristic, whether pictured as the Jeffersonian small farmer living by the sweat of his brow or the lordly planter dispatching his slave gangs. But in the end what made the South distinctive was its people's belief—and other people's belief—that the region *was* distinctive.

STAPLE CROPS   The idea of the Cotton Kingdom is itself something of a mythic stereotype. Although cotton was the most important of the "staple," or most profitable, crops, it was a latecomer. Tobacco, the first staple crop, had been the mainstay of Virginia and Maryland during the colonial era and common in North Carolina. After the Revolution, pioneers carried it over the mountains into Kentucky and as far as Missouri. Indigo, an important crop in colonial South Carolina, vanished with the loss of British bounties for this source of a valuable blue dye, but rice farming continued in a coastal strip that lapped over into North Carolina and Georgia. Rice production was limited to the tidewater areas of South Carolina and Georgia because it required the frequent flooding and draining of fields. Since rice production required substantial capital for floodgates, ditches, and machinery, the plantations that grew rice were large and relatively few in number.

Sugar, like rice, required a heavy capital investment—in machinery to grind the cane—and was limited to the Deep South because cane is susceptible to

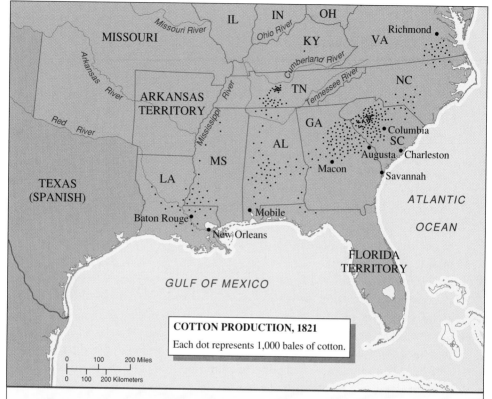

COTTON PRODUCTION, 1821
Each dot represents 1,000 bales of cotton.

Why was cotton an appealing staple crop? What regions produced the most cotton in 1821? Keeping in mind what you read about cotton in Chapter 12, what innovations would you suppose allowed farmers to move inland and produce cotton more efficiently?

frost. Since sugar needed the prop of a protective tariff to enable its farmers to compete with foreign suppliers, it produced the anomaly in southern politics of pro-tariff congressmen from Louisiana. Hemp had something of the same effect in the Kentucky Bluegrass region and in northwestern Missouri. Both flax and hemp were important to backcountry farmers at the end of the colonial era. Homespun clothing was most apt to be linsey-woolsey, a combination of linen and wool. But flax never developed more than a limited commercial market, and that mostly for linseed oil. Hemp, on the other hand, developed commercial possibilities in rope, cotton-baling cloth, and canvas for sails.

Cotton, the last of the major staple crops, eventually outpaced all the others put together. At the end of the War of 1812, annual cotton production

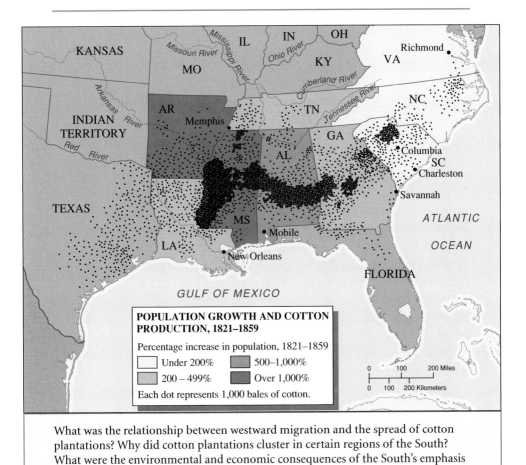

POPULATION GROWTH AND COTTON
PRODUCTION, 1821–1859

Percentage increase in population, 1821–1859

☐ Under 200%   ▨ 500–1,000%
▨ 200 – 499%   ■ Over 1,000%

Each dot represents 1,000 bales of cotton.

What was the relationship between westward migration and the spread of cotton plantations? Why did cotton plantations cluster in certain regions of the South? What were the environmental and economic consequences of the South's emphasis on cotton?

was estimated at less than 150,000 bales; in 1860 it was reported at 4 million. Two factors accounted for the dramatic growth: the voracious market for American cotton among British and French textile manufacturers and the cultivation of new lands in the Old Southwest (Alabama, Mississippi, Arkansas, and Louisiana). Much of the story of the southern people—white and black—from 1820 to 1860 was their movement from Virginia and the Carolinas to fertile cotton lands farther west. By 1860 the center of the cotton belt stretched from eastern North Carolina, South Carolina, and Georgia, through the fertile Alabama-Mississippi black belts (so called for the color of the soil), through Louisiana on to Texas, and up the Mississippi Valley as far as southern Illinois. Cotton prices fell sharply after the financial panic of 1837 and remained below 10¢ a pound through most of the 1840s but advanced above 10¢ late in 1855 and stayed there until 1860, reaching 15¢ in 1857.

AGRICULTURAL DIVERSITY   The focus on cotton and the other cash crops has obscured the degree to which the antebellum South fed itself from its own fields. With 30 percent of the country's landmass in 1860 and 39 percent of its population, the slave states produced 52 percent of the nation's corn, 29 percent of its wheat, 19 percent of its oats, 19 percent of its rye, 10 percent of its white potatoes, and 94 percent of its sweet potatoes. Livestock added to the diversity of the farm economy. In 1860 the South had half the nation's cattle, over 60 percent of its swine, nearly 45 percent of its horses, 52 percent of its oxen, 90 percent of its mules, and nearly 33 percent of its sheep, the last mostly in the upper South. Plantations and farms commonly raised livestock for home consumption.

Yet the story of the southern economy was hardly one of unbroken prosperity. The South's cash crops quickly exhausted the soil. In low-country South Carolina, Senator Robert Y. Hayne spoke of "fields abandoned; and hospitable mansions of our fathers deserted." The older farming lands had trouble competing with the newer soils farther west. But lands in the Old Southwest, too, began to show wear and tear. By 1855 an Alabama senator

Southern Agriculture

Planting sweet potatoes on James Hopkinson's plantation, Edisto Island, South Carolina, April 1862.

had noted, "Our small planters, after taking the cream off their lands . . . are going further west and south in search of other virgin lands which they may and will despoil and impoverish in like manner."

So the Southeast and then the Old Southwest faced a growing sense of economic crisis as the nineteenth century advanced. Proposals to deal with the crisis followed two lines. Some argued for agricultural reform and others for economic diversification through industry and trade. Edmund Ruffin of Virginia stands out as perhaps the greatest of the reformers. After studying the chemistry of soils, he reasoned that most of the exhausted fields of the upper South were too acidic. He discovered that marl from a seashell deposit in eastern Virginia could restore the fields' fertility. Ruffin published the results in his *Essay on Calcareous Manures* (1832). Such publications and farm magazines in general reached but a minority of farmers, however, mostly the larger and more successful planters.

MANUFACTURING AND TRADE   By 1840 many thoughtful southerners had concluded that the region desperately needed to develop its own manufacturing and trade. The cotton-growing mania had led the South to become increasingly dependent upon northern industry and commerce: cotton and tobacco were exported mainly in northern vessels; southerners also relied upon northern merchants for imported goods—economically the South had become a kind of colonial dependency of the North. The merchants of northern cities, a southerner said, "export our . . . valuable productions, and import our articles of consumption and from this agency they derive a profit which has enriched them . . . at our expense."

Southern concerns about dependence upon northern merchants and bankers prompted interest in a more diversified economy to allow native industries to balance agriculture and trade. Southern publicists called attention to the section's great resources: its raw materials, labor supply, waterpower, wood and coal, and markets. In Richmond the Tredegar Iron Works grew into the single most important manufacturing enterprise in the Old South. It used mostly slave labor to produce cannon, shot, and shell as well as axes, saws, bridge materials, boilers, and steam engines, including locomotives. Yet despite such efforts the region still lagged well behind the North in its industrial development and commercial network.

ECONOMIC DEVELOPMENT   During the antebellum years two major explanations were put forward for the lag in southern industrial development. First, blacks were presumed unsuited to factory work. Second, the ruling elite of the Old South had developed a lordly disdain for industrial

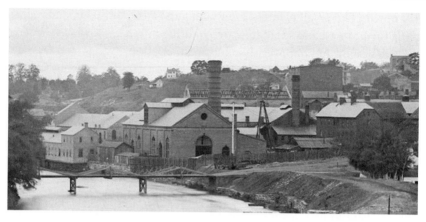

Iron Manufacturing

The Tredegar Iron Works in Richmond, Virginia.

production. A certain aristocratic prestige derived from owning land and holding slaves. But any argument that African-American labor was incompatible with industrial work simply flew in the face of the evidence, since factory owners bought or hired enslaved blacks to operate just about every kind of manufacture. Given the opportunity, any number of African Americans displayed managerial skills as overseers.

One should not take at face value the legendary indifference of aristocratic planters to profits. More often than not the successful planter was bent on maximizing profits. While the profitability of slavery has been a long-standing subject of controversy, in recent years economic historians have concluded that slaves on the average supplied about a 10 percent annual return on their cost. At the time that was an enticing profit margin, just as it is now. By a strictly economic calculation, slaves and land on which cotton could be grown were the most profitable investments available in the antebellum South. Some slaveholders, particularly in the newer cotton lands of the Old Southwest, were incredibly rich.

WHITE SOCIETY IN THE SOUTH

If an understanding of the Old South must begin with a knowledge of social myths, it must end with a sense of tragedy. White southerners had won short-term gains at the cost of both long-term development and moral

King Cotton Captured

An engraving showing cotton being trafficked in Louisiana.

isolation in the eyes of the world. The concentration on agriculture and slaves and the paucity of cities and immigrants deprived the South of the most dynamic sources of innovation. The slaveholding South hitched its wagon not to a star but to the (largely British) demand for cotton, which had not slackened since the start of the Industrial Revolution. During the late 1850s southern agricultural prosperity seemed never ending. The South, "safely entrenched behind her cotton bags . . . can defy the world—for the civilized world depends on the cotton of the South," said a Mississippi newspaper in 1860. "No power on earth dares to make war upon it," said James H. Hammond of South Carolina. "Cotton is king." What southern boosters could not perceive was what they could least afford: the imminent slackening of the world demand for cotton. The heyday of expansion in British textiles had ended by 1860, but by then the Deep South was locked into large-scale cotton production for generations to come.

PLANTERS   Although there were only a few giant plantations, they set the tone for southern economic and social life. What distinguished the plantation from the farm, in addition to its size, was the use of a large labor force, under separate control and supervision, to grow primarily staple crops (cotton, rice, tobacco, and sugarcane) for profit. A clear-cut distinction between management and labor set the planter apart from the small slaveholder, who often worked side by side with slaves at the same tasks.

If, to be called a planter, one had to hold 20 slaves, only 1 out of every 30 whites in the South in 1860 was a planter. Fewer than 11,000 held 50 or more slaves, and only 2,300 held over 100. The census listed only 11 planters with 500 slaves and just 1 with as many as 1,000. Yet this privileged elite tended to think of its class interests as the interests of the entire South and to perceive its members as community leaders and "natural aristocrats." The planter group, making up under 4 percent of the adult white men in the South, held more than half the slaves and produced most of the cotton, tobacco, and hemp and all of the sugar and rice. The number of slaveholders was only 383,637 out of a total white population of 8 million. But assuming that each family numbered five people, then whites with some proprietary interest in slavery came to 1.9 million, or roughly one fourth of the white population. While the preponderance of southern whites belonged to the small-farmer class, they tended to defer to the large planters. After all, many small farmers aspired to become planters themselves.

Often the planter did live in the splendor that legend attributes to him, with the wealth and leisure to cultivate the arts of hospitality, good manners, learning, and politics. More often the scene was less charming. Some of the mansions, on closer inspection, turned out to be modest houses with false fronts. The planter commonly had less leisure than legend would suggest, for he in fact managed a large enterprise. At the same time he often served as the patron to whom workers appealed the actions of their foremen. The quality of life for the enslaved workers was governed far more by the attitude of the master than by the formal slave codes, which were seldom strictly enforced except in times of trouble.

THE PLANTATION MISTRESS   The mistress of the plantation, like the master, seldom led a life of idle leisure. She supervised the domestic household in the same way the planter took care of the business, overseeing the supply and preparation of food and linens, the house-cleaning and care of the sick, and a hundred other details. Mary Boykin Chesnut of South Carolina complained that "there is no slave like a wife." The wives of all but the most wealthy planters were expected to supervise the domestic activities of the household and manage the slaves to boot. The son of a Tennessee slaveholder remembered that his mother and grandmother were "the busiest women I ever saw."

White women living in a slaveholding culture confronted a double standard in terms of moral and sexual behavior. While they were expected to behave as exemplars of Christian piety and sexual purity, their husbands, brothers, and sons often followed an unwritten rule of self-indulgent hedonism. "God forgive us," Mary Chesnut wrote in her diary,

> but ours is a monstrous system. Like the patriarchs of old, our men live all in one house with their wives and their [enslaved] concubines; and the mulattoes one sees in every family partly resemble the white children. Any lady is ready to tell you who is the father of all the mulatto children in everybody's household but her own. Those, she seems to think, drop from the clouds.

Such a double standard both illustrated and reinforced the arrogant authoritarianism displayed by many male planters. Yet for all their private complaints and daily burdens, few plantation mistresses engaged in public criticism of the prevailing social order and racist climate.

THE MIDDLE CLASS Overseers on the largest plantations generally came from the middle class of small farmers or skilled workers or were younger sons of planters. Most aspired to become slaveholders themselves, but others were constantly on the move in search of more lucrative opportunities. Occasionally there were black overseers, but the highest management position to which a slave could aspire was usually that of "driver," placed in charge of a small group of slaves with the duty of getting them to work without creating dissension.

The most numerous white southerners were the small farmers (yeomen), those who lived with their families in modest two-room cabins rather than columned mansions. They raised a few hogs and chickens, grew some corn and cotton, and traded with neighbors more than they bought from stores. The men in the family focused their energies on outdoor labors. Women worked in the fields during harvest time but spent most of their days attending to domestic chores. Many of these "middling" farmers held a handful of slaves, but most had none.

Southern farmers were typically mobile folk, ever willing to pull up stakes and move west or southwest in pursuit of better land. They tended to be fiercely independent and suspicious of government authority, and they overwhelmingly identified with the Democratic party of Andrew Jackson and the spiritual fervor of evangelical Protestantism. Even though only a minority of the middle-class farmers held slaves, most of them supported the slave system. They feared that the slaves, if freed, would compete with them for land, and they enjoyed the privileged status that racially based slavery afforded them. As one farmer told a northern traveler, "Now suppose they was free. You see they'd all think themselves as good as we." Such racist sentiments pervaded the border states as well as the Deep South.

"POOR WHITES"   Visitors to the Old South often had trouble telling yeomen apart from the true "poor whites," a degraded class relegated to the least desirable land, living on the fringes of polite society. The "poor whites," given over to hunting and fishing, to hound dogs and moonshine whiskey, were characterized by a pronounced lankness and sallowness. Speculation had it that they were descended from indentured servants or convicts transported to the colonies or that they were the weakest of the frontier population, forced to take refuge in the sand land, the pine barrens, and the swamps after having been pushed aside by the more enterprising and the more successful. But the problem was less heredity than environment, the consequence of infections and dietary deficiencies that gave rise to a trilogy of "lazy diseases": hookworm, malaria, and pellagra, all of which produced an overpowering lethargy. Many "poor whites" displayed a morbid craving to chew clay, from which they got the name dirt eaters; the cause was a dietary deficiency, although a folklore grew up about the nutritional and medicinal qualities of certain clays. Around 1900 modern medicine discovered the causes of and cures for these diseases. By 1930 they had practically disappeared, taking with them many of the stereotypes.

HONOR AND VIOLENCE   From colonial times most southern white men prided themselves on adhering to a moral code centered on a prickly sense of honor. Such a preoccupation with masculine honor was common among Germanic and Celtic peoples (the Scottish, Irish, Scotch-Irish, Cornish, and Welsh), from whom most white southerners were descended. It flourished in hierarchical rural societies, where face-to-face relations governed social manners. The dominant ethical code for the southern white elite included a combative sensitivity to slights; loyalty to family, locality, state, and region; deference to elders and social "betters"; and an almost theatrical hospitality. Southern men displayed a fierce defense of female purity and a propensity to magnify personal insults into capital offenses.

The preoccupation of southern white men with a sense of honor steeped in violence found outlets in several popular rituals. Like their Celtic and English ancestors, white southerners hunted, rode, and gambled—over cards, dice, horse racing, and cockfighting. All those activities provided arenas for masculine camaraderie as well as competition.

Southern men of all social classes were preoccupied with an often reckless manliness. Duels constituted the ultimate public expression of personal honor and manly courage. Although not confined to the South, dueling was much more common there than in the rest of the young nation, a fact that gave rise to the observation that southerners would be polite until they were angry enough to kill you. Dueling was outlawed in the northern states after Aaron Burr killed Alexander Hamilton in 1804, and a number of southern states and counties banned the practice as well—but the prohibition was rarely enforced. Amid the fiery antebellum political debates over nullification, abolition, and the fate of slavery in the territories,

Scene in Washington

This caricature of the prominent Whig newspaper editor James Watson Webb appeared after Webb provoked a duel between two congressmen in 1838. He is shown armed with a sword cane, a musket, a knife, and several pistols and is trailed by a turkey, a symbol of his arrogance.

clashing opinions often ended in duels. Many of the most prominent southern leaders engaged in duels—congressmen, senators, governors, editors, and planters. The roster of participants included Andrew Jackson, Henry Clay, Sam Houston, and Jefferson Davis.

Black Society in the South

Slavery was one of the fastest growing elements of American life during the first half of the nineteenth century. In 1790 there were fewer than 700,000 enslaved blacks in the United States. By 1830 there were more than 2 million, and by 1860 there were almost 4 million. From its American inception in 1619, the enslavement of Africans was a dynamic, ever-changing institution. Throughout the seventeenth and well into the eighteenth centuries, slavery was largely an uncodified system of forced labor practiced in most New World colonies. Black enslaved workers were treated largely like white indentured servants. After the Revolution, however, slavery increasingly became a highly regulated institution limited to the South. People referred to it as the peculiar institution because it so flagrantly violated the principle of individual freedom that served as the basis of the Declaration of Independence. During the antebellum era, slavery became such a powerful engine of economic development—for both the southern cotton crop and the New England textile industry—that its mushrooming significance defied domestic and international criticism. By 1860 the dollar value of southern slavery outstripped the value of all banks, railroads, and factories combined. Slavery was the most important force shaping American history in the first half of the nineteenth century. Yet by no means was it monolithic in character, nor was it necessarily inescapable.

"FREE PERSONS OF COLOR" In the Old South free persons of color occupied an uncertain status, balanced somewhere between slavery and freedom, subject to racist legal restrictions not imposed upon whites. Free blacks attained their status in a number of ways. Over the years some slaves were able to purchase their freedom, while some gained freedom as a reward for wartime military service. Others were simply freed by conscientious masters, either in their wills or during their lifetime. By 1860 there were 260,000 free blacks in the slave states.

Yarrow Mamout

Mamout, an African Muslim, was sold into slavery, purchased his freedom, acquired property, and settled in Georgetown (now part of Washington, D.C.). Charles Willson Peale executed this portrait in 1819, when Mamout was over 100 years old.

Among them were a large number of mulattoes, people of mixed racial ancestry. The census of 1860 reported 412,000 persons of mixed parentage in the United States, or about 10 percent of the black population, probably a drastic undercount. In urban centers like Charleston and especially New Orleans, "colored" society became virtually a third caste, a new people who occupied a status somewhere between that of blacks and that of whites. Some mulattoes built substantial fortunes and even became slaveholders. They often operated inns serving a white clientele. Jehu Jones, for instance, was the "colored" proprietor of one of Charleston's best hotels. In

Louisiana a mulatto, Cyprien Ricard, paid $250,000 for an estate that had ninety-one slaves. In Natchez, Mississippi, William Johnson, son of a white father and a mulatto mother, operated three barbershops, owned 1,500 acres of land, and held several slaves.

Black slaveholders were few in number, however. The 1830 census revealed that 3,775 free blacks, about 2 percent of the total free black population, held 12,760 slaves. Although most of the black slaveholders were in the South, some lived in Rhode Island, Connecticut, Illinois, New Jersey, New York, and the border states. Some blacks held slaves for humanitarian purposes. One minister, for instance, bought slaves and then enabled them to purchase their freedom from him on easy terms. Most often, black slaveholders were free blacks who bought their own family members with the express purpose of freeing them.

Free Blacks

This badge, issued in Charleston, South Carolina, was worn by a free black so that he would not be mistaken for someone's "property."

THE TRADE IN SLAVES   The rise in the slave population occurred mainly through a natural increase, the rate of which was very close to that of whites at the time. When the African slave trade was outlawed in 1808, it seemed to many a step toward the extinction of slavery, but the expansion of the cotton economy, with its voracious appetite for manual workers, soon created such a vested interest in slaves as to dash those hopes. Shutting off the importation of slaves only added to the value of those already present.

The rise in the cash value of enslaved workers brought better treatment. "Massa was purty good," one ex-slave recalled. "He treated us jus' 'bout like you would a good mule." Another said his master "fed us reg'lar on good, 'stantial food, jus' like you'd tend to you hoss, if you had a real good one." Some slaveholders hired wage laborers, often Irish immigrants, for ditching and other dangerous work rather than risk the lives of the more valuable slaves.

The end of the foreign slave trade gave rise to a flourishing domestic trade, with slaves moving mainly from the used-up lands of the Southeast into the booming new country of the Old Southwest. The slave trade peaked just before 1837, then slacked off, first because of economic depression, then

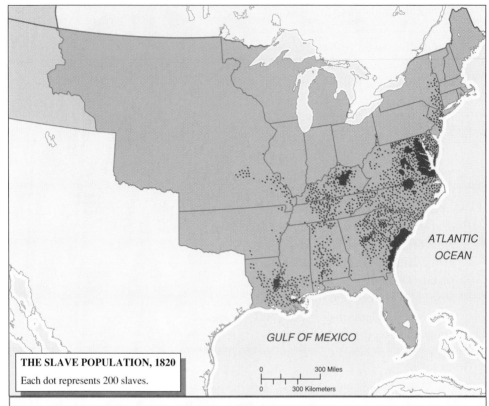

THE SLAVE POPULATION, 1820

Each dot represents 200 slaves.

ATLANTIC OCEAN

GULF OF MEXICO

0 ——— 300 Miles
0 ——— 300 Kilometers

Consider where the largest populations of slaves were clustered in the South in 1820. Why were most slaves clustered in these regions of the South and not in others? What were the limitations on the spread of slavery? How was the experience of plantation slavery different for men and women?

because agricultural reform and recovery renewed the demand for slaves in the upper South. Many slaves moved south and west with the planters, but there also developed an organized business, with brokers, pens, and auctioneers. The worst aspect of the domestic slave trade was the separation of children from parents and husbands from wives. Only Louisiana and Alabama (from 1852) forbade separating a child under ten from his or her mother, and no state forbade the separation of husband from wife.

PLANTATION SLAVERY Most slaves labored on plantations. The preferred jobs were as household servants and skilled workers, including blacksmiths and carpenters, or a special assignment, such as boatman or cook.

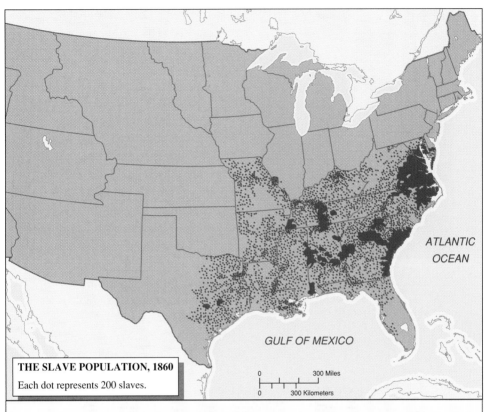

THE SLAVE POPULATION, 1860

Each dot represents 200 slaves.

ATLANTIC OCEAN

GULF OF MEXICO

0 — 300 Miles

0 — 300 Kilometers

Why did slavery spread west? Compare this map with the map of cotton production on page 535. What patterns do you see? Why would slaves have resisted migrating west?

Field hands were usually housed in one- or two-room wooden shacks with dirt floors, some without windows. A set of clothes was distributed twice a year, but shoes were generally provided only in winter. On larger plantations there was sometimes an infirmary and a regular sick call, but most planters resorted to doctors mainly in cases of severe illness. Based upon detailed records from eleven plantations in the lower South during the antebellum era, scholars have calculated that half of all slave babies died in the first year of life, a mortality rate more than twice that of whites. Field hands worked long hours, from dawn to dusk. The difference between a good owner and a bad one, according to one ex-slave, was the difference between one who did not "whip too much" and one who "whipped till he's bloodied you and

Jack, photographed by Joseph T. Zealy

Daguerreotype of a man identified only as Jack, a driver from Guinea, on the plantation of B. F. Taylor of Columbia, South Carolina, 1850.

blistered you." Over 50,000 slaves a year escaped. Those not caught often headed for Mexico, the northern states, or Canada.

THE EXPERIENCE OF SLAVE WOMEN Although black men and women often performed similar labors, they did not experience slavery in the same way. Slaveholders had different expectations for the men and women they controlled. During the colonial period male slaves vastly outnumbered females. By the mid–eighteenth century, however, the gender ratio had come into balance. Once slaveholders realized how profitable a fertile female slave could be over time, giving birth every two and a half years to a child who eventually could be sold, they began to encourage reproduction through a variety of incentives. Pregnant slaves were given less work to do and more food. Some plantation owners rewarded new mothers with dresses and silver dollars.

But if motherhood endowed enslaved women with stature and benefits, it also entailed exhausting demands. Within days after childbirth, the mother was put to work spinning, weaving, or sewing. A few weeks thereafter mothers were sent back to the fields; breast-feeding mothers were often forced to take their babies to the fields with them. Enslaved women were expected to do "man's work" outside: they cut trees, hauled logs, plowed fields with mules, dug ditches, spread fertilizer, slaughtered and dressed animals, hoed corn, and picked cotton. As a slave who escaped reported, "Women who do outdoor work are used as bad as men."

Once women passed their childbearing years, around the age of forty, their workload was increased. Slaveholders put middle-aged women to work full-time in the fields or performing other outdoor labor. On larger plantations elderly women, called grannies, kept the children during the day while their mothers worked outside. Enslaved women of all ages usually worked in sex-segregated gangs, which enabled them to form close bonds with one another. To enslaved African Americans, developing a sense of community and camaraderie meant emotional and psychological survival.

The Business of Slavery

The offices of Price, Birch and Company, dealers in slaves, Alexandria, Virginia.

Unlike enslaved men, enslaved girls and women faced the threat of sexual abuse. Sometimes a white master or overseer would rape a woman in the fields or cabins. Sometimes he would lock a woman in a cabin with a male slave whose task was to impregnate her. Female slaves responded to such sexual abuse in different ways. Some seduced their master away from his wife. Others fiercely resisted the sexual advances—and were usually whipped or even killed for their disobedience. Some women killed their babies rather than see them grow up in slavery.

Women had fewer opportunities than men to escape slavery. Women tended to lack the physical strength and endurance required to run away and stay ahead of relentless pursuers. An even greater impediment was a mother's responsibility to her children. A few enslaved women did escape, but most of them learned to cope and resist within the confines of captivity. For them resistance to slavery took forms other than flight. Some engaged in truancy, hiding for several days at a time. Many feigned illness to avoid work. Others sabotaged food or crops or stole from owners. Several slave women started fires. A few killed their masters, most often by poison.

CELIA   Occasionally a single historical incident involving ordinary people can illustrate the web of laws and customs within a society. Such is the case of a teenage girl named Celia. In 1850, fourteen-year-old Celia was purchased by Robert Newsom, a prosperous, respected Missouri farmer who had six other slaves, all males. Newsom told his daughters that he had bought Celia to work as their domestic servant. In fact, however, the recently widowed Newsom wanted a sexual slave. After purchasing Celia, he raped the girl while taking her back to his farm. For the next five years, Newsom treated Celia as his mistress, even building her a brick cabin fifty yards from his house. During that time she gave birth to two children, presumably his offspring. By 1855 Celia had fallen in love with another slave, George, who demanded that she "quit the old man." Desperate for relief from her tormentor, Celia appealed to Newsom's two grown daughters, but they either could not or would not provide assistance.

Soon thereafter, on June 23, 1855, the sixty-five-year-old Newsom entered Celia's cabin, ignored her frantic appeals, and kept advancing until she struck and killed him with a large stick. When family members and neighbors realized that Newsom had disappeared, they questioned George, who eventually pointed to Celia. She finally confessed but refused to implicate George or anyone else in Newsom's death.

Celia was not allowed to testify at her trial because she was a slave. Her attorneys, all of them slaveholders, argued that the right of white women to defend themselves against sexual assault should be extended to enslaved women. The prevailing public opinion in the slave states, however, stressed that the white rape of a slave was not a crime. At worst, it was trespassing. But Newsom could not be accused of trespassing upon his own property, so the judge and jury, all white men, agreed with prevailing sentiment; they pronounced Celia guilty. On December 21, 1855, after two months of trials and futile appeals, Celia was hanged.

The grim story of Celia's brief life and abused condition highlights the skewed power structure in southern society before the Civil War. Celia bore a double burden, that of a slave and that of a woman living in a male-dominated society.

SLAVE REBELLIONS   Organized slave resistance was rare in the face of overwhelming white authority and firepower. In the nineteenth century only three major slave insurrections were attempted, two of which were betrayed before they got under way. In 1800 a slave named Gabriel on a plantation near Richmond hatched a plot involving perhaps 1,000 others to seize key points in the city and start a general slaughter of whites. Twenty-five of his conspirators were executed and ten others deported to the West Indies.

The Denmark Vesey plot in Charleston, discovered in 1822, was believed to be a plan of a free black to assault the white population, seize ships in the harbor, burn the city, and head for Santo Domingo. It never got off the ground. Instead, thirty-five supposed slave rebels were executed and thirty-four were deported. The city also responded by curtailing the liberties of free blacks. In Charleston, blacks outnumbered whites, and the ruling elite was hysterically determined to quash any slave uprising. In the aftermath of the Vesey trial and executions, the South Carolina legislature appropriated funds to build a new arsenal and citadel in Charleston to deter any future unrest.

Only the Nat Turner insurrection of August 1831 in rural Southampton County, Virginia, got beyond the planning stage. Turner, a black overseer, was also a self-anointed religious exhorter who professed a divine mission in leading a slave rebellion. The revolt began when a small group of slaves killed the adults and children in Turner's master's household and set off down the road, repeating the process at other farmhouses, where other slaves joined in. Before it ended, at least fifty-five whites had been killed. The militia killed large numbers of slaves indiscriminately in the process of putting down the rebels. Seventeen slaves were hanged.

Most slaves, however, did not openly rebel or run away. Instead, they more often retaliated against oppression by malingering or engaging in outright sabotage. Yet there were constraints on such behavior, for laborers would likely eat better on a prosperous plantation than on one they had reduced to poverty. And the shrewdest slaveholders knew that they would more likely benefit from offering rewards than from inflicting pain. Plantations based upon the profit motive fostered mutual dependency between slaves and their masters, as well as natural antagonism. And in an agrarian society in which personal relations counted for much, blacks could win concessions that moderated the harshness of slavery, permitting them a certain degree of individual and community development.

FORGING A SLAVE COMMUNITY To generalize about slavery is to miss elements of diversity from place to place and time to time. The experience was as varied as people are. Enslaved African Americans were certainly victims, but to stop at so obvious a perception would be to miss an important story of endurance, resilience, and achievement. If ever there was an effective melting pot in American history, it may have been that in which Africans with a variety of ethnic, linguistic, and tribal origins fused to form a new community and a new culture as African Americans. Slave culture incorporated many African elements, especially in areas with few whites. Among the Gullahs of the South Carolina and Georgia coast, for example, a researcher found as late as the 1940s more than 4,000 words still in use from the languages of twenty-one African tribes. Elements of African culture have thus survived, adapted, and interacted with those of the other cultures with which they came in contact.

SLAVE RELIGION AND FOLKLORE   Among the most important manifestations of slave culture was its dynamic religion, a mixture of African and Christian elements. In religion, slaves found both balm for the soul and release for their emotions. Most Africans brought with them to the Americas a concept of a Creator, or Supreme God, whom they could recognize in the Christian Jehovah, and lesser gods, whom they might identify with Christ, the Holy Ghost, and the saints, thereby reconciling their African beliefs with Christianity. Alongside the church they maintained beliefs in spirits (many of them benign), magic, and conjuring. Belief in magic is in fact a common human response to conditions of danger or helplessness.

Slaves found great comfort in religion. Masters sought to instill lessons of Christian humility and obedience, but African Americans identified their plight with that of the Israelites in Egypt or of the Christ who suffered as they did. And the ultimate hope of a better world gave solace in this one. Some slaveholders encouraged religious meetings among their slaves, many of them believing that an enslaved Christian would be a better slave. "Church was what they called it," one former slave remembered, "but all that [white] preacher talked about was for us slaves to obey our masters and not to lie and steal."

Such a manipulated Christianity alienated many African Americans, and most sought to create a genuine faith that spoke to their own spiritual and human needs. This required many of them to worship in secret, stealing away from their quarters to hold "bush meetings." A slave preacher explained that the "way in which we worshiped is almost indescribable. The singing helped provoke a certain ecstasy of emotion, clapping of hands, tossing of heads, which would continue without cessation about half an hour. The old house partook of the ecstasy; it rang with their jubilant shouts, and shook in all its joints."

Slaves found the Bible edifying in its tributes to the poor and oppressed, and they embraced its promise of salvation through Jesus. Likewise, the lyrics of religious "spirituals" helped slaves endure the strain of field labor and provided them with a musical code with which to express their own desire for freedom on earth. The former slave Frederick Douglass stressed that "slaves sing most when they are most unhappy," and spirituals offered them deliverance from their worldly woes.

African culture influenced a music of rhythmic complexity, forms of dance and body language, spirituals and secular songs, and folk tales. Among oppressed peoples, humor often becomes a means of psychological release, and there was a lively humor in the adapted West African trickster tales of rabbits, tortoises, and Anansi the spider—relatively weak creatures who outwit stronger animals. African-American folklore tended to be realistic in its images of wish fulfillment. Until after emancipation there were few stories of superhuman heroes in American folklore, except for tales about captive Africans who escaped slavery by flying home across the ocean.

THE SLAVE FAMILY   That so many slaves were able to sustain familial bonds is a testament to their resourcefulness and resilience. Slave marriages had no legal status, but slaveholders generally seem to have accepted marriage as a stabilizing influence on the plantation. Sometimes they performed the marriages themselves or had a minister celebrate a formal wedding. Whatever the formalities, the norm for the slave community, as for the white, was the nuclear family, with the father regarded

Plantation of J. J. Smith, Beaufort, South Carolina, 1862

Several generations of a family raised in slavery.

as head of the household. Most slave children were socialized by means of the nuclear family, which afforded some degree of independence from white influence. Childhood was short for slaves. At five or six years of age, children were given work assignments: they collected trash and firewood, picked cotton, scared away crows, weeded, and ran errands. One observer noted that this "army of juveniles are in full training to take the places" of adult workers. By age ten they were full-time field hands. Children were often sold to new masters. In Missouri an enslaved woman saw six of her seven children, aged one to eleven, separated from her and sold to six separate masters.

THE CULTURE OF THE SOUTHERN FRONTIER

There was substantial social and cultural diversity within the South during the three decades before the Civil War. The region known as the Old Southwest, for example, is perhaps the least well known. It includes the states and territories west of Georgia—Alabama, Mississippi, Arkansas, Louisiana, and Texas—as well as the frontier areas of Tennessee, Kentucky, and Florida.

Largely unsettled until the 1820s, this region bridged the South and the West, exhibiting characteristics of both areas. Raw and dynamic, filled with dangers, uncertainties, and opportunities, it served as a powerful magnet, luring thousands of settlers from Virginia, Georgia, and the Carolinas when the seaboard economy faltered during the 1820s and 1830s. The migrating southerners carved out farms, built churches, raised towns, and eventually brought culture and order to a raw frontier. As they took up new lives and occupations, the southern pioneers transplanted many practices and institutions from the coastal states. But they also fashioned a distinct new set of cultural values and social customs.

THE DECISION TO MIGRATE By the late 1820s the agricultural economy of the upper South was suffering from depressed commodity prices and soil exhaustion. Large farm families in particular struggled to provide each child with sufficient land and resources with which to subsist and maintain the family legacy. Thus the dwindling economic opportunities available in the Carolinas and Virginia led many to migrate to the Old Southwest. Like their northern counterparts, restless southern sons of the planter and professional elite wanted to make it on their own, to be "self-made men," economically self-reliant and socially independent.

Women were underrepresented among migrants to the Old Southwest. Few were interested in relocating to a disease-ridden, violent, and primitive territory. The new region did not offer them independence or adventure. In general, women more than men regretted the loss of kinship ties that migration entailed. To them a stable family life was more important than the prospect of material gain. As a Carolina woman prepared to depart for Alabama, she confided to a friend that "you *cannot* imagine the state of despair that I am in." Another said that "my heart bleeds within me" at the thought of the "many tender cords [of kinship] that are now severed forever." Others feared that life on the frontier would produce a "dissipation" of morals. They heard vivid stories of lawlessness, drunkenness, gambling, and miscegenation.

Enslaved blacks had many of the same reservations. Almost 1 million captive blacks were taken to the Old Southwest during the antebellum era, most of them in the 1830s. Like the white women, they feared the harsh working conditions and torpid heat and humidity of the new territory. They were also despondent at the breakup of their family ties.

THE JOURNEY AND SETTLEMENT Most of the migrants to the Old Southwest headed for the fertile lands of Alabama, Mississippi, and central Tennessee. The typical trek was about 500 miles. Once in the new territory the pioneers bought land that had been appropriated from Indians. Parcels of 640 acres sold for as little as $2 an acre; land in Alabama's fertile black belt brought higher prices. As cotton prices soared in the 1830s, aspiring planters bought as much land and as many slaves as possible. As a result, the average size of the farms and plantations in the Old Southwest was larger than that in the Carolinas and Virginia. But the Old Southwest was much more unhealthy than the Carolina Piedmont. The hot climate, contaminated water, and poor sanitation spawned an epidemic of disease. Malaria was especially common. Women and slaves in particular found their harsh new surroundings uninviting. Life in tents and rude log cabins made many newcomers yearn for the material comforts they had left behind. A male settler reported that "all the men is very well pleased but the women is not very satisfied."

A MASCULINE CULTURE The southern frontier environment prompted important changes in sex roles, and relations between men and women became even more inequitable. Young adult men indulged themselves in activities that would have generated disapproval in the more settled seaboard society. They drank, gambled, fought, and gratified their sexual desires. In 1834 a South Carolina migrant urged his brother to move west and join him because "you can live like a fighting cock with us." Alcohol consumption hit new heights. Most Old Southwest plantations had their own stills to manufacture whiskey, and alcoholism ravaged frontier families. Violence was also commonplace. A Virginian who settled in Mississippi fought in fourteen duels, killing ten men in the process. The frequency of fights, stabbings, shootings, and murders shocked visitors. So, too, did the propensity of white men to take sexual advantage of enslaved women. An Alabama woman married to a lawyer and politician was outraged by the "beastly passions" of the white men who fathered slave children and then sold them like livestock. She also recorded in her diary instances of men regularly beating their wives. Wives, it seems, had little choice but to endure the mistreatment because, as one woman wrote about a friend whose husband abused her, she was "wholly dependent upon his care."

Anti-slavery Movements

EARLY OPPOSITION TO SLAVERY   Scattered criticism of slavery developed in the North and the South in the decades after the Revolution, but the first organized emancipation movement appeared with the formation, in 1817, of the American Colonization Society, which proposed to return freed slaves to Africa. Its supporters included such prominent figures as James Madison, James Monroe, Henry Clay, John Marshall, and Daniel Webster. Some backed it because of their opposition to slavery, while others saw it as a way to bolster slavery by getting rid of potentially troublesome free blacks. Leaders of the free black community denounced it from the start. America, they stressed, was their native land. Nevertheless, in 1821, agents of the American Colonization Society acquired from local chieftains in West Africa a parcel of land that became the nucleus of a new country. In 1822 the first freed slaves arrived there, and twenty-five years later the society relinquished control to the Free and Independent Republic of Liberia. But given its uncertain purpose, the African colonization movement received only meager support from either anti-slavery or pro-slavery elements. In all only about 15,000 blacks migrated to Africa up to 1860, approximately 12,000 with the help of the Colonization Society. The number was infinitesimal compared with the number of slave births.

FROM GRADUALISM TO ABOLITIONISM   Meanwhile, in the early 1830s the anti-slavery movement took a new route. Its initial efforts to promote a gradual end to slavery by prohibiting slavery in the new western territories and encouraging manumission gave way to demands for immediate abolition everywhere. In 1831 William Lloyd Garrison began publication in Boston of a new anti-slavery newspaper, the *Liberator.* Garrison, who rose from poverty in Newburyport, Massachusetts, had been apprenticed to a newspaper publisher and had edited a number of anti-slavery papers but had grown impatient with the strategy of moderation. In the first issue of the *Liberator,* he renounced "the popular but pernicious doctrine of gradual emancipation" and vowed, "I will be as harsh as truth, and as uncompromising as justice."

William Lloyd Garrison

Garrison was a vocal abolitionist and advocate for immediate emancipation.

Garrison's militancy elicited outraged retorts from slaveholders. Their angry defense gave the *Liberator* more exposure than anything the newspaper actually said. In the South literate blacks would more likely encounter Garrison's ideas in the local newspapers than in the few copies of the *Liberator* that found their way to them. Slaveholders' outrage mounted after the Nat Turner insurrection in August 1831. Garrison, they assumed, bore a large part of the responsibility for the affair, but there is no evidence that Nat Turner had ever heard of him, and Garrison said that he had not a single subscriber in the South at the time. What is more, however violent his language, Garrison was a pacifist, opposed to the use of force.

During the 1830s Garrison became the nation's most fervent, principled, and unyielding foe of slavery. In 1831 he and his followers set up the New England Anti-Slavery Society. Two years later two wealthy New York merchants, Arthur and Lewis Tappan, founded the American Anti-Slavery Society with the help of Garrison and others. They hoped to exploit the publicity generated when the British anti-slavery movement, also in 1833, induced Parliament to end slavery, and compensate slaveholders, throughout the British Empire.

The American Anti-Slavery Society sought to convince people "that Slaveholding is a heinous crime in the sight of God, and that the duty, safety, and best interests of all concerned, require its *immediate abandonment,* without expatriation." The society went beyond the issue of emancipation to argue that blacks should "share an equality with the whites, of civil and religious privileges." The group issued a barrage of propaganda for its cause, including periodicals, tracts, agents, lecturers, organizers, and fund-raisers.

A SPLIT IN THE MOVEMENT   As the anti-slavery movement spread, debates over tactics intensified. The Garrisonians, mainly New Englanders, were radicals who felt that American society had been corrupted from top to bottom and needed universal reform. Garrison embraced just about every important reform movement of the day: abolition, temperance, pacifism, and women's rights. He also championed equal social and legal rights for African Americans. He broke with the organized church, which to his mind was in league with slavery. The federal government was all the more so. The Constitution, he said, was "a covenant with death and an agreement with hell." Garrison therefore refused to vote.

Other reformers were less dogmatic. They saw American society as fundamentally sound and concentrated on purging it of slavery. Garrison struck them as an impractical fanatic. A showdown came in 1840 on the issue of women's rights. Women had joined the abolition movement from the start, but largely in groups without men. Then the activities of the Grimké sisters brought the issue of women's rights to center stage.

Sarah and Angelina Grimké, daughters of a prominent South Carolina slaveholding family, had broken with their parents and moved north to embrace Quakerism, abolitionism, feminism, and other reforms. Having attended a New York training conference for anti-slavery activists organized by Theodore Weld (whom Angelina later married), they set out speaking first to audiences of women and eventually to both men and women.

Their behavior inspired the Congregational clergy of Massachusetts to chastise the sisters for engaging in unfeminine activity. The chairman of the Connecticut Anti-Slavery Society declared, "No woman shall speak or vote where I am a moderator." Catharine Beecher reminded the activist sisters that women occupied "a subordinate relation in society to the other sex" and should therefore limit their activities to the "domestic and social circle." Angelina Grimké stoutly rejected the conventional arguments. "It is a woman's right," she insisted, "to have a voice in all laws and regulations by which she is to be governed, whether in church or in state."

The debate over the role of women in the anti-slavery movement crackled and simmered until it finally exploded in 1840. At the Anti-Slavery Society's meeting that year, the Garrisonians insisted on the right of women to participate equally in the organization and carried their point. They did not commit the group to women's rights in any other way, however. Contrary opinion, mainly from the Tappans' New York group, ranged from outright anti-feminism to the fear of scattering shots over too many re-forms. The New Yorkers thus broke away to form the American and Foreign Anti-Slavery Society.

BLACK ANTI-SLAVERY ACTIVITY   White male abolitionists also balked at granting full recognition to black abolitionists of either sex. Often blindly patronizing, white abolitionists expected free blacks to take a back-seat in the movement. Despite the invitation to form separate groups, African-American leaders were active in the white societies from the begin-ning. Three attended the organizational meeting of the American Anti-Slavery Society in 1833, and some—notably former slaves, who could speak from firsthand experience—became outstanding agents for the movement. Garrison pronounced such men as Henry Bibb and William Wells Brown, both escapees from Kentucky, and Frederick Douglass, who fled Maryland, "the best qualified to address the public on the subject of slavery."

Douglass, blessed with an imposing frame and a simple eloquence, became the best-known black man in America. "I appear before the immense assembly this evening as a thief and a robber," he told a Massachusetts group in 1842. "I stole this head, these limbs, this body from my master, and ran off with them." Fearful of capture after publishing his *Narrative of the Life of Frederick Douglass* (1845), he left for an extended lecture tour of the British Isles, returning two years later with enough money to purchase his freedom. He then started an abolitionist newspaper for blacks, the *North Star,* in Rochester, New York.

Douglass's *Narrative* was but the best known among hundreds of such accounts. Escapees often made it out of slavery on their own—Douglass borrowed a pass from a free black seaman—but many were aided by the Underground Railroad, which grew into a vast system that concealed run-aways and spirited them to freedom, often over the Canadian border. Levi Coffin, a North Carolina Quaker who moved to Cincinnati and helped many fugitives, was the reputed president. Actually, there seems to have been more spontaneity than system to the matter, and blacks contributed more than was credited in the legend. A few intrepid refugees actually returned to the slave states to organize escapes. Harriet Tubman, the most celebrated, ven-tured back nineteen times.

Equally courageous was the black abolitionist Sojourner Truth. Born to slaves in New York in 1797, she was given the name Isabella but renamed herself in 1843 after experiencing a mystical conversation with God, who told her "to travel up and down the land" preaching against the sins of slav-ery. She did just that, crisscrossing the country during the 1840s and 1850s, exhorting audiences to support abolition and women's rights. Having been a

Frederick Douglass (left) and Sojourner Truth (right)

Leading abolitionists.

slave until freed by a New York law in 1828, Sojourner Truth was able to speak with conviction and knowledge about the evils of the "peculiar institution" and the inequality of women. As she told a gathering of the Women's Rights Convention in Ohio in 1851, "I have plowed, and planted, and gathered into barns, and no man could head me—and ar'n't I a woman? I have borne thirteen children, and seen 'em mos' all sold off into slavery, and when I cried out with a mother's grief, none but Jesus heard—and ar'n't I a woman?"

Through such compelling testimony, Sojourner Truth demonstrated the powerful intersection of abolitionism and women's rights agitation, and in the process she tapped the distinctive energies that women brought to reformist causes. "If the first woman God ever made was strong enough to turn the world upside down all alone," she concluded in her address to the Ohio gathering, "these women together ought to be able to turn it back, and get it right side up again!"

REACTIONS TO ABOLITION   Even in the North, abolitionists had to face down hostile crowds who disliked blacks or found anti-slavery agitation bad for business. In 1837 a mob in Alton, Illinois, killed the anti-slavery editor Elijah P. Lovejoy, giving the movement a martyr to the causes of both abolition and freedom of the press.

In the 1830s abolition took a political turn, focusing at first on Congress. One shrewd strategy was to deluge Congress with petitions for abolition in the District of Columbia. Most such petitions were presented by former president John Quincy Adams, elected to the House from Massachusetts in 1830. In 1836, however, the House adopted a rule to lay abolition petitions automatically on the table, in effect ignoring them. Adams, "Old Man Eloquent," stubbornly fought this "gag rule" as a violation of the First Amendment and hounded its supporters until the rule was finally repealed in 1844.

Meanwhile, in 1840, the year of the schism in the anti-slavery movement, a small group of abolitionists organized a national convention in Albany, New York, and launched the Liberty party, with James G. Birney, onetime slaveholder of Alabama and Kentucky, as its candidate for president. Birney, converted to abolitionism by Theodore Weld, had moved to Ohio and in 1837 had become executive secretary of the American Anti-Slavery Society. In the 1840 election he polled only 7,000 votes, but in 1844 he won 60,000, and from that time forth an anti-slavery party contested every national election until Abraham Lincoln won the presidency in 1860.

THE DEFENSE OF SLAVERY James Birney was but one of several southerners propelled north during the 1830s by the South's growing hostility to emancipationist ideas. The anti-slavery movement in the upper South had its last stand in 1831–1832, when the Virginia legislature debated a plan of gradual emancipation and African colonization, then rejected it by a vote of seventy-three to fifty-eight. Thereafter leaders of southern thought worked out an elaborate intellectual defense of slavery, presenting it as a positive good.

The evangelical Christian churches, which had widely condemned slavery at one time, gradually turned pro-slavery, at least in the South. Biblical passages were cited to buttress slaveholding. Ministers of all denominations joined in the argument. Had not the patriarchs of the Hebrew Bible held people in bondage? Had not Saint Paul advised servants to obey their masters and told a fugitive servant to return to his master? And had not Jesus remained silent on the subject, at least so far as the Gospels reported his words? In 1843–1844 disputes over slavery split two great denominations along sectional lines and led to the formation of the Southern Baptist Convention and the Methodist Episcopal Church, South. Presbyterians, the only other major denomination to split, did not do so until the Civil War.

A more fundamental feature of the pro-slavery argument stressed the racial inferiority of blacks. Other arguments took a more "practical" view. Not only was slavery profitable, one argument went, but it was also a matter of social necessity. Thomas Jefferson, for instance, in his *Notes on the State of Virginia* (1785), had argued that whites and emancipated slaves could not live together without the risk of a race war triggered by the recollection of past injustices. What is more, it seemed clear to some defenders of slavery that blacks could not be expected to work under conditions of freedom. They were too shiftless and improvident, the argument went, and in freedom would be a danger to themselves as well as to others. White workers, on the other hand, feared the competition for jobs if slaves were freed.

A new argument on behalf of slavery arose in the late 1850s. The Virginian George Fitzhugh and others began to defend slavery as better for workers than freely chosen employment because it provided them with security in sickness and old age, unlike the "wage slavery" of northern industry, which exploited workers for profit and then cast them away. Within one generation such ideas had triumphed in the white South over the post-Revolutionary apology for slavery as an evil bequeathed by the nation's forefathers. Opponents of the orthodox faith in slavery as a positive good were either silenced or exiled. Freedom of thought in the Old South had become a victim of the region's growing obsession with the preservation and expansion of slavery—at all costs.

MAKING CONNECTIONS

- The abolition movement never represented the majority of northerners. As Chapter 16 shows, however, by the end of the 1850s most voters in the North supported the idea of limiting the expansion of slavery westward, if not the abolition of it in the southern states.

- The Civil War brought great changes to southerners, both black and white. Chapter 17 describes the effect of the war on southern society.

- There are striking contrasts between the Old South of this chapter and the New South of Chapter 19.

FURTHER READING

Those interested in the problem of discerning myth and reality in the southern experience should consult William R. Taylor's *Cavalier and Yankee: The Old South and American National Character* (1961). Two recent efforts to understand the mind of the Old South and its defense of slavery are Eugene D. Genovese's *The Slaveholders' Dilemma: Freedom and Progress in Southern Conservative Thought, 1820–1860* (1992) and Eric H. Walther's *The Fire-Eaters* (1992).

Contrasting analyses of the plantation system are Eugene D. Genovese's *The World the Slaveholders Made: Two Essays in Interpretation* (1988) and Gavin Wright's *The Political Economy of the Cotton South: Households, Markets, and Wealth in the Nineteenth Century* (1978). Stephanie McCurry's *Masters of Small Worlds: Yeoman Households, Gender Relations, and the Political Culture of the Antebellum South Carolina Low Country* (1995) greatly enriches our understanding of southern households, religion, and political culture.

Other essential works on southern culture and society include Bertram Wyatt-Brown's *Honor and Violence in the Old South* (1986), Elizabeth Fox-Genovese's *Within the Plantation Household: Black and White Women of the Old South* (1988), Catherine Clinton's *Plantation Mistress: Woman's World in the Old South* (1982), Joan E. Cashin's *A Family Venture: Men and Women on the Southern Frontier* (1991), and Theodore Rosengarten's *Tombee: Portrait of a Cotton Planter* (1986).

A provocative discussion of the psychology of African-American slavery can be found in Stanley M. Elkins's *Slavery: A Problem in American Institutional and Intellectual Life*, 3rd ed. (1976). John W. Blassingame's *The Slave Community: Plantation Life in the Antebellum South*, rev. and enlarged ed. (1979), Eugene D. Genovese's *Roll, Jordan, Roll: The World the Slaves Made* (1974), and Herbert G. Gutman's *The Black Family in Slavery and Freedom, 1750–1925* (1976) all stress the theme of a persisting and identifiable slave culture. On the question of slavery's profitability, see Robert William Fogel and Stanley L. Engerman's *Time on the Cross: The Economics of American Negro Slavery* (1974).

Other works on slavery include Lawrence W. Levine's *Black Culture and Black Consciousness: Afro-American Folk Thought from Slavery to Freedom* (1977); Albert J. Raboteau's *Slave Religion: The "Invisible Institution" in the Antebellum South* (1978); *We Are Your Sisters*, edited by Dorothy Sterling (1984); Deborah Gray White's *Ar'n't I a Woman? Female Slaves in the Plantation South* (1999); and Joel Williamson's *The Crucible of Race: Black-White Relations in the American South since Emancipation* (1984). Charles Joyner's

Down by the Riverside: A South Carolina Slave Community (1984) offers a vivid reconstruction of one community.

Useful surveys of abolitionism include James Brewer Stewart's *Holy Warriors: The Abolitionists and American Slavery* (1997) and Julie Roy Jeffrey's *The Great Silent Army of Abolitionism: Ordinary Women in the Antislavery Movement* (1998). On William Lloyd Garrison, see Henry Mayer's *All on Fire: William Lloyd Garrison and the Abolition of Slavery* (1998). For the pro-slavery argument as it developed in the South, see Larry E. Tise's *Proslavery: A History of the Defense of Slavery in America, 1701–1840* (1987) and James Oakes's *The Ruling Race: A History of American Slaveholders* (1982). The problems southerners had in justifying slavery are explored in Kenneth S. Greenberg's *Masters and Statesmen: The Political Culture of American Slavery* (1985).

16

THE CRISIS OF UNION

FOCUS QUESTIONS

- How did slavery become increasingly politicized?
- How did the Compromise of 1850 and the Kansas-Nebraska Act reflect sectional tensions?
- What led to the rise of a third-generation party system: Republicans and Democrats?
- What events led to the secession of the southern states?

To answer these questions and access additional review material, please visit www.wwnorton.com/studyspace.

John C. Calhoun of South Carolina and Ralph Waldo Emerson of Massachusetts had little in common, but both men sensed in the Mexican War the omens of a national disaster. Mexico was "the forbidden fruit; the penalty of eating it would be to subject our institutions to political death," Calhoun warned. "The United States will conquer Mexico," Emerson conceded, "but it will be as the man swallows the arsenic. . . . Mexico will poison us." Wars, as both men knew, have a way of corrupting ideals and breeding new wars, often in unforeseen ways. America's winning of the war with Mexico gave rise to quarrels over newly acquired land, quarrels that set in motion a series of disputes that led to a crisis of union.

SLAVERY IN THE TERRITORIES

THE WILMOT PROVISO The Mexican War was less than three months old when the seeds of a new political conflict began to sprout. On August 8, 1846, a freshman Democratic congressman from Pennsylvania, David Wilmot, delivered a provocative speech to the House in which he endorsed the annexation of Texas as a slave state. But slavery had come to an end in the rest of Mexico, and if new Mexican territory should be acquired, Wilmot declared, "God forbid that we should be the means of planting this institution upon it." Drawing upon the words of the Northwest Ordinance, he proposed that in any additional land acquired from Mexico, "neither slavery nor involuntary servitude shall ever exist."

The Wilmot Proviso politicized the festering debate over slavery once and for all. For a generation, since the Missouri controversy of 1819–1821, the issue had been lurking in the wings. Now, for the next two decades, it would never be far from center stage. The House adopted the Wilmot Proviso, but the Senate balked. When Congress reconvened in December 1846, President Polk, who believed a debate over slavery had no place in the conduct of the war in Mexico and dismissed the proviso as "mischievous and foolish," prevailed upon Wilmot to withhold his amendment to any effort to annex Mexican territory, but by then others were ready to take up the cause. When a New York congressman revived the proviso, he signaled a revolt by the Van Burenite Democrats in concert with the antislavery forces of the North. Once again the House approved the amendment; again the Senate refused to do so. In one form or another, however, Wilmot's idea kept cropping up. Abraham Lincoln later recalled that during his one term as a congressman, in 1847–1849, he voted for it "as good as forty times."

John Calhoun, meanwhile, devised a thesis to counter the proviso, which he set before the Senate on February 19, 1847. Calhoun began by reasserting his pride in being a slaveholding cotton planter. He made no apologies for holding slaves and insisted that slaveholders had an unassailable right to take their slaves into any territories acquired by the United States. Wilmot's effort to exclude slaves from Mexican territories, Calhoun declared, would violate the Fifth Amendment, which forbids Congress to deprive any person of life, liberty, or property without due process of the law, and slaves were property. By this clever stroke of logic, Calhoun took that basic guarantee of liberty, the Bill of Rights, and turned it into a basic guarantee of slavery. The irony was not lost on his critics, but the point became established southern dogma—echoed by his colleagues and formally endorsed by the Virginia legislature.

Senator Thomas Hart Benton of Missouri, himself a slaveholder but also a Jacksonian nationalist eager to calm sectional tensions, found in Calhoun's stance a set of abstractions "leading to no result." Wilmot and Calhoun between them, he said, had fashioned a pair of shears. Neither blade alone would cut very well, but joined together they could sever the ties of union.

POPULAR SOVEREIGNTY Senator Benton and others sought to bypass the brewing conflict over slavery in the new territories. President Polk was among the first to suggest extending the Missouri Compromise, dividing free and slave territory at the latitude of 36°30′ all the way to the Pacific Ocean. Senator Lewis Cass of Michigan suggested that the citizens of a territory "regulate their own internal concerns in their own way," like the citizens of a state. Such an approach would combine the merits of expediency and democracy. It would take the contentious issue of slavery in new territories out of the national arena and put it in the hands of those directly affected.

Popular sovereignty, or "squatter sovereignty," as the idea was also called, appealed to many Americans. Without directly challenging the slaveholders' access to the new lands, it promised to open them quickly to nonslaveholding farmers, who would almost surely dominate the territories. With this tacit understanding the idea prospered in the Midwest, where Stephen A. Douglas of Illinois and other prominent Democrats soon endorsed it.

When the Mexican War ended in 1848, the question of slavery in the new territories was no longer hypothetical. Nobody doubted that Oregon would become a free-soil (nonslave) territory, but it, too, was drawn into the growing controversy. Territorial status, pending since 1846, was delayed for Oregon because its provisional government had excluded slavery. To concede that provision would imply an authority drawn from the powers of Congress, since a territory was created by Congress. After much wrangling, an exhausted Congress let Oregon organize without slavery but postponed a decision on the Southwest. President Polk signed the bill on the principle that Oregon was north of 36°30′, the latitude that had formed the basis of the Missouri Compromise in 1820.

Polk had promised to serve only one term; exhausted and having accomplished his major goals, he refused to run again. At the 1848 Democratic convention, Lewis Cass won the presidential nomination, but the party refused to endorse Cass's "squatter sovereignty" plan. Instead, it simply denied the power of Congress to interfere with slavery in the states and criticized all efforts by anti-slavery activists to bring the question before Congress. The Whigs devised an even more artful shift. Once again, as in 1840, they passed over their party leader, Henry Clay, this time for a general, Zachary Taylor, whose fame had grown since the Battle of Buena Vista. Taylor was a resident of Louisiana who held more than 100 slaves, an apolitical figure who had never voted in a national election. Once again, as in 1840, the Whig party adopted no platform at all. Stunned that his party had deserted him in favor of a "wholly incompetent" general with no political experience, the crestfallen yet still vain Henry Clay concluded that the Whigs were on the verge of dissolution.

THE FREE-SOIL COALITION   But the anti-slavery impulse was not easily squelched. Congressman David Wilmot had raised a standard for resisting the expansion of slavery, to which a broad coalition could rally. Americans who shied away from abolition could readily endorse the exclusion of slavery from the western territories. The Northwest Ordinance and the Missouri Compromise supplied honored precedents. Free soil in the new territories, therefore, rather than abolition in the slave states, became the rallying point—and also the name of a new political party.

Three major groups entered the free-soil coalition: rebellious northern Democrats, anti-slavery Whigs, and members of the Liberty party, which dated from 1840. Disaffection among the Democrats centered in New York, where the Van Burenite "Barnburners" seized upon the free-soil issue as a moral imperative. Free-soil principles among the Whigs centered in Massachusetts, where a group of "Conscience" Whigs battled the "Cotton" Whigs, a coalition of northern businessmen and southern planters. Conscience Whigs rejected the slaveholding nominee of their party, Zachary Taylor.

In 1848 these groups—Van Burenite Democrats, Conscience Whigs, and followers of the Liberty party—organized the Free-Soil party at a convention at Buffalo, New York, and nominated Martin Van Buren for president. The platform of the Free-Soil party endorsed the Wilmot Proviso's declaration that slavery would not be allowed in the new territories acquired from Mexico. The Free-Soil party entered the campaign with the catchy slogan of "free soil, free speech, free labor, and free men." The new party infuriated the Democrat John Calhoun and other southerners committed to the expansion of slavery. Calhoun called Van Buren a "bold, unscrupulous and vindictive demagogue." Other Democrats, both northern and southern, denounced

Van Buren as a traitor and a hypocrite, while the New Yorker's supporters praised his service as a "champion of freedom."

The impact of the new Free-Soil party on the election was mixed. The Free-Soilers split the Democratic vote enough to throw New York to the Whig Zachary Taylor, and they split the Whig vote enough to give Ohio to the Democrat Lewis Cass, but Van Buren's total of 291,000 votes was far below the totals of 1,361,000 for Taylor and 1,222,000 for Cass. Taylor won with 163 to 127 electoral votes, and both major parties retained a national following. Taylor took eight slave states and seven free; Cass, just the opposite: seven slave and eight free.

THE CALIFORNIA GOLD RUSH Meanwhile, a new dimension had been introduced into the vexing question of the western territories: on January 24, 1848, gold was discovered in California. Word spread quickly, and the California gold rush constituted the greatest mass migration in American history. During 1849 some 80,000 gold seekers reached California,

California News (1850) by **William Sidney Mount**

During the California gold rush, San Francisco quickly became a cosmopolitan city as the population increased almost fiftyfold in a few months.

half of them Americans, and by 1854 the number would top 300,000. The "forty-niners" included people from every social class and every state and territory, as well as slaves brought by their masters. Most "forty-niners" went overland; the rest, by ship. After touring the gold region, the territorial governor reported that the influx of newcomers had "entirely changed the character of Upper California." The new Californians quickly reduced the 14,000 Mexicans to a minority, and sporadic conflicts with the Indians of the Sierra Nevada foothills decimated California's Native Americans.

Unlike the land-hungry pioneers who traversed the overland trails, the miners were mostly unmarried young men representing quite different ethnic and cultural backgrounds. Few were interested in establishing a permanent settlement. They wanted to strike it rich and return home. The mining camps in California's valleys and canyons and along its creek beds thus sprang up like mushrooms and disappeared almost as rapidly. As soon as rumors of a new strike made the rounds, miners converged on the area, joined soon thereafter by a hodgepodge of merchants and camp followers. When no more gold could be found, they picked up and moved on.

The mining shantytowns were disorderly, unsanitary, and often lawless communities; vigilante justice prevailed, and leisure time revolved around

Gold miners, ca. 1850

Daguerreotype of miners panning for gold at their claim.

saloons and gambling halls. One newcomer reported that "in the short space of twenty-four days, we have had murders, fearful accidents, bloody deaths, a mob, whippings, a hanging, an attempt at suicide, and a fatal duel." Within six months of arriving in California in 1849, one in every five of the gold seekers was dead. The goldfields and mining towns were so dangerous that insurance companies refused to provide coverage. The town of Marysville had seventeen murders in one week. Seemingly everyone carried weapons—usually pistols or bowie knives. Suicides were common, and disease was rampant. Cholera and scurvy plagued every camp.

Women were as rare in the mining camps as liquor was abundant. In 1850 less than 8 percent of California's population was female, and even fewer women hazarded life in the camps. Those who did could demand a premium for their work as cooks, laundresses, entertainers, and prostitutes. In the polyglot mining camps white Americans often looked with disdain upon the Latinos and Chinese, who were most often employed as wage laborers to help in the panning process, separating gold from sand and gravel. But the white Americans focused their contempt on the Indians. In the mining culture it was not a crime to kill Indians or work them to death. American miners tried several times to outlaw foreigners in the mining country but had to settle for a tax on foreign miners, which was applied to Mexicans in express violation of the treaty ending the Mexican War.

CALIFORNIA STATEHOOD   As civic leaders emerged within the burgeoning California population, they grew increasingly frustrated by the inability of military authorities to maintain law and order. In this context the new president, Zachary Taylor, thought he saw an ideal opportunity to use California statehood to end the stalemate in Congress brought about by the slavery issue.

Born in Virginia and raised in Kentucky, Taylor had been a soldier most of his life. Constantly on the move, he had acquired a home in Louisiana and a plantation in Mississippi. Southern Whigs had rallied to his support, expecting him to uphold the cause of slavery. Instead, he turned out to be a southern man who upheld Union principles and had no use for John Calhoun's proslavery abstractions. Innocent of politics Taylor might be, but Old Rough-and-Ready had a soldier's practical mind. Slavery should be upheld where it existed, he felt, but he had little patience with abstract theories about slavery in territories where it probably could not exist. Why not make California and New Mexico free states immediately, he reasoned, and bypass the whole issue?

But the Californians, in need of organized government, were ahead of him. By December 1849, without consulting Congress, California had put a free-state government into operation. New Mexico responded more slowly, but by 1850 Americans there had adopted a free-state constitution. The Mormons around Salt Lake, meanwhile, drafted a basic law for the state of Deseret, which embraced most of the Mexican cession, including a slice of the coast from Los Angeles to San Diego. In his annual message on December 4, 1849, President Taylor endorsed immediate statehood for California and enjoined Congress to avoid injecting slavery into the issue of statehood. The new Congress, however, was in no mood for simple solutions.

THE COMPROMISE OF 1850

The spotlight fell on the Senate, where a stellar cast—the triumvirate of Henry Clay, John Calhoun, and Daniel Webster with William Seward, Stephen A. Douglas, Jefferson Davis, and Thomas Hart Benton in supporting roles—enacted one of the great dramas of American politics: the Compromise of 1850. Seventy-three-year-old Henry Clay had become so concerned about the fate of the Union that he had come out of retirement to return to the Senate. After arriving in Washington, D.C., he observed that the "feeling for disunion among some intemperate Southern politicians is stronger than I supposed it could be." At the end of 1849, southerners fumed over President Taylor's efforts to bring California and New Mexico into the union as free states. After all, some of them reasoned, southerners had fought disproportionately in the Mexican War; their concerns about the expansion of slavery should be given more weight. Other southerners demanded a federal fugitive slave law that would require northern authorities to arrest and return runaways. For their part anti-slavery Whigs in the North called for the end of the slave trade throughout the United States and the end of slavery itself in the District of Columbia. Irate southerners responded by threatening secession. "I avow before this House and country, and in the presence of the living God," shouted Robert Toombs of Georgia, "that if by your legislation you seek to drive us [slaveholders] from the territories of California and New Mexico . . . and to abolish slavery in this District . . . *I am for disunion.*"

By 1850 the United States was facing its greatest political crisis, and Henry Clay, who for all his compulsive desire to be president, remained at heart devoted to the preservation of the Union and so was willing to alienate southern supporters by once again assuming the role of Great

Compromiser, which he had played in the Missouri and nullification controversies.

THE GREAT DEBATE   In January 1850, having gained the support of Daniel Webster, Clay presented to Congress a package of eight resolutions in ways that would settle the "controversy between the free and slave States." His proposals represented what he called a "great national scheme of compromise and harmony." He proposed to (1) admit California as a free state, (2) organize the territories of New Mexico and Utah without restrictions on slavery, allowing the residents to decide the issue for themselves, (3) deny Texas its extreme claim to much of New Mexico, (4) compensate Texas by having the federal government pay the pre-annexation Texas debts, (5) uphold slavery in the District of Columbia, but (6) abolish the slave trade across its boundaries, (7) adopt a more effective federal fugitive slave act, and (8) deny congressional authority to interfere with the interstate slave trade. His complex cluster of proposals became in substance the Compromise of 1850, but only after a prolonged debate, the most celebrated, if not the greatest, in the annals of Congress.

On February 5–6 Clay addressed a Senate chamber overflowing with spectators eager to hear the "lion of the day" speak. He did not disappoint the expectant audience. Although desperately ill, he summoned all his eloquence in a defense of the proposed settlement. In the interest of "peace, concord and harmony," he called for an end to "passion, passion—party, party—and intemperance." Otherwise, continued sectional bickering would lead to a "furious, bloody" civil war. To avoid such a catastrophe, he stressed, California should be admitted as a free state on the terms that its own citizens had approved. He begged the opposing sides "by all of their love of liberty—by all their veneration for their ancestors—by all their regard for posterity . . . to pause—solemnly to pause—at the edge of the precipice, before the fearful and disastrous leap is taken into the yawning abyss below." No sooner had Clay finished than a crowd rushed forward to shake his hand and kiss his cheek.

The debate continued sporadically through February, with the Texan Sam Houston rising to the support of Clay's compromise and Mississippi's Jefferson Davis defending the slavery cause on every point. President Taylor believed that slavery in the South could best be protected if southerners avoided injecting the issue into the dispute over new territories. Unlike John Calhoun he did not believe the new western territories were suitable for slave-based agriculture. Because in his mind the issue of bringing slaves into the territories was moot, he continued to urge Congress to admit California and New Mexico without reference to slavery. But few others embraced such a simple solution. In fact, a rising chorus of southern leaders, labeled Ultras, threatened to secede from the Union if slavery were not allowed in California.

On March 4 John Calhoun left his sickbed to sit in the Senate chamber, a gaunt figure draped in a black cloak, as a colleague read his defiant speech. "I have, Senators, believed from the first that the agitation of the subject of slavery would, if not prevented by some timely and effective measure, end in disunion," said James Mason on Calhoun's behalf. Neither Clay's compromise nor Taylor's efforts would serve the Union, he added. The South simply needed an acceptance of its rights: equality of treatment in the territories, the return of fugitive slaves, and some guarantee of "an equilibrium between the sections."

Three days later Calhoun returned to the Senate to hear Daniel Webster. The "Godlike Daniel" no longer possessed the thunderous voice of his youth, nor did his shrinking frame project its once magisterial aura, but he remained a formidable presence. He chose as the central theme of his three-hour speech the preservation of the Union: "I wish to speak today, not as a Massachusetts man, not as a Northern man, but as an American. . . . I speak today for the preservation of the Union." The geographic extent of slavery had already been determined, he insisted, by the Northwest Ordinance, by the Missouri Compromise, and in the new lands by the law of nature. The Wilmot Proviso was superfluous: "I would not take pains to reaffirm an ordinance of nature nor to re-enact the will of God." Both northerners and southerners, to be sure, had legitimate grievances: on the one hand the excesses of "infernal fanatics and abolitionists" in the North and on the other hand southern efforts to expand slavery and heap southern slurs on northern workingmen. But "Secession! Peaceable secession! Sir, your eyes and mine are never destined to see that miracle." Instead of looking into such "caverns of darkness," let "men enjoy the fresh air of liberty and union. Let them look to a more hopeful future."

Webster's March 7 speech was a supreme gesture of conciliation, and the Massachusetts senator had knowingly brought down a storm upon his head. New England anti-slavery leaders lambasted this new "Benedict Arnold" who had betrayed his region. On March 11 William H. Seward, the freshman Whig senator from New York, gave the anti-slavery reply to Webster. He declared that compromise with slavery was "radically wrong and essentially vicious." There was, he said, "a higher law than the Constitution" that demanded the abolition of slavery.

In mid-April a select committee of thirteen senators bundled Clay's suggestions (insofar as they concerned the Mexican cession) into one comprehensive bill, and presented it to the Senate early in May. President Taylor continued to oppose Clay's compromise, and their feud threatened to split the Whig party wide open. As the weeks and months passed, Clay worked tirelessly to convince his opponents that compromise by all parties was essential to preserving the Union. Yet as the stalemate continued and the atmosphere in Congress became more fevered and violent, he grew frustrated and peevish. "Mr. Clay with all his talents," Daniel Webster told a friend, "is not a good leader, for want of temper. He is irritable, impatient, and occasionally overbearing; & he drives people off." Another crisis loomed near the end of June when word came that New Mexico was applying for statehood, with President Taylor's support and on the basis of boundaries that conflicted with the Texas claim to the east bank of the Rio Grande.

TOWARD A COMPROMISE   On July 4, 1850, supporters of the Union staged a grand rally at the base of the unfinished Washington Monument. Zachary Taylor went to hear the speeches, lingering in the hot sun and humid heat. Five days later he died of a gastrointestinal affliction possibly caused by tainted food or water.

Taylor's sudden death strengthened the chances of a congressional compromise. The soldier in the White House was replaced by a politician, Vice President Millard Fillmore. The son of a poor upstate New York farmer, Fillmore had succeeded despite few opportunities or advantages. Largely self-educated, he had made his own way in the profession of law and the rough-and-tumble world of New York politics. Experience had taught him caution, which some interpreted as indecision, but he had made up his mind to support Henry Clay's compromise and had so informed Taylor. It was a strange switch: Taylor, the Louisiana slaveholder, had been ready to make war on his native region; Fillmore, who southerners thought was opposed to slavery, was ready to make peace.

Millard Fillmore

His support of the Compromise of 1850 helped the Union muddle through the crisis.

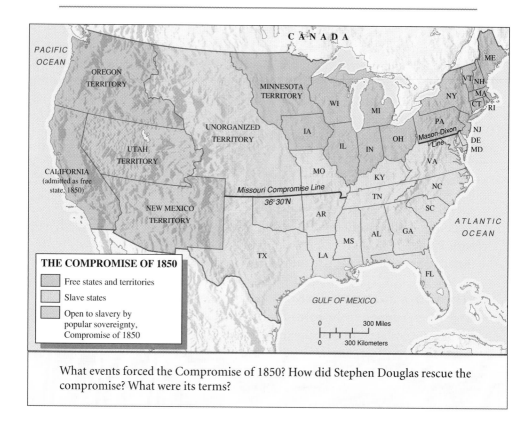

THE COMPROMISE OF 1850

- Free states and territories
- Slave states
- Open to slavery by popular sovereignty, Compromise of 1850

What events forced the Compromise of 1850? How did Stephen Douglas rescue the compromise? What were its terms?

At this point the young senator Stephen A. Douglas of Illinois, a rising star in the Democratic party, rescued Clay's faltering compromise. Short and stocky, brash and brilliant, Douglas was known as the Little Giant. His strategy was in fact the same one Clay had used to pass the Missouri Compromise thirty years before. Reasoning that nearly everybody objected to one or another provision of Clay's "comprehensive scheme," Douglas worked on the principle of breaking it up into six (later five) separate measures. Few members were prepared to vote for all of them, but from different elements Douglas hoped to mobilize a majority for each.

It worked. By September 20 President Fillmore had signed the last of the measures into law. The Union had muddled through, and the settlement went down in history as the Compromise of 1850. For a time it defused an explosive situation, settled each of the major points at issue, and postponed secession and civil war for ten years.

In its final version, the Compromise of 1850 included the following elements: *First,* California entered the Union as a free state, ending forever the old balance of free and slave states. *Second*, the Texas–New Mexico Act made New Mexico a territory and set the Texas boundary at its present location. In return for giving up its claims east of the Rio Grande, Texas was paid $10 million, which secured payment of the state's debt. *Third*, the Utah Act set up the Utah Territory. The territorial act in each case omitted reference to slavery except to give the territorial legislature authority over "all rightful subjects of legislation" with provision for appeal to the federal courts. For the sake of agreement, the deliberate ambiguity of the statement was its merit. Northern congressmen could assume that the territorial legislatures might act to exclude slavery; southern congressmen assumed that they could not.

Fourth, a new Fugitive Slave Act put the matter of apprehending runaway slaves wholly under federal jurisdiction and stacked the cards in favor of slave catchers. *Fifth*, as a gesture to anti-slavery forces, the slave trade, but not slavery itself, was abolished in the District of Columbia. The spectacle of chained-together slaves passing through the streets of the capital, to be sold at public auctions, was brought to an end.

President Millard Fillmore pronounced the five measures making up the Compromise of 1850 "a final settlement." Still, doubts lingered that both North and South could be reconciled to the measures permanently. In the South the disputes of 1846–1850 had transformed the abstract doctrine of secession into a movement animated by such "fire-eaters" as Robert Barnwell Rhett of South Carolina, William Lowndes Yancey of Alabama, and Edmund Ruffin of Virginia.

But once the furies aroused by the Wilmot Proviso had been spent, the compromise left little on which to focus pro-slavery agitation. The state of California was an accomplished fact and, ironically, tended to elect pro-slavery men to Congress. New Mexico and Utah were far away and in any case at least hypothetically open to slavery. Both in fact adopted slave codes, but the census of 1860 reported no slaves in New Mexico and only twenty-nine in Utah. The Fugitive Slave Act was something else again. It was the one clear-cut victory for the cause of slavery, but would the North enforce it?

THE FUGITIVE SLAVE ACT   Southern insistence on the Fugitive Slave Act presented abolitionists with an emotional new focus for their agitation. The act did more than strengthen the hand of slave catchers; it offered a strong temptation to kidnap free blacks. The law denied alleged fugitives a jury trial and provided that special commissioners get a fee of $10 when they certified delivery of an alleged slave but only $5 when they refused

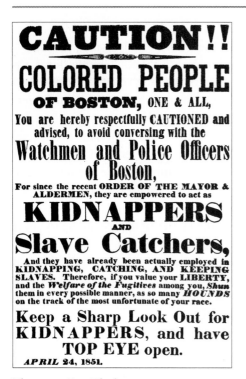

Threats to Free Blacks

An 1851 notice to the free blacks of Boston to avoid the "watchmen and police officers … empowered to act as kidnappers and slave catchers."

certification. In addition, federal marshals could require citizens to help in enforcement; violators could be imprisoned for up to six months and fined $1,000.

"This filthy enactment was made in the nineteenth century, by people who could read and write," Ralph Waldo Emerson marveled in his journal. He advised neighbors to break the new law "on the earliest occasion." The occasion soon arose in Detroit, where only military force stopped the rescue of an alleged fugitive by an outraged mob in October 1850.

There were relatively few such incidents, however. In the first six years of the fugitive act, only three fugitives were forcibly rescued from slave catchers. On the other hand, probably fewer than 200 were returned to bondage during the same years. The Fugitive Slave Act had the tremendous effect of deepening the anti-slavery impulse in the North.

UNCLE TOM'S CABIN Anti-slavery forces found their most persuasive appeal not in the Fugitive Slave Act but in the fictional drama of Harriet Beecher Stowe's *Uncle Tom's Cabin* (1852). The novel is a combination of unlikely saints and sinners, stereotypes, and melodramatic escapades—and was a smashing commercial success. The long-suffering Uncle Tom, the villainous Simon Legree, the angelic Eva, the desperate Eliza carrying her child to freedom across the icy Ohio River—all became stock characters of the American imagination. Slavery, seen through Stowe's eyes, was an abominable sin. It took time for the novel to work its effect on public opinion, however. Neither abolitionists nor fire-eaters fought for their sections of the country at the time of its publication. The country was enjoying a surge of prosperity, and the course of the presidential campaign in 1852 reflected a common desire to lay sectional quarrels to rest.

THE ELECTION OF 1852

In 1852 the Democrats chose Franklin Pierce of New Hampshire as their presidential candidate; their platform pledged them to abide by the measures enacted by the Compromise of 1850. The party's candidates and platform generated a surprising reconciliation of its factions. Pierce rallied both the southern rights' advocates and the Van Burenite Democrats. The third-party Free-Soilers, as a consequence, mustered only 156,000 votes, for John P. Hale, in contrast to the 291,000 they had tallied for Van Buren in 1848.

135,000 SETS, 270,000 VOLUMES SOLD.

UNCLE TOM'S CABIN

FOR SALE HERE.

AN EDITION FOR THE MILLION, COMPLETE IN 1 Vol. PRICE 37 1-2 CENTS.
" " IN GERMAN, IN 1 Vol. PRICE 50 CENTS.
" " IN 2 Vols. CLOTH, 6 PLATES, PRICE $1.50.
SUPERB ILLUSTRATED EDITION, IN 1 Vol. WITH 153 ENGRAVINGS,
PRICES FROM $2.50 TO $5.00.

The Greatest Book of the Age.

"The Greatest Book of the Age"

Uncle Tom's Cabin, as this advertisement indicates, was a best seller.

The Whigs repudiated the lackluster Fillmore, who had faithfully supported the Compromise of 1850, and once again tried to exploit martial glory. It took fifty-three ballots, but the convention finally chose General Winfield Scott, the hero of the Mexican War and a native of Virginia backed mainly by northern Whigs. The Whig convention dutifully endorsed the compromise, but with some opposition from the North. Scott, an able army commander but an inept politician, had gained a reputation for anti-slavery and nativist sentiments, alienating German- and Irish-American voters. In the end, Scott carried only Tennessee, Kentucky, Massachusetts, and Vermont. Pierce overwhelmed him in the Electoral College, 254 to 42, although the popular vote was close: 1.6 million to 1.4 million.

Franklin Pierce, an undistinguished but handsome, engaging figure, a former congressman, senator, and soldier in Mexico, was, like James Polk, touted as another Young Hickory. But the youngest president to date was unable to unite the warring factions of his party. After the election, Pierce wrote a poignant letter to his wife in which he expressed his frustration at the prospect of keeping North and South together. "I can do no right," he sighed. "What am I to do, wife? Stand by me." By the end of Pierce's first year in office, the leaders of his own party had decided he was a failure. By trying to be all things to all people, Pierce looked more and more like a "Northern man with Southern principles."

FOREIGN ADVENTURES

CUBA   During the early 1850s foreign diversions sporadically distracted attention from domestic quarrels. Cuba, one of Spain's last possessions in the New World, continued to be an object of American desire. In the early 1850s a crisis arose over expeditions launched from American soil and meant to incite Cubans to rebel against Spain. Spanish authorities retaliated by harassing American ships. In response the Pierce administration in 1854 instructed Pierre Soulé, the American minister in Madrid, to make an offer of $130 million for Cuba, which Spain peremptorily spurned. Soulé then joined the U.S. ministers to France and Britain in drafting the Ostend Manifesto, which declared that if Spain, "actuated by stubborn pride and a false sense of honor refused to sell," then the United States must ask itself, "Does Cuba, in the possession of Spain, seriously endanger our internal peace and the existence of our cherished Union?" If so, "then, by every law, human and divine, we shall be justified in wresting it from Spain." Publication of the supposedly confidential dispatch left the administration no choice but to disavow what northern opinion widely regarded as a "slaveholders' plot."

DIPLOMATIC GAINS IN THE PACIFIC   In the Pacific, U.S. diplomacy scored some important achievements. American trade with China dated from 1784–1785 but was allowed only through the port of Canton (Guangzhou). In 1844 the United States and China signed the Treaty of Wanghsia (Wanxian), which opened four ports, including Shanghai, to American trade. The Treaty of Tientsin (Tianjin, 1858) opened eleven more ports and granted Americans the right to travel and trade throughout China. Protestant missionaries had also developed a keen interest in China. About fifty were already there by 1855, and for nearly a century China remained the most active mission field for Americans.

Japan, meanwhile, had for two centuries remained closed to U.S. trade. Moreover, American whalers wrecked on the shores of Japan had been forbidden to leave the country. Mainly in their interest, President Fillmore entrusted a special Japanese expedition to Commodore Matthew Perry, who arrived in Tokyo in 1853. Negotiations led to the Treaty of Kanagawa (1854).

Japan agreed to allow a U.S. consulate, promised to treat castaways cordially, and permitted American ships to enter certain ports for supplies and repairs. Broader commercial relations came after the first U.S. envoy, Townsend Harris, negotiated the Harris Convention of 1858, which opened five Japanese ports to American trade.

THE KANSAS-NEBRASKA CRISIS

American commercial interests in Asia helped spark a growing desire for a transcontinental railroad line connecting the eastern seaboard with the Pacific coast. During the 1850s the only land added to the United States was a barren stretch of some 30,000 square miles south of the Gila River in present-day New Mexico and Arizona. This Gadsden Purchase of 1853, for which the United States paid Mexico $10 million, was made to acquire land offering a likely route for a transcontinental railroad. The idea of building a railroad linking the far-flung regions of the new continental domain of the United States reignited sectional rivalries and reopened the slavery issue. Among the many transcontinental routes projected, the four most important were a northern route from Milwaukee to the Columbia River in northern Oregon, a central route from

Expedition to Japan

A woodcut by the Japanese artist Hiroshige Utagawa depicts Commodore Perry's steamship.

Stephen Douglas, ca. 1852

Initiator of the Kansas-Nebraska Act.

St. Louis to San Francisco, another from Memphis to Los Angeles, and a more southerly route from Houston to Los Angeles via the Gadsden Purchase.

DOUGLAS'S PROPOSAL   In 1852 and 1853 Congress debated and dropped several likely proposals for a transcontinental rail line. For various reasons, including terrain, climate, and sectional interests, Secretary of War Jefferson Davis favored the southern route and encouraged the Gadsden Purchase. Any other route, moreover, would go through the territories granted to Indians which stretched from Texas to the Canadian border.

Senator Stephen Douglas of Illinois had an even better idea: Chicago should be the transcontinental railroad's eastern terminus. Since 1845, therefore, Douglas and his supporters had offered bills for a new territory west of Missouri and Iowa, bearing the Indian name Nebraska. In 1854, as chairman of the Committee on Territories, Senator Douglas proposed yet another Nebraska bill, which became the Kansas-Nebraska Act. Unlike the others this one included the entire unorganized portion of the Louisiana Purchase, extending to the Canadian border. Political necessity then began to transform Douglas's proposal from a railroad bill into a pro-slavery bill, thus reopening

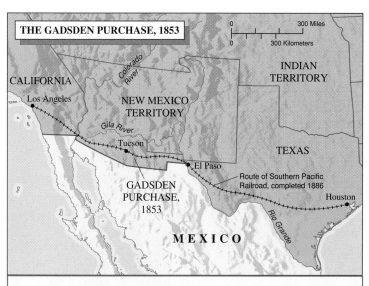

THE GADSDEN PURCHASE, 1853

Why did the U.S. government purchase this land from Mexico? What was the route of the new Southern Pacific Railroad? How did the debate over the national railroad open up sectional conflicts?

the controversy over the extension of slavery into the territories. To carry his point, Douglas needed the support of southerners, and to win that support he needed to make some concession on slavery in the new territories. This he did by writing the principle of popular sovereignty into the bill, allowing voters in each territory to decide for themselves whether to allow slavery.

It was a clever dodge, since the 1820 Missouri Compromise would exclude slaves until the territorial government had made a decision. Southerners quickly spotted the barrier, and Douglas as quickly made two more concessions. He supported an amendment for repeal of the Missouri Compromise insofar as it excluded slavery north of 36°30′, and he agreed to the creation of two territories, Kansas, west of Missouri, and Nebraska, west of Iowa and Minnesota.

Douglas's motives are unclear. Railroads were surely foremost in his mind, but he was also influenced by the desire to win support for his bill in the South, by the hope that his promotion of the principle of "popular sovereignty" would quiet the slavery issue and open the Northwest, or by a chance to split the Whigs. But whatever his reasoning, he had blundered, damaging his presidential chances and setting the country on the road to civil war. In replacing the Missouri Compromise boundary line with the concept of popular sovereignty, enabling territorial residents to decide the issue of slavery for themselves, Douglas fanned the flames of sectional discord and forced moderate political leaders to align with the extremes. In the end the Kansas-Nebraska Act would destroy the Whig party, fragment the Democratic party, and ignite a territorial civil war between pro- and anti-slavery settlers in Kansas.

The tragic flaw in Douglas's reasoning was his failure to appreciate the growing breadth and intensity of anti-slavery sentiment spreading across the country. Douglas himself preferred that the territories vote against slavery. Their climate and geography excluded plantation agriculture, he reasoned, and he could not comprehend how people could get so wrought up over the abstract right of taking their slaves into the territories. Yet he had in fact opened the possibility that slavery might gain a foothold in Kansas.

Douglas's proposal to repeal the long-standing Missouri Compromise was less than a week old when six anti-slavery congressmen published a protest, the "Appeal of the Independent Democrats." Their moral indignation quickly spread among those who opposed Douglas. The document dismissed his bill "as a gross violation of a sacred pledge" and as "part and parcel of an atrocious plot" to create "a dreary region of despotism, inhabited by masters and slaves." The anti-slavery Democrats called upon their fellow citizens to protest this "atrocious crime."

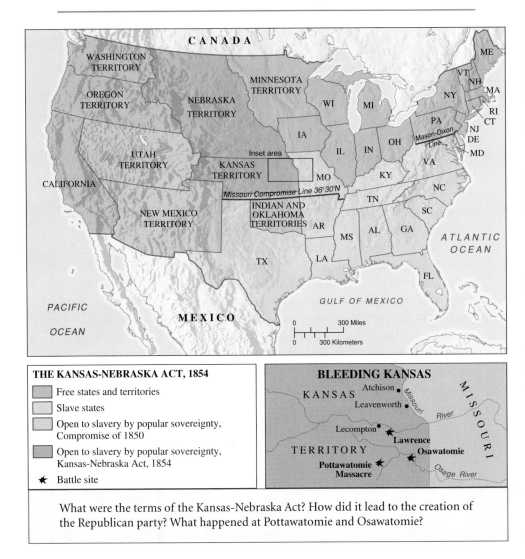

THE KANSAS-NEBRASKA ACT, 1854

- Free states and territories
- Slave states
- Open to slavery by popular sovereignty, Compromise of 1850
- Open to slavery by popular sovereignty, Kansas-Nebraska Act, 1854
- ★ Battle site

BLEEDING KANSAS

What were the terms of the Kansas-Nebraska Act? How did it lead to the creation of the Republican party? What happened at Pottawatomie and Osawatomie?

Across the North, editorials, sermons, speeches, and petitions echoed this indignation. What had been the opinion of a radical minority was fast becoming the common view of northerners. But in Congress, Douglas had the votes for his Kansas-Nebraska Act, and once committed, he forced the issue with tireless energy. President Pierce impulsively added his support. Southerners lined up behind Douglas, with notable exceptions such as Texas senator Sam Houston, who denounced the act's violation of two solemn compacts: the Missouri Compromise and the confirmation of the territory deeded to the Indians "as long as grass shall grow and water run." He was not the only one concerned about the Indians, however. Federal agents were already busy hoodwinking or bullying Indians into relinquishing their claims. Douglas and Pierce whipped reluctant Democrats into line (though about half the northern Democrats refused to yield), pushing the passage of the Kansas-Nebraska bill by a vote of 37 to 14 in the Senate and 113 to 100 in the House.

Very well, many in the North reasoned, if the Missouri Compromise was not a sacred pledge, then neither was the Fugitive Slave Act that was part of the Compromise of 1850. On June 2, 1854, Boston witnessed the most dramatic demonstration against the act. After several attempts had failed to rescue a fugitive slave named Anthony Burns, soldiers dispatched by President Pierce marched him to a waiting ship through streets lined with people shouting "Kidnappers!" Burns was the last southern slave to be returned from Boston and was soon freed through purchase by the African-American community of Boston. New Englanders blamed Pierce for the sorry episode. One sent a letter to the White House that read: "To the chief slave-catcher of the United States. You damned, infernal scoundrel, if only I had you here in Boston, I would murder you!"

THE EMERGENCE OF THE REPUBLICAN PARTY   By the mid-1850s the tensions over slavery were fracturing the nation. What John Calhoun had called the cords holding the Union together had begun to fray. The national organizations of Baptists and Methodists, for instance, had split over slavery by 1845 and formed new northern and southern organizations. The national parties were also beginning to buckle under the strain of slavery. The Democrats managed to postpone disruption for a while, but their congressional delegation lost heavily in the North, enhancing the influence of their southern wing.

The strain of the Kansas-Nebraska Act soon destroyed the Whig party. Southern Whigs now tended to abstain from voting, while northern Whigs gravitated toward two new parties. One was the American (Know-Nothing) party, which had raised the banner of nativism and the hope of serving the patriotic cause of Union. The other, which attracted even more northern Whigs, was formed in 1854 when those Whigs joined with independent Democrats and Free-Soilers to form the Republican party.

BLEEDING KANSAS   After passage of the Kansas-Nebraska Act in 1854, attention swung to the plains of Kansas, where opposing elements gathered to stage a rehearsal for civil war. Whereas all agreed that Nebraska would be a free state, Kansas soon exposed the potential for mischief in the idea of popular sovereignty. The ambiguity of the law, useful to Douglas in getting it passed, only added to the chaos. The people of Kansas were "perfectly free to form and regulate their domestic institutions in their own way, subject only to the Constitution." That in itself invited conflicting interpretations, but the law was completely silent as to the time of any decision, adding to each side's sense of urgency in getting political control of the 50-million-acre territory.

The settlement of Kansas therefore differed from the typical pioneering efforts. Groups sprang up in North and South to hurry right-minded transplants westward. Most of the settlers were from Missouri and its surrounding states. Although few of them held slaves, they were not sympathetic to militant abolitionism; racism was prevalent even among nonslaveholding whites. Many of the Kansas settlers wanted to keep all blacks, enslaved or free, out of the territory. "I kem to Kansas to live in a free state," declared a minister, "and I don't want niggers a-trampin' over my grave." By 1860 there were only 627 African Americans in the territory.

When Kansas's first federal governor arrived, in 1854, he found several thousand settlers there. He ordered a census and scheduled an election for a territorial legislature in 1855. When the election took place, several thousand "border ruffians" crossed over from Missouri, illegally swept the polls

The Border Ruffian Code in Kansas (1856)

This pamphlet, published by Horace Greeley's *New York Tribune*, features a map of the country divided into slave states (dark), free states (white), and those in the middle (gray). It attempts to "prove how the suffering South is oppressed by the North."

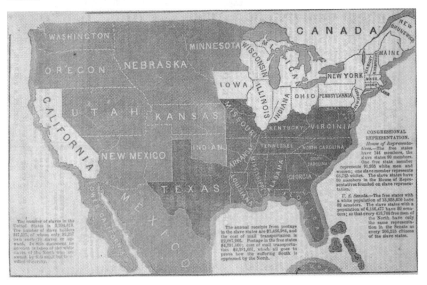

for pro-slavery forces, and vowed to kill every "God-damned abolitionist in the Territory." The governor denounced the vote as a fraud but did nothing to alter the results, for fear of being killed. The legislature expelled its few anti-slavery members, adopted a drastic slave code, and made it a capital offense to aid a fugitive slave and a felony even to question the legality of slavery in the territory.

Outraged free-state advocates rejected this "bogus" government and moved directly toward application for statehood. In 1855 a constitutional convention, the product of an extralegal election, met in Topeka, drafted a state constitution excluding both slavery and free blacks from Kansas, and applied for admission to the Union. By 1856 a free-state "governor" and "legislature" were functioning in Topeka; thus there were two illegal governments in the Kansas territory. The prospect of getting any government to command general authority seemed dim, and both sides began to arm.

Finally, the tense confrontation began to slip into violent conflict. In May 1856 a pro-slavery mob entered the free-state town of Lawrence, Kansas, destroyed newspaper presses, set fire to the free-state governor's home, stole property, and demolished the Free State Hotel.

The "sack of Lawrence" resulted in just one casualty, but the excitement aroused a fanatic Free-Soiler named John Brown, who had a history of mental instability. Two days after Lawrence was sacked, Brown set out with four of his sons and three other men for Pottawatomie, site of a pro-slavery settlement, where they dragged five men from their houses and hacked them to death in front of their screaming families.

The "Sack" of Lawrence

This sheet-music cover for an anti-slavery song portrays the burning of the Free-State Hotel in Lawrence, Kansas, by a proslavery mob in 1856. Shalor Eldridge, the hotel's owner, rebuilt the hotel in 1857 and again in 1865, after it was destroyed by William Quantrill and his raiders in 1863.

The Pottawatomie Massacre (May 24–25, 1856) set off a guerrilla war in the Kansas Territory that lasted through the fall. On August 30 Missouri ruffians raided the free-state settlement at Osawatomie, Kansas. They looted and burned the houses and shot John Brown's son Frederick through the heart. The elder Brown, who barely escaped, looked back at the site being devastated by "Satan's legions" and muttered, "God sees it." He then swore to his surviving sons and followers, "I have only a short time to live—only one death to die, and I will die fighting for this cause." Three years later he would do just that, in a futile uprising that inflamed sentiment in the North and the South. Altogether, by the end of 1856, about 200 settlers had been killed in Kansas and $2 million in property destroyed during the territorial civil war. Some 1,500 federal troops were dispatched to restore some semblance of order.

VIOLENCE IN THE SENATE   Combat in Kansas spilled over into Congress. On May 22, 1856, the day after the sack of Lawrence and two days before the Pottawatomie Massacre, a sudden flash of violence on the Senate floor electrified the whole country. Just two days earlier Senator Charles Sumner of Massachusetts had delivered an inflammatory speech on "The Crime against Kansas." Sumner, elected five years earlier by a coalition of Free-Soilers and Democrats, was a brilliant orator with a sharp tongue. His two-day speech, delivered from memory, was an exercise in studied insult. The pro-slavery Missourians who crossed into Kansas, he charged, were "hirelings picked from the drunken spew and vomit of an uneasy civilization."

"Bully" Brooks's Attack on Charles Sumner

The incident worsened the strains on the Union.

Their treatment of Kansas was "the rape of a virgin territory," he said, "and it may be clearly traced to a depraved longing for a new slave State, the hideous offspring of such a crime." Sumner singled out the elderly senator Andrew Pickens Butler of South Carolina for censure. Butler, Sumner charged, had "chosen a mistress . . . who . . . though polluted in the sight of the world, is chaste in his sight—I mean the harlot, Slavery."

Sumner's indignant rudeness might well have backfired had it not been for Butler's kinsman Preston S. Brooks, a fiery-tempered congressman from South Carolina. For two days, Brooks brooded over the insult to his relative, knowing that Sumner would refuse a challenge to a duel. On May 22 he found Sumner writing at his Senate desk after an adjournment, accused him of libel against South Carolina and Butler, and commenced beating him about the head with a cane while stunned colleagues looked on. Sumner, struggling to rise, wrenched the desk from the floor and collapsed. Brooks kept beating the unconscious Sumner until his cane broke.

Brooks had satisfied his rage but in doing so had created a martyr for the anti-slavery cause. For two and a half years, Sumner's empty Senate seat was a solemn reminder of the violence done to him. When the House censured Brooks, he resigned, only to return after being triumphantly re-elected. His southern admirers presented him with new canes. The editor of the Richmond *Enquirer* urged Brooks to cane Sumner again: "These vulgar abolitionists in the Senate . . . must be lashed into submission." Northerners hastened to Sumner's defense. The news of the beating drove John Brown "crazy," his eldest son remembered, "*crazy.*" People on each side, appalled at the behavior of the other, decided that North and South had developed into different civilizations with incompatible standards of honor. "I do not see," Ralph Waldo Emerson confessed, "how a barbarous community and a civilized community can constitute one state. We must either get rid of slavery, or get rid of freedom."

SECTIONAL POLITICS Within the span of five days in May of 1856, "Bleeding Kansas," "Bleeding Sumner," and "Bully Brooks" had set the tone for another presidential election. The major parties could no longer evade the slavery issue. Already in February it had split the infant American party wide open. Southern delegates, with help from New York, killed a resolution to restore the Missouri Compromise and nominated Millard Fillmore for president. Later what was left of the Whig party endorsed him as well. But as a friend wrote Fillmore, the "outrageous proceedings in Kansas & the assault on Mr. Sumner have contributed very much to strengthen the [new] Republican Party."

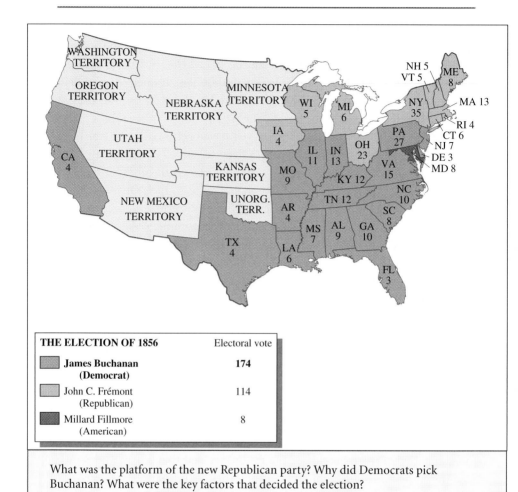

THE ELECTION OF 1856   Electoral vote

	James Buchanan (Democrat)	**174**
	John C. Frémont (Republican)	114
	Millard Fillmore (American)	8

What was the platform of the new Republican party? Why did Democrats pick Buchanan? What were the key factors that decided the election?

At its first national convention the Republican party passed over its lead-ing figure, William H. Seward, who was awaiting a better chance in 1860. Following the Whig tradition, the party sought out a military hero, John C. Frémont, the "Pathfinder" who had led the conquest of Mexican California. The Republican platform also owed much to the Whigs. It favored a transcontinental railroad and, in general, more government-financed internal improvements. It condemned the repeal of the Missouri Compromise, the Democratic policy of territorial expansion, and "those twin relics of bar-barism—Polygamy and Slavery." The campaign slogan echoed that of the Free-Soilers: "Free soil, free speech, and Frémont." It was the first time a major-party platform had taken a stand against slavery.

The Democrats, meeting two weeks earlier in June, had rejected Franklin Pierce, the hapless victim of so much turmoil. Stephen Douglas, too, was left out, because of the damage done by his Kansas-Nebraska Act. The party therefore turned to James Buchanan of Pennsylvania, who had long sought the nomination. The party and its candidate nevertheless supported Pierce's policies. The Democratic platform endorsed the Kansas-Nebraska Act, called for vigorous enforcement of the fugitive slave law, and stressed that Congress should not interfere with slavery in either states or territories. The party reached out to its newly acquired Irish and German voters by condemning nativism and endorsing religious liberty.

The campaign of 1856 resolved itself into a sectional contest in which parties vied for northern or southern votes. The Republicans had few southern supporters and only a handful in the border states, where fears of disunion held many Whigs in line. Buchanan thus went into the campaign as the candidate of the only remaining national party. Frémont swept the northernmost states with 114 electoral votes, but Buchanan added five free states—Pennsylvania, New Jersey, Illinois, Indiana, and California—to his southern majority for a total of 174.

The sixty-five-year-old Buchanan, America's only unmarried president, brought to the White House a portfolio of impressive achievements in politics and diplomacy. His career went back to 1815, when he served as a Federalist legislator in Pennsylvania before switching to Andrew Jackson's party in the 1820s. He had been in Congress for over twenty years, minister to Russia and Britain, and James K. Polk's secretary of state. His long quest for the presidency had been built on his commitment to states' rights and his aggressive promotion of territorial expansion. His political debts reinforced his belief that saving the Union depended upon concessions to the South. Republicans charged that he lacked the backbone to stand up to the southerners who dominated the Democratic majorities in Congress. His choice of four slave-state men and only three free-state men for his cabinet seemed another bad omen.

THE DEEPENING SECTIONAL CRISIS

During James Buchanan's first six months in office, three major events caused his undoing: (1) the Supreme Court decision in the *Dred Scott* case, (2) new troubles in Kansas, and (3) a financial panic that sparked a widespread economic depression. For all of Buchanan's experience as a legislator and diplomat, he failed to handle those and other key issues in a statesman-like manner. As one historian has recently concluded, the new president proved to be "an abysmal failure as a chief executive."

THE *DRED SCOTT* CASE   On March 6, 1857, two days after Buchanan's inauguration, the Supreme Court rendered a decision in the long-pending case of *Dred Scott v. Sandford*. Dred Scott, born a slave in Virginia about 1800, had been taken to St. Louis in 1830 and sold to an army surgeon, who took him to Illinois, then to the Wisconsin Territory (later Minnesota), and finally back to St. Louis in 1842. While in the Wisconsin Territory, Scott had met and married Harriet Robinson, and they eventually had two daughters.

After his master's death, in 1843, Scott had tried to buy his freedom. In 1846 Harriet Scott persuaded her husband to file suit in the Missouri courts, claiming that residence in Illinois and the Wisconsin Territory had made him free. A jury decided in his favor, but the state supreme court ruled against him. When the case rose on appeal to the Supreme Court, the country anxiously awaited its opinion on whether freedom once granted could be lost by returning to a slave state.

Eight of the nine justices filed separate opinions; one concurred with Chief Justice Roger B. Taney of Maryland. By different lines of reasoning, seven justices ruled that Scott remained a slave. The aging Taney, who wrote the Court's majority opinion, ruled that Scott lacked legal standing because he lacked citizenship. Taney argued that one became a U.S. citizen either by birth or by naturalization, and both of those methods ruled out any former slave. He then mistakenly argued that no state had ever accorded citizenship to blacks. At the time the Constitution was adopted, Taney further said, blacks "had for more than a century been regarded as . . . so far inferior, that they had no rights which the white man was bound to respect."

Taney declared that Scott's residency in a free state had not freed him since, in line with precedent, the decision of the state court governed. This left the question of residency in a free territory. On that point, Taney argued that the Missouri Compromise had deprived citizens of property by prohibiting slavery, an action "not warranted

Chief Justice Roger B. Taney

Taney played a critical role in the Supreme Court's decision in the *Dred Scott* case, which fanned the flames of sectional discord.

by the constitution." He strongly implied, but never said explicitly, that the Missouri Compromise had violated the due-process clause of the Fifth Amendment, as John C. Calhoun had earlier argued.

The upshot was that the Supreme Court had declared an act of Congress unconstitutional for the first time since *Marbury v. Madison* (1803) and had declared a major act of Congress unconstitutional for the first time ever. Congress had repealed the Missouri Compromise in the Kansas-Nebraska Act three years earlier, but the *Dred Scott* decision now challenged popular sovereignty. If Congress itself could not exclude slavery from a territory, then presumably neither could a territorial government created by an act of Congress.

By this decision the Supreme Court had tried to settle a question that Congress had dodged ever since the Wilmot Proviso had surfaced. But far from settling it, Taney's ruling had fanned the flames of dissension. Little wonder that Republicans protested: the Court had declared their anti-slavery program unconstitutional. It had also reinforced the suspicion that the slavocracy was hatching a conspiracy. Were not all but one of the justices who had joined Taney southerners? And President Buchanan had sought to influence the Court's decision both before and during his inaugural ceremony. Besides, if Dred Scott were not a citizen and had no standing in court, there was no case before the Court. The majority ruling was an obiter dictum—a statement not essential to deciding the case and therefore not binding, "entitled to just so much moral weight as would be the judgment of a majority of those congregated in any Washington bar-room."

Pro-slavery elements of course greeted the Court's opinion as binding. Now the most militant among them were emboldened to make yet another demand. It was not enough to deny Congress the right to interfere with slavery in the territories; Congress had an obligation to protect the property of slaveholders, making a federal slave code the next step.

THE LECOMPTON CONSTITUTION   Out in Kansas, meanwhile, the struggle over slavery continued. Just before Buchanan's inauguration the pro-slavery legislature called for a constitutional convention. Since no provision was made for a referendum on the constitution, however, the governor vetoed the measure, and then the legislature overrode his veto. The Kansas governor resigned on the day Buchanan took office, and the new president replaced him with Robert J. Walker. A native Pennsylvanian who had made a political career in Mississippi and a former member of Polk's cabinet, Walker had greater prestige than his predecessors, and he put the Union above slavery. In Kansas he scented a chance to advance the cause of both the Union and his party. Under popular sovereignty fair elections would produce a state that would be both free and Democratic.

Walker arrived in Kansas in 1857, and with Buchanan's approval the new governor pledged to the free-state Kansans that the new constitution would be submitted to a fair vote. But in spite of his pleas, he arrived too late to persuade free-state men to vote for convention delegates in elections they were sure had been rigged against them. Later, however, Walker did persuade the free-state leaders to vote in the election of a new territorial legislature.

As a result a polarity arose between an anti-slavery legislature and a pro-slavery constitutional convention. The convention, meeting at Lecompton, Kansas, drew up a constitution under which Kansas would become a slave state. Although Kansas had only about 200 slaves at the time, free-state men boycotted the vote on the new constitution on the claim that it, too, was rigged. At this point, President Buchanan took a fateful step. Influenced by southern advisers and politically dependent upon southern congressmen, he decided to renege on his pledge to Governor Walker and support the action of the Lecompton convention. Walker resigned, and the election went according to form: 6,226 for the constitution with slavery, 569 for the constitution without slavery. Meanwhile, the acting governor had convened the antislavery legislature, which called for another election to vote the Lecompton Constitution up or down. Most of the pro-slavery settlers boycotted this election, and the result, on January 4, 1858, was overwhelming: 10,226 against the constitution, 138 for the constitution with slavery, 24 for the constitution without slavery.

The combined results suggested a clear majority against slavery, but pro-southern Buchanan stuck to his support of the Lecompton Constitution, driving another wedge into the Democratic party. Senator Douglas, up for reelection, broke dramatically with the president in a tense confrontation, but Buchanan persisted in trying to get the Lecompton Constitution approved by Congress. In the Senate, administration forces held firm, and in 1858 Lecompton was passed. In the House enough anti-Lecompton Democrats combined to put through an amendment for a new and carefully supervised popular vote in Kansas. Enough senators went along to permit passage of the House bill. Southerners were confident the vote would favor slavery, because to reject slavery the voters would have to reject the constitution, which would postpone statehood until the population reached 90,000. On August 2, 1858, Kansas voters nevertheless rejected Lecompton, 11,300 to 1,788. With that vote, Kansas, now firmly in the hands of its anti-slavery legislature, largely ended its provocative role in the sectional controversy.

THE PANIC OF 1857   The third emergency of Buchanan's first half
year in office, a financial crisis, occurred in August 1857. It was brought on
by a reduction in foreign demand for American grain, a surge in manufacturing that outran the growth of markets, and the continued weakness and
confusion of the state bank-note system. The failure of the Ohio Life Insurance and Trust Company on August 24, 1857, precipitated the panic, which
was followed by a depression from which the country did not emerge until
1859.

Everything in those years seemed to get drawn into the vortex of sectional
conflict, and business troubles were no exception. Northern businessmen
tended to blame the depression on the Democratic tariff of 1857, which had
set rates on imports at their lowest level since 1816. The agricultural South
weathered the crisis better than the North. Cotton prices fell, but slowly, and
world markets for cotton quickly recovered. The result was an exalted notion
of King Cotton's importance to the world and apparent confirmation of the
growing argument that the southern system of slave-based agriculture was
superior to the free-labor system of the North.

DOUGLAS VERSUS LINCOLN   Amid the recriminations over the *Dred
Scott* decision, Kansas, and the depression, the center could not hold. The
Lecompton battle put severe strains on the most substantial cord of union
that was left, the Democratic party. To many, Senator Stephen Douglas
seemed the best hope for unity and union, one of the few remaining Democratic leaders with support in both the North and the South. But now Douglas was being whipsawed by the extremes. Kansas-Nebraska had cast him in
the role of a doughface, a southern sympathizer. Yet his opposition to
Lecompton, the fraudulent fruit of popular sovereignty, had alienated him
from Buchanan's southern junta. But for all his flexibility and opportunism,
Douglas had convinced himself that popular sovereignty was a point of
principle, a bulwark of democracy and local self-government. In 1858 he
faced reelection to the Senate against the opposition of both Buchanan Democrats and Republicans. The year 1860 would give him a chance for the
presidency, but first he had to secure his home base in Illinois.

To oppose him, Illinois Republicans named Abraham Lincoln of Springfield, the lanky, raw-boned former Whig state legislator and one-term congressman, a small-town lawyer. Lincoln's early life had been the hardscrabble
existence of the frontier farmer. Born in a Kentucky log cabin in 1809 and
raised on farms in Indiana and Illinois, the young Lincoln had worked at
various farm tasks, operated a ferry, and made two trips down to New Orleans as a flatboatman. Striking out on his own, he managed a general store

in New Salem, Illinois, learned surveying, served in the Black Hawk War in 1832, won election to the legislature in 1834 (at the age of twenty-five), read law, and was admitted to the bar in 1836. Lincoln stayed in the Illinois legislature until 1842 and in 1846 won a seat in Congress. After a single term he retired from active politics to cultivate his law practice in Springfield.

In 1854 the Kansas-Nebraska debate drew Lincoln back into the political arena. When Douglas appeared in Springfield to defend the idea of popular sovereignty, Lincoln countered from the same platform. Lincoln abhorred slavery but was no abolitionist. He did not believe the two races could coexist as equals, but he did oppose any further extension of slavery into new territories, assuming that over time the institution would die a "natural death." Slavery, he said in the 1840s, was a vexing but "minor question on its way to extinction." Now, in 1854 in Peoria, he preached an old but oft-neglected doctrine: hate the sin but not the sinner:

> When Southern people tell us they are no more responsible for the origin of slavery, than we, I acknowledge the fact. When it is said that the institution exists; and that it is very difficult to get rid of it, in any satisfactory way, I can understand and appreciate the saying. . . .
>
> But all this, to my judgment, furnishes no more excuses for permitting slavery to go into our own free territory, than it would for reviving the African slave trade by law.

At first Lincoln had held back from the rapidly growing Republican party, but in 1856 he had joined it and had given some fifty speeches for the Frémont ticket in Illinois and nearby states. By 1858, as the obvious choice to oppose Douglas for the Senate seat, he was resorting to the classic ploy of the underdog: he challenged the favorite to debate him. Douglas agreed to meet him in seven places around the state.

Thus the legendary Lincoln-Douglas debates took place, from August 21 to October 15, 1858. As they mounted the platform, the two men could not have presented a more striking contrast. Lincoln was well over six feet tall, sinewy and craggy featured with a singularly long neck and deep-set, brooding eyes. Unassuming in manner, dressed in homely, well-worn clothes, and walking with a shambling gait, he lightened his essentially serious demeanor with a refreshing sense of humor. To sympathetic observers he conveyed an air of simplicity, sincerity, and common sense. Douglas, on the other hand, was short, rotund, stern, and cocky, attired in the finest custom-tailored suits. A man of considerable abilities and even greater ambition, he strutted to the platform with the pugnacious air of a predestined champion.

At the time and since, much attention focused on the second debate, at Freeport, where Lincoln asked Douglas how he could reconcile popular sovereignty with the *Dred Scott* ruling that citizens had the right to carry slaves into any territory. Douglas's answer, thenceforth known as the Freeport Doctrine, was to state the obvious: whatever the Supreme Court might say about slavery, it could not exist anywhere unless supported by local police regulations.

Douglas tried to set some traps of his own. He intimated that Lincoln belonged to the fanatic sect of abolitionists who advocated racial equality. The question was a hot potato, which Lincoln handled with caution. There was, he said, "a physical difference between the white and black races" that would "forever forbid the two races living together on terms of social and political equality." But Lincoln insisted that blacks did have an "equal" right to freedom and the fruits of their labor. The basic difference between the two men, Lincoln insisted, lay in Douglas's professed indifference to the moral question of slavery.

If Lincoln had the better of the argument, at least in the long view, Douglas had the better of the election. Still, according to the Constitution, the voters actually had to choose their state's legislature, which would then elect the senator. Lincoln men won the larger total vote, but the distribution of votes gave Douglas the legislature, fifty-four to forty-one. As the returns trickled in from the 1858 fall elections—there was still no common election date—they recorded one loss after another for candidates aligned with Buchanan. When the elections were over, the Buchanan administration had lost control of the House.

JOHN BROWN'S RAID   The gradual return of prosperity in 1859 offered hope that the sectional storms of the 1850s might yet pass. But the slavery issue remained volatile. In October 1859 John Brown once again surfaced, this time in the East. Since the Pottawatomie Massacre in 1856, he had led a furtive existence, engaging in fund-raising and occasional bushwhacking. His commitment to abolish the "wicked curse of slavery," meanwhile, had intensified to a fever pitch. Self-righteous and demanding, he was driven by a sense of crusading zeal. His penetrating gray eyes and

John Brown

Although his anti-slavery efforts were based in Kansas, Brown was a native of Connecticut.

flowing beard and the religious certainty that he was an instrument of God struck fear into supporters and opponents alike.

On October 16, 1859, Brown launched his supreme gesture. From a Maryland farm he crossed the Potomac River with about twenty men, including five blacks. Under cover of darkness, they occupied the federal arsenal in Harpers Ferry, Virginia (now West Virginia). Brown planned to arm the slaves in the area, who he assumed would flock to his cause; then he would set up a black stronghold in the mountains of western Virginia, thus providing a nucleus of support for slave insurrections across the South.

What Brown actually did was to take the arsenal by surprise, seize eleven hostages, and hole up in the fire-engine house, where he was surrounded by militiamen and townspeople. The next morning, Brown sent his son Watson and another supporter out under a white flag, hoping to trade his hostages for his freedom, but the enraged crowd shot them both. Intermittent shooting continued, and another Brown son was wounded. He begged his father to kill him so as to end his suffering, but the righteous Brown lashed out, "If you must die, die like a man." A few minutes later the son was dead.

That night Lieutenant Colonel Robert E. Lee arrived with his aide, Lieutenant J.E.B. Stuart, and a force of marines, having been dispatched from Washington by President Buchanan. The following morning, October 18, Stuart and his troops, with thousands of spectators cheering, broke down the barricaded doors and rushed into the fire-engine house. A young lieutenant found Brown kneeling with his rifle cocked. Before Brown could fire, however, the marine plunged his dress sword into him with such force that the blade bent back double upon striking his breast bone. He then used the hilt to beat Brown unconscious. The siege was over. Altogether Brown's men had killed four people and wounded nine. Of their own force, ten died (including two of Brown's sons), seven were captured, and five escaped.

Brown, who recovered from his wounds, was quickly tried for treason and conspiracy to incite insurrection. He was convicted on October 31 and hanged on December 2. Six others died on the gallows later. If Brown had failed in his purpose—whatever it was—he had achieved two things: he had become a martyr for the anti-slavery cause, and he had set off a panic throughout the slaveholding South. At his sentencing he delivered one of America's classic speeches: "Now, if it is deemed necessary that I should forfeit my life for the furtherance of the ends of justice, and mingle my blood further with the blood of my children and with the blood of millions in this slave country whose rights are disregarded by wicked, cruel, and unjust enactments, I say, let it be done."

When Brown, still unflinching, met his end, there were solemn observances in the North. "That new saint," Ralph Waldo Emerson said, "will make the gallows as glorious as the cross." By far the gravest effect of Brown's raid was to encourage pro-slavery southerners to equate John Brown with the Republican party. All through the fall and winter of 1859–1860, rumors of abolitionist conspiracies and slave insurrections swept through the slave states. Every northern visitor, commercial traveler, or schoolteacher came under suspicion, and many were driven out. "We regard every man in our midst an enemy to the institutions of the South," said the *Atlanta Confederacy,* "who does not boldly declare that he believes African slavery to be a social, moral, and political blessing."

THE CENTER COMES APART

THE DEMOCRATS DIVIDE   Thus amid emotional hysteria and impossible demands the nation ushered in the year of another presidential election, destined to be the most fateful in its history. In April 1860 the Democrats gathered in Charleston, a pro-slavery hotbed, for their presidential convention. South Carolina itself had chosen a remarkably moderate delegation, but the radical southern states rights' men held the upper hand in the delegations from the Gulf states.

Illinois senator Stephen Douglas's supporters at the convention reaffirmed the platform of 1856, which simply promised congressional noninterference with slavery. Southern firebrands, however, demanded federal protection for slavery in the territories. Buchanan supporters, hoping to stop Douglas, encouraged the strategy. The platform debate reached a heady climax when the Alabama extremist William Yancey informed the northern Democrats that their error had been the failure to defend slavery as a positive good. An Ohio senator offered a blunt reply. "Gentlemen of the South," he said, "you mistake us—you mistake us. We will not do it."

When the pro-slavery planks lost, Alabama's delegates walked out of the convention, followed by those representing the other Gulf states as well as Georgia, South Carolina (except for two brave up-country Unionists), and parts of the Arkansas and Delaware delegations. "We say, go your way," exclaimed a Mississippi delegate to Douglas's supporters, "and we will go ours." The convention then decided to leave the overwrought atmosphere of Charleston and reassemble in Baltimore on June 18. The Baltimore convention finally nominated Stephen Douglas and reaffirmed the 1856 platform. The Charleston seceders met first in Richmond and then in Baltimore, where they adopted the slave-code platform defeated in Charleston and

Prospect of a Smash Up (1860)

This cartoon shows the Democratic Party—the last remaining national party—about to be split by sectional differences and the onrush of Republicans, led by Lincoln.

named Vice President John C. Breckinridge of Kentucky as their candidate for president. Thus another cord of union had snapped: the last remaining national party had fragmented.

LINCOLN'S ELECTION   The Republicans, meanwhile, gathered in Chicago. There everything suddenly came together for "Honest Abe" Lincoln, the uncommon common man. Lincoln had emerged on the national scene during his unsuccessful Illinois senatorial campaign two years before and had since taken a stance designed to make him available for the nomination. He was strong enough on the containment of slavery to satisfy the abolitionists yet moderate enough to seem less threatening than they were. In 1860 he had gone East to address an audience of influential Republicans at Cooper Union, a newly established art and engineering college in New York City, where he emphasized his view of slavery "as an evil, not to be extended, but to be tolerated and protected only because of and so far as its actual presence among us makes that toleration and protection a necessity."

At the Chicago Republican Convention, New York's William H. Seward was the early leader among the presidential nominees, but he had been tagged, perhaps wrongly, as an extremist for his earlier statements about a looming "irrepressible conflict" over slavery. On the first ballot, Lincoln finished in second place. On the next ballot he drew almost even with Seward, and when he came within one and a half votes of a majority on the third count, Ohio quickly switched four votes to put him over the top.

The Republican party platform denounced both the Supreme Court's *Dred Scott* decision allowing slavery in all federal territories and John Brown's raid as "among the gravest of crimes." It also promised "the right of each state to order and control its own domestic institutions." The party reaffirmed its resistance to the extension of slavery and, in an effort to gain broader support, endorsed a higher protective tariff for manufacturers, free federal homesteads for farmers, a more liberal naturalization law for immigrants, and internal improve-

Abraham Lincoln

Republican candidate for president, June 1860.

ments, including a transcontinental railroad. With this platform, Republicans made a strong appeal to eastern businessmen, western farmers, and the large immigrant population.

Both major conventions revealed that opinions tended to become more radical in the upper North and the Deep South. Attitude followed latitude. In the border states a sense of moderation aroused the die-hard Whigs to make one more try at reconciliation. Meeting in Baltimore a week before the Republicans met in Chicago, they reorganized into the Constitutional Union party and named John Bell of Tennessee for president. Their only platform was a vague statement promoting "the Constitution of the Country, the Union of the States, and the Enforcement of the Laws."

Of the four candidates not one generated a national following, and the campaign evolved into a choice between Lincoln and Douglas in the North (Lincoln was not even on the ballot in the South), Breckinridge and Bell in the South. One consequence of the separate campaigns was that each section gained a false impression of the other. The South never learned to distinguish Lincoln from the radicals; the North, and especially Lincoln, failed to gauge the force of southern intransigence. Lincoln stubbornly refused to offer the South assurances or to clarify his position, which he said was a matter of public record.

The one man who attempted to break through the veil that was falling between the North and the South was Douglas, who tried to mount the first nationwide campaign tour. Only forty-seven but weakened by excessive drink, ill health, and disappointments, he wore himself out in one final glorious campaign. Early in October 1860, at Cedar Rapids, Iowa, he learned of Republican victories in the Pennsylvania and Indiana state legislatures. "Mr. Lincoln is the next President," he said. "We must try to save the Union. I will go South." Down through the hostile states of Tennessee, Georgia, and Alabama, Douglas carried appeals on behalf of the Union. "I do not believe that every Breckinridge man is a disunionist," he said, "but I do believe that every disunionist is a Breckinridge man." He was in Mobile, Alabama, when the presidential election was held.

By midnight on November 6, Lincoln's victory was clear. In the final count he had about 40 percent of the total popular vote but a clear majority, with 180 votes in the Electoral College. He carried every one of the eighteen free states, and by a margin wide enough to elect him even if the votes for the other candidates had been combined. But hidden in the balloting was an ominous development: for the first time a president had been elected by a clear sectional vote. Among all the candidates, only Douglas had won electoral votes from both slave and free states, but his total of 12 was but a pitiful remnant of Democratic unionism. Bell took Virginia, Kentucky, and Tennessee for 39 votes, and Breckinridge swept the other slave states to come in second with 72.

SECESSION OF THE DEEP SOUTH   Soon after Lincoln's election, South Carolina held a special election to choose delegates to a state convention. In Charleston on December 20, 1860, the convention unanimously endorsed an Ordinance of Secession, declaring the state's ratification of the Constitution repealed and its union with the other states dissolved. A Declaration of the Causes of Secession reviewed the threats to slavery and asserted that a purely sectional (Republican) party had elected to the presidency a man "whose opinions and purposes are hostile to slavery," who had declared "government cannot endure permanently half slave, half free" and that slavery "is in the course of ultimate extinction."

By February 1, 1861, Mississippi, Florida, Alabama, Georgia, Louisiana, and Texas had also seceded. Three days later a convention of the seven states met in Montgomery, Alabama; on February 7 they adopted a provisional constitution for the Confederate States of America, and two days later they elected Mississippi's Jefferson Davis as president. He was inaugurated February 18, with Alexander Stephens of Georgia as vice president.

In all seven Deep South states a solid majority had voted for secessionist delegates, but their combined vote would not have been a majority of the presidential vote in November. What happened, it seemed, was what often

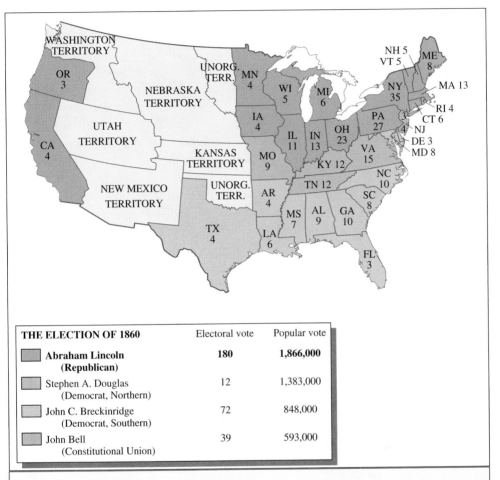

THE ELECTION OF 1860	Electoral vote	Popular vote
Abraham Lincoln (Republican)	**180**	**1,866,000**
Stephen A. Douglas (Democrat, Northern)	12	1,383,000
John C. Breckinridge (Democrat, Southern)	72	848,000
John Bell (Constitutional Union)	39	593,000

What caused the division in the Democratic party? How did Lincoln position himself to win the Republican nomination? What were the major factors that led to Lincoln's electoral victory?

happens in revolutionary situations: a determined minority acted quickly in an emotionally charged climate and carried out its program against a confused and indecisive opposition.

BUCHANAN'S WAITING GAME   History is full of might-have-beens. A bold stroke, even a bold statement, by the lame-duck president at this point might have changed the course of events. But James Buchanan lacked boldness. Besides, a bold stroke might simply have hastened the

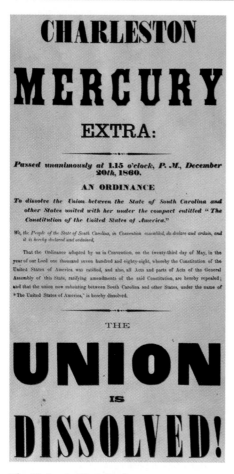

CHARLESTON

MERCURY

EXTRA:

Passed unanimously at 1.15 o'clock, P. M., December 20th, 1860.

AN ORDINANCE

To dissolve the Union between the State of South Carolina and other States united with her under the compact entitled "The Constitution of the United States of America."

We, the People of the State of South Carolina, in Convention assembled, do declare and ordain, and it is hereby declared and ordained,

That the Ordinance adopted by us in Convention, on the twenty-third day of May, in the year of our Lord one thousand seven hundred and eighty-eight, whereby the Constitution of the United States of America was ratified, and also, all Acts and parts of Acts of the General Assembly of this State, ratifying amendments of the said Constitution, are hereby repealed; and that the union now subsisting between South Carolina and other States, under the name of "The United States of America," is hereby dissolved.

THE

UNION

IS

DISSOLVED!

The Union is Dissolved

A handbill announcing South Carolina's secession from the Union.

conflict. No bold stroke came from Lincoln either, nor would he consult with the Buchanan administration during the months before his inauguration on March 4. He inclined all too strongly to the belief that secession was just another bluff and kept his public silence.

In his annual message on December 3, President Buchanan criticized northern agitators for trying to interfere with "slavery in the southern states." He then declared that secession was illegal but that he lacked the authority to coerce a state back into the Union. The president did reaffirm his duty to "take care that the laws be faithfully executed" insofar as he was able. If the president could enforce the law upon all citizens, he would have no need to "coerce" a state. Indeed, his position became the policy of the Lincoln administration, which ended up fighting a civil war on the theory that individuals but not states were in rebellion.

Buchanan held firmly to his resolve, with some slight stiffening by the end of December 1860, when secession became a fact, but he refrained from taking provocative actions. As the secessionists seized federal property, arsenals, and forts, this policy soon meant holding federal facilities at Fort Pickens in Pensacola Harbor, some remote islands off southern Florida, and Fort Sumter in Charleston Harbor.

Fort Sumter was commanded by Major Robert Anderson, a Kentucky Unionist, when South Carolina secessionists demanded withdrawal of all federal forces. Buchanan sharply rejected the South Carolina ultimatum. He dispatched a steamer, *Star of the West,* to Fort Sumter with reinforcements and provisions. As the ship approached Charleston Harbor, Confederate batteries opened fire on January 9, 1861, and drove it away. It was in fact an act of war, but Buchanan chose to ignore the challenge. He decided instead to hunker down and ride out the remaining weeks of his term, hoping against hope that one of several compromise efforts would prevail.

FINAL EFFORTS AT COMPROMISE   Desperate efforts at compromise continued in Congress. On December 18 Senator John J. Crittenden of Kentucky had proposed a series of amendments and resolutions that allowed for slavery in the territories south of 36°30′ and guaranteed to maintain slavery where it already existed. Meanwhile, a peace conference met at Willard's Hotel in Washington, D.C., in February 1861. Twenty-one states sent delegates, and former president John Tyler presided, but the convention's proposal, substantially the same as the Crittenden Compromise, failed to win the support of either house of Congress. The only proposal that met with any success was a constitutional amendment guaranteeing slavery where it existed. Many Republicans, including Lincoln, were prepared to go that far to save the Union, but they were unwilling to repudiate their stand against slavery in the territories. As it happened, after passing the House, the amendment passed the Senate without a vote to spare, by twenty-four to twelve, on the dawn of inauguration day. It would have become the Thirteenth Amendment, with the first use of the word *slavery* in the Constitution, but the states never ratified it. When a Thirteenth Amendment was ratified, in 1865, it did not guarantee slavery—it abolished it.

MAKING CONNECTIONS

- Through the 1850s most of the debate over slavery concerned the expansion of slavery into the territories; with Lincoln's Emancipation Proclamation, discussed in the next chapter, the issue shifted to slavery itself.

- Many of the Radical Republicans who designed Reconstruction (Chapter 18) had been anti-slavery Republicans before the war.

- The proposed transcontinental railroad that had brought about the Kansas-Nebraska crisis would finally be completed in 1869 (Chapter 20).

FURTHER READING

The best surveys of the forces and events leading to the Civil War include James M. McPherson's *Battle Cry of Freedom: The Civil War Era* (1988), Stephen B. Oates's *The Approaching Fury: Voices of the Storm, 1820–1861* (1997), Bruce Levine's *Half Slave and Half Free: The Roots of Civil War* (1992), and David M. Potter's *The Impending Crisis, 1848–1861* (1976). The most recent narrative of the political debate leading to secession is Michael A. Morrison's *Slavery and the American West: The Eclipse of Manifest Destiny and the Coming of the Civil War* (1997).

Mark J. Stegmaier's *Texas, New Mexico, and the Compromise of 1850: Boundary Dispute and Sectional Crisis* (1996) probes that crucial dispute while Michael F. Holt's *The Political Crisis of the 1850s* (1978) traces the demise of the Whigs. Eric Foner, in *Free Soil, Free Labor, Free Men: The Ideology of the Republican Party before the Civil War* (1970), shows how events and ideas combined in the formation of a new political party. A more straightforward study of the rise of the Republicans is William E. Gienapp's *The Origins of the Republican Party, 1852–1856* (1987). The economic, social, and political crises of 1857 are examined in Kenneth M. Stampp's *America in 1857: A Nation on the Brink* (1990).

Robert W. Johannsen's *Stephen A. Douglas* (1973) analyzes the issue of popular sovereignty. A more national perspective is provided in James A. Rawley's *Race and Politics: "Bleeding Kansas" and the Coming of the Civil War* (1969). On the role of John Brown in the sectional crisis, see Stephen B. Oates's *To Purge This Land with Blood: A Biography of John Brown* (1970). An excellent study of the South's journey to secession is William W. Freehling's *The Road to Disunion: Secessionists at Bay, 1776–1854* (1990).

On Lincoln's role in the coming crisis of war, see Don E. Fehrenbacher's *Prelude to Greatness: Lincoln in the 1850s* (1962). Harry V. Jaffa's *Crisis of the House Divided: An Interpretation of the Issues in the Lincoln-Douglas Debate* (1959) details the debates, and Maury Klein's *Days of Defiance: Sumter, Secession, and the Coming of the Civil War* (1997) treats the Fort Sumter controversy. An excellent collection of interpretive essays is *Why the War Came* (1996), edited by Gabor S. Boritt.

17

THE WAR OF THE UNION

FOCUS QUESTIONS

· What were the major strategies of the Civil War?

· How did the war affect the home front in the North and the South?

· What were the reasons for, and the results of, Lincoln's Emancipation Proclamation?

To answer these questions and access additional review material, please visit www.wwnorton.com/studyspace.

During the four long months between his election and his inauguration, Abraham Lincoln said little about future policies and less about past positions. "If I thought a repetition would do any good I would make it," he wrote to an editor in St. Louis. "But my judgment is it would do positive harm. The secessionists per se, believing they had alarmed me, would clamor all the louder." So he stayed in Illinois until mid-February 1861, biding his time. He then boarded a train for a long, roundabout trip to Washington and began to drop some hints about his shifting outlook to audiences along the way. He told the New Jersey legislature that he was "devoted to peace" but warned that "it may be necessary to put the foot down." At the end of the journey, reluctantly yielding to rumors of plots against his life, he passed unnoticed on a night train through Baltimore and slipped into Washington, D.C., before daybreak on February 23, 1861.

THE END OF THE WAITING GAME

In early 1861, as the possibility of civil war captured the attention of a divided nation, no one imagined that a conflict of horrendous scope and intensity awaited them. On both sides, people believed that any fighting would be over in little more than a month and that their daily lives would go on as usual.

LINCOLN'S INAUGURATION   In his inaugural address, Lincoln repeated his pledge not "to interfere with the institution of slavery in the States where it exists. I believe I have no lawful right to do so, and I have no inclination to do so." But the immediate question had shifted from slavery to secession, and most of the speech emphasized Lincoln's view that "the Union of these States is perpetual." The Union, he asserted, preceded the Constitution itself, dating from the Articles of Association drafted by the Continental Congress in 1774. It was "matured and continued" by the Declaration of Independence and the Articles of Confederation. Yet even if the United States were only a contractual association, "no State upon its own mere motion can lawfully get out of the Union." Lincoln promised to hold forts in the South belonging to the federal government, collect taxes, and deliver the mail unless repelled, but beyond that "there will be no invasion, no using of force against or among the people anywhere." In the final paragraph of the speech, Lincoln offered an eloquent appeal for regional harmony:

> I am loath to close. We are not enemies, but friends. We must not be enemies. Though passion may have strained, it must not break our bonds of affection. The mystic chords of memory, stretching from every battlefield and patriot grave to every living heart and hearthstone all over this broad land, will yet swell the chorus of the Union, when again touched, as surely they will be, by the better angels of our nature.

Lincoln not only entered office amid the gravest crisis yet faced by a president, but he also confronted unusual problems of transition. Republicans, in power for the first time, crowded Washington, hungry for office. Four of the seven new cabinet members had been rivals for the presidency: William H. Seward at the State Department, Salmon P. Chase at the Treasury Department, Simon Cameron at the War Department, and Edward Bates as attorney general. Four were former Democrats, and three were former Whigs. They formed a group of better-than-average ability, though most were so strong-minded they thought themselves better qualified to lead than Lincoln. Only later did they acknowledge with Seward that Lincoln "is the best man among us."

THE FALL OF FORT SUMTER   For the time being, Lincoln's combination of firmness and moderation differed little from James Buchanan's stance. The new president's only other choices were to accept the secession of seven states as an accomplished fact or use force right away. On the day after he took office, however, word arrived from Charleston that time was running out. Major Robert Anderson, in charge of the federal forces at Fort Sumter, had supplies for a month to six weeks, and Confederates were encircling the fort with a "ring of fire."

Events moved quickly to a climax in the next two weeks. On April 4, 1861, Lincoln decided to resupply the sixty-nine men at Fort Sumter. On April 9 President Jefferson Davis and his Confederate cabinet in Montgomery, Alabama, decided against permitting Lincoln to resupply the fort. On April 11 the Confederate general Pierre G. T. Beauregard, a dapper Louisiana Creole who had studied the use of artillery under Robert Anderson at West Point, demanded a speedy surrender of Fort Sumter. Anderson refused but said his supplies would be used up in three days. With the relief ships approaching, Anderson received an ultimatum to yield. He again refused, and at four-thirty on the morning of April 12 the shelling of Fort Sumter began. After more than thirty hours, his ammunition exhausted, Anderson lowered the flag.

The guns of Charleston signaled the end of the waiting game. On the day after Anderson's surrender, Lincoln called upon the loyal states to supply 75,000 militiamen to subdue the rebel states. Volunteers rallied around the flag at the recruiting stations. On April 19 Lincoln proclaimed a blockade of southern ports, which, as the Supreme Court later ruled, confirmed the existence of war.

TAKING SIDES   Lincoln's war proclamation swept four more states into the Confederacy. Virginia acted first. Its convention passed an Ordinance of Secession on April 17. The Confederate Congress then chose Richmond, Virginia, as its new capital, and the government moved there in June. Three other states followed Virginia in little over a month: Arkansas on May 6, Tennessee on May 7, and North Carolina on May 20. All four of the holdout states, especially Tennessee and Virginia, had areas (mainly in the mountains) where slaves were scarce and Union support ran strong. In east Tennessee the mountain counties would supply more volunteers to the Union than to the Confederate

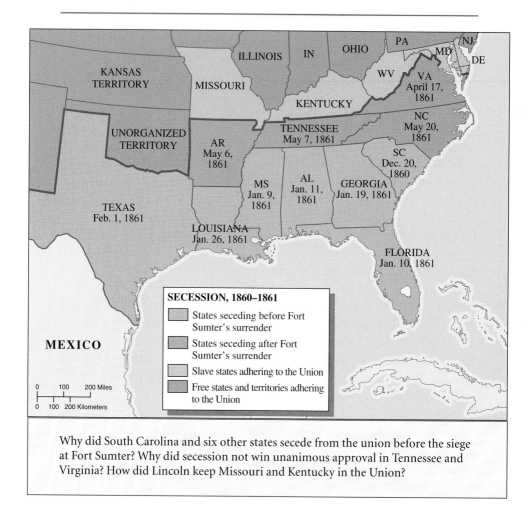

SECESSION, 1860–1861

- ☐ States seceding before Fort Sumter's surrender
- ■ States seceding after Fort Sumter's surrender
- ☐ Slave states adhering to the Union
- ■ Free states and territories adhering to the Union

Why did South Carolina and six other states secede from the union before the siege at Fort Sumter? Why did secession not win unanimous approval in Tennessee and Virginia? How did Lincoln keep Missouri and Kentucky in the Union?

cause. Unionists in western Virginia, bolstered by a Union army from Ohio under General George B. McClellan, contrived a loyal government of Virginia that formed a new state. In 1863 Congress admitted West Virginia to the Union with a constitution that provided for gradual emancipation of the few slaves there.

Of the other slave states, Delaware remained firmly in the Union, but Maryland, Kentucky, and Missouri went through bitter struggles to decide which side to support. The secession of Maryland would have isolated Washington, D.C., within the Confederacy. To hold on to that state, Lincoln took drastic measures of dubious legality: he suspended the writ of habeas corpus (under which judges could require arresting officers to produce their prisoners and justify their arrest) and rounded up pro-Confederate leaders and threw them in jail. The fall elections ended the threat of Maryland's secession by returning a solidly Unionist majority in the state.

Kentucky, native state of both Abraham Lincoln and Jefferson Davis, harbored divided loyalties. Its fragile neutrality lasted until September 3, when a Confederate force occupied several towns. General Ulysses S. Grant then moved Union soldiers into Paducah. Thereafter, Kentucky, though divided in allegiance, for the most part remained with the Union. It joined the Confederacy, some have said, only after the war.

Lincoln's effort to hold a middle course in Missouri ran afoul of the maneuvers of less patient men in the state. Elections for a convention brought an overwhelming Union victory, whereas a pro-Confederate militia under the state governor began to gather near St. Louis. In that city, Unionist forces rallied, and on May 10 they surprised and disarmed the rebel militia at its camp. They pursued the pro-Confederate forces into the southwestern part of the state, and after a temporary setback on August 10 the Unionists pushed the Confederates back again, finally breaking their resistance at the Battle of Pea Ridge (March 6–8, 1862), just over the state line in Arkansas. Thereafter border warfare continued in Missouri, pitting against each other rival bands of gunslingers who kept up their feuding and banditry for years after the war was over.

CHOOSING SIDES   Robert E. Lee's decision epitomized the agonizing choice facing many residents of the border states. Son of "Light-Horse Harry" Lee, a Revolutionary War hero, and married to a descendant of Martha Washington's, Lee had served in the U.S. Army for thirty years. When Fort Sumter was attacked, he was summoned by General Winfield Scott, another Virginian, and offered command of the Federal forces. After a sleepless night spent pacing the floor, Lee told Scott that he could not go against his "country," meaning Virginia. Although Lee failed to "see the good of secession," he could not "raise my hand against my birthplace, my home, my children." Lee resigned his army commission, retired to his estate, and soon answered a call to the Virginia—later the Confederate—service.

Many southerners made great sacrifices to remain loyal to the Union. Some left their native region once the fighting began. Others who remained in the South found ways to support the Union. In every Confederate state except South Carolina, whole regiments were organized to fight for the Union. Some 100,000 men from the southern states fought against the Confederacy. One out of every five soldiers from Arkansas killed in the war fought on the Union side.

THE BALANCE OF FORCE

Shrouded in an ever-thickening mist of larger-than-life mythology, the Union triumph in the Civil War has acquired an aura of inevitability. The Confederacy's fight for independence, on the other hand, has taken on the aura of a romantic lost cause, doomed from the start by the region's sparse industrial development, smaller pool of able-bodied men, paucity of capital resources and warships, and spotty transportation network.

But in 1861 the military situation seemed by no means so clear-cut. For all of the South's obvious disadvantages, it initially enjoyed a captive labor force and the benefits of fighting a defensive campaign on familiar territory. Jefferson Davis and other Confederate leaders were genuinely confident that their cause would prevail on the battlefield. The outcome of the Civil War was not inevitable: it was determined as much by human decisions and human willpower as by physical resources.

ECONOMIC ADVANTAGES   The South seceded in part out of a growing awareness of its minority status in the nation; a balance sheet of the sections in 1861 shows the accuracy of that perception. The Union held twenty-three states, including four border slave states, while the Confederacy had eleven.

Union Soldiers at Harpers Ferry, Virginia, in 1862

Neither side in the Civil War was prepared for the magnitude of this first "modern" war.

The population count was about 22 million in the Union to 9 million in the Confederacy, and about 4 million of the latter were enslaved. The Union therefore had an edge of about four to one in potential human resources. To help redress the imbalance, the Confederacy mobilized 80 percent of its military-age white men, one third of whom would die during the prolonged war.

An even greater advantage for the North was its industrial development. The states that joined the Confederacy produced just 7 percent of the nation's manufactures on the eve of the war. The Union states produced 97 percent of the firearms and 96 percent of the railroad equipment. They had most of the trained mechanics, most of the shipping and mercantile firms, and the bulk of the banking and financial resources. The North's advantage in transportation weighed heavily as the war went on. The Union had more wagons, horses, and ships than the Confederacy and an impressive edge in railroads.

As the Civil War began, the Confederacy enjoyed a major geographic advantage: it could fight a defensive war on its own territory. In addition, the South had more experienced military leaders. Some of those advantages were soon countered, however, by the Union navy's effective blockade of the major southern ports. On the inland waters navy gunboats and transports played an even more direct role in securing the Union's control of the Mississippi River and its larger tributaries, which provided easy invasion routes into the center of the Confederacy.

The U.S. Watervliet Arsenal in Watervliet, New York

The North had an advantage in industrial development, and its foundries turned out most of the nation's firearms.

THE WAR'S EARLY COURSE

After the fall of Fort Sumter, partisans on both sides hoped that the war might end with one sudden bold stroke, the capture of Washington or the fall of Richmond. Nowhere was this naive optimism more clearly displayed than at the First Battle of Bull Run (or Manassas).* An eager public pressured both sides to strike quickly and decisively. Jefferson Davis allowed the battle-hungry General P.G.T. Beauregard to hurry the main Confederate army to the railroad center at Manassas Junction, Virginia, about twenty-five miles west of Washington. Lincoln decided that General Irvin McDowell's hastily assembled Union army of some 37,000 might overrun the outnumbered Confederates and quickly march on to Richmond, the Confederate capital.

It was a hot, dry day on July 21, 1861, when McDowell's raw recruits encountered Beauregard's army dug in behind a meandering little stream called Bull Run. The two generals, former classmates at West Point, adopted markedly similar plans: each would try to turn the other's left flank. The Federals almost achieved their purpose early in the afternoon, but Confederate reinforcements, led by General Joseph E. Johnston, poured in to check the Union offensive. Amid the fury a South Carolina officer rallied his men by pointing to Thomas Jackson's brigade of Virginians: "Look, there is Jackson with his Virginians, standing like a stone wall." The reference thereafter served as Jackson's nickname.

After McDowell's last assault faltered, his army's frantic retreat turned into a panic as fleeing soldiers and terrified civilians clogged the Washington road. An Ohio congressman and several colleagues tried to rally the frenzied soldiers. "We called them cowards, denounced them in the most offensive terms, pulled out our heavy revolvers and threatened to shoot them, but in vain; a cruel, crazy, mad, hopeless panic possessed them." But the Confederates were about as disorganized and exhausted by the battle as the Yankees were, and they failed to give chase. It would have been futile anyway, for the next day a summer downpour turned roads into quagmires.

The Battle of Bull Run was a sobering experience for both sides. Much of the romance—the splendid uniforms, bright flags, rousing songs—gave way

---

*The Federals most often named battles for natural features; the Confederates, for nearby towns—thus Bull Run (Manassas), Antietam (Sharpsburg), Stones River (Murfreesboro), and the like.

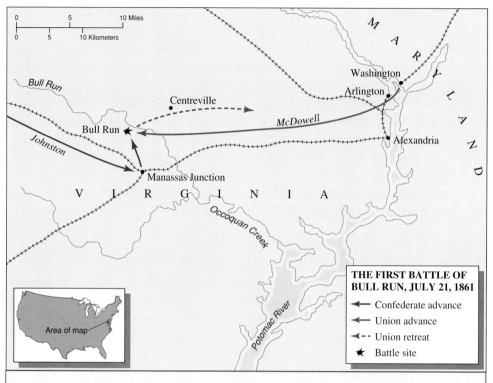

0 · 5 · 10 Miles
0 · 5 · 10 Kilometers

MARYLAND

Bull Run

Centreville

Washington

Arlington

Bull Run ★

McDowell

Johnston

Alexandria

Manassas Junction

V I R G I N I A

Occoquan Creek

Potomac River

THE FIRST BATTLE OF BULL RUN, JULY 21, 1861
→ Confederate advance
← Union advance
◄-- Union retreat
★ Battle site

Area of map

Why did the Confederate and Union armies rush to battle before they were ready? How did Beauregard win the first Battle of Bull Run? Why did Jackson not pursue the Union army?

to the agonizing realization that this would be a long and costly struggle. *Harper's Weekly* bluntly warned: "From the fearful day at Bull Run dates war. Not polite war, not incredulous war, but war that breaks hearts and blights homes." The sobering Union defeat "will teach us in the first place . . . that this war must be prosecuted on scientific principles."

THE WAR'S EARLY PHASE   The Battle of Bull Run demonstrated that the war would not be decided with one sudden stroke. General Winfield Scott, the seventy-five-year-old commander of the Union armies, had predicted as much, and now Lincoln fell back upon Scott's three-pronged "anaconda" strategy. It called first for the Army of the Potomac to defend Washington, D.C., and exert constant pressure on the Confederate capital at Richmond.

At the same time the navy would blockade the southern ports and dry up the Confederacy's access to foreign goods and weapons. The final component of the plan would divide the Confederacy by invading the South along the main water routes: the Mississippi, Tennessee, and Cumberland rivers. This strategy would slowly entwine and crush the southern resistance.

The Confederate strategy was simpler. If the Union forces could be stalemated, Jefferson Davis and others hoped, then the cotton-hungry British or French might be persuaded to join their cause, or perhaps public sentiment in the North would force Lincoln to seek a negotiated settlement. So at the same time that armies were forming in the South, Confederate diplomats were seeking assistance in London and Paris, and Confederate sympathizers in the North were urging an end to the North's war effort.

NAVAL ACTIONS   After Bull Run, for the rest of 1861 and into early 1862, the most important military actions involved a naval war and blockade. The one great threat to the Union navy's blockade of southern ports proved to be short-lived. The Confederates in Norfolk, Virginia, fashioned an ironclad ship from an abandoned Union steam frigate, the *Merrimack*. Rechristened the *Virginia*, it ventured out on March 8, 1862, and began attacking Union ships. But as luck would have it, a new Union ironclad, the *Monitor*, arrived from New York in time to engage the *Virginia* on the next day. They fought to a draw, and the *Virginia* returned to port, where the Confederates destroyed it when they had to give up Norfolk soon afterward.

Thereafter the Union navy tightened its grip on the South. In late 1861 a Federal flotilla appeared at Port Royal, South Carolina, pounded the fortifications into submission, and seized the port and nearby sea islands. The navy extended its bases farther down the Carolina coast in the late summer and fall of 1862. From there its progress extended southward along the Georgia-Florida coast. In the spring of 1862, Admiral David Farragut forced open the lower Mississippi near its mouth and surprised the Confederate defenders of New Orleans.

FORMING ARMIES   Once the fighting began, the Federal Congress recruited 500,000 more men and after the Battle of Bull Run added another 500,000. By the end of 1861, the first half million had enlisted. This rapid mobilization left the army with a large number of "political" officers, commissioned by state governors or elected by the recruits.

The nineteenth-century army often organized its units along community and ethnic lines. The Union army, for example, included a Scandinavian regiment (the 15th Wisconsin Infantry), a Scottish Highlander unit (the

The U.S. Army Recruiting Office in City Hall Park, New York City

The sign advertises the money offered those willing to serve: $677 to new recruits, $777 to veteran soldiers, and $15 to anyone who brought in a recruit.

79th New York Infantry), a French regiment (the 55th New York Infantry), and a mixed unit of Poles, Hungarians, Germans, Spaniards, and Italians (the 39th New York Infantry).

In the Confederacy, Jefferson Davis initially called up 100,000 twelve-month volunteers. Once the fighting started, he was authorized to raise up to 400,000 three-year volunteers "without the delay of a formal call upon the respective states." Thus by early 1862 most of the veteran Confederate soldiers were nearing the end of their enlistment without having encountered much significant action. They were also resisting the incentives of bonuses and furloughs for reenlistment. The Confederate government thus turned to conscription. By an act passed on April 16, 1862, all white male citizens aged eighteen to thirty-five were declared members of the army for three years, and those already in service were required to serve out three years. In 1862 the upper age was raised to forty-five, and in 1864 the age limit was further extended from seventeen to fifty, with those under eighteen and over forty-five reserved for state defense.

The conscription law included two loopholes, however. First, a draftee might escape service either by providing an able-bodied substitute who was not of draft age or by paying $500 in cash. Second, exemptions, designed to protect key civilian work, were subject to abuse by men seeking "bombproof" jobs. The exemption of one white man for each plantation with twenty or more slaves led to bitter complaints about "a rich man's war and a poor man's fight."

The Union took nearly another year to force men into service. In 1863 the government began to draft men aged twenty to forty-five. Exemptions were granted to specified federal and state officeholders and to others on medical or compassionate grounds. For $300 one could avoid service. In both the North and the South, conscription spurred men to volunteer, either to collect bounties or to avoid the disgrace of being drafted.

The Civil War draft flouted an American tradition of voluntary service and was widely held to be arbitrary and unconstitutional. Widespread public opposition impeded its enforcement in both the North and the South. In New York City the announcement of a draft lottery on July 11, 1863, incited a week of rioting in which roving bands of working-class toughs, many of them Irish Catholic immigrants, took control of the streets. Although provoked by feelings that the draft loopholes catered to the wealthy, the riots also exposed racial and ethnic tensions. The mobs set upon conscription offices, factories, docks, and the homes of prominent Republicans. But they directed their wrath most furiously at African Americans. They blamed blacks for causing the war and for threatening to take their own unskilled jobs. The violence ran completely out of control; over 100 people were killed before five regiments of battle-weary soldiers brought from Gettysburg restored order.

CONFEDERATE DIPLOMACY   While the Union and the Confederate armies mobilized, Confederate diplomacy focused on gaining foreign supplies, diplomatic recognition, and perhaps even military intervention. The Confederates indulged the pathetic hope that official diplomatic recognition by England and France would prove decisive, when in fact it more likely would have followed a decisive victory in the field, which never came. An equally fragile illusion was the conviction that King Cotton would lure military aid and political sympathy from countries around the world dependent upon the fiber.

The first Confederate emissaries to England and France took hope when the British foreign minister received them informally after their arrival in London in 1861; they even won a promise from France's Napoléon III to recognize the Confederacy if Britain would lead the way. But the British foreign minister refused to receive the Confederates again, partly in response to Union pressure and partly out of British self-interest.

One incident early in the war threatened to upset British neutrality. In November 1861 a Union warship stopped a British ship, the *Trent,* and took into custody two Confederate agents, James M. Mason and John Slidell. Celebrated as a heroic deed by a northern public still starved for victories, the

Trent affair roused a storm of protest in Britain. The British government sent Lincoln an ultimatum for the captives' release. To interfere with a neutral ship on the high seas violated a long-settled American principle, and federal officials finally decided to release the two agents, much to their own chagrin. Mason and Slidell were more useful as martyrs to their own cause than they could ever be in London and Paris.

Confederate agents in Europe were far more successful in getting supplies than in gaining official government recognition of the Confederacy as a sovereign nation. The most spectacular feat was the purchase of raiding ships designed to attack Union vessels around the world. Although British law forbade the sale of warships to belligerents, a Confederate commissioner contrived to have ships built and then, on trial runs, escape to the Azores or elsewhere to be outfitted with guns. In all, eighteen such ships were activated and saw action in the Atlantic, Pacific, and Indian oceans, where they sank hundreds of Yankee ships and terrified the rest. The most spectacular of the Confederate raiders were the first two, the *Florida* and the *Alabama*, which captured thirty-eight and sixty-four Union ships, respectively.

THE WEST AND THE CIVIL WAR   During the Civil War western settlement continued unabated. New discoveries of gold and silver along the eastern slopes of the Sierra Nevadas and in Montana and Colorado lured thousands of prospectors and their suppliers. New transportation and communication networks emerged to serve the growing population in the West. Telegraph lines sprouted above the plains, and stagecoach lines fanned out to serve the new communities. Dakota, Colorado, and Nevada gained territorial status in 1861, Idaho and Arizona in 1863, and Montana in 1864. Silver-rich Nevada gained statehood in 1864.

With the firing on Fort Sumter, many of the regular army units assigned to frontier outposts in the West began to head east to meet the Confederate threat. In Texas, the Indian Territory (Oklahoma), and southern New Mexico, Union soldiers left altogether. Elsewhere they left behind skeleton units. Texas was the only western state to join the Confederacy. For the most part, the federal government maintained its control of the other western territories during the war. But it was not easy. Fighting in Kansas and the Indian Territory was widespread and furious. By 1862 Lincoln had been forced to dispatch new volunteer units to the West. He had two primary concerns: to protect the shipments of gold and silver and to win over western political support for the war and his presidency.

The most intense fighting in the West occurred along the Kansas-Missouri border. There the disputes between the pro-slavery and anti-slavery settlers of the 1850s turned into brutal guerrilla warfare. The most prominent pro-Confederate leader in the area was William Quantrill. He and his pro-slavery followers, mostly teenagers, fought under a black flag, meaning that they gave no quarter. In destroying Lawrence, Kansas, in 1863, Quantrill ordered his forces to "kill every male and burn every house." By the end of the day, 182 boys and men had been killed. Their opponents, the Jayhawkers, responded in kind. They tortured and hanged pro-Confederate prisoners, burned houses, and destroyed livestock.

Many Indian tribes found themselves caught up in the war. Indian regiments fought on both sides, and in Oklahoma they fought against each other. Indians among the "Five Civilized Tribes" held black slaves and felt a natural bond with southern whites. Oklahoma's proximity to Texas influenced the Choctaws and Chickasaws to support the Confederacy. The Cherokees, Creeks, and Seminoles were more divided in their loyalties. For those tribes the Civil War served as a wedge that fractured their unity. The Cherokees, for example, split in two, some supporting the Union and others supporting the South.

ACTIONS IN THE WESTERN THEATER   Little happened of military significance in the eastern theater (east of the Appalachians) before May 1862. On the other hand, the western theater (from the mountains to the Mississippi River) flared up with several encounters and an important penetration of the Confederate states. In western Kentucky, the Confederate general Albert Sidney Johnston had perhaps 40,000 men stretched over some 150 miles.

Early in 1862 General Ulysses S. Grant made the first Union thrust against the weak center of Johnston's overextended lines. Moving out of Cairo, Illinois, and Paducah, Kentucky, with a gunboat flotilla, he swung southward up the Tennessee River and captured Fort Henry on February 6. Grant then moved quickly overland to attack nearby Fort Donelson. On February 16 a force of 12,000 Confederates surrendered.

SHILOH   After suffering defeats in Kentucky and Tennessee, General Albert Johnston regrouped the Confederate forces and moved to Corinth, in northern Mississippi, near the Tennessee border. Ulysses Grant, meanwhile, moved his Union army southward along the Tennessee River during the early spring of 1862. Grant then made a costly mistake. While planning his attack on Corinth, he exposed his 42,000 troops on a rolling plateau between two creeks flowing into the Tennessee River and failed to dig defensive trenches. Johnston shrewdly recognized Grant's oversight, and on the morning of April 6 the Kentuckian ordered an attack on the vulnerable Federals,

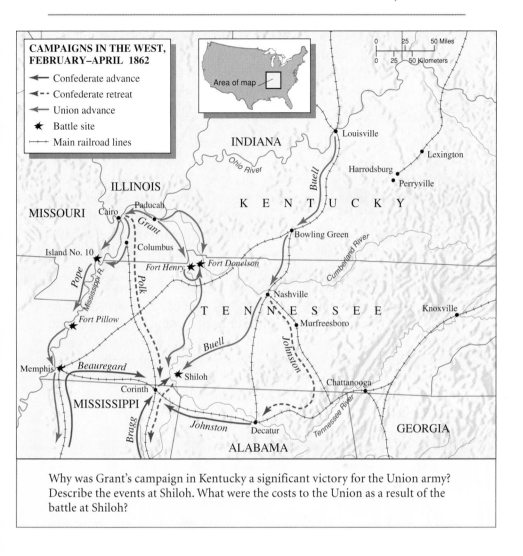

CAMPAIGNS IN THE WEST,
FEBRUARY–APRIL 1862

◄─── Confederate advance
◄─ ─ ─ Confederate retreat
◄─── Union advance
★ Battle site
├──┤ Main railroad lines

Area of map

Why was Grant's campaign in Kentucky a significant victory for the Union army? Describe the events at Shiloh. What were the costs to the Union as a result of the battle at Shiloh?

urging his men to be "worthy of your race and lineage; worthy of the women of the South."

The 44,000 Confederates struck suddenly at Shiloh, the site of a log church in the center of the Union camp in southwestern Tennessee. They found most of Grant's troops still sleeping or eating breakfast; many died in their bedrolls. After a day of carnage and confusion, the Union soldiers were pinned against the river. At the height of the battle, a wounded Union soldier was told to leave his rifle and go to the rear. He soon returned, saying, "Gimme another gun. This blame fight ain't got any rear." The Union army might well have been totally defeated had the Confederate commander, General Johnston, not been mortally wounded at the peak of the battle; his second in command called off the attack. Bolstered by reinforcements, Grant took the offensive the next day, and the Confederates glumly withdrew to Corinth, leaving the Union army too battered to pursue. Casualties on both sides totaled over 20,000.

Shiloh, a Hebrew word meaning "Place of Peace," was the costliest battle in which Americans had ever engaged, although worse was yet to come. Grant observed that the ground was "so covered with dead one could walk across the field without touching the ground." Like so many battles thereafter, Shiloh was a story of missed opportunities and debated turning points punctuated by lucky incidents and accidents. Throughout the Civil War winning armies would fail to pursue their retreating foes, thus allowing the wounded opponent to slip away and fight again.

After the battle at Shiloh, General Henry Halleck, already jealous of Grant's success, spread the false rumor that Grant had been drinking during the battle. Some called upon Lincoln to fire Grant, but the president refused: "I can't spare this man; he fights." Halleck, however, took Grant's place as field commander, and as a result the Union thrust southward ground to a halt. For the remainder of 1862, the chief action in the western theater was a series of inconclusive maneuvers punctuated by sharp engagements.

MCCLELLAN'S PENINSULAR CAMPAIGN   The eastern theater remained fairly quiet for nine months after Bull Run. In the wake of the Union defeat, Lincoln had replaced McDowell with General George B. McClellan, Stonewall Jackson's classmate at West Point. As head of the Army of the Potomac, McClellan set about building a powerful, well-trained army that would be ready for its next battle. When General Winfield Scott retired in November, Lincoln appointed McClellan general in chief. McClellan exuded confidence and poise. Yet for all his organizational ability and dramatic flair, his innate caution would prove crippling.

Time passed, and McClellan kept building and training his army to meet the superior numbers he claimed the Confederates were deploying. Lincoln wanted the army to move directly toward Richmond, but McClellan, who dismissed the president as a "well-meaning baboon," sought to enter Richmond by the side door, so to speak, up the neck of land between the York and James rivers, site of Jamestown, Williamsburg, and Yorktown.

In mid-March 1862 McClellan's army finally moved down the Potomac River and Chesapeake Bay to the Virginia peninsula southeast of Richmond.

Camp Winfield Scott

McClellan's headquarters during the siege of Yorktown, 1862.

This bold move put the Union forces within sixty miles of the Confederate capital. Thousands of Richmond residents fled the city in panic, but McClellan waited to strike, failing to capitalize on his advantages.

President Jefferson Davis, at the urging of his adviser Robert E. Lee, sent Stonewall Jackson's army into the Shenandoah Valley on what proved to be a brilliant diversionary action. From March 23 to June 9, Jackson's 18,000 men pinned down two separate Union armies with more than twice their numbers in the western Virginia mountains. While the Union army under General McDowell braced to defend Washington, Jackson hastened back to defend Richmond against McClellan.

On May 31 the Confederate general Joseph E. Johnston struck at McClellan's forces along the Chickahominy River. In the Battle of Seven Pines (Fair Oaks), only the arrival of federal reinforcements, who somehow crossed the swollen river, prevented a disastrous Union defeat. Both sides took heavy casualties, and General Johnston was severely wounded.

At this point, Robert E. Lee assumed command of the Army of Northern Virginia, a development that changed the course of the war. Tall, erect, and broad shouldered, Lee projected a commanding presence. At the start of the Civil War, the West Point graduate was considered the most promising army officer in the United States. Dignified yet fiery, Lee was an audacious commander. He led by example, and his men loved him. Unlike Johnston, Lee enjoyed Jefferson Davis's trust. More important, he knew how to use the talents of his superb field commanders: Stonewall Jackson, the pious, fearless mathematics professor from the Virginia Military Institute; James Longstreet, Lee's deliberate but tireless "warhorse"; sharp-tongued D.H. Hill, the former engineering professor at Davidson College; Ambrose P. Hill, the consummate fighter who challenged one commander to a duel and feuded with Stonewall Jackson; and J.E.B. Stuart, the colorful young cavalryman who once said, "All I ask of fate is that I may be killed leading a cavalry charge." He would get his wish.

Once in command, Lee attacked the Union lines east of Richmond but failed to dislodge the Union forces. McClellan's army was still near Richmond. On July 9, when Lincoln visited McClellan's headquarters, the general complained that the administration had failed to support him adequately and instructed the president at length on war policies. It was ample reason to remove McClellan. Lincoln returned to Washington and on July 11 called Henry Halleck from the West to take charge as general in chief. Miffed at his demotion, McClellan angrily dismissed Halleck as an officer "whom I know to be my inferior."

SECOND BULL RUN Lincoln and Halleck ordered McClellan to leave the peninsula and join the Washington defense force, now under the command of the bombastic John Pope, who had been called back from the West for a new overland assault on Richmond. In a letter to his wife, McClellan predicted that "Pope will be thrashed and disposed of" by Lee. As McClellan's Army of the Potomac began to pull out of the Tidewater, Lee moved northward to strike Pope before McClellan's troops arrived. Dividing his forces, Lee sent Jackson's "foot cavalry" around Pope's right flank to attack his supply lines. At Cedar Mountain, Virginia, Jackson pushed back an advance party of Federals and went on to seize and destroy the Federal supply base at Manassas Junction. At the Second Battle of Bull Run (or Manassas), fought on almost the same site as the earlier battle, Pope assumed that he faced only Jackson, but Lee's main army by that time had joined in. On August 30 a crushing attack on Pope's flank drove the Federals from the field. In the next few days the Union forces pulled back to the fortifications around Washington, where McClellan once again took command and reorganized. He displayed his unflagging egotism in a letter to his wife: "Again I have been called upon to save the country." The disgraced Pope was dispatched to Minnesota to fight Indians.

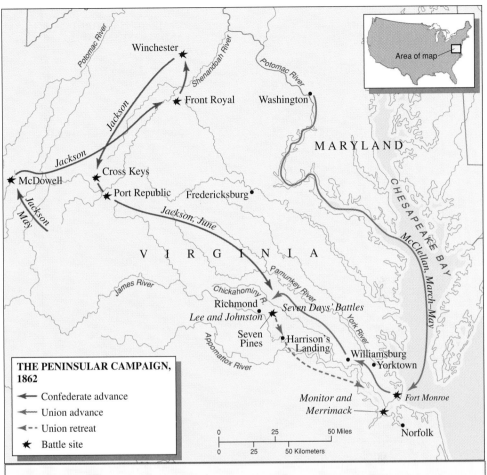

THE PENINSULAR CAMPAIGN, 1862

← Confederate advance

← Union advance

◄-- Union retreat

★ Battle site

What was McClellan's strategy for attacking Richmond? How did Jackson divert the attention of the Union army? Why did Lincoln demote McClellan after the Peninsular campaigns?

ANTIETAM Still on the offensive, Lee decided to invade the North and perhaps thereby gain foreign recognition and military supplies for the Confederacy. He and his battle-tested troops pushed into western Maryland in September 1862, headed for Pennsylvania. But Lee's bold strategy was uncovered when a Union soldier picked up a bundle of cigars and discovered a secret order from Lee wrapped around them. The paper revealed that Lee had again divided his army, sending Stonewall Jackson off to take Harpers Ferry, Virginia. McClellan boasted upon seeing the captured document,

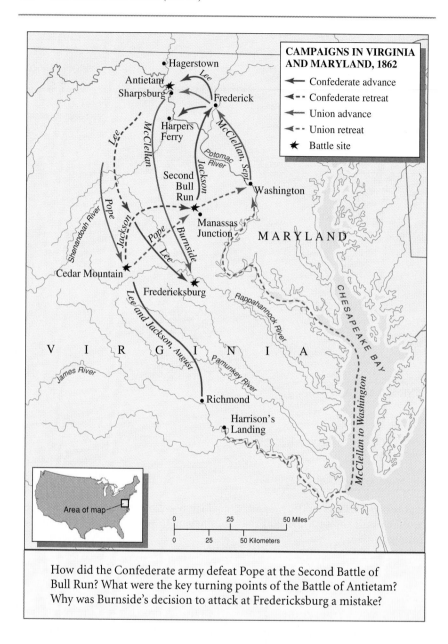

CAMPAIGNS IN VIRGINIA
AND MARYLAND, 1862

← — Confederate advance
◄- - Confederate retreat
← — Union advance
◄- - Union retreat
★ Battle site

Hagerstown

Antietam
Sharpsburg
Frederick

Harpers
Ferry

Second
Bull
Run

Washington

Manassas
Junction

MARYLAND

Cedar Mountain

Fredericksburg

Rappahannock River

CHESAPEAKE BAY

VIRGINIA

Pamunkey River

James River

Richmond

Harrison's
Landing

McClellan to Washington

Area of map

0   25   50 Miles
0   25   50 Kilometers

How did the Confederate army defeat Pope at the Second Battle of
Bull Run? What were the key turning points of the Battle of Antietam?
Why was Burnside's decision to attack at Fredericksburg a mistake?

"Here is a paper with which, if I cannot whip Bobby Lee, I will be willing to
go home." Instead of seizing his unexpected opportunity, however, he delayed
for sixteen crucial hours, still worried—as always—about enemy strength,
and Lee was thereby able to reassemble most of his tired army behind Antietam Creek. Still, McClellan was optimistic, and Lincoln, too, relished the

chance for a truly decisive blow. "God bless you and all with you," he wired McClellan. "Destroy the rebel army if possible."

On September 17, 1862, McClellan's forces attacked Confederate units near Sharpsburg, Maryland, along Antietam Creek, commencing the furious Battle of Antietam (Sharpsburg). With the Confederate lines ready to break, Ambrose P. Hill's division arrived from Harpers Ferry, having marched sixteen miles to the battlefield. Bone weary and footsore, they nevertheless plunged immediately into the fray, battering the Union army's left flank. Still outnumbered more than two to one, the Confederates forced a standoff in the most costly day of the Civil War, a day participants thought would never end. The next day the battered Confederates slipped south across the Potomac River to the safety of Virginia. General Lee's northern invasion had failed. The Battle of Antietam was the bloodiest single day in American history. Some 6,400 soldiers on both sides were killed and another 15,000 wounded. Surveying the battlefield afterward, a Union officer counted "hundreds of dead bodies lying in rows and in piles." The scene was "sickening, harrowing, horrible. O what a terrible sight!"

The vainglorious McClellan insisted that he had "fought the battle splendidly" and that "our victory was complete," but Lincoln thought otherwise. Disgusted by McClellan's failure to gain a truly decisive victory, the

The Early Campaigns

Lincoln and McClellan confer at Antietam, October 4, 1862.

president sent a curt message to the general: "I have just read your dispatch about sore-tongued and fatigued horses. Will you pardon me for asking what the horses of your army have done . . . that fatigues anything?" Failing to receive a satisfactory answer, Lincoln removed McClellan from command and assigned him to recruiting duty in New Jersey. Never again would he command troops.

FREDERICKSBURG   The Battle of Antietam was the turning point in the war. It revived sagging Northern morale, emboldened Abraham Lincoln to issue the Emancipation Proclamation, freeing all slaves in the Confederate states, and dashed the Confederacy's hopes of foreign recognition. Yet the war was far from over. In his search for a fighting general, Lincoln now made the worst choice of all. He turned to Ambrose E. Burnside, who had twice before turned down the job on the grounds that he felt unfit for so large a command. But if the White House wanted him to fight, he would attack, even in the face of the oncoming winter.

On December 13, 1862, Burnside sent the Army of the Potomac across the icy Rappahannock River to assault Lee's forces, who were well entrenched on ridges and behind stone walls west of Fredericksburg, Virginia. Confederate artillery and muskets chewed up the blue columns as they crossed a mile of open land outside the town. It was, a Federal general sighed, "a great slaughter-pen." The scene was both awful and awesome, prompting Lee to remark, "It is well that war is so terrible—we should grow too fond of it." After taking more than 12,000 casualties, compared with fewer than 6,000 for the Confederates, Burnside wept as he gave the order to withdraw.

The year 1862 ended with forces in the East deadlocked and the Union advance in the West stalled since midyear. Union morale plummeted: northern Democrats were calling for a negotiated peace. At the same time, Lincoln was under pressure from the so-called Radical Republicans, who were pushing for more stringent war measures and questioning the president's competence. General Burnside, too, was under fire, with some of his own officers ready to testify publicly to his shortcomings.

But amid the dissension the deeper currents of the war were turning in favor of the Union: in the lengthening war its superior resources began to tell. In both the eastern and the western theaters the Confederate counterattack had been repulsed. And while the armies clashed, Lincoln by the stroke of a pen changed the conflict from a war to restore the Union into a revolutionary struggle for the abolition of slavery. On January 1, 1863, he signed the Emancipation Proclamation.

EMANCIPATION

At the war's outset, Lincoln had promised to restore the Union but maintain slavery where it existed. Congress, too, endorsed that position. Once fighting began, the need to hold the border states in the Union dictated caution on the volatile issue of emancipation. Beyond that, several other considerations deterred action. For one, Lincoln had to cope with a deep-seated racial prejudice in the North. Whereas most abolitionists promoted both complete emancipation and the social integration of the races, many anti-slavery activists wanted slavery prohibited only in the new western territories and states. They were willing to allow slavery to continue in the South and were uneasy about racial integration. Lincoln himself harbored doubts about his authority to emancipate slaves so long as he clung to the view that the rebellious states remained legally in the Union. The only way around the problem would be to justify emancipation as a military necessity.

A MEASURE OF WAR   The expanding war forced the issue. As Federal forces pushed into the Confederacy, fugitive slaves began to turn up in Union army camps, and generals did not know whether or not to declare them free. Some put the "contrabands" to work building fortifications; others set them free. Lincoln, meanwhile, began to edge toward emancipation. In March 1862 he proposed that federal compensation be offered any state

Contrabands

Former slaves on a farm in Cumberland Landing, Virginia, 1862.

that began gradual emancipation. The plan failed in Congress because of border-state opposition, but on April 16, 1862, Lincoln signed an act that abolished slavery in the District of Columbia; on June 19 another act excluded slavery from the territories, without offering owners compensation. A Second Confiscation Act, passed on July 17, liberated the slaves of all persons aiding the rebellion. Still another act forbade the army to help return runaways to their border-state owners.

To save the Union, Lincoln finally decided, emancipation of Confederate slaves would be required for several reasons: slave labor bolstered the Rebel war effort, sagging morale in the North needed the boost of a moral cause, and public opinion was swinging toward emancipation as the war dragged on. Proclaiming a war on slavery, moreover, would end forever any chance that France or Britain would support the Confederacy. In July 1862 Lincoln first confided to his cabinet that he was considering issuing a proclamation that under his war powers would free the slaves of the enemy. At the time, Secretary of State William Seward advised him to wait for a Union victory in order to avoid any semblance of desperation.

The time to act finally came after the Battle of Antietam. On September 22, 1862, Lincoln issued a preliminary Emancipation Proclamation, in which he repeated that his object was mainly to restore the Union and that he favored proposals for paying slaveholders for their losses. But the main burden of the document was his warning that on January 1, 1863, "all persons held as slaves within any state, or designated part of a state, the people whereof shall be in rebellion against the United States, shall be then, thenceforward and forever free." On January 1, 1863, Lincoln signed the second Emancipation Proclamation, again emphasizing that this was a war measure based upon his war powers. He also urged blacks to abstain from violence except in self-defense, and he added that free blacks would now be received into the armed services of the United States. As he wrote his name on the document, Lincoln said, "I never, in my life, felt more certain that I was doing the right thing than I do in signing this paper."

Reactions to Emancipation

Among the Confederate states, Tennessee and the Union-controlled parts of Virginia and Louisiana were exempted from the Emancipation Proclamation. Thus no slaves who were within Union lines at the time were freed. But many enslaved African Americans in those areas claimed

Two Views of the Emancipation Proclamation

The Union view (top) shows a thoughtful Lincoln composing the proclamation, the Constitution and the Holy Bible in his lap. The Confederate view (bottom) shows a demented Lincoln, his foot on the Constitution and his inkwell held by the devil.

their freedom anyway. "In a document proclaiming liberty," wrote the historian Benjamin Quarles, "the unfree never bother to read the fine print."

BLACKS IN THE MILITARY

Lincoln's Emancipation Proclamation sparked new efforts to organize all-black Union military units, to be led by white officers. Massachusetts organized the first all-black unit, the 54th Massachusetts Regiment under Colonel Robert Gould Shaw. Rhode Island and other states soon followed suit. In May 1863 the War Department authorized general recruitment of African Americans across the country. This was a momentous decision, for it changed a war to preserve the Union into a revolution to transform the social, economic, and racial status quo in the South.

By mid-1863 African-American units were involved in significant action in both the eastern and the western theaters. On July 18, 1863, Colonel Shaw, a Harvard graduate and the son of a prominent abolitionist, led his troops in a

The 107th U.S. Colored Infantry

From early in the war, Union commanders found "contrabands" useful as informants and guides to unfamiliar terrain.

courageous assault against Fort Wagner, a massive earthwork barrier guarding Charleston, South Carolina. During the battle almost half the members of the 54th Regiment were killed, including Colonel Shaw. The courageous performance of the 54th Regiment did much to win acceptance for both black soldiers and emancipation. Commenting on Union victories at Port Hudson and Milliken's Bend, Louisiana, Lincoln reported that "some of our commanders . . . believe that . . . the use of colored troops constitutes the heaviest blow yet dealt to the rebels, and that at least one of these important successes could not have been achieved . . . but for the aid of black soldiers."

By the end of the war, almost 180,000 African Americans had served in the regiments of the U.S. Colored Troops, providing around 10 percent of the Union army total. Some 80 percent of the "colored troops" were former slaves or free blacks from the South. Some 38,000 gave their lives. In the navy, blacks accounted for about one fourth of all enlistments; of these more than 2,800 died.

"Drummer" Jackson

This photograph of a former slave who served in the 79th U.S. Colored Troops, was used to encourage African Americans to enlist.

As the war entered its final months, freedom emerged more fully as a legal reality. Three major steps occurred in January 1865, when both Missouri and Tennessee abolished slavery by state action and the U.S. House of Representatives passed an abolition amendment. Upon ratification by three fourths of the reunited states, the Thirteenth Amendment became part of the Constitution on December 18, 1865, and removed any lingering doubts about the legality of emancipation. By then, in fact, slavery remained only in the border states of Kentucky and Delaware.

WOMEN AND THE WAR

While breaking the bonds of slavery, the Civil War also loosened traditional restraints on female activity. "No conflict in history," a journalist wrote at the time, "was such a woman's war as the Civil War." Women on both sides played prominent roles in the conflict. They sewed uniforms, composed uplifting poems and songs, and raised money and supplies. Thousands of northern women worked with the U.S. Sanitary Commission, which organized medical relief and other services for soldiers. Others, black and white, supported the freedmen's aid movement to help impoverished freed slaves.

In the North alone, some 20,000 women served as nurses or other health-related volunteers. A nurse working at a Maryland hospital recorded that she and her peers "endured the cold without sufficient bedding for our hard beds, and with no provision made for our fires. On bitter mornings we rose shivering, broke the ice in our pails, and washed our numb hands and faces, then went out into the raw air, up to our mess room, also without fire, thence to the wards." The most famous nurses were Dorothea Dix and Clara Barton, both untiring volunteers in service to the wounded and dying. Dix, the veteran reformer of the nation's insane asylums, became the Union army's first superintendent of women nurses. She soon found herself flooded with applications from around the country. Dix explained that nurses should be "sober, earnest, self-sacrificing, and self-sustained" women between the ages of thirty-five and fifty who could "bear the presence of suffering and exercise entire self control" and who could be "calm, gentle, quiet, active, and steadfast in duty."

Nursing and the War

Clara Barton oversaw the distribution of medicines to Union troops and later helped found the American Red Cross. Instead of accepting an assignment to a general hospital during the war, she followed the troops on her own, working in makeshift field hospitals.

The departure of hundreds of thousands of men for the battlefield forced women to assume the public and private roles the men left behind. In many southern towns and counties the home front became a world of white women, children, and slaves. A resident of Lexington, Virginia, reported in 1862 that there were "no men left" in town by mid-1862. Women suddenly found themselves farmers or plantation managers, clerks, munitions-plant workers, and schoolteachers. Some 400 women disguised themselves as men and fought in the war; dozens served as spies; others traveled with the armies, cooking meals, writing letters, and assisting with amputations.

The war's unrelenting carnage took a terrible toll on the nation's women. A North Carolina mother lost seven sons in the fighting; another lost four. Women who bore such losses or who witnessed daily suffering while serving as nurses were permanently altered by the experience. The number of widows, spinsters, and orphans mushroomed. Many bereaved women on both sides came to look upon the war with what the poet Emily Dickinson called a "chastened stare."

GOVERNMENT DURING THE WAR

Freeing 4 million slaves and loosening the restraints on female activity constituted a momentous social and economic revolution. But an even broader revolution began as power in Congress shifted from South to North. Before the war southern congressmen exercised a great deal of influence, but once the secessionists had abandoned Congress to the Republicans, a dramatic change occurred. Several projects that had been stalled by sectional controversy were adopted before the end of 1862. A new protective tariff was passed. A transcontinental railroad was approved, to run through Omaha, Nebraska, to Sacramento, California. A homestead act granted 160 acres to settlers who agreed to work the land for five years. The National Banking Act followed in 1863. Two other key pieces of legislation were the Morrill Land Grant Act (1862), which provided federal aid to state colleges of "agriculture and mechanic arts," and the Contract Labor Act (1864), which encouraged the importation of immigrant labor. All of these had long-term significance for the expansion of the national economy—and the federal government.

UNION FINANCES Congress focused on three options to finance the war: raising taxes, printing paper money, and borrowing. The taxes came chiefly in the form of the Morrill tariff on imports and excise taxes on manufactures and nearly every profession. A butcher, for example, had to pay 30¢ for every head of beef he slaughtered, 10¢ for every hog, 5¢ for every sheep. On top of the excises came an income tax. In 1862 Congress passed the Internal Revenue Act, which created an Internal Revenue Service.

But federal tax revenues trickled in so slowly—in the end they would meet only 21 percent of wartime expenditures—that Congress in 1862 resorted to printing paper money. Beginning with the Legal Tender Act of 1862, Congress ultimately authorized $450 million in paper currency, which soon became known as greenbacks because of the bills' color. The congressional decision to allow the Treasury to print paper money was a profoundly important development for the U.S. economy, then and since. Unlike previous paper currencies issued by local banks, the federal greenbacks could not be exchanged for gold or silver. Instead, their value relied upon public trust in the government. Many bankers were outraged by the advent of the greenbacks. "Gold and silver are the only true measure of value," one financier declared. "These metals were prepared by the Almighty." But the crisis of the Union and the desperate need to finance the expanding war demanded such a solution. As the months passed, the greenbacks helped ease the Union's financial crisis without causing the ruinous inflation that the unlimited issue of paper money caused in the Confederacy.

The federal government also relied upon the sale of bonds. A Philadelphia banker named Jay Cooke (sometimes tagged the Financier of the Civil War) mobilized a nationwide campaign to sell government bonds to private investors. Eventually bonds generated $2 billion in federal revenue.

For many businessmen, war-related ventures brought quick riches. Some suppliers and financiers bilked the government or provided shoddy goods. Not all the wartime fortunes were made dishonestly, however. And the war-related expenditures by the Union helped promote the capital accumulation with which businesses fueled later expansion. Wartime business thus laid the groundwork for the postwar economic boom and for the fortunes of tycoons such as J. P. Morgan, John D. Rockefeller, Andrew Mellon, and Andrew Carnegie.

CONFEDERATE FINANCES Confederate finances were a disaster from the start. In the first year of its existence, the Confederacy levied export and import duties, but exports and imports were too low to generate much revenue. It then enacted a tax of one half of 1 percent on most forms of property, which should have yielded a hefty income, but the Confederacy farmed out its collection of the taxes to the states. The result was chaos. In 1863 the desperate Confederate Congress began taxing nearly everything. Enforcement of the taxes was poor and evasion easy. Altogether taxes covered no more than 5 percent of Confederate costs; bond issues accounted for less than 33 percent; and Treasury notes (paper money), for more than 66 percent. Altogether the Confederacy turned out more than $1 billion in paper money and sparked a steep inflation. By 1864 a turkey sold in the Richmond market for $100, flour brought $425 a barrel, and bacon was $10 a pound.

UNION POLITICS AND CIVIL LIBERTIES   On the home fronts, the crisis of war brought no moratorium on partisan politics, northern or southern. Within his own party, Lincoln faced a Radical wing composed mainly of prewar abolitionists. Led by House members such as Thaddeus Stevens and George Washington Julian and senators such as Charles Sumner, Benjamin Franklin Wade, and Zachariah Chandler, the Radical Republicans pushed for confiscation of plantations, immediate emancipation of slaves, and a more vigorous prosecution of the war. The majority of Republicans, however, continued to back Lincoln's more cautious approach. The party was generally united on economic policy.

The Democratic party suffered the loss of its southern wing and the death of its leader, Stephen A. Douglas, in June 1861. By and large, northern Democrats supported a war for the "Union as it was" before 1860, giving reluctant support to Lincoln's policies but opposing restraints on civil liberties and the new economic legislation. "War Democrats," such as Tennessee Senator Andrew Johnson and Secretary of War Edwin M. Stanton fully supported Lincoln's policies, while a peace wing of the party preferred an end to the fighting, even if that meant risking the Union. An extreme fringe of the peace wing even flirted with outright disloyalty. The Copperheads, as they were called, were strongest in states such as Ohio, Indiana, and Illinois, all leavened with native southerners, some of whom were pro-Confederate.

Such open sympathy for the enemy provoked Lincoln to crack down hard. Early in the war he assumed emergency powers, including the power to suspend the writ of habeas corpus, which guarantees arrested citizens a speedy hearing. The Constitution states that habeas corpus may be suspended only in cases of rebellion or invasion, but congressional leaders argued that Congress alone had the authority to take such action. By the Habeas Corpus Act of 1863, Congress authorized the president to suspend the writ.

There were probably more than 14,000 arrests made without recourse to a writ of habeas corpus. Most of those arrested were Confederate citizens accused of slipping vessels through the Union blockade, or they were foreign nationals. But Union citizens were also detained. One celebrated case arose in 1863 when Federal soldiers hustled the Democrat Clement L. Vallandigham out of his home in Dayton, Ohio; a military court condemned Ohio's most prominent Confederate sympathizer to confinement for the duration of the war. The muzzling of a political opponent proved such an embarrassment to Lincoln that he commuted the sentence, but only by another irregular device: banishment behind Confederate lines. Vallandigham eventually found his way to Canada.

At their 1864 national convention in Chicago, the Democrats called for an immediate end to the war, to be followed by a national convention that would restore the Union. They named General George B. McClellan as their candidate, but McClellan distanced himself from the peace platform by declaring that agreement on Union would have to precede peace.

Radical Republicans, who still regarded Lincoln as soft on treason, tried to thwart his nomination for a second term, but he outmaneuvered them at every turn. Lincoln promoted the vice-presidential nomination of Andrew Johnson, a "war Democrat" from Tennessee, on the "National Union" ticket, so named to minimize partisanship. As the war dragged on through 1864,

Abraham's Dream

This cartoon depicts Lincoln having a nightmare about the election of 1864. Lady Liberty brandishes the severed head of a black man at the door of the White House as General McClellan walks up the steps and Lincoln runs away.

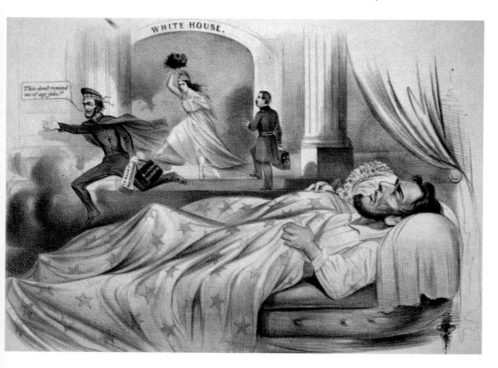

however, with Grant's army taking heavy losses in Virginia, Lincoln fully expected to lose the 1864 election. Then Admiral David Farragut's capture of Mobile in August and General William Tecumseh Sherman's capture of Atlanta on September 2, 1864, turned the tide. McClellan carried only New Jersey, Delaware, and Kentucky, with 21 electoral votes to Lincoln's 212, and he won only 1.8 million popular votes (45 percent) to Lincoln's 2.2 million (55 percent).

CONFEDERATE POLITICS   Unlike Lincoln, Jefferson Davis never had to face a presidential contest. He and his vice president, Alexander Stephens, were elected without opposition in 1861 for a six-year term. But discontent flourished as the war dragged on. Food grew scarce, and prices skyrocketed. A bread riot in Richmond on April 2, 1863, ended only when Davis himself threatened to shoot the protesters (mostly women). After the Confederate congressional elections of 1863, about one third of the legislators were ardent critics of Davis. Although parties as such did not figure in the elections, it was noteworthy that many ex-Whigs and other opponents of secession were chosen.

Davis's greatest challenge came from the politicians who had embraced secession and then guarded states' rights against the central government of the Confederacy as zealously as they had against the Union. Georgia and, to a lesser degree, North Carolina were strongholds of such sentiments. The states' rights advocates challenged, among other things, the legality of the military draft, taxes on farm produce, and above all the suspension of habeas corpus. Vice President Alexander Stephens carried on a running battle against Davis's effort to establish "military despotism," and he eventually left Richmond to sulk at his Georgia home for eighteen months.

Among other fatal flaws the Confederacy suffered from an excess of dogma. Where Lincoln was the consummate pragmatist, Davis was a brittle ideologue with a waspish temper. Once he made a decision, nothing could change his mind. One southern politician said that Davis was "as stubborn as a mule." Davis could never

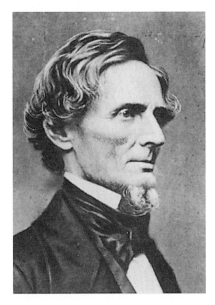

Jefferson Davis
President of the Confederacy.

find it in himself to admit that he had made a mistake. Such a personality was ill suited to the chief executive of an infant—and fractious—nation.

THE CIVIL WAR AND THE ENVIRONMENT Wars not only kill and maim people; they also transform the environment. The Civil War devastated the ecology of the South. While well over a half million soldiers died of wounds, disease, or accidents, equally appalling numbers of animals, especially horses and mules but also cattle and pigs, were killed in battle or for food. During the final year of the war, nearly 500 horses a day died of shell fire, starvation, overwork, or disease. Pork was the staple of the southern diet before the Civil War, and the region produced enough hogs to feed itself. After the war, however, the southern hog population was so decimated that the region had to import pigs and pork from the Midwest. Because midwestern hogs were bred for weight, their high fat content contributed to higher rates of heart disease and strokes in the postwar South.

Fighting during the Civil War also destroyed much of the landscape. In 1864 a Confederate major wrote that near Chickamauga, Georgia, just south of Chattanooga, Tennessee, the road was "covered with the skeletons of horses, and every tree bears the mark of battle. Many strong trunks were broken down by artillery fire." Hundreds of bridges and levees were also destroyed during the war, as were endless miles of fences, which foraging soldiers used for firewood. The loss of levees caused massive flooding; the loss of fencing meant that much of the postwar South would revert to open-range grazing. Craters gouged out by cannonballs pockmarked the landscape and provided breeding grounds for mosquitoes. The loss of so many animals meant that the mosquitoes focused on humans for their blood meal, thus increasing the spread of malaria. Hundreds of miles of trenches dug for military defense scarred the land and accelerated erosion. All told, the environment was as much a victim of the warfare as were the soldiers, and it would take years to heal nature's wounds across the South.

THE FALTERING CONFEDERACY

CHANCELLORSVILLE After the Union disaster at Fredericksburg at the end of 1862, Lincoln's search for a capable general had turned to one of Burnside's disgruntled lieutenants, Joseph Hooker, whose pugnacity had earned him the nickname Fighting Joe. With a force of 130,000 men, the largest Union army yet gathered, and a brilliant plan, Hooker failed his leadership test at Chancellorsville, Virginia, on May 1–5, 1863. Robert E. Lee, with perhaps half that number of troops, staged what became a textbook example of daring and maneuver. Hooker's plan was to leave his base, opposite Fredericksburg, on a sweeping movement upstream across the Rappahannock and Rapidan rivers to flank Lee's position. A diversionary force was to cross below the town. Lee, however, sniffed out the ruse and pulled his main forces back to meet Hooker. The Union general lost sight of his opponent and panicked. At Chancellorsville, after a preliminary skirmish, Lee divided his army again, sending Stonewall Jackson's famous foot soldiers on a long march to hit the enemy's exposed right flank.

On May 2, toward evening, Jackson surprised the Federals at the edge of a densely wooded area called the Wilderness, but the fighting died out in confusion as darkness fell. General Jackson rode out beyond the skirmish line to locate the Union forces. Fighting erupted in the darkness, and nervous Confederates mistakenly opened fire on Jackson, who was struck by three bullets that shattered his left arm and right hand. The next day a surgeon amputated his arm. The indispensable Jackson seemed to be recovering well but then contracted the dreaded pneumonia and died. Jackson had been an utterly fearless general famous for leading rapid marches, bold flanking movements, and furious assaults. "I have lost my right arm," Lee lamented, and "I do not know how to replace him." The next day, Lee forced Hooker's army back across the Rappahannock. It was the peak of Lee's career, but Chancellorsville was his last significant victory.

VICKSBURG   While Lee's army held the Federals at bay in the East, Ulysses Grant, his command reinstated, had been inching his army down the Mississippi River toward the Confederate stronghold of Vicksburg, in western Mississippi. If Union forces could gain control of the Mississippi River, they could split the Confederacy in two. Grant marched his army into Louisiana, and while the navy ran gunboats and transports past the Confederate batteries along the river at Vicksburg, he moved south to meet them at the end of April 1863. From there Grant swept eastward on a campaign that Lincoln later called "one of the most brilliant in the world," taking Jackson, Mississippi, where he seized or destroyed supplies, and then turning westward and on May 18 pinning the 30,000 Confederates inside Vicksburg. He resolved to wear them down by bombarding and starving them.

GETTYSBURG   The plight of besieged Vicksburg put the Confederate high command in a quandary. Joseph E. Johnston, now in charge of the

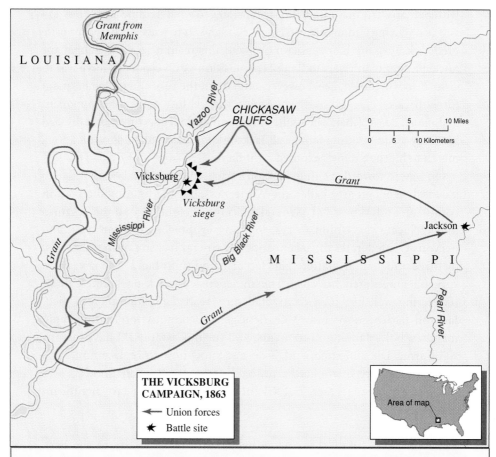

LOUISIANA

Grant from Memphis

Yazoo River

CHICKASAW BLUFFS

Vicksburg

Vicksburg siege

Mississippi River

Big Black River

Grant

Grant

Grant

MISSISSIPPI

Jackson

Pearl River

THE VICKSBURG CAMPAIGN, 1863

← Union forces
★ Battle site

Area of map

0   5   10 Miles
0   5   10 Kilometers

Why was the capture of Vicksburg an important strategic victory? Why was Vicksburg difficult to seize from the Confederacy? How did Lee hope to save Vicksburg from the Union siege?

western Confederate forces, wanted to lure Grant's army into Tennessee and thereby relieve the siege of Vicksburg. Lee had another idea for a diversion. If he could win a major battle on northern soil, he might do more than save Vicksburg; he might also persuade northern public opinion to end the war. In June he again moved his army northward across Maryland.

Neither side chose Gettysburg, Pennsylvania, as the site for the war's climactic battle, but a Confederate scavenging party entered the town in search of shoes and encountered units of Union cavalry on June 30, 1863. The main forces quickly converged on that point. On July 1 the Confederates pushed

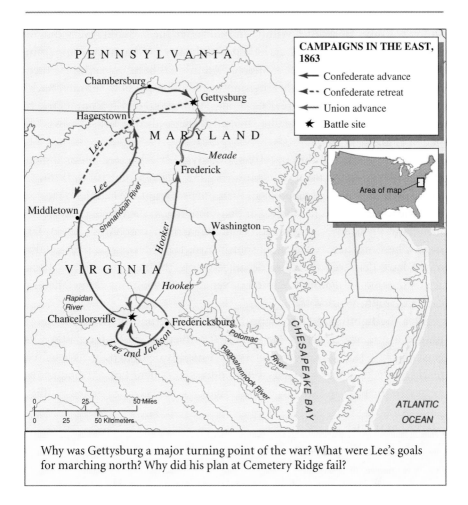

CAMPAIGNS IN THE EAST, 1863

⬅ Confederate advance
◄-- Confederate retreat
⬅ Union advance
★ Battle site

Area of map

PENNSYLVANIA

Chambersburg

Gettysburg

Hagerstown

MARYLAND

Lee

Meade

Frederick

Middletown

Shenandoah River

Hooker

Washington

VIRGINIA

Hooker

Rapidan River

Chancellorsville

Fredericksburg

Lee and Jackson

Potomac

Rappahannock River

CHESAPEAKE BAY

ATLANTIC OCEAN

0   25   50 Miles
0   25   50 Kilometers

Why was Gettysburg a major turning point of the war? What were Lee's goals for marching north? Why did his plan at Cemetery Ridge fail?

the Federals out of the town, but into stronger positions on high ground to the south. The new Union commander, General George Meade, hastened reinforcements to his new lines along the heights. On July 2 Confederate units assaulted the extreme left and right flanks of Meade's army, but in vain.

The next day, July 3, Lee staked everything on one final assault on the Union center at Cemetery Ridge. At about two in the afternoon, General George Pickett's 15,000 Confederate troops emerged from the woods into the brilliant sunlight, formed neat ranks, and began their suicidal advance uphill across open ground commanded by Union artillery. The few Confederates who got within range of hand-to-hand combat were quickly overwhelmed. At the head of Pickett's division were the University Greys, thirty-one college students from Mississippi. Within an hour after their assault, every one of them was killed or wounded. As he watched the few survivors returning from the bloody field, General Lee muttered, "All this has been my fault." He then ordered Pickett to regroup his division to repulse a possible counterattack, only to have Pickett tartly reply, "General Lee, I have no division now." Pickett never forgave Lee. Years later he charged, "That old man had my division slaughtered."

With nothing left to do but retreat, on July 4 Lee's dejected and mangled army, with about one third of its number gone, began to slog south through a driving rain. They had failed in all their purposes, not the least being to relieve the pressure on Vicksburg. On that same July 4, the Confederate commander at Vicksburg surrendered his entire garrison after a forty-seven-day siege. The Confederacy was now split in two. Had Meade pursued Lee, he might have delivered the coup de grâce before the Rebels could get back across the flooded Potomac River, but yet again the winning army failed to capitalize on its victory.

After the fighting at Gettysburg had ended, a group of northern states funded a military cemetery for the 6,000 soldiers killed in the battle. On November 19, 1863, the new cemetery was officially dedicated. In his brief remarks, since known as the Gettysburg Address, President Lincoln eloquently expressed the pain and sorrow of the brutal civil war. The prolonged conflict

Harvest of Death

Timothy H. O'Sullivan's grim photograph of the dead at Gettysburg.

was testing whether a nation "dedicated to the proposition that all men are created equal . . . can long endure." Lincoln declared that all living Americans must ensure that the "honored dead" had not "died in vain." In stirring words that continue to inspire, Lincoln predicted that "this nation, under God, shall have a new birth of freedom—and that government of the people, by the people, and for the people, shall not perish from the earth."

CHATTANOOGA   The third great Union victory of 1863 occurred in fighting around Chattanooga, the railhead of eastern Tennessee and gateway to northern Georgia. In the late summer a Union army led by General William Rosecrans took Chattanooga and then rashly pursued General Braxton Bragg's Rebel forces into Georgia, where they met at Chickamauga. The battle (September 19–20) had the makings of a Union disaster, since it was one of the few times the Confederates had a numerical advantage (about 70,000 to 56,000). Only the stubborn stand of Union troops under George H. Thomas (thenceforth dubbed the Rock of Chickamauga) prevented a rout. The battered Union forces fell back into Chattanooga while Bragg held the city virtually under siege from the heights to the south and the east.

Rosecrans seemed stunned and apathetic, but Lincoln urged him to hang on: "If we can hold Chattanooga, and East Tennessee, I think rebellion must dwindle and die." The Union command sent reinforcements. General Grant, given overall command of the western theater of operations, replaced Rosecrans with Thomas. On November 24 the Federal troops took Lookout Mountain in what was mainly a feat of mountaineering. The next day Union forces dislodged the Rebels atop Missionary Ridge.

Bragg was unable to regroup his Confederates until they were many miles to the south, and the Battle of Chattanooga was the end of his active career. Jefferson Davis reluctantly replaced Bragg with Joseph E. Johnston. The Union victory at Missionary Ridge confirmed the impression of Grant's genius. Lincoln had at last found his general. In 1864 Grant arrived in Washington to assume the rank of lieutenant general and a new position as general in chief.

THE CONFEDERACY'S DEFEAT

During the winter of 1863–1864, Confederates began to despair of victory. A War Department official in Richmond noted in his diary a spreading "sense of hopelessness." At the same time, Mary Chesnut of South Carolina reported that "gloom and despondency hang like a pall everywhere." Union

Ulysses S. Grant

At his headquarters in City Point (now Hopewell), Virginia.

leaders, sensing the momentum swinging their way, stepped up their pressure on Confederate forces.

The Union command's main targets now were Lee's army in Virginia and General Joseph Johnston's forces in Georgia. Grant personally would accompany George Meade, who retained direct command over the Army of the Potomac; operations in the West were entrusted to Grant's longtime lieutenant, William T. Sherman. As Sherman put it later, Grant "was to go for Lee, and I was to go for Joe Johnston."

Grant brought with him a new strategy against Lee. Where all his predecessors had hoped for the climactic single battle, he adopted a policy of attrition. Grant's military strategy was brutally simple: "Find out where your enemy is. Get at him as soon as you can. Strike him as hard as you can and as often as you can, and keep moving on." The Union general's unimpressive physical appearance belied his greatness. Although short and stocky, slouching and grubby, he was coolly efficient and unflappable. Like Lincoln he had an indomitable will to fight and an unblinking focus on essentials. Grant's unyielding faith that the Union armies were destined for victory enabled him to impose his tenacious will upon his troops; his violent and unflappable calmness in the face of adversity and danger inspired his troops, enabling them to survive defeats and endure savage losses. With the benefit of far more soldiers and better supplies than Lee, Grant planned to attack, attack, attack, keeping the pressure on the Confederates, grinding down their numbers and their will to fight. As he ordered Meade, "Wherever Lee goes, there you will go also." Grant would wage total war, confiscating or destroying civilian property of use to the military. It was a brutal and costly—but effective—plan.

GRANT'S PURSUIT OF LEE In May 1864 Grant's Army of the Potomac, numbering about 115,000 to Lee's 65,000, moved south across the Rappahannock and Rapidan rivers into the Wilderness of eastern Virginia,

Sheridan's Ride

This sketch, attributed to Alfred Waud, depicts General Philip Sheridan's ride at the Battle of Cedar Creek, Virginia, October 19, 1864. Artists traveling with the soldiers rendered quick, accurate sketches of battle scenes.

where Hooker had come to grief in the Battle of Chancellorsville. In the nightmarish Battle of the Wilderness (May 5–6), the armies fought blindly through the woods, the horror and suffering of the scene heightened by crackling brushfires. Grant's men suffered heavier casualties than the Confederates, but the Rebels were running out of replacements. Always before when bloodied by Lee's troops, Union forces had pulled back to nurse their wounds, but Grant slid off to his left and continued to push southward, engaging Lee's men near Spotsylvania Court House. "Whatever happens," he assured Lincoln, "we will not retreat."

Again Grant's forces slid off to the left of Lee's army and kept moving. Along the banks of the Chickahominy River, the two sides clashed again at Cold Harbor (June 1–3), ten miles east of Richmond. Grant ordered his troops to assault the heavily entrenched Confederate lines. As the Confederates had discovered at Gettysburg, such a frontal assault was murder. The Union army was massacred at Cold Harbor: in twenty minutes almost 7,000 attacking Federals were killed or wounded. Grant later admitted that the attack was his greatest mistake. Critics called him the Butcher after Cold Harbor. Yet the relentless Grant brilliantly maneuvered his battered forces around Lee and headed for Petersburg, south of Richmond, where the major railroads converged.

The Tattered Colors of the 56th and 36th Massachusetts Regiments

Union soldiers march through Virginia in 1864.

The two armies then dug in for a siege along lines that extended for twenty-five miles above and below Petersburg. Grant telegraphed Lincoln that he intended "to fight it out on this line if it takes all summer." Lincoln replied, "Hold on with a bulldog grip, and chew and choke as much as possible." For nine months the two armies faced each other down while Grant kept pushing toward his left flank to break the railroad arteries that were Lee's lifeline. During that time, Grant's troops, twice as numerous as the Confederate army, were generously supplied by Union vessels moving up the James River while Lee's forces, beset by hunger, cold, and desertion, wasted away. Petersburg had become Lee's prison while disasters piled up for the Confederacy elsewhere.

SHERMAN'S MARCH   When Grant headed south, so did General William T. Sherman—toward the railroad hub of Atlanta, with 90,000 men against Joseph Johnston's 60,000. Johnston's skillful defensive tactics caused an impatient President Jefferson Davis to replace him with the reckless John B. Hood, a natural fighter but an inept strategist who did not know the meaning of retreat. Having had an arm crippled by a bullet at Gettysburg and most of one leg shot off at Chickamauga, he had to be strapped to his horse.

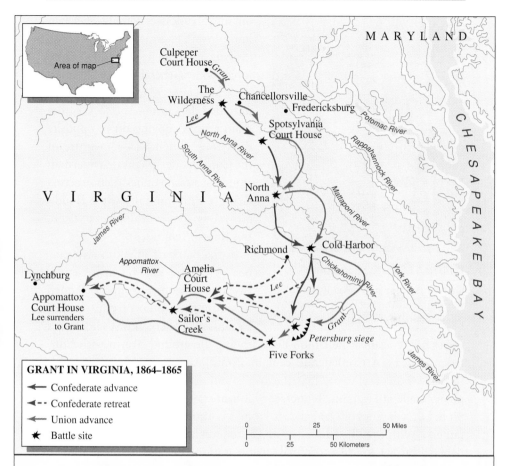

GRANT IN VIRGINIA, 1864–1865
← Confederate advance
←-- Confederate retreat
← Union advance
★ Battle site

How were Grant's tactics in the Battle of the Wilderness different from the Union's previous encounters with Lee's army? Why did Grant have the advantage at Petersburg? How did Grant eventually force Lee to surrender?

Three times in eight days, Hood's Confederate army lashed out at the Union lines, each time meeting a bloody rebuff. Sherman at first resorted to a siege of Atlanta, then slid off to the right again, cutting the rail lines below the city. Hood evacuated the city on September 1 but kept his army intact.

Sherman now laid plans for a march through central Georgia, where no organized Confederate armies remained. His intention was to "whip the rebels, to humble their pride, to follow them into their inmost recesses, and make them fear and dread us." Hood, meanwhile, had hatched an equally audacious plan: he would slip out of Georgia into northern Alabama and push

William Tecumseh Sherman

Sherman's campaign developed into a war of maneuver, but without the pitched battles of Grant's campaign.

on into Tennessee, forcing Sherman into pursuit. Sherman refused to take the bait, although he did send a Union force, led by General George Thomas, back to Tennessee to keep watch. So unfolded the curious spectacle of the main armies' moving off in opposite directions. But it was a measure of the Confederates' plight that Sherman could cut a swath of destruction across Georgia with impunity while Hood's army was soon outnumbered again, this time in Tennessee.

In the Battle of Franklin (November 30), Hood sent his army across two miles of open ground defended by entrenched Union troops backed by massed artillery. It was suicide. Six waves broke against the Union lines, leaving the ground strewn with Confederate dead. A Confederate captain from Texas, scarred by the battle's senseless butchery, wrote that the "wails and cries of the widows and orphans made at Franklin, Tennessee will heat up the fires of the bottomless pit to burn the soul of General J. B. Hood for murdering their husbands and fathers." With what he had left, Hood dared not attack Nashville, nor did he dare withdraw for fear of final disintegration. Finally, in the Battle of Nashville (December 15–16), the Federals broke and scattered what was left of the Confederate Army of Tennessee. The Confederate front west of the Appalachians had collapsed.

During all this William T. Sherman's Union army was marching through Georgia, waging war against the people's resources and their will to resist. In his effort to demoralize the civilian populace, Sherman was determined to "make Georgia howl." The Union army moved southeast from Atlanta, living off the land and destroying any provisions that might serve Confederate forces. Bands of stragglers and deserters from both armies joined in looting along the flanks while Union cavalry destroyed Rebel supplies to keep them out of enemy hands.

More than any other Civil War general, Sherman recognized the connection between the South's economy, its morale, and its ability to wage war. He explained that "we are not only fighting hostile armies, but a hostile people" who must be made to "feel the hard hand of war." He wanted the Rebels to

Ruins of Depot, Blown Up on Sherman's Departure (1864)

In the wake of Sherman's march, abandoned locomotives and twisted rails marked Atlanta's destruction.

"fear and dread us." When, after a month of ravaging the Georgia country-side, Sherman's army arrived in Savannah, on the coast, his forces had destroyed over $100 million in property, freed over 40,000 slaves, and burned many plantations. A Macon, Georgia, newspaper wrote that Sherman was a "demon" willing to plumb the "depths of depravity" in wreaking his campaign of vengeance. Yet Sherman scoffed at such criticism. "Those people made war on us, defied and dared us to come south to their country, where they boasted they would kill us and do all manner of terrible things. We accepted their challenge, and now for them to whine and complain of the natural and necessary results is beneath contempt." Sherman's troops, in fact, rarely committed the atrocities later attributed to them. To be sure, they confiscated food and livestock, destroyed railroads and mills, and burned plantations, but most houses were left untouched, and Union soldiers committed few serious crimes against individuals. Sherman's goal was to defeat Confederate morale and reunite the nation, not destroy Georgia or the South physically. After the war a Confederate officer acknowledged that Sherman's march through Georgia was in fact well conceived and well managed. "I don't think there was ever an army in the world that would have behaved better, in a similar expedition, in an enemy country. Our army certainly wouldn't."

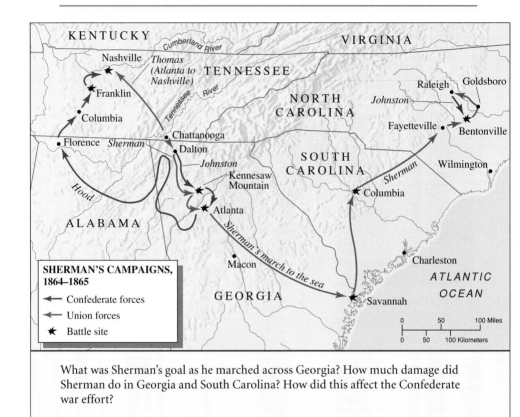

What was Sherman's goal as he marched across Georgia? How much damage did Sherman do in Georgia and South Carolina? How did this affect the Confederate war effort?

Pushing across the Savannah River into South Carolina, that "hell-hole of secession," Sherman's men wrought even greater destruction. More than a dozen towns were burned in whole or part, including the state capital of Columbia, captured on February 17, 1865. Meanwhile, Charleston's defenders abandoned the city and headed north to join a ragtag Rebel army that Joseph E. Johnston was desperately pulling together in North Carolina. Johnston mounted one final attack on Sherman's army at Bentonville (March 19–20), but that would be his last major battle.

During the late winter and early spring of 1865, the Confederacy found itself besieged on all sides. Defeat was in the air. Some Rebel leaders argued that it was time to negotiate a peace settlement. Confederate secretary of war John C. Breckinridge, a Kentuckian who had served as vice president under James Buchanan and had run for president in 1860, urged Robert E. Lee to negotiate an honorable end to the war. "This has been a magnificent epic," he said. "In God's name, let it not terminate in a farce." But Jefferson Davis dismissed any talk of surrender. If the Confederate armies should be defeated, he wanted the soldiers to disperse and fight a guerrilla war. "The war came and now it must go on," he stubbornly insisted, "till the last man of this generation falls in his tracks, and his children seize his musket and fight our battle."

While Confederate forces made their last stands, Abraham Lincoln prepared for his second term as president. He was the first president since Andrew Jackson to have been reelected. The weary commander in chief had weathered constant criticism during his first term, but with the war nearing its end, Lincoln now garnered deserved praise. The *Chicago Tribune* observed that the president "has slowly and steadily risen in the respect, confidence, and admiration of the people."

On March 4, 1865, amid rumors of a Confederate attempt to abduct or assassinate the president, the six-foot-four-inch, rawboned Lincoln, dressed in a black suit and stovepipe hat, his face weathered by prairie wind and political worry, delivered his brief but eloquent second inaugural address on the East Portico of the Capitol. Not a hundred feet away, looking down on Lincoln from the Capitol porch, was a twenty-six-year-old actor named John Wilkes Booth, who five weeks later would kill the president in a desperate attempt to do something "heroic" for his beloved South.

The nation's capital had long before become an armed camp and a massive military hospital. Sick and wounded soldiers were scattered everywhere: in hotels, warehouses, schools, businesses, and private homes. Thousands of Confederate deserters roamed the streets. After a morning of torrential rains, the sun broke through the clouds just as Lincoln began to speak to the mud-spattered audience of some 35,000, half of whom were African Americans. While managing a terrible civil war, the president had experienced personal tragedy (the loss of a second child and a wife plagued by mental instability) and chronic depression. What kept him from unraveling was a principled pragmatism and godly foundation that endowed his life with purpose.

Lincoln's address was more a sermon than a speech, the reflections of a somber statesman still struggling to understand the relation between divine will and human endeavor. Rather than detailing the progress of the war effort or indulging in self-congratulatory celebration, Lincoln focused on the origins and paradoxes of the war. Slavery, he said, had "somehow" caused the war, and everyone bore some guilt for the national shame of racial injustice and its bloody expiation. Both sides had known before the fighting began that war was to be avoided at all costs, but "one of them would *make* war rather than let the nation survive; and the other would *accept* war rather than let it perish."

The weary but resolute commander in chief longed for peace. "Fondly do we hope—fervently do we pray—that this mighty scourge of war may speedily pass away." He wondered aloud why the war had lasted so long and had been so brutal. "The Almighty," he acknowledged, "has His own purposes." Lincoln noted the paradoxical irony of both sides in this civil war reading the same Bible, praying to the same God, and appealing for divine support in its fight against the other. The God of Judgment, however, would not be misled or denied. If God willed that the war continue until "every drop of blood drawn with the lash, shall be paid with another drawn by the sword, as was said three thousand years ago, so still it must be said 'the judgments of the Lord are true and righteous altogether.'" After four years of escalating combat, the war had grown "incomprehensible" in its scope and horrors. Now the president, looking gaunt and tired, urged the Union forces "to finish the work we are in," bolstered with "firmness in the right insofar as God gives us to see the right."

As Lincoln looked ahead to the end of the fighting and a "just and lasting peace," he stressed the need to "bind up the nation's wounds" by exercising the Christian virtues of forgiveness and mercy. Vengeance must be avoided at all costs. Reconciliation must be pursued "with malice toward none; with charity for all." Those eight words marvelously captured Lincoln's hopes for a restored Union. His simple but powerful and profound speech, only 700 words long, endures because it manifests the extraordinary humility and complex faith of a president too humane to be vengeful or partisan. Redemption was his goal; victory was less important than peace. The sublime majesty of Lincoln's brief speech revealed how the rigors of war had transformed and elevated him from the obscure congressman who had entered the White House in 1861. The abolitionist leader Frederick Douglass proclaimed Lincoln's second inaugural address "a sacred effort."

APPOMATTOX During the spring of 1865, General Grant's army kept pushing, probing, and battering the entrenched Rebels around Petersburg, Virginia, twenty miles south of Richmond. The badly outnumbered Confederates were slowly starving. Their trenches were filled with rats and lice; scurvy and dysentery were rampant. News of Sherman's progress through Georgia and South Carolina added to the gloom and heightened the impulse of weary Rebels to desert. Lee began to lay plans for his starving forces to escape and join Johnston's army in North Carolina. On April 2, 1865, Lee's army abandoned Richmond and Petersburg in a desperate flight southwest toward Lynchburg and railroads leading south. President Davis, exhausted but still defiant, too stubborn and vain to concede, gathered what archives and treasure he could and fled by train ahead of the advancing Federals, only to be captured in Georgia by Union cavalry on May 10.

By then the Confederacy was dead. Lee had moved out of Petersburg with Grant in hot pursuit and soon found his escape route cut off. Lee recognized that there was no need to prolong the inevitable. As he told the Union officer who delivered the terms of a proposed surrender, "There is nothing left for me to do but go and see General Grant, and I would rather die a thousand deaths." On April 9 (Palm Sunday) the tall, stately Lee donned a crisp dress uniform and met the mud-spattered Grant in the parlor of Wilmer McLean's home at Appomattox Court House to tender his surrender. Grant, at Lee's request, let the Rebel officers keep their sidearms and permitted soldiers to keep their personal horses and mules. As the gaunt,

Robert E. Lee

Mathew Brady took this photograph in Richmond eleven days after Lee's surrender at Appomattox.

hungry Confederate troops formed ranks for the last time, Joshua Chamberlain, the Union general in charge of the surrender ceremony, ordered his Federal soldiers to salute their foes as they paraded past. His Confederate counterpart signaled his men to do likewise. General Chamberlain remembered that there was not a sound—no trumpets or drums, no cheers or jeers, simply an "awed stillness . . . as if it were the passing of the dead." On April 18 General Joseph Johnston surrendered his Confederate army to General Sherman near Durham, North Carolina. The remaining Confederate forces surrendered during May.

A MODERN WAR

The Civil War was in many respects the first modern war. Its scope was unprecedented. One out of every twelve adult American men served in the war, and few families were unaffected by the event. Over 620,000 Americans died in the conflict from wounds or disease, 50 percent more than in World War II. Because battlefield surgeons were constantly overworked and frequently lacked equipment, supplies, and knowledge, almost any stomach or head wound proved fatal, and gangrene was rampant. Of the survivors, 50,000 returned home with one or more limbs amputated. Disease, however, was the greatest threat to soldiers, killing twice as many as were lost in battle.

The Civil War was also modern in that much of the killing was distant, impersonal, and mechanical. The opposing forces used an array of new weapons and instruments of war: artillery with "rifled," or grooved, barrels for greater accuracy, repeating rifles, ironclad ships, observation balloons, and wire entanglements. Men were killed without knowing who had fired the shot that felled them.

Historians have provided conflicting assessments of the reasons for the Union victory. Some have focused on the inherent weaknesses of the Confederacy: its lack of industry, the fractious relations between the states and the central government in Richmond, poor political and military leadership, faulty coordination and communication, the burden of slavery, and the disparities in population and resources compared with those of the North. Still others have highlighted the erosion of Confederate morale in the face of chronic food shortages and horrific human losses. The debate over why the North won and the South lost the Civil War will probably never end, but as in other modern wars, firepower and manpower were essential factors. Robert E. Lee's own explanation of the Confederate defeat retains an enduring legitimacy: "After four years of arduous service marked by unsurpassed courage and fortitude, the Army of Northern Virginia has been compelled to yield to overwhelming numbers and resources."

MAKING CONNECTIONS

- Certain fiscal measures enacted during the Civil War (when southerners were not in Congress to block them) helped fuel the postwar economic growth (discussed in Chapter 20).

- The Confederacy's defeat had a tremendous impact on all dimensions of life in the South, as Chapter 19 (on the New South) demonstrates.

FURTHER READING

The best one-volume overview of the Civil War period is James M. McPherson's *Battle Cry of Freedom: The Civil War Era* (1988). A good introduction to the military events is Herman Hattaway's *Shades of Blue and Gray* (1997). The outlook and experiences of the common soldier are explored in James M. McPherson's *For Cause and Comrades: Why Men Fought in the Civil War* (1997) and Earl J. Hess's *The Union Soldier in Battle: Enduring the Ordeal of Combat* (1997).

For emphasis on the South, turn first to Gary W. Gallagher's *The Confederate War* (1997). For a sparkling account of the birth of the Rebel nation, see William C. Davis's *"A Government of Our Own": The Making of the Confederacy* (1994). The same author provides a fine biography of the Confederate president in *Jefferson Davis: The Man and His Hour* (1991). On the best Confederate commander, see John M. Taylor's *Duty Faithfully Performed: Robert E. Lee and His Critics* (2000). On the key Union generals, see Lee Kennett's *Sherman: A Soldier's Life* (2001) and Josiah Bunting III's *Ulysses S. Grant* (2004).

Analytical scholarship on the military conflict includes Joseph L. Harsh's *Confederate Tide Rising: Robert E. Lee and the Making of Southern Strategy, 1861–1862* (1998), Steven E. Woodworth's *Jefferson Davis and His Generals: The Failure of Confederate Command in the West* (1990), and Paul D. Casdorph's *Lee and Jackson: Confederate Chieftains* (1992). Lonnie R. Speer's *Portals to Hell: Military Prisons of the Civil War* (1997) details the ghastly experience of prisoners of war.

The history of the North during the war is surveyed in Philip Shaur Paludan's *A People's Contest: The Union and Civil War, 1861–1865* (1996) and J. Matthew Gallman's *The North Fights the Civil War: The Home Front* (1994).

The central northern political figure, Abraham Lincoln, is the subject of many books. See Harry V. Jaffa's *A New Birth of Freedom: Abraham Lincoln and the Coming of the Civil War* (2000). On Lincoln's great speeches, see Ronald C. White Jr.'s *The Eloquent President: A Portrait of Lincoln through His Words* (2005). The election of 1864 is treated in John C. Waugh's *Reelecting Lincoln: The Battle for the 1864 Presidency* (1997). On Lincoln's assassination, see William Hanchett's *The Lincoln Murder Conspiracies* (1983).

Concerning specific military campaigns, see Larry J. Daniel's *Shiloh: The Battle That Changed the Civil War* (1997), Thomas Goodrich's *Black Flag: Guerrilla Warfare on the Western Border, 1861–1865* (1995), Stephen W. Sears's *To the Gates of Richmond: The Peninsula Campaign* (1992), James M.

McPherson's *Crossroads of Freedom: Antietam 1862* (2002), James Lee McDonough and James Pickett Jones's *War So Terrible: Sherman and Atlanta* (1988), Robert Garth Scott's *Into the Wilderness with the Army of the Potomac* (1985), Albert Castel's *Decision in the West: The Atlanta Campaign of 1864* (1992), and Ernest B. Furgurson's *Not War but Murder: Cold Harbor, 1864* (2000). On the final weeks of the war, see William C. Davis's *An Honorable Defeat: The Last Days of the Confederate Government* (2001).

The experience of the African-American soldier is surveyed in Joseph T. Glatthaar's *Forged in Battle: The Civil War Alliance of Black Soldiers and White Officers* (1990) and Ira Berlin, Joseph P. Reidy, and Leslie S. Rowland's *Freedom's Soldiers: The Black Military Experience in the Civil War* (1998). For the African-American woman's experience, see Jacqueline Jones's *Labor of Love, Labor of Sorrow: Black Women, Work, and the Family from Slavery to the Present* (1985).

Recent gender and ethnic studies include *Divided Houses: Gender and the Civil War*, edited by Catherine Clinton and Nina Silber (1992), Drew Gilpin Faust's *Mothers of Invention: Women of the Slaveholding South in the American Civil War* (1996), George C. Rable's *Civil Wars: Women and the Crisis of Southern Nationalism* (1989), and William L. Burton's *Melting Pot Soldiers: The Union's Ethnic Regiments,* 2nd ed. (1998).

18

RECONSTRUCTION: NORTH AND SOUTH

FOCUS QUESTIONS

· What were the different approaches to Reconstruction?

· How did Congress try to reshape southern society?

· What was the role of African Americans in the postwar South?

· What were the main issues in national politics in the 1870s?

To answer these questions and access additional review material, please visit www.wwnorton.com/studyspace.

In the spring of 1865, the Civil War was over. At a frightful cost of 620,000 lives and the destruction of the southern economy and much of its landscape, American nationalism had emerged triumphant, and some 4 million enslaved Americans had seized their freedom. Ratification of the Thirteenth Amendment in December 1865 abolished slavery throughout the Union. Now the nation faced the task of reuniting, coming to terms with the abolition of slavery, and "reconstructing" a ravaged and resentful South.

THE WAR'S AFTERMATH

In the war's aftermath important questions faced the victors: Should the Confederate leaders be tried for treason? How should new governments be formed? How and at whose expense was the South's economy to be rebuilt?

Should debts incurred by the Confederate state governments be honored? Who should pay to rebuild the South's railroads and public buildings, dredge the clogged southern harbors, and restore damaged levees? What was to be done for the freed slaves? Were they to be given land? social equality? education? voting rights? Such complex questions required sober reflection and careful planning, but policy makers did not have the luxury of time or the benefits of consensus. Some wanted the former Confederate states returned to the Union with little or no changes in the region's social, political, and economic life. Others wanted southern society punished and transformed. The editors of the nation's foremost magazine, *Harper's Weekly*, expressed the vengeful attitude when they declared at the end of 1865 that "the forgive-and-forget policy . . . is mere political insanity and suicide."

DEVELOPMENT IN THE NORTH   To some Americans the Civil War had been more truly a social revolution than the War of Independence, for it reduced the once-dominant power of the South's planter elite in national politics and elevated the power of the northern "captains of industry." Government, both federal, and state, became more friendly to business leaders and more unfriendly to those who would probe into their activities. The wartime Republican Congress had delivered on the major platform promises of 1860, which had cemented the allegiance of northeastern businessmen and western farmers to the party of free labor.

In the absence of southern members, Congress during the war had centralized national power and enacted the Republican economic agenda. It passed the Morrill tariff, which doubled the average level of import duties. The National Banking Act created a uniform system of banking and bank-note currency and helped finance the war. Congress also passed legislation guaranteeing that the first transcontinental railroad would run along a north-central route, from Omaha, Nebraska, to Sacramento, California, and it donated public land and public bonds to ensure its financing. In the Homestead Act of 1862, moreover, Congress voted free federal homesteads of 160 acres to settlers, who had only to occupy the land for five years to gain title. No cash was needed. The Morrill Land Grant Act of the same year conveyed to each state 30,000 acres of federal land per member of Congress from the state. The sale of some of the land provided funds to create colleges of "agriculture and mechanic arts." Such measures helped stimulate the North's economy in the years after the Civil War.

DEVASTATION IN THE SOUTH   The postwar South offered a sharp contrast to the victorious North. Along the path of General William T. Sherman's army, one observer reported in 1866, the countryside "looked for many miles like a broad black streak of ruin and desolation." Columbia, South Carolina, said another witness, was "a wilderness of ruins," Charleston a place of "vacant houses, of widowed women, of rotting wharves, of deserted warehouses, of weed-wild gardens, of miles of grass-grown streets, of acres of pitiful and voiceless barrenness."

Throughout the South, property values had collapsed. Confederate bonds and paper money were worthless; most railroads were damaged or destroyed. Cotton that had escaped destruction was seized by federal troops. Emancipation wiped out $4 billion invested in human flesh and left the labor system in disarray. The great age of expansion in the cotton market was over. Not until 1879 would the cotton crop again equal the record harvest of 1860; tobacco production did not regain its prewar level until 1880; the sugar crop of Louisiana not until 1893; and the old rice industry of the Tidewater and the hemp industry of the Kentucky Bluegrass never regained their prewar status.

A Street in the "Burned District"

Ruins of Richmond, Virginia, spring 1865.

A TRANSFORMED SOUTH   The defeat of the Confederacy transformed much of southern society. The freeing of slaves, the destruction of property, and the collapse of land values left many planters destitute and homeless. Amanda Worthington, a planter's wife from Mississippi, saw her whole world destroyed. In the fall of 1865, she assessed the damage: "None of us can realize that we are no longer wealthy—yet thanks to the yankees, the cause of all unhappiness, such is the case."

After the Civil War many former Confederates were so embittered that they abandoned their native region rather than submit to "Yankee rule." Some migrated to Canada, Europe, Mexico, South America, or Asia. Others preferred the western territories and states. Still others settled in northern and midwestern cities on the assumption that educational and economic opportunities would be better among the victors.

Those who remained in the South found old social roles reversed. One Confederate army captain reported that on his father's plantation "our negroes are living in great comfort. They were delighted to see me with overflowing affection. They waited on me as before, gave me breakfast, splendid dinners, etc. But they firmly and respectfully informed me: 'We own this land now. Put it out of your head that it will ever be yours again.'"

Union troops who fanned out across the defeated South to impose order were cursed and spat upon. A Virginia woman expressed a spirited defiance common among her circle of friends: "Every day, every hour, that I live increases my hatred and detestation, and loathing of that race. They [Yankees] disgrace our common humanity. As a people I consider them vastly inferior to the better classes of our slaves." Fervent southern nationalists, both men and women, implanted in their children a similar hatred of Yankees and a defiance of northern rule. One mother said that she trained her children to "fear God, love the South, and live to avenge her."

LEGALLY FREE, SOCIALLY BOUND   In the former Confederate states the newly freed slaves suffered most of all. According to the African-American abolitionist Frederick Douglass, the former slave remained dependent: "He had neither money, property, nor friends. He was free from the old plantation, but he had nothing but the dusty road under his feet. . . . He was turned loose, naked, hungry, and destitute to the open sky." A few northerners argued that what the ex-slaves needed most was their own land. But even dedicated abolitionists shrank from proposals to confiscate white-owned land and distribute it to the freed slaves. Citizenship and

Freedmen in Richmond, Virginia

According to a former Confederate general, freed blacks had "nothing but freedom."

legal rights were one thing, wholesale confiscation of property and land redistribution quite another. Nonetheless, discussions of land distribution fueled false rumors that freed slaves would get "forty acres and a mule," a slogan that swept the South at the end of the war. Instead of land or material help, the freed slaves more often got advice about proper behavior.

THE FREEDMEN'S BUREAU   On March 3, 1865, while the war was still raging, Congress set up within the War Department the Bureau of Refugees, Freedmen, and Abandoned Lands to provide "such issues of provisions, clothing, and fuel" as might be needed to relieve "destitute and suffering refugees and freedmen and their wives and children." Agents of the Freedmen's Bureau were entrusted with negotiating labor contracts (something new for both blacks and planters), providing medical care, and setting up schools, often in cooperation with such northern agencies as the American Missionary Association and the Freedmen's Aid Society. The bureau had its own courts to deal with labor disputes and land titles, and its agents were authorized to supervise trials involving blacks in other courts.

White intransigence and the failure to grasp the intensity of racial prejudice increasingly thwarted the efforts of Freedmen's Bureau agents to protect and

Freedmen's School in Virginia

Throughout the former Confederate states the Freedmen's Bureau set up schools such as this one.

assist the former slaves. Congress was not willing to strengthen the powers of the bureau to reflect those problems. Beyond temporary relief measures, no program of Reconstruction ever incorporated much more than constitutional and legal rights for freedmen. These were important in themselves, of course, but the extent to which even they should go was very uncertain, to be settled more by the course of events than by any clear-cut commitment to social and economic equality.

THE BATTLE OVER RECONSTRUCTION

The problem of reconstructing the South politically centered on deciding what governments would constitute authority in the defeated states. This problem arose first in Virginia at the very beginning of the Civil War, when the state's thirty-five western counties refused to go along with secession. In 1861 a loyal state government of Virginia was proclaimed at Wheeling, and that government in turn formed a new state, called West Virginia, which was admitted to the Union in 1863. As Union forces advanced into the South, President Lincoln in 1862 named military governors for Tennessee, Arkansas, and Louisiana. By the end of the following year, he had formulated a plan for regular governments in those states and any others that might be liberated from Confederate rule.

LINCOLN'S PLAN AND CONGRESS'S RESPONSE   In late 1863, President Lincoln had issued a Proclamation of Amnesty and Reconstruction, under which any rebel state could form a Union government whenever a number equal to 10 percent of those who had voted in 1860 took an oath of allegiance to the Constitution and the Union and had received a presidential pardon. Participants also had to swear support for laws and proclamations dealing with emancipation. Certain groups, however, were excluded from the pardon: civil and diplomatic officers of the Confederacy; senior officers of the Confederate army and navy; judges, congressmen, and military officers of the United States who had left their federal posts to aid the rebellion; and those accused of failure to treat captured black soldiers and their officers as prisoners of war.

Under this plan, governments loyal to the Union appeared in Tennessee, Arkansas, and Louisiana, but Congress recognized them neither in terms of representation nor in counting the electoral votes of 1864. In the absence of specific provisions for Reconstruction in the Constitution, politicians disagreed as to where authority properly rested. Lincoln claimed the right to direct Reconstruction under the clause that set forth the presidential power to grant pardons and under the constitutional obligation of the United States to guarantee each state a republican form of government. Republican congressmen, however, argued that this obligation implied that Congress, not the president, should supervise Reconstruction.

A few conservative and most moderate Republicans supported Lincoln's program of immediate restoration. The small but influential group of Radical Republicans, however, favored a sweeping transformation of southern society based upon granting freed slaves full-fledged citizenship. The Radicals hoped to reconstruct southern society so as to dismantle the old planter class and the Democratic party.

The Radicals were talented, earnest men who insisted that Congress control the Reconstruction program. To this end in 1864 they helped pass the Wade-Davis bill, sponsored by Senator Benjamin Wade of Ohio and Representative Henry Winter Davis of Maryland. In contrast to Lincoln's 10 percent plan, the Wade-Davis bill required that a majority of white male citizens declare their allegiance and that only those who could take an "ironclad" oath (required of federal officials since 1862) attesting to their *past* loyalty could vote or serve in the state constitutional conventions. The conventions, moreover, would have to abolish slavery, exclude from political rights high-ranking civil and military officers of the Confederacy, and repudiate debts incurred during the conflict.

Passed during the closing day of the session, the Wade-Davis bill never became law: Lincoln vetoed it. In retaliation furious Republicans penned the Wade-Davis Manifesto, which accused the president of usurping power and attempting to use readmitted states to ensure his reelection, among other sins. Lincoln offered his last view of Reconstruction in his final public address, on April 11, 1865. Speaking from the White House balcony, he pronounced that the Confederate states had never left the Union. Those states were simply "out of their proper practical relation with the Union," and the object was to get them "into their proper practical relation." At a cabinet meeting, Lincoln proposed the creation of new southern state governments before Congress met in December. He shunned the vindictiveness of the Radicals. He wanted "no persecution, no bloody work," no radical restructuring of southern social and economic life.

THE ASSASSINATION OF LINCOLN   On the evening of April 14, Lincoln went to Ford's Theater and his rendezvous with death. With his trusted bodyguard called away to Richmond and the policeman assigned to his box away from his post, watching the play, Lincoln was helpless as John Wilkes Booth slipped into the unguarded presidential box. Booth, a crazed actor and Confederate zealot, fired his derringer point-blank at the president's head. He then stabbed Lincoln's aide and jumped from the box onto the stage, crying "*Sic semper tyrannis*" (Thus always to tyrants), the motto of Virginia. The president died nine hours later. Accomplices of Booth had also targeted Vice President Andrew Johnson and Secretary of State William Seward. Seward and four others, including his son, were victims of severe but not fatal stab wounds. Johnson escaped injury, however, because his would-be assassin got cold feet and wound up tipsy in the barroom of the vice president's hotel.

The nation extracted a full measure of vengeance from the conspirators. Booth was pursued into Virginia and killed in a burning barn. Three of his collaborators were convicted by a military court and hanged, along with the woman at whose boardinghouse they had plotted. Three others got life sentences, including a Maryland doctor who set the leg Booth had broken when he jumped to the stage. President Johnson eventually pardoned them all, except one who died in prison. Apart from those cases, however, there was only one other execution in the aftermath of war: that of the Confederate Henry Wirz, who commanded the infamous prison at Andersonville, Georgia.

Presidential Assassination

The funeral procession for President Lincoln.

JOHNSON'S PLAN   Lincoln's death elevated to the White House Andrew Johnson of Tennessee, a man who lacked most presidential virtues. When General Ulysses Grant learned that Lincoln had died and Johnson was president, he said that he "dreaded the change" because the new commander in chief was vindictive toward his native South. Essentially illiterate, Johnson was provincial and bigoted—he harbored fierce prejudices. He was also short-tempered and lacking in self-control. At the inaugural ceremonies in early 1865, he had delivered his address in a state of slurring drunkenness that embarrassed Lincoln and the nation. Johnson was a war (pro-Union) Democrat who had been put on the Union ticket in 1864 as a gesture of unity. Of origins as humble as Lincoln's, Johnson had moved as a youth from his birthplace in Raleigh, North Carolina, to Greeneville, Tennessee, where he became the proprietor of a tailor shop. Self-educated with the help of his wife, he had served as mayor, congressman, governor, and senator, then as military governor of Tennessee before he became vice president. In the process he had become an advocate of the small farmers in opposition to the privileges of the large planters—"a bloated, corrupted aristocracy." He also

Andrew Johnson

A pro-Union Democrat from Tennessee.

shared the racist attitudes of most white yeomen. "Damn the negroes," he exclaimed to a friend during the war, "I am fighting those traitorous aristocrats, their masters."

Some of the Radicals at first thought Johnson, unlike Lincoln, to be one of them. Johnson had, for example, once asserted that treason "must be made infamous and traitors must be impoverished." Senator Benjamin Wade loved such vengeful language. "Johnson, we have faith in you," he promised. "By the gods, there will be no trouble now in running this government." But Wade would soon find Johnson as unsympathetic as Lincoln, if for different reasons.

Johnson's loyalty to the Union sprang from a strict adherence to the Constitution and a fervent belief in limited government. When discussing what to do with the former Confederate states, Johnson preferred the term *restoration* to *reconstruction*. He held that the rebellious states should be quickly brought back into their proper relation to the Union because the states and the Union were indestructible. In 1865 Johnson declared that "there is no such thing as reconstruction. Those States have not gone out of the Union. Therefore reconstruction is unnecessary." Like many other whites he found it hard to accept the growing Radical sentiment to grant the vote to blacks.

Johnson's plan to restore the Union thus closely resembled Lincoln's. A new Proclamation of Amnesty (May 1865) excluded not only those Lincoln had excluded from pardon but also everybody with taxable property worth more than $20,000. Those wealthy planters, bankers, and merchants were the people Johnson believed had led the South to secede. Those in the excluded groups might make special applications for pardon directly to the president, and before the year was out Johnson had issued some 13,000 pardons.

Johnson followed up his amnesty proclamation with his own plan for readmitting the former Confederate states. In each state a native Unionist became provisional governor with authority to call a convention of men elected by loyal voters. Lincoln's 10 percent requirement was omitted. Johnson called upon the state conventions to invalidate the secession ordinances, abolish slavery, and repudiate all debts incurred to aid the Confederacy. Each state, moreover, was to ratify the Thirteenth Amendment. Lincoln had privately advised the governor of Louisiana to consider giving the vote to some blacks, "the very intelligent and those who have fought gallantly in our ranks." In his final public address he had also endorsed a limited black suffrage. Johnson repeated Lincoln's advice. He reminded the provisional governor of Mississippi, for example, that the state conventions might "with perfect safety" extend suffrage to blacks with education or with military service so as to "disarm the adversary," the adversary being "radicals who are wild upon" giving all blacks the right to vote.

The state conventions for the most part met Johnson's requirements. But Carl Schurz, a German immigrant and war hero who became a prominent Missouri politician, found during his visit to the South "an *utter absence of national feeling* . . . and a desire to preserve slavery . . . as much and as long as possible." Southern whites had accepted the situation because they thought so little had changed after all. Emboldened by Johnson's indulgence, they ignored his pleas for moderation and conciliation. Suggestions of black suffrage were scarcely raised in the state conventions and promptly squelched when they were.

SOUTHERN INTRANSIGENCE   When Congress met in December 1865, for the first time since the end of the war, it faced the fact that the new state governments in the postwar South were remarkably like the old ones. Southern voters had acted with extreme disregard for northern feelings. Among the new members presenting themselves to Congress were Georgia's Alexander Stephens, former vice president of the Confederacy, now claiming a seat in the Senate, four Confederate generals, eight colonels, and six cabinet members. The Congress forthwith denied seats to all members from the eleven former Confederate states. It was too much to expect, after four bloody years, that the Unionists in Congress would welcome back ex-Confederates.

Furthermore, the new southern state legislatures, in passing repressive "black codes" restricting the freedom of African Americans, demonstrated that they intended to preserve slavery as nearly as possible. As one white southerner stressed, "The ex-slave was not a free man; he was a free Negro," and the black codes were intended to highlight the distinction.

The black codes varied from state to state, but some provisions were common. Existing marriages, including common-law marriages, were recognized (although interracial marriages were prohibited), and testimony of blacks was accepted in legal cases involving blacks—and in six states in all cases. Blacks could own property. They could sue and be sued in the courts. On the other hand, they could not own farmland in Mississippi or city lots in South Carolina; they were required to buy special licenses to practice certain trades

(?) Slavery Is Dead (?)

Thomas Nast's cartoon suggests that in 1866 slavery was dead only legally.

in Mississippi. They were required to enter into annual labor contracts. Unemployed ("vagrant") blacks were punished with severe fines, and if unable to pay, they were forced to labor in the fields of those who paid the courts for this source of cheap labor. Aspects of slavery were simply being restored in another guise. The new Mississippi penal code virtually said so: "All penal and criminal laws now in force describing the mode of punishment of crimes and misdemeanors committed by slaves, free negroes, or mulattoes are hereby reenacted, and decreed to be in full force."

Faced with such blatant evidence of southern intransigence, moderate Republicans in Congress drifted toward the Radicals' views. Having excluded the "reconstructed" southern members, the new Congress set up a Joint Committee on Reconstruction, with nine members from the House and six from the Senate, to gather evidence of southern efforts to thwart Reconstruction. Initiative fell to determined Radical Republicans who knew what they wanted: Benjamin Wade of Ohio, George Julian of Indiana, and—most conspicuously of all—Thaddeus Stevens of Pennsylvania and Charles Sumner of Massachusetts.

THE RADICAL REPUBLICANS   Most Radical Republicans had been connected with the anti-slavery cause for decades. In addition, few could escape the bitterness bred by the long and bloody war or remain unaware of the partisan advantage that would come to the Republican party from black suffrage. The Republicans needed African-American votes to maintain their control of Congress and the White House. They also needed to disenfranchise former Confederates to keep them from helping to elect Democrats who would restore the old southern ruling class to power. In public, however, the Radical Republicans rarely disclosed such partisan self-interest. Instead, they asserted that the Republicans, the party of Union and freedom, could best guarantee the fruits of victory and that extending voting rights to blacks would be the best way to promote their welfare.

Senator Charles Sumner

A leading Radical Republican.

The growing conflict of opinion over Reconstruction policy brought about an inversion in constitutional reasoning. Secessionists—and Andrew Johnson—were now arguing that the Rebel states had in fact remained in the Union, and some Radical Republicans were contriving arguments that they had left the Union after all. Thaddeus Stevens argued that the Confederate states were now conquered provinces, subject to the absolute will of the victors, and that the "whole fabric of southern society must be changed." Charles Sumner maintained that the southern states, by their pretended acts of secession, had reverted to the status of unorganized territories and thus were subject to the will of Congress. Most Republicans, however, converged instead on the "forfeited-rights theory," later embodied in the report of the Joint Committee on Reconstruction. This held that the states as entities continued to exist, but by the acts of secession and war they had forfeited "all civil and political rights under the Constitution." And Congress, not the president, was the proper authority to determine how and when such rights might be restored.

JOHNSON'S BATTLE WITH CONGRESS A long year of political battling remained, however, before this idea triumphed. By the end of 1865, the Radical Republicans' views had gained a majority in Congress, if one not yet large enough to override presidential vetoes. But the critical year of 1866 saw the gradual waning of Andrew Johnson's power and influence, much of which was self-induced. Johnson first challenged Congress in 1866, when he vetoed a bill to extend the life of the Freedmen's Bureau. The measure, he said, assumed that wartime conditions still existed, whereas the country had returned "to a state of peace and industry." Because it was no longer valid as a war measure, the bill violated the Constitution in several ways, he declared: it made the federal government responsible for the care of indigents, it was passed by a Congress in which eleven states had been denied seats, and it used vague language in defining the "civil rights and immunities" of blacks. For the time being, Johnson's prestige remained sufficiently intact that the Senate upheld his veto.

Three days after the veto, however, during an impromptu speech, Johnson undermined his already weakening authority with a fiery assault upon Radical Republican leaders. From that point forward, moderate Republicans backed away from a president who had opened himself to counterattack. The Radical Republicans took the offensive. Johnson was "an alien enemy of a foreign state," Stevens declared. Sumner called him "an insolent drunken brute"—and Johnson was open to the charge because of his behavior at the 1865 inauguration. Weakened by illness, he had taken a belt of brandy to get through the ceremony and, under the influence of fever and alcohol, had been incoherent.

In mid-March 1866 the Radical-led Congress passed the Civil Rights Act. A response to the black codes created by unrepentant southern state legislatures, this bill declared that "all persons born in the United States and not subject to any foreign power, excluding Indians not taxed," were citizens entitled to "full and equal benefit of all laws." The granting of citizenship to native-born blacks, Johnson fumed, exceeded the scope of federal power. It would, moreover, "foment discord among the races." Johnson vetoed the bill, but this time, on April 9, Congress overrode the presidential veto. On July 16 it enacted a revised Freedmen's Bureau bill, again overriding a veto. From that point on, Johnson steadily lost both public and political support.

The Cruel Uncle

A cartoon depicting Andrew Johnson leading two children, "Civil Rights" and "the Freedmen's Bureau," into the "Veto Wood."

THE FOURTEENTH AMENDMENT   To remove all doubt about the constitutionality of the new Civil Rights Act, the joint committee recommended a new constitutional amendment, which passed Congress on June 16, 1866, and was declared by Congress to have been ratified by the states on July 28, 1868. The Fourteenth Amendment went far beyond the Civil Rights Act, however. It reaffirmed the state and federal citizenship of persons born or naturalized in the United States, and it forbade any state (the word *state* would be important in later litigation) to "abridge the privileges or immunities of citizens," to deprive any *person* (again an important term) "of life, liberty, or property, without due process of law," or to "deny any person . . . the equal protection of the laws." These three clauses have been the subject of many lawsuits, resulting in applications not widely, if at all, foreseen at the time. The "due-process clause" has come to mean that state as well as federal power is subject to the Bill of Rights, and it has been used to protect corporations, as legal "persons," from "unreasonable" regulation by the states. Other provisions of the amendment have had less far-reaching effects. One section specified that the debt of the United States "shall not be questioned" by the former Confederate states and declared "illegal and void" all debts contracted in aid of the rebellion. The final sentence specified the power of Congress to pass laws enforcing the amendment.

Johnson's home state was among the first to ratify the Fourteenth Amendment. In Tennessee, which had harbored more Unionists than any other Confederate state, the government had fallen under Radical Republican control. The state's governor, in reporting the results to the secretary of the Senate, added, "Give my respects to the dead dog of the White House." His words illustrate the growing acrimony on both sides of the Reconstruction debates. In May and July, race riots in Memphis and New Orleans added fuel to the flames. Both incidents involved indiscriminate massacres of blacks by local police and white mobs. The carnage, Radical Republicans argued, was the natural fruit of Johnson's policy. "Witness Memphis, witness New Orleans," Senator Charles Sumner cried. "Who can doubt that the President is the author of these tragedies?"

RECONSTRUCTING THE SOUTH

THE TRIUMPH OF CONGRESSIONAL RECONSTRUCTION   As 1866 drew to an end, the congressional elections promised to be a referendum on the growing split between Andrew Johnson and the Radical Republicans. Johnson sought to influence voters with a speaking tour of the Midwest, a "swing around the circle," which turned into an undignified shouting contest between Andrew Johnson and his critics. In Cleveland he described the Radical Republicans as "factious, domineering, tyrannical" men, and he foolishly exchanged hot-tempered insults with a heckler. At another stop, while Johnson was speaking from an observation car, the engineer mistakenly pulled the train out of the station, making the president appear quite the fool. Such incidents tended to confirm his image as a "ludicrous boor" and a "drunken imbecile," which Radical Republicans promoted. In the 1866 congressional elections the Republicans won more than a two-thirds majority in each house, a comfortable margin with which to override presidential vetoes.

Congress in fact enacted a new program even before the new members took office. Two acts passed in 1867 extended the suffrage to African Americans in the District of Columbia and the territories. Another law provided that the new Congress would convene on March 4 instead of the following December, depriving Johnson of a breathing spell. On March 2, 1867, two days before the old Congress expired, it passed over Johnson's vetoes three basic laws promoting congressional Reconstruction: the Military Reconstruction Act, the Command of the Army Act (an amendment to an army appropriation), and the Tenure of Office Act.

The first of the three acts prescribed conditions under which the formation of southern state governments should begin all over again. The other two sought to block any effort by the president to obstruct the process. The Command of the Army Act required that all orders from the commander in chief go through the headquarters of the general of the army, then Ulysses Grant. The Radical Republicans trusted Grant, who was already leaning their way. The Tenure of Office Act required Senate permission for the president to remove any officeholder whose appointment the Senate had confirmed. The purpose of at least some congressmen was to retain Secretary of War Edwin Stanton, the one Radical Republican sympathizer in Johnson's cabinet. But an ambiguity crept into the wording of the act. Cabinet officers, it said, should serve during the term of the president who appointed them—and Lincoln had appointed Stanton, although, to be sure, Johnson was serving out Lincoln's term.

The Military Reconstruction Act was hailed—or denounced—as the triumphant victory of "Radical" Reconstruction. The act declared that "no legal state governments or adequate protection for life and property now exists in the rebel States." One state, Tennessee, which had ratified the Fourteenth Amendment, was exempted from the application of the new act. The other ten states were divided into five military districts, and the commanding officer of each was authorized to keep order and protect the "rights of persons and property." The Johnson governments remained intact for the time being, but new constitutions were to be framed "in conformity with the Constitution of the United States," in conventions elected by male citizens aged twenty-one and older "of whatever race, color, or previous condition." Each state constitution had to provide the same universal male suffrage. Then, once the constitution was ratified by a majority of voters and accepted by Congress, other criteria had to be met. The state legislature had to ratify the Fourteenth Amendment, and once the amendment became part of the Constitution, any given state would be entitled to representation in Congress. Persons excluded from officeholding by the proposed amendment were also excluded from participation in the process.

Johnson reluctantly appointed military commanders under the act, but the situation remained uncertain for a time. Some people expected the Supreme Court to strike down the act, and no machinery existed at the time for the new elections. Congress quickly remedied that on March 23, 1867, with the Second Reconstruction Act, which directed the army commanders to register all adult men who swore they were qualified. A Third Reconstruction Act, passed on July 19, directed registrars to go beyond the loyalty oath and determine each person's eligibility to take it and authorized district army commanders to remove and replace officeholders of any existing "so-called state" or division thereof. Before the end of 1867, new elections had been held in all the states but Texas.

Having clipped the president's wings, the Republican Congress moved a year later to safeguard its southern program from possible interference by the Supreme Court. On March 27, 1868, Congress simply removed the power of the Supreme Court to review cases arising under the Military Reconstruction Act, which Congress clearly had the right to do under its power to define the Court's appellate jurisdiction. The Court accepted this curtailment of its authority on the same day it affirmed the principle of an "indestructible union" in *Texas v. White* (1869). In that case the Court also asserted the right of Congress to reframe state governments, thus endorsing the Radical Republican point of view.

THE IMPEACHMENT AND TRIAL OF JOHNSON By 1868 Radical Republicans were convinced not only that the power of the Supreme Court and the president needed to be curtailed but also that Andrew Johnson himself had to be removed from office. Horace Greeley, the prominent editor of the *New York Tribune,* called Johnson "an aching tooth in the national jaw, a screeching infant in a crowded lecture room. There can be no peace or comfort till he is out."

Johnson, though hostile to the congressional Reconstruction program, had gone through the motions required of him. He continued, however, to pardon former Confederates and transferred several of the district military commanders who had displayed Radical sympathies. Johnson was revealing himself to be a man of limited ability and narrow vision. He lacked Lincoln's resilience and pragmatism. He also allowed his temper to get the better of his judgment. He castigated the Radical Republicans as "a gang of cormorants and bloodsuckers who have been fattening upon the country." During 1867 newspapers had reported that the differences between Johnson and the Republicans had become irreconcilable.

The Republicans unsuccessfully tried to impeach Johnson early in 1867, alleging a variety of flimsy charges, none of which represented an indictable crime. Then Johnson himself provided the occasion for impeachment when he deliberately violated the Tenure of Office Act in order to test its constitutionality. Secretary of War Edwin Stanton had become a thorn in the president's side, refusing to resign despite his disagreements with Johnson's Reconstruction policy. On August 12, 1867, during a congressional recess, Johnson suspended Stanton and named General Ulysses S. Grant in his place. When the Senate refused to confirm Johnson's action, however, Grant returned the office to Stanton.

The Radical Republicans now saw their chance to remove the president. As Charles Sumner declared, "Impeachment is a political proceeding before a political body with a political purpose." The debate in the House was vicious. One congressman said Johnson had dragged the robes of his office through the "filth of treason." Another denounced the president as "an ungrateful, despicable, besotted traitorous man—an incubus." Still another called Johnson's advisers "the worst men that ever crawled like filthy reptiles at the footstool of power." On February 24, 1868, the Republican-dominated House passed eleven articles of impeachment by a party-line vote of 126 to 47.

Of the eleven articles of impeachment, eight focused on the charge that Johnson had unlawfully removed Stanton. Article 9 accused the president of issuing orders in violation of the Command of the Army Act. The last two articles in effect charged him with criticizing Congress by "inflammatory and scandalous harangues." Article 11 also accused him of "unlawfully devising and contriving" to violate the Reconstruction Acts, contrary to his obligation to execute the laws. At the very least, it stated, Johnson had tried to obstruct Congress's will while observing the letter of the law.

The Senate trial began on March 5, 1868, and continued until May 26, with Chief Justice Salmon P. Chase presiding. It was a great spectacle before a packed gallery. Witnesses were called, speeches made, and rules of order

The Trial of Andrew Johnson

House of Representatives managers of the impeachment proceedings. Among them were Benjamin Franklin Butler (Republican of Massachusetts, seated left) and Thaddeus Stevens (Republican of Pennsylvania, seated with cane).

debated. Johnson wanted to plead his case in person, but his attorneys refused, fearing that his short temper might erupt and hurt his cause. The president thereupon worked behind the scenes to win over undecided Republican senators, offering them a variety of political incentives.

As the weeks passed, the trial grew tedious. Senators slept during the proceedings, spectators passed out in the unventilated room, and poor acoustics prompted repeated cries of "We can't hear." Debate eventually focused on Stanton's removal, the most substantive impeachment charge. Johnson's lawyers argued that Lincoln, not Johnson, had appointed Stanton, so the Tenure of Office Act did not apply to him. At the same time they claimed (correctly, as it turned out) that the law was unconstitutional.

As the five-week trial ended and the voting began in May 1868, the Senate Republicans could afford only six defections from their ranks to ensure the two-thirds majority needed to convict. In the end seven moderate Republicans and all twelve Democrats voted to acquit. The final tally was thirty-five to nineteen for conviction, one vote short of the two thirds needed for removal from office. The renegade Republicans offered two primary reasons for their controversial votes: they feared damage to the separation of powers among the branches of government if Johnson were removed, and they were assured by Johnson's attorneys that he would stop obstructing congressional policy in the South.

Although the Senate failed to remove Johnson, the trial crippled his already weak presidency. During the remaining ten months of his term, he initiated no other clashes with Congress. In 1868 Johnson sought the Democratic presidential nomination but lost to New York governor Horatio Seymour, who then lost to Republican Ulysses Grant in the general election. A bitter Johnson refused to attend Grant's inauguration. His final act as president was to issue a pardon to former Confederate president Jefferson Davis. In 1874, after failed bids for the Senate and the House, Johnson won a measure of vindication with election to the Senate, the only former president ever to do so, but he died a few months later. He was buried with a copy of the Constitution tucked under his head.

As for the impeachment trial, only two weeks after it ended, a Boston newspaper reported that Americans were amazed at how quickly "the whole subject of impeachment seems to have been thrown into the background and dwarfed in importance" by other events. Moreover, the impeachment of Johnson was in the end a great political mistake, for the failure to remove the president damaged Radical Republican morale and support. Nevertheless, the Radical cause did gain something. To blunt the opposition, Johnson agreed not to obstruct the process of Reconstruction, and thereafter Radical Reconstruction began in earnest.

REPUBLICAN RULE IN THE SOUTH In June 1868 Congress agreed that seven southern states had met the conditions for readmission to the Union, all but Virginia, Mississippi, and Texas. Congress rescinded Georgia's admission, however, when the state legislature expelled twenty-eight African-American members and seated former Confederate leaders. The federal military commander in Georgia then forced the legislature to reseat the black members and remove the Confederates, and the state was compelled to ratify the Fifteenth Amendment before being admitted in July 1870. Mississippi, Texas, and Virginia had returned earlier in 1870, under the added requirement that they, too, ratify the Fifteenth Amendment. That amendment, submitted to the states in 1869, and ratified in 1870, forbade the states to deny any person the vote on grounds of "race, color, or previous condition of servitude."

Long before the new governments had been established, Republican groups began to spring up in the South, chiefly sponsored by the Union League, founded in Philadelphia in 1862 to promote support for the Union. League recruiters enrolled African Americans and loyal whites, initiated them into the secrets and rituals of the order, and instructed them "in their rights and duties." Their recruiting efforts were so successful that in 1867, on the eve of South Carolina's choice of convention delegates, the league reported eighty-eight chapters, which claimed to have enrolled almost every adult black male in the state.

THE RECONSTRUCTED SOUTH

THE FREED SLAVES   To focus solely on what white Republicans did to reconstruct the defeated South creates the false impression that the freed slaves were simply pawns in the hands of others. In fact, however, southern blacks were active agents in affecting the course of Reconstruction. It was not an easy road, though. Many former Confederates continued to harbor deeply ingrained racial prejudices. They resisted and resented federally imposed changes in southern society. During the era of Reconstruction, whites used terror, intimidation, and violence to suppress black efforts to gain social and economic equality. In July 1866, for instance, a black woman in Clinch County, Georgia, was arrested and given sixty-five lashes for "using abusive language" during an encounter with a white woman. A month later another black woman suffered the same punishment. The Civil War had brought freedom to enslaved African Americans, but it did not bring them protection against exploitation or abuse. Many former slaves found themselves liberated but destitute after the fighting ended. The mere promise of freedom, however, raised their hopes of achieving a biracial democracy, equal justice, and economic opportunity. "Most anyone ought to know that a man is better off free than as a slave, even if he did not have anything," said the Reverend E. P. Holmes, a black Georgia preacher and former domestic servant. "I would rather be free and have my liberty."

Participation in the Union army or navy had provided many freedmen with training in leadership. Black military veterans would form the core of the first generation of African-American political leaders in the postwar South. Military service provided many former slaves with the first opportunities to learn to read and write. Army life also alerted them to new opportunities for economic advancement and social respectability. Fighting for the Union cause also instilled a fervent sense of nationalism. A Virginia freedman explained that the United States was "now *our* country—made emphatically so by the blood of our brethren."

Former slaves established independent churches after the war, and such churches quickly formed the foundation of African-American community life. Blacks preferred the Baptist denomination, in part because of the decentralized structure that allowed each congregation to worship in its own way.

The First African Church

Richmond, Virginia, 1874.

By 1890 there were over 1.3 million black Baptists in the South, nearly three times as many as any other black denomination. In addition to forming viable new congregations, freed blacks organized thousands of fraternal, benevolent, and mutual-aid societies, clubs, lodges, and associations. Memphis, for example, had over 200 such organizations; Richmond boasted twice that number.

The freed slaves also hastened to reestablish their families. Marriages that had been prohibited during slavery were now legitimized through the assistance of the Freedmen's Bureau. By 1870 a preponderant majority of former slaves were living in two-parent households. One white editor in Georgia, lamenting the difficulty of finding black women to serve as house servants, reported that "every negro woman wants to set up house keeping" for herself and her family. With little money or technical training, freed slaves faced the prospect of becoming wage laborers. Yet in order to retain as much autonomy as possible over their productive energies and those of their children on a daily and a seasonal basis, many husbands and wives chose sharecropping, in which the crop produced was divided between the tenant and the landowner. This choice enabled mothers and wives to devote more of their time to domestic needs while still contributing to the family's income.

African-American communities in the postwar South also sought to establish schools. The antebellum planter elite had denied education to blacks because they feared that literate slaves would organize uprisings. After the war the white elite worried that education programs would encourage poor whites and poor blacks to leave the South in search of better social and economic opportunities. Economic leaders wanted to protect the competitive advantage afforded by the region's low-wage labor market. "They didn't want us to learn nothin'," one former slave recalled. "The only thing we had to learn was how to work." White opposition to education for blacks made it all the more important to African Americans. South Carolina's Mary McLeod Bethune, the fifteenth child of former slaves and one of the first children in the household born after the Civil War, reveled in the opportunity to gain an education: "The whole world opened to me when I learned to read." She walked five miles to school as a child, earned a scholarship to college, and went on to become the first black woman to found a school that became a four-year college, Bethune-Cookman, in Daytona Beach, Florida.

The general resistance among the former slaveholding class to new education initiatives forced the freed slaves to rely on northern assistance or take their own initiative. A Mississippi Freedmen's Bureau agent noted in 1865 that when he told a gathering of some 3,000 former slaves that they "were to have the advantages of schools and education, their joy knew no bounds. They fairly jumped and shouted in gladness." African-American churches and individuals helped raise the money and often built the schools and paid the teachers. Soldiers who had acquired some literacy skills often served as the teachers, and the students included adults as well as children.

BLACKS IN SOUTHERN POLITICS   In the postwar South the new role of African Americans in politics caused the most controversy. If largely illiterate and inexperienced in the rudiments of politics, southern blacks were little different from the millions of propertyless whites or immigrants. Some freedmen frankly confessed their disadvantages. Beverly Nash, a black delegate to the South Carolina convention of 1868, told his colleagues: "I believe, my friends and fellow-citizens, we are not prepared for this suffrage. But we can learn. Give a man tools and let him commence to use them, and in time he will learn a trade. So it is with voting."

Several hundred African-American delegates participated in the statewide political conventions. Most had been selected by local political meetings or by churches, fraternal societies, Union Leagues, or black army units from the North, although a few simply appointed themselves. The African-American delegates "ranged all colors and apparently all conditions," but free mulattoes

Freedmen Voting in New Orleans

The Fifteenth Amendment, passed in 1870, guaranteed at the federal level the right of citizens to vote regardless of "race, color, or previous condition of servitude." But former slaves had been registering to vote—and voting in large numbers—in state elections since 1867, as in this scene.

from the cities played the most prominent roles. At Louisiana's Republican state convention, for instance, nineteen of the twenty black delegates had been born free.

By 1867, however, former slaves began to gain political influence and vote in large numbers, and this development revealed emerging tensions within the African-American community. Some southern blacks resented the presence of northern brethren who moved south after the war, while others complained that few ex-slaves were represented in black leadership positions. Northern blacks and the southern free black elite, most of whom were urban dwellers, opposed efforts to redistribute land to the rural freedmen, and many insisted that political equality did not mean social equality. As an Alabama black leader stressed, "We do not ask that the ignorant and degraded shall be put on a social equality with the refined and intelligent." In general, however, unity rather than dissension prevailed, and blacks focused on common concerns such as full equality under the law.

Brought suddenly into politics in times that tried the most skilled of statesmen, many African Americans served with distinction. Nonetheless, the derisive label "black Reconstruction" used by later critics exaggerates

African-American Political Figures of the Reconstruction

Blanche K. Bruce (left) and Hiram Revels (right) served in the U.S. Senate. Frederick Douglass (center) was a major figure in the abolitionist movement.

African-American political influence, which was limited mainly to voting, and overlooks the political clout of the large number of white Republicans, especially in the mountain areas of the upper South, who also favored the Radical plan for Reconstruction. Only one of the new state conventions, South Carolina's, had a black majority, seventy-six to forty-one. Louisiana's was evenly divided racially, and in only two other conventions were more than 20 percent of the members black: Florida's, with 40 percent, and Virginia's, with 24 percent. The Texas convention was only 10 percent black, and North Carolina's was 11 percent—but that did not stop a white newspaper from calling it a body consisting of "baboons, monkeys, mules . . . and other jackasses."

In the new state governments any African-American participation was a novelty. Although some 600 blacks—most of them former slaves—served as state legislators, no black man was ever elected governor, and only a few served as judges. In Louisiana, however, Pinckney Pinchback, a northern black and former Union soldier, won the office of lieutenant governor and served as acting governor when the white governor was indicted for corruption. Several blacks were elected lieutenant governor, state treasurer, or secretary of state. There were two black senators in Congress, Hiram Revels and Blanche K. Bruce, both Mississippi natives who had been educated in the North, and fourteen black members of the House of Representatives during Reconstruction.

CARPETBAGGERS AND SCALAWAGS   The top positions in southern state governments went for the most part to white Republicans, whom the opposition whites soon labeled carpetbaggers and scalawags, depending upon their place of birth. The northern opportunists who allegedly rushed South with all their belongings in carpetbags to grab the political spoils were more often than not Union veterans who had arrived as early as 1865 or 1866, drawn South by the hope of economic opportunity and other attractions that many of them had seen in their Union service. Many other so-called carpetbaggers were teachers, social workers, or preachers animated by a missionary impulse.

The "scalawags," or native white Republicans, were even more reviled and misrepresented. A Nashville editor called them the "merest trash that could be collected in a civilized community, of no personal credit or social responsibility." Most "scalawags" had opposed secession, forming a Unionist majority in many mountain counties as far south as Georgia and Alabama, and especially in the hills of eastern Tennessee. Among the "scalawags" were several distinguished figures, including the former Confederate general James Longstreet, who decided after Appomattox that the Old South must change its ways. He became a successful cotton broker in New Orleans, joined the Republican party, and supported the Radical Reconstruction program. Other "scalawags" were former Whigs attracted by the Republican party's economic program of industrial and commercial expansion.

THE RADICAL REPUBLICAN RECORD   Former Confederates also resented the new state constitutions because of their provisions allowing for black suffrage and civil rights. Yet most remained in effect for some years after the end of Radical Republican control, and later constitutions incorporated many of their features. Conspicuous among Radical innovations were such steps toward greater democracy as requiring universal manhood suffrage, reapportioning legislatures more nearly according to population, and making more state offices elective.

Given the hostile circumstances under which the Radical governments operated, their achievements are remarkable. They constructed an extensive

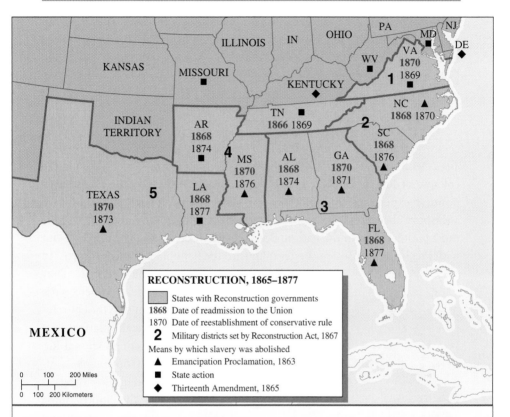

RECONSTRUCTION, 1865–1877

States with Reconstruction governments
1868 Date of readmission to the Union
1870 Date of reestablishment of conservative rule
2 Military districts set by Reconstruction Act, 1867
Means by which slavery was abolished
▲ Emancipation Proclamation, 1863
■ State action
◆ Thirteenth Amendment, 1865

How did the Military Reconstruction Act reorganize government in the South in the late 1860s and 1870s? What did the former Confederate states have to do to be readmitted to the Union? Why did "Conservative" parties gradually regain control of the South from the Republicans in the 1870s?

railroad network and established state school systems. Some 600,000 black pupils were enrolled in southern schools by 1877. State governments under the Radicals also gave more attention to the poor and to orphanages, asylums, and institutions for the deaf and the blind of both races. Public roads, bridges, and buildings were repaired or rebuilt. Blacks achieved new rights and opportunities that would never again be taken away, at least in principle: equality before the law and the rights to own property, carry on business, enter professions, attend schools, and learn to read and write.

Yet several of these Republican state regimes also engaged in corrupt practices. Bids for contracts were accepted at absurdly high prices, and public officials took their cut. Public money and public credit were often awarded to privately owned corporations, notably railroads, under conditions that invited influence peddling. Corruption was not invented by the Radical Republican regimes, nor did it die with them. Louisiana's "carpetbag" governor recognized as much. "Why," he said, "down here everybody is demoralized. Corruption is the fashion."

THE GRANT YEARS

THE ELECTION OF 1868   Ulysses S. Grant, who presided during the collapse of Republican rule in the South, brought to the White House little political experience. But in 1868 northern voters supported "the Lion of Vicksburg" because of his record as the Union army commander. He was the most popular man in the nation. Both parties wooed him, but his falling-out with President Johnson pushed him toward the Republicans and built trust in him among the Radicals. They were, as Thaddeus Stevens said, ready to "let him into the church."

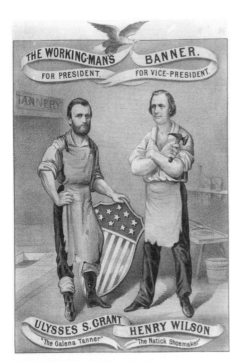

The Working-Man's Banner

This campaign banner makes reference to the working-class origins of Ulysses S. Grant and his vice-presidential candidate, Henry Wilson, by depicting Grant as a tanner and Wilson as a shoemaker.

The Republican platform of 1868 endorsed congressional Reconstruction. One plank cautiously defended black suffrage as a necessity in the South but a matter each northern state should settle for itself. Another urged payment of the national debt "in the utmost good faith to all creditors," which meant in gold. More important than the platform were the great expectations of a soldier-president and his slogan, "Let us have peace."

The Democrats took opposite positions on both Reconstruction and the debt. The Republican Congress, the Democratic platform charged, instead of restoring the Union had "so far as in its power, dissolved it, and subjected ten states, in the time of profound peace, to military despotism and

Negro supremacy." As for the federal debt, the party endorsed Representative George H. Pendleton's "Ohio idea" that, since most war bonds had been bought with depreciated greenbacks, they should be paid off in greenbacks. With no conspicuously available candidate in sight, the Democratic convention turned to Horatio Seymour, war governor of New York and chairman of the convention. His friends had to hustle him out of the hall to prevent his withdrawal. Seymour neither sought nor embraced the nomination, leading opponents to call him "the Great Decliner." Yet the Democrats made a closer race of it than the electoral vote revealed. Eight states, including New York and New Jersey, went for Seymour. While Grant swept the Electoral College by 214 to 80, his popular majority was only 307,000 out of a total of over 5.7 million votes. More than 500,000 African-American voters accounted for Grant's margin of victory.

Grant had proved himself a great leader in the war, but as the youngest president ever (forty-six years old at the time of his inauguration), he was blind to the political forces and influence peddlers around him. He was awestruck by men of wealth and unaccountably loyal to some who betrayed his trust, and he passively followed the lead of Congress. This approach at first endeared him to Republican party leaders, but it at last left him ineffective and left others disillusioned with his leadership.

At the outset, Grant consulted nobody on his seven cabinet appointments. Some of his choices indulged personal whims; others simply displayed bad judgment. In some cases, appointees learned of their nomination from the newspapers. As time went by, Grant betrayed a fatal gift for losing men of talent and integrity from his cabinet. Secretary of State Hamilton Fish of New York turned out to be a happy exception; Fish guided foreign policy throughout the Grant presidency. Other than Fish, however, the Grant cabinet overflowed with incompetents.

THE GOVERNMENT DEBT   Financial issues dominated Grant's presidency. After the war the Treasury had assumed that the $432 million worth of greenbacks issued during the conflict would be retired from circulation and that the nation would revert to a "hard-money" currency—gold coins. Many agrarian and debtor groups resisted any contraction of the money supply resulting from the elimination of greenbacks, believing that it would mean lower prices for their crops and would make it harder for them to repay long-term debts. They were joined by a large number of Radical Republicans who thought a combination of high tariffs and inflation would generate more rapid economic growth. As Senator John Sherman explained, "I prefer gold to paper money. But there is no other resort. We must have money or a fractured government." In 1868 congressional supporters of such a "soft-money" policy halted the retirement of greenbacks. There matters stood when Grant took office.

The "sound," or hard-money, advocates, mostly bankers and merchants, claimed that Grant's election was a mandate to save the country from the Democrats' "Ohio idea" of using greenbacks to repay government bonds. Quite influential in Republican circles, the sound-money advocates also had the benefit of agreeing with the deeply ingrained popular assumption that hard money was morally preferable to paper currency. Grant agreed as well, and in his inaugural address he endorsed payment of the national debt in gold as a point of national honor. On March 18, 1869, the Public Credit Act, which endorsed that principle, became the first act of Congress that Grant signed. Under the Refunding Act of 1870, the Treasury was able to replace 6 percent Civil War bonds with a new bond issue promising purchasers a return of 4 to 5 percent in gold.

SCANDALS   The complexities of the "money question" exasperated Grant, but that was the least of his worries, for his administration soon fell into a cesspool of scandal. In the summer of 1869, two financial buccaneers, the crafty Jay Gould and the flamboyant con man James Fisk, connived with the president's brother-in-law to corner the nation's gold market. That is, they would create a public craze for gold by purchasing massive quantities of the yellow metal and convincing traders and the general public that the price would keep climbing. As more buyers joined the frenzy, the value of gold would soar. The only danger to the scheme was the federal Treasury's selling large amounts of gold. Gould concocted an argument that the government should refrain from selling gold on the market because the resulting rise in gold prices would raise temporarily depressed farm prices. Grant apparently smelled a rat from the start, but he was seen in public with the speculators. As the rumor spread on Wall Street that the president had bought the argument, gold rose from $132 to $163 an ounce. When Grant finally persuaded his brother-in-law to pull out of the deal, Gould began quietly selling out. Finally, on "Black Friday," September 24, 1869, Grant ordered the Treasury to sell a large quantity of gold, and the bubble burst. Fisk got out by repudiating his agreements and hiring thugs to intimidate his creditors. "Nothing is lost save honor," he said.

The plot to corner the gold market was only the first of several scandals that rocked the Grant administration. During the campaign of 1872, the public first learned about the financial crookery of the Crédit Mobilier, a sham construction company composed of directors of the Union Pacific Railroad who had milked the Union Pacific for exorbitant fees in order to line the pockets of the insiders who controlled both firms. Union Pacific shareholders were left holding the bag. The schemers bought political support by giving congressmen stock in the enterprise. This chicanery had transpired before Grant's election in 1868, but it now touched a number of prominent Republicans. The beneficiaries had included Speaker of the House Schuyler Colfax, later vice president, and Representative James A. Garfield, later president. Of the thirteen members of Congress involved, only two were censured.

Even more odious disclosures soon followed, some involving the president's cabinet. The secretary of war, it turned out, had accepted bribes from merchants who traded with Indians at army posts in the West. He was impeached, but he resigned in time to elude a Senate trial. Post-office contracts, it was revealed, went to carriers who offered the highest kickbacks. The Secretary of the Treasury had awarded a political friend a commission of 50 percent for the collection of overdue taxes. In St. Louis a "whiskey ring" bribed tax collectors to bilk the government of millions of dollars in revenue. Grant's private secretary was enmeshed in that scheme, taking large sums of money and other valuables in return for inside information. There is no evidence that Grant himself was ever involved in, or personally profited from, any of the fraud, but his poor choice of associates and his gullibility earned him widespread criticism.

WHITE TERROR   President Grant initially fought hard to enforce the federal efforts to reconstruct the postwar South. By the time he became president, southern resistance had turned violent. In Grayson County, Texas, three whites murdered three freed slaves because they felt the need to "thin the niggers out and drive them to their holes."

The prototype of all the terrorist groups was the Ku Klux Klan (KKK), first organized in 1866 by some young men of Pulaski, Tennessee, as a social club, with the costumes and secret rituals common to fraternal groups. At first a

Worse Than Slavery

This Thomas Nast cartoon chides the Ku Klux Klan and the White League for promoting conditions "worse than slavery" for southern blacks after the Civil War.

group of pranksters, its members soon turned to intimidation of blacks and white Republicans, and the KKK and its imitators, like Louisiana's Knights of the White Camelia, spread rapidly across the South in answer to the Republican party's Union League. Klansmen rode about the countryside, hiding behind masks and under robes, spreading horrendous rumors, issuing threats, harassing African Americans, and occasionally wreaking violence and destruction.

Klansmen focused their terror on prominent Republicans, black and white. In Mississippi they killed a black Republican leader in front of his family. Three white "scalawag" Republicans were murdered in Georgia in 1870. That same year an armed mob of whites assaulted a Republican political rally in Alabama, killing four blacks and wounding fifty-four. In South Carolina the Klan was especially active. Virtually the entire white male population of York County joined the organization, and they were responsible for eleven murders and hundreds of whippings. In 1871 some 500 masked men laid siege to the Union County jail and eventually lynched eight black prisoners.

At the urging of President Grant, Congress struck back with three Enforcement Acts (1870–1871) to protect black voters. The first of these measures levied penalties on persons who interfered with any citizen's right to vote. A second placed the election of congressmen under surveillance by federal election supervisors and marshals. The third (the Ku Klux Klan Act) outlawed the characteristic activities of the Klan—forming conspiracies, wearing disguises, resisting officers, and intimidating officials—and authorized the president to suspend habeas corpus where necessary to suppress "armed combinations." In 1871 the federal government singled out nine counties in up-country South Carolina as an example, suspended habeas corpus, and pursued mass prosecutions. In general, however, the federal Enforcement Acts suffered from weak and inconsistent execution. As time passed, President Grant vacillated between clamping down on the Klan and capitulating to racial intimidation. The strong tradition of states' rights and local autonomy in the South resisted federal force.

CONSERVATIVE RESURGENCE   The Klan's impact on southern politics varied from state to state. In the upper South it played only a modest role in facilitating a Democratic resurgence. But in the Deep South, Klan violence and intimidation had more substantial effects. In overwhelmingly black Yazoo County, Mississippi, vengeful whites used violence to reverse the political balance of power. In the 1873 elections the Republicans cast 2,449 votes and the Democrats 638; two years later the Democrats polled

4,049 votes, the Republicans 7. Throughout the South the activities of the Klan weakened black and Republican morale, and in the North they encouraged a growing weariness with the whole southern question. "The plain truth is," noted the *New York Herald,* "the North has got tired of the Negro."

The erosion of northern interest in civil rights resulted from more than weariness, however. Western expansion, Indian wars, new economic opportunities, and political controversy over the tariff and the currency distracted attention from southern outrages against Republican rule and black rights. In addition, after a business panic that occurred in 1873 and an ensuing depression, desperate economic circumstances in the North and the South created new racial tensions that helped undermine already inconsistent federal efforts to promote racial justice in the former Confederacy. Republican control in the South gradually loosened as "Conservative" parties—a name used by Democrats to mollify former Whigs—mobilized the white vote. Prewar political leaders reemerged to promote the antebellum Democratic goals of limited government, states' rights, and free trade. They politicized the race issue to excite the white electorate and intimidate black voters. The Republicans in the South became increasingly an organization limited to blacks and federal officials. Many "scalawags" and carpetbaggers drifted away from the Radical Republican ranks under pressure from their white neighbors. Few of them had joined the Republicans out of concern for black rights in the first place. And where persuasion failed to work, Democrats were willing to use chicanery. As one enthusiastic Democrat boasted, "The white and black Republicans may outvote us, but we can outcount them."

Republican political control collapsed in Virginia and Tennessee as early as 1869; in Georgia and North Carolina it collapsed in 1870, although North Carolina had a Republican governor until 1876. Reconstruction lasted longest in the Deep South states with the largest black population, where whites abandoned Klan masks for barefaced intimidation in paramilitary groups such as the Mississippi Rifle Club and the South Carolina Red Shirts. By 1876 Radical Republican regimes survived only in Louisiana, South Carolina, and Florida, and those collapsed after the elections of that year.

REFORM AND THE ELECTION OF 1872   Long before Grant's first term ended, a reaction against Radical Reconstruction and incompetence and corruption in the administration had incited mutiny within the Republican ranks. A new faction, called Liberal Republicans, favored free trade, the redemption of greenbacks with gold, a stable currency, an end to federal Reconstruction efforts in the South, the restoration of the rights of former

What I Know about Raising the Devil

With the tail and cloven hoof of the devil, Horace Greeley (center) leads a small band of Liberal Republicans in pursuit of incumbent president Ulysses S. Grant and his supporters in this 1872 cartoon.

Confederates, and civil service reform. Open revolt first broke out in Missouri, where Carl Schurz led a group of Liberal Republicans who elected a governor with Democratic help in 1870 and sent Schurz to the Senate. In 1872 the Liberal Republicans held their own national convention at Cincinnati, which produced a compromise platform condemning the Republicans' Reconstruction policy and favoring civil service reform but remained silent on the protective tariff. The delegates embraced a quixotic presidential candidate: Horace Greeley, the prominent editor of the *New York Tribune,* a longtime champion of just about every reform available. Greeley's image as a visionary eccentric was complemented by his record of hostility to the Democrats, whose support the Liberals needed. The Democrats nevertheless swallowed the pill and gave their nomination to Greeley as the only hope of beating Grant.

The result was a foregone conclusion. Republican regulars duly endorsed Radical Reconstruction and the protective tariff. Grant still had seven southern carpetbag states in his pocket, generous contributions from business and banking interests, and the stalwart support of the Radical Republicans. Above all, he still evoked the imperishable glory of the Union victory in the war. Greeley, despite an exhausting tour of the country—still unusual for a presidential candidate—carried only six southern and border states and none in the North. Grant won by 3,598,235 votes to Greeley's 2,834,761.

PANIC AND REDEMPTION   Economic distress followed close upon the public scandals besetting the Grant administration. Such developments help explain why northerners lost interest in Reconstruction. A contraction of the nation's money supply resulting from the withdrawal of greenbacks and investments in new railroads made investors cautious and helped precipitate a financial crisis. During 1873 the market for railroad bonds turned sour as some twenty-five railroads defaulted on their interest payments. The prestigious investment bank of Jay Cooke and Company went bankrupt on September 18, 1873. The ensuing stampede of investors eager to exchange securities for cash forced the stock market to close for ten days. The panic of 1873 set off a depression that lasted six years, the longest and most severe that Americans had yet suffered. Thousands of businesses went bankrupt, millions of people lost their jobs, and as usually occurs, voters blamed the party in power for their economic woes.

Hard times and political scandals hurt Republicans in the midterm elections of 1874. The Democrats won control of the House of Representatives and gained seats in the Senate. The new Democratic House immediately launched inquiries into the scandals and unearthed further evidence of corruption in high places. The financial panic, meanwhile, focused attention once more on greenback currency.

Since the value of greenbacks was lower than that of gold, greenbacks had become the chief circulating medium. Most people spent greenbacks first and held their gold or used it to settle foreign accounts, thereby draining much gold out of the country. The postwar reduction of greenbacks in circulation, from $432 million to $356 million, had made for tight money. To relieve the currency shortage and stimulate business expansion, the Treasury reissued $26 million in greenbacks that had previously been withdrawn. As usually happened during economic hard times in the nineteenth century, debtors, the people hurt most by depression, called upon the federal government to inflate the money supply so as to make it easier for them to pay their obligations.

For a time the advocates of paper money were riding high. But in 1874 Grant vetoed a bill to issue more greenbacks. Then, in his annual message, he called for the gradual resumption of specie payments—that is, the redemption of greenbacks in gold, making greenbacks "good as gold" and raising their value to a par with that of the gold dollar. Congress obliged by passing the Specie Resumption Act of 1875. The payment in gold to people who turned in their paper money began on January 1, 1879, after the Treasury had built a gold reserve for that purpose and reduced the value of the greenbacks in circulation. This act infuriated those promoting an inflationary monetary policy and prompted the formation of the Greenback party, which elected fourteen congressmen in 1878. The much-debated and very complex "money question" was destined to remain one of the most divisive issues in American politics.

THE COMPROMISE OF 1877   President Grant, despite the controversies swirling around him, wanted to run again in 1876, but many Republicans were not enthusiastic about the prospect of Grant as the nation's first three-term president. After all, the Democrats had devastated the Republicans in the 1874 congressional elections: the decisive Republican majority in the House had evaporated, and the Democrats had taken control. In the summer of 1875, Grant acknowledged the growing opposition to his renomination and announced his retirement. James G. Blaine of Maine, former Speaker of the House and one of the nation's favorite orators, emerged as the Republican front-runner, but he, too, bore the taint of scandal. Letters in the possession of James Mulligan of Boston linked Blaine to some dubious railroad dealings, and the "Mulligan letters" found their way into print.

The Republican convention therefore eliminated Blaine and several other hopefuls in favor of Ohio's favorite son, Rutherford B. Hayes. Three times elected governor of Ohio, most recently as an advocate of hard money, Hayes had also made a name as a civil service reformer. But his chief virtue was that he offended neither Radicals nor reformers. As a journalist put it, he was "a third rate nonentity, whose only recommendation is that he is obnoxious to no one."

The Democratic Convention was abnormally harmonious from the start. The nomination went on the second ballot to Samuel J. Tilden, a millionaire corporation lawyer and reform governor of New York who had directed a campaign to overthrow the notorious Tweed ring controlling New York City politics and the canal ring in Albany, which had bilked the state of millions.

The 1876 campaign generated no burning issues. Both candidates favored the trend toward relaxing federal authority and restoring white conservative rule in the South. In the absence of strong differences, Democrats aired the Republicans' dirty linen. In response, Republicans waved the "bloody shirt," which is to say that they engaged in verbal assaults on former Confederates, linking the Democratic party to secession and the outrages committed against Republicans in the South. As one Republican speaker insisted, "Every man that tried to destroy this nation was a Democrat. . . . The man that assassinated Abraham Lincoln was a Democrat. . . . Soldiers, every scar you have on your heroic bodies was given you by a Democrat!"

Early election returns pointed to a Tilden victory. Tilden enjoyed a 254,000-vote edge in the balloting and had won 184 electoral votes, just one short of a majority. Hayes had 165 electoral votes, but the Republicans also claimed 19 doubtful votes from Florida, Louisiana, and South Carolina. The Democrats laid a counterclaim to 1 electoral vote from Oregon, but the Republicans had clearly carried that state. In the South the outcome was less certain, and given the fraud and intimidation perpetrated on both sides, nobody will ever know what might have happened if, to use a slogan of the day, "a free ballot and a fair count" had prevailed.

In all three of the disputed southern states, rival canvassing boards sent in different returns. In Florida, Republicans conceded the state election, but in Louisiana and South Carolina rival state governments appeared. The Constitution offered no guidance in this unprecedented situation. Even if Congress were empowered to sort things out, the Democratic House and the Republican Senate proved unable to reach an agreement.

Finally, on January 29, 1877, the two houses decided to set up a special Electoral Commission with fifteen members, five each from the House, the Senate, and the Supreme Court. Members were chosen such that there were seven from each major party, with Justice David Davis of Illinois as the swing vote. Davis, though appointed to the Court by Lincoln, was no party regular and was in fact thought to be leaning toward the Democrats. Thus, the panel appeared to be stacked in favor of Tilden.

But as it turned out, the panel got restacked the other way. Short-sighted Democrats in the Illinois legislature teamed up with minority Greenbackers to name Davis their senator. Davis accepted, no doubt with a sense of relief. From the remaining justices, all Republicans, the panel chose Joseph P. Bradley to fill the vacancy. The decision on each state went by a vote of eight to seven along party lines, in favor of Hayes. After much bluster and the threat of a filibuster by the Democrats, the House voted on March 2 to accept the report and declared Hayes elected by an electoral vote of 185 to 184.

Critical to this outcome was the defection of southern Democrats, who, seeing the way the wind was blowing in the composition of the Electoral Commission, had made several informal agreements with the Republicans. On February 26, 1877, prominent Ohio Republicans (including James A.

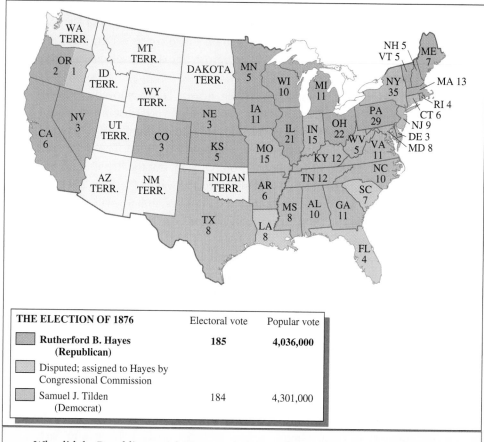

THE ELECTION OF 1876	Electoral vote	Popular vote
Rutherford B. Hayes (Republican)	185	4,036,000
Disputed; assigned to Hayes by Congressional Commission		
Samuel J. Tilden (Democrat)	184	4,301,000

Why did the Republicans pick Hayes as their presidential candidate? Why were the electoral votes of several states disputed? What was the Compromise of 1877?

Garfield) and powerful southern Democrats struck a bargain at Wormley's Hotel in Washington. The Republicans promised that if elected, Hayes would withdraw the last federal troops from Louisiana and South Carolina, letting the Republican governments there collapse. In return, the Democrats promised to withdraw their opposition to Hayes, accept in good faith the Reconstruction amendments (including civil rights for blacks), and refrain from partisan reprisals against Republicans in the South.

Southern Democrats could now justify deserting Tilden because this so-called Compromise of 1877 brought a final "redemption" from the Radicals and a return to "home rule," which actually meant rule by white Democrats. As a former slave observed in 1877, "The whole South—every state in the South—has got [back] into the hands of the very men that held us as slaves." Other, more informal promises, less noticed by the public, bolstered the "Wormley Conference." Hayes's friends pledged more support for rebuilding Mississippi River levees and other internal improvements, including a federal subsidy for a transcontinental railroad along a southern route. Southerners extracted a further promise that Hayes would name a white southerner as postmaster general, the cabinet position with the most patronage jobs at hand. In return, southerners would let the Republicans make James Garfield the Speaker of the new House. Such a deal illustrates the relative weakness of the presidency compared with Congress during the postwar era.

THE END OF RECONSTRUCTION   In 1877 President Hayes withdrew federal troops from Louisiana and South Carolina, and the Republican governments there collapsed soon thereafter—along with much of Hayes's claim to legitimacy. Hayes chose a Tennessean and former Confederate as postmaster general. But after southern Democrats failed to permit the choice of James Garfield as Speaker of the House, Hayes expressed doubt about any further subsidy for railroad building, and none was voted. Most of the other Wormley Conference promises were either renounced or forgotten.

As for southern promises regarding the civil rights of blacks, only a few Democratic leaders, such as the new governors of South Carolina and Louisiana, remembered them for long. Over the next three decades the protection of black civil rights crumbled under the pressure of restored white rule in the South and the force of Supreme Court decisions narrowing the application of the Reconstruction amendments. Radical Reconstruction never offered more than an uncertain commitment to black civil rights and social equality. Yet it left an enduring legacy, the Thirteenth, Fourteenth, and Fifteenth Amendments—not dead but dormant, waiting to be awakened. If Reconstruction did not provide social equality or substantial economic opportunities for African Americans, it did create the foundation for future advances. It was a revolution, sighed former governor of North Carolina Jonathan Worth, and "nobody can anticipate the action of revolutions."

MAKING CONNECTIONS

- The political, economic, and racial policies of the conservatives who overthrew the Republican governments in the southern states are described in Chapter 19.

- Several of the political scandals mentioned in this chapter were related to the railroads, a topic discussed in greater detail in Chapter 20.

- This chapter ended with the election of Rutherford B. Hayes; for a discussion of Hayes's administration, see Chapter 22.

FURTHER READING

The most comprehensive treatment of Reconstruction is Eric Foner's *Reconstruction: America's Unfinished Revolution, 1863–1877* (1988). On Andrew Johnson, see Hans L. Trefousse's *Andrew Johnson: A Biography* (1989). An excellent brief biography of Grant is Josiah Bunting III's *Ulysses S. Grant* (2004).

Scholars have been fairly sympathetic to the aims and motives of the Radical Republicans. See, for instance, Herman Belz's *Reconstructing the Union: Theory and Policy during the Civil War* (1969) and Richard Nelson Current's *Those Terrible Carpetbaggers: A Reinterpretation* (1988). The ideology of the Radicals is explored in Michael Les Benedict's *A Compromise of Principle: Congressional Republicans and Reconstruction, 1863–1869* (1974).

The intransigence of southern white attitudes is examined in Michael Perman's *Reunion without Compromise* (1973) and Dan T. Carter's *When the War Was Over: The Failure of Self-Reconstruction in the South, 1865–1867* (1985). Allen W. Trelease's *White Terror: The Ku Klux Klan and Southern Reconstruction* (1971) covers the various organizations that practiced vigilante tactics. The difficulties former slaves had in adjusting to the new labor system are documented in James L. Roark's *Masters without Slaves: Southern Planters in the Civil War and Reconstruction* (1977). Books on southern politics during Reconstruction include Michael Perman's *The Road to Redemption: Southern Politics, 1869–1879* (1984), Terry L. Seip's *The South Returns to Congress: Men, Economic Measures, and Intersectional Relationships, 1868–1879* (1983), and Mark W. Summer's *Railroads, Reconstruction, and the Gospel of Prosperity: Aid under the Radical Republicans, 1865–1877* (1984).

Numerous works study the freed blacks' experience in the South. Start with Leon F. Litwack's *Been in the Storm So Long: The Aftermath of Slavery* (1979). Joel Williamson's *After Slavery: The Negro in South Carolina during Reconstruction, 1861–1877* (1965) argues that South Carolina blacks took an active role in pursuing their political and economic rights. The Freedmen's Bureau is explored in William S. McFeely's *Yankee Stepfather: General O. O. Howard and the Freedmen* (1968). The situation of freed slave women is discussed in Jacqueline Jones's *Labor of Love, Labor of Sorrow: Black Women, Work, and the Family, from Slavery to the Present* (1985).

The politics of corruption outside the South is depicted in William S. McFeely's *Grant: A Biography* (1981). The political maneuvers of the election of 1876 and the resultant crisis and compromise are explained in C. Vann Woodward's *Reunion and Reaction: The Compromise of 1877 and the End of Reconstruction* (1951) and William Gillette's *Retreat from Reconstruction, 1869–1879* (1979).

Part Five

GROWING
PAINS

he Federal victory in 1865 restored the Union and in the process helped accelerate America's transformation into a modern nation-state. A distinctly national consciousness began to displace the sectional emphases of the antebellum era. During and after the Civil War the Republican-led Congress pushed through legislation to foster industrial and commercial development and western expansion. In the process the United States abandoned the Jeffersonian dream of a decentralized agrarian republic and began to forge a dynamic new industrial economy nurtured by an increasingly national and even international market.

After 1865 many Americans turned their attention to the unfinished business of settling a continent and completing an urban-industrial revolution begun before the war. Huge national corporations based upon mass production and mass marketing began to dominate the economy. As the prominent sociologist William Graham Sumner remarked, the process of industrial development "controls us all because we are all in it. It creates the conditions of our own existence, sets the limits of our social activity, and regulates the bonds of our social relations."

The Industrial Revolution was not only an urban phenomenon; it transformed rural life as well. Those who got in the way of the new emphasis on large-scale, highly mechanized commercial agriculture and ranching were brusquely pushed aside. Farm folk, as one New Englander stressed, "must understand farming as a business; if they do not it will go hard with them." The friction between new market forces and traditional folkways generated political revolts and social unrest during the last quarter of the nineteenth century. Fault lines appeared throughout the social order, and they unleashed tremors that exerted what one writer called "a seismic shock, a cyclonic violence" upon the body politic.

The clash between tradition and modernity peaked during the 1890s, one of the most strife-ridden decades in American history. A deep depression, agrarian unrest, and labor violence unleashed fears of class warfare. This turbulent situation transformed the presidential-election campaign of 1896 into a clash between rival visions of America's future. The Republican candidate, William McKinley, campaigned on behalf of modern urban-industrial values. By contrast, William Jennings Bryan, the nominee of the Democratic and Populist parties, was an eloquent defender of America's rural past. McKinley's victory proved to be a watershed in American political and social history. By 1900 the United States would emerge as one of the world's greatest industrial powers, and it would thereafter assume a new leadership role in world affairs.

19

THE SOUTH AND THE WEST
TRANSFORMED

FOCUS QUESTIONS

· What were the economic and political policies of the states in the post-Reconstruction South?

· How did segregation and political disenfranchisement shape race relations in the New South?

· What were the experiences of farmers, miners, and cowboys in the West?

· What were the consequences of late-nineteenth-century Indian policy?

To answer these questions and access additional review material, please visit www.wwnorton.com/studyspace.

After the Civil War the South and the West provided enticing opportunities for American inventiveness and entrepreneurship. Before 1860 most people had viewed the region between the Mississippi River and California as a barren landscape unfit for human habitation or cultivation, an uninviting land suitable only for Indians and animals. Half the state of Texas, for instance, was still not settled at the end of the Civil War. After 1865, however, the federal government encouraged western settlement and economic exploitation. The construction of transcontinental railroads, the military conquest of the Indians, and a liberal land-distribution policy combined to help lure thousands of pioneers and expectant capitalists westward. Charles Goodnight, a Texas cattleman, recalled that "we were adventurers in a great land as fresh and full of the zest of darers."

Although the first great wave of railroad building occurred in the 1850s, the most spectacular growth took place during the quarter century after the Civil War. From about 35,000 miles of track in 1865, the national rail network grew to nearly 200,000 miles by 1897. The transcontinental rail lines led the way, and they helped populate the plains and the Far West. Of course, such a sprawling railroad system was expensive, and the long-term debt required to finance it would become a major cause of the financial panic of 1893 and the ensuing depression.

In the postwar South, rail lines were rebuilt and supplemented with new branch lines. The defeated Confederacy offered a fertile new ground for investment and industrial development. Proponents of a "New South" after 1865 argued that the region must abandon its single-minded preoccupation with agriculture and pursue industrial and commercial development. As a result, the South as well as the West experienced dramatic social and economic changes during the last third of the nineteenth century. By 1900 the South and the West had been transformed in ways that few could have predicted, and fourteen new states were created out of the western territories.

The New South

A FRESH VISION   Amid the pains of defeat and the ruins of war, many southerners looked wistfully to the plantation life that had dominated their region before the firing on Fort Sumter in 1861. A few prominent leaders, however, insisted that the postwar South must liberate itself from nostalgia and create a modern society of small farms, thriving industries, and bustling cities. The major prophet of this New South was Henry W. Grady, editor of the *Atlanta Constitution*. During the 1880s Grady set forth the vision that inspired a generation of southerners. "The Old South," he said, "rested everything on slavery and agriculture, unconscious that these could neither give nor maintain healthy growth." The New South, on the other hand, "presents a perfect democracy" of small farms and diversifying industries. The postwar South, Grady believed, held the promise of a real democracy, one no longer run by the planter aristocracy and no longer dependent upon slave labor.

Henry Grady's compelling vision of a New South attracted many supporters, who preached with evangelical fervor the gospel of industrial development. The Confederacy, they reasoned, had lost the war because it had relied too much upon King Cotton. In the future the South must follow the North's example and industrialize. From that central belief flowed certain corollaries: that a more diversified and efficient agriculture would be a foundation for economic growth, that more widespread education, especially vocational training, would promote material success, and that sectional peace and racial harmony would provide a stable environment for economic growth.

ECONOMIC GROWTH   The chief accomplishment of the New South movement was an expansion of the region's textile production. From 1880 to 1900, the number of cotton mills in the South grew from 161 to 400, the number of mill workers (among whom women and children outnumbered men) increased fivefold, and the demand for cotton went up eightfold.

Tobacco growing also increased significantly. Essential to the rise of the tobacco industry was the Duke family of Durham, North Carolina. At the end of the Civil War, the story goes, Washington Duke took a barnful of tobacco and, with the help of his three sons, beat it out with hickory sticks, stuffed it into bags, hitched two mules to his wagon, and set out across the state, selling tobacco as he went. By 1872 the Dukes had a factory producing 125,000

The Heroes of the Civil War

Ulysses S. Grant and Robert E. Lee share this 1889 album cover, issued by
W. Duke, Sons and Company to promote their cigarettes.

pounds of tobacco annually, and Washington Duke prepared to settle down and enjoy success.

His son Buck (James Buchanan Duke) wanted even greater success, however. He recognized that the tobacco industry was "half smoke and half ballyhoo," so he poured large sums into advertising schemes. Duke also undersold competitors in their own markets and cornered the supply of ingredients. Eventually his competitors agreed to join forces, and in 1890 Duke brought most of them into the American Tobacco Company, which controlled nine tenths of the nation's cigarette production and, by 1904, about three fourths of all tobacco production. In 1911 the Supreme Court ruled that the company was in violation of the Sherman Anti-Trust Act and ordered it broken up, but by then Duke had found new worlds to conquer, in hydroelectric power and aluminum.

Systematic use of other natural resources helped revitalize the area along the Appalachian Mountain chain from West Virginia to Alabama. Coal production in the South (including West Virginia) grew from 5 million tons in 1875 to 49 million tons by 1900. At the southern end of the mountains, Birmingham, Alabama, sprang up during the 1870s in the shadow of Red Mountain, so named for its iron ore, and boosters soon tagged the city the Pittsburgh of the South.

Industrial growth spawned a need for housing, and after 1870 lumbering became a thriving industry in the South. Lumber camps sprouted across the mountains and flatlands. By the turn of the century, their product, mainly southern pine, had outdistanced textiles in value. Tree cutting seemed to know no bounds, despite the resulting ecological devastation. In time the lumber industry would be saved only by the warm climate, which fostered quick growth of replanted forests, and the rise of scientific forestry.

The South still had far to go to achieve the diversified industry that Henry Grady envisioned in the mid-1880s, but a profusion of other products poured from southern plants: phosphate fertilizers from coastal South Carolina and Florida; oysters, vegetables, and fruits from widespread canneries; ships, including battleships, from the Newport News Shipbuilding and Drydock Company; leather products; liquors and other beverages; and clay, glass, and stone products.

AGRICULTURE OLD AND NEW At the turn of the century, however, most of the South remained undeveloped, at least by northeastern standards. Despite the optimistic rhetoric of Henry Grady and other New South spokesmen, the typical southerner was less apt to be tending a textile loom or iron forge than, as the saying went, facing the eastern end of a west-

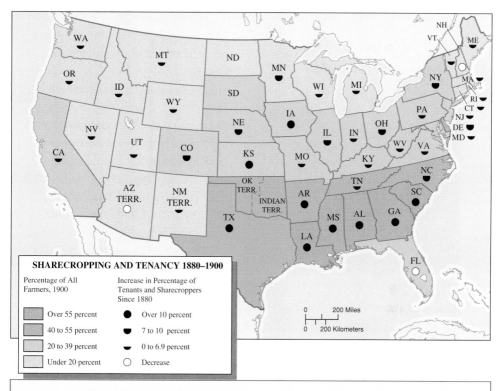

SHARECROPPING AND TENANCY 1880–1900

Why was there a dramatic increase in sharecropping and tenancy in the late nineteenth century? Why did the South have more sharecroppers than other parts of the country? Why do you think the rate of sharecropping was lowest in western states like New Mexico and Arizona?

bound mule. King Cotton survived the Civil War and expanded over new acreage even as its export markets leveled off. Louisiana cane sugar, probably the most war devastated of all crops, was flourishing again by the 1890s.

In the old rice belt of coastal South Carolina and elsewhere, vegetable farming blossomed with the advent of the railroads and refrigerated railcars. But the majority of southern farmers were not flourishing. A prolonged deflation in crop prices affected the entire Western world during the last third of the nineteenth century. Sagging prices for farm crops made it more difficult than ever to own land. Sharecropping and tenancy among blacks and whites grew increasingly prevalent. By 1890 most southern farms were worked by people who did not own the land. Rates of farm ownership in the Deep South belied Henry Grady's dream of a southern democracy of small landowners: South Carolina,

Picking Cotton in Mississippi, 1870

Tenant farming was extremely inefficient, as the tenant lacked incentive to care for the land, and the owner was largely unable to supervise the work.

39 percent; Georgia, 40 percent; Alabama, 42 percent; Mississippi, 38 percent; and Louisiana, 42 percent.

How did sharecropping and tenancy work? Sharecroppers, who had nothing to offer the landowner but their labor, worked the owner's land in return for supplies and a share of the crop, generally about half. Tenant farmers, hardly better off, might have their own mule, plow, and line of credit with the country store. They were entitled to claim a larger share of the crops. The sharecropper-tenant system was horribly inefficient and corrupting. It was in essence a post–Civil War version of land slavery. Tenants and landowners developed an intense suspicion of each other. Landlords often swindled the farm workers by not giving them their fair share of the crops.

The postwar South suffered from an acute shortage of capital; people had to devise ways to operate without cash. One innovation was the crop-lien system: country merchants furnished supplies to small farmers in return for liens (or mortgages) on their crops. The credit offered a way out of dependency for some farmers, but to most it offered only a hopeless cycle of perennial debt. The merchant, who assumed great risks, generally charged interest that ranged, according to one publication, "from 24 percent to grand larceny." The merchant, like the planter (often the same man), required his farmer clients to grow a cash crop that could be readily sold at harvest time. So for all the wind and ink expended by promoters of a New South based upon diversified agriculture, the routines of tenancy and sharecropping geared the marketing, supply, and credit systems to a staple crop, usually cotton. The stagnation of rural life thus held millions, white and black, in bondage to privation and ignorance.

TENANCY AND THE ENVIRONMENT The pervasive use of tenancy and sharecropping unwittingly caused profound environmental damage.

Growing commercial row crops like cotton on the same land year after year leached the nutrients from the soil. Tenants had no incentive to take care of farmland by manuring or rotating crops because it was not their own. They used fertilizer to accelerate the growing cycle, but the extensive use of phosphate fertilizers only accelerated soil depletion, by enabling multiple plantings each year. Fertilizer, said an observer, seduced southern farmers into believing that there was a "short cut to prosperity, a royal road to good crops of cotton year after year. The result has been that their lands have been cultivated clean year after year, and their fertility has been exhausted."

Once the soil had lost its fertility, the tenants moved on to another farm, leaving behind rutted fields whose topsoil washed away with each rain. The silt and mud flowed into creeks and rivers, swamping many lowland fields and filling millponds and lakes. By the early twentieth century much of the rural South resembled a ravaged land: deep gullies sliced through bare eroded hillsides, and streams and deep lakes were clogged with silt. As far as the eye could see, red clay devoid of nutrients dominated the landscape.

THE BOURBON REDEEMERS In post–Civil War southern politics, habits of social deference and political elitism still prevailed. "Every community," one Union officer noted in postwar South Carolina, "had its great man, or its little great man, around whom his fellow citizens gather when they want information, and to whose monologues they listen with a respect akin to humility." After Reconstruction southern politics was dominated by small groups of such men, collectively known as redeemers, or Bourbons. The supporters of these postwar Democratic leaders referred to them as redeemers because they supposedly redeemed, or saved, the South from Yankee domination as well as from the straitjacket of a purely rural economy. The redeemers included a rising class of entrepreneurs who were eager to promote a more diversified economy based upon industrial development and railroad expansion. The opponents of the redeemers labeled them Bourbons in an effort to depict them not as progressives but as reactionaries. Like the French royal family that, Napoléon had said, forgot nothing and learned nothing in the ordeal of revolution, Bourbons of the postwar South were said to have forgotten nothing and to have learned nothing in the ordeal of the Civil War.

The Bourbons of the New South perfected a political alliance with northern conservatives and an economic alliance with northern capitalists. They generally pursued a government fiscal policy of retrenchment and frugality, except for the tax exemptions and other favors they offered business. The

Bourbon governors and legislators slashed state expenditures, including those for the public-school systems started during Reconstruction. In 1871 the southern Atlantic states were spending $10.27 per pupil; by 1880 the figure was down to $6, and in 1890 it stood at $7.63. In 1882 there were 3,183 schools in South Carolina but only 3,413 teachers. Illiteracy rates in the South at the time ran at about 12 percent of the native-born white population and 50 percent of the black population.

The urge to reduce state expenditures created in the penal system one of the darkest blots on the Bourbon record: convict leasing. The wartime destruction of prisons and the poverty of state treasuries combined with the demand for cheap labor to make the leasing of convict workers a way for southern states to avoid penitentiary expenses and generate revenue. Convict leasing, in the absence of state supervision, allowed inefficiency, neglect, and disregard for human life to proliferate. White political and economic leaders often used a racial argument to rationalize the leasing of convicts, most of whom were African American. An "inferior" and "shiftless" race, they claimed, required the regimen of such coercion to elevate it above its idle and undisciplined ways.

The Bourbons reduced not only state expenditures but also the public debt, and by a simple means: they repudiated a vast amount of it. The corruption and extravagance of Radical rule were commonly advanced as justification for the process, but repudiation did not stop with Reconstruction debts. Altogether nine states repudiated more than half of what they owed to bondholders and creditors.

Despite their penny-pinching ways, the frugal Bourbon regimes, so ardently devoted to free enterprise, did respond to the demand for commissions to regulate the rates charged by railroads for commercial transport. They also established boards of agriculture and public health, stations for agricultural experimentation, agricultural and mechanical colleges, teacher-training schools and women's colleges, and even state colleges for African Americans.

Nor can any simplistic interpretation encompass the variety of Bourbon leaders. The Democratic party of the time was a mongrel coalition that threw Unionists, secessionists, businessmen, small farmers, hillbillies, planters, and even some Republicans together in an alliance against the Reconstruction Radicals. Democrats, therefore, even those who bore the Bourbon label, often marched to different drummers. And once they gained control, Bourbon regimes never achieved complete unity in philosophy or government.

Perhaps the ultimate paradox of the Bourbons' rule was that these paragons of white supremacy tolerated a lingering black voice in politics and

The Effects of Radical and Bourbon Rule in the South

This 1880 cartoon shows the South staggering under the oppressive weight of military Reconstruction (left) and flourishing under the "Let 'Em Alone Policy" of President Rutherford B. Hayes and the Bourbons (right).

showed no haste to raise the barriers of racial separation. In the 1880s southern politics remained surprisingly open and democratic, with 64 percent of eligible voters, blacks and whites, participating in elections. African Americans sat in the state legislature of South Carolina until 1900 and in the state legislature of Georgia until 1908; some of them were Democrats. The South sent African-American congressmen to Washington in every election except one until 1900, though they always represented gerrymandered districts into which most of the state's African-American voters had been placed. Under the Bourbons the disenfranchisement of African-American voters remained inconsistent, a local matter brought about mainly by fraud and intimidation, but it occurred often enough to ensure white control of the southern states.

A like flexibility applied to other aspects of race relations. The color line was drawn less strictly immediately after the Civil War than it would be in the twentieth century. In some places, to be sure, racial segregation appeared before the end of Reconstruction, especially in schools, churches, hotels and rooming houses, and private social relations. In places of public accommodation such as trains, depots, theaters, and soda fountains, discrimination was more sporadic.

The ultimate achievement of the New South prophets and their allies, the Bourbons, was that they reconciled tradition with innovation. Their relative moderation in racial policy, at least before the 1890s, allowed them to embrace just enough of the new to disarm adversaries and keep control. By promoting the growth of industry, the Bourbons led the South into a new economic era, but without sacrificing a mythic reverence for the Old South. Bourbon rule left a permanent mark on the South. As the historian C. Vann Woodward noted, "It was not the Radicals nor the Confederates but the Redeemers who laid the lasting foundations in matters of race, politics, economics and institutions for the modern South."

DISENFRANCHISING AFRICAN AMERICANS   During the 1890s the attitudes that permitted moderation in race relations evaporated. A violent "Negrophobia" swept across the South and much of the nation at the end of the century. One reason for it was that many whites resented signs of black success and social influence. An Alabama newspaper editor declared that "our blood boils when the educated Negro asserts himself politically. We regard each assertion as an unfriendly encroachment upon our native superior rights, and a dare-devil menace to our control of the affairs of the state."

Education did bring enlightenment—as it was supposed to do. In 1889 the student newspaper at all-black Fisk University in Nashville predicted a profound change in race relations at the end of the century. It stressed that a new generation of African Americans born since the end of the Civil War and educated in schools and colleges were determined to gain true equality. They were more assertive and less patient than their parents. "We are not the Negro from whom the chains of slavery fell a quarter century ago, most assuredly not," the editor announced. A growing number of young white adults, however, were equally determined to keep "Negroes in their place."

Racial violence and repression surged to the fore during the last decade of the nineteenth century and the first two decades of the twentieth. By the end of the nineteenth century, the so-called New South had come to resemble the Old South. Ruling whites ruthlessly imposed their will over all areas of black life, imposing racial subjugation and segregation by preventing blacks from voting and by enacting "Jim Crow" laws mandating public separation of the races. This development was not the logical culmination of the Civil War and emancipation but rather the result of a calculated campaign by white elites and thugs to limit African-American political, economic, and social life.

The political dynamics of the 1890s exacerbated racial tensions. The rise of populism, a farm-based protest movement that crystallized into a third political party in the 1890s, divided the white vote to such an extent that in some places the black vote became the balance of power. Some populists courted black votes and brought African Americans prominently into their leadership councils. In response the Bourbons revived the race issue, which they exploited with seasoned finesse, all the while controlling for their ticket a good part of the black vote in plantation areas. Nevertheless, the Bourbons soon reversed themselves and began arguing in the 1890s that the black vote should be eliminated from southern elections. The affluent and well-educated Democrats in southern counties with large African-American populations led the way in promoting disenfranchisement. They wanted to eliminate the voting of poor whites as well as blacks. It was imperative, said the governor of Louisiana in 1894, that "the mass of ignorance, vice and venality without any proprietary interest in the State" be denied the vote. Some farm leaders hoped that disenfranchisement of blacks would make it possible for whites to divide politically without raising the specter of "Negro domination." But since the Fifteenth Amendment made it impossible simply to deny African Americans the right to vote, disenfranchisement was accomplished indirectly, through such devices as poll taxes (or head taxes) and literacy tests.

Mississippi led the way to near-total disenfranchisement of blacks and many poor whites as well. The state called a constitutional convention in 1890 to change the suffrage provisions of the Radical constitution of 1868. The Mississippi plan set the pattern that seven more states would follow over the next twenty years. First, a residence requirement—two years in the state, one year in an election district—struck at those African-American tenant farmers who were in the habit of moving yearly in search of better opportunities. Second, voters were disqualified if convicted of certain crimes. Third, all taxes, including a poll tax, had to be paid before a person could vote. This proviso fell most heavily on poor whites and blacks. Fourth and finally, all voters had to be literate. The alternative, designed as a loophole for otherwise-disqualified whites, was an "understanding" clause. The voter, if unable to read the Constitution, could qualify by being able to "understand" it—to the satisfaction of the registrar. Not surprisingly, registrars declared far more blacks ineligible than whites.

Other states added variations on the Mississippi plan. In 1895 South Carolina tacked on the proviso that owning property assessed at $300 would qualify an illiterate voter. In 1898 Louisiana invented the "grandfather clause," which allowed illiterates to vote if their fathers or grandfathers had been eligible to vote on January 1, 1867, when African Americans were still excluded. By 1910 Georgia, North Carolina, Virginia, Alabama, and Oklahoma had adopted the grandfather clause. Every southern state, moreover, adopted a statewide Democratic primary between 1896 and 1915, which

Jim Crow

This stock character in old minstrel shows became a synonym for racial segregation in the twentieth century.

became the only meaningful election outside isolated areas of Republican strength. With minor exceptions the Democratic primaries excluded African-American voters altogether. The effectiveness of these measures can be seen in a few sample figures. Louisiana in 1896 had 130,000 black voters registered. By 1900 the number was only 5,320. Alabama in 1900 had 121,159 literate black men over twenty-one, according to the census; only 3,742, however, were registered to vote.

THE SPREAD OF SEGREGATION What came to be called Jim Crow social segregation followed political disenfranchisement and in some states came first. The symbolic first target was the railway train. In 1885 the novelist George Washington Cable noted that in South Carolina blacks "ride in first class [rail] cars as a right" and "their presence excites no comment." From 1875 to 1883, in fact, any racial segregation violated a federal Civil Rights Act, which forbade discrimination in places of public accommodation. But in 1883 the Supreme Court ruled on seven civil rights cases involving discrimination against blacks by corporations or individuals. The Court held, with only one dissent, that the force of federal law could not extend to individual action because the Fourteenth Amendment, which provided that "no State" could deny citizens equal protection of the law, stood as a prohibition only against *state* action.

This interpretation left as an open question the validity of state laws *requiring* separate racial facilities under the rubric of "separate but equal," a slogan popular with the New South prophets. In 1881 Tennessee had required railroads in the state to maintain separate first-class railcars for blacks and whites. In 1888 Mississippi went a step further by requiring passengers to occupy the car set aside for their race. When Louisiana followed suit in 1890, dissidents challenged the law in the case of *Plessy v. Ferguson,* which the Supreme Court decided in 1896.

The test case originated in New Orleans when Homer Plessy, an octoroon (a person having one-eighth African ancestry), refused to leave a whites-only railroad car when told to do so. He was convicted of violating the law, and the case rose on appeal to the Supreme Court. The Court ruled that segregation laws "have been generally, if not universally recognized as within the competency of state legislatures in the exercise of their police power."

Very soon the principle of racial segregation extended to every area of southern life, including streetcars, hotels, restaurants, hospitals, recreation, sports, and employment. In 1900 the editor of the *Richmond Times* expressed the prevailing view:

> It is necessary that this principle be applied in every relation of Southern life. God Almighty drew the color line and it cannot be obliterated. The negro must stay on his side of the line and the white man must stay on his side, and the sooner both races recognize this fact and accept it, the better it will be for both."

Unashamed and unregulated violence accompanied the Jim Crow laws. From 1890 to 1899, lynchings in the United States averaged 188 per year, 82 percent of which occurred in the South; from 1900 to 1909, they averaged 93 per year, with 92 percent in the South. Whites constituted 32 percent of the victims during the former period but only 11 percent in the latter. A young Episcopal priest in Montgomery, Alabama, said that extremists had proceeded "from an undiscriminating attack upon the Negro's ballot to a like attack upon his schools, his labor, his life."

By the end of the nineteenth century, legalized racial discrimination—segregation of public facilities, political disenfranchisement, and vigilante justice punctuated by brutal public lynchings and race riots—had elevated government-sanctioned bigotry to an official way of life in the South. South Carolina senator Benjamin Tillman declared in 1892 that blacks "must remain subordinate or be exterminated."

How did African Americans respond to the resurgence of racism and statutory segregation? Some left the South in search of equality and opportunity, but the vast majority stayed in their native region. In the face of overwhelming force and prejudicial justice, most accommodated themselves to the realities of white supremacy and segregation. "Had to walk a quiet life," explained James Plunkett, a Virginia black. "The least little thing you would do, they [whites] would kill ya."

Yet accommodation did not mean total submission. Excluded from the dominant white world and eager to avoid confrontations, black southerners after the 1890s increasingly turned inward and constructed their own culture and nurtured their own pride. A young white visitor to Mississippi in 1910 noticed that nearly every black person he met had "two distinct social selves, the one he reveals to his own people, the other he assumes among the whites."

African-American churches continued to provide the hub for black community life. Often the only public buildings available for African Americans, churches were used not only for worship but also for activities that had nothing to do with religion: social gatherings, club meetings, political activities. For men especially, churches offered leadership roles and political status. Serving as a deacon was one of the most prestigious roles an African-American man could achieve. Churches fostered racial pride and personal dignity and enabled African Americans of all classes to interact and exercise roles denied them in the larger society. Religious life provided great comfort to people worn down by the daily hardships and abuses associated with segregation.

One irony of state-enforced segregation is that it opened up new economic opportunities for blacks. A new class of African-American entrepreneurs emerged to provide services—insurance, banking, funerals, barbering, hair salons—to the black community in the segregated South. At the same time, African Americans formed their own social and fraternal clubs and organizations, all of which helped bolster black pride and provide fellowship and opportunities for service. For example, the Independent Order of Odd Fellows, the largest of the African-American fraternal orders, had over 400,000 members in 1904.

Middle-class black women formed a network of thousands of racial-uplift organizations across the South and around the nation. The women's clubs were engines of social service in their communities. They cared for the aged and the infirm, the orphaned and the abandoned. They created homes for single mothers and provided nurseries for working mothers. They sponsored health clinics and classes in home economics for women. In 1896 the leaders of such women's clubs from around the country converged to form the National Association of Colored Women, an organization meant to combat racism and segregation. Its first president, Mary Church Terrell, told members that they had an obligation to serve the "lowly, the illiterate, and even the vicious to whom we are bound by the ties of race and sex, and put forth every effort to uplift and reclaim them."

Ida B. Wells

While raising four children, Wells sustained her commitment to ending racial and gender discrimination.

IDA B. WELLS   One of the most outspoken African-American activists of the time was Ida B. Wells. Born into slavery in 1862 in Mississippi, she attended a school staffed by white missionaries. In 1878 an epidemic of yellow fever killed both her parents as well as an infant brother. At age sixteen, Wells assumed responsibility for her five younger siblings and secured a job as a country schoolteacher. In about 1880 she moved to nearby Memphis, then fast emerging as a commercial hub and cultural center. In Memphis she taught in segregated country and city schools and soon gained entrance to the social life of the city's striving African-American middle class.

In 1883 Wells confronted the reality and power of white supremacy. After being denied a seat in a railroad car because she was black, she became the first African American to file suit against such discrimination. The circuit court decided in her favor and fined the railroad, but the Tennessee Supreme Court overturned the ruling. Wells thereafter discovered "[my] first and [it] might be said, my only love"—journalism—and, through it, a weapon with which to wage her crusade for justice. Writing under the pen name Iola, she became a prominent editor of *Memphis Free Speech*, a newspaper focusing on African-American issues.

In 1892, when three of her friends were lynched by a white mob, Wells launched a lifelong crusade against lynching. Angry whites responded by destroying her office and threatening to lynch her. She moved to New York and continued to use her fiery journalistic talent to criticize Jim Crow laws and demand that blacks have their voting rights restored. In the spring of 1898, the lynching of an African-American postmaster in South Carolina so incensed Wells that she spent five weeks in Washington, D.C., fruitlessly trying to persuade the federal government to intervene. She helped found the National Association for the Advancement of Colored People (NAACP) in 1909 and worked to promote women's suffrage. In promoting full equality, Wells often found herself in direct opposition to the accommodationist views of Booker T. Washington.

Booker T. Washington

Founder of the Tuskegee Institute.

WASHINGTON AND DU BOIS

Booker T. Washington, born in Virginia of a slave mother and a white father, fought extreme adversity to get an education at Hampton Institute, one of the postwar missionary schools, and went on to build at Tuskegee, Alabama, a leading college for African Americans. By the 1890s Washington had become the foremost black educator in the nation. He argued that blacks should first establish an economic base for their advancement before striving for social equality. In a speech at the Atlanta Cotton States and International Exposition in 1895 that propelled him to fame, Washington advised fellow African Americans: "Cast down your bucket where you are—cast it down in making friends . . . of the people of all races by whom we are surrounded. Cast it down in agriculture, mechanics, in commerce, in domestic service, and in the professions." He conspicuously omitted politics from that list and offered an oblique endorsement of segregation: "In all things that are purely social we can be as separate as the five fingers, yet one as the hand in all things essential to mutual progress."

Some people bitterly criticized Washington, then and since, for making a bad bargain: the sacrifice of broad education and civil rights for the dubious acceptance of white conservatives and economic opportunities. W. E. B. Du Bois led blacks in this criticism. A native of Massachusetts, Du Bois first experienced southern racial practices as an undergraduate at Fisk University in Nashville. Later he earned a doctorate in history from Harvard and briefly attended the University of Berlin. In addition to an active career in racial protest, he left a distinguished record as a scholar and author. Trim and dapper in appearance, sporting a goatee, cane, and gloves, Du Bois possessed a combative spirit. Not long after he began his teaching career at Atlanta University in 1897, he began to assault Booker T. Washington's accommodationist philosophy and put forward his own program of "ceaseless agitation" for civil rights.

W.E.B. Du Bois

A fierce advocate for black education.

Washington, Du Bois argued, preached "a gospel of Work and Money to such an extent as . . . to overshadow the higher aims of life." The education of blacks, Du Bois maintained, should not be merely vocational but should nurture bold leaders willing to challenge segregation and discrimination through political action. He demanded that disenfranchisement and legalized segregation cease immediately and that the laws of the land be enforced. Du Bois minced no words in criticizing Washington's philosophy: he called Washington's 1895 speech the Atlanta Compromise and said that he would not "surrender the leadership of this race to cowards." The dispute between Washington and Du Bois came to define the tensions that would divide the civil rights movement: militancy versus conciliation, separatism versus assimilation, social justice versus economic advances.

THE NEW WEST

Like the South the West is a region wrapped in myths and constricted by stereotypes. The land west of the Mississippi River contains remarkable geographic extremes: majestic mountains, roaring rivers, searing deserts, and dense forests. For vast reaches of western America, the great epics of Civil War and Reconstruction were remote events hardly touching the lives of the Indians, Mexicans, Asians, trappers, miners, and Mormons scattered through the plains and mountains. There the march of settlement and exploitation continued, propelled by a lust for land and a passion for profit. On one level the settlement of the West beyond the Mississippi River constitutes a colorful drama of determined pioneers and two-fisted gunslingers overcoming all obstacles to secure their vision of freedom and opportunity amid the region's awesome vastness. The post–Civil War West offered the promise of democratic individualism, economic opportunity, and personal freedom that had long before come to define the American dream. On another level, however, the colonization of the Far West was a tragedy of shortsighted greed and irresponsible behavior, a story of reckless exploitation that scarred the land, decimated its wildlife, and nearly exterminated the culture of Native Americans.

In the second tier of trans-Mississippi states—Iowa, Kansas, Nebraska—and in western Minnesota, farmers began spreading across the Great Plains after midcentury. From California, miners moved east through the mountains with one new strike after another. From Texas nomadic cowboys migrated northward into the plains and across the Rockies into the Great Basin.

As they moved west, the settlers encountered a markedly different climate and landscape. The Great Plains were arid, and the scarcity of water and timber rendered useless or impossible the familiar trappings of the pioneer: the ax, the log cabin, the rail fence, and the accustomed methods of tilling the soil. For a long time the region had been called the Great American Desert, a barren barrier to cross on the way to the Pacific, unfit for human habitation and therefore, to white Americans, the perfect refuge for Indians. But that pattern changed in the last half of the nineteenth century as a result of newly discovered gold, silver, and other minerals, the completion of transcontinental railroads, the destruction of the buffalo, the collapse of Indian resistance, the rise of the range-cattle industry, and the dawning realization that the arid region need not be a sterile desert. With the use of what water was available, new techniques of dry farming and irrigation could make the land fruitful after all.

THE MIGRATORY STREAM   During the second half of the nineteenth century, an unrelenting stream of migrants flowed into the largely Indian and Latino West. Millions of Anglo-Americans, African Americans, Mexicans, and European and Chinese immigrants transformed the patterns of western society and culture. Most of the settlers were relatively prosperous white, native-born farming families. Because of the expense of transportation, land, and supplies, the very poor could not afford to relocate. Three quarters of the western migrants were men.

The largest number of foreign immigrants came from northern Europe and Canada. In the northern plains, Germans, Scandinavians, and Irish were especially numerous. In the new state of Nebraska in 1870, one quarter of the 123,000 residents were foreign-born. In North Dakota in 1890, 45 percent of the residents were immigrants. Compared with European immigrants, those from China and Mexico were much less numerous but nonetheless significant. More than 200,000 Chinese arrived in California between 1876 and 1890.

In the aftermath of the collapse of Radical Republican rule in the South, thousands of African Americans began migrating west from Kentucky, Tennessee, Louisiana, Arkansas, Mississippi, and Texas. Some 6,000 southern blacks arrived in Kansas in 1879 alone, and as many as 20,000 may have come the following year. They came to be known as Exodusters, making their exodus from the South in search of a haven from racism and poverty.

The foremost promoter of black migration to the West was Benjamin "Pap" Singleton. Born a slave in Tennessee in 1809, he escaped and settled in Detroit. After the Civil War he returned to Tennessee, convinced that God was calling him to rescue his brethren. When Singleton learned that land in Kansas could be had for $1.25 an acre, he led his first party of 200 colonists to Kansas in 1878, bought 7,500 acres that had been an Indian reservation, and established the Dunlop community.

Nicodemus, Kansas

A colony founded by southern blacks in the 1860s.

Over the next several years, thousands of African Americans followed Singleton into Kansas, leading many southern leaders to worry about the loss of laborers in the region. In 1879 whites closed access to the Mississippi River and threatened to sink all boats carrying black colonists to the West. An army officer reported to President Rutherford B. Hayes that "every river landing is blockaded by white enemies of the colored exodus; some of whom are mounted and armed, as if we are at war."

The black exodus to the West died out by the early 1880s. Many of the settlers were unprepared for the living conditions on the plains. Their homesteads were not large enough to be self-sufficient, and most of the black farmers were forced to supplement their income by hiring themselves out to white ranchers. Drought, grasshoppers, prairie fires, and dust storms led to crop failures. The sudden influx of so many people taxed resources and patience. Many of the black pioneers in Kansas soon abandoned their land and moved to the few cities in the state. Life on the frontier was not the "promised land" that settlers had been led to expect. Nonetheless, by 1890, some 520,000 African Americans lived west of the Mississippi River. As many as 25 percent of the cowboys who participated in the Texas cattle drives were African Americans.

In 1866 Congress passed legislation establishing two "colored" cavalry units and dispatched them to the western frontier. Nicknamed buffalo soldiers by the Indians, they were mostly Civil War veterans from Louisiana and Kentucky. They built and maintained forts, mapped vast areas of the Southwest, strung hundreds of miles of telegraph lines, protected railroad construction crews, subdued hostile Indians, and captured outlaws and rustlers. Eighteen of the buffalo soldiers won Congressional Medals of Honor for their service.

MINING THE WEST   Valuable mineral deposits continued to lure people to the West after the Civil War. The California miners of 1849 (forty-niners) set the typical pattern, in which the sudden, disorderly rush of prospectors to a new find was quickly joined by camp followers—a motley crew of peddlers, saloon keepers, prostitutes, cardsharps, hustlers, and assorted desperadoes out to mine the miners. If a new field panned out, the forces of respectability and more subtle forms of exploitation slowly worked their way in. Lawlessness gave way to vigilante rule and, finally, to a stable community.

The drama of the 1849 gold rush was reenacted time and again in the following three decades. Along the South Platte River, not far from Pikes Peak in Colorado, a prospecting party found gold in 1858, and stories of success brought perhaps 100,000 "fifty-niners" into the country by the next year. New discoveries in Colorado kept occurring: near Central City in 1859, at Leadville in the 1870s, and the last important strikes in the West, again gold and silver,

at Cripple Creek in 1891–1894. During those years, farming and grazing had given the economy a stable base, and Colorado became the Centennial State in 1876.

While the early miners were crowding around Pikes Peak, the Comstock Lode was discovered near Gold Hill, Nevada. H. T. P. Comstock, a Canadian-born fur trapper, had drifted to the Carson River diggings, which opened in 1856. He talked his way into a share in a new discovery made by two other prospectors in 1859 and gave it his own name. The lode produced gold and silver. Within twenty years the Comstock Lode had yielded more than $300 million from shafts

Deadwood, Dakota Territory

A gold-rush town in 1876, before the Dakotas became states.

that reached hundreds of feet into the mountainside. In 1861, largely on account of the settlers attracted to the Comstock Lode, Nevada became a territory, and in 1864 the state of Nevada was admitted to the Union in time to give its three electoral votes to Abraham Lincoln.

The growing demand for orderly government in the West led to the hasty creation of new territories and eventually the admission of a host of new states. After Colorado's admission in 1876, however, there was a long hiatus because of party divisions in Congress: Democrats were reluctant to create states out of territories that were heavily Republican. After the sweeping Republican victory of 1888, however, Congress admitted the Dakotas, Montana, and Washington in 1889 and Idaho and Wyoming in 1890, completing a tier of states from coast to coast. Utah entered the Union in 1896 (after the Mormons abandoned the practice of polygamy) and Oklahoma in 1907, and in 1912 Arizona and New Mexico finally rounded out the forty-eight contiguous states.

MINING AND THE ENVIRONMENT   During the second half of the nineteenth century, the nature of mining changed drastically. It became a mass-production industry as individual prospectors gave way to large companies. The first wave of miners who rushed to California in 1849 sifted gold dust and nuggets out of riverbeds by means of "placer" mining, or "panning." But once the placer deposits were exhausted, efficient mining required large-scale operations and huge investments. Companies shifted from surface digging to hydraulic mining, dredging, or deep-shaft "hard-rock" mining.

Hydraulicking, dredging, and shaft mining transformed vast areas of vegetation and landscape. Huge hydraulic cannons shot an enormous stream of water under high pressure, stripping the topsoil and gravel from

Yuba County, California, 1866

Miners look on as water pours into a sluice.

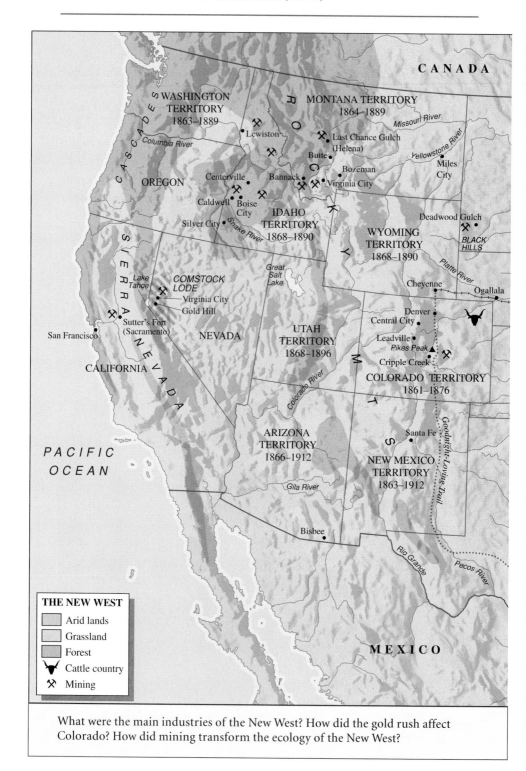

CANADA

WASHINGTON TERRITORY 1863–1889

Columbia River

Lewiston

OREGON

Centerville

Caldwell Boise City

Silver City

Snake River

IDAHO TERRITORY 1868–1890

MONTANA TERRITORY 1864–1889

Missouri River

Last Chance Gulch (Helena)

Butte

Bozeman

Bannack Virginia City

Yellowstone River

Miles City

ROCKY

Deadwood Gulch

WYOMING TERRITORY 1868–1890

BLACK HILLS

Platte River

Lake Tahoe

COMSTOCK LODE

Virginia City

Gold Hill

Great Salt Lake

Cheyenne

Ogallala

Denver

Central City

Sutter's Fort (Sacramento)

San Francisco

SIERRA NEVADA

NEVADA

UTAH TERRITORY 1868–1896

Leadville

Pikes Peak

Cripple Creek

Colorado River

COLORADO TERRITORY 1861–1876

CALIFORNIA

MTS

Goodnight-Loving Trail

ARIZONA TERRITORY 1866–1912

PACIFIC OCEAN

Santa Fe

NEW MEXICO TERRITORY 1863–1912

Gila River

Bisbee

Rio Grande

Pecos River

MEXICO

THE NEW WEST
- Arid lands
- Grassland
- Forest
- Cattle country
- Mining

What were the main industries of the New West? How did the gold rush affect Colorado? How did mining transform the ecology of the New West?

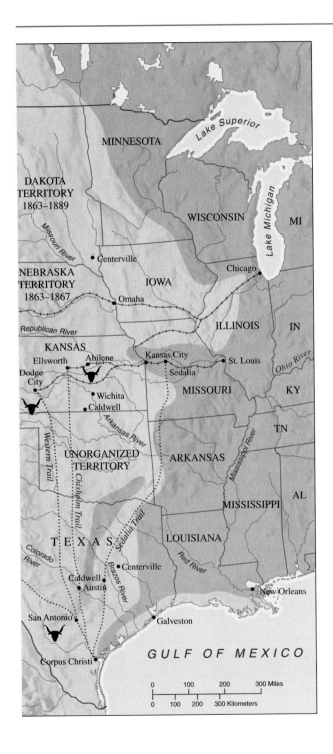

the bedrock and creating steep-sloped barren canyons that could not sustain plant life. The tons of dirt and debris unearthed by the water cannons covered rich farmland downstream and created sandbars that clogged rivers and killed fish. In 1880 alone some 40,000 acres of farmland and orchards were destroyed by the effects of hydraulic mining while another 270,000 acres were severely damaged. All told, some 12 billion tons of earth were blasted out of the Sierra Nevadas and washed into local rivers. At the massive Malakoff Diggings in northeastern California, hydraulic mining removed an estimated 41 million cubic yards of soil and rock and left a lifeless canyon over a mile long and up to 350 feet deep. The mine used three huge nozzles and 30.5 million gallons of water, twice as much water as was used by the entire city of San Francisco. The sprawling complex had over 150 miles of ditches, dams, and associated reservoirs to supply its gigantic operations.

Irate California farmers in the fertile Central Valley bitterly protested the damage done downstream by the industrial mining operations. In 1878 they formed the Anti-Debris Association, with its own militia, to challenge the powerful mining companies. Efforts to pass state legislation restricting hydraulic mining repeatedly failed because mining companies controlled the votes. The Anti-Debris Association then turned to the courts. On January 7, 1884, the farmers won their case when federal judge Lorenzo Sawyer, a former miner, outlawed the dumping of mining debris where it could reach farmland or navigable rivers. Thus *Woodruff v. North Bloomfield Gravel Mining Company* became the first major environmental ruling in the nation. As a result of the ruling, hydraulic mining dried up, leaving a legacy of abandoned equipment, ugly ravines, ditches, gullies, and mountains of discarded rock and gravel.

THE INDIAN WARS As the frontier pressed in from east and west, Indians were forced into what was supposed to be their last refuge. Perhaps 250,000 Indians on the Great Plains and in the mountain regions lived mainly off the buffalo herds, which provided food and, from their hides, clothing and shelter. In 1851 the chiefs of the Plains tribes had gathered at Fort Laramie in what would become Wyoming Territory, where they agreed to accept definite tribal borders and leave white emigrants on their trails unmolested. The treaty worked for a while, with wagon trains passing safely through Indian lands and the army building roads and forts without resistance. Fighting resumed, however, as the emigrants began to encroach upon Indian land on the plains rather than merely pass through it.

From the early 1860s until the late 1870s, the frontier raged with Indian wars. In 1864 Colorado's governor persuaded most of the warring Indians in his territory to gather at Fort Lyon, on Sand Creek, where they were promised protection. Despite that promise, Colonel John M. Chivington's untrained militia fell upon an Indian camp flying a white flag of truce, slaughtering 200 peaceful Indians—men, women, and children—in what one general called the "foulest and most unjustifiable crime in the annals of America."

With other scattered battles erupting, a congressional committee in 1865 began to gather evidence on the grisly Indian wars and massacres. Its 1867 "Report on the Condition of the Indian Tribes" led to an act to establish an Indian Peace Commission charged with removing the causes of Indian wars. Congress decided that this would be best accomplished at the expense of the Indians, by persuading them to take up life on out-of-the-way reservations. Yet the persistent encroachment on Indian hunting grounds continued.

In 1867 a conference at Medicine Lodge, Kansas, ended with the Kiowas, Comanches, Arapahos, and Cheyennes reluctantly accepting land in western Oklahoma. The following spring the Sioux agreed to settle within the Black Hills reservation in Dakota Territory. But Indian resistance in the southern plains continued until the Red River War of 1874–1875, when General Philip Sheridan forced the Indians to disband in the spring of 1875. Seventy-two Indian chiefs were imprisoned for three years.

Meanwhile, trouble was brewing again in the north. In 1874 Lieutenant Colonel George A. Custer, a reckless, glory-seeking officer, led an exploratory expedition into the Black Hills, accompanied by gold seekers. Miners were soon filtering into the Sioux hunting grounds despite promises that the army would keep them out. The army had done little to protect Indian land, but when ordered to move against wandering bands of Sioux hunting on the range according to their treaty rights, it moved vigorously.

What became the Great Sioux War was the largest military event since the end of the Civil War and one of the largest campaigns against Indians in American history. The war lasted fifteen months and entailed fifteen battles in a vast area of present-day Wyoming, Montana, South Dakota, and Nebraska. In 1876, after several indecisive encounters, Custer found the main encampment of Sioux and their Northern Cheyenne allies on the Little Bighorn River. Separated from the main body of soldiers and surrounded by 2,500 warriors, Custer's detachment of 210 men was annihilated.

Instead of following up their victory, the Indians celebrated and renewed their hunting. The army soon regained the offensive and compelled the Sioux to give up their hunting grounds and goldfields in return for payments.

The Battle of Little Bighorn

A painting by Amos Bad Heart Bull, an Oglala Sioux, 1876.

Forced onto reservations situated on the least valuable land in the region, the Indians soon found themselves struggling to subsist under harsh conditions. Many of them died of starvation or disease. When a peace commission imposed a settlement, Chief Spotted Tail said: "Tell your people that since the Great Father promised that we should never be removed, we have been moved five times. . . . I think you had better put the Indians on wheels and you can run them about wherever you wish."

In the Rocky Mountains and to the west the same story of hopeless resistance was repeated. The Blackfeet and Crows had to leave their homes in Montana. In a war along the California-Oregon boundary, the Modocs held out for six months in 1871–1872 before they were overwhelmed. In 1879 the Utes were forced to give up their vast territories in western Colorado after a brief battle. In Idaho the peaceful Nez Perces refused to surrender land along the Salmon River. Chief Joseph steadfastly tried to avoid war, but when fighting erupted, he directed a masterful campaign against overwhelming odds. After a retreat of 1,500 miles, through mountains and plains, he was caught thirty miles short of the Canadian border and exiled to Oklahoma. The heroic Joseph maintained strict discipline among his followers, countenanced no scalpings or outrages against civilians, paid for supplies that he could have confiscated, and kept his dignity to the end. His eloquent speech of surrender was an epitaph to the Indians' efforts to withstand the march of empire: "I am tired of fighting. Our chiefs are killed. . . . The old men are all

INDIAN WARS, 1864–1890

What was the Great Sioux War? What happened at Little Bighorn, and what were the consequences? Why were hundreds of Indians killed at Wounded Knee?

dead. . . . I want to have time to look for my children, and see how many of them I can find. . . . Hear me, my chiefs! I am tired. My heart is sick and sad. From where the sun now stands I will fight no more forever."

A generation of Indian wars virtually ended in 1886 with the capture of Geronimo, a chief of the Chiricahua Apaches who had fought white settlers in the Southwest for fifteen years. But there would be a tragic epilogue. Late in 1888 Wovoka (or Jack Wilson), a Paiute in western Nevada, fell ill and in a delirium imagined he had visited the spirit world, where he learned of a deliverer coming to rescue the Indians and restore their lands. To hasten the day, he said, they had to take up a ceremonial dance at each new moon. The Ghost Dance craze fed upon old legends of a coming messiah and spread

Indian Wars

Chief Joseph of the Nez Perce.

rapidly. In 1890 the Lakota Sioux took it up with such fervor that it alarmed white authorities. They banned the Ghost Dance on Lakota reservations, but the Indians defied the order and a crisis erupted. On December 29, 1890, a bloodbath occurred at Wounded Knee, South Dakota. An accidental rifle discharge led nervous soldiers to fire into a group of Indians who had come to surrender. Nearly 200 Indians and 25 soldiers died in the Battle of Wounded Knee. The Indian wars had ended with characteristic brutality and misunderstanding.

THE DEMISE OF THE BUFFALO   Over the long run the collapse of Indian resistance in the face of white settlement on the Great Plains resulted as much from the decimation of the buffalo herds as from the actions of federal troops. In 1750 there were an estimated 30 million buffalo; by 1850 there were less than 10 million; by 1900 only a few hundred were left. What happened to them? The conventional story focuses on intensive harvesting of buffalo by white hunters after the Civil War. Americans east of the Mississippi River developed a voracious demand for buffalo robes and buffalo leather. The average white commercial hunter killed 100 animals a day, and the hides and bones (to be ground into fertilizer) were shipped east on railroad cars. Some army officers encouraged the slaughter. "Kill every buffalo you can!" Colonel Richard Dodge told a sport hunter in 1867. "Every buffalo dead is an Indian gone."

This conventional explanation tells only part of a more complicated story, however. The buffalo disappeared from the western plains for a variety of environmental reasons, including a significant change in climate; competition for forage with horses, sheep, and cattle; and cattle-borne disease. A prolonged drought in the Great Plains during the late 1880s and 1890s, the same drought that would help spur the agrarian political revolt and the rise of populism, also devastated the buffalo herds by reducing the grasslands upon which the animals depended. At the same time the buffalo had to compete for forage with other grazing animals. By the 1880s over 2 million horses were roaming on buffalo lands. In addition, the Plains Indians themselves, empowered by horses and guns and spurred by the profits reaped from selling hides and meat to white traders, accounted for much of the devastation of the buffalo herds after 1840. White hunters who killed buffaloes by the millions in the 1870s and 1880s played a major role in the animal's demise, but only as the final catalyst. If there had been no white hunters, the buffalo would probably have lasted only another thirty years because their numbers had been so greatly reduced by other factors.

INDIAN POLICY   The slaughter of buffalo and Indians ignited widespread criticism. Politicians and religious leaders spoke out against the persistent mistreatment of Indians. In his annual message of 1877 President Rutherford B. Hayes joined the protest: "Many, if not most, of our Indian wars have had their origin in broken promises and acts of injustice on our part." Helen Hunt Jackson, a novelist and poet, focused attention on the Indian cause in *A Century of Dishonor* (1881). Indian policy gradually became more benevolent, but this change did little to ease the plight of the Indians and actually helped destroy the remnants of their culture. The reservation policy inaugurated by the Peace Commission in 1867 did little more than extend a practice that dated from colonial Virginia. Partly humanitarian in motive, it also saved money: housing and feeding Indians on reservations cost less than fighting them.

Well-intentioned reformers sought to "Americanize" Indians by dealing with them as individuals rather than tribes. The fruition of reform efforts came with the Dawes Severalty Act of 1887. Sponsored by Senator Henry L. Dawes of Massachusetts, the act divided the land of any tribe, granting 160 acres to each head of a family and lesser amounts to others. To protect the Indians' property, the government held it in trust for twenty-five years, after which the owner won full title and became a U.S. citizen. Under the Burke Act of 1906, Indians who took up life apart from their tribes became citizens immediately. Members of the tribes who were granted land titles were subject to state and federal laws like all other residents of the United States. In 1901 citizenship was extended to the Five Civilized Tribes of Oklahoma and, in 1924, to all Indians.

But the more it changed, the more Indian policy remained the same. Despite the best of intentions, the Dawes Act created opportunities for more white plundering of Indian land and disrupted what remained of the traditional culture. The Dawes Act broke up reservations and often led to the loss of Indian land to whites. Land not distributed to Indian families was sold, and some of the land the Indians did receive they lost to land sharks because of the Indians' inexperience with private ownership or simply their weakness in the face of fraud. Between 1887 and 1934, Indians lost an estimated

86 million of their 130 million acres. Most of what remained was unsuited to agriculture.

CATTLE AND COWBOYS   While the West was being taken from the Indians, cattle entered the grasslands where the buffalo had roamed. The cowboy enjoyed his brief heyday before fading into the folklore of the Wild West. From colonial times, especially in the South, cattle raising had been a common enterprise just beyond the fringe of settlement. In many cases, slaves took care of the livestock. Later, in the West, African-American cowboys were common.

Much of the romance of the open-range cattle industry derived from its Mexican roots. The Texas longhorns and the cowboys' horses had in large part descended from stock brought to the New World by the Spaniards, and many of the industry's trappings had been worked out in Mexico first: the cowboy's saddle, chaps (*chaparreras*) to protect the legs, spurs, and lariat.

For many years wild cattle competed with the buffalo in the Spanish borderlands. Natural selection and contact with Anglo-American scrub cattle produced the Texas longhorns: lean and rangy, they were noted more for speed and endurance than for yielding a choice steak. They had little value, moreover, because the largest markets for beef were too far away. At the end of the Civil War, as many as 5 million cattle roamed the grasslands of Texas, still neglected—but not for long. In the upper Mississippi River valley, where herds had been depleted by the war, cattle were in great demand, and the Texas cattle could be had just for the effort of rounding them up.

New opportunities arose as railroads pushed farther west, where cattle could be driven through relatively vacant lands. Joseph G. McCoy, an Illinois livestock dealer, recognized the possibilities for moving the cattle trade west. In 1867 in Abilene, Kansas, he bought 250 acres for a stockyard; laid plans for a barn, an office building, livestock scales, a hotel, and a bank; and sent an agent into Indian territory to cultivate owners of herds bound north. Over the next few years, Abilene flourished as the first successful Kansas cowtown. But as the railroads moved west, so did the cowtowns and the trails: Ellsworth, Wichita, Caldwell, and Dodge City, in Kansas; farther north Ogallala, Nebraska; Cheyenne, Wyoming; and Miles City, Montana.

During the twenty years after the Civil War, some 40,000 cowboys roamed the Great Plains. They were young—the average age was twenty-four—and from diverse backgrounds. Some 30 percent were either Mexican or African American, and hundreds were Indians. Many others were Civil War veterans from North and South, and still others were immigrants from Europe. The life of a cowboy, for the most part, was rarely as exciting as has been depicted

The Cowboy Era

Cowboys herd cattle near Cimarron, Colorado, 1905.

by movies and television shows. Working as a ranch hand involved grueling, dirty wage labor interspersed with drudgery and boredom, often amid terrible weather conditions.

The thriving cattle industry spurred rapid growth in the region, however. The population of Kansas increased from 107,000 in 1860 to 365,000 ten years later and reached almost 1 million by 1880. Nebraska witnessed similar increases. During the 1860s cattle would be delivered to rail depots, loaded onto freight cars, and shipped east. By the time the animals arrived in New York or Massachusetts, some would be dead or dying, and all would have lost significant weight. The secret to higher profits for the cattle industry was to devise a way to slaughter the cattle in the Midwest and ship the dressed carcasses east and west. That process required refrigeration to keep the meat from spoiling. In 1869 G. H. Hammond, a Chicago meat packer, shipped the first refrigerated beef in an air-cooled car from Chicago to Boston. Eight years later Gustavus Swift developed a more efficient system of mechanical

Langtry, Texas, 1900

Judge Roy Bean's courthouse and saloon.

refrigeration, an innovation that earned him a fortune and provided the cattle industry with a major stimulus.

The flush times of the cowtown soon passed, however, and the long cattle drives played out too, because they were economically unsound. The dangers of the trail, the wear and tear on men and cattle, the charges levied on drives across Indian territory, and the advance of farms across the trails combined to persuade cattlemen that they could function best near railroads. As railroads spread out into Texas and across the plains, the cattle business spread with them over the High Plains as far as Montana and on into Canada.

In the absence of laws governing the open range, cattle ranchers at first worked out a code of action largely dictated by circumstances. As cattle often wandered onto other ranchers' claims, cowboys would "ride the line" to keep as many of the animals as they could off the adjoining ranches. In the spring they would "round up" the herds that invariably got mixed up and sort out ownership by identifying the distinctive ranch symbols "branded," or burned, into the cattle. All that changed in 1873, when Joseph Glidden, an Illinois farmer, invented the first effective barbed wire, which ranchers used to fence off their claims at relatively low cost. Ranchers rushed to buy the new wire fencing, and soon the open range was no more. Cattle raising, like mining, evolved from a romantic adventure into a big business dominated by giant enterprises.

THE END OF THE OPEN RANGE A combination of factors put an end to the open range. Farmers kept crowding in and laying out homesteads, waging "barbed-wire wars" with ranchers by cutting the ranchers' fences or policing their own. The boundless range was being overstocked with cattle by 1883, and expenses mounted as stock breeders formed associations to keep intruders off overstocked ranges, establish and protect land titles, deal with railroads and buyers, fight prairie fires, and cope with rustlers and predatory beasts. The rise of sheepherding by 1880 caused still another conflict with the cattle ranchers. A final blow to the open-range industry came with two unusually severe winters in 1886 and 1887, followed by ten long years of drought.

Surviving the hazards of the range required establishing legal title and fencing in the land, limiting the herds to a reasonable size, and providing shelter and hay during the rigors of winter. Moreover, as the long cattle drives gave way to more rail lines and refrigerated railcars, the cowboy settled into a more sedentary existence. Within merely two decades, from 1866 to 1886, the era of the cowboy had come and gone.

RANGE WARS   Conflicting claims over land and water rights ignited violent disputes between ranchers and farmers. Ranchers often tried to drive off neighboring farmers, and farmers in turn tried to sabotage the cattle barons, cutting their fences and spooking their herds. The cattle ranchers also clashed with sheepherders over access to grassland. A strain of ethnic and religious prejudice heightened the tension between ranchers and herders. In the Southwest, shepherds were typically Mexican Americans; in Idaho and Nevada they were from the Basque region of Spain or Mormons. Many Anglo-American cattle ranchers and cowboys viewed those ethnic and religious groups as un-American and inferior, adopting an attitude that helped them rationalize the use of violence against the sheepherders. Warfare gradually faded, however, as the sheep for the most part found refuge in the high pastures of the mountains, leaving the grasslands of the plains to the cattle ranchers.

Yet there also developed a perennial tension between large and small cattle ranchers. The large ranchers fenced in huge tracts of public land, leaving the smaller ranchers with too little pasture. To survive, the smaller ranchers cut the fences. In central Texas this practice sparked the Fence-Cutters' War of 1883–1884. Several ranchers were killed and dozens wounded before the state ended the conflict by passing legislation outlawing fence cutting.

FARMERS AND THE LAND   Among the legendary figures of the West, the sodbusters projected an unromantic image in contrast to that of the cowboys, cavalrymen, and Indians. Farming has always been a hard life, and it was made more so on the Great Plains by the region's unforgiving environment and mercurial weather. After 1865, on paper at least, the federal land laws offered farmers favorable terms. Under the Homestead Act of 1862, a settler could realize the old dream of free land simply by staking out a claim and living on it for five years, or he could buy land at $1.25 an acre after six months. But such land legislation was predicated upon the tradition of farming the fertile lands east of the Mississippi River, and the laws were never adjusted to the fact that much of the prairie was suited only for cattle raising. Cattle ranchers were forced to obtain land by gradual acquisition from homesteaders or land-grant railroads.

As so often happens, environmental forces shaped development. The unchangeable fact of aridity, rather than new land laws, shaped institutions in the West after the Civil War. Where farming was impossible, ranchers simply established dominance by control of the water, regardless of the law. Belated legislative efforts to develop irrigable land finally achieved a major success when the 1901 Newlands Reclamation Act (after the aptly named Senator Francis G. Newlands of Nevada) set up the Bureau of Reclamation. The proceeds of public land sales in sixteen states created a fund for irrigation projects, and the Reclamation Bureau set about building such major projects as the Boulder (later Hoover) Dam on the Nevada-Arizona line, the Roosevelt Dam in Arizona, the Elephant Butte Dam in New Mexico and the Arrowrock Dam in Idaho.

The lands of the New West, like those on previous frontiers, passed to their ultimate owners more often from private hands than directly from the government. Many of the 274 million acres claimed under the Homestead Act passed quickly to ranchers or speculators and thence to settlers. The land-grant railroads got some 200 million acres of the public domain between 1851 and 1871 and sold much of it to create towns along the lines. The West of ranchers and farmers was in fact largely the product of the railroads.

The first arrivals on the sod-house frontier faced a grim struggle against danger, adversity, and monotony. Though land was relatively cheap, horses, livestock, wagons, wells, lumber, fencing, seed, and fertilizer were not. Freight rates and interest rates on loans seemed criminally high. As in the South, declining crop prices produced chronic indebtedness, leading strapped western farmers to embrace virtually any plan to inflate the money supply. The virgin land itself, although fertile, resisted planting; the heavy sod broke many a plow. Since wood was almost nonexistent on the prairie, pioneer families used buffalo chips (dried dung) for fuel.

Farmers and their families also fought a constant battle with the elements: tornadoes, hailstorms, droughts, prairie fires, blizzards, and pests. Swarms of locusts would cloud the horizon, occasionally covering the ground six inches deep. A Wichita newspaper reported in 1878 that the grasshoppers devoured "everything green, stripping the foliage off the bark and from the tender twigs of the fruit trees, destroying every plant that is good for food or pleasant to the eyes, that man has planted."

As the railroads arrived bearing lumber from the East, farmers could leave their sod houses (homes built of sod) to build more comfortable frame dwellings. New machinery helped provide fresh opportunities. In 1868 James Oliver, a Scottish immigrant living in Indiana, made a successful chilled-iron plow. This "sodbuster" plow greatly eased the task of breaking the tough grass roots of the plains. Improvements and new inventions in threshing machines, hay mowers, planters, manure spreaders, cream separators, and other devices lightened the burden of farm labor but added to the farmers' capital outlay. In Minnesota, the Dakotas, and central California, the gigantic "bonanza farms," with machinery for mass production, became the marvels of the age. On one farm in North Dakota, 13,000 acres of wheat made a single field. Another bonanza farm employed over 1,000 migrant workers to tend 34,000 acres.

To get a start on a family homestead required a minimum capital investment of $1,000. While the overall value of farmland and farm products increased in the late nineteenth century, small farmers did not keep up with the march of progress. Their numbers grew but decreased in proportion to the population at large. Wheat, like cotton in the antebellum period, was the great export crop that spurred economic growth. For a variety of reasons, however, few small farmers prospered. By the 1890s they were in open revolt against the "system" of corrupt processors and greedy bankers who they believed conspired against them.

PIONEER WOMEN The West remained a largely male society throughout the nineteenth century. In Texas, for example, the ratio of men to women in 1890 was 110 to 1. Women continued to face traditional legal barriers and social prejudice. A wife could not sell property without her husband's approval. Texas women could not sue except for divorce, nor could they serve on juries, act as lawyers, or witness a will.

But the fight for survival in the trans-Mississippi West made men and women more equal partners than were their eastern counterparts. Many women who lost their mates to the deadly toil of sod busting thereafter assumed complete responsibility for their farms. In general, women on the prairie became more independent than women leading domestic lives back East. Explained one Kansas woman: "The outstanding fact is that the environment was such as to bring out and develop the dominant qualities of individual character. Kansas women of that day learned at an early age to depend on themselves—to do whatever work there was to be done, and to face danger when it must be faced, as calmly as they were able."

Women of the Frontier

A woman and her family in front of their sod house. The difficult life on the prairie led to more egalitarian marriages than were found in other regions of the country.

THE END OF THE FRONTIER American life reached an important juncture at the end of the nineteenth century. After the 1890 population count, the superintendent of the national census noted that he could no longer locate a continuous frontier line beyond which population thinned out to fewer than two people per square mile. This fact inspired the historian Frederick Jackson Turner to develop his influential frontier thesis, first outlined in "The Significance of the Frontier in American History," a paper delivered to the American Historical Association in 1893. "The existence of an area of free land," Turner wrote, "its continuous recession, and the advance of American settlement westward, explain American development." The frontier, he added, had shaped the national character in fundamental ways. It was

> to the frontier [that] the American intellect owes its striking characteristics. That coarseness and strength combined with acuteness and acquisitiveness; that practical, inventive turn of mind, quick to find expedients; that masterful grasp of material things, lacking in the artistic but powerful to effect great ends; that restless, nervous energy; that dominant individualism,

working for good and for evil, and withal that buoyancy and exuberance which comes with freedom—these are traits of the frontier, or traits called out elsewhere because of the existence of the frontier.

In 1893, Turner concluded, "four centuries from the discovery of America, at the end of a hundred years under the Constitution, the frontier has gone and with its going has closed the first period of American history."

Turner's "frontier thesis" guided several generations of scholars and students in their understanding of the distinctive characteristics of American history. His view of the frontier as the westward-moving source of the nation's democratic politics, open society, unfettered economy, and rugged individualism, far removed from the corruptions of urban life, gripped the popular imagination as well. But it left out much of the story. The frontier experience Turner described exaggerated the homogenizing effect of the frontier environment and virtually ignored the role of women, African Americans, Indians, Mormons, Latinos and Asians in shaping the diverse human geography of the western United States. Turner also implied that the West would be fundamentally different after 1890 because the frontier experience was essentially over. But in many respects that region has retained the qualities associated with the rush for land, gold, timber, and water rights during the post–Civil War decades. The mining frontier, as one historian has recently written, "set a mood that has never disappeared from the West: the attitude of extractive industry—get in, get rich, get out."

MAKING CONNECTIONS

- The problems of southern and western farmers described in this chapter set the stage for the rise of the Populists, as discussed in Chapter 22.

- The late nineteenth century was a crucial period in the evolution of race relations in the South, bridging the antebellum period and the twentieth century.

- This chapter closed with the observation that as of 1890, according to the superintendent of the census and the historian Frederick Jackson Turner, the frontier has disappeared. Where would Americans now look to fulfill their expansionist urges?

Further Reading

The classic study of the emergence of the New South remains C. Vann Woodward's *Origins of the New South, 1877–1913* (1951). A more recent treatment of southern society after the end of Reconstruction is Edward L. Ayers's *Southern Crossing: A History of the American South, 1877–1906* (1995). A good survey of industrialization in the South is James C. Cobb's *Industrialization and Southern Society, 1877–1984* (1984).

C. Vann Woodward's *The Strange Career of Jim Crow,* 3rd ed. (2002), remains the standard on southern race relations. Some of Woodward's points are challenged in Howard N. Rabinowitz's *Race Relations in the Urban South, 1865–1890* (1978). Leon Litwack's *Trouble in Mind: Black Southerners in the Age of Jim Crow* (1998) treats the rise of legal segregation while Michael Perman's *Struggle for Mastery: Disfranchisement in the South, 1888–1908* (2001) surveys efforts to keep African Americans from voting. An award-winning study of white women and the race issue is Glenda Elizabeth Gilmore's *Gender and Jim Crow: Women and the Politics of White Supremacy in North Carolina, 1896–1920* (1996).

For stimulating reinterpretations of the frontier and the development of the West, see William Cronon's *Nature's Metropolis: Chicago and the Great West* (1991), Patricia Nelson Limerick's *The Legacy of Conquest: The Unbroken Past of the American West* (1987), Richard White's *"It's Your Misfortune and None of My Own": A New History of the American West* (1991), and Walter Nugent's *Into the West: The Story of Its People* (1999).

The role of African Americans in western settlement is the focus of William Loren Katz's *The Black West: A Documentary and Pictorial History of the African-American Role in the Westward Expansion of the United States* (1996) and Nell Irvin Painter's *Exodusters: Black Migration to Kansas after Reconstruction* (1977). The best account of the conflicts between Indians and whites is Robert Utley's *The Indian Frontier of the American West, 1846–1890* (1984). For a presentation of the Native American side of the story, see Peter Nabokov's *Native American Testimony: A Chronicle of Indian-White Relations from Prophecy to the Present, 1492–2000,* rev. ed.(1999). On the demise of the buffalo herds, see Andrew C. Isenberg's *The Destruction of the Bison: An Environmental History, 1750–1920* (2000).

20

BIG BUSINESS AND ORGANIZED LABOR

FOCUS QUESTIONS

- What factors fueled the growth of the post–Civil War economy?
- What were the methods and achievements of major entrepreneurs?
- What led to the rise of large labor unions?

To answer these questions and access additional review material, please visit www.wwnorton.com/studyspace.

America emerged as an industrial and agricultural giant in the late nineteenth century. Between 1869 and 1899 the nation's population nearly tripled, farm production more than doubled, and the value of manufactures grew sixfold. Within three generations after the Civil War, the predominantly rural nation burst forth as the world's preeminent industrial power. Bigness became the prevailing standard of corporate life, and social tensions and political chicanery worsened with the rising scale of business enterprise.

THE RISE OF BIG BUSINESS

The Industrial Revolution created huge corporations that came to dominate the economy—as well as political and social life—during the late nineteenth century. As businesses grew, their owners sought to integrate all the processes of production and distribution into single companies, thus creating even larger firms. Others joined forces with their competitors in an effort to dominate entire industries. This process of industrial combination and concentration transformed the nation's economy and social order. It also sparked widespread dissent and the emergence of an organized labor movement.

Many factors converged to help launch the dramatic business growth after the Civil War. A nationwide shortage of labor served as a powerful incentive, motivating inventors and business owners to develop more efficient labor-saving machinery. Technological innovations not only created new products but also brought about improved machinery and equipment, spurring dramatic advances in productivity. As the volume of production increased, the larger businesses and industries expanded into numerous states and in the process developed standardized machinery and parts which became available nationwide. A group of shrewd, determined, and energetic entrepreneurs took advantage of fertile business opportunities to create huge enterprises. Federal and state politicians after the Civil War actively encouraged the growth of business by imposing high tariffs on foreign manufacturers as a means of blunting competition and by providing land and cash to finance railroads and other internal improvements.

The American agricultural sector, by 1870 the world's leader, fueled the rest of the economy by providing wheat and corn to be milled into flour and meal. With the advent of the cattle industry, the processes of slaughtering and packing meat themselves became major industries. So the farm sector directly stimulated the industrial sector of the economy. A national government-subsidized network of railroads connecting the East and West coasts played a crucial role in the development of related industries and in the evolution of a national market for goods and services. Industry in the United States also benefited from an abundance of power sources—water, wood, coal, oil, and electricity—that were inexpensive compared with those of the other nations of the world.

THE SECOND INDUSTRIAL REVOLUTION The Industrial Revolution "controls us all," said Yale sociologist William Graham Sumner, "because we are all in it." Sumner and other Americans living during the second half of the nineteenth century experienced what economic historians have termed the Second Industrial Revolution. The First Industrial Revolution began in Britain during the late eighteenth century. It was propelled by the convergence of three new technologies: the coal-powered steam engine, textile machines for spinning thread and weaving cloth, and blast furnaces to produce iron.

The Second Industrial Revolution began in the mid–nineteenth century and was centered in the United States and Germany. It was spurred by an array of innovations and inventions in the production of metals, machinery, chemicals, and foodstuffs. While the First Industrial Revolution helped accelerate the growth of the early American economy, the second transformed the economy and the society into their modern urban-industrial form.

The Second Industrial Revolution involved three related developments. The first was the creation of an interconnected national transportation and communication network, which facilitated the emergence of a national and even an international market for American goods and services. Contributing to this development were the completion of the national telegraph and railroad systems, the emergence of steamships, and the laying of the undersea telegraph cable, which spanned the Atlantic Ocean and connected the United States with Europe.

During the 1880s a second major breakthrough—the use of electric power—accelerated the pace of change. Electricity created dramatic advances

The Hand of Man (1902)

Photogravure by Alfred Stieglitz.

in the power and efficiency of industrial machinery. It also spurred urban growth through the addition of electric trolleys and subways, and it greatly enhanced the production of steel and chemicals.

The third major aspect of the Second Industrial Revolution was the systematic application of scientific research to industrial processes. Laboratories staffed by graduates of new research universities sprouted up across the country, and scientists and engineers discovered dramatic new ways in which to improve industrial processes. Researchers figured out, for example, how to refine kerosene and gasoline from crude oil. They also improved techniques for refining steel from iron and spawned new products—telephones, typewriters, adding machines, sewing machines, cameras, elevators, and farm machinery—and lowered consumer prices. These advances in turn expanded the scope and scale of industrial organizations. Capital-intensive industries such as steel and oil, as well as processed food and tobacco, took advantage of new technologies to gain economies of scale that emphasized maximum production and national as well as international marketing and distribution.

BUILDING THE TRANSCONTINENTAL RAILROADS   Railroads were the first big business, the first magnet for the great financial markets, and the first industry to develop a large-scale management bureaucracy. The railroads opened the western half of the nation to economic development, connected raw materials to factories and retailers, and in so doing created an interconnected national market. At the same time the railroads were themselves gigantic consumers of iron, steel, lumber, and other capital goods.

The renewal of railroad building after the Civil War filled out the rail network east of the Mississippi River. Gradually tracks in the South were rebuilt and a spiderweb of new trunk lines was added throughout the country. But the most spectacular exploits were the monumental transcontinental lines built through granite mountains, over roaring rivers and deep canyons, and across desolate plains. Running through sparsely settled land, the railroads promised little quick return on investment but served the national purpose of binding the country together and so received generous government support in the form of huge loans, land grants, and cash subsidies.

Before the Civil War, sectional differences over the choice of routes had held up the start of a transcontinental line. Secession and the departure of southern congressmen finally permitted passage of the Pacific Railroads Act, which Abraham Lincoln signed into law in 1862, authorizing a line along a north-central route, to be built by the Union Pacific Railroad westward from Omaha and by the Central Pacific Railroad eastward from Sacramento. Both railroads began construction during the war, but most of the work was done after 1865 as the companies raced to get the most out of the federal subsidy, paid per mile of track. The Union Pacific pushed across the plains at a rapid pace, avoiding the Rocky Mountains by going through Evans Pass in Wyoming. Construction of the rail line and bridges was hasty and much of it so flimsy it had to be redone later, but the Union Pacific pushed on to its celebrated rendezvous with the Central Pacific in 1869. The buccaneering executives and financiers directing the transcontinental railroads were shrewd entrepreneurs so driven by dreams of great wealth that they often cut corners and bribed legislators. They also ruthlessly used federal troops to suppress the Plains Indians. But their shenanigans do not diminish the heroic efforts of the workers and engineers who built the rail lines, erected the bridges, and gouged out the tunnels under terrible conditions. Building the transcontinental railroads was an epic feat of daring that tied a nation together, changed the economic and political landscape, and enabled the United States to emerge as a world power.

The Union Pacific work crews, composed of ex-soldiers, former slaves, and Irish and German immigrants, had to cope with bad roads, water shortages, extreme weather conditions, and Indian attacks. The Central Pacific crews were composed mainly of Chinese workers lured to America first by the California gold rush and then by railroad jobs. Most of these "coolie" laborers were single men intent upon accumulating money and returning to their homeland, where they could then afford to marry and buy a parcel of land. Their temporary status and dream of a good life back in China apparently made them more willing than American laborers to endure the dangerous working conditions and low pay of railroad work, as well as the blatant racism. Many Chinese laborers died on the job.

All sorts of issues delayed the effort to finish the transcontinental line. Iron prices spiked. Broken treaties prompted Indian raids. Blizzards shut down work for weeks. Fifty-seven miles east of Sacramento, construction crews encountered the towering Sierra Nevadas, through which they had to cut before reaching more level terrain in Nevada. The Union Pacific had built 1,086 miles compared with the Central Pacific's 689 when the race ended on the salt plains at Promontory, Utah. There, on May 10, 1869, former California governor Leland Stanford drove a gold spike symbolizing the railroad's completion.

The next transcontinental line, completed in 1881, linked the Atchison, Topeka, and Santa Fe Railroad with the Southern Pacific Railroad at Needles in southern California. The Southern Pacific, which had absorbed the Central Pacific, pushed through Arizona to Texas in 1882, where it made

The Union Pacific

The celebration of the completion of the first transcontinental railroad, Promontory, Utah, May 10, 1869.

connections to St. Louis and New Orleans. To the north the Northern Pacific had connected Lake Superior with Oregon by 1883, and ten years later the Great Northern, which had slowly and carefully been building westward from St. Paul, Minnesota, thrust its way to Tacoma, Washington. Thus, before the turn of the century, five major trunk lines existed, supplemented by connections that afforded other transcontinental routes.

FINANCING THE RAILROADS The railroads were built by private companies that raised money for construction primarily by selling railroad bonds to American and foreign investors. Until 1850 constitutional scruples had constrained the granting of federal aid for internal improvements, although many states had subsidized railroads within their borders. But in 1850 Senator Stephen Douglas secured from Congress a grant of public lands to subsidize a north-south railroad connecting Chicago and Mobile. Over the next twenty years, federal land grants, mainly to transcontinental railroad companies, totaled 129 million acres. In addition to land, the railroads

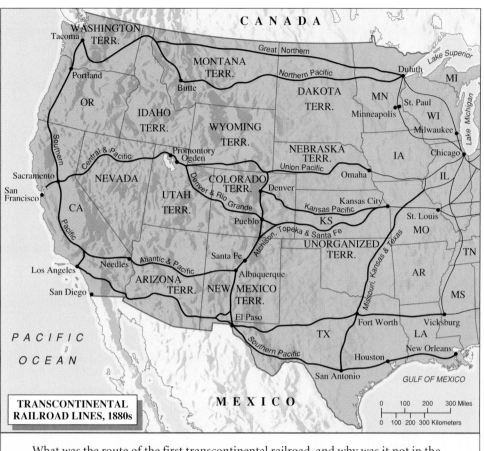

TRANSCONTINENTAL
RAILROAD LINES, 1880s

What was the route of the first transcontinental railroad, and why was it not in the South? Who built the railroads? How were they financed?

received massive financial aid from federal, state, and local governments. Altogether the railroads received about $707 million in cash and $335 million in land.

In the long run the federal government recovered much of its investment in transcontinental railroads and accomplished the purpose of linking the country together. As farms, ranches, and towns sprouted around the rail lines, the value of the government land on either side of the tracks skyrocketed. The railroads also benefited the public by hauling government freight, military personnel and equipment, and the mail at half fare or for free.

Moreover, by helping to accelerate the creation of a national market, the railroads spurred economic growth and thereby increased government revenues.

But that is only part of the story. The shady financial practices of railroad executives earned them the label of robber barons, an epithet soon extended to other "captains of industry" as well. These were shrewd, determined, often dishonest men, driven more by greed than by glory. The building of both the Union Pacific and the Central Pacific—as well as other transcontinental lines—induced shameless profiteering by construction companies controlled by insiders who overcharged the railroad companies. Crédit Mobilier of America, according to congressional investigators, bribed congressmen and charged the Union Pacific $94 million for a construction project that cost at most $44 million.

The prince of the railroad robber barons was Jay Gould, a secretive trickster who mastered the fine art of buying rundown railroads, making cosmetic improvements, and selling out at a profit, meanwhile using corporate funds for personal investment and judicious bribes. Ousted by a reform group after having looted New York's Erie Railroad, Gould moved on to richer spoils in western railroads. Nearly every enterprise he touched was compromised or ruined; Gould, meanwhile, was building a fortune that amounted to $100 million upon his death at age fifty-six.

Few railroad fortunes were built in those freewheeling times by purely honest methods, but compared with opportunists such as Gould most railroad owners were saints. They at least took some interest in the welfare of their companies, if not always in that of the public. Cornelius Vanderbilt, called Commodore by virtue of his early exploits in steamboating, stands out among the railroad barons. Already rich before the Civil War, he decided to give up the hazards of wartime shipping in favor of land transport. Under his direction the first of the major eastern railroad consolidations took form.

Jay Gould

Prince of the railroad buccaneers.

Vanderbilt merged separate trunk lines connecting Albany and Buffalo, New York, into a single powerful rail network led by the New York Central.

This accomplished, he forged connections to New York City and then tried to corner the stock of his chief competitor, the Erie Railroad. But the directors of that line fended him off by printing new Erie stock faster than Vanderbilt could buy it. In 1873, however, he bought the Lake Shore and Michigan Southern Railroad, which gave his lines connections to the lucrative Chicago market. After the Commodore's death, in 1877, his son William Henry extended the Vanderbilt railroads to include more than 13,000 miles in the Northeast. The consolidation trend was nationwide: about two thirds of the nation's railroad mileage were under the control of only seven major groups by 1900.

"Commodore" Cornelius Vanderbilt
Vanderbilt consolidated control of the vast New York Central Railroad in the 1860s.

MANUFACTURING AND INVENTIONS   The story of manufacturing after the Civil War shows much the same pattern of expansion and merger in old and new industries. The U.S. Patent Office, which had recorded only 276 inventions during its first decade of existence, the 1790s, registered almost 235,000 in the 1890s. New processes in steelmaking and oil refining enabled those industries to flourish. The refrigerated railcar allowed the beef, mutton, and pork of the New West to reach a national market, giving rise to great packinghouse enterprises. Corrugated rollers that could crack the hard, spicy wheat of the Great Plains provided impetus to the flour milling that centered in Minneapolis under the control of the Pillsbury Company and others.

The list of innovations after the Civil War can be extended nearly indefinitely: barbed wire, farm implements, George Westinghouse's air brake for trains (1868), steam turbines, gas distribution and electrical devices, Christopher Sholes's typewriter (1867), Ives W. McGaffey's vacuum cleaner (1869), and countless others. Before the end of the century, the internal-combustion engine and the motion picture were stimulating new industries that would emerge in the twentieth century.

These technological advances altered the daily lives of ordinary people far more than did activities in the political and intellectual realms. In no field was this more true than in the application of electricity to power and

New Technologies

Alexander Graham Bell being observed by businessmen at the New York end of the first long-distance telephone call to Chicago, 1892.

communications. Few if any inventions of the time could rival the importance of the telephone, which Alexander Graham Bell patented in 1876. To promote the new device, the inventor and his supporters formed the Bell Telephone Company. Its stiffest competition came from Western Union, which after turning down a chance to buy Bell's "toy," employed Thomas Edison to develop an improved version. Bell sold its rights and properties for a tidy sum, clearing the way for the creation of the American Telephone and Telegraph Company. By 1899 it was a huge holding company controlling forty-nine licensed subsidiaries and an operating company for long-distance lines.

In the development of electrical industries, the name Thomas Alva Edison stands above those of other inventors. Edison invented the phonograph in 1877 and the first successful incandescent lightbulb in 1879. Altogether he created or perfected hundreds of new devices and processes, including the storage battery, Dictaphone, mimeograph, electric motor, electric transmission, and the motion picture. Edison thus demonstrated the significance of "research and development" activities to business expansion.

In 1882, with the backing of J. P. Morgan, the Edison Electric Illuminating Company began to supply electrical current to eighty-five customers in New York City, beginning the great electric utility industry. A number of companies making lightbulbs merged into the Edison General Electric Company in 1888. But the use of direct current limited Edison's lighting system to a radius of about two miles. To cover greater distances required an alternating current, which could be transmitted at high voltage and then stepped down by transformers. George Westinghouse, inventor of the air brake for railroads, developed the first alternating-current electric system in 1886 and set up the Westinghouse Electric Company to manufacture the equipment. Edison resisted the new method as too risky, but the Westinghouse system won the "battle of the currents," and the Edison companies had to switch over. After the invention of the alternating-current motor by a Serbo-Croatian immigrant named Nikola Tesla, Westinghouse improved upon it. This invention enabled factories to locate wherever they wished; they no longer had to cluster around waterfalls and coal deposits for a ready supply of energy.

ENTREPRENEURS

Thomas Edison and George Westinghouse were rare examples of inventors with the luck and foresight to get rich from the industries they created. The great captains of commerce were more often pure entrepreneurs rather than inventors, men skilled mainly in organizing and promoting big business. Several post–Civil War entrepreneurs stand out for both their achievements and their special contributions: John D. Rockefeller and Andrew Carnegie for their innovations in organization, J. Pierpont Morgan for his development of investment banking, and Richard Sears and Alvah Roebuck, pioneers of mail-order retailing.

ROCKEFELLER AND THE OIL TRUST   Born in New York State, the son of a flamboyant con man and a devout Baptist mother, John D. Rockefeller moved as a youth to Cleveland. Soon thereafter his father abandoned the family and started a new life under an assumed name with a second wife. Raised by his mother, John Rockefeller developed a passion for systematic organization and self-discipline. He was obsessed with precision, order, and tidiness. And early on he decided to bring order and rationality to the chaotic oil industry.

The railroad and shipping connections around Cleveland, Ohio, made it a strategic location for servicing the oil fields of western Pennsylvania. The first oil well had been struck in 1859 in Titusville, Pennsylvania, and led to the Pennsylvania oil rush of the 1860s. As oil could be refined into kerosene, which could be used in lighting, heating, and cooking, the economic importance of the oil rush soon came to outweigh that of the

John D. Rockefeller

His Standard Oil Company dominated the oil industry.

The Rise of Oil

Wooden derricks crowd the farm of John Benninghoff in Oil Creek, Pennsylvania, in the 1860s.

California gold rush of just ten years before. Well before the end of the Civil War, derricks checkered western Pennsylvania, and refineries sprang up in Pittsburgh and Cleveland. Of the two cities, Cleveland had the edge in transportation, and Rockefeller focused his energies there.

Rockefeller recognized the potential profits in refining oil, and in 1870 he incorporated his various interests as the Standard Oil Company of Ohio. Although Rockefeller was the largest refiner, he wanted all of the business. So he decided to weed out the competition, which he perceived as flooding the market with too much refined oil, bringing down prices and reducing profits. Rockefeller approached his Cleveland competitors and offered to buy them out at his own price. Those who resisted were forced out. In less than six weeks, Rockefeller had taken over twenty-two of his twenty-six competitors. By 1879 Standard Oil was controlling 90 to 95 percent of the oil refining in the country.

Much of Rockefeller's success was based upon his determination to "pay nobody a profit." Instead of depending upon the products or services of other firms, known as middlemen, Standard Oil undertook the production of its own barrels, cans, staves, and whatever else it needed—in economic terms this is called vertical integration. The company also kept large amounts of cash reserves to make it independent of banks in case of a crisis.

In line with this policy, Rockefeller also set out to control his transportation needs. With Standard Oil owning most of the pipelines leading to railroads, plus the railroad tank cars and the oil-storage facilities, it was able to dissuade the railroads from serving its eastern competitors. Those rivals that insisted on holding out then faced a giant marketing organization capable of driving them to the wall with price wars.

Eventually, in order to consolidate scattered business interests under more efficient control, Rockefeller and his advisers resorted to a new legal device: the trust. Long established in law to enable one or more persons to manage property belonging to others, such as children or the mentally incompetent, the trust was now used for another purpose: centralized control of business. Thus in 1882 Rockefeller organized the Standard Oil Trust. All thirty-seven stockholders in various Standard Oil enterprises would convey their stock to nine trustees, receiving "trust certificates" in return. The nine trustees would thus be empowered to give central direction to all the scattered Standard Oil companies.

But the trust device, widely copied in the 1880s, proved legally vulnerable to prosecution under state laws against monopoly or restraint of trade. In 1892 Ohio's supreme court ordered the Standard Oil Trust dissolved. For a while the company managed to unify control by the simple device of interlocking directorates, through which the board of directors of one company was made identical or nearly so to the boards of the others. Gradually, however, Rockefeller perfected the idea of the holding company: a company that controlled other companies by holding all or at least a majority of their stock. He was convinced that big business was a natural result of capitalism at work. "It is too late," he declared in 1899, "to argue about the advantages of industrial combinations. They are a necessity." That year, Rockefeller brought his empire under the direction of the Standard Oil Company of New Jersey, a gigantic holding company. Though less vulnerable to prosecution under state law, some holding companies were broken up by the Sherman Anti-Trust Act of 1890.

Rockefeller not only made a colossal fortune, but he also gave much of it away, mostly to support advances in education and medicine. A man of simple tastes, who opposed the use of tobacco and alcohol and believed his fortune was a public trust awarded by God, he became the world's leading philanthropist. He donated more than $500 million during his ninety-eight-year lifetime. "I have always regarded it as a religious duty," Rockefeller said late in life, "to get all I could honorably and to give all I could."

CARNEGIE AND THE STEEL INDUSTRY   Andrew Carnegie, like Rockefeller, experienced an atypical rise from poverty to riches. Born in

Andrew Carnegie

Steel magnate and business icon.

Scotland, he migrated in 1848 with his family to Allegheny County, Pennsylvania. Then thirteen, he started work as a bobbin boy in a textile mill at wages of $1.20 per week. At fourteen he was earning $2.50 per week as a telegraph messenger. In 1853 he became personal secretary and telegrapher to Thomas Scott, then district superintendent of the Pennsylvania Railroad and later its president. When Scott moved up, Carnegie took his place as superintendent. During the Civil War, when Scott became assistant secretary of war in charge of transportation, Carnegie went with him and developed a military telegraph system.

Carnegie kept on moving—from telegraphy to railroading to bridge building and then to steelmaking and investments. In 1873 Carnegie resolved to concentrate on steel. Steel was the miracle material of the post–Civil War era, not because it was new but because it was suddenly cheap. Until the mid–nineteenth century, steel could be made only from wrought iron—itself expensive—and only in small quantities. Then, in 1855, Sir Henry Bessemer invented what became known as the Bessemer converter, a process by which steel could be produced directly and quickly from pig iron (crude iron made in a blast furnace). As more steel was produced, its price dropped and use soared. In 1860 the United States had produced only 13,000 tons of steel. By 1880 production had reached 1.4 million tons.

Carnegie was never a technical expert on steel. He was a promoter, salesman, and organizer with a gift for hiring men of expert ability. He insisted on up-to-date machinery and equipment and used times of recession to expand cheaply by purchasing struggling companies. He also preached to his employees a philosophy of continual innovation in order to reduce operating costs.

Carnegie stood out from other business titans as a thinker who fashioned and publicized a philosophy for big business, a conservative rationale that became deeply implanted in the conventional wisdom of some Americans. He believed that however harsh their methods at times, he and other captains of industry were on the whole public benefactors. In his best-remembered essay, "The Gospel of Wealth" (1889), he argued that in the evolution of society the contrast between the millionaire and the laborer measures the distance

Carnegie's Empire

The Carnegie steel plant at Homestead, Pennsylvania.

society has come. "Not evil, but good, has come to the race from the accumulation of wealth by those who have the ability and energy that produces it." The process had been costly in many ways, but the law of competition is "best for the trade, because it insures the survival of the fittest in every department."

When he retired from business at age sixty-five, Carnegie devoted himself to dispensing his fortune for the public good, out of a sincere desire to promote social welfare and further world peace. He called himself a "distributor" of wealth (he disliked the term *philanthropy*). He gave money to universities, libraries, hospitals, parks, halls for meetings and concerts, swimming pools, and church buildings.

J. P. MORGAN, FINANCIER Unlike Rockefeller and Carnegie, J. Pierpont Morgan was born to wealth, increasing it enormously through his bold innovations. His father was a partner in a London banking house, which he later came to direct. Young Pierpont attended boarding school in Switzerland and university in Germany. After a brief apprenticeship he was

J. Pierpont Morgan

Morgan is shown here in a famous 1903 portrait by Edward Steichen.

sent in 1857 to work in a New York firm representing his father's interests and in 1860 set himself up as its New York agent under the name of J. Pierpont Morgan and Company. That firm, under various names, channeled European capital into the United States and grew into a financial power in its own right.

Morgan was an investment banker, which meant that he would buy corporate stocks and bonds wholesale and sell them at a profit. The growth of large corporations put Morgan's and other investment firms in an increasingly strategic position in the economy. Since the investment business depended upon the general good health of client companies, investment bankers became involved in the operation of their clients' firms, demanding seats on the boards of directors so as to influence company policies.

Like John Rockefeller, J.P. Morgan viewed competition as wasteful and chaotic and sought to consolidate rival firms into giant trusts. Morgan early realized that railroads were the key to the times, and he acquired and reorganized one line after another. By the 1890s he alone controlled one sixth of the nation's railway system. To Morgan, an imperious, domineering man, the stability brought by his operations helped the economy and the public. His crowning triumph was consolidation of the steel industry. After a rapid series of mergers in the iron and steel industry, he bought out Andrew Carnegie's huge steel and iron holdings in 1901. In rapid succession, Morgan added other steel interests and the Rockefeller iron ore holdings in Minnesota's Mesabi Range and a Great Lakes shipping fleet. The new United States Steel Corporation, a holding company for these varied interests, was a marvel of the new century, the first billion-dollar corporation, the climactic event in the age of business consolidation.

SEARS AND ROEBUCK American inventors helped manufacturers after the Civil War produce a vast number of new products, but the most important challenge was extending the reach of national commerce to the millions of people who lived on isolated farms and in small towns. In the

The Rise of Business

A lavish dinner celebrated the merger of the Carnegie and Morgan interests, in 1901. The shape of the table is meant to symbolize a rail.

aftermath of the Civil War, a traveling salesman from Chicago named Aaron Montgomery Ward decided that he could reach more people by mail than on foot and in the process could eliminate the middlemen whose services increased the retail price of goods. Beginning in the early 1870s, Montgomery Ward and Company began selling goods at a 40 percent discount through mail-order catalogs.

By the end of the century, a new retailer had come to dominate the mail-order industry: Sears, Roebuck and Company, founded by two young midwestern entrepreneurs, Richard Sears and Alvah Roebuck, who began offering a cornucopia of goods by mail in the early 1890s. The Sears, Roebuck and Company catalog in 1897 was 786 pages long. It featured groceries, drugs, tools, bells, furniture, iceboxes, stoves and household utensils, musical instruments, farm implements, boots and shoes, clothes, books, and sporting goods. The company's ability to buy goods in high volume from wholesalers enabled it to sell items at prices below those offered in rural general stores. By 1907 Sears, Roebuck and Company had become one of the largest business enterprises in the nation.

The Sears catalog helped create a truly national market and in the process transformed the lives of millions of people. With the advent of free rural

Cover of the 1897 Sears, Roebuck and Company Catalog

Sears's extensive mail-order business and discounted prices allowed its many products to reach customers in cities and the backcountry.

mail delivery in 1898 and the widespread distribution of Sears catalogs, families on farms and in small towns and villages could purchase by mail the products that heretofore were either prohibitively expensive or available only to city dwellers. By the turn of the century, 6 million Sears catalogs were being distributed each year, and the catalog had become the single most widely read book in the nation after the Bible.

Labor Conditions and Organization

SOCIAL TRENDS   Accompanying the spread of huge corporations during the so-called Gilded Age was a rising standard of living for most people. If the rich were still getting richer, a lot of other people were at least better off. This, of course, is far from saying that disparities in the distribution of wealth had disappeared. One set of estimates reveals that in both 1860 and 1900 the richest 2 percent of American families owned more than one third of the nation's physical wealth, while the top 10 percent owned almost three fourths of it. Studies of social mobility in towns across the country, however, show that while the rise from rags to riches was rare, "upward mobility both from blue-collar to white-collar callings and from low-ranked to high-ranked manual jobs was quite common."

The continuing demand for unskilled or semiskilled workers, meanwhile, attracted new groups entering the workforce at the bottom: immigrants above all, but also growing numbers of women and children. Because of a long-term decline in prices and the cost of living, real wages and earnings in manufacturing went up about 50 percent between 1860 and 1890 and another 37 percent from 1890 to 1914. By modern-day standards, however, working conditions were dreary. At the turn of the century, the average hourly wage in manufacturing was about $3.50 in 2005 constant dollars. The average workweek was fifty-nine hours, or nearly six ten-hour days, but that was only an average. Most steelworkers put in a twelve-hour day, and as late as the 1920s a great many worked a seven-day, eighty-four-hour week.

Although wage levels were rising overall, working and living conditions remained precarious. In the crowded tenements and immigrant neighborhoods of major cities, the death rate ran substantially higher than that in the countryside. Factories often maintained poor health and safety conditions. In 1913, for instance, there were some 25,000 workplace fatalities and 700,000 job-related injuries that required at least four weeks' disability. The United States was the only industrial nation in the world that had no workmen's compensation program to provide support for workers injured on the job. And American industry had the highest accident rate in the world. The new industrial culture was also impersonal. Ever-larger numbers of people were dependent upon the machinery and factories of owners whom they seldom if ever saw. In the simpler world of small shops, workers and employers could enter into close relationships; the larger corporation, on the other hand, was likely governed by a bureaucracy in which ownership was separate from management. Much of the social history of the modern world in fact turns upon the transition from a world of personal relationships to one of impersonal, contractual relationships.

CHILD LABOR   A growing number of wage laborers after the Civil War were children—boys and girls who worked full-time for meager wages amid unhealthy conditions. Young people had of course, always worked in America: farms required everyone to pitch in. After the Civil War, however, millions of children took up work outside the home, operating machines, digging coal, stitching clothes, shucking oysters, peeling shrimp, canning food, blowing glass, and tending looms. Parents desperate for income believed they had no choice but to put their children to work. By 1880 one out of every six children in the nation was working full-time. And by 1900 there were almost 2 million child laborers in the United States. In southern cotton mills, where few African Americans were hired, one fourth of the employees were below the age of fifteen, with half of the children below age twelve. Children as young as eight were laboring alongside adults twelve hours a day, six days a week. This meant they received little or no education and had little time for play or parental nurturance.

Factories, mills, mines, and canneries were dangerous places, especially for children. Few machines had safety devices, and few factories or mills had ventilating fans or fire escapes. Throughout Appalachia, thousands of

Children in Industry

Four young boys who did the dangerous work of mine helpers in West Virginia in 1900.

soot-smeared boys worked deep in the coal mines. In New England and the South, thousands of young girls worked in dusty textile mills, brushing away lint from the clacking machines and retying broken threads. Foremen kept children awake by dousing them with water. Children suffered three times as many on-the-job accidents as adult workers, and respiratory diseases were common in the unventilated buildings. A child working in a textile mill was only half as likely to reach the age of twenty as a child outside a mill. Although some states passed laws limiting the number of hours children could work and establishing minimum-age requirements, they were rarely enforced and often ignored. By 1881 only seven states, mostly in New England, had laws requiring children to be at least twelve before they worked for wages. Yet the only proof required by employers in such states was a statement from a child's parents. Working-class and immigrant parents were often so desperate for income that they forged work permits for their children or taught their children to lie about their age to keep a job.

DISORGANIZED PROTEST Under these circumstances it was very difficult for workers to organize unions. Civic leaders respected property rights more than the rights of labor. Many businessmen believed that a "labor supply" was simply another commodity to be procured at the lowest possible price. Among workers recently removed from an agrarian world, the idea of labor unions was slow to take hold. And much of the workforce was made up of immigrant workers from a variety of cultures. They spoke different languages and harbored ethnic animosities. Many, if not most, saw their jobs as transient, the first rung on the ladder to success. They hoped to move on to a homestead or return with their earnings to the old farms of their European homeland. Nonetheless, with or without unions, workers staged impromptu strikes in response to wage cuts and other grievances. Such action often led to violence, however, and three incidents of the 1870s colored much of the public's view of labor unions thereafter.

THE MOLLY MAGUIRES   The decade's early years saw a reign of terror in the Pennsylvania coalfields, attributed to an Irish group called the Molly Maguires. The Mollies took their name from an Irish patriot who had directed violent resistance against the British. They were motivated by the dangerous working conditions in the mines and the owners' brutal efforts to suppress union activity. Convinced of the justness of their cause, the Mollies used intimidation, beatings, and killings to right perceived wrongs against Irish workers. Later investigations have shown that agents of the mine operators themselves stirred up some of the trouble. The terrorism reached its peak in 1874–1875, and mine owners hired Pinkerton detectives to stop the movement. One of the agents who infiltrated the Mollies produced enough evidence to have the leaders indicted. At trials in 1876, twenty-four of the Molly Maguires were convicted; ten were hanged. The trials also resulted in a wage reduction in the mines and the final destruction of the Miners' National Association, a weak union the Mollies had dominated.

THE RAILROAD STRIKE OF 1877   A far more widespread labor incident was the Great Railroad Strike of 1877, the first major interstate strike in American history. After the panic of 1873 and the ensuing depression, the major rail lines in the East had cut wages. In 1877 they made another 10 percent cut, which led most of the railroad workers at Martinsburg, West Virginia, to walk off the job and block the tracks. Without organized direction, however, the group of picketers degenerated into a mob that burned and plundered railroad property.

Walkouts and sympathy demonstrations spread spontaneously from Maryland to San Francisco. The strike engulfed hundreds of cities and towns, leaving in its wake over 100 people dead and millions of dollars in property destroyed. Militiamen called in from Philadelphia managed to disperse one crowd at the cost of twenty-six lives but then found themselves besieged in the railroad's roundhouse, where they disbanded and shot their way out.

Federal troops finally quelled the violence. Looting, rioting, and burning went on for another day until the frenzy wore itself out. A reporter described the scene as "the most horrible ever witnessed, except in the carnage of war. There were fifty miles of hot rails, ten tracks side by side, with as many miles of ties turned into glowing coals and tons on tons of iron car skeletons and wheels almost at white heat." Public opinion, sympathetic at first, tended to blame the workers for the looting and violence. Eventually the strikers, lacking organized bargaining power, had no choice but to drift back to work. Everywhere the strikes failed.

For many Americans the railroad strike raised the specter of a worker-based social revolution. As a Pittsburgh newspaper warned, "This may be the beginning of a great civil war in this country between labor and capital." Equally disturbing to those in positions of corporate and political power was the presence of many women among the protesters. A Baltimore journalist noted that the "singular part of the disturbances is the very active part taken by the women, who are the wives and mothers of the [railroad] firemen." From the point of view of organized labor, however, the Great Railroad Strike demonstrated potential union strength and the need for tighter organization.

THE SAND-LOT INCIDENT   In California the railroad strike indirectly gave rise to a working-class political movement. At a San Francisco sand lot a meeting to express sympathy for the strikers ended with attacks on some passing Chinese. Within a few days sporadic anti-Chinese riots had led to a mob attack on Chinatown. The depression of the 1870s had hit the West Coast especially hard, and the Chinese were handy scapegoats for frustrated white laborers who believed the Asians had taken their jobs.

Soon an Irish immigrant, Denis Kearney, had organized the Workingmen's Party of California, whose platform called for an end to further Chinese immigration. A gifted agitator, himself only recently naturalized, Kearney harangued the "sand lotters" about the "foreign peril" and assaulted the rich railroad barons for exploiting the poor—sometimes at gatherings outside their mansions on Nob Hill. In 1878 his new party won a hefty number of seats to a state constitutional convention but managed to incorporate into the state's basic law little more than ineffective attempts to regulate the railroads. The workingmen's movement peaked in 1879, when it elected many members to the state legislature and the mayor of San Francisco. Kearney lacked the gift for building a durable movement, but as his party went to pieces, his anti-Chinese theme became a national issue—in 1882 Congress voted to prohibit Chinese immigration for ten years.

TOWARD PERMANENT UNIONS   Meanwhile, efforts to build a national labor-union movement had begun to bear fruit. Earlier efforts, in the 1830s and 1840s, had largely been dominated by reformers with schemes that ranged from free homesteads to utopian socialism. But the 1850s had seen the beginning of "job-conscious" unions in selected skilled trades. By 1860 there were about twenty such craft unions. During the Civil War, because of the demand for labor, those unions grew in strength and number.

Yet there was no overall federation of these groups until 1866, when the National Labor Union (NLU) convened in Baltimore. The NLU was composed of congresses of delegates from labor and reform groups more interested in political and social reform than in bargaining with employers. The groups espoused such ideas as the eight-hour workday, workers' cooperatives, greenbackism (the printing of paper money to inflate the currency and thereby relieve debtors), and equal rights for women and African Americans. After the head of the union died suddenly, its support fell away quickly, and by 1872 the NLU had disbanded. The National Labor Union was not a total failure, however. It was influential in persuading Congress to enact an eight-hour workday for federal employees and to repeal the 1864 Contract Labor Act, passed during the Civil War to encourage the importation of laborers by allowing employers to pay for their passage to America. Employers had taken advantage of the Contract Labor Act to recruit foreign laborers willing to work for lower wages than their American counterparts.

THE KNIGHTS OF LABOR   Before the National Labor Union collapsed, another labor group of national standing had emerged: the Noble Order of the Knights of Labor, a name that evoked the aura of medieval guilds. The founder of the Knights of Labor, Uriah S. Stephens, a Philadelphia tailor, was a habitual "joiner" involved with several secret orders, including the Masons. His early training for the Baptist ministry also affected his outlook. Secrecy, he felt, along with a semireligious ritual, would protect members from retaliation by employers and create a sense of solidarity.

The Knights of Labor, started in 1869, grew slowly, but during the years of depression, as other unions collapsed, it spread more rapidly. In 1878 its first general assembly established it as a national organization. Its preamble and platform endorsed the reforms advanced by previous workingmen's groups, including the creation of bureaus of labor statistics and mechanics' lien laws (to ensure payment of salaries), elimination of convict-labor competition,

Members of the Knights of Labor

This national union was more egalitarian than most of its contemporaries.

the eight-hour day, and paper currency. One plank in the platform, far ahead of the times, called for equal pay for equal work by men and women.

Throughout its existence the Knights of Labor emphasized reform measures and preferred boycotts to strikes as a way to put pressure on employers. The Knights allowed as members all who had ever worked for wages, except lawyers, doctors, bankers, and those who sold liquor. Theoretically it was one big union of all workers, skilled and unskilled, regardless of race, color, creed, or sex.

In 1879 Stephens was succeeded as head of the Knights of Labor by Terence V. Powderly, the thirty-year-old mayor of Scranton, Pennsylvania. Born of Irish immigrant parents, Powderly had started working for a railroad at age sixteen. In many ways he was unsuited to his new job as head of the Knights of Labor. He was frail, sensitive to criticism, and indecisive at critical moments. He was temperamentally opposed to strikes, and when they did occur, he did not always support the local groups involved. Yet the Knights owed their greatest growth to strikes that occurred under his leadership. In the 1880s the Knights increased their membership from about 100,000 to more than 700,000. In 1886, however, the organization peaked and went into rapid decline after the failure of a railroad strike.

ANARCHISM The tensions between labor and management during the late nineteenth century in both the United States and Europe helped generate the doctrine of anarchism. Anarchists believed that government—any government—was in itself an abusive device used by the rich and powerful to oppress and exploit the working poor. Anarchists dreamed of the eventual disappearance of government altogether, and many of them believed that the transition to such a stateless society could be hurried along by promoting revolutionary action among the masses. One favored tactic was the use of dramatic acts of violence against representatives of the government. Many European anarchists emigrated to the United States during the last quarter of the nineteenth century, bringing with them their belief in the impact of "propaganda of the deed."

THE HAYMARKET AFFAIR   Labor-related violence increased during the 1880s. The Haymarket affair, for instance, grew indirectly out of agitation for an eight-hour workday. In 1884 Knights of Labor organizers set May 1, 1886, as the deadline for the institution of the eight-hour workday in all trades. Chicago became the center of the movement, and on May 3, 1886, the International Harvester plant became the site of an unfortunate clash between strikers and policemen in which one striker was killed.

Leaders of a minuscule anarchist movement in Chicago scheduled an open meeting the following night at Haymarket Square to protest the killing. After listening to long speeches promoting socialism and anarchism, the crowd was beginning to break up when a group of policemen arrived and called upon the meeting to disperse. At that point somebody threw a bomb at the police, killing one officer and wounding others. The police then fired into the crowd. Subsequently, in a trial marked by prejudice and hysteria, seven anarchist leaders were sentenced to death despite the lack of any evidence linking them to the bomb thrower, whose identity was never established. Of these, two were reprieved, one committed suicide in prison, and four were hanged. All but one of the group were German speaking, and that one held a membership card in the Knights of Labor.

The violent incident at Haymarket Square triggered widespread revulsion at the Knights of Labor and labor groups in general. Despite his best efforts, Terence Powderly could never dissociate in the public mind the Knights from the anarchists. He clung to leadership until 1893, but after that the union evaporated. By the turn of the century, it was but a memory. A number of problems accounted for the Knights' decline, besides fear of their supposed radicalism: a leadership devoted more to reform than to the nuts and bolts of organization, the failure of the Knights' cooperative enterprises, and a preoccupation with politics that led the Knights to sponsor labor candidates in hundreds of local elections.

The Knights nevertheless attained some lasting achievements, among them the creation of the federal Bureau of Labor Statistics in 1884 as well as several state labor bureaus; the Foran Act of 1885, which, though weakly enforced, penalized employers who imported contract labor (an arrangement similar to the indentured servitude of colonial times, in which workers were committed to a term of labor in exchange for transportation to America); and an 1880 national law providing for the arbitration of labor disputes. The Knights by example also spread the idea of unionism and initiated a new type of union organization: the industrial union, an industrywide union of skilled and unskilled workers.

GOMPERS AND THE AFL   The craft unions opposed industrial unionism. They organized workers who shared special skills, such as typographers or cigar makers. Leaders of the craft unions feared that joining with unskilled laborers would mean a loss of their craft's identity and a loss of the skilled workers' bargaining power. Thus in 1886 delegates from twenty-five craft unions organized the American Federation of Labor (AFL). Its structure differed from that of the Knights of Labor in that it was a federation of national organizations, each of which retained a large degree of autonomy and exercised greater leverage against management.

Samuel Gompers

Head of the American Federation of Labor, striking an assertive pose.

Samuel Gompers served as president of the AFL from its start until his death in 1924, with only one year's interruption. Born in London of Dutch Jewish ancestry, Gompers came to the United States as a teenager, joined the Cigarmakers' Union in 1864, and became president of his New York local in 1877. Unlike Terence Powderly and the Knights of Labor, Gompers focused on concrete economic gains—higher wages, shorter hours, better working conditions—and avoided involvement with utopian ideas or politics.

Gompers was temperamentally more suited than Powderly to the rough-and-tumble world of unionism. He had a thick hide, liked to talk and drink with workers in the back room, and willingly used the strike to achieve favorable trade agreements, including provisos for union recognition in the form of closed shops (which could hire only union members) or union-preference shops (which could hire others only if no union members were available).

The AFL at first grew slowly, but by 1890 it had surpassed the Knights of Labor in membership. By the turn of the century, it claimed 500,000 members in affiliated unions; in 1914, on the eve of World War I, it had 2 million; and in 1920 it reached a peak of 4 million. But even then it embraced less than 15 percent of the nation's nonagricultural workers. All unions, including the unaffiliated railroad brotherhoods, accounted for little more than 18 percent of those workers. Organized labor's strongholds were in transportation and the building trades. Most of the larger manufacturing industries—including steel, textiles, tobacco, and packinghouses—remained almost untouched. Gompers never frowned upon industrial unions, and several became important affiliates of the AFL: the United Mine Workers, the International Ladies Garment Workers, and the Amalgamated Clothing Workers. But the AFL had its greatest success in organizing skilled workers.

Union Workers

A cigar-box label celebrating union workers, ca. 1898.

THE HOMESTEAD STRIKE   Two violent incidents in the 1890s stalled the emerging industrial-union movement and set it back for the next forty years: the Homestead steel strike of 1892 and the Pullman strike of 1894. The Amalgamated Association of Iron and Steel Workers, founded in 1876, had by 1891 a membership of more than 24,000 and was probably the largest craft union at the time. But it excluded unskilled steelworkers and had failed to organize the larger steel plants. The Homestead Works at Pittsburgh was an important exception. There the union had enjoyed friendly relations with Andrew Carnegie's company until Henry Clay Frick became its president in 1889. A showdown was delayed until 1892, however, when the union contract came up for renewal. Carnegie, who had expressed sympathy for unions in the past, had gone to Scotland and left matters in Frick's hands. Carnegie, however, knew what was afoot: a cost-cutting reduction in the number of workers through the use of labor-saving devices and a deliberate attempt to smash the union. "Am with you to the end," he wrote to Frick.

As negotiations dragged on, the company announced it would treat workers as individuals unless an agreement with the union was reached by June 29. A strike—or, more properly, a lockout of unionists—began on that date. In no mood to negotiate, Frick built a twelve-foot fence around the entire plant and hired 300 union-busting Pinkerton detectives to protect what was soon dubbed Fort Frick. On the morning of July 6, 1892, when the Pinkertons floated up the Monongahela River on barges, unionists were waiting behind breastworks on shore. Who fired the first shot remains unknown, but a battle broke out in which six workers and three Pinkertons died. In the end the Pinkertons surrendered and were marched away, subjected to taunts from crowds in the street. Six days later the state militia appeared at the plant to protect the strikebreakers hired by Frick to restore production. The strike dragged on until November, but by then the union was dead at Homestead. Its cause was not helped when an anarchist, a Lithuanian immigrant, tried to assassinate Frick. Much of the local sympathy for the strikers evaporated.

THE PULLMAN STRIKE   The Pullman strike of 1894 was perhaps the most notable walkout in American history. It paralyzed the economies of twenty-seven states and territories making up the western half of the nation. It involved a dispute at Pullman, Illinois, a model town built on 4,000 acres outside Chicago, where workers of the Pullman Palace Car Company were housed. The town's idyllic appearance was deceptive, however. Employees were required to live there, pay rents and utility costs that were higher than those in nearby towns, and buy goods from company stores. During the depression of 1893, George Pullman laid off 3,000 of 5,800 employees and cut wages

25 to 40 percent, but not his rents and other charges. After Pullman fired three members of a workers' grievance committee, a strike began on May 11, 1894.

During this tense period, Pullman workers had been joining the American Railway Union, founded the previous year by Eugene V. Debs. The tall, gangly Debs was a man of towering influence and charismatic appeal. A child of working-class immigrants, he quit school in 1869, at age fourteen, and began working for an Indiana railroad. By the early 1890s Debs had become a tireless spokesman for labor radicalism, and he launched a crusade to organize *all* railway workers—skilled or unskilled—into the American Railway Union. Soon he was in charge of a powerful new labor organization, and he quickly turned his attention to the Pullman controversy.

In June 1894, after George Pullman refused Debs's plea for arbitration, the union workers stopped handling Pullman railcars and by the end of July had tied up most of the railroads in the Midwest. Railroad executives then brought strikebreakers to connect mail cars to Pullman cars so that interference with Pullman cars would entail interference with the federal mail. The U.S. attorney general, a former railroad attorney himself, swore in 3,400 special deputies to keep the trains running. When clashes occurred between those deputies and some of the strikers, angry workers ignored Debs's plea for an orderly boycott. They assaulted employees and destroyed property.

The Pullman Strike

Troops guarding the railroads, 1894.

Finally, on July 3, 1894, President Grover Cleveland sent federal troops into the Chicago area, where the strike was centered. The Illinois governor insisted that the state could keep order, but Cleveland claimed authority and a duty to ensure delivery of the mail. Meanwhile, the attorney general won an injunction forbidding any interference with the mail or any effort to restrain interstate commerce; the principle was that a strike or boycott violated the Sherman Anti-Trust Act. On July 13 the union called off the strike. A few days later the district court cited Debs for violating the injunction and he served six months in jail. The Supreme Court upheld the decree in the case of *In re Debs* (1895) on broad grounds of national sovereignty: "The strong arm of the national government may be put forth to brush away all obstructions to the freedom of interstate commerce or the transportation of the mails." Debs served his jail term, during which he read deeply in socialist literature, and emerged to devote the rest of his life to socialism.

MOTHER JONES   One of the most colorful and beloved labor agitators at the end of the nineteenth century was a remarkable woman known simply as Mother Jones. White haired, pink cheeked, and dressed in matronly black dresses and hats, she was a tireless champion of the working poor and a rabble-rouser who used fiery rhetoric to excite crowds and attract media attention. She led marches, dodged bullets, served jail terms, and confronted business titans and police with disarming courage. In 1913 a district attorney called her the "most dangerous woman in America."

Born in Cork, Ireland, in 1837, Mary Harris was the second of five children in a poor Catholic family that fled the Irish potato famine at midcentury and settled in Toronto. In 1861 she moved to Memphis and began teaching. There, as the Civil War was erupting, she met and married George Jones, an iron molder and staunch union member. They had four children, and then disaster struck. In 1867 a yellow fever epidemic devastated Memphis, killing Mary Jones's husband and four children. The grief-stricken thirty-seven-year-old widow moved to Chicago and took up dressmaking, only to see her shop, home, and belongings destroyed in the great fire of 1871. Having lost her family and her finances and angry at the social inequality and injustices she saw around her, Mary Jones drifted into the labor movement and soon emerged as its most passionate advocate. Chicago was then the seedbed of labor radicalism, and the union culture nurtured in Mary Jones a lifelong dedication to the cause of wage workers and their families.

The gritty woman who had lost her family now declared herself the "mother" of the fledgling labor movement. She joined the Knights of Labor as an organizer and public speaker. In the late 1880s she became an ardent speaker for the United Mine Workers (UMW), various other unions, and the Socialist party. For the next thirty years she crisscrossed the nation, recruiting union members, supporting strikers (her "boys"), raising funds, walking picket lines, defying court injunctions, berating politicians, and spending time in prison.

Mother Jones

A pioneer of the labor movement.

Wherever Mother Jones went, she promoted higher wages, shorter hours, safer workplaces, and restrictions on child labor. Coal miners, said the UMW president, "have had no more staunch supporter, no more able defender than the one we all love to call Mother." During a miners' strike in West Virginia, Jones was arrested, convicted of "conspiracy that resulted in murder," and sentenced to twenty years in prison. The outcry over her plight helped spur a Senate committee to investigate conditions in the coal mines; the governor set her free.

Mother Jones was especially determined to end the exploitation of children in the workplace. In 1903 she organized a highly publicized, weeklong march of child workers from Pennsylvania to the New York home of President Theodore Roosevelt. The children were physically stunted and mutilated, most of them missing fingers or hands from machinery accidents. President Roosevelt refused to see the ragtag children, but as Mother Jones explained, "Our march had done its work. We had drawn the attention of the nation to the crime of child labor." Soon the Pennsylvania state legislature raised the legal working age to fourteen.

Mother Jones lost most of the strikes she participated in, but over the course of her long life she saw average wages increase, working conditions improve, and child labor diminish. Her commitment to the cause of social justice never wavered. At age eighty-three she was arrested after joining a miners' strike in Colorado and jailed in solitary confinement. At her funeral in 1930, one speaker urged people to remember her famous rallying cry: "Pray for the dead and fight like hell for the living."

Eugene V. Debs

Founder of the American Railway Union and later candidate for president as head of the Socialist Party of America.

SOCIALISM AND THE UNIONS The major unions, for the most part, never allied themselves with the socialists, as many European labor movements did. But socialist ideas had been circulating in the country at least since the 1820s. Marxism, one strain of socialism, was imported mainly by German immigrants. Karl Marx's International Workingmen's Association, founded in 1864 and later called the First International, inspired only a few affiliates in the United States. In 1872, at Marx's urging, the headquarters was moved from London to New York. In 1877 followers of Marx in America organized the Socialist Labor party, a group so dominated by immigrants that German was initially its official language.

The movement gained little notice before the rise of Daniel De Leon in the 1890s. As editor of a Marxist newspaper, *The People*, he became the dominant figure in the Socialist Labor party. He proposed to organize industrial unions with a socialist purpose and to build a political party that would abolish the government once it gained power, after which the unions of the Socialist Trade and Labor Alliance, formed under his supervision, would become the units of control. De Leon preached revolution at the ballot box, not by violence.

Eugene Debs was more successful than De Leon at building a socialist movement in America, however. In 1897 Debs announced that he was a socialist and organized the Social Democratic party from the remnants of the American Railway Union; he got over 96,000 votes as its candidate for president in 1900. The next year his followers joined a number of secessionists from De Leon's party to set up the Socialist Party of America. In 1904 Debs polled over 400,000 votes as the party's candidate for president and in 1912 more than doubled that, to more than 900,000 votes, or 6 percent of the popular vote. In 1910 Milwaukee elected a socialist mayor and congressman.

By 1912 the Socialist party seemed well on the way to becoming a permanent fixture in American politics. Thirty-three cities had socialist mayors. The party sponsored five English-language daily newspapers, eight foreign-language dailies, and a number of weeklies and monthlies. In the Southwest the party built a sizable grassroots following among farmers and tenants. Oklahoma, for instance, had more paid-up party members in 1910 than any other state except New York and in 1912 gave 16.5 percent of its popular vote to Debs, a greater proportion than any other state ever gave him. But the Socialist party reached its peak in 1912. It would be wracked by disagreements over America's participation in World War I and was split thereafter by desertions to the new Communist party.

THE WOBBLIES During the years of Socialist party growth, a parallel effort to revive industrial unionism emerged, led by the Industrial Workers of the World (IWW). The chief base for this group was the Western Federation of Miners, organized at Butte, Montana, in 1893. Over the next decade the Western Federation was the storm center of violent confrontations with unyielding mine operators who mobilized private armies against it in Colorado, Idaho, and elsewhere. In 1905 the founding convention of the IWW drew a variety of delegates who opposed the AFL's philosophy of organizing unions made up only of skilled workers. Eugene Debs participated, although many of his comrades preferred to work within the AFL. Daniel De Leon seized this chance to strike back at craft unionism. He argued that the IWW "must be founded on the class struggle" and "the irrepressible conflict between the capitalist class and the working class."

But the IWW waged class war better than it articulated class ideology. Like the Knights of Labor, it was designed to be "one big union," including all workers, skilled or unskilled. Its roots were in the mining and lumber camps of the West, where unstable conditions of employment created a large number of nomadic workers, to whom neither the AFL's pragmatic approach nor the socialists' political appeal held much attraction. The revolutionary goal of the Wobblies, as they came to be called, was an idea labeled syndicalism by its French supporters: the ultimate destruction of the government and its replacement by one big union. But just how that union would govern remained vague.

Like other radical groups the IWW was split by sectarian disputes. Because of policy disagreements all the major founders withdrew, first the Western Federation of Miners, then Debs, then De Leon. William D. "Big Bill" Haywood of the Western Federation remained, however, and as its leader held the group together. Haywood was an imposing figure. Well over six feet tall, handsome and muscular, he commanded the attention and respect of his listeners. This hard-rock miner, union organizer, and socialist from Salt Lake City despised the AFL and its conservative labor philosophy. He called Samuel Gompers "a squat specimen of humanity" who was "conceited, petulant, and vindictive." Instead of following Gompers's advice to organize only skilled workers, Haywood promoted the concept of one all-inclusive union dedicated to a socialism "with its working clothes on."

Haywood and the Wobblies, however, were reaching out to the fringe elements with the least power and influence, chiefly the migratory workers of the West and the ethnic groups of the East. Always ambivalent about diluting their revolutionary principles, Wobblies scorned the usual labor agreements even when they participated in them. Consequently, they engaged in spectacular battles with employers but scored few victories. The largest was a textile strike at Lawrence, Massachusetts, in 1912 that garnered wage raises, overtime pay, and other benefits. But the next year a strike of silk workers at Paterson, New Jersey, ended in disaster, and the IWW entered a rapid decline.

The fading of the Wobblies was accelerated by the hysterical opposition they aroused. Its members branded as anarchists, bums, and criminals, the IWW was effectively destroyed during World War I, when most of its leaders were jailed for conspiracy because of their militant opposition to the war. Big Bill Haywood fled to the Soviet Union, where he married a Russian woman, died in 1928, and was honored by burial in the Kremlin wall. The short-lived Wobblies left behind a rich folklore of nomadic workingmen and a gallery of heroic agitators such as Elizabeth Gurley Flynn, a dark-haired Irishwoman who at age eighteen chained herself to a lamppost to impede her arrest during a strike. The movement also bequeathed martyrs such as the Swedish-American singer and labor organizer Joe Hill, framed (so the faithful assumed) for murder and executed by a Utah firing squad. His last words were written to Haywood: "Goodbye, Bill. I die like a true blue rebel. Don't waste any time mourning. Organize." The intensity of conviction and devotion to a cause shown by Hill, Flynn, and others ensured that the IWW's ideal of a classless society did not die.

MAKING CONNECTIONS

- The Darwinian ideas implicit in the attitudes of many leading entrepreneurs, especially Andrew Carnegie, are described in greater detail in the next chapter.

- In response to the growth of the railroads, reformers in the 1880s and 1890s began to push for government regulation of the industry, a trend explored in Chapter 22.

- The economic and industrial growth described in this chapter was an important factor in America's "new imperialism" of the late nineteenth century, as shown in Chapter 23.

- The socialist approach to reform was a significant influence on the Progressive movement, covered in Chapter 24.

FURTHER READING

For a masterful synthesis of post–Civil War industrial development, see Walter Licht's *Industrializing America: The Nineteenth Century* (1995). On the growth of railroads, see Albro Martin's *Railroads Triumphant: The Growth, Rejection, and Rebirth of a Vital American Force* (1992). A monumental study of the transcontinental railroad is David Haward Bain's *Empire Express: Building the First Transcontinental Railroad* (1999). On the 1877 railroad strike, see David O. Stowell's *Streets, Railroads, and the Great Strike of 1877* (1999).

On entrepreneurship in the iron and steel sector, see Thomas J. Misa's *A Nation of Steel: The Making of Modern America, 1865–1925* (1995). The best biographies of the leading business tycoons are Ron Chernow's *Titan: The Life of John D. Rockefeller, Sr.* (1998) and Jean Strouse's *Morgan, American Financier* (1999). Nathan Rosenberg's *Technology and American Economic Growth* (1972) documents the growth of invention during the period.

Much of the scholarship on labor stresses the traditional values and the culture of work that people brought to the factory. Herbert G. Gutman's

Work, Culture, and Society in Industrializing America: Essays in American Working-Class History (1975) best introduces these themes. The leading survey remains David Montgomery's *The Fall of the House of Labor: The Workplace, the State, and American Labor Activism, 1865–1925* (1987).

For the role of women in the changing workplace, see Alice Kessler-Harris's *Out to Work: A History of Wage-Earning Women in the United States* (1982) and Susan E. Kennedy's *If All We Did Was to Weep at Home: A History of White Working-Class Women in America* (1979).

As for the labor unions, Gerald N. Grob's *Workers and Utopia: A Study of Ideological Conflict in the American Labor Movement, 1865–1900* (1961) examines the difference in outlook between the Knights of Labor and the American Federation of Labor. For the Knights, see Leon Fink's *Working-men's Democracy: The Knights of Labor and American Politics* (1983). Also useful is Susan Levine's *Labor's True Woman: Carpet Weavers, Industrialization, and Labor Reform in the Gilded Age* (1984), on the role of women in the Knights. On Mother Jones, see Elliott J. Gorn's *Mother Jones: The Most Dangerous Woman in America* (2001). To trace the rise of socialism among organized workers, see Nick Salvatore's *Eugene V. Debs: Citizen and Socialist* (1982). The key strikes are discussed in Paul Avrich's *The Haymarket Tragedy* (1984) and Paul Krause's *The Battle for Homestead, 1880–1892: Politics, Culture, and Steel* (1992).

21

THE EMERGENCE
OF URBAN AMERICA

FOCUS QUESTIONS

· How did immigration affect the growth of the modern city?

· What led to the rise of powerful reform movements?

· What was the impact of Darwinian thought on the social sciences?

· What were the literary and philosophical trends of the late nineteenth century?

To answer these questions and access additional review material, please visit www.wwnorton.com/studyspace.

During the second half of the nineteenth century, the United States experienced an urban transformation unparalleled in world history. The late nineteenth century, declared an economist in 1899, was "not only the age of cities, but the age of great cities." Between 1860 and 1910 the urban population mushroomed from 6 million to 44 million. By 1920 more than half the population lived in urban areas.

The rise of big cities during the nineteenth century created a distinctive urban culture. People from different ethnic and religious backgrounds and representing every walk of life poured into the high-rise apartment buildings and ramshackle tenements springing up in every major city. They came in search of jobs, wealth, and excitement.

Not surprisingly, the rise of metropolitan America created an array of new social problems. Rapid urban development produced widespread poverty and political corruption. The question of how to feed, clothe, shelter, and educate the new arrivals taxed the imagination—and patience—of urban leaders. Further complicating efforts to improve the quality of life in the nation's cities was the pattern of increasing residential segregation according to racial and ethnic background and social class.

AMERICA'S MOVE TO TOWN

The prospect of good jobs and social excitement in the cities lured workers by the millions from the countryside and overseas. City people became distinctively urban in demeanor and outlook, and the contrasts between farm and city life grew more vivid with each passing year.

EXPLOSIVE URBAN GROWTH   The frontier was a societal safety valve, the historian Frederick Jackson Turner said in his influential thesis on American development. Its cheap lands afforded a release for the population pressures mounting in the cities. If there was such a thing as a safety valve in his own time, however, he had it exactly backward. The flow of population toward cities was greater than the flow toward the West.

Much of the westward movement in fact was itself an urban movement, spawning new towns near the mining digs or at the railheads. On the Pacific coast a greater portion of the population was urbanized than anywhere else; its major concentrations were around San Francisco Bay at first and then in Los Angeles, which became a boomtown after the arrival of the Southern Pacific and Santa Fe Railroads in the 1880s. In the Northwest, Seattle grew quickly, first as the terminus of three transcontinental railroad lines and, by the end of the century, as the staging area for the Yukon gold rush. Minneapolis, St. Paul, Omaha, Kansas City, and Denver were no longer the mere villages they had been in 1860. The South, too, produced new cities: Durham, North Carolina, and Birmingham, Alabama, which were centers of tobacco and iron manufactures, and Houston, Texas, which handled cotton and cattle and, later, oil.

While the Far West had the greatest proportion of urban population, the Northeast had far greater numbers of people in its teeming cities. These city dwellers were increasingly landless and homeless: they had nothing but their labor to sell. By 1900 more than 90 percent of the residents in New York City's Manhattan lived in rented houses or congested apartment buildings called tenements.

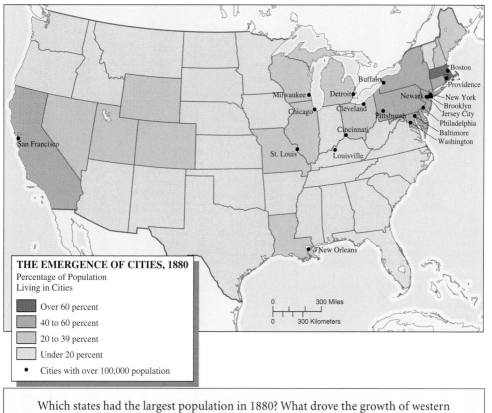

THE EMERGENCE OF CITIES, 1880
Percentage of Population
Living in Cities

- Over 60 percent
- 40 to 60 percent
- 20 to 39 percent
- Under 20 percent
- Cities with over 100,000 population

Which states had the largest population in 1880? What drove the growth of western cities? How were western cities different from eastern cities?

Several technological innovations allowed cities to expand vertically to accommodate their surging populations. In the 1870s developments in heating, such as steam circulating through radiators, enabled the construction of large apartment buildings, since fireplaces were no longer needed. In 1889 the Otis Elevator Company installed the first electric elevator, which made possible the erection of taller buildings—before the 1860s few structures had gone higher than three or four stories. And during the 1880s engineers developed cast-iron and steel-frame construction techniques. Because such materials were stronger than brick, they allowed developers to erect high-rise buildings.

Cities also expanded horizontally after the introduction of important transportation innovations. Before the 1890s the chief power sources of urban transport were either animals or steam. Horse- and mule-drawn

THE EMERGENCE OF CITIES, 1920

Percentage of Population
Living in Cities

Over 60 percent

40 to 60 percent

20 to 39 percent

Under 20 percent

• Cities with over 100,000 population

How did technology change life in cities in the early twentieth century? What was
the role of mass transit in expanding the urban population? How did the demographics of these new cities change between 1880 and 1920?

streetcars had appeared in antebellum cities, but they were slow and cumbersome, and cleaning up after the animals added to the cost. In 1873 San
Francisco became the first city to use cable cars that clamped onto a moving underground cable driven by a central power source. Some cities used
steam-powered trains on elevated tracks, but by the 1890s electric trolleys
were preferred. Mass transit received an added boost when subways were
built in Boston, New York City, and Philadelphia.

The spread of mass transit allowed large numbers of people to become
commuters, and a growing middle class retreated to quieter tree-lined
"streetcar suburbs," whence they could travel into the central city for business
or entertainment (though working folk generally stayed put, unable to afford
even the nickel fare). Urban growth often became a sprawl, since it usually took

Urban Mass Transit

A horse-drawn streetcar moving along rails in New York City.

place without plan, in the interest of a fast buck, and without thought to the need for parks and public services.

The use of horse-drawn railways, cable cars, and electric trolleys helped transform the social character of cities. Until the introduction of such new transportation systems, people of all classes lived and worked together in the central city. After the Civil War, however, the emergence of suburbs began to segregate people according to their economic standing. The more affluent moved outside the city, leaving behind the working folk, many of whom were immigrants or African Americans. The poorer districts of a city became more congested and crime ridden as the population grew, fueled by waves of newcomers from abroad.

THE ALLURE AND PROBLEMS OF THE CITIES   The wonder of the cities—their glittering new electric lights, their streetcars, telephones, department stores, vaudeville shows and other amusements, newspapers and magazines, and a thousand other attractions—cast a magnetic lure on rural youth. The new cities threw into stark contrast the frustration of unending toil and the isolation and loneliness of country life. In times of rural depression, thousands left for the cities in search of opportunity and personal freedom. The exodus from the countryside was especially evident in the East, where the census documented the shift in population from country to city and stories were told of entire regions where abandoned buildings were going to ruin and the wilderness was reclaiming farms that had been wrested from it during the previous 250 years.

Yet those who moved to the city often traded one set of problems for another. Workers in the big cities often had no choice but to live in crowded apartments, most of which were poorly designed. In 1900 Manhattan's 42,700 tenements housed almost 1.6 million people. Such unregulated urban growth created immense problems of health and morale.

During the last quarter of the nineteenth century, cities became so cramped and land so scarce that designers were forced to build upward. In New York City this resulted in "dumbbell" tenement houses. These structures, usually six to eight stories tall and jammed tightly against one another, derived their name from the fact that housing codes required a two-foot-wide air shaft between buildings. The fronts and the backs of adjoining buildings abutted each other, but the midsections were narrower, giving the structures the appearance of dumbbells when viewed from overhead. Twenty-four to thirty-two families would cram into each building. Some city blocks housed almost 4,000 people. The tiny air shafts provided little ventilation; instead, they proved to be a fire hazard, fueling and conveying flames from building to building.

The early tenements were poorly heated and had communal toilets outside in a yard or alley. By the end of the century, tenements featured two toilets to a floor. Shoehorned into their quarters, families had no privacy, free space, or sunshine; children had few places to play except in the city streets; infectious diseases and noxious odors were rampant. Not surprisingly, the mortality rate among the urban poor was much higher than that of the general population. In one poor Chicago district at the end of the century, three out of five babies died before their first birthday.

CITY POLITICS   After the Civil War, the sheer size of the cities helped create a new form of politics. Because local government was often fragmented and beset by parochial rivalries, a need grew for a central organization to coordinate citywide services such as public transportation, sanitation, and utilities. Urban political machines developed, consisting of local committeemen, district captains, and culminating in a political boss. While the bosses granted patronage favors and engaged in graft, buying and selling votes, taking kickbacks and payoffs, they also provided needed services. They distributed food, coal, and money to the poor; found jobs for those who were out of work; sponsored English-language classes for immigrants; organized sports teams, social clubs, and neighborhood gatherings; and generally helped newcomers adjust to their new life. As one ward boss in Boston said, "There's got to be in every ward somebody that any bloke can come to—no matter what he's done—and get help. Help, you understand, none of your law and justice, but help." In return the political professionals felt entitled to some reward for having done the grubby work of the local organization.

CITIES AND THE ENVIRONMENT   Nineteenth-century urban communities were generally filthy and disease ridden, noisy and smelly. They overflowed with garbage, contaminated water, horse manure, roaming pigs, and untreated sewage. Providing clean water was a chronic problem, and raw sewage was dumped into streets and waterways. Epidemics of water-related diseases such as cholera, typhoid fever, and yellow fever ravaged populations. Animal waste was pervasive. In 1900, for example, there were over 3.5 million horses in American cities, each of which generated 20 pounds of manure and several gallons of urine daily. In Chicago alone, 82,000 horses produced 300,000 tons of manure each year. The life expectancy of urban draft horses was only two years, which meant that thousands of horse carcasses had to be disposed of each year. In New York City alone, 15,000 dead horses were removed annually.

During the late nineteenth century, municipal reformers organized to clean up the cities. Their goal was not only to improve the appearance of metropolises but also to remove the environmental causes of disease. The "sanitary reformers," public health officials, and municipal engineers persuaded city governments to banish hogs and cattle, pushed through cleanup campaigns, government-financed water and sewage systems, city trash collection, and electric streetcars to replace horses. By 1900, 94 percent of American cities had developed regular trash-collection services.

Yet such improvements in public health had important social and ecological trade-offs and caused unanticipated problems. Waste that once had been put into the land was now dumped into waterways. Urban populations had to deal with the waste dumped upstream; rural populations had to deal with the urban waste sent downstream.

Similarly, solving the horse-manure problem involved trade-offs. The manure dropped on city streets did cause stench and breed countless flies, many of which carried diseases such as typhoid fever. But urban horse manure also had benefits. Farmers living on the outskirts of cities used it to fertilize hay and vegetable crops. City-generated manure was the agricultural lifeblood of the vegetable farms outside New York, Baltimore, Philadelphia, and Boston. Likewise, human waste was used on farm fields. In the nineteenth century most cities converted the "night soil" from outhouses into agricultural fertilizer.

Urbanization and the Environment

A garbage cart retrieves trash in New York City, ca. 1890.

Ultimately, however, the development of public water and sewer systems and flush toilets separated urban dwellers and their waste from the agricultural cycle at the same time that the emergence of refrigerated railcars and massive meatpacking plants separated most people from their sources of food. While the advances provided great benefits, a flush-and-forget-it mentality emerged. Well into the twentieth century, people presumed that running water purified itself and consequently dumped massive amounts of untreated waste into rivers and bays. What they failed to calculate was the carrying capacity of the waterways. No longer were they contributing to soil fertility. And the high phosphorous content of bodily waste dumped into streams led to algae blooms that sucked the oxygen out of the water and unleashed a string of environmental reactions that suffocated fish and affected marine ecology. By the 1930s, Lake Erie was coated with algae; the fish population had plummeted.

THE NEW IMMIGRATION

The Industrial Revolution brought to American shores waves of new immigrants from every part of the globe. By 1900 nearly 30 percent of the residents of major cities were foreign-born. These newcomers provided much-needed labor, but their arrival created ugly racial and ethnic tensions.

AMERICA'S PULL   The migration of foreigners to the United States has been one of the most powerful forces shaping American history, and this was especially true between 1860 and 1920. In steadily rising numbers European immigrants moved from the great agricultural areas of eastern and southern Europe directly to the foremost cities of America. They wanted to live with others of like language, customs, and religion. Ethnic neighborhoods in American cities preserved familiar folkways and shielded newcomers from the shocks of a strange culture. In 1890 four out of five New Yorkers were foreign-born, a higher proportion than in any other city in the world. New York had twice as many Irish as Dublin, as many Germans as Hamburg, and half as many Italians as Naples. In 1893 Chicago claimed the largest Bohemian (Czech) community in the world, and by 1910 the size of its Polish population ranked behind only the population of Warsaw and Lodz.

This nation of immigrants continued to draw new inhabitants for much the same reasons as always and from much the same segments of society. Immigrants took flight from famine or the dispiriting lack of opportunity in their native lands. They fled racial, religious, and political persecution and compulsory military service. Yet more immigrants were probably pulled by America's promise than were pushed out by conditions at home. American industries, seeking cheap labor, sent recruiting agents abroad. Railroads, eager to sell land and build up the traffic on their lines, put out tempting propaganda in a medley of languages. Many of the western and southern states set up official bureaus and agents to attract immigrants. Under the Contract Labor Act of 1864, the federal government itself encouraged immigration by helping to pay an immigrant's passage. The law was repealed in 1868, but not until 1885 did the government forbid companies to import contract labor, a practice that put immigrant workers under the control of their employers.

After the Civil War the tide of immigration rose from just under 3 million in the 1870s to more than 5 million in the 1880s, then fell to a little over 3.5 million in the depression decade of the 1890s and rose to its high-water mark of nearly 9 million in the first decade of the new century. The numbers declined to 6 million in the 1910s and to 4 million in the 1920s, after which official restrictions cut the flow of immigrants to a negligible level.

Before 1880 immigrants were mainly from northern and western Europe. By the 1870s, however, that pattern had begun to change. The proportion of Slavs and Jews from southern and eastern Europe rose sharply. After 1890 these groups made up a majority of the newcomers, and by the first decade of the

Steerage Deck of the S.S. Pennland, 1893

These immigrants are about to arrive at Ellis Island in New York Harbor. Many newcomers to America settled in cities because they lacked the means to take up farming.

new century they formed 70 percent of the immigrants to this country. Among the new immigrants were Italians, Hungarians, Czechs, Slovaks, Poles, Serbs, Croats, Slovenes, Russians, Romanians, and Greeks—all people whose culture and language were markedly different from those of western Europe and whose religion for the most part was Judaism or Catholicism.

ELLIS ISLAND   As the number of immigrants passing through the port of New York soared during the late nineteenth century, the state-run Castle Garden receiving center overflowed with corruption. Money changers cheated new arrivals, railroad agents overcharged them for tickets, and baggage handlers engaged in blackmail. With reports of these abuses filling the newspapers, Congress ordered an investigation, which resulted in the closure of Castle Garden in 1890. Thereafter the federal government's new Bureau of Immigration took over the business of admitting newcomers to New York City.

To launch this effort, Congress funded the construction of a new reception center on a tiny island off the New Jersey coast, a mile south of Manhattan, near the Statue of Liberty. In 1892 Ellis Island opened its doors to the

The Registry Room at Ellis Island

Inspectors asked arriving passengers twenty-nine probing questions, including "Are you a polygamist?"

"huddled masses" of the world. In 1907 the reception center's busiest year, more than 1 million new arrivals passed through the receiving center, an average of about 5,000 per day; in one day alone immigration officials processed some 11,750 arrivals. These were the immigrants who arrived crammed into the steerage compartments deep in the ships' hulls. Those refugees who could afford first- and second-class cabins did not have to visit Ellis Island; they were examined on board, and most of them simply walked down the gangway onto the docks in lower Manhattan.

Among the arrivals at Ellis Island were many youngsters who would distinguish themselves in their new country: the songwriter Irving Berlin (from Russia), football legend Knute Rockne (from Norway), Supreme Court justice Felix Frankfurter (from Austria), entertainer Al Jolson (from Lithuania), and comedian Bob Hope (from England). But many others found America's opportunities harder to grasp. An old Italian saying expresses the disillusionment that was felt by many: "I came to America because I heard the streets were paved with gold. When I got here, I found out three things: First, the streets weren't paved with gold; second, they weren't paved at all; and third, I was expected to pave them."

MAKING THEIR WAY   Once on American soil in Manhattan or New Jersey, immigrants felt exhilaration, exhaustion, and usually a desperate need for work. Many were greeted by family and friends who had come over before them, others by representatives of the many immigrant-aid societies or by hiring agents offering jobs in mines, mills, or sweatshops. Since most immigrants knew little if any English and nothing about American employment practices, they were easy subjects for exploitation. In exchange for a bit of whiskey and a job, obliging hiring agents claimed a healthy percentage of their wages. Among Italians and Greeks these agents were known as padrones, and they came to dominate the labor market in New York. Other contractors provided train tickets to inland cities such as Buffalo, Pittsburgh, Cleveland, Chicago, Milwaukee, Cincinnati, and St. Louis.

Strangers in a new land, most of the immigrants naturally gravitated to neighborhoods populated by their own kind. The immigrant enclaves—nicknamed Little Italy, Little Hungary, Chinatown, and so on—served as crucial transitional communities between the newcomers' Old World past and their New World future. By 1920 Chicago had some seventeen separate Little Italy colonies scattered across the city, representing various home provinces. In such kinship communities, immigrants practiced their religion, clung to their native customs, conversed in their native tongue, and filled an aching loneliness. But they paid a price for such community solidarity. When the "new immigrants" moved into an area, older residents typically moved out, taking with them whatever social prestige and political influence they had achieved. The quality of living conditions quickly deteriorated as housing and sanitation codes went unenforced.

THE NATIVIST RESPONSE   Many native-born Americans saw the new immigration as a threat to their way of life and their jobs. "Immigrants work for almost nothing," groused one laborer. Others felt that the newcomers threatened traditional American culture. A Stanford University professor called them "illiterate, docile, lacking in self-reliance and initiative, and not possessing the Anglo-Teutonic conceptions of law, order, and government." Cultural differences confirmed in the minds of nativists the assumption that the Nordic peoples of the old immigration were superior to the Slavic and Latin peoples of the new immigration. Many of the new immigrants were illiterate, and more appeared so because they could not speak English. Some resorted to crime, encouraging suspicions that criminals were being quietly helped out of Europe just as they had once been transported from England to the colonies.

Religious prejudice, mainly anti-Catholic and anti-Semitic sentiments, also underlay hostility toward the latest newcomers. During the 1880s

Mulberry Street, Little Italy, New York City, ca. 1900

Immigrants established ethnic enclaves in which they could carry on Old-World traditions.

nativist prejudices spawned groups devoted to stopping the flow of immigrants. The most successful of the nativist groups, the American Protective Association (APA), operated mainly in Protestant strongholds of the upper Mississippi River valley. Its organizer harbored paranoid fantasies of Catholic conspiracies and was especially eager to keep public schools free from Jesuit control. The association grew slowly from its start in 1887 until 1893, when leaders took advantage of a severe depression to draw large numbers of the frustrated to its ranks. The APA promoted restrictions on immigration, more stringent naturalization requirements, workplaces that refused to employ aliens or Catholics, and the teaching of the "American" language in the schools.

IMMIGRATION RESTRICTION   In 1891 the prominent Representative Henry Cabot Lodge of Massachusetts took up the cause of excluding illiterate foreigners—a measure that would have affected much of the new wave of immigrants even though literacy in English was not required. Bills embodying the restriction were vetoed by three presidents on the grounds that they penalized people for lack of opportunity: Grover Cleveland in 1897, William H. Taft in 1913, and Woodrow Wilson in 1915 and 1917. The last time, however, Congress overrode the veto.

Proponents of immigration restriction during the late nineteenth century did succeed in excluding the Chinese, who were victims of every discrimination the European immigrants suffered plus color prejudice as well. By 1880 there were some 75,000 Chinese in California, about one ninth of the state's population. Their nemesis was himself an immigrant (from Ireland), Denis Kearney, leader of the Workingmen's party. Many white workers resented the Chinese for accepting lower wages, but the Asians' greatest sin, the editor of the *New York Nation* opined, was perpetuating "those disgusting habits of thrift, industry, and self-denial."

In 1882 Congress passed over President Chester A. Arthur's veto of the Chinese Exclusion Act. It shut the door to Chinese immigrants for ten years. The legislation received overwhelming support. One congressman explained that because the "industrial army of Asiatic laborers" was increasing the tension between workers and management, "the gate must be

Anti-Chinese Protest, California, 1880

Widespread racism and prejudice against the Chinese resulted in the Chinese Exclusion Act (1882), which banned Chinese immigration.

closed." The Chinese Exclusion Act was periodically renewed before being extended indefinitely in 1902. Not until 1943 were barriers to Chinese immigration finally removed.

The West Coast counterpart to Ellis Island was the Immigration Station on rugged Angel Island, six miles offshore from San Francisco. Opened in 1910, it served as a processing center for tens of thousands of Asian immigrants, most of them Chinese. Although the Chinese Exclusion Act had sharply reduced the flow of Chinese immigrants, it did not stop the influx completely. Those arrivals who could claim a Chinese-American parent were allowed to enter, as were certain officials, teachers, merchants, and students. The powerful prejudice the Chinese immigrants encountered helps explain why over 30 percent of the arrivals at Angel Island were denied entry.

POPULAR CULTURE

The influx of people into large towns and cities created new patterns of recreation and leisure. Whereas people in rural areas were tied to the rituals of the harvest season and intimately connected to their neighbors and extended families, most middle-class urban whites were more mobile and primarily connected to the other members of their nuclear family (made up only of parents and children), and their affluence enabled them to enjoy greater leisure time and an increasing discretionary income. Middle- and upper-class urban families spent much of their leisure time together at home, usually in the parlor, singing around a piano, reading novels, or playing cards, dominoes, backgammon, chess, and checkers.

In the congested metropolitan areas, politics became as much a form of public entertainment as it was a means of providing civic representation and public services. People flocked to hear visiting candidates give speeches in cavernous halls, on outdoor plazas, or from railway cars. In cities such as New York, Philadelphia, Boston, and Chicago, membership in a political party was akin to belonging to a social club. In addition, labor unions provided activities that were more social than economic in nature, and members often visited the union hall as much to socialize as to discuss working conditions. The sheer number of people congregated in cities also helped generate a market for new forms of mass entertainment, such as traveling Wild West shows, vaudeville shows, and spectator sports.

VAUDEVILLE Growing family incomes and innovations in urban transportation—cable cars, subways, electric streetcars and streetlights—enabled more people to take advantage of urban cultural life. Attendance at theaters, operas, and dance halls soared. Those interested in serious music could attend concerts by symphony orchestras appearing in every major city by the end of the nineteenth century. But by far the most popular—and most diverse—form of theatrical entertainment in the late nineteenth century was vaudeville. The term derives from a French word for a play accompanied by music. It emerged in the United States in saloons whose owners sought to attract more customers by offering a free show.

Vaudeville "variety" shows featured comedians, singers, musicians, blackface minstrels, farcical plays, animal acts, jugglers, gymnasts, dancers, mimes, and magicians. Vaudeville houses attracted all social classes and types—men, women, and children—all of whom were expected to behave according to middle-class standards of gentility and decorum. Raucous cheering, booing, and tobacco spitting were prohibited. The shows included something to please every taste and, as such, reflected the heterogeneity of city life. To commemorate the opening of a palatial new Boston theater in 1894, an actress read a dedicatory poem in which she announced that "all are equals here." The vaudeville house was the people's theater; it knew "no favorites, no class." She promised the spectators that the producers would "ever seek the new" in providing entertainers who epitomized "the spice of life, Variety," with its motto, "ever to please—and never to offend."

SALOON CULTURE   The most popular destinations for working-class Americans with free time were saloons and dance halls. The saloon was the poor-man's social club during the late nineteenth century. By 1900 there were more saloons in the United States than there were grocery stores and meat markets. New York City alone had 10,000, or one for every 500 residents. Chicago had one saloon for every 335 people; Houston, one for every 300; and San Francisco, one for every 215. Often sponsored by beer brewers and frequented by local politicians, saloons offered a free lunch to encourage patrons to visit and buy 5¢ beer or 15¢ whiskey.

Saloons provided much more than food and drink, however; they were in effect public homes, offering haven and fellowship to people who often worked ten hours a day, six days a week. Saloons were especially popular among male immigrants seeking friends and companionship in a new land. Saloons served as busy social hubs and were often aligned with local political machines. In New York City in the 1880s, most of the primary elections and local political caucuses were conducted in saloons.

Men went to saloons to learn about jobs, engage in labor-union activities, cash paychecks, mail letters, read newspapers, and gossip about neighborhood affairs. Because saloons were heated, and open long hours and offered public restrooms, they also served as places of refuge for poor people whose own slum tenements or cramped lodging houses were not as accommodating. Many saloons included gymnasiums. Patrons could play handball, chess, billiards, darts, cards, or dice. They could also bet on sporting events. Group singing was an especially popular activity among saloon goers.

Saloons were also defiantly male enclaves. Although women and children occasionally entered a saloon—through a side door—in order to carry home a pail of beer (called "rushing the growler") or to drink at a backroom party, the main bar at the front of the saloon was for men only. Some saloons provided "snugs," small separate rooms for female patrons.

Saloons aroused intense criticism. Anti-liquor societies such as the Women's Christian Temperance Union and the Anti-Saloon League charged that saloons contributed to alcoholism, divorce, crime, and absenteeism from work. The reformers demanded that saloons be closed down. Yet drunkenness in saloons was the exception rather than the rule. To be sure, most patrons of working-class saloons had little money to waste, and recent studies have revealed that the average amount of money spent on liquor was no more than 5 percent of a man's annual income. Saloons were the primary locus of the workingman's leisure time and political activity. As a journalist

A Workingman's Social Center

Men gather at a neighborhood saloon in New York City, ca. 1895.

observed, "The saloon is, in short, the social and intellectual center of the neighborhood."

OUTDOOR RECREATION   The congestion and disease associated with city life led many people to participate in forms of outdoor recreation intended to restore their vitality and improve their health. A movement to create urban parks flourished after the construction of New York's Central Park in 1858. Its designer, Frederick Law Olmsted, viewed city parks as much more than recreational centers; Olmsted sought to create oases of culture that would promote social stability and cohesion. He was convinced that Central Park would exercise "a distinctly harmonizing and refining influence upon the most unfortunate and lawless classes of the city—an influence favorable to courtesy, self-control, and temperance." Olmsted went on to design parks for Boston, Brooklyn, Chicago, Philadelphia, and San Francisco.

Although originally intended as places where people could walk and commune with nature, parks soon offered more vigorous forms of exercise and recreation—for men and women. During most of the nineteenth century, prevailing social attitudes scoffed at the notion of "proper" young women participating in even the lightest athletic endeavors. Women were deemed too delicate for such behavior. Before the Civil War, women essentially had only one exercise option: pedestrianism, the formal name for outdoor walking. After the war, however, women enrolled in colleges in growing numbers, began to participate in physical education, and they in turn demanded access to more vigorous sports.

Croquet and tennis courts were among the first additions to city parks because they took up little space and required little maintenance. Because croquet could be played by both sexes, it combined the virtues of sport with the opportunities of courtship. Croquet as a public sport suffered a setback in the 1890s, however, when Boston clergymen lambasted the drinking, gambling, and licentious behavior associated with it.

Lawn tennis was invented by an Englishman in 1873 and arrived in the United States a year later. By 1885 Central Park had thirty courts. Lawn tennis was originally viewed as a leisurely sport best suited for women. The Harvard student newspaper declared in 1878 that the sport was "well enough for a lazy or *weak* man, but men who have rowed or taken part in a nobler sport should blush to be seen playing Lawn Tennis."

Even more popular than croquet or tennis was cycling, or "wheeling." In the 1870s bicycles began to be manufactured in the United States, and by the end of the century a bicycle craze had swept the country. Bicycles were especially popular with women who chafed at the restricting conventions of the Victorian era. The new vehicles offered exercise, freedom, and access to the countryside. Female cyclists were able to discard their cumbersome corsets and full dresses in favor of "bloomers" and split skirts.

The urban working poor could not afford to acquire a bicycle or join a croquet club, however. Nor did they have as much free time as the affluent. At the end of their long days and on Sundays they eagerly sought recreation and fellowship on street corners or on the front stoops of their apartment buildings. Organ grinders and musicians would perform on the sidewalks among the food vendors. Many ethnic groups, especially the Germans and the Irish, formed male singing, drinking, or gymnastic clubs. Working folk also attended bare-knuckle boxing matches or baseball games and on Sundays would gather for picnics. By the end of the century, large-scale amusement

Tandem Tricycle

In spite of the danger and discomfort of early bicycles, "wheeling" became a popular form of recreation and mode of transportation.

Steeplechase Park, Coney Island, Brooklyn, New York

Members of the working-class could afford the inexpensive rides at this popular amusement park.

parks such as Brooklyn's Coney Island provided entertainment for the entire family. Yet many inner-city youth could not afford the trolley fare, so the crowded streets and dangerous alleys became their playgrounds.

WORKINGWOMEN AND LEISURE   In contrast to the male public culture centered in saloons, the leisure activities of working-class women, many of them immigrants, were more limited at the end of the nineteenth century. Married women were so encumbered by housework and maternal responsibilities that they had little free time. As a social worker noted, "The men have the saloons, political clubs, trade-unions or [fraternal] lodges for their recreation . . . while the mothers have almost no recreation, only a dreary round of work, day after day, with occasionally doorstep gossip to vary the monotony of their lives." Married working-class women could not afford domestic help or sitters for their children, so they usually had to combine entertainment with their work. They often used the streets as their public space. Washing clothes, supervising children, or shopping at the local market provided opportunities for fellowship with other women.

Single women had more opportunities for leisure and recreation than did working mothers. As the average workday gradually declined from twelve hours in the 1880s to nine or ten hours in 1914, all working people had more free time. In the cities young factory hands, domestic servants, office workers, and retail clerks eagerly sought access to urban pleasures. City amusements enticed women from their congested and drab tenements. Women flocked to dance halls, theaters, amusement parks, and picnic grounds. On hot summer days many working-class folk went to public beaches. For young workingwomen in and around New York City, for example, an excursion to Coney Island was a special treat. Not only could they swim, but they could also experience the sideshow attractions, vaudeville shows, dance pavilions, restaurants, and boardwalk. By 1900 as many as 500,000 people converged on Coney Island on Saturdays and Sundays. With the advent of movie theaters during the second decade of the twentieth century, the cinema became the most popular form of entertainment for women.

Young single women participated in urban amusements for a variety of reasons: escape, pleasure, adventure, companionship, and autonomy. As a promotional flyer for a movie theater promised, "If you are tired of life, go to the movies. If you are sick of troubles rife, go to the picture show. You will forget your unpaid bills, rheumatism and other ills, if you stow your pills and go to the picture show." Urban recreational and entertainment activities also allowed opportunities for romance and sexual relationships. Not surprisingly, young women eager for such recreation encountered far more obstacles than did young men. Just as reformers sought to shut down saloons, parental and societal concerns tried to restrict the freedom of young single women to engage in "cheap amusements." Daughters of immigrants confronted "Old World" notions of leisure and pleasure that conflicted with those of modern American culture. Yet many young women followed their own wishes and in so doing helped carve out their own social sphere.

SPECTATOR SPORTS   In the last quarter of the nineteenth century, new spectator sports such as college football and basketball and professional baseball gained mass popularity, reflecting the growing urbanization of life. People could gather easily for sporting events in the large cities. And news of the games could be conveyed quickly by newspapers and specialized sports magazines that relied upon telegraph reports. Saloons also posted the scores. Athletic rivalries between distant cities were made possible by the network of railroads spanning the continent. Spectator sports became urban extravaganzas, unifying the diverse ethnic groups in the large cities and attracting people with the leisure time and cash to spend on watching others perform— or bet on the outcome.

Football emerged as a modified form of soccer and rugby. The College of New Jersey (Princeton) and Rutgers played the first college football game in 1869. By the end of the century, scores of colleges and high schools had football teams, and some college games attracted more than 50,000 spectators. Basketball was invented in 1891, when Dr. James Naismith, a physical-education instructor, nailed two peach baskets to the walls of the Young Men's Christian Association training school in Springfield, Massachusetts. Naismith wanted to create an indoor winter game that could be played between the fall football and spring baseball seasons. Basketball quickly grew in popularity among boys and girls. Vassar and Smith Colleges added the sport in 1892. In 1893, Vanderbilt University, in Nashville, became the first college to field a men's team.

Baseball Card, 1887

The excitement of rooting for the home team united all classes.

Baseball laid claim to being America's national pastime at midcentury. Contrary to popular opinion, Abner Doubleday did not invent the game. Instead, Alexander Cartwright, a New York bank clerk and sportsman, is recognized as the father of organized baseball. In 1845 he gathered a group of merchants, stockbrokers, and physicians to form the Knickerbocker Base Ball Club of New York.

The first professional baseball team was the Cincinnati Red Stockings, which made its appearance in 1869. In 1900 the American League was organized, and two years later the first World Series was held. Baseball became the "national pastime" and the most democratic sport in America. People from all social classes (mostly men) attended the games, and ethnic immigrants were among the most faithful fans. The *St. Louis Post-Dispatch* reported in 1883 that "a glance at

the audience on any fine day at the ball park will reveal . . . telegraph operators, printers who work at night, travelling men [salesmen] . . . men of
leisure . . . men of capital, bank clerks who get away [from work] at 3 P.M.,
real estate men . . . barkeepers . . . hotel clerks, actors and employees of the
theater, policemen and firemen on their day off . . . butchers and bakers."
Cheering for a city baseball team gave rootless people a common loyalty and
a sense of belonging.

Only white players were allowed in the major leagues. African
Americans played on "minor-league" teams or in all-black Negro leagues.
In 1887, the Cuban Giants, an exhibition team made up of black players,
traveled the country. A few major-league white teams agreed to play them.
An African-American-owned newspaper announced in early 1888 that
the Cuban Giants "have defeated the New Yorks, 4 games out of 5, and are
now virtually champions of the world." But, it added, "the St. Louis
Browns, Detroits and Chicagos, afflicted by Negrophobia and unable to
bear the odium of being beaten by colored men, refused to accept their
challenge."

By the end of the nineteenth century, sports of all kinds had become a major cultural phenomenon in the United States. A writer for *Harper's Weekly*
announced in 1895 that "ball matches, football games, tennis tournaments, bicycle races, [and] regattas, have become part of our national life." They "are
watched with eagerness and discussed with enthusiasm and understanding by
all manner of people, from the day-laborer to the millionaire." One reporter in
the 1890s referred to the "athletic craze" that was sweeping the American
imagination. Moreover, it was in 1892 that a Frenchman, Pierre de Coubertin,
called for the revival of the ancient Olympic Games, and the first modern
olympiad was held four years later.

EDUCATION AND THE PROFESSIONS

THE SPREAD OF PUBLIC EDUCATION   The spread of public education, spurred partly by the determination to "Americanize" immigrant
children, helped quicken the emergence of a new urban culture. In 1870
there were 7 million pupils in public schools; by 1920 the number had risen
to 22 million. The percentage of school-age children in attendance went
from 57 to 78 during those years.

The spread of secondary schools accounted for much of the increased enrollment in public schools. In antebellum America private academies prepared those who intended to enter college. At the beginning of the Civil War,

there were only about 100 public high schools in the whole country, but their number grew to about 800 in 1880 and to 6,000 at the turn of the century. Their curricula at first copied the academies' emphasis on higher mathematics and classical languages, but the public schools gradually accommodated their programs to those not going on to college, devising vocational training in such arts as bookkeeping, typing, drafting, and the use of tools.

VOCATIONAL TRAINING   Vocational training was most intensely promoted after the Civil War by missionary schools for African Americans in the South, such as the Hampton Institute in Virginia, which trained Booker T. Washington. Congress had supported vocational training at the college level for many years. The Morrill Act of 1862 granted each state 30,000 acres per representative and senator, the income from which was to be applied to teaching agriculture and the mechanic arts in what came to be known as the land-grant colleges. Among the new institutions were Clemson University, Pennsylvania State University, and Iowa State University. In 1890 a second Morrill Act provided federal grants to these colleges.

Vocational Education for African Americans

Students in a current-events class at Virginia's Hampton Institute, 1899.

HIGHER EDUCATION American colleges at this time, whether church schools or state universities, sought to instill discipline and morality. They offered a curriculum stressing mathematics and the classics (and, in church schools, theology), along with ethics and rhetoric. History, modern languages and literature, and some science were tolerated, although laboratory work was usually limited to a professor's demonstration to his class.

Nevertheless, the demand for higher learning led to an increase in the college-student population, from 52,000 in 1870 to 157,000 in 1890 and 600,000 in 1920. To accommodate the diverse needs of these growing numbers, colleges moved from rigidly prescribed courses toward an elective system. The new approach allowed students to favor their strong points and colleges to expand their scope. But as Henry Cabot Lodge complained, it also allowed students to "escape without learning anything at all by a judicious selection of unrelated subjects taken up only because they were easy or because the burden imposed by those who taught them was light."

Colleges remained largely male bastions, but women's access to higher education improved markedly in the late nineteenth century. Before the Civil War a few men's colleges had admitted women, and most state universities in the West were open to women from the start. But colleges in the South and

Women as Students

An astronomy class at Vassar College, 1880.

the East fell in line very slowly. Vassar, opened in 1865, was the first women's college to teach by the same standards as the best of the men's colleges. In the 1870s two more excellent women's schools appeared in Massachusetts: Wellesley and Smith, the latter being the first to set the same admission requirements as men's colleges. By the end of the century, women made up more than one third of all college students.

The dominant new trend in American higher education after the Civil War was the rise of the graduate school. The versatile professors of the antebellum era had a knowledge more broad than deep. They engaged in little research, nor were they expected to advance the frontiers of knowledge. But gradually more and more Americans experienced a different system at the German universities, where training was more systematic and focused. After the Civil War the German system became the basis for the modern American university. Yale awarded its first doctorate of philosophy in 1861, and Harvard awarded its in 1872.

The Johns Hopkins University, opened in Baltimore in 1876, set a precedent by making graduate work its chief concern. Graduate students gathered in seminar rooms or laboratories, where under the guidance of an experienced scholar they learned a craft, much as journeymen had in the medieval guilds. The crowning achievement, signifying admission to full membership in the craft, was a masterpiece—in this case the doctoral dissertation, which was expected to make an original contribution to knowledge.

THEORIES OF SOCIAL CHANGE

Every field of thought in the post–Civil War years felt the impact of Charles Darwin's *On the Origin of Species* (1859), which argued that existing species, including humanity itself, had evolved through a long process of "natural selection" from less complex forms of life: those species that adapted to survival by reason of quickness, shrewdness, or other advantages reproduced their kind, while others fell by the wayside.

The idea of species evolution shocked people who held conventional religious views by contradicting a literal interpretation of the biblical creation stories. Heated arguments arose between scientists and clergymen. Some of the faithful rejected Darwin's doctrine while others found their faith severely shaken not only by evolutionary theory but also by the urging of professional scholars to apply the critical standards of scholarship to the Bible itself. Most of the faithful, however, came to reconcile science and religion. They viewed evolution as the divine will, one of the secondary causes through which God worked.

SOCIAL DARWINISM Though Charles Darwin's theory of evolution applied only to biological phenomena, other thinkers drew broader inferences from it. The temptation to apply evolutionary theory to the social (human) world proved irresistible. Darwin's fellow Englishman Herbert Spencer became the first major prophet of social Darwinism and an important influence on American thought. Spencer argued that human society and institutions, like organ-

Charles Darwin

Darwin's theories influenced more than a century of political debate.

isms, passed through the process of natural selection, which resulted, in Spencer's chilling phrase, in the "survival of the fittest." For Spencer, social evolution implied progress, ending "only in the establishment of the greatest perfection and the most complete happiness."

If, as Spencer believed, society naturally evolved for the better, then government interference with the process of social evolution was a serious mistake. Social Darwinism implied a government policy of hands off; it decried the regulation of business, the graduated income tax, sanitation and housing regulations, and even protection against medical quacks. Such intervention, Spencer charged, would help the "unfit" survive and thereby impede progress. The only acceptable charity was voluntary, and even that was of dubious value. Spencer warned that "fostering the good-for-nothing at the expense of the good, is an extreme cruelty."

For Spencer and his many American supporters, successful businessmen and corporations were the engines of social progress. If small businesses were crowded out by trusts and monopolies, that, too, was part of the evolutionary process. John D. Rockefeller told his Baptist Sunday-school class that the "growth of a large business is merely a survival of the fittest. . . . This is not an evil tendency in business. It is merely the working-out of a law of nature and a law of God."

The ideas of Darwin and Spencer spread quickly. *Popular Science Monthly,* founded in 1872, became the chief medium for popularizing Darwinism. That same year, Spencer's chief academic disciple, William Graham Sumner,

Lester Frank Ward

Proponent of reform Darwinism.

took up the new chair of political and social science at Yale and preached the gospel of natural selection. Sumner's most lasting contribution, made in his book *Folkways* (1907), was to argue that it would be a mistake for government to interfere with established customs in the name of ideals of equality or natural rights.

REFORM DARWINISM Efforts to use Darwinism to promote "rugged individualism" did not go without challenge. Reform found its major philosopher in an obscure Washington civil servant, Lester Frank Ward, who fought his way up from poverty and never lost his empathy for the underdog. Ward's book *Dynamic Sociology* (1883) singled out one product of evolution that Darwin and Spencer had neglected: the human brain. People, unlike animals, had minds that could shape social evolution. Far from being the helpless pawn of evolution, Ward argued, humanity could control the process. Ward's reform Darwinism challenged Sumner's conservative social Darwinism, holding that cooperation, not competition, would better promote progress. According to Ward, Sumner's "irrational distrust of government" might have been justified in an earlier day of autocracy but was not applicable under a representative system. Government could become the agency of progress by striving to reach two main goals: to ameliorate poverty, which impeded the development of the mind, and to promote the education of the masses. "Intelligence, far more than necessity," Ward wrote, "is the mother of invention," and "the influence of knowledge as a social factor, like that of wealth, is proportional to the extent of its distribution." Intellect, rightly informed by science, could promote social improvement.

PRAGMATISM Around the turn of the century, the concept of evolutionary development found expression in a philosophical principle set forth in mature form by William James in his book *Pragmatism: A New Name for Some Old Ways of Thinking* (1907). James, a professor of philosophy and psychology at Harvard, shared Lester Frank Ward's focus on the role of ideas in the process of evolution. Pragmatists, said James, believed that ideas gain their validity not from their inherent truth but from their social consequences and practical applications. Thus scientists could test the validity of their ideas in the laboratory and judge their import by their applications. Pragmatism reflected a quality often looked upon as genuinely American: the inventive, experimental spirit that judged ideas on their results and their ability to adapt to changing social needs and environments.

John Dewey, who would become the chief philosopher of pragmatism after James, preferred the term *instrumentalism,* by which he meant that ideas were instruments for action, especially for social reform. Dewey, unlike James, threw himself into movements for the rights of labor and women, the promotion of peace, and the reform of education. He believed that education was the process through which society would gradually progress toward the goal of economic democracy.

William James

The conceptual founder of pragmatism.

THE LOCAL COLORISTS   Writers of fiction in the post–Civil War decades responded in different ways to the changes in life and thought. What came to be called the local-color movement expressed the nostalgia of people moving from a rural culture to an urban one and longing for those places where the old folkways survived. Sarah Orne Jewett depicted the down-easters of her native Maine most enduringly in the stories and sketches collected in *The Country of the Pointed Firs* (1896). Jewett's creative vision was always backward looking and affectionate. She looked upon her parents' generation "as the one to which I really belong—I who was brought up with grandfathers and granduncles and aunts for my best playmates."

CLEMENS   The best of the local colorists could find universal truths in common life, and Samuel Langhorne Clemens (Mark Twain) transcended them all. A native of Missouri, he was impelled to work at age twelve, becoming first a printer and then a Mississippi riverboat pilot. When the Civil War shut down the river traffic, he briefly joined a Confederate militia company, then left with his brother, Orion, for Nevada. He moved on to California in 1864 and first gained widespread notice with his tall tale of the gold country, "The Celebrated

A Tramp Abroad (1880)

Mark Twain in the frontispiece to his travel narrative.

Jumping Frog of Calaveras County" (1865). In 1867 the San Francisco *Alta Californian* staked him to a tour of the Mediterranean, and his humorous reports on the trip, revised and collected as *The Innocents Abroad* (1869), established him as a funny man much in demand on the lecture circuit. With the success of *Roughing It* (1872), an account of his western years, he moved to Hartford, Connecticut, and was able to establish himself as a full-time author and hilarious lecturer.

Clemens was the first great American writer born and raised west of the Appalachians. His early writings accentuated his western background, but for his greatest books he drew heavily upon his boyhood in a border slave state and the tall-tale tradition of southwestern humor. In *The Adventures of Tom Sawyer* (1876), he evoked in fiction the prewar Hannibal, Missouri, where his own boyhood was cut so short. Clemens's masterpiece, *The Adventures of Huckleberry Finn* (1884), created unforgettable characters in Huck Finn, his shiftless father, the slave Jim, the Widow Douglas, "the King," and "the Duke." The product of an erratic upbringing, Huck Finn embodied the instinct of every red-blooded American boy to "light out for the territory" whenever polite society set out to civilize him. Huck's effort to help his friend Jim escape bondage expressed well the moral dilemmas imposed by slavery on everyone. Many years later another great American writer, Ernest Hemingway, would claim that "all modern American literature comes from one book by Mark Twain, called *Huckleberry Finn*."

LITERARY NATURALISM   During the 1890s a new literary school, known as naturalism, shocked genteel sensibilities. The naturalists were young literary rebels who imported scientific determinism into literature, viewing humanity as part of the animal world, prey to natural forces and internal drives without control over them or even a full understanding of them.

Stephen Crane in *Maggie: A Girl of the Streets* (1893) and *The Red Badge of Courage* (1895) portrayed people caught up in environments that were beyond their control. *Maggie* depicts a tenement girl driven to prostitution and death amid scenes so sordid that Crane had to finance the book's publication himself. *The Red Badge of Courage,* his masterpiece, tells the story of a young man going through his baptism of fire in the Civil War and thus evokes nobility and courage amid the ungovernable carnage of war.

Two naturalists achieved a degree of popular success: Jack London and Theodore Dreiser. London was both a professed socialist and a believer in the German philosopher Friedrich Nietzsche's doctrine of the superman. In adventure stories such as *The Call of the Wild* (1903) and *The Sea Wolf* (1904), London celebrated the triumph of brute force and the will to survive. He reinforced his point about animal force in *The Call of the Wild.* The novel's protagonist is not a superman but a superdog that reverts to the wild in Alaska and runs with a wolf pack.

Theodore Dreiser shocked the genteel public probably more than the others, presenting protagonists who sinned without remorse and without punishment. *Sister Carrie* (1900), a counterpoint to Crane's *Maggie,* departed from it by having Carrie Meeber survive illicit loves and go on to success on the stage. In *The Financier* (1912) and *The Titan* (1914), Dreiser's main character is a sexual athlete and a man of elemental force who rises to a dominant position in business and society.

SOCIAL CRITICISM   Behind their dogma of determinism, the naturalists harbored intense outrage at human misery and social injustice. Other writers shared their indignation but addressed themselves more directly to protest and reform. One of the most influential of these activists was Henry George, a California printer and journalist. During a visit to New York, he was shocked by the contrast the city offered between wealth and poverty. The basic social problem, he reasoned, was the "unearned increment" in wealth that came to those who owned land. The fruit of his thought, *Progress and Poverty* (1879), a thick and difficult book, sold slowly at first but by 1905 had sold about 2 million copies in several languages.

George held that everyone had as much right to the use of the land as to the air. Nobody had a right to the value that accrued from the land, since that was created by the community, not by its owner. George proposed simply to tax the "unearned" increment in the value of the land, or the rent. His idea was widely propagated and actually affected tax policy here and there, but his influence on the thinking of the day came less from his "single-tax" panacea than from the paradox he posed in his title, *Progress and Poverty.*

Another social critic, Thorstein Veblen, brought to his work a background of formal training in economics and the purpose of making economics more an evolutionary or historical science. By all accounts he taught miserably, even inaudibly, and seldom held a job for long, but he wrote brilliantly. In his best-known work, *The Theory of the Leisure Class* (1899), he examined the pecuniary values of the middle classes and introduced phrases that have since become almost clichés: *conspicuous consumption* and *conspicuous leisure*. With the advent of industrial society, Veblen argued, property became the conventional basis of reputation. For the upper classes, moreover, it became necessary to consume time nonproductively as evidence of the ability to afford a life of leisure. In this and later works, Veblen held that the division between industrial experts and business managers was widening to a dangerous point. The businessman's interest in profits, combined with his ignorance of efficiency, produced wasteful organization and a failure to realize the full potential of modern technology.

THE SOCIAL GOSPEL

During the late nineteenth century more and more people took action to address the complex social problems generated by rapid urban and industrial growth. Some reformers focused on legislative solutions to social problems; others stressed philanthropy or organized charity. A few militants promoted socialism or anarchism. Whatever the method or approach, however, social reformers were on the march at the turn of the century, and their activities gave to American life a new urgency and energy.

THE RISE OF THE INSTITUTIONAL CHURCH   Churches responded slowly to the mounting social concerns, for American Protestantism had become one of the main props of the established order. The Reverend Henry Ward Beecher, pastor of the fashionable Plymouth Congregational Church in Brooklyn, preached success, social Darwinism, and the unworthiness of the poor. As the middle classes moved out to the streetcar suburbs, their churches followed. From 1868 to 1888, for instance, seventeen Protestant churches abandoned the area below Fourteenth Street in Manhattan. In the center of Chicago, 60,000 residents had no church, Protestant or Catholic. Where churches became prosperous, they fell easily under the spell of respectability and do-nothing social Darwinism.

Many churches responded to the human needs of the time, however, by devoting their resources to community service and care of the unfortunate. The Young Men's Christian Association (YMCA) entered the United States from England in the 1850s and grew rapidly after 1870; the Salvation Army, founded in London in 1878, came to the United States a year later. Churches in

Social Service

A Salvation Army Group in Flint, Michigan, 1894.

urban districts began to develop institutional features that were more social than strictly religious in function. After the Civil War, churches acquired gymnasiums, libraries, lecture rooms, and other facilities for social programs. Russell Conwell's Baptist Temple in Philadelphia included, among other features, a night school for working people that grew into Temple University.

RELIGIOUS REFORMERS   Church leaders who feared that Christianity was losing influence in the cities preached what came to be called the social gospel. Washington Gladden of Columbus, Ohio, preached that true Christianity lies not in rituals, dogmas, or even the mystical experience of God but in the principle that "thou shalt love thy neighbor as thyself." Christian law should govern the workplace, with worker and employer united in serving each other's interest. Gladden argued for labor's right to organize and complained that class distinctions split congregations as well.

The acknowledged intellectual leader of the social-gospel movement, however, was the Baptist Walter Rauschenbusch, professor at the Colgate-Rochester Theological Seminary. In *Christianity and the Social Crisis* (1907) and other works, he developed a theological basis for the movement in the kingdom of God. This kingdom existed in the churches themselves, Rauschenbusch held, but it embraced far more than these: "It is the Christian transfiguration of the social order. The church is one social institution alongside of the family, the industrial organization of society, and the State. The Kingdom of God is in all these, and realizes itself through them all." The church was indispensable to religion, but "the greatest future awaits religion in the public life of humanity."

EARLY EFFORTS AT URBAN REFORM

THE SETTLEMENT-HOUSE MOVEMENT   While preachers of the social gospel dispensed inspiration, other dedicated reformers attacked the problems of the slums from residential and community centers called settlement houses. By 1900 perhaps 100 settlement houses existed in the United States, some of the best known being Jane Addams and Ellen Starr's Hull-House in Chicago (1889), Robert A. Woods's South End House in Boston (1891), and Lillian Wald's Henry Street Settlement (1893) in New York.

The settlement houses were staffed mainly by young middle-class idealists, a majority of them college-trained women who had few other outlets for meaningful work outside the home. Settlement workers sought to broaden the horizons and improve the lives of slum dwellers in diverse ways. At Hull-House, for instance, Jane Addams rejected the "do-goodism" spirit of religious reformers and tried to avoid the assumption that she and the other social workers knew what was best for the poor immigrants. Her approach used pragmatism rather than preaching, focusing on the practical needs of the working poor. She and her staff helped enroll neighborhood children in clubs and kindergartens and set up a nursery to care for the infant children of working mothers. The program gradually expanded as Hull-House sponsored health clinics, lectures, music and art studios, an employment bureau, men's clubs, training in skills such as bookbinding, a gymnasium, and a savings bank.

Settlement-house leaders realized, however, that the spreading slums made their work as effective as bailing out the ocean with a teaspoon. They therefore organized political support for housing laws, public playgrounds, juvenile courts, mothers' pensions, workers' compensation laws, and legislation prohibiting child labor. Lillian Wald promoted

Jane Addams

By the end of the century, religious groups were taking up the settlement-house movement.

the establishment of the federal Children's Bureau in 1912, and Jane Addams, for her work in the peace movement, received the Nobel Peace Prize for 1931. When Addams died, in 1935, she was the most venerated woman in America.

WOMEN'S EMPLOYMENT AND SUFFRAGE   Settlement-house workers, insofar as they were paid, made up but a fraction of all gainfully employed women. With the growth of the population, the number of employed women steadily increased, as did the percentage of women in the labor force and in the population. The greatest leaps forward came in the 1880s and the 1900s, which were also peak decades of immigration, a correlation that can be explained by the immigrants' need for income. The number of employed women went from over 2.6 million in 1880 to 4 million in 1890, then from 5.1 million in 1900 to 7.8 million in 1910. "Between 1880 and 1900 the employment of women in most parts of the economy became an established fact," wrote one historian. "This was surely the most significant event in the modern history of women." Through all those years domestic work remained the largest category of employment for women; teaching and nursing also remained among the leading fields. The main change was that clerical work (bookkeeping, stenography, and the like) and sales jobs became increasingly available to women.

These changes in occupational status had little connection to the women's rights movement, which increasingly focused on the issue of suffrage. Immediately after the Civil War, Susan B. Anthony, a seasoned veteran of the movement, demanded that the Fifteenth Amendment guarantee the vote for women as well as black men. She made little impression on the defenders of a man's prerogative, however, who insisted that women belonged in the domestic sphere.

In 1869 the unity of the women's movement was broken in a manner reminiscent of the anti-slavery rift three decades before. The question once again was whether the movement should concentrate on one overriding issue. Susan B. Anthony and Elizabeth Cady Stanton founded the National Woman Suffrage Association to promote a women's suffrage amendment to the Constitution, but they looked upon the vote as but one among many feminist causes to be promoted. Later that year, activists formed the American Woman Suffrage Association, which focused single-mindedly on the suffrage as the first and basic reform.

It would be another half century before the battle would be won, and the long struggle focused the women's cause ever more on the primary objective of the vote. In 1890, after three years of negotiation, the rival groups united as the National American Woman Suffrage Association, with Elizabeth Cady Stanton as president for two years, to be followed by Susan B. Anthony until 1900. The work thereafter was carried on by a new generation of activists, led by Anna

Elizabeth Cady Stanton

In this 1870s engraving, Stanton speaks at a meeting of the National Woman's Suffrage Association.

Howard Shaw and Carrie Chapman Catt. Over the years the movement achieved some local and partial victories as a few states granted women suffrage in school-board or municipal elections or bond referenda. In 1869 the territory of Wyoming granted full suffrage to women, and after 1890 it retained women's suffrage when it became a state. Three other western states soon followed suit: Colorado in 1893, Utah and Idaho in 1896. But women's suffrage lost in a California referendum in 1896 by a dishearteningly narrow margin.

The movement remained in the doldrums until the cause easily won a Washington State referendum in 1910 and then carried California by a close majority in 1911. The following year three more western states—Arizona, Kansas, and Oregon—joined in to make a total of nine western states with full suffrage. In 1913 Illinois granted women suffrage in presidential and municipal elections. Yet not until New York acted in 1917 did a state east of the Mississippi adopt universal suffrage. In 1878 California's Senator A. A. Sargent introduced the "Anthony amendment," a women's suffrage provision that remained before Congress until 1896 and then vanished until 1919, when it was finally passed by Congress and ratified a year later.

Despite the focus on the vote, women did not confine their public work to that issue. In 1866 the Young Women's Christian Association (YWCA), a parallel to the YMCA, appeared in Boston and spread elsewhere. The New England

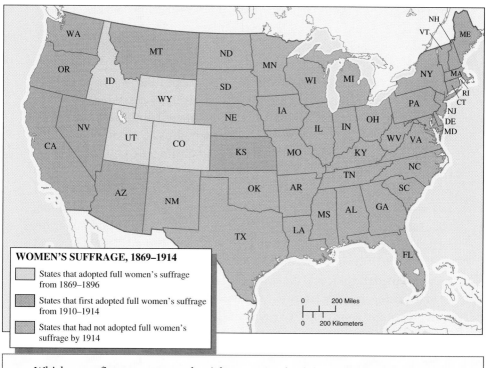

WOMEN'S SUFFRAGE, 1869–1914

☐ States that adopted full women's suffrage from 1869–1896

☐ States that first adopted full women's suffrage from 1910–1914

☐ States that had not adopted full women's suffrage by 1914

0   200 Miles

0   200 Kilometers

Which states first gave women the right to vote? Why did it take fifty-one years, from Wyoming's grant of full suffrage to women until Congress's ratification of the Nineteenth Amendment, for women to receive the rigth to vote? How was suffrage part of a larger women's reform movement?

Women's Club, started in 1868 by Julia Ward Howe and others, was an early example of the women's clubs that proliferated to the extent that a General Federation of Women's Clubs tied them together in 1890. Many women's clubs confined themselves to "literary" and social activities, but others became deeply involved in charities and reform. The New York Consumers' League, formed in 1890, and the National Consumers' League, formed nine years later, sought to make the buying public, chiefly women, aware of labor conditions. One of its devices was the "White List" of firms that met its minimum standards. The National Women's Trade Union League, founded in 1903, performed a similar function of bringing educated and middle-class women together with workingwomen for the benefit of women unionists.

These and the many other women's groups of the time may have aroused the fear in opponents to women's suffrage that voting women would tilt the nation toward reform. This was the fear of the brewing and liquor interests, large business interests generally, and political-machine bosses. Others, mainly in the South, opposed national women's suffrage on the ground that black women would be enfranchised or that it would violate states' rights.

TOWARD A WELFARE STATE   Even without the support of voting women in most places, the states adopted rudimentary measures to regulate big business and labor conditions in the public interest. By the end of the century, nearly every state had begun to regulate railroads, if not always effectively, and had moved to supervise banks and insurance companies. By one count the states and territories passed over 1,600 laws between 1887 and 1897 relating to conditions of work: limiting the number of hours required of workers, providing special protection for women, limiting or forbidding child labor, requiring that wages be paid regularly and in cash, and calling for factory inspections. Nearly all states had boards or commissioners of labor, and some had boards of conciliation and arbitration. Still, conservative judges limited the practical impact of the laws.

In thwarting new regulatory efforts, the Supreme Court used a revised interpretation of the Fourteenth Amendment clauses forbidding the states to "deprive any person of life, liberty, or property, without due process of law" or to deny any person "the equal protection of the laws." Two significant steps of legal reasoning turned the due-process clause into a bulwark of private property. First, the judges reasoned that the word *person* in the clause included corporations, which in other connections were legally artificial persons with the rights to own property, buy and sell, and sue and be sued like natural persons. Second, the courts moved away from the old view that "due process" referred only to correct procedures, adopting instead the doctrine of "substantive due process," which allowed courts to review the substance of an action. The principle of substantive due process enabled judges to overturn laws that deprived persons of property to an unreasonable degree and thereby violated due process.

From the due-process clause the Court also derived a new doctrine of "liberty of contract," defined as being within the liberties protected by the due-process clause. Liberty, the Court ruled in 1897, involved "not only the right of the citizen to be free from the mere physical restraint of his person, . . . but the term is deemed to embrace the right of the citizen to be free in the enjoyment of all his faculties" and to be free "to enter into all contracts" to carry out such purposes. When it came to labor laws, this translated into an employee's "liberty" to contract for work under the most oppressive conditions without interference from the state. The courts continued to apply such an interpretation well into the twentieth century.

At the end of the nineteenth century, opinion in the country stood poised between such conservative rigidities and a growing sense that new corporate structures and social problems required more progressive action. "By the last two decades of the century," wrote one observer, "many thoughtful men had begun to march under various banners declaring that somewhere and somehow the promise of the American dream had been lost—they often said 'betrayed'—and that drastic changes needed to be made to recapture it."

The last two decades of the nineteenth century had already seen a slow erosion of laissez-faire values, which had found their most secure home in the courts. From the social philosophy of the reformers, social gospelers, and Populists there emerged a concept of the general-welfare state, which, in the words of one historian, sought "to promote the general welfare not by rendering itself inconspicuous but by taking such positive action as is deemed necessary to improve the condition under which its citizens live and work." The reformers supplied no agreed-upon blueprint for a general-welfare utopia, but "simply assumed that government could promote the public interest by appropriate positive action ... whenever the circumstances indicated that such action would further the common weal." The conflict between this notion and laissez-faire values went on into the new century, but by the mid–twentieth century, after the Progressive movement, the New Deal, and the Fair Deal, the conflict would be "resolved in theory, in practice, and in public esteem in favor of the general-welfare state."

MAKING CONNECTIONS

- As the next chapter shows, the presidential election of 1896 was in many ways a contest between the new urban values discussed in this chapter and those of a more traditional rural society.

- The reform impulse discussed in this chapter finds voice again in the discussion of the Progressive movement in Chapter 24.

- The nativist thinking discussed in this chapter fueled the restrictive immigration laws of the 1920s, discussed in Chapter 26.

FURTHER READING

For a survey of urbanization, see David R. Goldfield's *Urban America: A History*, 2nd ed. (1989). Gunther Barth discusses the emergence of a new urban culture in *City People: The Rise of Modern City Culture in Nineteenth-Century America* (1980). John Bodnar offers a synthesis of the urban immigrant experience in *The Transplanted: A History of Immigrants in Urban America* (1985). See also Roger Daniels's *Guarding the Golden Door: American Immigration Policy and Immigrants since 1882* (2004). Walter Nugent's *Crossings: The Great Transatlantic Migrations, 1870–1914* (1992) provides a wealth of demographic information and insight.

On urban environments and sanitary reforms, see Martin V. Melosi's *The Sanitary City: Urban Infrastructure in America from Colonial Times to the Present* (2000), Joel A. Tarr's *The Search for the Ultimate Sink: Urban Pollution in Historical Perspective* (1996), and Suellen Hoy's *Chasing Dirt: The American Pursuit of Cleanliness* (1995).

For the growth of urban leisure and sports, see Roy Rosenzweig's *Eight Hours for What We Will: Workers and Leisure in an Industrial City, 1870–1920* (1983) and Steven A. Riess's *City Games: The Evolution of American Urban Society and the Rise of Sports* (1989). Saloon culture is examined in Madelon Powers's *Faces along the Bar: Lore and Order in the Workingman's Saloon, 1870–1920* (1998).

Richard Hofstadter's *Social Darwinism in American Thought,* rev. ed. (1969) and Cynthia Eagle Russett's *Darwin in America: The Intellectual Response, 1865–1912* (1976) examine the impact of the theory of evolution. On the rise of realism in thought and the arts during the second half of the nineteenth century, see David E. Shi's *Facing Facts: Realism in American Thought and Culture, 1850–1920* (1995).

Eleanor Flexner and Ellen Fitzpatrick's *Century of Struggle: The Woman's Rights Movement in the United States* (1996) surveys the condition of women in the late nineteenth century. The best study of the settlement-house movement is Jean Bethke Elshtain's *Jane Addams and the Dream of American Democracy: A Life* (2002).

22

GILDED AGE POLITICS
AND AGRARIAN REVOLT

FOCUS QUESTIONS

· What were the political developments of the Gilded Age?

· What problems, real and perceived, affected American farmers of the era?

· What factors precipitated the rise of the agrarian revolt and the Populists?

· What was significant about the election of 1896?

To answer these questions and access additional review material, please visit www.wwnorton.com/studyspace.

In 1873 the writers Mark Twain and Charles Dudley Warner created an enduring label for the post–Civil War era when they collaborated on a novel titled *The Gilded Age*, a depiction of widespread political corruption and personal greed. Perspectives on the times would eventually mellow, but generations of political scientists and historians have since reinforced the two novelists' judgment. As a young college graduate in 1879, Woodrow Wilson described the state of the American political system: "No leaders, no principles; no principles, no parties." Indeed, the real movers and shakers of the Gilded Age were not the men who sat in the White House or Congress but the captains of industry who crisscrossed the continent with railroads and decorated its cities with plumed smokestacks and gaudy mansions.

PARADOXICAL POLITICS

Throughout the last third of the nineteenth century, political inertia reigned at the national level. A close division between Republicans and Democrats in Congress created a sense of stalemate. Neither party was willing to embrace controversial issues or take bold initiatives because each one's relative strength was so precarious. Many observers then and since considered this a time of political mediocrity, in which the parties refused to confront "real issues" such as the runaway growth of an unregulated economy and its attendant social injustices. Voters of the time nonetheless thought politics was very important. Voter turnout during the Gilded Age was commonly about 70 to 80 percent, even in the South, where the disenfranchisement of African Americans was not yet complete. (By contrast, the turnout for the 2004 presidential election was 56 percent.) The paradox of such a high rate of voter participation in the face of the inertia at the national political level raises an obvious question: How was it that leaders who failed to address the "real issues" of the day presided over the most highly organized and politically active electorate in U.S. history?

The answer is partly that the politicians and the voters believed that they *were* dealing with crucial issues: tariff rates, the regulation of corporations, monetary policy, Indian disputes, civil service reform, and immigration. But the answer also reflects the extreme partisanship of the times and the essentially local nature of political culture during the Gilded Age.

PARTISAN POLITICS   Most Americans after the Civil War were intensely loyal to one of the two major parties, Democratic or Republican. Political parties gave people an anchor for their activity and loyalty in an unstable world. Local party officials took care of those who voted their way and distributed appointive public offices and other favors to party loyalists. These "city machines" used patronage and favoritism to keep the loyalty of business supporters while providing jobs or food or fuel to working-class voters who had fallen on hard times. The party faithful eagerly took part in rallies and picnics, deriving a sense of camaraderie as well as an opportunity for recreation that offered a welcome relief from their usual workday routine.

Party loyalties and voter turnout in the late nineteenth century reflected religious and ethnic divisions as well as geographic differences. The Republican party attracted mainly Protestants of British descent. Their native seat was New England, and their other strongholds were New York and the upper

Midwest, both of which were populated with Yankee stock. The Republicans, the party of Abraham Lincoln, could also rely upon the votes of African Americans and Union veterans of the Civil War.

The Democrats, by contrast, tended to be a heterogeneous, often unruly coalition embracing southern whites, immigrants and Catholics of any origin, Jews, freethinkers, skeptics, and all those repelled by the "party of morality." As one Chicago Democrat explained, "A Republican is a man who wants you t' go t' church every Sunday. A Democrat says if a man wants to have a glass of beer on Sunday he can have it."

Republicans pressed nativist causes, calling for restrictions on both immigration and the employment of foreigners and greater emphasis on the teaching of the "American" language in the schools. Prohibitionism revived along with nativism in the 1880s. Among the immigrants who crowded into the growing cities were many Irish, Germans, and Italians who enjoyed alcoholic beverages. Republicans increasingly saw saloons as the central social evil around which all others revolved, including vice, crime, political corruption, and neglect of families, and they associated these problems with the ethnic groups that frequented the saloons.

POLITICAL STALEMATE AT THE NATIONAL LEVEL   Between 1869 and 1913, from the presidency of Ulysses S. Grant to that of William Howard Taft, Republicans monopolized the White House except for the two nonconsecutive terms of the Democrat Grover Cleveland, but Republican domination was more apparent than real. Between 1872 and 1896 no president won a majority of the popular vote. In each of those presidential elections, sixteen states invariably voted Republican and fourteen voted Democratic, leaving a pivotal six states whose results might change. The important swing-vote role played by two of those states, New York and Ohio, helps explain the election of eight presidents from those states from 1872 to 1912.

No chief executive between Lincoln and Theodore Roosevelt could be described as a "strong" president. None challenged the prevailing view that Congress, not the White House, should formulate policy. Senator John Sherman of Ohio expressed the widely held notion that the legislative branch should take initiative in a republic: "The President should merely obey and enforce the law."

Republicans controlled the Senate, and Democrats controlled the House during the Gilded Age. Only during 1881–1883 and 1889–1891 did a Republican president coincide with a Republican Congress, and only between 1893 and 1895 did a Democratic president enjoy a Democratic Congress.

Political stasis thus led Congress to postpone making major decisions or launching new programs and to concentrate instead on partisan maneuvering over procedural issues. Because most bills required bipartisan support to pass both houses and legislators tended to vote along party lines, the Democrats and the Republicans pursued a policy of evasion on the national issues of the day. Only the tariff created clear-cut divisions between protectionist Republicans and low-tariff Democrats, but there were individual exceptions even on that. On the important questions of the currency, regulation of big business, farm problems, civil service reform, and immigration, the parties differed very little. As a result, they primarily became vehicles for seeking office and dispensing patronage in the form of government jobs and contracts.

STATE AND LOCAL INITIATIVES   Unlike today, Americans during the Gilded Age expected little direct support from the federal government; most significant political activity occurred at the state and local levels. Residents of the western territories were largely forced to fend for themselves rather than rely upon federal authorities. They formed towns, practiced vigilante justice, and made laws on their own. Once incorporated into the Union, the former territories retained much of their autonomy.

Thus state governments after the Civil War were dynamic centers of political activity and innovation. Over 60 percent of the nation's spending and taxing were exercised by state and local authorities. Then, unlike today, the large cities spent far more on local services than did the federal government. And three fourths of all public employees worked for state and local governments. Local issues such as prohibition, Sunday closing laws, and parochial-school funding generated far more excitement than complex debates over tariffs and monetary policies. It was the state and local governments that first sought to curb the power and restrain the abuses of corporate interests.

CORRUPTION AND REFORM

After the Civil War, states made rudimentary attempts to regulate big business; most of these regulations were overturned by the courts, however. A close alliance developed between business and political leaders. As a congressman, James G. Blaine of Maine, for example, and many of his supporters, saw nothing wrong in his accepting stock certificates from an Arkansas railroad after helping it win a land grant from Congress. Railroad passes, free entertainment, and a host of other favors were freely provided to politicians, newspaper editors, and other leaders in positions to influence public opinion or affect legislation.

The Bosses of the Senate

This 1889 cartoon bitingly portrays the period's alliance between big business and politics.

On the local level the exchange of favors for votes was not perceived as improper either. People voted for their party out of intense partisan loyalty. Although they looked to their parties to supply them with favors, entertainment, and even jobs, they did not see themselves as "selling their vote." This was simply the practice of patronage democracy, in which local party officials awarded party loyalists with contracts and public jobs, such as heading customhouses and post offices.

Both Republican and Democratic leaders squabbled over the "spoils" of office, the appointive offices at the local and the national levels. After each election it was expected that the victorious party would throw out the defeated party's appointees and appoint their own men to office. Each party had its share of corrupt officials willing to buy and sell government appointments or congressional votes, yet each also witnessed the emergence of factions promoting honesty in government. The struggle for clean government soon became one of the foremost issues of the day.

HAYES AND CIVIL SERVICE REFORM   In the aftermath of Reconstruction, President Rutherford B. Hayes admirably embodied the "party of morality." Hayes brought to the White House in 1877 a new style of uprightness, in sharp contrast to the graft and corruption of the Grant administration. The son of an Ohio farmer, Hayes became one of the early Republicans, was wounded four times in the Civil War, and was promoted to the rank of major general. Elected governor of Ohio in 1867, he served three terms. Honest and respectable, competent and dignified, he lived in a modest style with his wife, who was nicknamed Lemonade Lucy because of her refusal to serve alcohol at White House functions.

Yet Hayes's presidency suffered from the supposed secret deal that awarded him victory over the Democrat Samuel Tilden in the contested 1876 election. Snide references to him as "His Fraudulence" denied him any chance at a second term, which he renounced from the beginning. Hayes's own party was split between so-called Stalwarts and Half-Breeds, led respectively by Senators Roscoe Conkling of New York and James G. Blaine of Maine. The difference between these Republican factions was murkier than that between the parties. The Stalwarts had been stalwart in their support of President Grant during the furor over the behavior of his cabinet members. They also promoted Radical Reconstruction of the South and the "spoils system" of distributing federal political jobs to party loyalists. The Half-Breeds acquired their name because they were only half loyal to Grant and half committed to reform of the spoils system.

For the most part the two Republican factions were loose alliances designed to advance the careers of Conkling and Blaine. The two men could not abide each other. Blaine once referred to the haughty Conkling as displaying a "majestic, supereminent, overpowering, turkey-gobbler strut." Tall and lordly, with a pointed beard, thick, auburn hair, and upturned jaw and nose, Conkling boasted good looks, fine clothes, and an arrogant manner. Yet underneath his glamorous facade he was a ruthless power broker willing to reward friends and punish enemies. Conkling viewed politics as a brute struggle for control. Politics "is a rotten business," he declared. "Nothing counts except to win."

By contrast, Hayes aligned himself with the growing public discontent over the corruption that characterized the political process. American leaders were just learning about the merit system for public employees, which was long established in the bureaucracies of France and Germany, and the new British practice in which civil service jobs were filled by competitive examination. Prominent leaders such as James A. Garfield in the House and Carl Schurz in the Senate embraced civil service reform, and Hayes raised the issue during the campaign of 1876.

Although Hayes failed to get civil service legislation, he did mandate his own rules for political appointments based on merit: those already in office would be dismissed only for the good of the government and not for political reasons; party members would have no more influence in appointments than other respectable citizens; no assessments of government employees for political contributions would be permitted; and no officeholder could manage election campaigns for political organizations, although all could vote and express opinions.

The issue of nonpartisan government administration culminated in a dispute over the federal customhouses, notorious centers of corrupt politics, filled with political appointees with little or nothing to do but draw salaries and run political machines. An inquiry into operations at the New York Customhouse, the largest federal operation in the nation, revealed that both collector Chester A. Arthur and naval officer Alonzo Cornell were guilty of "laxity" and of using the customhouse to reward political favors and jobs on behalf of Roscoe Conkling's organization. When Hayes hinted that resignations would be welcomed, Conkling accused the president and other civil service reformers of being blinded by a "canting self-righteousness."

On October 15, 1877, after removing Arthur and Cornell from office, Hayes named replacements, only to have the nominees rejected when Conkling appealed to the "courtesy of the Senate," an old custom whereby senators might control political appointments in their own states. During a recess in the summer of 1878, however, Hayes appointed new replacements. When Congress reassembled, the administration put pressure on the Senate, and with Democratic support the nominations were approved. Even this, however, did not end the New York Customhouse episode; it would flare up again under the next president.

For all of Hayes's efforts to clean house, his vision of government's role remained limited. On the economic issues of the day, he held to a conservative line that would guide his successors for the rest of the century. His solution to labor troubles, demonstrated in the Great Railroad Strike of 1877, was to send in federal troops and break the strike. Yet Hayes privately expressed misgivings about using troops to suppress labor unrest. He told his cabinet that "if railroad workers were to be subjected to governmental force, perhaps the railroads should be subjected to governmental supervision of their labor policies." In his diary he concluded that the best remedy would be "judicious control of the capitalists." But Hayes never found a way to implement such regulation.

Hayes's answer to demands for an expansion of the currency was to veto the 1878 Bland-Allison Act, which provided for a limited expansion of silver money through the government's purchase of $2 million to $4 million worth in silver coins per month. (The act passed anyway when Congress overrode Hayes's veto.) A bruised president confided in his diary that he had lost the support of his own party. There was "a very decided opposition to the Administration in both houses of Congress among the Republican members," and their objections extended to "all of my principal acts." Congressional leader James Garfield echoed Hayes's assessment, noting that the president had pursued "a suicidal policy toward Congress and is almost without a friend." In 1879, with a year still left in his term, Hayes was ready to leave the White House. "I am now in my last year of the Presidency," he wrote a friend, "and look forward to its close as a schoolboy longs for the coming vacation."

GARFIELD AND ARTHUR   With Hayes out of the running for a second term, the Republicans were forced to look elsewhere in 1880. The Stalwarts, led by Conkling, brought Ulysses S. Grant forward for a third time, still a strong contender despite the tarnish of his administration's scandals. For two days the Republican Convention in Chicago was deadlocked, with Grant holding a slight lead over Blaine. When Wisconsin's delegates suddenly switched their votes to Senator-elect James A. Garfield, the convention stampeded to the dark-horse candidate, carrying him to the nomination. As a sop to the Stalwarts, the convention named Chester A. Arthur, the deposed collector of the New York Customhouse, as the candidate for vice president.

The Democrats selected Winfield Scott Hancock, a Union commander at Gettysburg, to counterbalance the Republicans' "bloody-shirt" attacks on their party as the vehicle of rebellion. Former Confederates nevertheless advised their constituents to "vote as you shot"—that is, against Republicans. In an election characterized by widespread bribery, Garfield eked out a plurality of only 39,000 votes, or 48.5 percent of the vote, but with a comfortable margin of 214 to 155 in the Electoral College.

A native of Ohio and an early foe of slavery, Garfield distinguished himself during the Civil War and was mustered out as a major general when he went to Congress in 1863. Noted for his oratorical and parliamentary skills, he became one of the outstanding leaders in the House.

On July 2, 1881, after only four months in office, President Garfield was walking through the Washington, D.C., railroad station when a deranged man, Charles Guiteau shot him in the back. "I am a Stalwart," Guiteau explained to the arresting officers. "Arthur is now President of the United States," an announcement that would prove crippling to the Stalwarts. "The dreadful tragedy," ex-president Hayes wrote in his diary, "has occupied our

Invitation to the Inaugural Reception for President James A. Garfield

Garfield, on the left, and Chester Arthur, on the right, flank a portrait of George Washington.

thoughts." He and others were grieving not only for the mortally wounded president. They were mortified at the prospect that Vice President Chester Arthur, the compliant lieutenant of the Stalwart leader Senator Roscoe Conkling, might become commander in chief. "The death of the President at this time would be a national calamity whose consequence we can not now confidently conjecture. Arthur for President! Conkling the power behind the throne!" Garfield lingered near death for two months. On September 19 he died of complications resulting from the shooting. Chester Arthur was now President.

Little in Arthur's past, except for his record as an abolitionist lawyer who helped secure the freedom of a fugitive slave, raised hopes that he would rise above customhouse politics. But Arthur proved to be a surprisingly competent president. He distanced himself from Conkling and the Stalwarts and established a genuine independence. He vigorously prosecuted the Star Route postal frauds, a kickback scheme on contracts for postal routes that involved his old political cronies. The president further surprised old-guard Republicans in 1882 with the veto of an $18-million river and harbors bill, a pork-barrel measure that included something for most congressional districts. He also vetoed the Chinese Exclusion Act (1882), which in his view violated the Burlingame Treaty of 1868 by excluding Chinese immigrants for twenty years. Congress proceeded to override both vetoes.

Most startling of all was Arthur's emergence as something of a civil service and tariff reformer. Stalwarts had every reason to expect him to oppose a merit system of government appointments, but instead he allied himself with the reformers. The assassin Guiteau had unwittingly stimulated widespread public support of reform. In 1883 a reform bill sponsored by "Gentleman George" Pendleton, a Democratic senator from Ohio, set up a three-member Civil Service Commission independent of the cabinet departments, the first such federal agency established on a permanent basis. About 14 percent of all government jobs would now be filled on the basis of competitive examinations rather than political favoritism. What was more, the president could enlarge the class of affected jobs at his discretion. This development would have important consequences over the years because after each of the next four presidential elections the party out of power emerged as victors. Each new president thus had a motive to enlarge this category of government jobs because it would shield his own appointees from political removal. The Pendleton Act was thus a vital step in a new approach to government administration that valued merit over partisanship.

The high protective tariff, a heritage of the Civil War designed to deter foreign imports by taxing them, had by the early 1880s raised federal revenues to a point where the government was enjoying an embarrassment of riches, a surplus that drew money into the Treasury and out of circulation, thus constricting economic growth. Some argued that lower tariff rates would reduce prices by enabling foreign competition and at the same time leave more money in circulation to fuel economic growth. In 1882 Arthur named a special commission to study the problem. The Tariff Commission recommended a 20 to 25 percent rate reduction, which gained Arthur's support, but any attempt at tariff reform ran up against swarms of lobbyists and organized interest groups representing different industries determined to keep the rate on their particular commodity high. Congress's effort to enact the proposal was marred by logrolling (the trading of votes to benefit different legislators' local interests), resulting in the "mongrel tariff" of 1883, so called because of its diverse rates for different commodities. Overall, the tariff provided for a slight rate reduction, perhaps by 5 percent, but it actually raised the duty on some articles.

THE SCURRILOUS CAMPAIGN   When the 1884 presidential campaign began, Chester Arthur's record might have commended him to the voters, but it did not please leaders of his party. So the Republicans dumped Arthur and turned to the glamorous senator James Gillespie Blaine of Maine, longtime leader of the Half-Breeds. Blaine was the consummate politician.

He never forgot a name or a face, he inspired the party faithful with his oratory, and at the same time he knew how to wheel and deal in the back rooms. Blaine did have his enemies, however. Democratic newspapers, for example, turned up evidence of his corruption. Based on references in the "Mulligan letters," they once again claimed that Blaine was in the pocket of the railroad barons and that while Speaker of the House he had sold his votes on measures favorable to their interests.

Senator James G. Blaine of Maine

The Republican candidate in 1884.

During the campaign more letters surfaced with disclosures embarrassing to Blaine. For the reform element of the Republican party, this was too much, and prominent leaders and supporters of the party bolted the ticket. Party regulars scorned them as goo-goos—the good-government crowd who ignored partisan realities—and the editor of the *New York Sun* jokingly called them mugwumps, after an Algonquian word for a self-important chieftain. To party regulars, in what soon became a stale joke, mugwumps were unreliable Republicans who had their mugs on one side of the fence and their "wumps" on the other. The mugwumps were centered in the large cities and major universities. Mostly educators or editors, they shared an opposition to tariffs and championed free trade. They disdained efforts to inflate the money supply by coining more silver, were hostile to efforts at regulating railroads, and were suspicious of excessive democracy. Their foremost goal was to enact civil service reform by removing from the party in power the ability to distribute federal jobs to its supporters.

The rise of the mugwumps influenced the Democrats to nominate the New Yorker Stephen Grover Cleveland as a reform candidate. Cleveland rose rapidly from obscurity to the White House. One of many children in the family of a small-town Presbyterian minister, he had first attracted national attention when, in 1881, he was elected as the anti-corruption mayor of Buffalo. In 1882 he was elected governor, and he continued to build a reform record by fighting New York City's corrupt Tammany Hall organization. As mayor and as governor, he repeatedly vetoed what he considered special-privilege bills serving selfish interests.

A stocky 270-pound man, Cleveland seemed the stolid opposite of Blaine. He possessed little charisma but impressed the public with his stubborn

Another Voice for Cleveland

This 1884 cartoon attacks "Grover the Good" for fathering an illegitimate child.

integrity. Then a scandal erupted when the *Buffalo Evening Telegraph* revealed that as a bachelor Cleveland had had an affair with an attractive Buffalo widow, who had named him as the father of a child born to her in 1874. Cleveland responded by providing financial support for the child. The respective escapades of Blaine and Cleveland provided some of the most colorful battle cries in political history: "Blaine, Blaine, James G. Blaine, the continental liar from the state of Maine," Democrats chanted; Republicans countered with "Ma, ma, where's my pa? Gone to the White House, ha, ha, ha!"

Near the end of the brutal campaign, Blaine and his supporters committed two fateful blunders. The first occurred at New York's fashionable Delmonico's restaurant, where Blaine went to a private dinner with several millionaire bigwigs to discuss campaign finances. Cartoons and accounts of "Belshazzar's feast" festooned the opposition press for days. The second fiasco occurred when one member of a delegation of Protestant ministers visiting Republican headquarters in New York referred to the Democrats as the party of "rum, Romanism, and rebellion." Blaine, who was present, let pass the implied insult to Catholics—a fatal oversight, since he had always cultivated Irish-American support with his anti-British talk and public reminders that his mother was Catholic. Democrats spread the word that Blaine was at heart anti-Irish and anti-Catholic. The incident may have tipped the election. The electoral vote in Cleveland's favor, stood at 219 to 182, but the popular vote ran far closer: Cleveland's plurality was fewer than 30,000 votes.

CLEVELAND AND THE SPECIAL INTERESTS   For all of Cleveland's hostility to the spoils system and politics as usual, he represented no sharp break with the conservative policies of his predecessors, except in opposing government favors to business. "A public office is a public trust" was one of his favorite mottoes. He held to a strictly limited view of government's role in both economic and social matters, a rigid philosophy illustrated by his 1887 veto of the Texas seed bill, an effort to appropriate funds to meet drought victims' urgent need for seed grain. Back to Congress it went with a lecture on the need to limit the powers and functions of government. "Though the people support the government, the government should not support the people," Cleveland asserted.

Despite his strong philosophical convictions, Cleveland had a mixed record on civil service. He had good intentions as the first Democratic president since James Buchanan's term from 1856 to 1860, but he also led a party hungry for partisan appointments. Before his inauguration, Cleveland repeated his support for the Pendleton Civil Service Reform Act: he would not remove able government workers simply on partisan grounds. But he inserted one significant exception: those who had used federal jobs to forward the interests of the opposition party. In many cases, especially in the post office, he thus had ample excuse to remove people who had practically made their offices into Republican headquarters.

Party pressures gradually forced Cleveland's hand. When he left office, about two thirds of the federal officeholders were Democrats, including all Internal Revenue collectors and nearly all the heads of customhouses. At the same time, however, Cleveland had extended the number of federal jobs subject to civil service regulation to about 27,000 employees, almost double the number that had been covered when he came in. Yet he satisfied neither mugwumps nor spoilsmen; indeed, he managed to antagonize both.

On other matters, Cleveland's stubborn courage and concern for protecting the public Treasury led him into conflicts with predatory interests that eventually cost him the White House. One such dispute arose over misuse of government-owned land in the West. Cleveland's secretary of the interior and the commissioner of the General Land Office uncovered one case after another of fraud and mismanagement: bogus surveys filed by government surveyors; public lands used fraudulently by lumber companies, mine operators, and cattle ranchers with the collusion of government officials; and at least 30 million acres of land grants given to railroads that never built the agreed-upon lines. The administration sued the railroads to recover the land. It also nullified exploitive leases of Indian lands. Cattle barons were ordered to remove fences enclosing water holes and grasslands on the open range. In all, during Cleveland's first term about 81 million acres of public land were restored to the federal government.

Cleveland incurred the wrath of Union war veterans by his firm stand against their pension raids on the Treasury. Congress had passed the first Civil War pension law in 1862 to provide for Union veterans disabled in service and for the widows, orphans, and dependents of veterans. By 1882 the Grand Army of the Republic, an organization of Union veterans and a powerful pressure group, was trying to get pensions paid for any disability, even if unrelated to military service. Meanwhile, many veterans succeeded in pushing private pension bills through an obliging Congress. In Washington, D.C., lawyers built careers on filing claims and pressing for special laws to benefit veterans.

Insofar as time permitted, Cleveland examined such bills critically and vetoed the dubious ones. Although he signed more pension bills than any of his predecessors, he also vetoed more. A climax came in 1887 when Congress passed the dependent-pension bill, which provided funds for veterans dependent upon manual labor and unable to work, whether or not the reason was connected to military service. Cleveland sent it back with a ringing veto, declaring that the pension list would become a refuge for frauds rather than a "roll of honor."

In about the middle of his term, Cleveland launched a new assault on special interests, leading to the adoption of an important new policy: railroad regulation. Since the late 1860s states had adopted laws regulating railroads, and from the early 1870s Congress had debated federal legislation. In 1886 a Supreme Court decision finally spurred action. In the case of *Wabash, St. Louis, and Pacific Railroad Company v. Illinois*, the Court denied the state's power to regulate rates on interstate traffic. Cleveland thereupon urged that since this "important field of control and regulation [has] thus been left entirely unoccupied," Congress should act.

It did, and in 1887 Cleveland signed into law an act creating the Interstate Commerce Commission (ICC), the first such independent federal regulatory commission. The law empowered the ICC's five members to investigate railroads and prosecute violators. All freight rates had to be "reasonable and just." Railroads were forbidden to grant secret rebates to preferred shippers; discriminate against persons, places, and commodities; or enter into pools (secret agreements among competing companies to fix rates). The commission's actual powers proved to be weak, however, when first tested in the courts. Though creating the ICC seemed to conflict with Cleveland's fear of big government, it accorded with his fear of big business. The Interstate Commerce Act, to his mind, was a legitimate exercise of sovereign power.

THE TARIFF   President Cleveland's most dramatic challenge to special interests focused on tariff reform. Why was the tariff such an important and controversial issue? By the late nineteenth century, Republicans and business leaders had come to assume that prosperity and high tariffs were tightly linked. Others disagreed. Many observers had concluded that the formation of huge corporate "trusts" was not a natural development of a maturing capitalist system. Instead, critics charged that government tariff policies had fostered big business at the expense of small producers and retailers by effectively shutting out foreign imports, thereby enabling corporations to dominate their American markets and charge higher prices for their products. "The heart of the trust problem is in our tariff system of plunder," declared the head of the New England Free Trade League. "The quickest and most certain way of reaching the evils of trusts is . . . by the abolition of tariff duties."

Cleveland agreed. He concluded that the tariff rates were too high and included many inequities. Near the end of 1887, the president devoted his entire annual message to the subject. He did so despite the warnings of his advisers and fully aware that he was focusing attention on a political minefield on the eve of an election year. "What is the use of being elected or reelected if you don't stand for something?" he asked.

Cleveland's message noted that tariff revenues had bolstered the federal surplus, making the Treasury "a hoarding place for money needlessly withdrawn from trade and the people's use." By reducing foreign competition the tariff pushed up prices for everybody. And while it was supposed to protect

Grover Cleveland

As President, he made the issue of tariff reform central to the politics of the late 1880s.

American workers against the competition of cheap foreign labor, the most recent census had shown that of the 17.4 million Americans gainfully employed, only 2.6 million were in "such manufacturing industries as are claimed to be benefitted by a high tariff."

It was evident, moreover, that competition in every industry produced better prices for consumers. Business combinations could push prices up to the artificial level set by the prices of dutied foreign goods, but prices often fell below that level when domestic producers were in competition, "proof that someone is willing to accept lower prices for such commodity and that such prices are remunerative." Congress, Cleveland argued, should reduce the tariff rates. Blaine and other Republicans denounced Cleveland's message as pure "free trade," a doctrine all the more suspect because it was also British policy. If Cleveland's talk accomplished his purpose of drawing party lines more firmly, it also confirmed the fears of his advisers. The election of 1888 for the first time in years highlighted a difference between the major parties on an issue of substance.

Cleveland was the obvious nominee of his party. The Republicans, now calling themselves the GOP (Grand Old Party), turned to the obscure Benjamin Harrison, who had all the attributes of availability. The grandson of President William Henry Harrison, and a lawyer with a flourishing practice in Indiana, Harrison resided in a pivotal state and had a good war record. There was little in his political record to offend any voter. He had lost a race for governor and served one term in the Senate (1881–1887). The Republican platform accepted Cleveland's challenge to make the protective tariff the chief issue and promised generous pensions to veterans.

The Republicans enjoyed a huge advantage over the Democrats in funding and organization. To fend off Cleveland's efforts to reduce the tariff, business owners contributed over $3 million to the Republican campaign. Harrison was also willing to campaign actively for the presidency, while Cleveland stuck to the tradition of sitting presidents' not stumping for themselves. He also prohibited his cabinet members to campaign on his behalf.

On the eve of the election, Cleveland suffered a more devastating blow. A California Republican had written the British minister to the United States, Sir Lionel Sackville-West, using the false name Charles F. Murchison. Posing as an English immigrant, he asked advice on how to vote in the presidential election. Sackville-West, engaged at the time in sensitive negotiations over British and U.S. access to Canadian fisheries, hinted that the man should vote for Cleveland. The letter aroused a storm of protest against foreign intervention and further linked Cleveland to British free traders. The Democrats' explanations never caught up with the public's sense of outrage.

Still, the outcome was incredibly close. Cleveland won the popular vote by 5,538,000 to 5,447,000, but that was little comfort. The distribution of votes was such that Harrison, with the key states of Indiana and New York on his side by virtue of the sordid but common practice of paying voters, carried the Electoral College by 233 to 168. When his campaign manager reported the election returns, Harrison exclaimed fervently, "Providence has given us the victory." The cynical adviser later remarked that Harrison "ought to know that Providence hadn't a damn thing to do with it" and opined that the president "would never know how close a number of men were compelled to approach a penitentiary to make him president."

REPUBLICAN REFORM UNDER HARRISON As president, Benjamin Harrison was a competent and earnest figurehead overshadowed by his flamboyant secretary of state, James G. Blaine. Harrison had aroused the hopes of civil service reformers when he declared that "fitness and not party service should be the essential and discriminating test" for government employment. Nevertheless, he appointed a wealthy Philadelphia merchant as his postmaster general, allegedly as a reward for a generous compaign contribution. The first assistant postmaster general announced less than a year later, "I have changed 31,000 out of 55,000 fourth-class postmasters and I expect to change 10,000 more before I finally quit." Harrison made a few feckless efforts to resist partisan pressures, but the party leaders had their way. His most significant gesture at reform was to name young Theodore Roosevelt to the Civil Service Commission.

Harrison owed a heavy debt to Union Civil War veterans, which he discharged by naming an officer of the Grand Army of the Republic to the position of pension commissioner. "God help the surplus," the new commissioner reportedly exclaimed. He proceeded to approve pensions for military veterans with such abandon that the secretary of the interior removed him six months and several million dollars later. In

BILLION- DOLLARISM) HOLE

A Billion-Dollar Hole

In an attack on Benjamin Harrison's spending policies, Harrison is shown pouring Cleveland's huge surplus down a hole.

1890 Congress passed, and Harrison signed, the Dependent Pension Act, substantially the same measure that Cleveland had vetoed. The pension rolls almost doubled between 1889 and 1893.

During the first two years of Harrison's term, the Republicans controlled the presidency and both houses of Congress for only the second time in the twenty years between 1875 and 1895. They were positioned to have pretty much their own way, and they made the year 1890 memorable for some of the most significant legislation enacted in the entire period. In addition to the Dependent Pension Act, Congress and the president approved the Sherman Anti-Trust Act, the Sherman Silver Purchase Act, the McKinley Tariff Act, and the admission of Idaho and Wyoming as new states, which followed the admission of the Dakotas, Montana, and Washington in 1889.

Both parties had pledged to do something about the growing power of trusts and monopolies. The Sherman Anti-Trust Act, named for Ohio senator John Sherman, chairman of the Senate committee that drafted it, sought to incorporate into federal law a long-standing principle opposing activities in "restraint of trade." It forbade contracts, combinations, or conspiracies in restraint of trade or in the effort to establish monopolies in interstate or foreign commerce. A broad consensus put the vague law through, but its passage turned out to be largely symbolic. During the next decade successive administrations rarely enforced the new law, in part because of the ambiguity about what constituted "restraint of trade." From 1890 to 1901, only eighteen lawsuits were instituted, and four of those were against labor unions.

Congress meanwhile debated currency legislation against the backdrop of growing economic distress in the farm regions of the West and the South. Hard-pressed farmers demanded an increased coinage of silver to inflate the currency, which would raise commodity prices, making it easier for them to earn the money with which to pay their debts.

The farmers found allies, especially in the Senate, among members from the new western states. All six of the states admitted to the Union in 1889 and 1890 had substantial silver mines, and their new congressional delegations—largely Republican—were eager to promote legislation requiring the federal government to mint more silver. Thus Congress passed the Sherman Silver Purchase Act in 1890, replacing the Bland-Allison Act of 1878. It required the Treasury to purchase 4.5 million ounces of silver each month and to issue in payment paper money redeemable in gold or silver. Although the amount of silver purchased doubled, it was still too little to have an inflationary impact on the national economy. Yet eastern business and financial groups saw a threat to the gold reserve in the growth of paper currency that holders could redeem for gold at the Treasury. The stage was set for the currency issue to eclipse all others in a panic that would sweep the country three years later.

Republicans viewed their victory over Cleveland in 1888 as a mandate not just to maintain the protective tariff but to raise it. Piloted through Congress by Ohio representative William McKinley, chairman of the committee on Ways and Means, and by Senator Nelson W. Aldrich, the McKinley tariff of 1890 raised duties on manufactured goods to their highest level ever and included three new departures. First, the protectionists reached out for farmers' votes by putting high duties on imported agricultural products. Second, they sought to lessen the tariff's impact on consumers by putting sugar, a universal necessity, on the duty-free list—thus reducing its cost—and then compensating sugar growers with a bounty of 2¢ a pound out of the federal Treasury. And third, they included a reciprocity section, which empowered the president to hike duties on sugar, molasses, tea, coffee, and hides to pressure countries exporting those items to reduce unreasonably high duties on American goods imported into their countries.

The absence of a public consensus for higher tariffs became clearly visible in the 1890 midterm elections. The voters repudiated the McKinley tariff with a landslide of Democratic votes. In the new House, Democrats outnumbered Republicans by almost three to one; in the Senate the Republican majority was reduced to eight.

One of the election casualties was Congressman McKinley himself, the victim of tricks the Democrats used to reinforce the widespread revulsion against the increased tariff duties. But there was more to the election than the tariff. Voters also reacted to the baldly partisan measures of the Harrison administration and the "billion-dollar" Republican Congress's extravagant expenditures on military pensions and other programs. With expenditures rising and revenues dropping, largely because the McKinley tariff was so high as to discourage imports, the nation's Treasury surplus was rapidly shrinking.

The large Democratic vote in 1890 may also have been a reaction to Republican efforts to legislate against alcohol. Between 1880 and 1890 sixteen out of twenty-one states outside the South held referenda on a constitutional prohibition of alcoholic beverages, although only six states voted for prohibition. Teetotaling Republicans were playing a losing game, arousing wets (anti-prohibitionists) on the Democratic side. Another issue that served to mobilize Democratic resistance was the Republican attempt to eliminate funding for state-supported Catholic schools. In 1889 Wisconsin Republicans pushed through a law that held that a school could be accredited only if it taught the basic subjects in English. That was the last straw: it turned large numbers of outraged immigrants into Democratic activists. In 1889 and 1890 the Democrats swept state after state.

THE FARM PROBLEM AND AGRARIAN PROTEST MOVEMENTS

The 1890 election reflected more than a reaction against the Republican tariff, patronage politics, extravagant spending, and moralizing. The Democratic victory revealed a deep-seated unrest in the farming communities of the South and the West. In drought-devastated Kansas, Populists took over five Republican congressional seats. As the congressional Democrats took power, the beginnings of an economic crisis appeared on the horizon. Farmers' debts mounted as crop prices plummeted.

Frustrated by the unwillingness of Congress to meet their demands and ease their plight, disgruntled farmers began to focus on political action. Like so many of their counterparts laboring in urban factories, they realized that social change required demonstrations of power, and power lay in numbers. Unlike labor unions, however, the farm organizations faced a more complex array of economic variables affecting their livelihood. They had to deal with more than just management. Bankers, food processors, railroad and grain-elevator operators, as well as the world commodities market, all affected the agricultural sector. So, too, did the unpredictable forces of nature: droughts, blizzards, insects, and erosion.

There were also important obstacles to collective action by farmers. Farmers' rugged individualism and physical isolation made communication and organization especially difficult. American farmers had long prided themselves on their self-reliant hardihood, and many balked at sacrificing their independence. Another hurdle was the fact that after the Civil War agricultural interests had diverged and in some cases conflicted with one another. In the Great Plains, for example, the railroads were the largest landowners. In addition, there were large absentee landowners, some foreign, who leased out vast tracts of land. There were also huge "bonanza" farms that employed hundreds of seasonal workers. Yet the majority of farmers were simple rural folk in the South and West who were moderate-size landowners, small land speculators, small landowners, tenant farmers, sharecroppers, and hourly wage workers. It was the middle-size landowners who experienced rapidly rising land values and rising indebtedness. Those

"I Feed You All"

This 1875 poster shows the farmer at the center of society.

farmers were concerned with land values and crop prices, while tenants, sharecroppers, and farmhands supported land-distribution schemes that would give them access to their own land.

Given such a diversity of interests, farm activists discovered that it was often difficult to develop and maintain a cohesive organization. Yet for all the difficulties, they persevered, and the results were dramatic, if not completely successful. Thus, for example, the deep-seated unrest in the farming communities of the South and the West began to find voice in the Granger movement, the Farmers' Alliances, and the new People's party, agrarian movements of considerable political and social significance.

ECONOMIC CONDITIONS   Since the end of the Civil War, farmers in the South and Midwest had been subject to worsening economic and social conditions. The source of their problems was a long decline in commodity prices, from 1870 to 1898, the product of domestic overproduction and growing international competition for world markets. The vast new land brought under cultivation in the West poured an ever-increasing supply of farm products into the market, driving prices down. This effect was reinforced as innovations in transportation and communications brought American farmers ever more into international competition, further increasing the supply of farm commodities. Considerations of abstract economic forces puzzled many farmers, however. How could one speak of overproduction when so many remained in need? Instead, they reasoned, there must be a screw loose somewhere in the system.

The railroads and the processors who handled the farmers' products were seen as the prime villains. Farmers resented the high railroad rates that prevailed in farm regions with no alternative forms of transportation. Individual farmers could not get the rebates on freight charges that the big corporations could extract from the railroads, and they could not exert the political influence wielded by the railroad lobbies. In other ways, farmers found themselves with little bargaining power as either buyers or sellers. When they tried to sell wheat or cotton, the buyer set the price; when they went to buy a plow point, the seller set the price.

High tariffs operated to farmers' disadvantage because they protected manufacturers from foreign competition, allowing them to raise the prices of factory goods upon which farmers depended. Farmers, however, had to sell their wheat, cotton, and other staples in foreign markets, where competition lowered prices. Tariffs inflicted a double blow on farmers because insofar as they hampered imports, they indirectly hampered exports by making it harder for foreign buyers to get the U.S. currency or exchange necessary to purchase American crops.

Debt, too, had been a perennial problem of agriculture. After the Civil War, farmers became ever more enmeshed in debt: western farmers incurred mortgages to cover the costs of land and machinery, while southern farmers used crop liens. As commodity prices dropped, the burden of debt grew because farmers had to cultivate more wheat or cotton to raise the same amount of money; and by growing more, they furthered the vicious cycle of surpluses and price declines.

THE GRANGER MOVEMENT   When the Department of Agriculture sent Oliver H. Kelley on a tour of the postbellum South in 1866, it was the isolation of farm folk that most impressed him. Resolving to do something about it, Kelley and some government clerks in 1867 founded the National Grange of the Patrons of Husbandry, better known as the Grange (an old word for granary), as each chapter was called. In the next few years the

Grange mushroomed, reaching a membership as high as 1.5 million by 1874. The Grange started as a social and educational response to the farmers' isolation, but as it grew, it began to promote farmer-owned cooperatives for the buying and selling of crops. The Grangers' long-range ideal was to free themselves from the high fees charged by grain elevators and processors.

The Grange soon became indirectly involved in politics, through independent third parties, especially in the Midwest during the early 1870s. The Grange's chief political goal was to regulate the rates charged by railroads and warehouses. In five states they brought about the passage of "Granger laws," which at first proved relatively ineffective but laid a foundation for stronger legislation. Owners subject to their regulation challenged the laws in cases that soon advanced to the Supreme Court, where the plaintiffs in the "Granger cases" claimed to have been deprived of property without due process of law. In a key case involving warehouse regulation, *Munn v. Illinois* (1877), the Supreme Court ruled that the state, under its "police powers," had the right to regulate property where that property was clothed in a public interest. If regulatory power were abused, the ruling said, "the people must resort to the polls, not the courts." Later, however, the courts would severely restrict state regulatory powers.

The Granger movement gradually declined (but never vanished) as members' energies were drawn off into both cooperatives, many of which failed, and political action. Out of the independent political movements of the time, there grew in 1875 a party calling itself the Independent National party, more commonly known as the Greenback party because of its emphasis on the virtues of paper money. In the 1878 midterm elections it polled over 1 million votes and elected fifteen congressmen. But in 1880 the party's fortunes declined, and it disintegrated after 1884.

FARMERS' ALLIANCES   As the Grange lost energy, other farm organizations, known as Farmers' Alliances, grew in size and significance. Like the Grange, the Farmers' Alliances offered social and recreational opportunities, but they also emphasized political action. Farmers throughout the South and Midwest, where tenancy rates were highest, rushed to join the Alliance movement. They saw in collective action a way to seek relief from the hardships created by chronic indebtedness, declining prices, and devastating droughts. Unlike the Grange, which was a national organization that tended to attract larger and more prosperous farmers, the Alliance was a grassroots local organization representing marginal farmers.

The Alliance movement swept across the cotton belt in the South and established strong positions in Kansas and the Dakotas. In 1886 a white minister in

Texas, which had one of the largest and most influential Alliance movements, responded to the appeals of African-American farmers by organizing the Colored Farmers' National Alliance. The white leadership of the Alliance movement in Texas endorsed this development because the Colored Alliance stressed that its objective was economic justice, not social equality. By 1890 the Alliance movement had members from New York to California, numbering about 1.5 million, and the Colored Farmers' National Alliance claimed over 1 million members.

A powerful attraction for many isolated, struggling farmers and their families was the sense of community provided by the Alliance. The Alliance movement welcomed rural women and men over sixteen years of age who displayed a "good moral character," believed in God, and demonstrated "industrious habits." The slogan of the Southern Alliance was "equal rights to all, special privileges to none." Women eagerly embraced the chance to engage in economic and political issues. One North Carolina woman expressed her appreciation for the "grand opportunities" the Alliance provided women, allowing them to emerge from traditional domesticity. "Drudgery, fashion, and gossip," she declared, "are no longer the bounds of woman's sphere." One Alliance publication made the point explicitly: "The Alliance has come to redeem woman from her enslaved condition, and place her in her proper sphere." The number of women in the movement grew rapidly, and many assumed key leadership roles in the "grand army of reform."

The Alliance movement sponsored an ambitious social and educational program and about 1,000 affiliated newspapers. Unlike the Grange, however, the Alliance also proposed an elaborate economic program. In 1890 Alliance agencies and exchanges in some eighteen states claimed a business of $10 million, but they soon went the way of the Granger cooperatives, victims of both discrimination by wholesalers, manufacturers, railroads, and bankers—as well as their own inexperienced management and overextended credit.

In 1887 Charles W. Macune, the new Alliance president, proposed that Texas farmers create their own Alliance Exchange in an effort to free themselves from their dependence upon food processors and banks. Members of the exchange would sign joint notes, borrow money from banks, and purchase their goods and supplies from a new corporation created by the Alliance in Dallas. The exchange would also build its own warehouses to store and market members' crops. While their crops were being stored, member farmers would be able to obtain credit from the warehouse cooperative so that they could buy household goods and supplies.

This grand cooperative scheme collapsed when Texas banks refused to accept the joint notes from Alliance members. Macune and others then focused their energies on what Macune called a "subtreasury plan." Under this plan,

Members of the Texas Alliance, 1880s

Alliances united local farmers, fostered a sense of community, and influenced political policies.

farmers would be able to store their crops in new government warehouses and obtain government loans for up to 80 percent of the value of their crops at 1 percent interest. Besides providing immediate credit, the plan would allow the farmer the leeway to hold a crop for a better price later, since he would not have to sell it at harvest time to pay off debts. The plan would also promote inflation because the loans to farmers would be made in new legal-tender notes.

The subtreasury plan went before Congress in 1890 but was never adopted. Its defeat as well as setbacks to other proposals convinced many farm leaders that they needed more political power in order to secure railroad regulation, currency inflation, state departments of agriculture, antitrust laws, and farm credit.

FARM POLITICS   In the West, where hard times had descended after the blizzards of 1887, farmers agitated for third-party political action. In the South, however, white Alliance members hesitated to bolt the Democratic party, seeking instead to influence or control it. Both approaches gained startling success. Independent parties under various names upset the political balance in western states, almost electing a governor under the banner of the People's party (also known as the Populist party) in Kansas (where a Populist was elected governor in 1892) and taking control of one house of

Mary Elizabeth Lease, 1890

A charismatic leader in the farm protest movement.

the state legislature there and both houses in Nebraska. In South Dakota and Minnesota, Populists gained a balance of power in the state legislatures, and Kansas sent a Populist to the Senate.

The farm protest movement produced colorful leaders, especially in Kansas, where Mary Elizabeth Lease advised farmers "to raise less corn and more hell." Born in Pennsylvania, Lease migrated to Kansas, taught school, raised a family, and failed at farming in the mid-1880s. She then studied law, "pinning sheets of notes above her wash tub," and through strenuous effort became one of the state's first female lawyers. At the same time, she took up public speaking on behalf of various causes, including Irish nationalism, temperance, and women's suffrage. By the end of the 1880s, Lease had joined the Alliance as well as the Knights of Labor, and she soon applied her gifts as a fiery speaker to the cause of free silver. A tall, proud, and imposing woman, Lease drew attentive audiences. "The people are at bay," she warned in 1894, "let the bloodhounds of money beware."

Jeremiah Simpson was an equally charismatic agrarian radical. Born in Canada, he served as a seaman on Great Lakes steamships before buying a farm in northern Kansas. He, his wife, and their young daughter made a go of the farm, but when he saw his child crushed to death in a sawmill accident, he and his wife relocated to the southern part of the state. There Simpson raised cattle for several years before losing his herd in a blizzard. Simpson embraced the Alliance movement, and in 1890 he campaigned for Congress. A shrewd man with huge, callused hands, he simplified the complex economic and political issues of the day. "Man must have access to the land," he maintained, "or he is a slave." He warned Republicans: "You can't put this movement down by sneers or by ridicule, for its foundation was laid as far back as the foundation of the world. It is a struggle between the robbers and the robbed." Simpson dismissed his Republican opponent, a wealthy railroad lawyer, as an indulgent pawn of the corporations whose "soft white hands" and "silk hosiery" betrayed his true priorities. His outraged opponent thereupon shouted that it was better to have silk socks than none at all, providing Simpson with his folksy nickname. Sockless Jerry won a seat in Congress, and so too did many other friends of "the people" in the Midwest.

In the South the Alliance won equal if not greater success by forcing the Democrats to nominate candidates pledged to their program. The southern states elected four pro-Alliance governors, seven pro-Alliance legislatures, forty-four pro-Alliance congressmen, and several senators. Among the most respected of the southern Alliance leaders was Thomas E. Watson of Georgia. The son of prosperous slaveholders who had lost everything after the Civil War, Watson became a successful lawyer and orator on behalf of the Alliance cause. He took the lead in urging African-American tenant farmers and sharecroppers to join with their white counterparts in ousting the white political elite. "You are kept apart," he told black and white farmers, "that you may be separately fleeced of your earnings."

THE POPULIST PARTY AND THE ELECTION OF 1892 The success of the Alliances led many politicians to consider the formation of a third political party on the national level. In 1891 a conference in Cincinnati brought together delegates from farm, labor, and reform organizations to discuss strategy. The meeting endorsed a national third party and formed a national executive committee of the People's party. Few southerners attended the Cincinnati conference, but many approved of the third-party idea after their failure to move the Democratic party toward the subtreasury plan. In 1892 a larger meeting in St. Louis called for a national

The Populist Party

A Populist gathering in Callaway, Nebraska, 1892.

convention of the People's party at Omaha to adopt a platform and choose candidates. The Populist Convention opened on July 4, 1892. It was like "a religious revival, said a participant, "a crusade, a Pentecost of politics in which a tongue of flame sat upon every man, and each spoke as the spirit gave him utterance."

The Populist platform focused on issues of finance, transportation, and land. Its financial program demanded implementation of the subtreasury plan, unlimited coinage of silver, an increase in the amount of money in circulation to $50 per capita, a graduated income tax whose rates would rise with personal income levels, and postal savings banks to protect depositors who otherwise risked disastrous losses in small-town banks vulnerable to farm depressions. As for transportation, the time had come "when the railroad corporations will either own the people or the people must own the railroads." Let government therefore nationalize the railroads, and the telephone and telegraph systems as well. The Populists called for the government to reclaim from railroads and other corporations lands "in excess of their actual needs" and to forbid land ownership by immigrants who had not gained citizenship. Finally, the platform endorsed the eight-hour workday and restriction of immigration. The party took these last positions to win support from the urban workers, whom Populists looked upon as fellow "producers." The party's platform turned out to be more exciting than its candidate. Iowa's James B. Weaver, an able, prudent man, carried the stigma of his defeat on the Greenback ticket twelve years before. To balance Weaver, who had been a Union general, the party named a former Confederate general for vice president.

The Populist party was the startling new feature of the 1892 campaign. The major parties renominated the candidates of 1888: Democrat Grover Cleveland and Republican Benjamin Harrison. The tariff issue monopolized their attention. Both major candidates polled over 5 million votes, but Cleveland carried a plurality of the popular votes and a majority of the Electoral College. Weaver polled over 1 million votes and carried Colorado, Kansas, Nevada, and Idaho, for a total of twenty-two electoral votes. Alabama was the banner Populist state of the South, with 37 percent of its vote going to Weaver.

THE ECONOMY AND THE SILVER SOLUTION

While the farmers were funneling their discontent into politics and businessmen were consolidating their holdings, a fundamental weakness in the economy was about to cause a major collapse.

INADEQUATE CURRENCY   The nation's money supply in the late nineteenth century lacked the flexibility to grow along with the expanding economy. From 1865 to 1890, the amount of currency in circulation per capita decreased about 10 percent. Currency deflation raised the cost of borrowing money, as a tight money supply caused bankers to hike interest rates on loans.

Metallic money dated from the Mint Act of 1792, which authorized free and unlimited coinage of silver and gold at a ratio of 15 to 1, meaning that the amount of precious metal in a silver dollar weighed fifteen times as much as that in a gold dollar, a reflection of the relative value of gold and silver at the time. "Free and unlimited coinage" simply meant that owners of precious metals could have any quantity of their gold or silver coined free, except for a nominal fee to cover costs.

A fixed ratio of values between gold and silver did not reflect fluctuations in the shifting market value of the metals, however. When gold rose to a market value higher than that reflected in the official ratio, owners ceased to present it for coinage. The country was actually on a silver standard until 1837, when Congress changed the ratio to 16 to 1, which soon reversed the situation. Silver became more valuable in the open market than in coinage, and the country drifted to a gold standard. This state of affairs prevailed until 1873, when Congress passed a general revision of the coinage laws and dropped the then-unused provision for the coinage of silver.

This occurred just when silver production in the western states began to increase, however, reducing its market value through the growth in supply. Under the old laws that development would have induced owners of silver to present it at the mint for coinage. Soon advocates of currency inflation began to denounce the "crime of '73," which they had scarcely noticed at the time. Gradually suspicion grew that bankers and merchants had conspired in 1873 to stop coining silver so as to ensure a scarcity of money. But the pro-silver forces had little more legislative success than the advocates of greenback inflation. The Bland-Allison Act of 1878 and the Sherman Silver Purchase Act of 1890 provided for some silver coinage, but too little in each case to offset the overall contraction of the currency as the population and economy grew.

THE DEPRESSION OF 1893   Just before Grover Cleveland started his second term, in 1893, one of the most devastating business crises in history erupted when the Philadelphia and Reading Railroad declared bankruptcy, setting off a panic on Wall Street. Other overextended railroads collapsed, taking many banks with them. Not only was business affected, but entire farm regions were also devastated by the spreading depression. One quarter of the cities' unskilled workers lost their jobs, and by the fall of 1893 over 600 banks had closed. By 1894 the nation's economy had reached bottom. That year some 750,000 workers went on strike, millions found themselves unemployed, and railroad construction workers, laid off in the West, began tramping east and talked of marching on Washington, D.C.

Few of them made it to the capital. One protest group that did reach Washington was "Coxey's Army," led by Jacob S. Coxey, a wealthy Ohio quarry owner turned Populist who demanded that the federal government provide the unemployed with meaningful work. Coxey, his wife, and their son, Legal Tender Coxey, rode in a carriage ahead of some 400 hardy protesters who finally straggled into Washington. There Coxey was arrested for walking on the grass. Although his ragtag army dispersed peacefully, the march on Washington, as well as the growing political strength of populism, struck fear into the hearts of many Americans. Critics portrayed Populists as "hayseed socialists" whose election would endanger property rights.

The 1894 congressional elections, taking place amid this climate of anxiety, produced a severe setback for the Democrats, who paid politically for the economic downturn, and the Republicans were the chief beneficiaries. The third-party Populists emerged with six senators and seven representatives. They had polled 1.5 million votes for their congressional candidates and expected the festering discontent to carry them to national power in 1896.

SILVERITES VERSUS GOLDBUGS   The course of events would dash that hope, however. In the mid-1890s events conspired to focus all concerns on the currency issue. One of the causes of the 1893 depression was the failure of a major British bank, which had led many British investors to unload their American holdings in return for gold. Soon after Grover Cleveland's inauguration the U.S. gold reserve had fallen below $100 million. To plug the drain on the Treasury by stopping the issuance of silver notes redeemable in gold, the president sought repeal of the Sherman Silver Purchase Act. Cleveland won the repeal in 1893, but at the cost of irreparable division in his own party. One embittered pro-silver Democrat labeled the president a Benedict Arnold.

Western silver interests now escalated their demands for silver coinage, presenting a strategic dilemma for Populists: Should the party promote the long list of varied reforms it had originally advocated, or should it try to ride the silver issue into power? The latter seemed the practical choice. As a consequence, the Populist leaders decided, over the protests of more radical members, to hold their 1896 nominating convention last, confident that the two major parties would at best straddle the silver issue and they would then reap a harvest of bolting silverite Republicans and Democrats.

THE ELECTION OF 1896   Contrary to these expectations, the major parties took opposite positions on the currency issue. The Republicans, as expected, chose William McKinley on a gold-standard platform. McKinley, a former congressman and governor of Ohio, symbolized the mainstream Republican values that had served the party well. After the convention, a friend told McKinley that the "money question" would determine the election. The Republican candidate dismissed the notion, insisting that the tariff would continue to govern national elections. But one of McKinley's advisers disagreed. "In my opinion," said Judge William Day of Ohio, "in thirty days you won't hear of anything else" but the money question. He was right.

On the Democratic side the pro-silver forces captured the convention for their platform. William Jennings Bryan arranged to give the closing speech for the silver plank. A fervent Baptist moralist, Bryan was a two-term congressman from Nebraska who had been swept out of office in the Democratic losses of 1894. In the months before the convention, he had traveled throughout the South and the West, speaking for free silver and against Cleveland's "do-nothing" response to the depression. Bryan's rehearsed phrases swept the convention into a frenzy:

> I come to speak to you in defense of a cause as holy as the cause of liberty—the cause of humanity.... We have petitioned, and our petitions have been scorned. We have entreated, and our entreaties have been disregarded. We have begged, and they have mocked when our calamity came. We beg no longer; we entreat no more; we petition no more. We defy them!

By the time the messianic Bryan reached his free-silver conclusion—"You shall not press down upon the brow of labor this crown of thorns. You shall not crucify mankind upon a cross of gold!"—there was little doubt that he would get the nomination.

The next day, Bryan won the nomination on the fifth ballot, and in the process the Democratic party was fractured beyond repair. Disappointed pro-gold, pro-Cleveland Democrats were so alienated by Bryan's inflationary program and Jacksonian rhetoric that they walked out of the convention and nominated their own candidate, Senator John M. Palmer of Illinois. "Fellow Democrats," Palmer announced, "I will not consider it any great fault if you decide to cast your vote for [the Republican] William McKinley."

William Jennings Bryan

His "cross of gold" speech at the 1896 Democratic Convention roused the delegates and secured him the party's presidential nomination.

When the Populists met in St. Louis two weeks later, they faced an impossible choice. They could name their own candidate and divide the silver vote, or they could endorse Bryan and probably lose their identity as an independent party. In the end they backed Bryan but chose their own vice presidential candidate, former representative Thomas E. Watson of Georgia, and invited the Democrats to drop their vice-presidential nominee—an action that Bryan refused to countenance.

The thirty-six-year-old Bryan crisscrossed the country, exploiting his spellbinding eloquence on behalf of "the struggling masses" of workers, farmers, and small-business owners and promising the panacea of the unlimited coinage of silver. McKinley, meanwhile, conducted a "front-porch campaign," receiving selected delegations of supporters at his home in Canton, Ohio, and giving only prepared responses. McKinley's campaign manager, Mark Hanna, shrewdly portrayed Bryan as a radical whose "communistic spirit" would ruin the capitalist system. Many observers agreed with the portrait. The *New York Tribune* denounced Bryan as a "wretched rattle-pated boy, posing in vapid vanity and mouthing resounding rottenness." Theodore Roosevelt had equally strong opinions. "The silver craze surpasses belief," he wrote a friend. "Bryan's election would be a great calamity."

By preying upon such fears, the McKinley campaign raised vast sums of money to finance an army of Republican speakers who traveled the country in his support. In the end the Democratic-Populist-silverite candidates were overwhelmed by the well-organized and well-financed Republican campaign. McKinley won the popular vote by 7.1 million to 6.5 million and the Electoral College vote by 271 to 176.

Bryan carried most of the West and the South but found little support in the metropolitan centers east of the Mississippi and north of the Ohio and Potomac rivers. In the critical midwestern battleground, from Minnesota and Iowa eastward to Ohio, Bryan carried not a single state. Many Catholic

	WA 4										NH 4		
OR 4		MT 3	ND 3		MN 9						VT 4	ME 6	
	ID 3		SD 4			WI 12	MI 14			NY 36		MA 15	
	WY 3			NE 8	IA 13					PA 32		RI 4	
NV 3	UT 3					IL 24	IN 15	OH 23			CT 6		
CA 7 (+1 Dem.)		CO 4	KS 10	MO 17			KY 11 (+1 Dem.)	WV 8	VA 12		NJ 10 DE 3 MD 8		
AZ TERR.	NM TERR.		OK TERR. IND. TERR.	AR 8		TN 12			NC 11				
			TX 15		LA 8	MS 9	AL 11	GA 13	SC 9				
									FL 4				

THE ELECTION OF 1896	Electoral vote	Popular vote
William McKinley (Republican)	271	7,100,000
William J. Bryan (Democrat)	176	6,500,000

How did Bryan's "cross of gold" speech divide the Democratic party? How did McKinley's strategy differ from Bryan's? Why was Bryan able to carry the West and the South but unable to win in cities and the northeast?

voters, normally drawn to the Democrats, were repelled by Bryan's evangelical style. Farmers in the Northeast, moreover, were less attracted to agrarian radicalism than were farmers in the wheat and cotton belts, where there were higher rates of tenancy and a narrower range of crops. Among factory workers in the cities, Bryan found even less support. Wage laborers found it easier to identify with McKinley's "full dinner pail" pledge than with Bryan's freesilver panacea. Some workers, moreover, may have been intimidated by business owners' threats to close shop if the "Demopop" heresies triumphed.

A NEW ERA   The election of 1896 was a climactic political struggle. Urban-industrial values had indeed taken firm hold of the political system.

The first important act of the McKinley administration was to call a special session of Congress to raise the tariff again. The Dingley Tariff of 1897 became the highest ever. By 1897 economic prosperity was returning, helped along by inflation of the currency, which bore out the arguments of the greenbackers and silverites. But the inflation came, in one of history's many ironies, not from greenbacks or silver but from a new flood of gold into the market and into the mints. During the 1880s and 1890s discoveries of gold in South Africa, the Canadian Yukon, and Alaska led to spectacular new gold rushes. In 1900 Congress passed a Gold Standard Act, which marked an end to the silver movement.

At the close of the nineteenth century, the old issues of tariff and currency policy, which had dominated national politics since the Civil War, gave way to global concerns: the outbreak of the Spanish-American War and the acquisition of territories outside the Western Hemisphere. At the same time the advent of a new century brought new social and political developments. Even though the Populist movement faded with William Jennings Bryan's defeat, most of the agenda promoted by Bryan Democrats and Populists, dismissed as too radical and controversial in 1896, would be implemented over the next two decades. Bryan's impassioned candidacy helped transform the Democratic party into a vigorous instrument of "progressive" reform during the early twentieth century. Democrats began to promote anti-trust prosecutions, state laws to limit the working hours of women and children, the establishment of a minimum wage, and measures to support farmers and protect labor-union organizers. As the United States looked ahead to a new century, it began to place more emphasis on the role of the national government in society and the economy.

MAKING CONNECTIONS

- The laissez-faire policies of the Gilded Age were challenged by Progressive reform activists, as will be discussed in Chapter 24.
- William Jennings Bryan was one of the most prominent figures in American politics and political culture for thirty years. He will be discussed again in Chapters 24 and 26.

FURTHER READING

A good overview of the Gilded Age is Vincent P. De Santis's *The Shaping of Modern America, 1877–1920* (1973). Nell Irvin Painter's *Standing at Armageddon: The United States, 1877–1919* (1987) focuses on the experience of the working class. Excellent presidential biographies include Hans L. Trefousse's *Rutherford B. Hayes* (2002), Zachary Karabell's *Chester Alan Arthur* (2004), Henry F. Graff's *Grover Cleveland* (2002), and Kevin Phillips's *William McKinley* (2003).

Scholars have also examined various Gilded Age issues and interest groups. Gerald W. McFarland's *Mugwumps, Morals, and Politics, 1884–1920* (1975) examines the issue of reforming government service. Tom E. Terrill's *The Tariff, Politics, and American Foreign Policy, 1874–1901* (1973) lends clarity to that complex issue. The finances of the Gilded Age are covered in Walter T. K. Nugent's *Money and American Society, 1865–1880* (1968).

One of the most controversial works on populism is Lawrence Goodwyn's *The Populist Movement: A Short History of the Agrarian Revolt in America* (1978). A more balanced account is Robert C. McMath Jr.'s *American Populism: A Social History, 1877–1898* (1992).

Part Six

MODERN AMERICA

The United States entered the twentieth century on a wave of unrelenting change. In 1800 the nation was a rural, agrarian society largely detached from the concerns of international affairs. By 1900, the United States had become a highly industrialized urban culture with a growing involvement in world politics and commerce. In other words, the nation was on the threshold of modernity.

The prospect of modernity both excited and scared Americans. Old truths and beliefs clashed with unsettling scientific discoveries and social practices. People debated the legitimacy of Darwinism, the existence of God, the dangers of jazz, and the federal effort to prohibit the sale of alcoholic beverages. The automobile and airplane helped shrink distance, and such communications innovations as radio and film contributed to a national consciousness. In the process the United States began to emerge from its isolationist shell. Throughout most of the nineteenth century, policy makers had sought to isolate America from the intrigues and conflicts of the great European powers. As early as 1780, John Adams had warned Congress against involving the United States in the affairs of Europe. "Our business with them, and theirs with us," he wrote, "is commerce, not politics, much less war." George Washington echoed this sentiment in his farewell address upon leaving the presidency, warning Americans to avoid "entangling alliances" with foreign governments.

With only a few exceptions, statesmen during the nineteenth century followed such advice. Noninvolvement in foreign wars and nonintervention in the internal affairs of foreign governments formed the pillars of American foreign policy until the end of the century. During the 1890s, however, expanding commercial interests around the world led Americans to expand the horizons of their concerns. Imperialism was the order of the day among the great European powers, and a growing number of American expansionists demanded that the United States also adopt a global ambition and join in the hunt for new territories and markets. Such motives helped spark the Spanish-American War of 1898 and helped to justify the resulting acquisition of colonies outside the continental United States. Entangling alliances with European powers soon followed.

The outbreak of the Great War in Europe in 1914 posed an even greater challenge to the tradition of isolation and nonintervention. The prospect of a German victory over the French and the British threatened the European balance of power, which had long ensured the security of the United States. By 1917 it appeared that Germany might emerge triumphant and begin to menace the Western Hemisphere. Woodrow Wilson's crusade to use American intervention in World War I to transform the world order in accordance with his idealistic principles dislodged foreign policy from its isolationist moorings. It also spawned a prolonged debate about the role of the United States in world affairs, a debate that World War II would resolve for a time on the side of internationalism.

While the United States was entering the world stage as a formidable military power, it was also settling into its role as a great industrial power. Cities and factories sprouted across the landscape. An abundance of new jobs served as a magnet attracting millions of immigrants from nearly every landmass on the globe. They were not always welcomed, nor were they readily assimilated. Ethnic and racial strife, as well as labor agitation, increased at the turn of the century. In the midst of such social turmoil and unparalleled economic development, reformers made their first sustained attempt to adapt their political and social institutions to the realities of the industrial age. The worst excesses and injustices of urban-industrial development—corporate monopolies, child labor, political corruption, hazardous working conditions, urban ghettos—were finally addressed in a comprehensive way. During the Progressive Era (1900–1917), local, state, and federal governments sought to rein in the excesses of industrial capitalism and develop a more rational and efficient public policy.

A conservative Republican resurgence challenged the notion of the new regulatory state during the 1920s. Free enterprise and corporate capitalism witnessed a dramatic revival. But the stock market crash of 1929 helped propel the United States and the world into the worst economic downturn in history. The unprecedented severity of the Great Depression renewed public demands for federal programs to protect the general welfare. "This nation asks for action," declared President Franklin D. Roosevelt in his  1933 inaugural address. The many New Deal initiatives and agencies instituted by Roosevelt and his Democratic administration created the framework for a welfare state that has since served as the basis for public policy.

The New Deal helped revive public confidence and put people back to work, but it did not end the Great Depression. It took a world war to restore full employment. The necessity of mobilizing the nation in support of the Second World War also served to accelerate the growth of the federal government. And the unparalleled scope of the war helped catapult the United States into a leadership role in world politics. The use of atomic bombs ushered in a new era of nuclear diplomacy that held the fate of the world in the balance. For all of the new creature comforts associated with modern life, Americans in 1945 found themselves living amid an array of new anxieties.

23

AN AMERICAN EMPIRE

FOCUS QUESTIONS

· What were the circumstances that led to America's "new imperialism"?

· What were the causes of the Spanish-American War?

· What were the main tenets of Theodore Roosevelt's foreign policy in Asia and Latin America?

To answer these questions and access additional review material, please visit www.wwnorton.com/studyspace.

Throughout the nineteenth century most Americans displayed what one senator called "only a languid interest" in foreign affairs. The overriding priorities were industrial development, western settlement, and domestic politics. Foreign relations simply were not important to the vast majority of Americans. After the Civil War an isolationist mood swept across the United States as the country basked in its geographic advantages: wide oceans as buffers, the British navy situated between America and the powers of Europe, and militarily weak neighbors in the Western Hemisphere.

Yet the notion of America's having a Manifest Destiny ordained by God to expand its territory and its influence remained alive in the decades after the end of the Civil War. Several prominent political and business leaders argued that the rapid industrial development of the United States required the acquisition of foreign territories to gain easier access to vital raw materials. In addition, as their exports grew, American companies and farmers became increasingly intertwined in the world economy. This, in turn, required an expanded naval presence to protect the shipping lanes. And a modern steam-powered navy needed bases where its ships could replenish their supplies of coal and water. For these reasons and others the United States during the last quarter of the nineteenth century began to expand its military presence beyond the Western Hemisphere.

TOWARD THE NEW IMPERIALISM

By the late nineteenth century, European powers had already unleashed a new surge of imperialism in Africa and Asia, where they had seized territory, established colonies, and promoted economic exploitation and Christian evangelism. Writing in 1902, the British economist J. A. Hobson declared that imperialism was "the most powerful factor in the current politics of the Western world."

IMPERIALISM IN A GLOBAL CONTEXT Western imperialism had economic roots and racist overtones. The new imperialism was above all a quest for markets and raw materials. The Second Industrial Revolution generated such dramatic increases in production that business leaders felt compelled to find new markets for their burgeoning supply of goods and new sources of investment for their growing supply of capital. Manufacturers, on the other hand, were eager to find new sources of raw materials to supply their expanding needs. At the same time, the aggressive nationalism and bitter rivalries of the European powers made all of them compete with one another as they expanded their empires.

The result was a widespread process of imperial expansion into Africa and Asia. Beginning in the 1880s, the British, French, Belgians, Italians, Dutch, Spanish, and Germans used military force and political guile to conquer those continents. Each of the imperial nations, including the United States, dispatched Christian missionaries to convert native peoples. By 1900 some 18,000 Christian missionaries were scattered around the world. Often the conversion to Christianity was the first step in the loss of a culture's indigenous traditions. The Western religious efforts also influenced the colonial power structure. A British nationalist explained the global ambitions of the imperialist nations: "Today, power and domination rather than freedom and independence are the ideas that appeal to the imagination of the masses— and the national ideal has given way to the imperial." This imperial outlook set in motion clashes among the Western powers that would lead to unprecedented conflict in the twentieth century.

AMERICAN IMPERIALISM As the European nations expanded their control over much of the rest of the world, the United States also began to acquire new territories. Most Americans became increasingly aware of world markets as developments in transportation and communication quickened the pace of commerce and diplomacy. From the first, agricultural exports had been the basis of economic growth. Now the conviction grew that manufacturers had matured to the point where they could outsell foreign competitors in the world market. But should the expansion of markets lead to territorial expansion as well? or to intervention in the internal affairs of other countries? On such points, Americans disagreed, but a small yet vocal and influential group of public officials embraced the idea of overseas possessions, regardless of the implications. These expansionists included Senators Albert J. Beveridge of Indiana and Henry Cabot Lodge of Massachusetts, Theodore Roosevelt, and not least of all, naval captain Alfred Thayer Mahan.

During the 1880s Captain Mahan had become a leading advocate of sea power and Western imperialism. In 1890 he published *The Influence of Sea Power upon History, 1660–1783*, in which he argued that national greatness and prosperity flowed from maritime power. To Mahan modern economic development called for a powerful navy, a strong merchant marine, foreign commerce, colonies, and naval bases. A self-described imperialist, Mahan championed America's "destiny" to control the Caribbean, build an isthmian canal to connect the Pacific and the Caribbean, and spread Western civilization in the Pacific. His ideas were widely circulated in popular journals and within the U.S. government. Theodore Roosevelt, the assistant secretary of the navy, ordered a copy of Mahan's book for every American ship. Yet even before Mahan's writings became influential, a gradual expansion of the navy had begun. In 1880 the nation had fewer than 100 seagoing vessels, many of them rusting or rotting at the docks. By 1896, eleven powerful new battleships had been built or authorized.

IMPERIALIST THEORY Claims of racial superiority bolstered the new imperialist spirit. Spokesmen in each Western country, including the United States, used the arguments of social Darwinism to justify economic exploitation and territorial conquest. Among nations as among individuals, expansionists claimed, the fittest survive and prevail. John Fiske, a historian and popular lecturer on Darwinism, developed racial corollaries from Darwin's ideas. In *American Political Ideas Viewed from the Standpoint of Universal*

History (1885), he stressed the superior character of "Anglo-Saxon" institutions and peoples. The English "race," he argued, was destined to dominate the globe and transform the institutions, traditions, language—even in the blood—of the world's peoples. Josiah Strong, a Congregationalist minister, added the sanction of religion to theories of racial and national superiority. In his book *Our Country: Its Possible Future and Its Present Crisis* (1885), Strong asserted that "Anglo-Saxon" embodied two great ideas: civil liberty and "a pure spiritual Christianity." The Anglo-Saxon was "divinely commissioned to be, in a peculiar sense, his brother's keeper."

Expansion in the Pacific

For Josiah Strong and other expansionists, Asia offered an especially alluring temptation. President Andrew Johnson's secretary of state, William H. Seward, had predicted in 1866 that the United States must inevitably exercise commercial domination "on the Pacific Ocean, and its islands and continents." Eager for American manufacturers to exploit Asian markets, Seward believed the United States first had to remove all foreign interests from the northern Pacific coast and gain access to that region's valuable ports. To that end, he cast covetous eyes on the British crown colony of British Columbia, sandwiched between Russian America (Alaska) and the Washington Territory.

Late in 1866, while encouraging British Columbians to consider making their colony a U.S. territory, Seward learned of Russia's desire to sell Alaska. He leaped at the opportunity, and in 1867 the United States bought Alaska for $7.2 million, thus removing Russia, the most recent colonial power, from the New World. Critics scoffed at "Seward's folly" of buying the Alaskan "icebox," but it proved in time to be the biggest bargain since the Louisiana Purchase. Seward's successors at the State Department sustained his expansionist vision. Acquiring key ports in the Pacific Ocean was the major focus of overseas activity through the rest of the nineteenth century. Two island groups occupied especially strategic positions: Samoa and Hawaii (the Sandwich Islands). Both had major harbors, Pago Pago and Pearl Harbor, respectively. In the years after the Civil War, American interest in those islands gradually deepened.

SAMOA In 1878, the Samoans signed a treaty with the United States that granted a naval base at Pago Pago and extraterritoriality for Americans (meaning that in Samoa, Americans remained subject only to U.S. law),

American Expansion

In a critical comment on William Seward's 1867 purchase of Alaska, this cartoon represents the territory as a block of ice labeled "Russian America."

exchanged trade concessions, and called for the United States to extend its good offices in case of a dispute with another nation. The Senate ratified this accord, and in the following year the German and British governments worked out similar arrangements with other islands of the Samoan group. There matters rested until civil war broke out in 1887. A peace conference in Berlin in 1889 established a tripartite protectorate over Samoa, with Germany, Great Britain, and the United States in an uneasy partnership.

HAWAII   In Hawaii the Americans had a clearer field to exploit. The islands, a united kingdom since 1795, had a sizable settlement of American missionaries and planters and were strategically more important to the United States than Samoa. In 1875 the kingdom signed a reciprocal trade agreement under which Hawaiian sugar would enter the United States duty-free and Hawaii promised that none of its territory would be leased or granted to a third power. This agreement resulted in a boom in sugar production, and American settlers in Hawaii soon formed an economic elite. White planters in Hawaii built their fortunes on cheap immigrant labor, mainly Chinese, Japanese, and Portuguese. By the 1890s, the native population had been reduced to a minority by smallpox and other foreign diseases, and Asians quickly became the most numerous group in Hawaii.

Queen Liliuokalani

The Hawaiian queen sought to preserve her nation's independence.

In 1885 President Grover Cleveland called the Hawaiian Islands "the stepping-stone to the growing trade of the Pacific." Two years later Americans in Hawaii forced the king to accept a constitutional government, which they dominated. In 1890, however, the McKinley Tariff destroyed Hawaii's favored position in the sugar trade by putting the sugar of all countries on the duty-free list and granting growers in the continental United States a 2¢ subsidy per pound of sugar. This change led to an economic crisis in Hawaii and brought political turmoil as well.

In 1891, when the king's sister, Liliuokalani, ascended the throne, she tried to eliminate white control of the government. Two years later Hawaii's white population revolted and seized power. The American ambassador brought in marines to support the coup. As he cheerfully reported to Washington, "The Hawaiian pear is now fully ripe, and this is the golden hour for the United States to pluck it." Within a month a committee of the new white government in Hawaii turned up in Washington with a treaty calling for the island nation to be annexed to the United States.

The treaty appeared just weeks before President Benjamin Harrison left office, however, and Democratic senators blocked its ratification. President Cleveland then withdrew the treaty and sent a special commissioner to investigate. The commissioner removed the U.S. Marines and reported that the Americans in Hawaii had acted improperly. Most Hawaiians opposed annexation to the United States, the commissioner found. He concluded that the revolution had been engineered mainly by the American planters hoping to take advantage of the subsidy for sugar grown in the United States. Cleveland proposed to restore the queen to power in return for amnesty to the revolutionists. The provisional government controlled by the sugar planters refused to give up power, however, and on July 4, 1894, it proclaimed the islands the Republic of Hawaii, which included in its constitution a standing provision for American annexation. When William McKinley became president in 1897, he was looking for an excuse to annex the islands. "We need Hawaii," he claimed, "just as much and a good deal more than we did California. It is manifest destiny." When the Japanese, also hoping to take over the islands, sent warships to Hawaii, McKinley responded by sending U.S. warships and asked the Senate to approve a treaty to annex the islands. When the Senate could not muster the two-thirds majority needed to approve the treaty, McKinley used a joint resolution of the House and the Senate to achieve his aims. The resolution passed by simple majorities in both houses, and Hawaii was annexed in the summer of 1898.

THE SPANISH-AMERICAN WAR

Until the 1890s, a certain ambivalence about overseas possessions had checked America's drive to expand. Suddenly, in 1898 and 1899, the inhibitions collapsed, and the United States thrust its way to the far reaches of the Pacific. The occasion for this explosion of imperialism lay neither in the Pacific nor in the quest for bases and trade but to the south, in Cuba. Ironically, the chief motive was a sense of outrage at another country's imperialism.

"CUBA LIBRE"   Throughout the second half of the nineteenth century, Cubans had repeatedly revolted against Spanish rule, only to be ruthlessly suppressed. One of Spain's oldest colonies, Cuba was a major export market for the mother country. Yet American investments in Cuba, mainly in sugar and mining, were steadily increasing. The United States in fact traded more with Cuba than Spain did.

On February 24, 1895, insurrection broke out again. Simmering discontent with Spanish rule had been aggravated by the Wilson-Gorman Tariff of 1894, which took sugar off the duty-free list in the midst of a depression already damaging the market for Cuban sugar. Raw-sugar prices collapsed, putting Cubans out of work and thereby rekindling their desire for rebellion. Public feeling in the United States supported the Cuban rebels.

Cuban insurrectionists waged guerrilla warfare against Spanish troops and sought to damage the economic life of the island, which they expected would excite the concern of American investors. The strategy dictated hit-and-run attacks on trains, railways, and plantations. Americans often compared the insurrection to their own War of Independence. In 1896 the Spanish general Valeriano Weyler y Nicolau adopted a policy of gathering Cubans behind Spanish lines, often in detention (*reconcentrado*) centers so that no one could join

José Martí y Perez

Leader of the Cuban revolt against Spanish rule.

the insurrections by night and appear peaceful by day. In some of the centers, a combination of tropical climate, poor food, and unsanitary conditions quickly produced a heavy toll of disease and death. The American press promptly christened the Spanish commander "Butcher" Weyler.

Events in Cuba supplied exciting copy for the popular press. William Randolph Hearst's *New York Journal* and Joseph Pulitzer's *New York World* were at the time locked in a monumental competition for readers. "It was a battle of gigantic proportions," one journalist later wrote, "in which the sufferings of Cuba merely chanced to furnish some of the most convenient ammunition." The newspaper sensationalism came to be called yellow journalism.

At the outset the Cleveland administration tried to protect American rights in Cuba but avoided involvement beyond an offer of mediation. Mounting public sympathy for the rebel cause prompted concern in Congress, however. By concurrent resolution on April 6, 1896, the two houses endorsed official recognition of the Cuban rebels and urged the president to help them gain independence. Cleveland, however, offered only to cooperate with Spain in bringing peace on the basis of allowing Cubans a measure of self-governance. The Spanish politely refused.

PRESSURE FOR WAR   America's posture of neutrality changed sharply when William McKinley became president in 1897. He had been elected on a platform that endorsed Cuban independence as well as American control of Hawaii and the construction of an isthmian canal connecting the Caribbean Sea to the Pacific Ocean. In 1897 Spain offered Cuba autonomy (self-government without formal independence) in return for peace. The Cubans rejected the offer. Spain was impaled on the horns of a dilemma, unable to end the rebellion and unready to give up Cuba.

Early in 1898 events moved rapidly to arouse American opinion against Spain. On January 25, the U.S. battleship *Maine* docked in Havana Harbor, ostensibly on a courtesy call. On February 9 the *New York Journal* released the text of a letter from the Spanish ambassador Depuy de Lôme to a friend in Havana, stolen from the post office by a Cuban spy. In the letter, de Lôme called President McKinley "weak and a bidder for the admiration of the crowd, besides being a would-be politician who tries to leave a door open behind himself while keeping on good terms with the jingoes of his party." This was hardly more extreme than what McKinley's outspoken assistant secretary of the navy, Theodore Roosevelt, had said about him: that the "white-livered" president had "no more backbone than a chocolate eclair." But that comment had remained private. De Lôme resigned to prevent further embarrassment to his government.

Six days later, during the night of February 15, 1898, the *Maine* exploded and sank in Havana Harbor, with a loss of 260 men. The ship's captain, one of only 84 survivors, scribbled a telegram to Washington: "*Maine* blown up in Havana Harbor at nine forty tonight and destroyed. Many wounded and doubtless more killed or drowned. . . . Public opinion should be suspended until further report."

The Sinking of the *Maine* in Havana Harbor

The uproar created by the incident and its coverage in the "yellow press" helped to push President William McKinley to declare war.

But those eager for a war with Spain saw no need to withhold judgment. Theodore Roosevelt called the sinking "an act of dirty treachery on the part of the Spaniards." The United States, he claimed, "needs a war." A naval court of inquiry reported that an external mine had set off an explosion in the ship's munitions magazine. Lacking hard evidence, the court made no effort to fix the blame, but the yellow press had no need of evidence. The outcry against Spain rose in a crescendo with the words "Remember the *Maine!*" Never mind that Spain could have derived little benefit from such an act. A comprehensive study in 1976 concluded that the sinking of the *Maine* was an accident, the result of an internal explosion triggered by a fire in its coal bunker.

The weight of outraged public opinion and the influence of Republican militants such as Theodore Roosevelt and the president's closest friend, Senator Henry Cabot Lodge, eroded McKinley's neutrality. On March 9 the president coaxed from Congress a $50-million appropriation for defense. Still McKinley sought to avoid war, as did most business leaders. Their caution infuriated Roosevelt. "We will have this war for the freedom of Cuba," he fumed on March 26, "in spite of the timidity of the commercial interests."

The Spanish government, sensing the growing militancy in the United States, announced a unilateral cease-fire in early April. On April 10 the Spanish ambassador to the United States gave the State Department a message that amounted to a surrender: Cuba would have an autonomous government, and the question of the sinking of the *Maine* would go to arbitration. The United States minister to Spain then cabled from Madrid: "I hope nothing will now be done to humiliate Spain, as I am satisfied that the present government is going, and is loyally ready to go, as fast and as far as it can." McKinley, he predicted, could win a settlement by August 1 on any terms: autonomy, independence, or cession of Cuba to the United States.

But the message came too late. The following day, McKinley asked Congress for power to use armed forces in Cuba to protect U.S. property and trade. On April 20 a joint resolution of Congress declared Cuba independent and demanded withdrawal of Spanish forces. The Teller Amendment, added on the Senate floor, disclaimed any U.S. designs on Cuban territory. McKinley signed the war resolution, and a copy went off to the Spanish government, with notice that McKinley would execute it unless Spain gave a satisfactory response by noon on April 23. Meanwhile, on April 22 the president announced a blockade of Cuba's northern coast and the port of Santiago. Under international law this was an act of war. Rather than give in to an ultimatum, the Spanish government declared war on April 24. Determined to be first, Congress declared war on April 25, retroactive to April 21, 1898.

Why such a rush to war after the American ambassador had predicted that Spain would cave in before the summer was out? Chiefly because too much momentum and popular pressure had built up for a confidential message to change the course of events. Also, leaders of the business community were now demanding a quick resolution of the problem. Many of them lacked faith in the willingness or ability of the Spanish government to carry out a moderate policy in the face of hostile public opinion. Still, it is fair to ask why McKinley did not take a stronger stand for peace. He might have defied Congress and public opinion, but in the end he decided that the political risk was too high. The ultimate blame for war, if blame must be levied, belongs to the American people for letting themselves be whipped into such a hostile frenzy.

MANILA   The war itself lasted only 114 days. John Hay, soon to be secretary of state, called it "a splendid little war." The conflict's end was also the end of Spain's once-great New World empire. It marked as well the emergence of the United States as a world power. The United States liberated Spain's colonies, yet in some cases it would substitute Spanish oppression with its own. If war with Spain saved many lives by ending the insurrection in Cuba, it also led to U.S. involvement in another insurrection, in the Philippines, and created a host of festering problems that persisted into the twentieth century.

The Spanish-American War was barely under way before the U.S. Navy produced a spectacular victory in an unexpected quarter: Manila Bay. While public attention focused on Cuba, young Theodore Roosevelt was thinking of the Spanish-controlled Philippines. As assistant secretary of the navy, he ordered Commodore George Dewey, commander of the small squadron in Asia, to engage Spain in the Philippines in case of war. President McKinley had approved the orders.

Arriving late on April 30 with four cruisers and two gunboats, Dewey destroyed or captured all the Spanish warships in Manila Bay. The Spanish force lost 381 men while in Dewey's squadron only eight men were wounded. Dewey, without an occupation force, was now in awkward possession of Manila Bay. Promised reinforcements, he stayed while German and British warships hung about the scene like watchful vultures, ready to take over the Philippines if the United States did not do so. American troops finally arrived, and with the help of Filipino insurrectionists under Emilio Aguinaldo, Dewey's forces entered Manila on August 13.

THE CUBAN CAMPAIGN   While these events transpired halfway around the world, the fighting in Cuba reached a surprisingly quick climax.

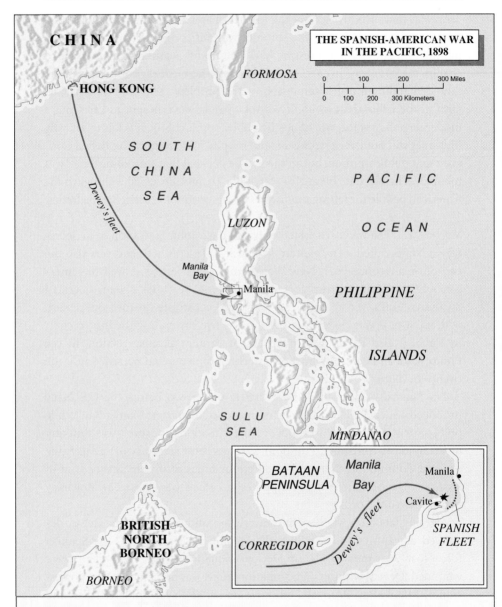

THE SPANISH-AMERICAN WAR IN THE PACIFIC, 1898

Why did Roosevelt order Dewey to take Manila? What role did Emilio Aguinaldo play? Why were many Americans opposed to the acquisition of the Philippines?

The U.S. Navy blockaded the Spanish navy at Santiago. A force of some 17,000 American troops hastily assembled at Tampa, Florida. One significant unit was the First Volunteer Cavalry, better known as the Rough Riders and best remembered because Lieutenant Colonel Theodore Roosevelt was second in command. Eager to get "in on the fun" and "to act up to my preachings," Roosevelt had quit the Navy Department soon after war was declared. He ordered a custom-fitted powder-blue army uniform from Brooks Brothers and rushed to help organize a volunteer regiment of Ivy League athletes, leathery ex-convicts, Indians, and southwestern sharpshooters. Their landing at the southeastern tip of Cuba was a mad scramble, as the horses were mistakenly sent elsewhere, leaving the Rough Riders to become the "Weary Walkers." Only Roosevelt had a horse.

Land and sea battles around Santiago broke Spanish resistance. On July 1, about 7,000 U.S. soldiers took the fortified village of El Caney. While a much larger force attacked San Juan Hill, a smaller unit, including the dismounted Rough Riders together with African-American soldiers from two cavalry units, seized the enemy position atop nearby Kettle Hill. Roosevelt later claimed that he "would rather have led that charge than served three terms in the U.S. Senate." A friend wrote to Roosevelt's wife that her husband was "revelling in victory and gore." Roosevelt's oversized ego and penchant for self-promotion led him to lobby Congress—unsuccessfully—to award him a Congressional Medal of Honor for his headlong gallop at the head of his troops in Cuba. (President Bill Clinton finally awarded Roosevelt the medal in 2001.)

The two battles put American forces atop heights from which, to the west and south, they could bring Santiago and the Spanish fleet under siege. On July 3 the Spanish navy made a gallant run for it, but its decrepit ships were little more than sitting ducks for the newer American fleet. The casualties were as one-sided as those at Manila: 474 Spanish were killed and wounded and 1,750 were taken prisoner, while only one American was killed and one wounded. Santiago surrendered on July 17. On July 25 an American force moved into Spanish-held Puerto Rico, meeting only minor resistance.

The next day the Spanish government sued for peace. After discussions lasting two weeks, an armistice was signed on August 12, less than four months after the war's start and the day before Americans entered Manila. The peace protocol specified that Spain should give up Cuba and that the United States should annex Puerto Rico and occupy Manila pending the transfer of power in the Philippines.

In all, over 60,000 Spanish soldiers died of disease or wounds in the four-month war. Among the Americans who served during the war and the

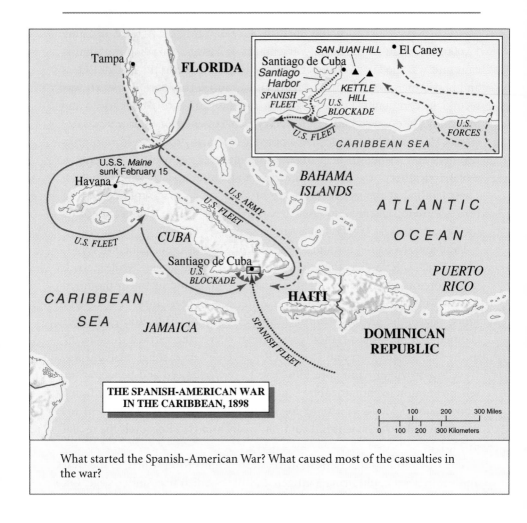

SAN JUAN HILL • El Caney
Santiago de Cuba
Santiago
Harbor
SPANISH
FLEET
KETTLE
HILL
U.S.
BLOCKADE
U.S. FLEET
U.S.
FORCES
CARIBBEAN SEA

Tampa
FLORIDA

U.S.S. *Maine*
sunk February 15
Havana

U.S. ARMY
U.S. FLEET

BAHAMA
ISLANDS

ATLANTIC

OCEAN

U.S. FLEET
CUBA

Santiago de Cuba
U.S.
BLOCKADE

PUERTO
RICO

CARIBBEAN

SEA   JAMAICA

HAITI

SPANISH FLEET

DOMINICAN
REPUBLIC

**THE SPANISH-AMERICAN WAR
IN THE CARIBBEAN, 1898**

0   100   200   300 Miles

0   100   200   300 Kilometers

What started the Spanish-American War? What caused most of the casualties in
the war?

ensuing demobilization, more than 274,000, some 6,000 died, but only
379 in battle. Most succumbed to malaria, typhoid, dysentery, or yellow
fever. At such a cost the United States was launched onto the world scene
as a great power, with all the benefits—and burdens—of a new colonial
power.

THE DEBATE OVER ANNEXATION   The United States and Spain
signed the Treaty of Paris on December 10, 1898, but the status of the Philippines remained unresolved. There had been no demand for annexation of
the Philippines before the war, but Commodore Dewey's victory quickly
kindled expansionist fever. Business leaders began thinking of the commercial

possibilities in the nearby continent of Asia, such as oil for the lamps of China and textiles for its millions of people. Missionary societies saw the chance to bring Christianity to "the little brown brother." The Philippines promised to provide a useful base for all such activities. It was neither the first nor the last time that Americans would get caught up in fantasies of "saving" Asia or getting rich there. McKinley pondered the alternatives and later explained his reasoning to a group of his fellow Methodists:

> And one night late it came to me this way—I don't know how it was, but it came: (1) that we could not give them back to Spain—that would be cowardly and dishonorable; (2) that we could not turn them over to France or Germany—our commercial rivals in the Orient—that would be bad business and discreditable; (3) that we could not leave them to themselves—they were unfit for self-government—and they would soon have anarchy and misrule over there worse than Spain's was; and (4) that there was nothing left for us to do but to take them all, and to educate the Filipinos, and uplift and civilize and Christianize them, and by God's grace do the very best we could by them, as our fellowmen for whom Christ also died. And then I went to bed, and went to sleep and slept soundly.

In one brief statement McKinley had summarized the motivating ideas of imperialism: (1) national glory, (2) commerce, (3) racial superiority, and (4) altruism. Spanish negotiators raised the delicate point that American forces had no claim by right of conquest and had even occupied Manila after the armistice. American negotiators finally offered the Spanish compensation of $20 million. The treaty thus added to U.S. territory Puerto Rico, Guam (a Spanish-controlled island in the Pacific), and the Philippines.

Meanwhile Americans had taken other giant steps in the Pacific. Hawaii had been annexed in the midst of the war. In 1899, after another outbreak of fighting over the royal succession in Samoa, Germany and the United States agreed to partition the Samoa Islands. The United States annexed the easternmost islands; Germany took the rest, including the largest. Meanwhile, in 1898 the United States had laid claim to Wake Island, located between Guam and the Hawaiian Islands, which would become a vital link in a future transpacific cable line.

The Treaty of Paris had yet to be ratified in the Senate, where most Democrats and Populists and some Republicans opposed it. Anti-imperialists argued that acquisition of the Philippines would undermine democracy. They stressed traditional isolationism, American principles of self-government, the inconsistency of liberating Cuba and annexing the Philippines, the involvement in foreign entanglements that would undermine the logic of the Monroe Doctrine, and the danger that the Philippines would become impossible to defend. The prospect of incorporating so many alien peoples was not the least of some Americans' worries. "Bananas and self-government cannot grow on the same piece of land," one senator claimed.

The opposition might have been strong enough to kill the treaty had not the populist Democrat William Jennings Bryan influenced the vote for approval. Ending the war, he argued, would open the way for the future independence of Cuba and the Philippines. Finally, ratification came on February 6, 1899, by the narrowest of margins: only one vote more than the necessary two thirds. Senator Henry Cabot Lodge of Massachusetts described his efforts to gain approval of the treaty as "the closest, hardest fight" he had witnessed in the Senate. He also admitted that if U.S. troops had not provoked a clash with Filipino insurgents the weekend before, the treaty would have been rejected and the Philippines would have been set free.

American troops had engaged the Filipino insurrectionists near Manila. The Filipino leader, Emilio Aguinaldo, had been in exile until Commodore Dewey brought him back to Luzon to make trouble for the Spanish. Since Aguinaldo's forces were more or less in control of the islands outside Manila, what followed was largely an American war of conquest that lasted more

Turmoil in the Philippines

Emilio Aguinaldo (seated third from right) and other leaders of the Filipino insurgence.

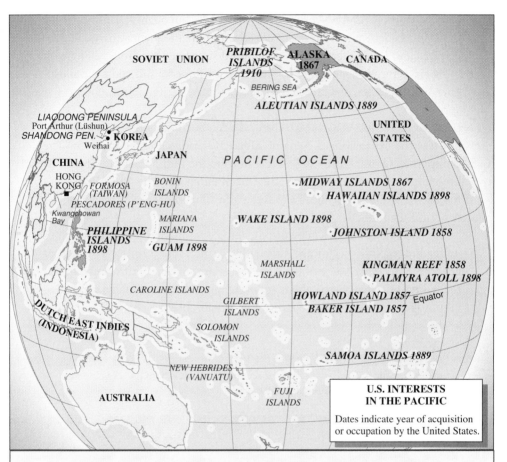

SOVIET UNION

PRIBILOF ISLANDS 1910

ALASKA 1867

CANADA

BERING SEA

ALEUTIAN ISLANDS 1889

LIAODONG PENINSULA
Port Arthur (Lüshun)
SHANDONG PEN. KOREA
Weihai

UNITED STATES

CHINA

JAPAN

PACIFIC OCEAN

HONG KONG
FORMOSA (TAIWAN)
PESCADORES (P'ENG-HU)
Kwangchowan Bay

BONIN ISLANDS

MIDWAY ISLANDS 1867

HAWAIIAN ISLANDS 1898

MARIANA ISLANDS

WAKE ISLAND 1898

JOHNSTON ISLAND 1858

PHILIPPINE ISLANDS 1898

GUAM 1898

MARSHALL ISLANDS

KINGMAN REEF 1858

PALMYRA ATOLL 1898

CAROLINE ISLANDS

GILBERT ISLANDS

HOWLAND ISLAND 1857
BAKER ISLAND 1857

Equator

DUTCH EAST INDIES (INDONESIA)

SOLOMON ISLANDS

NEW HEBRIDES (VANUATU)

SAMOA ISLANDS 1889

AUSTRALIA

FIJI ISLANDS

U.S. INTERESTS IN THE PACIFIC

Dates indicate year of acquisition or occupation by the United States.

Why was McKinley eager to acquire territory in the Pacific and the Caribbean? What kind of political system did the U.S. government create in Hawaii and in the Philippines? How did Filipinos and Hawaiians resist the Americans?

than two years. Organized Filipino resistance collapsed by the end of 1899, but even after the American capture of Aguinaldo in 1901, sporadic guerrilla action lasted until mid-1902. It was a sordid conflict, with massacres and torture on both sides. In the end it took 63,000 American troops, 4,300 American deaths, and almost three years to crush the revolt.

Against the backdrop of this nasty guerrilla war, the great debate over imperialism continued in the United States. The treaty debates inspired a number of anti-imperialist groups, which united in 1899 as the American Anti-Imperialist League. The league attracted members representing many shades of opinion; the main thing they had in common was that most belonged to an older generation. Andrew Carnegie footed the bills, but on imperialism, at least, the union leader Samuel Gompers agreed with him. Presidents Charles Eliot of Harvard and David Starr Jordan of Stanford supported the group, along with the social reformer Jane Addams. The drive for imperialism, said the philosopher William James, had caused the nation to "puke up its ancient soul."

ORGANIZING THE ACQUISITIONS Such criticism, however, did not faze the expansionists. Senator Albert Beveridge boasted in 1900: "The Philippines are ours forever. And just beyond the Philippines are China's illimitable markets. We will not retreat from either. . . . The power that rules the Pacific is the power that rules the world. That power will forever be the American Republic."

In 1900 President McKinley dispatched a commission to the Philippines under Judge William Howard Taft with instructions to set up a system of government. Unlike some of the Americans on the scene, Taft seemed to like the Filipinos, encouraged them to participate, and eventually persuaded Filipino representatives to sit on the commission itself.

"Well, I Hardly Know Which to Take First."

At the end of the nineteenth century, it seemed that Uncle Sam had developed a considerable appetite for foreign territory.

On July 4, 1901, the U.S. military government in the Philippines came to an end. Under an act of Congress, Judge William H. Taft became the civil governor. The Philippine Government Act, passed by Congress in 1902, declared the Philippine Islands an "unorganized territory" and made the inhabitants citizens of the Philippines. In 1917 the Jones Act affirmed America's intention to grant the Philippines independence on an unspecified date. Finally, the Tydings-McDuffie Act of 1934 offered independence after ten more years. A constitution was drafted and ratified, and in September 1934 Manuel Quezon y Molina was elected the first president of the Philippines. Independence finally took effect on July 4, 1946.

Closer to home, Puerto Rico had been acquired in part to serve as a U.S. outpost on the approach to the Caribbean and any future isthmian canal. On April 12, 1900, the Foraker Act established a civil government on the island. The president appointed a governor and eleven members of an executive council, and an elected House of Delegates made up the lower house of the legislature. Residents of the island were declared citizens of Puerto Rico but were not made citizens of the United States until 1917, when the Jones Act granted them U.S. citizenship and made both houses of the legislature elective. In 1947 the governor also became elective, and in 1952 Puerto Rico became a commonwealth with its own constitution and elected officials, a unique status. Like a state, Puerto Rico is free to change its constitution insofar as it does not conflict with the U.S. Constitution.

The Foraker Act of 1900 also levied a temporary duty on imports from Puerto Rico. The tariff was challenged in the federal courts on the grounds that the island had become part of the United States, but the Supreme Court upheld it. In this and other "insular cases" federal judges faced a question that went to the fundamental nature of the Union and to the civil and political rights of the people in America's new possessions: Does the Constitution follow the flag? The Court ruled in effect that it did not apply in U.S. territories abroad unless Congress extended it to those possessions.

Having liberated the Cubans from Spanish rule, the Americans found themselves propping up a shaky new Cuban government whose economy was in a state of collapse. Bad relations between U.S. soldiers and Cubans erupted almost immediately. When McKinley set up a military government for the island late in 1898, it was at odds with rebel leaders from the start. The United States finally fulfilled the promise of independence for Cuba after the military regime had restored order, gotten schools under way, and improved sanitary conditions. The problem of disease in Cuba prompted the work of Dr. Walter Reed, who made an outstanding contribution to health in tropical climates around the world. Named head of the Army

Yellow Fever Commission in 1900, he proved that yellow fever was carried by mosquitoes. The commission's experiments led the way to effective control of the worldwide disease.

In 1900, on President McKinley's order, a Cuban convention drafted a constitution modeled on that of the United States. The Platt Amendment to the army-appropriations bill passed by Congress in 1901 sharply restricted the independence of the new government, however. The amendment required that Cuba never impair its independence by signing a treaty with a third power, that it keep its debt within the government's power to repay it out of ordinary revenues, and that it acknowledge the right of the United States to intervene in Cuba for the preservation of Cuban independence and the maintenance of "a government adequate for the protection of life, property, and individual liberty." Finally, Cuba was called upon to sell or lease to the United States lands to be used for coaling or naval stations—a proviso that led to an American naval base at Guantánamo Bay, a base still in operation.

Under pressure the Cuban delegates made the Platt Amendment an appendix to their own constitution. As early as 1906, an insurrection arose against the new government, and President Theodore Roosevelt responded by sending Secretary of War William Howard Taft to suppress the rebels. Backed by U.S. armed forces, Taft assumed full government authority, as he had in the Philippines, and the American army stayed until 1909, when a new Cuban president was peacefully elected. Further interventions by U.S. troops would follow for more than two decades.

Imperial Rivalries in East Asia

During the 1890s not only the United States but also Japan emerged as a world power. Commodore Matthew Perry's voyage of 1853–1854 had opened Japan to Western ways, and the country had begun modernization in earnest after the 1860s. Flexing its new muscles, Japan defeated China's stagnant empire in the First Sino-Japanese War (1894–1895) and as a result picked up the Pescadores Islands and the island of Formosa (modern-day Taiwan). China's weakness, demonstrated in the war, brought the European powers into a scramble for "spheres of influence" on that remaining frontier of imperialist expansion. Russia secured the privilege of building a railroad across Manchuria and established itself in Port Arthur (Lü-shun) and on the Liao-tung Peninsula. The Germans moved into Shan-tung, the French into Kwangchow Bay, the British into Wei-hai.

The bright prospect of American trade with China dimmed with the possibility that the great powers would throw up tariff barriers in their own spheres of influence. The British, embroiled in Hong Kong since 1840, had more to lose though, for they already had the largest foreign trade with China. Just before the Spanish-American War, in 1898, the British suggested joint action with the United States to preserve the integrity of China and renewed the proposal early in 1899. Both times the Senate rejected the request because it risked an entangling alliance.

THE "OPEN DOOR" In its origins and content, what soon came to be known as the Open Door policy resembled the Monroe Doctrine. In both cases the United States unilaterally proclaimed a hands-off policy, this time in China, that the British had earlier proposed as a joint statement. The policy outlined in Secretary of State John Hay's Open Door Note, dispatched in 1899 to London, Berlin, and St. Petersburg (Russia) and a little later to Tokyo, Rome, and Paris, proposed to keep China open to trade with all countries on an equal basis. More specifically it called upon foreign powers, within their spheres of influence, (1) to refrain from interfering with any treaty port (a port open to all by treaty) or any vested interest, (2) to permit Chinese authorities to collect tariffs on an equal basis, and (3) to show no favors to their own nationals in the matter of harbor dues or railroad charges. As it turned out, none of the European powers except Britain accepted Hay's principles, but none rejected them either. So Hay simply announced that all powers had accepted the policy.

The Open Door policy, if rooted in the self-interest of American businesses eager to exploit Chinese markets, also tapped the deep-seated sympathies of those who opposed imperialism, especially as it endorsed China's territorial integrity. But it had little legal standing. When the Japanese, concerned about Russian pressure in Manchuria, asked how the United States intended to enforce the policy, Hay replied that America was "not prepared . . . to enforce these views." So it would remain for forty years, until continued Japanese expansion in China would bring America to war in 1941.

THE BOXER REBELLION A new Asian crisis arose in 1900, when a group of Chinese nationalists known to the Western world as Boxers ("Fists of Righteous Harmony") rebelled against foreign encroachments on China and laid siege to foreign embassies in Peking (Beijing). An international expedition of British, German, Russian, Japanese, and American forces mobilized to relieve the embassy compound. Hay, fearful that the intervention might become an excuse to dismember China, took the opportunity to further refine the Open

Trade with China

U.S. troops marching in Peking after quelling the Boxer Rebellion.

Door policy. The United States, he said in a letter of July 3, 1900, sought a solution that would "preserve Chinese territorial and administrative integrity" as well as "equal and impartial trade with all parts of the Chinese Empire." Six weeks later the expedition reached Peking and quelled the Boxer Rebellion.

BIG-STICK DIPLOMACY

More than any other American of his time, Theodore Roosevelt transformed the role of the United States in world affairs. The nation had emerged from the Spanish-American War a world power, and he insisted that this status entailed major new responsibilities. To ensure that his country accepted its international obligations, Roosevelt stretched both the Constitution and executive power to the limit. In the process he pushed a reluctant nation onto the center stage of world affairs.

ROOSEVELT'S RISE   Born in 1858, the son of a wealthy New York merchant and a Georgia belle, Roosevelt had grown up in Manhattan in cultured comfort, had visited Europe as a child, spoke German fluently, and had graduated from Harvard with honors in 1880. A sickly, scrawny boy with poor eyesight and chronic asthma, he built himself up into a physical and intellectual athlete, a lifelong practitioner of the "strenuous life." Rigorous exercise and outdoor activities became integral to his life. A boxer, wrestler, mountain climber, hunter, and outdoorsman, he was also possessed of extraordinary intellectual curiosity. He became a dedicated bird-watcher, a renowned historian and essayist, and a zealous moralist. He wrote thirty-eight books on a wide variety of subjects. His boundless energy and fierce competitive spirit were inexhaustible and infectious, and he was ever willing to express an opinion on any subject. Within two years of graduating from Harvard, Roosevelt won election to the New York legislature. "I rose like a rocket," he later observed.

But with the world seemingly at his feet, disaster struck. In 1884 his beloved mother, only forty-eight years old, died. Eleven hours later, in the same house, his twenty-two-year-old wife struggled with kidney failure and died in his arms, having recently given birth to their only child. Roosevelt was distraught and bewildered. The double funeral was so wrenching that the officiating minister wept throughout his prayer. In an attempt to recover from this "strange and terrible fate," Roosevelt turned his baby daughter over to his sister, quit his political career, sold the family house, and moved west to take up cattle ranching in the Badlands of the Dakota Territory. The blue-blooded New Yorker relished hunting, leading roundups, capturing outlaws, fighting Indians—and reading novels by the campfire. When a drunken cowboy, a gun in each hand, tried to bully the tinhorn Roosevelt, teasing him about his glasses, the feisty Harvard dude laid him out with one punch. Although his western career lasted only two years, he never quite got over being a cowboy.

Back in New York City, Roosevelt remarried and ran unsuccessfully for mayor in 1886; he later served six years as civil service commissioner and two years as New York City's police commissioner. In 1896 Roosevelt campaigned hard for McKinley, and the new president was asked to reward him with the position of assistant secretary of the navy. McKinley initially balked, saying that young Roosevelt was too "hotheaded" and "too pugnacious. I want peace." But he eventually relented and appointed the war-loving aristocrat. After serving in Cuba and hastening into print his self-promoting account of the Rough Riders, Roosevelt easily won the governorship of New York, arousing audiences with his impassioned speeches and powerful personality.

In the 1900 presidential contest, the Democrats turned once again to William Jennings Bryan, who sought to make imperialism the "paramount

Mr. Imperialism

This 1900 cartoon shows the Republican vice-presidential candidate, Theodore Roosevelt, overshadowing his running mate, President William McKinley.

issue" of the campaign. The Democratic platform condemned the Philippine conflict as "an unnecessary war" that had "placed the United States, previously known and applauded throughout the world as the champion of freedom, in the false and un-American position of crushing with military force the efforts of our former allies to achieve liberty and self-government."

The Republicans welcomed the issue. They renominated McKinley and named Roosevelt his running mate. After his role in the military action in the Philippines and Cuba, Roosevelt had virtually become Mr. Imperialism. McKinley outpolled Bryan, by 7.2 million to 6.4 million popular votes and 292 to 155 electoral votes. Less than a year later, on September 6, 1901, at a reception at the Pan-American Exposition in Buffalo, a fanatic anarchist named Leon Czolgosz (pronounced chole-gosh) approached the fifty-eight-year-old president with a gun concealed in a bandaged hand and fired at point-blank range. McKinley died eight days later, and Theodore Roosevelt was elevated to the White House. "Now look," Mark Hanna, the Ohio businessman and politico, erupted, "that damned cowboy is President of the United States!"

Six weeks short of his forty-third birthday, Roosevelt was the youngest man ever to reach the White House, but he had more experience in public affairs than most and perhaps more vitality than any. One observer compared him to Niagara Falls, "both great wonders of nature." Roosevelt's glittering spectacles, glistening teeth, and overflowing gusto were a godsend to the cartoonists, who added another trademark when he pronounced the adage "Speak softly, and carry a big stick."

Along with Roosevelt's boundless energy went an unshakable righteousness that led him to cast every issue in moral and patriotic terms. He considered the presidency his "bully pulpit," and he delivered fist-pumping speeches on the virtues of righteousness, honesty, civic duty, and strenuosity. Yet his moral earnestness cloaked a cautious pragmatism. Roosevelt could get carried away, but as he said of his foreign-policy steps, this was likely to happen only when "I am assured that I shall be able eventually to carry out my will by force." Nowhere was President Roosevelt's forceful will more evident than in his conduct of foreign affairs.

THE PANAMA CANAL   After the Spanish-American War, the United States became more deeply involved in the Caribbean. One issue overshadowed every other in the region: the Panama Canal. The narrow isthmus of Panama had long excited dreams of an interoceanic canal. Alfred Thayer Mahan, now an admiral, regarded a canal as crucial to commerce and naval power, a point dramatized in 1898 by the long voyage of the battleship *Oregon* around South America's Cape Horn to join the U.S. fleet off Cuba.

Transit across the isthmus had first become a major concern of the United States in the late 1840s, when it became an important route to the California goldfields. Two treaties dating from that period loomed years later as obstacles to the construction of a canal. The Bidlack Treaty (1848) with Colombia (then New Granada) guaranteed both Colombia's sovereignty over Panama and the neutrality of the isthmus. In the Clayton-Bulwer Treaty (1850) the British agreed to acquire no more Central American territory, and the United States joined them in agreeing to build or fortify a canal only by mutual consent.

After the Spanish-American War, Secretary of State John Hay commenced talks with the British ambassador to establish such consent. The outcome was the Hay-Pauncefote Treaty of 1900, but the Senate rejected it on the grounds that it forbade fortification of the canal and required that the canal be neutral even in time of war. By then a bill for a Nicaraguan canal was pending in Congress, and the British apparently decided to accept the inevitable. In 1901 the Senate ratified a second Hay-Pauncefote Treaty, which simply omitted reference to the former limitations.

Other obstacles remained, however. From 1881 to 1887 a French company under Ferdinand de Lesseps, who had engineered the Suez Canal between 1859 and 1869, had spent nearly $300 million and some 20,000 lives to dig less than one third of a canal through Panama, then under the control of Colombia. The company now wanted $109 million for its holdings. An Isthmian Canal Commission, appointed by President McKinley, reported in 1901 that a Nicaraguan route would be cheaper. When the House of Representatives quickly passed an act for construction there, the French company lowered its price to $40 million, and the Canal Commission switched its focus to Panama.

Meanwhile, Secretary Hay had opened negotiations with Ambassador Tomás Herrán of Colombia. In return for a Canal Zone six miles wide, the

United States agreed to pay $10 million in cash and a rental fee of $250,000 a year. The U.S. Senate ratified the Hay-Herrán Treaty in 1903, but the Colombian senate held out for $25 million in cash. In response to this act by those "foolish and homicidal corruptionists in Bogotá," Theodore Roosevelt, by then president, flew into a rage punctuated by references to "dagos" and "contemptible little creatures." Meanwhile in Panama, an isolated province long at odds with the remote Colombian authorities in Bogotá, feeling was heightened by Colombia's rejection of the treaty. Manuel Amador Guerrero, an employee of the French canal company, then hatched a plot in close collusion with the company's wily representative, Philippe Bunau-Varilla. After Bunau-Varilla visited Roosevelt and Hay and apparently obtained inside information, Amador informed his conspirators that the U.S.S. *Nashville* would arrive at Colón, Panama, on November 2.

With an army of some 500 Panamanians, Amador staged a revolt the next day. Colombian troops, who could not penetrate the overland jungle, found U.S. ships blocking the sea-lanes. On November 13 the Roosevelt administration received its first ambassador from Panama, whose name happened to be Philippe Bunau-Varilla, and he signed a treaty that extended the Canal Zone

Digging the Canal

President Theodore Roosevelt operating a steam shovel during his 1906 visit to the Panama Canal.

from six to ten miles in width. For $10 million down and $250,000 a year, the United States received "in perpetuity the use, occupation and control" of the Canal Zone. The U.S. attorney general, asked to supply a legal opinion upholding Roosevelt's actions, responded wryly, "No, Mr. President, if I were you I would not have any taint of legality about it."

In 1904 Congress created a new Isthmian Canal Commission to direct construction, and Roosevelt instructed its members to make the "dirt fly." He later explained, "I took the Canal Zone and let Congress debate; and while the debate goes on the Canal does also." By needlessly offending Latin American sensibilities, Roosevelt had committed one of the greatest

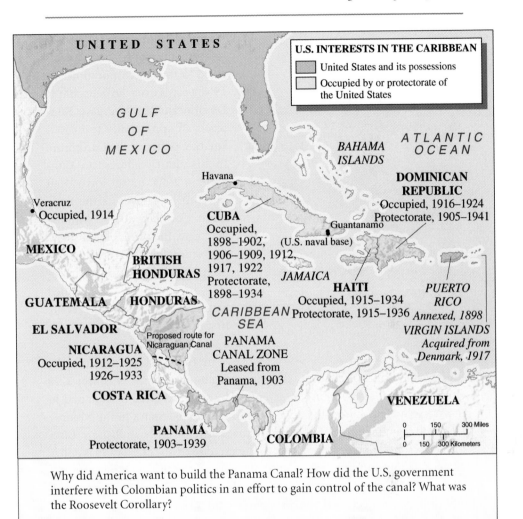

U.S. INTERESTS IN THE CARIBBEAN

- United States and its possessions
- Occupied by or protectorate of the United States

UNITED STATES

GULF OF MEXICO

BAHAMA ISLANDS

ATLANTIC OCEAN

Havana

Veracruz
Occupied, 1914

MEXICO

DOMINICAN REPUBLIC
Occupied, 1916–1924
Protectorate, 1905–1941

CUBA
Occupied, 1898–1902, 1906–1909, 1912, 1917, 1922
Protectorate, 1898–1934

Guantanamo (U.S. naval base)

BRITISH HONDURAS

GUATEMALA   HONDURAS

JAMAICA

HAITI
Occupied, 1915–1934
Protectorate, 1915–1936

PUERTO RICO
Annexed, 1898

EL SALVADOR

CARIBBEAN SEA

NICARAGUA
Occupied, 1912–1925
1926–1933

Proposed route for Nicaraguan Canal

PANAMA CANAL ZONE
Leased from Panama, 1903

VIRGIN ISLANDS
Acquired from Denmark, 1917

COSTA RICA

PANAMA
Protectorate, 1903–1939

COLOMBIA

VENEZUELA

0   150   300 Miles
0   150   300 Kilometers

Why did America want to build the Panama Canal? How did the U.S. government interfere with Colombian politics in an effort to gain control of the canal? What was the Roosevelt Corollary?

blunders in American foreign policy. Colombia eventually got its $25 million, from the Harding administration in 1921, but only once America's interest in Colombian oil had lubricated the wheels of diplomacy. There was no apology, but the payment was made to remove "all misunderstandings growing out of the political events in Panama, November, 1903." The canal opened on August 15, 1914, two weeks after the outbreak of World War I in Europe.

THE ROOSEVELT COROLLARY   Even without the canal the United States would have been concerned with the stability of the Caribbean region, and particularly with the activities of any hostile power there. A prime excuse

The World's Constable

President Theodore Roosevelt wields "the big stick," symbolizing his approach to diplomacy.

for intervention in those days was to force the collection of debts owed to foreign corporations. In 1904 a crisis over the debts of the Dominican Republic gave Roosevelt an opportunity to formulate U.S. policy in the Caribbean. In his annual address to Congress in 1904, he set forth what came to be known as the Roosevelt Corollary to the Monroe Doctrine: the principle, in short, that since the Monroe Doctrine prohibited intervention in the region by Europeans, the United States was justified in intervening first to forestall the actions of outsiders.

In the president's words the Roosevelt Corollary held that "chronic wrongdoing . . . may in America, as elsewhere, ultimately require intervention by some civilized nation, and in the Western Hemisphere the adherence of the United States to the Monroe Doctrine may force the United States, however reluctantly, in flagrant cases of such wrongdoing or impotence, to the exercise of an international police power." As put into practice by mutual agreement with the Dominican Republic in 1905, the Roosevelt Corollary called for the United States to install and protect a collector of customs who would apply 55 percent of the nation's revenues to debt payments owed to American companies.

THE RUSSO-JAPANESE WAR   In East Asia, meanwhile, the principle of equal trading rights embodied in the Open Door policy received a serious challenge when rivalry between Russia and Japan flared into a fight. By 1904 the Japanese had grown convinced that the Russians threatened their ambitions in China and Korea. On February 8 Japan therefore launched a surprise attack that devastated the Russian fleet. The Japanese then occupied Korea and drove the Russians back into Manchuria. But neither side could score a knockout blow, and neither relished a prolonged war. Roosevelt sought to maintain a balance between the two powers and offered to mediate their conflict. When the Japanese signaled that they would welcome a negotiated settlement, Roosevelt agreed to sponsor a peace conference in Portsmouth, New Hampshire. In the

Treaty of Portsmouth, signed on September 5, 1905, the concessions all went to the Japanese. Russia acknowledged Japan's "predominant political, military, and economic interests in Korea" (Japan would annex the kingdom in 1910), and both powers agreed to evacuate Manchuria.

RELATIONS WITH JAPAN Japan's show of strength against Russia raised doubts among American leaders about the security of the Philippines. During the Portsmouth talks, Roosevelt sent William Howard Taft to meet with the Japanese foreign minister in Tokyo. The two men negotiated the Taft-Katsura Agreement of July 29, 1905, in which the United States accepted Japanese control of Korea and Japan disavowed any designs on the Philippines. Three years later the Root-Takahira Agreement, negotiated by Secretary of State Elihu Root and the Japanese ambassador, endorsed the status quo and reinforced the Open Door policy by supporting "the independence and integrity of China" and "the principle of equal opportunity for commerce and industry in China."

Behind the diplomatic facade of goodwill, however, lay mutual distrust. For many Americans the Russian threat in east Asia now gave way to "yellow peril" (a term apparently coined by Kaiser Wilhelm II of Germany). Racial animosities on the West Coast helped sour relations with Japan. In 1906 San Francisco's school board ordered students of Chinese, Japanese, and Korean descent to attend a separate public school. The Japanese government sharply protested the show of prejudice, and President Roosevelt managed to talk the school board into changing its policy after making sure that Japanese authorities would not issue passports to "laborers," except former residents of the United States; the parents, wives, or children of residents; or those who already possessed an interest in an American farming enterprise. This "Gentlemen's Agreement" of 1907, the precise terms of which have never been revealed, halted the influx of Japanese immigrants and brought some respite to racial agitation in California.

THE UNITED STATES AND EUROPE During the years of expansionism, the United States cast its gaze westward and southward. But events in Europe also required attention. While Roosevelt was moving toward mediation of the Russo-Japanese War in 1905, a dangerous crisis was brewing in Morocco. There, on March 31, 1905, the German kaiser, Wilhelm II, stepped ashore at Tangier and gave a saber-rattling speech criticizing French and British interests in North Africa. The kaiser's speech aroused a diplomatic storm of dangerous proportions. Roosevelt felt that the United States had a huge stake in preventing the outbreak of a major war. At the kaiser's behest he talked the French and the British into attending an international conference at Algeciras, Spain, with U.S. delegates present. Roosevelt then maneuvered the Germans into accepting his lead.

The Act of Algeciras, signed in 1906, affirmed the independence of Morocco and guaranteed an open door for trade there but provided for the training and control of Moroccan police by France and Spain. The U.S. Senate ratified the agreement, but only with the proviso that it was not to be construed as a departure from America's traditional policy of noninvolvement in European affairs. It was a departure, of course, and one that may well have prevented a general war, or at least postponed it until 1914. Roosevelt received the Nobel Peace Prize in 1906 for his work at Portsmouth and Algeciras. Despite his bellicosity on other occasions, he had earned it.

Before Roosevelt left the White House, he celebrated America's rise to the status of a world power with one great flourish. In 1907 he sent the entire U.S. Navy, by then second in strength only to the British fleet, on a grand tour around the world, their commander announcing that he was ready for "a feast, a frolic, or a fight." He got mostly the first two and none of the last. At every port of call, the "Great White Fleet" set off rousing celebrations, down the Atlantic coast of South America, up the west coast, out to Hawaii, and down to New Zealand and Australia. The triumphal procession continued home by way of the Mediterranean and steamed back into American waters in 1909, just in time to close out Roosevelt's presidency on a note of success.

Yet it was a success that would have mixed consequences. Roosevelt's ability to project American power abroad was burdened by a racist ideology shared by many prominent political figures of the time. He once told the graduates of the Naval War College that all "the great masterful races have been fighting races, and the minute that a race loses the hard fighting virtues ... it has lost the right to stand as equal to the best." On another occasion he called war the best way to promote "the clear instinct for race selfishness" and insisted that "the most ultimately righteous of all wars is a war with savages." Such a belligerent and bigoted attitude would come back to haunt the United States in world affairs—and at home.

MAKING CONNECTIONS

- The Spanish-American War marked a turning point in U.S. foreign policy. America's emergence as a global power is a central theme of the twentieth century.

- Theodore Roosevelt's foreign policy displayed an activist approach to the presidency. The next chapter describes connections between his foreign policies and his approach to domestic affairs.

FURTHER READING

An excellent survey of the diplomacy of the era is Charles Soutter Campbell's *The Transformation of American Foreign Relations, 1865–1900* (1976). For background on the events of the 1890s, see Walter LaFeber's *The American Search for Opportunity, 1865–1913* (1993) and D. Healy's *U.S. Expansionism: The Imperialist Urge in the 1890s* (1970). The dispute over American policy in Hawaii is covered in Thomas J. Osborne's *"Empire Can Wait": American Opposition to Hawaiian Annexation, 1893–1898* (1981).

Ivan Musicant's *Empire by Default: The Spanish-American War and the Dawn of the American Century* (1998) is the most comprehensive volume on the conflict. For the war's aftermath in the Philippines, see Stuart Creighton Miller's *"Benevolent Assimilation": The American Conquest of the Philippines, 1899–1903* (1982). Robert L. Beisner's *Twelve against Empire: The Anti-Imperialists, 1898–1900* (1968) handles the debate over annexation.

A good introduction to American interest in China is Michael H. Hunt's *The Making of a Special Relationship: The United States and China to 1914* (1983). Kenton J. Clymer's *John Hay: The Gentleman as Diplomat* (1975) examines the role of this key secretary of state in forming policy.

For U.S. policy in the Caribbean and Central America, see Walter LaFeber's *Inevitable Revolutions: The United States in Central America*, 2nd ed. (1993). David McCullough's *The Path between the Seas: The Creation of the Panama Canal, 1870–1914* (1977) presents the fullest account of how the United States secured the Panama Canal.

24

THE PROGRESSIVE ERA

FOCUS QUESTIONS

- From what social bases did progressivism emerge?
- What were the basic elements of Progressive reform?
- What events shaped the presidencies of Theodore Roosevelt, William H. Taft, and Woodrow Wilson?
- Why was the election of 1912 so significant?

To answer these questions and access additional review material, please visit www.wwnorton.com/studyspace.

Theodore Roosevelt's emergence as a national leader coincided with the onset of what historians have labeled the Progressive Era (1900–1917). The Progressive movement arose in response to many societal changes, the most powerful of which were the devastating depression of the 1890s and its attendant social unrest. The depression brought hard times to the cities, deepened distress in the rural areas, and aroused both the fears and the conscience of the rapidly growing middle and upper-middle classes. By the turn of the century, so many activists were at work seeking to improve social conditions that people began to speak of a Progressive Era, a time of fermenting idealism and sweeping social, economic, and political change.

ELEMENTS OF REFORM

Progressivism was a reform movement so varied and comprehensive it almost defies definition. Political Progressives crusaded against the abuses of urban political bosses and corporate robber barons. Their goals were greater democracy, honest and efficient government, more effective regulation of business, and greater social justice for working people. They believed that the scope of local, state, and federal government authority should be expanded to accomplish these goals. Doing so, they hoped, would ensure the "progress" of American society. The "real heart of the movement," declared one reformer, was "to use the government as an agency of human welfare."

The Progressive movement contained an element of conservatism. In some cases the regulation of business turned out to be regulation proposed *by* business leaders who preferred regulated stability to the chaos and uncertainty of unrestrained competition. In addition, many reformers were motivated by religious beliefs that led them to concentrate on moral reforms such as the prohibition of alcoholic beverages and Sunday closing laws. In sum, progressivism was diverse in both its origins and its agenda. Few people adhered to all of the varied Progressive causes. What reformers shared was a common assumption that the complex social ills and tensions generated by the urban-industrial revolution required new responses. Governments were now called upon to extend a broad range of direct services: schools, good roads (a movement propelled first by cyclists and then by automobilists), environmental conservation, public health and welfare, care of the disabled, and farm loans and demonstration agents (county workers who visited farms to demonstrate new technology), among others. Such initiatives represented the first tentative steps toward what would become known during the 1930s and thereafter as the welfare state.

THE ANTECEDENTS OF PROGRESSIVISM   Populism was one of the catalysts of progressivism. The Populist platform of 1892 outlined many reforms that would be accomplished in the Progressive Era. After the collapse of the farmers' movement and the revival of the agricultural economy at the turn of the century, the reform spirit shifted to the cities, where middle-class activists had for years attacked the problems of political bossism and urban development. The mugwumps, those gentlemen reformers who had fought the spoils system and insisted that government jobs be awarded on the basis of merit, supplied the Progressive movement with an important element of its thinking: the honest-government ideal. Over the years their ranks had been supplemented, and the honest-government outlook had been broadened by leaders who confronted urban problems such as crime, vice, and the efficient provision of gas, electricity, water, sewers, mass transit, and garbage collection.

Finally, another significant force in fostering the spirit of Progressivism was the growing familiarity with socialist doctrines and their critiques of living and working conditions. The Socialist party of the time served as the left wing of Progressivism. Most progressives found socialist remedies unacceptable, and the Progressive reform impulse arose in part from a desire to counter the growing influence of socialist doctrines. More important in spurring progressive reform were social critics who dramatized the need for reform.

THE MUCKRAKERS   Poverty, unsafe working conditions, and child labor in mills, mines, and factories were complex social issues; remedying them required raising public awareness, which would in turn spur political action. The "muckrakers," writers who thrived on exposing social ills, got their name when Theodore Roosevelt compared them to a character in John Bunyan's *Pilgrim's Progress:* "A man that could look no way but downwards with a muckrake in his hands." "Muckrakers are often indispensable to . . . society," Roosevelt said, "but only if they know when to stop raking the muck."

Henry Demarest Lloyd is sometimes cited as the first of the muckrakers, for his critical examination of the Standard Oil Company and other monopolies in his book *Wealth Against Commonwealth* (1894). Another early muckraker was Jacob Riis, a Danish immigrant who exposed slum conditions in *How the Other Half Lives* (1890). The chief outlets for these social critics were the inexpensive popular magazines that began to flourish in the 1890s, such as the *Arena* and *McClure's*.

The golden age of muckraking is sometimes dated from 1902, when *McClure's* began to run articles by the reporter Lincoln Steffens on municipal corruption, later collected into a book, *The Shame of the Cities* (1904). *McClure's* also ran Ida M. Tarbell's *History of the Standard Oil Company* (1904). Other reform-minded books that began as magazine articles exposed corruption in the stock market, the meat industry, the life-insurance business, and the political world.

Without the muckrakers, Progressivism surely would never have achieved widespread popular support. In feeding the public's appetite for sordid facts about the new urban-industrial society, the muckrakers demonstrated one of the salient features of the Progressive movement, and one of its central failures: the Progressives were stronger on diagnosis than on remedy. They professed a naive faith in the power of democracy. Give the people the facts, expose corruption, and bring government close to the people, reformers believed, and the correction of evils would follow automatically. The cure for the ills of democracy, it seemed, was a more informed and more active democracy.

FEATURES OF PROGRESSIVISM

DEMOCRACY   The most important reform that political Progressives promoted to democratize government was the direct primary, or the nomination of candidates by the vote of all party members. Under the traditional convention system, only a small proportion of voters attended the local caucuses or precinct meetings that sent delegates to county, and in turn to state and national, conventions. While this traditional method allowed seasoned leaders to sift the candidates, it also lent itself to domination by political professionals. Direct primaries at the local level had been held sporadically since the 1870s, but after South Carolina adopted the first statewide primary in 1896, the movement spread within two decades to nearly every state.

The party primary was but one expression of a broad movement for greater public participation in the political process. In 1898 South Dakota became the first state to adopt the *initiative* and *referendum,* procedures that allow voters to enact laws directly. If a designated number of voters petitioned to have a measure put on the ballot (the initiative), the electorate could then vote it up or down (the referendum). Oregon adopted a spectrum of reform measures, including a voter-registration law (1899), the initiative and referendum (1902), the direct primary (1904), a sweeping corrupt-practices act (1908), and the recall (1910), whereby corrupt or incompetent public officials could be removed by a public petition and vote. Within a decade nearly twenty states had adopted the initiative and referendum, and nearly a dozen had accepted the recall.

Most states adopted the party primary even in the choice of U.S. senators, heretofore selected by state legislatures. Nevada was first, in 1899, to let voters express a choice that state legislators of their party were expected to follow in choosing senators. The popular election of senators required a constitutional amendment, and the House of Representatives, beginning in 1894, four times adopted such an amendment, only to see it defeated in the Senate, which came under increasing attack as a "millionaires' club." In 1912 the Senate finally accepted the inevitable and agreed to the Seventeenth Amendment, authorizing popular election of senators. The amendment was ratified in 1913.

EFFICIENCY A second major theme of Progressivism was the "gospel of efficiency." In the business world during the early twentieth century, Frederick W. Taylor, the original "efficiency expert," was developing the techniques he summed up in his book *The Principles of Scientific Management* (1911). "Taylorism," as scientific management came to be known, promised to reduce waste through the careful analysis of labor processes. By breaking down the production process into sequential steps and meticulously studying the time it took each worker to perform a task, Taylor prescribed the optimum technique for the average worker and establish detailed performance standards for each job classification. The promise of higher wages, he believed, would motivate workers to exceed the "average" expectations.

Instead, many workers resented Taylor's innovations. They saw in scientific management a tool for employers to make people work faster than was healthy or fair. Yet Taylor's controversial system brought concrete improvements in productivity—especially among those industries whose production processes were highly standardized and whose jobs were rigidly defined. "In the future," Taylor predicted in 1911, "the system [rather than the individual workers] will be first."

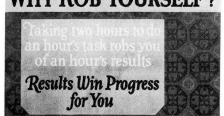

WHY ROB YOURSELF?

Taking two hours to do an hour's task robs you of an hour's results

Results Win Progress for You

Why Rob Yourself?

Poster from the 1920s encouraging on-the-job productivity. With a series of posters, the Mather Poster Company aimed to keep workers focused, productive, and loyal.

In government the efficiency movement demanded the reorganization of agencies to eliminate redundancy, to establish clear lines of authority, and to assign responsibility and accountability to specific officials. Two new ideas for making municipal government more efficient gained headway in the first decade of the new century. The commission system, first adopted by Galveston, Texas, in 1901, when local government there collapsed in the aftermath of a devastating hurricane and tidal wave, placed ultimate authority in a board composed of elected administrative heads of city departments—commissioners of sanitation, police, utilities, and so on. The more durable idea, however, was the city-manager plan, under which a professional administrator ran the municipal government in accordance with policies set by the elected council and mayor. Staunton, Virginia, first adopted the plan in 1908. By 1914 the National Association of City Managers had heralded the arrival of a new profession.

When America was a pre-industrial society, Andrew Jackson's notion that any reasonably intelligent citizen could perform the duties of any public office may have been true. By the early twentieth century, however, many functions of government and business had come to require specialists. This principle of government by experts was promoted by Governor Robert M. La Follette of Wisconsin, who established a Legislative Reference Bureau to provide research, advice, and help in the drafting of legislation. The "Wisconsin idea" of efficient government was widely publicized and copied. La Follette also pushed for such reforms as the direct primary, stronger railroad regulation, the conservation of natural resources, and workmen's compensation programs to support laborers injured on the job.

Robert M. La Follette

A proponent of expertise in government.

REGULATION   Of all the problems facing American society at the turn of the century, one engaged a greater diversity of reformers, and elicited more solutions, than any other: the regulation of giant corporations, which became a third major theme of Progressivism. Bipartisan concern over the concentration of economic power had brought passage of the Sherman Anti-Trust Act in 1890, but the act had turned out to be more symbolic than effective.

The problem of concentrated economic power and its abuse offered a dilemma for progressives. Four broad solutions were available, but of these, two were extremes that had limited support: letting business work out its own destiny under a policy of laissez-faire and adopting a socialist program of public ownership of big businesses. At the municipal level, however, the socialist alternative was rather widely adopted for public utilities and transportation— so-called gas and water socialism; otherwise, it was not seriously considered as a general policy. The other choices were either to adopt a policy of trust-busting in the belief that restoring old-fashioned competition would best prevent economic abuses or to accept big business in the belief that it brought economies of scale but to regulate it to prevent abuses.

Efforts to restore the competition of small firms proved unworkable, however, partly because breaking up large corporations was complex and therefore difficult. To some extent, regulation and "stabilization" won acceptance among business leaders; whatever respect they paid to competition in the abstract, they preferred not to face it in practice. As time passed, however, regulatory agencies often came under the influence or control of those they were supposed to regulate. Railroad executives, for instance, generally had more intimate knowledge of the intricate details involved in their business, giving them the advantage over the outsiders who might be appointed to the Interstate Commerce Commission.

SOCIAL JUSTICE   A fourth important feature of the Progressive spirit was the impulse toward social justice, which motivated diverse actions—from the promotion of private charities to campaigns against child labor and liquor. The settlement-house movement of the late nineteenth century had spawned a corps of social workers and genteel reformers devoted to the uplift of slum dwellers. But with time it became apparent that social evils extended beyond the reach of private charities and demanded government intervention.

Child Labor

A young girl working as a spinner in a cotton mill in Vermont, 1910.

Labor legislation was perhaps the most significant reform to emerge from the drive for social justice. It emerged first at the state level. The National Child Labor Committee, organized in 1904, led a movement for laws banning the still-widespread employment of young children. Through publicity, the organization of state and local committees, and a graphic documentation of the evils of child labor by the photographer Lewis W. Hine, the committee within ten years brought about legislation in most states banning the labor of underage children (the minimum age varying from twelve to sixteen) and limiting the hours older children might work.

Closely linked to the child-labor reform movement was a concerted effort to regulate the hours of work for women. Spearheaded by Florence Kelley, the head of the National Consumers' League, this Progressive crusade prompted the passage of state laws to address the distinctive hardships that long working hours imposed on women who were wives and mothers. Many states also outlawed night work and labor in dangerous occupations for both women and children. But numerous exemptions and inadequate enforcement often virtually nullified those laws.

The Supreme Court pursued a curiously erratic course in ruling on state labor laws. In *Lochner v. New York* (1905), the Court voided a ten-hour-workday law because it violated workers' "liberty of contract" to accept any terms they chose. But in *Muller v. Oregon* (1908), the high court upheld a ten-hour-workday law for women largely on the basis of sociological data regarding the effects of long hours on the health and morals of women. In *Bunting v. Oregon* (1917), the Court accepted a ten-hour day for both men and women but for twenty more years held out against state minimum-wage laws.

Legislation to protect workers against avoidable accidents gained impetus from disasters such as the 1911 fire at the Triangle Shirtwaist Company in New York City, in which 146 people, mostly young women, died because the owner kept the stairway doors locked to prevent theft. Workers trapped on the three upper floors of the ten-story building died in the fire or leaped to their death. Stricter building codes and factory-inspection acts followed. One of the most important advances along these lines was the series of workers' compensation laws enacted after Maryland led the way in 1902. Accident-insurance systems replaced the old common-law principle that an injured worker was entitled to compensation only if he could prove employer negligence, a costly and capricious procedure from which the worker was likely to win nothing or be granted excessive awards from an overly sympathetic jury.

PROHIBITION   For many activists the cause of liquor prohibition was a fifth area of action. Opposition to strong drink was an ideal cause in which to merge the older religious-based ethics with the new social ethics. Given the importance of saloons as arenas for local politics, prohibitionists could equate the "liquor traffic" with Progressive suspicion of bossism and "special interests." When reform pressures mounted, prohibition offered an easy outlet, bypassing the complexities of corporate regulation.

The battle against booze dated back to the nineteenth century. The Women's Christian Temperance Union had promoted the cause since 1874, and a Prohibition party had entered the elections in 1876. But the most successful political action followed the formation in 1893 of the Anti-Saloon League, an organization that pioneered the strategy of the single-issue pressure group. Through its singleness of purpose it forced the prohibition issue into the forefront of state and local elections. At its "Jubilee Convention" in 1913, the bipartisan Anti-Saloon League endorsed a prohibition amendment to the Constitution, adopted by Congress in 1917. By the time it was ratified two years later, state and local action had already dried up areas occupied by nearly three fourths of the nation's population.

ROOSEVELT'S PROGRESSIVISM

While most Progressive initiatives originated at the state and local levels, calls for national reform efforts began to appear around 1900. Theodore Roosevelt brought to the White House in 1901 an expansive vision of the presidency that well suited the cause of progressive reform. In one of his first addresses to Congress, he stressed the need for a new political approach. When the Constitution was first drafted, he explained, the nation's social and economic conditions were quite unlike those at the dawn of the twentieth century. "The conditions are now wholly different and wholly different action is called for."

More than any other president since Lincoln, Roosevelt possessed an activist bent. Still, his initial approach to reform was cautious. He sought to avoid the extremes of socialism on the one hand and laissez-faire individualism on the other. A skilled political maneuverer, Roosevelt greatly expanded the role and visibility of the presidency, as well as the authority and scope of the federal government. His capacity for hard work was boundless; his boyish energy was infectious. He thrived on crises and took the leadership role in negotiating major legislation and labor disputes. Always a self-promoter, Roosevelt craved the spotlight. As one of his sons explained, "Father always wanted to be the bride at every wedding and the corpse at every funeral." He also cultivated party leaders in Congress and steered away from such divisive issues as the tariff and regulation of the banks. And when he did approach the explosive issue of regulating the trusts, he took care to reassure the business community. For him politics was the art of the possible. Unlike the more radical Progressives and the doctrinaire "lunatic fringe," as he called it, he would take half a loaf rather than none at all.

EXECUTIVE ACTION   At the outset of Roosevelt's presidency in 1901, he promised to sustain McKinley's policies. He worked with Republican leaders in Congress, against whom the minority of new progressives was as yet powerless. Yet Roosevelt would accomplish more by vigorous executive action than by passing legislation, and in the exercise of presidential power he would not be inhibited by points of legal detail. He argued that as president he might do anything not expressly forbidden by the Constitution.

In 1902 Roosevelt endorsed a "square deal" for all, calling for enforcement of existing anti-trust laws and stricter controls on big business. "Of all forms of tyranny," Roosevelt asserted, "the least attractive and the most vulgar is the tyranny of mere wealth." From the outset, however, Roosevelt balked at wholesale trust-busting. Effective regulation of corporate giants was better than a futile effort to restore small business, which might be achieved only at a cost to the efficiencies of scale gained in larger operations. Because Congress balked at regulatory legislation, Roosevelt sought to force the issue by a more vigorous prosecution of the Sherman Anti-Trust Act. He chose his target carefully. In the case against the sugar trust (*United States v. E. C. Knight and Company,* 1895), the Supreme Court had declared manufacturing strictly an intrastate activity. Railroads, however, were beyond question engaged in interstate commerce and thus subject to federal authority.

In 1902 Roosevelt ordered his attorney general to break up the Northern Securities Company, a giant conglomerate of railroads. The company, formed the previous year, had taken shape during a gigantic battle between E. H. Harriman of the Union Pacific and James J. Hill and J. P. Morgan of the Great Northern over the Northern Pacific, which was crucial to shipping in the Northwest. The stock battle had raised the threat of a panic on the New York Stock Exchange and so led to a settlement in which the chief contenders made peace by forming Northern Securities, a holding company that controlled the Great Northern and the Northern Pacific. The merger of such rival rail lines essentially ended competition by forging a monopoly. In 1904 the Supreme Court ordered the railroad combination dissolved.

THE 1902 COAL STRIKE   Support for Roosevelt's use of the "big stick" against corporations was strengthened by the stubbornness of mine owners in the anthracite coal strike of 1902. On May 12 some 150,000 members of the United Mine Workers walked off the job in Pennsylvania and West Virginia, demanding a 20 percent wage increase, a reduction in daily hours from ten to nine, and official recognition of the union by the mine owners. The mine operators, having granted a 10 percent raise two years

Roosevelt's Duality

Theodore Roosevelt as an "apostle of prosperity" (top) and as a Roman tyrant (bottom). Roosevelt's energy, self-righteousness, and impulsiveness elicited sharp reactions.

before, dug in their heels and shut down the mines in preparation for a long struggle to starve out the miners, many of whom were immigrants from eastern Europe. One mine owner expressed the attitude of many of them when he proclaimed, "The miners don't suffer—why, they can't even speak English."

Previous presidents such as Hayes and Cleveland had responded to labor unrest by dispatching federal troops. But the coal strike had not become violent when Roosevelt aggressively intervened. He was concerned about the approach of winter amid a nationwide coal shortage and the effects of the strike on the fall congressional elections—he told a friend that the public would blame the Republicans if coal were in short supply. By October 1902 the price of coal had soared, and hospitals and schools reported empty coal bins. Roosevelt thus decided upon a bold move: he invited leaders of both sides to a conference in Washington, where he appealed to their "patriotism, to the spirit that sinks personal considerations and makes individual sacrifices for the public good." The mine owners attended the conference but arrogantly refused even to speak to the UMW leaders. The "extraordinary stupidity and temper" of the "wooden-headed" owners infuriated Roosevelt. The president wanted to grab the spokesman for the mine owners "by the seat of his breeches" and "chuck him out" a window. With the conference ending in an impasse, Roosevelt reluctantly threatened to take over the mines and send in the army to run them. When a congressman questioned the constitutionality of such a move, an exasperated Roosevelt roared, "To hell with the Constitution when the people want coal!" Militarizing the mines would have been an act of dubious legality, but the owners feared that Roosevelt might do it and that public opinion would support him.

The coal strike ended on October 23, 1902, with an agreement to submit the issues to an arbitration commission named by the president. The agreement enhanced Roosevelt's prestige, although it produced only a partial victory for the miners. By the arbitrators' decision in 1903, the miners won a nine-hour day but only a 10 percent wage increase and no union recognition.

EXPANDING FEDERAL POWER   Roosevelt continued to use his executive powers to enforce the Sherman Anti-Trust Act, but he shrank from further anti-trust legislation. Altogether his administration initiated about twenty-five anti-trust suits; the most notable victory came in *Swift and Company v. United States* (1905), a decision against the "beef trust" through which most of the meat packers had avoided competitive bidding in the purchase of livestock. In this decision the Supreme Court put forth the "stream-of-commerce" doctrine, which overturned its previous holding that

The Presidential Lion Tamer

Theodore Roosevelt confronts the beasts of the steel trust, the oil trust, the beef trust, and others, in the arena of Wall Street.

manufacturing was strictly intrastate. Since both livestock and the meat products of the packers moved in the stream of interstate commerce, the Court reasoned, both were subject to federal regulation. This interpretation of the interstate commerce power would be broadened in later years until few enterprises would remain beyond the reach of federal regulation.

In 1903 Congress passed the Elkins Act, which made it illegal for railroads to take, as well as to give, secret rebates from freight charges to their favorite customers. All shippers would be charged the same price. That same year, Congress created a new Bureau of Corporations to report on the activities of interstate corporations. Its findings could lead to anti-trust suits, but its purpose was rather to help corporations correct malpractices and avoid the need for lawsuits. Many companies, among them United States Steel and International Harvester, worked closely with the bureau, but others held back. When Standard Oil refused to turn over its records, the government brought an anti-trust suit that resulted in the breakup of the huge company in 1911. The Supreme Court broke up the American Tobacco Company at the same time. This approach fell short of the direct regulation that Roosevelt preferred, but without a congressional will to pass such laws, little more was possible. Trusts that cooperated were left alone; others had to run the gauntlet of anti-trust suits.

ROOSEVELT'S SECOND TERM

Roosevelt's policies built a coalition of Progressive- and conservative-minded voters who assured his election in his own right in 1904. The Republican Convention chose him by acclamation. The Democrats, having lost with William Jennings Bryan twice, turned to Alton B. Parker, who as chief justice of New York had upheld labor's right to the closed shop (requiring that all employees be union members) and the state's right to limit hours of work. Despite Parker's liberal record, party leaders presented him as a safe conservative, and his acceptance of the gold standard as "firmly and irrevocably established" bolstered such a view. The effort to present a candidate more conservative than Roosevelt proved a futile gesture for the party that had twice nominated Bryan. Despite Roosevelt's trust-busting proclivities, most business executives, according to the *New York Sun,* preferred the "impulsive candidate of the party of conservatism to the conservative candidate of the party which the business interests regard as permanently and dangerously impulsive." Even business tycoons J. P. Morgan and E. H. Harriman contributed handsomely to Roosevelt's campaign chest.

An invincible popularity plus the sheer force of his personality swept Roosevelt to an impressive victory by a popular vote of 7.6 million to 5.1 million. Parker carried only the Solid Democratic South of the former Confederacy and two border states, Kentucky and Maryland, with an electoral vote of 336 for Roosevelt and 140 for Parker. Roosevelt was surprised by his lopsided victory. The president told his wife that he was "no longer a political accident." He now had a popular mandate. On the eve of his inauguration in March 1905, Roosevelt announced: "Tomorrow I shall come into office in my own right. Then watch out for me!" On election night, Roosevelt had announced that he would not run again, a statement he later would regret.

LEGISLATIVE LEADERSHIP   Elected in his own right, Roosevelt approached his second term with heightened confidence and a stronger commitment to Progressive reform. In 1905 he devoted most of his annual message to the regulation and control of big business. This understandably irked many of his corporate contributors and congressional Republican leaders. Said steel baron Henry Frick, "We bought the son of a bitch and then he did not stay bought." The independent-minded Roosevelt took aim at the railroads first. The Elkins Act of 1903, finally outlawing rebates, had been a minor step. Railroad executives themselves welcomed it as an escape from shippers clamoring for special favors.

But a new proposal for railroad regulation endorsed by Roosevelt was something else again. It sought to extend the authority of the Interstate Commerce Commission, giving it effective control over freight rates. Enacted in 1906, the Hepburn Act for the first time gave the ICC power to set maximum freight rates. The commission no longer had to go to court to enforce its decisions. While the carriers could challenge the rates in court, the burden of proof now rested upon them rather than upon the ICC. In other ways, too, the Hepburn Act enlarged the mandate of the ICC. Its reach now extended beyond railroads, to pipelines, express companies, sleeping-car companies, bridges, and ferries, and it could prescribe a uniform system of bookkeeping to provide uniform statistics.

Regulating railroads was Roosevelt's first priority, but a growing movement for the regulation of meat packers, food processors, and makers of drugs and patent medicines reached fruition, as it happened, on the very day after passage of the Hepburn Act. Discontent with abuses in these industries had grown rapidly as a result of the muckrakers' revelations. Journalists supplied evidence of harmful preservatives and adulterants in the preparation of "embalmed meat" and other food products. The *Ladies' Home Journal* and *Collier's* published evidence of false claims and dangerous ingredients in patent medicines. One of the more notorious "medicines," Lydia Pinkham's vegetable compound, was advertised to work wonders in the relief of "female complaints"; that was no wonder, for the compound was 18 percent alcohol.

Perhaps the most telling blow against such abuses was struck by Upton Sinclair's novel *The Jungle* (1906). Sinclair meant the book to promote socialism, but its main impact came from its portrayal of filthy conditions in Chicago's meat-packing industry:

The Meat Industry

Pigs strung up along the hog-scraping rail at Armour's packing plant in Chicago, ca. 1909.

It was too dark in these storage places to see well, but a man could run his hand over these piles of meat and sweep off handfuls of the dried dung of rats. These rats were nuisances, and the packers would put poisoned bread out for them, they would die, and then rats, bread, and meat would go into the hoppers together.

Roosevelt read *The Jungle*—and reacted quickly. He sent two agents to Chicago, and their report confirmed all that Sinclair had said: "We saw meat shovelled from filthy wooden floors, piled on tables rarely washed, pushed from room to room in rotten box carts, in all of which processes it was in the way of gathering dirt, splinters, floor filth, and the expectoration of tuberculous and other diseased workers."

Congress and Roosevelt responded by creating the Meat Inspection Act of 1906. It required federal inspection of meats destined for interstate commerce and empowered officials in the Agriculture Department to impose sanitation standards within processing plants. The Pure Food and Drug Act, enacted the same day, placed restrictions on the makers of prepared foods and patent medicines and forbade the manufacture, sale, or transportation of adulterated, misbranded, or harmful foods, drugs, and liquors.

CONSERVATION   One of the most enduring legacies of Roosevelt's leadership was his energetic support for the emerging conservation movement. Roosevelt was the first president to challenge the long-standing myth of America's having inexhaustible natural resources. In fact, Roosevelt came to believe that conservation of natural resources was the "great material question of the day." He and other early conservationists were convinced that the tradition of freewheeling individual and corporate exploitation of the environment must be supplanted by the scientific management of the nation's natural resources for the *long-term* public benefit. "The things that will destroy America," he said, "are prosperity at any price, peace at any price, safety first instead of duty first, the love of soft living and the get-rich-quick theory of life."

After the Civil War a growing number of individuals and organizations had begun to oppose the unregulated exploitation of natural resources and sought to preserve wilderness areas. Timber companies stripped forests and moved on, leaving debris and erosion behind. Ranchers abused the native grasslands by overgrazing, and farmers depleted the soil by excessive planting. Commercial hunters, trappers, and fishermen decimated game animals. Industries polluted streams, rivers, and air.

Such reckless abuse of the environment eventually generated intense concern and organized opposition. George Perkins Marsh, a Vermont diplomat and one of the first advocates of government conservation efforts, published a best-selling book, *Man and Nature* (1864), in which he observed that man was "everywhere a disturbing agent. Wherever he plants his foot, the harmonies of nature are turned to discords." Marsh urged Americans to intervene to protect the long-term health of the environment.

By the end of the nineteenth century, many people were heeding Marsh's warning. Just as reformers promoted the regulation of business and industry for the public welfare, activists championed efforts to manage and preserve the natural environment for future generations. The first promoters of resource conservation were ardent sport hunters and anglers among the social elite (including Theodore Roosevelt), who worried that rapacious commercial hunters and trappers were killing game animals to the point of extermination. In 1886, for example, the sportsman-naturalist George Bird Grinnell, editor of *Forest and Stream*, founded the Audubon Society to protect wild birds from being killed for their plumage. Two years later Grinnell, Roosevelt, and a dozen other recreational hunters formed the Boone and Crockett Club, named in honor of Daniel Boone and Davy Crockett, the two legendary frontiersmen. The club's goal was to ensure that big-game animals were protected for posterity. Those goals were shared and promoted by national monthly newspapers such as *American Sportsman*, *Forest and Stream*, and *Field and Stream*. By 1900 most states had enacted laws regulating game hunting and had created game refuges and wardens to enforce the new rules, much to the chagrin of local hunters, including Indians, who now were forced to abide by state laws designed to protect the interests of wealthy recreational hunters.

Along with industrialists concerned about water quality, Roosevelt and the sportsmen conservationists formed a powerful coalition promoting the rational government management of natural resources: rivers and streams,

Nathaniel Pitt Langford

The first superintendent of Yellowstone National Park, on Jupiter Terrace at Mammoth Hot Springs, ca. 1875.

forests, minerals, and natural wonders. Those concerns, as well as the desire of railroad companies to transport tourists to destinations featuring majestic scenery, led the federal government to displace Indians in order to establish the 2-million-acre Yellowstone National Park in 1872 at the junction of the Montana, Wyoming, and Idaho territories (the National Park Service would be created in 1916 after other parks had been established). In 1881 Congress created a Division of Forestry (now the U.S. Forest Service) within the Department of the Interior. At the same time, New York State officials established a Forest Commission in 1885 to manage timber in the vast state-owned acreage of the Adirondack Mountains. Seven years later the legislature created the 5-million-acre Adirondack Park. The legislature also imposed restrictions on hunting in state forests and created a "forest police" to enforce the new regulations. As president, Theodore Roosevelt created fifty federal wildlife refuges, approved five new national parks, and designated as national monuments unfit for economic use such natural treasures as the Grand Canyon.

In 1898 Roosevelt, while serving as vice president, had endorsed the appointment of Gifford Pinchot, a close friend and the nation's first professional forester, as the head of the Division of Forestry. Pinchot and Roosevelt believed that conservation entailed the scientific management of natural resources to serve the public interest. In his first State of the Union address, delivered in 1901, Roosevelt explained that conservationists were concerned not simply with protecting national forests for their beauty; their foremost objective was utilitarian: to ensure that there would always be forests to "increase and sustain the resources of our country and the industries which depend upon them." Pinchot explained that the conservation movement sought to promote the "greatest good for the greatest number for the longest time."

Gifford Pinchot

Pinchot is seen here with two children at the edge of a larch grove.

Roosevelt and Pinchot championed the Progressive notion of

efficiency and government regulation. They were not romantics about nature, nor were they ecologists; they did not understand the complex interdependence of trees, plants, insects, and animals, nor did they appreciate the environmental benefits of natural fires. Instead, they were utilitarian Progressives determined to ensure that entrepreneurs and industrialists exploited nature in appropriate ways. As Pinchot insisted, "The first principle of conservation is development." He sought to ensure the wisest "use of the natural resources now existing on this continent for the benefit of the people who live here now."

Pinchot and the president were especially concerned about the millions of acres of public land still owned by the government. Over the years vast tracts of federal land had been given away or sold at discount prices to large business enterprises. Roosevelt and Pinchot were determined to end such carelessness and exploitation. They championed the systematic management of natural resources by government experts trained to promote the most efficient public use of the environment. This meant, for example, that commercial loggers must abide by forestry regulations; otherwise there would be no trees for future generations to exploit. "Forestry," Pinchot explained, "is handling trees so that one crop follows another." He and Roosevelt opposed the mindless clear-cutting of entire forests for short-term profit and sought to restrict particular forests from any economic development. In fact, Roosevelt as president used the Forest Reserve Act (1891) to protect some 172 million acres of timberland. Lumber companies were furious, but Roosevelt held firm. As he bristled, "I hate a man who skins the land."

Congressional resistance to Pinchot and Roosevelt's environmental proposals led them to publicize the cause through a White House Conference on Conservation in 1908 and later that year by setting up a National Conservation Commission, which proposed a thorough survey of the nation's mineral, water, forest, and soil resources. Within eighteen months some forty-one state conservation commissions had sprung up, and a number of private groups took up the cause. The infant environmental movement remained divided, however, between those who wanted to conserve resources for continuous human use and those who wanted to set aside areas as wilderness preserves.

Pinchot, for instance, provoked the wrath of the famous naturalist John Muir in 1906 when he endorsed a water reservoir in the wild Hetch Hetchy Valley of Yosemite National Park to supply the needs of San Francisco. The Hetch Hetchy project had forced President Roosevelt to choose between preserving a beautiful mountain valley and providing water to a bustling city 200 miles away. Convinced by Pinchot and other government experts, Roosevelt declared that "domestic use, especially for a municipal water supply, is the highest use to which water and available storage basins can be put." The president's stance excited a firestorm of criticism from Muir, the Sierra Club he had founded, and other preservationists. When a congressional committee voted against the Hetch Hetchy bill, the House report noted that it had been opposed by "an exceedingly widespread, earnest, and vigorous protest voiced by scientists, naturalists, mountain climbers, travelers, and others in person, by letters and telegrams, and in newspapers and magazine articles." A stunned Roosevelt postponed a decision, turning the volatile issue over to his successors. In 1913 President Woodrow Wilson signed the Raker Act approving construction of the Hetch Hetchy Reservoir. By then a clear split between utilitarians and preservationists had occurred within the conservation movement.

Theodore Roosevelt's far-flung conservation efforts also encompassed reclamation and irrigation projects. In 1902 the president signed the Reclamation Act (also known as the Newlands Act, after its sponsor, Nevada senator Francis Newlands). The Reclamation Act established a new agency within the Interior Department, called the Reclamation Service (renamed the Bureau of Reclamation in 1923), to administer a massive new program designed to bring water to arid western states. Using funds from the sale of federal land in sixteen states in the West, the Reclamation Service constructed dams and irrigation systems to transform barren desert acreage into farmland. Farms of no more than 160 acres were eligible to purchase the water provided by the irrigation systems, but over time the restrictions were ignored, and large commercial farms tended to dominate the program. Agribusiness thus became the main beneficiary of the federal irrigation policy.

Federal and state initiatives to conserve the nation's natural resources and manage them for the public welfare brought many improvements during the Progressive Era but also generated unexpected consequences. The efforts to set aside national parks and forests, for example, often came at the expense of Indians and local rural whites who were pushed off the property and denied traditional hunting rights. Conservation efforts to satisfy the desires of affluent Americans, as one historian has written, meant for poorer Americans "fines and jail time, and empty bellies." Government efforts to suppress fires in national forests and destroy predators such as mountain lions, wolves, coyotes, and bobcats that preyed upon popular game animals unwittingly disrupted natural ecological cycles and often caused more harm than good. Yet the progressive conservation movement, for all its unexpected complexities and ironies, did succeed in reining in the unregulated exploitation of natural resources for private gain. As Pinchot recalled late in life, "Launching the Conservation movement was the most significant achievement of the T.R. Administration, as he himself believed."

FROM ROOSEVELT TO TAFT

Toward the end of his second term, Roosevelt declared, "I have had a great time as president." Although eligible to run again, he opted for retirement. He decided that the heir to the White House should be Secretary of War William Howard Taft, and the Republican Convention ratified the choice on its first ballot in 1908. The Democrats, whose conservative strategy had backfired in 1904, decided to give William Jennings Bryan one more chance at the highest office. Still vigorous at forty-eight, Bryan retained a faithful following but struggled to attract a national following. Roosevelt advised Taft: "Do not answer Bryan; *attack* him. Don't let him make the issues." Taft followed Roosevelt's advice, declaring that Bryan's election would result in a "paralysis of business."

The Republican platform declared its support for Roosevelt's policies, including conservation and further strengthening of the Interstate Commerce Commission. The Democratic platform hardly differed on regulation, but it endorsed a lower tariff and an AFL-supported plank opposing court injunctions against labor actions. In the end, voters opted for Roosevelt's chosen successor: Taft swept the Electoral College, 321 to 162. The real surprise of the election, however, was the strong showing of the Socialist party candidate, labor hero Eugene V. Debs. His 421,000 votes revealed the depth of working-class resentment in the United States.

Out of office, the fifty-year-old Roosevelt set off on a prolonged safari in Africa, prompting his old foe J. P. Morgan to mutter, "Let every lion do his duty." The new president he left behind was an entirely different political animal—in fact, he was hardly a political animal at all. The offspring of a prominent Cincinnati family—his father had been Ulysses Grant's attorney general—Taft had progressed through appointive offices, from judge in Ohio to solicitor in the Justice Department, federal judge, commissioner and governor general in the Philippines, and secretary of war. As secretary of war, Taft had overseen construction of the Panama Canal. The presidency was the only elective office he ever held. Later he would be

William Howard Taft

Speaking at Manassas, Virginia, in 1911.

chief justice of the Supreme Court (1921–1930), a job more suited to his temperament.

Taft detested the give-and-take of backroom politics and never felt comfortable in the White House. He once observed that whenever someone said "Mr. President," he looked around for Roosevelt. The political dynamo in the family was his wife, Helen, who had wanted the White House more than he. One of the major tragedies of Taft's presidency was that Nellie Taft suffered a debilitating stroke soon after they entered the White House, and for most of his term she remained unable to serve as his political adviser.

TARIFF REFORM   Taft's domestic policies generated a storm of controversy within his own party. Contrary to Republican tradition, Taft preferred a lower tariff, and he made this the first important issue of his presidency. But if Taft, in pressing an issue that Roosevelt had skirted, seemed the bolder of the two, he proved less skillful in dealing with Congress. A tariff bill passed the House with surprising ease. It lowered rates less than Taft would have preferred but made some important reductions and enlarged the number of items that were duty-free. But the chairman of the Senate Finance Committee, Nelson W. Aldrich, guided through the upper chamber a drastically revised bill, one that included more than 800 changes. What came out of the conference committee was a measure close to the final Senate version, although Taft did get some reductions on important items: hides, iron ore, coal, oil, cottons, boots, and shoes.

In response to the higher rates in Aldrich's bill, a group of midwestern Republicans took the Senate floor to fight what they considered a corrupt throwback to the days when the Republican party had done the bidding of big business. In all, ten progressive Republicans joined the Democrats in an unsuccessful effort to defeat the bill. Taft at first agreed with them; then, fearful of a party split, he backed the majority and agreed to an imperfect bill. He lacked Roosevelt's love of a grand battle as well as his gift for working both sides of the street. Temperamentally conservative, inhibited by scruples about interfering too much with the legislative process, he drifted into the orbit of the Republican Old Guard and quickly alienated the Progressive wing of his party, whom he tagged "assistant Democrats."

BALLINGER AND PINCHOT   In 1910 Taft's policies drove the wedge deeper between the conservative and Progressive Republican factions. What came to be called the Ballinger-Pinchot controversy made Taft appear to be a less reliable custodian of Roosevelt's conservation policies than he actually was. Taft's secretary of the interior, Richard A. Ballinger of Seattle, was well aware that many westerners opposed conservation programs on the grounds that they held back full development of the region. The strongest conservation leaders, such as Roosevelt and Gifford Pinchot of Pennsylvania, were often easterners. Ballinger threw open to commercial use more than 1 million acres of waterpower sites that Roosevelt had withdrawn in the guise of ranger stations. Ballinger's reasoning was that the withdrawal had "gone far beyond legal limitations," and Taft agreed. At about the same time, Ballinger turned over certain federal coal lands in Alaska to a group of Seattle tycoons, some of whom he had represented as a lawyer. Apparently without Ballinger's knowledge, this group had already agreed to sell part of the land to a banking syndicate.

As chief of forestry, Pinchot reported the collusion to Taft, who refused to intervene. When Pinchot went public with the controversy early in 1910, Taft fired him for insubordination. A joint congressional investigation exonerated Ballinger of all charges of fraud or corruption, but Progressive suspicions created such pressure that he resigned in 1911. In firing Pinchot, Taft had acted according to the strictly legal view that his training had taught him to value, but circumstances tarnished his image in the public mind. "In the end," one historian has written, "the Ballinger-Pinchot affair had more impact on politics than it did on conservation." Taft had been elected to carry out the Roosevelt policies, his opponents said, and he was carrying them out—"on a stretcher."

Meanwhile, in the House of Representatives, rebellion had broken out among the more progressive Republicans. When the regular session opened in 1910, the insurgents joined Democrats in voting to investigate Ballinger. Flushed with that victory, they resolved to clip the wings of Speaker Joseph G. Cannon, Republican of Illinois, a conservative who held almost a stranglehold on procedures with his power to appoint all committees and their chairmen and especially with his control of the Rules Committee, of which he was a member. A coalition of Democrats and progressive Republicans overrode a ruling by the Speaker and proceeded to adopt new rules offered by George W. Norris, Republican of Nebraska, that enlarged the Rules Committee from five to fifteen members, made them elective by the House, and excluded the Speaker as a member. About forty Republicans joined the Democratic minority in the move. In the next Congress the rules would be further changed to make all committees elective.

Events had conspired to cast Taft in a conservative role at a time when progressive sentiment was riding high in the country. The result was a severe rebuke of the president in the congressional elections of 1910, first by the widespread defeat of pro-Taft candidates in the Republican primaries, then by the election of a Democratic majority in the House and enough Democrats in the Senate to allow Progressive Republicans to wield the balance of power.

TAFT AND ROOSEVELT   In 1910 Theodore Roosevelt returned from his extended travels abroad. He had been reading news accounts and letters about the Taft "betrayal," but unlike some of his supporters, he refused to break with his successor. With rather severe politeness, however, Roosevelt refused an invitation to visit the White House. He wrote Taft, "I shall keep my mind open as I keep my mouth shut." Neither was easy for Roosevelt, whose followers urged him to act. Roosevelt was finding it much less fulfilling to be a former president than to be a president. He also was growing increasingly concerned about Taft's administration. His handpicked successor had replaced many of Roosevelt's cabinet members with corporate attorneys, and Taft's dismissal of Pinchot infuriated Roosevelt, who decided that Taft had fallen under the spell of the Republican Old Guard leadership. During the fall of 1910, Roosevelt made several speeches promoting "sane and progressive" Republican candidates in the congressional elections. In Kansas he gave a catchy name to his latest principles, the "New Nationalism." Roosevelt issued a stirring call for an array of new federal regulatory laws, a social-welfare program, and new measures of direct democracy, including the old Populist demands for the initiative, recall, and referendum. His purpose was not to revolutionize the political system but to save it from the threat of revolution. "What I have advocated," he explained a few days later, "is not wild radicalism. It is the highest and wisest kind of conservatism."

Relations between Roosevelt and Taft remained tense, but it was another year before they came to an open break. The split happened in the fall of 1911, when the Taft administration announced an anti-trust suit against United States Steel, citing specifically as its cause the company's acquisition of the Tennessee Coal and Iron Company in 1907, a move to which Roosevelt had given tacit approval in the belief that it would avert a business panic. In mid-November, Roosevelt published a sharp attack on Taft's "archaic" attempt to restore competition. The only sensible response to the problem, he argued, was to accept business combinations under modern circumstances but to enlarge the government's power to regulate them. Roosevelt's entry into the next presidential campaign was now only a matter of time.

Many progressive Republicans who assumed that Roosevelt would not run again proposed to back Wisconsin senator Robert La Follette in 1912, but they were ready to switch if Roosevelt entered the race. An opening came on February 2, 1912, when La Follette showed signs of nervous exhaustion in a rambling speech in Philadelphia. As his following began to drop away, a group of seven Republican governors met in Chicago and called upon Roosevelt to become a candidate. On February 24 Roosevelt decided to enter the race. "I hope that so far as possible the people may be given the chance, through direct primaries," Roosevelt wrote the governors, "to express their preference." He had decided that Taft had "sold the Square Deal down the river," and he now dismissed Taft as a "hopeless fathead."

The rebuke implicit in Roosevelt's decision to run against Taft, his chosen successor, was in many ways undeserved. During Taft's first year in office, one political tempest after another had left his image irreparably damaged. The three years of solid achievement that followed came too late to restore its luster or reunite his divided party. Taft had at least attempted tariff reform, which Roosevelt had never dared. He replaced Ballinger and Pinchot with men of impeccable credentials in the arena of conservation. He won from Congress the power to protect public lands for any reason and was the first president to withdraw oil reserves from use. Under the Appalachian Forest Reserve Act (1911), he enlarged the national forest by purchasing land in the East. In the end his administration withdrew more public land in four years than Roosevelt's had in nearly eight and brought more anti-trust suits, by a score of eighty to twenty-five.

In 1910, with Taft's support, Congress passed the Mann-Elkins Act, which empowered the Interstate Commerce Commission for the first time to initiate railroad freight rate changes, extended regulation to telephone and telegraph companies, and set up the Commerce Court to expedite appeals of ICC rulings. Taft also established the Bureau of Mines and the federal Children's Bureau (1912), and he called for statehood for Arizona and New Mexico and territorial government for Alaska (1912). The Sixteenth Amendment (1913), authorizing a federal income tax, was ratified with Taft's support before he left office, and the Seventeenth Amendment (1913), providing for the popular election of senators, was ratified soon after he left office.

Despite this Progressive record, Roosevelt now hastened Taft's demise. Senator Elihu Root, formerly Roosevelt's secretary of state, and one of Taft's closest advisers and the chairman of the Republican Convention, told a friend that Roosevelt would not gain the party's nomination but would "succeed in so damaging Taft that he can't be elected." In all but two of the thirteen states that held presidential primaries, Roosevelt won, even in Taft's Ohio. But the groundswell of popular support was no match for Taft's decisive position as sitting president and party leader. In state nominating conventions the party regulars held the line, and so Roosevelt entered the Republican National Convention about 100 votes short of victory. The Taft forces proceeded to nominate their man by the same steamroller tactics that had nominated Roosevelt in 1904.

Outraged at such "naked theft," the Roosevelt delegates—mostly social workers, reformers, intellectuals, insurgents, and executives who favored the new nationalism—assembled in a rump convention. "If you wish me to make the fight I will make it," Roosevelt told the delegates, who then issued a call for a Progressive party convention, which assembled in Chicago on August 5. Roosevelt appeared before the

The Bull Moose Candidate in 1912

A skeptical view of Theodore Roosevelt.

delegates, feeling "fit as a bull moose." He was "stripped to the buff and ready for the fight," he said. "We stand at Armageddon and we battle for the Lord." But few professional politicians turned up. Progressive Republicans decided to preserve their party credentials and fight another day. For the time being, with the disruption of the Republican party, the progressive torch was about to be passed to the Democrats.

WILSON'S PROGRESSIVISM

WILSON'S RISE   The emergence of Thomas Woodrow Wilson as the Democratic nominee in 1912 climaxed a political rise even more rapid than that of Grover Cleveland. In 1910, before his nomination and election as governor of New Jersey, Wilson had been president of Princeton University, but he had never run for public office. Born in Staunton, Virginia, in 1856, the son of a "noble-saintly mother" and a stern Presbyterian minister, he had grown up in Georgia and the Carolinas during the Civil War and Reconstruction.

Young Wilson, tall and slender, with a lean, long, sharply chiseled face, inherited his father's unquestioning piety, once declaring that "so far as religion is concerned, argument is adjourned." Wilson also developed a consuming ambition to "serve" humankind. Driven by a sense of providential destiny and self-righteous moralism, he coupled a rigid sense of rectitude with chronic emotional fragility. He once confessed that "I am too intense." Wilson nurtured a stubborn commitment to principle that would prove to be his undoing.

Wilson graduated from Princeton in 1879, and after law school at the University of Virginia he had a brief, unfulfilling, and profitless legal practice in Atlanta. From there he went to the new Johns Hopkins University in Baltimore, where he found his calling in the study of history and political science. As a college student he had said that he loved nothing more than "writing and talking."

Wilson's doctoral dissertation, *Congressional Government*, published in 1885, argued that the president, like the British prime minister, should be the leader of party government, as active in directing legislation as in the administration and enforcement of laws. In calling for a strong presidency, he expressed views closer to those of Roosevelt than those of Taft. He also shared Roosevelt's concern that government should promote the general welfare rather than narrowly serve special interests. And like Roosevelt he was critical of big business, organized labor, socialists, and agrarian radicalism.

After Johns Hopkins, Wilson taught at Bryn Mawr, in Pennsylvania, and then at Wesleyan College in Connecticut, before moving to Princeton in 1890. There he quickly earned renown for his polished lectures, vigorous mind, and sharp debating skills. In 1902 he was unanimously elected president of the university. In that position he showed the first evidence of reform views. "We are not put into this world to sit still and know," he stressed in his inaugural address. "We are put into it to act." And act he did. At Princeton, Wilson modernized the curriculum, expanded and improved the faculty, introduced the tutorial system, and raised admissions standards. But he failed in his attempt to restructure the elitist student social clubs.

Wilson's urge for reform increasingly antagonized university administrators and alumni, however, and when the Democratic boss of New Jersey offered Wilson his support for the 1910 gubernatorial nomination, Wilson accepted. The party leaders sought a respectable candidate to help them ward off Progressive challengers, but they discovered too late that the professor actually had an iron will of his own. Like Roosevelt, Wilson had come to shed some of his original conservatism and view progressive reform as a necessary expedient in order to stave off more radical social change. Elected as a reform candidate, Governor Wilson promoted Progressive measures and pushed them through the legislature. He pressured lawmakers to enact a workers' compensation law, a corrupt-practices law, measures to regulate public utilities, and ballot reforms. Such strong leadership in a state known as the home of the trusts because of its lenient corporation laws brought Wilson to national attention.

In the spring of 1911, a group of southern Democrats in New York opened a Wilson presidential-campaign headquarters, and Wilson set forth on strenuous tours across the country, denouncing special privilege and political bossism. Despite a fast start, however, the Wilson campaign seemed headed for defeat by Speaker of the House Champ Clark of Missouri. Clark had enough support for a majority in the early ballots, but the Wilson forces combined with supporters of Oscar Underwood of Alabama to prevent a two-thirds majority. On the fourteenth ballot, William Jennings Bryan went over to Wilson. When the Democratic boss

Wilson's Reforms

Woodrow Wilson campaigning from a railroad car.

of Illinois deserted Clark on the forty-second ballot and the Underwood delegates went over to Wilson on the forty-sixth, he clinched the nomination.

THE ELECTION OF 1912 The 1912 presidential campaign involved four candidates: Wilson and Taft represented the two major parties while Eugene Debs ran as a Socialist and Roosevelt headed the Progressive party ticket. They all shared a basic assumption that the old notion of do-nothing government was bankrupt; modern conditions required active measures to promote the general welfare. But they differed in the nature and extent of their activism.

No sooner did the formal campaign open than Roosevelt's candidacy almost ended. While entering a car on his way to deliver a speech in Milwaukee, he was shot by John Schrank, a mentally disturbed New Yorker who believed any president seeking a third term should be shot. The bullet went through Roosevelt's overcoat, spectacles case, and fifty-page speech, then fractured a rib before lodging just below his right lung. "Stand back, don't hurt the man," he yelled at the crowd as they mobbed the attacker. Roosevelt demanded that he be driven to the auditorium to deliver his speech. In a dramatic gesture, he showed the audience his bloodstained shirt and punctured text and vowed, "It takes more than this to kill a bull moose."

As the campaign developed, Taft quickly lost ground. "There are so many people in the country who don't like me," he lamented. The contest settled down to a running debate over the competing ideologies of the two front-runners: Roosevelt's New Nationalism and Wilson's New Freedom. The inchoate ideas that Roosevelt fashioned into his New Nationalism had first been presented systematically in *The Promise of American Life* (1909) by Herbert Croly, a then-obscure New York journalist. Its central point was often summarized in a useful catchphrase: "Hamiltonian means to achieve Jeffersonian ends," meaning that Alexander Hamilton's program of government activism on behalf of business interests should be used to achieve democratic and egalitarian Jeffersonian goals. The times required Americans to give up Jeffersonian prejudices against big government and use a strong central government to achieve democratic ends in the interest of the people. Big business, in other words, required big government.

The old nationalism had been used "by the sinister . . . special interests," Roosevelt said. His New Nationalism would enable government to promote social justice and effect such reforms as graduated income and inheritance taxes, workers' compensation, regulation of the labor of women and children, and a stronger Bureau of Corporations. These ideas and more went into the platform of the Progressive party, which called for a federal trade commission with sweeping authority over business and a tariff commission to set rates on a "scientific basis."

Before the end of his administration, Wilson would be swept into the current of New Nationalism, too. But initially he adhered to the decentralizing anti-trust traditions of his party. Before the start of the campaign, Wilson conferred with Louis D. Brandeis, a Progressive lawyer from Boston who focused Wilson's thought much as Croly had focused Roosevelt's. Brandeis's design for the New Freedom differed from Roosevelt's New Nationalism in its belief that the federal government should restore the competition among small economic units rather than regulate huge monopolies. Where Roosevelt admired the power and efficiency of large corporations that behaved themselves, Wilson was convinced that all huge industries needed to be broken up. This required a vigorous anti-trust policy, lowering tariffs to allow competition with foreign goods, and breaking up the concentration of financial power in Wall Street. But Brandeis and Wilson saw the vigorous expansion of federal power as only a temporary necessity, not a permanent condition. Roosevelt, who was convinced that both corporate concentration and an expanding federal government were permanent developments, dismissed the New Freedom as mere fantasy. For his part, Taft attacked his two progressive opponents by reminding them that the federal government "cannot create good times. It cannot make the rain to fall, the sun to shine or the crops to grow," but too many "meddlesome" regulations could deny the nation the prosperity it deserved.

The Republican schism between Taft and Roosevelt opened the way for Woodrow Wilson to win, by 435 electoral votes to 88 for Roosevelt and 8 for Taft. But in popular votes, Wilson had only 42 percent of the total. Roosevelt received 27 percent, Taft 23 percent, and Debs 6 percent. After learning of his election, Wilson told the chairman of the Democratic party that "God ordained that I should be the next president of the United States." Perhaps. But had the Republican party not been split in two, Wilson would have lost. His was the victory of a minority over a divided opposition.

The 1912 election was significant in several ways. First, it was a high-water mark for Progressivism. The election was the first to feature presidential primaries. The two leading candidates debated the basic issues of Progressivism in a campaign unique in its focus on vital alternatives and in its highly philosophical tone. Taft, too, despite his temperament and associations, showed his own progressive instincts. And the Socialist party, the left wing of Progressivism, polled over 900,000 votes for Eugene V. Debs, its highest proportion ever.

Second, the election gave Democrats effective national power for the first time since the Civil War. For two years during the second administration of

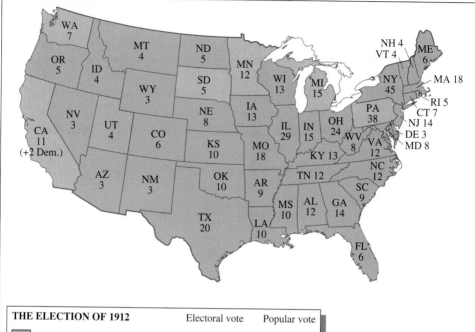

THE ELECTION OF 1912	Electoral vote	Popular vote
Woodrow Wilson (Democrat)	**435**	**6,293,000**
Theodore Roosevelt (Progressive)	88	4,119,000
William H. Taft (Republican)	8	3,486,000

Why was Taft so unpopular? How did the division between Roosevelt and Taft give Wilson the victory? Why was Wilson's victory in 1912 significant?

Grover Cleveland, 1893–1895, they had held the White House and majorities in both houses of Congress, but they had fallen quickly out of power during the severe depression of the 1890s. Now, under Wilson, they again held the presidency and were the majority in both the House of Representatives and the Senate.

Third, the election of Wilson brought southerners back into the orbit of national and international affairs in a significant way for the first time since the Civil War. Five of Wilson's ten cabinet members were born in the South, three still resided there, and William Jennings Bryan, the secretary of state, was an idol of the southern masses. At the president's right hand,

and one of the most influential members of the Wilson circle, at least until 1919, was "Colonel" Edward M. House of Texas. Wilson described House as "my second personality. He is my independent self." On Capitol Hill, southerners, by virtue of their seniority, held the lion's share of committee chairmanships. As a result, much of the Progressive legislation of the Wilson era would bear the names of the southerners who guided it through Congress.

Fourth and finally, the election of 1912 had begun to alter the character of the Republican party. Even though most party professionals remained, the defection of the Bull Moose Progressives had weakened the party's progressive wing. The leaders of the Republican party that would return to power in the 1920s would be more conservative in tone and temperament.

WILSONIAN REFORM   Wilson's inaugural address voiced in eloquent tones the ideals of social justice that animated many Progressives. "We have been proud of our industrial achievements," he said, "but we have not hitherto stopped thoughtfully enough to count the human cost . . . the fearful physical and spiritual cost to the men and women and children upon whom the dead weight and burden of it all has fallen pitilessly the years through." He promised specifically a lower tariff and a new banking system. "This is not a day of triumph; it is a day of dedication. Here muster, not the forces of party, but the forces of humanity."

If Roosevelt had been a strong president by force of personality, Wilson became a strong president by force of conviction. The president, he wrote in *Congressional Government*, "is . . . the political leader of the nation, or has it in his choice to be. The nation as a whole has chosen him, and is conscious that it has no other political spokesman. His is the only national voice in affairs." Wilson courted popular support, but he also courted members of Congress through personal contacts, invitations to the White House, and speeches in the Capitol. He used patronage power to reward friends and punish enemies. He might have acted through a Progressive coalition, but chose instead to rely upon party loyalty. "I'd rather trust a machine Senator when he is committed to your program," he told his navy secretary, "than a talking Liberal who can never quite go along with others because of his admiration of his own patented plan of reform." Wilson therefore made use of the party caucus, in which disagreements among Democrats were settled.

THE TARIFF   Wilson's leadership faced its first big test on the issue of tariff reform. Tariffs were originally needed to protect infant industries from foreign competition. Now, however, Wilson believed, tariffs were abused by corporations to suppress foreign competition and keep prices high. He often claimed that the "tariff made the trusts," believing that tariffs had encouraged the growth of monopolies and degraded the political process by producing armies of paid lobbyists who invaded Congress each year. In attacking high tariffs, Wilson sought to strike a blow for consumers and honest government. He acted quickly and boldly, summoning Congress into special session and addressing it in person—the first president to do so since John Adams. (Roosevelt was said to have asked, "Why didn't I think of that?") Congress acted vigorously on tariff reductions. Only four Democrats crossed the party line, and the new bill passed the House easily.

The crunch came in the Senate, the traditional graveyard of tariff reform. Swarms of lobbyists got so thick in Washington, Wilson said, that "a brick couldn't be thrown without hitting one of them." The president turned the tables with a public statement that focused the spotlight on the "industrious and insidious" tariff lobby.

The Underwood-Simmons Tariff became law in 1913. It reduced import duties on most goods and lowered the overall average duty from about 37 percent to about 29 percent. A list of some 300 items exempted from tariff duties included important consumer goods and raw materials: sugar, wool, iron ore, steel rails, agricultural implements, cement, coal, wood and wood pulp, and many farm products. The act lowered tariff rates but raised federal revenues with the first income tax levied under the newly ratified Sixteenth Amendment: 1 percent on income over $3,000 ($4,000 for married couples) and a surtax graduated from 1 percent on income of about $20,000 to 6 percent on income above $500,000. The highest total tax rate would thus be 7 percent.

THE FEDERAL RESERVE ACT Before the new tariff had cleared the Senate, the administration proposed the first major banking and currency reform since the Civil War. Ever since Andrew Jackson had killed the second Bank of the United States in the 1830s, the nation had been without a central bank. Instead, the country's money supply was provided by hundreds of private banks. Such a decentralized system brought instability and inefficiency. By 1913 virtually everyone agreed that the banking system needed restructuring. Wilson told the Congress that a federal banking system was needed to ensure that "the banks may be the instruments, not the masters, of business and of individual enterprise and initiative."

The Federal Reserve Act of 1913 created a new national banking system, with regional reserve banks supervised by a central board of directors. There would be twelve Federal Reserve banks, each owned by member banks in its district, which could issue Federal Reserve notes (currency) to member banks.

All national banks became members; state banks and trust companies could join if they wished. Each member bank had to subscribe 6 percent of its capital to the Federal Reserve bank and deposit a portion of its reserves there. This arrangement made it possible to expand both the money supply and bank credit in times of high business activity or as the level of borrowing increased.

This new system corrected three great defects in the previous arrangement: now bank reserves could be pooled, affording greater security; both the currency and bank credit became more elastic; and the concentration of reserves in New York was decreased. The new national banking system represented a new step in active government intervention and control in one of the most sensitive segments of the economy.

Reading the Death Warrant

Woodrow Wilson's plan for banking and currency reform spells the death of the "money trust," according to this cartoon.

ANTI-TRUST LAWS   Wilson made trust-busting the central focus of the New Freedom. The concentration of economic power had continued to grow despite the Sherman Anti-Trust Act and the federal watchdog agency, the Bureau of Corporations. Wilson's solution to the problem was a revision of the Sherman Act to define more explicitly what counted as restraint of trade. He decided to make a strong Federal Trade Commission (FTC) the cornerstone of his anti-trust program. Created in 1914, the five-member commission replaced Roosevelt's Bureau of Corporations and assumed new powers to define "unfair trade practices" and issue "cease-and-desist" orders when it found evidence of unfair competition.

Henry D. Clayton, a Democrat from Alabama, of the House Judiciary Committee, drafted an anti-trust bill in 1914 that outlawed practices such as price discrimination (charging different customers different prices for the same goods); "tying" agreements, which limited the right of dealers to handle the products of competing manufacturers; interlocking directorates connecting corporations with a capital of more than $1 million (or banks with more than $5 million); and corporations' acquisition of stock in competing corporations. In every case, however, conservative forces in the Senate qualified these provisions by tacking on the weakening phrase "where the effect may be to substantially lessen competition" or words of similar effect. And conservative southern Democrats and northern Republicans amended the Clayton Anti-Trust Act to allow for broad judicial review of the FTC's decisions, thus further weakening its freedom of action. In accordance with the president's recommendation, however, corporate officials were made individually responsible for any violations. Victims of price discrimination and tying agreements could sue for compensation equaling three times the amount of the damages suffered.

Agrarian activists in alliance with organized labor won a stipulation that declared farm-labor organizations were not unlawful combinations in restraint of trade. Injunctions in labor disputes, moreover, were not to be handed down by federal courts unless "necessary to prevent irreparable injury to property." Though hailed by union leaders as labor's Magna Carta, these provisions were actually little more than pious affirmations, as later court decisions would demonstrate. Wilson himself remarked that the act did little more than affirm the right of unions to exist by forbidding their dissolution for acting in restraint of trade.

Administration of the anti-trust laws generally proved disappointing to the more vehement Progressives under Wilson. The president reassured business that his purposes were friendly. As his secretary of commerce put it later, Wilson hoped to "create in the Federal Trade Commission a counsellor and friend to the business world." But its first chairman lacked forcefulness, and under its next head, a Chicago industrialist, the FTC practically abandoned its function as watchdog. The Justice Department, meanwhile, offered help and advice to businessmen interested in arranging matters so as to avoid anti-trust prosecutions. The appointment of conservative men to the Interstate Commerce Commission and the Federal Reserve won plaudits from the business world and profoundly disappointed Progressives.

SOCIAL JUSTICE   Wilson had never been a strong Progressive of the social-justice persuasion. He had carried out promises to lower the tariff, reorganize the banking system, and strengthen the anti-trust laws. Swept along by the course of events and the pressures of more far-reaching progressives, he was pushed further than he intended to go on some points. The New Freedom was now complete, he wrote late in 1914; the future would be "a time of healing because [it would be] a time of just dealing." Although

Wilson endorsed state action for women's suffrage, he declined to support a federal suffrage amendment because his party platform had not done so. He withheld support from federal child-labor legislation because he regarded it as a state matter. He opposed a bill for federal support of rural credits (low-interest loans to farmers) on the grounds that it was "unwise and unjustifiable to extend the credit of the government to a single class of the community."

Not until the second anniversary of his inauguration (March 4, 1915) did Wilson sign an important piece of social-justice legislation, the La Follette Seamen's Act. The product of stubborn agitation by the eloquent president of the Seamen's Union, the act strengthened shipboard safety requirements, reduced the power of captains, set minimum food standards, and required regular wage payments. Seamen who jumped ship before their contracts expired, moreover, were relieved of the charge of desertion.

PROGRESSIVISM FOR WHITES ONLY   Like many other Progressives, Woodrow Wilson showed little interest in the plight of African Americans. In fact, he shared many of the racist attitudes prevalent at the time. Although Wilson denounced the Ku Klux Klan's "reign of terror," he sympathized with its motives of restoring white rule in the postwar South and relieving whites of the "ignorant and hostile" power of the black vote. As a student at Princeton, Wilson had detested the enfranchisement of blacks, arguing that Americans of Anglo-Saxon origin would always resist domination by "an ignorant and inferior race."

Later, as a politician, Wilson courted African-American voters, but he rarely consulted black leaders and repeatedly avoided opportunities to associate with them in public. Many of the southerners he appointed to his cabinet were uncompromising racists who systematically began segregating the employees in their agencies even though the agencies had been integrated for over fifty years. Workplaces were segregated by race, as were toilets, drinking fountains, and areas for work breaks. When black leaders protested these actions, Wilson replied that such racial segregation was intended to eliminate "the possibility of friction" in federal offices.

PROGRESSIVE RESURGENCE   The need to weld a winning coalition in 1916 pushed Wilson back onto the road of reform. Progressive Democrats were restless, and after war broke out in Europe in August 1914, further divisions arose over defense and foreign policy. At the same time the Republicans were repairing their own rift, as the "Bull Moose" Progressive party showed little staying power in the midterm elections and Roosevelt showed little will to preserve it. Wilson could gain reelection only by courting Progressives of all parties. In 1916 Wilson scored points with them when he nominated Louis D. Brandeis to the Supreme Court. Conservatives waged a vigorous battle against Brandeis, but Senate Progressives rallied to win confirmation of the social-justice champion, the first Jewish member of the Court.

Meanwhile, Wilson began to promote a broad program of farm and labor reforms. The agricultural sector continued to suffer from a shortage of capital. To address the problem, Wilson supported a proposal to set up special banks to sponsor long-term farm loans. The Federal Farm Loan Act became law in 1916. Under the control of the Federal Farm Loan Board, twelve Federal Land banks paralleled the regional Federal Reserve banks and offered farmers loans of five to forty years' duration at low interest rates.

Thus the dream of federal rural loans, sponsored by a generation of Alliance members and Populists, finally came to fruition. Democrats had never embraced the Populist subtreasury plan, but they made a small step in that direction with the Warehouse Act of 1916. This measure authorized federal licensing of private warehouses, and federal backing made their receipts for stored produce more acceptable as collateral for short-term bank loans to farmers. Other concessions to farm demands came in the Smith-Lever Act of 1914 and the Smith-Hughes Act of 1917, both of which passed with little controversy. The first provided federal grants-in-aid for farm-demonstration agents under the supervision of land-grant colleges. The measure made permanent a program that had started a decade before in Texas and had already spread to many localities. The second measure extended agricultural and mechanical education to high schools through grants-in-aid.

Farmers with automobiles had more than a passing interest as well in the Federal Highways Act of 1916, which provided dollar-matching contributions to states with highway departments that met certain federal standards. The measure authorized distribution of $75 million over five years and marked a sharp departure from Jacksonian opposition to internal improvements at federal expense, just as the Federal Reserve System departed from Jacksonian banking principles. Although the argument that highways were one of the nation's defense needs weakened constitutional scruples against the act, it still restricted support to "post roads" used for the delivery of mail. A renewal act in 1921 would mark the beginning of a systematic network of numbered U.S. highways.

The Progressive resurgence of 1916 broke the logjam on labor reforms as well. Advocates of child-labor legislation persuaded Wilson that social-justice progressives would regard his stand on the issue as an important test of his humanitarian concerns, and Wilson overcame doubts about its constitutionality to support and sign the Keating-Owen Act, which excluded from interstate commerce goods manufactured by children under the age of fourteen. Both the Keating-Owen Act and a later act of 1919 to achieve the same purpose with a prohibitory tax were ruled unconstitutional by the Supreme Court on the grounds that regulation of interstate commerce could not extend to the conditions of labor. Effective action against the social evil of child labor had to await the New Deal of the 1930s, although it seems likely that discussion of the issue contributed to the sharp reduction in the number of underage workers during the next few years.

Another important accomplishment was the eight-hour workday for railroad workers, a measure that the Supreme Court upheld. The Adamson Act of 1916 was brought about by a threatened strike of railroad unions demanding an eight-hour workday and other concessions. Wilson, who objected to some of the demands, nevertheless went before Congress to request action on the hours limitation. The resulting Adamson Act required an eight-hour workday, with time and a half for overtime, and appointed a commission to study the problem of working conditions in the railroad industry.

In Wilson's first term, Progressivism reached its zenith. Progressivism had conquered the old dictum that the government is best that governs least. From two decades of ferment (three if the Populist years are counted) the great contribution of Progressive politics was the firm establishment and general acceptance of the public-service concept of government.

LIMITS OF PROGRESSIVISM

The Progressive Era was an optimistic age in which all sorts of reformers assumed that no problem lay beyond solution. But like all great historic movements, Progressivism displayed elements of paradox and irony. Despite its talk of greater democracy, it was the age of disenfranchisement for southern blacks—an action seen by many whites as progressive. The first two decades of the twentieth century also witnessed a new round of anti-immigrant prejudice. The initiative and referendum, supposedly democratic reforms, proved subject to manipulation by well-financed publicity campaigns. And much of the public policy of the time came to be formulated by experts and members of appointed boards, not by broad segments of the population. There is a fine irony in the fact that the drive to increase the political role of ordinary people paralleled efforts to strengthen executive leadership and exalt government expertise. This age of efficiency and bureaucracy, in business as well as government, brought into being a society in which more and more of the decisions affecting people's lives were made by unelected policy makers.

Progressivism was largely a middle-class movement in which the poor and unorganized had little influence. The supreme irony was that a movement so dedicated to the rhetoric of democracy should experience so steady a decline in voter participation. In 1912, the year of the Bull Moose campaign, voting dropped off by between 6 and 7 percent. The new politics of issues and charismatic leaders proved to be less effective in turning out voters than traditional party organizations and bosses had been. And by 1916 the optimism of an age that looked to infinite progress was already confronted by a vast slaughter. Europe had stumbled into war, and America would soon be drawn in. The twentieth century, which dawned with such bright hopes, held in store episodes of unparalleled horror.

MAKING CONNECTIONS

- Many of the Progressive reforms described in this chapter— particularly business regulation and the growth of the welfare state—provided the seeds for the New Deal reforms of the 1930s (Chapter 28).

- After World War I the Progressive impulse manifested itself in reforms such as Prohibition and women's suffrage, but the moralistic strain in progressivism would take an ugly turn in the Red Scare and immigration restriction.

- The next chapter shows how Wilson's foreign policy in Latin America and Europe reflected the same moralism that guided his domestic policy.

FURTHER READING

A splendid analysis of Progressivism is John Whiteclay Chambers II's *The Tyranny of Change: America in the Progressive Era, 1890–1920* (1992).

The evolution of government policy toward business is examined in Martin J. Sklar's *The Corporate Reconstruction of American Capitalism, 1890–1916: The Market, the Law, and Politics* (1988). Mina Carson's *Settlement Folk: Social Thought and the American Settlement Movement, 1885–1930* (1990) and Jack M. Holl's *Juvenile Reform in the Progressive Era: William R. George and the Junior Republic Movement* (1971) examine the social problems in the cities. An excellent study of the role of women in Progressivism's emphasis on social justice is Kathryn Kish Sklar's *Florence Kelley and the Nation's Work: The Rise of Women's Political Culture, 1830–1900* (1995). On the tragic fire at the Triangle Shirtwaist Company, see David Von Drehle's *Triangle: The Fire That Changed America* (2003).

There is a rich body of scholarship focused on the conservation movement. See especially Rebecca Conard's *Places of Quiet Beauty: Parks, Preserves, and Environmentalism* (1997), Samuel P. Hays's *Conservation and the Gospel of Efficiency: The Progressive Conservation Movement, 1890–1920* (1959), Karl Jacoby's *Crimes against Nature: Squatters, Poachers, Thieves, and the Hidden History of American Conservation* (2001), John F. Reiger's *American Sportsmen and the Origins of Conservation* (1975), and Ted Steinberg's *Down to Earth: Nature's Role in American History* (2002). Robert Kanigel's *The One Best Way: Frederick Winslow Taylor and the Enigma of Efficiency* (1997) highlights the role of efficiency in the Progressive Era.

On the pivotal election of 1912, see James Chace's *1912: Wilson, Roosevelt, Taft, and Debs—The Election That Changed the Country* (2004). Excellent biographies include Kathleen Dalton's *Theodore Roosevelt: A Strenuous Life* (2002) and H. W. Brands's *Woodrow Wilson* (2003). For banking developments, see Allan H. Meltzer's *A History of the Federal Reserve*, vol. 1, *1913–1951* (2003).

25

AMERICA AND
THE GREAT WAR

FOCUS QUESTIONS

- How did Wilson's foreign policy lead to American involvement in Latin America?
- What were the causes of the Great War in Europe?
- Why did America enter the Great War, and what was its role?
- How did Wilson promote his peace plan?
- What were the consequences of the war in America and Europe?

To answer these questions and access additional review material, please visit www.wwnorton.com/studyspace.

Throughout the nineteenth century the United States reaped the benefits of its distance from the wars that plagued Britain and Europe. The Atlantic Ocean provided a welcome buffer. During the early twentieth century, however, events combined to end the nation's comfortable isolation. Ever-expanding world trade entwined American national interests with the fate of Europe. In addition, the development of steam-powered ships and submarines meant that foreign navies could threaten American security. At the same time the election of Woodrow Wilson in 1912 brought to the White House a stern moralist determined to impose his standards for right conduct on renegade nations. This combination of circumstances made the outbreak of war in Europe in 1914 a profound crisis for the United States, a crisis that would transform the nation's role in international affairs.

WILSON AND FOREIGN AFFAIRS

Woodrow Wilson brought to the presidency little background in international relations. The former college professor admitted as much when he remarked just before taking office, "It would be an irony of fate if my administration had to deal chiefly with foreign affairs." But events in Latin America and Europe were to make the irony all too real. From the summer of 1914, when a catastrophic world war erupted, foreign relations increasingly overshadowed all else, including Wilson's ambitious domestic program.

AN IDEALIST'S DIPLOMACY   Although lacking in international experience, Wilson did not lack ideas or convictions about global issues. He saw himself as a man of destiny who would help create a new world order governed by morality and idealism rather than national interests. Both Wilson and Secretary of State William Jennings Bryan believed that America had a religious duty to advance democracy and moral progress in the world. As Wilson had declared a few years before becoming president, "Every nation of the world needs to be drawn into the tutelage of America." In many respects Wilson and Bryan developed a diplomatic policy based on pious idealism. During 1913–1914 Bryan negotiated some thirty "cooling-off" treaties under which participating nations pledged not to go to war over any disagreement for a period of twelve months pending discussion by an international arbitration panel. The treaties were of little consequence, however. They were soon forgotten in the revolutionary sweep of world events that would make the twentieth century the bloodiest in recorded history.

INTERVENTION IN MEXICO   Mexico, which had been in the throes of rival revolutions for nearly three years, presented a thorny problem for Wilson soon after he took office in 1913. Between 1876 and 1910, Porfirio Díaz had dominated Mexico. As military dictator he had suppressed opposition and showered favors on wealthy allies and foreign investors, who piled up holdings in Mexican mines, petroleum, railroads, and agriculture. But eventually the dictator's hold slipped, and in 1910 popular resentment boiled over into revolt. Revolutionary armies occupied Mexico City, and in 1911 Díaz fled.

The leader of the rebellion, Francisco Madero, proved unable to manage the tough adversaries attracted by the scramble for power. In 1913 Madero's chief of staff, General Victoriano Huerta, assumed power, and Madero was murdered soon afterward. Confronted with a military dictator across the nation's southern border, Wilson enunciated a new diplomatic doctrine of nonrecognition: "We hold . . . that just government rests upon the consent of the governed." Official recognition by the U.S. government, formerly extended routinely to governments that exercised de facto power, now would depend upon judgments of their legality; an immoral government presumably would not pass muster.

Wilson expressed sympathy with the revolutionary movement in Mexico and began to put diplomatic pressure on the "desperate brute" Huerta. Early in 1914 he removed an embargo on arms to Mexico in order to help an insurgent faction under Venustiano Carranza of the Constitutionalist party and stationed U.S. warships off Veracruz (formerly Vera Cruz) to halt arms shipments to Huerta. "I am going to teach the South American republics to elect good men," Wilson vowed to a British diplomat. On April 9, 1914, several American sailors gathering supplies in Tampico, Mexico, strayed into a restricted area and were arrested. Mexican officials quickly released them and sent an apology to the American naval commander. There the incident might have ended, but the naval officer demanded that the Mexicans salute the American flag. Wilson backed him up and won from Congress authority to use force to bring Huerta to terms. Before the Tampico incident could be resolved, Wilson sent some 6,000 U.S. marines and sailors ashore at Veracruz on April 21, 1914, and they occupied the city at a cost of 19 American lives. At least 200 Mexicans were killed.

In Mexico the American occupation of Veracruz aroused the opposition of all factions, and Huerta tried to rally support against a foreign invasion. At this juncture, Wilson accepted an offer of mediation by the ABC powers (Argentina, Brazil, and Chile), which proposed the withdrawal of U.S. forces, the removal of Huerta, and the installation of a provisional government sympathetic to reform. Huerta refused to step down, but the moral effect of the proposal and the growing strength of his foes soon forced him to leave office. The Carranzistas entered Mexico City, and the Americans left Veracruz in late 1914. A year later the United States and several Latin American governments recognized Carranza as president of Mexico.

Still the troubles south of the border continued. Bickering among various revolutionary factions erupted in chaotic civil war. The prolonged upheaval had spawned independent gangs of bandits, Francesco "Pancho" Villa's among the wildest. All through 1915 fighting between the forces of Villa and the forces of Carranza continued sporadically. In 1916 the charismatic Villa seized a train and murdered sixteen American mining engineers in a deliberate attempt to trigger U.S. intervention, discredit Carranza, and build himself up as an opponent of the "gringos." That failing, he crossed the border

Pancho Villa

Villa (center) and his followers rebelled against the president of Mexico and antagonized the United States with attacks against "gringos."

on raids into Texas and New Mexico. On March 9 he entered Columbus, New Mexico, burned the town, and killed seventeen Americans.

A furious Woodrow Wilson abandoned his policy of "watchful waiting." With the reluctant consent of Carranza, he sent General John J. Pershing across the border with a force of 11,000 men and mobilized 150,000 national guardsmen. For nearly a year, Pershing's troops went on a fruitless chase after Villa through northern Mexico. They had no luck and were ordered home in 1917. Carranza then pressed his own war against the bandits and in 1917 put through a new liberal constitution. Mexico was on its way to a more orderly government, almost in spite of Wilson's actions rather than because of them.

PROBLEMS IN THE CARIBBEAN   In the Caribbean, Wilson found it as hard to act on his ideals as in Mexico. The "dollar diplomacy" practiced by the Taft administration had encouraged bankers in the United States to aid debt-plagued governments in Haiti, Guatemala, Honduras, and Nicaragua. Despite Wilson's public stand against using military force to back up American investments, he kept the marines in Nicaragua, where they had been sent by President Taft in 1912, to prevent renewed civil war. Then, in 1915, he dispatched more marines to Haiti after two successive revolutions and subsequent government disarray. "I suppose," Wilson told Secretary of State Bryan, "there is nothing to do but to take the bull by the horns and restore order." The American forces stayed in Nicaragua until 1933 and in Haiti until 1934. Disorders in the Dominican Republic brought U.S. marines to that country in 1916; they remained until 1924. The repeated use of military force only exacerbated the hatred many Latin Americans felt toward the United States. And as the *New York Times* charged, Wilson's frequent interventions made Taft's dollar diplomacy look like "ten cent diplomacy."

AN UNEASY NEUTRALITY

During the summer of 1914, problems in Latin America and the Caribbean, as well as family tragedy, loomed larger in Wilson's thinking than the gathering storm in Europe. During his first year as president, his beloved wife, Ellen, contracted kidney disease. By the summer of 1914, her condition was critical, and on August 6 she died. President Wilson was devastated. "Oh, my God! What am I to do?" he exclaimed. He sobbed throughout the funeral service and for days thereafter would weep uncontrollably. His family doctor said he had never witnessed a "sadder picture." The president is a "man with his heart torn out." Yet six months later the president met Edith Bolling Galt, a Washington widow, and was smitten by her charm and beauty. In December 1915 they were married.

Ellen Wilson had died just as another tragedy was erupting overseas. When the thunderbolt of war struck Europe in the summer of 1914, most Americans, one North Carolinian wrote, saw it "as lightning out of a clear sky." Whatever the troubles in Mexico, whatever disorders and interventions agitated other countries, it seemed unreal that civilized Europe could descend into such an orgy of destruction. Since the fall of Napoléon in 1815, Europe had known local wars, but only as interruptions of a general peace that contributed to a century of unprecedented material progress.

The peace ended when an Austrian citizen of Serbian descent who wanted an independent Serbia assassinated the Austrian archduke Franz Ferdinand. Austria-Hungary's vengeful determination to punish Serbia for the murder led Russia to mobilize its army in sympathy with its Slavic friends in Serbia. That in turn triggered a European system of alliances: the Triple Alliance, or Central Powers (Germany, Austria-Hungary, and Italy), and the Triple Entente, or Allied Powers (France, Great Britain, and Russia). When Russia refused to stop its army's mobilization, Germany, which backed Austria-Hungary, declared war on Russia on August 1, 1914, and on Russia's ally France two days later. Germany then invaded Belgium to get at France, which brought Great Britain into the war on August 4. Japan, eager to seize German holdings in the Pacific, declared war on August 23, and Turkey entered on the side of the Central Powers in October. Although allied with the Central Powers, Italy initially stayed out of the war and then struck a bargain under which it joined the Allied powers in 1915.

As the fighting unfolded, it quickly became apparent that the First World War was unlike any previous conflict in its scope and carnage. Machine guns, high-velocity rifles, aerial bombing, poison gas, flame throwers, land mines, long-range artillery, and armored tanks changed the nature of warfare and produced massive casualties and widespread destruction. Over 61 million men served in the armed forces on both sides, and over 9 million combatants were killed in action. Another 19 million were wounded. The war produced 3 million widows and 6 million orphans.

The battlefields of World War I were surreal in their horrors. What began as a war of quick movement bogged down into a stalemated war of senseless attrition led by mediocre generals. During the Battle of Verdun, in northeast France, which lasted from February to December 1916, some 32 million artillery shells were fired—1,500 shells for every square meter of the battlefield. Such devastating firepower ravaged the landscape, turning farmland and forests into wasteland. The casualties were staggering. Some 162,000 French soldiers died at Verdun; German losses were 143,000.

Trench warfare gave the First World War its lasting character. Most of the great battles of the war involved hundreds of thousands of men crawling out of their muddy, rat-infested trenches and then crossing a no-man's-land to attack enemy positions, only to be pushed back a day or a week later. The 475 miles of trenches provided protection and living space as well as a jumping-off point for large- and small-scale attacks by day or night. Life in the trenches was miserable. In addition to the dangers of enemy fire, soldiers on both sides were forced to deal with flooding and such diseases as trench fever and trench foot, which could lead to amputation. Lice and rats were constant companions. The stench was unbearable. Soldiers on both sides ate, slept, and fought among the dead and amid the reek of death.

INITIAL REACTIONS   As the trench war along the western front in Belgium and France stalemated, the casualties soared and pressure for American intervention increased. On the first day of the Battle of the Somme, on July 1, 1916, 20,000 British soldiers were killed and 40,000 others were wounded—all in less than twenty-four hours. Shock in the United

The Samson-like "War" Pulls Down the Temple of "Civilization"

Most Americans tended to support the Allied Powers, but everyone was shocked at the carnage of the Great War.

States over the war in Europe gave way to gratitude that an ocean stood between America and the killing fields. "Our isolated position and freedom from entangling alliances," said the *Literary Digest,* ensure that "we are in no peril of being drawn into the European quarrel." President Wilson repeatedly urged the public to be "neutral in thought as well as in action."

That was more easily said than done. More than one third of American were "hyphenated Americans," first- or second-generation immigrants who retained ties to their old country. Among the 13 million immigrants from the countries at war, by far the largest group was German American, numbering 8 million. And 4 million Irish Americans harbored a deep-rooted enmity toward England. These groups instinctively leaned toward the Central Powers. But old-line Americans, largely of British origin, supported the Allied Powers. American leaders were pro-British from the outset of the war. Robert Lansing, first counselor of the State Department; Walter Hines Page, ambassador to London; and "Colonel" Edward House, Wilson's close adviser, saw in German militarism a potential danger to America.

A STRAINED NEUTRALITY   At first the war in Europe brought a slump in American exports and the threat of a depression, but by the spring of 1915 the Allies' demand for food and war supplies generated an economic boom. The Allies at first financed their purchases by disposing of American securities, but ultimately they needed loans. Early in the war, Secretary of State William Jennings Bryan declared that loans to any warring nation were "inconsistent with the true spirit of neutrality." Yet Wilson quietly began approving short-term credit to sustain trade with the desperate Allies. When in the fall of 1915 it became apparent that the Allies could no longer carry on

WORLD WAR I IN EUROPE, 1914

- Central Powers (Triple Alliance)
- Allied Powers (Triple Entente)
- Neutral countries

How did the European system of alliances spread conflict across all of Europe? How was World War I different from previous wars? How did the war in Europe lead to ethnic tensions in the United States?

without long-term credit, the administration removed all restrictions, and American investors would eventually advance over $2 billion to the Allies before the United States entered the war, and only $27 million to Germany.

The administration nevertheless clung to the fond hope of neutrality through two and a half years of warfare in Europe and tried to uphold the traditions of "freedom of the seas," which had guided American policy since the Napoleonic Wars of the early nineteenth century. As the German army's advance through Belgium toward Paris ground down into the stalemate of trench warfare, trade on the high seas assumed a new importance. In a war of attrition, survival depended upon access to supplies, and in such a war British naval power counted for a great deal.

On August 6, 1914, Secretary of State Bryan called upon the belligerents to accept the Declaration of London, drafted and signed in 1909 by leading powers but never ratified by the British. That document reduced the list of contraband (war-related) items and specified that a blockade was legal only when effective just outside enemy ports. The Central Powers promptly accepted the declaration. The British almost as promptly refused to, lest they lose some of their advantage in sea power. Britain gradually extended the list of contraband goods to include all sorts of items formerly excluded, such as food, cotton, wood, and certain ores. In November 1914 the British declared the whole North Sea a war zone, sowed it with mines, and ordered neutral ships to submit to searches. In March 1915 they announced that they would seize ships carrying goods to Germany. American protests were ignored.

NEUTRAL RIGHTS AND SUBMARINES   British actions, including blacklisting American companies that traded with the enemy and censoring the mail, raised some old issues of neutral rights, but the German reaction introduced an entirely new question. With the German fleet bottled up by the British blockade, the German government proclaimed a war zone around the British Isles. Enemy merchant ships in those waters were liable to sinking by submarines, the Germans declared, and "it may not always be possible to save crews and passengers." As the chief advantage of U-boat (*Unterseeboot*) warfare was in surprise, it violated the established procedure of stopping an enemy vessel on the high seas and providing for the safety of passengers and crew before sinking it. Since the British sometimes flew neutral flags as a ruse, neutral ships in this war zone would also be in danger.

The United States pronounced the German policy "an indefensible violation of neutral rights" and warned that Germany would be held to "strict accountability" for any destruction of American lives and property. Then, on May 7, 1915, the captain of a German submarine sighted a huge oceanliner moving slowly through the Irish Sea and fired a torpedo. The ship exploded and sank within a few minutes. Only as it tipped into the waves was the German commander able to make out the name *Lusitania* on the stern. Before the *Lusitania* had left New York, bound for Liverpool, the German embassy had published warnings in the American press against travel to the war zone, but 128 Americans were nevertheless among the 1,198 persons lost.

The New York Times.

THE WEATHER
Fair today and Sunday; fresh to strong southwest to west winds

VOL. LXIV...NO. 20,923.   NEW YORK, SATURDAY, MAY 8, 1915.—TWENTY-FOUR PAGES.   ONE CENT   TWO CENTS

LUSITANIA SUNK BY A SUBMARINE, PROBABLY 1,000 DEAD; TWICE TORPEDOED OFF IRISH COAST; SINKS IN 15 MINUTES; AMERICANS ABOARD INCLUDED VANDERBILT AND FROHMAN; WASHINGTON BELIEVES THAT A GRAVE CRISIS IS AT HAND

THE LOST CUNARD STEAMSHIP LUSITANIA

The *Lusitania*

Americans were outraged when a German torpedo sank the *Lusitania* on May 7, 1915.

Americans were outraged. The sinking was an act of piracy, Theodore Roosevelt declared. To quiet the uproar, Wilson urged patience: "There is such a thing as a man being too proud to fight. There is such a thing as a nation being so right that it does not need to convince others by force that it is right." Wilson immediately knew he had misspoken. Critics lambasted his lame response to the death of 128 Americans. "I have a bad habit of thinking out loud," he confessed to a friend the day after his "too proud to fight" speech. The language, he admitted, had "occurred to me while I was speaking, and I let it out. I should have kept it in." But his previous demand for "strict accountability" forced him to make a stronger response. On May 13 Secretary of State Bryan reluctantly signed a note demanding that the Germans abandon unrestricted submarine warfare, disavow the sinking, and pay reparations. The Germans responded that the ship was armed (which it was not) and secretly carried a cargo of rifles and ammunition (which it did). A second note on June 9 repeated American demands in stronger terms. The United States, Wilson asserted, was "contending for nothing less high and sacred than the rights of humanity." Bryan, unwilling to risk war over the issue, resigned in protest. He groused to Wilson that Colonel House "has been [acting as] secretary of state, not I, and I have never had your full confidence." Edith Galt, not yet Wilson's wife, took great delight in Bryan's resignation. "Hurrah! Old Bryan is out!" she told the president. "I could shout and sing that at last the world will *know* just what he is." Bryan's

Stand by the President

In this 1915 cartoon, Woodrow Wilson holds to the middle course between the pacifism of Bryan (whose sign reads, "Let Us avoid Unnecessary Risks") and the belligerence of Roosevelt (whose sign reads, "Let Us Act Without Unnecessary Delay").

successor, Robert Lansing, signed the note to the Germans.

In response to the uproar over the *Lusitania,* the German government had secretly ordered U-boat captains to avoid sinking large passenger vessels. When, despite the order, two American lives were lost in the sinking of the New York–bound British liner *Arabic,* the Germans paid an indemnity and offered a public assurance on September 1, 1915: "Liners will not be sunk by our submarines without warning and without safety of the lives of noncombatants, provided that the liners do not try to escape or offer resistance." With this *Arabic* pledge, Wilson's resolute stand seemed to have resulted in a victory for his policy.

During early 1916 Wilson's trusted adviser Colonel House visited London, Paris, and Berlin in an effort to negotiate an end to the war but found neither side ready to begin serious negotiations. In 1916 peace advocates in Congress introduced resolutions in the House and Senate warning Americans against traveling on armed belligerent vessels. Such surrender to the German threat, Wilson asserted, would be a "deliberate abdication of our hitherto proud position as spokesmen, even amidst the turmoil of war, for the law and the right." He warned that if the United States accepted a single abatement of neutral rights, "the whole fine fabric of international law might crumble under our hands piece by piece." The administration managed to defeat both resolutions by a solid margin. On March 24, 1916, a U-boat torpedoed the French steamer *Sussex,* injuring two Americans. When Wilson threatened to break off relations, Germany renewed its pledge that U-boats would not torpedo merchant and passenger ships. This *Sussex* pledge implied the virtual abandonment of submarine warfare.

THE DEBATE OVER PREPAREDNESS   The *Lusitania* incident and, more generally, the quarrels over neutral commerce contributed to a growing demand for a stronger army and navy. On December 1, 1914, champions of preparedness organized the National Security League to promote their cause. After the *Lusitania* sinking, Wilson asked the War and Navy Departments to draft proposals for military expansion.

Progressives and pacifists, however, as well as many residents of the rural South and West, were opposed to a defense buildup. Their anti-war sentiments tapped into the traditional American suspicion of military establishments, especially of standing armies, which dated back to the colonial period. The new Democratic leader in the House spoke for many Americans when he declared his opposition to "the big Navy and big Army program of the jingoes and war traffickers." The administration's plan to enlarge the regular army and create a national reserve force of 400,000 ran into stubborn opposition in the House Military Affairs Committee. Wilson was forced to accept a compromise between advocates of an expanded force under federal control and advocates of a traditional citizen army. The National Defense Act of 1916 expanded the regular federal army from 90,000 to 175,000 and permitted gradual enlargement to 223,000. It also increased the national guard to 440,000, made provision for training, and gave federal funds for summer training camps for civilians.

The bill for an increased navy aroused less opposition because of the general feeling expressed by the navy secretary that there was "no danger of militarism from a relatively strong navy such as would come from a big standing army." The Naval Construction Act of 1916 authorized between $500 million and $600 million for a three-year expansion program.

Forced to relent on military preparedness, opponents of a buildup insisted that the financial burden should rest upon the wealthy people they held responsible for promoting the military expansion. The income tax became their weapon. Supported by a groundswell of popular support, they wrote into the Revenue Act of 1916 changes that doubled the basic income tax rate from 1 to 2 percent, lifted the surtax to a maximum of 13 percent (for a total of 15 percent) on income over $2 million, added an estate tax, levied a 12.5 percent tax on gross receipts of munitions makers, and added a new tax on excess corporate profits. The new taxes amounted to the most clear-cut victory of radical Progressives in the entire Wilson period, a victory further consolidated and advanced after America entered the war. It was the capstone to the Progressive legislation that Wilson supported in preparation for the upcoming presidential election.

THE ELECTION OF 1916 As the 1916 election approached, Republicans hoped to regain their normal electoral majority, and Theodore

Roosevelt hoped to be their leader again. But he had committed the deadly sin of bolting his party in 1912, and what was more, his eagerness for the United States to enter the war scared many voters. Needing somebody who would draw Bull Moose Progressives back into the fold, the Republican regulars turned to Justice Charles Evans Hughes, who had a Progressive record as governor of New York from 1907 to 1910. On the Supreme Court since then, he had neither endorsed a candidate in 1912 nor spoken out on foreign policy. The remnants of the Progressive party gathered in Chicago at the same time as the Republicans. Roosevelt had held out the vain hope of getting both nominations, but he now declined to lead a third party. Two weeks later the Progressive National Committee disbanded the party and endorsed Hughes.

The Democrats, as expected, chose Wilson again and in their platform endorsed a program of social-welfare legislation, neutrality as far as the war in Europe, and reasonable military preparedness. The party further commended women's suffrage to the states and pledged support for a postwar league of nations to enforce peace with collective-security measures against aggressors. The Democrats' most popular issue, however, was an insistent pledge to keep the nation out of the war in Europe. The peace theme, refined in the slogan "He kept us out of war," became the rallying cry of the Wilson campaign.

Peace with Honor

Woodrow Wilson's policies of neutrality proved popular in the 1916 campaign.

The candidates in the 1916 presidential election were remarkably similar. Both Wilson and Hughes were the sons of preachers; both were attorneys and former professors; both had been Progressive governors; both were known for their pristine integrity. Theodore Roosevelt highlighted the similarities between them when he called the bearded Hughes a "whiskered Wilson." Wilson, however, proved to be the better campaigner. In the end, his twin pledges of peace and Progressivism, a unique combination of issues forged in the legislative and diplomatic crucibles of 1916, brought a narrow victory. Early returns showed a Republican sweep in the East and the Midwest, signaling a victory for Hughes, but the outcome remained in doubt until word came that Wilson had carried California by a scant 3,772 votes. The final vote showed a Democratic sweep of the Far West and the South, enough for victory in the Electoral College, by 277 to 254, and in the popular vote, by 9 million to 8.5 million.

LAST EFFORTS FOR PEACE   Immediately after the election, Wilson again offered to mediate an end to the war in Europe, but neither side was willing to abandon its major war aims. Wilson then decided to make one more appeal, in the hope that public opinion would force the hands of the warring governments. Speaking before the Senate on January 22, 1917, he asserted the right of the United States to a share in laying the foundations for a lasting peace, which would have to be a "peace without victory," for only a "peace among equals" could endure. The peace must be based upon the principles of democratic government, freedom of the seas, and disarmament, and those ideals must be enforced by an international league for peace established to make another such catastrophe impossible.

Although Wilson did not know it, he was already too late. Exactly two weeks before he spoke, impatient German military leaders had decided to wage unrestricted submarine warfare. They took the calculated risk of arousing American anger in the hope of scoring a quick knockout. On January 31 the new policy was announced, effective the next day. All vessels would be sunk without warning. "Freedom of the seas," said the *Brooklyn Eagle,* "will now be enjoyed [only] by icebergs and fish."

On February 3, 1917, Wilson told a joint session of Congress that the United States had broken diplomatic relations with the German government. Three weeks later he asked for authority to arm merchant ships and "to employ any other instrumentalities or methods" necessary and "to protect our ships and our people." There was little quarrel with arming merchant ships, but there was bitter opposition to Wilson's vague reference to "any other instrumentalities or methods." A group of eleven or twelve die-hard noninterventionists in

Congress filibustered the measure until the legislative session expired on March 4. A furious Wilson decided to outflank Congress. On March 12 the State Department announced that a forgotten law of 1792 allowed the arming of merchant ships regardless of congressional inaction.

On February 25 Wilson learned that the British had intercepted and decoded an important message from the German foreign secretary Arthur Zimmermann to his ambassador in Mexico. The note instructed the envoy to offer an alliance and financial aid to Mexico in case of war between the United States and Germany. In return for diversionary action against the United States, Mexico would recover "the lost territory in Texas, New Mexico, and Arizona." On March 1, news of the Zimmermann telegram broke in the American press and infuriated the public. Then, later in March, a revolution overthrew Russia's czarist government and established the provisional government of a Russian republic. The fall of the czarist autocracy allowed Americans the illusion that all the major Allied powers were now fighting for constitutional democracy. Not until November 1917 was that illusion shattered, when the Bolsheviks, led by Vladimir Lenin, seized power in Russia and began establishing a Communist dictatorship.

AMERICA'S ENTRY INTO THE WAR

In March 1917 German submarines sank five U.S. merchant vessels in the North Atlantic. On March 20 Wilson's cabinet unanimously endorsed a declaration of war, and the following day the president called a special session of Congress. When it met on April 2, Wilson asked Congress to recognize the war that imperial Germany was already waging against the United States. The German government had revealed itself as a natural foe of liberty, and therefore "the world must be made safe for democracy." The war resolution passed the Senate by a vote of 82 to 6 on April 4. The House concurred, 373 to 50, and Wilson signed the measure on April 6, 1917.

How had matters come to this less than three years after Wilson's proclamation of neutrality? Prominent among the various explanations of America's entrance into the war were the effects of British propaganda in the United States and America's deep involvement in trade with the Allies, which some observers then and later credited to the intrigues of war profiteers and munitions makers. Some proponents of war thought German domination of Europe would be a threat to American security, especially if it meant the destruction of the British navy. But whatever the influence of such factors, they likely would not have been decisive without the issue of submarine warfare. Once Wilson had taken a stand for the traditional rights of neutrals and noncombatants on the high seas, he was to some extent at the mercy of decisions by the German high command.

AMERICA'S EARLY ROLE   War had been declared, but the scope of America's role in the European conflict remained unclear. Few on either side of the Atlantic expected more from the United States than a token military effort. Despite Congress's preparedness measures, the army remained small and untested. The navy also was largely undeveloped. The Americans made two important contributions to Allied naval strategy, however. Merchant ships had previously survived submarine attacks by means of speed and evasive action. Now, Rear Admiral William S. Sims, commander of American ships in European waters, persuaded the Allies to adopt a convoy system of escorting merchant ships in groups. The result was a sharp decrease in Allied shipping losses. As its second contribution, the U.S. Navy laid a gigantic minefield across the North Sea, limiting U-boat access to the North Atlantic.

Within a month of the declaration of war, British and French officials arrived in the United States. They first requested money with which to buy American supplies, a request Congress had anticipated in the Liberty Loan Act, which added $5 billion to the national debt in "liberty bonds." Of this amount, $3 billion could be lent to the Allied powers. The United States was also willing to furnish naval support, financial credits, supplies, and munitions. But to raise and train a large army, equip it, and send it across a submarine-infested ocean seemed out of the question. The French nevertheless insisted that the United States send a token military force to bolster morale, and on June 26, 1917, the first contingent of U.S. soldiers, about 14,500 men commanded by General John J. Pershing, dis-

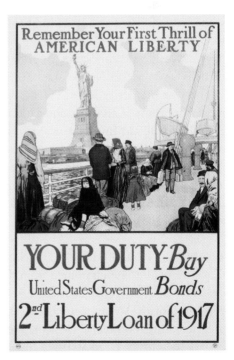

The Thrill of American Liberty

This Liberty Loan poster urges immigrants to do their duty for their new country by buying government bonds.

embarked on the French coast. Pershing and his troops reached Paris by July 4. Pershing soon advised the War Department to send 1 million American troops by the following spring. It was done—but only through strenuous efforts.

When the United States entered the war, the combined strength of the regular army and national guard was only 379,000; at the end it would be 3.7 million. The need for such large numbers of troops forced Wilson to embrace conscription. Under the Selective Service Act of 1917, all men aged twenty-one to thirty (later, eighteen to forty-five) had to register to be drafted for military service. All told, about 2 million American troops crossed the Atlantic, and about 1.4 million saw some combat.

MOBILIZING A NATION   Complete economic mobilization on the home front was also necessary to conduct the war efficiently. The Army Appropriation Act of 1916 had created a Council of National Defense, which in turn led to the creation of other wartime agencies. The Lever Food and Fuel Control Act of 1917 created a Food Administration, headed by Herbert Hoover, a future president, who sought to raise agricultural production while reducing civilian use of foodstuffs. "Food will win the war" was the slogan. Hoover directed a propaganda campaign promoting "meatless Tuesdays," "wheatless Wednesdays," "porkless Saturdays," the planting of victory gardens, and the creative use of leftovers.

The War Industries Board (WIB), established in 1917, soon became the most important of all the mobilization agencies. It was headed by Bernard Baruch, a brilliant financier who exercised a virtual dictatorship over the economy. Under Baruch the purchasing bureaus of the United States and Allied governments submitted their needs to the board, which set priorities and planned production. The board could allocate raw materials, tell manufacturers what to produce, order construction of new plants, and with the approval of the president, fix prices.

A NEW LABOR FORCE   The closing off of foreign immigration and the movement of 4 million men from the workforce into the armed services created a labor shortage. To meet it, women, African Americans, and other ethnic minorities were encouraged to enter industries and agricultural activities heretofore dominated by white men. Northern businesses sent recruiting agents into the Deep South to find workers for their factories and mills, and over 400,000 southern blacks began the Great Migration northward during the war years, a mass movement that continued unabated through the 1920s. Mexican Americans followed the same migratory pattern. Recruiting agents and newspaper editors protrayed the North as the "land of promise" for southern blacks suffering from their region's depressed agricultural economy and rising racial intimidation and violence. The African-American *Chicago Defender* exclaimed: "To die from the bite of frost is far more glorious than at the hands of a mob." By 1930 the number of African Americans living in the North was triple that of 1910.

But the newcomers were not always welcomed above the Mason-Dixon line. Many native white workers resented the new arrivals, and racial tensions sparked riots in cities across the country. In 1917 over forty African Americans and nine whites were killed during a riot over employment in a defense plant in East St. Louis. Two years later the toll of a Chicago race riot was nearly as high, with twenty-three African Americans and fifteen whites left dead. In these and other incidents of racial violence, the pattern was the same: whites angered by the influx of blacks into their communities would seize upon an incident as an excuse to rampage through black neighborhoods, killing, burning, and looting while white policemen looked the other way or encouraged the hooliganism.

For women, intervention in World War I had more positive effects. Initially women supported the war effort in traditional ways. They helped organize war-bond and war-relief drives, conserved foodstuffs and war-related materials, supported the Red Cross, and joined the army nurse corps. But as the scope of the war widened, both government and industry sought to

Women Aid the War Effort

Women working at the Bloomfield International Fuse Company, New Jersey, 1918.

mobilize women workers for service on farms, loading docks, and railway crews, as well as in armaments industries, machine shops, steel and lumber mills, and chemical plants. Many women leaders saw such opportunities as a breakthrough. "At last, after centuries of disabilities and discrimination," said a speaker at a Women's Trade Union League meeting in 1917, "women are coming into the labor and festival of life on equal terms with men." An African-American woman who exchanged her job as a live-in servant for work in a factory declared: "I'll never work in nobody's kitchen but my own any more. No indeed, that's the one thing that makes me stick to this job."

In fact, however, war-generated changes in female employment were limited and brief. About 1 million women participated in "war work," but most of them were young and single and already working outside the home. Most returned to their previous jobs once the war ended. In fact, male-dominated unions encouraged women to revert to their stereotypical domestic roles after the war ended. The Central Federated Union of New York insisted that "the same patriotism which induced women to enter industry during the war should induce them to vacate their positions after the war." The anticipated gains of women in the workforce failed to materialize. In fact, in 1920 the 8.5 million working women made up a smaller percentage of the labor force than women had in 1910. Still, one lasting result of women's contributions to the war effort was Woodrow Wilson's decision to endorse women's suffrage. In the fall of 1918, he told the Senate that giving women the vote was "vital to the winning of the war."

WAR PROPAGANDA   The war effort led the government to mobilize more than economic life: the progressive gospel of efficiency suggested mobilizing public opinion as well. On April 14, 1917, eight days after the declaration of war, an executive order established the Committee on Public Information, composed of the secretaries of state, war, and the navy. Its executive head, George Creel, a Denver newsman, sold Wilson on the idea that the best approach to influencing public opinion was "expression, not repression"—propaganda instead of censorship. Creel organized a propaganda machine to convey the Allies' war aims to the people and, above all, to the enemy, where it might help sap their morale. To sell the war, Creel gathered a remarkable group of journalists, photographers, artists, entertainers, and others useful to his purpose. A film division produced such pictures as *The Beast of Berlin*. Hardly any public group escaped a harangue by one of the 75,000 "four-minute men" organized to give short speeches on liberty bonds, the need to conserve food and fuel, and other timely topics.

CIVIL LIBERTIES   By arousing public opinion to such a frenzy, the war effort channeled the zeal of Progressivism into grotesque campaigns of "Americanism" and witch-hunting. Wilson had foreseen these consequences. "Once lead this people into war," he said, "and they'll forget there ever was such a thing as tolerance." Popular prejudice equated anything German with disloyalty. Symphonies refused to perform Bach and Beethoven, schools dropped courses in the German language, and patriots translated *sauerkraut* into "liberty cabbage," *German measles* into "liberty measles," and *dachshunds* into "liberty pups."

Under the Espionage and Sedition Acts, Congress in effect outlawed criticism of government leaders and war policies. The Espionage Act of 1917 set penalties of up to $10,000 and twenty years in prison for anyone who gave aid to the enemy; who tried to incite insubordination, disloyalty, or refusal of duty in the armed services; or who circulated false reports and statements with intent to interfere with the war effort. The postmaster general could bar from the mail anything that violated the act or advocated treason, insurrection, or forcible resistance to any U.S. law. The Sedition Act of 1918 extended the penalties to those who did or said anything to obstruct the sale of liberty bonds or to advocate cutbacks in production, and—just in case something had been overlooked—for saying, writing, or printing anything "disloyal, profane, scurrilous, or abusive" about the American form of government, the Constitution, or the army and navy.

The Espionage and Sedition Acts generated more than 1,000 convictions. Socialists and other radicals were the primary targets. Victor Berger, a Socialist congressman from Milwaukee, received a twenty-year sentence for editorials in the Milwaukee *Leader* that called the war a capitalist conspiracy. Eugene V. Debs, who had polled over 900,000 votes for president in 1912, ardently opposed intervention in the war. He repeatedly urged men to refuse to serve in the military, even though he knew he could be prosecuted for such remarks under the Espionage Act. "I would a thousand times rather be a free soul in jail than a sycophant and a coward in the streets," he told a Socialist gathering in 1918. He received his wish. Two weeks later Debs was arrested and eventually given a ten-year prison sentence for encouraging draft resistance. In 1920, still in jail, he polled nearly 1 million votes for president.

In two important decisions just after the war, the Supreme Court upheld the Espionage and Sedition Acts. *Schenck v. United States* (1919) reaffirmed the conviction of a man for circulating anti-draft leaflets among members of the armed forces. In this case, Justice Oliver Wendell Holmes said, "Free speech would not protect a man in falsely shouting fire in a theater, and causing a panic." The act applied where there was "a clear and present danger" that speech in wartime might create evils Congress had a right to prevent. In *Abrams v. United States* (1919), the Court upheld the conviction of a man who circulated pamphlets opposing American intervention in Russia to oust the Bolsheviks. Here Holmes and Louis Brandeis dissented from the majority view. The "surreptitious publishing of a silly leaflet by an unknown man," they argued, posed no danger to government policy.

"THE DECISIVE POWER"

American troops played little more than a token role in the European fighting until early 1918. Before that they were parceled out in quiet sectors mainly for training purposes. All through 1917 the Allies remained on the defensive, and late in the year their situation turned desperate. In October the Italian lines collapsed and were overrun by Austrian forces. With the help of Allied troops from France, the Italians finally held their ground. In November the Bolshevik revolution overthrew the infant Russian republic, and the new Soviet government dropped out of the war. With the Central Powers free to concentrate their forces on the western front, the American war effort became a "race for France," to restore the balance of strength.

Fighting on the Western Front

A gun crew firing on entrenched German positions, 1918.

French premier Georges Clemenceau appealed to the Americans to accelerate their mobilization. "A terrible blow is imminent," he predicted to a journalist. "Tell your Americans to come quickly."

THE WESTERN FRONT   On March 21, 1918, Clemenceau's prediction came true when the Germans began the first of several offensives in France and Belgium to try to end the war before the Americans arrived in force. On May 27 the Germans began their next drive along the Aisne River, took Soissons, and pushed on to the Marne River along a forty-mile front. By May 1918 there were 1 million fresh U.S. troops in Europe, and for the first time they made a difference. In a counterattack, American forces retook Cantigny on May 28 and held it. During the first week in June, a marine brigade blocked the Germans at Belleau Wood, and army troops took Vaux and opposed the Germans at Château-Thierry. Though these actions had limited military significance, their effect on Allied morale was immense. Each was a solid American success, and together they reinforced General Pershing's demand that the U.S. Army retain its independence and not be integrated with Allied forces.

Before that could come to pass, the turning point in the western campaign came, on July 15, 1918, in the Second Battle of the Marne. On both sides of

America at War

U.S. soldiers fire an artillery gun in Argonne, France.

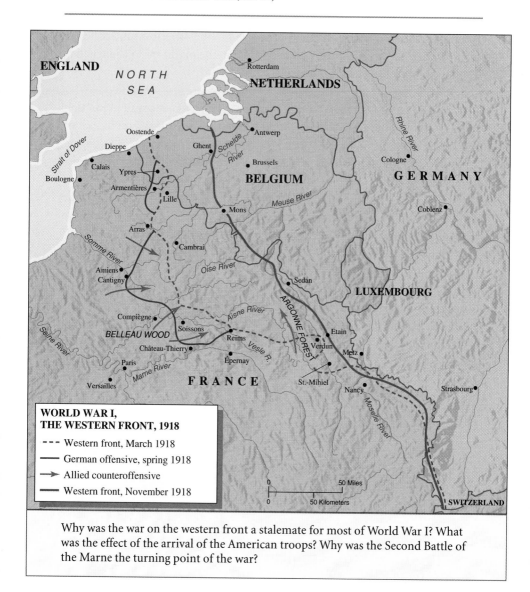

England
NORTH SEA
Rotterdam
NETHERLANDS
Rhine River
Oostende
Dieppe
Ghent
Schelde River
Antwerp
Cologne
GERMANY
Calais
Ypres
Brussels
Boulogne
Armentières
BELGIUM
Lille
Mons
Meuse River
Coblenz
Arras
Cambrai
Oise River
Sedan
LUXEMBOURG
Somme River
Amiens
Cantigny
Compiègne
Aisne River
ARGONNE FOREST
Etain
Soissons
Reims
Verdun
Metz
BELLEAU WOOD
Château-Thierry
Vesle R.
Strait of Dover
Seine River
Paris
Marne River
Épernay
FRANCE
St.-Mihiel
Nancy
Strasbourg
Versailles
Moselle River
SWITZERLAND

WORLD WAR I, THE WESTERN FRONT, 1918

- - - Western front, March 1918
—— German offensive, spring 1918
→ Allied counteroffensive
—— Western front, November 1918

0 ____ 50 Miles
0 ____ 50 Kilometers

Why was the war on the western front a stalemate for most of World War I? What was the effect of the arrival of the American troops? Why was the Second Battle of the Marne the turning point of the war?

Reims, the Germans assaulted the French lines. Within three days, however, they had stalled, and soon the British, French, and Americans began to roll the German front back into Belgium. Then, on August 10, the U.S. First Army was organized and assigned the task of liquidating the Germans at St.-Mihiel, southeast of Verdun. There, on September 12, an army of more than 500,000 staged the first strictly American offensive of the war. Within three days the Germans had pulled back. The great Meuse-Argonne offensive, begun on September 26, then employed American divisions in a drive toward

Sedan and its railroad, which supplied the entire German front. The largest American action of the war, it involved 1.2 million U.S. troops and resulted in 117,000 American casualties, including 26,000 dead. But along the entire front from Sedan to Flanders, the Germans were in retreat. "America," wrote German general Erich Ludendorff, "thus became the decisive power in the war."

American Casualties

A Salvation Army worker writing a letter home for a wounded soldier.

THE BOLSHEVIKS When the war broke out in 1914, Russia was one of the Allied powers. Over the next three years the Russians suffered some 5.5 million casualties. By 1917 there were shortages of ammunition for the Russian troops and food for the Russian people. The czarist government was in disarray, and after the czar's abdication, it first gave way to a provisional republican government, which succumbed, in November 1917, to a revolution led by Vladimir Lenin and his Bolshevik party, who promised warweary Russians "peace, land, and bread."

Once in control of the government, the Bolsheviks unilaterally stopped fighting in World War I. With German troops deep in Russian territory and with armies of "White" Russians (anti-Bolsheviks) organizing resistance to their power, on March 3, 1918, the Bolsheviks concluded a separate peace with Germany, the Treaty of Brest-Litovsk. In an effort to prevent military supplies from falling into German hands and encourage anti-Bolshevik forces in the developing Russian Civil War, Wilson sent American forces into Russia's Arctic ports. Troops were also sent to eastern Siberia, where they remained until April 1920 in an effort to curb the growing Japanese ambitions there. The Allied intervention in Russia failed because the Bolsheviks were able to consolidate their power. Russia took no further part in World War I and did not participate in the peace settlement. The intervention largely served to generate among Soviets a long-lasting suspicion of the West.

THE FOURTEEN POINTS   As the conflict in Europe was ending, neither the Allies nor the Central Powers, despite Wilson's prodding, had stated openly what they hoped to gain through the fighting. Wilson repeated that the Americans had no selfish ends. "We desire no conquest, no dominion," he stressed in his war message of 1917. "We seek no indemnities for ourselves, no material compensation for the sacrifices we shall freely make. We are but one of the champions of the rights of mankind." Unfortunately for his idealistic purpose, after the Bolsheviks seized power in Russia in 1917, they published copies of secret treaties in which the Allies had promised territorial gains in order to win Italy, Romania, and Greece to their side. When an Interallied Conference in Paris late in 1917 failed to agree on a statement of war aims, Colonel House advised Wilson to formulate his own.

During 1917 House had been drawing together an informal panel of American experts, called the Inquiry, to formulate plans for peace. With advice from these experts, Wilson himself drew up a statement that would come to be called the Fourteen Points. These he delivered to a joint session of Congress on January 8, 1918, "as the only possible program" for peace. The first five points in general terms called for open diplomacy rather than secret treaties, freedom of the seas, removal of trade barriers, reduction of armaments, and an impartial adjustment of the victor's colonial claims based upon the desires of the populations involved. Most of the remaining points dealt with territorial claims: they called on the Central Powers to evacuate occupied lands and to allow self-determination for various nationalities, a crucial principle for Wilson. Point 13 proposed an independent Poland with access to the sea. Point 14, the capstone in Wilson's thinking, called for the creation of a "league" of nations to secure guarantees of independence and territorial integrity to all countries, great and small.

The Fourteen Points embodied Wilson's sincere commitments, but they also served the purpose of psychological warfare. One of their aims was to keep Russia in the war by a more liberal statement of purpose—a vain hope, as it turned out. Another was to reassure the Allied peoples that they were involved in a noble cause. A third was to drive a wedge between the governments of the Central Powers and their people by offering a reasonable peace. Wilson's promise of "autonomous development" for the subject nationalities of Austria-Hungary (point 10) might have weakened the polyglot Hapsburg Empire, though he did not intend to break it up. But the chaos into which Central Europe descended in 1918, and the national aspirations of the Hapsburg Empire's peoples, took matters out of his hands.

On September 29, 1918, German general Ludendorff advised his government to seek the best peace terms possible. On October 3 a new chancellor made the first German overtures for peace on the basis of the Fourteen Points. A month of diplomatic fencing followed between Colonel House and Allied representatives. Finally, when House threatened to pursue separate negotiations with Germany, the Allies accepted the Fourteen Points as a basis of peace, but with two significant reservations: they reserved the right to discuss limiting freedom of the seas, and they demanded reparations for war damages.

Allied Victory

Celebration of the armistice ending World War I, New York City, November 1918.

Meanwhile the German home front was being torn apart by a loss of morale, culminating in a naval mutiny at Kiel. Germany's allies dropped out of the war: Bulgaria on September 29, 1918, Turkey on October 30, and Austria-Hungary on November 3. On November 9 the kaiser abdicated, and a German republic was proclaimed. On November 11 at 5 A.M., an armistice was signed. Six hours later, at the eleventh hour of the eleventh day of the eleventh month, the guns fell silent. Under the armistice the Germans had to evacuate occupied territories, pull back behind the Rhine River, and surrender their naval fleet and railroad equipment. The Germans were assured that the Fourteen Points would be the basis for the peace conference.

THE FIGHT FOR THE PEACE

DOMESTIC UNREST   Woodrow Wilson made a fateful decision to attend in person the peace conference that convened in Paris on January 18, 1919. It shattered precedent for a president to leave the country for so long, but it dramatized all the more Wilson's messianic vision and his desire to ensure his goal of a lasting peace. From one viewpoint it was a shrewd move, for his prestige and determination made a difference in Paris. But during his prolonged trip abroad he lost touch with political developments at home. His progressive coalition was already unraveling under the pressures of wartime discontent. Western farmers complained about the government's control of wheat prices while southern cotton producers rode the wartime inflation. Eastern businessmen chafed at revenue policies designed, according to the *New York Sun,* "to pay for the war out of taxes raised north of the Mason and Dixon Line." Organized labor, despite manifest gains, was unhappy with inflation and the problems of reconversion to a peacetime economy.

In the midterm elections of 1918, Wilson made matters worse when he defied the advice of his wife and aides and urged voters to elect a Democratic Congress to support his foreign policies. Republicans, who for the most part had supported war measures, took affront. In elections held on November 5, a week before the armistice, the Democrats lost control of both houses of Congress. With an opposition majority in the new Congress, Wilson further weakened his standing by failing to involve a single prominent Republican in the peace negotiations. Former president Taft groused that Wilson's real intention in going to Paris was "to hog the whole show."

When Wilson reached Europe in December 1918, enthusiastic demonstrations greeted him in Paris. The cheering millions saw in the American idealist a prophet of peace and a spokesman for humanity. Their heartfelt support no doubt strengthened his hand at the conference, but Wilson had to deal with some tough-minded statesmen who did not share his utopian zeal.

The Paris Peace Conference included delegates from all countries that had declared war or broken diplomatic relations with Germany. It was controlled by the Big Four: the prime ministers of Britain, France, and Italy and the president of the United States. Japan restricted its interests to Asia and the Pacific. French premier Georges Clemenceau was a stern realist who had little patience with Wilson's utopianism. "God gave us the Ten Commandments and we broke them," Clemenceau sneered. "Wilson gave us the Fourteen Points—we shall see." The French insisted on harsh measures to weaken Germany. British prime minister David Lloyd George was a gifted politician fresh from electoral victory following a campaign whose slogan declared "Hang the kaiser." Vittorio Orlando, prime minister of Italy, was there to pick up the spoils promised in the secret Treaty of London (1915), in which the Allies had promised Italy the Austrian province of Dalmatia in exchange for its entry into the war.

The Big Four

Woodrow Wilson (second from left) with Georges Clemenceau of France and Arthur Balfour of Great Britain at the Paris Peace Conference.

THE LEAGUE OF NATIONS   Woodrow Wilson insisted that his cherished League of Nations come first, in the conference and in the treaty. Whatever compromises he might have to make regarding territorial boundaries and financial claims, whatever mistakes might result, Wilson believed that a league of nations committed to collective security would ensure international stability. Wilson presided over the commission set up to work out its charter. Article X of the covenant, which Wilson called "the heart of the League," pledged members to impose military and economic sanctions against aggressors. The use of armed force would be a last (and an improbable) resort. The League, it was assumed, would exercise enormous moral influence, making military action unnecessary. The League structure would allow each member an equal voice in the Assembly; the Big Five (Britain, France, Italy, Japan, and the United States) and four other nations would make up the Council; the administrative staff, with headquarters in Geneva, would make up the Secretariat; and a Permanent Court of International Justice (set up in 1921 and usually called the World Court) could "hear and determine any dispute of an international character."

The League of Nations Argument in a Nutshell

J. N. "Ding" Darling's summation of the League controversy.

On February 14, 1919, Wilson presented the finished draft of the League covenant to the plenary session of the conference and departed the next day for a month-long visit home. Already he faced rumblings of opposition. Wilson's proposed League of Nations, Theodore Roosevelt grumbled, would revive German militarism and undermine American morale. "To substitute internationalism for nationalism," the former president argued, "means to do away with patriotism." Roosevelt's close friend Henry Cabot Lodge, chairman of the Senate Foreign Relations Committee, also scorned Wilson's naive idealism. He announced that the League's covenant was unacceptable. His statement bore the signatures of thirty-nine Republican senators or senators-elect, more than enough to block ratification.

TERRITORY AND REPARATIONS   Back in Paris, Wilson grudgingly acceded to French demands for territorial concessions and reparations from Germany that would keep it weak for years to come. Yet Wilson clashed sharply with Clemenceau, and after the American president threatened to leave the conference, they settled on a demilitarized Rhineland (up to thirty-one miles beyond the Rhine River), Allied occupation of this zone for fifteen years, and League administration of Germany's Saar Basin. France could use Saar coal mines for fifteen years, after which the region's residents would vote to determine their status.

In other territorial matters, Wilson had to compromise his principle of national self-determination. There was in fact no way to make Europe's boundaries correspond to ethnic divisions. The folk wanderings of centuries had left mixed populations scattered throughout Central Europe. In some areas, moreover, national self-determination yielded to other interests: the Polish Corridor, for instance, gave Poland its much-needed outlet to the sea through German territory, and the South Tyrol, home to some 200,000 German-speaking Austrians, gave Italy a more defensible frontier at the Brenner Pass. One part of the Austro-Hungarian Empire became Czechoslovakia, which included the German-speaking Sudetenland, an area favored with good defenses. Another part united with Serbia to create the kingdom of Yugoslavia. Still other substantial parts passed to Poland (Galicia), Romania (Transylvania), and Italy (Trentino–Alto Adige and Trieste). All in all, despite aberrations, the new boundaries more nearly followed the ethnic divisions of Europe than had the prewar lines.

The discussion of reparations (payments by the vanquished to the victors) was among the longest and most bitter at the conference. Despite a pre-armistice agreement that Germany would be liable only for civilian damages, Clemenceau and Lloyd George proposed reparations for the entire cost of the war, including veterans' pensions. On this point, Wilson made perhaps his most fateful concessions. He accepted in the treaty a clause by which Germany confessed responsibility for the war and thus for its entire cost. The "war guilt" clause offended Germans and made for persistent bitterness.

On May 7, 1919, the victorious powers presented the treaty to the German delegates, who returned three weeks later with 443 pages of criticism protesting that the terms violated the Fourteen Points. A few changes were made, but when the Germans still refused to sign, the French prepared to move their army across the Rhine. Finally, on June 28, 1919, the Germans gave up and signed the treaty in the Hall of Mirrors at Versailles.

WILSON'S LOSS AT HOME   The force of Wilson's idealism struck deep, and on July 8, 1919, he returned home with the Versailles Treaty amid a great clamor of popular support. One third of the state legislatures had endorsed the League, as had thirty-three of the nation's forty-eight governors. Two days later Wilson called upon the Senate to accept "this great duty." He dismissed critics of the League as "blind and little provincial people."

Yet Senator Henry Cabot Lodge insisted that the treaty exhibited weakness in its "beautiful scheme of making mankind virtuous by a statute or a written constitution." Americans, thought Lodge, were too prone to promise more than they could deliver when great principles entailed great sacrifices. Foreign policy had to be built up from what the public would sustain rather than be imposed from above. A staunch Republican with an intense dislike for Wilson, Lodge sharpened his partisan knives. He knew the undercurrents already stirring up opposition to the treaty: the resentment of German, Italian, and Irish groups in the United States, the disappointment of liberals with Wilson's compromises on reparations and territories, the distractions

EUROPE AFTER THE TREATY OF VERSAILLES, 1918

- ········ 1914 boundaries
- New nations
- Plebiscite areas
- Occupied area

Why was self-determination difficult for states in Central Europe? How did territorial concessions weaken Germany? Why might territorial changes like the creation of the Polish Corridor or the concession of the Sudetenland to Czechoslovakia have created problems in the future?

of demobilization and the resulting domestic problems, and the revival of isolationism. Theodore Roosevelt, still a popular figure, continued to lambast the League, noting that he keenly distrusted a "man who cares for other nations as much as his own." Some Republicans claimed that Wilson's preoccupation with his cherished League of Nations revealed that he really wanted to be president of the world.

Others agreed. In the Senate a group of "irreconcilables," fourteen Republicans and two Democrats, was unwilling to allow America to enter the League on any terms. They were mainly western and midwestern Progressives who feared that foreign commitments threatened domestic reforms. The irreconcilables would be useful to Lodge's purpose, but he belonged to a larger group of "reservationists," who insisted upon limiting American participation in the League. Wilson pointed out to them that the agreement already stipulated that with its veto in the League Council, the United States could not be obligated to do anything against its will.

Lodge, who set more store by the old balance of power than by the new idea of collective security, proposed a set of amendments, or reservations. Wilson responded by agreeing to interpretive reservations but to nothing that would reopen the negotiations in Europe. He especially opposed weakening Article X of the League covenant, which provided for collective action against aggression.

By September, with momentum for the treaty slackening, Wilson decided to go to the people and, as he put it, "purify the wells of public opinion." Against the advice of doctors and friends, he set forth on a railroad tour through the Midwest to the West Coast. In all he traveled 8,000 miles in twenty-two days, giving thirty-two major addresses and eight informal ones. For a while, Wilson seemed to be regaining the initiative, but on October 2, 1919, he suffered a severe stroke, leaving him paralyzed on his left side and an invalid for the rest of his life. For seventeen months his protective wife, Edith, kept him isolated from all but the most essential business. Wilson's disability intensified his stubbornness. He might have done better to secure the best compromise possible, but now he refused to yield. As he scoffed to an aide, "Let Lodge compromise." The president's hardened arteries seemed to have hardened his outlook.

Lodge was determined to amend the treaty before it was ratified. The Senate adopted fourteen of his reservations, most having to do with the League. Wilson especially opposed the revision of Article X, which, he said, "does not provide for ratification but, rather, for the nullification of the treaty." As a result, the Wilsonians found themselves thrown into an unlikely combination with the irreconcilables, who opposed the treaty under any circumstances. The Senate vote was thirty-nine for and fifty-five against. On the question of taking the treaty without reservations, irreconcilables and reservationists combined to defeat ratification again, with thirty-eight for and fifty-three against.

In the face of public reaction, however, the Senate voted to reconsider. But the stricken Wilson remained adamant: "Either we should enter the League fearlessly, accepting with responsibility and not fearing the role of leadership which we now enjoy, contributing our efforts toward establishing a just and permanent peace, or we should retire as gracefully as possible from the great concert of powers by which the world was saved." On March 19, 1920, twenty-one Democrats deserted the intransigent Wilson and joined the reservationists, but the treaty once again fell short of a two-thirds majority, by a vote of forty-nine yeas and thirty-five nays. The real winner was the smallest of the three groups in the Senate, neither the Wilsonians nor the reservationists but the irreconcilables.

When Congress declared the war at an end by joint resolution on May 20, 1920, Wilson vetoed the action; it was not until July 2, 1921, after he left office, that a joint resolution ended the state of war with Germany and Austria-Hungary. Peace treaties with Germany, Austria, and Hungary were ratified on October 18, 1921, but by then Warren Gamaliel Harding was president of the United States.

LURCHING FROM WAR TO PEACE

The Versailles Treaty, for all the time it spent in the Senate, was but one issue clamoring for public attention in the turbulent period after the war. Demobilization of the armed forces and war industries proceeded in haphazard fashion. The sudden cancellation of war contracts left workers and business leaders to cope with reconversion on their own. Wilson's leadership was missing. He had been preoccupied by the war and the League, and once bedridden by his illness, he became strangely grim and peevish. His administration floundered through its last two years.

THE SPANISH FLU   Amid the confusion of postwar life many Americans confronted a virulent menace that produced far more casualties than the war itself. It became known as the Spanish flu, and its contagion spread around the globe. Erupting in the spring of 1918 and lasting a year, the pandemic killed more than 22 million people throughout the world, twice as many as the number who died in World War I. In the United States alone the flu accounted for 675,000 deaths, nearly seven times the number of American combat deaths in France.

American soldiers and sailors returning from France brought the flu with them, and it raced through the congested army camps and naval bases. Some 43,000 servicemen died of influenza in 1918. By September the epidemic had spread to the civilian population. In that month alone 10,000 Americans died from the disease. "Nobody seemed to know what the disease was, where

Influenza Epidemic

Office workers wearing gauze masks during the Spanish flu epidemic of 1918.

it came from or how to stop it," observed the editors of *Science* magazine in 1919. Millions of people began wearing surgical masks to work. Phone booths were locked up, as were dance halls, poolrooms, and theaters. Even churches and saloons in many communities were declared off-limits. Still the death toll rose. In Philadelphia 528 people were buried in a single day. Life-insurance companies nearly went bankrupt, hospitals were besieged, and cemeteries ran out of burial space.

By the spring of 1919, the pandemic had run its course. It ended as suddenly—and as inexplicably—as it had begun. Although another outbreak occurred in the winter of 1920, the population had grown more resistant to its assaults. No disease, plague, war, famine, or natural catastrophe in world history killed so many people in such a short time. The most remarkable aspect of the flu pandemic was that people for the most part took it in stride; they seemed resigned to biological forces beyond their control while issues of war and peace in Europe and the home-front economy continued to dominate the headlines.

THE ECONOMIC TRANSITION   The problems of postwar readjustment were worsened by general labor unrest. Prices continued to rise after the war, and discontented workers, released from wartime constraints, were more willing to strike for their demands. In 1919 more than 4 million workers went on strike in thousands of disputes. Some workers in the East won their demands early in the year, but after a general strike in Seattle, public opinion began to turn against labor's demands. Seattle's mayor denounced the walkout of 60,000 workers as evidence of Bolshevik influence. The strike lasted only five days, but public alarm over the affair damaged the cause of unions across the country.

An American Federation of Labor campaign to organize steelworkers suffered from charges of radicalism against its leader, William Z. Foster, who had joined the Socialists in 1900 and later emerged as a Communist. The focus on Foster's radicalism obscured the squalid conditions and long hours that had marked the steel industry since the Homestead strike of 1892: the twelve-hour day, often combined with a seven-day week, was common. On September 22, 1919, after U.S. Steel refused to talk, about 340,000 workers walked out. When information about working conditions became widely known, public opinion turned in favor of the steelworkers, but too late: the strike had ended after four months. Steelworkers remained unorganized until the 1930s.

The most celebrated postwar labor dispute was the Boston police strike. Though less significant than the steel strike in the numbers involved, it inadvertently launched a presidential career. On September 9, 1919, most of Boston's police force went out on strike. Massachusetts governor Calvin Coolidge mobilized the national guard to keep order, and after four days the strikers were ready to return, but the police commissioner refused to take them back. When labor leader Samuel Gompers appealed for their reinstatement, Coolidge responded in words that suddenly turned him into a national figure: "There is no right to strike against the public safety by anybody, anywhere, any time."

Domestic Unrest

A victim of racial rioting in Chicago, July 1919.

RACIAL FRICTION The summer of 1919 also brought a season of race riots, both in the North and in the South. What African-American leader James Weldon Johnson called the Red Summer (*Red* here signified blood) began in July, when whites invaded the black section of Longview, Texas, in search of a teacher who had allegedly accused a white woman of a liaison with a black man. They burned shops and houses and ran several African Americans out of town. A week later in Washington, D.C., reports of black assaults on white women aroused white mobs, and for four days gangs of white and black rioters waged race war in the streets until soldiers and driving rains ended the fighting. These were but preliminaries to the Chicago riot of late July, in which 38 people were killed and 537 injured. The climactic disorders of the summer occurred in the rural area around Elaine, Arkansas, where African-American tenant farmers tried to organize a union. According to official reports, 5 whites and 25 blacks died, but whites told one reporter in the area that in reality more than 100 blacks had died. Altogether twenty-five race riots erupted in 1919.

THE RED SCARE   Public reaction to the wave of labor strikes and race riots reflected the impact of the Bolshevik revolution. A minority of radicals thought America's domestic turbulence, like that in Russia, was the first scene in a drama of world revolution. A much larger public was persuaded that they might be right. After all, a tiny faction in Russia, the Bolsheviks, had exploited confusion to impose its will. In 1919 the Socialist party, already depleted by wartime persecution, suffered the further defection of radicals inspired by the Russian example. Left-wing members formed the Communist party and the short-lived Communist Labor party. Wartime hysteria against all things German was readily transformed into a postwar Red Scare against Communists.

Fears of revolution in America might have remained latent except for the actions of a lunatic fringe. In April 1919 the post office intercepted nearly forty homemade letter bombs addressed to prominent citizens. One slipped through and blew off the hands of a Georgia senator's maid. In June another bomb destroyed the front of Attorney General A. Mitchell Palmer's house in Washington. Palmer and many other Americans were convinced that a well-organized Communist terror campaign was being unleashed in America. "Like a prairie fire," Palmer wrote, the blaze of revolution was sweeping over every American institution of law and order."

Soon the government was promoting witch hunts. In 1919 the Justice Department decided to deport radical aliens, and Attorney General Palmer set up as the head of the new General Intelligence Division the young J. Edgar Hoover, who began to collect files on radicals. Raids began on November 7, 1919, when agents swooped down on the Union of Russian Workers in twelve cities. On December 22 the transport ship *Buford,* dubbed the Soviet ark, left New York for Finland with 249 passengers, including assorted anarchists, criminals, and public charges. All were deported to Russia without benefit of a court hearing. On January 2, 1920, a series of police raids in dozens of cities swept up some 5,000 suspects, many taken from their homes without arrest warrants, of whom more than half were kept in custody. That same month the New York State legislature expelled five duly elected Socialist members.

Basking in popular approval, Palmer continued to warn of the Red menace, but like other fads and alarms, the mood passed. By the summer of 1920 the Red Scare had begun to evaporate. Communist revolutions in Europe died out, leaving Bolshevism isolated in Russia. Bombings tapered off; the wave of strikes and race riots receded. The paranoid attorney general began to seem more threatening to civil liberties than a handful of radicals. By September 1920, when a bomb explosion at the corner of Broad and Wall Streets in New York City killed thirty-eight people, Americans were ready to take it for what it was: the work of a crazed mind and not the start of a revolution. The Red Scare nevertheless left a lasting mark on American life. Part of its legacy was the continuing crusade for "100 percent Americanism" and restrictions on immigration. It left a stigma on labor unions and contributed to the anti-union open-shop campaign—the American plan, its sponsors called it. But for many Americans the chief residue of the Great War, President Wilson's physical collapse, and its disordered aftermath was a profound disillusionment that pervaded cultural life in the postwar decade.

MAKING CONNECTIONS

- The Red Scare at the end of World War I led to a wave of nativism and to immigration restriction, outlined in the next chapter.

- This chapter ends by noting the "profound disillusionment" Americans felt with efforts to reform the world. The political aspect of that disillusionment—the turn to "normalcy" in the 1920s—is discussed in Chapter 27.

- The treaty ending World War I was designed to cripple Germany's military strength. But as Chapter 29 shows, within two decades Adolf Hitler was leading a rebuilt German military force into World War II.

FURTHER READING

A lucid overview of international events covered in this chapter is Robert H. Ferrell's *Woodrow Wilson and World War I, 1917–1921* (1985). On Wilson's stance toward war, see Ross Gregory's *The Origins of American Intervention in the First World War* (1971). An excellent brief biography is H. W. Brands's *Woodrow Wilson* (2003).

Edward M. Coffman's *The War to End All Wars: The American Military Experience in World War I* (1968) is a detailed presentation of America's military involvement. David M. Kennedy's *Over Here: The First World War and American Society* (1980) surveys the impact of the war on the home front. Maurine Weiner Greenwald's *Women, War, and Work: The Impact of World War I on Women Workers in the United States* (1980) discusses the role of women. Ronald Schaffer's *America in the Great War: The Rise of the War Welfare State* (1991) shows the effect of war mobilization on business organization. Richard Polenberg's *Fighting Faiths: The Abrams Case, the Supreme Court, and Free Speech* (1987) examines the prosecution of a case under the 1918 Sedition Act.

How American diplomacy fared in the making of peace has received considerable attention. Thomas J. Knock interrelates domestic affairs and foreign relations in his explanation of Wilson's peacemaking in *To End All Wars: Woodrow Wilson and the Quest for a New World Order* (1992).

The problems of the immediate postwar years are chronicled by a number of historians. On the Spanish flu, see John M. Barry's *The Great Influenza: The Epic Story of the Deadliest Plague in History* (2004). Labor tensions are examined in David E. Brody's *Labor in Crisis: The Steel Strike of 1919* (1965) and Francis Russell's *A City in Terror: The 1919 Boston Police Strike* (1975). On racial strife, see William M. Tuttle Jr.'s *Race Riot: Chicago in the Red Summer of 1919* (1970). The fear of Communists is analyzed in Robert K. Murray's *Red Scare: A Study in National Hysteria, 1919–1920* (1955).

26

THE MODERN TEMPER

FOCUS QUESTIONS

- Why did reactionary forces emerge in the 1920s?
- What characterized the social ferment of the 1920s?
- How did modernism influence American culture?

To answer these questions and access additional review material, please visit
www.wwnorton.com/studyspace.

The horrors of World War I dealt a shattering blow to the widespread belief that Western civilization was progressing. The editors of *Presbyterian* magazine announced in 1919 that the "world has been convulsed . . . and every field of thought and action has been disturbed. . . . The most settled principles and laws of society have been attacked."

The war's unimaginable carnage produced a postwar disillusionment among young intellectuals that challenged old values and spurred a new "modernist" sensibility among artists, writers, and intellectuals. At once a mood and a movement, modernism appeared first in Europe at the end of the nineteenth century and became a pervasive international force by 1920. It arose out of a widespread recognition that Western civilization had entered an era of bewildering change. New technologies, new modes of transportation and communication, and new scientific discoveries such as quantum mechanics and relativity theory combined to rupture perceptions of reality and generate new forms of artistic expression. "One must never forget," declared Gertrude Stein, the experimentalist poet, "that the reality of the twentieth century is not the reality of the nineteenth century, not at all." Modernism introduced a whole series of intellectual and artistic movements: impressionism, futurism, Dadaism, surrealism, Freudianism. As the French painter Paul Gauguin acknowledged, the upheavals of modernism produced "an epoch of confusion."

Just as the war, with its turbulent aftermath, provided an accelerant for modernism, it also stimulated political and social radicalism. The postwar wave of strikes, bombings, anti-Communist hysteria, and race riots symbolized a frightening new era of turmoil and change. Defenders of tradition located the germs of radicalism in the polyglot cities teeming with immigrants and foreign ideas. The defensive mood of the 1920s fed on a growing tendency to connect American nationalism with nativism, Anglo-Saxon racism, and militant Protestantism.

REACTION IN THE TWENTIES

NATIVISM The foreign connections of so many political radicals strengthened the sense that the seeds of sedition were foreign-born. In the early 1920s over half of the white men and one third of the white women working in manufacturing industries were immigrants, most of them from central or eastern Europe. That socialism and anarchism were popular in those regions made immigrant workers from there especially suspicious in the eyes of "old stock" Americans.

The most celebrated criminal case of the times seemed to prove the connection. It involved two Italian-born anarchists, Nicola Sacco and Bartolomeo Vanzetti, who were arrested on May 5, 1920, for a robbery and murder in South Braintree, Massachusetts. They were brought for trial before a judge who privately referred to the defendants as "those anarchist bastards." People then and since claimed that Sacco and Vanzetti were sentenced for their political ideas and ethnic origins rather than for any crime they had committed. The case became a great radical and liberal cause célèbre of the 1920s, but despite public demonstrations around the world on behalf of the two men, the evidence convicting them was compelling; they went to the electric chair on August 23, 1927.

The surging postwar nativism generated new efforts to restrict immigration. The flow of immigrants, slowed by the war, rose again at its end. From June 1920 to June 1921, more than 800,000 immigrants entered the country, 65 percent of them from southern and eastern Europe, and more were on

Sacco and Vanzetti

Painting from a series by Ben Shahn (1931–1932).

the way. An alarmed Congress passed the Emergency Immigration Act of 1921, which restricted new arrivals each year to 3 percent of the foreign-born of any nationality as shown in the 1910 census. A new quota law in 1924 reduced the number to 2 percent based on the 1890 census, which included fewer of the "new" immigrants. This law set a permanent limitation, which became effective in 1929, of slightly over 150,000 new arrivals per year based on the "national origins" of the U.S. population as of 1920. However inexact the quotas, their purpose was clear: to tilt the balance in favor of immigrants from northern and western Europe, who were assigned about 85 percent of the total. The law completely excluded people from east Asia—a gratuitous insult to the Japanese, who were already kept out of the United States by their Gentlemen's Agreement with Theodore Roosevelt.

On the other hand, the law left the gate open to new arrivals from Western Hemisphere countries, so that an ironic consequence was a substantial increase in the Hispanic Catholic population of the United States. Legal arrivals from Mexico peaked at 89,000 in 1924. Lower figures after that date reflect the Mexican government's policies of clamping down on the outflow of labor and stronger U.S. enforcement of old regulations such as the 1882 exclusion of immigrants likely to become public charges. Waves of illegal immigrants continued to flow across the border, however, in response to southwestern agriculture's demand for "stoop" labor. People of Latin American descent (chiefly Mexicans, Puerto Ricans, and Cubans) became the fastest-growing ethnic minority in the country.

THE KLAN   During the postwar years the nativist tradition took on a new form, a revived Ku Klux Klan modeled on the group founded during Reconstruction. The new Klan was devoted to "100 percent Americanism" and restricted its membership to native-born white Protestants. It was determined to protect its warped notion of the American way of life not only from African Americans, but also from Roman Catholics, Jews, and immigrants. The United States was no melting pot, the modern Klan's founder, William J. Simmons, warned: "It is a garbage can! . . . When the hordes of aliens walk to the ballot box and their votes outnumber yours, then that alien horde has got you by the throat." A habitual joiner and promoter of fraternal orders, Simmons had gathered a hooded group of bigots near Atlanta on Thanksgiving night 1915. There, "bathed in the sacred glow of the fiery cross, the invisible empire was called from its slumber of half a century to take up a new task."

The revived Klan was no longer restricted to the South. Its appeal reached states as widely scattered as Oregon and Maine. Its appeal to bigotry thrived in small towns and cities in the North and especially in the Midwest. The robes, the flaming crosses, the eerie processionals, the kneeling recruits, the occult liturgies—all tapped a deep urge toward mystery and brought drama into the dreary routine of a thousand small communities. The Klan was a vicious reaction to shifting moral standards, the declining influence

Klan Rally

In 1925 the Ku Klux Klan staged a huge parade down Pennsylvania Avenue in Washington, D.C.

of churches, and the broad-mindedness of city dwellers and college students. Estimates of its peak membership range from 3 million to 8 million, but the Klan's influence evaporated as quickly as its numbers grew. For one thing the Klan suffered from a decline in nativist excitement after passage of the 1924 immigration law. For another, it suffered recurrent factional quarrels and schisms, and its willing use of violence tarnished its moral pretensions.

FUNDAMENTALISM   While the Klan saw a threat mainly in the "alien menace," many adherents of the old-time religion saw threats from modernism in the churches: new ideas held that the Bible should be studied in the light of modern scholarship (the "higher criticism") or that it could be reconciled with biological theories of evolution. Fearing that such notions had infected schools and even pulpits, orthodox Christians took on a militant new fundamentalism, which was distinguished less by a faith that many others shared than by a posture of hostility toward any other belief.

Among rural fundamentalist leaders only former secretary of state William Jennings Bryan had the following, prestige, and eloquence to make the movement a popular crusade. In 1921 Bryan sparked a drive for state laws to prohibit the teaching of evolution in the public schools. He denounced Charles Darwin with the same zeal he had once directed against William McKinley. "Evolution," he said, "by denying the need or possibility of spiritual regeneration, discourages all reforms, for reform is always based upon the regeneration of the individual." Anti-evolution bills began to turn up in legislatures, but the only victories came in the South—and there were few of those. Some officials took direct action without legislation. Governor Miriam "Ma" Ferguson of Texas outlawed textbooks upholding Darwinism. "I am a Christian mother," she declared, "and I am not going to let that kind of rot go into Texas schoolbooks."

The climax came in Tennessee, where in 1925 the legislature passed a bill outlawing the teaching of evolution in public schools and colleges. The governor, unwilling to endanger a pending school program, signed the bill with the hope that it would probably never be applied. He was wrong. In Dayton, Tennessee, citizens persuaded a young high-school teacher, John T. Scopes, to accept an offer from the American Civil Liberties Union to defend a test case—chiefly to put their town on the map. They succeeded beyond their wildest hopes: the publicity was worldwide and enduring. Before the opening day of the "monkey trial," July 10, 1925, the streets of Dayton swarmed with publicity hounds, curiosity seekers, evangelists, atheists, hot-dog and soda-pop hucksters, and a miscellany of reporters.

Courtroom Scene during the Scopes Trial

The media, food vendors, and others flocked to Dayton, Tennessee, for the case against John Scopes, the teacher who taught evolution.

The two stars of the show—William Jennings Bryan, who had offered his services to the prosecution, and Clarence Darrow, renowned trial lawyer of Chicago and confessed agnostic—united at least in their determination to make the trial an exercise in public education. When the judge ruled out scientific testimony, however, the defense called Bryan as an expert witness on biblical interpretation. In his dialogue with Darrow, he repeatedly trapped himself in literal-minded interpretations and revealed his ignorance of biblical history and scholarship. He insisted that a "great fish" had swallowed Jonah, that Joshua had made the sun stand still, that the world was created in 4004 B.C.—all, according to Darrow, "fool ideas that no intelligent Christian on earth believes." It was a bitter scene. At one point the two men, their patience exhausted in the broiling summer heat, lunged at each other, shaking their fists, prompting the judge to adjourn court.

At the end of the twelve-day trial, the only issue before the court, the judge ruled, was whether Scopes had taught evolution, and no one denied that he had. He was found guilty, but the Tennessee Supreme Court, while upholding the state's anti-evolution statute, overruled the $100 fine on a technicality. The chief prosecutor accepted the higher court's advice against "prolonging the life of this bizarre case" and dropped the issue. With more prescience than he knew, Bryan had described the trial as a "duel to the death." A few days after it closed, he died of a heart condition aggravated by heat and fatigue.

PROHIBITION   Prohibition of alcoholic beverages offered another example of reforming zeal channeled into a drive for moral righteousness and social conformity. Around 1900 the leading temperance organizations, the Women's Christian Temperance Union and the Anti-Saloon League, had launched a campaign for a national prohibition law. By the 1910s the Anti-Saloon League had become one of the most effective pressure groups in history, mobilizing Protestant churches behind its single-minded battle to elect "dry" candidates.

At its Jubilee Convention in 1913, the league endorsed a prohibition amendment to the Constitution. The 1916 elections finally produced two-thirds majorities for prohibition in both houses of Congress. Soon the wartime spirit of sacrifice, the need to use grain for food, and wartime hostility to German-American brewers transformed the cause into a virtual test of patriotism. On December 18, 1917, Congress sent to the states the Eighteenth Amendment, which one year after ratification, on January 16, 1919, banned the manufacture, sale, or transportation of intoxicating liquors.

But the new amendment did not persuade people to stop drinking. Instead, it motivated them to use ingenious—and illegal—ways to satisfy their thirst for alcohol. Congress never supplied adequate enforcement, if such was indeed possible given the public thirst, the spotty support of local officials, and the profits to be made in bootlegging. In Detroit the liquor industry during the Prohibition era was second in size only to the auto industry. Speakeasies, hip flasks, and cocktail parties were among the social innovations of Prohibition, along with increased drinking by women.

It would be too much to say that Prohibition gave rise to organized crime, but it supplied criminals with an enormous source of new income while the automobile and the submachine gun provided greater mobility and firepower. Gangland leaders showed remarkable gifts for exploiting loopholes in the law when they did not simply bribe policemen and politicians.

The most celebrated gangster was "Scarface" Al Capone. In 1927 his Chicago-based bootlegging, prostitution, and gambling empire brought him an income of $60 million, which he flaunted in expensive suits and silk pajamas, a custom-upholstered bulletproof Cadillac, an entourage of bodyguards,

Prohibition

A 1926 police raid on a speakeasy.

and lavish support for city charities. Capone always insisted that he was merely providing the public with goods and services it demanded: "They say I violate the prohibition law. Who doesn't?" He neglected to say that he had also bludgeoned to death several police lieutenants and ordered the execution of dozens of his rival criminals. Law-enforcement officials led by Federal Bureau of Investigation agent Eliot Ness began to smash his bootlegging operations in 1929, but they were unable to pin anything on him until a Treasury agent infiltrated his gang and uncovered evidence that nailed him for tax evasion. Tried in 1931, Capone was sentenced to eleven years in prison.

The Roaring Twenties

In many ways the reactionary temper of the 1920s and the repressive movements it spawned arose as reactions to a social and intellectual revolution that threatened to rip America from its old moorings. As described by various labels given to the times, it was an era of excess, the Jazz Age, and the Roaring Twenties. During those years a cosmopolitan urban America confronted an insular, rural America, and cultural conflict reached new levels of tension.

Leading young urban intellectuals disdained the old-fashioned rural and small-town values of the hinterlands. Sinclair Lewis's novel *Main Street* (1920), for example, portrayed the stifling, mean, cramped life of the prairie town, depicting a "savorless people, gulping tasteless food, and sitting afterward, coatless and thoughtless, in rocking chairs prickly with inane decorations, listening to mechanical music, saying mechanical things about the excellence of Ford automobiles, and viewing themselves as the greatest race in the world." The Baltimore journalist H. L. Mencken was the most merciless in his attacks on the "booboisie." The daily panorama of America, he wrote, had become "so inordinately gross and preposterous . . . that only a man who was born with a petrified diaphragm can fail to laugh himself to sleep every night, and to awake every morning with all the eager, unflagging expectation of a Sunday-school superintendent touring the Paris peep-shows." The hinterlands responded with images of cities infested with vice, crime, corruption, and foreigners.

THE JAZZ AGE   The writer F. Scott Fitzgerald dubbed the postwar era the Jazz Age because daring young people were willing to experiment

Frankie "Half Pint" Jackson and His Band at the Sunset Cafe, Chicago, 1920s

Jazz emerged in the 1920s as an especially American expression of the modernist spirit. African-American artists bent musical conventions to give fuller rein to improvisation and sensuality.

with new forms of recreation and sexuality. The new music bubbling to the surface in New Orleans, Kansas City, Memphis, New York City, and Chicago blended African and European traditions to form a distinctive sound characterized by improvisation, "blue notes," and polyrhythm. The syncopated rhythms of jazz were immensely popular among rebellious young adults and helped create carefree new dance steps such as the Charleston and the black bottom, gyrations that shocked guardians of morality.

THE NEW MORALITY   Much of the shock to old-timers during the Jazz Age came from the revolution in manners and morals, evidenced first among young people, and especially on college campuses. In *This Side of Paradise* (1920) a novel of student life at Princeton, F. Scott Fitzgerald wrote of "the great current American phenomenon, the 'petting party.'" None of the Victorian mothers, he said, "had any idea how casually their daughters were accustomed to be kissed." From such novels and from magazine pieces, the heartland learned about the wild parties, bathtub gin, promiscuity, speakeasies, "shimmy dancers," and new uses to which automobiles were put on secluded lovers' lanes.

Writers also informed the nation about the "new woman" eager to exercise new freedoms. These independent women discarded corsets and sported bobbed hair, heavy makeup, and skirts above the ankle; they smoked cigarettes and drank beer, drove automobiles, and in general defied Victorian expectations of womanly behavior.

Sex came to be discussed with a new frankness during the 1920s. Much of the talk derived from a spreading awareness of Dr. Sigmund Freud, the Viennese father of psychoanalysis. When in 1909 Freud visited Clark University in Massachusetts, he was surprised to find himself so well known "even in prudish America." By the 1920s, his ideas had begun to percolate among the public, and in society and literature there was talk of about libido, inhibitions, Oedipus complexes, and repression.

Fashion also reflected the rebellion against prudishness and a loosening of inhibitions. In 1919 women's skirts were typically six inches above the ground; by 1927 they were at the knees, and the "flapper" was providing a shocking model of the new feminism. The name derived from the way fashionable women allowed their galoshes to flap around their ankles. Conservative moralists saw the flappers as just another sign of a degenerating society. Others saw in the "new women" an expression of American individualism. "By sheer force of violence," explained the *New York Times* in 1929, the

The "New Woman" of the 1920s

Two flappers dance atop the Sherman Hotel in Chicago, 1926.

flapper has "established the feminine right to equal representation in such hitherto masculine fields of endeavor as smoking and drinking, swearing, petting, and upsetting the community peace."

MARGARET SANGER AND BIRTH CONTROL Perhaps the most controversial women's issue of the Jazz Age was birth control. Margaret Sanger, a New York nurse and midwife in the working-class tenements on the Lower East Side of Manhattan, saw many struggling young mothers who often did not have enough money to provide for their growing families. She also witnessed firsthand the consequences of unwanted pregnancies, tragic miscarriages, and amateur abortions. Sanger began to distribute birth-control information to working-class women in 1912 and resolved to spend the rest of her life helping women gain control of their bodies.

In 1921 Sanger organized the American Birth Control League, which in 1942 changed its name to Planned Parenthood. The Birth Control League distributed birth-control information to doctors, social workers, women's clubs, and the scientific community, as well as to thousands of women. In the 1920s, however, Sanger alienated supporters then and since by endorsing sterilization for the mentally incompetent and for people with certain hereditary conditions. Birth control, she stressed, was "the most constructive and necessary of the means to racial health." In 1928 Sanger angrily resigned as president of the American Birth Control League over issues related to the eugenics movement and her own autocratic style of leadership. For all of her faults, Sanger never lost her focus on women's freedom and its wider implications for social justice. She insisted that women should direct their own lives. Although Sanger did not succeed in legalizing the distribution of contraceptives and contraceptive information through the mail, she had laid the foundation for such efforts. In 1936 a federal court ruled that physicians could prescribe contraceptives—a vital step in Sanger's efforts to realize her slogan, "Every child a wanted child."

THE WOMEN'S MOVEMENT Voting rights for women arrived in 1920. The suffrage movement, which had been in the doldrums since 1896, sprang back to life in the second decade of the new century. In 1912 Alice Paul, a Quaker social worker, returned from an apprenticeship with the militant suffragists of England and became head of the National American Woman Suffrage Association's Congressional Committee. Paul instructed female activists to picket state legislatures, target and "punish" politicians who failed to endorse suf-

Margaret Sanger

The birth-control activist opened the nation's first family-planning clinic in Brooklyn in 1916.

frage, chain themselves to public buildings, incite police to arrest them, and undertake hunger strikes. By 1917 she and her followers were picketing the White House and deliberately provoking arrests, after which they went on hunger strikes in prison. The authorities obligingly cooperated in making martyrs. They arrested them by the hundreds.

For several years, President Woodrow Wilson had evaded the issue of an amendment but had supported a plank in the 1916 Democratic platform endorsing state action for women's suffrage. He also addressed the National Woman Suffrage Association that year, which was once again headed by Carrie Chapman Catt, and thereafter worked closely with its leaders.

Finally, in 1918, after the House had passed the "Susan B. Anthony amendment," President Wilson went before the Senate to plead for its passage. The Senate fell short of the needed two-thirds majority by two votes, but the focus on the issue helped defeat two antisuffrage senators. On June 4, 1919, the Senate finally adopted the amendment, by a bare two-thirds majority. Ratification of the Nineteenth Amendment took another fourteen months. The Tennessee legislature had the distinction of completing the ratification, on August 21, 1920. It was one of the climactic achievements of the Progressive Era.

Votes for Women

Suffragettes march in New York City in 1912, their children by their side.

Alice Paul and the National Woman's party set a new feminist goal, first introduced in Congress in 1923: an equal-rights amendment that would eliminate any remaining legal distinctions between the sexes—including the special legislation for the protection of working women put on the books over the previous fifty or so years. It would be another fifty years before Alice Paul would see Congress adopt her amendment in 1972; she did not live to see it fall short of ratification, however.

The sharp increase in the number of women in the workforce during World War I proved short-lived, but in the longer view a steady increase in the number of employed women occurred in the 1920s and 1930s. By 1910 women made up almost one quarter of all nonagricultural workers, and in 1920 women were found in all but 35 of the 572 job categories listed by the census. The continued entry of women into the workforce brought their numbers up from 8 million in the 1920 census to 10 million in 1930 and 13 million in 1940. Still, working women remained concentrated in traditional occupations, working as domestics, office workers, teachers, clerks, salespeople, dressmakers, milliners, and seamstresses. On the eve of World War II, women's work was little more diversified than it had been at the turn of the century, but by 1940 it was on the verge of a major transformation.

THE "NEW NEGRO"   The most significant development in African-American life during the early twentieth century was the Great Migration northward. The movement of blacks to the North began in 1915–1916, when rapidly expanding war industries were experiencing a labor shortage and the war prevented replacement by foreign immigrants; legal restrictions on immigration continued the movement in the 1920s. Altogether between 1910 and 1920 the Southeast lost some 323,000 African Americans, or 5 percent of the native black population, and by 1930 it had lost another 615,000, or 8 percent of the native black population in 1920. With the migration a slow but steady growth in black political influence set in. African Americans were freer to speak and act in a northern

A Negro Family Just Arrived in Chicago from the Rural South, 1922

Between 1910 and 1930 almost 1 million African Americans left the South.

setting; they also gained political leverage by concentrating in large cities in states with many electoral votes.

Along with political activity came a bristling spirit of protest, a spirit that received cultural expression in a literary and artistic movement known as the Harlem Renaissance. Claude McKay, a Jamaican immigrant, was the first significant writer of the movement, which featured a rediscovery of black folk culture and bolder treatment of controversial topics. Poems collected in McKay's *Harlem Shadows* (1922) expressed defiance in such titles as "If We Must Die" and "To the White Fiends." Other emergent writers included Langston Hughes, Zora Neale Hurston, Countee Cullen, and James Weldon Johnson. Perhaps the greatest single creation of the time was Jean Toomer's novel *Cane* (1923), which pictured the lives of simple folk in Georgia's black belt and the sophisticated African-American middle class in Washington, D.C.

The spirit of the "New Negro" also found expression in what came to be called Negro nationalism, which exalted blackness, black cultural expression, and black exclusiveness. The leading spokesman for such views was the flamboyant Marcus Garvey. In 1916 Garvey brought to New York the Universal Negro Improvement Association (UNIA), which he had started in his native Jamaica two years before. His organization grew rapidly amid the racial tensions of the postwar years. Garvey told African Americans to liberate themselves from the surrounding white culture. He saw every white person as a "potential Klansman" and therefore endorsed the "social and political separation of all peoples to the extent that they promote their own ideals and civilization."

Marcus Garvey

Garvey was the founder of the Universal Negro Improvement Association and a leading spokesman for "Negro nationalism" in the 1920s.

Such a separatist message appalled other African-American leaders. W.E.B. Du Bois, for example, labeled Garvey "the most dangerous enemy of the Negro race." Garvey and his aides created their own black version of Christianity, organized their own fraternal lodges and community cultural centers, started their own businesses, and published their own newspaper. Garvey's message of racial pride and self-reliance appealed to many blacks who had arrived in the northern cities during the Great Migration and had grown frustrated and embittered with the hypocrisy of American democracy during the postwar economic slump.

Delivering the keynote address at the first convention of the UNIA in 1920, Garvey declared that the only lasting hope for blacks was to flee America and build their own republic in Africa. Garvey quickly enlisted half a million members in the UNIA and claimed as many as 6 million by 1923. At that point he was charged with fraudulent use of the mail in fund-raising. Found guilty, he was sent to prison in 1925, where he remained until President Calvin Coolidge pardoned him, deporting him to Jamaica in 1927. Garvey died in obscurity in London in 1940, but the memory of his movement kept alive an undercurrent of racial nationalism that would reemerge later under the slogan of black power.

A more lasting and influential force for racial equality was the National Association for the Advancement of Colored People, founded in 1910 by white liberals and black activists. Black participants came mainly from a group associated with W.E.B. Du Bois, called the Niagara movement, which had met each year since 1905 at places associated with the anti-slavery movement (Niagara Falls, Oberlin, Boston, Harpers Ferry) and issued defiant statements against discrimination.

Although most white progressives did not embrace the NAACP, the new group took seriously the progressive idea that the solution to social problems begins with informing the people, and it planned an active press bureau to accomplish this. Du Bois became its director of publicity and research and editor of its journal, the *Crisis*. The NAACP's main strategy was to focus on legal action designed to bring the Fourteenth and Fifteenth Amendments back to life. One early victory came with *Guinn v. United States* (1915), in which the Supreme Court struck down Oklahoma's grandfather clause, used to deprive African Americans of the vote. In *Buchanan v. Worley* (1917) the Court invalidated a residential segregation ordinance in Louisville, Kentucky.

In 1919 the NAACP launched a campaign against lynching, then a still-common form of vigilante racism. An anti-lynching bill to make mob murder a federal offense passed the House in 1922 but lost to a filibuster by southern senators. The bill stayed before the House until 1925, and NAACP field secretary James Weldon Johnson believed the continued agitation on the issue did more than the bill's passage would have to reduce lynchings, which decreased to one third of what they had been in the previous decade.

THE CULTURE OF MODERNISM

After 1920, changes in the realms of science and social thought were perhaps even more dramatic than those affecting women and African Americans. As the twentieth century advanced, the easy faith in progress and reform expressed by Progressives fell victim to a series of frustrations and disasters, including the Great War, the failure of the League of Nations, Woodrow Wilson's physical and political collapse, and the failure of Prohibition. Startling new findings in physics further shook prevailing assumptions of order and certainty.

SCIENCE AND SOCIAL THOUGHT   Physicists of the early twentieth century altered the image of the cosmos in bewildering ways. Since the eighteenth century, conventional wisdom had held that the universe was governed by laws that the scientific method could ultimately uncover. This rational world of order and certainty disintegrated at the turn of the century

Albert Einstein

Widely regarded as one of the most influential scientists of the twentieth century, Einstein was awarded a Nobel Prize in 1921.

when Albert Einstein, a young German physicist, announced his theory of relativity, which maintained that space, time, and mass were not absolutes but relative to the location and motion of the observer. Sir Isaac Newton's laws of mechanics, according to Einstein's relativity theories, worked well enough at relatively slow speeds, but the more nearly one approached the velocity of light (about 186,000 miles per second), the more all measuring devices would change accordingly, so that yardsticks would become shorter, clocks and heartbeats would slow down, even the aging process would ebb.

The farther one reached out into the universe and the farther one reached inside the minute world of the atom, the more certainty dissolved. The discovery of radioactivity in the 1890s showed that atoms were not irreducible units of matter and that some of them emitted particles of energy. This meant, Einstein noted, that mass and energy were not separate phenomena but interchangeable.

Meanwhile, the German physicist Max Planck had discovered that electromagnetic emissions of energy, whether as electricity or light, came in little bundles that he called quanta. The development of quantum theory suggested that atoms were far more complex than once believed and, as another pioneering German physicist, Werner Heisenberg, stated in his uncertainty principle in 1927, ultimately indescribable. One could never know both the position and the velocity of an electron, Heisenberg concluded, because the very process of observation would inevitably affect the behavior of the particle, altering its position or velocity.

Heisenberg's thesis meant that human knowledge had limits. "The physicist thus finds himself in a world from which the bottom has dropped clean out," a Harvard mathematician wrote in 1929. The scientist had to "give up his most cherished convictions and faith. The world is not a world of reason, understandable by the intellect of man, but as we penetrate ever deeper, the very law of cause and effect, which we had thought to be a formula to which we could force God Himself to subscribe, ceases to have any meaning." Hard for the public to grasp, such findings proved too troubling even for Einstein, who spent much of the rest of his life in search of an explanation that would unify the relativity and quantum theories. "I shall never believe that God plays dice with the world," Einstein asserted.

Just as Enlightenment thinkers drew on Isaac Newton's laws of gravitation two centuries before to formulate their views on the laws governing society, the ideas of relativity and uncertainty in the twentieth century led people to deny the relevance of absolute values in any sphere of society, thus undermining the concepts of personal responsibility and absolute standards. Anthropologists aided the process by transforming the word *culture*, which had before meant "refinement," into a term for the whole system of ideas, folkways, and institutions within which any group lives. Even the most primitive groups had cultures, and all things being relative, one culture should not impose its value judgments on another. Two anthropologists, Ruth Benedict and Margaret Mead, were especially effective in spreading this viewpoint.

MODERNIST ART AND LITERATURE   The cluster of scientific ideas associated with Charles Darwin, Sigmund Freud, and Albert Einstein inspired a revolution in the minds of intellectuals and creative artists, which they expressed in the new modernism. The modernist world was one in which, as Karl Marx said, "all that is solid melts into air." Whereas nineteenth-century writers and artists took for granted an accessible world that could be readily observed and accurately represented, self-willed modernists viewed reality as something to be created rather than copied, expressed rather than reproduced. They thus concluded that the subconscious regions of the psyche were more interesting and potent than reason, common sense, and logic.

In the various arts, related technical features appeared: abstract painting that represented an inner mood rather than a recognizable image of an object, atonal music, free verse in poetry, stream-of-consciousness narrative, and interior monologues in stories and novels. Writers showed an intense concern with new forms in language in an effort to avoid outmoded forms and structures and to violate expectations and shock their audiences.

The search for the new centered in America's first major artistic bohemias, in Chicago and New York, especially in the area of lower Manhattan known as Greenwich Village. In 1913 an international art exhibit at a National Guard building in New York, known as the Armory Show, which went on to Chicago,

Gertrude Stein

Pablo Picasso's 1906 portrait of the writer.

Philadelphia, and Boston, shocked traditionalists with its display of the latest works by experimental and nonrepresentational artists: postimpressionists, expressionists, primitives, and cubists. Pablo Picasso's work made its American debut there. The show aroused shock, indignation, and not a little good-natured ridicule, but it was a huge success.

The chief prophets of modernism were neither in Chicago nor in New York but were expatriates in Britain and Europe: Ezra Pound and T. S. Eliot in London and Gertrude Stein in Paris, all deeply concerned with creating new and often difficult styles of modernist expression. Pound, as foreign editor of *Poetry,* became the conduit through which many American poets achieved publication. Eliot's *The Waste Land* (1922) made few concessions to readers in its arcane allusions, its juxtaposition of unexpected metaphors, its deep sense of postwar disillusionment and melancholy, and its suggestion of a burned-out civilization, but it became for a generation almost the touchstone of the modern temper, along with the Irishman James Joyce's stream-of-consciousness novel *Ulysses,* published the same year. As poet and critic writing for the *Criterion,* which he founded in 1922, Eliot became the arbiter of modernist taste in Anglo-American literature.

Gertrude Stein, in voluntary exile since 1903, was, with her brother, Leo, an early champion of modern art and a collector of works by Paul Cézanne, Henri Matisse, and Picasso. Long regarded as no more than the literary eccentric who wrote "a rose is a rose is a rose is a rose," Stein came to be recognized as one of the chief promoters of the modernist prose style, beginning with *Three Lives* (1909). She sought to capture interior moods in her writing, developing in words the equivalent of nonrepresentational painting.

But Stein was long known chiefly through her influence on other expatriates, such as Ernest Hemingway, whom she told, "All of you young people who served in the war, you are the lost generation." The earliest chronicler of that generation,

The Fitzgeralds Celebrate Christmas

F. Scott Fitzgerald and his wife, Zelda, lived in and wrote about the "greatest, gaudiest spree in history."

F. Scott Fitzgerald, blazed up brilliantly and then quickly flickered out like all the tinseled, sad young characters who peopled his novels. Successful and famous at age twenty-four, having published *This Side of Paradise* in 1920, Fitzgerald, along with his wife, Zelda, lived in and wrote about the "greatest, gaudiest spree in history," and then both had their crack-ups during the Great Depression. What gave depth to the best of his work was what a character in *The Great Gatsby* (1925), Fitzgerald's finest novel, called "a sense of the fundamental decencies" amid all the surface gaiety—and almost always a sense of impending doom.

Ernest Hemingway's novels *The Sun Also Rises* (1926) and *A Farewell to Arms* (1929) depict a desperate search for "real" life and the doomed, war-tainted love affairs of young Americans of the "lost generation." These novels feature the frenetic, hard-drinking lifestyle and the cult of athletic masculinity (epitomized by the bullfighter) that became the stuff of the public image Hemingway cultivated for himself. Hundreds of writers tried to imitate Hemingway's terse style but few had his gift, which lay less in what he had to say than in the way he said it.

THE SOUTHERN RENAISSANCE As modernist literature arose in response to the changes taking place in the United States and Europe, so southern literature of the twenties reflected a mythic world in the midst of rebirth. A southern renaissance in writing emerged from the conflict between the dying world of tradition and the modern commercial world struggling to come to life in the aftermath of the Great War. While in the South the conflict of values aroused the Ku Klux Klan and fundamentalist furies, both of which tried desperately to bring back the world of tradition, it also inspired the vitality and creativity of the South's young writers.

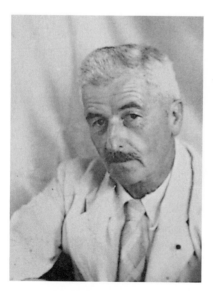

William Faulkner

Faulkner discovered that his "own little postage stamp of native soil was worth writing about."

"One may reasonably argue," wrote a critic in 1930, "that the South is the literary land of promise today." Just the previous year two vital figures had emerged: Thomas Wolfe, with *Look Homeward, Angel,* and

William Faulkner, with *Sartoris* and *The Sound and the Fury*. Fame rushed in first on Wolfe and his native Asheville, North Carolina, which became in the 1920s a classic example of the scandalized community. "Against the Victorian morality and the Bourbon aristocracy of the South," Wolfe had "turned in all his fury," wrote newspaper editor Jonathan Daniels, a former classmate. Daniels's reaction was not an uncommon response to the works of the southern renaissance, created by authors who had outgrown their "provincial" hometowns and looked back from new perspectives acquired through travel and education.

William Faulkner's achievement, more than Wolfe's, was rooted in the coarsely textured social world that produced him. Born near Oxford, Mississippi, Faulkner transmuted his hometown into the fictional Jefferson, in Yoknapatawpha County. With *The Sound and the Fury*, Faulkner created one of the triumphs of the modernist style.

Modernism and the southern literary renaissance, both of which emerged from the crucible of the Great War and its aftermath, were products of the 1920s. But the widespread alienation felt by the artists of the 1920s did not survive the decade. The onset of the Great Depression in 1929 sparked a renewed sense of commitment and affirmation in the arts, as if people could no longer afford the art-for-art's-sake affectations of the 1920s. Alienation would give way to social activism in the decade to come.

MAKING CONNECTIONS

- The next chapter discusses the growing consumer culture of the 1920s, an economic offshoot of the Roaring Twenties described in this chapter.

- Chapter 28 touches on the changes in literary culture wrought by the Great Depression—from the modernism discussed in this chapter to a recognition of the social role of literature and the cultural "rediscovery of America" in the 1930s.

- The status of women in the workforce did not improve in the 1920s despite the successes of the women's movement. It did change, however, at least temporarily, during World War II. In Chapter 30 the increase in women in the workforce is discussed.

FURTHER READING

For a lively survey social and cultural changes during the interwar period, start with William E. Leuchtenburg's *The Perils of Prosperity, 1914–32*, 2nd ed. (1993). The best introduction to the culture of the 1920s remains Loren Baritz's *The Culture of the Twenties* (1970). See also Lynn Dumenil's *The Modern Temper: American Culture and Society in the 1920s* (1995).

John Higham's *Strangers in the Land: Patterns of American Nativism, 1860–1925*, 2nd ed. (1988) details the story of immigration restriction. The controversial Sacco and Vanzetti case is thoroughly explored in *Kill Now, Talk Forever: Debating Sacco and Vanzetti*, edited by Richard Newby (2002). For analysis of the revival of Klan activity, see Nancy MacLean's *Behind the Mask of Chivalry: The Making of the Second Ku Klux Klan* (1994).

Women's suffrage is treated extensively in Eleanor Flexner's *Century of Struggle: The Woman's Rights Movement in the United States*, enlarged ed. (1996). See Charles F. Kellogg's *NAACP: A History of the National Association for the Advancement of Colored People* (1967) for his analysis of the pioneering court cases against racial discrimination. Nathan Irvin Huggins's *Harlem Renaissance* (1971) assesses the cultural impact of the Great Migration on New York. On the African-American migration to Chicago, see James R. Grossman's *Land of Hope: Chicago, Black Southerners, and the Great Migration* (1989). Nicholas Lemann's *The Promised Land: The Great Black Migration and How it Changed America* (1991) is a fine exposition of the changes brought about by the migration in both the South and the North.

On southern modernism, see Daniel Joseph Singal's *The War Within: From Victorian to Modernist Thought in the South, 1919–1945* (1982). Stanley Coben's *Rebellion against Victorianism: The Impetus for Cultural Change in 1920s America* (1991) surveys the appeal of modernism among writers, artists, and intellectuals.

27

REPUBLICAN
RESURGENCE
AND DECLINE

FOCUS QUESTIONS

· What characterized the conservatism in the presidencies of
Harding, Coolidge, and Hoover?

· What drove the growth in the American economy in the 1920s?

· What were the causes of the Great Depression?

To answer these questions and access additional review material, please visit
www.wwnorton.com/studyspace.

By 1920 the Progressive political coalition that reelected
Woodrow Wilson in 1916 had fragmented. It unraveled
for several reasons. Radicals and other opponents of the
war were disaffected by America's participation in the conflict and the war's
aftermath. Organized labor resented the Wilson administration's unsympathetic attitude toward the strikes of 1919–1920. Farmers of the Great Plains
and the West thought that wartime price controls had discriminated against
them. Liberal intellectuals also drifted away from their former support of
Progressivism. They became disillusioned with grassroots democracy because of popular support for Prohibition and religious fundamentalism.
movements. The larger middle class became preoccupied with building a
new business civilization "based not upon monopoly and restriction," in the
words of one historian, "but upon a whole new set of business values—mass
production and consumption, short hours and high wages, full employment, welfare capitalism." Progressivism's final triumphs at the national

level were already pretty much foregone conclusions before the war's end: the Eighteenth Amendment, ratified in 1919, which imposed national prohibition, and the Nineteenth Amendment, ratified in 1920, which extended women's suffrage to the entire country.

Progressivism did not disappear in the 1920s, however. Progressives dominated key leadership positions in Congress during much of the decade even while conservative Republicans occupied the White House. The Progressive impulse for "good government" and broader public services remained strong, especially at the state and local levels, where movements for good roads, education, public health, and social welfare gained momentum during the decade.

"NORMALCY"

THE ELECTION OF 1920   After World War I most Americans had grown weary of idealistic crusades and were suspicious of leaders promoting widespread reforms. Woodrow Wilson himself recognized this. "It is only once in a generation," he remarked, "that a people can be lifted above material things. That is why conservative government is in the saddle two-thirds of the time."

When the Republicans met in Chicago in 1920, the party regulars found their man in the affable Ohio senator Warren Gamaliel Harding, who had set the tone of his campaign when he told a Boston audience: "America's present need is not heroics, but healing; not nostrums, but normalcy; not revolution, but restoration; not agitation, but adjustment; not surgery, but serenity; not the dramatic, but the dispassionate." In contrast to Wilson's grandiose internationalism, Harding promised to "safeguard America first . . . to exalt America first, to live for and revere America first."

Harding's vanilla promise of a "return to normalcy" reflected his own conservative values and folksy personality. The son of an Ohio farmer, he described himself as "just a plain fellow" who was "old-fashioned and even reactionary in matters of faith and morals." But far from being an old-fashioned moralist in his personal life, Harding drank bootleg liquor in the midst of Prohibition, smoked and chewed tobacco, relished weekly poker games, and had several affairs with women other than his austere wife, whom he called Duchess. The general public, however, remained unaware of Harding's escapades. Instead, voters saw him as a handsome, charming, lovable politician. A man of self-confessed limitations in vision, leadership, and intellectual power, he once admitted that "I cannot hope to be one of the great presidents, but perhaps I may be remembered as one of the best loved."

The Democrats in 1920 hoped that Harding would not be president at all. James Cox, a former newspaper publisher and former governor of Ohio, won the presidential nomination of an increasingly fragmented Democratic party on the forty-fourth ballot. For vice president the convention named Franklin D. Roosevelt, who as assistant secretary of the navy occupied the same position his Republican cousin Theodore Roosevelt had once held.

The Democrats suffered from the breakup of the Wilsonian coalition and the conservative postwar mood. In the words of the Progressive journalist William Allen White, Americans in 1920 were "tired of issues, sick at heart of ideals, and weary of being noble." The country voted overwhelmingly for Harding's promised "return to normalcy." Harding got 16 million votes to 9 million for Cox, who carried no state outside the Democratic South.

EARLY APPOINTMENTS AND POLICY   Harding in office had much in common with Ulysses Grant. His cabinet, like Grant's, mixed some of the "best minds" in the party, whom he had promised to seek out, with a few of the worst, cronies who sought him out. Charles Evans Hughes, like Grant's Hamilton Fish, became a distinguished secretary of state. Herbert Hoover in the Commerce Department, Andrew Mellon in the Treasury Department, and Henry Wallace in the Agriculture Department functioned efficiently and made policy on their own. Other cabinet members and administrative appointees, however, were not so conscientious. The secretary of the interior landed in prison, and the attorney general narrowly escaped serving time. Many lesser offices went to members of the "Ohio gang," a group with which Harding met in a house on K Street to get away from the pressures of the White House.

Until he became president, Harding had loved politics. He was the party hack par excellence, "bloviating" (a favorite verb of his, which means "speaking with gaseous eloquence") on the stump, jollying it up in the clubhouse and cloakroom, hobnobbing with the great and near great in Washington. As president, however, Harding was simply in over his head, and self-doubt overwhelmed him. "I don't think I'm big enough for the Presidency," he confided to a friend. Harding much preferred to relax with the Ohio gang, who shared his taste for whiskey, poker, and women.

Harding and his friends set about dismantling or neutralizing many of the social and economic components of Progressivism. The president took advantage of four Supreme Court vacancies by appointing conservatives, including Chief Justice William Howard Taft, who announced that he had been "appointed to reverse a few decisions." During the 1920s the Taft court struck down a federal child-labor law and a minimum-wage law for women, issued numerous injunctions against striking unions, and passed rulings limiting the powers of federal regulatory agencies.

The Harding administration established a pro-business tone reminiscent of the McKinley White House. To deal with the postwar recession and generate economic growth, Secretary of the Treasury Mellon reduced government spending and lowered taxes. To get a better handle on expenditures, he persuaded Congress to pass the Budget and Accounting Act of 1921, which created a new Bureau of the Budget to prepare a unified federal budget and a General Accounting Office to audit the accounts. This act realized a long-held progressive desire to bring greater efficiency and nonpartisanship to the budget preparation process. General tax reductions from the wartime level were warranted, but Mellon insisted that they should go mainly to the rich, on the principle that wealth in the hands of the few would augment the general welfare through increased capital investment. Mellon's admirers tagged him the greatest secretary of the Treasury since Alexander Hamilton.

In Congress a group of western Republicans and southern Democrats fought a dogged battle to preserve the graduated scale (higher rates on higher income) built into wartime taxes, but Mellon, in office through the 1920s, eventually won out. At his behest, Congress in 1921 repealed the wartime excess-profits tax and lowered the maximum rate on personal income from 65 to 50 percent. Subsequent revenue acts lowered the maximum rate to 40 percent in 1924 and to 20 percent in 1926. The Revenue Act of 1926 extended further benefits to high-income groups by lowering estate taxes and repealing the gift tax. Unfortunately, much of the tax money released to the wealthy seems to have fueled the speculative excess of the late 1920s as much as it fostered gainful enterprise. Mellon, however, did balance the federal budget for a time. Government expenditures fell, as did the national debt.

In addition to tax cuts, Mellon—the third richest man in the United States, after John D. Rockefeller and Henry Ford—favored the time-honored Republican policy of high tariffs. The Fordney-McCumber Tariff of 1922 increased rates on chemical and metal products as a safeguard against the revival of German industries that had previously commanded the field. To please the farmers, who historically benefited little from tariffs, the new act further extended the duties on agricultural imports.

Higher tariffs had unexpected consequences, however. During the war the United States had been transformed from a debtor nation to a creditor nation. Foreign capital had long flowed into the United States, playing an important role in the economic expansion of the nineteenth century. But the private and public credits given the Allies to purchase American supplies during the war had reversed the pattern. Mellon insisted that the European powers repay all that they had borrowed. But the high American tariffs made it all the harder for other nations to sell their products in the United States and thus acquire the dollars or credits with which to repay their war debts. For nearly a decade further extensions of American loans and investments sent more dollars abroad, postponing the reckoning.

Rounding out the Republican economic program of the 1920s was a more lenient attitude toward government regulation of corporations. Neither Harding nor his successor, Calvin Coolidge, could dissolve the regulatory agencies, but they named commissioners who promoted "friendly" regulation. Harding appointed conservative advocates of big business to the Interstate Commerce Commission, the Federal Reserve Board, and the Federal Trade Commission. Senator George Norris characterized the new appointments as "the nullification of federal law by a process of boring from within." Senator Henry Cabot Lodge agreed, boasting that "we have torn up Wilsonism by the roots." In one area, however, Warren Harding proved to be much more progressive than Woodrow Wilson. He reversed the Wilson administration's policy of excluding African Americans from federal positions. He also spoke out against vigilante racism. In his first speech to a joint session of Congress in 1921, Harding insisted that the nation must deal with the festering "race question." The ugly racial incidents during and after World War I were a stain on American ideals. The new president, unlike his Democratic predecessor, attacked the Ku Klux Klan for fomenting "hatred and prejudice and violence," and he urged Congress "to wipe the stain of barbaric lynching from the banners of a free and orderly, representative democracy." The Senate, however, failed to pass the bill Harding was promoting.

ADMINISTRATIVE CORRUPTION   Republican conservatives such as Lodge and Mellon operated out of a philosophical conviction intended to benefit the nation. Members of the Ohio gang, however, used White House connections to line their own pockets. Early in 1923 Harding learned that the head of the Veterans Bureau was systematically looting medical and hospital supplies. In February, realizing he had been found out, the official resigned. A few weeks later the legal adviser to the Veterans Bureau committed suicide. Not long afterward a close friend of the attorney general's also shot himself. The corrupt crony held no government appointment but had set up an office in the Justice Department from which he peddled influence for a fee. The attorney general himself was implicated in the fraudulent handling of German assets seized after the war. When discovered, he refused to testify on the grounds that he might incriminate himself. Twice brought to court, he was never indicted, for want of evidence, possibly because he had destroyed pertinent records. These were but the most visible among the many scandals that touched the Justice Department, the Prohibition Bureau, and other agencies under Harding.

One major scandal rose above all the others, however. Teapot Dome, like the Watergate break-in fifty years later, became the catchphrase for the climate of corruption surrounding the Harding administration. An oil deposit under the sandstone in Wyoming, Teapot Dome had been set aside as a naval oil reserve administered by the Interior Department under Albert B. Fall. At the time the move seemed a sensible attempt to unify control of public reserves. But once Fall had control, he signed sweetheart contracts letting petroleum companies exploit the deposits. Fall argued that these contracts were in the government's interest. But suspicions were aroused, however, when Fall's standard of living suddenly rose. It turned out that he had taken bribes of about $400,000 (which came in "a little black bag") from oil tycoons.

Juggernaut of Corruption

This 1924 cartoon alludes to the dimensions of the Teapot Dome scandal.

Harding himself avoided public disgrace. How much he knew of the scandals swirling about him is unclear, but he knew enough to give the appearance of being troubled. "My God, this is a hell of a job!" he confided to a friend. "I have no trouble with my enemies, I can take care of my enemies all right. But my damn friends, my God-damn friends. . . . They're the ones that keep me walking the floor nights!" In 1923 Harding left on what would be his last journey, a western speaking tour and a trip to the Alaska Territory. In Seattle he suffered an attack of food poisoning, recovered briefly, then died in a San Francisco hotel.

The nation was heartbroken. Not since the death of Abraham Lincoln had there been such an outpouring of grief for a "beloved president," for the kindly, ordinary man who found it in his heart (as Woodrow Wilson had not) to pardon Eugene Debs, the Socialist who had been jailed for opposing U.S. entry into World War I. As the black-streamered funeral train moved toward Washington, D.C., then back to Ohio, millions stood by the tracks to honor their lost leader. Eventually, however, grief yielded to scorn and contempt. For nearly a decade, the revelations of scandal within the Harding administration were paraded before investigating committees and then the courts. In 1927 an Ohio woman named Nan Britton published a sensational book in which she claimed to have had a long affair with Harding. She wrote that they had had numerous trysts in the White House and that Harding was the father of her daughter. Harding's love letters to another man's wife also surfaced.

As a result of Harding's amorous detours and corrupt associates, his foreshortened administration came to be viewed as one of the worst in American history. More recent assessments of Harding's presidency, however, suggest that the scandals obscured accomplishments. Some historians credit Harding with leading the nation out of the turmoil of the postwar years and creating the foundation for the decade's remarkable economic boom. These revisionists also stress that Harding was a hardworking president who played a far more forceful role than previously assumed in shaping his administration's economic and foreign policies and in shepherding legislation through Congress. Harding also promoted diversity and civil rights. He appointed Jews to key federal positions and spoke out forcefully against the Ku Klux Klan as well as other "factions of hatred and prejudice and violence." No previous president had promoted women's rights as forcefully as did Harding. But even Harding's foremost scholarly defender admits that he lacked good judgment and "probably should never have been president."

"SILENT CAL" The news of Harding's death found Vice President Calvin Coolidge visiting his father in the isolated mountain village of

Conservatives in the White House

Warren Harding (left) and Calvin Coolidge (right).

Plymouth, Vermont, his birthplace. There, at 2:47 A.M. on August 3, 1923, by the light of a kerosene lamp, Colonel John Coolidge administered the oath of office to his son. The rustic simplicity of Plymouth, the very name itself, evoked just the image of traditional roots and solid integrity that the country would long for amid the coming disclosures of corruption and carousing in the Harding administration.

Coolidge brought to the White House his provincial background and a clear conviction that the presidency should revert to its Gilded Age stance of passive deference to Congress. "Four-fifths of our troubles," Coolidge predicted, "would disappear if we would sit down and keep still." He abided by this rule, insisting on twelve hours of sleep and an afternoon nap. The satirist H. L. Mencken asserted that Coolidge "slept more than any other president, whether by day or by night. Nero fiddled, but Coolidge only snored."

Americans embraced the unflappability of Silent Cal. He was simple and direct, a man of strong principles and few words. After being reelected president of the Massachusetts State Senate, he delivered that office's shortest inaugural address ever. His four-sentence speech urged his colleagues: "Conserve the foundations of our institutions. Do your work with the spirit of a soldier in the public service. Be loyal to the Commonwealth, and to yourselves. And be brief—above all things, be brief." Although a man of few words, he was not as bland or as dry as critics claimed. Yet he was conservative. Even more than Harding, Coolidge identified the nation's welfare with the success of big business. "The chief business of the American people is business," he preached. "The man who builds a factory builds a temple. The man who works there worships there." Where Harding had sought to balance the interests of labor, agriculture, and industry, Coolidge focused on industrial development. Even more than Harding he strove to end government regulation of business and industry and reduce taxes as well as the national debt. His fiscal frugality and pro-business stance led the *Wall Street Journal* to exult: "Never before, here or anywhere else, has a government been so completely fused with business."

THE ELECTION OF 1924   In filling out Harding's unexpired term, Calvin Coolidge successfully distanced himself from the scandals of the administration and put in charge of the prosecutions two lawyers of undoubted integrity. A man of honesty and ability, a good administrator who delegated well and managed Republican factions adroitly, he quietly took control of the party machinery and seized the initiative in the campaign for nomination, which he won with only token opposition.

Meanwhile, the Democrats fell victim to continuing dissension, which prompted the humorist Will Rogers's classic statement that "I am a member of no organized political party. I am a Democrat." The Democratic party's fractiousness illustrated the deep divisions between the new urban culture of the 1920s and the more traditional hinterland. After much factional fighting it took the Democrats 103 ballots to bestow the tarnished nomination on John W. Davis, a Wall Street lawyer from West Virginia who could nearly outdo Coolidge in conservatism.

While the Democrats bickered, a new farmer-labor coalition was creating a new political party. Meeting in Cleveland on July 4, 1924, activists organized the Progressive party and nominated Robert M. La Follette for president. The Wisconsin reformer also won the support of the Socialist party and the American Federation of Labor.

In the 1924 campaign, Coolidge focused on La Follette, whom he called a dangerous radical who would turn America into a "communistic and socialistic state." The voters preferred to "keep cool with Coolidge," who swept both the popular and the electoral votes by decisive majorities. Davis took only the solidly Democratic South, and La Follette carried only his native Wisconsin. The popular vote went 15.7 million for Coolidge, 8.4 million for Davis, and 4.8 million for La Follette—the largest popular vote ever polled by a third-party candidate. The Electoral College result was 382 to 136 to 13, respectively.

THE NEW ERA

Business executives interpreted the Republican victory in 1924 as a vindication of their leadership, and Coolidge saw the economy's surging prosperity as a confirmation of his efforts to promote the interests of big business. In fact, the prosperity and technological achievements of the time known as the New Era had much to do with Coolidge's victory over the Democrats and Progressives. Those in the large middle class who before had formed an important segment of the Progressive party coalition were now absorbed instead into the prosperous New Era created by advances in communications, transportation, and business organization.

THE GROWING CONSUMER CULTURE   Economic and social life was transformed during the 1920s. More people than ever had the money and leisure to indulge their consumer fancies, and a growing advertising industry fueled the appetites of this expanding moneyed class. By the mid-1920s advertising had become a huge enterprise with powerful social significance. Old-time values of thrift and saving gave way to a new ethic of consumption that made spending a virtue. The innovation of installment buying made an increase in consumption feasible for many. A newspaper editorial insisted that the American's "first importance to his country is no longer that of citizen but that of consumer. Consumption is a new necessity in response to dramatic increases in productivity."

Consumer-goods industries fueled much of the economic boom from 1922 to 1929. Moderately priced creature comforts, including items such as handheld cameras, wristwatches, cigarette lighters, vacuum cleaners, washing machines, and linoleum, became more widely available. Inventions in communications and transportation, such as motion pictures, radio, telephones, and automobiles, fueled the boom and triggered social transformations.

Motion Pictures

A dispirited Charlie Chaplin in a still image from his classic 1921 film *The Kid.*

In 1896 a New York audience viewed the first moving-picture show. By 1908 there were nearly 10,000 movie theaters scattered across the nation. Hollywood became the center of movie production, grinding out cowboy Westerns and the timeless comedies of Mack Sennett's Keystone Company, where a raft of slapstick comedians, most notably Charlie Chaplin, perfected their art, transforming it into a form of social criticism.

Birth of a Nation, directed in 1915 by D. W. Griffith, became a triumph of cinematic art that marked the arrival of the modern motion picture and at the same time perpetuated a grossly distorted image of Reconstruction. Based on Thomas Dixon's novel *The Clansman,* the movie featured stereotypes of villainous carpetbaggers, sinister mulattoes, blameless white southerners, and faithful "darkies." The blatantly racist film grossed $18 million and revealed the movie industry's enormous potential as a social force. By the mid-1930s every city and most small towns had movie theaters, and movies became the nation's chief form of mass entertainment. A further advancement in technology came with the "talkies"—movies with soundtracks.

Radio broadcasting had an even more spectacular growth. Except for experimental broadcasts, radio served only for basic communication until 1920. In

The Rise of Radio

The radio brings this farm family together and connects them to the outside world. By the end of the 1930s, millions would tune in to newscasts, soap operas, sports events, and church services.

that year, station WWJ in Detroit began transmitting news bulletins from the *Detroit Daily News,* and KDKA in Pittsburgh, owned by the Westinghouse Electric and Manufacturing Company, began broadcasting regularly scheduled programs. The first radio commercial aired in New York in 1922. By the end of that year, there were 508 stations and some 3 million receivers in use. In 1926 the National Broadcasting Company (NBC), a subsidiary of the Radio Corporation of America (RCA), began linking stations into a network; the Columbia Broadcasting System (CBS) entered the field the next year. In 1927 a Federal Radio Commission was established to regulate the industry; in 1934 it became the Federal Communications Commission (FCC), with authority over other forms of communication as well. Calvin Coolidge was the first president to address the nation by radio, and he did so monthly, paving the way for Franklin Roosevelt's influential "fireside chats."

AIRPLANES, AUTOMOBILES, AND THE ECONOMY Advances in transportation were equally significant. Wilbur and Orville Wright of Dayton, Ohio, owners of a bicycle shop, built and flew the first airplane at Kitty Hawk, North Carolina, in 1903. But the use of planes advanced slowly

First Flight

Orville Wright pilots the first flight of a power-driven airplane while his brother, Wilbur, runs alongside.

until the outbreak of war in 1914, after which the Europeans rapidly developed the airplane as a military weapon. When the United States entered the war, it had no combat planes—American pilots flew British or French planes. An American aircraft industry developed during the war but foundered in the postwar demobilization. Under the Kelly Act of 1925, however, the federal government began to subsidize the industry through airmail contracts. The Air Commerce Act of 1926 provided federal funds to aid in the advancement of air transportation and navigation; among the projects it supported was the construction of airports.

The infant aviation industry received a psychological boost in 1927 when Charles A. Lindbergh Jr. made the first solo transatlantic flight, traveling from New York to Paris in thirty-three and a half hours. The heroic deed, which won him $25,000, was dramatic. He flew through a dense fog for part of the way and dropped to within ten feet of the ocean's surface before sighting the Irish coast and regaining his bearings. The New York City parade in Lindbergh's honor surpassed even the celebration of the armistice.

Five years later New York honored another pioneering aviator—Amelia Earhart, who in 1932 became the first woman to fly solo across the Atlantic Ocean. Born in Kansas in 1897, she made her first solo flight in 1921 and began working as a stunt pilot at air shows across the country. Earhart's popularity soared after her transatlantic solo flight. The fifteen-hour feat led Congress to award her the Distinguished Flying Cross, and she was named Outstanding American Woman of the Year in 1932.

In 1937 Earhart and a navigator left Miami, Florida, heading east on a round-the-world flight. The voyage went smoothly until July 2, 1937, when they attempted the most difficult leg: from New Guinea to a tiny Pacific island 2,556 miles away. The plane disappeared, and despite extensive searches, no trace of it or the aviators was ever found. It remains the most intriguing mystery in aviation history. The accomplishments of Lindbergh and Earhart helped catapult aviation industry to prominence. By 1930 there were forty-three airline companies in operation in the United States.

Nevertheless, by far the most significant economic and social development of the early twentieth century was the automobile. The first motor car had been manufactured for sale in 1895, but the founding of the Ford Motor Company in 1903 revolutionized the infant industry. Ford's reliable Model T (the celebrated Tin Lizzie) came out in 1908 at a price of $850 (in 1924 it would sell for $290). Henry Ford vowed "to democratize the automobile. When I'm through everybody will be able to afford one, and about everyone will have one."

He was right. In 1916 the total number of cars manufactured passed 1 million; by 1920 more than 8 million were registered, and in 1929 there were more than 23 million. The production of automobiles stimulated other industries by consuming large amounts of steel, rubber, glass, and textiles, among other materials. It gave rise to a gigantic market for oil products just as the Spindletop gusher (drilled in 1901 in Texas) heralded the opening of vast southwestern oil fields. It quickened the movement for good roads, financed in large part from a gasoline tax; speeded transportation; encouraged suburban sprawl; and sparked real-estate booms in California and Florida.

By virtue of its size and importance, the automobile industry became the leading example of modern mass-production techniques and efficiency. When the Model T first came out, demand ran far ahead of production. Henry Ford then hired a factory expert who, by rearranging the plant and installing new equipment, met Ford's production goal of 10,000 cars in twelve months. The next year, 1909, Ford's new Highland Park plant outside of Detroit was planned with job analysis in mind. In 1910 gravity slides were installed to move parts from one workbench to the next, and by the end of 1913 the system was complete, with seemingly endless chain conveyors pulling the parts along feeder lines and the chassis down the final assembly line.

STABILIZING THE ECONOMY   During the 1920s, the drive for efficiency, which had been a prominent feature of the Progressive impulse, powered the wheels of mass production and consumption and became a cardinal belief of Republican leaders. Herbert Hoover, who served as secretary

Ford Motor Company's Highland Park Plant, 1913

Gravity slides and chain conveyors contributed to the mass production of automobiles.

of commerce in the Harding and Coolidge cabinets, was an engineer who had made a fortune in mining operations in Australia, China, Russia, and elsewhere. Out of his experiences in business and his management of the Food Administration and other wartime activities, he had developed a philosophy that he set forth in book, *American Individualism* (1922). The idea might best be called cooperative individualism or *associationalism,* one of Hoover's favorite terms. The principle also owed something to Hoover's Quaker upbringing, which taught him the virtue of the work ethic and mutual help. When he applied it to the relations of government and business, Hoover prescribed a kind of middle way between the regulatory and trust-busting traditions, a way of voluntary cooperation among businesses.

As secretary of commerce under Harding and Coolidge, Hoover transformed the trifling Commerce Department into the government's most dynamic agency. During a period of government retrenchment, he was engaged in expansion. Through an enlarged Bureau of Foreign and Domestic Commerce, he sought out new markets for business. A Division of Simplified Practice in the Bureau of Standards sponsored more than 1,000 conferences on more efficient design, production, and distribution, carrying forward the wartime move toward standardization of everything to include, for example, automobile tires, paving bricks, bedsprings, and toilet paper. In 1926 Hoover created a Bureau of Aviation and the next year established the Federal Radio Commission.

Hoover's priority was the burgeoning trade-association movement. Through trade associations, business leaders competing in a given industry would share information on everything: sales, purchases, shipments, production, and prices. This information allowed them to make plans with more confidence, the advantages of which included predictable costs, prices, and markets, as well as more stable employment and wages. Sometimes abuses crept in as associations engaged in price-fixing and other monopolistic practices, but the Supreme Court in 1925 held the practice of sharing information as such to be within the law.

THE BUSINESS OF FARMING   During the 1920s agriculture remained the weakest sector in the economy. Briefly after the war, farmers' hopes soared on wings of prosperity. The wartime boom fed by sales abroad lasted into 1920, and then commodity prices collapsed as world agricultural production returned to prewar levels. Overproduction brought lower prices for crops. Wheat went in eighteen months from $2.50 a bushel to less than $1; cotton from 35¢ per pound to 13¢. Low crop prices persisted into 1923, especially in the wheat and corn belts, and after that improvement was spotty. A bumper cotton crop in 1926 resulted only in a price collapse and an early taste of depression in much of the South, where foreclosures and bankruptcies spread.

Yet the most successful farms, like corporations, were getting larger, more efficient, and more mechanized. By 1930 about 13 percent of all farmers had tractors, and the proportion was even higher on the western plains. Better plows, harvesters, and other machines were part of the mechanization process that accompanied improved crop yields, fertilizers, and methods of animal breeding.

Yet most farmers in the 1920s were simply struggling to survive. And like their predecessors they sought political remedies. In 1924 Senator Charles L. McNary of Oregon and Representative Gilbert N. Haugen of Iowa introduced the first McNary-Haugen bill. It sought to secure "equality for agriculture in the benefits of the protective tariff." Complex as it would have been in operation, it was simple in conception: in short, it was a plan to dump farm surpluses on the world market in order to raise prices in the home market. The goal was to achieve "parity"—that is, to raise domestic farm prices to a point where they would have the same purchasing power relative to other prices they had had between 1909 and 1914, a time viewed in retrospect as a golden age of American agriculture.

Farming Technology

Mechanization became increasingly important in early-twentieth-century agriculture. Here a silo leader stands at the center of this Wisconsin farm scene.

A McNary-Haugen bill passed both houses of Congress in 1927, only to be vetoed by President Coolidge. The president explained that "no complicated scheme of relief, no plan for government fixing of prices, no resort to the public treasury" would help the farm sector. He dismissed the McNary-Haugen bill as unsound and unconstitutional. The process was repeated in 1928. Coolidge pronounced the measure an unsound effort at price-fixing and un-American and unconstitutional to boot. In a broader sense, however, McNary-Haugenism did not fail. The debates over the bill made the farm problem a national-policy issue and defined it as a problem of surpluses. Moreover, the evolution of the McNary-Haugen plan revived the idea of a political alliance between the rural South and the West, a coalition that in the next decade became a dominant influence on national farm policy.

SETBACKS FOR UNIONS   Urban workers more than farmers shared in the affluence of the 1920s. "A workman is far better paid in America than anywhere else in the world," a French visitor wrote in 1927, "and his standard of living is enormously higher." Nonfarmworkers gained about 20 percent in real wages between 1921 and 1928 while farm income rose only 10 percent.

Organized labor, however, did no better than organized agriculture in the 1920s. Even though President Harding had endorsed collective bargaining and tried to reduce the twelve-hour workday and the six-day workweek so that the working class "may have time for leisure and family life," he ran into stiff opposition in Congress. Overall, unions suffered a setback after the growth years of the war. The Red Scare and strikes of 1919 left the uneasy impression that unions practiced subversion, an idea that the enemies of unions promoted. The brief postwar depression of 1921 further weakened the unions, and they felt the severe impact of open-shop associations that proliferated across the country after the war, led by chambers of commerce and other business groups. In 1921 business groups in Chicago designated the open shop the "American plan" of employment. Although the open shop in theory implied only an employer's right to hire anyone, in practice it meant discrimination against unionists and a refusal to recognize unions even in shops where most of the workers belonged to one.

To suppress unions, employers often required "yellow-dog" contracts that forced workers to agree to stay out of a union. Owners also used labor spies, blacklists, intimidation, and coercion. Some employers tried to kill the unions with kindness. They introduced programs of "industrial democracy" guided by company unions or various schemes of "welfare capitalism," such as profit sharing, bonuses, pensions, health programs, recreational activities, and the like. The benefits of such programs were often considerable.

Prosperity, propaganda, welfare capitalism, and active hostility combined to cause union membership to drop from about 5 million in 1920 to 3.5 million in 1929. In 1924 Samuel Gompers, founder and longtime president of the AFL, died; William Green of the United Mine Workers, who took his place, embodied the conservative, even timid, attitude of unions during the period. The outstanding exception to the anti-union policies of the decade was passage of the Railway Labor Act in 1926, which abolished the Railway Labor Board and substituted a new Board of Mediation. The act also provided for the formation of railroad unions "without interference, influence, or coercion," a statement of policy not extended to other workers until the 1930s.

THE GASTONIA STRIKE OF 1929 Anti-union sentiment was fiercest in the South during the 1920s. In 1929 a wave of violent strikes swept across the region. Most of the unrest centered in the large textile mills that had come to dominate the southern economy. During World War I the desperate need for military clothing brought rapid expansion and high profits to the textile industry. After the war, however, demand for cotton cloth sagged and prices plummeted. Military demobilization, changing women's fashions—rising hemlines—and foreign competition eroded the profit margins of the textile companies. In response, owners closed mills, slashed wages, and raised production quotas. They operated the mills around the clock and established rigid production quotas (piecework) for each worker.

This onerous "stretch-out" system finally provoked workers to rebel. Many of them joined the AFL's United Textile Workers (UTW). Strikes and work stoppages followed, and the powerful mill owners, supported by security guards, local police, and state militias, forcefully suppressed the union efforts. Few of the strikes lasted more than a week, but the 1929 walkout at the huge Loray Mill in Gastonia, North Carolina, escalated into a prolonged conflict that involved two deaths.

Gaston County then had more textile plants than any other county in the nation. The red-brick Loray Mill was the largest in the South. At its peak it employed 3,500 workers, almost half of them women. During 1927 and 1928, however, the workforce was slashed. Those who kept their jobs were required to work longer (eleven hours a day six days a week) and tend more machines for lower wages. A night shift was also added. On April 1, 1929, over 1,000 exhausted Loray workers walked off the job. They were encouraged to do so by the National Textile Workers Union (NTWU), a Communist party–led rival of the UTW. Local officials were outraged that mill workers were collaborating with Communists. Equally shocking was the large number of young women among the strikers. Gastonia, a Charlotte newspaper reported, had discovered that "militant women were within its bounds."

But perhaps most upsetting to local prejudices was the NTWU's commitment to racial equality. Only 1 percent of the Loray employees were black, but the Communist party organizers who traveled to Gastonia insisted that racial justice be included among the strike's demands. In fact, however, few of the white strikers embraced racial equality, and some of them abandoned the union and the strike because of their racial prejudices. While willing to allow African Americans to join the union, local leaders required them to meet in a separate room. Leaders in the black community, especially the clergy, feared a racial backlash and discouraged African Americans from

The Gastonia Strike

These female textile workers pit their strength against that of a national guardsman during the strike at the Loray Mill in Gastonia, North Carolina, in 1929.

joining the strike or the union. Race remained a more divisive issue than class in the twentieth-century South.

The Loray Mill's managers refused to negotiate or even meet with the strikers. As tensions rose, the North Carolina governor, himself a textile-mill owner, dispatched national guard units to break the strike. Vigilante groups took matters into their own hands. A gang of masked men destroyed the union's strike headquarters and assaulted workers. When police entered the strikers' tent city to search for weapons, a skirmish erupted and someone shot and killed Gastonia's police chief. Police then arrested seventy-five of the strike leaders, thirteen of whom were eventually charged with murder. Reporters from across the nation and around the world descended on Gastonia. Vigilantes again attacked the union headquarters and later assaulted a convoy of strikers headed to a rally. Shots were fired, and twenty-nine-year-old Ella May Wiggins, a folk-singing labor organizer and mother of nine, was killed.

Despite a lack of concrete evidence, seven strikers were eventually convicted of conspiracy to commit murder in the death of the police chief and sentenced to long prison terms. By contrast, those accused of shooting Ella May Wiggins were found not guilty. The Loray strike had collapsed by the end of May 1929. The infant NTWU did not have enough funds to feed the strikers. Within a few months the mill's owners were sponsoring an essay contest, inviting workers to compete for prizes by describing "Why I Enjoy Working at the Loray."

PRESIDENT HOOVER, THE ENGINEER

HOOVER VERSUS SMITH   On August 2, 1927, while on vacation in the Black Hills of South Dakota, President Coolidge, without consulting anyone, passed out to reporters slips of paper with the curious statement "I do not choose to run for President in 1928." His retirement surprised the nation and cleared the way for Herbert Hoover to mount an active campaign for the nomination. He was the party's only strong candidate. The platform took credit for prosperity, cost cutting, debt and tax reduction, and the protective tariff ("as vital to American agriculture as it is to manufacturing"). It rejected the McNary-Haugen program but promised a farm board to manage surpluses more efficiently.

The Democratic nomination went to Governor Alfred E. Smith of New York. The party's farm plank, while not endorsing the McNary-Haugen plan, did pledge "economic equality of agriculture with other industries." Like the

Republicans the Democrats promised to enforce the Volstead Act, which provided for the enforcement of Prohibition, and, aside from calling for stricter regulation of water power, promised nothing that departed from the conservative position of the Republicans.

The two candidates' sharply different images obscured the essential similarities of their programs. Hoover was the Quaker son of middle America, the successful engineer and businessman, the architect of Republican prosperity, while Smith was the prototype of those things rural and small-town America distrusted: the son of Irish immigrants, Catholic, and anti-Prohibition. Outside the large cities all those attributes were handicaps he could scarcely surmount, for all his affability and wit. Militant members of the religious right launched a furious assault on him. The Ku Klux Klan, for example, mailed thousands of postcards proclaiming that the Catholic New Yorker was the Antichrist.

In the election of 1928, more people voted than ever before. Hoover won in the third consecutive Republican landslide, with 21 million popular votes to Smith's 15 million and an even more top-heavy electoral-vote majority of 444 to 87. Hoover even cracked the Democrats' Solid South, leaving Smith only six Deep South states plus Massachusetts and Rhode Island. The election was above all a vindication of Republican prosperity, although Calvin Coolidge was skeptical that his successor could sustain the good times. He derisively called Hoover the Wonder Boy, and had quipped in 1928 that the new president had "offered me unsolicited advice for six years, all of it bad."

The shattering defeat of the Democrats concealed a portentous realignment in the making. Al Smith had nearly doubled the vote for John W. Davis, the Democratic candidate of four years before. Smith's image, though a handicap in the hinterlands, swung big cities back into the Democratic column. In the farm states of the West, there were signs that some disgruntled farmers had switched over to the Democrats. A coalition of urban workers and unhappy farmers was in the making.

HOOVER IN CONTROL   The milestone year 1929 dawned with high hopes. Business seemed good, income was rising, and the chief architect of Republican prosperity was about to enter the White House. "I have no fears for the future of our country," Hoover told the audience at his inauguration. "It is bright with hope."

Hoover's program to stabilize business carried over into his program for agriculture, the weakest sector of the economy. To treat the malady of glutted markets, he offered two main remedies: federal help for cooperative marketing and higher tariffs on imported farm products. In 1929 he pushed

Herbert Hoover

"I have no fears for the future of our country," Hoover told the nation at his inauguration in 1929.

through Congress the Agricultural Marketing Act, which set up a Federal Farm Board to help farm cooperatives market the major commodities. The act also provided a program in which the Farm Board could set up "stabilization corporations" empowered to buy surpluses. Unluckily for any chance of success the plan might have had, it got under way almost simultaneously with the onset of the Great Depression that fall.

Farmers gained even less from tariff revision. What Hoover won after fourteen months of struggle with competing local interests in Congress was in fact a general upward revision of duties on manufactures as well as farm goods. The Hawley-Smoot Tariff of 1930 carried duties to an all-time high. Rates went up on some 70 farm products and more than 900 manufactured items. More than 1,000 economists petitioned Hoover to veto the bill because, they said, it would raise prices paid by consumers, damage the export trade and thus hurt farmers, promote inefficiency, and incite foreign reprisals. Events proved them right, but Hoover felt that he had to go along with his party in an election year.

THE ECONOMY OUT OF CONTROL   The tariff did nothing to check a deepening crisis of confidence in the economy. After the postwar slump of 1921, the idea grew that the economy had entered a new era of *permanent* growth. Greed then propelled a growing contagion of get-rich-quick schemes. Speculative mania fueled the Florida real-estate boom that began when the Coolidge prosperity combined with Henry Ford's Tin Lizzies to give people extra money and make Florida an accessible playground. Thousands of people invested in Florida real estate, eager for quick profits in the nation's fastest growing state. In the fanfare of fast turnover, the reckless speculator was, if anything, more likely to gain than the prudent investor. In mid-1926, however, the Florida real-estate bubble burst.

For the losers it was a sobering lesson, but it proved to be but an audition for the great bull market in stocks. Until 1927 stock values had gone up with profits, but then they began to soar on wings of pure speculation. Treasury Secretary Andrew Mellon's tax reductions had given people more discretionary income, which with the help of aggressive brokerage houses, found its way to Wall Street. Instead of speculating in real estate, one could buy stock on margin—that is, make a small down payment (the "margin") and borrow the rest from a broker, who held the stock as security against a down market. If the stock declined and the buyer failed to meet a margin call for more funds, the broker could sell the stock to cover his loan. Brokers' loans more than doubled from 1927 to 1929.

Gamblers in the market ignored warning signs. By 1927 residential construction and automobile sales were catching up to demand, business inventories had risen, and the rate of consumer spending had slowed. By mid-1929 production, employment, and other measures of economic activity were declining. Still the stock market rose.

By 1929 the stock market had entered a fantasy world. Conservative financiers and brokers who counseled caution were ignored. President Hoover voiced concern about the "orgy of mad speculation," and he urged stock exchange and Federal Reserve officers to discourage speculation in stocks. But to no avail. On September 4 stock prices wavered, and the day after that they dropped, opening a season of fluctuations. The great bull market staggered on into October, trending downward but with enough good days to keep hope alive. On October 22 a leading bank president assured reporters, "I know of nothing fundamentally wrong with the stock market or with the underlying business and credit structure."

THE CRASH AND ITS CAUSES   The next day, stock values tumbled, and the day after that a wild scramble to unload stocks lasted until word arrived that leading bankers had formed a pool to buy stocks to halt the slide. Prices steadied for the rest of the week, but after a weekend to think the situation over, stockholders began to unload. On Tuesday, October 29, the most devastating single day in the market's history, brokers reported sales of 16.4 million shares (at the time the trading of 3 million shares was a busy day). The plunge in prices fed on itself as brokers sold the shares they held for buyers who failed to meet their margin calls. During October, stocks on the New York Stock Exchange fell in value by 37 percent.

Business and government leaders initially expressed confidence that the markets would rebound. According to President Hoover, "the fundamental business of the country" was sound. Some speculators who had gotten out of the market went back in for bargains but only found themselves caught in a slow, tedious erosion of values. By March 1933, the value of stocks on the

Stock Market Crash

Apprehensive crowds gather on the steps of the Subtreasury Building, opposite the New York Stock Exchange, as news of a stock collapse spreads on October 29, 1929.

New York Stock Exchange was less than one fifth of the value at the market's peak. The *New York Times* stock average, which stood at 452 in September 1929, bottomed at 52 in July 1932.

The collapse of the stock market revealed that the much-trumpeted economic prosperity of the 1920s was built on weak foundations. From 1929 to 1932, personal income declined by more than half. Unemployment soared. Farmers, already in trouble, faced catastrophe. More than 9,000 banks closed during the period, hundreds of factories and mines shut down, and thousands of farms were foreclosed for debt and sold at auction. A cloak of gloom fell over the nation.

The stock-market crash did not cause the Great Depression, but it did reveal major structural flaws in the economy and in government policies. Too many businesses had maintained retail prices and taken large profits while holding down wages. As a result, about one third of personal income went to only 5 percent of the population. By plowing most profits back into expansion rather than wage increases, the business sector brought on a growing imbalance between rising productivity and declining purchasing power. As public consumption of goods declined, the rate of investment in new plants also plummeted. For a time the erosion of consumer purchasing power was concealed by an increase in installment buying, and the deflationary effects of the high tariffs were concealed by the volume of foreign loans and investments that supported foreign demand for American goods. But the flow of American capital abroad began to dry up when the stock market began to look more attractive. Swollen profits and corporate dividends, together with the Treasury Secretary Mellon's business-friendly tax policies, enticed the rich into stock-market speculation. When trouble came, the bloated corporate structure collapsed.

Government policies also contributed to the economic debacle. Mellon's tax reductions led to oversaving by the general public, which helped diminish the demand for consumer goods. Hostility toward labor unions discouraged collective bargaining and may have worsened the prevalent imbalances in income. High tariffs discouraged foreign trade. Lax enforcement of antitrust laws also encouraged high prices.

Another culprit was the gold standard. The world monetary system remained fragile throughout the 1920s. When economic output, prices, and savings began dropping in 1929, policy makers—certain that they had to keep their currencies tied to gold at all costs—often tightened money supplies at the very moment that economies needed an expanding money supply to keep growing. The only way to restore economic stability within the constraints of the gold standard was to let prices and wages continue to fall, allowing the downturn, in Andrew Mellon's words, to "purge the rottenness out of the system." What happened instead was that passivity among government and financial leaders turned a recession into the world's worst depression.

THE HUMAN TOLL OF THE DEPRESSION The devastating collapse of the economy caused immense social hardships. By 1933 over 13 million people were out of work. Millions more who kept their jobs saw their hours and wages reduced. Factories shut down, banks closed, farms went bankrupt, and millions of people found themselves not only jobless but also homeless and penniless. Hungry people lined up at churches and soup kitchens; others rummaged through trash cans behind restaurants. Many slept on park benches or in back alleys. Others congregated in makeshift shelters in vacant lots. Thousands of desperate men in search of jobs rode the rails. These hobos or tramps, as they were derisively called, sneaked onto empty railway cars and rode from town to town, looking for work. During the winter homeless people wrapped themselves in newspapers to keep warm, sarcastically referring to their coverings as Hoover blankets. Some grew so weary of their grim fate that they ended their lives. The suicide rate soared during the 1930s. America had never before experienced social distress on such a scale.

HOOVER'S EFFORTS AT RECOVERY   Although the policies of public officials helped to bring on economic collapse, few leaders even acknowledged that there was an unprecedented crisis: all that was needed, they claimed, was a slight correction of the market. Those who held to the dogma of limited government thought the economy would cure itself. The best policy, Treasury Secretary Mellon advised, would be to "liquidate labor, liquidate stocks, liquidate the farmers, liquidate real estate." Yet Hoover was unwilling to sit by and let events take their course. He in fact did more than any president had ever done before in such dire economic circumstances. Still, his own philosophy, now hardened into dogma, set firm limits on government action, and he was unready to set that philosophy aside even to meet an unprecedented national emergency.

Hoover believed that the nation's fundamental business structure was sound and that the country's main need was confidence. In speech after speech, he exhorted people to keep up hope, and he asked business owners to keep their mills and shops open, maintain wage rates, and spread out the work to avoid layoffs—in short, to let the first shock of depression fall on corporate profits rather than on wage earners. In return, union leaders, who had little choice, agreed to refrain from making wage demands and staging strikes. As it happened, however, uplifting words were not enough, and the prediction that good times were just around the corner (actually made by the vice president, though attributed to Hoover) eventually became a sardonic joke.

Hoover did more than try to reassure the public, however. He hurried the commencement of government construction projects in order to provide jobs, but state and local cutbacks more than offset the new federal spending. At Hoover's demand the Federal Reserve returned to an easier credit policy, and Congress passed a modest tax reduction to put more cash into people's pockets. The Federal Farm Board stepped up its loans and its purchases of farm surpluses, only to face bumper crops in 1930 despite droughts in the Midwest and Southwest. The high Hawley-Smoot Tariff, proposed at first to help farmers, brought reprisals against American exports abroad, thus devastating foreign trade.

As always, a depressed economy hurt the party in power. Democrats exploited Hoover's predicament for all it was worth. The squalid settlements that sprouted across the country to house the destitute and homeless became known as Hoovervilles; a Hoover flag was an empty pocket turned inside out. In November 1930 the Democrats gained their first national victory since 1916, winning a majority in the House and enough gains in the Senate to control it in coalition with western agrarians.

In the first half of 1931, economic indicators rose, renewing hope for an upswing. Then, as recovery beckoned, another shock occurred. In May 1931

Impact of the Depression

Two children set up shop in a Hooverville in Washington, D.C.

the failure of Austria's largest bank triggered a financial panic in central Europe. To ease concerns, President Hoover proposed a one-year moratorium on both reparations and war-debt payments by the European nations. European leaders accepted the moratorium as well as a later temporary "standstill" on the settlement of private obligations between banks. The general shortage of monetary exchange drove Europeans to withdraw their gold from American banks and dump their American securities. One European country after another abandoned the gold standard and devalued its currency. Even the Bank of England went off the gold standard. The United States, meanwhile, slid into the third bitter winter of deepening depression.

CONGRESSIONAL INITIATIVES   With a new Congress in session, demands for federal action impelled Hoover to stretch his individualistic philosophy to its limits. He was ready now to use government resources to at least shore up the financial institutions of the country. In 1932 the new Congress set up the Reconstruction Finance Corporation (RFC) with $500 million (and authority to borrow $2 billion more) for emergency loans to banks, life-insurance companies, building-and-loan societies, farm-mortgage associations, and railroads. Under former vice president Charles G. Dawes, it authorized $1.2 billion in loans within six months. The RFC staved off bankruptcies, but Hoover's critics found in it favoritism to business, the most damaging instance of which was a $90 million loan to Dawes's own Chicago bank, made soon after he left the RFC in 1932. The RFC nevertheless remained a key agency through the mid-1940s.

Further help to the financial structure came with the Glass-Steagall Act of 1932, which broadened the definition of commercial loans that the Federal Reserve would support. The new arrangement also released about $750 million in gold formerly used to back Federal Reserve notes, countering the effect of foreign withdrawals and domestic hoarding of gold at the same time that it enlarged the supply of credit. For homeowners the Federal Home Loan Bank Act of 1932 created with Hoover's blessing a series of discount banks for home mortgages. They provided to savings-and-loan and other mortgage agencies with a service much like the one that the Federal Reserve System provided to commercial banks.

Hoover's critics said all these measures reflected a dubious "trickle-down" theory. If government could help banks and railroads, asked New York senator Robert F. Wagner, "is there any reason why we should not likewise extend a helping hand to that forlorn American, in every village and every city of the United States, who has been without wages since 1929?" The contraction of credit devastated such debtors as farmers and those who made purchases on the installment plan or held balloon-style mortgages, whose monthly payments increased over time.

By 1932 members of Congress were filling the hoppers with bills for federal measures to provide relief to individuals. At that point, Hoover might have pleaded "dire necessity" and taken the leadership of the relief movement and salvaged his political fortunes. Instead, he held back and only grudgingly edged toward federal-directed relief of human distress. On July 21, 1932, he signed the Emergency Relief Act, which avoided a direct federal dole (cash payment) to individuals but gave the RFC $300 million for relief loans to the states, authorized loans of up to $1.5 billion for state and local public works, and appropriated $322 million for federal public works.

FARMERS AND VETERANS IN PROTEST Government relief for farmers had long since been abandoned. In mid-1931 the government quit buying crop surpluses and helplessly watched prices slide. Faced with the loss of everything, desperate farmers began to defy the law. Angry mobs stopped foreclosures and threatened to lynch the judges sanctioning them. In Nebraska, farmers burned corn to keep warm. Iowans formed the militant Farmers' Holiday Association, which called a farmers' strike.

Anger and Frustration

Unemployed military veterans, members of the Bonus Expeditionary Force, clash with Washington, D.C., police at Anacostia Flats in July 1932.

In the midst of the crisis, there was even desperate talk of revolution. "Folks are restless," Mississippi governor Theodore Bilbo told reporters in 1931. "Communism is gaining a foothold. . . . In fact, I'm getting a little pink myself." Across the country the once-obscure Communist party began to draw crowds to its rallies and willing collaborators to its "hunger marches." Yet for all the sound and fury, few Americans were converted to communism during the 1930s. Party membership in the United States never rose much above 100,000.

Fears of organized revolt arose when unemployed veterans converged on the nation's capital in the spring of 1932. The "Bonus Expeditionary Force" grew quickly to more than 15,000. Their purpose was to get immediate payment of the bonus to veterans of World War I that Congress had voted in 1924. The House approved a bonus bill, but when the Senate voted it down, most of the veterans went home. The rest, having no place to go, camped in vacant government buildings and in a shantytown at Anacostia Flats, within sight of the Capitol.

Eager to disperse the squatters, Hoover persuaded Congress to pay for their tickets home. More left, but others stayed even after Congress adjourned, hoping at least to meet with the president. Late in July the administration ordered the government buildings cleared. In the ensuing melee a policeman panicked, fired into the crowd, and killed two veterans. The president then dispatched about 700 soldiers under General Douglas MacArthur, who was aided by junior officers Dwight D. Eisenhower and George S. Patton. The soldiers drove out the unarmed veterans and their families, injuring dozens and killing one, an eleven-week-old boy born at Anacostia, who died from exposure to tear gas.

General MacArthur claimed that the "mob," animated by "the essence of revolution," was about to seize control of the government. The administration insisted that the Bonus Army consisted mainly of Communists and criminals, but neither a grand jury nor the Veterans Administration could find evidence to support the charge. One observer wrote before the incident: "There is about the lot of them an atmosphere of hopelessness, of utter despair, though not of desperation. . . . They have no enthusiasm whatever and no stomach for fighting."

Their mood, and the mood of the country, echoed that of Hoover himself. He worked very hard, but the stress took its toll on his health and morale. "I am so tired," he said, "that every bone in my body aches." Presidential news conferences became more strained and less frequent. When friends urged him to seize the reins of leadership, he said, "I can't be a Theodore Roosevelt" or "I have no Wilsonian qualities." Hoover's deepening sense of futility became increasingly evident to the country. In a mood more despairing than rebellious, Americans in 1932 eagerly anticipated what the next presidential campaign would produce.

MAKING CONNECTIONS

- This chapter discussed setbacks suffered by labor unions during the 1920s. In the next chapter, unions win new protections under Franklin Roosevelt's New Deal.

- An element of the "normalcy" discussed in this chapter was American isolation from global affairs. Chapter 29 discusses that isolationism in the context of the coming of World War II.

- The characteristics of American society in the 1920s may be compared with the postwar society and culture of the 1950s, discussed in Chapter 32.

FURTHER READING

A fine synthesis of events immediately following the First World War is Ellis W. Hawley's *The Great War and the Search for a Modern Order: A History of the American People and Their Institutions, 1917–1933* (1979).

On Harding, see Robert K. Murray's *The Harding Era: Warren G. Harding and His Administration* (2000). On Coolidge, see Robert H. Ferrell's *The Presidency of Calvin Coolidge* (1998). On Hoover, see Martin L. Fausold's *The Presidency of Herbert C. Hoover* (1985).

Overviews of the depressed economy are found in Charles P. Kindleberger's *The World in Depression, 1929–1939*, rev. and enlarged ed. (1986) and Peter Fearon's *War, Prosperity, and Depression: The U.S. Economy, 1917–1945* (1987). John A. Garraty's *The Great Depression: An Inquiry into the Causes, Course, and Consequences of the Worldwide Depression of the Nineteen-Thirties* (1986) describes how people survived the Depression.

28

NEW DEAL AMERICA

FOCUS QUESTIONS

- What were the social effects of the Great Depression and Franklin Roosevelt's efforts at relief, recovery, and reform?

- Why did the New Deal draw criticism from both the right and the left?

- How did the New Deal expand the federal government's authority and responsibilities?

- What were the major cultural changes of the 1930s?

To answer these questions and access additional review material, please visit www.wwnorton.com/studyspace.

Upon arriving in the White House in 1933, Franklin Roosevelt inherited a nation mired in the third year of an unprecedented economic depression. No other business slump had been so deep, so long, or so painful. One out of every four Americans in 1932 was unemployed, and in many large cities nearly half the adults were out of work. Some 500,000 Americans had lost homes or farms because they could not pay their mortgages. Thousands of banks had failed; millions of depositors had lost their life savings. The worldwide depression had also helped accelerate the rise of fascism and communism. Totalitarianism was on the march. "The situation is critical," the prominent political analyst Walter Lippmann warned President-elect Roosevelt. "You may have to assume dictatorial powers."

Roosevelt did not become a dictator, but he did take decisive action. He and a supportive Congress immediately adopted bold measures to relieve the human suffering and promote economic recovery. Such initiatives provided the foundation for what came to be called welfare capitalism.

FROM HOOVERISM TO THE NEW DEAL

THE ELECTION OF 1932 On June 14, 1932, while the ragtag Bonus Army was still encamped in Washington, D.C., Republicans gathered in Chicago to renominate Herbert Hoover. The delegates went through the motions in a mood of defeat. By contrast, the Democrats converged on Chicago confident that they would nominate the next president. New York governor Franklin D. Roosevelt was already the front-runner, with most of the delegates lined up, and he went over the top on the fourth ballot.

In a bold gesture, Roosevelt appeared in person to accept the nomination instead of awaiting formal notification. "Let it . . . be symbolic that . . . I broke traditions," he told the delegates. "Republican leaders not only have failed in material things, they have failed in national vision, because in disaster they have held out no hope. . . . I pledge you, I pledge myself to a new deal for the American people." What the New Deal would be in practice Roosevelt had little idea as yet, but he was much more willing to experiment than Hoover. What was more, his upbeat personality communicated joy, energy, and hope. Roosevelt's campaign song was "Happy Days Are Here Again."

Born in 1882 into a wealthy family, educated by governesses and tutors at his father's rambling estate along the Hudson River in New York, Roosevelt led the cosmopolitan life of a young patrician. After attending an elite Connecticut boarding school, he earned degrees from Harvard and Columbia Law School. While a law student, he married his distant cousin, Anna Eleanor Roosevelt, a niece of his fifth cousin, Theodore Roosevelt, then president of the United States.

In 1910 Franklin Roosevelt won a Democratic seat in the New York State Senate. As a freshman legislator he displayed the contradictory qualities that would characterize his political career: he was an aristocrat with a sincere empathy for common folk, a traditionalist with a penchant for experimenting, an affable charmer with a buoyant smile and upturned chin who harbored profound convictions, and a skilled political tactician with a shrewd sense of timing and a distinctive willingness to listen to and learn from others.

Tall, handsome, and athletic, Roosevelt seemed destined for greatness. In 1912 he backed Woodrow Wilson, and for both of Wilson's terms he served as assistant secretary of the navy. Then, in 1920, largely on the strength of his name, he became James Cox's running mate on the Democratic ticket. The following year, at age thirty-nine, his career seemed destined to be cut short by an attack of polio that left him permanently disabled, unable to stand or walk without braces. But the battle for recovery transformed the young aristocrat. He became less arrogant, less superficial, more focused, and more interesting. A friend recalled that Roosevelt emerged from his struggle with polio "completely warm-hearted, with a new humility of spirit" that led him to identify with the poor and the suffering. Justice Oliver Wendell Holmes later summed up his qualities this way: "a second-class intellect—but a first-class temperament."

For seven years, aided by his talented wife, Eleanor, Roosevelt strengthened his body to compensate for his disability, and in 1928 he won the governorship of New York. Reelected by a whopping majority of 700,000 in 1930, Roosevelt became the favorite for president in 1932.

Partly to dispel doubts about his health, nominee Roosevelt set forth on a grueling campaign tour. He blamed the Depression on Hoover and the Republicans, and he began to define what he meant by the New Deal. Like Hoover, Roosevelt promised to balance the budget, but he was willing to incur short-term deficits to prevent starvation and revive the economy. On the tariff he was evasive. On farm policy he offered several options pleasing to farmers and ambiguous enough not to alarm city dwellers. He called for strict regulation of utilities and for at least some government development of electricity, and he consistently stood by his party's pledge to repeal the Prohibition amendment. Perhaps most important, he recognized that a revitalized economy would require national planning and new ideas. "The country needs, and, unless I mistake its temper, the country demands bold, persistent experimentation," he said. "Above all, try something."

What came across to voters, however, was less the content of Roosevelt's speeches than his uplifting confidence. By contrast, Hoover lacked vitality and assurance. Democrats, Hoover argued, ignored the international causes of the Depression. They were also taking a reckless course. Roosevelt's proposals, he warned, "would destroy the very foundations of our American system." Pursue them, and "grass will grow in the streets of a hundred cities, a thousand towns." But few were listening. Amid the persistent depression the country wanted a new course, a new leadership, a new deal.

Some disillusioned voters took a dim view of both major candidates. Those who believed that only a radical departure would suffice supported

The "New Deal" Candidate

Governor Franklin D. Roosevelt, the Democratic nominee for president in 1932, campaigning in Topeka, Kansas. Roosevelt's confidence inspired voters.

the Socialist party candidate, Norman Thomas, who polled 882,000 votes, and a few preferred the Communist party candidate, who won 103,000. The wonder is that a desperate people did not turn in greater numbers to radical candidates. Instead, they swept Roosevelt into office with 23 million votes to Hoover's 16 million. Hoover carried only four states in New England plus Pennsylvania and Delaware and lost decisively in the Electoral College by 472 to 59.

THE INAUGURATION For the last time the country waited four months, until March 4, for a new president and Congress to take office. The Twentieth Amendment, ratified on January 23, 1933, provided that presidents would thereafter take office on January 20 and the newly elected Congress on January 3.

The bleak winter of 1932–1933 witnessed spreading destitution and misery. Unemployment continued to spread, and panic struck the banking system. As bank after bank collapsed, people rushed to their own banks to remove their deposits. Many discovered that they, too, were caught short of cash. When the Hoover administration ended, four fifths of the nation's banks were closed, and the country teetered on the brink of economic paralysis.

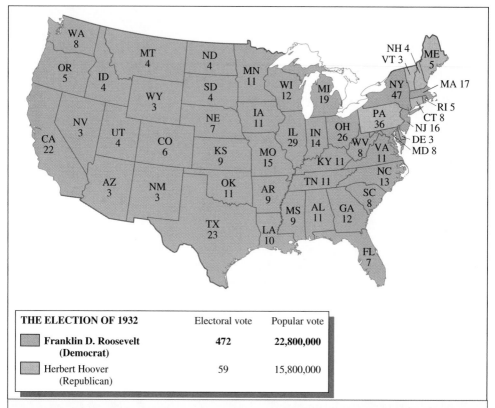

THE ELECTION OF 1932	Electoral vote	Popular vote
Franklin D. Roosevelt (Democrat)	472	22,800,000
Herbert Hoover (Republican)	59	15,800,000

Why did Roosevelt appeal to voters struggling during the Depression? What were Hoover's criticisms of Roosevelt's "New Deal"? What policies defined Roosevelt's New Deal during the presidential campaign?

The profound crisis of confidence that greeted Roosevelt when he took the oath of office on March 4, 1933, gave way to a mood of expectancy. The new president asserted "that the only thing we have to fear is fear itself— nameless, unreasoning, unjustified terror which paralyzes needed efforts to convert retreat into advance." If need be, he said, "I shall ask the Congress for . . . broad executive power to wage a war against the emergency as great as the power that would be given me if we were in fact invaded by a foreign foe." It was a measure of the country's mood that this call for unprecedented presidential power received the loudest applause.

COMPETING SOLUTIONS   When Roosevelt and his corps of New Dealers arrived in Washington, they confronted three major challenges: reviving the economy, relieving the human misery, and rescuing the farm sector and its desperate families. His "brain trust" of advisers offered conflicting opinions about how best to rescue the economy from depression. Some promoted vigorous enforcement of the anti-trust laws as a means of restoring business competition; others argued for the opposite, saying that anti-trust laws should be suspended so as to enable large corporations to collaborate with the federal government and thereby better manage the overall economy. Still others called for a massive expansion of welfare programs and a prolonged infusion of increased government spending to address the profound human crisis and revive the economy.

Roosevelt was willing to try some elements of each approach without ever embracing one completely. In part his flexible outlook reflected the political reality that conservative southern Democrats controlled the Congress and the president could not risk alienating these powerful proponents of balanced budgets and limited government. Roosevelt's inconsistencies also reflected his own outlook. He was a pragmatist rather than an ideologue. As he once explained, "Take a method and try it. If it fails admit it frankly and try another." Roosevelt's New Deal would therefore take the form of a series of trial-and-error actions.

Roosevelt and his advisers initially settled on a three-pronged strategy to address the problems facing the nation. First, they sought to remedy the banking crisis and to provide short-term emergency relief for the jobless. Second, they tried to promote industrial recovery through increased federal spending and cooperative agreements between management and organized labor. Third, they attempted to raise depressed commodity prices (and thereby farm income) by paying farmers to reduce the size of crops and herds. By reducing the overall supply of farm products, prices for grain and meat would rise. None of these initiatives worked perfectly, but their combined effect was to restore hope and energy to a nation paralyzed by fear and uncertainty.

STRENGTHENING THE MONETARY SYSTEM   On his second day in office, Roosevelt called upon Congress to meet in a special session on March 9 and then declared a four-day bank holiday to allow the panic to subside. It took Congress only seven hours to pass the Emergency Banking Relief Act, which permitted sound banks to reopen and provided managers for those that remained in trouble. On March 12, in the first of his radio-broadcast "fireside chats," the president insisted that it was safer to "keep your money in a reopened bank than under the mattress." His reassurances soothed a nervous nation. The following day, deposits in reopened banks exceeded withdrawals. The banking crisis had ended, and the new administration was ready to get on with its broader program.

Roosevelt next followed through on two pledges in the Democratic platform. At his behest, Congress passed an Economy Act, granting the executive branch the power to cut government salaries, reduce payments to military veterans for non-service-connected disabilities, and reorganize federal agencies in the interest of reducing federal expenses. The Beer-Wine Revenue Act amended the Volstead Act to permit the sale of beverages with an alcohol content of 3.2 percent. The Twenty-first Amendment, already submitted by Congress to the states, would be declared ratified on December 5, thus ending the "noble experiment" of alcohol prohibition.

The measures of March were but the beginning of an avalanche of new legislation. During a session that lasted from March 9 to June 16, the so-called Hundred Days, Congress received from the president, and enacted, fifteen major proposals with a speed unlike any seen before in American history:

March 9	Passage of the Emergency Banking Relief Act
March 20	Passage of the Economy Act
March 31	Establishment of the Civilian Conservation Corps
April 19	Abandonment of the gold standard
May 12	Passage of the Federal Emergency Relief Act
May 12	Passage of the Agricultural Adjustment Act, including the Thomas amendment, which gave the president powers to expand the money supply
May 12	Passage of the Emergency Farm Mortgage Act, providing for the refinancing of farm mortgages
May 18	Passage of the Tennessee Valley Authority Act, providing federal funds for the unified hydroelectric development of the Tennessee River valley
May 27	Passage of the Federal Securities Act, requiring full disclosure in the issuing of new securities
June 13	Passage of the Home Owners' Loan Act, setting up the Home Owners' Loan Corporation to refinance home mortgages
June 16	Passage of the National Industrial Recovery Act, providing for a system of industrial self-regulation under federal supervision and for a $3.3-billion public-works program
June 16	Passage of the Banking Act, separating commercial and investment banking and establishing the Federal Deposit Insurance Corporation
June 16	Passage of the Farm Credit Act, which reorganized federal agricultural subsidies

With the banking crisis over, an acute debt problem remained for farmers and homeowners, along with a lingering distrust of the banks. By executive decree, Roosevelt reorganized all federal farm credit agencies into the Farm Credit Administration. By the Emergency Farm Mortgage Act and the Farm Credit Act, Congress authorized extensive refinancing of farm mortgages at lower interest rates to stem the tide of foreclosures.

The Home Owners' Loan Act provided a similar service to city dwellers through the Home Own-ers' Loan Corporation, which re-

The Galloping Snail

A vigorous Roosevelt drives Congress to action in this *Detroit News* cartoon from March 1933.

financed mortgage loans at lower monthly payments for strapped home-owners, again helping to slow the rate of foreclosures. The Banking Act further shored up confidence in the banking system. Its Federal Deposit Insurance Corporation guaranteed personal bank deposits up to $5,000. To prevent speculative abuses, it separated investment and commercial banking corporations and extended the Federal Reserve Board's regulatory power over credit. The Federal Securities Act required the full disclosure of information about new stock and bond issues, at first by registration with the Federal Trade Commission and later with the Securities and Exchange Commission, which was created to regulate the chaotic stock and bond markets.

Throughout 1933 Roosevelt tinkered with devaluation of the currency as a way to raise prices and thus ease the debt burden on strapped investors and farmers. With the government's official abandonment of the gold standard on April 19, the decline in the value of the dollar increased the prices of commodities and corporate stocks.

RELIEF MEASURES   Another urgent priority in 1933 was relieving the widespread personal distress caused by the Great Depression. Hoover had stubbornly resisted using the federal government to provide direct relief for the unemployed and homeless. Roosevelt was more flexible. He asked Congress to create the Civilian Conservation Corps (CCC), which was designed to give work to unemployed and unmarried young men age eighteen to twenty-five.

Nearly 3 million men were hired to work at a variety of CCC jobs in forests, parks, and recreational areas and on soil-conservation projects. CCC workers built roads, bridges, campgrounds, and fish hatcheries; planted trees; taught farmers how to control soil erosion; and fought fires. They were paid a nominal sum of $30 a month, of which $25 went home to their families. The enrollees could also take education courses and earn high-school diplomas.

The Federal Emergency Relief Administration (FERA) addressed the broader problems of human distress. Harry L. Hopkins, a tough-talking, big-hearted social worker who had directed Roosevelt's relief efforts in New York State, pushed the program with a boundless energy. The FERA expanded the assistance to the unemployed that had begun under Hoover's RFC, but with a difference. Federal money flowed to the states in grants rather than "loans." Hopkins pushed an "immediate work instead of dole" approach on state and local officials, but they preferred the dole (direct cash payments to individuals) as a quicker way to reach the needy.

Federal Relief Programs

Civilian Conservation Corps enrollees in 1933, on a break from work. Directed by army officers and foresters, the CCC adhered to a semimilitary discipline.

The first large-scale experiment with *federal* work relief, which put people directly on the government payroll at competitive wages, came with the formation of the Civil Works Administration (CWA). Created in November 1933, when it had become apparent that the state-sponsored programs funded by the FERA were inadequate, the CWA provided federal jobs and wages to those unable to find work that winter. It was hastily conceived and implemented but during its four-month existence put to work over 4 million people. The agency organized a variety of useful projects, from making highway repairs and laying sewer lines to constructing or improving more than 1,000 airports and 40,000 schools and providing 50,000 teaching jobs that helped keep rural schools open. As the number of people employed by the CWA soared, the program's costs skyrocketed to over $1 billion. Roosevelt balked at the expenditures and worried that people would become dependent upon federal jobs. So in the spring of 1934, he ordered the CWA dissolved. By April some 4 million workers were again unemployed.

Roosevelt nevertheless continued to favor work relief over the dole. He thought the dole was an addictive "narcotic, a subtle destroyer of the human spirit." Real jobs, on the other hand, nurtured "self-respect and self-reliance." In 1935 he asked for an array of new federal job programs, and Congress responded by passing a $4.8-billion Emergency Relief Appropriation Act, providing work relief for the jobless. To manage these programs, Roosevelt created the Works Progress Administration (WPA), headed by Harry Hopkins, to replace the FERA. Hopkins was told to provide millions of jobs quickly, and as a result some of the new jobs appeared to be make-work or mere "leaning on shovels." But before the WPA died during World War II, it left permanent monuments on the landscape in the form of buildings, bridges, hard-surfaced roads, airports, and schools.

The WPA also employed a wide range of talented Americans in the Federal Theatre Project, the Federal Art Project, the Federal Music Project, and the Federal Writers' Project. Writers such as Ralph Ellison, John Cheever, and Saul Bellow found work writing travel guides to the United States, and Orson Welles directed Federal Theatre Project's productions. Critics charged that these programs were frivolous, but Hopkins replied that writers and artists needed "to eat just like other people." The National Youth Administration (NYA), also under the WPA, provided part-time employment to students, set up technical training programs, and aided jobless youths. Twenty-seven-year-old Lyndon Johnson was director of an NYA program in Texas, and Richard Nixon, a penniless Duke University law student, found work through the NYA at 35¢ an hour. Although the WPA took care of only about 3 million out of some 10 million jobless at any

City Life

This mural, painted by WPA artist Victor Arauntoff, depicts a bustling New Deal–era street scene.

one time, in all it helped some 9 million clients weather desperate times before it expired in 1943.

RECOVERY THROUGH REGULATION

In addition to rescuing the banks and providing immediate relief to the unemployed, Roosevelt and his advisers promoted the long-term recovery of agriculture and business. The languishing economy needed a boost— a big one. There were 13 million people without jobs. Members of Franklin Roosevelt's brain trust were largely heirs to Theodore Roosevelt's New Nationalism. Like the earlier progressives, members of the brain trust insisted that the trend toward economic concentration was inevitable. Big businesses were not going to go away. They also believed that the mistakes of the 1920s showed that the only way to operate an integrated economy at capacity and in the public interest was through efficient regulation and organized central planning, not by breaking up huge corporations. The success of government-led economic planning during World War I reinforced such ideas, and new recovery programs sprang from those beliefs.

AGRICULTURAL RECOVERY   The sharp decline in commodity prices after 1929 meant that many farmers could not afford to plant or harvest their crops. Farm income had plummeted from $6 billion in 1929 to $2 billion in 1932. The Agricultural Adjustment Act of 1933 created a new federal agency, the Agricultural Adjustment Administration (AAA), which sought to control farm production by compensating farmers for voluntary cutbacks in production. Its goal was to raise farm prices by reducing supply. The money for benefit payments came from a processing tax levied on certain basic commodities—at the cotton gin, for example, or at the flour mill.

By the time Congress acted, however, the growing season was already under way. The prospect of another bumper cotton crop forced the AAA to sponsor a plow-under program. To destroy a growing crop was a "shocking commentary on our civilization," Agriculture Secretary Henry A. Wallace lamented. "I could tolerate it only as a cleaning up of the wreckage from the old days of unbalanced production." Moreover, given the oversupply of hogs, some 6 million pigs were slaughtered. It could be justified, Wallace said, only as a means of helping farmers do with pigs what steelmakers did with pig iron—cut production to fit the market and thereby raise prices.

For a while these farm measures worked. By the end of 1934, Secretary of Agriculture Wallace could report significant declines in wheat, cotton, and corn production and a simultaneous increase in commodity prices. Farm income increased by 58 percent between 1932 and 1935. The AAA was only partially responsible for the gains, however. A devastating drought that settled over the plains states between 1932 and 1935 played a major role in reducing production and creating the epic "dust-bowl" migrations so poignantly evoked in John Steinbeck's *Grapes of Wrath*. Many migrant families had actually been driven off the land by AAA benefit programs that encouraged large farmers to take the lands worked by tenants and sharecroppers out of cultivation.

Although it created unexpected problems, the AAA achieved successes in boosting the overall farm economy. But conservatives opposed its sweeping powers. On January 6, 1936, in *United States v. Butler*, the Supreme Court, by a vote of six to three, declared the AAA's tax on food processors unconstitutional. The administration hastily devised a new plan in the Soil Conservation and Domestic Allotment Act, which it pushed through Congress in six weeks. The new act omitted processing taxes and acreage quotas but provided benefit payments for soil-conservation practices that took land out of soil-depleting staple crops, thus indirectly achieving crop reduction.

The act was an almost unqualified success as an engineering and educational project because it helped heal the scars of erosion and the plague of dust storms. But soil conservation nevertheless failed as a device for limiting production. With their worst lands taken out of production, farmers cultivated their fertile acres more intensively. In response, Congress passed the Agricultural Adjustment Act of 1938, which reestablished the earlier programs but left out the processing taxes. Benefit payments would come from general federal funds. By the time the second AAA reached a test in the Supreme Court, changes in the Court's personnel had altered its outlook. This time the law was upheld as a legitimate exercise of the power to regulate interstate commerce. Agriculture, like manufacturing, was now held to be in the stream of commerce.

INDUSTRIAL RECOVERY The industrial counterpart to the AAA was the National Industrial Recovery Act (NIRA), the two major parts of which dealt with economic recovery and public-works projects. The latter part created the Public Works Administration (PWA), granting $3.3 billion for public buildings, highway programs, flood control, and other improvements. Under the direction of Interior Secretary Harold L. Ickes, the PWA indirectly served the purpose of work relief. Ickes focused it on well-planned permanent improvements, and he used private contractors rather than workers on the government payroll. PWA workers built Virginia's Skyline Drive, New York's Triborough Bridge, the Overseas Highway from Miami to Key West, and Chicago's subway system.

The more controversial and ambitious part of the NIRA created the National Recovery Administration (NRA), headed by Hugh S. Johnson, a colorful retired army general. Its purpose was twofold: to stabilize business by reducing chaotic competition through the implementation of industry-wide codes that set wages and prices and to generate more purchasing power for consumers by providing jobs, defining labor standards, and raising wages. In each major industry, committees representing management, labor, and government drew up the codes of fair practice. The labor standards featured in every code set a forty-hour workweek and minimum weekly wages of $13 ($12 in the South, where living costs were lower), which more than doubled earnings in some cases. Announcement of a proviso prohibiting child labor under the age of sixteen did "in a few minutes what neither law nor constitutional amendment had been able to do in forty years," Johnson said.

Labor unions, already hard pressed by the economic downturn and a loss of members, were understandably concerned about the NRA's efforts to reduce competition by allowing competing businesses to cooperate in fixing

The Spirit of the New Deal!

In this cartoon, employer and employee agree to cooperate in the spirit of unity that inspired the National Recovery Administration.

wages and prices. To gain their support, the NRA included a provision that guaranteed the right of workers to organize unions. But while prohibiting employers from interfering with labor-organizing efforts, the NRA did not create adequate enforcement measures, nor did it require employers to bargain in good faith with labor representatives.

For a time the NRA worked, perhaps because an air of confidence had overcome the depression blues and the downward spiral of wages and prices had subsided. But as soon as economic recovery began, business owners expressed growing hostility toward NRA codes. Charges mounted that the larger companies dominated the code authorities and that price-fixing robbed small producers of the chance to compete. In 1934 an investigating committee substantiated some of the charges. Moreover, limiting industrial production had discouraged capital investment. And because the NRA wage codes excluded agricultural and domestic workers, three out of every four employed African Americans derived no direct benefit from the program. By 1935 the NRA had developed more critics than friends. When it effectively died, in May 1935, struck down by the Supreme Court as unconstitutional, few paused to mourn.

Yet the NRA experiment left an enduring mark. With dramatic suddenness the industry codes had set new workplace standards, such as the forty-hour workweek and the abolition of child labor. The NRA's endorsement of collective bargaining spurred the growth of unions. Moreover, the codes advanced trends toward stabilization and rationalization that were becoming the standard practice of business at large and that, despite misgivings about the concentration of power, would be further promoted by trade associations. Yet as 1934 ended, economic recovery was nowhere in sight.

REGIONAL PLANNING   The wide-ranging scope of the New Deal embraced several pathbreaking ideas. The creation of the Tennessee Valley Authority (TVA) was a truly bold and original venture designed to bring electrical power and jobs to one of the poorest regions in the nation. In May 1933 Congress created the TVA as a multipurpose public corporation. By 1936 it had six dams completed or under way and a master plan to build nine high dams on the Tennessee River, which would create the "Great Lakes of the South," and other dams on the tributaries. The agency, moreover,

Norris Dam

The massive dam in Tennessee, completed in 1936, was essential to the TVA's effort to expand power production.

opened the rivers to navigation, fostered soil conservation and forestry, experimented with fertilizers, drew new industry to the region, encouraged the formation of labor unions, improved schools and libraries, and sent cheap electric power pulsating through the valley for the first time. But the construction of dams and the creation of huge power-generating lakes also meant the destruction of homes and communities. "I don't want to move," said an elderly East Tennessee woman. "I want to sit here and look out over these hills where I was born."

Cheap electricity became more and more the TVA's reason for being—a purpose that would become all the more important during World War II. The TVA's success at generating greater power consumption and lowering utility rates in distressed areas awakened private utilities to the mass consumer

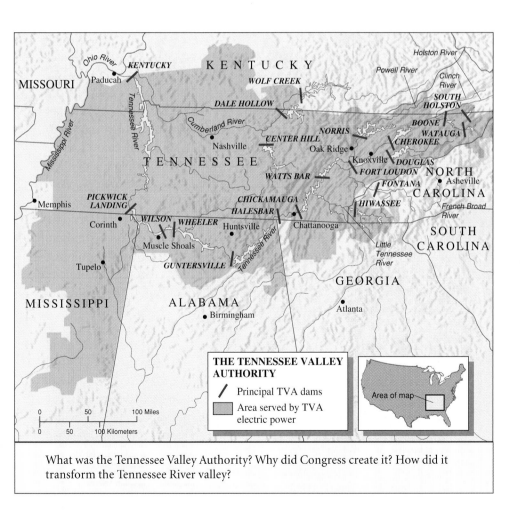

What was the Tennessee Valley Authority? Why did Congress create it? How did it transform the Tennessee River valley?

markets. Cheap power transported farmers of the valley from the age of kerosene to the age of electricity. The TVA's first rural cooperative, set up at Corinth, Mississippi, in 1934, pointed the way to the electrification of the nation's farms in the decade that followed.

THE HUMAN COST OF THE DEPRESSION

Although New Deal programs helped ease the devastation wrought by the Depression, they did not restore prosperity or end the widespread human suffering. The Depression continued to take a toll on ordinary Americans: factory workers, farmers, bankers, and professionals remained in the throes of a shattered economy that was only slowly working its way back to health.

CONTINUING HARDSHIPS   As late as 1939, some 9.5 million workers (17 percent of the labor force) remained unemployed. Prolonged economic hardship continued to create personal tragedies and tremendous social strains. Poverty led desperate people to do desperate things. Petty theft soared during the 1930s, as did street-corner begging and prostitution. Although the divorce rate dropped during the decade, in part because couples could not afford to live separately or pay the legal fees to obtain a divorce, all too often husbands down on their luck simply deserted their wives. A 1940 survey revealed that 1.5 million husbands had left home. With their future uncertain, married couples often decided not to have children; the birthrate plummeted. Parents sometimes could not support their children. In 1933 the Children's Bureau reported that one out of every five children was not getting enough to eat. Often struggling parents sent their children to live with relatives or friends. Some 900,000 children simply left home and joined the army of homeless "tramps."

DUST-BOWL MIGRANTS   In the southern plains of the Midwest and the Mississippi River valley, a decade-long drought during the 1930s helped produce an environmental and human catastrophe known as the dust bowl. Colorado, New Mexico, Kansas, Nebraska, Texas, and Oklahoma were the hardest hit. Crops withered and income plummeted. Unrelenting winds swept across the treeless plains, scooping up millions of tons of parched topsoil into billowing dark clouds that floated east across entire states, engulfing farms and towns in what were called black blizzards. A massive dust storm in May 1934 darkened skies from Colorado to the Atlantic seaboard, depositing silt on porches and rooftops as well as on ships in the Atlantic Ocean. In 1937 there were seventy-two such major dust storms. The worst of them killed livestock and people and caused railroads to derail and automobiles to career off roads. By 1938 over 25 million acres of prairie land had lost most of its topsoil.

What made these dust storms worse than normal was the transition during the early twentieth century from scattered subsistence farming to widespread industrial agriculture, in which "factory farms" used dry-farming techniques to plant vast acres of wheat, corn, and cotton. The advent of powerful tractors, deep-furrow plows, and mechanical harvesters greatly increased the scale and intensity of farming—and the indebtedness of farmers. The mercurial cycle of falling crop prices and rising indebtedness led farmers to plant as much and as often as they could. Overfarming and overgrazing disrupted the fragile ecology of the plains by decimating the native prairie grasses that stabilized the nutrient-rich topsoil. Constant plowing loosened vast amounts of dirt that were easily swept up by powerful winds during the devastating drought of the 1930s. Hordes of grasshoppers followed the gigantic dust storms and devoured what meager crops were left standing.

Human misery paralleled the environmental devastation. The dust storms penetrated windows and doors. A Kansas woman reported that the grit "got into cupboards and clothes closets; our faces were as dirty as if we had rolled in the dirt; our hair was gray and stiff and we ground dirt between our teeth." Parched farmers could not pay mortgages, and banks foreclosed on their property. Suicides and divorces soared. With each year, millions of people abandoned their farms. Uprooted farmers and their families formed a migratory stream rushing from the South and the Midwest toward California, buoyed by currents of hope and desperation. The West Coast was rumored to have plenty of jobs. So off they went on a cross-country trek in pursuit of new opportunities. Although frequently lumped together as "Okies," most of the dust-bowl refugees were actually from cotton belt communities in Arkansas, Texas, and Missouri, as well as Oklahoma. During the 1930s and 1940s, some 800,000 people left those four states and headed to the Far West. Not all were farmers; many were white-collar workers and retailers whose jobs had been tied to the health of the agriculture sector. Most of the dust-bowl migrants were white, and most were young adults in their twenties and thirties who relocated with spouses and children. Some traveled on trains or buses; others hopped a freight train or hitched a ride; most rode in their own cars, the trip taking four to five days on average.

Dust Storm Approaching, 1930s

When a dust storm blew in, it brought utter darkness, as well as the sand and grit that soon covered every surface, both indoors and out.

Most of the dust bowl migrants who had come from cities gravitated to California's urban areas—Los Angeles, San Diego, or San Francisco. Many of the newcomers, however, moved into the San Joaquin Valley, the agricultural heartland of the state. There they discovered that California was no paradise. Only a few of the migrants could afford to buy land. Most found themselves competing with local Latinos and Asians for seasonal work as pickers in the cotton fields or orchards of large corporate farms. Living in tents or crude cabins and frequently on the move, they suffered from exposure and poor sanitation.

They also felt the sting of social prejudice. John Steinbeck explained that "Okie us'ta mean you was from Oklahoma. Now it means you're a dirty son-of-a-bitch. Okie means you're scum. Don't mean nothing in itself, it's the way they say it." Such hostility toward the migrants drove one third of the "Okies" to return to their home states. Most of the farmworkers who stayed tended to fall back upon their old folkways rather than assimilate themselves into their new surroundings. These gritty "plain folk" had brought with them their own prejudices against blacks and ethnic minorities, as well as a potent tradition of evangelical Protestantism and a distinctive style of music variously labeled country, hillbilly, or cowboy. This "Okie" subculture remains a vivid part of California society.

MINORITIES AND THE NEW DEAL   The Depression was especially traumatic for the most disadvantaged groups in American society. However progressive Franklin Roosevelt was on social issues, he failed to assault long-standing patterns of racism and segregation for fear of alienating conservative southern Democrats in Congress. As a result, many of the New Deal programs were for whites only. The Federal Housing Administration, for example, re-fused to guarantee mortgages on houses purchased by blacks in white neigh-borhoods. Both the CCC and the TVA practiced racial segregation.

The efforts of the Roosevelt administration to raise crop prices by reducing production proved especially devastating for African Americans and Mexican Americans. To earn the federal payments for reducing crops as provided by the AAA and other New Deal agriculture programs, many farm owners would first take out of cultivation the marginal lands worked by tenants and sharecroppers. The effect was to drive the landless off farms and eliminate the jobs of many migrant workers. Over 200,000 black tenant farmers na-tionwide were displaced by the AAA.

Mexican Americans suffered even more. Thousands of Mexicans had migrated to the United States during the 1920s, most of them settling in California, New Mexico, Arizona, Colorado, Texas, and the midwestern states. But because many Mexican Americans were unable to prove their cit-izenship, either out of ignorance of the regulations or because their migra-tory work hampered their ability to meet residency requirements, they were denied access to the new federal relief programs under the New Deal. As economic conditions worsened, government officials called for the depor-tation of Mexican-born Americans to avoid the cost of providing them with public services and relief. By 1935, over 500,000 Mexican Americans and their American-born children had returned to Mexico. The state of Texas alone returned over 250,000 people.

Deportation became a popular solution in part because of the rising level of involvement of Mexican-American workers in union activities. In 1933 Mexican-American women in El Paso, Texas, formed the Society of Female Manufacturing Workers to protest wages as low as 75¢ a day. In the same year some 18,000 Mexican cotton pickers went on strike in California's San Joaquin Valley. Police crushed the strike by burning the workers' camps.

Native Americans were also devastated by the Great Depression. They ini-tially were encouraged by Roosevelt's appointment of John Collier as the commissioner of the Bureau of Indian Affairs (BIA). Collier steadily in-creased the number of Native Americans employed by the BIA and strove to ensure that Indians gained access to the various relief programs. Collier's primary objective, however, was passage of the Indian Reorganization Act.

He wanted the new legislation to replace the provisions of the General Allotment Act (1887), known as the Dawes Act, which had sought to "Americanize" the Indians by breaking up their tribal land and allocating it to individuals. Collier insisted that the Dawes Act had produced only widespread poverty and demoralization. He hoped to reinvigorate Indian cultural traditions by restoring land to tribes, granting Indians the right to charter business enterprises and establish self-governing constitutions, and providing federal funds for vocational training and economic development. The act that Congress finally passed was a much-diluted version of Collier's original proposal, however, and the "Indian New Deal" brought only a partial improvement to the lives of Native Americans.

COURT DECISIONS AND CIVIL RIGHTS   Although the NAACP's legal campaign against racial prejudice gathered momentum during the 1930s, a major setback occurred in *Grovey v. Townsend* (1935), which upheld the Texas Democrats' white primary. But the *Grovey* decision held for only nine years and marked the end of the major decisions that for half a century had narrowed application of the Reconstruction amendments. A reversal had already set in. Two important precedents rose from the celebrated Scottsboro case in 1931, in which nine black youths were convicted of raping two white women while riding a freight train in Alabama. The first verdict failed, the high court ruled in *Powell v. Alabama* (1932), because the judge had not

The Scottsboro Case

Heywood Patterson (center), one of the defendants in the case, is seen here with his attorney, Samuel Liebowitz (left) in Decatur, Alabama, in 1933.

ensured that the accused were provided adequate defense attorneys. In *Norris v. Alabama* (1935), another verdict fell to the judgment that the systematic exclusion of African Americans from Alabama juries had denied the defendants equal protection of the law—a principle that had significant and widespread impact on state courts.

Like Woodrow Wilson, Franklin Roosevelt did not give a high priority to racial issues. As a consequence many of his New Deal programs failed to help minorities, and in a few instances the new initiatives discriminated against those least able to help themselves. Nevertheless, Roosevelt included in his administration people who did care deeply about racial issues. As his first term drew to a close, Roosevelt found that there was a de facto "black cabinet" of some thirty to forty advisers in government departments and agencies, people who were very concerned about racial issues and the plight of African Americans. Moreover, by 1936, many black voters were fast transferring their political loyalty from the Republicans to the Democrats and would vote accordingly in the coming presidential election.

CULTURE IN THE THIRTIES

In view of the celebrated—if exaggerated—alienation of writers, artists, and intellectuals rebelling against the materialism of the 1920s, one might have expected the onset of the Great Depression to have deepened their despair. Instead, it brought a renewed sense of militancy and affirmation, as if society could no longer afford the art-for-art's-sake outlook of the 1920s. Said one writer early in 1932: "I enjoy the period thoroughly. The breakdown of our cult of business success and optimism, the miraculous disappearance of our famous American complacency, all this is having a tonic effect."

In the early 1930s the "tonic effect" of commitment sometimes took the form of allegiance to revolution. By the summer of 1932, even the "golden boy" of the lost generation, the writer F. Scott Fitzgerald, had declared that "to bring on the revolution, it may be necessary to work within the Communist party." But few remained Communists for long. Being a notoriously independent lot, most writers rebelled at demands to hew to a shifting party line. And many abandoned communism upon learning that the Soviet leader Joseph Stalin practiced a tyranny more horrible than anything under the czars.

LITERATURE AND THE DEPRESSION   Among the writers who addressed themes of immediate social significance two novelists deserve special notice: John Steinbeck and Richard Wright. The single piece of fiction that best captured the ordeal of the Depression, Steinbeck's *The Grapes of Wrath* (1939), treated workers as people rather than just a variable in a political formula. Steinbeck had traveled with displaced "Okies" driven from the Oklahoma dust bowl by bankers and farm machines to pursue the illusion of good jobs in the fields of California's Central Valley. This firsthand experience allowed him to create a vivid tale of the Joad family's painful journey west from Oklahoma.

Among the most talented of the young novelists emerging in the 1930s was Richard Wright, an African American born near Natchez, Mississippi. The grandson of former slaves and the son of a Mississippi sharecropper who deserted his family, Wright ended his formal schooling with the ninth grade (as valedictorian of his class). He then worked in Memphis and greedily devoured books he borrowed on a white friend's library card, all the while saving up to go north to escape the racism of the segregated South. In Chicago, where he arrived on the eve of the Depression, the Federal Writers' Project gave him a chance to develop his talent. His period as a Communist, from 1934 to 1944, gave him an intellectual framework that did not overpower his fierce independence.

Native Son (1940), Wright's masterpiece, is set in the Chicago he had come to know before moving to New York. It is the story of Bigger Thomas, a product of the ghetto, a man hemmed in, and finally impelled to murder, by forces beyond his control. Somehow Wright managed to sublimate into literary power his bitterness and rage at what he called "the Ethics of Living Jim Crow."

POPULAR CULTURE   While many writers and artists dealt directly with the human suffering and social tensions aroused by the Great Depression, the more popular cultural outlets, such as radio programs and movies, provided patrons with a welcome escape from the decade's grim realities. By the 1930s radio had become a major source of family entertainment. More than 10 million families owned a radio, and by the end of the decade the number had tripled. "There is radio music in the air, every night, everywhere," reported a San Francisco newspaper. "Anybody can hear it at home on a receiving set which any boy can put up in an hour." Franklin Roosevelt was the first president to take full advantage of the popularity of radio broadcasting. He hosted sixteen "fireside chats" to generate public support for his New Deal initiatives.

In the late 1920s, what had been silent films were transformed by the introduction of sound. The "talkies" made movies by far the most popular form of entertainment during the 1930s—much more popular than they are today. The introduction of double features in 1931 and the construction of outdoor drive-in theaters in 1933 boosted interest and attendance. More than 60 percent of the population—70 million people—saw at least one movie each week.

The movies of the 1930s rarely dealt directly with hard times. Exceptions were the film version of *The Grapes of Wrath* (1940) and the classic documentaries of Pare Lorentz, *The Plow That Broke the Plains* (1936) and *The River* (1937). Much more popular were movies intended for pure entertainment; they transported viewers into the realm of adventure, spectacle, and fantasy. People relished shoot-'em-up gangster films, animated cartoons, spectacular musicals, "screwball" comedies, and horror films such as *Dracula* (1931), *Frankenstein* (1931), *The Mummy* (1932), and *Werewolf of London* (1935).

But the best way to escape the daily troubles of the Depression was to watch one of the zany comedies of the Marx Brothers, former vaudeville performers. As one Hollywood official explained, the movies of the 1930s were intended to "laugh the big bad wolf of the depression out of the public mind." *The Cocoanuts* (1929), *Animal Crackers* (1930), and *Monkey Business* (1931) introduced Americans to the anarchic antics of Chico, Groucho, Harpo, and

The Marx Brothers

In addition to their vaudeville antics, the Marx Brothers satirized social issues such as Prohibition.

Zeppo Marx, who combined slapstick humor with verbal wit to create plot-less masterpieces of irreverent satire.

The Second New Deal

During Roosevelt's first year in office, his programs and his personal charms generated massive support. The president's travels and speeches, his twice-weekly press conferences, and his radio-broadcast fireside chats brought vitality and warmth from a once-remote White House. In the congressional elections of 1934, the Democrats increased their strength in both the House and the Senate, an almost unprecedented midterm victory for a party in power. Only seven Republican governors remained in office throughout the country.

ELEANOR ROOSEVELT   One of the reasons for Roosevelt's unprecedented popularity was his wife, Eleanor, who had become an enormous political asset and would prove to be one of the most influential and revered leaders of her time. From an early age, Eleanor Roosevelt had embraced social service and shown ardent concern for the rights of women and blacks. Her compassion resulted in part from the loneliness she had experienced as she was growing up and in part from the sense of betrayal she felt upon learning in 1918 that her husband was engaged in an extramarital affair with Lucy Mercer, her personal secretary. "The bottom dropped out of my own particular world," she recalled. In the face of personal setbacks, Eleanor Roosevelt "lived to be kind." Compassionate without being maudlin, more stoic than sentimental, she exuded warmth and sincerity, and she challenged the complacency of the comfortable and the affluent. "No woman," observed a friend, "has ever so comforted the distressed or so distressed the comfortable."

The First Lady

An intelligent, principled, and candid woman, Eleanor Roosevelt became a political figure in her own right. Here she is serving as guest host for a radio program, ca. 1935.

Eleanor Roosevelt was an activist who redefined the role of the presidential spouse. She was the first woman to address a national political convention, to write a nationally syndicated column, and to hold regular press conferences. A tireless advocate and agitator, Eleanor crisscrossed the nation, representing the president and the New Deal, defying local segregation ordinances to meet with African-American leaders, supporting women's causes and organized labor, highlighting the plight of unemployed youth, and imploring Americans to live up to their egalitarian and humanitarian ideals.

Eleanor Roosevelt also became her husband's most visible and effective liaison with many liberal groups, bringing labor leaders, women activists, and black spokesmen to the White House after hours and serving to deflect criticism of the president by taking progressive stands and running political risks he himself dared not attempt. He was the politician, she once remarked, and she was the agitator.

CRITICISM   Public criticism of the New Deal during Roosevelt's first year in office was muted, but not for long. The Depression's downward slide had been halted, but unemployment remained high (10 million were out of work in 1935, more than 20 percent of the workforce), and prosperity remained elusive. "We have been patient and long suffering," said a farm leader in October 1933. "We were promised a New Deal. . . . Instead we have the same old stacked deck." Even more unsettling to some was the dramatic growth of executive power and the emergence of welfare capitalism, whereby workers developed a sense of entitlement to federal support programs. In 1934 a group of conservative businessmen and politicians, including Alfred E. Smith and John W. Davis, two former Democratic presidential candidates, formed the American Liberty League to oppose New Deal measures as violations of personal and property rights.

"The Kingfish"

Huey Long, governor of Louisiana. Although he often led people to believe he was a country bumpkin, Long was a shrewd lawyer and consummate politician.

More potent threats to Roosevelt came from the hucksters of social panaceas. The most flamboyant of the group was Louisiana's "Kingfish," Senator Huey P. Long. A short, strutting man, Long sported pink suits and pastel shirts, red ties, and two-toned shoes. He was a brilliant but unscrupulous reformer driven by a compulsive urge for power and attention. First as Louisiana's governor, then as political boss of the state, Long had delivered tax favors, roads, schools, free textbooks, charity hospitals, and better public services. That he had become a sort of state dictator in the process, using bribery, physical intimidation, and blackmail to achieve his ends, seemed irrelevant to many of his supporters.

In 1933 Long arrived in Washington as a Democratic senator. He initially supported Roosevelt and the New Deal but quickly grew suspicious of the NRA's collusion with big business. He had also grown jealous of Roosevelt's mushrooming popularity, having developed his own presidential aspirations. Promoting himself as a radical egalitarian, a true if self-indulgent friend of the people, Long had his own plan for dealing with the Great Depression.

Long's Share-the-Wealth program proposed to confiscate large personal fortunes so as to guarantee every poor family a cash grant of $5,000 and every worker an annual income of $2,500, provide pensions to the aged, reduce working hours, pay veterans' bonuses, and ensure a college education for every qualified student. It did not matter to him that his figures failed to add up or that his program offered little to promote an economic recovery. As he told a group of distressed Iowa farmers, "Maybe somebody says I don't understand it. Well, you don't have to. Just shut your damn eyes and believe it. That's all." Whether he had a workable plan or not, by early 1935 the charismatic Long was claiming 7.5 million supporters.

Another popular social scheme was hatched by a gray-haired California doctor, Francis E. Townsend. Outraged by the sight of three elderly women raking through garbage cans for scraps of food, Townsend proposed government pensions for the aged. In 1934 he began promoting the Townsend Recovery Plan, which would pay $200 a month to every citizen over sixty who retired from employment and promised to spend the money within the month. The plan had the lure of providing financial security for the aged and stimulating economic growth. Critics noted that the cost of his program for 9 percent of the population would be more than half the national income. Yet Townsend, like Long, was indifferent to details and balanced budgets. "I'm not in the least interested in the cost of the plan," he blandly told a House committee.

A third huckster of panaceas, Father Charles E. Coughlin, the Roman Catholic "radio priest," founded the National Union for Social Justice in 1935. In broadcasts over the CBS network, he promoted schemes for the coinage of silver to increase the money supply and made attacks on bankers that increasingly hinted at anti-Semitism.

Coughlin, Townsend, and Long drew support largely from desperate lower-middle-class Americans. Of the three, Long had the widest following. A 1935 survey showed that he could draw 5 million to 6 million votes as a third-party candidate for president in 1936, perhaps enough to undermine Roosevelt's chances of reelection. Beset by pressures from both ends of the political spectrum, Roosevelt hesitated for months before deciding to "steal the thunder" from the left by instituting new programs of reform and social security. "I'm fighting Communism, Huey Longism, Coughlinism, Townsendism," Roosevelt told a reporter in early 1935. He needed "to save our system, the capitalist system," from such "crackpot ideas." Political pressures impelled Roosevelt to move to the left, but so did the growing influence within the administration of jurists Louis Brandeis and Felix Frankfurter. These powerful advisers urged Roosevelt to be less cozy with big business and to push for restored competition in the market place and heavy taxes on large corporations.

OPPOSITION FROM THE COURT   A series of Supreme Court decisions finally galvanized the president to act. On May 27, 1935, the Court killed the National Industrial Recovery Act by a unanimous vote. The defendants in *Schechter Poultry Corporation v. United States*, quickly tagged the sick-chicken case, had been convicted of selling an "unfit chicken" and violating other NRA code provisions. The high court ruled that Congress had delegated too much power to the executive branch when it granted the code-making authority to the NRA and Congress had exceeded its power under the commerce clause by regulating intrastate commerce. The poultry in question, the Court decided, had "come to permanent rest within the state," although earlier it had been moved across state lines. In a press conference soon afterward, Roosevelt fumed: "We have been relegated to the horse-and-buggy definition of interstate commerce." The same line of reasoning, he warned, might endanger other New Deal programs.

LEGISLATIVE ACHIEVEMENTS OF THE SECOND NEW DEAL To rescue his legislative program from such judicial and political challenges, Roosevelt in 1935 launched the second phase of the New Deal. He demanded several pieces of "must" legislation, most of which Congress passed within a few months. The National Labor Relations Act, often called the Wagner Act for its sponsor, New York senator Robert Wagner, gave workers the right to bargain through unions of their own choice and prohibited employers from interfering with union activities. A National Labor Relations Board of five members could supervise plant elections and certify unions as bargaining agents where a majority of the workers approved. The board could also investigate the actions of employers and issue "cease-and-desist" orders against specified unfair practices.

The Social Security Act of 1935, Roosevelt announced, was the New Deal's "cornerstone" and "supreme achievement." Indeed, it has proved to be the most significant and far-reaching of all the New Deal initiatives. The basic concept was by no means new. Progressives during the early 1900s had proposed a federal system of social security for the aged, indigent, disabled, and unemployed. Other nations had already enacted such programs, but the United States remained steadfast in its tradition of individual self-reliance. The hardships caused by the Great Depression revived the idea, however, and Roosevelt masterfully guided the legislation through Congress.

The Social Security Act included three major provisions. Its centerpiece was a pension fund for retired people over the age of sixty-five and their survivors. Beginning in 1937, workers and employers contributed payroll taxes to establish the fund. Benefit payments started in 1940 and averaged $22 per month, a modest sum even for those depressed times. Roosevelt stressed that the pension program was not intended to guarantee a comfortable retirement; it was designed to supplement other sources of income and protect the elderly from some of the "hazards and vicissitudes of life." Only later did voters and politicians come to view Social Security as the *primary* source of retirement income for most of the aged. By 2006 the average monthly payment was over $900.

Social Security

A poster distributed by the government to educate the public about the new Social Security Act.

The Social Security Act also set up a shared federal-state unemployment-insurance program, financed by a payroll tax on employers. In addition, the new legislation committed the national government to a broad range of social-welfare activities based upon the assumption that "unemployables"—people who were unable to work—would remain a state responsibility while the national government would provide work relief for the able-bodied. To that end the law inaugurated federal grants-in-aid for three state-administered public-assistance programs — old-age assistance, aid to dependent children, aid for the blind—and further aid for maternal, child-welfare, and public health services.

Relatively speaking, the new federal program was quite conservative. It was the only government pension program in the world financed by taxes on the earnings of workers: most other countries funded such programs out of general revenues. The Social Security payroll tax was also a regressive tax in that it entailed a single fixed rate for all, regardless of income level. It thus pinched the poor more than the rich, and it also impeded Roosevelt's efforts to revive the economy because it removed from circulation a significant amount of money: the new Social Security tax took money out of workers' pockets and placed it into a retirement trust fund, exacerbating the shrinking money supply that was one of the main causes of the Depression. By taking discretionary income away from workers, the government blunted the sharp increase in public consumption needed to restore the health of the economy. In addition, the Social Security system initially excluded 9.5 million workers who most needed the new program: farm laborers, domestic workers, and the self-employed, a disproportionate percentage of whom were African Americans.

Roosevelt regretted the limitations, but he knew that they were necessary compromises in order to see the Social Security Act through Congress and enable it to withstand court challenges. As he replied to an aide who criticized funding the pension program through employee contributions:

> I guess you're right on the economics, but those taxes were never a problem of economics. They are politics all the way through. We put those payroll contributions there so as to give the contributors a moral, legal, and political right to collect their pensions and their unemployment benefits. With those taxes in there, no damn politician can ever scrap my Social Security program.

Another major bill making up the second phase of the New Deal was the Revenue Act of 1935, sometimes called the Wealth-Tax Act but popularly known as the soak-the-rich tax. The Revenue Act raised tax rates on income above $50,000. Estate and gift taxes also rose, as did the corporate tax on all but small corporations (those with an annual income below $50,000).

Business leaders fumed over Roosevelt's tax and spending policies. They railed against the New Deal and Roosevelt, whom they called a traitor to his own class. By "soaking" the rich, Roosevelt stole much of the thunder from the political left, although the results of his tax policy fell short of the promise. The new soak-the-rich tax failed to increase federal revenue significantly, nor did it result in a significant redistribution of income. Still, the prevailing view among conservatives was that Roosevelt had moved in a radical direction. The newspaper editor William Randolph Hearst growled that the wealth tax was "essentially communism. This bastard proposal should be ascribed to a composite personality which might be labeled Stalin Delano Roosevelt." Roosevelt countered by stressing his own basic conservatism and asserted that he had no love for socialism: "I am fighting communism. . . . I want to save our system, the capitalistic system." Yet he added that to save it from revolutionary turmoil required a more equal "distribution of wealth."

ROOSEVELT'S SECOND TERM

THE ELECTION OF 1936   On June 27, 1936, Roosevelt accepted the Democratic party's presidential nomination for a second term. He promised to continue to promote a government motivated by "a spirit of charity" rather than a government "frozen in the ice of its own indifference." The popularity of Roosevelt and the New Deal impelled the Republican Convention in 1936 to avoid candidates too closely identified with the "hate-Roosevelt" contingent. The party chose Governor Alfred M. Landon of Kansas, a former Progressive Republican who had endorsed many New Deal programs. He was probably more liberal than most of his backers and clearly more so than the party's platform, which accused the New Deal of overextending federal power.

The Republicans hoped that the followers of Long, Coughlin, Townsend, and other dissidents would combine to draw enough Democratic votes away from Roosevelt to throw the election to them. But that possibility faded when an assassin, the son-in-law of a Louisiana judge whom Long had sought to remove, gunned down the Kingfish in 1935. In the 1936 election Coughlin, Townsend, and a remnant of the Long movement supported Representative William Lemke of North Dakota on a Union party ticket, but it was a forlorn effort, polling only 882,000 votes.

In 1936 Roosevelt forged a new electoral coalition that would affect national politics for years to come. While holding the support of most traditional Democrats, North and South, the president made strong gains in the West among beneficiaries of New Deal agricultural programs. In the northern cities he held on to the ethnic groups helped by New Deal welfare measures. Middle-class voters, whose property had been saved by New Deal measures, flocked to support Roosevelt, as did intellectuals stirred by the ferment of new ideas coming from the government. The revived labor movement threw its support to Roosevelt, and in the most profound new departure of all, African-American voters for the first time cast the majority of their ballots for a Democratic president. "My friends, go home and turn Lincoln's picture to the wall," a Pittsburgh journalist told black Republicans. "That debt has been paid in full." The final tally in the 1936 election revealed that 81 percent of those with an income under $1,000 a year opted for Roosevelt, as did 79 percent of those earning between $1,000 and $2,000. By contrast, only 46 percent of those earning over $5,000 voted for Roosevelt. He later claimed that never before had business leaders been "so united against one candidate." They were "unanimous in their hate for me—and I welcome their hatred." In the 1936 election, Roosevelt wound up carrying every state except Maine and Vermont, with a popular vote of 27.7 million to Landon's 16.7 million. Democrats would also dominate Republicans in the new Congress, by 77 to 19 in the Senate and 328 to 107 in the House.

THE COURT-PACKING PLAN   Soon after his landslide reelection, however, Roosevelt found himself deluged in a sea of troubles. His second inaugural address, delivered on January 20, 1937, promised even greater reforms. The challenge to American democracy, he maintained, was that millions of citizens "at this very moment are denied the greater part of what the very lowest standards of today call the necessities of life. . . . I see one-third of a nation ill-housed, ill-clad, ill-nourished." The election of 1936 had been a mandate for even more extensive government action, he argued, and the overwhelming Democratic majorities in Congress ensured the passage of new legislation to buttress the Second New Deal. But one major roadblock stood in the way: the Supreme Court.

By the end of its 1936 term, the Court had ruled against New Deal programs in seven of the nine major cases it reviewed. Suits against the Social Security and Wagner Acts were pending. Given the conservative tenor of the Court, the Second New Deal seemed in danger of being nullified, just as much of the original New Deal had been.

For that reason, Roosevelt resolved to change the Court's philosophy by enlarging it, a move for which there was ample precedent and power. Congress, not the Constitution, determines the size of the Court, which at different times has numbered six, seven, eight, nine, and ten justices, and in 1937 numbered nine. On February 5 Roosevelt sent his plan to Congress, without having consulted congressional leaders. He wanted to create up to fifty new federal judges, including six new Supreme Court justices, and diminish the power of the judges who had served ten or more years or reached the age of seventy.

But the "Court-packing" maneuver, as opponents quickly tagged the president's scheme, backfired. It was a shade too contrived, much too brazen, and far too political. The normally pro–New Deal *New York World-Telegram* dismissed it as "too clever, too damned clever." By implying that some judges were impaired by senility, Roosevelt affronted the elder statesmen of Congress and the Court, especially Justice Louis D. Brandeis, who was both the oldest

"Court-Packing"

An editorial cartoon commenting on Roosevelt's grandiose plan to enlarge the Supreme Court. He is speaking to Harold Ickes, director of the Public Works Administration (PWA).

and the most liberal of the Supreme Court judges. Roosevelt's Court-packing plan also ran headlong into a deep-rooted public veneration of the courts and aroused fears that another president might use the precedent for quite different purposes.

As it turned out, unforeseen events blunted Roosevelt's drive to change the Court. A sequence of Court decisions during the spring of 1937 reversed previous judgments in order to uphold the Wagner and Social Security Acts. In addition, a conservative justice resigned, and Roosevelt named to the vacancy one of the most consistent New Dealers, Senator Hugo Black of Alabama.

Roosevelt later claimed he had lost the battle but won the war. The Court had reversed itself on important New Deal legislation, and the president was able to appoint justices in harmony with the New Deal. But the episode created dissension within the Democratic party and blighted Roosevelt's prestige. For the first time, Democrats in large numbers, especially southerners, opposed the president, and the Republican opposition found a powerful new issue to use against the administration. During the first eight months of 1937, the momentum of Roosevelt's 1936 landslide victory was lost. As Secretary of Agriculture Henry Wallace later remarked, "The whole New Deal really went up in smoke as a result of the Supreme Court fight."

A NEW DIRECTION FOR LABOR   Rebellions erupted on other fronts even while the Court-packing bill pended. Under the impetus of the New Deal, the dormant labor-union movement stirred anew. When the National Industrial Recovery Act demanded that every industry code include a statement of the workers' right to organize a union, alert unionists quickly translated it to mean "the president wants you to join the union."

John L. Lewis, head of the United Mine Workers, was among the first to exploit the spirit of the NIRA. Leading a union decimated by the depression, he rebuilt it from 150,000 members to 500,000 within a year. Spurred by the mine workers' example, Sidney Hillman of the Amalgamated Clothing Workers and David Dubinsky of the International Ladies Garment Workers joined Lewis in promoting a campaign to organize workers in the mass-production industries. As leaders of some of the few industrial unions (made up of all types of workers) in the AFL, they found the more restrictive craft unions (made up only of skilled male workers) to be obstacles to organizing the basic industries.

In 1935, with passage of the Wagner Act, the industrial unionists formed a Committee for Industrial Organization (CIO), and craft unionists began to fear submergence by the mass unions. Jurisdictional disputes divided them, and in 1936 the AFL expelled the CIO unions, which then formed a permanent structure, called after 1938 the Congress of Industrial Organizations (also known by the initials CIO). The rivalry spurred both groups to greater efforts.

The CIO's major organizing drives in the automobile and steel industries began in 1936, but until the Supreme Court upheld the Wagner Act in 1937, companies had failed to cooperate with its provisions. Employers used blacklisting, private detectives, labor spies, vigilante groups, and other forms of intimidation to fight the infant unions. Early in 1937 automobile workers spontaneously adopted a new technique, the "sit-down strike," in which workers refused to leave a workplace until employers granted collective-bargaining rights to their union.

Led by the fiery young autoworker and union organizer Walter Reuther, thousands of employees at the General Motors assembly plants in Flint, Michigan, occupied the factories and stopped all production. Female workers supported their male counterparts by picketing at the plant entrances. The wives, daughters, and mothers of the strikers formed a Women's Auxiliary to feed the "sit-down" strikers who slept at the plants. Management refused to recognize the union efforts. Company officials called in police to harass the strikers, sent spies to union meetings, and threatened to fire the

Organized Labor

CIO pickets jeer as nonstriking workers enter a mill, 1941.

workers. They also pleaded with President Roosevelt to dispatch federal troops. He refused, while expressing his displeasure with the sit-down strike. The standoff lasted over a month. Then, on February 11, the company relented and signed a contract recognizing the United Automobile Workers as a legitimate union. Other automobile manufacturers soon followed suit. And the following month, U.S. Steel capitulated to the Steel Workers Organizing Committee (later the United Steelworkers of America), granting it recognition, a 10 percent wage hike, and a forty-hour workweek.

The Wagner Act put the power of the federal government behind the principle of unionization. Roosevelt himself, however, had come late to the support of unions and sometimes took exception to their behavior. In the fall of 1937, he became so irritated with the warfare between the mercurial John L. Lewis and the Republic Steel Corporation that he pronounced "a plague on both your houses." The pompous Lewis, who for a year had been trying to organize a union for steelworkers, responded, "It ill behooves one who has supped at labor's table and who has been sheltered in labor's house to curse with equal fervor and fine impartiality both labor and its adversaries when they become locked in a deadly embrace." In 1940 an angry Lewis would back the Republican presidential candidate, but he would be unable to carry the labor vote with him. As wage workers became more organized, they more closely identified with the Democratic party. By August 1937 the CIO claimed over 3.4 million members, more than the AFL. The unions made a difference in the lives of workers and in the political scene. Through their efforts, wages rose and working conditions improved. Whether by design or accident, Roosevelt and the Democratic party were the beneficiaries of the labor movement. Workers became active voters and reliable Democrats. But unions made little headway in the South, where conservative Democrats and mill owners stubbornly opposed efforts to organize workers.

A SLUMPING ECONOMY   During the years 1935 and 1936 the economy finally showed signs of revival. By the spring of 1937, output had moved above the 1929 level. The prosperity of early 1937 was achieved largely through government spending. But in 1937 Roosevelt, worried about federal deficits and rising inflation, ordered sharp cuts in government spending. At the same time the Treasury began to diminish disposable income by collecting $2 billion in Social Security payroll taxes. Private spending could not fill the gap left by reductions in government spending, and business still lacked the faith to risk large investments. The result was that the economy suddenly stalled and then slid into a business slump deeper than that of 1929. The Dow Jones stock average fell some 40 percent between

August and October of 1937. By the end of the year, 2 million more people had been thrown out of work.

The 1937 recession ignited a fierce debate within the administration. One group, led by Treasury Secretary Henry Morgenthau Jr., favored less spending and a balanced budget. The slow pace of recovery, Morgenthau thought, resulted from the reluctance of business to invest, which resulted in turn from a fear that federal spending would bring inflation and heavy taxes. The other group, which included Harry Hopkins and Harold Ickes, argued for renewed government spending. The recession, they noted, had come just when the budget was brought into balance. Their view echoed that of the English economist John Maynard Keynes, who had explored the idea in his book *The General Theory of Employment, Interest, and Money* (1935). Keynesian economics offered a convenient theoretical justification for what New Dealers had already done in pragmatic response to existing conditions.

ECONOMIC POLICY AND LATER REFORMS   Roosevelt waited as the rival theorists sought his approval. When the spring of 1938 failed to bring economic recovery, he endorsed the ideas of the spenders. On April 14, 1938, he asked Congress to adopt a large-scale federal spending program, and Congress voted $3.3 billion in new expenditures. In a short time the increase in spending reversed the economy's decline, but the recession and Roosevelt's reluctance to adopt the truly massive, sustained government spending called for in Keynesian theory forestalled the achievement of full recovery. Only during World War II would employment reach pre-1929 levels.

The Court-packing fight, the sit-down strikes, and the 1937 recession all undercut Roosevelt's prestige and dissipated the mandate of the 1936 elections. When the 1937 congressional session ended, the only major new reforms enacted were the Wagner-Steagall National Housing Act and the Bankhead-Jones Farm Tenant Act. In 1938 the Democratic Congress enacted three more major reforms, the last of the New Deal era: the second Agricultural Adjustment Act; the Food, Drug and Cosmetic Act; and the Fair Labor Standards Act.

The Housing Act set up the U.S. Housing Authority (USHA) in the Department of the Interior, which extended long-term loans to local agencies willing to assume part of the cost of slum clearance and public housing. The agency also subsidized rents for poor people. Later, during World War II, it financed housing in connection with new defense plants.

The Farm Tenant Act addressed the epidemic of rural poverty. In some ways the New Deal's larger farm program, the AAA, had aggravated agrarian distress;

although tenants were supposed to be kept on in spite of government-sponsored cutbacks in production, landlords often simply evicted workers and pocketed their share of benefit payments. The Farm Tenant Act was administered by a new agency, the Farm Security Administration (FSA). The program made available rehabilitation loans to shore up marginally profitable farmers and prevent their sinking into tenancy. It also made loans to tenants for the purchase of their own farms. In the end, however, the FSA proved to be little more than another relief operation that tided a few farmers over difficult times. Sadly, a more effective answer to the problem awaited national mobilization for war, which landed many tenants in the military services or defense industries, broadened their horizons, and taught them new skills.

The Agricultural Adjustment Act of 1938 was a response to the renewed crop surpluses and price declines of the recession. It reenacted the basic devices of the earlier AAA. The new Food, Drug, and Cosmetic Act broadened the coverage of the 1906 Pure Food and Drug Act and forbade the use of false or misleading advertising. Enforcement of the advertising provision became the responsibility of the Federal Trade Commission. The Fair Labor Standards Act applied only to enterprises that operated in or affected *interstate* commerce. It set a minimum wage of 40¢ an hour and a maximum workweek of forty hours, to be put into effect over several years. The act also prohibited child labor under the age of sixteen.

THE LEGACY OF THE NEW DEAL

SETBACKS FOR THE PRESIDENT   By the late 1930s the Democratic party was fragmenting. The conservative southern wing felt threatened when in 1936 the Democratic Convention eliminated the two-thirds rule for nominations, thereby removing the South's veto power, and seated African-American delegates. Many southern Democrats balked at the national party's growing dependence on organized labor and northern blacks. Ellison "Cotton Ed" Smith of South Carolina and several other southern delegates walked out of the 1936 convention, with Smith declaring that he would not support any party that views "the Negro as a political and social equal." Other critics believed that Roosevelt was exercising too much power and opposed his deficit-spending philosophy. Some disgruntled southern Democrats drifted toward a coalition with conservative Republicans. By the end of 1937, a bipartisan conservative bloc had coalesced against the New Deal.

In 1938 the conservative opposition stymied an attempt by Roosevelt to reorganize the executive branch, claiming that it would lead to dictatorship.

Members of the opposition also secured drastic cuts in the undistributed-profits and capital-gains taxes to help restore business "confidence." That year the House of Representatives set up a Committee on Un-American Activities, chaired by Martin Dies of Texas, who took to the warpath against Communists. Soon he began to brand New Dealers as Red dupes. "Stalin baited his hook with a 'progressive' worm," Dies wrote in 1940, "and New Deal suckers swallowed the bait, hook, line, and sinker."

As the political season of 1938 advanced, Roosevelt unfolded a new idea as momentous as the Court-packing plan—a proposal to reshape the Democratic party in the image of the New Deal. He announced his purpose to intervene in Democratic primaries as the party leader, "charged with the responsibility of carrying out the definitely liberal declaration of principles set forth in the 1936 Democratic platform." He wanted his own supporters nominated in the state primaries. Instead of succeeding, however, the effort backfired and broke the spell of Roosevelt's invincibility, or what was left of it. As in the Court-packing fight, the president had risked his prestige while handing his adversaries a combustible issue to use against him. His opponents tagged his intervention in the primaries an attempt to "purge" the Democratic party of its southern conservatives; the word evoked visions of Adolf Hitler and Joseph Stalin, tyrants who had purged their Nazi and Communist parties with blood.

The elections of November 1938 handed the administration another setback, a result partly of the friction among the Democrats. Roosevelt had failed utterly in his efforts to liberalize the party by ousting southern conservatives. The Democratic dominance in the House fell from 229 to 93, in the Senate from 56 to 42. The margins remained large, but the president now headed a divided party. In his State of the Union message in 1939, Roosevelt for the first time proposed no new reforms but spoke of the need "to invigorate the process of [economic] recovery, in order to *preserve* our reforms." In the same year the administration won an extension of Social Security and finally put through a diluted version of its reorganization plan. Under the Administrative Reorganization Act the president could "reduce, coordinate, consolidate, and reorganize" government agencies. Thereafter, however, Roosevelt lost widespread congressional and popular support. The conservative coalition of Republicans and southern Democrats had stalemated the Roosevelt juggernant. As one observer noted, the New Deal "has been reduced to a movement with no program, with no effective political organization, with no vast popular party strength behind it."

A HALFWAY REVOLUTION   The New Deal had lost momentum, but it had wrought several enduring changes. By the end of the 1930s, the power of the national government was vastly enlarged over what it had been in 1932, and hope had been restored to people who had grown disconsolate. But the New Deal entailed more than just bigger government and revived public confidence. It also constituted a significant change from the older liberalism embodied in the Progressivism of Theodore Roosevelt and Woodrow Wilson. Those reformers, despite their sharp differences, had assumed that the function of progressive government was to use aggressive regulation of industry and business to ensure that the people had an equal opportunity to pursue their notions of happiness.

Franklin Roosevelt and the New Dealers went beyond this concept of a regulatory state by insisting that the government not simply *respond* to social crises but also take positive steps to *avoid* them. To this end the New Deal's various welfare and benefit programs conferred on the government the responsibility to ensure a minimum level of well-being for all Americans. The New Deal had established minimum qualitative standards for labor conditions and public welfare and helped middle-class Americans hold on to their savings, their homes, and their farms. The protection afforded by bank-deposit insurance, unemployment pay, and Social Security pensions would come to be universally accepted as a safeguard against future depressions.

The old Progressive formulation of regulation versus trust-busting was now superseded by the rise of the "broker state," a powerful federal government that mediated among major interest groups. Government's role was to act as an honest broker protecting a variety of interests, not just big business but workers, farmers, consumers, small business, the unemployed, and retirees.

In implementing his domestic program, Roosevelt steered a zigzag course between the extremes of laissez-faire capitalism and socialism. The first New Deal had experimented for a time with a managed economy under the NRA but had abandoned that experiment for a turn toward enforcing competition and priming the economy with increased government spending. This tactic finally produced full employment during World War II.

Roosevelt himself, impatient with political theory, was flexible in developing policy: he kept what worked and discarded what did not. The result was, paradoxically, both profoundly revolutionary and profoundly conservative. Roosevelt sharply increased the regulatory functions of the federal government and laid the foundation for what would become an expanding welfare system. Despite what his critics charged, however, his initiatives fell far short of socialism; they left the basic capitalist structure in place. In the process of such bold experimentation and dynamic preservation, the New Deal represented a "halfway revolution" that permanently altered the nation's social and political landscape.

MAKING CONNECTIONS

- In the mid-1930s, just as Roosevelt was getting the New Deal into place, the growing conflict in Europe began to consume more and more of his (and America's) attention: Chapter 29 shows how Roosevelt went from combating the Depression to leading the United States into World War II.

- Harry Truman, Roosevelt's successor in the White House, tried unsuccessfully to expand the New Deal into new areas (national health insurance and federal aid to education, for example), a topic covered in Chapter 31.

FURTHER READING

A comprehensive overview of the New Deal is David M. Kennedy's *Freedom from Fear: The American People in Depression and War, 1929–1945* (1999). On the critics of the New Deal, see Alan Brinkley's *Voices of Protest: Huey Long, Father Coughlin, and the Great Depression* (1982).

James N. Gregory's *American Exodus: The Dust Bowl Migration and Okie Culture in California* (1989) describes the migratory movement's effect on American culture. On the environmental and human causes of the dust bowl, see Donald Worster, *Dust Bowl: The Southern Plains in the 1930s* (1979).

29

FROM ISOLATION
TO GLOBAL WAR

FOCUS QUESTIONS

- What was the impact of isolationism and peace movements on American politics between the two world wars?

- How did the United States respond to German aggression in Europe during the late 1930s?

- How did events in Asia lead to Japan's attack on Pearl Harbor and America's entry into the global war?

To answer these questions and access additional review material, please visit www.wwnorton.com/studyspace.

In the late 1930s, as the winds of war swept across Asia and Europe, the focus of American politics moved abruptly from domestic to foreign affairs. Another Democratic president had to shift attention from social reform to military preparedness and war. And the public again had to wrestle with a painful choice: involve the country in volatile world affairs or remain aloof and officially neutral.

POSTWAR ISOLATIONISM

THE LEAGUE AND THE UNITED STATES Between Woodrow Wilson and Franklin Roosevelt lay two decades of relative isolation from foreign entanglements. The postwar mood of detached indifference to global affairs expressed in the election of 1920 set the pattern. The voters yearned for a restored isolationism, and President-elect Harding lost little time in disposing of the League of Nations. "You just didn't want a surrender of the United States," he stressed in his victory speech. "That's why you didn't care for the League, which is now deceased." The spirit of isolation found other expressions as well: the higher tariff walls, the Red Scare, and restrictive immigration laws with which the nation all but shut the door to newcomers.

The United States may have felt the urge to insulate itself from a wicked world, but it could hardly ignore its own expanding global interests. American business now had worldwide connections. American investments and loans abroad put in circulation the dollars that purchased American exports. Overseas possessions, moreover, directly involved the country in world affairs, especially in the Pacific. Even the League of Nations was too great a fact to ignore. By the end of 1922, the United States had "unofficial observers" at the League's headquarters in Geneva, and after 1924 American diplomats gradually entered into joint efforts with the League on such matters as the international trade in illegal drugs and arms and the criminal traffic in women and children, and they took part in a variety of economic, cultural, and technical conferences.

WAR DEBTS AND REPARATIONS   Probably nothing did more to heighten American isolationism—or anti-American feeling in Europe—than the war-debt tangle. When in 1917 the Allies had begun to exhaust their ability to pay for American military supplies, the U.S. government had advanced them billions of dollars, first for the war effort and then for postwar reconstruction.

Most Americans expected the debts to be paid back, but Europeans had a different perception. In the first place, Americans who thought their loaned money had flowed to Europe were wrong: most of it went toward purchases of military supplies in the United States, which fueled American prosperity. Then, too, the Allies held off the Germans at great cost while the United States was raising an army. American states, the British noted, had repudiated debts to British investors after the American Revolution; the French pointed out that they had never been repaid for helping the Americans win the Revolution and gain their independence. But most difficult were the practical problems of repayment. To get dollars to use to pay their war debts, European nations had to sell their goods to the United States, but American tariff walls went higher in 1921 and 1922 and again in 1930, making European goods more expensive and debts harder to pay.

The French and the British had insisted that they could pay America only as they collected reparations from defeated Germany. Twice during the 1920s the resulting financial strain on Germany brought the structure of international payments to the verge of collapse, and both times the Reparations Commission called in private American bankers to work out rescue plans.

The whole structure finally did collapse during the Great Depression. In 1931 President Hoover negotiated a moratorium on both German reparations and Allied payment of war debts, thereby indirectly accepting the connection between the two. The purpose was in part to shore up American private loans of several billion dollars in Germany, which for the time had kept the international credit structure intact. Once the United States had accepted the connection between reparations and war debt, the Allies virtually canceled German reparations. At the end of 1932, after Hoover's debt moratorium ended, most of the European countries defaulted on their war debts to the United States. In retaliation, Congress passed the Johnson Debt Default Act of 1934, which prohibited even private loans to any government that had defaulted on its debts to the United States.

ATTEMPTS AT DISARMAMENT   After World War I many Americans decided that excessive armaments had caused the terrible conflict and that arms limitations would bring lasting peace. The United States had no intention of maintaining a large army, but under the building program begun in 1916, it constructed a navy second only to that of Britain. Neither the British nor the Americans had much stomach for the cost of a naval armaments race, but both shared a common concern with the alarming growth of Japanese power.

During and after the war, Japanese-American relations grew increasingly strained. The United States objected to continued Japanese encroachments in Asia. During the war, Japan had tried to expand its presence in China. In 1915 the cabinet in Tokyo issued what came to be known as the Twenty-one Demands, which would virtually have brought China under Japanese control. The United States protested, and fortunately the Japanese decided not to force their most rigorous demands. In 1917, after the United States entered the war, Viscount Kikujirō Ishii visited Washington to secure American recognition of Japan's expanding claims in Asia. Secretary of State Robert Lansing entered an ambiguous agreement that recognized Japan's "special interests" (translated by the Japanese as "paramount interests") in China. Americans were unhappy with the Lansing-Ishii Agreement, but it seemed the only way to preserve the appearance of friendship.

After the war ended, Japanese-American relations worsened. To address the problem, President Warren Harding invited eight principal foreign powers to the Washington Conference in 1921. U.S. secretary of state Charles Evans Hughes, in what was expected to be a perfunctory greeting, announced that the only way out of an armaments race "is to end it now." It was one of the most dramatic moments in American diplomatic history. In less than fifteen minutes, one electrified reporter said, Hughes had destroyed more tonnage "than all the admirals of the world have sunk in a cycle of centuries."

Delegates from the United States, Britain, Japan, France, and Italy signed a Five-Power Treaty (1922), incorporating Hughes's plan for tonnage limits on their navies and a moratorium of ten years, during which no battleships would be built. The five major powers also agreed to refrain from further fortification of their Pacific possessions. The agreement in effect partitioned the world: U.S. naval power became supreme in the Western Hemisphere, Japanese power in the western Pacific, and British power from the North Sea to Singapore.

Two other significant agreements emerged from the Washington Armaments Conference. With the Four-Power Treaty, the United States, Britain, Japan, and France agreed to respect one another's possessions in the Pacific. The Nine-Power Treaties for the first time pledged the signers to support the principle of the Open Door enunciated by Secretary of State John Hay at

The Washington Conference, 1921

The Big Five at the conference were (from left) Iyesato Tokugawa (Japan), Arthur Balfour (Great Britain), Charles Evans Hughes (United States), Aristide Briand (France), and Carlo Schanzer (Italy).

the turn of the century. The Open Door enabled all nations to compete for trade and investment opportunities in China on an equal footing rather than allow individual nations to create economic monopolies in particular regions of the country. The signers of the Nine-Power Treaties also promised to respect the territorial integrity of China. The nations involved, in addition to those signing the Five-Power Treaty, were China, Belgium, Portugal, and the Netherlands.

With these agreements in hand, Harding could boast of a brilliant diplomatic stroke that relieved citizens of the need to pay for an enlarged navy and warded off potential conflicts in the Pacific. Yet the agreements were without obligation and without teeth. The signers of the Four-Power Treaty agreed only to consult, not to help one another militarily. The formal endorsement of the Open Door in the Nine-Power Treaties was just as ineffective, and the American people remained unwilling to uphold the principle with anything but pious affirmation. The naval-disarmament treaty set tonnage limits only on capital ships (battleships and aircraft carriers); the race to build cruisers, destroyers, submarines, and other smaller craft continued. Expansionist Japan withdrew from the agreement in 1934. Thus twelve years after the Washington Conference, the dream of naval disarmament died.

THE KELLOGG-BRIAND PACT   During and after World War I the fanciful ideal of simply abolishing war captured the American imagination. In 1921 a wealthy Chicagoan founded the American Committee for the Outlawry of War. "We can outlaw this war system just as we outlawed slavery and the saloon," said one of the more enthusiastic converts.

The glorious vision of abolishing war at the stroke of a pen culminated in the signing of the Kellogg-Briand Pact in 1928. This unique treaty started with an initiative from the French foreign minister Aristide Briand, who in 1927 proposed to Secretary of State Frank B. Kellogg an agreement whereby the two countries would never go to war against each other. This innocent-seeming proposal was actually a clever ploy to draw the United States into the French security system by the back door. In any future war, for instance, such a pact would inhibit the United States from seeking reprisals in response to any French intrusions on neutral rights. Kellogg gave the idea a cool reception and was outraged to discover that Briand had urged leaders of the American peace movement to put pressure on the government to sign the accord.

Finally Kellogg turned the tables on Briand. He countered with a scheme to have all nations sign the pact. Caught in a trap of his own making, the French foreign minister finally relented. The Pact of Paris (its official name), signed on August 27, 1928, declared that the signatories "condemn recourse to war . . . and renounce it as an instrument of national policy." Eventually sixty-two nations adhered to the pact, but all reserved "self-defense" as an escape hatch. The U.S. Senate included a reservation declaring the preservation of the Monroe Doctrine necessary to self-defense and then ratified the agreement by a vote of eighty-five to one. One senator who voted for "this worthless, but perfectly harmless peace treaty" wrote a friend later that he feared it would "confuse the minds of many good people who think that peace may be secured by polite professions of neighborly and brotherly love."

THE "GOOD NEIGHBOR" POLICY   In Latin America the spirit of peace and noninvolvement helped allay long-festering resentments against "Yankee imperialism," which had been freely practiced in the Caribbean during the first two decades of the century. The Harding administration agreed in 1921 to pay the republic of Colombia the $25 million it had once demanded for America's use of Panama Canal rights. In 1924 American troops left the Dominican Republic, occupied since 1916, although U.S. officials continued to collect customs duties there for another twenty-five years.

César Augusto Sandino

The rebel leader objected to U.S. intervention in Nicaragua.

The marines left Nicaragua in 1925, but returned a year later at the outbreak of disorders and civil war. There, in 1927, the Coolidge administration brought both parties into an agreement for U.S.-supervised elections, but one rebel leader, César Augusto Sandino, held out, and the marines stayed until 1933.

The troubles in Nicaragua increased strains between the United States and Mexico. Relations had already been soured by repeated Mexican threats to expropriate American oil properties in Mexico. In 1928, however, the U.S. ambassador negotiated an agreement protecting American rights acquired before 1917. Expropriation did in fact occur in 1938, but the Mexican government agreed to reimburse American owners.

In 1928, with problems apparently clearing up in Mexico and Nicaragua, President Calvin Coolidge traveled to Havana to open the Pan-American Conference. It was an unusual gesture of friendship, and so was the choice of Charles Evans Hughes, the former secretary of state, to head the American delegation. Hughes announced the United States' intention to withdraw its marines from Nicaragua and Haiti as soon as possible, although he did block a resolution declaring that "no state has the right to intervene in the affairs of another."

At the end of 1928, President-elect Herbert Hoover toured ten Latin American nations. Once in office he reversed Woodrow Wilson's policy of refusing to recognize "bad" regimes and reverted to the older policy of recognizing governments in power, regardless of their actions. In 1930 he generated more goodwill by permitting publication of a memorandum drawn up in 1928 by Undersecretary of State J. Reuben Clark. The Clark Memorandum denied that the Monroe Doctrine justified U.S. intervention in Latin America. Although Hoover never endorsed the memorandum, he never intervened in the region. Before he left office, steps had been taken to withdraw American forces from Nicaragua and Haiti.

Franklin D. Roosevelt likewise embraced the policy of the "good neighbor" and soon advanced it in practice. In 1933, at the Seventh Pan-American Conference, the United States supported a resolution declaring that no nation "has the right to intervene in the internal or external affairs of another." Under President Franklin Roosevelt the marines completed their withdrawal from Nicaragua and Haiti, and in 1934 the president negotiated with Cuba a treaty that abrogated the Platt Amendment and thus ended the last formal claim to a right to intervene in Latin America. Roosevelt reinforced hemispheric goodwill in 1936, when he opened the Eighth Pan-American Conference with a speech declaring that outside aggressors "will find a Hemisphere wholly prepared to consult together for our mutual safety and our mutual good."

WAR CLOUDS

JAPANESE INCURSIONS INTO CHINA Improving U.S. relations in the Western Hemisphere during the 1930s proved an exception in an otherwise dismal world scene as war clouds thickened over Europe and Asia. Actual conflict erupted first in Asia, where unsettled conditions in China had invited foreign encroachments since before the turn of the century. In

1929 Chinese nationalist aspirations and China's subsequent clashes with Russia convinced the Japanese that their own extensive investments in Manchuria, including the South Manchurian Railway, were in danger.

Japanese occupation of Manchuria, a vast, contested region in northeast Asia, began with the Mukden incident of 1931, when an explosion destroyed a section of railroad track near that city (modern-day Shenyang). The Japanese army based in Manchuria to guard the railway blamed the incident on the Chinese and used it as a pretext to occupy all of Manchuria. In 1932 the Japanese converted much of Manchuria into the puppet empire of Manchukuo.

The Manchuria incident, as the Japanese called their undeclared war, flagrantly violated the Nine-Power Treaty, the Kellogg-Briand Pact, and Japan's pledges as a member of the League of Nations. But when China asked the League and the United States for help, neither responded. President Hoover was unwilling to invoke military or economic sanctions. Secretary of State Henry Stimson, who would have preferred to do more, warned in 1932 that the United States refused to recognize any treaty, agreement, or situation

Japan and China

Japan's seizure of Manchuria in 1931 prompted this American condemnation.

that violated American treaty rights, the Open Door, the territorial integrity of China, or any situation brought about by violation of the Kellogg-Briand Pact. This statement, later known as the Stimson Doctrine, had no effect on Japanese action, for soon the Japanese navy attacked and briefly occupied Shanghai, China's great port city.

Indiscriminate bombing of Shanghai's civilian population aroused indignation but no further Western action. When the League of Nations condemned Japanese aggression in 1933, Japan withdrew from the League. During the spring of 1933, hostilities in Manchuria gradually subsided and ended with a truce. Then an uneasy peace settled upon east Asia for four years, during which time Japanese military leaders further extended their political sway in Tokyo.

ITALY AND GERMANY   The rise of the Japanese militarists paralleled the rise of fascist dictators in Italy and Germany. In 1922 Benito Mussolini had seized power in Italy. After returning from World War I as a wounded veteran, he had organized the Fascist movement, a hybrid of nationalism and socialism. The Fascist program, and above all Mussolini's promise to restore order and pride in a country fragmented by dissension, enjoyed a wide appeal. Once in power, Mussolini largely abandoned the socialist part of his platform and gradually suppressed all political opposition. By 1925 he was wielding dictatorial power as Il Duce (the Leader).

There was always something ludicrous about the strutting Mussolini. Italy, after all, was a declining power. But Germany was another matter, and Americans were not amused, even at the beginning, by Il Duce's German counterpart, Adolf Hitler. Hitler's National Socialist German Workers' (Nazi) party duplicated the major features of Italian fascism, including the ancient Roman salute. The impotence of Germany's democratic Weimar Republic in the face of world depression offered Hitler his opening. Made chancellor on January 30, 1933, he swiftly won dictatorial powers from a subservient Reichstag (parliament). In 1934 he assumed the title of Reichsführer (national leader), along with absolute powers. The Nazi police state cranked up the engines of tyranny, persecuting socialists and Jews, whom Hitler blamed for Germany's troubles, and rearming in defiance of the Versailles Treaty. Hitler flouted international agreements, pulled Germany out of the League of Nations in 1933, and threatened to extend control over all German-speaking peoples. Despite one provocation after another, the European democracies lacked the will to resist his bold grab for power.

THE MOOD IN AMERICA   Most Americans, absorbed by the problems of the Depression, retreated all the more into isolationism during the

Axis Leaders

Mussolini and Hitler in Munich, June 1940.

early 1930s. In the 1932 presidential campaign, Roosevelt renounced his earlier support for the United States' joining the League of Nations. The chief exception to the administration's isolationism was Secretary of State Cordell Hull's grand scheme of reciprocal trade agreements. Hull believed that free trade among all nations would advance understanding and preserve peace. In 1934 the administration threw its support behind Hull's pet project. Over the objections of business interests and Republicans, Congress adopted the Trade Agreements Act, which authorized the president to lower tariff rates as much as 50 percent for countries that made similar concessions on American products. Agreements were made with fourteen countries by the end of 1935 and with a total of twenty-nine by 1945.

Another effort to build foreign markets involved diplomatic recognition of Soviet Russia. By 1933 the reasons for America's refusal to recognize the Bolshevik regime had grown stale. Japanese expansionism in Asia, moreover, gave Russia and the United States a common concern. Given an opening by the shift of opinion, Roosevelt invited Maksim Litvinov, Soviet commissar for foreign affairs, to visit Washington, D.C. After nine days of talks, a formal exchange of notes on November 16, 1933, signaled the renewal of diplomatic relations. Litvinov promised that his country would abstain from promoting Communist propaganda in the United States, extend religious freedom to Americans in the Soviet Union, and reopen the question of unpaid czarist debts to America.

THE EXPANDING AXIS   As the 1930s unfolded, a catastrophic chain of events in Asia and Europe sent the world hurtling toward disaster. In 1934 Japan renounced the Five-Power Treaty. The next year, Mussolini commenced an Italian conquest of Ethiopia. That same year a referendum in Germany's Saar Basin, held in accordance with the Versailles Treaty, delivered the coal-rich region into the hands of Hitler. In 1936 Hitler reoccupied the Rhineland with armed forces, a direct violation of the Versailles Treaty. The French, however, failed to summon the courage to oust the German force. The year 1936 also brought the Spanish Civil War, which began with an uprising of the Spanish armed forces in Morocco, led by General Francisco Franco. In three years, Franco had established a fascist dictatorship with help from Hitler and Mussolini while the European democracies stood by and left the Spanish republic to its fate.

On July 7, 1937, Japanese and Chinese troops clashed at the Marco Polo Bridge, west of Beijing. The incident quickly developed into a full-scale war. World War II had begun in Asia two years before it would erupt in Europe. That same year, Japan joined Germany and Italy in the "Anti-Comintern Pact," allegedly directed at the Communist threat, thus establishing the Rome-Berlin-Tokyo "Axis."

By 1938 the peace of Europe trembled in the balance. Having rebuilt the German military force, Hitler forced the *Anschluss* (union) of Austria with Germany in March 1938 and six months later took the Sudeten (German-speaking) territory from Czechoslovakia after signing an agreement at Munich, according to which Britain and France abandoned Czechoslovakia, a country that probably had the second-best army in central Europe. The mountainous Sudetenland, largely German in population, was vital to the defense of Czechoslovakia. Having promised that this was his last territorial demand, Hitler in March 1939 brazenly violated his pledge: the German army occupied the remainder of Czechoslovakia and seized formerly German territory from Lithuania. In quick succession the Spanish republic collapsed, and Mussolini conquered the kingdom of Albania. During the summer, Hitler heated up a "war of nerves" over control of the free city of Danzig (Gdánsk) and the Polish Corridor, and on September 1 Germany invaded Poland. A few days before, Hitler had signed a nonaggression pact with Soviet Russia. Having deserted

Keeping in mind the terms of the Treaty of Versailles (see page 000), explain why Hitler began his campaign of expansion by invading the Rhineland and the Sudetenland. Why would Hitler have wanted to retake the Polish Corridor? Why did the attack on Poland begin World War II whereas Hitler's previous invasions of his European neighbors did not?

Czechoslovakia, Britain and France now honored their commitment to go to war if Poland were invaded.

DEGREES OF NEUTRALITY   During these years of deepening crisis, the Western democracies seemed paralyzed, hoping in vain that each concession would appease the appetites of fascist dictators. The Americans retreated more deeply into isolation. The prevailing mood was reinforced by a Senate inquiry into the role of bankers and munitions makers in World War I. Under Senator Gerald P. Nye of North Dakota, a progressive Republican, the committee sat from 1934 to 1937 and at last concluded that bankers and munitions makers had made scandalous profits from the war. Although Nye never showed that greed for profit had impelled Woodrow Wilson to lead the U.S. into war, millions of Americans became convinced that Uncle Sam had been duped by the "merchants of death."

During the 1930s, the United States moved toward complete isolation from the quarrels of Europe. In 1935 President Roosevelt signed the first of five formal neutrality laws intended to keep the United States out of war. The Neutrality Act of 1935 forbade the sale of arms and munitions to all warring nations whenever the president proclaimed that a state of war existed, and it declared that Americans who traveled on belligerents' ships did so at their own risk. Roosevelt would have preferred discretionary authority to levy an embargo only against aggressors but reluctantly accepted the act because it would be in effect for only six months.

Yet on October 3, 1935, just weeks after Roosevelt signed the legislation, Italy invaded Ethiopia and the president invoked the act. One shortcoming became apparent right away: the key problem was neither weapons traffic nor passenger travel but trade in material not covered by the Neutrality Act. While Italy did not need to buy arms, it did need to buy raw materials, such as oil, which was not covered by the Neutrality Act. So the sanctions imposed under the act had no deterrent effect on Mussolini or his suppliers. In the summer of 1936, Italy conquered Ethiopia.

When Congress reconvened in 1936, it extended the arms embargo and added a provision forbidding loans to nations at war. Then, in July 1936, while Italian troops mopped up the last resistance in Ethiopia, the Spanish army, led by Franco, revolted against the democratic government in Madrid. Roosevelt now became an even greater isolationist than some of the country's most extreme isolationists. Although the Spanish Civil War involved a fascist uprising against a recognized democratic government, Roosevelt accepted the French and British position that only nonintervention would localize the fight. There existed, moreover, a strong bloc of pro-Franco Catholics in America, who worried that the Spanish republic was a threat to the Roman Catholic Church; they feared an atheistic Communist influence in the Spanish government. Intrigues by Spanish Communists did prove divisive, and the Soviet Union did supply aid to the republic, but it was nothing in comparison to the German and Italian assistance to Franco.

The conflict in Spain led Roosevelt to seek another "moral embargo" on the arms trade, and he asked Congress to extend the neutrality laws to cover civil wars. Congress did so in 1937 with only one dissenting vote. The Western democracies then stood by as German and Italian soldiers, planes, and armaments supported Franco's overthrow of Spanish democracy, which was completed in 1939.

In the spring of 1937, isolationist sentiment peaked in the United States. A Gallup poll found that 94 percent of its respondents preferred efforts to keep out of war over efforts to prevent war. That spring, Congress passed a fourth neutrality law. This one maintained restraints on arms sales and loans, forbade Americans to travel on the ships of nations at war, and prohibited the arming of U.S. merchant ships trading with those nations. The president also won discretionary authority to require that goods other than arms or munitions exported to warring nations be sold on a cash-and-carry basis (that is, a purchaser would have to pay cash and then carry the goods away in its own ships). This was an ingenious scheme to preserve a profitable trade without running the risk of war.

The new law faced its first test in July 1937, when Japanese and Chinese forces clashed at the Marco Polo Bridge. Since neither side declared war,

Neutrality

A 1938 cartoon shows U.S. foreign policy entangled by the serpent of isolationism.

Roosevelt was able to use his discretion in invoking the neutrality law. He decided to wait and in fact never invoked it because its net effect would have favored the Japanese. Trade in munitions to China flourished as ships carried arms across the Atlantic to England, where they were reloaded onto British ships bound for Hong Kong. Roosevelt, by his inaction, had challenged strict isolationism.

Then, on December 12, 1937, Japanese planes bombed and sank the American gunboat *Panay,* which had been lying at anchor in China, on the Yangtze (Chang) River, prominently flying the American flag; Japan also attacked three American oil tankers. Two members of the *Panay* crew and an Italian journalist died; thirty more were injured. Though the Japanese government apologized and paid reparations, the incident reinforced American animosity toward Japan. The private boycott of Japanese goods spread, but isolationist sentiment continued strong, as was vividly demonstrated by support for the Ludlow amendment in Congress. The proposed constitutional amendment would have required a public referendum for a declaration of war except in case of attack on U.S. territory. Only by the most severe pressure from the White House, and a vote of 209 to 188, was consideration of the measure tabled in 1938.

July 1937

Japanese troops enter Peking (Beijing) after the clash at the Marco Polo Bridge.

After the German occupation of Czechoslovakia in 1939, Roosevelt no longer pretended impartiality in the deepening European struggle. Hitler's violation of his Munich pledge convinced Roosevelt that the German ruler was not simply a dictator but a mad international gangster who must be stopped. Throughout late 1938 and 1939 Roosevelt struggled to educate the American public about the menace of fascism. He urged Congress to repeal the embargo and permit the United States to sell arms on a cash-and-carry basis to Britain and France, but to no avail. When the Germans attacked Poland on September 1, 1939, Roosevelt proclaimed neutrality but in a radio talk said that he would not, like Woodrow Wilson in 1914, ask Americans to remain neutral in thought because "even a neutral has a right to take account of the facts."

Roosevelt summoned Congress into special session and asked once again for amendments to the Neutrality Act. "I regret the Congress passed the Act," the president said. "I regret equally that I signed the Act." This time he got what he wanted, however. Under the Neutrality Act of 1939, Britain and France could send their own freighters to the United States, buy supplies with cash, and take away arms or anything else they wanted. American ships, on the other hand, were excluded from the ports of warring nations and from specified war zones. Roosevelt then designated as a war zone the Baltic Sea and the waters around Great Britain and Ireland from Norway south to the coast of Spain. One unintended effect of this move was to relieve Hitler of any inhibitions about using unrestricted submarine warfare to blockade Britain.

Once the great democracies of western Europe faced war, American public opinion, appalled at Hitler's tyranny, supported measures short of war to help their cause. "What the majority of the American people want," an editor wrote in the *Nation*, "is to be as un-neutral as possible without getting into war." After Hitler overran Poland in less than a month, the war in Europe settled into a stalemate during early 1940 that began to be called the phony war. What lay ahead, it seemed, was a long war of attrition in which Britain and France would have the resources to outlast Hitler. That illusion lasted through the winter.

THE STORM IN EUROPE

BLITZKRIEG   In the spring of 1940, the winter's long *Sitzkrieg*—sitting war—suddenly erupted into *Blitzkrieg*—lightning war. At dawn on April 9, without warning, Nazi troops occupied Denmark and landed along the

Norwegian coast. Denmark fell in a day, Norway within a few weeks. On May 10 Hitler unleashed dive bombers and tank divisions on neutral Belgium and the Netherlands. On May 21 German troops reached the English Channel, cutting off a British force sent to help the Belgians and the French. A desperate evacuation from the French beaches at Dunkirk enlisted every available British boat, from warship to tug. Amid the chaos some 338,000 soldiers, about one third of them French, escaped to England.

Having outflanked the forts on France's eastern perimeter of defense, the Maginot Line, the German forces rushed ahead, cutting the French armies to pieces and spreading panic. On

The Blitz

In London, St. Paul's Cathedral looms above the destruction wrought by German bombs during the Blitz. Winston Churchill's response: "We shall never surrender."

June 14 the German swastika flew over Paris. Eight days later French delegates, in the presence of Hitler, submitted to his surrender terms in the same railroad car in which German delegates had been forced to sign the armistice of 1918.

AMERICA'S GROWING INVOLVEMENT   Britain now stood alone, but in Parliament the new prime minister, Winston Churchill, breathed defiance. "We shall go on to the end," he said; "we shall never surrender." Nevertheless, America seemed suddenly vulnerable as Hitler turned his air force against Britain. After World War I the U.S. Army had been reduced to a small force; by 1939 it numbered only 175,000 and ranked sixteenth in the world, just behind Romania. It would take time to create a viable military force to stop fascism. President Roosevelt called for a military buildup and the production of 50,000 combat planes a year. By October 1940, Congress had voted more than $17 billion for defense. In response to Churchill's appeal for military supplies, the War and Navy Departments reluctantly followed Roosevelt's orders and began releasing stocks of arms, planes, and munitions to the British.

The world crisis transformed Roosevelt. Having been stalemated for much of his second term by congressional opposition, he was revitalized by the war in Europe. Nervous cabinet officers, military leaders, and diplomats now encountered a decisive and forceful president willing to exert executive authority on behalf of Britain. Roosevelt acted with remarkable boldness in the face of an American public that still held staunchly to the doctrine of isolationism. In June 1940 the president set up the National Defense Research Committee to coordinate military research, including a top-secret effort to develop an atomic bomb, suggested the previous fall by Albert Einstein and other scientists. To bolster national unity, Roosevelt named two Republicans to the defense posts in his cabinet: Henry L. Stimson as secretary of war and Frank Knox as secretary of the navy.

The summer of 1940 brought the desperate Battle of Britain, in which the Royal Air Force, with the benefit of radar, a new technology, outfought the numerically superior German Luftwaffe and finally forced the Germans to postpone plans to invade England. Submarine warfare meanwhile strained the resources of the battered Royal Navy. To relieve the pressure, Churchill urgently requested the transfer of American destroyers. Secret negotiations led to an executive agreement under which fifty "overaged" U.S. destroyers went to the British in return for ninety-nine-year American leases on naval and air bases in British territories in the Caribbean. Roosevelt disguised the action as necessary for defense of the hemisphere. On September 16 Roosevelt signed the first peacetime conscription in American history, requiring the registration of all 16 million men aged twenty-one to thirty-five for a year's military service within the United States.

The new state of affairs prompted vigorous debate between "internationalists," who believed national security demanded aid to Britain, and isolationists, who charged that Roosevelt was drawing the United States into a needless war. In 1940 internationalists organized the nonpartisan Committee to Defend America by Aiding the Allies. It drew its strongest support from the East and West Coasts and the South. On the other hand, isolationists formed the America First Committee, which included among its members Herbert Hoover and Charles A. Lindbergh Jr. The isolationists argued that the war involved, in Senator William E. Borah's words, "nothing more than another chapter in the bloody volume of European power politics." Borah and others argued that a Nazi victory, while distasteful, would pose no threat to national security.

FDR'S THIRD TERM In the midst of these terrible global crises, the quadrennial presidential campaign came due. Isolationist sentiment was strongest in the Republican party and both leading Republican candidates were noninterventionists, but neither man was of sufficient stature to challenge Roosevelt. Senator Robert A. Taft of Ohio, son of the former president, lacked popular appeal, and New York district attorney Thomas E. Dewey, who had won fame as a "racket buster," at thirty-eight seemed young and unseasoned. This left an opening for an inspired group of political amateurs to promote the dark-horse candidacy of Wendell L. Willkie of Indiana.

Willkie seemed at first an unlikely choice: a former Democrat who had voted for Roosevelt in 1932 and a utilities president who had fought the TVA, but he was also a Hoosier farm boy whose disheveled charm inspired strong loyalty. Unlike the Republican front-runners, he openly supported aid to the Allies, and the Nazi blitzkrieg had brought many other Republicans to the same viewpoint. When the Republicans met at Philadelphia on June 28, six days after the French surrender, the convention was stampeded by cries of "We want Willkie" from the galleries.

The Nazi victory in France also ensured Roosevelt's nomination. Had war not erupted in Europe, Roosevelt would probably have followed custom and retired after his second term. But the crisis led him to run again, for an unprecedented third term. The president cultivated party unity with his foreign policy and kept a sphinxlike silence about his intentions regarding the war. The world crisis reconciled southern conservatives to the man whose foreign policy, at least, they supported. At the July convention in Chicago, Roosevelt won nomination for a third term with only token opposition.

Through the summer of 1940, Roosevelt assumed the role of a man above the political fray, busy rather with urgent matters of defense and diplomacy: pan-American agreements for mutual defense, the destroyer-bases deal, and visits to defense facilities that took the place of campaign trips. Willkie was reduced to attacks on New Deal red tape and promises to run the new federal programs better. In the end, however, he switched to an attack on Roosevelt's conduct of foreign policy. In October he warned: "If you re-elect him you may expect war in April, 1941." To this Roosevelt responded, "I have said this before, but I shall say it again and again and again: Your boys are not going to be sent into any foreign wars." Neither man distinguished himself with such hollow statements, since both knew the risks of all-out aid to Britain, which they both supported.

Roosevelt won the election by a comfortable margin of 27 million votes to Willkie's 22 million and by a wider margin, of 449 to 82, in the Electoral College. Even so it was Roosevelt's narrowest victory. Willkie polled 5 million more votes than Alf Landon had four years before, a telling indicator of Roosevelt's declining stature. But given the dangerous world situation, a majority of the voters still agreed with the Democrats' slogan: "Don't switch horses in the middle of the stream."

THE "ARSENAL OF DEMOCRACY"   Bolstered by the mandate for an unprecedented third term, Roosevelt moved quickly for greater measures to aid Britain, whose cash was running out. Since direct American loans would arouse memories of earlier war-debt defaults—the Johnson Debt Default Act of 1934 forbade such loans anyway—the president created an ingenious device to bypass that issue and yet supply British needs, the "lend-lease" program. In a fireside radio chat, Roosevelt told the nation that it must become "the great arsenal of democracy" because of the threat of Britain's fall to the Nazis. And to do so it must make new efforts to help the British purchase American supplies. The lend-lease bill, introduced in Congress on January 10, 1941, proposed authorizing the president to sell, transfer, exchange, lend, lease, or otherwise dispose of arms and other equipment and supplies to "any country whose defense the President deems vital to the defense of the United States."

For two months a bitter debate over the lend-lease bill raged in Congress and across the country. Isolationists saw it as the point of no return. "The lend-lease-give program," said Senator Burton K. Wheeler, "is the New Deal's triple A foreign policy; it will plow under every fourth American boy." Roosevelt pronounced this "the rottenest thing that has been said in public life in my generation." Administration supporters denied that lend-lease would lead to war, but they knew that it did increase the risk. Lend-lease became law in March. Almost all of the dissenting votes were Republican senators and congressmen from the staunchly isolationist Midwest.

While the nation debated, the war expanded. Italy had officially entered the war in June 1940 as Germany's ally. In October 1940, when the American presidential campaign was approaching its climax, Mussolini launched attacks on Greece and, from Italian Libya, on the British in Egypt. But he miscalculated, and his forces had to fall back in both cases. In the spring of 1941, German forces under General Erwin Rommel joined the Italians in Libya, forcing the British to withdraw to Egypt, their resources having been drained to help Greece. In April 1941 Nazi armored divisions overwhelmed Yugoslavia and Greece, and by the end of May German airborne forces had subdued the Greek island of Crete, putting Hitler in a position to menace the entire Middle East.

With Hungary, Romania, and Bulgaria forced into the Axis fold, Hitler controlled nearly all of Europe. But his ambition was unbounded. On June 22, 1941, German armies suddenly fell upon Soviet Russia, their ally. Frustrated

Lend-Lease

Members of the "Mother's Crusade," urging defeat of the lend-lease program, kneel in prayer in front of the Capitol. They feared that the program would bring the United States into the European war.

in the purpose of subduing Britain, Hitler sought to eliminate the potential threat on his rear with another lightning stroke. The Russian plains offered an ideal theater for blitzkrieg, or so it seemed. With Romanian and Finnish allies, the Nazis massed 3.6 million troops and thousands of tanks and planes along a 2,000-mile front from the Arctic to the Black Sea. Then, after four months of grudging retreat, the Russian soldiers rallied in front of Leningrad (formerly St. Petersburg), Moscow, and Sevastopol. During the winter of 1941–1942, Hitler's legions began to learn the bitter lesson the Russians had taught Napoleon and the French army in 1812. Invading armies had to contend with Russian weather. Still, in the summer of 1941, the Nazi juggernaut appeared unstoppable.

Winston Churchill had already decided to offer British support to the Soviet Union in case of such an attack. "If Hitler invaded Hell," he said, "I would make at least a favorable reference to the Devil in the House of Commons." Roosevelt adopted the same policy, offering American aid to Russia two days after the German attack. Stalinist Russia, so long as it held out against the Nazis, ensured the survival of Britain. American aid was now indispensable to Europe's defense, and the logic of lend-lease led to deeper American involvement. To deliver aid to Britain, convoys of supply ships had to maneuver through the German U-boat "wolf packs" in the North Atlantic. So in April 1941 Roosevelt informed Churchill that the U.S. Navy would extend its patrols in the North Atlantic nearly all the way to Iceland.

In August 1941 Roosevelt and Churchill held a secret meeting off Newfoundland, where they drew up a statement of principles known as the Atlantic Charter. Their joint statement called for the self-determination of all peoples, equal access to raw materials, economic cooperation, freedom of the seas, and a new system of international security. In September it was announced that eleven anti-Axis nations, including the Soviet Union, had endorsed the charter.

Thus Roosevelt had led the United States into a joint statement of war aims with the anti-Axis powers. It was not long before shooting incidents involved Americans in the North Atlantic. The first attack on an American warship occurred on September 4, when a German submarine fired two torpedoes at the destroyer *Greer*. The president announced a week later orders to "shoot on sight" any German or Italian raiders ("rattlesnakes of the Atlantic") that ventured into American waters. Five days later, the U.S. Navy began convoying merchant vessels all the way to Iceland.

Then, on October 17, 1941, while the destroyer *Kearny* was attacking German submarines, it sustained severe damage from a German torpedo, and eleven lives were lost. Two weeks later a German submarine torpedoed and sank the destroyer *Reuben James,* with a loss of 115 seamen, while it was on convoy duty west of Iceland. This action spurred Congress to make the changes in the 1939 Neutrality Act already requested by the president. On November 17 the legislation was in effect repealed when the bans on arming merchant vessels and allowing them to enter combat zones and the ports of nations at war were removed. Step-by-step the United States had given up neutrality and embarked on naval warfare against Germany. Still the American people hoped to avoid taking the final step into all-out war. The decision to go to war would be made in response to aggression in an unexpected quarter—the Pacific.

THE STORM IN THE PACIFIC

JAPANESE AGGRESSION   After the Nazi victories in the spring of 1940, U.S. relations with Japan took a turn for the worse. Japanese militarists, bogged down in the vastness of China, now eyed new temptations in south Asia: French Indochina (Vietnam, Laos, Cambodia), the Dutch East Indies (Indonesia), British Malaya (Malaysia), and Burma (Myanmar), where they could cut off one of China's last links to the West, the Burma Road. What was more, they could incorporate into their "Greater East Asia Co-Prosperity Sphere" the oil, rubber, and other strategic materials that the crowded Japanese homeland lacked. As it was, Japan depended upon the United States for important supplies, including 80 percent of its fuel.

In 1940 Japan and the United States began a series of moves, each of which aggravated but failed to restrain the other, all the while pushing each other toward war. During the summer of 1940, Japan forced the helpless French government, under German control at Vichy, to permit the construction of Japanese airfields in French-controlled northern Indochina and to cut off the railroad into south China. The United States responded with a loan to China and the Export Control Act of July 2, 1940, which authorized the president to restrict the export of American arms and other strategic materials to Japan. Gradually Roosevelt extended embargoes on aviation gas, scrap iron, and other supplies.

On September 27, 1940, the Tokyo government signed a Tripartite Pact with Germany and Italy, by which each pledged to declare war on any nation that attacked any of them. On April 13, 1941, while the Nazis were sweeping through the Balkans, Japan signed a nonaggression pact with the Soviet Union, and once the Nazis invaded Russia in June, the Japanese were freed of any threat from the north.

In July 1941 Japan announced that it was assuming a protectorate over all of French Indochina. Roosevelt took three steps in response: he froze all Japanese assets in the United States, he restricted oil exports to Japan, and he merged the armed forces of the Philippines with the U.S. Army and put their commander, General Douglas MacArthur, in charge of all U.S. forces in east Asia. By September the oil restrictions had tightened into an embargo. The Japanese estimated that their oil reserves would last two years at most. Forced by the American embargo to secure other oil supplies, the Japanese army and navy began planning attacks on the Dutch and British colonies to the south.

Actions by both sides put the United States and Japan on a collision course leading to a war that neither wanted. In his regular talks with the Japanese ambassador, Secretary of State Cordell Hull demanded that Japan withdraw from Indochina and China as the price of renewed trade with the United States. A more flexible position might have strengthened the moderates in Japan. The Japanese were not then pursuing a concerted plan of aggression comparable to Hitler's. The Japanese military leadership had stumbled crazily from one act of aggression to another without approval from the government in Tokyo. Prime Minister Fumimaro Konoe, however, while known as a man of liberal principles who preferred peace, caved in to pressures from the militants. Perhaps he had no choice.

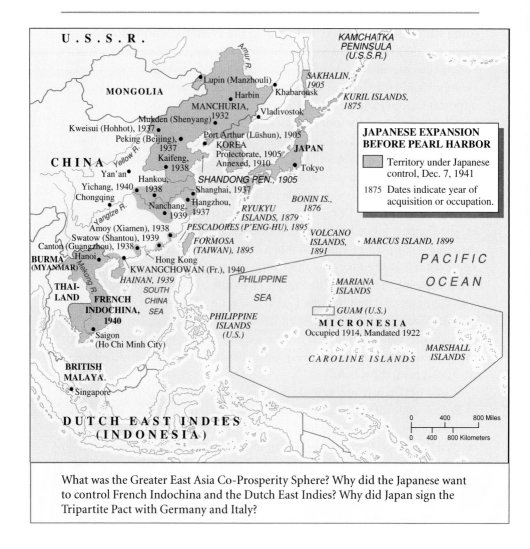

What was the Greater East Asia Co-Prosperity Sphere? Why did the Japanese want to control French Indochina and the Dutch East Indies? Why did Japan sign the Tripartite Pact with Germany and Italy?

The Japanese warlords, for their part, seriously misjudged the United States. The desperate wish of the Americans to stay out of the war might have enabled the Japanese to conquer the British and Dutch colonies in the Pacific. But the warlords decided that they dared not leave the U.S. Navy intact and the Philippines untouched on the flank of their new lifeline to the south.

TRAGEDY AT PEARL HARBOR   Thus a tragedy began to unfold with a fatal certainty—mostly out of sight of the American people, whose attention was focused on the war in the Atlantic. Late in August 1941 Prime Minister Konoe proposed a meeting with President Roosevelt. Secretary of State Hull urged the president not to meet Konoe unless an agreement on fundamental issues could be reached in advance. Soon afterward, on September 6, a Japanese imperial conference approved preparations for a surprise attack on Hawaii and gave Prime Minister Konoe six weeks in which to reach a settlement.

The Japanese emperor's concern about the risks of an attack afforded the prime minister one last chance to pursue a compromise, but the stumbling block was still the presence of Japanese troops in China. In October, Konoe urged War Minister Hideki Tōjō to consider withdrawal while saving face by keeping some troops in north China. Tōjō countered with his "maximum concession": Japanese troops would stay no longer than twenty-five years if the United States stopped aiding China. Faced with this rebuff and with Tōjō's threat to resign and bring down the cabinet, Konoe himself resigned on October 15; Tōjō became prime minister the next day. The war party had now assumed complete control of the government.

On the very day that Tōjō became prime minister, a special Japanese envoy conferred with Hull and Roosevelt in Washington. The envoy's arrival was largely a cover for Japan's war plans, although neither he nor the Japanese ambassador knew that. On November 20 they presented Tōjō's final proposal: Japan would occupy no more territory in Asia if the United States would cut off aid to China, restore trade, and help Japan get supplies from the Dutch East Indies. Tōjō expected the United States to refuse the demands. On November 26 Hull insisted that Japan withdraw from China altogether. War now seemed inevitable. "The question," Secretary of War Stimson thought, "was how we should maneuver them into the position of firing the first shot without allowing too much danger to ourselves." That same day a Japanese naval force began heading secretly across the North Pacific toward Pearl Harbor, the key American military base in the Pacific.

Officials in Washington knew that war was imminent. Reports of Japanese troop transports moving south from Formosa prompted them to send warnings to U.S. commanders in the Pacific, and to the British government. The massive movements southward clearly signaled attacks on the British and the Dutch possessions. American leaders had every reason to expect war in the southwest Pacific, but none expected that Japan would commit most of its aircraft carriers to another attack 5,000 miles away, at Pearl Harbor.

In the early morning of December 7, 1941, American servicemen decoded the last part of a fourteen-part Japanese message breaking off the diplomatic negotiations. Japan's ambassador was instructed to deliver the message at 1 P.M. (7:30 A.M. in Honolulu), about a half hour before the Japanese attack, but delays held up delivery by more than an hour. The War Department sent out an alert at noon that something was about to happen, but the message, which went by commercial telegraph because radio contacts were broken, arrived in Hawaii eight and a half hours later. Even so, the decoded Japanese message had not mentioned Pearl Harbor, and everyone still assumed that any Japanese attack would be in Southeast Asia.

It was still a sleepy Sunday morning in Hawaii when the first Japanese planes roared down the west coast and the central valley of Oahu to begin their assault. For nearly two hours the Japanese planes pummeled an unsuspecting Pacific Fleet. Of the eight battleships in Pearl Harbor, three were sunk, one grounded, one capsized, and the others badly battered. Altogether nineteen ships were sunk or disabled. At the adjoining Hickam Field and other airfields on the island, the Japanese found planes parked wing to wing and destroyed about 180 of them. The raid killed more than 2,400 American servicemen and civilians and wounded 1,178 more.

The surprise attack fulfilled the dreams of its planners, but it fell short of total success in two ways. The Japanese ignored the onshore facilities and oil

The Attack on Pearl Harbor

This view from an army airfield shows the destruction and confusion brought on by the surprise attack.

tanks in Hawaii that supported the U.S. fleet, without which the surviving ships might have been forced back to the West Coast, and they missed the aircraft carriers that had fortuitously left port a few days earlier. In the naval war to come, these aircraft carriers would prove decisive.

Later that day (December 8 in the western Pacific), Japanese forces invaded the Philippines, Guam, Midway, Hong Kong, and the Malay Peninsula. With one stroke the Japanese had silenced America's debate on neutrality—a suddenly unified and vengeful nation prepared for war. The next day, President Roosevelt delivered his war message to Congress: "Yesterday, December 7, 1941—a date which will live in infamy—the United States of America was suddenly and deliberately attacked by naval and air forces of the Empire of Japan." Congress voted for the war resolution with near unanimity, the sole exception being Representative Jeannette Rankin, a Montana pacifist who was unable to vote for war in good conscience in 1917 or 1941. For several days it was uncertain whether war with the other Axis powers would follow. The Tripartite Pact was ostensibly for defense only, and it carried no obligation for Germany and Italy to take part, but Hitler, impatient with continuing American aid to Britain, willingly joined his Asian allies. On December 11, Germany and Italy impetuously declared war on the United States. The separate wars that were being waged by armies in Asia and Europe had become one global conflict—and American isolationism was cast aside.

MAKING CONNECTIONS

- During the 1930s the United States tried to stake out a neutral position in the growing world conflict. Compare that effort with earlier American attempts at neutrality, from the Napoleonic Wars of Jefferson's administration onward.

- The American alliance with the Soviet Union described in this chapter proved to be temporary: after the war the Americans and the Soviets would be adversaries in a prolonged cold war, the beginnings of which are outlined in Chapter 31.

- The Japanese conquest of French Indochina (Vietnam) would play an important role in the events leading to American involvement in that region, a topic discussed in Chapter 34.

FURTHER READING

The best overview of interwar diplomacy remains Selig Adler's *The Uncertain Giant, 1921–1941: American Foreign Policy between the Wars* (1965). Joan Hoff's *American Business and Foreign Policy, 1920–1933* (1971) highlights the efforts of Republican administrations during the 1920s to promote international commerce. Robert Dallek's *Franklin D. Roosevelt and American Foreign Policy, 1932–1945* (1979) provides a judicious assessment of Roosevelt's foreign policy during the 1930s.

A noteworthy study of America's entry into World War II is Waldo Heinrichs's *Threshold of War: Franklin D. Roosevelt and American Entry into World War II* (1988). See also David Reynolds's *From Munich to Pearl Harbor: Roosevelt's America and the Origins of the Second World War* (2001). Bruce M. Russett's *No Clear and Present Danger: A Skeptical View of the United States Entry into World War II* (1972) provides a critical account of American actions.

On Pearl Harbor, see Gordon W. Prange's *Pearl Harbor: The Verdict of History* (1986). Japan's perspective is described in Akira Iriye's *The Origins of the Second World War in Asia and the Pacific* (1987).

30

THE SECOND WORLD WAR

FOCUS QUESTIONS

· What were the social and economic effects of World War II, especially in the West?

· How did the Allied forces win the war?

· What efforts did the Allies make to shape the postwar world?

To answer these questions and access additional review material, please visit www.wwnorton.com/studyspace.

The Japanese attack on Pearl Harbor ended a period of tense neutrality for the United States, and it launched the nation into a global conflict that would cost the lives of over 400,000 Americans. The war would also transform the nation's social and economic life, as well as its position in international affairs. The Second World War would become the most destructive and far-reaching conflict in history. It was so terrible in its intensity and obscene in its cruelties that it altered the image of war itself. Devilish new instruments of destruction were invented—plastic explosives, flame throwers, proximity fuses, rockets, jet airplanes, and atomic weapons— and systematic genocide emerged as an explicit war aim of the Nazis. Racist propaganda flourished on both sides, and excited hatred of the enemy caused many military and civilian prisoners to be executed. The scorching passions of such an all-out war blanched many moral niceties from the conduct of war. Over 50 million deaths resulted from the worldwide war, and the physical destruction was incalculable. Whole cities were leveled, nations dismembered, and societies transformed. The world is still coping with the consequences.

AMERICA'S EARLY BATTLES

SETBACKS IN THE PACIFIC   For months after the attack on Pearl Harbor, the news from the Pacific was "all bad," as President Roosevelt confessed. In quick sequence the Japanese captured numerous Allied outposts before the end of December 1941: Guam, Wake Island, the Gilbert Islands, and Hong Kong. The fall of Rangoon (present-day Yangon), in Burma, cut off the Burma Road, the main supply route to China. In the Philippines, where General Douglas MacArthur abandoned Manila on December 27, the main U.S. forces, outmanned and outgunned, held out on the Bataan peninsula until April 9 and then retreated to the fortified island of Corregidor. General MacArthur slipped away in March, when he was ordered to Australia to take command of the Allied forces in the southwest Pacific. By May 6, 1942, when American forces surrendered Corregidor, Japan controlled a new empire that stretched from Burma eastward through the Dutch East Indies and extending to Wake Island and the Gilbert Islands.

Early Defeats

U.S. prisoners of war, captured by the Japanese in the Philippines, 1942.

The Japanese might have consolidated an almost impregnable empire with the resources they had seized. But leaders of the Japanese navy succumbed to what one of its admirals later called victory disease: lusting for more conquests, they pushed on into the South Pacific, intending to isolate Australia, and strike again at Hawaii. Japanese planners hoped to destroy the American navy before the productive power of the United States could be brought to bear on the war effort.

A Japanese mistake and a stroke of American luck enabled the U. S. Navy to frustrate the plan, however. Japan's failure to destroy the shore facilities at Pearl Harbor left the base relatively intact, and most of the ships damaged on December 7 lived to fight another day. The aircraft carriers that were luckily at sea during the attack spent several months harassing Japanese outposts. Their most spectacular exploit, an air raid on Tokyo itself, was launched on April 18, 1942. B-25 bombers took off from the carrier *Hornet* and, unable to land on its deck, proceeded to China after dropping their bombs over Tokyo. The raid caused only token damage but did much to lift American morale amid a series of defeats elsewhere.

CORAL SEA AND MIDWAY   U.S. forces finally halted the Japanese advance toward Australia in two decisive naval battles. The Battle of the Coral Sea (May 7–8, 1942) stopped a fleet convoying Japanese troop transports toward New Guinea. Planes from the *Lexington* and *Yorktown* sank one Japanese carrier, damaged another, and destroyed smaller ships. American losses were greater, but the Japanese threat against Australia was repulsed.

Less than a month after the Coral Sea engagement, Admiral Isoroku Yamamoto, the Japanese naval commander, steered his fleet for Midway Island, from which he hoped to render Pearl Harbor helpless. This time it was the Japanese who were the victims of surprise. American cryptanalysts had by then broken the Japanese naval code, and Admiral Chester Nimitz, commander of the central Pacific, knew what was up. He reinforced Midway with planes and carriers.

The first Japanese foray against Midway, on June 4, 1942, severely damaged the island's defenses, but at the cost of about one third of the Japanese planes. American torpedo planes and dive bombers struck back before another Japanese attack could be mounted. The Japanese lost their four best aircraft carriers; the Americans, a carrier and a destroyer. The Japanese navy was forced into retreat less than six months after the attack on Hawaii. The Battle of Midway was the turning point of the Pacific war. It demonstrated that aircraft carriers, not battleships, were the decisive elements of modern naval warfare, and it bought time for the United States to mobilize for war.

SETBACKS IN THE ATLANTIC   Early American setbacks in the Pacific were matched by setbacks in the Atlantic. Since the blitzkrieg of 1940, German submarine "wolf packs" had wreaked havoc in the North Atlantic. In 1942 German submarines appeared off American shores and began to attack coastal shipping. Nearly 400 ships were lost before effective countermeasures brought the problem under control. The naval command accelerated the building of small escort vessels, meanwhile pressing into patrol service all kinds of surface craft and planes, some of them civilian. During the second half of 1942, the losses to Nazi submarines diminished substantially.

MOBILIZATION AT HOME

The attack on Pearl Harbor ended not only the long public debate on isolation and intervention but also the long depression that had ravaged the economy during the 1930s. The war effort would require all of America's immense productive capacity and full employment of the workforce. Mobilization was in fact already further along than preparedness had been in 1916–1917. The army had grown to more than 1.4 million men by July 1941. With the declaration of war, men between the ages of eighteen and forty-five were now subject to the draft. The average soldier or sailor was twenty-six years old, stood five feet eight, and weighed 144 pounds, an inch taller and eight pounds heavier than the typical recruit in World War I. Less than half the soldiers and sailors had finished high school. Altogether more than 15 million men and women would serve in the armed forces over the course of the conflict.

ECONOMIC CONVERSION The economy, too, was already partially mobilized for war, by the lend-lease and defense preparedness efforts. The War Powers Act of 1941 had given the president the authority to reshuffle government agencies, and a second War Powers Act empowered the government to allot materials and facilities as needed for defense, with penalties for those who failed to comply.

The War Production Board, created in 1942, directed the conversion of industrial manufacturing to war production. Roosevelt established staggering production goals: 60,000 warplanes in 1942 and twice as many the following year; 55,000 anti-aircraft guns; and tens of thousands of tanks. His purpose was to confront the enemy with a "crushing superiority of equipment."

The war effort required conservation as well as production. "Use it up, wear it out, make do, or do without" became the prevailing slogan encouraging the public to sacrifice on behalf of the war effort. People collected scrap metal and grew their own food in backyard "victory gardens." Tire and gasoline rationing began in earnest. Through the Office of Scientific Research and Development, Dr. Vannevar Bush mobilized thousands of scientists to create and modify radar, sonar, the proximity fuse, the bazooka, means to isolate blood plasma, and numerous other innovations spurred by the war effort.

The pressure of wartime needs and the stimulus of government spending sent the gross national product soaring from $100 billion in 1940 to $214 billion in 1945. The figure for total government expenditures was twice as great as the total of all previous federal spending in the history of the republic, about 10 times what America had spent in World War I and 100 times the expenditures during the Civil War.

FINANCING THE WAR   To cover the war's huge cost, the president preferred raising taxes to borrowing. The wartime Congress, however, dominated by conservatives, feared taxes more than deficits and refused to go more than halfway with Roosevelt's fiscal prudence. The Revenue Act of 1942 provided for only about $7 billion in increased revenue, less than half that recommended by the Treasury. It also greatly broadened the tax structure. Whereas in 1939 only about 4 million people filed returns, the new act made everyone a taxpayer.

The federal government paid for about 45 percent of its 1939–1946 costs with tax revenues. To cover the rest of its expenses, the government borrowed from the public. War-bond drives, including a Victory drive in 1945, induced citizens to invest more than $150 billion in government bonds. Financial institutions picked up most of the rest of the government's debt. In all, by the end of the war the national debt had grown to about $260 billion, about six times its size at the start of the war.

The basic economic problem was no longer finding jobs but finding workers for the booming shipyards, aircraft factories, and gunpowder mills. Millions of people who had lived on the margins of the economic system, especially women, were now brought fully into the economy. Stubborn pockets of poverty did not disappear, but for most civilians the war spelled neither hardship nor suffering but a better life than ever before, despite shortages and rationing.

ECONOMIC CONTROLS   Increased family income and government spending during the war raised fears of inflation. Some of the available money went into taxes and war bonds, but even so, more was sent chasing after scarce consumer goods just as production was converting to war needs. Consumer durables such as cars, washing machines, and nondefense housing in fact ceased to be produced at all. It was apparent that only strict restraints would keep prices from soaring out of sight. In 1942, therefore, Congress authorized the Office of Price Administration to set price ceilings. With prices frozen, goods had to be allocated through rationing, with coupons doled out for sugar, coffee, gasoline, automobile tires, and meats.

Wages and farm prices were not controlled, however, and this complicated things. War prosperity offered farmers a chance to recover from two decades of distress, and farm-state congressmen raised both floors and ceilings on farm prices. Higher food prices reinforced workers' demands for higher wages, and the Stabilization Act of 1942 gave the president authority to control wages and farm prices. At the same time, he set up the Office of Economic Stabilization under James F. Byrnes, who left his seat on the Supreme Court to coordinate the effort.

Businesses and workers chafed at the wage and price controls. On occasion the government seized industries threatened by strikes. Both coal mines and railroads came under government operation for a short time in 1943, and in 1944 the government briefly took over the Montgomery-Ward Company. Soldiers had to carry its chairman out of his office when he stubbornly defied orders of the National War Labor Board. Despite these problems the government effort to stabilize wages and prices succeeded. By the end of the war, consumer prices had risen about 31 percent, a record far better than the World War I rise of 62 percent.

DOMESTIC CONSERVATISM Despite government efforts to promote patriotic sacrifice among the public, discontent with price controls, labor shortages, rationing, and a hundred other petty vexations spread. In 1942 the congressional elections registered a national swing against the Democrats. Republicans gained forty-six seats in the House and nine in the Senate, chiefly in the farm areas of the midwestern states. Democratic losses outside the South strengthened the southern delegation's position within the party, and the delegation itself reflected conservative victories in southern primaries. A coalition of conservatives dismantled "nonessential" New Deal agencies. In 1943 Congress abolished the Work Projects Administration (originally the Works Progress Administration), the National Youth Administration, the Civilian Conservation Corps, and the National Resources Planning Board.

Organized labor, despite substantial gains during the war, felt the impact of the conservative trend. In the spring of 1943, when John L. Lewis led the coal miners out on strike, Congress passed the Smith-Connally War Labor Disputes Act, which authorized the government to seize plants and mines useful to the war effort. In 1943 a dozen states adopted laws variously restricting picketing and other union activities, and in 1944 Arkansas and Florida set in motion a wave of "right-to-work" legislation that outlawed the closed shop (requiring that all employees be union members).

Social Effects of the War

MOBILIZATION AND THE DEVELOPMENT OF THE WEST The dramatic expansion of defense production after 1940 and the mobilization

Changing Focus

With mobilization for war the nation's priority, many New Deal programs were allowed to expire.

of millions of people in the armed forces accelerated economic development and a population boom in the western states. Nearly 8 million people moved into the states west of the Mississippi River between 1940 and 1950. The Far West experienced the fastest rate of urban growth in the country. Small cities such as Phoenix and Albuquerque mushroomed while Seattle, San Francisco, Los Angeles, and San Diego witnessed dizzying growth. San Diego's population, for example, increased by 147 percent between 1941 and 1945.

The migration of workers to new defense jobs in the West had significant demographic effects. Lured by news of job openings and higher wages, African Americans from Texas, Oklahoma, Arkansas, and Louisiana headed west. During the war years, Seattle's African-American population jumped from 4,000 to 40,000, Portland's from 2,000 to 15,000.

CHANGING ROLES FOR WOMEN   The war marked an important watershed in the changing status of women. With millions of men going into military service, the demand for labor shook up old prejudices about sex roles in the workplace—and in the military. Nearly 200,000 women served in the Women's Army Corps (WAC) and the navy's equivalent, Women Accepted for Volunteer Emergency Service (WAVES). Lesser numbers joined the Marine Corps, the Coast Guard, and the Army Air Force. Over 6 million women entered the workforce during the war, an increase of more than 50 percent overall and in manufacturing alone an increase of some 110 percent. Old barriers fell overnight as women became toolmakers, machinists, crane operators, lumberjacks, stevedores, blacksmiths, and railroad workers.

The government launched an intense publicity campaign to draw women into traditional male jobs. "Do your part, free a man for service," one ad pleaded. "Rosie the Riveter," a beautiful model dressed in overalls, became the cover girl for the recruiting campaign. One striking feature of the new labor scene was the larger proportion of older, married women in the workforce. In 1940 about 15 percent of married women were gainfully employed; by 1945 about 24 percent were.

Many men opposed the trend. One disgruntled male legislator asked what would happen to traditional domestic tasks if women flocked to factories: "Who will do the cooking, the washing, the mending, the humble homey tasks to which every woman has devoted herself; who will rear and nurture the children?" Many women, however, were eager to get away from the grinding routine of domestic life. One female welder remembered that her wartime job "was the first time I had a chance to get out of the kitchen and work in industry and make a few bucks. This was something I had never dreamed

Women in the Military

This navy recruiting poster urged women to join the WAVES (Women Accepted for Volunteer Emergency Service).

would happen." And it was something that many women did not want to relinquish after the war.

AFRICAN AMERICANS IN WORLD WAR II   The most volatile issue ignited by the war was African-American participation in the military. From the start black leaders demanded equality in the armed forces and defense industries. Eventually about 1 million African Americans served in the armed forces, but usually in segregated units. Every army camp had segregated facilities—and periodic racial "incidents." The most important departure was a 1940 decision to integrate officer-candidate schools, except those for air force cadets. A separate flight school at Tuskegee, Alabama, trained about 600 African-American pilots, many of whom distinguished themselves in combat.

War industries were even less hospitable to integration. "We will not employ Negroes," said the president of North American Aviation. But black leaders refused to accept such racist stances. In 1941 A. Philip Randolph, the tall, gentlemanly head of the Brotherhood of Sleeping Car Porters, planned a March on Washington to demand an end to racial discrimination in defense industries. The Roosevelt administration then struck a bargain. The Randolph group called off its march in return for an executive order that forbade discrimination in defense work and training

Tuskegee Airmen, 1942

One of the last segregated military training schools, the flight school at Tuskegee trained African-American men for combat during World War II.

programs and set up the Fair Employment Practices Commission (FEPC). The FEPC's authority was chiefly moral, since it had no power to enforce directives. It nevertheless offered willing employers the chance to say they were following government policy in giving jobs to black citizens.

African-American leaders quickly began to challenge more openly all kinds of discrimination, including racial segregation itself. Membership in the NAACP grew during the war from 50,000 to 450,000. African Americans could look forward to greater political participation after the Supreme Court, in *Smith v. Allwright* (1944), struck down Texas's whites-only primary on the grounds that Democratic primaries were part of the election process and thus subject to the Fifteenth Amendment.

Racial violence did not approach the level of that during World War I, but growing tensions on a hot summer afternoon in Detroit sparked incidents at a park. Fighting raged through June 20–21, 1943, until federal troops arrived on the second evening. Twenty-five blacks and nine whites had been killed.

LATINOS IN THE LABOR FORCE   As rural dwellers moved to the western cities during the war, many farm counties experienced a labor shortage. In an ironic about-face, local and federal government authorities who before the war had striven to force undocumented Mexican laborers back across the border now recruited them to harvest crops. Before it would assist in providing the needed workers, however, the Mexican government insisted that the United States ensure minimum working and living conditions. The result was the creation of the bracero program in 1942. Mexico agreed to provide seasonal farmworkers in exchange for a promise by the U.S. government not to draft them into military service. The workers were hired on year-long contracts, and American officials provided transportation from the border to their job sites. Under the bracero program some 200,000 Mexican farmworkers entered the western United States. At least that many more crossed the border as undocumented workers.

The rising tide of Mexican Americans in Los Angeles prompted a growing stream of anti-Latino editorials and incidents. Even though Mexican Americans fought in the war with great valor, earning seventeen Congressional Medals of Honor, there was constant conflict between servicemen and Mexican-American gang members and teenage "zoot-suiters" in southern California. In 1943 several thousand off-duty sailors and soldiers, joined by hundreds of local white civilians, rampaged through downtown Los Angeles streets, assaulting Latinos, African Americans, and Filipinos. The violence

lasted a week and came to be labeled the zoot
flamboyant suits popular in the 1940s and
American men.)

NATIVE AMERICANS AND THE WA
the war effort more fully than any other g
one third of eligible Native American men
armed forces. Another one fourth worked i
sands of Indian women volunteered as nurses
case with African Americans, Indians benefited from the experience
by the war. Those who left reservations to work in defense plants or to join the
military gained new vocational skills as well as a greater awareness of mainstream society and how to succeed within it.

Why did so many Native Americans fight for a nation that had stripped
them of their land and decimated their heritage? Some felt that they had no
choice. Mobilization for the war effort ended many New Deal programs
that had provided Indians with jobs. Reservation Indians thus faced the necessity of finding new jobs elsewhere. Many viewed the Nazis and Japanese
warlords as threats to their own homeland. The most common sentiment,
however, seems to have been a genuine sense of patriotism. Whatever the
reasons, Indians distinguished themselves in the military. Unlike their
African-American counterparts, Indian servicemen were integrated into
regular units. Perhaps the most distinctive activity performed by Indians
was their service as "code talkers": every military branch used Indians to
encode and decipher messages using Indian languages.

INTERNMENT OF JAPANESE AMERICANS   The record on civil
liberties during World War II was on the whole better than that during
World War I, if only because there was virtually no domestic opposition to
the war effort after the attack on Pearl Harbor. Neither German Americans
nor Italian Americans faced the harassments meted out to their counterparts
in the previous war; few had much sympathy for Hitler or Mussolini. The
shameful exception to an otherwise improved record was the treatment accorded to more than 100,000 Americans of Japanese descent (nisei), who
were forcibly removed from their homes and businesses on the West Coast
and transported to "war relocation camps" in the interior. Caught up in the
war hysteria and racial prejudice aroused by the attack on Pearl Harbor, President Roosevelt initiated the removal of Japanese Americans when he issued
Executive Order 9066 on February 19, 1942. More than 60 percent of the internees were U.S. citizens; one third were under the age of nineteen. Forced

Internment

This young Japanese American and her parents were forced to relocate from Los Angeles to an internment camp in eastern California in 1942.

to sell their farms and businesses at great losses, the internees lost not only their property but also their liberty. Few if any were disloyal, but all were victims of fear and racial prejudice. Following the attack on Pearl Harbor, Idaho's governor declared, "A good solution to the Jap problem would be to send them all back to Japan, then sink the island." Such vengeful attitudes help explain why the U.S. government pursued a policy that represented a mass violation of civil liberties. Not until 1983 did the government recognize the injustice of the internment policy. That year it authorized granting those nisei still living $20,000 each in compensation.

THE ALLIED DRIVE TOWARD BERLIN

By mid-1942, the "home front" had begun to get encouraging news from the war fronts. Japanese naval losses at the battles of Coral Sea and Midway had secured Australia and Hawaii. By midyear a motley fleet of American air and sea subchasers was ending six months of successful hunting for German U-boats off the Atlantic coast. This was all the more important because war plans called for the defeat of Germany first.

WAR AIMS AND STRATEGY   There were good reasons for giving top priority to defeating Hitler. Nazi forces in western Europe and the Atlantic posed a more direct threat to the Western Hemisphere than did Japan, and Germany's war potential was greater than Japan's. Yet Japanese attacks involved Americans directly in the Pacific war from the start, and as a consequence during the first year of fighting more American troops went to the Pacific than across the Atlantic.

The Pearl Harbor attack brought British prime minister Winston Churchill to Washington, D.C., for lengthy talks about a common war plan. Thus began a crucial wartime alliance between the United States and Great Britain, a partnership marked almost as much by disagreement and suspicion as it was by common purposes. As Churchill later remarked, "There is only one thing worse than fighting with allies, and that is fighting without them." Although he and Roosevelt admired each other, they often disagreed about military strategy and the likely makeup of the postwar world.

Initially, at least, such differences of opinion were masked by the need to make basic decisions related to the conduct of the war. On January 1, 1942, representatives of twenty-six governments then at war with the Axis signed the Declaration of the United Nations, affirming the principles of the Atlantic Charter, pledging their full resources to the war, and promising not to make a separate peace with Germany, Italy, or Japan. The meetings between Churchill and Roosevelt in Washington in 1942 produced several major decisions, including the one to name a supreme allied commander in each major theater of war. Each commander would be subject to orders from the British-American Combined Chiefs of Staff. Other joint boards allotted munitions, raw materials, and shipping. Finally, in the course of their talks, the British and American leaders reaffirmed the priority of the war against Germany.

Agreement on war aims did not bring agreement on strategy, however. Roosevelt and Churchill, meeting at the White House again in June 1942, could not agree on where to hit first. U.S. military planners wanted to strike directly across the English Channel before the end of 1942, secure a beachhead in German-occupied France, and move against Germany itself in 1943. The British preferred to keep the Germans off balance with hit-and-run raids and air attacks while continuing to build up their forces. With vivid memories of the last war, the British feared a mass bloodletting in trench warfare if they struck prematurely. The Russians, bearing the brunt of the massive German attack in the east, insisted that the Western Allies must do something to relieve the pressure. Finally, the Americans accepted Churchill's proposal to invade French North Africa, which had been captured by German and Italian armies.

THE NORTH AFRICA CAMPAIGN On November 8, 1942, British and American forces commanded by U.S. general Dwight D. Eisenhower landed at Casablanca in Morocco and at Oran and Algiers in Algeria. Completely surprised, French forces under the Vichy government (which collaborated with the Germans) had little will to resist. Hitler, in response, occupied the whole of France and sent German forces into Tunisia, a French protectorate.

What was the Atlantic Charter? Compare and contrast the alliances in the First World War (see page 937) and the Second World War. How were the Germans able to seize most of the Allied territory so quickly?

Farther east, General Bernard Montgomery's British forces were pushing the brilliant German tank commander General Erwin Rommel back across Libya, and green American forces were confronting seasoned Nazis pouring into Tunisia. Before spring, however, the British forces had taken Libya, and the Germans were caught in a gigantic pair of pincers. Hammered from all sides, unable to retreat across the Mediterranean, an army of over 200,000 Germans and Italians surrendered on May 12, 1943, leaving all of North Africa in Allied hands.

While the Battle of Tunisia unfolded, in January 1943 Roosevelt, Churchill, and the Combined Chiefs of Staff met at Casablanca, Morocco. Stalin declined to leave besieged Russia for the meeting but continued to press for a second front in western Europe to relieve the pressure on Russia. Since the German invasion of Russia in 1941, over 90 percent of German military casualities had occurred on the Russian front. The British and American engagements with German forces in North Africa were minuscule in comparison with the scope and fury of the fighting in Russia.

Churchill and Roosevelt spent eight days at Casablanca hammering out key strategic decisions. The Americans wanted to invade German-occupied France as soon as possible, but the British insisted that such a major assault was premature. They convinced the Americans that they should follow up a victory in North Africa with an assault on Sicily and Italy. Roosevelt and Churchill also decided to step up the bombing of Germany and to increase shipments of military supplies to the Soviet Union and the Nationalist Chinese forces fighting the Japanese. The two allied leaders ordered Admiral Chester Nimitz and General Douglas MacArthur to dislodge the Japanese from the Pacific islands. Top priority, however, went to an anti-submarine campaign against the Germans in the Atlantic.

Before leaving Casablanca, Roosevelt announced, with Churchill's endorsement, that the war would end only with the "unconditional surrender" of all enemies. This decision was designed to quiet Soviet suspicions that the Western Allies might negotiate separately with the enemy. The announcement also reflected Roosevelt's determination that "every person in Germany should realize that this time Germany is a defeated nation." This dictum was later criticized for having stiffened enemy resistance, but it probably had little effect; in fact, neither the Italian nor the Japanese surrender would be totally unconditional. But the decision did have one unexpected result: it opened an avenue for eventual Soviet control of eastern Europe because it required Russian armies to pursue Hitler's forces all the way to Germany. And as they liberated the countries of eastern Europe, the Soviets created new Communist governments under their control.

THE BATTLE OF THE ATLANTIC   While fighting raged in North Africa, the more crucial Battle of the Atlantic reached its climax on the high seas. By early 1943 in the western portion of the North Atlantic, there were at any one time an average of 31 convoys with 145 escorts and 673 merchant ships, as well as a number of heavily escorted troopships. None of the troopships going to Britain or the Mediterranean was lost. The U-boats kept up the Battle of the Atlantic until the war's end; when Germany finally collapsed, at least forty-nine submarines were still at sea. But their commander later admitted that the battle had been lost by the end of May 1943. He credited the difference largely to radar. What he did not know then was that the Allies had a

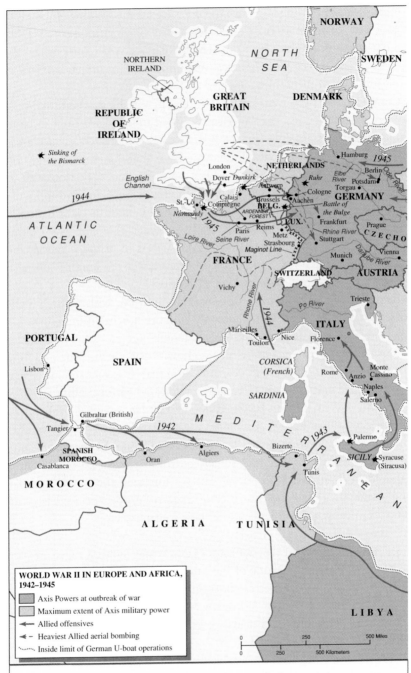

WORLD WAR II IN EUROPE AND AFRICA, 1942–1945

Axis Powers at outbreak of war
Maximum extent of Axis military power
◄— Allied offensives
◄ – Heaviest Allied aerial bombing
⋯⋯ Inside limit of German U-boat operations

What was the Allies' strategy in North Africa, and why was it important for the invasion of Italy? Why did Eisenhower's plan on D-day succeed? What was the Battle of the Bulge? What was the role of strategic bombing in the war? Was it effective?

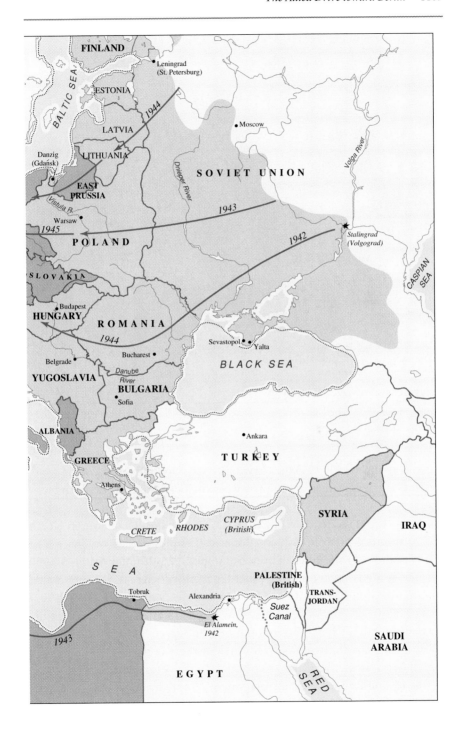

Major General George S. Patton

Patton commanded the U.S. invasion of Sicily, the largest amphibious action in the war up to that point.

secret weapon: by early 1943 their cryptanalysts were routinely decoding secret messages and telling their sub-hunters where to look for German U-boats.

SICILY AND ITALY   On July 10, 1943, after the Allied victory in North Africa, about 250,000 British and American troops landed on Sicily. The entire island was in Allied hands by August 17, although some 40,000 German soldiers escaped to the mainland. Allied success in Sicily ended Mussolini's twenty years of Fascist rule. On July 25, 1943, Italy's King Victor Emmanuel III dismissed Mussolini as prime minister. A new regime startled the Allies when it offered not only to surrender but also to switch sides in the war. Unfortunately, mutual suspicions prolonged talks until September 3, while the Germans poured reinforcements into Italy. In the confusion the Italian army disintegrated, although most of the navy escaped to Allied ports. A few army units later joined the Allied effort. Mussolini, plucked from imprisonment by a daring German airborne raid, became head of a puppet government in northern Italy.

Although American and British troops secured beachheads in Italy and captured Naples, fighting stalled in the Apennine Mountains. Finally, on June 4, 1944, the U.S. Fifth Army entered Rome. The capture of Rome provided only a brief moment of glory, however, for the long-awaited cross-Channel landing in France came two days later. Italy, always a secondary front, faded from the world's attention.

THE STRATEGIC BOMBING OF EUROPE Behind the long-postponed landings on the Normandy beaches lay months of preparation. While waiting, the U.S. Army Air Force (AAF) and the British Royal Air Force (RAF) had attacked the German-controlled areas of Europe. Early

Willie and Joe

"Joe, yestiddy ya saved my life an' I swore I'd pay ya back. Here's my last pair of dry socks." From Bill Mauldin's cartoon strip about two infantrymen slogging their way through the Italian campaign that appeared in the army newspaper *Yank.*

in 1943 Americans launched their first air raid on Germany itself. Thereafter, American strategic bombers were full-fledged partners of the RAF in the effort to pound Germany into submission. The RAF confined itself mostly to night raids. The Americans preferred high-level daylight "precision" bombing.

Yet while causing widespread damage, the strategic air offensive had failed to devastate German industrial production; the strikes also, some contend, were unable to break civilian morale. Heavy Allied air losses persisted through 1943. By the end of that year, however, jettisonable gas tanks permitted fighters to escort the bombers all the way to Berlin and back, thus reducing the number of bombers lost to German fighters. Berlin suffered repeated Allied raids. With air supremacy assured, the Allies were free to concentrate on their primary urban and industrial targets and, when the time came, to provide cover for the Normandy landings. On April 14, 1944, General Eisenhower assumed control of the Strategic Air Forces for the invasion of German-controlled France. On D-Day, June 6, 1944, he told the troops, "If you see fighting aircraft over you, they will be ours."

THE TEHRAN MEETING   Late in the fall of 1943, Churchill and Roo-sevelt finally had their first joint meeting with Joseph Stalin, in Tehran, Iran. Prior to the conference, when Britain and America promised a cross-Channel invasion, the Soviets pledged to enter the war against Japan af-ter Germany's defeat. On the way to the Tehran meeting with Stalin, Churchill and Roosevelt met in Cairo with China's general Chiang Kai-shek from November 22 to 26. The resultant Declaration of Cairo (De-cember 1, 1943) affirmed that war against Japan would continue until Japan's unconditional surrender, that all Chinese territories taken by Japan would be restored to China, that Japan would lose the Pacific islands acquired after 1941, and that "in due course Korea shall become free and independent."

From November 28 to December 1, the Big Three leaders conferred in Tehran. Their chief subject was the planned invasion of France and a Russian offensive timed to coincide with it. Stalin repeated his promise to enter the war against Japan, and the three leaders agreed to create an international organization (the United Nations) to maintain peace after the war.

D-DAY AND AFTER   In early 1944 General Dwight D. Eisenhower, smart, efficient, and well organized, arrived in London to take command at the Supreme Headquarters of the Allied Expeditionary Force (SHAEF). Al-ready battle-tested in North Africa and the Mediterranean, he now faced the daunting task of planning and conducting Operation Overlord, the cross-Channel assault on Hitler's "Atlantic Wall," what seemed to be an impreg-nable series of fortifications along the French coastline that German forces had created using captive Europeans for laborers.

The prospect of an amphibious assault against such defenses in a single huge battle unnerved some Allied planners. As D-Day approached, Eisen-hower's chief of staff predicted only a fifty-fifty chance of success. Operation Overlord prevailed largely because it was the most carefully planned operation in military history and because Eisenhower and the Allies surprised the Ger-mans. They fooled Hitler's generals into believing that the invasion would come at Pas de Calais, on the French-Belgian border, where the English Channel was narrowest. Instead, the landings occurred in Normandy, almost 200 miles south. In April and May 1944, while the vast invasion forces made final preparations, the Allied air forces disrupted the transportation network of northern France, smashing railroads and bridges. By early June all was ready, and D-Day fell on June 6, 1944.

On the evening of June 5, Eisenhower visited some of the 16,000 American paratroopers preparing to land behind the German lines in France to create

Operation Overlord

General Dwight D. Eisenhower instructing paratroopers before they boarded their airplanes to launch the D-Day assault.

chaos and disrupt communications. The men noticed his look of grave concern and tried to lift his spirits. "Now quit worrying, General," one of them said, "we'll take care of this thing for you." After the planes took off, Eisenhower returned to his car with tears in his eyes. "Well," he said quietly to his driver, "it's on." He knew that many of his troops would die within a few hours.

Airborne forces dropped behind the beaches while planes and battleships pounded the coastal defenses. At dawn the invasion fleet of some 4,000 ships carrying 150,000 men (57,000 Americans) filled the horizon off the Normandy coast. Overhead, thousands of Allied planes supported the invasion force. Sleepy German soldiers awoke to see the vast armada arrayed before them. For several hours the local German commanders interpreted the Normandy landings as merely a diversion for the "real" attack at Pas de Calais. When Hitler learned of the Allied landings, he boasted that "the news couldn't be better. As long as they were in Britain, we couldn't get at them. Now we have them where we can destroy them."

Despite Eisenhower's meticulous planning and the imposing array of Allied troops and firepower, the D-Day invasion almost failed. Thick clouds and German anti-aircraft fire caused many of the paratroopers and glider

The Landing at Normandy

D-Day, June 6, 1944. Before they could huddle under a seawall and begin to root out the region's Nazi defenders, soldiers on Omaha Beach had to cross a fifty-yard stretch that exposed them to bullets fired from machine guns housed in concrete bunkers.

pilots to miss their landing zones. Oceangoing landing craft delivered their troops to the wrong locations. Low clouds led the Allied planes to drop their bombs too far inland. The naval bombardment was equally ineffective. Rough seas made many soldiers seasick and capsized dozens of landing craft. Over 1,000 men drowned. On Utah Beach the American invaders landed against relatively light opposition, but farther east, on a four-mile segment designated Omaha Beach, bombardment failed to take out the German defenders, and the Americans were caught in heavily mined water. The first units ashore lost over 90 percent of their troops. In one rifle company 197 of the 205 men were killed or wounded within ten minutes. By nightfall the bodies of some 5,000 killed or wounded Allied soldiers were strewn across the sand and surf of Normandy.

German losses were even more incredible. Entire units were decimated or captured. Operation Overlord was the greatest military invasion in the annals of warfare and the climactic battle of World War II. With the beachhead secured, the Allied leaders knew that victory was now in their grasp. "What a plan!" Churchill exclaimed to the British Parliament. Stalin, who had been clamoring for the cross-Channel invasion for years, applauded the Normandy operation, declaring that the "history of warfare knows no other like undertaking from the point of view of its scale, its vast conception and its orderly execution."

Within two weeks the Allies had landed 1 million troops, 556,000 tons of supplies, and 170,000 vehicles. They had seized a beachhead sixty miles wide and five to fifteen miles deep. As the weeks passed, they continued to pour men and supplies onto the beaches and to edge inland through the marshes and hedgerows. A stubborn Hitler issued disastrous orders to contest every inch of land. General Rommel, convinced that all was lost, began to intrigue for a separate peace. Other like-minded German officers, sure that the war was hopeless, tried to kill Hitler at his headquarters on July 20, 1944, but the Führer survived the bomb blast and ordered hundreds of conspirators and suspects tortured to death. Rommel was granted the option of suicide, which he took.

Meanwhile, the Führer's tactics brought calamity to the German forces in western France. On July 25 American units broke out westward into Brittany and eastward toward Paris. On August 15 a joint American-French invasion force landed on the French Mediterranean coast and raced up the Rhone Valley. German resistance in France collapsed. A division of the Free French Resistance, aided by American forces, had the honor of liberating Paris on August 25. Nazi forces retired pell-mell toward the German border, and by mid-September most of France and Belgium were cleared of enemy troops.

SLOWING MOMENTUM   Events had moved so much faster than expected, in fact, that the Allies were running out of gasoline. Neither their plans nor their supply system could keep up with the rapid movement of tanks and troops. British and Canadian forces under General Bernard Montgomery had moved into Belgium, where they took Antwerp on September 4. From there, Montgomery argued, a quick thrust toward Berlin could end things. On the right flank, General George Patton was just as sure he could take the American Third Army all the way to Berlin. Eisenhower reasoned, however, that a swift, narrow thrust into Germany would be cut off, counterattacked, and defeated. Instead he advocated advancing along a broad front. Prudence demanded getting his supply lines in order first, which required clearing out stubborn German forces and opening a supply channel to Antwerp—a long, hard battle that lasted until the end of November 1944.

LEAPFROGGING TO TOKYO

Even in the Pacific, relegated to a lower priority, Allied forces had brought the war within reach of the enemy's homeland by the end of 1944. The Pacific war's first American offensive, in fact, had been in the southwest Pacific. There the Japanese, stopped at the Coral Sea and Midway, had captured the southern Solomon Islands and were building an airstrip on Guadalcanal, from which they would be able to attack Allied transportation routes to Australia. On August 7, 1942, two months before the North Africa landings, the First Marine Division landed on Guadalcanal and seized the airstrip.

MacARTHUR IN NEW GUINEA   Meanwhile, American and Australian forces under General Douglas MacArthur had begun to push the Japanese out of their positions on the northern coast of New Guinea. These battles, fought through some of the hottest, most humid, and most mosquito-infested swamps in the world, bought advances at a heavy cost, but by the end of January 1943 the eastern tip of New Guinea had been secured.

At this stage, U.S. strategists made a critical decision. The egotistical MacArthur, sometimes accused of being a legend in his own mind, proposed to move westward along the northern coast of New Guinea toward the Philippines and ultimately to Tokyo. Admiral Chester Nimitz, with headquarters at Pearl Harbor, argued for a sweep through the islands of the central Pacific to Formosa and China. In March 1943 the combined chiefs of staff agreed to pursue both plans.

During the Battle of the Bismarck Sea (March 2–3, 1943), American bombers sank eight Japanese troopships and ten warships carrying reinforcements. Thereafter the Japanese dared not risk sending transports to reinforce points under siege, thereby making it possible for the Allies to use the tactic of neutralizing Japanese strongholds with air and sea power and moving on, leaving them to die on the vine. Some called it leapfrogging, and Japanese leaders later acknowledged the strategy as a major factor contributing to the Allied victory. Meanwhile, in mid-April, before the offensive got under way, U.S. fighter planes shot down a Japanese plane that code breakers knew was carrying Admiral Yamamoto, Japan's naval commander and the planner of the Pearl Harbor attack. His death shattered Japanese morale.

NIMITZ IN THE CENTRAL PACIFIC   Admiral Nimitz's advance through the central Pacific had as its first target two tiny islands, Makin (Butaritari) and Tarawa. After advance bombing raids, a fleet of 200 ships delivered infantry and marines at dawn on November 20, 1943. Makin, where the

Japanese had only a small force, was soon cleared. Tarawa, however, was one of the most heavily protected islands in the Pacific. There nearly 1,000 American soldiers, sailors, and marines lost their lives rooting out Japanese soldiers who refused to surrender.

Invasion of the Marshall Islands, the next step up the ladder to Tokyo, began on January 31, 1944. American forces took Saipan, in the Marianas, on June 15, bringing the new American B-29 bombers within striking distance of Japan itself. In the Battle of the Philippine Sea, fought mostly in the air on June 19–20, 1944, the Japanese lost 3 more aircraft carriers, 2 submarines, and over 300 planes. The battle secured the Marianas, and soon B-29s were winging their way from Saipan to bomb the Japanese homeland. Defeat in the Marianas convinced General Tōjō that the war was lost. On July 18, 1944, he and his entire cabinet resigned.

THE BATTLE OF LEYTE GULF With New Guinea and the Mariana Islands all but conquered, President Roosevelt met with General MacArthur and Admiral Nimitz in Honolulu on July 27–28, 1944. They decided next to liberate the Philippine Islands from Japanese control. MacArthur's forces

MacArthur's Triumphant Return

General Douglas MacArthur (center) theatrically comes ashore at the island of Leyte in the Philippines, October 1944.

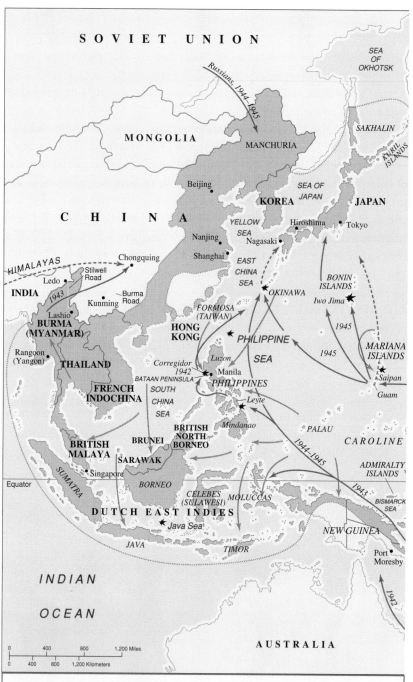

SOVIET UNION

SEA
OF
OKHOTSK

SAKHALIN

Russians 1944–1945

MONGOLIA

MANCHURIA

KURIL ISLANDS

Beijing

KOREA *SEA OF JAPAN*

JAPAN

C H I N A

YELLOW
SEA

Hiroshima

Tokyo

HIMALAYAS

Chongqing

Nanjing

Nagasaki

Stilwell Road

Ledo

Shanghai

EAST CHINA SEA

1943

Burma Road

Kunming

OKINAWA

BONIN ISLANDS

Iwo Jima

INDIA

Lashio

BURMA
(MYANMAR)

FORMOSA (TAIWAN)

1945

1945

MARIANA
ISLANDS

Rangoon
(Yangon)

THAILAND

HONG
KONG

PHILIPPINE

Saipan

*Corregidor
1942*

Luzon

SEA

Guam

FRENCH
INDOCHINA

BATAAN PENINSULA

Manila

*SOUTH
CHINA
SEA*

PHILIPPINES

Leyte

BRITISH
NORTH
BORNEO

Mindanao

PALAU

CAROLINE

BRITISH
MALAYA

BRUNEI

SARAWAK

1944–1945

ADMIRALTY
ISLANDS

Singapore

BORNEO

Equator

SUMATRA

*CELEBES
(SULAWESI)*

MOLUCCAS

1943

*BISMARCK
SEA*

DUTCH EAST INDIES

Java Sea

NEW GUINEA

JAVA

TIMOR

Port
Moresby

INDIAN

1942

OCEAN

AUSTRALIA

| 0 | 400 | 800 | 1,200 Miles |
| 0 | 400 | 800 | 1,200 Kilometers |

What was "leapfrogging"? Why were the battles in the Marianas a major
turning point in the war? What was the significance of the Battle of Leyte
Gulf? How did the battle at Okinawa affect how both sides proceeded in
the war? Why did Truman decide to drop atomic bombs on Hiroshima and
Nagasaki?

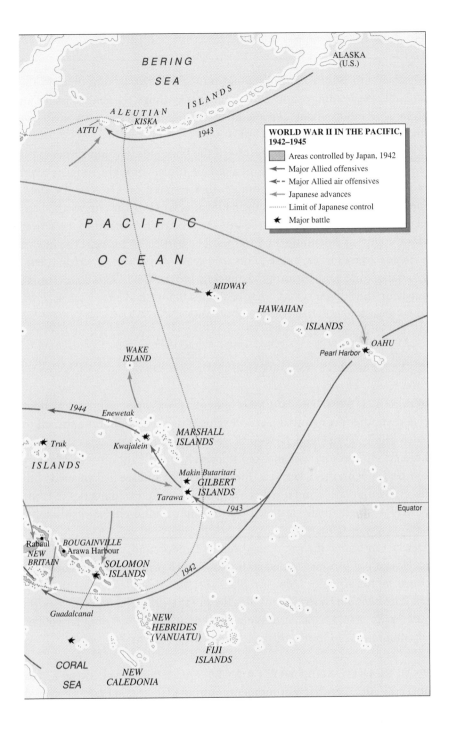

BERING

SEA

ALASKA
(U.S.)

ALEUTIAN ISLANDS
KISKA
ATTU   1943

PACIFIC

OCEAN

MIDWAY

HAWAIIAN

ISLANDS

OAHU
Pearl Harbor

WAKE
ISLAND

1944   Enewetak

Truk   Kwajalein

ISLANDS

MARSHALL
ISLANDS

Makin Butaritari
GILBERT
ISLANDS

Tarawa

1943   Equator

Rabaul
NEW
BRITAIN

BOUGAINVILLE
Arawa Harbour

SOLOMON
ISLANDS   1942

Guadalcanal

NEW
HEBRIDES
(VANUATU)

FIJI
ISLANDS

CORAL

SEA

NEW
CALEDONIA

WORLD WAR II IN THE PACIFIC,
1942–1945

Areas controlled by Japan, 1942
Major Allied offensives
Major Allied air offensives
Japanese advances
Limit of Japanese control
Major battle

made their move into the Philippines on October 20, landing first on the island of Leyte. Wading ashore behind the first landings, the general issued an emotional announcement: "People of the Philippines: I have returned. . . . Rally to me. . . . Let no heart be faint."

The Japanese, knowing that the loss of the Philippines would cut them off from the essential raw materials of the East Indies, brought in fleets from three directions. The three encounters that resulted on October 25, 1944, came to be known collectively as the Battle of Leyte Gulf, the largest naval engagement in history. The Japanese lost most of their remaining sea power and the ability to defend the Philippines. The battle also brought the first of the suicide attacks by Japanese pilots who crash-dived into American carriers, sinking one and seriously damaging others. The "kamikaze" units, named for the "divine wind" that centuries before had saved Japan from Mongol invasion, inflicted considerable damage.

A New Age Is Born

ROOSEVELT'S FOURTH TERM   In 1944, war or no war, the calendar dictated another presidential election. This time the Republicans turned to former crime fighter and New York governor Thomas E. Dewey as their candidate. No Democrat challenged Roosevelt, but a fight did develop over the second spot on the ticket. Vice-President Henry Wallace had angered both southern conservative and northern city bosses, who feared his ties to labor unions. Roosevelt finally fastened on the compromise choice of Missouri senator Harry S. Truman.

Dewey ran under the same handicap as Landon and Willkie had before him. He did not propose to dismantle Roosevelt's programs but argued that it was time for younger men to replace the "tired" old leaders of the New Deal. Roosevelt did show signs of illness and exhaustion, but nevertheless, on November 7, 1944, he was once again elected, this time by a popular vote of 25.6 million to 22 million and an electoral vote of 432 to 99.

CONVERGING MILITARY FRONTS   After their quick sweep across France, the Allied armies lost momentum in the fall of 1944 as they neared Germany. The Germans sprang a surprise in the rugged Ardennes Forest, where the Allied line was thinnest. Attacking on December 16, 1944, the Germans advanced along a fifty-mile bulge in Belgium and Luxembourg—hence the Battle of the Bulge. In ten days they penetrated nearly to the Meuse River on their way to Antwerp, but they stalled at Bastogne. Reinforced by the Allies just before it was surrounded, Bastogne held for six days against relentless German attacks. On December 22 the American general Tony McAuliffe gave his memorable answer to the demand for surrender: "Nuts." When a German major asked what the term meant, an American officer said, "It's the same as 'Go to Hell.' And I will tell you something else—if you continue to attack, we will kill every goddamn German that tries to break into this city." The American situation remained desperate until the next day, when the clouds lifted, allowing Allied airpower to hit the Germans and drop in supplies. On December 26, U.S. forces broke through to relieve Bastogne, but it would be mid-January 1945 before the previous lines were restored.

Germany's sudden counterattack upset Eisenhower's timetable, but the outcome shook the Nazis' power and morale. Their desperate effort at Bastogne had weakened the eastern front, and in January 1945 the Russians began their final offensive westward. The destruction of Hitler's last reserve units at the Battle of the Bulge had also left open the door to Germany's heartland from the west. By early March the Allies had reached the banks of the Rhine River, which runs from Switzerland to Holland. On March 6 they took Cologne, and the next day, by remarkable luck, the Allies seized the bridge at Remagen before the Germans could blow it up. Troops poured across the Rhine. The Allies then encircled the Ruhr Valley, center of Germany's heavy industry. By mid-April resistance there had been overcome. Meanwhile the Soviet offensive had also reached Germany, after taking Warsaw, Poland, on January 17 and Vienna, Austria, on April 13.

With the British and American armies racing across western Germany and the Soviets moving in from the east, the attention of the war planners turned to Berlin. Churchill had grown suspicious of the Soviets and worried that if they arrived in Berlin first, they would gain dangerous leverage in deciding the postwar map of Europe. He urged Eisenhower to get to Berlin first. Eisenhower, however, refused to mix politics with military strategy. He was convinced the Soviets would get to Berlin first. He also knew that the Allied leaders were envisioning separate occupation zones for Germany, and Berlin was in the Soviet zone. Why rush to liberate the German capital only to turn it over to the Soviets? Berlin, he decided, was no longer of military significance. His purpose remained the destruction of German ground forces. Churchill disagreed and appealed to Roosevelt, but the American president, now seriously ill, left the decision to the supreme commander. Eisenhower then asked his trusted lieutenant, General Omar Bradley, to estimate what it would take to liberate Berlin before the Soviets. Bradley predicted that it would cost 100,000 Allied casualties, which he described as a

The War's End

German prisoners of war being corralled by U.S. soldiers in 1945.

"pretty stiff price to pay for a prestige objective." Eisenhower agreed, and they left Berlin to the Soviets.

YALTA AND THE POSTWAR WORLD   As the final offensives against Germany got under way, the Yalta Conference (February 4–11, 1945) brought the Big Three leaders together again, this time in a czar's palace at a Crimean resort (the only place in Russia both warm enough in February and undamaged enough to be hospitable). While the focus at Tehran in 1943 had been on wartime strategy, the leaders now discussed the shape of the postwar world. Stalin was self-confident, assertive, demanding, and sarcastic. He knew that the Soviet forces' control of key areas would ensure that his demands were met. Two aims loomed large in Roosevelt's thinking. One was the need to ensure that the Soviet Union would join the war against Japan. The other was based upon the lessons he had drawn from the previous world war. Chief among the mistakes to be remedied this time were the failure of the United States to join the League of Nations and the failure of the Allies to maintain a united front against the German aggressors after the war.

The Yalta meeting began by calling for a conference to create a new world security organization, to be held in the United States beginning on April 25, 1945.

The Yalta Conference

Churchill, Roosevelt, and Stalin confer on the shape of the postwar world in February 1945.

Arrangements for the postwar governance of Germany were also made at Yalta. The war map dictated the basic pattern of occupation zones: the Soviets would control eastern Germany, and the Western Allies would control the rich industrial areas of the west. Berlin, isolated within the Soviet zone, would be subject to joint occupation. Similar arrangements were made for Austria, with Vienna, like Berlin, under joint occupation within the Soviet zone. At the behest of Churchill and Roosevelt, liberated France was granted an occupation zone along its border with Germany and in Berlin. Soviet demands that defeated Germany pay in reparations, $20 billion, half of which would go to the Soviet Union, were referred to a reparations commission in Moscow. The commission never reached agreement, however, although the Soviets appropriated massive amounts of German machinery and equipment from their occupation zone.

With respect to Eastern Europe, where Soviet forces were advancing on a broad front, there was little the Western Allies could do to influence events. Roosevelt was inhibited by his wish to win Soviet cooperation in the fight against Japan and in the effort to build the proposed United Nations. Poland became the main focus of Western concern. Britain and

France had gone to war in 1939 to defend Poland, and now, six years later, the course of the war had left Poland's fate in the hands of the Soviets.

When Soviet forces reentered Poland in 1944, they placed civil administration under a Polish Committee of National Liberation in Lublin, a puppet Communist regime representing few Poles. As Soviet troops reached the gates of Warsaw, the underground resistance in the city, supporters of the Polish government-in-exile in London, rose up against the Nazi occupiers. The Soviet armies then stopped their offensive for two months while the Nazis wiped out thousands of Poles, potential rivals of the Soviets' Lublin puppet government.

The belief that postwar cooperation among the Allies could survive such events was a triumph of hope over experience. The Western Allies could do no more than acquiesce to Soviet demands or stall at Yalta. On the Soviet proposal to expand the Lublin committee into a provisional government together with representatives of the London Poles, Roosevelt and Churchill acquiesced. On the issue of Poland's boundaries, they stalled. The Soviets proposed to keep eastern Poland for themselves, offering land taken from Germany as compensation. Roosevelt and Churchill accepted the proposal but considered the western boundary at the Oder and Neisse rivers only provisional. The peace conference at which the western boundary of Poland was to be settled never took place, however, because of later disagreements. The presence of the London Poles in the provisional government lent a tone of legitimacy to a Polish regime dominated by Communists, who soon ousted their rivals.

At Yalta the Big Three promised to sponsor free elections, democratic governments, and constitutional safeguards of freedom throughout the rest of Europe. The Yalta Declaration of Liberated Europe reaffirmed faith in the principles of the Atlantic Charter, but in the end it made little difference. It may have postponed takeovers in Eastern Europe for a few years, but before long Communist members of coalition governments had ousted the opposition. Russia, twice invaded by Germany in the twentieth century, was determined to create buffer states between it and the Germans.

YALTA'S LEGACY   Critics later attacked the Yalta agreements for "giving" Eastern Europe over to Soviet domination. But the course of the war shaped the actions at Yalta. The Soviet army controlled the region. By suppressing opposition in the occupied territories, moreover, the Soviets were acting not under the Yalta accords, but in violation of them.

Perhaps the most bitterly criticized of the Yalta accords was a secret agreement on the Far East, not made public until after the war. As the Big Three met, fighting still raged against the Japanese in the Philippines and Burma. The combined chiefs of staff estimated that Japan could hold out for eighteen months after the defeat of Germany. Costly campaigns lay ahead, and the atomic bomb was still an untested gamble. Roosevelt therefore accepted Stalin's demands on postwar arrangements in the Far East, subject technically to agreement later by Chiang Kai-shek. Stalin wanted continued Soviet control of Outer Mongolia through its puppet People's Republic, acquisition of the Kuril Islands from Japan, and recovery of rights and territory lost after the Russo-Japanese War of 1905. Stalin in return promised to enter the war against Japan two or three months after the German defeat, recognize Chinese sovereignty over Manchuria, and conclude a treaty of friendship and alliance with the Chinese Nationalists. Roosevelt's concessions would later appear in a different light, but given their geographic advantages in Asia, as in Eastern Europe, the Soviets were in a position to get what they wanted in any case.

THE COLLAPSE OF THE THIRD REICH   By 1945 the collapse of Nazi resistance was imminent, but President Roosevelt did not live to join the celebrations. Throughout 1944 his health had been declining, and photographs from early 1945 reveal a very sick man. In the spring of 1945 he went to his second home, in Warm Springs, Georgia, to rest up for the charter conference of the United Nations in San Francisco. On April 12, 1945, he died from a cerebral hemorrhage.

Hitler's Germany collapsed less than a month later. The Allied armies rolled up almost unopposed to the Elbe River, where they met advance detachments of Soviets on April 25. Three days later Italian partisans caught and killed Mussolini as he tried to flee. In Berlin, which was under siege by the Soviets, Hitler married his mistress, Eva Braun, in an underground bunker on the last day of April. He then killed her and himself. On May 2 Berlin fell to the Soviets. That same day German forces in Italy surrendered. Finally, on May 7, General Alfred Jodl, chief of staff of the German armed forces, signed an unconditional surrender in the Allied headquarters at Reims, France. So ended the Thousand-Year Reich, little more than twelve years after its führer came to power.

Massive victory celebrations in Europe on V-E day, May 8, 1945, were tempered by the tragedies that had engulfed the world: mourning for the lost American president and the death and mutilation of untold millions. Most shocking was the realization of the extent of the Holocaust, scarcely believable until the Allied armies came upon the death camps in which the Nazis had sought to apply their "final solution" to the "Jewish problem": the wholesale

May 8, 1945

The celebration in New York's City's Times Square on V-E Day.

extermination of some 6 million Jews along with more than 1 million others. During the war, testimony from relief agencies had piled up growing evidence of the Nazis' systematic genocide against the Jews of Europe. Reports appeared in major American newspapers as early as 1942 but were nearly always buried on inside pages. The falsehoods of World War I propaganda had conditioned too many people to doubt all atrocity stories, and rumors of such horror seemed beyond belief.

American government officials, even some Jewish leaders, dragged their feet for fear that relief for Jewish refugees might stir up latent anti-Semitism at home. Under pressure, Roosevelt had set up a War Refugee Board early in 1944. It managed to rescue about 200,000 European Jews and some 20,000 others. More might have been done by broadcasts warning people in Europe that Nazi "labor camps" were in fact death traps. The Allies rejected a plan to bomb the rail lines into the largest concentration camp, Auschwitz, in Poland, although American planes hit industries five miles away. And few refugees were accepted into the United States. The Allied handling of the Holocaust was inept at best and disgraceful at worst.

Holocaust Survivors

U.S. troops encounter survivors of the Nazis' Wöbbelin concentration camp in Germany, May 1945.

A GRINDING WAR AGAINST JAPAN   The sobering thought that the defeat of Japan remained to be accomplished cast a further pall over the victory celebrations in Europe in the spring of 1945. American forces continued to assault the Japanese Empire in the early months of 1945, but at a heavy cost. While fighting continued in the Philippines, marines invaded Japanese-controlled Iwo Jima island on February 19, 1945, a speck of volcanic rock 760 miles from Tokyo that was needed to provide a fighter escort for bombers over Japan and a landing strip for disabled B-29 bombers. Nearly six weeks were required to secure an island five miles square from defenders hiding in underground caves. The cost was more than 20,000 American casualties, including nearly 7,000 dead.

The fight for Okinawa, beginning on Easter Sunday, April 1, was even bloodier. The largest island in the Ryukyu chain, Okinawa was large enough to afford a staging area for the planned invasion of Japan. Assaulting Okinawa would be the largest amphibious operation of the Pacific war, involving some 300,000 troops. The fight for Okinawa raged until late June. An estimated 140,000 Japanese died. Casualties also included about 42,000 Okinawans.

When resistance on Okinawa collapsed, the Japanese emperor instructed his new prime minister to seek peace terms.

THE ATOMIC BOMB By that time, however, President Truman had learned of the first successful test explosion of an atomic bomb, the result of intensive research and development, begun in 1940, when President Roosevelt had set up a committee to study atomic weaponry. Army and navy funds were soon diverted to fund the research that ultimately grew into the $2-billion top-secret Manhattan Project. On December 2, 1942, Dr. Enrico Fermi and other scientists achieved the first atomic chain reaction at the University of Chicago, removing any remaining doubts about the bomb's feasibility. Gigantic plants sprang up at Oak Ridge, Tennessee, and Hanford, Washington, to provide material for atomic bombs, while a group of physicists under J. Robert Oppenheimer worked out the scientific and technical problems of bomb construction in a laboratory at Los Alamos, New Mexico. On July 16, 1945, the first atomic fireball rose from the desert. Oppenheimer said later that in the observation bunker "a few people laughed, a few people cried, most people were silent."

How to use this awful new weapon posed a profound dilemma. Some scientists favored a demonstration in a remote area, but military use was decided upon because only two bombs were available, and even those might misfire. More consideration was given to the choice of targets. Four Japanese cities were potential targets. Priority went to Hiroshima, a port city of 400,000 people in southern Japan, which was a major assembly point for Japanese naval convoys, a center of war industries, and head-quarters of the Second General Army.

On July 25, 1945, President Harry S. Truman, who had been thrust into office after Roosevelt's death in April, ordered the atomic bomb dropped if Japan did not surrender before August 3. Although an intense scholarly debate has emerged over the decision to drop the atomic bomb, it is clear that Truman be-lieved that the bomb was "a military weapon and never had any doubt that it should be used." He was convinced that the atomic bomb would save lives by avoiding a costly American invasion against defenders who would fight like "savages, ruthless, merciless, and fanatic."

The ferocious Japanese defense of Okinawa had convinced military plan-ners that an amphibious invasion of Japan itself, scheduled to begin on No-vember 1, 1945, could cost as many as 250,000 Allied casualties and even more Japanese losses. Moreover, some 100,000 Allied prisoners of war being held in Japan would most likely be executed when an invasion began. It is important to remember as well that the bombing of cities and the consequent killing of civilians had become accepted military practice during 1945. Once the Japanese navy was destroyed, American ships had roamed the Japanese coastline, shelling targets onshore. American planes had bombed at will and mined the waters of the Inland Sea. Tokyo, Nagoya, and other major cities had been devastated by firestorms created by incendiary bombs. The firebomb raids on Tokyo on a single night in March 1945 killed over 100,000 civilians and left over 1 million people homeless. By July more than sixty of Japan's largest cities had been firebombed, resulting in 500,000 deaths and 13 million civilians left homeless. The use of atomic bombs on Japanese cities was thus seen as a logical next step to end the war without an invasion of Japan. As it turned out, American scientists greatly underestimated the physical effects of the atomic bomb. They predicted that 20,000 people would be killed.

On July 26 the heads of the American, British, and Russian governments issued the Potsdam Declaration, demanding that Japan surrender or face "prompt and utter destruction." The deadline passed, and on August 6, 1945, a B-29 bomber named the *Enola Gay* took off at 2 A.M. from the island of Tinian and headed for Hiroshima. At 8:15 A.M., flying at 31,600 feet, the *Enola Gay* released the five-ton uranium bomb nicknamed Little Boy. Forty-three seconds later, as the *Enola Gay* turned sharply to avoid the blast, the bomb tumbled to an altitude of 1,900 feet, where it exploded as planned with the force of 20,000 tons of TNT. A blinding flash of light was followed by a fireball towering to 40,000 feet. The tail gunner on the *Enola Gay* described the scene: "It's like bubbling molasses down there . . . the mushroom is spreading out . . . fires are springing up everywhere . . . it's like a peep into hell."

The shock wave, firestorm, cyclonic winds, and radioactive rain killed some 80,000 people, including thousands of Japanese soldiers assigned to the Second General Army headquarters and 23 American prisoners of war housed in the city. Dazed survivors wandered the streets, so painfully burned that their skin began to peel off in large strips. By the end of the year, the death toll had reached 140,000 as the effects of radiation burns and infection took their toll. In addition, 70,000 buildings were destroyed, and four square miles of the city turned to rubble.

In the United States, Americans greeted the first news with elation: the bombing promised a quick end to the long nightmare of war. "No tears of sympathy will be shed in America for the Japanese people," the *Omaha World-Herald* predicted. "Had they possessed a comparable weapon at Pearl Harbor, would they have hesitated to use it?" Others were more circumspect. "Yesterday," the journalist Hanson Baldwin wrote in the *New York Times*, "we clinched victory in the Pacific, but we sowed the whirlwind."

The Bomb

This image shows the wasteland that remained after the atomic bomb "Little Boy" decimated Hiroshima in 1945.

Two days after the Hiroshima bombing, an opportunistic Soviet Union, eager to share in the spoils of victory, hastened to enter the war in Asia. Truman and his aides, frustrated by the stubborn refusal of Japanese military and political leaders to surrender and fearful that the Soviet Union's entry into the war would complicate negotiations, ordered the second atomic bomb dropped. On August 9, a B-29 aircraft named *Bockscar*, carrying a bomb dubbed Fat Man, flew over its primary target, Kokura. However, the city was so shrouded in haze and smoke from an earlier air raid that the plane turned to its secondary target, Nagasaki, where it dropped its bomb at 11:02 A.M., killing 36,000 people. That night the Japanese emperor urged his cabinet to surrender on the sole condition that he remain as sovereign. The next day the U.S. government announced its willingness to let the emperor keep his throne, but under the authority of an Allied supreme commander. Frantic exchanges ended with Japanese acceptance of the terms on August 14, 1945, when the emperor himself broke with precedent to record a radio message announcing the surrender to the public.

On September 2, 1945, General Douglas MacArthur and other Allied representatives accepted Japan's formal surrender on board the battleship *Missouri* in Tokyo Bay. MacArthur then settled in at his occupation headquarters across from the imperial palace in Tokyo.

The Final Ledger

Thus ended the costliest conflict in human history. One estimate has it that 70 million fought in the war, at a cost of 25 million military dead and more than 24 million civilian dead, including Jews and others murdered in Nazi concentration camps. The Soviet Union suffered the greatest losses of all: over 13 million military deaths, over 7 million civilian deaths, and at least 25 million left homeless. World War II was more costly for the United States than any other foreign war: 292,000 battle deaths and 114,000 other deaths. But in proportion to its population, the United States suffered a far smaller loss than any of the other major Allies or their enemies, and American territory escaped the devastation visited on so many other parts of the world.

World War II had profound effects on American life and society. Mobilization for the war stimulated a phenomenal increase in productivity and brought full employment, thus ending the Great Depression and laying the foundation for an era of unprecedented prosperity. New technologies and products developed for military purposes—radar, computers, electronics, plastics and synthetics, jet engines, rockets, atomic energy—began to transform the private sector as well. And new opportunities for women as well as for African Americans and other minorities set in motion changes that would culminate in the civil rights movement of the 1960s and the feminist movement of the 1970s.

The Democratic party benefited from the war effort by solidifying its control of both the White House and Congress. The dramatic expansion of the federal government occasioned by the war continued after 1945. Presidential authority and prestige increased enormously at the expense of congressional and state power. The isolationist sentiment in foreign relations that had been so powerful in the 1920s and 1930s disintegrated as the United States emerged from the war with global responsibilities and interests.

The war's end opened a new era for the United States in the world arena. It accelerated the growth of American power while devastating all other world powers, leaving the United States economically and militarily the strongest nation on earth. But the Soviet Union, despite its human and material losses, emerged from the war with much new territory and enhanced influence, making it the greatest power on the whole Eurasian landmass. Just a little over a century after the Frenchman Alexis de Tocqueville had predicted that western Europe would be overshadowed by the power of the United States and Russia, his prophecy came to pass.

MAKING CONNECTIONS

- The impact of World War II on the home front was much more extensive than that of World War I, especially in the effects of war on race and gender relations.

- The growing domestic conservatism of the war years continued into the 1950s, a topic discussed in the next chapter.

- Dwight D. Eisenhower's success as a military commander and the Allied leader led to his nomination and election as president in 1952. Compare Eisenhower's experience to that of General Grant's in and after the Civil War and to the political experience of other American military leaders.

FURTHER READING

John Keegan's *The Second World War* (1989) surveys the European conflict, while Charles B. MacDonald's *The Mighty Endeavor: The American War in Europe* (1986) concentrates on U.S. involvement. Roosevelt's wartime leadership is analyzed in Eric Larrabee's *Commander in Chief: Franklin Delano Roosevelt, His Lieutenants, and Their War* (1987).

Books on specific European campaigns include Stephen E. Ambrose's *D-Day, June 6, 1944: The Climactic Battle of World War II* (1994) and Charles B. MacDonald's *A Time for Trumpets: The Untold Story of the Battle of the Bulge* (1985). On the Allied commander, see Carlo D'Este's *Eisenhower: A Soldier's Life* (2002).

For the war in the Far East, see John Costello's *The Pacific War, 1941–1945* (1981), Ronald H. Spector's *Eagle against the Sun: The American War with Japan* (1985), John W. Dower's award-winning *War without Mercy: Race and Power in the Pacific War* (1986), and Dan van der Vat's *The Pacific Campaign: The U.S.-Japanese Naval War, 1941–1945* (1991).

An excellent overview of the war's effects on the home front is Michael C. C. Adams's *The Best War Ever: America and World War II* (1994). On economic effects, see Harold G. Vatter's *The U.S. Economy in World War II* (1985).

Susan M. Hartmann's *The Home Front and Beyond: American Women in the 1940s* (1982) treats the new working environment for women. Neil A. Wynn looks at the participation of blacks in *The Afro-American and the Second World War* (1976). The story of the oppression of Japanese Americans is told in Peter Irons's *Justice at War: The Story of the Japanese American Internment Cases* (1983).

A sound introduction to U.S. diplomacy during the conflict can be found in Gaddis Smith's *American Diplomacy during the Second World War, 1941–1945* (1965). To understand the role that Roosevelt played in policy making, consult Warren F. Kimball's *The Juggler: Franklin Roosevelt as Wartime Statesman* (1991).

The issues and events that led to the deployment of atomic weapons are addressed in Martin J. Sherwin's *A World Destroyed: The Atomic Bomb and the Grand Alliance* (1975).

Part Seven

THE
AMERICAN
AGE

he United States emerged from World War II the preeminent military and economic power in the world. America enjoyed a commanding position in international trade and was the only nation in possession of the atomic bomb. While much of Europe and Asia struggled to recover from the horrific physical devastation of the war, the United States was virtually unscathed, its economic infrastructure intact and operating at peak efficiency. Jobs that had been scarce in the 1930s were now available for the taking. By 1955 the United States, with only 6 percent of the world's population, was producing half of the world's goods. American capitalism not only demonstrated its economic strength but became a dominant cultural force as well. In Europe, Japan, and elsewhere, American products, forms of entertainment, and fashion attracted excited attention.

Yet the specter of a "cold war" cast a pall over the buoyant revival of the American economy. The ideological contest with the Soviet Union and Communist China produced numerous foreign crises and sparked a domestic witch hunt for American Communists that far surpassed earlier episodes of political and social repression in the nation's history.

Both major political parties accepted the geopolitical assumptions embedded in the ideological cold war with international communism. Both Republican and Democratic presidents affirmed the need to "contain" the spread of Communist influence around the world. This bedrock assumption eventually embroiled the United States in a costly war in Southeast Asia, which destroyed Lyndon Johnson's presidency and revived neo-isolationist sentiments. The Vietnam War was also the catalyst for a countercultural movement in which young idealists of the "baby-boom" generation provided energy for many overdue social reforms, including the civil rights and environmental movements. But the youth revolt also contributed to an array of social ills, from street riots to drug abuse to sexual license. The social upheavals of the 1960s and early 1970s also provoked a conservative backlash. Richard Nixon's paranoid reaction to his critics led to the Watergate affair and destruction of his presidency.

Through all of this turmoil, however, the basic premises of welfare-state capitalism that Franklin Roosevelt had instituted with his New Deal programs remained essentially intact. With only a few exceptions, both Republicans and Democrats after 1945 accepted the notion that the federal government must assume greater responsibility for the welfare of individuals than had heretofore been the case. Even Ronald Reagan, a sharp critic of liberal social-welfare programs, recognized the need for the federal government to provide a "safety net" for those who could not help themselves.

Yet this fragile consensus on public policy began to disintegrate in the late 1980s amid stunning international developments and less visible domestic events. The surprising collapse of the Soviet Union and the disintegration of European communism sent policy makers scurrying to respond to a post–cold war world, in which the United States remained the only legitimate superpower. After forty-five years, American foreign policy was no longer keyed to a single adversary, and world politics lost its bipolar quality. During the early 1990s the two Germany reunited, apartheid in South Africa ended, and Israel and the Palestinians signed a previously unimaginable peace treaty.

At the same time, American foreign policy began to focus less on military power and more on economic competition and technological development. In those arenas, Japan and a reunited Germany challenged the United States for preeminence. By reducing the public's fear of nuclear annihilation, the end of the cold war also reduced American interest in foreign affairs. The presidential election of 1992 was the first since 1936 in which foreign-policy issues played virtually no role. This was an unfortunate development, for post–cold war world affairs remained volatile and dangerous. The implosion of Soviet communism after 1989 unleashed a series of ethnic, nationalist, and separatist conflicts. In the face of inertia among other governments and pleas for assistance, the United States found itself being drawn into crises in faraway lands such as Bosnia, Somalia, Afghanistan, and Iraq.

As the new multipolar world careened toward the end of a century and the start of a new millennium, fault lines began to appear in the American social and economic landscape. A gargantuan federal debt and rising annual deficits threatened to bankrupt a nation that was becoming top-heavy with retirees. Without fully realizing it, much less appreciating its cascading consequences, the American population was becoming disproportionately old. The number of people aged ninety-five to ninety-nine doubled between 1980 and 1990, and the number of centenarians increased 77 percent. The proportion of the population aged sixty-five and older rose steadily during the 1990s. By the year 2000 half of the elderly population was over seventy-five. This demographic fact harbored profound social and political implications. It exerted increasing stress on health-care costs, nursing-home facilities, and the very survival of the Social Security system.

At the same time that the gap between young and old was increasing, so, too, was the disparity between rich and poor. This trend threatened to stratify a society already experiencing rising levels of racial and ethnic tension. Between 1960 and 1990 the gap between the richest 20 percent of the population and the poorest 20 percent doubled. Over 20 percent of all American children in 1990 lived in poverty, and the infant-mortality rate rose. The infant-death rate in Japan was less than half that in the United States. Despite the much-ballyhooed "war-on-poverty" programs initiated by Lyndon Johnson and continued in one form or another by all of his successors, the chronically poor at the end of the twentieth century were more numerous and more bereft of hope than in 1964.

31

THE FAIR DEAL
AND CONTAINMENT

FOCUS QUESTIONS

· What was the economic, social, and political aftermath of
World War II, and what were the origins and early
developments of the cold war?

· What was Truman's Fair Deal?

· What was the extent of U.S. involvement in the Korean War?

· What were the roots of McCarthyism?

To answer these questions and access additional review material, please visit
www.wwnorton.com/studyspace.

 o sooner did the Second World War end than a "cold war"
began. The uneasy wartime alliance between the United
States and the Soviet Union had collapsed by the fall of
1945. The two strongest nations to emerge from the carnage of World War II
could not bridge their ideological differences over such basic issues as human rights, individual liberties, and religious beliefs. Mutual suspicion and a
race to gain influence and control over the so-called third world countries
further polarized the two nations. The defeat of Japan and Germany had created power vacuums that sucked the Soviet Union and the United States into
an unrelenting war of words fed by clashing strategic interests. At the same
time the devastation wrought by the war in western Europe and the exhaustion of its peoples led to anti-colonial uprisings in Asia and Africa that
threatened to strip Britain and France of their empires. The postwar world

was thus an unstable one in which international tensions shaped the contours of domestic politics and culture as well as foreign relations.

DEMOBILIZATION UNDER TRUMAN

TRUMAN'S UNEASY START   "Who the hell is Harry Truman?" Roosevelt's chief of staff asked the president in the summer of 1944. The question was on more lips when, after less than twelve weeks as vice president, Harry Truman took the presidential oath on April 12, 1945. Clearly he was not Franklin Roosevelt, and that was one of the burdens he would bear.

Roosevelt and Truman came from quite different backgrounds. For Truman there had been no inherited wealth, no early contact with the great and near great, no European travel, no Harvard—indeed, no college at all. Born in 1884 in western Missouri, Truman grew up in Independence, an unglamorous town near Kansas City. Bookish and withdrawn, he moved to his grandmother's farm after high school, spent a few years working in Kansas City banks, and grew into an outgoing young man.

During World War I, Truman served in France as captain of an artillery battery. Afterward he and a partner went into the clothing business, but it failed miserably in the recession of 1922, and Truman then became a professional politician under the tutelage of Kansas City's Democratic machine. In 1934 Missouri sent him to the U.S. Senate, where he remained fairly obscure until he became chairman of a committee to investigate fraud in the war-mobilization effort.

Truman lacked Roosevelt's dash and charm, his brilliance and creativity. He was terribly nearsighted and a clumsy public speaker. Yet he had virtues of his own. Something about Harry Truman evoked the spirit of Andrew Jackson: his decisiveness, his feisty character, his family loyalty. But that was a side of the man that the public came to know only as he settled into the presidency. On his first full day as president, he remained awestruck. "Boys, if you ever pray, pray for me now," he told a group of reporters. "I don't know whether you fellows ever had a load of hay fall on you, but when they told me yesterday what had happened, I felt like the moon, the stars and all the planets had fallen on me." But Truman was up to the challenges. Despite his lack of executive experience, he was confident and self-assured—and he needed to be. Managing the transition from war to peace was a monumental task.

Truman favored much of the New Deal and was even prepared to extend its scope, but he was uneasy with many New Dealers. Within ninety days he had replaced much of the Roosevelt cabinet with his own choices. On the

whole they were more conservative in outlook and included several medi-
ocrities. Truman suffered the further handicap of seeming to be a caretaker
for the remainder of Roosevelt's term. Few, including Truman himself at
first, expected him to run in 1948.

Truman gave a significant clue to his domestic policies on September 6,
1945, when he sent Congress a comprehensive peacetime program that in
effect proposed to enlarge the New Deal. Its twenty-one points included expansion of unemployment insurance, a higher minimum wage, a permanent
Fair Employment Practices Committee, slum clearance and low-rent housing, regional development of the nation's river valleys, and a public-works
program. "Not even President Roosevelt asked for so much at one sitting,"
said the House Republican leader. "It's just a plain case of out-dealing the
New Deal." Beset by other problems, Truman soon saw his new domestic
proposals mired in disputes over the transition to a peacetime economy.

CONVERTING TO PEACE The raucous celebrations that greeted
Japan's surrender in the summer of 1945 signaled the habitual American response to military victory: a rapid demobilization of the armed forces and a
return to more congenial pursuits. The public demanded that the president and

The Eldridge General Store, Fayette County, Illinois

Postwar America quickly demobilized, turning its attention to the pursuit of
abundance.

Congress bring the troops home. By 1947 the total armed forces had shrunk from 12 million to 1.5 million. In his memoirs, Truman termed this "the most remarkable demobilization in the history of the world, or 'disintegration' if you want to call it that." By early 1950 the army had been reduced to 600,000 troops.

The military veterans eagerly returned to schools, jobs, wives, and babies. Population growth, which had dropped off sharply in the 1930s, now soared. Americans born during this postwar period composed what came to be known as the baby-boom generation, and that oversize generation would become a dominant force in the nation's social and cultural life.

The end of the war, with its sudden demobilization and conversion to a peacetime economy, brought sharp dislocations but not the postwar depression that many had feared. Several shock absorbers cushioned the economic impact of demobilization: unemployment insurance and other Social Security benefits; the Servicemen's Readjustment Act of 1944, known as the GI Bill of Rights, under which $13 billion was spent for military veterans on education, vocational training, medical treatment, unemployment insurance, and loans for building houses and going into business; and most important, the pent-up demand for consumer goods that was fueled by wartime deprivation. The gross national product first exceeded the 1929 level in 1940, when it reached $101 billion; by annual increases (except in 1946) it had grown to $347 billion by 1952, Truman's last full year in office.

CONTROLLING INFLATION   The most acute economic problem Truman faced was not depression but inflation. Released from wartime restraints, the demands of business owners and workers combined to frustrate efforts at controlling rising prices. Truman endorsed wage increases to sustain purchasing power. He felt that there was "room in the existing price structure" for business to grant such pay increases, a point management refused to concede. Within six weeks of the war's end, corporations had confronted a wave of union demands for higher wages and better benefits.

A series of strikes followed. The United Automobile Workers walked out on General Motors, with union chief Walter Reuther arguing that the company could afford a 30 percent pay hike without raising the prices of its cars. (The company denied this claim.) A strike in the steel industry generalized a formula for settling most of the disputes. President Truman suggested a pay raise of 18.5¢ per hour, which the United Steelworkers accepted but management refused. To break the logjam, the administration in 1946 agreed to let the company increase its prices. That sequence of events became the pattern for settlements in other industries and set a dangerous precedent of price-wage spirals that would plague consumers in the postwar world.

Major disputes soon developed in the coal and railroad industries. John L. Lewis, head of the United Mine Workers, wanted more than the 18.5¢-per-hour wage increase. He also demanded improved safety regulations and a health and welfare fund for union members. Mine owners refused the demands, and a strike followed. The government used its wartime powers to seize the mines; Truman's interior secretary then accepted nearly all of the union's demands.

Truman also seized control of the railroads and won a five-day postponement of a strike. But when the union leaders refused to budge further, the president lashed out against their "obstinate arrogance" and demanded authority from Congress to draft strikers into the armed forces. In the midst of his speech on the issue, the president learned that the strike had been settled, but after informing Congress, he went on with his message. The House passed a bill including the president's demands, but with the strike settled, it died in the Senate.

Into 1946 the wartime Office of Price Administration maintained some restraint on price increases while gradually ending the rationing of most consumer goods, and Truman asked for a one-year renewal of its powers. During the winter and spring of 1946, however, business leaders campaigned against price controls and other restraints. After the congressional elections of 1946, Truman gave up the battle, ending all price controls except those on rent, sugar, and rice.

PARTISAN COOPERATION AND CONFLICT   The legislative history of 1946 was not all deadlock and frustration, however. Amid the turmoil, Congress and the administration worked out two important initiatives, the Employment Act of 1946 and the Atomic Energy Commission. A program of "full employment" had been a Democratic promise in the campaign of 1944, a pledge reaffirmed by Truman in 1945. Thus the administration backed an employment bill proposing that the government make an annual estimate of the investment and production necessary to ensure full employment and calibrate federal spending to that estimate in order to raise production to full-employment levels. Conservatives objected to what they denounced as carte blanche for deficit spending and proposed a nonpartisan commission to advise the president on the economy. Compromise resulted in the Employment Act of 1946, which dropped the commitment to full employment and set up a three-member Council of Economic Advisers to make appraisals of the economy and advise the president in an annual economic report. A new congressional Joint Committee on the Economic Report would propose legislation.

With regard to the new force that atomic scientists had released upon the world, there was little question that the public welfare required the control of atomic energy through a government monopoly. Disagreements over military versus civilian control were resolved when Congress in 1946 created the civilian Atomic Energy Commission. The president alone was given power to order the use of atomic weapons in warfare. Technical problems and high costs would delay for two decades the construction of nuclear power plants, however.

As congressional elections approached in the fall of 1946, public discontent ran high, with most of it focusing on the administration. Both sides held Truman responsible for labor problems. A speaker at the national convention of the Congress of Industrial Organizations (CIO) had tagged Truman "the No. 1 strikebreaker," while much of the public, angry at striking unions, also blamed the strikes on the White House. Earlier in the year, Truman had fired Henry A. Wallace as secretary of commerce in a disagreement over foreign policy, thus offending the Democratic left. At the same time, Republicans charged that Communists had infiltrated the government. Republicans had a field day coining partisan slogans. "To err is Truman" was credited to Martha Taft, wife of Senator Robert Taft. In the elections, Republicans won majorities in both houses of Congress for the first time since 1928.

"To the Rescue!"

Organized labor is being pulled under by the Taft-Hartley Act as Congress, which passed the bill over Truman's veto, makes sure there is no rescue.

Given the head of steam built up against organized labor, the new Republican Congress sought to curb the power of the unions. The result was the Taft-Hartley Labor Act of 1947, which banned the closed shop (in which non-union workers could not be hired) but permitted a union shop (in which workers newly hired were required to join the union) unless banned by state law. It included provisions against "unfair" union practices such as secondary boycotts, jurisdictional strikes (by one union to exclude another from a given company or field), "featherbedding" (paying for work not done), refusal to bargain in good faith, and contributing to political campaigns.

Unions' political action committees were allowed to function on a voluntary basis only, and union leaders had to take oaths declaring that they were not members of the Communist party. Employers were permitted to sue unions for breaking contracts, petition the National Labor Relations Board for votes for or against the use of specific unions as collective-bargaining agents, and speak freely during union campaigns. The act forbade strikes by federal employees and imposed a "cooling-off" period of eighty days on any strike that the president found to be dangerous to the national health or safety.

Truman's veto of the Taft-Hartley bill, which unions called the slave-labor act, restored his credit with labor, and many unionists who had gone over to the Republicans in 1946 returned to the Democrats. The bill passed over Truman's veto, however. Its most severe impact probably was on the CIO's Operation Dixie, a drive to win unions a more secure foothold in the South. By 1954 fifteen states, mainly in the South, had used the Taft-Hartley Act's authority to enact "right-to-work" laws forbidding the union shop.

Truman clashed with the Republicans on other domestic issues, including tax reduction. He vetoed a tax cut on the principle that in times of high production and high employment the federal debt should be reduced. In 1948, however, Congress succeeded in overriding his veto of a $5-billion tax cut even as the government debt was still running high.

Yet the conflicts between Truman and Congress obscured the high degree of bipartisan cooperation marking matters of government reorganization and foreign policy. In 1947 Congress passed the National Security Act, which created a National Military Establishment, headed by the secretary of defense with sub-cabinet departments of army, navy, and air force, and the National Security Council (NSC), which included the president, heads of the defense departments, and the secretary of state, among others. The act made permanent the Joint Chiefs of Staff, a wartime innovation, and established the Central Intelligence Agency (CIA) to coordinate global intelligence-gathering activities.

THE COLD WAR

BUILDING THE UN   The hope that the wartime military alliance would carry over into the postwar world proved but another great illusion. The pragmatic Roosevelt had shared no such hope. To the contrary, he expected that the great powers in the postwar world would have separate spheres of influence but felt he had to support an organization "which would satisfy widespread demand in the United States for new idealistic or universalist arrangements for assuring the peace."

On April 25, 1945, two weeks after Roosevelt's death and two weeks before the German surrender, delegates from fifty nations at war with the Axis met in San Francisco's opera house to draw up the Charter of the United Nations. Additional members would be admitted by a two-thirds vote of the General Assembly. This body, one of the two major agencies set up by the charter, included delegates from all member nations and was to meet annually to approve the budget, receive annual reports from UN agencies, and choose members of the Security Council and other bodies. The Security Council, the other major charter agency, would remain in permanent session and would have "primary responsibility for the maintenance of international peace and security." Its eleven members (fifteen after 1965) included six (later ten) members elected for two-year terms and five permanent members: the United States, the Soviet Union, Britain, France, and the Republic of China (replaced by the People's Republic of China in 1971). Each permanent member had a veto on any question of substance. The Security Council might investigate any dispute, recommend settlement or reference to an International Court at The Hague, in the Netherlands, and take measures, including a resort to military force. The Senate ratified the UN charter by a vote of eighty-nine to two. The organization held its first meeting in London in 1946, pending completion of its permanent home in New York City.

TRYING WAR CRIMINALS   The Allies agreed that those responsible for the atrocities of World War II should face trial and punishment. Both German and Japanese officials were tried for crimes against peace, humanity, and the established rules of war. At Nuremberg, site of the annual Nazi party rallies, twenty-one major German offenders faced an international military tribunal. After a ten-month trial filled with massive documentation of Nazi atrocities, the court acquitted three and sentenced eleven to death, three to life imprisonment, and four to shorter terms. In Tokyo a similar tribunal put twenty-five Japanese leaders on trial in 1946 and sentenced seven to death, sixteen to life imprisonment, and two to lesser prison terms. Other international tribunals tried thousands of others.

DIFFERENCES WITH THE SOVIETS   Since the end of World War II, historians have debated which side held greater responsibility for the onset of the cold war. The conventional, or "orthodox," view argues that the Soviets, led by a paranoid dictator, tried to dominate the globe and the United States had no choice but to stand firm in defense of democratic capitalist values. By contrast, scholars known as revisionists argue that Truman and American economic imperialists were the culprits. Instead of continuing

Nazi Leaders

Hermann Goering (far left, leaning forward) and Rudolf Hess (second from left, covering his eyes) in 1945 at Nuremberg, where they were on trial for war crimes.

Roosevelt's efforts to collaborate with Stalin and the Soviets, revisionists assert, Truman adopted an unnecessarily belligerent stance and an aggressive foreign policy that sought to create American spheres of influence around the world. Truman and his military advisers exaggerated the Soviet threat, in part to justify an American military buildup. Their provocative policies thus crystallized the tensions between the two countries. Yet such an interpretation fails to recognize that Truman inherited a deteriorating relationship with the Soviets. Events of 1945 made compromise and conciliation more difficult, whether for Roosevelt or for Truman.

There were signs of trouble in the Grand Alliance of Britain, the Soviet Union, and the United States as early as the spring of 1945, as the Soviet Union installed compliant governments in Eastern Europe, violating the Yalta promises of democratic elections. On February 1 the Polish Committee of National Liberation, a puppet group already claiming the status of provisional government, moved from Lublin to Warsaw. In March the Soviets installed a puppet prime minister in Romania. Protests against such actions led to Soviet counterprotests that the British and Americans were negotiating a German surrender in Italy "behind the back of the Soviet Union" and that German forces were being concentrated against the Soviet Union.

Such was the atmosphere when Truman entered the White House. A few days before the San Francisco conference to organize the United Nations, Truman gave Soviet foreign minister Vyacheslav Molotov a dressing-down in Washington on the Polish situation. "I have never been talked to like that in my life," Molotov said. "Carry out your agreements," Truman snapped, "and you won't get talked to like that."

On May 12, 1945, four days after victory in Europe, Winston Churchill sent a telegram to Truman: "What is to happen about Europe? An iron curtain is drawn down upon [the Russian] front. We do not know what is going on behind [it]. . . . Surely it is vital now to come to an understanding with Russia, or see where we are with her, before we weaken our armies mortally." Nevertheless, as a gesture of goodwill, and over Churchill's protest, U.S. forces withdrew from the German occupation zone assigned to the Soviet Union at Yalta. American diplomats still hoped that the Yalta agreements would be carried out, at least after a fashion, and that the Soviet Union would help defeat Japan.

Although the Soviets admitted British and American observers to their sectors of occupied Eastern Europe, there was little the Western powers could do to prevent Soviet control of the region, even if they had not let their military forces dwindle. The presence of Soviet armed forces frustrated the efforts of non-Communists to gain political influence in Eastern European countries. The leaders of those opposed to Soviet influence were either exiled, silenced, executed, or imprisoned.

Secretary of State James F. Byrnes struggled through 1946 with the problems of postwar treaties. In early 1947 the Council of Foreign Ministers finally produced treaties for Italy, Hungary, Romania, Bulgaria, and Finland. In effect these treaties confirmed Soviet control over Eastern Europe, which in Russian eyes seemed but a parallel to American control over Japan and Western control over most of Germany and all of Italy. The Yalta guarantees of democracy in Eastern Europe had turned out much like the Open Door policy in China, little more than pious rhetoric sugarcoating the realities of raw power and national interest.

Byrnes's impulse to pressure Soviet diplomats by brandishing the atomic bomb only added to the irritations, intimidating no one. As early as April 1945, he had suggested to Truman that possession of the new weapon "might well put us in position to dictate our own terms at the end of the war." After becoming secretary of state, he had threatened Soviet diplomats with America's growing arsenal of nuclear weapons. But they paid little notice.

CONTAINMENT By the beginning of 1947, relations with the Soviet Union had become even more troubled. A year before, Stalin had pronounced international peace impossible "under the present capitalist development of the world economy." His statement impelled George F. Kennan, counselor of the American embassy in Moscow, to send the secretary of state an 8,000-word dispatch in which he sketched the roots of Soviet policy and warned that Stalinists were "committed fanatically to the belief that . . . it is desirable and necessary that the internal harmony of our society be disrupted, our traditional way of life be destroyed, the international authority of our state be broken, if Soviet power is to be secure."

More than a year later Kennan, now back at the State Department in Washington, spelled out his ideas for a proper response to the Soviets in a 1947 article published anonymously in *Foreign Affairs*. Kennan provided a brilliant psychological analysis of Soviet insecurity and intentions. He predicted that the Soviets would try to fill "every nook and cranny available . . . in the basin of world power." Yet their insecurity also meant that in general they would act cautiously and seek to reduce their risks. Therefore, he insisted, "the main element of any United States policy toward the Soviet Union must be that of a long-term, patient but firm and vigilant *containment* of Russian expansive tendencies . . . by the adroit application of counterforce as a series of constantly shifting geopolitical and political points, corresponding to the shifts and maneuvers of Soviet policy." Kennan predicted "that Soviet power, like the capitalist world of its conception, bears within it the seeds of its own decay, and that the sprouting of those seeds is well advanced."

George F. Kennan

Kennan's 1947 *Foreign Affairs* article spelled out the doctrine of containment.

Kennan's containment concept dovetailed with the outlook of Truman and his advisers. They all harbored a growing fear that Soviet aims reached beyond Eastern Europe, posing dangers in the eastern Mediterranean, the Middle East, and western Europe itself. Indeed, the Soviet Union sought to gain access to the Mediterranean, long important to Russia for purposes of trade and defense. After the war the Soviet Union pressed Turkey for territorial concessions and the right to build naval bases on the Bosporus, an important gateway between the Black Sea and the Mediterranean. In 1946 civil war broke out in Greece between a government backed by the British and a Communist-led faction that held the northern part of the country and drew supplies from Soviet-dominated Yugoslavia, Bulgaria, and Albania. In 1947 the British ambassador informed the American government that the British could no longer bear the economic and military burden of aiding Greece. When Truman conferred with congressional leaders on the situation, the chairman of the Senate Foreign Relations Committee recommended a strong presidential appeal to the American people.

THE TRUMAN DOCTRINE AND THE MARSHALL PLAN   On March 12, 1947, President Truman appeared before Congress to request $400 million in economic aid to Greece and Turkey and the authority to send U.S. military personnel to train their soldiers. In his speech the president enunciated what quickly came to be known as the Truman Doctrine. It justified aid to Greece and Turkey in terms more provocative than George Kennan's ambiguous idea of containment and more general than this specific case warranted. "I believe," Truman declared, "that it must be the policy of the United States to support free peoples who are resisting attempted subjugation by armed minorities or by outside pressures." George Kennan blanched at Truman's indiscriminate commitment to "contain" communism everywhere.

In 1947 Congress passed the Greek-Turkish aid bill and by 1950 had spent $659 million on the program. Turkey achieved economic stability, and Greece defeated the Communist insurrection in 1949, partly because President Tito of Yugoslavia had broken with the Soviets in the summer of 1948 and cut off aid to the Greek Communists. But the principles embedded in the Truman Doctrine committed the United States to intervene throughout the world in order to "contain" the spread of communism, and this global commitment would produce failures as well as successes in the years to come.

The Truman Doctrine marked the beginning, or at least the open acknowledgment, of a contest that the former government official Bernard Baruch named in a 1947 speech to the legislature of South Carolina: "Let us not be deceived—today we are in the midst of a cold war." Greece and Turkey were but the front lines of an ideological struggle that was spreading to western Europe. There wartime damage and dislocation had devastated factory production, and severe drought in 1947, followed by a harsh winter, had destroyed crops. Coal shortages in London left only enough fuel to heat and light homes for a few hours each day. In Berlin, people were freezing or starving to death. The transportation system in Europe was in shambles. Bridges were out, canals clogged, and rail networks destroyed. Amid the chaos the Communist parties of France and Italy were flourishing. Aid from the United Nations had staved off mass starvation but provided little basis for economic recovery.

In the spring of 1947, former general George C. Marshall, who had replaced James Byrnes as secretary of state, called for a program of massive aid to rescue western Europe from disaster. The retired chairman of the Joint Chiefs of Staff and orchestrator of the Allied victories over Germany and Japan, Marshall had been the highest-ranking general during World War II. "He is the great one of the age," said Truman. Marshall used the occasion of the 1947 Harvard graduation ceremonies to outline his plan for the reconstruction of Europe. "Our policy," he said, "is directed not against country or doctrine, but against hunger, poverty, desperation, and chaos." Marshall offered aid to all European countries, including the Soviet Union, and called upon them to take the lead in judging their own needs. On June 27 the foreign ministers of France, Britain, and the Soviet Union met in London to discuss Marshall's overture. Soviet foreign minister Molotov arrived with eighty advisers but during the talks got word from Moscow to withdraw from the "imperialist" scheme.

In December 1947 Truman submitted his proposal for the European Recovery Program to Congress. Two months later a Communist insurgency in Czechoslovakia ended the last remaining coalition government in Eastern Europe. The Communist seizure of power in Prague ensured congressional passage of the Marshall Plan. From 1948 until 1951, the Economic Cooperation Administration, which managed the Marshall Plan, poured $13 billion into European economic recovery.

DIVIDING GERMANY   The Marshall Plan drew the nations of western Europe closer together, but the breakdown of the wartime alliance between the United States and the Soviet Union left the problem of postwar Germany unsettled. The German economy had stagnated, requiring the U.S. Army to support a staggering burden of civilian relief. Slowly zones of occupation evolved into functioning governments. In 1948 the British, French, and Americans united their zones. The "West Germans" then organized state governments and elected delegates to a federal constitutional convention.

"IT'S THE SAME THING WITHOUT MECHANICAL PROBLEMS"

MARSHALL PLAN

MARSHAL STALIN PLAN

"It's the Same Thing"

The Marshall Plan, which distributed aid throughout Europe, is represented in this 1949 cartoon as a modern tractor driven by a prosperous farmer. In the foreground a poor, overworked man is yoked to an old-fashioned "Soviet" plow, forced to go over the ground of the "Marshal Stalin Plan," while Stalin himself tries to persuade others that "it's the same thing without mechanical problems."

Soviet leaders resented the Marshall Plan and the political unification of West Germany. In April 1948 the Soviets began to restrict road and rail traffic into West Berlin; on June 23 they stopped all traffic. The next day, Stalin cut electricity to the western sector of the city. The Soviets hoped the blockade would force the Allies to give up either Berlin or the plan to unify West Germany. It was war by starvation and intimidation. But the American commander in Germany proposed to stand firm. "When Berlin falls, Western Germany will be next," he declared. "If we mean . . . to hold Europe against communism, we must not budge."

Truman agreed, saying, "We are going to stay—period." After considering the use of armed convoys to supply West Berlin, he opted for a massive airlift. At the time this seemed an impossible task. But the Allied air forces quickly brought in planes from around the world and by October 1948 were flying in up to 13,000 tons of food, medicine, coal, and equipment a day. The massive Berlin airlift went on for months. Finally, on May 12, 1949, after extended talks, the Soviets lifted the blockade. Before the end of the year, the Federal Republic of Germany had a government functioning under Chancellor Konrad Adenauer. At the end of May 1949, an independent German "Democratic" republic arose in the Soviet-controlled eastern zone, formalizing the division of Germany. West Germany gradually acquired more authority, until the Western powers recognized its full sovereignty in 1955.

BUILDING NATO   As relations between the Soviets and western Europe chilled, transatlantic unity ripened into formal military alliance. On April 4,

THE OCCUPATION OF GERMANY AND AUSTRIA

French zone · U.S. zone · British zone · Soviet zone

How did the Allies divide Germany and Austria at the Yalta Conference (see page 1120)? What was the "iron curtain"? Why did Truman airlift supplies to Berlin?

1949, the North Atlantic Treaty was signed by representatives of twelve nations: the United States, Britain, France, Belgium, the Netherlands, Luxembourg, Canada, Denmark, Iceland, Italy, Norway, and Portugal. Greece and Turkey joined the alliance in 1952, Germany in 1955, Spain in 1982. Senate ratification of the North Atlantic Treaty by a vote of eighty-two to thirteen demonstrated that the isolationism of the prewar period had disappeared in the face of Soviet communism. The treaty pledged that an attack against any one of the members would be considered an attack against all and provided

NATO

NATO is depicted as a symbol of renewed strength for a battered Europe.

for a council of the North Atlantic Treaty Organization (NATO).

The eventful year of 1948 produced another foreign-policy decision with long-term consequences. Palestine, as the biblical Holy Land had come to be known, had been under Turkish rule until the League of Nations made it a British mandate after World War I. Over the early years of the twentieth century, many Zionists, who advocated a Jewish nation in the region, had migrated there. More arrived after the British gained control, and a greatly increased number arrived during the Nazi persecution of European Jews and just after the Second World War ended. The British having offered the promise of a national homeland, the Jews of Palestine demanded their own state. Efforts to create a Jewish nation in Palestine benefited from the earnest support of American Jews and worldwide Jewish organizations.

Late in 1947, the UN General Assembly voted to partition Palestine into Jewish and Arab states, but this plan met fierce Arab opposition. Finally, the British mandate expired on May 14, 1948, and Jewish leaders proclaimed the independence of Israel. President Truman, who had been in close touch with Jewish leaders, ordered recognition of Israel within minutes—the United States became the first nation to act. The neighboring Arab states thereupon attacked Israel, which held its own. UN mediators gradually worked out truce agreements with Israel's Arab neighbors, and an uneasy peace was restored by May 11, 1949, when Israel joined the United Nations. But the hard feelings and intermittent warfare between Israel and the Arab states have festered ever since, complicating U.S. foreign policy, which has tried to maintain friendship with both sides but has tilted toward Israel.

CIVIL RIGHTS DURING THE 1940s

The social tremors triggered by World War II and the onset of the cold war transformed America's racial landscape. The government-sponsored racism of the German Nazis, the Italian Fascists, and the Japanese imperialists focused attention on the need for the United States to improve its own race relations and to provide for equal rights under the law. As a *New York Times* editorial explained in early 1946, "This is a particularly good time to campaign against the evils of bigotry, prejudice, and race hatred because we have witnessed the defeat of enemies who tried to found a mastery of the world upon such cruel and fallacious policy." The postwar confrontation with the Soviet Union gave Americans an added incentive to improve race relations at home. In the ideological contest with communism for influence in Africa, American diplomats were at a disadvantage as long as racial segregation continued in the United States; the Soviets often compared official racial segregation in the American South to the Nazis' treatment of the Jews.

For most of his political career, Harry Truman had shown little concern with the plight of African Americans. He had grown up in western Missouri assuming that blacks and whites preferred to be segregated from one another. As president, however, he began to reassess his convictions. In the fall of 1946, Truman hosted a delegation of civil rights activists, who urged the president to issue a public statement condemning the resurgence of the Ku Klux Klan and the lynching of African Americans. The delegation graphically described incidents of torture and intimidation against blacks in the South. Truman was aghast. He soon appointed a Committee on Civil Rights to investigate violence against African Americans and to recommend preventive measures. In its recommendations the committee urged the renewal of the Fair Employment Practices Committee (FEPC) and the creation of a permanent civil rights commission to investigate abuses. It also argued that federal aid be denied to any state that mandated segregated schools and public facilities.

On July 26, 1948, Truman banned racial discrimination in the hiring of federal employees. Four days later he issued an executive order ending racial segregation in the armed forces. The air force and navy quickly complied, but the army dragged its feet until the early 1950s. By 1960 the armed forces were the most racially integrated of all national organizations. Desegregating the military was, Truman claimed, "the greatest thing that ever happened to America."

JACKIE ROBINSON Meanwhile, racial segregation was being confronted in a much more public field of endeavor: professional baseball. In April 1947, as the baseball season opened, the National League's Brooklyn Dodgers included on its roster the first African-American player to cross the color line in major-league baseball: Jackie Robinson. Born in Georgia and raised in California, Robinson was an army veteran and baseball player in the Negro leagues. Teammates and opposing players viciously baited

Jackie Robinson, 1949

Racial discrimination remained widespread throughout the postwar period. In 1947 Jackie Robinson of the Brooklyn Dodgers became the first black to play major-league baseball.

Robinson, pitchers threw at him, base runners spiked him, and spectators booed him in every city. Hotels refused him rooms, and restaurants denied him service. Hate mail arrived by the bucket load. On the other hand, black spectators were electrified by Robinson's courageous example; they turned out in droves to watch him play. As time passed, Robinson won over many fans and opposing players through his quiet courage, self-deprecating wit, and determined performance. Soon other teams began to sign black players. Baseball's path-breaking efforts stimulated other professional sports to integrate their rosters. Jackie Robinson vividly demonstrated that racism, not inferiority, impeded African-American advancement in the postwar era and that segregation need not be a permanent condition of American life.

SHAPING THE FAIR DEAL   The determination Truman projected in foreign affairs did not alter his weak image on the domestic front. By early 1948, after three years in the White House, he had yet to shake the impression that he was not up to the job. The Democratic party seemed about to fragment: southern conservatives resented Truman's outspoken support of civil rights, while the left had flared up in 1946 over his firing of Secretary of Commerce Henry Wallace after a speech critical of the administration's policy. "Getting tough [with the Soviet Union]," Wallace had argued, "never brought anything real and lasting—whether for schoolyard bullies or world powers. The tougher we get, the tougher the Russians will get." The left itself was splitting between the Progressive Citizens of America, formed in 1946, which supported Wallace, and the Americans for Democratic Action, formed in 1947, which also criticized Truman but endorsed his firm anti-Communist stance.

By 1948 most political analysts presumed that Truman would be defeated in the November election. Such gloomy predictions did not faze the combative president, however. He resolved to mount a furious reelection campaign. His first step was to shore up the major elements of the New Deal coalition. He needed the midwestern and western farm belts and enjoyed strong support among farmers. In metropolitan areas he needed to carry the labor-union and African-American vote, which he wooed by working closely with unions and liberals and pressing the cause of civil rights.

"I Stand Pat!"

Truman's support of civil rights for African Americans had its political costs, as this 1948 cartoon suggests.

Like other presidents, Truman used his State of the Union message to set the agenda for an election year. The 1948 speech offered something to nearly every group the Democrats hoped to attract. The first goal, Truman said, was "to secure fully the essential human rights of our citizens," and he promised a special message later on civil rights. "To protect human resources," he proposed federal aid to education, increased and extended unemployment and retirement benefits, a comprehensive system of health insurance, more federal support for housing, and extension of rent controls. He continued to pile on the demands: for more rural electrification, for a higher minimum wage, for the admission of thousands of international refugees to the United States, for money for the Marshall Plan, and for a "cost-of-living" tax credit.

THE ELECTION OF 1948   The Republican-controlled Congress for the most part spurned the Truman program, an action it would later regret. At the Republican Convention, New York governor Thomas E. Dewey won the nomination on the third ballot. The platform endorsed most of the New Deal reforms and approved the administration's bipartisan foreign policy; Dewey promised to run things more efficiently, however.

In July a glum Democratic Convention gathered in Philadelphia expecting to do little more than go through the motions but found itself doubly surprised: first by the battle over the civil rights plank and then by Truman's acceptance speech. To keep from stirring southern hostility, the administration sought a platform plank that opposed racial discrimination only in general terms. Liberal Democrats, however, sponsored a plank that called on Congress to take specific action and commended Truman "for his courageous stand on the issue of civil rights." Minneapolis mayor Hubert H. Humphrey electrified the delegates and set off a ten-minute demonstration when he declared, "The time has arrived for the Democratic party to get out of the shadow of states' rights and walk forthrightly into the bright sunshine of human rights." Segregationist delegates from Alabama and Mississippi instead walked out of the convention.

After the Democratic Convention had nominated Truman, the feisty president pledged to "win this election and make the Republicans like it" and added, "Don't you forget it!" He also vowed to call Congress back into session "to get the laws the people need," many of which the Republican platform had endorsed.

On July 17 a group of rebellious southern Democrats met in Birmingham, Alabama, and nominated South Carolina governor Strom Thurmond on a States' Rights Democratic ticket, quickly dubbed the Dixiecrat party. The

Picketing in Philadelphia

The opening of the 1948 Democratic National Convention was marked by demonstrations against racial segregation, led by A. Philip Randolph (left).

The Dixiecrats

The Dixiecrats nominated South Carolina governor Strom Thurmond (center) to lead their ticket in the 1948 election.

Dixiecrats hoped to draw enough electoral votes to preclude a majority for either major party, throwing the election into the House of Representatives, where they might strike a sectional bargain. A few days later, on July 23, the left wing of the Democratic party gathered in Philadelphia to nominate Henry A. Wallace on a Progressive party ticket. These splits in the Democratic ranks seemed to spell the final blow to Truman. The special session of Congress petered out in futility.

But Truman, undaunted, set out on a 31,000-mile "whistle-stop" train tour, during which he castigated the "do-nothing" Eightieth Congress. Friendly audiences shouted, "Pour it on, Harry!" and "Give 'em hell, Harry." Truman responded: "I don't give 'em hell. I just tell the truth and they think it's hell." Dewey, in contrast, ran a restrained campaign, designed to avoid rocking the boat. By so doing, he may have snatched defeat from the jaws of victory.

The polls and the pundits predicted a sure win for Dewey, but on election day Truman chalked up the biggest upset in American history, taking 24.2 million votes (49.5 percent) to Dewey's 22 million (45.1 percent) and winning a thumping margin of 303 to 189 in the Electoral College. Thurmond and Wallace each got more than 1 million votes, but the revolt of right and left had worked to Truman's advantage. The Dixiecrat rebellion backfired by

"Dewey Defeats Truman"

Truman's victory in 1948 was a huge upset, so much so that even the early edition of the *Chicago Daily Tribune* was caught off guard, running this presumptuous headline.

angering black voters, while the Progressive party's radicalism made it hard to tag Truman as soft on communism. Thurmond carried four Deep South states (South Carolina, Mississippi, Alabama, and Louisiana) with 39 electoral votes, including one from a Tennessee elector who repudiated his state's decision for Truman. Thurmond's success hastened a momentous disruption of the Democratic Solid South. But Truman's victory carried Democratic majorities into Congress, where the new group of senators included Hubert Humphrey and, by eighty-seven disputed votes, "Landslide Lyndon" Johnson of Texas.

Truman viewed his victory as a vindication for the New Deal and a mandate for moderate liberalism. "We have rejected the discredited theory that the fortunes of the nation should be in the hands of a privileged few," he said. His State of the Union message repeated the agenda he had set forth the year before. "Every segment of our population and every individual," he declared, "has a right to expect from his government a fair deal." Whether deliberately or not, he had invented a tag, the Fair Deal, to distinguish his program from the New Deal.

Some of Truman's Fair Deal proposals became law, but most of them were mainly extensions or enlargements of New Deal programs already in

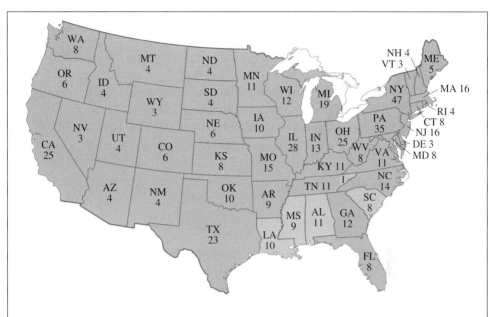

THE ELECTION OF 1948	Electoral vote	Popular vote
Harry S. Truman (Democrat)	**303**	**24,200,000**
Thomas E. Dewey (Republican)	189	22,000,000
J. Strom Thurmond (States' Rights Democrat)	39	1,200,000

Why did the political pundits predict a Dewey victory? Why was civil rights a divisive issue at the Democratic Convention? How did the candidacies of Thurmond and Wallace help Truman?

place: a higher minimum wage, expansion of Social Security coverage to workers not included in the original bill, extension of rent controls, increased farm subsidies, and a sizable slum-clearance and public-housing program. Despite Democratic majorities, however, the conservative coalition of southern Democrats and Republicans thwarted any drastic new departures in domestic policy. Congress rejected civil rights bills, national health insurance, federal aid to education, and a plan to provide subsidies that would hold up farm income rather than farm prices. Congress also turned down Truman's demand for repeal of the Taft-Hartley Act.

THE COLD WAR HEATS UP

Global concerns, never far from center stage in the postwar world, plagued Truman's second term, as they had his first. Americans began to fear that Communists were infiltrating their society. In his inaugural address, Truman called for a vigilant anti-Communist foreign policy to rest on four pillars: the United Nations, the Marshall Plan, NATO, and a "bold new plan" for technical assistance to underdeveloped parts of the world, a global Marshall Plan that came to be known simply as Point Four. This program to aid the postwar world never accomplished its goals, in part because other international problems soon diverted Truman's attention.

"LOSING" CHINA AND THE BOMB   One of the most intractable problems, the China tangle, was fast unraveling in 1949. The Chinese Nationalists, led by Chiang Kai-shek, had been fighting Mao Tse-tung* and the Communists since the 1920s. The outbreak of war with Japan in 1937 had halted this civil war, and both Roosevelt and Stalin believed that the Nationalists would control China after the war. But the commanders of U.S. forces in China during World War II concluded that Chiang's government was hopelessly corrupt, tyrannical, and inefficient. After the war, American forces nevertheless ferried Nationalist Chinese armies back into the eastern and northern provinces of China as the Japanese withdrew. U.S. policy during and immediately after the war promoted peace between the factions in China, but sporadic civil war broke out late in 1945.

It soon became a losing fight for the Nationalists as the Communists won over the land-hungry peasantry. By the end of 1949, the Nationalist government had fled to the island of Formosa, which it renamed Taiwan. Truman's critics now asked bitterly, "Who lost China?" A State Department study blamed Chiang for his failure to hold on to the support of the Chinese people. In fact it is hard to imagine how the U.S. government could have prevented a Communist victory short of getting involved in a massive military intervention, which would have been risky and unpopular. The United States continued to recognize the Nationalist government on Taiwan as the rightful government of China, delaying formal relations with Communist China for thirty years. Seeking to shore up friendly regimes in Asia, in 1950 the United States recognized the French-supported government of Emperor Bao Dai in

---

*The traditional (Wade-Giles) spelling is used here. In 1958 the Chinese government adopted the "pinyin" transliteration that became more widely used after Mao's death in 1976, so that, for example, Mao Tse-tung became Mao Zedong, and Peking became Beijing.

Vietnam and shortly afterward extended aid to the French in their battle against Ho Chi Minh's guerrillas there.

As Mao and the Communists were gaining control of China, U.S. intelligence found an unusual level of radioactivity in the air, evidence that the Soviets had successfully tested an atomic bomb. The American nuclear monopoly had lasted just four years. The discovery of the Soviet bomb in 1949 triggered an intense reappraisal of the strategic balance of power in the world, causing Truman in 1950 to order the construction of a hydrogen bomb, a weapon far more powerful than the atomic bombs dropped on Japan, lest the Soviets make one first.

The discovery that the Soviets had atomic weapons led the National Security Council to produce a top-secret document, known as NSC-68, that called for rebuilding America's conventional military forces to provide options other than nuclear war. Such a plan represented a major departure from America's time-honored aversion to keeping large standing armies in peacetime. It was also an expensive proposition. But the public was growing more receptive to the nation's new role as world leader, and an invasion of South Korea by Communist forces from the north clinched the issue for most Americans.

WAR IN KOREA   The Japanese had occupied Korea since 1910, and after their defeat and withdrawal in 1945 the victorious Allies faced the difficult task of creating a new Korean nation. Complicating that task was the fact that Soviet troops had advanced into northern Korea and accepted the surrender of Japanese forces above the 38th parallel, while U.S. forces had done the same south of that line. The Soviets quickly organized a Korean government in the north along Stalinist lines, while the Americans set up a Western-style regime in the south.

The division of Korea at the end of World War II, like the division of Germany, began as a temporary expedient and ended as a permanent deed. In the hectic days of August 1945, the Soviets accepted an American proposal to divide Korea at the 38th parallel until steps could be taken to unify the war-torn country. With the onset of the cold war, however, it became clear that agreement on unification was no more likely in Korea than in Germany, and by the end of 1948 separate regimes had appeared in the two sectors and occupation forces had withdrawn. The weakened state of the U.S. military contributed to the impression that South Korea was vulnerable to a Communist assault. A growing body of evidence later gleaned from Soviet archives reveals that Stalin encouraged the North Koreans to use force to unify their country and oust the Americans from the peninsula. The

Soviets helped design a war plan that called for North Korean forces to seize South Korea within a week. Stalin apparently assumed that the United States would not intervene.

Over 80,000 North Korean soldiers crossed the boundary on June 25, 1950, and swept down the peninsula. President Truman responded decisively. He and his advisers assumed that the North Korean attack was directed by Moscow and was a brazen indication of the aggressive designs of Soviet communism. "The attack upon Korea makes it plain beyond all doubt," Truman told Congress, "that communism has passed beyond the use of subversion to conquer independent nations and will now use armed invasion and war." Truman then made two critical decisions. First, he decided to wage war under the auspices of the United Nations rather than unilaterally. Second, he decided to wage war without asking Congress for a formal declaration of war.

An emergency meeting of the UN Security Council quickly censured the North Korean "breach of peace." The Soviet delegate, who held a veto power, was at the time boycotting the council because it would not seat Communist China in place of Nationalist China. On June 27, its first resolution having been ignored, the Security Council called on UN members to "furnish such assistance to the Republic of Korea as may be necessary to repel the armed attack and to restore international peace and security in the area." Truman ordered American air, naval, and ground forces into action. In all, some fourteen other nations contributed token military units. General Douglas MacArthur was put in command. The American defense of South Korea set a precedent of profound consequence: war by order of a president rather than by vote of Congress. Yet it had the sanction of the UN Security Council and could technically be considered a "police action," not a war. To be sure, other presidents had ordered U.S. troops into action without a declaration of war, but never on such a scale.

Truman's conviction that the invasion of South Korea was orchestrated by Stalin prompted two other decisions that had far-reaching consequences. First, Truman was convinced that the Korean conflict was actually a diversion for a Soviet invasion of western Europe, so he ordered a major expansion of American forces in Europe. Second, he increased assistance to French troops in Indochina, creating the Military Assistance Advisory Group for Indochina—the start of America's deepening military involvement in Vietnam.

For three months the fighting in Korea went badly for the Republic of Korea and the UN forces. By September they were barely hanging on to the Pusan perimeter in the southeast corner of Korea. Then, in a brilliant maneuver on September 15, 1950, MacArthur landed a new force to the North Korean rear

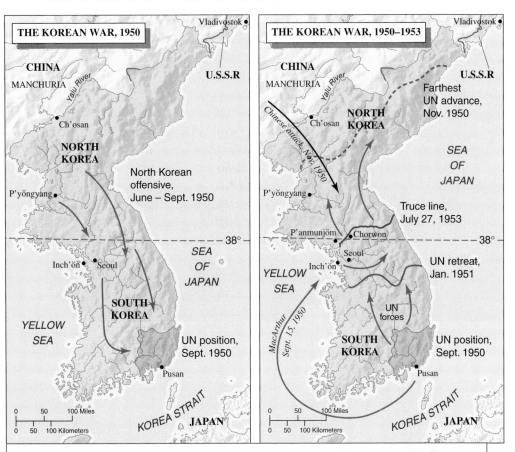

THE KOREAN WAR, 1950

Vladivostok

CHINA

MANCHURIA

Yalu River

Ch'osan

NORTH KOREA

U.S.S.R

North Korean offensive, June – Sept. 1950

P'yŏngyang

38°

SEA OF JAPAN

Inch'ŏn · Seoul

SOUTH KOREA

YELLOW SEA

UN position, Sept. 1950

Pusan

KOREA STRAIT JAPAN

0 50 100 Miles
0 50 100 Kilometers

THE KOREAN WAR, 1950–1953

Vladivostok

CHINA

MANCHURIA

Yalu River

Chinese attack, Nov. 1950

Ch'osan

NORTH KOREA

U.S.S.R

Farthest UN advance, Nov. 1950

SEA OF JAPAN

P'yŏngyang

P'anmunjŏm · Chorwon

Truce line, July 27, 1953

38°

Seoul

Inch'ŏn

YELLOW SEA

UN retreat, Jan. 1951

MacArthur Sept. 15, 1950

UN forces

SOUTH KOREA

UN position, Sept. 1950

Pusan

KOREA STRAIT JAPAN

0 50 100 Miles
0 50 100 Kilometers

How did the surrender of the Japanese in Korea set up the conflict between Soviet-influenced North Korea and U.S.-influenced South Korea? What was MacArthur's strategy for retaking Korea? Why did Truman remove MacArthur from command?

at Inch'ŏn, the port city for Seoul. Synchronized with a breakout from Pusan, the sudden blow stampeded the enemy back across the border. At that point, MacArthur persuaded Truman to allow him to push north and seek to reunify Korea. By now the Soviet delegate was back in the Security Council, wielding his veto. So on October 7 the United States won approval for this course from the UN General Assembly, where the veto did not apply. U.S. forces had crossed the North Korean boundary by October 1 and were continuing northward. President Truman, concerned about intervention by Communist China, flew 7,000 miles to Wake Island for a conference with General MacArthur on

September 1950

Soldiers engaged in the recapture of Seoul from the North Koreans.

October 15. There the general discounted chances that the Chinese Red Army would act, but if it did, he predicted, "there would be the greatest slaughter."

That same day Peking announced that China "cannot stand idly by." On October 20 UN forces had entered P'yŏngyang, the North Korean capital, and on October 26 advance units had reached Ch'osan' on the Yalu River, Korea's border with China. MacArthur predicted total victory by Christmas. On the night of November 25, however, some 260,000 Chinese "volunteers" counterattacked, and massive "human-wave" attacks, with the support of tanks and planes, turned the tables on the UN troops, sending them into a desperate retreat just at the onset of winter. It had become "an entirely new war," MacArthur said. He criticized the administration for requiring that he conduct a limited war. He asked for thirty-four atomic bombs and proposed air raids on China's "privileged sanctuary" in Manchuria, a naval blockade of China, and an invasion of the Chinese mainland by the Taiwan Nationalists.

Truman opposed leading the United States into the "gigantic booby trap" of war with China, and the UN forces soon rallied. By January 1951 over 900,000 UN troops under General Matthew B. Ridgway finally secured their lines below Seoul and then launched a counterattack that in some places carried them back across the 38th parallel in March. When Truman seized the chance and offered negotiations to restore the prewar boundary, General MacArthur undermined the move by issuing an ultimatum for China to make peace or suffer an attack. Truman then decided that MacArthur, whom he called Mr. Prima Donna, would have to go. On April 5, on the floor of the Congress, the Republican minority leader read a letter in which MacArthur criticized the president and said that "there is no substitute for victory." Such an act of open insubordination left the commander in chief no choice but to accept MacArthur's demands or fire him. Civilian control of the military was at stake, Truman later said, and he acted swiftly. On April 11, 1951, the president removed the popular MacArthur from all his commands and replaced him with Ridgway.

Truman's action ignited an immediate uproar in the country, and a tumultuous reception greeted MacArthur upon his first return home since 1937. MacArthur's emotional speech to a joint session of Congress provided the climactic event. He recalled a barracks ballad of his youth "which proclaimed most proudly that old soldiers never die, they just fade away." And like the old soldiers of that ballad, he said, "I now close my military career and just fade away, an old soldier who tried to do his duty as God gave him the light to see that duty." A Senate investigation brought out the administration's arguments, best summarized by General Omar Bradley, chairman of the Joint Chiefs of Staff. "Taking on Red China," he explained, would lead only "to a larger deadlock at greater expense." The MacArthur strategy "would involve us in the wrong war at the wrong place at the wrong time and with the wrong enemy." Most Americans found General Bradley's logic persuasive.

On June 24, 1951, the Soviet representative at the United Nations proposed a cease-fire in Korea along the 38th parallel; Secretary of State Dean Acheson accepted the cease-fire a few days later with the consent of the United Nations. China and North Korea responded favorably—at the time, General Ridgway's "meat-grinder" offensive was inflicting severe losses—and truce talks started on July 10, 1951, at P'anmunjo˘m, only to drag on for two years while the fighting continued. The chief snags were exchanges of prisoners and the South Korean president's insistence on unification. By the time a truce was finally reached, on July 27, 1953, Truman had relinquished the White House to Dwight D. Eisenhower. The truce line followed the war front at that time, mostly a little north of the 38th parallel, with a demilitarized zone of two and a half miles separating the forces; repatriation of prisoners would be voluntary, supervised by a neutral commission. No final peace conference ever took place, and Korea, like Germany, remained divided. The war had cost the United States more than 33,000 battle deaths and

103,000 wounded or missing. South Korean casualties, all told, were about 1 million, and North Korean and Chinese casualties an estimated 1.5 million.

ANOTHER RED SCARE   In calculating the costs of the Korean War, one must add in the far-reaching consequences of a second Red Scare, which had grown since 1945 as the domestic counterpart to the cold war abroad and reached a climax during the Korean conflict. Since 1938 the House Un-American Activities Committee (HUAC) had kept up a drumbeat of accusations about supposed subversives in the federal government. On March 21, 1947, just nine days after he announced the Truman Doctrine, the president signed an executive order setting up procedures for an employee loyalty program in the federal government. Every person entering federal service would be subject to a background investigation. By early 1951 the Civil Service Commission had cleared over 3 million people, while over 2,000 had resigned and 212 had been dismissed for doubtful loyalty.

Perhaps the case most damaging to the administration involved Alger Hiss, president of the Carnegie Endowment for International Peace, who had served in several government departments. Whittaker Chambers, a former Soviet agent and later an editor of *Time* magazine, told the HUAC in 1948 that Hiss had given him secret documents ten years earlier, when Chambers was spying for the Soviets and Hiss was working in the State Department. Hiss sued for libel, and Chambers produced microfilms of the State Department documents that he said Hiss had passed to him. Hiss denied the accusation, whereupon he was indicted and, after one mistrial, convicted in 1950. The charge was perjury, but he was convicted of lying about espionage, for which he could not be tried because the statute of limitations on that crime had expired.

Alger Hiss

Accused of leading a Soviet spy ring, Hiss testifies before the House Un-American Activities Committee in August 1948.

Most damaging to the administration was that President Truman, taking at face value the many testimonials to Hiss's integrity, had called the charges against him a "red herring." The Hiss affair had another political consequence: it raised to national prominence a young

California congressman, Richard M. Nixon, who doggedly insisted on pursuing the case and then exploited an anti-Communist stance to win election to the Senate in 1950.

More cases of Communist infiltration surfaced. In 1949 eleven top leaders of the Communist party in the United States were convicted under the Smith Act of 1940, which outlawed any conspiracy to advocate the overthrow of the government. The Supreme Court upheld the law under the doctrine of a "clear and present danger," which overrode the right to free speech. What was more, in 1950 the government unearthed the existence of a British-American spy network that had fed information about the development of the atomic bomb to the Soviet Union. These disclosures led to the arrest of, among others, Klaus Fuchs in Britain and Julius and Ethel Rosenberg in the United States.

MCCARTHY'S ANTI-COMMUNIST WITCH HUNT   Revelations of Soviet spying encouraged politicians to exploit the public's fears. If a man of such respectability as Hiss was guilty, many wondered, who then could be trusted? The United States, which bestrode the world like a colossus in 1945, had since "lost" Eastern Europe and Asia to communism and its atomic secrets to Russia. Early in 1950 a little-known Republican senator, Joseph R. McCarthy of Wisconsin, suddenly surfaced as the shrewdest and most

Joseph McCarthy

Senator McCarthy (left) and his aide Roy Cohn (right) exchange comments during testimony.

ruthless exploiter of such anxieties. He took up the cause of anti-communism with an incendiary speech at Wheeling, West Virginia, on February 9, 1950, in which he claimed that the State Department was infested with Communists and that he was in possession of a list of their names. Later there was confusion as to whether he had said there were 205, 81, 57, or "a lot" of names on the list and even whether the sheet of paper he brandished contained any such list. Confusion typically surrounded McCarthy's charges.

Despite his outlandish claims, McCarthy never uncovered a single Communist agent in the government. But with the United States at war with Korean Communists in mid-1950, it was easy for him to mobilize true believers. By 1951 he had outrageously called General George Marshall a traitor. His smear campaign went unchallenged until the end of the Korean War.

Fears of Communist espionage led Congress in 1950 to pass the McCarran Internal Security Act over President Truman's veto, making it unlawful "to combine, conspire, or agree with any other person to perform any act which would substantially contribute to . . . the establishment of a totalitarian dictatorship." Communist and Communist-front organizations had to register with the attorney general. Aliens who had belonged to totalitarian parties were barred from admission to the United States. The McCarran Act, Truman said in his veto message, would "put the Government into the business of thought control." He might in fact have said as much about the Smith Act of 1940 or even his own program of loyalty investigations. Yet documents recently uncovered in Russian archives and U.S. security agencies reveal that the Soviets did indeed operate an extensive espionage ring in the United States. Russian agents recruited several hundred American spies to ferret out secrets regarding atomic weapons, defense systems, and military intelligence.

ASSESSING THE COLD WAR   In retrospect, the onset of the cold war takes on an appearance of terrible inevitability. American and Soviet misunderstanding of each other's motives was virtually unavoidable. America's preference for international principles, such as self-determination and democracy, conflicted with the Soviet Union's preference for international spheres of influence and totalitarianism. Russia, after all, had been invaded by Germany twice in the first half of the twentieth century, and Soviet leaders wanted tame buffer states on their borders for protection. The people of Eastern Europe were again caught in the middle. But the Communists themselves held to a universal principle: world revolution.

If international conditions set the stage for the cold war, the actions of political leaders and thinkers set events in motion. President Truman may have erred in seeming to include all the world in his 1947 doctrine of Communist containment. The government loyalty program, following on the heels of the Truman Doctrine, may have incited the anti-Communist hysteria. Containment itself proved hard to contain, its author, George Kennan, later confessed, in part because he failed at the outset to spell out its limits.

The years after World War II were unlike any other postwar period in American history. Having taken on global burdens, the nation had become if not a "garrison state" at least a country committed to a permanent national military establishment, along with the attendant National Security Council and Central Intelligence Agency and, by presidential directive in 1952, the enormous National Security Agency, entrusted with monitoring media and communications for foreign intelligence.

The policy initiatives of the Truman years led the country to abandon its long-standing aversion to peacetime alliances. It was a far cry from the world of 1796, when George Washington in his farewell address warned his countrymen against "those overgrown military establishments which . . . are inauspicious to liberty" and advised his country "to steer clear of permanent alliances with any portion of the foreign world." But then Washington had warned only against participation in the "ordinary" combinations and collusions of Europe, and surely the postwar years had seen extraordinary events and unprecedented new alliances.

MAKING CONNECTIONS

- The cold war had a major impact on American society: among other things, it helped create the "conforming culture" described in the next chapter.
- The New Frontier and Great Society programs of Presidents Kennedy and Johnson, discussed in Chapter 34, accomplished much of what Truman tried to do through his Fair Deal policies.
- The world seemed a dangerous place at the height of the cold war, but when seen from the perspective of the post–cold war world of the 1990s (discussed in Chapters 36 and 37), it had a certain stability that discouraged political violence.

Further Reading

The cold war remains a hotly debated topic. The traditional interpretation is best reflected in John Lewis Gaddis's *The United States and the Origins of the Cold War, 1941–1947* (1972) and *We Now Know: Rethinking Cold War History* (1997). Both superpowers, Gaddis argues, were responsible for causing the cold war, but the Soviet Union was more culpable. The revisionist perspective is represented by Gar Alperovitz's *Atomic Diplomacy: Hiroshima and Potsdam: The Use of the Atomic Bomb and the American Confrontation with Soviet Power*, 2nd ed. (1994). Alperovitz places primary responsibility for the conflict on the United States. Also see H. W. Brands's *The Devil We Knew: Americans and the Cold War* (1993) and Melvyn P. Leffler's *A Preponderance of Power: National Security, the Truman Administration, and the Cold War* (1992). On the architect of containment, see David Mayers's *George Kennan and the Dilemmas of U.S. Foreign Policy* (1988).

Arnold A. Offner indicts Truman for clumsy statesmanship in *Another Such Victory: President Truman and the Cold War, 1945–1953* (2002). For a positive assessment of Truman's leadership, see Alonzo L. Hamby's *Beyond the New Deal: Harry S. Truman and American Liberalism* (1973). The domestic policies of the Fair Deal are treated in William C. Berman's *The Politics of Civil Rights in the Truman Administration* (1970), Richard M. Dalfiume's *Desegregation of the U.S. Armed Forces: Fighting on Two Fronts, 1939–1953* (1969), and Maeva Marcus's *Truman and the Steel Seizure Case: The Limits of Presidential Power* (1977). The most comprehensive biography of Truman is David McCullough's *Truman* (1992).

For an introduction to the tensions in Asia, see Akira Iriye's *The Cold War in Asia: A Historical Introduction* (1974). For the Korean conflict, see Callum A. MacDonald's *Korea: The War before Vietnam* (1986) and Max Hasting's *The Korean War* (1987).

The anti-Communist syndrome is surveyed in David Caute's *The Great Fear: The Anti-Communist Purge under Truman and Eisenhower* (1978). Arthur Herman's *Joseph McCarthy: Reexamining the Life and Legacy of America's Most Hated Senator* (2000) covers McCarthy himself. For a well-documented account of how the cold war was sustained by superpatriotism, intolerance, and suspicion, see Stephen J. Whitfield's *The Culture of the Cold War*, 2nd ed. (1996).

32

THROUGH THE PICTURE WINDOW: SOCIETY AND CULTURE, 1945–1960

FOCUS QUESTIONS

· Why did the American economy expand during the postwar period?

· In what ways were contrasting strains of conformity and innovation characteristic of the 1950s?

· What were the characteristics of America's burgeoning consumer culture?

To answer these questions and access additional review material, please visit www.wwnorton.com/studyspace.

Americans emerged from World War II elated, proud of their military strength and industrial might, and eager to pursue peacetime prosperity. As the editors of *Fortune* magazine proclaimed in 1946, "This is a dream era, this is what everyone was waiting through the blackouts for. The Great American Boom is on." So it was, from babies to Buicks to Admiral television sets. A society that had known mostly deprivation and sacrifice for a decade and a half began to enjoy unprecedented economic growth and rising social contentment. Divorce and homicide rates fell, the birthrate soared, and the prevailing mood seemed aggressively upbeat—at least on the surface.

Amid the rising affluence and comfortable domesticity, however, many social critics, writers, and artists expressed a growing sense of unease. Was postwar society becoming too complacent, too conformist, too materialistic?

Such questions reflected the perennial tension in American life between idealism and materialism, a tension that arrived with the first settlers and remains with us today. Americans have always struggled to accumulate goods and cultivate goodness. During the postwar era the nation again tried to do both. For a while, at least, it appeared to succeed.

PEOPLE OF PLENTY

The dominant feature of post–World War II society was its remarkable prosperity. After a surprisingly brief postwar recession, the economy soared to record heights. The gross national product nearly doubled between 1945 and 1960, and the 1960s witnessed an even more spectacular expansion of the economy. By 1970 the gap between the living standard in the United States and in the rest of the world had become a chasm: with 6 percent of the world's population, America produced and consumed two thirds of its goods.

During the 1950s government officials assured the citizenry that they should not fear another economic collapse. "Never again shall we allow a depression in the United States," President Eisenhower promised. Several factors contributed to the prolonged economic surge that fueled his optimism. The massive federal expenditures to meet military needs during the war had catapulted the economy out of the Great Depression. High government spending continued in the postwar era, thanks to the tensions generated by the cold war. The military budget after 1945 represented the single most important stimulant to the postwar economic boom. Military research also helped spawn the new glamour industries of the postwar era: chemicals, electronics, and aviation.

Most of the other major industrial nations of the world—England, France, Germany, Japan, the Soviet Union—had been physically devastated during the war, which meant that American manufacturers enjoyed a virtual monopoly on international trade. In addition, technological innovations contributed to the "automation" of the workplace and thereby created spectacular increases in productivity. The widespread use of new and more efficient machinery and computers led to a 35 percent jump in worker productivity between 1945 and 1955.

The major catalyst in promoting economic expansion after 1945 was the unleashing of pent-up consumer demand. During the war, Americans had postponed purchases of such major items as cars and houses and in the process had saved over $150 billion. Now they were eager to buy. The United States after World War II experienced a purchasing frenzy.

THE GI BILL OF RIGHTS   Part of the purchasing frenzy was indirectly financed by the federal government. Fears that a sharp drop in military spending and the sudden influx of veterans into the workforce would send the economy into a downward spiral and produce widespread unemployment led Congress to pass the Servicemen's Readjustment Act of 1944. Popularly known as the GI Bill of Rights (*GI* meaning "government issue" a phrase that was stamped on military uniforms and became slang for "serviceman"), it led to the creation of a new government agency, the Veterans Administration, and included provisions for mustering out pay, unemployment pay for veterans for one year, preference for government jobs, loans for home construction, access to government hospitals, and generous subsidies for college or professional training.

Between 1944 and 1956, almost 8 million veterans took advantage of $14.5 billion in GI Bill subsidies to attend college or job-training programs. Some 5 million veterans bought new homes with GI Bill mortgage loans, which required no down payment and provided up to twenty years for repayment. Before World War II approximately 160,000 Americans graduated from college each year. By 1950 the figure had risen to 500,000. In 1949 veterans accounted for 40 percent of all college enrollments, and the United States could boast the world's best-educated workforce.

The GI Bill democratized higher education. It provided a generation of working-class Americans with an opportunity to earn a college degree for the first time. In turn a college education served as a lever into the middle class. But while the GI Bill helped erode class barriers, it was less successful in dismantling racial barriers. Many African-American veterans could not take equal advantage of the education benefits. Most colleges and universities after the war remained racially segregated, either by regulation or by practice. Of the 9,000 students enrolled at the University of Pennsylvania in 1946, for example, only 46 were African Americans. Those blacks who did manage to gain admission to white colleges or universities were barred from playing on athletic teams, attending dances and other social events, and joining fraternities or sororities.

The historically black colleges, most of which were in the South, could not expand quickly enough to meet the demand. In 1940 African-American colleges enrolled 43,000 students; in 1950 the number had soared to 77,000. Yet over 20,000 black veterans were denied admission because of overcrowded facilities. In 1946 only one fifth of the 100,000 African Americans who had applied for education benefits had enrolled.

The return of some 12 million veterans to private life also helped generate a postwar baby boom, which peaked in 1957. Many young married couples

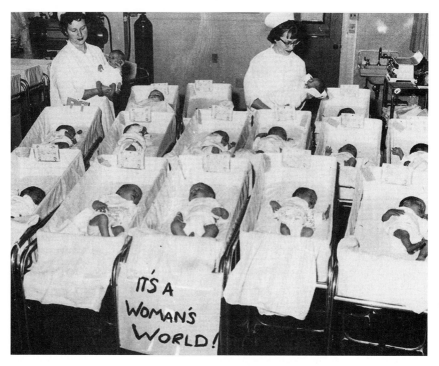

The Baby Boom

Much of America's social history since the 1940s has been the story of the baby-boom generation.

who had delayed having children were intent on making up for lost time. Between 1945 and 1960, the total population grew by some 40 million, an increase of almost 30 percent. Much of America's social history since the 1940s has been the story of this unusually large baby-boom generation and its progress through the stages of life. The postwar baby boom created a massive demand for diapers, baby food, toys, medicines, schools, books, teachers, furniture, and housing.

AN EXPANDING CONSUMER CULTURE   The baby boom was accompanied by a postwar construction boom. The proportion of homeowners in the population increased by 50 percent between 1945 and 1960. And those new homes filled up with the latest appliances: refrigerators, washing machines, sewing machines, vacuum cleaners, freezers, electric mixers, electric carving knives, electric shoe polishers.

By far the most popular new household product was the television set. In 1946 there were only 7,000 primitive black-and-white TV sets in the country;

by 1960 there were 50 million high-quality sets. Nine out of ten homes had one, and by 1970, 38 percent of homes had one of the new color sets. *TV Guide* was the fastest-growing new periodical of the 1950s. Watching television displaced listening to the radio as an essential daily activity for millions of people.

What differentiated the affluence of the post–World War II era from earlier periods of prosperity was its ever-widening dispersion. Although rural and urban poverty persisted in every state, few commentators noticed such exceptions to the prevailing affluence during the 1950s. When George Meany was sworn in as head of the American Federation of Labor–Congress of Industrial Organizations (AFL-CIO) in 1955, he proclaimed that "American labor never had it so good."

On the surface many blacks were also beneficiaries of the wave of prosperity that swept over postwar society. By 1950 African Americans were earning on average more than four times their 1940 wages. One journalist declared in 1951 that "the progressive improvement of race relations and the economic rise of the Negro in the United States is a flattering example of democracy in action." But while gains had been made, African Americans and members of other minority groups lagged behind whites in their rate of improvement. The gap between the average yearly income of whites and blacks widened during the decade of the 1950s. Yet such trends were rarely noticed amid the boosterism of the day. The need to present a united front against communism led commentators to ignore or gloss over issues of racial and economic injustice. Such corrosive neglect would fester and explode during the 1960s, but for now the emphasis was on consensus, conformity, and economic growth.

To perpetuate the postwar prosperity, marketing specialists targeted consumers' desires and social envy. An advertisement for Ford automobiles assured customers, "You'll bask in the envious glances which Ford's Thunderbird styling draws." It then added, "Why not own two?" Expenditures for TV advertising increased 1,000 percent during the 1950s. Such startling rates led the president of NBC to claim in 1956 that the primary reason for the postwar prosperity was that "advertising has created an American frame of mind that makes people want more things, better things, and newer things."

Paying for such "things" was no problem; the age of the credit card had arrived. Between 1945 and 1957, consumer credit soared 800 percent. Where families in other industrialized nations were typically saving 10 to 20 percent of their income, American families by the 1960s were saving only 5 percent. "Never before have so many owed so much to so many," *Newsweek* announced in 1953. "Time has swept away the Puritan conception of immorality in debt and godliness in thrift." This consumer revolution had

A Mink Coat for Father

An advertisement for a Ford Thunderbird claims that "what a mink coat does to perk up a lady, a Thunderbird does for a male."

far-reaching cultural effects. Shopping became a major recreational activity. In 1945 there were only 8 "shopping centers" in the entire country; by 1960 there were 3,840. Much as life in a medieval town revolved around the cathedral, life in postwar America centered on the new giant shopping centers.

THE SUBURBAN FRONTIER   The postwar era witnessed a mass migration to a new frontier—the suburbs. The burgeoning population created new communities and required an array of new services. Almost the entire population increase of the 1950s and 1960s (97 percent) was an urban or suburban phenomenon. Dramatic new technological advances in agricultural production reduced the need for manual laborers. Almost 20 million people left farms and villages for the city between 1940 and 1970.

Much of the urban population growth occurred in the South, the Southwest, and the West, in an arc that stretched from the Carolinas to California, a region that by the 1970s was being lumped together into the "sunbelt." Air-conditioning, developed by Willis Haviland Carrier in the first decade of the century, became a common household fixture in the 1950s and enhanced the appeal of living in warm climates. But the Northeast remained the most densely populated area; by the early 1960s, 20 percent of the nation's population lived in the corridor that stretched from Boston to Norfolk, Virginia.

While more concentrated in cities, post–World War II Americans were simultaneously spreading out within the metropolitan areas. During the 1950s suburbs grew six times faster than cities. By 1970 more people lived in suburbs (76 million) than in central cities (64 million). "Suburbia," proclaimed the *Christian Century* in 1955, "is now a dominant social group in American life." Suburban development required cars, highways, and government-guaranteed mortgages. It also required visionary entrepreneurs.

William Levitt, a brassy New York developer, led the suburban revolution. In 1947, on 1,200 acres of Long Island farmland, he built 10,600 houses, to be inhabited by more than 40,000 people—mostly adults under thirty-five and their children. Within a few years there were similar Levittowns in Pennsylvania and New Jersey, and other developers soon followed suit across the country. This suburban revolution benefited greatly from government assistance. By insuring loans for up to 95 percent of the value of a house, the Federal

Levittown

Identical, mass-produced houses in Levittown, New York, and other suburbs across the country provided veterans and their families with affordable homes.

Housing Administration made it easy for a builder to construct low-cost homes. Veterans got added benefits: a veteran could buy a Levitt house with no down payment and monthly mortgage installments of $56.

Expanded automobile production and highway construction also facilitated the rush to the suburbs as more and more people were able to commute longer distances to work. Car production soared, and a "car culture" soon transformed social behavior. As one commentator observed, the proliferation of automobiles "changed our dress, manners, social customs, vacation habits, the shape of our cities, consumer purchasing patterns, [and] common tastes." Widespread car ownership also necessitated an improved road network. Local and state governments built many new roads, but the guiding force was the federal government. In 1947 Congress authorized the construction of 37,000 miles of highways, and nine years later it funded over 42,000 additional miles in a new national system of interstate expressways.

Cars and roads provided access to the suburbs, and Americans—mostly middle-class white Americans—rushed to take advantage of the new living spaces. The motives for moving to the suburbs were numerous. The availability of more spacious homes and yards, greater security, and better educational opportunities for children played a role. Racial considerations were also a factor. After World War II, African Americans from the South migrated to the cities of the North and the Midwest. As they moved in, many white residents moved out. Those engaged in "white flight" were usually eager to maintain residential segregation in their new suburban communities. As William Levitt explained, "We can solve a housing problem or we can try to solve a racial problem. But we can't combine the two." Contracts for houses in Levittown, Long Island, specifically excluded "members of other than the Caucasian race." Such discrimination, whether explicit or implicit, was widespread; the nation's suburban population in 1970 was 95 percent white.

THE GREAT BLACK MIGRATION   The mass migration of rural southern blacks to the urban North and Midwest after World War II was much larger than that after World War I, and its social consequences were much more dramatic. After 1945 more than 5 million southern blacks, mostly farm folk, left their native regions in search of better jobs, higher wages, decent housing, and greater social equality. During the 1950s, for example, the African-American population of Chicago more than doubled. The South Side of Chicago soon became known as the capital of black America. It remains the neighborhood with the largest concentration of African Americans in the nation.

Most black migrants were sharecroppers and farm laborers from the Mississippi Delta, the richest cotton-producing land in the world. For over a century the Delta cotton culture had been dependent upon black workers, first as slaves and then as sharecroppers and wage laborers. But a mechanical cotton picker invented in 1944 changed all that. The new machine could do the work of fifty people, making many farmworkers superfluous. Displaced southern blacks, many of them illiterate and provincial, streamed northward in search of a new promised land only to see many of their dreams dashed. The writer Richard Wright, himself a migrant from the Delta to Chicago, observed that "never in history has a more utterly unprepared folk wanted to go to the city." In northern cities such as Chicago, Philadelphia, Newark, Detroit, New York, Boston, and Washington, D.C., rural African Americans from the South confronted harsh new realities. Slumlords gouged them for rent, employers refused to hire them, and union bosses denied them membership. Soon the promised land had become for many an ugly nightmare of slum housing, joblessness, illiteracy, dysfunctional families, welfare dependency, street gangs, pervasive crime, and racism.

The unexpected tidal wave of African-American migrants severely taxed the resources of urban governments and the patience of white racists. For several nights during 1951, a white mob in a Chicago suburb assaulted a building into which a black family had moved. The National Guard had to quell the disturbance and disperse the crowd. Like other northern cities, Chicago sought to deal with the migrants and alleviate racial stress by constructing massive all-black public-housing projects to accommodate the newcomers. These overcrowded racial enclaves soon became segregated prisons. To be sure, many black migrants and their children did manage through extraordinary determination and ingenuity to "clear"—to climb out of the teeming ghettos and into the middle class. But most did not. As a consequence the great black migration produced a web of complex social problems in northern cities that in the 1960s would erupt into a crisis.

A Conforming Culture

In the 1950s, social commentators mostly ignored people and cultures outside the middle-class mainstream. As evidenced in many of the new look-alike suburbs sprouting up across the land, much of middle-class social life during the two decades after the end of World War II exhibited an increasingly homogenized character. Fears generated by the cold war initially played a key role in encouraging orthodoxy. But McCarthyism was simply the most visible symbol of the many political and social forces promoting common standards of behavior. Suburban life itself encouraged uniformity. In new communities of strangers, people felt a need for companionship and a sense of belonging. Changes in corporate life as well as the influence of the consumer culture also played an important socializing role. "Conformity," predicted an editor in 1954, "may very well become the central social problem of this age."

CORPORATE LIFE   The composition of the workforce and the very nature of work itself were dramatically changing during the postwar era. Fewer people were self-employed, and manual labor was rapidly giving way to mental labor. By the mid-1950s white-collar (salaried) workers outnumbered blue-collar (hourly wage) workers for the first time in history. During World War II big business had grown bigger. The government relaxed its anti-trust activity, and huge defense contracts promoted corporate concentration and consolidation. In 1940, for example, the 100 largest companies were responsible for 30 percent of all manufacturing output; three years later they were providing 70 percent. After the war a wave of mergers occurred, and dominant corporate giants appeared in every major industry, providing the primary source of new jobs. By 1960, 38 percent of the workforce was employed

Office in a Small City

Edward Hopper's 1953 painting suggests the alienation associated with white-collar work and the corporate atmosphere of the 1950s.

by organizations with more than 500 employees. In such huge companies, as well as similarly large government agencies and universities, the working atmosphere promoted conformity rather than individualism.

WOMEN'S "PLACE"   Increasing conformity in the middle-class workplace was mirrored in the middle-class home. A special issue of *Life* magazine in 1956 featured the "ideal" middle-class woman, a thirty-two-year-old "pretty and popular" white suburban housewife, mother of four, who had married at age sixteen. She was described as an excellent wife, mother, volunteer, and "home manager" who made her own clothes, hosted dozens of dinner parties each year, sang in her church choir, worked with the parent-teacher association and the Campfire Girls, and was devoted to her husband. "In her daily round," *Life* reported, "she attends club or charity meetings, drives the children to school, does the weekly grocery shopping, makes ceramics, and is planning to study French."

   Life's description of the middle-class woman was symptomatic of a cult of feminine domesticity that witnessed a dramatic revival in the postwar era. The soaring birthrate reinforced the deeply embedded notion that a woman's place was in the home. "Of all the accomplishments of the American

The New Household

A Tupperware party in a middle-class suburban home.

woman," the *Life* cover story proclaimed, "the one she brings off with the most spectacular success is having babies."

Even though millions of women had responded to wartime appeals and joined the traditionally male workforce, afterward they were encouraged—and even forced—to turn their jobs over to the returning male veterans and resume their full-time commitment to home and family. A 1945 article in *House Beautiful* lectured women on their postwar responsibilities. The returning veteran, it said, was "head man again. . . . Your part in the remaking of this man is to fit his home to him, understanding why he wants it this way, forgetting your own preferences." Women were also to forget wartime-generated thoughts of their own career in the workplace. "Women must boldly announce," a Barnard College trustee asserted in 1950, "that no job is more exacting, more necessary, or more rewarding than that of housewife and mother."

THE SEARCH FOR COMMUNITY   In a number of respects, Americans were on the move after World War II. Not only were they moving from the central cities to the suburbs, but they were also moving from farm to city, suburb to suburb, state to state. Some 20 percent of the population changed their place of residence each year. The major cause of the mobility was the largest corporations' standard policy of relocating their sales and managerial employees. Executives of International Business Machines (IBM) Corporation told friends that the company initials actually stood for "I've Been Moved." Such flux led people to search for a sense of community and rootedness. Hence middle-class Americans, even more than usual, tended to be joiners; they joined civic clubs, garden clubs, bridge clubs, carpools, and babysitting groups.

They also joined churches and synagogues in record numbers. The postwar era witnessed a massive renewal of religious participation. In 1940 less than half the adult population belonged to a church; by 1960 over 65 percent were official communicants. Sales of Bibles soared during the postwar era, and books, movies, and songs with religious themes were pervasive.

President Eisenhower repeatedly promoted a patriotic crusade to bring Americans back to God. "Recognition of the Supreme Being," he declared, "is the first, the most basic, expression of Americanism. Without God, there could be no American form of government, nor an American way of life." The president had himself joined a church only in 1953, but he characterized himself as the "most intensely religious man I know." Not to be outdone, Congress in 1954 added the phrase one nation "under God" to the Pledge of Allegiance and the following year made the statement "In God We Trust"

Billy Graham Preaches to Thousands, 1955

The Baptist evangelist used radio and television to promote his huge crusades, as droves of Americans, encouraged by the president, Congress, and billboard advertising, joined churches and attended revival meetings.

mandatory on all currency. A godly nation, it was widely assumed, would better withstand the march of godless communism.

The prevailing tone of the popular religious revival of the 1950s was upbeat and soothing. Many ministers assumed that people were not interested in fire-and-brimstone harangues from the pulpit; they did not want their consciences overburdened with a sense of personal sin or social guilt about such issues as racial segregation or inner-city poverty. Instead, they wanted to be reassured that their comfortable way of life was indeed God's will. As the Protestant Council of New York City explained to its corps of radio and television speakers, their addresses "should project love, joy, courage, hope, faith, trust in God, goodwill. Generally avoid condemnation, criticism, controversy. In a very real sense we are 'selling' religion, the good news of the Gospel."

The best salesman of this gospel of reassuring "good news" was the Reverend Norman Vincent Peale, champion of feel-good theology. No speaker was more in demand during the 1950s, and no writer was more widely read. Peale's book *The Power of Positive Thinking* (1952) was a phenomenal best-seller throughout the decade—and for good reason. It offered a simple how-to course in personal happiness. "Flush out all depressing, negative, and tired thoughts," Peale advised. "Start thinking faith, enthusiasm, and joy." By following this simple formula for success, he pledged, the reader could become "a more popular, esteemed, and well-liked individual."

NEO-ORTHODOXY   "Stop worrying and start living" was Peale's simple credo. But was it too simplistic? The "peace-of-mind" and "positive-thinking" psychology struck some members of the religious community as shallow and misleading. They argued that the gospel of good news was primarily a way of promoting sociability or a sense of "belonging." These advocates of "neo-orthodoxy" criticized those who identified the United States as the only truly providential society and who used faith as a sanction for the social status quo.

The most significant spokesman for such neo-orthodoxy was Reinhold Niebuhr. A brilliant preacher-professor at New York's Union Theological Seminary, Niebuhr lambasted the "undue complacency and conformity" that had settled over postwar life. He disdained the popular religion of self-assurance and material success. Spiritual peace, Niebuhr insisted, involves not the cheap comfort and sedating reassurance offered by Peale and other popular evangelists but the reality of pain, a pain "caused by love and responsibility" for the well-being of the entire human race.

CRACKS IN THE PICTURE WINDOW

Reinhold Niebuhr was one of many critics who challenged the moral complacency and social conformity of American life during the 1950s and early 1960s. The widely publicized evidence of middle-class prosperity masked festering poverty in rural areas and urban ghettos. Moreover, one of the most striking aspects of postwar culture was the sharp contrast between the buoyant public mood and the increasingly bitter social criticism coming from intellectuals, theologians, novelists, playwrights, poets, and artists.

THE LONELY CROWD   The criticism of postwar life and values began in the early 1950s and quickly gathered momentum. Scores of books and articles decried virtually every area of social life. The critics shared a common fear: America in the age of Eisenhower was becalmed in a sea of conformity, content to succumb to the soul-denying demands of the corporate "rat race" and eager to wallow in the consumer culture. In *The Affluent Society* (1958), for example, the economist John Kenneth Galbraith attacked the prevailing notion that sustained economic growth would solve chronic social problems. The public sector was starved for funds, Galbraith argued, and public enterprises were everywhere deteriorating. He reminded readers that for all of America's vaunted postwar prosperity, the nation had yet to eradicate poverty.

Postwar cultural critics also questioned the supposed bliss of middle-class corporate and suburban life. John Keats, in *The Crack in the Picture Window* (1956), launched the most savage assault on life in the huge new suburban developments. He ridiculed Levittown and other mass-produced communities as having been "conceived in error, nurtured in greed, corroding everything they touch." Locked into a monotonous routine, hounded by financial insecurity, and engulfed by mass mediocrity, suburbanites, he concluded, were living in a "homogeneous, postwar Hell."

Mass-produced suburban developments did exhibit a startling sameness. Levittown, for example, encouraged and even enforced uniformity. The houses all sold for the same price—$7,990—and featured the same floor plan and accessories. Each had a picture window, a living room, bathroom, kitchen, and two bedrooms. A tree was planted every twenty-eight feet.

Suburban Life

A woman vaccums her living room in Queens, New York, 1953, illustrating the 1950s ideal of domestic perfection.

Homeowners were required to cut their grass once a week, fences were pro-hibited, and laundry could not be hung out on weekends. However, Levit-town was in many ways distinctive rather than representative. There were thousands of suburbs by the mid-1950s, and few were as regimented or as unvarying as Keats and other critics implied. Keats also failed to recognize the benefits that the suburbs offered those who otherwise would have remained in crowded urban apartments.

Still, there was more than a grain of truth to the charge that postwar American life was becoming regimented, and the huge modern corporation was repeatedly cited by social critics as the primary villain. The most comprehensive analysis of the new corporate character was David Ries-man's *The Lonely Crowd* (1950). Riesman and his research associates de-tected a fundamental shift in the dominant American personality from what they called the "inner-directed" type to the "other-directed" type. Inner-directed people possess a deeply internalized set of basic values im-planted by strong-minded parents or other elders. These values act as a built-in stabilizer that keeps them on course. Such an assured, self-reliant personality, Riesman argued, had prevailed throughout the nineteenth century. But during the mid–twentieth century an other-directed person-ality had displaced it. The new corporate culture demanded employees who could win friends and influence people rather than rugged individu-alists indifferent to personal popularity. Other-directed people were concerned more with being well liked than with being independent. In the workplace they were always smiling, always glad-handing, always trying to please the boss.

Riesman amassed considerable evidence to show that the other-directed personality was not just an aspect of the business world; its premises were widely dispersed throughout middle-class life. Dr. Benjamin Spock's advice on raising children, Riesman pointed out, had become immensely influen-tial. Spock's popular manual, *The Common Sense Book of Baby and Child Care*, sold 1 million copies a year between its first appearance in 1946 and 1960. Spock said that parents should foster in their children qualities and skills that would enhance their chances in what Riesman called the "popu-larity market."

By the mid-1950s social commentators were growing increasingly con-cerned about the negative effects of such a managerial personality. In his influential study *White Collar Society* (1951), the sociologist C. Wright Mills attacked the attributes and influence of modern corporate life. "When white-collar people get jobs," Mills explained, "they sell not only their time and energy, but their personalities as well. They sell by the week or month their smiles and their kindly gestures, and they must practice the prompt repression of resentment and aggression."

ALIENATION AND LIBERATION

THE STAGE   Many of the best theatrical productions of the postwar period reinforced David Riesman's image of modern American society as a "lonely crowd" of individuals without internal values, hollow at the core, groping for a sense of belonging and affection. Arthur Miller's play *Death of a Salesman* (1949), for example, was a powerful exploration of the theme. The play's protagonist, Willy Loman, an aging, confused salesman in decline, has centered his life and that of his family on the notion that material success is secured through personal popularity, only to be abruptly told by his boss that he is in fact a failure. Loman insists that it is "not what you say, it's how you say it—because personality always wins the day." Yet Willy, for all his puffery about being well liked, admits in a fit of candor that he is "terribly lonely." He has no real friends; even his relations with his family are neither honest nor intimate. When Willy finally realizes that he has been leading a counterfeit existence, he is so dumbfounded that he decides he can endow his life with meaning only by ending it.

THE NOVEL   The most enduring novels of the postwar period display a preoccupation with the individual's struggle for survival amid the smothering and disorienting forces of mass society. The characters in novels such as James Jones's *From Here to Eternity* (1951), Saul Bellow's *Dangling Man* (1944) and *Seize the Day* (1956), William Styron's *Lie Down in Darkness* (1951), and John Updike's *Rabbit, Run* (1961), among many others, tend to be like Willy Loman— restless, tormented, and often socially impotent individuals who can find neither contentment

Death of a Salesman (1949)

In Arthur Miller's play, Willy Loman (center, played by Lee J. Cobb) destroys his life and his family with the credo "be liked and you will never want."

Ralph Ellison

Ellison is best remembered for his 1952 novel *Invisible Man*.

nor respect in an overpowering or un-interested world.

The African-American writer Ralph Ellison explored the theme of the lonely individual imprisoned in privacy in his kaleidoscopic novel *Invisible Man* (1952). By using a black narrator struggling to find and liberate himself in the midst of an oppressive white society, Ellison forcefully accentuated the problem of alienation. The narrator opens by confessing: "All my life I had been looking for something, and everywhere I turned someone tried to tell me what it was. I accepted their answers too, though they were often in contradiction and even self-contradictory. I was naive. I was looking for myself and asking everyone except myself questions which I, and only I, could answer."

PAINTING   The artist Edward Hopper also explored the theme of desolate loneliness in postwar urban-industrial American life. Virtually all of his paintings of the period depict isolated individuals, melancholy, anonymous, motionless. The silence of his scenes is deafening, the monotony striking, the alienation absorbing. (For an example of Hopper's work, see p. 1180.)

A younger group of painters in New York City decided that postwar society was so chaotic that it precluded any attempt at literal representation. As the artist Jackson Pollock maintained, "the modern painter cannot express this age—the airplane, the atomic bomb, the radio—in the old form of the Renaissance or of any past culture. Each age finds its own technique." The anarchic technique Pollock adopted came to be called abstract expressionism, and during the late 1940s and 1950s it dominated not only the American art scene but the international field as well. In addition to Pollock, its adherents included Robert Motherwell, Willem de Kooning, and Mark Rothko. "Abstract art," Motherwell explained, "is an effort to close the void that modern men feel." In practice this meant that the *act* of painting was as important as the result.

THE BEATS   In Saul Bellow's novel *Dangling Man*, a character concludes that the essence of life is the "desire for pure freedom." The desire to liberate

self-expression, to surmount organizational constraints and discard traditional conventions, was an abiding goal of the abstract expressionists. It was
also the central concern of a small but highly visible and controversial group
of young writers, poets, painters, and musicians known as the Beats. These
angry young men—Jack Kerouac, Allen Ginsberg, Gary Snyder, William
Burroughs, and Gregory Corso, among others—rebelled against the regimented horrors of war and the mundane horrors of middle-class life.

The self-described Beats grew out of the bohemian underground in New
York's Greenwich Village. There they began their quest for a visionary sensibility and a spontaneous way of life. Essentially apolitical throughout the
1950s, they were more interested in transforming themselves than in reforming the world. They sought personal rather than social solutions to
their anxieties. As Kerouac insisted, his friends were not beat in the sense of
beaten; they were "mad to live, mad to talk, mad to be saved." Their road to
salvation lay in hallucinogenic drugs and alcohol, sex, a penchant for jazz
and the street life of urban ghettos, an affinity for Buddhism, and a restless,
vagabond spirit that took them speeding back and forth across the country
between San Francisco and New York during the 1950s.

This existential mania for intense experience and frantic motion provided
the subject matter for the Beats' writing. Ginsberg's long prose poem *Howl,*

Allen Ginsberg

Ginsberg, considered the poet laureate of the Beat generation, reads his uncensored
poetry to a crowd in Washington Square Park in New York City.

published in 1956, features an explicit sensuality as well as an impressionistic attempt to catch the color, movement, and dynamism of modern life. Kerouac issued his autobiographical novel *On the Road* a year later. In frenzied prose and plotless ramblings, it portrays the Beats' life of "bursting ecstasies" and maniacal traveling.

Howl and *On the Road* elicited sarcasm and anger from many reviewers, but the books enjoyed brisk sales, especially among young people. *On the Road* made the best-seller list, and soon the terms *Beat generation* and *beatnik* referred to almost any young rebel who openly dissented from the comfortable ethos of middle-class life. Defiant, unruly actors such as James Dean and Marlon Brando were added to the pantheon of Beat "anti-heroes." The anarchic gaiety of the Beats played an important role in preparing for the more widespread youth revolt of the 1960s.

YOUTH CULTURE AND DELINQUENCY   Young people occupied a distinctive place in postwar life. The children of the baby boom were becoming adolescents during the 1950s, and in the process a distinctive "teen" subculture began to emerge. Living amid such a prosperous era, teenagers had more money and more free time than any previous generation. A vast new teen market arose for goods ranging from transistor radios, Hula-Hoops, and rock-and-roll records to cameras, surfboards, *Seventeen* magazine, and Pat Boone movies. Teenagers in the postwar era knew nothing of economic depressions or wartime rationing; immersed in abundance from an early age, the children of prospering parents took the notion of carefree consumption for granted.

To be sure, most young people during the 1950s embraced the values of their parents and the capitalist system. It was "the reassuring truth," reported *Collier's* magazine in 1951, "that the average young American is probably more conservative than you or your neighbor." One critic labeled the college students of the postwar era "the silent generation," content to cavort at fraternity parties and "sock hops" before landing a job with a large corporation, marrying, and settling down to the routine of middle-class suburban life.

Yet such general descriptions masked a great deal of turbulence. During the 1950s a wave of juvenile delinquency swept across middle-class society. By 1956 over 1 million teens a year were being arrested each year. Car theft was the leading offense, but larceny, rape, beatings, and even murder were not uncommon. What was causing the delinquency? J. Edgar Hoover, head of the Federal Bureau of Investigation, insisted that the root of the problem was a lack of religious training. Others pointed to the growing number of urban slums. Such "bad" and "brutish" environments almost ensured that children

Youth Culture

A drug store soda fountain, a popular outlet for teenagers' consumerism in the 1950s.

would become criminals. The problem with those explanations was that they failed to explain why so many middle-class kids from God-fearing families were becoming delinquents. One contributing factor may have been the unprecedented mobility of young people. Access to automobiles enabled teens to escape parental control, and in the words of one journalist, cars provided "a private lounge for drinking and for petting or sex episodes."

ROCK AND ROLL   Many concerned observers blamed the teen delinquency problem on a new form of music that emerged during the postwar era: rock and roll. In 1955 *Life* magazine published a long article about a mysterious new "frenzied teenage music craze" that was creating "a big fuss." Alan Freed, a Cleveland disc jockey, had coined the term *rock and roll* in 1951. At a record store he had noticed white teenagers buying rhythm and blues (R&B) records that had heretofore been purchased only by African Americans and Hispanic Americans. Freed began playing R&B records but labeled the music *rock and roll* (a phrase used in African-American communities to refer to dancing and sex) to surmount the racial barrier. Freed's radio program was an immediate success, and its popularity helped bridge the gap between "white" and "black" music. African-American singers such as Chuck Berry, Little Richard, and Ray Charles and Hispanic-American performers such as Ritchie Valens (Richard Valenzuela) were suddenly the rage among young white middle-class audiences eager to claim their own cultural style and message.

At the same time, Elvis Presley, a young white truck driver and aspiring singer from Memphis, Tennessee, began experimenting with "rockabilly" music, his unique blend of gospel, country-and-western, and R&B rhythms and lyrics. In 1956 the twenty-one-year-old Presley released his smash hit "Heartbreak Hotel," and over the next two years emerged as the most popular musician entertainer in American history. Presley's long hair and sideburns, his knowing grins and disobedient sneers, his leather jacket and tight blue jeans—all shouted defiance of adult conventions. His sexually suggestive stage performances, featuring twisting hips and a gyrating pelvis, drove teenagers wild.

Such hysterics prompted cultural conservatives to urge parents to destroy Presley's records because they promoted "a pagan concept of life." A Catholic cardinal denounced Presley as a vile symptom of a teenage "creed of dishonesty, violence, lust and degeneration." Patriotic groups claimed that rock-and-roll music was a tool of Communist insurgents designed to corrupt youth. Yet rock and roll survived the assaults, and in the process it gave adolescents a self-conscious sense of belonging to a unique social group with distinctive characteristics. It also represented an unprecedented intermingling of racial, ethnic, and class identities.

Elvis Presley, 1956

The teenage children of middle-class America made rock and roll a thriving industry in the 1950s and Elvis its first star. The strong beat of rock music combined with the electric guitar, its signature instrument, produced a distinctive new sound.

A PARADOXICAL ERA

Rock and roll would become one of the major vehicles of the youth revolt of the 1960s. In the 1950s, however, it had little impact on the prevailing patterns of social and cultural life. The same held true for most of the critics who attacked the smug conformity and excessive materialism they saw pervading their society. The public had become weary of larger social or political concerns in the aftermath of the Depression and the war. Instead, Americans eagerly focused on personal and family goals and material achievements.

Yet those achievements, considerable as they were, eventually created a new set of problems. The benefits of abundance were by no means equally distributed during the 1950s, and millions of people still lived in poverty. For those more fortunate, unprecedented affluence and security fostered greater leisure and independence, which in turn provided opportunities for pursuing more varied notions of what the good life entailed. Yet the conformist mentality of the cold war era discouraged experimentation. By the mid-1960s tensions between innovation and convention would erupt into open conflict. Members of the baby-boom generation would become the leaders of the 1960s rebellion against the corporate and consumer cultures. Ironically, the person who would warn Americans of the 1960s of the mounting dangers of the burgeoning "military-industrial complex" was the president who had long symbolized its growth: Dwight D. Eisenhower.

MAKING CONNECTIONS

- The culture of the 1950s laid the groundwork for the counterculture of the 1960s, discussed in Chapters 34 and 35.

- There are fruitful comparisons between American culture in the 1950s and the earlier postwar period, the 1920s, which was described in Chapter 26.

- The women's movement of the 1970s, discussed in Chapter 35, was led by women who rejected the cult of domesticity described in this chapter.

- The baby boom of the postwar period would have continuing economic, social, political, and cultural significance as it moved through the life cycle. Follow along in coming chapters.

FURTHER READING

Two excellent overviews of social and cultural trends in the postwar era are William H. Chafe's *The Unfinished Journey: America since World War II,* 5th ed. (2003) and William E. Leuchtenburg's *A Troubled Feast: America Since 1945* (1973). For insights into the cultural life of the 1950s, see Jeffrey Hart's *When the Going Was Good!: American Life in the Fifties* (1982) and David Halberstam's *The Fifties* (1993).

The baby-boom generation and its impact are vividly described in Paul C. Light's *Baby Boomers* (1988). The emergence of the television industry is discussed in Erik Barnouw's *Tube of Plenty: The Evolution of American Television* (1975) and Ella Taylor's *Prime-Time Families: Television Culture in Postwar America* (1989).

A comprehensive account of the process of suburban development is Kenneth T. Jackson's *Crabgrass Frontier: The Suburbanization of the United States* (1985). Equally good is Tom Martinson's *American Dreamscape: The Pursuit of Happiness in Postwar America* (2000).

The middle-class ideal of family life in the 1950s is examined in Elaine Tyler May's *Homeward Bound: American Families in the Cold War Era* (1988). Thorough accounts of women's issues are found in Wini Breines's *Young, White, and Miserable: Growing Up Female in the Fifties* (1992). For an overview of the resurgence of religion in the 1950s, see George M. Marsden's *Religion and American Culture* (1990).

A lively discussion of movies of the 1950s can be found in Peter Biskind's *Seeing Is Believing: How Hollywood Taught Us to Stop Worrying and Love the Fifties* (1983). The origins and growth of rock and roll are surveyed in Carl Belz's *The Story of Rock,* 2nd ed. (1972). Thoughtful interpretive surveys of postwar literature include Josephine Hendin's *Vulnerable People: A View of American Fiction since 1945* (1978) and Malcolm Bradbury's *The Modern American Novel* (1983). The colorful Beats are brought to life in Steven Watson's *The Birth of the Beat Generation: Visionaries, Rebels, and Hipsters, 1944–1960* (1995).

33

CONFLICT AND DEADLOCK: THE EISENHOWER YEARS

FOCUS QUESTIONS

- What were the main characteristics of Eisenhower's "dynamic conservatism"?
- What events shaped American foreign policy in the 1950s?
- Why did the civil rights movement emerge in the 1950s?
- What events in Southeast Asia led to the Vietnam War?

To answer these questions and access additional review material, please visit www.wwnorton.com/studyspace.

The New Deal political coalition established by Franklin Roosevelt and sustained by Harry Truman posed a formidable challenge to Republicans after World War II. To counter the potent combination of Solid South white Democrats, African Americans, members of other minority groups, and organized labor, the Grand Old Party turned to General Dwight David Eisenhower, a military hero with an infectious grin capable of attracting independent voters as well as some Democrats. Eisenhower's commitment to a "moderate Republicanism" promised to slow the rate of government expansion while retaining many of the coveted social programs established by Roosevelt and Truman. Eisenhower's two terms as president are often characterized as representing a lull between two eras of Democratic activism. In Eisenhower's view, however, his administration would restore the authority of state and local governments and restrain the executive branch from political and social "engineering." In the process, the former general sought to renew traditional virtues and inspire Americans with a vision of a brighter future.

"TIME FOR A CHANGE"

By 1952 the Truman administration had piled up a heavy burden of political liabilities. Its bold stand in Korea had brought a bloody stalemate in the war, renewed wage and price controls at home, charges of Communist subversion and disloyalty, and the exposure of corrupt lobbyists and influence peddlers who rigged favors in Washington. The disclosure of corruption led Truman to fire nearly 250 employees of the Internal Revenue Service and, among others, an assistant attorney general in charge of the Justice Department's Tax Division. But doubts lingered that Truman would ever finish the housecleaning.

THE POLITICAL RISE OF EISENHOWER It was, Republicans claimed, "time for a change," and they saw public sentiment turning their way as the 1952 election approached. Republican leaders recruited General Dwight D. Eisenhower to be their candidate. Eisenhower, then the commander of NATO, inspired confidence. His leadership had been tested in war, but as a professional soldier he had escaped the scars of political combat. He stood, therefore, outside and above the arena of public life, although his political instincts and skills were sharpened during his successful army career. In 1952 Eisenhower affirmed that he was a Republican, left his NATO post, and permitted his name to be entered in party primaries. An outpouring of public enthusiasm greeted his candidacy. Bumper stickers announced simply, "I Like Ike." Eisenhower won the presidential nomination on the first ballot. He balanced the ticket with a youthful Californian, the thirty-nine-year-old senator Richard M. Nixon, who had built a career on opposition to left-wing "subversives" and gained his greatest notoriety as the member of Congress most eager in the pursuit of Alger Hiss.

THE ELECTION OF 1952 The Twenty-second Amendment, ratified in 1951, forbade any president from serving more than two terms. The amendment exempted the current incumbent, Harry Truman, but weary of the war in Korea and harassed by charges of subversion and corruption in his administration, Truman withdrew and endorsed Governor Adlai E. Stevenson of Illinois, who roused the Democratic delegates with an eloquent speech welcoming them to Chicago.

The 1952 campaign matched two of the most magnetic personalities ever pitted against each other in a presidential contest. Eisenhower, though a political novice, was a world hero who had been in the public eye for a decade. Stevenson was hardly known outside Illinois and was never able to escape the burden of Truman's liabilities. The genial general, who had led the crusade against Hitler, now opened a domestic crusade to clean up "the mess in Washington." To this he added a promise, late in the campaign, that as president-elect he would secure "an early and honorable" peace in Korea. Stevenson possessed a lofty eloquence spiced with a quick wit, but he came across as just too aloof, a shade too intellectual. The Republicans labeled him an egghead in contrast to Eisenhower, the man of the people, the general of decisive action.

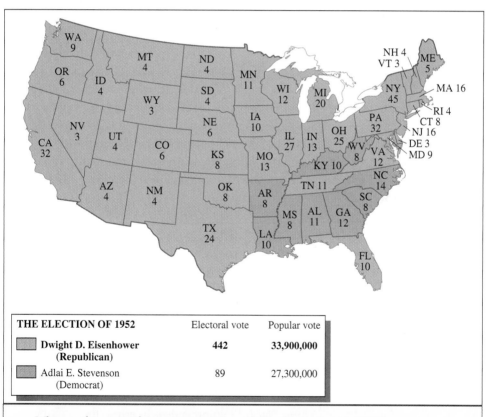

THE ELECTION OF 1952	Electoral vote	Popular vote
Dwight D. Eisenhower (Republican)	442	33,900,000
Adlai E. Stevenson (Democrat)	89	27,300,000

Why was the contest between Stevenson and Eisenhower lopsided? Why was Eisenhower's victory in the South remarkable? Did Eisenhower's broad appeal help congressional Republicans win more seats?

Good First Impression

In the 1952 election the Republican party won significant support in the South for the first time.

In the end, Stevenson's humor and intellect were no match for Eisenhower's popularity. The war hero triumphed in a landslide of 34 million votes to Stevenson's 27 million and 442 electoral votes to Stevenson's 89. The election marked a turning point in Republican fortunes in the South: for the first time since the 1850s, the South was moving toward a two-party system. Stevenson carried only eight southern states plus West Virginia. He also failed to win his home state of Illinois. Eisenhower picked up five states on the periphery of the Deep South: Florida, Oklahoma, Tennessee, Texas, and Virginia. In the former Confederacy the Republican ticket captured 49 percent of the votes. The "nonpolitical" Eisenhower had made it respectable, even fashionable, to vote Republican in the South. Elsewhere, too, the former general made inroads into the New Deal coalition, attracting supporters among the ethnic and religious minorities in the major cities who had long identified with the Democratic party.

The voters, it turned out, liked Ike better than they liked his party. Democrats retained most of the governorships, lost control of the House by only eight votes, and broke even in the Senate, where only the vote of the vice president ensured Republican control. The congressional elections two years later would weaken the Republican grip on Congress, and Eisenhower would have to work with a Democratic Congress until he left office.

EISENHOWER'S HIDDEN-HAND PRESIDENCY

IKE Born in Denison, Texas, on October 14, 1890, Dwight David Eisenhower grew up in Abilene, Kansas and attended the U.S. Military Academy at West Point, New York. During World War II he commanded American forces in the European theater and directed the invasion of North Africa in 1942. Two years later he assumed the post of supreme commander of Allied forces in preparation for the invasion of Nazi-controlled Europe. After the war, by then a five-star general of the army, he became chief of staff and supreme commander of NATO forces, with a brief interlude as president of Columbia University.

Far from being a "do-nothing" president, as some have charged, Eisenhower was in fact an effective leader. The art of leadership, he once explained, did not require "hitting people over the head. Any damn fool can do that. . . . It's persuasion—and conciliation—and education—and patience. That's the only kind of leadership I know—or believe in—or will practice." Ike was a midwestern middle-of-the-road patriot, a common man with a winning smile who read little, was uninformed about trends in intellectual and artistic life, and was prone to giving folksy advice. A diplomat labeled him "the nation's number one Boy Scout." But those who were closer to Ike have presented another side. When provoked, the genial general could show a fiery temper and release a stream of scalding profanity. One student of Eisenhower's leadership techniques has spoken of a "hidden-hand presidency," in which Ike deliberately cultivated a public image of passivity to hide his active involvement in policy decisions.

"DYNAMIC CONSERVATISM" AT HOME   Like Ulysses Grant, Eisenhower enjoyed hobnobbing with rich men. The president of General Motors became secretary of defense, one auto distributor became secretary of the interior, and another became postmaster general. The New Dealers, Adlai Stevenson wryly remarked, "have all left Washington to make way for the car dealers."

Eisenhower called his domestic program dynamic conservatism, which meant being "conservative when it comes to money and liberal when it comes to human beings." Budget cutting was a high priority for the new administration, which set out to slash both domestic programs and national defense spending. Eisenhower warned repeatedly against the dangers of "creeping socialism," "huge bureaucracies," and perennial budget deficits. He abolished the Reconstruction Finance Corporation, ended wage and price controls, and reduced farm-price subsidies.

In 1954 the administration formulated tax reductions that resembled the Republican programs of the 1920s in providing benefits mainly to corporations and wealthy individuals. The new budget slashed expenditures by $6.5 billion, nearly 10 percent, and the Federal Reserve Board reinforced administration policy by tightening credit and raising interest rates to avert inflation. But a business slump followed, which reduced government revenues, making it harder to balance the budget. Eisenhower's fiscal and monetary policies thereafter became more flexible. The government accepted easier credit and deficits as necessary "countercyclical" methods.

Although Eisenhower chipped away at several Democratic programs, his presidency in the end kept the basic structure and premises of the New Deal. In a letter to his brother in 1954, Eisenhower observed, "Should any political party attempt to abolish Social Security and eliminate labor laws and farm programs, you would not hear of that party again in our political history." In some ways the Eisenhower administration expanded the New Deal, especially after 1954, when it had the help of Democratic Congresses. Amendments to the Social Security Act in 1954 and 1956 brought coverage to millions formerly excluded: professional people, domestic and clerical workers, farmworkers, and members of the armed forces. In 1959 the program's benefits went up 7 percent. Federal expenditures for public health rose steadily in the Eisenhower years, and the president went so far as to endorse federal participation in health insurance, but Congress twice refused to act on such a plan. Low-income housing continued to be built with federal funds, although on a much reduced scale.

Some farm-related aid programs were expanded during the Eisenhower years as well. The president also continued to support federal construction projects that served national needs. Two such programs left major monuments to his presidency: the St. Lawrence Seaway and the interstate highway system. The St. Lawrence Seaway opened the Great Lakes to oceangoing ships by means of locks and dredging. Even more important, in 1956 a new highway-construction act authorized the federal government to put up 90 percent of the cost of building 42,500 miles of interstate highways to serve the needs of commerce and defense, as well as the convenience of private citizens. The states put up the remaining 10 percent. It was only afterward that Americans realized that the huge national commitment to the automobile might have come at the expense of the nation's railroad system, already in a state of advanced decay.

CONCLUDING AN ARMISTICE   America's new global responsibilities in the postwar world absorbed much of Eisenhower's attention. The most pressing problem when he entered office was the painful deadlock in the Korean peace talks. UN negotiators refused to agree to return Communist prisoners of war who did not want to go back to the North. North Korean and Chinese negotiators insisted that all prisoners be returned regardless of their wishes. To break the stalemate, Eisenhower resolved upon a bold stand. In mid-May 1953 he stepped up aerial bombardment of North Korea, then had Secretary of State John Foster Dulles secretly threaten to use atomic warfare. Whether for that reason or others, negotiations moved quickly toward an armistice along the established border just above the 38th parallel and toward a complicated arrangement for an exchange of prisoners that allowed captives to accept or refuse repatriation.

On July 26, 1953, President Eisenhower announced the end of fighting in Korea. Whether he had pulled a masterful bluff in getting the agreement has never become clear; no one knows whether he would have used atomic weapons. Perhaps the more decisive factors in bringing about a settlement were rising Chinese losses, which China's leaders increasingly found unacceptable, and the spirit of uncertainty and caution felt by the Soviet Communists after the death of Joseph Stalin on March 5, 1953—six weeks after Ike's inauguration.

CONCLUDING A WITCH HUNT   The Korean armistice helped to end the meteoric career of Senator Joseph McCarthy. Convinced that the government was infested with Communists and spies, the Wisconsin senator launched a one-man crusade to root them out. Eventually McCarthy's unscrupulous tactics led to his self-destruction, but not before he had left still more careers and reputations in ruins. The Republicans thought their victory in 1952 would curb his recklessness, but McCarthy actually grew more outlandish in both his charges and his investigative methods.

The freewheeling McCarthy finally overreached himself when he made the absurd charge that the U.S. Army itself was "soft" on communism. From April 22 to June 17, 1954, televised Senate hearings displayed McCarthy at his capricious worst, bullying witnesses, dragging out lengthy irrelevances, repeatedly

The Army-McCarthy Hearings, June 1954

The attorney Joseph Welch (hand on head) listening incredulously to Senator McCarthy's claims of Communist infiltration of the U.S. Army.

calling "point of order." He became the perfect foil for the Army's gentle but unflappable counsel, Joseph Welch of Boston, whose rapier wit repeatedly drew blood. When McCarthy tried to smear one of Welch's young associates, the counsel went into a cold rage: "Until this moment, Senator, I think I never really gauged your cruelty or your recklessness. . . . Have you no sense of decency, sir, at long last?" When the audience burst into applause, the confused, skulking senator was reduced to whispering, "What did I do?"

On December 2, 1954, the Senate voted sixty-seven to twenty-two to "condemn" McCarthy for contempt of the Senate. McCarthy's political career collapsed, and he began drinking heavily. Three years later, at the age of forty-eight, he was dead. To the end, Eisenhower refused to "get down in the gutter with that guy" and sully the dignity of the presidency, but he did work resolutely against McCarthy behind the scenes. Eisenhower recognized, however, that Communist espionage posed a real danger to national security. He denied clemency to Julius and Ethel Rosenberg, who were convicted of transmitting atomic secrets to the Russians, on the grounds that they "may have condemned to death tens of millions of innocent people." The Rosenbergs were electrocuted on June 19, 1953.

INTERNAL SECURITY   The anti-Communist crusade survived the downfall of McCarthy. Eisenhower stiffened the government security program that Truman had set up in 1947. In 1953 an executive order broadened the basis for firing subversive government workers by replacing Truman's criterion of "disloyalty" with the new category of "security risk." Under the new edict, federal workers could lose their jobs because of dubious political associations or personal behavior that might make them careless or vulnerable to blackmail. The Supreme Court modified some of the more extreme expressions of the Red Scare, however.

In 1953 Eisenhower appointed former governor Earl Warren of California as chief justice, a decision he later pronounced the "biggest damnfool mistake I ever made." Warren, who had seemed safely conservative while active in politics, proved to have a social conscience and a streak of libertarianism that was shared by another Eisenhower Court appointee, William J. Brennan Jr. The Warren Court (1953–1969), under the chief justice's influence, became an important agency of social and political change through the 1960s. In connection with security programs and loyalty requirements, the Court upheld traditional individual rights. A 1957 opinion narrowly construed the Smith Act of 1940, aimed at conspirators against the government, to apply only to those advocating "revolutionary" action. Merely teaching a revolutionary doctrine in the abstract could not be construed as a crime under the act.

This, along with decisions setting rigid standards for admissible evidence, rendered the Smith Act a dead letter.

FOREIGN INTERVENTION

DULLES AND FOREIGN POLICY   The Eisenhower administration promised new departures in foreign policy under the direction of Secretary of State John Foster Dulles. Grandson of one former secretary of state and nephew of another, Dulles had pursued a lifetime career as an international lawyer and sometime diplomat. As counselor to the Truman State Department, he had negotiated the Japanese peace treaty. Son of a minister and himself an active Presbyterian layman, Dulles, in the words of the British ambassador, resembled those old zealots of the wars of religion who "saw the world as an arena in which the forces of good and evil were continuously at war." Dulles gave the appearance of dour sternness and Calvinist righteousness, but he was a man of immense energy, intelligence, and experience.

The foreign-policy planks of the 1952 Republican platform, which Dulles wrote, showed both the moralist and the tactician at work. The Democratic policy of containment was needlessly defensive, Dulles thought. Americans should instead work toward the "liberation" of Eastern Europe from Soviet domination. Eisenhower was quick to explain, however, that liberating Eastern Europe from Soviet control would not involve military force. He would promote independence "by every peaceful means, but only by peaceful means."

Yet for all his bold talk of liberating Eastern Europe, Dulles made no significant departure from the strategy of containment created under Truman. Instead, he institutionalized containment in the rigid mold of his cold war rhetoric and extended it to the military strategy of deterrence. His endorsement of "massive retaliation" was an effort to get, in the slogan soon current, "more bang for the buck." Budgetary considerations lay at the root of any military plans, for Eisenhower and his cabinet feared that in the effort to build superior war power the country could spend itself into bankruptcy. During 1953 members of the Joint Chiefs of Staff began planning a new military posture. The heart of their so-called New Look was the assumption that nuclear weapons could be used in limited-war situations, allowing reductions in conventional forces and thus budgetary savings. Dulles, who announced the policy in early 1954, explained that savings would come "by placing more reliance on deterrent power, and less dependence on local defensive power."

"Don't Be Afraid—I Can Always Pull You Back."

Secretary of State John Foster Dulles pushes a reluctant America to the brink of war.

By this time both the United States and the Soviet Union had developed hydrogen bombs. With the new policy of deterrence, what Winston Churchill called a "balance of terror" had replaced the old balance of power. The threat of nuclear holocaust was terrifying, but the notion that the United States would risk such a disaster in response to local wars had little credibility.

Dulles's policy of "brinkmanship" depended for its strategic effect upon those very fears of nuclear disaster. Dulles argued in 1956 that in following a tough policy of confrontation with communism, a nation sometimes had to "go to the brink" of war. Such a firm stand, he believed, had halted further aggression in Korea in 1953 when America threatened to break the stalemate by removing restraints from the armed forces. Dulles had also employed brinkmanship in 1954 in Indochina, when the United States sent aircraft carriers into the South China Sea "both to deter any Red Chinese attack against Indochina and to provide weapons for instant retaliation."

INDOCHINA: THE BACKGROUND TO WAR Dulles's use of brinkmanship in Indochina neglected the complexity of the situation there, which presented a special case of the nationalism that swept through the old colonial world of Asia and Africa after World War II. By the early 1950s most of British Asia was independent or on its way to independence: India, Pakistan, Ceylon (later Sri Lanka), Burma (later Myanmar), and the Malay States (later the Federation of Malaysia). The Dutch and French, however, were less ready than the British to give up their colonies, a situation that created a dilemma for U.S. policy makers. Americans sympathized with the colonial nationalists but also wanted Dutch and French help fending off incursions of communism. For the Dutch and the French to maintain control of their colonial possessions, they had to reconquer areas that had passed from Japanese occupation into the hands of local patriots. The Truman administration had felt obliged to answer their pleas for aid.

In the Dutch East Indies the Japanese had created a puppet Indonesian republic, which emerged from World War II virtually independent. The Dutch effort to regain control met with resistance that exploded into open warfare. Eventually American pressure persuaded the Dutch to accept Indonesian self-government under a Dutch-Indonesian union in 1949, but that lasted only until 1954, when the Republic of Indonesia became independent.

In 1955 the Bandung Conference in Indonesia, attended by delegates from twenty-nine independent countries of Asia and Africa, signaled the emergence of a "third world" of underdeveloped countries, unaligned with either the United States or the Soviet bloc. Among other actions, the conference denounced "colonialism in all its manifestations," a statement that implicitly condemned both the Soviet Union and the West.

French Indochina, created in the nineteenth century out of the old kingdoms of Cambodia, Laos, and Vietnam, offered a variation on colonial nationalism. During World War II, when the Japanese controlled the region, they supported French civil servants and opposed the local nationalists. Chief among the latter were members of the Viet Minh (League for the Independence of Vietnam), which fell under the influence of Communists led by Ho Chi Minh, a seasoned revolutionary and passionate Vietnamese nationalist obsessed by a single goal: independence for his country. At the end of the war, Ho's followers controlled part of northern Vietnam, and on September 2, 1945, Ho Chi Minh proclaimed a Democratic Republic of Vietnam, with its capital in Hanoi.

Ho's declaration of Vietnamese independence borrowed from Thomas Jefferson, opening with the words "We hold these truths to be self-evident. That all men are created equal." Ho had secretly received American help against

Ho Chi Minh

A seasoned revolutionary, Ho Chi Minh cultivated a humble, proletarian image of himself as Uncle Ho, a man of the people.

the Japanese during the war, but his bids for additional aid after the war went unanswered. Vietnam was a low priority in U.S. diplomatic concerns at the time, and Truman could not stomach aiding a professed Communist.

In 1946 the French recognized Ho's new government as a "free state" within the French union. Before the year was out, however, Ho's forces had challenged French efforts to restore their colonial regime in the southern provinces, and this clash soon expanded into the First Indochina War. In 1949, having set up puppet rulers in Laos and Cambodia, the French reinstated former emperor Bao Dai as head of state in Vietnam. The victory of the Communists in China later in 1949 was followed by China's diplomatic recognition of the Viet Minh government in Hanoi and then the recognition of Bao Dai by the United States and Britain.

The Viet Minh movement thereafter became more dependent on the Soviet Union and Communist China for help. In 1950, with the outbreak of fighting in Korea, the struggle in Vietnam became a major battleground in the cold war. When the Korean War ended, U.S. aid to the French in Vietnam, begun by the Truman administration, continued. By the end of 1953, the Eisenhower administration was paying about two thirds of the cost of the French military effort in Indochina, and the United States had found itself at the "brink" to which Dulles later referred. A major French force had been sent to Dien Bien Phu, near the Laos border, in the hope of luring Viet Minh guerrillas into the open and overwhelming them with superior firepower. The French instead found themselves trapped by a Viet Minh force that threatened to overrun their stronghold.

In March 1954 the French government requested an American air strike to relieve the pressure on Dien Bien Phu. Eisenhower seemed to endorse forceful action, but when congressional leaders expressed reservations, he opposed U.S. intervention unless the British joined the effort. When they refused, he backed away from unilateral military action in Vietnam.

On May 7, 1954, the Viet Minh overwhelmed the last French resistance at Dien Bien Phu. It was the very eve of the day that an international conference at Geneva took up the question of Indochina. Six weeks later, as French forces continued to suffer defeats in Vietnam, a new French government promised to get an early settlement. On July 20 representatives of France, Britain, the Soviet Union, the People's Republic of China, and the Viet Minh signed the Geneva Accords. The agreement proposed to make Laos and Cambodia independent and to divide Vietnam at the 17th parallel. The Viet Minh would take power in the north, and the French would remain south of the line until elections in 1956 would reunify Vietnam. American and South Vietnamese representatives refused to join in the accord, leading the Soviet

Union and China to back away from earlier hints that they would guarantee the Geneva settlement.

Dulles responded to the growing Communist influence in Vietnam by organizing mutual defense agreements for Southeast Asia. On September 8, 1954, at a meeting in Manila, the United States joined seven other countries in forming the Southeast Asia Treaty Organization (SEATO). The impression that it paralleled NATO was false, for SEATO was neither a common defense organization like NATO nor was it primarily Asian. The signers agreed that in case of attack on one, the others would act according to their "constitutional practices," and in case of threats or subversion they would "consult immediately." The members included only three Asian countries— the Philippines, Thailand, and Pakistan—together with Britain, France, Australia, New Zealand, and the United States. India and Indonesia, the two most populous countries in the region, refused to join. A special protocol added to the treaty extended coverage to Indochina. The treaty reflected what Dulles's critics called pactomania, which by the end of the Eisenhower administration contracted the United States to defend forty-three other countries.

Eisenhower announced that though the United States "had not itself been party to or bound by the decision taken at the [Geneva] Conference," any renewal of Communist aggression in Southeast Asia "would be viewed by us as a matter of grave concern." (He failed to note that the United States had agreed at Geneva to "refrain from the threat or use of force to disturb" the agreements.) In Vietnam, when Ho Chi Minh took over the north, those who wished to leave for South Vietnam, mostly Catholics, did so with American aid. Power in the south gravitated to a new premier imposed on Emperor Bao Dai by the French at American urging: Ngo Dinh Diem, a Catholic who had opposed both the French and the Viet Minh. In 1954 Eisenhower offered to assist Diem "in developing and maintaining a strong, viable state, capable of resisting attempted subversion or aggression through military means." In return the United States expected Diem to enact democratic reforms and distribute land to the peasants. U.S. aid took the form of CIA and military advisers charged with training Diem's armed forces and police. Eisenhower remained opposed to the use of U.S. combat troops. He was convinced that such military intervention would bog down into a costly stalemate—as it eventually did.

Instead of instituting political and economic reforms, however, Diem suppressed his political opponents on both the right and the left, offering little or no land distribution and permitting widespread corruption. In 1956 he refused to join in the elections to reunify Vietnam. After the French

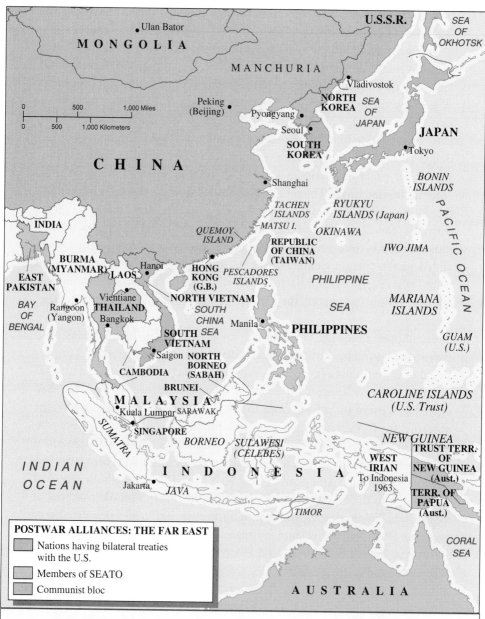

How did the United States become increasingly involved in Vietnam? Why did the installation of Ngo Dinh Diem by the French and the Americans backfire and generate more conflict in Vietnam? Why was the protection of Taiwan important to the United States?

withdrawal from the country, he ousted Bao Dai and declared himself president. His efforts to eliminate all opposition played into the hands of the Communists, who found recruits among the discontented. By 1957 guerrilla forces known as the Viet Cong had begun attacks on the Diem government, and in 1960 the resistance groups coalesced as the National Liberation Front. As guerrilla warfare gradually disrupted South Vietnam, the Eisenhower administration was helpless to do anything but "sink or swim with Ngo Dinh Diem."

PROTECTING TAIWAN   Just before the Manila conference in 1954, Chinese artillery began shelling the islands of Quemoy and Matsu, in Taiwan Strait, held by Chiang Kai-shek's Nationalists. On his way back from Manila, Secretary of State Dulles stopped in Taipei, Taiwan's capital, and worked out a mutual defense treaty that bound the United States to defend Taiwan and the nearby Pescadores Islands. In 1955 the president secured a congressional resolution giving him full power to defend Taiwan and the Pescadores and authorizing him to secure and protect "related positions of that area now in friendly hands" in order to defend Taiwan. Congress's endorsement was overwhelming—the resolution drew only three negative votes in each house—for so sweeping a grant of power to wage war if deemed necessary.

The Communist Chinese kept up their provocative activity nonetheless, and Quemoy and Matsu became symbols of the American will to protect Taiwan. The U.S. chief of naval operations "leaked" word to journalists that the administration was considering a plan "to destroy Red China's military potential and thus end its expansionist tendencies." Soon afterward the Chinese backed away from the brink. At the Bandung Conference in April, with diplomatic encouragement from other Asian nations, the Chinese premier, Chou En-lai, declared that the People's Republic of China was ready to discuss the Taiwan Strait issue directly with the United States. In 1955 representatives of the two governments began meetings in Geneva, and the guns fell silent.

REELECTION AND FOREIGN CRISES

As the United States continued to forge cold war alliances and bring pressure to bear on foreign governments by practicing brinkmanship, a new presidential campaign unfolded. Despite having suffered a coronary seizure in the fall of 1955 and undergoing an operation for ileitis (an intestinal inflammation) in early 1956, Eisenhower decided to run for reelection. He retained widespread public support and confidence, although the Democrats controlled Congress. Meanwhile, new crises in foreign and domestic affairs required him to take decisive action.

A LANDSLIDE FOR IKE   In 1956 the Republican Convention renominated Eisenhower by acclamation and again named Richard Nixon the vice-presidential candidate. The party platform endorsed Eisenhower's "modern Republicanism." The Democrats turned again to Adlai Stevenson. The platform revived old Democratic issues: less "favoritism" to big business, repeal of the Taft-Hartley Act, and tax relief for those in low-income brackets.

Neither candidate generated much excitement. During the last week of the campaign, however, fighting erupted along the Suez Canal in Egypt and in the streets of Budapest, Hungary. These two unrelated events in combination caused a profound international crisis. The attack on Egypt by Britain, France, and Israel disrupted the Western alliance and damaged any claim to moral outrage at the Soviet Union's actions in Hungary. For the Soviets, the Suez War afforded both a smoke screen for the subjugation of rebellious Hungary and a chance to enlarge their influence in the Middle East, an increasingly important source of oil.

The two crises led Adlai Stevenson to declare the administration's foreign policy "bankrupt." Most voters, however, reasoned that the foreign turmoil spelled a poor time to switch leaders, and they handed Eisenhower a landslide victory. The president lost one border state, Missouri, but in carrying Louisiana became the first Republican to win a Deep South state since Reconstruction; nationally he carried all but seven states. The decision was unmistakably clear: Eisenhower won more than 35.5 million popular votes to a little over 26 million for Stevenson, 457 electoral votes to the Democrat's 73.

A beaming Eisenhower declared on election night "that modern Republicanism has now proved itself. And America has approved of modern Republicanism." Eisenhower Republicans, it seemed clear, had assimilated the New Deal as an accomplished fact. But Eisenhower's decisive win failed to swing a congressional majority for his party in either house, the first time events had worked out this way since the election of Zachary Taylor in 1848.

CRISIS IN THE MIDDLE EAST   To forestall Soviet penetration in the Middle East, Dulles in 1955 completed his series of alliances across the northern tier of the region. Under American sponsorship, Britain had joined the Middle Eastern states of Turkey, Iraq, Iran, and Pakistan in the Middle East Treaty Organization (METO), or Baghdad Pact Organization, as the treaty was commonly called. By linking the easternmost NATO state (Turkey) to the westernmost SEATO state (Pakistan), METO had a certain

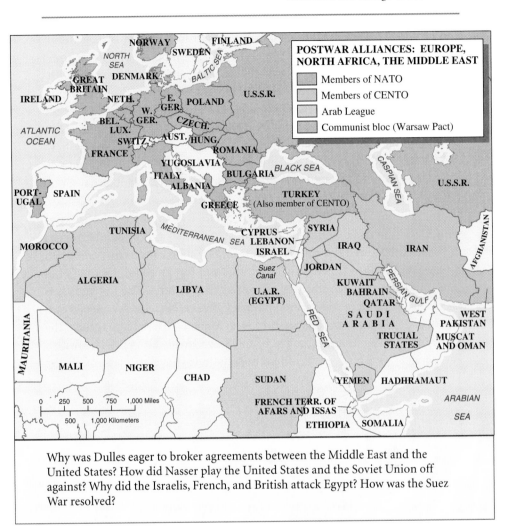

POSTWAR ALLIANCES: EUROPE, NORTH AFRICA, THE MIDDLE EAST

Members of NATO
Members of CENTO
Arab League
Communist bloc (Warsaw Pact)

Why was Dulles eager to broker agreements between the Middle East and the United States? How did Nasser play the United States and the Soviet Union off against? Why did the Israelis, French, and British attack Egypt? How was the Suez War resolved?

superficial logic, but after Iraq, the only Arab member, withdrew in 1959, the alliance lost its cohesion and its credibility. The neighboring Arab states remained aloof from the organization. These were the states of the Arab League (Egypt, Iraq, Jordan, Lebanon, Saudi Arabia, Syria, and Yemen), which had warred on Israel in 1948–1949 and remained committed to its destruction.

The most fateful developments in the Middle East turned on the rise of the Egyptian general Gamal Abdel Nasser after the overthrow of King Farouk in 1952. The bone of contention was the Suez Canal, which had opened in 1869 as a joint French-Egyptian venture. But in 1875 the British government had acquired the largest block of shares, and from 1882 on British troops were posted along the canal to protect the British Empire's "lifeline" to India and other colonies. When Nasser's nationalist regime pressed for the withdrawal of British forces from the canal zone, Eisenhower and Dulles supported the demand, and in 1954 an Anglo-Egyptian treaty provided for British withdrawal within twenty months. Nasser, like other leaders of the third world, remained unaligned in the cold war and sought to play both sides off against each other. The United States, meanwhile, courted Egyptian support by offering a loan to build a huge hydroelectric plant at Aswān on the Nile River.

From the outset the administration's proposal was opposed by Jewish constituencies concerned with Egyptian threats to Israel and by southern congressmen who feared the competition from Egyptian cotton. In 1956, when Nasser increased trade with the Soviet bloc and recognized the People's Republic of China, Dulles abruptly canceled the loan offer. The outcome was far from a triumph of American diplomacy. The chief victims, it turned out, were Anglo-French interests in the Suez. Unable to retaliate against the United States, Nasser took control of the Suez Canal Company. The British and French were furious. Fruitless negotiations dragged on through the

General Moshe Dayan

Commander of the Israeli forces during the Sinai campaign in 1956, Dayan (with eye patch) receives bread on the noon chow line, along with soldiers who volunteered to strengthen Israel's defenses on the Gaza Strip.

summer, and finally, on October 29, Israeli forces invaded the Gaza Strip and the Sinai peninsula. The Israelis invaded ostensibly to root out Arab guerrillas but actually to synchronize with the British and the French, who began bombing Egyptian air bases and occupied Port Said.

The Suez War put the United States in a quandary. Either the administration could support its European allies and see the troublesome Nasser crushed, or it could defend the UN charter and champion Arab nationalism against imperialist aggression. Eisenhower opted for the latter course, with the unusual result that the Soviet Union sided with the United States. Once American pressure had forced the Anglo-French-Israeli capitulation, the Soviets capitalized on the situation by threatening to use missiles against the Western aggressors. This belated bravado won for the Soviet Union in the Arab world some of the credit actually owed the United States.

REPRESSION IN HUNGARY   In the Soviet Union, Nikita Khrushchev had come out on top in the post-Stalin power struggles. Khrushchev in 1956 had delivered a "secret" speech on the crimes of the Stalin era before a Communist Party congress and had hinted at relaxed policies and "different roads to socialism" that different countries might take. This new policy of "de-Stalinization" put Stalinist leaders in the satellite countries of Eastern Europe on the defensive and emboldened the more independent leaders to take action. Riots in the Polish city of Poznań led to the rise of Wladyslaw Gomulka, a Polish nationalist, as leader of the Polish Communist party. Gomulka managed to win a degree of independence by avoiding an open break with the Soviets.

In Hungary, however, a similar movement got out of hand. On October 23, 1956, fighting broke out in Budapest, followed by the installation of Imre Nagy, a moderate Communist, as head of the government. Again the Soviets seemed content to let de-Stalinization follow its course, and on October 28 they withdrew their forces from Budapest. But Nagy's announcement three days later that Hungary would withdraw from the Warsaw Pact (a military alliance linking the Eastern European countries under Soviet control) brought Soviet tanks back into Budapest. Although Khrushchev was willing to relax relations with the Eastern European satellites, he refused to allow them to break with the Soviet Union or abandon their mutual defense obligations. The Soviets installed a more compliant leader in Hungary, János Kádár, and hauled Nagy off to Moscow, where a firing squad executed him in 1958. It was a tragic ending to an independence movement that at the outset promised the sort of moderation that might have vindicated George Kennan's policy of containment, if not Dulles's notion of liberation.

REACTIONS TO *SPUTNIK* On October 4, 1957, the Soviets launched the first satellite, called *Sputnik*. Americans, until then complacent about their technical superiority, panicked. If the Soviets were so advanced in rocketry, then perhaps they could hit American cities with armed missiles. A Democratic senator demanded that Eisenhower call a special session of Congress to address the *Sputnik* crisis. The president refused, not wanting to heighten anxieties. All along Eisenhower had known that the "missile gap" was more illusory than real, but he could not reveal that high-altitude spy planes were gathering that information. Even so, American missile development was in a state of disarray, with a tangle of agencies and committees creating waste and duplication.

The Soviet Union's success with *Sputnik* led to efforts in the United States to increase defense spending, offer NATO allies intermediate-range ballistic missiles pending development of long-range intercontinental ballistic missiles (ICBMs), set up a new agency to coordinate space efforts, and establish a crash program in science education and military research. The "*Sputnik* syndrome," compounded by a sharp recession through the winter of 1957–1958, loosened the purse strings of frugal legislators, who added to the new budget more than Eisenhower wanted for both defense and domestic programs. During 1958 Britain, Italy, and Turkey accepted U.S. missiles on their territory. Also in 1958 Congress created the National Aeronautics and Space Administration (NASA) to coordinate research and development in the field. Before the end of the year, NASA had unveiled a program to put a manned craft in orbit, but the first manned flight, by Commander Alan B. Shepard Jr., did not take place until May 5, 1961. Finally, in 1958 Congress enacted the National Defense Education Act, which authorized federal grants for training in mathematics, science, and modern languages, as well as for student loans and fellowships.

By the Rocket's Red Glare

The Soviet success in space shocked Americans and created concerns about a "missile gap."

FESTERING PROBLEMS ABROAD

Once the Suez and Hungary crises faded from the front pages, Eisenhower enjoyed eighteen months of smooth sailing in foreign affairs. Nonetheless, a brief flurry occurred in 1958 over hostile demonstrations in Peru and Venezuela against Vice President Richard Nixon, who was on a goodwill tour of eight Latin American countries. Meanwhile, tensions in the Middle East and Europe continued to simmer, only to boil over in 1958.

CRISIS IN THE MIDDLE EAST   In 1958 Congress approved what came to be called the Eisenhower Doctrine, a resolution that promised to extend economic and military aid to Middle East nations and to use armed forces if necessary to assist any such nation against armed aggression by any Communist country.

President Gamal Abdel Nasser of Egypt, meanwhile, had emerged from the Suez crisis with heightened prestige, and in 1958 he created the United Arab Republic by (a short-lived) merger with Syria. Then, on July 14, a leftist coup in Iraq, supposedly inspired by Nasser and the Soviets, threw out the pro-Western government and killed the king, the crown prince, and the premier. In Lebanon, already unsettled by internal conflict, the government appealed to the United States for support to fend off a similar fate. Eisenhower immediately ordered 5,000 marines into Lebanon. British forces meanwhile went into Jordan at the request of King Hussein. Once the situation stabilized and the Lebanese factions reached a compromise, U.S. forces (up to 15,000 at one point) withdrew in October 1958.

CRISIS IN EAST ASIA   East Asia heated up again in 1958 when, on August 23, the People's Republic of China renewed its shelling of the Chinese Nationalists on the offshore islands of Quemoy and Matsu. In September the U.S. Seventh Fleet began to escort Nationalist convoys but stopped short of entering Chinese territorial waters. On October 1 Eisenhower suggested that a cease-fire would provide "an opportunity to negotiate in good faith." China ordered such a cease-fire on October 6 and on October 25 said that it would reserve the right to bombard the islands on alternate days. With that strange stipulation the worst of the crisis passed, but the tensions between Communist China and Taiwan continued to fester.

CRISIS IN BERLIN   The problem of Berlin, an island of Western capitalism deep in Soviet-controlled East Germany, festered too: Soviet premier Nikita Khrushchev called Berlin a "bone in his throat." After World War II, West

Nikita Khrushchev

The Soviet premier speaks on the problem of Berlin, 1959.

Berlin served as a "showplace" of Western democracy and prosperity, a listening post for Western intelligence gathering, and a funnel through which news and propaganda from the West penetrated what British leader Winston Churchill had called the iron curtain. Although East Germany had sealed its western frontiers, refugees could still pass from East to West Berlin. On November 10, 1958, however, at a Soviet-Polish friendship rally in Moscow, Khrushchev threatened to give East Germany control of East Berlin and the air lanes into West Berlin. After the deadline he set, May 27, 1959, Western occupation authorities would have to deal with the East German government, in effect recognizing it, or face the possibility of another blockade.

Eisenhower refused to budge from his position on Berlin but sought a settlement. Khrushchev, it turned out, was no more eager for confrontation than Eisenhower. In talks with British prime minister Harold Macmillan, Khrushchev suggested that the main thing was to begin discussions of the Berlin issue, postponing for the moment talks about the May 27 deadline. Macmillan in turn won Eisenhower's consent to a meeting of the Big Four foreign ministers representing the United States, Great Britain, France, and the Soviet Union.

There was little hope of resolving the conflicting views on Berlin and German reunification, but the talks distracted attention from Khrushchev's deadline of May 27: it passed almost unnoticed. In September 1959, after the Big Four talks had adjourned, Premier Khrushchev visited the United States, stopping in New York, Washington, D.C., Los Angeles, San Francisco, and Iowa. In talks with Eisenhower, Khrushchev endorsed "peaceful coexistence," and Eisenhower admitted that the Berlin situation was "abnormal." They agreed that the time was ripe for a summit meeting in the spring.

THE U-2 SUMMIT   The planned summit meeting blew up in Eisenhower's face, however. On May 1, 1960, a Soviet rocket brought down an American spy plane. Such planes had been flying secret missions over the Soviet Union for three and a half years. Khrushchev set out to entrap Eisenhower and succeeded. At first the Soviets announced only that the plane had been shot down. When the State Department insisted that there had been no attempt to violate Soviet airspace, Khrushchev disclosed that the Soviets had American pilot Francis Gary Powers "alive and kicking" and also had his pictures of Soviet military installations. On May 11 Eisenhower abandoned his efforts to cover up the incident and finally took personal responsibility—an unprecedented action for a head of state—justifying the aerial spying on grounds of national security. In Paris five days later Khrushchev withdrew an invitation for Eisenhower to visit the Soviet Union and called upon the president to repudiate the spy flights. When Eisenhower refused, Khrushchev cut off discussion. (Later, in 1962, Powers was exchanged for a captured Soviet spy.)

CASTRO'S CUBA   Yet for all of Eisenhower's crises in foreign affairs, the greatest thorn in his side was the regime of Fidel Castro, which came to power in Cuba on January 1, 1959, after two years of guerrilla warfare against the dictator Fulgencio Batista. In their struggle against Batista, Castro's forces

Fidel Castro

Castro (center) became Cuba's Communist premier in 1959, following three years of guerrilla warfare against the Batista regime. He planned a social and agrarian revolution and opposed foreign control of the Cuban economy.

had the support of many Americans who hoped for a democratic government in Cuba. When American television covered unfair political trials and summary executions conducted by the victorious Castro, however, those hopes were dashed. Castro's programs of land redistribution and nationalization of foreign-owned property worsened relations with the United States. Some observers believed, however, that by rejecting Castro's requests for loans and other help, the U.S. government lost a chance to influence the direction of the Cuban revolution, and by acting on the assumption that Communists already had the upper hand in his movement, the administration may have ensured that fact.

Castro, on the other hand, readily embraced Soviet support. In 1960 he entered a trade agreement to swap Cuban sugar for Soviet oil and machinery. Then, after Cuba had seized three British-American oil refineries that refused to process Soviet oil, Eisenhower ordered strict limits on imports of Cuban sugar. Premier Khrushchev warned in response that any American military intervention in Cuba would trigger a Soviet response. The United States next suspended imports of Cuban sugar and embargoed most trade from America to Cuba. One of Eisenhower's last acts as president, on January 3, 1961, was to suspend diplomatic relations with Cuba. The president also authorized the CIA to begin secretly training a force of Cuban refugees to oust Castro. But the final decision on the use of that force would rest with the next president, John F. Kennedy.

The Early Years of the Civil Rights Movement

While the cold war had produced a tense stalemate by the mid-1950s, race relations in the United States threatened to explode the domestic tranquility masking years of injustice. Eisenhower entered office committed to civil rights in principle, and he pushed the issue in areas of federal authority. During his first three years, public services in Washington, D.C., were desegregated, as were navy yards and veterans' hospitals. Beyond that, however, two aspects of the president's philosophy limited progress in civil rights: his preference for state or local action over federal involvement and his doubt that laws could change racial attitudes. "I don't believe you can change the hearts of men with laws or decisions," he said. Eisenhower's stance meant that leadership in the civil rights field would come from the judiciary more than from the executive or legislative branch of the government.

Civil Rights Stirrings

In the late 1930s the NAACP began to test the constitutionality of racial segregation.

In the mid-1930s the NAACP had resolved to test the separate-but-equal doctrine that had upheld racial segregation since the *Plessy* decision in 1896. Charles H. Houston, dean of the Howard University Law School, laid the plans, and his former student Thurgood Marshall served as chief NAACP lawyer. They decided to begin their efforts to integrate society by focusing on higher education. But it took almost fifteen years to convince the courts that segregation must end. In *Sweatt v. Painter* (1950), the Supreme Court ruled that a separate black law school in Texas was not equal in quality to the state's whites-only schools. The Court ordered the state to remedy the situation.

THE *BROWN* DECISION   By the early 1950s challenges to state laws mandating segregation in the public schools were rising through the appellate courts. Five such cases, from Kansas, Delaware, South Carolina, Virginia, and the District of Columbia—usually cited by reference to the first, *Brown v. Board of Education of Topeka, Kansas*—came to the Supreme Court for joint argument by NAACP attorneys in 1952. Chief Justice Earl Warren wrote the opinion, handed down on May 17, 1954, in which a unanimous Court declared that "in the field of public education the doctrine of 'separate but equal' has no place." In support of its opinion, the Court cited sociological and psychological findings—demonstrating that even if separate facilities were equal in quality, the mere fact of separating students by race engendered feelings of inferiority. A year later, after further argument, the Court directed that the process of racial integration should move "with all deliberate speed."

Eisenhower refused to force states to comply with the Court's decisions, however. Privately he maintained "that the Supreme Court decision *set back* progress in the South *at least fifteen years.* The fellow who tries to tell me you can do these things by *force* is just plain *nuts.*" While token integration began as early as 1954 in the border states of Kentucky and Missouri, hostility mounted in the Deep South and Virginia, led by the newly formed Citizens' Councils. The Citizens' Councils were middle- and upper-class versions of the Ku Klux Klan that spread quickly across the region and eventually enrolled 250,000 members. Instead of physical violence and intimidation, the Councils used economic coercion to discipline blacks who crossed racial boundaries. African Americans who defied white supremacy would lose their jobs, have their insurance policies canceled, or be denied personal loans or home mortgages. The Citizens' Councils grew so powerful in many communities that membership became almost a prerequisite for an aspiring white politician.

Before the end of 1955, opponents of court-ordered integration grew dangerously belligerent. Virginia senator Harry F. Byrd supplied a rallying cry: "Massive Resistance." In 1956, 101 members of Congress signed a "Southern Manifesto" denouncing the Court's decision in the *Brown* case as "a clear abuse of judicial power." At the end of 1956 in six southern states, not a single black child attended school with whites.

THE MONTGOMERY BUS BOYCOTT The essential role played by the NAACP and the courts in providing a legal lever for the civil rights movement often overshadows the courageous contributions of individual African Americans who took great personal risks to challenge segregation. In Montgomery, Alabama, for example, on December 1, 1955, Mrs. Rosa Parks, a black seamstress, was arrested for refusing to give up her seat on a city bus to a white man. (As was the case in many southern communities, Montgomery had a local ordinance that required blacks to give up their bus or train seat to a white when asked.) The next night black community leaders met in the Dexter Avenue Baptist Church to organize a massive bus boycott.

In Dexter Avenue's twenty-six-year-old pastor, Martin Luther King Jr., the boycott movement found a charismatic leader. Born in Atlanta, the grandson of a slave and the son of a minister, King was endowed with intelligence, courage, and eloquence. After graduating from Morehouse College in

Atlanta, he attended divinity school, earned a doctorate in philosophy from Boston University, and accepted a call to preach in Montgomery. He inspired the civil rights movement with a compelling call for nonviolent disobedience based upon the Gospels, the writings of Henry David Thoreau, and the example of Mahatma Gandhi in India. "We must use the weapon of love," King told his supporters. "We must realize so many people are taught to hate us that they are not totally responsible for their hate." To his antagonists he said, "We will soon wear you down by our capacity to suffer, and in winning our freedom we will so appeal to your heart and conscience that we will win you in the process."

The Montgomery bus boycott achieved a remarkable solidarity. For months African Americans formed carpools, hitchhiked, or simply walked. But the white civic leaders held out against the boycott and against the pleas of a bus company tired of losing money. The boycotters finally won a federal case they had initiated against bus segregation, and in 1956 the Supreme Court affirmed that "the separate but equal doctrine can no longer be safely

Montgomery, Alabama

Martin Luther King Jr., here facing arrest for leading a civil rights march, advocated nonviolent resistance to racial segregation.

followed as a correct statement of the law." The next day, King and other African Americans boarded the buses, but they still had a long way to travel before segregation ended.

To keep alive the spirit of the bus boycott, King and a group of associates in 1957 organized the Southern Christian Leadership Conference. Several days later King found an unexploded dynamite bomb on his front porch. Two hours later he addressed his congregation:

> I'm not afraid of anybody this morning. Tell Montgomery they can keep shooting and I'm going to stand up to them; tell Montgomery they can keep bombing and I'm going to stand up to them. If I had to die tomorrow morning I would die happy because I've been to the mountain top and I've seen the promised land and it's going to be here in Montgomery.

THE CIVIL RIGHTS ACT   Despite President Eisenhower's reluctance to take the lead in desegregating schools, he supported the right of African Americans to vote. In 1956, hoping to exploit divisions between northern and southern Democrats and to reclaim some of the black vote for the Republicans, Eisenhower proposed legislation that became the Civil Rights Act of 1957. The first civil rights law passed since Reconstruction, it finally got through the Senate, after a year's delay, with the help of majority leader Lyndon B. Johnson, a Texas Democrat who won southern acceptance by watering it down. The Civil Rights Act established the Civil Rights Commission, which was later extended indefinitely, and a new Civil Rights Division in the Justice Department, which could seek injunctions to prevent interference with the right to vote. Yet by 1959 the Civil Rights Act had not added a single southern black to the voting rolls. Neither did the Civil Rights Act of 1960, which provided for federal court referees to register African Americans to vote in districts where a court found a "pattern and practice" of discrimination, and made it a federal crime to interfere with any court order. This bill, too, lacked teeth and depended upon vigorous presidential enforcement to achieve any tangible results.

DESEGREGATION IN LITTLE ROCK   A few weeks after the Civil Rights Act of 1957 passed, Arkansas governor Orval Faubus called out the national guard to prevent nine black students from entering Little Rock's Central High School under a federal court order. A conference between the president and the governor proved fruitless, but on court order Governor Faubus withdrew the national guard. When the African-American students tried to enter the school, an hysterical white mob forced local authorities to remove the students. At that point, Eisenhower, who had said two months before that he could not "imagine any set of circumstances that would ever induce me to send federal troops," ordered 1,000 paratroopers to Little Rock to protect the black students, and he placed the national guard on federal service. The soldiers stayed through the school year.

In the summer of 1958, Faubus decided to close the Little Rock high schools rather than allow integration, and court proceedings dragged on into 1959 before the schools could be reopened. In that year, massive resistance to integration in Virginia collapsed when both state and federal courts struck down state laws that had cut off funds to integrated schools. Thereafter, "massive resistance" for the most part was confined to the Deep South, where five states—from South Carolina west through Louisiana—still opposed even token integration.

Assessing the Eisenhower Years

During President Eisenhower's second term the country added Alaska and Hawaii as states (1959), experienced an economic slump, a drop in tax revenues, and a large federal deficit. The country also suffered the embarrassments of the U-2 spy-plane incident and Cuba's falling into the Communist orbit. Emotional issues such as civil rights, defense policy, and corrupt aides also compounded Eisenhower's troubles. The president's reluctance to enforce civil rights rulings and his unwillingness to speak out on behalf of racial equality undermined his efforts to promote the general welfare. One observer called the Eisenhower years "the time of the great postponement," during which the president left domestic and foreign policies "about where he found them in 1953."

Yet opinion of Eisenhower's presidency has improved with time. Even critics now grant that Eisenhower succeeded in ending the war in Korea and muzzling Joseph McCarthy. If Eisenhower failed to end the cold war and in fact institutionalized global confrontation, he did sense the limits of American power and kept its application to low-risk situations. He also tried to restrain the arms race. If he took few initiatives in addressing social and racial problems, he did sustain the major innovations of the New Deal. If he tolerated unemployment of as much as 7 percent at times, he saw to it that inflation remained minimal during his two terms.

Eisenhower's January 17, 1961, farewell address to the American people showed his remarkable foresight in his own area of expertise, the military. Like George Washington, Eisenhower couched his wisdom largely in the form of warnings: that America faced in communism "a hostile ideology, global in scope, atheistic in character, ruthless in purpose, and insidious in method"; that America's "leadership and prestige depend, not merely upon our unmatched material strength, but on how we use our power in the interests of world peace and human betterment"; that the temptation to find easy answers should take into account "the need to maintain balance in and among national problems"; and above all that Americans "must avoid the impulse to live only for today, plundering, for our own ease and convenience, the precious resources of tomorrow."

As a former soldier, Eisenhower highlighted, perhaps better than anyone else could have, the dangers of a large military establishment in a time of peace: "In the councils of government we must guard against the acquisition of unwarranted influence, whether sought or unsought, by the military-industrial complex. The potential for the disastrous rise of misplaced power exists and will persist." Eisenhower confessed that his great disappointment was that he could affirm only that "war has been avoided," not that "a lasting peace is in sight."

MAKING CONNECTIONS

- The civil rights movement of the 1950s aimed to achieve the racial integration of public services and equal access to political rights. This struggle would continue into the 1960s and then move in several new directions, as discussed in Chapter 34.

- U.S. involvement in Vietnam grew in the 1950s but remained limited to an advisory role. Escalation to an active fighting role came under Lyndon Johnson in 1965, a topic also covered in Chapter 34.

- Eisenhower's hands-off approach to the presidency was reminiscent of the Gilded Age presidencies and those of the 1920s. See Chapters 18, 22, and 27.

FURTHER READING

Scholarship on the Eisenhower years is extensive. A carefully balanced overview of the period is Chester J. Pach Jr. and Elmo Richardson's *The Presidency of Dwight D. Eisenhower,* rev. ed. (1991). For the manner in which Eisenhower conducted foreign policy, see Robert A. Divine's *Eisenhower and the Cold War* (1981). Tom Wicker deems Eisenhower a better person than a president in *Dwight D. Eisenhower* (2002).

For the buildup of U.S. involvement in Indochina, consult Lloyd C. Gardner's *Approaching Vietnam: From World War II through Dien Bien Phu, 1941–1954* (1988) and David L. Anderson's *Trapped by Success: The Eisenhower Administration and Vietnam, 1953–1961* (1991). How the Eisenhower Doctrine came to be implemented is traced in Stephen E. Ambrose and Douglas G. Brinkley's *Rise to Globalism: American Foreign Policy since 1938,* 8th ed. (1997).

The impact of the Supreme Court during the 1950s is the focus of Archibald Cox's *The Warren Court: Constitutional Decision as an Instrument of Reform* (1968). A masterful study of the important Warren Court decision on school desegregation is James T. Patterson's *Brown v. Board of Education: A Civil Rights Milestone and Its Troubled Legacy* (2001).

For the story of the early years of the civil rights movement, see Taylor Branch's *Parting the Waters: America in the King Years, 1954–1963* (1988) and Robert Weisbrot's *Freedom Bound: A History of America's Civil Rights Movement* (1990).

34

NEW FRONTIERS: POLITICS AND SOCIAL CHANGE IN THE 1960s

FOCUS QUESTIONS

- What were the goals of Kennedy's New Frontier and Johnson's Great Society programs?
- What were the achievements of the civil rights movement and the ensuing splinter movements?
- Why did the United States increasingly involve itself in Vietnam, and why was there rising opposition to the war?
- How did Kennedy try to combat communism in Cuba?

To answer these questions and access additional review material, please visit www.wwnorton.com/studyspace.

For those pundits who considered the social and political climate of the 1950s dull, the following decade would provide a striking contrast. The 1960s were years of extraordinary social turbulence and innovation in public affairs—as well as sudden tragedy and prolonged trauma. Many social ills that had been festering for decades suddenly forced their way onto the national agenda. At the same time the deeply entrenched assumptions of cold war ideology led the country into the longest, most controversial, and least successful war in the nation's history.

THE NEW FRONTIER

KENNEDY VERSUS NIXON   In 1960 there was little awareness of such dramatic change on the horizon. The presidential election of that year pitted two candidates—Richard M. Nixon and John F. Kennedy—who symbolized the bland politics of the 1950s. Though better known than Kennedy because of his eight years as Eisenhower's vice president, Nixon had also developed the reputation of a cunning chameleon, the Tricky Dick who concealed his duplicity behind a series of masks. "Nixon doesn't know who he is," Kennedy told an aide, "and so each time he makes a speech he has to decide which Nixon he is, and that will be very exhausting."

But Nixon could not be so easily dismissed. He possessed a shrewd intelligence and a compulsive love for politics, the more combative the better. Born in suburban Los Angeles in 1913, he grew up in a working-class Quaker family struggling to make ends meet. In 1946, having completed law school and a wartime stint in the navy, Nixon jumped into the political arena as a Republican and won election to Congress. Four years later he became a senator.

Nixon arrived in Washington eager to reverse the tide of New Deal liberalism. As a campaigner he unleashed scurrilous personal attacks on his opponents, employing half-truths, lies, and rumors, and he shrewdly manipulated and fed the growing anti-Communist hysteria. Yet Nixon became both a respected and an effective member of Congress, and by 1950 he was the most requested Republican speaker in the country. The reward for his rapid rise to political stardom was the vice-presidential nomination in 1952, which led to successive terms as the partner of the popular Eisenhower.

In comparison to his Republican opponent, John F. Kennedy was inexperienced. He boasted an abundance of assets, including a record of heroism in World War II, a glamorous young wife, a bright, agile mind and Harvard education, a rich, powerful family, a handsome face, movie-star charisma, and a robust outlook. Yet the forty-three-year-old candidate had not distinguished himself in the House or the Senate. His political rise owed not so much to his abilities or his accomplishments as to the effective public relations campaign engineered by his ambitious father, Joseph Kennedy, a self-made tycoon.

During his campaign for the Democratic nomination, Kennedy had shown that he had the energy and wit to match his grace and ambition, even though he suffered from serious spinal problems, Addison's disease (a debilitating disorder of the adrenal glands), recurrent blood disorders, venereal disease, and fierce fevers. He took medicine daily, sometimes hourly. Like

Franklin Roosevelt, he and his aides and family members successfully masked his physical ailments from the public.

By the time of the Democratic Convention in 1960, Kennedy had traveled over 65,000 miles, visited twenty-five states, and made over 350 speeches. In his acceptance speech he found the stirring, muscular rhetoric that would stamp the rest of his campaign and his presidency: "We stand today on the edge of a New Frontier—the frontier of unknown opportunities and perils—a frontier of unfulfilled hopes and threats." Kennedy and his staff fastened upon the frontier metaphor as the label for their domestic program because Americans had always been adventurers, eager to conquer and exploit new frontiers. Kennedy promised to use his administration to get the country "moving again."

Three events shaped the presidential campaign that fall. First, as the only Catholic to run for the presidency since Al Smith in 1928, Kennedy strove to dispel the impression that his religion was a major political liability. In a speech before the Greater Houston Ministerial Association in 1960, he stressed that "the separation of church and state is absolute," and "no Catholic prelate would tell the President—should he be a Catholic—how to act and no Protestant minister should tell his parishioners for whom to vote." The religious question thereafter drew little public attention; Kennedy's candor had neutralized it.

Second, Richard Nixon violated one of the cardinal rules of politics when he agreed to debate his less prominent opponent on television. During the first of four debates, few significant policy differences surfaced, allowing viewers to shape their opinions more on matters of style. Some 70 million people watched this first-ever televised debate. They saw an obviously uncomfortable Nixon, still weak from a recent illness, perspiring heavily and looking haggard, uneasy, and even sinister before the camera. Kennedy, on the other hand, projected a cool poise and offered crisp answers that made him seem equal, if not superior, in his fitness for the office. Kennedy's popularity immediately shot up in the polls. In the words of a bemused southern senator, Kennedy combined "the best qualities of Elvis Presley and Franklin D. Roosevelt."

Still, the momentum created by the first debate was not enough to ensure a Kennedy victory. The third key event in the campaign involved the civil rights issue. Democratic strategists knew that in order to offset the loss of southern conservatives suspicious of Kennedy's Catholicism and strong civil rights positions, they had to increase the registration of minority voters and generate a high turnout among African Americans.

Perhaps the most crucial incident of the campaign occurred when Martin Luther King Jr. and some fifty demonstrators were arrested in Atlanta for

Kennedy versus Nixon

John Kennedy's poise and precision in the debates with Richard Nixon impressed viewers and voters.

"trespassing" in an all-white restaurant. Although the other demonstrators were soon released, King was sentenced to four months in prison, ostensibly because of an earlier traffic violation. Robert Kennedy, the candidate's younger brother and campaign manager, phoned the judge handling King's case, imploring him with the argument "that if he was a decent American, he would let King out of jail by sundown." King was soon released on bail, and the Kennedy campaign seized full advantage of the outcome, distributing some 2 million pamphlets in African-American neighborhoods extolling Kennedy's efforts on behalf of Dr. King.

When the votes were counted, Kennedy and his running mate, Lyndon B. Johnson of Texas, had won the closest presidential election since 1888. The winning margin was only 118,574 votes out of 68 million cast. Kennedy's wide lead in the electoral vote, 303 to 219, belied the paper-thin margin in several key states. Nixon had in fact carried more states than Kennedy, sweeping most of the West and holding four of the six southern states that Eisenhower had carried in 1956. Kennedy's majority was built on victories in southern New England, the populous middle Atlantic states, and key states in the South where African-American voters provided the critical margin of

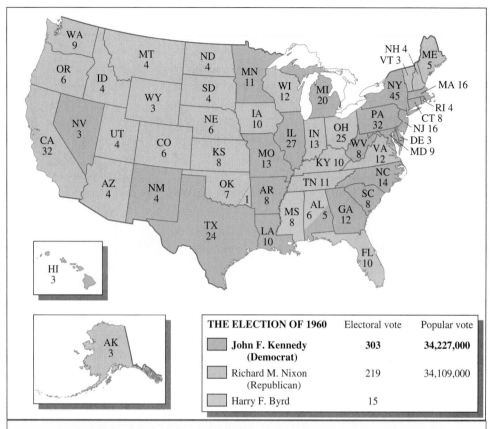

THE ELECTION OF 1960	Electoral vote	Popular vote
John F. Kennedy (Democrat)	**303**	**34,227,000**
Richard M. Nixon (Republican)	219	34,109,000
Harry F. Byrd	15	

How did the election of 1960 represent a sea change in American presidential politics? What three events shaped the campaign? How did Kennedy win the election in spite of winning fewer states than Nixon?

victory. Yet ominous rumblings of discontent appeared in the once-solid Democratic South, as all eight of Mississippi's electors and six of Alabama's eleven (as well as one elector from Oklahoma) defied the national ticket and voted for Virginia senator Harry Byrd, the arch segregationist.

THE NEW ADMINISTRATION   John F. Kennedy was the youngest person ever elected president, and his cabinet appointments put an accent on youth. He was determined to attract the "best and the brightest" minds available, individuals who would provide new ideas and fresh thinking—and inject a tough, pragmatic, and vigorous outlook into government affairs. Adlai Stevenson was favored by liberal Democrats for the post of secretary of state, but Kennedy chose Dean Rusk, a career diplomat. Stevenson received the post of ambassador to the United Nations. Robert McNamara, one of the whiz kids who had reorganized the Ford Motor Company, was asked to bring his managerial magic to bear on the Department of Defense. C. Douglas Dillon, a Republican banker, was made secretary of the Treasury in an effort to reassure conservative business executives. When critics attacked the appointment of Kennedy's thirty-five-year-old brother Robert as attorney general, the president quipped, "I don't see what's wrong with giving Bobby a little experience before he goes into law practice." McGeorge Bundy, whom Kennedy called "the second smartest man I know," was made special assistant for national security affairs, lending additional credence to the impression that foreign policy would remain under tight White House control.

The inaugural ceremonies set the tone of elegance and youthful vigor that would come to be called the Kennedy style. Kennedy dazzled listeners with uplifting rhetoric. "Let the word go forth from this time and place," he proclaimed. "Let every nation know, whether it wishes us well or ill, that we shall pay any price, bear any burden, meet any hardship, support any friend, oppose any foe, to assure the survival and success of liberty. And so, my fellow Americans: ask not what your country can do for you—ask what you can do for your country." Spines tingled at the time; the glittering atmosphere and inspiring language of the inauguration seemed to herald an era of fresh promise and youthful energy.

THE KENNEDY RECORD   Despite his idealistic rhetoric, however, Kennedy called himself a realist or "an idealist without illusions," and he had a difficult time launching his New Frontier domestic program. Elected by a razor-thin margin, he did not enjoy a popular mandate. "Great innovations," Kennedy said, quoting Thomas Jefferson, "should not be forced on slender majorities." The new president did not show much skill in shepherding legislation through a Congress controlled by a conservative southern coalition that blocked his efforts to increase federal aid to education, provide health insurance for the aged, and create a Department of Urban Affairs. The Senate killed his initiatives on behalf of unemployed youths, migrant workers, and mass transit. When Kennedy finally followed the advice of his advisers in 1963 and submitted a drastic tax cut, Congress blocked that as well.

Administration proposals did nevertheless win some notable victories in Congress. Legislators readily approved broad Alliance for Progress programs to help Latin America and the celebrated Peace Corps, created in 1961 to supply volunteers who would provide educational and technical services abroad. Kennedy's greatest legislative accomplishment, however, may have been the Trade Expansion Act of 1962, which eventually led to tariff cuts averaging 35 percent on goods traded between the United States and the European Economic Community (the Common Market).

In the field of domestic social legislation, the Kennedy administration scored a few more victories. They included a Housing Act that earmarked nearly $5 billion for urban renewal over four years; an increase in the minimum wage and its application to more than 3 million additional workers; the Area Redevelopment Act of 1961, which provided nearly $400 million in loans and grants to "distressed areas"; an increase in Social Security benefits; and additional funds for sewage-treatment plants. Kennedy also won support for an accelerated space program with the goal of landing on the moon before the end of the decade.

THE WARREN COURT   Under Chief Justice Earl Warren the Supreme Court continued to be a decisive influence on domestic life. In 1962 the Court ruled that a school prayer adopted by the New York State Board of Regents violated the constitutional prohibition against an established religion. In *Gideon v. Wainwright* (1963), the Court required that every felony defendant be provided a lawyer regardless of the defendant's ability to pay. In 1964 the Court ruled in *Escobedo v. Illinois* that a person accused of a crime must also be allowed to consult a lawyer before being interrogated by police. Two years later, in *Miranda v. Arizona,* the Court issued perhaps its most bitterly criticized ruling when it ordered that an accused person in police custody must be informed of certain basic rights: the right to remain silent; the right to know that anything said can be used against the individual in court; and the right to have a defense attorney present during interrogation. In addition, the Court established rules for police to follow in informing suspects of their legal rights before questioning could begin.

Expansion of the Civil Rights Movement

The most important development in domestic life during the 1960s occurred in civil rights. John F. Kennedy entered the White House reluctant to challenge conservative southern Democrats on the race issue. He was never as personally committed to the cause of civil rights as his brother Robert, the attorney general. Despite a few dramatic gestures of support toward African-American leaders, President Kennedy only belatedly grasped the moral and emotional significance of the most widespread reform movement of the decade. Like Franklin Roosevelt, he celebrated equality but did little to promote it. Eventually, however, his conscience was pricked by the grass-roots civil rights movement led by Martin Luther King Jr.

SIT-INS AND FREEDOM RIDES   After the Montgomery bus boycott of 1955–1956, King's philosophy of "militant nonviolence" inspired others to challenge the deeply entrenched patterns of racial segregation in the South. At the same time, lawsuits to desegregate the public schools got thousands of parents and young people involved. The momentum generated the first genuine mass movement in African-American history when four black college students sat down and demanded service at a "whites-only" Woolworth's lunch counter in Greensboro, North Carolina, on February 1, 1960. Within a week, the "sit-in" movement had spread to six more towns in the state, and within two months demonstrations had occurred in fifty-four cities in nine states.

In 1960 student activists, black and white, formed the Student Nonviolent Coordinating Committee (SNCC), which worked with King's Southern

Sit-in at Woolworth's Lunch Counter, Greensboro, North Carolina

Four of the protesters, students at North Carolina A&T College, were (from left) Joseph McNeil, Franklin McCain, Billy Smith, and Clarence Henderson.

Christian Leadership Conference to broaden the civil rights movement. The sit-ins became "kneel-ins" at churches and "wade-ins" at segregated public swimming pools.

Most of the activists practiced King's concept of nonviolent protest. They refused to retaliate, even when struck with clubs or poked with cattle prods. The conservative white editor of the *Richmond News Leader* conceded his admiration for their courage:

> Here were the colored students, in coats, white shirts, ties, and one of them was reading Goethe, and one was taking notes from a biology text. And here, on the sidewalk, was a gang of white boys come to heckle, a ragtail rabble, slack-jawed, black-jacketed, grinning fit to kill, and some of them, God save the mark, were waving the proud and honored flag of the Southern States in the last war fought by gentlemen.

During the year after the Greensboro sit-ins, over 3,600 black and white activists spent time in jail. In many communities they were pelted with rocks, burned with cigarettes, and subjected to unending verbal abuse.

In May 1961 the Congress of Racial Equality sent a group of black and white "freedom riders" on buses to test a federal court ruling that had banned segregation on buses and trains and in terminals. In Alabama, mobs attacked the travelers with fists and pipes, burned one of the buses, and assaulted Justice Department observers, but the demonstrators persisted and drew national attention, generating new respect and support for their cause. Yet President Kennedy was not inspired by the courageous freedom riders. Preoccupied with the Berlin crisis, he ordered an aide to tell them to "call it off." Former president Herry Truman called the bus activists northern "busybodies." It fell to Attorney General Robert Kennedy to use federal marshals to protect the freedom riders during the summer of 1961.

FEDERAL INTERVENTION   In 1962 Governor Ross Barnett of Mississippi, who believed that God made "the Negro different to punish him," defied a court order and refused to allow James Meredith, an African-American student whose grandfather had been a slave, to enroll at the University of Mississippi. Attorney General Robert Kennedy intervened again dispatching federal marshals to enforce the law. When the marshals were assaulted by a white mob, federal troops had to intervene, but only after two deaths and many injuries. Meredith was registered at Ole Miss a few days later.

In 1963 Martin Luther King launched a series of demonstrations in Birmingham, Alabama, where Police Commissioner Eugene "Bull" Connor served

Birmingham, Alabama, May 1963

Eugene "Bull" Connor's police unleash dogs on civil rights demonstrators.

as the perfect foil for King's tactic of nonviolent civil disobedience. Connor used dogs, tear gas, electric cattle prods, and fire hoses on the protesters while millions of outraged Americans watched the confrontations on television.

King, who was arrested and jailed during the demonstrations, wrote his now-famous Letter from Birmingham City Jail, a stirring defense of the nonviolent strategy that became a classic document of the civil rights movement. "One who breaks an unjust law," he stressed, "must do so openly, lovingly, and with a willingness to accept the penalty." In his letter, King signaled a shift in his strategy for social change. Heretofore he had emphasized the need to educate southern whites about the injustice of segregation and other patterns of discrimination. Now he focused more on gaining federal enforcement of the law and new legislation by provoking racists to display their violent hatred in public. As King admitted in his letter, he sought through organized nonviolent protest to "create such a crisis and foster such a tension that a community which has constantly refused to negotiate is forced to confront the issue." This concept of confrontational civil disobedience outraged

J. Edgar Hoover, the powerful head of the FBI, who labeled King "the most dangerous Negro of the future in this nation." He ordered agents to follow King, bugged his telephones and motel rooms, and circulated scandalous rumors to discredit him.

The sublime courage that King and many other protesters displayed helped mobilize national support for their integrationist objectives. (In 1964 King would be awarded the Nobel Peace Prize.) Nudged by his brother Robert, a man of greater conviction, compassion, and vision, President Kennedy finally decided that enforcement of existing statutes was not enough; new legislation was needed to deal with the race question. In 1963 he told the nation that racial discrimination "has no place in American life or law." He then endorsed an ambitious civil rights bill intended to end discrimination in public facilities, desegregate public schools, and protect African-American voters. But the bill was quickly blocked in Congress by southern conservatives who had become increasingly resistant to social change since mobilizing to thwart Roosevelt's New Deal in the late 1930s. As Kennedy told Martin Luther King: "This is a very serious fight. We're in this up to the neck. The worst trouble would be to lose the fight in Congress. . . . A good many programs I care about may go down the drain as a result of this [bill]—We may all go down the drain . . . so we are putting a lot on the line."

Throughout the Deep South, traditionalists defied efforts at racial integration. In the fall of 1963, the cocky and confrontational governor George Wallace dramatically stood in the doorway of a building at the University of Alabama to block the enrollment of African-American students, but he stepped aside in the face of insistent federal marshals. That night, President Kennedy for the first time highlighted the *moral* issue facing the nation: "If an American, because his skin is black, cannot enjoy the full and free life which all of us want, then who among us would be content to have the color of his skin changed and stand in his place? Who among us would be content with the counsels of patience and delay?" Later the same night, NAACP official Medgar Evers was shot to death as he returned to his home in Jackson, Mississippi.

The high point of the integrationist phase of the civil rights movement occurred on August 28, 1963, when over 200,000 blacks and whites marched down the Mall in Washington, D.C., toward the Lincoln Memorial, singing "We Shall Overcome." The March on Washington for Jobs and Freedom was the largest civil rights demonstration in history. Standing in front of Lincoln's statue, Martin Luther King Jr. delivered one of the century's most memorable speeches:

"I Have a Dream," August 28, 1963

Protesters in the March on Washington make their way to the Lincoln Memorial, where Martin Luther King Jr. delivered his now-famous speech.

I say to you today, my friends, that in spite of the difficulties and frustrations of the moment I still have a dream. It is a dream deeply rooted in the American dream.

I have a dream that one day this nation will rise up and live out the true meaning of its creed: "We hold these truths to be self-evident; that all men are created equal."

I have a dream that one day . . . the sons of former slaves and the sons of former slaveowners will be able to sit together at the table of brotherhood.

Such racial harmony had not yet arrived, however. Two weeks later a bomb exploded in a Birmingham church, killing four black girls. Yet King's dream—shared and promoted by thousands of other activists—survived. The intransigence and violence that civil rights workers encountered won converts to their cause all across the country. Moreover, corporate and civic leaders in large southern cities promoted civil rights advances in large part because the continuing protests threatened economic development. Atlanta, for example, described itself as "the city too busy to hate."

Foreign Frontiers

EARLY SETBACKS   John Kennedy's record in foreign relations, like that in domestic affairs, was mixed, but more spectacularly so. Although he had made the existence of a missile gap between the United States and the Soviet Union a major part of his 1960 election campaign, he learned upon taking office that there was no missile gap: the United States remained far ahead of the Soviets in nuclear weaponry. Kennedy also discovered that there was in the works a secret CIA operation training 1,500 anti-Castro Cubans for an invasion of their homeland. The Joint Chiefs of Staff assured the inexperienced Kennedy that the plan was feasible in theory; CIA analysts predicted that the invasion would inspire Cubans to rebel against Castro.

In retrospect the scheme, poorly planned and poorly executed, had little chance of succeeding. When the ragtag invasion force landed at the Bay of Pigs in Cuba on April 17, 1961, it was brutally subdued in two days; more than 1,100 men were captured. A *New York Times* columnist lamented that the United States "looked like fools to our friends, rascals to our enemies, and incompetents to the rest." It was hardly an auspicious way for the new president to demonstrate his mastery of foreign policy. Kennedy called the bungled Bay of Pigs invasion a "colossal mistake." The planners had underestimated Castro's popularity and his ability to react to the surprise attack. The invasion also suffered from poor communication, inaccurate maps, faulty equipment, and ineffective leadership. The Cuban rebels had been told they would receive American air cover, but the invaders had been left defenseless on the beach. As one of them told a comrade on the beach, "Eddie, don't you realize we have been abandoned?" Former President Eisenhower characterized Kennedy's role in the clumsy invasion as a "Profile in Timidity and Indecision." a sarcastic reference to Kennedy's book *Profiles in Courage* (1956). Kennedy responded to the Bay of Pigs fiasco by firing the CIA director and the CIA officer who coordinated the invasion.

Two months after the Bay of Pigs debacle, Kennedy met Soviet premier Nikita Khrushchev in Vienna. The volatile Khrushchev bullied and browbeat the inexperienced Kennedy and threatened to limit Western access to Berlin, the divided city located 100 miles within Communist East Germany. Khrushchev decided that Kennedy was "a youngster who had a great deal to learn and not much to offer." Kennedy was stunned by the aggressive Soviet stand. Upon his return home, he demonstrated his resolve by calling up army reserve and national guard units. The Soviets responded by erecting the Berlin Wall, cutting off movement between East and West Berlin. The Berlin Wall plugged the most accessible escape hatch for East Germans,

The Berlin Wall

Two West Berliners communicate with family members (visible in the open window on the upper right side of the apartment building) on the East Berlin side of the newly constructed Berlin wall. The wall physically divided the city and served as a wedge between the United States and the Soviet Union.

showed Soviet willingness to challenge American resolve in Europe, and became another intractable barrier to improved relations between East and West.

THE CUBAN MISSILE CRISIS   A year later, in the fall of 1962, Khrushchev and the Soviets posed another challenge, this time ninety miles off the coast of Florida. Kennedy's unwillingness to commit the forces necessary to overthrow Fidel Castro at the Bay of Pigs seemed to signify a failure of will, and the Soviets reasoned that they could install their ballistic missiles in Cuba without U.S. opposition. Their motives were to protect Cuba from another American-backed invasion, which Castro believed to be imminent, and to redress the strategic imbalance caused by the presence of U.S. missiles in Turkey aimed at the Soviet Union. Khrushchev relished the idea of throwing "a hedgehog at Uncle Sam's pants."

U.S. officials feared that Soviet missiles in Cuba represented a real threat to American security. Kennedy also worried that acquiescence to a Soviet military presence in Cuba would weaken the credibility of the American

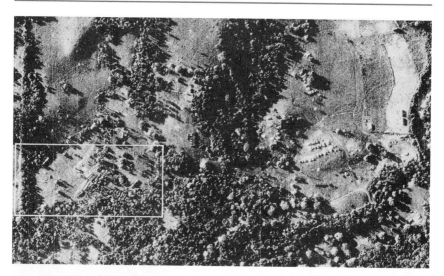

The Cuban Missile Crisis

Photographs taken from a U.S. surveillance plane on October 14, 1962, revealed both missile launchers and missile shelters in San Cristóbal, Cuba.

nuclear deterrent among Europeans and demoralize anti-Castro elements in Latin America. At the same time the installation of Soviet missiles served Khrushchev's purpose of demonstrating his toughness to both Chinese and Soviet critics of his earlier advocacy of peaceful coexistence. But he misjudged the American response.

On October 14, 1962, U.S. intelligence analysts discovered Soviet missile sites under construction in Cuba. From the beginning, even though the Soviet actions violated no law or treaty, the administration decided that the weapons had to be removed; the only question was how. As the air force chief of staff told Kennedy, "you're in a pretty bad fix, Mr. President." In a grueling series of secret meetings, the Executive Committee of the National Security Council narrowed the options to a choice between a "surgical" air strike and a naval blockade of Cuba. President Kennedy wisely opted for a blockade, which was carefully disguised by the euphemism *quarantine*, since a blockade was technically an act of war. A blockade offered the advantage of forcing the Soviets to shoot first, if it came to that, and left open the options of stronger action. Monday, October 22, began the most perilous week in world history. On that day the president announced the discovery of the missile sites in Cuba and the naval quarantine of the island nation. The United States and the Soviet Union now headed toward their closest encounter with nuclear war.

Tensions grew as Khrushchev blustered that Kennedy had pushed humankind "to the abyss of a world missile-nuclear war." Soviet ships, he declared, would ignore the quarantine. But on Wednesday, October 24, five Soviet ships, presumably with missiles aboard, stopped short of the quarantine line. Two days later the Soviets offered to withdraw the missiles in return for a public pledge by the United States not to invade Cuba. Secretary of State Dean Rusk replied that the administration was interested but stressed to a newscaster, "Remember, when you report this, that eyeball to eyeball, they [the Soviets] blinked first."

That same evening, Kennedy received two messages from Khrushchev, the first repeating the original offer and the second demanding the removal of American missiles from Turkey. The two messages probably reflected divided counsels in the Kremlin. Ironically, Kennedy had already ordered removal of the outmoded missiles from Turkey, but he refused now to act under the gun. Instead, he followed Robert Kennedy's suggestion that he respond favorably to the first letter and ignore the second. On Sunday, October 28, Khrushchev agreed to remove the Soviet missiles from Cuba.

In the aftermath of the crisis, tensions between the United States and the Soviet Union quickly subsided, relaxed in part by several symbolic steps: an agreement to sell the Soviet Union surplus American wheat, the installation of a "hot-line" telephone between Washington and Moscow to provide instant contact between the heads of government, and the removal of obsolete American missiles from Turkey, Italy, and Britain. On June 10, 1963, President Kennedy revealed that direct discussions with the Soviets would soon begin, and he called upon the nation to reexamine its attitude toward peace, the Soviet Union, and the cold war. Those discussions resulted in a treaty with the Soviet Union and Britain to end nuclear testing in the atmosphere, oceans, and outer space. The treaty, ratified in September 1963, was an important symbolic and substantive move toward détente. As Kennedy put it, "A journey of a thousand miles begins with one step."

KENNEDY AND VIETNAM As tensions with the Soviet Union were easing, a crisis was growing in Southeast Asia. Events there were moving toward what would become the greatest American foreign-policy calamity of the century. During John Kennedy's "thousand days" in office, the turmoil of Indochina never preoccupied public attention for any extended period, but it dominated international diplomatic debates from the time the administration entered office.

The landlocked kingdom of Laos, along with neighboring Cambodia to the south, had been declared neutral in the Geneva Accords of 1954, but thereafter Laos had fallen into a complex struggle for power between the Communist Pathet Lao insurgents and the inept Royal Laotian Army. There matters stood when Eisenhower left office and told Kennedy, "You might have to go in there and fight it out." The chairman of the Joint Chiefs of Staff favored combat against the Pathet Lao. After a lengthy consideration of alternatives, Kennedy and his advisers decided to promote a neutral coalition government that would include Pathet Lao representatives yet prevent a Pathet Lao victory and would avoid U.S. military involvement. The Soviets, who were extending aid to the Pathet Lao, indicated a readiness to negotiate, and in 1961 talks began in Geneva. After more than a year of tangled negotiations, all parties agreed to a neutral coalition. American and Soviet aid to the opposing parties was supposed to end, but both countries in fact continued covert operations while North Vietnam kept open the Ho Chi Minh Trail through eastern Laos, which it used to supply its Viet Cong allies in South Vietnam.

The situation in South Vietnam worsened thereafter under the leadership of Premier Ngo Dinh Diem. At the time the problem was less the scattered Communist guerrilla attacks than Diem's failure to deliver promised social and economic reforms and his inability to rally popular support. His repressive tactics, directed not only against Communists but also against the Buddhist majority and other critics, played into the hands of his enemies. In 1961 White House assistant Walt Rostow and General Maxwell Taylor, the first in a long train of presidential emissaries to South Vietnam's capital,

Ngo Dinh Diem

The Vietnamese premier in 1962, celebrating the anniversary of Vietnam's independence from colonial rule.

proposed a major increase in the U.S. military presence. Kennedy refused but continued to dispatch more military "advisers" in the hope of stabilizing the situation: when he took office, there had been 2,000 U.S. troops in Vietnam; by the end of 1963, there were 16,000, none of whom had been officially committed to battle.

By 1963 Kennedy was receiving sharply divergent reports from the South Vietnamese countryside. American military advisers expressed confidence in the Army of the Republic of Vietnam. On-site political reporters, however, watching the reactions of the Vietnamese people, predicted civil turmoil as long as Diem remained in power. By midyear, growing Buddhist demonstrations ignited the discontent in the south. The spectacle of Buddhist monks setting themselves on fire in protest against government tyranny stunned Americans. By the fall of 1963, the Kennedy administration had decided that the autocratic Diem was a lost cause. When dissident generals proposed a coup d'état, the U.S. ambassador assured them that America would not stand in the way. On November 1 they seized the South Vietnamese government and murdered Diem. But the rebel generals provided no more stability than had earlier regimes, and successive coups set the fragile country spinning from one military leader to another.

KENNEDY'S ASSASSINATION   By the fall of 1963, President Kennedy seemed to acknowledge the intractability of the situation in Vietnam. In September 1963 he declared of the South Vietnamese: "In the final analysis it's their war. They're the ones who have to win it or lose it. We can help them as advisers but they have to win it." The following month he announced the administration's intention to withdraw U.S. forces from South Vietnam by the end of 1965. What Kennedy would have done thereafter has remained a matter of endless controversy, endless because it is unanswerable, and it is unanswerable because on November 22, 1963, while visiting Dallas, Texas, Kennedy was shot in the neck and head by Lee Harvey Oswald.

Oswald's motives remain unknown. Although a blue-ribbon federal commission appointed by President Johnson and headed by Chief Justice Earl Warren concluded that Oswald acted alone, debate still swirls around various conspiracy theories. Kennedy's death and then the murder of Oswald by Jack Ruby, a Dallas nightclub owner, were shown over and over again on television, the medium that had so helped Kennedy's rise to the presidency and now captured his death and the moving funeral at Arlington National Cemetery. Kennedy's assassination enshrined him in the public imagination as a martyred leader cut down in the prime of his life.

Lyndon Johnson and the Great Society

Lyndon Johnson took the presidential oath of office on board the plane that brought John Kennedy's body back to Washington from Dallas. Fifty-five years old, he had spent twenty-six years on the Washington scene and had served nearly a decade as Democratic leader in the Senate, where he had displayed the greatest gift for compromise since Henry Clay.

Johnson brought to the White House a marked change of style from Kennedy. A self-made and self-centered man who had worked his way out of a hardscrabble rural Texas environment to become one of Washington's most powerful figures, Johnson had none of the Kennedy elegance. He was a bundle of conflicting elements: earthy, idealistic, domineering, insecure, gregarious, suspicious, affectionate, manipulative, ruthless, and compassionate. Johnson's ego was as huge as his ambition. He had to be at the center of things, directing and dominating. He craved both political power and public affection. Like another southern president, Andrew Johnson, he harbored a sense of being the perpetual outsider despite his long experience with legislative power. And indeed he was so regarded by Kennedy "insiders." He, in turn, had "detested" the way Kennedy and his aides ignored him as vice president.

Presidential Assassination

John F. Kennedy's vice president, Lyndon B. Johnson, takes the presidential oath in Air Force One before its return from Dallas with Jacqueline Kennedy (right), the presidential party, and the body of the assassinated president.

Those who viewed Johnson as a stereotypical southern conservative failed to appreciate his long-standing admiration for Franklin Roosevelt, the depth of his concern for the poor, and his commitment to the cause of civil rights. "I'm going to be the best friend the Negro ever had," he told a member of the White House staff. In foreign affairs, however, he was, like Woodrow Wilson, a novice. Johnson wanted to be the greatest American president, the one who did the most good for the most people. And he would let nothing stand in his way. In the end, however, the grandiose Johnson ended up promising far more than he could accomplish, raising false hopes and stoking fiery resentments.

The Johnson Treatment

Lyndon Johnson used powerful body language to intimidate and manipulate anyone who dared disagree with him.

POLITICS AND POVERTY   Domestic policy was Johnson's first priority. Amid the national grief after the assassination, he declared that Kennedy's legislative program, stymied in congressional committees, would be passed. Johnson loved the kind of political infighting and legislative detail that Kennedy had loathed. The logjam in the Congress that had blocked Kennedy's legislative efforts broke under Johnson's forceful leadership, and a torrent of legislation poured through.

Before 1963 was out, Congress had approved a pending foreign-aid bill and a plan to sell wheat to the Soviet Union. But America's commitment to foreign aid drew attention to its own people's needs. In 1964 the Council of Economic Advisers reported that 9.3 million American families, about 20 percent of the population, were living below the "poverty line." "Unfortunately, many Americans live on the outskirts of hope," Johnson told Congress in his first State of the Union message, "some because of their poverty and some because of their color, and all too many because of both." At the top of his agenda, he put Kennedy's stalled measures for tax reductions and civil rights. In 1962 Kennedy had announced an unusual plan to jump-start the sluggish economy: a tax cut designed to stimulate consumer spending. Congressional Republicans opposed the idea because it would increase the federal budget deficit. And polls showed that public opinion was also skeptical. So Kennedy postponed the proposed tax cut a year. It was still bogged down in Congress when the president was assassinated, but Lyndon Johnson was able to break the logjam. The Revenue Act of 1964 did provide a needed boost to the economy.

Likewise, the Civil Rights Act that Kennedy had presented to Congress in 1963 was brought to fruition in 1964 by Johnson's forceful leadership. It prohibited racial segregation in public facilities such as bus terminals, restaurants, theaters, and hotels. And it outlawed long-standing racial discrimination in the registration of voters and the hiring of employees. The civil rights bill passed the House in February 1964. In the Senate, however, southern legislators launched a filibuster that lasted two months. Johnson finally prevailed and the bill became law on July 2. But the new president knew it had come at a political price. On the night after signing the bill, Johnson told an aide that "we have just delivered the South to the Republican Party for a long time to come."

In addition to fulfilling Kennedy's major promises, Johnson launched an ambitious legislative program of his own. In his 1964 State of the Union address, he added to his must-do list a bold new idea that bore the Johnson brand: "This Administration today, here and now, declares unconditional war on poverty in America." The particulars of this "war on poverty" were to come later, the product of a task force that was at work before Johnson took office.

Americans had rediscovered poverty when the social critic Michael Harrington published a powerful exposé titled *The Other America* (1962). Harrington argued that more than 40 million people were mired in a "culture of poverty." Unlike the upwardly mobile immigrant poor at the turn of the century, the modern poor lacked hope. "To be impoverished," he asserted, "is to be an internal alien, to grow up in a culture that is radically different from the one that dominates the society." President Kennedy asked his advisers to investigate the poverty problem and suggest solutions. Upon taking office as president, Lyndon Johnson announced that he wanted an anti-poverty package that was "big and bold, that would hit the nation with real impact." Money for the program would come from the tax revenues generated by corporate profits made possible by the tax reduction of 1964, which had led to one of the longest sustained economic booms in history.

The administration's war on poverty was embodied in an economic-opportunity bill that incorporated a wide range of programs: a Job Corps for inner-city youths aged sixteen to twenty-one, a Head Start program for disadvantaged preschoolers, work-study programs for college students, grants to farmers and rural businesses, loans to employers willing to hire the chronically unemployed, the Volunteers in Service to America (a domestic Peace Corps), and the Community Action Program, which would provide "maximum feasible participation" of the poor in directing neighborhood programs designed for their benefit. Speaking at Ann Arbor, Michigan, in 1964, Johnson called for a "Great Society" resting on "abundance and liberty for all. The Great Society demands an end to poverty and racial injustice, to which we are fully committed in our time."

THE ELECTION OF 1964   Johnson's well-intentioned but hastily conceived "war on poverty" and Great Society social program provoked a Republican counterattack. For years, conservatives had come to fear that the Republican party had fallen into the hands of an "eastern establishment" that had given in to the same internationalism and big-government policies as liberal Democrats. Ever since 1940, so the theory went, the party had nominated "me-too" candidates who merely promised to run more efficiently the programs that Democrats designed. Offer the Republican voters "a choice, not an echo," they reasoned, and a true conservative majority would assert itself.

By 1960 Arizona senator Barry Goldwater, a millionaire department-store magnate, had emerged as the leader of the Republican right. In his book *The Conscience of a Conservative* (1960), Goldwater proposed the abolition of the income tax, sale of the Tennessee Valley Authority, and a drastic overhaul of Social Security. Almost from the time of Kennedy's victory in 1960, a movement to draft Goldwater had begun, mobilizing right-wing activists to capture party caucuses and contest primaries. In 1964 they took an early lead, and they swept the all-important California primary. Thus Goldwater's forces controlled the Republican Convention when it gathered in San Francisco. "I would remind you," Goldwater told the delegates, "that extremism in the defense of liberty is no vice."

During the 1964 campaign, Goldwater displayed a gift for frightening voters. He urged wholesale bombing of North Vietnam and left the impression of being trigger-happy. He savaged Johnson's war on poverty and the entire New Deal tradition. At times he was foolishly candid. In Tennessee he proposed the sale of the Tennessee Valley Authority; in St. Petersburg, Florida, a major retirement community, he questioned the value of Social Security. He also opposed the nuclear test ban and the 1964 Civil Rights Act. To Republican campaign buttons that claimed, "In your heart, you know he's right," Democrats responded, "In your guts, you know he's nuts."

Barry Goldwater

Many voters feared that the Republican presidential candidate in 1964, senator Barry Goldwater, was trigger-happy. In this cartoon, Goldwater wields in one hand his book *The Conscience of a Conservative* and in the other a hydrogen bomb.

Johnson, on the other hand, portrayed himself as a responsible centrist. He chose as his running mate Hubert Humphrey from Minnesota, a prominent liberal senator who had long promoted the cause of civil rights. In contrast to Goldwater's bellicose rhetoric on Vietnam, Johnson pledged, "We are not about to send American boys nine or ten thousand miles from home to do what Asian boys ought to be doing for themselves."

The result was a landslide. Johnson polled 61 percent of the total votes; Goldwater carried only Arizona and five states in the Deep South, where race remained the salient issue. Vermont went Democratic for the first time ever in a presidential election. Johnson won the electoral vote by a whopping 486 to 52. In the Senate the Democrats increased their majority by two (68 to 32) and in the House by thirty-seven (295 to 140). Johnson knew, however, that such a mandate could quickly erode. He shrewdly told his aides, "Every day I'm in office, I'm going to lose votes. I'm going to alienate somebody. . . . We've got to get this legislation fast. You've got to get it during my honeymoon." Goldwater's success in the Deep South also continued that traditionally Democratic region's shift to the Republican party.

LANDMARK LEGISLATION   In 1965 Johnson flooded the new Congress with Great Society legislation that, he promised, would end poverty, revitalize the decaying central cities, provide every young American with the chance to attend college, protect the health of the elderly, enhance cultural life, clean up the air and water, and make the highways safer and prettier. The scope of Johnson's legislative program was unparalleled since Franklin Roosevelt's Hundred Days.

Priority went to federal health insurance and aid to education, proposals that had languished since President Truman had proposed them in 1945. For twenty years a comprehensive medical-insurance program had been stalled by the steadfast opposition of the American Medical Association. But now that Johnson had the votes, the AMA joined Republicans in supporting a bill serving those over age sixty-five. The AMA proposed, in addition to hospital insurance, a program for the payment of doctors' bills and drug costs, with the government footing half the premium. The act that finally emerged went well beyond the original program. It not only incorporated the new proposal into the Medicare program for the aged but also added another program, dubbed Medicaid, for federal grants to states to help cover medical payments for the indigent. President Johnson signed the bill on July 30, 1965, in Independence, Missouri, with eighty-one-year-old Harry Truman looking on.

Five days after he submitted his Medicare program, Johnson sent to Congress a massive program of federal aid to elementary and secondary education. Such proposals had been ignored since the 1940s, blocked alternately by issues of segregation and separation of church and state. The first issue had been laid to rest, legally at least, by the Civil Rights Act of 1964. Now Congress devised a means of extending aid to "poverty-impacted" school districts regardless of their public or parochial character.

The momentum generated by these measures had already begun to carry others along, and it continued through the following year. Before the Eighty-ninth Congress adjourned, it had established a record in the passage of landmark legislation unequaled since the time of the New Deal. Altogether the tide of Great Society legislation had carried 435 bills through the Congress. Among them was the Appalachian Regional Development Act of 1966, which provided $1 billion for programs in remote mountain areas that had long been pockets of desperate poverty. The Housing and Urban Development Act of 1965 provided for construction of 240,000 public housing units and $3 billion for urban renewal. Funds for rent supplements for low-income families followed in 1966, and in that year a new Department of

Housing and Urban Development appeared, headed by Robert C. Weaver, the first African-American cabinet member. Lyndon Johnson had, in the words of one Washington reporter, "brought to harvest a generation's backlog of ideas and social legislation."

THE IMMIGRATION ACT   Little noticed in the stream of legislation flowing from Congress was a major new immigration bill that had originated in the Kennedy White House. President Johnson signed the Immigration and Nationality Services Act of 1965 in a ceremony held on Liberty Island in New York Harbor. In his speech he stressed that the new law would redress the wrong done to those "from southern and eastern Europe" and the "developing continents" of Asia, Africa, and Latin America. It would do so by abolishing the discriminatory quotas based on national origin that had governed immigration policy since the 1920s. The new law treated all nationalities and races equally. In place of national quotas, it created hemispheric ceilings on visas issued: 170,000 for persons from outside the Western Hemisphere, 120,000 for persons from within. It also stipulated that no more than 20,000 people could come from any one country each year. The new act allowed the entry of immediate family members of American residents without limit. Most of the annual visas were to be given on a first-come, first-served basis to "other relatives" of American residents, and only a small proportion (about 10 percent) were allocated to those with special talents or job skills. During the 1960s Asians and Latin Americans became the largest contingent of new Americans.

ASSESSING THE GREAT SOCIETY   The Great Society programs included several successes. The Highway Safety Act and the Traffic Safety Act (1966) established safety standards for automobile manufacturers and highway design, and the scholarships provided for college students under the Higher Education Act (1965) were quite popular. Many Great Society initiatives aimed at improving the health, nutrition, and education of poor Americans, young and old, made some headway. So, too, did federal efforts to clean up air and water pollution. Several of Johnson's most ambitious programs, however, were ill conceived, others were vastly underfunded, and many were mismanaged. Medicare, for example, removed incentives for hospitals to control costs, and medical bills skyrocketed. The Great Society helped reduce the number of people living in poverty, but it did so largely by providing federal welfare payments, not by finding them productive jobs. The war on poverty ended up being as disappointing as the war in Vietnam. Often funds appropriated for various programs never made it through the tangled bureaucracy to the needy. Widely publicized cases of welfare fraud became a powerful weapon in the hands of those who were opposed to liberal social programs. By 1966 middle-class resentment over the cost and waste of the Great Society programs helped to generate a conservative backlash that fueled a Republican resurgence at the polls.

FROM CIVIL RIGHTS TO BLACK POWER

CIVIL RIGHTS LEGISLATION   Early in 1965, Martin Luther King Jr. announced a drive to enroll the 3 million African Americans in the South who had not registered to vote. In Selma, Alabama, civil rights protesters began a march to Montgomery, about forty miles away, only to be violently dispersed by state troopers and a mounted posse. A federal judge agreed to allow the march, and President Johnson provided troops for protection. By March 25, when the demonstrators reached Montgomery, some 35,000 people were with them, and King delivered a rousing address from the steps of the state capitol.

Several days before the march, President Johnson went before Congress with a moving plea that reached its climax when he slowly intoned the words of the movement's hymn: "And we shall overcome." The resulting Voting Rights Act of 1965 ensured all citizens the right to vote. It authorized the attorney general to dispatch federal examiners to register voters. In states or counties where fewer than half the adults had voted in 1964, the act suspended literacy tests and other devices commonly used to defraud citizens of the vote. By the end of the year, some 250,000 African Americans were newly registered.

BLACK POWER   Amid this success, however, the civil rights movement began to fragment. On August 11, 1965, less than a week after the passage of the Voting Rights Act, Watts, a predominantly black and poor community in Los Angeles, exploded in a frenzy of riots and looting. When the uprising ended, thirty-four were dead, almost 4,000 rioters were in jail, and property damage exceeded $35 million. Chicago and Cleveland, along with forty other American cities, experienced similar race riots in the summer of 1966. The following summer, Newark and Detroit burst into flames.

In retrospect, it was predictable that the civil rights movement would shift its focus to the plight of urban blacks. By the middle 1960s, about 70 percent of the black population lived in metropolitan areas, most of them in central-city ghettos that had been bypassed by the postwar prosperity. And again it seemed clear, in retrospect, that the nonviolent tactics that had worked in the rural South would not work as readily in northern cities. "It may be," wrote a contributor to *Esquire*, "that looting, rioting and burning . . . are really nothing more than radical forms of urban renewal, a response not only to the frustrations of the ghetto but the collapse of all ordinary modes of change, as if a body despairing of the indifference of doctors sought to rip a cancer out of itself." A special Commission on Civil Disorders noted that, unlike earlier race riots, the urban upheavals of the middle 1960s were initiated by blacks themselves; earlier riots had been started by whites, which had then prompted black counterattacks. Now blacks visited violence and destruction on themselves in an effort to destroy what they could not stomach and what civil rights legislation seemed unable to change.

By 1966 "black power" had become the new rallying cry. When Stokely Carmichael, a twenty-five-year-old graduate of Howard University, became head of the Student Nonviolent Coordinating Committee (SNCC) in 1966, he made the separatist philosophy of black power the official objective of the organization and ousted whites from the organization. H. Rap Brown, who succeeded Carmichael as head of SNCC in 1967, urged blacks to "get you some guns" and "kill the honkies." Carmichael, meanwhile, had moved on to the Black Panther party, a self-professed group of urban revolutionaries founded in Oakland, California, in 1966. Headed by Huey P. Newton and Eldridge Cleaver, the provocative, armed Black Panthers terrified the public, but eventually fragmented in spasms of violence.

The most articulate spokesman for black power was Malcolm X (formerly Malcolm Little, with the X denoting his lost African surname). Malcolm had risen from a ghetto childhood of narcotics and crime to become the chief disciple of Elijah Muhammad, the Black Muslim leader in the United States. "Yes, I'm an extremist," Malcolm acknowledged in 1964. "The black race in the United States is in extremely bad shape. You show me a black man who isn't an extremist and I'll show you one who needs psychiatric attention." By 1964 Malcolm had broken with Elijah Muhammad and founded an organization committed to the establishment of alliances between African Americans and the nonwhite peoples of the world. But shortly after the publication of his *Autobiography* in 1964, Malcolm was gunned down in Harlem by assassins representing a rival faction of Black Muslims. With him went the most effective voice for urban black militancy since Marcus Garvey in the 1920s. What made the assassination of Malcolm X especially tragic was that he had just months before begun to abandon his strident anti-white rhetoric and to preach a biracial message of social change.

Although widely publicized and highly visible, the black power movement never attracted more than a small minority of African Americans. Only about 15 percent of blacks labeled themselves separatists. The preponderant majority continued to identify with the philosophy of nonviolent integration promoted by Martin Luther King Jr. and with organizations such as the NAACP. King

Malcolm X

Malcolm X was the black power movement's most influential spokesman.

dismissed black separatism and the promotion of violent social change. He reminded his followers that "we can't win violently."

The black power philosophy, despite its hyperbole, violence, and small number of adherents, had two positive effects upon the civil rights movement. First, it helped African Americans take greater pride in their racial heritage. As Malcolm X often pointed out, prolonged slavery and institutionalized racism had eroded the self-esteem of many blacks in the United States. "The worst crime the white man has committed," he declared, "has been to teach us to hate ourselves." He and others helped blacks appreciate their African roots and their American accomplishments. In fact, it was Malcolm X who insisted that blacks call themselves African Americans as a symbol of pride in their roots and as a spur to learn more about their history as a people. As the popular singer James Brown urged, "Say it loud—I'm black and I'm proud."

Second, the black power phenomenon forced King and other mainstream black leaders and organizations to launch a new stage in the civil rights movement to focus attention on the plight of poor inner-city blacks. Legal access to restaurants, schools, and other public accommodations, King pointed out, meant little to people mired in a culture of urban poverty. They needed jobs and decent housing as much as they needed legal rights. To this end, King began to emphasize the economic plight of the black urban underclass. The time had come for radical measures "to provide jobs and income for the poor." Yet as King and others sought to heighten the war on poverty at home, the escalating war in Vietnam was consuming more and more of America's resources and energies.

The Tragedy of Vietnam

As racial violence erupted in America's cities, the war in Vietnam reached new levels of intensity and destruction. In November 1963, when John Kennedy was assassinated, there were 16,000 American military "advisers" in South Vietnam. Lyndon Johnson inherited a commitment to prevent a Communist takeover in Indochina as well as a reluctance on the part of American presidents to assume primary responsibility for fighting the Viet Cong (Communist-led guerrillas in South Vietnam) and their North Vietnamese allies. Beginning with Harry Truman, one president after another had done just enough to avoid being charged with having "lost" Vietnam to communism. Johnson initially sought to do the same, fearing that any other course of action would undermine his political influence and jeopardize his Great Society programs in

"How Deep Do You Figure We'll Get Involved, Sir?"

Although U.S. soldiers were first sent to Vietnam as noncombatant advisers, they soon found themselves involved in a quagmire of fighting.

Congress. But this path took him and the United States deeper into an expanding military commitment in Southeast Asia. Early on Johnson doubted that Vietnam was worth military involvement. In May 1964 he told national security adviser, McGeorge Bundy, that he had spent a sleepless night worrying about Vietnam: "It looks to me like we are getting into another Korea. . . . I don't think we can fight them 10,000 miles away from home. . . . I don't think it's worth fighting for. And I don't think we can get out. It's just the biggest damned mess that I ever saw."

Yet Johnson's fear of appearing weak abroad was stronger than his misgivings and forebodings. By the end of 1965, there were 184,000 U.S. troops in Vietnam; in 1966 there were 385,000; and by 1969, the height of the American presence, 542,000. By the time the last troops left, in March 1973, some 58,000 Americans had died and another 300,000 had been wounded. The war had cost the taxpayers $150 billion, siphoned away funding from many Great Society programs, produced 570,000 draft offenders and 563,000 less-than-honorable military discharges, toppled Johnson's administration, and divided the country as no event in history had since the Civil War.

ESCALATION   The official sanction for military "escalation" in Southeast Asia—a Defense Department term favored in the Vietnam era—was the Tonkin Gulf resolution, voted by Congress on August 7, 1964. On that day, Johnson told a national television audience that two destroyers, the U.S.S. *Maddox* and the *C. Turner Joy,* had been attacked by North Vietnamese vessels on August 2 and 4 in the Gulf of Tonkin, off the coast of North Vietnam. Although Johnson described the attack as unprovoked, in truth the destroyers had been monitoring South Vietnamese attacks against two North Vietnamese islands—attacks planned by American advisers. Even though there was no tangible evidence of an attack on the U.S. ships, the Tonkin Gulf resolution authorized the president to "take all necessary measures to repel any armed attack against the forces of the United States and to prevent further aggression." Only Senator Wayne Morse of Oregon and Senator Ernest Gruening of Alaska voted against the resolution, which Johnson thereafter interpreted as equivalent to a congressional declaration of war.

Soon after his landslide victory over Goldwater in 1964, Johnson, while still plagued with private doubts, made the crucial decisions that shaped policy in Vietnam for the next four years. On February 5, 1965, Viet Cong guerrillas killed 8 and wounded 126 Americans at Pleiku, in South Vietnam. Further attacks later that week led Johnson to order Operation Rolling Thunder, the first sustained bombing of North Vietnam, which was intended to stop the flow of soldiers and supplies into the south. Six months later an extensive study concluded that the bombing had not slowed the supplies pouring down the Ho Chi Minh Trail from North Vietnam through Laos and into South Vietnam.

In March 1965 the new U.S. commander in Vietnam, General William C. Westmoreland, greeted the first installment of combat troops. By the summer, American forces were engaged in "search-and-destroy" operations throughout South Vietnam. As combat operations increased, so did casualties, announced each week on the nightly news, along with the "body count" of alleged Viet Cong dead. "Westy's war," although fought with helicopter

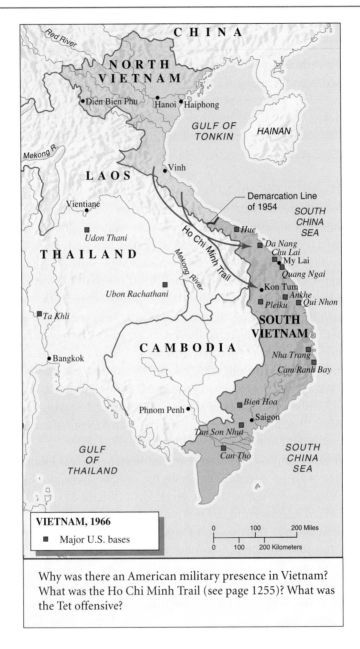

VIETNAM, 1966
■ Major U.S. bases

Why was there an American military presence in Vietnam? What was the Ho Chi Minh Trail (see page 1255)? What was the Tet offensive?

gunships, chemical defoliants, and napalm, became like the trench warfare of World War I—a war of attrition.

THE CONTEXT FOR POLICY   Lyndon Johnson's decision to "Americanize" the Vietnam War, so ill-starred in retrospect, was consistent with the foreign-policy principles pursued by all presidents after World War II. The version of the containment theory articulated in the Truman Doctrine, endorsed by Eisenhower throughout the 1950s, and reaffirmed by Kennedy, pledged U.S. opposition to the advance of communism anywhere in the world. "Why are we in Vietnam?" Johnson asked rhetorically at Johns Hopkins University in 1965. "We are there because we have a promise to keep. . . . To leave Vietnam to its fate would shake the confidence of all these people in the value of American commitment." Secretary of State Dean Rusk frequently repeated this rationale, warning that Thailand, Burma, and the rest of Southeast Asia would fall "like dominoes" to communism if American forces withdrew from Vietnam. Military intervention was thus a logical culmination of the assumptions that were widely shared by the foreign-policy establishment and the leaders of both political parties since the early days of the cold war.

At the same time, Johnson and his advisers presumed that military involvement in Vietnam must not reach levels that would cause the Chinese or Soviets to intervene directly. And that meant, in effect, that a complete military victory was never possible. The goal of the United States was not to win the war in any traditional sense but to prevent the North Vietnamese and the Viet Cong from winning and, eventually, to force a negotiated settlement with the North Vietnamese. This meant that the United States would have to maintain a military presence as long as the enemy retained the will to fight.

As it turned out, public support for the war eroded faster than the will of the North Vietnamese leaders to tolerate devastating casualties and destruction. Systematic opposition to the war on college campuses began in 1965 with "teach-ins" at the University of Michigan. The following year, Senator J. William Fulbright of Arkansas, chairman of the Senate Foreign Relations Committee, began congressional investigations into American policy in Vietnam. George Kennan, the author of the containment doctrine, told Senator Fulbright's committee that the doctrine was appropriate for Europe but not for Southeast Asia. And a respected general testified that General Westmoreland's military strategy had no chance of achieving victory. By 1967 anti-war demonstrations attracted massive support. Nightly television accounts of the fighting—Vietnam was the first war to receive extended television coverage and hence was dubbed the living-room war—called into question the official optimism. By May 1967 even Secretary of Defense Robert McNamara was wavering: "The picture of the world's greatest superpower killing or injuring 1,000 noncombatants a week, while trying to pound a tiny backward nation into submission on an issue whose merits are hotly disputed, is not a pretty one."

In a war of political will, North Vietnam had the advantage. Johnson and his advisers grievously underestimated the tenacity of the North Vietnamese commitment to unify Vietnam and expel American forces. While the United States fought a limited war for limited objectives, the Vietnamese Communists fought an all-out war for their very survival. Just as General Westmoreland was assuring Johnson and the public that the war effort in early 1968 was on the verge of gaining the upper hand, the Communists again displayed their cunning and tenacity.

THE TURNING POINT   On January 31, 1968, the first day of the Vietnamese New Year (Tet), the Viet Cong defied a holiday truce to launch ferocious assaults on American and South Vietnamese forces throughout South Vietnam. The old capital city of Hue fell to the Communists, and Viet Cong units temporarily occupied the grounds of the U.S. embassy in Saigon, the capital of South Vietnam. General Westmoreland proclaimed the Tet offensive a major defeat for the Viet Cong, and most students of military

The Tet Offensive

Many Vietnamese were driven from their homes during the bloody street battles of the 1968 Tet offensive. Here, following a lull in the fighting, civilians carrying a white flag approach U.S. Marines.

strategy later agreed with him. While Viet Cong casualties were enormous, however, the impact of the surprise attacks on the American public was more telling. The scope and intensity of the offensive contradicted upbeat claims by U.S. commanders that the war was going well. *Time* and *Newsweek* magazines soon ran anti-war editorials urging withdrawal. Polls showed that Lyndon Johnson's popularity had declined to 35 percent, lower than that of any president in polling history since Truman's darkest days. Civil rights leaders and social activists felt betrayed as they saw federal funds earmarked for the war on poverty gobbled up by the expanding war. In 1968 the United States was spending $322,000 on every Communist killed in Vietnam; the poverty programs at home received only $53 per person.

During 1968 Lyndon Johnson grew increasingly embittered and isolated. He suffered from depression and bouts of paranoia. It had become painfully evident that the Vietnam War was a never-ending stalemate that was fragmenting the nation and undermining the Great Society programs. Clark Clifford, Johnson's new secretary of defense, reported to the president that a task force of prominent soldiers and civilians saw no prospect for a military victory. Robert Kennedy, now a senator from New York, was considering a run for the presidency in order to challenge Johnson's Vietnam policy.

Senator Eugene McCarthy of Minnesota had already decided to oppose Johnson in the Democratic primaries. With anti-war students rallying to his candidacy, McCarthy polled 42 percent of the vote to Johnson's 48 percent in New Hampshire's March primary. It was a remarkable showing for a little-known senator. Each presidential primary now promised to become a referendum on Johnson's Vietnam policy. The war in Vietnam had become Lyndon Johnson's war; as more and more voters soured on the fighting, he saw his public support evaporate. In Wisconsin, scene of the next Democratic primary, the president's political advisers forecast a humiliating defeat.

Johnson and Vietnam

The Vietnam War sapped the spirit of Lyndon Johnson, who decided not to run for reelection in 1968.

On March 31 Johnson made a dramatic decision. He appeared on national television to announce a limited halt to the bombing of North Vietnam and fresh initiatives for a negotiated cease-fire. Then he added a stunning postscript: "I shall not seek, and I will not accept the nomination of my party for another term as your President." Although U.S. troops would remain in Vietnam for five more years and the casualties would continue, the quest for military victory had ended. Now the question was how the most powerful nation in the world could extricate itself from Vietnam with a minimum of damage to its prestige.

Sixties Crescendo

A TRAUMATIC YEAR   Change moved at a fearful pace throughout the 1960s, but 1968 was the most turbulent and traumatic year of all. On April 4, only four days after Johnson's withdrawal from the presidential race, Martin Luther King Jr. was gunned down in Memphis, Tennessee. The assassin, James Earl Ray, had expressed hostility toward blacks, but debate still continues over whether he was a pawn in an organized conspiracy. King's death set off an outpouring of grief among whites and blacks. It also ignited riots in over sixty cities.

Two months later, on June 5, Robert Kennedy was shot in the head by a young Palestinian, Sirhan Sirhan, who resented Kennedy's strong support of Israel. Kennedy's death occurred at the end of the day on which he had convincingly defeated Eugene McCarthy in the California Democratic primary, thereby assuming leadership of the anti-war forces in the race for the presidential nomination. Political reporter David Halberstam of the *New York Times* thought back to the assassinations of John Kennedy and Malcolm X, then the violent end of King, the most influential African-American leader of the twentieth century, and then Robert Kennedy, the heir to leadership of the Kennedy clan. "We could make a calendar of the decade," Halberstam wrote, "by marking where we were at the hours of those violent deaths."

CHICAGO AND MIAMI   In August 1968 Democratic delegates gathered inside a Chicago convention hall to nominate for president Johnson's faithful vice president, Hubert Humphrey, while almost 20,000 police officers and national guardsmen and a small army of television reporters stood watch over a gathering of eclectic protesters herded together miles away in a public park. Chicago mayor Richard J. Daley, who had given "shoot-to-kill" orders to police during the April riots protesting the King assassination, warned that he would not tolerate disruptions. Nonetheless, riots broke out and were televised nationwide. As police tear gas and billy clubs struck demonstrators, others chanted, "The whole world is watching."

The Democratic party's liberal tradition was clearly in disarray, a fact that gave heart to the Republicans, who gathered in Miami Beach to nominate Richard Nixon. Only six years earlier, after he had lost the California gubernatorial race, Nixon had vowed never again to run for public office. But by 1968 he had changed his mind and had become a spokesman for the values of "Middle America." Nixon and the Republicans offered a vision of stability and order that appealed to a majority of Americans—soon to be called the silent majority.

George Wallace, the Democratic governor of Alabama who had made his reputation as an outspoken defender of segregation, ran as a third candidate in the campaign, on the American Independent party ticket. Wallace moderated his position on the race issue but appealed even more candidly than Nixon to voters' concerns about rioting anti-war protesters, the welfare

The 1968 Election

Richard Nixon (left) and running mate Spiro Agnew (right).

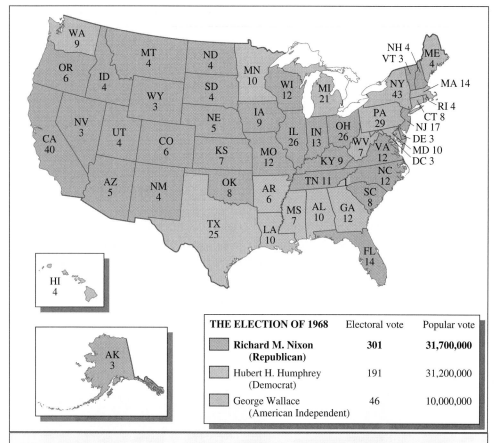

THE ELECTION OF 1968	Electoral vote	Popular vote
Richard M. Nixon (Republican)	**301**	**31,700,000**
Hubert H. Humphrey (Democrat)	191	31,200,000
George Wallace (American Independent)	46	10,000,000

How did the riots at the Chicago Democratic Convention affect the 1968 presidential campaign? How did Nixon engineer his political comeback? What was Wallace's appeal to over 10 million voters?

system, and the growth of the federal government. Wallace's reactionary candidacy generated considerable appeal outside his native South, especially among white working-class communities, where resentment flourished against Lyndon Johnson's Great Society liberalism. Although never a possible winner, Wallace did pose the possibility of denying Humphrey or Nixon an electoral majority and thereby throwing the choice into the House of Representatives, which would have provided an appropriate climax to a chaotic year.

NIXON AGAIN It did not happen that way. Nixon enjoyed an enormous lead in the polls, which narrowed as the 1968 election approached. Wallace's campaign was hurt by his outspoken running mate, retired air force general Curtis LeMay, who favored expanding the war in Vietnam and using nuclear weapons. In October 1968 Hubert Humphrey infuriated Johnson when he announced that, if elected, he would stop bombing North Vietnam "as an acceptable risk for peace."

Nixon and Governor Spiro Agnew of Maryland, his running mate, eked out a narrow victory of about 500,000 votes, a margin of about 1 percentage point. The electoral vote was more decisive, 301 to 191. George Wallace received 10 million votes, 13.5 percent of the total. It was the best showing by a third-party candidate since Robert La Follette ran on the Progressive ticket in 1924. All but one of Wallace's 46 electoral votes were from the Deep South. Nixon swept all but four of the states west of the Mississippi. Humphrey's support came almost exclusively from the Northeast.

So at the end of a turbulent year near the end of a traumatic decade, a nation on the verge of violent chaos looked to Richard Nixon to provide what he had promised in the campaign: "peace with honor" in Vietnam and a middle ground on which a majority of Americans, silent or otherwise, could come together.

MAKING CONNECTIONS

- The reform movements of the 1960s galvanized the baby-boom generation into a new youth movement, described in the next chapter, that continued through the early 1970s.

- The conflict in Vietnam, America's longest war, would come to a bitter end for U.S. forces, but the divisions it spawned still echo today.

- The Immigration and Nationality Act of 1965 would have profound and unexpected consequences on American society, described in Chapter 37.

- The success of the civil rights movement in the 1960s led to similar movements by women, gays, Native Americans, and Latinos, as we will see in the next chapter.

Further Reading

A dispassionate analysis of John Kennedy's life is Thomas C. Reeves's *A Question of Character: A Life of John F. Kennedy* (1991). The best study of the Kennedy administration's domestic policies is Irving Bernstein's *Promises Kept: John F. Kennedy's New Frontier* (1991). For details on the still swirling conspiracy theories about the assassination, see David W. Belin's *Final Disclosure: The Full Truth about the Assassination of President Kennedy* (1988).

The most comprehensive biography of Johnson is Robert Dallek's two-volume work, *Lone Star Rising: Lyndon Johnson and His Times, 1908–1960* (1991) and *Flawed Giant: Lyndon B. Johnson and His Times, 1960–1973* (1998). On the Johnson administration, see Vaughn Davis Bornet's *The Presidency of Lyndon B. Johnson* (1984).

Among the works that interpret liberal social policy during the 1960s, John Schwarz's *America's Hidden Success: A Reassessment of Twenty Years of Public Policy* (1983) offers a glowing endorsement of Democratic programs. For a contrasting perspective, see Charles Murray's *Losing Ground: American Social Policy, 1950–1980,* rev. ed. (1994).

On foreign policy, see *Kennedy's Quest for Victory: American Foreign Policy, 1961–1963* (1989), edited by Thomas G. Paterson. To learn more about Kennedy's problems in Cuba, see Mark White's *Missiles in Cuba: Kennedy, Khrushchev, Castro and the 1962 Crisis* (1997). See also Aleksandr Fursenko and Timothy Naftali's *"One Hell of a Gamble": Khrushchev, Castro and Kennedy, 1958–1964* (1997).

American involvement in Vietnam has received voluminous treatment from all political perspectives. For an excellent overview, see Larry Berman's *Planning a Tragedy: The Americanization of the War in Vietnam* (1982) and *Lyndon Johnson's War: The Road to Stalemate in Vietnam* (1989), as well as Stanley Karnow's *Vietnam: A History,* rev. ed. (1991). An analysis of policy making concerning the Vietnam War is David M. Barrett's *Uncertain Warriors: Lyndon Johnson and His Vietnam Advisors* (1993). A fine account of the military involvement is Robert D. Schulzinger's *A Time for War: The United States and Vietnam, 1941–1975* (1997). On the legacy of the Vietnam War, see Arnold R. Isaacs's *Vietnam Shadows: The War, Its Ghosts, and Its Legacy* (1997).

Many scholars have dealt with various aspects of the civil rights movement and race relations of the 1960s. See especially Carl M. Brauer's *John F. Kennedy and the Second Reconstruction* (1977), David Garrow's *Bearing the Cross: Martin Luther King, Jr., and the Southern Christian Leadership Conference* (1986), Adam Fairclough's *To Redeem the Soul of America: The Southern*

Christian Leadership Conference and Martin Luther King, Jr. (1987). William H. Chafe's *Civilities and Civil Rights: Greensboro, North Carolina, and the Black Struggle for Freedom* (1980) details the original sit-ins. An award-winning study of racial and economic inequality in a representative American city is Thomas J. Sugrue's *The Origins of the Urban Crisis: Race and Inequality in Postwar Detroit* (1996).

35

REBELLION AND REACTION IN THE 1960s AND 1970s

FOCUS QUESTIONS

- What characterized the social rebellion and struggles for rights in the 1960s and 1970s?
- How did the war in Vietnam end?
- What was Watergate, and why did Nixon resign?
- How did the Carter administration deal with the foreign policy crises in the Middle East?

To answer these questions and access additional review material, please visit www.wwnorton.com/studyspace.

As Richard Nixon entered the White House in early 1969, he faced a nation whose social fabric was in tatters. Everywhere, it seemed, traditional institutions and notions of authority were under attack. The traumatic events of 1968 revealed how deeply divided society had become and how difficult a task Nixon faced in carrying out his pledge to restore social harmony. The stability he promised proved elusive. His policies and his combative temperament served to heighten rather than reduce societal tensions. Those tensions reflected profound fissures in the postwar consensus promoted by Eisenhower and inherited by Kennedy and Johnson. Ironically, many of the same forces that had enabled the flush times of the Eisenhower years helped generate the social upheavals of the 1960s and 1970s.

THE ROOTS OF REBELLION

YOUTH REVOLT   By the early 1960s the baby boomers were maturing. Now young adults, they differed from their elders in that they had experienced neither economic depression nor a major war. In record numbers they were attending colleges and universities: college enrollment quadrupled between 1945 and 1970. Many universities had become gigantic institutions dependent upon research contracts from corporations and the federal government. As these "multiversities" grew more bureaucratic and hierarchical, they unknowingly invited resistance from a generation of students wary of involvement in what President Eisenhower had labeled the military-industrial complex.

The Greensboro sit-ins in 1960 not only precipitated a decade of civil rights activism but also signaled an end to the supposed apathy that had enveloped college campuses and social life during the 1950s. Although most immediately concerned with the rights and status of African Americans, the sit-ins, marches, protests, principles, and sacrifices associated with the civil rights movement provided the model and inspiration for other groups that demanded justice, freedom, and equality as well: women, Native Americans, Hispanics, and homosexuals.

During 1960–1961 a small but significant number of white students joined African Americans in the sit-in movement. They and many others were also inspired by President Kennedy's direct appeals to their youthful idealism. Thousands enrolled in the Peace Corps and VISTA (Volunteers in Service to America), and others continued to participate in civil rights demonstrations. But as it became clear that politics was mixed with principle in the president's position on civil rights and later, as criticism of escalating military involvement in Vietnam mounted, more and more young people grew disillusioned with the government. By the mid-1960s a full-fledged youth revolt had broken out across the country. Rebellious students began to flow into two distinct yet frequently overlapping movements: the New Left and the counterculture.

THE NEW LEFT   The explicitly political strain of the youth revolt had its official origin when Tom Hayden and Al Haber, two University of Michigan students, formed the Students for a Democratic Society (SDS) in 1960. In 1962 Hayden and Haber convened a meeting of sixty activists at Port Huron, Michigan, where Hayden drafted what became known as the Port Huron Statement which began by saying: "We are the people of this generation, bred in at least moderate comfort, housed in universities, looking uncomfortably to the world we inherit."

Hayden's manifesto focused on the absence of individual freedom in modern life. The country, he insisted, was dominated by huge organizational structures—governments, corporations, unions, universities—all of which conspired to oppress and alienate the individual. Inspired by the example of African-American activism in the South, Hayden declared that students had the power to restore "participatory democracy" by wresting "control of the educational process from the administrative bureaucracy" and then forging links with other dissident movements. He and others adopted the term New Left to distinguish their efforts at grassroots democracy from the Old Left of the 1930s, which had espoused an orthodox Marxism and embraced Stalinism.

In the fall of 1964, students at the University of California at Berkeley took Hayden's program to heart. Several of them had returned to the campus after spending the summer working with the SNCC black voter-registration project in Mississippi, where three volunteers had been killed, dozens shot, and nearly 1,000 arrested. When UC-Berkeley chancellor Clark Kerr announced that political demonstrations would no longer be allowed, several hundred students staged a sit-in. Soon thereafter over 2,000 more joined in. After a tense thirty-two-hour standoff the administration relented. Student groups then formed the free-speech movement.

Led by Mario Savio, a philosophy major and compelling public speaker, the free-speech movement initially protested on behalf of student rights. But it quickly escalated into a more general criticism of the modern university and what Savio called the "depersonalized, unresponsive bureaucracy" infecting American life. In 1964 Savio led hundreds of students into UC-Berkeley's administration building and organized a sit-in. In the early-morning hours 600 policemen, dispatched by the governor, arrested the protesters.

The goals and tactics of the free-speech movement and SDS soon spread to colleges throughout the country. Issues large and small became the subject of student protest: unpopular faculty tenure decisions, mandatory ROTC (Reserve Officers' Training Corps) programs, dress codes, curfews, dormitory regulations.

Escalating U.S. involvement in Vietnam soon changed the student agenda. With the dramatic expansion of the war after 1965, millions of young men faced the grim prospect of being drafted to fight in an increasingly unpopular Asian war. In fact, however, the Vietnam conflict, like virtually every other war, was primarily a poor man's fight. Deferments enabled college students to postpone military service until they received their degree or reached the age of twenty-four; in 1965–1966 college students made up only 2 percent of all military inductees. In 1966, however, the Selective Service System modified the provisions so that even under-graduates were eligible for the draft.

As the war dragged on and opposition mounted, 200,000 young men simply refused to obey their draft notices, and some 4,000 of them served prison sentences. Another 56,000 men qualified for conscientious-objector status during the Vietnam War, compared with only 7,600 during the Korean conflict. Still others left the country altogether—several thousand fled to Canada or Sweden—to avoid military service. The most popular way to avoid the draft was to flunk the physical examination. Whatever the preferred method, many students succeeded in avoiding military service. Of the 1,200 men in the Harvard senior class of 1970, only fifty-six served in the military, and just two of those went to Vietnam.

In the spring of 1967, 500,000 war protesters of all ages converged on Manhattan's Central Park, where the most popular chant was "Hey, hey, LBJ, how many kids did you kill today?" Dozens ceremoniously burned their draft cards, and the so-called resistance phase of the anti-war movement was born. Thereafter a coalition of draft-resistance groups around the country sponsored draft-card-burning rallies and sit-ins that led to numerous arrests. Meanwhile, some SDS leaders were growing even more militant. Inspired by the rhetoric and violence of black power spokesmen such as Stokely Carmichael, H. Rap Brown, and Huey Newton, Tom Hayden abandoned his earlier commitment to passive civil disobedience. Rap Brown told the white radicals to remember the heritage of John Brown: "Take up a gun and go shoot the enemy." As the SDS became more militant, it grew more centralized and authoritarian. Capitalist imperialism replaced university bureaucracy as the primary foe.

Throughout 1967 and 1968, the anti-war movement grew more volatile as inner-city ghettos were exploding in flames of racial violence. Frustration over patterns of discrimination in employment and housing and staggering rates of joblessness among inner-city African-American youths exploded into violence. "There was a sense everywhere, in 1968," the journalist Garry Wills wrote, "that things were giving way. That man had not only lost control of his history, but might never regain it."

During the eventful spring of 1968—when Lyndon Johnson announced that he would not run for reelection and when Martin Luther King Jr. was assassinated—campus unrest enveloped the country. Over 200 major demonstrations took place. The turmoil reached a climax with the disruption of Columbia University. There Mark Rudd, an SDS leader, led a small cadre of radicals in occupying the president's office and classroom buildings. They also kidnapped a dean—all in protest of the university's decision to displace

Students for a Democratic Society Take Over Columbia University

Mark Rudd, leader of the SDS at Columbia University, talking to representatives of the media during student protests of university policies, April 1968.

neighboring African-American housing in order to build a new gymnasium. During the next week, more buildings were occupied, faculty and administrative offices were ransacked, and classes were canceled. University officials finally called in the New York City police. In the process of arresting the protesters, the police injured a number of innocent bystanders. Their excessive force aroused the anger of many unaligned students, who then staged a strike that shut down the university for the remainder of the semester. The chaotic events at Columbia buoyed militants across the nation. Similar clashes among students, administrators, and police occurred at Harvard, Cornell, and San Francisco State.

At the 1968 Democratic Convention in Chicago, the polarization of society reached a bizarre climax. Inside the tightly guarded convention hall, Democrats nominated Hubert Humphrey while on Chicago's streets the whole spectrum of anti-war dissenters gathered, from the earnest supporters of Senator Eugene McCarthy to the nihilistic Yippies, members of the new Youth International party. The Yippies were determined to create anarchy in the streets of Chicago. Abbie Hoffman, one of their leaders, explained that their "conception of revolution is that it's fun." The Yippies distributed a leaflet at the convention calling for the immediate legalization of marijuana and all psychedelic drugs, the abolition of money, student-run schools, and promiscuous sex.

The outlandish behavior of the Yippies and the other demonstrators provoked an equally outlandish response by Mayor Richard J. Daley and his army of city police. As a horrified television audience watched, many police officers went berserk, clubbing and gassing demonstrators as well as bystanders caught up in the melee. The spectacle lasted three days and seriously damaged Humphrey's presidential candidacy. The Chicago riots also generated a wave of anger among many middle-class Americans, anger that Richard Nixon and the

Upheaval in Chicago

The violence that accompanied the 1968 Democratic National Convention in Chicago seared the nation.

Republicans exploited at their nominating convention in Miami Beach. At the same time, the riots helped to fragment the anti-war movement. Those groups committed to nonviolent protest, while castigating the reactionary policies of Mayor Daley and the police, felt betrayed by the actions of the Yippies and other anarchistic militants.

In 1968 the SDS fractured into rival factions, the most extreme of which called itself the Weathermen, a name derived from a lyric written by the protest singer Bob Dylan: "You don't need a weatherman to know which way the wind blows." These hardened young activists embarked on a campaign of violence and disruption, firebombing university buildings and killing innocent people—as well as several of their own. Government forces arrested most of the Weathermen, and the rest went underground. By 1971 the New Left was dead as a political movement. In large measure it had committed suicide by abandoning the democratic and pacifist principles that had originally inspired participants and given the movement moral legitimacy. The larger anti-war movement also began to fade. There would be a wave of student protests against the Nixon administration in 1970–1971, but thereafter campus unrest virtually disappeared.

If the social mood was changing during the early 1970s, a large segment of the public continued the quest for social justice. The burgeoning environmental movement attested to the continuity of sixties idealism. A *New York Times* survey of college campuses in 1969 revealed that many students were refocusing their attention on the environment. This new ecological awareness would blossom in the 1970s into one of the most compelling items on the nation's social agenda.

THE COUNTERCULTURE   The numbing events of 1968 led other disaffected activists away from radical politics altogether, toward another manifestation of the sixties youth revolt: the counterculture. Long hair, blue jeans, tie-dyed shirts, sandals, mind-altering drugs, rock music, and experimental living arrangements were more important than revolutionary ideology to the hippies, the direct descendants of the Beats of the 1950s. These advocates of the counterculture were, like their New Left peers, primarily well-educated, middle-class young whites alienated by the Vietnam War, racism, political and parental demands, runaway technology, and a crass corporate mentality that equated the good life with material goods. In their view a complacent materialism had settled over urban and suburban life. But they were not attracted to organized political action. Instead, they eagerly embraced the credo outlined by the zany Harvard professor Timothy Leary: "Tune in, turn on, drop out."

For some the counterculture entailed the study and practice of Asian mysticism. For many it meant the daily use of hallucinogenic drugs. Collective living in urban enclaves such as San Francisco's Haight-Ashbury district, New York's East Village, and Atlanta's Fourteenth Street was the rage for a time among hippies, until conditions grew so crowded, violent, and depressing that residents migrated elsewhere. Rural communes also attracted bourgeois rebels. During the 1960s and early 1970s thousands of inexperienced romantics flocked to the countryside, eager to be liberated from parental and institutional restraints, to live in harmony with nature, and coexist in an atmosphere of love and openness.

But only a handful of their utopian homesteads survived more than a few months. Rooted in the pleasure principle, rustic hippies often produced more babies than bread. Initially intent upon rejecting conventional society, many found themselves utterly dependent upon it, and they were soon panhandling on street corners or lined up at government offices, collecting welfare, unemployment compensation, and food stamps to help them survive the rigors of natural living.

Huge outdoor rock-music concerts were also a popular source of community for hippies. The largest of these was the Woodstock Music and Art Fair. In August 1969 some 500,000 young people converged on a 600-acre farm near the tiny rural town of Bethel, New York. For three days the assembled flower

Woodstock

The Woodstock music festival drew nearly half a million people to a farm in Bethel, New York. The concert was billed as three days of "peace, music, . . . and love."

children reveled in good music, cheap marijuana, and casual sex. "Everyone swam nude in the lake," a journalist reported. The country had never "seen a society so free of repression."

But the carefree spirit of the Woodstock festival was short-lived. When other promoters tried to replicate the scene four months later, this time at Altamont Speedway forty miles east of San Francisco, the counterculture encountered the criminal culture. The Rolling Stones hired Hells Angels motorcycle-gang members to provide the "security" for their show. During the band's performance of "Under My Thumb," drunken white motorcyclists beat to death an eighteen-year-old African-American man wielding a gun in front of the stage. Three other spectators were accidentally killed that night; much of the vitality and innocence of the counterculture died with them.

After 1969 the hippie phenomenon began to wane. The counterculture had become counterproductive and had developed both faddish and fashionable overtones. Entrepreneurs were quick to see profits in protest.

Retailers developed a banner business in faded blue jeans, surplus army jackets, beads, incense, and sandals. Health-food stores and "head" shops appeared in shopping malls alongside Neiman Marcus and Sears. Rock-music groups, for all their lyrical protests against the capitalist system, made millions from it. The search on the part of alienated youth for a better society and a good life was strewn with both comic and tragic aspects.

FEMINISM   The seductive ideal of liberation spawned during the sixties helped accelerate a powerful women's rights crusade. Like the New Left the new feminism drew much of its inspiration and many of its tactics from the civil rights movement. Its aim was to challenge the "cult of female domesticity" that had prevailed since the 1950s.

The mainstream of the women's movement was led by Betty Friedan. Her influential book, *The Feminine Mystique* (1963), launched the new phase of female protest on a national level. During the 1950s Friedan, a Smith College graduate, raised three children in a New York suburb. Still politically active but now socially domestic, she mothered her children, pampered her husband, "read *Vogue* under the hair dryer," and occasionally did some freelance writing. In 1957 she conducted a poll of her fellow Smith alumnae and discovered that, despite the prevailing rhetoric about the happy suburban housewife, many women were in fact miserable. This revelation led to more research, which culminated in the publication of *The Feminine Mystique*.

Betty Friedan

Author of *The Feminine Mystique*.

Women, Friedan wrote, had actually lost ground during the years after World War II, when many left wartime employment and settled down in suburbia. A propaganda campaign engineered by advertisers and women's magazines encouraged them to do so by creating the "feminine mystique" of blissful domesticity. This notion that women were "gaily content in a world of bedroom, kitchen, sex, babies, and home" thus served to imprison women. In Friedan's view the middle-class home had become "a comfortable concentration camp" where women suffocated and stagnated in an atmosphere of mindless materialism, daytime television, and neighborhood gossip.

The Feminine Mystique, an immediate best seller, inspired many women who felt trapped in a rut with no way out. Moreover, Friedan discovered that there were far more women working outside the home than the pervasive "feminine mystique" suggested. Many of these working women were frustrated by the demands of holding "two full-time jobs instead of just one—underpaid clerical worker and unpaid housekeeper."

In 1966 Friedan and other activists founded the National Organization for Women (NOW). It initially sought to end discrimination in the workplace on the basis of sex and went on to spearhead efforts to legalize abortion and obtain federal and state support for child-care centers.

In the early 1970s Congress, the Supreme Court, and NOW advanced the cause of gender equality. Under Title IX of the Educational Amendments Act of 1972, colleges were required to institute "affirmative action" programs to ensure equal opportunities for women. In the same year, Congress overwhelmingly approved the equal-rights amendment, which had been bottled up in a House committee for almost half a century. In 1973 the Supreme Court, in *Roe v. Wade*, struck down state laws forbidding abortions during the first three months of pregnancy. Meanwhile, the educational bastions of male segregation, including Yale and Princeton, led a new movement for coeducation that swept the country. "If the 1960s belonged to blacks," said one feminist, "the next ten years are ours."

Feminist Awakenings

In 1967 Syracuse University student Kathy Switzer challenged the Boston Marathon's tradition of excluding women. Officials tried to pull Switzer from the course, but with the aid of fellow runners she completed the race. Women did not become official entrants until 1971.

By the end of the 1970s, however, sharp disputes between moderate and radical feminists fragmented the women's movement. The movement's failure to broaden its appeal much beyond the confines of the middle class also caused reform efforts to stagnate. The equal-rights amendment, which had once seemed a straightforward assertion of equal opportunity ("Equality of rights under the law shall not be denied or abridged by the United States or by any State on account of sex") and assured of ratification, was stymied in several state legislatures. By 1982 it had died, several states short of passage. And the very success of NOW's efforts to liberalize local and state abortion laws generated a powerful backlash, especially among Catholics and fundamentalist Protestants, who mounted a potent "right-to-life" crusade.

Yet the success of the women's movement endured long after the militant rhetoric had evaporated. Women's growing presence in the labor force brought them a greater share of economic and political influence. By 1976 over half the married women and nine out of ten female college graduates were employed outside the home, a development that one economist called "the single most outstanding phenomenon of this century." Most career women, however, did not regard themselves as feminists; they took jobs because they and their families needed the money to achieve higher levels of material comfort. Whatever the motives, traditional gender roles and childbearing practices were being changed to accommodate the two-career family and the sexual revolution.

THE SEXUAL REVOLUTION AND THE PILL   The feminist movement coincided with the so-called sexual revolution, a much-discussed loosening of traditional restrictions on social behavior. Young people opposed to the conflict in Vietnam chanted "Make Love, Not War." Other members of the counterculture promoted "free love" as an alternative to what they claimed was a repressive, materialistic capitalist society. Activists promoting more permissive sexual attitudes staged rallies, formed organizations, engaged in civil disobedience, filed suits against prevailing laws, and flouted social norms.

The publicity given to the sexual revolution exaggerated its scope and depth, but the movement did help generate two major cultural changes: society became more tolerant of premarital sex, and women became more sexually active. Between 1960 and 1975 the number of college women reporting having had sexual intercourse doubled, from 27 percent to 50 percent. What facilitated this change was a scientific breakthrough in contraception: the birth-control pill.

Approved by the Food and Drug Administration in 1960, the pill, as it came to be known, blocks ovulation by releasing synthetic hormones into a woman's body. Initially birth-control pills were available only to married

Birth Control

In an effort to spread the word about birth-control options, Planned Parenthood in 1967 displayed posters like this one in New York City buses.

couples, but that restriction soon ended. Widespread access to the pill gave women a greater sense of sexual freedom than any previous contraceptive device. It also contributed to a rise in sexually transmitted diseases. Yet many women viewed the birth-control pill as a godsend. "When the pill came out, it was a savior," recalled Eleanor Smeal, president of the Feminist Majority Foundation. "The whole country was waiting for it. I can't even describe to you how excited people were."

The pill quickly became the most popular birth-control method. In 1960 the U.S. birth rate was 3.6 children per woman. By 1970 it had plummeted to 2.5 children, and since 1980 it has remained slightly below 2. Eight out of ten women have taken birth-control pills at some time in their lives. Clare Boothe Luce, the congresswoman, ambassador, journalist, and playwright, viewed the advent of the pill as a key element in the broader women's movement: "Modern woman is at last free as a man is free, to dispose of her own body, to earn her living, to pursue the improvement of her mind, to try a successful career."

HISPANIC RIGHTS   The activism that animated the student revolt, the civil rights movement, and the crusade for women's rights soon spread to various ethnic minority groups. *Hispanic,* a term used in the United States to refer to people who are from, or trace their ancestry to, Spanish-speaking Latin America or Spain, came into increasing use after 1945 in conjuction with growing efforts to promote economic and social justice for such people. (Although frequently used as a synonym for Hispanic, the term *Latino* technically refers only to people of Latin American descent.) The labor shortages during World War II had led defense industries to offer Hispanic Americans their first significant access to skilled-labor jobs. And as was the case with African Americans, service in the military during the war years helped to heighten an American identity among Hispanic Americans and excite their desire for equal rights and opportunities.

But equality was elusive. After World War II, Hispanic Americans still faced widespread discrimination in hiring, housing, and education. Poverty was widespread. In 1960, for example, the median income of a Mexican-American family was only 62 percent of the median income of a family in the general population. Hispanic-American activists during the 1950s and 1960s mirrored the efforts of black civil rights leaders. They, too, denounced segregation, promoted efforts to improve the quality of public education, and struggled to increase Hispanic-American political influence and economic opportunities.

One of the most popular initiatives was the use of the term *Chicano* as an inclusive label for all Mexican immigrants, Spanish Americans in New Mexico as well as old Californios (descendants of the inhabitants of California before it was seized by the United States, most of whom were Indians or of mixed ancestry) and Tejanos (descendants of the inhabitants of Texas before it became independent). The word *Chicano* was originally Mexican slang for a clumsy person. Over the years, Anglo Americans had fastened upon the term as a pejorative reference. Now *Chicano* took on a positive connotation. In southern California, students formed Young Chicanos for Community Action, a social-service group designed to promote greater self-reliance and local involvement within Chicano neighborhoods. Wearing brown berets, the members protested the disproportionate number of Hispanics being killed in the Vietnam War and demanded improvements in their neighborhood schools.

Unlike their African-American counterparts, however, Chicano leaders faced an awkward dilemma: what should they do about the continuing stream of undocumented Mexicans flowing across the border? Many Mexican Americans argued that their hopes for economic advancement and social equality were put at risk by the daily influx of undocumented Mexican laborers willing to accept low-paying jobs. Mexican-American leaders thus helped end the bracero program in 1964 (which trucked in contract day laborers from Mexico at harvest time) and formed the United Farm Workers (UFW, originally the National Farm Workers Association) in 1962 to represent Mexican-American migrant workers.

The founder of the UFW was Cesar Chavez. Born in Yuma, Arizona, in 1927 to Mexican immigrant parents, Chavez moved with his family to California in 1939. There they joined thousands of other migrant farmworkers traversing the state, moving from job to job, living in tents, cars, or ramshackle cabins. In 1944, at age seventeen, Chavez joined the navy. After the war he married and found work, first as a sharecropper raising strawberries and then as a migrant laborer in apricot orchards. In 1952 Chavez joined the Community Service Organization (CSO), a social-service group that sought to educate and organize the migrant poor so that they could become self-reliant. He founded new CSO chapters and was named general director in 1958.

Chavez left the organization in 1962 when it refused to back his proposal to establish a union for farmworkers. Other CSO leaders believed that it was impossible to organize migrant workers into an effective union. They thought migrants were too mobile, too poor, too illiterate, too ethnically diverse, and too easily replaced by braceros. Moreover, farmworkers did not enjoy protected status under the National Labor Relations Act of 1935 (the Wagner Act). Unlike industrial laborers they were not guaranteed the right to organize or the right to receive a minimum wage. Nor did federal regulations govern the safety of their workplace.

Despite such obstacles, Chavez resolved to organize the migrant farmworkers. His fledgling National Farm Workers Association gained national attention in 1965 when it joined a strike by Filipino farmworkers against the corporate grape farmers in

United Farm Workers

Cesar Chavez (center) with organizers of the grape boycott. In 1968 Chavez ended a three-week fast by taking communion and breaking bread with Senator Robert Kennedy.

California's San Joaquin Valley. Chavez's charisma and Catholic piety, his insistence upon nonviolent tactics and his reliance upon college-student volunteers, his skillful alliance with organized labor and religious groups—all combined to attract media interest and popular support. Soon the UFW began organizing migrant workers in the fields of the Salinas Valley.

Still, the grape strike itself brought no tangible gains. So Chavez organized a nationwide consumer boycott of grapes. Two years later, in 1970, the grape strike and consumer boycott brought twenty-six grape growers to the bargaining table. They signed formal contracts recognizing the UFW, and soon migrant workers throughout the West were benefiting from Chavez's strenuous efforts on their behalf. Wages increased, and working conditions improved. In 1975 the California state legislature passed a bill that required growers to bargain collectively with the elected representatives of the farmworkers.

The chief strength of the Hispanic movement lay less in the duplication of civil rights strategies than in the rapid growth of the Hispanic population. In 1960 Hispanics in the United States numbered slightly more than 3 million; by 1970 they had increased to 9 million, and by 2006 they numbered over 40 million, making them the country's largest minority. By 1980 aspiring presidential candidates were openly courting the Hispanic vote, promising support for urban-renewal projects in New York and amnesty programs for illegal immigrants in Texas and delivering rousing anti-Castro speeches in Miami. The voting power of Hispanics and their concentration in states with key electoral votes has helped give the Hispanic point of view significant political clout.

NATIVE AMERICANS   American Indians—many of whom had begun calling themselves Native Americans—also emerged as a political force in the late 1960s. Two conditions combined to make Indian rights a priority: first, whites felt a persistent sense of guilt for the destructive policies of their ancestors toward a people who had, after all, been here first; second, the plight of the Native American minority was more desperate than that of any other group in the country. Indian unemployment was 10 times the national rate, life expectancy was 20 years lower than the national average, and the suicide rate was a whopping 100 times higher than the rate for whites.

Although President Lyndon Johnson recognized the poverty of the Native Americans and attempted to funnel federal anti-poverty-program funds into reservations, militants within the Indian community became impatient with the pace of change. They organized protests and demonstrations against local,

Wounded Knee

Instigating a standoff with the FBI, members of AIM and local Oglala Sioux occupied the town of Wounded Knee, South Dakota, in March 1973 in an effort to focus attention on poverty and rampant alcoholism among Indians on reservations.

state, and federal agencies. In 1963 two Chippewas (or Ojibwas) living in Minneapolis, George Mitchell and Dennis Banks, founded the American Indian Movement (AIM) to promote "red power." The leaders of AIM occupied Alcatraz Island in San Francisco Bay in 1969, claiming the site "by right of discovery." And in 1972 a sit-in at the Department of the Interior's Bureau of Indian Affairs (BIA) in Washington attracted national attention to their cause. The BIA, then and since, has been widely viewed as the worst-managed federal agency. Instead of finding creative ways to promote tribal autonomy and economic self-sufficiency, the BIA has served as a classic example of government inefficiency and paternalism gone awry.

In 1973 AIM led 200 Sioux in occupying the tiny village of Wounded Knee, South Dakota, where the Seventh Cavalry had massacred a Sioux village in 1890. Outraged by the light sentences given a group of local whites who had killed a Sioux in 1972, the organizers also sought to draw attention to the plight of the Indians living on the reservation there. Half of the families were dependent upon government welfare checks, alcoholism was rampant, and over 80 percent of the children had dropped out of school.

After the militants took eleven hostages, federal marshals and FBI agents surrounded the encampment. For ten weeks the two sides engaged in a tense standoff. When AIM leaders tried to bring in food and supplies, a shoot-out resulted, with one Indian killed and another wounded. Soon thereafter the tense confrontation ended with a government promise to re-examine Indian treaty rights.

Indian protesters subsequently discovered a more effective tactic than di-rect action and sit-ins: they went into federal courts armed with copies of old treaties and demanded that these become the basis for restitution. In Alaska, Maine, South Carolina, and Massachusetts they won significant set-tlements that provided legal recognition of their tribal rights and financial compensation at levels that upgraded the standard of living on several reservations.

GAY RIGHTS   The liberationist impulses of the 1960s also encouraged homosexuals to organize and assert their right to equal treatment. On June 27, 1969, New York City police raided the Stonewall Inn, a male gay bar in Greenwich Village. The patrons fought back, and the struggle spilled into the streets. Hundreds of other gays and their supporters joined the fracas against the police. Rioting lasted throughout the weekend. When it ended, homo-sexuals had forged a new sense of solidarity and a new organization, the Gay Liberation Front. "Gay is good for all of us," proclaimed one of its mem-bers. "The artificial categories 'heterosexual' and 'homosexual' have been laid on us by a sexist society."

As news of the Stonewall riots spread across the country, the gay rights movement assumed national proportions. One of its main tactics was to encourage people to "come out," to make public their homosexuality. This was by no means an easy decision, for professing gays faced social os-tracism, physical assault, exclusion from the military and civil service, and discrimination in the workplace. Yet despite the risks, thousands of homo-sexuals did come out. By 1973 almost 800 gay and lesbian organizations had been formed across the country, and every major city had a visible gay com-munity and cultural life.

As was the case with the civil rights crusade and the women's movement, however, the campaign for gay rights soon suffered from internal divisions and a conservative backlash. Gay activists engaged in fractious disputes over tactics and objectives, and conservative moralists and Christian fundamen-talists launched a nationwide counterattack. By the end of the 1970s, the gay movement had lost its initial momentum and was struggling to salvage many of its hard-won gains.

NIXON AND VIETNAM

The numerous liberation movements of the 1960s fundamentally changed the tone and texture of social life. By the early 1970s, however, the pendulum of national mood was swinging back. The election of Richard Nixon and Spiro Agnew in 1968 and the rise of George Wallace as a serious political force reflected the emergence of the "silent majority"—those predominantly white working-class and middle-class citizens who were determined to regain control of a society they feared was awash in permissiveness, anarchy, and tyranny by the minority. Many among the "silent majority" also believed that Lyndon Johnson's Great Society programs were ineffective and inefficient. Such attitudes were highlighted in one of the period's most popular television shows, *All in the Family,* whose central character, Archie Bunker, was a reactionary lower-middle-class husband and father outraged by the permissiveness of modern society and the radicalism of young people. Large as the gap was between the "silent majority" and the forces of dissent, both sides agreed that the Vietnam War remained the dominant event of the time. Until the war was ended and all troops had returned home, the nation would find it difficult to achieve the equilibrium that the new president had promised.

GRADUAL WITHDRAWAL Looking back on the Vietnam War, former secretary of state and national security adviser Henry Kissinger called it a "nightmare": "We should have never been there at all." But when Richard Nixon was inaugurated as president in January 1969, he inherited the nightmare; there were 530,000 U.S. troops in Vietnam. Nixon believed that "there's no way to win the war. But we can't say that of course" because the United States needed to "keep some bargaining leverage" at the negotiating table. During the 1968 presidential campaign, he had claimed to have a secret plan that would bring "peace with honor" in Vietnam. He insisted that the United States could not simply "cut and run," leaving the 17 million South Vietnamese to a cruel fate under Communist tyranny. Yet he assured an aide that "I'm not going to end up like LBJ, holed up in the White House afraid to show my face on the street. I'm going to stop that war. Fast."

Peace, however, was long in coming and not very honorable. Nixon and Kissinger overestimated the ability of the Soviets to expert pressure on the North Vietnamese to sign a negotiated settlement, just as they misread their own ability to manipulate the South Vietnamese government. By the time a settlement was finally reached in 1973, another 20,000 Americans had died, the morale of the U.S. military had been shattered, millions of

The Trauma of Vietnam

Even as the Nixon administration began a phased withdrawal of U.S. troops from Vietnam, the war took a heavy toll on Vietnamese and Americans alike.

Asians had been killed or wounded, and fighting continued in Southeast Asia. In the end, Nixon's policy gained nothing he could not have accomplished in 1969.

The new Vietnam policy of the Nixon administration moved along three separate fronts. First, U.S. negotiators in Paris demanded the withdrawal of Communist forces from South Vietnam and the preservation of the U.S.-backed regime of President Nguyen Van Thieu. The North Vietnamese and Viet Cong negotiators insisted on the retention of a Communist military presence in the south and the reunification of the Vietnamese people under a government dominated by the Communists. There was no common ground on which to come together. Hidden from public awareness and from America's South Vietnamese allies were secret meetings between Henry Kissinger, Nixon's national security adviser, and the North Vietnamese.

Second, Nixon tried to quell domestic unrest over the war. He labeled the anti-war movement a "brotherhood of the misguided, the mistaken, the well-meaning, and the malevolent." But he could not ignore the growing opposition to the war. Instead, he resolved to defuse it by reducing the number of U.S. troops in Vietnam, justifying the reduction as the natural result of "Vietnamization"—the equipping and training of the South Vietnamese to assume the burden of ground combat in place of Americans. From a peak of 560,000 in 1969, American combat troops were withdrawn at a steady pace that matched almost precisely the pace of the buildup from 1965 to 1969. By 1973 only 50,000 troops remained in Vietnam. In 1969 Nixon also established a draft lottery system that eliminated many inequities and clarified the likelihood of being drafted—only nineteen-year-olds with low lottery numbers would have to go—and in 1973 the president did away with the draft altogether by creating an all-volunteer military. Nixon was more successful in achieving the goal of reducing anti-war activity than in forcing concessions from the North Vietnamese in Paris.

Third, while reducing the number of U.S. combat troops, Nixon and Henry Kissinger expanded the air war over Vietnam in an effort to persuade the enemy to come to terms. Heavy bombing of North Vietnam was part of what Nixon called his "madman theory." He wanted the North Vietnamese leaders to believe that he "might do *anything* to stop the war." In March 1969 the United States began a fourteen-month-long bombing campaign aimed at Communist forces in Cambodia. Congress did not learn of these secret raids until 1970, although the total tonnage of bombs dropped was four times that dropped on Japan during World War II. But Hanoi's leaders did not flinch. Then, on April 30, 1970, Nixon announced what he called an "incursion" into "neutral" Cambodia by U.S. troops to "clean out" North Vietnamese military staging areas. The head of Cambodia's government for two decades, Prince Norodom Sihanouk, had previously objected to raids into his country, but a coup by General Lon Nol had replaced Sihanouk earlier in the spring, clearing the way for the American invasion. Nixon knew that sending troops into Cambodia would ignite ferocious criticism. Secretary of State William Rogers predicted that "this will make the [anti-war] students puke." Nixon told his national security adviser, Henry Kissinger, who strongly endorsed the decision to extend the fighting into Cambodia, "If this doesn't work, it'll be your ass, Henry."

DIVISIONS AT HOME   Nixon's slow withdrawal from Vietnam had a devastating effect on the military's morale and reputation. "No one wants to be the last grunt to die in this lousy war," said one soldier. Between 1969 and 1971 there were 730 reported fragging incidents, efforts by troops to kill or injure their own officers, usually with fragmentation grenades. Drug abuse became a major problem in the armed forces. In 1971 four times as many troops were hospitalized for drug abuse as for combat-related wounds.

Back on the home front, revelations of previously suppressed reports of atrocities in Vietnam caused even the staunchest supporters of the war to wince. Late in 1969 the story of the My Lai Massacre broke in the press, plunging the country into two years of exposure to the gruesome tale of Lieutenant William Calley, who ordered the murder of 347 civilians in the village of My Lai in 1968. Twenty-five army officers were charged with complicity in the massacre and subsequent cover-up, but only Calley was convicted; Nixon later granted him parole.

The loudest public outcry against Nixon's Indochina policy occurred in the wake of the Cambodian "incursion." In the spring of 1970, campuses across the country exploded in what the president of Columbia University called "the most disastrous month of May in the history of American higher education."

Kent State University

National guardsmen shot and killed four bystanders during antiwar demonstrations on the campus of Kent State University in Ohio.

Large, angry student protests led to the closing of hundreds of colleges and universities. At Kent State University, the Ohio National Guard was called in to quell rioting in which the campus' ROTC building was burned down by anti-war protesters. The poorly trained guardsmen panicked and opened fire on the rock-throwing demonstrators, killing four student bystanders. Nixon was visibly shaken by what one aide called the "absolute public hysteria" unleashed by the Cambodian invasion. Although an official investigation of the Kent State episode condemned the "casual and indiscriminate shooting," polls indicated that the public supported the National Guard; students had "got what they were asking for." Eleven days after the Kent State tragedy, on May 15, Mississippi highway patrolmen riddled a dormitory at Jackson State College with bullets, killing two students. In New York City, anti-war demonstrators who gathered to protest the deaths at Kent State and the invasion of Cambodia were attacked by "hard-hat" construction workers, who forced the protesters to disperse and then marched on City Hall to raise the flag, which had been lowered to half staff in mourning for the Kent State victims.

The following year in June, the *New York Times* began publishing excerpts from *The History of the U.S. Decision Making Process in Vietnam,* a secret Defense Department study commissioned by Robert McNamara before his resignation as secretary of defense in 1968. The so-called Pentagon Papers, leaked to the press by a former Defense Department official, Daniel Ellsberg, confirmed what many critics of the war had long suspected: Congress and the public had not received the full story on the Gulf of Tonkin incident of 1964, and contingency plans for American entry into the war were being drawn up while President Johnson was promising that combat troops would never be sent to Vietnam. Moreover, there was no plan for bringing the war to an end so long as the North Vietnamese persisted. Although the Pentagon Papers dealt with events only up to 1965, the Nixon administration attempted to block their publication, arguing that they endangered national security and that their publication would prolong the war. By a vote of six to three, the Supreme Court ruled against the government. Newspapers throughout the country began publication of the controversial documents the next day.

WAR WITHOUT END The mounting social divisions at home and the approach of the 1972 presidential election combined to produce a shift in the American negotiations in Paris with representatives of North Vietnam. In the summer of 1972, Henry Kissinger again began meeting privately with Le Duc Tho, the North Vietnamese negotiator, and he now dropped his insistence upon the removal of all North Vietnamese troops from the south before the withdrawal of the remaining U.S. troops. On October 26, only a week before the American presidential election, Kissinger announced, "Peace is at hand." But this was a cynical ploy to win votes. Several days earlier the Thieu regime in South Vietnam had rejected the Kissinger plan for a cease-fire, fearful that the presence of North Vietnamese troops in the south virtually guaranteed an eventual Communist victory. The Paris peace talks broke off on December 16, and two days later the re-elected Nixon ordered massive bombing of Hanoi and Haiphong, the two largest cities in North Vietnam. These so-called Christmas bombings and the simultaneous mining of North Vietnamese harbors aroused worldwide protest.

But the bombings also made the North Vietnamese more flexible at the negotiating table. The "Christmas bombings" stopped on December 29, and the talks in Paris soon resumed. On January 27, 1973, the United States, North and South Vietnam, and the Viet Cong signed an "agreement on ending the war and restoring peace in Vietnam." While Nixon and Kissinger claimed that the bombing had brought North Vietnam to its senses, in truth the North Vietnamese never altered their basic stance; they kept 150,000 troops in the south and remained committed to the reunification of Vietnam under one government. What had changed since the previous fall was the willingness of the South Vietnamese, who were never allowed to participate in the negotiations, to accept these terms, albeit reluctantly, on the basis of Nixon's promise that the United States would respond "with full force" to any Communist violation of the agreement. Kissinger had little confidence that the treaty provisions would enable South Vietnam to survive on its own. He told a White House staffer, "If they're lucky, they can hold out for a year and a half."

On March 29, 1973, the last U.S. combat troops left Vietnam. On that same day 87 American prisoners of war, most of them downed pilots, were released from Hanoi. Within a period of months, however, the cease-fire in Vietnam collapsed, the war between north and south resumed, and the Communist forces gained the upper hand. In Cambodia (renamed the Khmer Republic after it fell to the Communists and now called Cambodia or Kampuchea) and Laos, where fighting had been more sporadic, Communist

Withdrawal from Saigon

Soldiers block people from climbing over the walls of the U.S. embassy in Saigon, South Vietnam, in 1975. They were seeking to flee before the Communist forces seized the city.

victory also seemed inevitable. In 1975 the North Vietnamese launched a full-scale armored invasion against the south, and South Vietnamese president Thieu appealed to Washington for the promised U.S. assistance. Congress refused. The much-mentioned "peace with honor" had proved to be, in the words of one CIA official, only a "decent interval"—enough time for the United States to extricate itself from Vietnam before the collapse of the South Vietnamese government. On April 30, 1975, Americans watched on television as North Vietnamese tanks rolled into Saigon, soon to be renamed Ho Chi Minh City, and helicopters lifted the officials in the U.S. embassy to ships waiting offshore. In those last desperate moments, terrified South Vietnamese fought to get on board the departing helicopters, for they knew that the Communists would be merciless victors.

The longest war in American history was finally over, leaving in its wake a bitter legacy. During the period of U.S. involvement in the fighting, almost 2 million combatants and civilians were killed on both sides. North Vietnam absorbed incredible losses—some 600,000 soldiers and countless civilians killed. More than 58,000 Americans died in Vietnam, 300,000 were wounded, 2,500 were declared missing, almost 100,000 returned missing one or more limbs, and over 150,000 combat veterans suffered drug or alcohol addiction or severe psychological disorders. Most of the Vietnam veterans readjusted well to civilian life, but even they carried for years the stigma of a lost war.

The "loss" of the war and revelations of American atrocities such as those at My Lai eroded respect for the military so thoroughly that many young people came to regard military service as corrupting and ignoble. The Vietnam War, initially described as a noble crusade on behalf of democratic ideals, instead suggested that democracy was not easily transferable to third world regions that lacked any historical experience with representative government. Fought to show the world that the United States would be steadfast in containing the spread of communism, instead the war sapped the national will and fragmented the national consensus that had governed foreign affairs since 1947. It also changed the balance of power in domestic politics. Not only did the war undermine Lyndon Johnson's presidency; it also created enduring fissures in the Democratic party. Said anti-war senator and 1972 Democratic presidential candidate George McGovern, "The Vietnam tragedy is at the root of the confusion and division of the Democratic party. It tore up our souls."

Little wonder that most people at war's end wanted to put Vietnam behind them and forget. Although subsequent debates over foreign policy in the Middle East, Africa, and Latin America frequently referred to "the lessons of Vietnam," the phrase was used by different factions for diametrically opposed purposes, ranging from refusal to commit any American troops and re-sources in El Salvador and Nicaragua to an insistence on massive military commitments unfettered by any presidential restrictions that might preclude outright victory. "In the end, then," one journalist wrote concerning the Vietnam era, "there was no end at all."

NIXON AND MIDDLE AMERICA

Richard Nixon had been elected in 1968 as the representative of Mid-dle America, those middle-class citizens fed up with the liberal politics and cultural radicalism of the 1960s. Nixon selected men for his cabinet and White House staff who would restore conservative values and carry out his orders with blind obedience. John Mitchell, the gruff attorney general who had been a senior partner in Nixon's New York law firm, was the new presi-dent's closest confidant. H. R. "Bob" Haldeman, an imperious former adver-tising executive, served as Nixon's chief of staff. As Haldeman explained, "Every President needs a son of a bitch, and I'm Nixon's. I'm his buffer, I'm his bastard." He was succeeded in 1973 by General Alexander Haig, whom Nixon described as "the meanest, toughest, most ambitious son of a bitch I ever knew." John Ehrlichman, a Seattle attorney and college schoolmate of Haldeman's, served as chief domestic-policy adviser. As secretary of state, Nixon tapped his old friend William Rogers, who had served as attorney general under Eisenhower. Rogers's control over foreign policy was quickly preempted by Henry Kissinger, a distinguished Harvard political scientist who served as national security adviser before becoming secretary of state in 1973. Kissinger came to dominate the Nixon administration's diplo-matic planning and emerged as one of the most respected and internation-ally famous members of the staff. Nixon often had to mediate the tensions between Rogers and Kissinger, noting that the secretary of state considered the German-born Kissinger "Machiavellian, deceitful, egotistical, arrogant, and insulting," while Kissinger viewed Rogers as "vain, emotional, unable to keep a secret, and hopelessly dominated by the State Department bureaucracy."

DOMESTIC AFFAIRS A major reason for Richard Nixon's election in 1968 was the effective "southern strategy" fashioned by his campaign staffers. To garner support among Republican delegates from the South and then to win over southern voters in the election, Nixon had assured southern conservatives that he would slow federal enforcement of civil rights laws and appoint pro-southern justices to the Supreme Court. Once in office, Nixon strove to follow through on his pledges. He appointed no African Americans to his cabinet and refused to meet with the Congressional Black Caucus. In 1970 he launched a concerted effort to block congressional renewal of the Voting Rights Act of 1965 and to delay implementation of court orders requiring the desegregation of school districts in Mississippi. Sixty-five lawyers in the Justice Department signed a letter of protest against the administration's stance. The Democratic Congress then extended the Voting Rights Act over Nixon's veto. The Supreme Court, in the first decision made under the new chief justice, Warren Burger—a Nixon appointee—mandated the integration of the Mississippi public schools. In *Alexander v. Holmes County Board of Education* (1969), a unanimous Court ordered a quick end to segregation. During Nixon's first term and despite his wishes, more schools were desegregated than in all the Kennedy-Johnson years combined.

Nixon's attempts to block desegregation efforts in urban areas also failed. The Burger Court ruled unanimously in *Swann v. Charlotte-Mecklenburg Board of Education* (1971) that school systems must bus students out of their neighborhoods if necessary to achieve racial integration. Protest over desegregation now began to erupt more in the North, the Mid west, and the Southwest than in the South, as white families in Boston, Denver, and other cities denounced the destruction of "the neighborhood school" and angry parents in Pontiac, Michigan, firebombed school buses.

Nixon asked Congress to impose a moratorium on all busing orders by the federal courts. The House of Representatives, equally attuned to voter outrage at busing to achieve racial integration, went along. But a Senate filibuster blocked the president's anti-busing bill. Busing opponents won a limited victory when the Supreme Court ruled, in *Milliken v. Bradley* (1974), that desegregation plans in Detroit requiring the transfer of students

The End of Segregation

Demonstrators at the Boston Statehouse protest forced integration of the school system, May 1973.

from the inner city to the suburbs were unconstitutional. This landmark case, along with the *Regents of the University of California v. Bakke* (1978) decision, which restricted the use of quotas to achieve racial balance, marked the transition of desegregation from an issue of simple justice to a more tangled thicket of conflicting group and individual rights.

President Nixon invented several names for his domestic program. At one point it was called the New Federalism and promised to "start resources and power flowing back from Washington to the states and to the people." To that end, in 1972 he pushed through Congress a five-year revenue-sharing plan that would distribute $30 billion of federal revenues to the states for use as they saw fit. At another point, Nixon called for a New American Revolution to revive traditional values. These catchphrases never caught on as the New Frontier or the Great Society had, most likely because Nixon's domestic program was a hodgepodge of reactionary and progressive initiatives. His speechwriter William Safire explained that although Nixon's "heart was on the right, his head was, with FDR, slightly left of center." Nixon was a shrewd—and often devious—pragmatist who juggled opposing positions in an effort to maintain public support. He was, said the journalist Tom Wicker, "at once liberal and conservative, generous and begrudging, cynical and idealistic, choleric and calm, resentful and forgiving." Nixon also had to deal with a stern fact: the Democrats controlled both houses of Congress during his first term.

The Democratic Congress moved forward with new legislation: the right of eighteen-year-olds to vote in national elections (1970), and in all elections under the Twenty-sixth Amendment (1971); increases in Social Security benefits indexed to the inflation rate and a rise in food-stamp funding; the Occupational Safety and Health Act (1970); the Clean Air Act (1970); new bills to control water pollution (1970 and 1972); and the Federal Election Campaign Act (1972), which modified the rules of campaign finance. These measures accounted for a more rapid rise in spending on social programs than President Lyndon Johnson's Great Society programs had.

ECONOMIC MALAISE The major domestic development during the Nixon years was a floundering economy. Overheated by the expense of the Vietnam War, the annual inflation rate began to rise in 1967, when it was 3 percent. By 1973 it was at 9 percent; a year later it was at 12 percent, and it remained in double digits for most of the 1970s. The Dow Jones average of major industrial stocks fell by 36 percent between 1968 and 1970, its steepest decline in more than thirty years. Meanwhile unemployment, at a low of 3.3 percent when Nixon took office, climbed to 6 percent by the end of 1970 and threatened to keep rising. Somehow the economy was undergoing a recession and an inflation at the same time. Economists coined the term *stagflation* to describe the syndrome that defied the orthodox laws of economics.

The economic malaise had at least three deep-rooted causes. First, the Johnson administration had attempted to pay for both the Great Society social-welfare programs and the war in Vietnam without a major tax increase, thereby generating larger federal deficits, a major expansion of the money supply, and price inflation. Second and more important, by the late 1960s U.S. goods faced stiff competition in international markets from West Germany, Japan, and other emerging industrial powers. American technological and economic superiority was no longer unchallenged. Third, the economy had depended heavily upon cheap sources of energy; no other nation was more dependent upon the automobile and the automobile industry, and no other nation was more careless in its use of fossil fuels in factories and homes.

Just as domestic petroleum reserves began to dwindle and dependence upon foreign sources increased, the Organization of Petroleum Exporting Countries (OPEC) resolved to use its huge oil supplies as a political and economic weapon. In 1973, after the United States sent massive aid to Israel after a devastating Syrian-Egyptian attack on Yom Kippur, the holiest day on the Jewish calendar, OPEC announced that it would not sell oil to nations supporting Israel and that it was raising its prices by 400 percent. Motorists thereafter faced long lines at gas stations, and factories cut production.

Another condition leading to stagflation was the flood of new workers—mainly baby boomers and women—entering the labor market. From 1965 to 1980, the workforce grew by 40 percent, almost 30 million workers, a number greater than the total labor force of France or West Germany. The number of new jobs could not keep up, leaving many unemployed. At the same time, worker productivity declined, further increasing inflation in the face of rising demand.

Stagflation posed a new set of economic problems, but Nixon responded erratically and ineffectively, trying old remedies for a new problem. First he tried to reduce the federal deficit by raising taxes and cutting the budget. When the Democratic Congress refused to cooperate with that approach, he encouraged the Federal Reserve Board to reduce the money supply by raising interest rates. The stock market immediately collapsed, and the economy plunged into the "Nixon recession."

A sense of desperation seized the White House. In 1969, when asked about government restrictions on wages and prices, Nixon had been unequivocal: "Controls. Oh, my God, no! . . . We'll never go to controls." But in 1971 he reversed himself. He froze all wages and prices for ninety days and announced that the United States would no longer convert dollars into gold for foreign banks. The dollar, its link to gold severed, now drifted lower on world currency exchanges. After ninety days, Nixon established mandatory guidelines for subsequent wage and price increases under the supervision of a federal agency. Still the economy floundered. By 1973 the wage and price guidelines were made voluntary, and therefore almost entirely ineffective.

ENVIRONMENTAL PROTECTION   The widespread recognition that America faced limits to economic growth fueled broad support for environmental protection in the early 1970s. The realization that cities and industrial development were damaging the environment and altering the earth's ecology was not new: Rachel Carson's pathbreaking book *Silent Spring* (1962) had sounded the warning years earlier. But in Nixon's first term the Democratic-controlled Congress took concerted action, passing several acts to protect and clean up the environment. Bowing to pressure from both parties, Nixon told an aide to "keep me out of trouble on environmental issues." Ever the pragmatic politician, the president recognized that the public mood was shifting toward greater environmental protections. So he reluctantly signed the Endangered Species Act in late 1969 and the National Environmental Policy Act in early 1970. The latter legislation created a Council on Environmental Quality in the White House that reported annually to Congress and required environmental-impact studies prior to any federal construction project. In 1970 Nixon signed legislation creating a federal Environmental Protection Agency and a National Oceanic and Atmospheric Administration.

The OPEC oil boycott and price increase led to an energy crisis in the United States. People began to realize that natural resources were not infinitely expendable. "Although it's positively un-American to think so," said one sociologist, "the environmental movement and energy shortage have forced us all to accept a sense of our limits, to lower our expectations, to seek prosperity through conservation rather than growth."

Environmental Awareness

An Earth Day demonstration dramatizing the dangers of air pollution, April 1972.

As stagflation persisted into the middle and late 1970s, corporate criticism that environmental regulations were cutting into jobs and profit margins began to sound more persuasive, especially when the staggering cost of cleaning up accumulated toxic wastes became known. "Why worry about the long run," said one unemployed steelworker in 1976, "when you're out of work right now." Polls showed that protection of the environment remained a high priority among a majority of Americans but few were willing to suffer a cutback in their standard of living to achieve that goal. People still lived for the moment. "It was," bemoaned one journalist, "as if passengers knew they were boarding the *Titanic,* but preferred to jostle with one another for first class accommodations so they might enjoy as much of the voyage as possible."

NIXON TRIUMPHANT

Richard Nixon was the first president since Eisenhower in 1957 to confront a Congress in which both houses were under the control of the opposition party. It followed that he focused his energies on foreign policy, where presidential initiatives were less encumbered, and thus he, in tandem with Henry Kissinger, achieved several major breakthroughs. He also continued to support the Apollo space program to beat the Soviets to the moon. In July 1969 astronaut Neil Armstrong became the first person to walk on the moon.

Race to the Moon

In July 1969 a program begun by President Kennedy reached its goal: putting a man on the moon.

This extraordinary achievement buoyed American spirits at a time when troops were mired in Vietnam, cities were boiling over in racial unrest, and the economy was languishing. Similarly, Nixon's foreign-policy successes gave Americans some measure of confidence in their government. His administration managed to improve relations with the major powers of the Communist world—China and the Soviet Union—and to shift fundamentally the pattern of the cold war.

By 1969 Nixon had perceived that a new multipolar world order was emerging to replace the conventional cold war confrontation between the United States and the Soviet Union. Since 1945 the United States had lost its monopoly on nuclear weapons and its overwhelming economic dominance and geopolitical influence. The rapid rise of competing power centers in Europe, China, and Japan complicated international relations—China had replaced the United States as the Soviet Union's most threatening competitor—but also provided strategic opportunities, which Nixon and Kissinger seized.

In early 1970 Nixon announced a significant alteration in foreign policy. The United States could no longer be the world's policeman against communism; the long-standing containment policy developed by President Truman must be revised: "America cannot—and will not—conceive *all* the plans, design *all* the programs, execute *all* the decisions, and undertake *all* the defense of the free nations of the world." In explaining what became known as the Nixon Doctrine, the president declared that "our interests must shape our commitments, rather than the other way around." The United States, he and Kissinger stressed, must become more strategic and more realistic in its commitments, and it would begin to establish selected partnerships with Communist countries in areas of mutual interest.

CHINA   In 1971 Henry Kissinger made a secret trip to Peking to explore the possibility of U.S. recognition of Communist China. Since 1949, when Mao Tse-tung's revolutionary movement established control in China, the United States had refused to recognize Communist China, preferring to regard Chiang Kai-shek's exiled regime on Taiwan as the legitimate Chinese government. In one simple but stunning stroke, Nixon and Kissinger ended two decades of diplomatic isolation of the People's Republic of China. In 1972 Americans watched on television as Nixon visited famous Chinese landmarks and drank toasts with Premier Chou En-lai and Mao Tse-tung. The United States and China agreed to scientific and cultural exchanges, steps toward the resumption of trade, and the eventual reunification of Taiwan with the mainland. A year after the Nixon visit, "liaison offices" were established in Washington and Beijing that served as unofficial embassies, and in 1979 diplomatic recognition was formalized. Richard Nixon, the former anti-Communist crusader who had condemned the State Department for "losing" China in 1949, had accomplished a diplomatic feat that his Democratic predecessors could not.

DÉTENTE   In truth, China welcomed the breakthrough in relations with the United States because its festering rivalry with the Soviet Union, with which it shares a long border, had become more bitter than its rivalry with the West. The Soviet leaders, troubled by the Sino-American

The United States and China

With President Richard Nixon's visit to China in 1972, the United States formally recognized China's Communist government. Here Nixon and Chinese premier Chou En-lai drink a toast.

agreements, were also eager for an easing of tensions with the United States now that they had, as the result of a huge arms buildup following the Cuban missile crisis, achieved virtual parity with the United States in nuclear weapons. Once again President Nixon surprised the world, announcing that he would visit Moscow in 1972 for discussions with Leonid Brezhnev, the Soviet premier. The high theater of the China visit was repeated in Moscow, with toasts and elegant dinners attended by world leaders who had previously regarded each other as incarnations of evil.

What became known as détente with the Soviets offered the promise of a more orderly and restrained competition between the two superpowers. Nixon and Brezhnev signed agreements reached at the Strategic Arms Limitation Talks (SALT), which negotiators had been working on since 1969. The SALT agreement did not end the arms race, but it did limit both the number of ICBMs each nation could possess and the construction of antiballistic missile systems. In effect the Soviets were allowed to retain a greater number of missiles with greater destructive power while the United States retained a lead in the total number of warheads. No limitations were placed on new weapons systems, though each side agreed to work toward a permanent freeze on all nuclear weapons. The Moscow summit also produced new trade agreements, including an arrangement whereby the United States sold almost one quarter of its wheat crop to the Soviets at a favorable price. American farmers rejoiced, since the wheat deal assured them a high price for their crop, but domestic critics grumbled that the deal would raise food prices in the United States, serving mainly to rescue the Soviets from troublesome economic problems. The Moscow summit revealed the dramatic easing of tensions between the two cold war superpowers. For Nixon and Kissinger the agreements with China and the Soviet Union represented monumental changes in the global order.

SHUTTLE DIPLOMACY   The Nixon-Kissinger initiatives in the Middle East were less dramatic and less conclusive than the agreements with China and the Soviet Union, but they did show that America recognized Arab power in the region and its own dependence upon oil from Middle Eastern states, which were fundamentally opposed to the existence of Israel. In the Six-Day War of 1967, Israeli forces routed the armies of Egypt, Syria, and Jordan and seized territory from all three nations. Moreover, the number of Palestinian refugees, many of them homeless since the creation of Israel in 1948, increased after the 1967 Israeli victory. When Israel recovered from the initial shock of the surprise Yom Kippur War of 1973, Henry Kissinger negotiated a cease-fire and exerted pressure to prevent Israel from taking additional Arab territory. He also promoted closer ties with Egypt and its president, Anwar el-Sadat, and more restrained support for Israel. In an attempt to broker a lasting settlement, Kissinger made numerous flights among the capitals of the Middle East. This "shuttle diplomacy" won acclaim from all sides, but Kissinger failed to find a comprehensive formula for peace in the troubled region and ignored the Palestinian problem. He did, however, lay groundwork for the accord between Israel and Egypt in 1977.

THE ELECTION OF 1972   Nixon's foreign-policy achievements allowed him to stage the presidential campaign of 1972 as a triumphal procession. The main threat to his reelection came from Alabama's Democratic governor George Wallace, who had the potential as a third-party candidate to deprive the Republicans of conservative votes and thereby throw the election to the Democrats or the Democratic-controlled Congress. On May 15, 1972, however, Wallace was shot and left paralyzed below the waist by a man eager to achieve a grisly brand of notoriety. Wallace was forced to withdraw from the campaign.

Meanwhile, the Democrats were further ensuring Nixon's victory by nominating Senator George S. McGovern of South Dakota, a steadfast liberal who embodied anti-war principles and embraced progressive social-welfare policies. At the Democratic Convention in Miami Beach, McGovern benefited from party reforms that increased the representation of women, African Americans and other minorities. But those changes alienated party regulars. Mayor Richard Daley of Chicago was actually ousted from the convention, and the AFL-CIO refused to endorse the liberal Democratic candidate.

The 1972 campaign was an exercise in futility for McGovern, while Nixon made only a few formal political trips and cast himself in the role of "global peacekeeper." Nixon won the greatest victory of any Republican presidential candidate in history, capturing 520 electoral votes to only 17 for McGovern. The popular vote was equally decisive: 46 million to 28 million, a proportion of the total vote (60.8 percent) that was second only to Lyndon Johnson's victory over Bany Goldwater in 1964.

Nonetheless, Nixon's easy victory did not ensure an easy—or complete—second term. During the course of the presidential campaign, George McGovern had complained about the numerous "dirty tricks" orchestrated by members of the Nixon administration. On several occasions Nixon sought to coerce the Internal Revenue Service to investigate and intimidate his opponents. McGovern was especially disturbed by a curious incident on June 17, when five burglars were caught breaking into the Democratic campaign committee headquarters in the Watergate apartment complex in Washington, D.C. The burglars were former CIA agents, one of whom, James W. McCord, worked for the Nixon campaign. At the time, McGovern's Watergate accusations seemed shrill and biased, the lamentations of a candidate running far behind in the polls. Nixon and his staff ignored the news of the burglary. The president said that no one cares "when somebody bugs somebody else." Privately, however, he and his aides Bob Haldeman, John Dean, and John Ehrlichman began feverish efforts to cover up the Watergate break-in so as not to endanger his reelection campaign. The White House offered legal assistance to the burglars in an effort to buy their silence and tried to keep the FBI out of the investigation. Nixon and his closest aides also discussed using the CIA to derail the Justice Department investigation.

WATERGATE

During the trial of the accused Watergate burglars in January 1973, the relentless prodding of Judge John J. Sirica led one of the accused to tell the full story of the Nixon administration's complicity in the Watergate episode. James McCord, a former CIA agent and security chief of the Committee to

Re-elect the President (CREEP), was the first in a long line of informers in a melodrama that unfolded over the next two years. It ended in the first resignation of a president in American history, the conviction and imprisonment of twenty-five officials of the Nixon administration, including four cabinet members, and the most serious constitutional crisis since the impeachment trial of President Andrew Johnson.

UNCOVERING THE COVER-UP The trail of evidence pursued first by Judge Sirica, then by a grand jury, and then by a Senate investigation committee headed by Democratic Senator Samuel J. Ervin Jr. of North Carolina led directly to the White House. There was never any evidence that Nixon ordered the break-in or that he was aware of plans to burglarize the Democratic National Committee. From the start, however, Nixon was personally involved in the cover-up of the incident. He used his presidential powers to discredit and block the investigation. And most alarming, the Watergate burglary was merely one small part of a larger pattern of corruption and criminality sanctioned by the Nixon White House.

The White House had adopted illegal tactics in 1970 when the *New York Times* disclosed that the secret American bombings in Cambodia had been going on for years. In response, Nixon had ordered illegal telephone taps on several journalists and government employees suspected of leaking the story. The covert activity against the press and critics of Nixon's Vietnam policies increased in 1971, during the crisis generated by the publication of the Pentagon Papers, when a team of burglars under the direction of White House adviser John Ehrlichman had broken into Daniel Ellsberg's psychiatrist's office in an effort to obtain damaging information on Ellsberg, the man who had given the Pentagon Papers to the press. By the spring of 1972, Ehrlichman was in command of a team of "dirty tricksters" who performed various acts of sabotage against prospective Democratic candidates—for example, falsely accusing Senators Hubert Humphrey and Henry Jackson of sexual improprieties, forging press releases, setting off stink bombs at Democratic rallies, and associating the opposition candidates with racist remarks. By the time of the Watergate break-in, the money to finance these pranks was being illegally collected through CREEP and had been placed under the control of the White House staff.

The Watergate cover-up began to unravel as various people, including John Dean, legal counsel to the president, began to cooperate with prosecutors. It unraveled further in 1973 when L. Patrick Gray, acting director of the FBI, resigned after confessing that he had confiscated and destroyed several incriminating documents. On April 30 Ehrlichman and Haldeman resigned, together with Attorney General Richard Kleindienst. A few days later the president nervously assured the public in a television address, "I am not a crook." Then John Dean, whom Nixon had dismissed because of his cooperation with prosecutors, testified to the Ervin Committee that there had been a cover-up and Nixon had approved it. Nixon, meanwhile, refused to provide the Ervin committee with documents it requested, citing "executive privilege" to protect national security and the operations of the government. In another bombshell disclosure, a White House aide told the committee that Nixon had installed a taping system in the White House and that many of the conversations about the Watergate burglary and cover-up had been recorded.

A year-long legal battle for the "Nixon tapes" began. Harvard law professor Archibald Cox, whom Nixon's new attorney general, Elliot Richardson, had appointed as special prosecutor to investigate the Watergate case, took the president to court in October 1973 in order to obtain the tapes. Nixon refused to release the recordings and ordered Cox fired. In what became known as the Saturday Night Massacre, on October 20 Attorney General Elliot Richardson and Deputy Attorney General William Ruckelshaus resigned rather than execute the order. Solicitor General Robert Bork finally fired Cox. Nixon's firing of Cox produced a firestorm of public indignation. Numerous newspaper and magazine editorials, as well as a growing chorus of legislators, called for the president to be impeached for obstructing justice. A Gallup poll revealed that Nixon's approval rating had plunged to 17 percent, its lowest level ever. And the firing of Cox failed to end Nixon's legal troubles. Cox's replacement as special prosecutor, Leon Jaworski, also took the president to court. In March 1974 the Watergate grand jury indicted John Ehrlichman, H.R. Haldeman, and John Mitchell for obstruction of justice and named Nixon as an "unindicted co-conspirator." By the summer of 1974 Nixon was in full retreat, besieged on all fronts and unpredictably combative, melancholy, or petty, at times talking of resignation and on other occasions expressing determination to fight impeachment efforts. In December 1973 Senator Barry Goldwater reported that the president "jabbered incessantly, often incoherently." He seemed "to be cracking."

On July 24, 1974, the Supreme Court ruled unanimously, in *United States v. Richard M. Nixon*, that the president must surrender all of the tapes. A few days later the House Judiciary Committee voted to recommend three articles of impeachment: obstruction of justice through the payment of "hush money" to witnesses and the withholding of evidence, abuse of power through the use of federal agencies to deprive citizens of their constitutional rights, and defiance of Congress by withholding the tapes. But before the

Nixon's Resignation

Having resigned his office, Richard Nixon waves farewell outside the White House on August 9, 1974.

House of Representatives could meet to vote on impeachment, Nixon handed over the complete set of White House tapes. Investigators then learned that sections of certain recordings were missing, including eighteen minutes of a key conversation in June 1972 during which Nixon first mentioned the Watergate burglary. The president's loyal secretary tried to accept blame for the erasure, claiming she accidentally pushed the wrong button, but experts later concluded that the missing segments had been intentionally deleted. On August 9, 1974, fully aware that the evidence on the tapes implicated him in the cover-up, Richard Nixon resigned from office, the only president ever to do so. Nixon had begun his presidency hoping to heal America. He left the presidency having deeply wounded the nation. The credibility gap between the presidency and the public that had developed under Lyndon Johnson had become a chasm under Nixon.

THE EFFECTS OF WATERGATE   Vice President Spiro Agnew did not succeed Nixon because he had been forced to resign in October 1973 for having accepted bribes from contractors before and during his term as vice president. The vice president at the time of Nixon's resignation was Gerald Ford, the former Michigan congressman and House minority leader whom Nixon had appointed, with the approval of Congress, under the provisions of the Twenty-fifth Amendment. Ratified in 1967, the amendment provided for the appointment of a vice president when the office became vacant. President Ford initially insisted that he had no intention of pardoning Nixon, who was still liable for criminal prosecution. "I do not think the public would stand for it," he said. But a month after Nixon's resignation, on September 8, the new president did issue the pardon, explaining that it was necessary to end the national obsession with the Watergate scandals. Many Americans, however, were not in a forgiving mood. After the pardon was announced,

Ford's approval rating plummeted from 71 percent to 49 percent in one day, the steepest drop ever recorded. Even the president's press secretary resigned in protest. Ford was devastated by the "hostile reaction" to the pardon, and the new president never recovered the public's confidence. Many Americans suspected that Nixon and Ford had made a deal, though there was no evidence to confirm the speculation. President Ford testified personally to a congressional committee: "There was no deal, period."

If there was a silver lining in the dark cloud of Watergate, it was the vigor and resilience of the institutions that had brought a president down—the press, Congress, the courts, and an aroused public opinion. Congress responded to the Watergate revelations with several pieces of legislation designed to curb executive power. Already nervous about possible efforts to renew American military assistance to South Vietnam, the Democratic-led Congress passed the War Powers Act (1973), which requires a president to inform Congress within forty-eight hours if U.S. troops are deployed in combat abroad and to withdraw troops after sixty days unless Congress specifically approves their stay. In an effort to correct abuses of campaign funds, Congress enacted legislation in 1974 that set new ceilings on political contributions and expenditures. And in reaction to the Nixon claim of "executive privilege" as a means of withholding evidence, Congress strengthened the 1966 Freedom of Information Act to require prompt responses to requests for information from government files and to place on government agencies the burden of proof for classifying information as secret.

With Nixon's resignation, the nation had weathered a profound constitutional crisis, but the aftershock of the Watergate episode produced a deep sense of disillusionment with the so-called imperial presidency. Apart from Nixon's illegal actions, the vulgar language used in the White House and made public on the tapes stripped away the veils of mystery surrounding national leaders and left even the die-hard defenders of presidential authority shocked at the crudity and duplicity of Nixon and his subordinates. Coming on the heels of the erosion of public confidence generated by the Vietnam War, the Watergate affair renewed public cynicism toward a government that had systematically lied to the people and violated their civil liberties.

AN UNELECTED PRESIDENT

During Richard Nixon's last year in office, the Watergate crisis so dominated the Washington scene that major domestic and foreign problems received little executive attention. The perplexing combination of inflation and recession worsened, as did the oil crisis. At the same time, Henry Kissinger, who assumed control over the management of foreign policy, watched helplessly as the South Vietnamese forces began to crumble before North Vietnamese attacks, attempted with limited success to establish a framework for peace in the Middle East, and supported a CIA role in the overthrow of Salvador Allende Gossens, the popularly elected Marxist president of Chile. Allende was subsequently murdered and replaced by General Augusto Pinochet Ugarte, a military dictator supposedly friendly to the United States.

THE FORD YEARS   Gerald Ford inherited those simmering problems when he assumed office after Nixon's resignation. An amiable, honest man, Ford candidly admitted upon becoming vice president, "I am a Ford, not a Lincoln." "Jerry Ford," explained the *Washington Post*, "is the most normal, sane, down-to-earth individual to work in the Oval Office since Harry Truman left." As president, Gerald Ford soon adopted the posture he had developed as a conservative minority leader in the House: nay-saying leader of the opposition who believed that the federal government exercised too much power over domestic affairs. In his fifteen months as president, Ford vetoed thirty-nine bills, thereby outstripping Herbert Hoover's veto record in less than half the time. By resisting congressional pressure to reduce taxes and increase federal spending, he succeeded in plummeting the economy into the deepest recession since the Great Depression. Unemployment jumped to 9 percent in 1975, and the federal deficit hit a record the next year. Ford rejected wage and price controls to curb inflation, preferring voluntary restraints that he tried to bolster by passing out WIN buttons, symbolizing his campaign to Whip Inflation Now. The WIN buttons instead became a national joke and a popular symbol of Ford's ineffectiveness in the fight against stagflation.

In foreign policy, Ford retained Henry Kissinger as secretary of state and attempted to pursue Nixon's goals of stability in the Middle East, rapprochement with China, and détente with the Soviet Union. Late in 1974 Ford met with Soviet leader Leonid Brezhnev at Vladivostok, in Siberia, and accepted the framework for another arms-control accord that was to serve as the basis for SALT II. Meanwhile, Kissinger's tireless shuttling between Cairo and Tel Aviv produced an important agreement: Israel promised to return to Egypt most of the Sinai territory captured in the 1967 war, and the two nations agreed to rely upon negotiations rather than force to settle future disagreements. These limited but significant achievements should have enhanced Ford's image, but they were drowned in the sea of criticism and carping that followed the collapse of South Vietnam to the Communists in May 1975.

Not only had a decade of American effort in Vietnam proved futile, but the Khmer Rouge, the Cambodian Communist movement, had also won a resounding victory, plunging that country into a bloodbath. The Khmer Rouge organized a genocidal campaign to destroy their opponents, killing almost one third of the population. Meanwhile, the OPEC oil cartel was threatening another worldwide boycott, and various third world nations denounced the United States as a depraved and declining imperialistic power. Ford lost his patience when he sent marines to rescue the crew of the American merchant ship *Mayaguez,* which had been captured by the Cambodian Communists. This vigorous move won popular acclaim until it was disclosed that the Cambodians had already agreed to release the captured Americans: the forty-one Americans killed in the operation had died for no purpose.

THE ELECTION OF 1976   In the midst of the turmoil, the Democrats could hardly wait for the 1976 election. At the Republican Convention, Ford managed to fend off a powerful challenge for the nomination from the former California governor and Hollywood actor Ronald Reagan. The Democrats chose an obscure former naval officer and engineer turned peanut farmer who had served one term as governor of Georgia. Jimmy Carter campaigned harder than any of the other Democratic hopefuls; he capitalized on the post-Watergate cynicism by promising "I will never tell a lie to the American people" and by citing his inexperience in the byways of Washington politics as an asset. Facing the prospect of the first president from the Deep South since 1849, reporters marveled at a Baptist candidate who claimed to be "born again."

To the surprise of many pundits, the little-known Carter revived the New Deal coalition of southern whites, blacks, urban labor, and ethnic groups to win 41 million votes to Ford's 39 million and a narrow electoral-vote majority of 297 to 240. A heavy turnout of African Americans in the South enabled Carter to sweep every state in the region except Virginia. Carter also benefited from the appeal of Walter F. Mondale, his liberal running mate and a favorite among blue-collar workers and the urban poor. Carter lost most of the trans-Mississippi West, but no Democratic candidate had made much headway there since Harry Truman in 1948. The big story of the election was the low voter turnout. "Neither Ford nor Carter won as many votes as Mr. Nobody," said one reporter, commenting on the fact that almost half the eligible voters, apparently alienated by Watergate and the lackluster candidates, chose to sit out the election.

The Carter Interregnum

POLICY STALEMATE   Once in office, Jimmy Carter suffered the fate of all presidents since Kennedy: after an initial honeymoon, during which he displayed folksy charm by walking down Pennsylvania Avenue after his inauguration rather than riding in a limousine and by wearing cardigan sweaters during televised "fireside chats," his popularity and political effectiveness waned. Like Ford before him, Carter faced an almost insurmountable set of domestic and international problems. He was expected to cure the economic recession and reduce inflation at a time when all industrial economies were shaken by a shortage of energy and confidence. He was expected to reassert America's global power at a time of waning respect for America's international authority. And he was expected to do this, as well as buoy the national spirit, through a set of political institutions in which many Americans had lost faith.

Yet during the first two years of his term, Carter enjoyed several successes. His administration included more African Americans and women than ever

The Carter Administration

President Jimmy Carter and his wife, Rosalynn, forgo the traditional limousine and walk down Pennsylvania Avenue after the inauguration, January 20, 1977.

before. Carter created a federal task force to study the problem of Vietnam-era draft evaders and eventually offered amnesty to the thousands of young men who had fled the country rather than serve in Vietnam. He reformed the civil service to provide rewards for merit, and he created new cabinet-level Departments of Energy and Education. He also pushed through Congress several significant environmental initiatives, including a bill to establish controls over strip mining, a "superfund" of $1.6 billion to clean up chemical waste sites, and a proposal to protect over 100 million acres of Alaskan land from development.

But success was short-lived. Carter's political predicament surfaced in the protracted debate over energy policy. Carter had a distaste for stroking legislators or wheeling and dealing to get legislation passed. The energy bill that Carter signed in 1978 was a gutted version of the original legislation proposed by the administration, reflecting the power of both conservative and liberal special-interest lobbies. One Carter aide said that the energy bill looked like it had been "nibbled to death by ducks." The clumsy political maneuvers that plagued Carter and his inexperienced aides repeatedly frustrated efforts to remedy the energy crisis.

In the summer of 1979, when renewed violence in the Middle East produced a second fuel shortage in the United States, motorists were again forced to wait in long lines for limited supplies of gas that they regarded as excessively expensive. Opinion polls showed Carter with an approval rating of only 26 percent.

Several of Carter's early foreign-policy initiatives also got caught in political crossfires. Soon after his inauguration, Carter vowed that "the soul of our foreign policy" should be the defense of human rights abroad. This human rights campaign aroused opposition from two sides, however: those who feared it sacrificed a detached appraisal of national interest for high-level moralizing and those who believed that human rights were important but that the administration was applying the standard inconsistently.

Similarly, Carter's successful negotiation of treaties to turn over control of the Panama Canal to the government of Panama generated intense criticism. Republican Ronald Reagan claimed that the Canal Zone was sovereign American soil purchased "fair and square" in Theodore Roosevelt's administration. (In the congressional debate one senator quipped, "We stole it fair and square, so why can't we keep it?") Carter argued that the limitations on U.S. influence in Latin America and the deep resentment of American colonialism in Panama left the United States with no other choice. The Canal Zone would revert to Panama in stages, with completion of the process in 1999. The Senate ratified the treaties by a paper-thin margin (sixty-eight to thirty-two, two votes more than the required two thirds), but conservatives lambasted Carter for surrendering American authority in a strategically critical part of the world.

THE CAMP DAVID ACCORDS   Carter's crowning foreign-policy achievement, which even his most bitter critics applauded, was the arrangement of a peace agreement between Israel and Egypt. In 1977 Egyptian president Anwar el-Sadat flew to Tel Aviv at the invitation of Israeli prime minister Menachem Begin. Sadat's bold act, and his accompanying announcement that Egypt was willing to recognize the legitimacy of the Israeli state, opened up diplomatic opportunities that Carter and Secretary of State Cyrus Vance quickly pursued.

The Camp David Accords

Egyptian president Anward el-Sadat (left), Jimmy Carter (center), and Israeli prime minister Menachem Begin (right) at the announcement of the Camp David Accords, September 1978.

In 1978 Carter invited Sadat and Begin to the presidential retreat at Camp David, Maryland, for two weeks of difficult negotiations. The first part of the eventual agreement called for Israel to return all land in the Sinai in exchange for Egyptian recognition of Israel's sovereignty. This agreement was successfully implemented in 1982, when the last Israeli settler vacated the peninsula. But the second part of the agreement, calling for Israel to negotiate with Sadat to resolve the Palestinian refugee dilemma, began to unravel soon after the Camp David summit.

By March 26, 1979, when Begin and Sadat returned to Washington to sign the formal treaty, Begin had already made clear his refusal to block new Israeli settlements on the West Bank of the Jordan River, which Sadat had regarded as a prospective homeland for the Palestinians. In the wake of the Camp David Accords, most of the Arab nations condemned Sadat as a traitor. Islamic extremists assassinated him. Still, Carter and Vance were responsible for a dramatic display of high-level diplomacy that, whatever its limitations, made an all-out war between Israel and the Arab world less likely in the foreseeable future.

MOUNTING TROUBLES Carter's crowning failure, which even his most avid supporters acknowledged, was his mismanagement of the economy. In effect he inherited a bad situation and made it worse. Carter employed the same economic policies as Nixon and Ford to fight stagflation, but he reversed the order of the federal "cure," preferring first to fight unemployment with a tax cut and increased public spending. Unemployment declined slightly, from 8 to 7 percent in 1977, but inflation soared; at 5 percent when he took office, it reached 10 percent in 1978 and kept going. During one month in 1980, it measured at an annual rate of no less than 18 percent. Like previous presidents, Carter then reversed himself to fight the other side of the economic malaise: budget deficits caused by the sagging economy. By midterm he was delaying tax reductions and vetoing government spending programs that he had proposed in his first year. The result was the worst of both possible worlds: a deepened recession and inflation averaging between 12 and 13 percent per year.

The signing of a controversial new Strategic Arms Limitation Talks treaty with the Soviets (SALT II) put Carter's leadership to the test just as the mounting economic problems made him the subject of biting editorial cartoons nationwide. The new agreement placed a ceiling of 2,250 bombers and missiles on each side and set limits on the number of warheads and new weapons systems each power could assemble. But the proposed SALT II treaty became moot in 1979 when the Soviet army invaded Afghanistan to prop up the faltering Communist government there, which was being challenged by Muslim rebels. Carter immediately shelved SALT II, suspended grain shipments to the Soviet Union, and called for an international boycott of the 1980 Olympics, which were to be held that summer in Moscow.

IRAN Then came the Iranian crisis, a year-long cascade of unwelcome events that epitomized the inability of the United States to control world affairs and heightened public perceptions of Carter's weak leadership. The crisis began with the fall of the shah of Iran in 1979. The revolutionaries who toppled the shah's government rallied around Ayatollah Ruhollah Khomeini, a fundamentalist Muslim religious leader who symbolized the orthodox Islamic values the shah had tried to replace with Western ways. Khomeini's hatred of the United States dated back to the CIA-sponsored overthrow of the government of Mohammed Mossadegh in 1953. Nor did it help the American image that the CIA had trained SAVAK, the shah's ruthless secret-police force. Late in 1979 the exiled shah was allowed to enter the United States in order to undergo treatment for cancer. A few days later, in November 4, a frenzied mob stormed the U.S. embassy in Tehran and seized the diplomats and staff. Khomeini endorsed the mob action and demanded the return of the shah along with all his wealth in exchange for the release of the fifty-two hostages still held captive.

Tehran, 1979

Iranian militants stormed the U.S. embassy in Tehran and held fifty-two Americans hostage for over a year. Here one of the hostages (face covered) is paraded before a camera.

Indignant Americans demanded a military response, but Carter's range of options was limited. He appealed to the United Nations, but Khomeini scoffed at UN requests for the release of the hostages. Carter then froze all Iranian assets in the United States and appealed to American allies for a trade embargo of Iran. The trade restrictions were only partially effective—even America's most loyal European allies did not want to lose their access to Iranian oil—so a frustrated and besieged Carter authorized a risky rescue attempt by commandos in 1980. Secretary of State Cyrus Vance resigned in protest against the rescue attempt and Carter's sharp turn toward a more hawkish foreign policy. The commando raid was aborted because of helicopter failures and ended on April 25, 1980, with eight fatalities when a helicopter collided with a transport plane in the desert. Nightly television coverage of the taunting Iranian rebels generated widespread popular craving for action and a near obsession with the falling fortunes of the United States and the fate of the hostages. The end finally came after 444 days of captivity, on January 20, 1981, when Carter released several billion dollars of Iranian assets to ransom the kidnapped hostages. By then however, Ronald Reagan had been elected president, and Carter was headed into retirement.

The turbulent and often tragic events of the 1970s—the Communist conquest of South Vietnam, the Watergate scandal and Nixon's resignation, the energy shortage and stagflation, the Iranian hostage episode—generated what Carter labeled a "crisis of confidence." By 1980 American power and prestige seemed to be on the decline, the economy remained in a shambles, and the sexual revolution launched in the 1960s, with the questions it raised for the family and other basic social and political institutions, had sparked a backlash of resentment among Middle America. With theatrical timing, Ronald Reagan emerged to tap the growing reservoir of public frustration and transform his political career into a crusade to make America "stand tall again." He told his supporters that there was "a hunger in this land for a spiritual revival, a return to a belief in moral absolutes." The United States, he declared, remained the "greatest country in the world. We have the talent, we have the drive, we have the imagination. Now all we need is the leadership."

MAKING CONNECTIONS

- Foreign affairs in the 1970s showed the changing patterns of the cold war. The next chapter details the end of both the cold war and the Soviet Union.

- Presidents Nixon and Ford tried, with limited success, to decrease the power of the federal government over domestic affairs. President Reagan was much more successful at advancing the conservative agenda, another topic covered in the next chapter.

- The rebellion and turbulence of the 1960s and 1970s became less apparent in the following decade; as Chapter 37 shows, however, that turbulence reappeared, in a somewhat different form, in the 1990s.

FURTHER READING

An engaging overview of the cultural trends of the 1960s is Maurice Isserman and Michael Kazin's *America Divided: The Civil War of the 1960s* (1999). The New Left is assessed in Irwin Unger's *The Movement: A History of the American New Left, 1959–1972* (1974). On the Students for a Democratic

Society, see Kirkpatrick Sale's *SDS* (1973) and Allen J. Matusow's *The Unraveling of America: A History of Liberalism in the 1960s* (1984). Also useful is Todd Gitlin's *The Sixties: Years of Hope, Days of Rage*, rev. ed. (1993).

Two influential assessments of the counterculture by sympathetic commentators are Theodore Roszak's *The Making of a Counterculture: Reflections on the Technocratic Society and Its Youthful Opposition* (1969) and Charles A. Reich's *The Greening of America* (1970). A good scholarly analysis of the hippies that takes them seriously is Timothy Miller's *The Hippies and American Values* (1991).

The best study of the women's liberation movement is Ruth Rosen's *The World Split Open: How the Modern Women's Movement Changed America* (2000). The organizing efforts of Cesar Chavez are detailed in Ronald B. Taylor's *Chavez and the Farm Workers* (1975). The struggles of Native Americans for recognition and power are sympathetically described in Stan Steiner's *The New Indians* (1968).

On Nixon, see Melvin Small's *The Presidency of Richard Nixon* (1999). For a solid overview of the Watergate scandal, see Stanley I. Kutler's *The Wars of Watergate: The Last Crisis of Richard Nixon* (1990). For the way the Republicans handled foreign affairs, consult Tad Szulc's *The Illusion of Peace: Foreign Policy in the Nixon Years* (1978).

The loss of Vietnam and the end of American involvement there are traced in Larry Berman's *No Peace, No Honor: Nixon, Kissinger, and Betrayal in Vietnam* (2001). William Shawcross's *Sideshow: Kissinger, Nixon and the Destruction of Cambodia*, rev. ed. (2002), deals with the broadening of the war, while Larry Berman's *Planning a Tragedy: The Americanization of the War in Vietnam* (1982) assesses the final impact of U.S. involvement. The most comprehensive treatment of the anti-war movement is Tom Wells's *The War Within: America's Battle over Vietnam* (1994).

A comprehensive treatment of the Ford administration is contained in John Robert Greene's *The Presidency of Gerald R. Ford* (1995). The best overview of the Carter administration is Burton I. Kaufman's *The Presidency of James Earl Carter, Jr.* (1993). A work more sympathetic to the Carter administration is John Dumbrell's *The Carter Presidency: A Re-evaluation* (1993). Gaddis Smith's *Morality, Reason, and Power: American Diplomacy in the Carter Years* (1986) provides an overview. Background on how the Middle East came to dominate much of American policy is found in William B. Quandt's *Decade of Decisions: American Policy toward the Arab-Israeli Conflict, 1967–1976* (1977).

36
A CONSERVATIVE
INSURGENCY

FOCUS QUESTIONS

· What were the demographic, social, and economic reasons for
  the rise of Ronald Reagan and Republican conservatism?

· How did relations between the United States and the Soviet
  Union change and lead to the end of the cold war?

· What characterized the economy and society of the 1980s?

· What were the causes and consequences of the Gulf War?

To answer these questions and access additional review material, please visit
www.wwnorton.com/studyspace.

 hile the lackluster Carter administration was founder-
ing, Republican conservatives were forging an ag-
gressive plan to win the White House in 1980 and to
assault the New Deal welfare-state mentality in Washington. Those plans
centered on the popularity and charisma of Ronald Reagan, the Hollywood actor turned California governor and prominent political commentator. Reagan was not a deep thinker, but he was a superb analyst of the
public mood, an unabashed patriot, and a committed champion of conservative principles. He was also charming and cheerful, a likable politician
renowned for his relentless anecdotes and optimistic outlook. Where the
dour Carter denounced the evils of free-enterprise capitalism and scolded
Americans in an attempt to get them to revive long-forgotten virtues of
frugality, a sunny Reagan promised a "revolution of ideas" designed to

unleash the capitalist spirit, restore national pride, and regain international respect.

During the late 1970s Reagan's simple message promoting a restoration of pride and prosperity offered an uplifting alternative to Carter's strident moralism. Reagan wanted to increase military spending, dismantle the "bloated" federal bureaucracy, reduce taxes and regulations, and in general, shrink the role of the federal government. He also wanted to affirm old-time religious values by banning abortions and reinstituting prayer in public schools. Reagan's appeal derived from his remarkable skills as a public speaker and his dogmatic commitment to a few overarching ideas and simple themes. As a true believer and an able compromiser, he combined the fervor of a revolutionary with the pragmatism of a diplomat.

Such attributes won Reagan two presidential terms, in 1980 and 1984, and ensured the election of his successor, George H. W. Bush, in 1988. Just how revolutionary the Reagan era was remains a subject of intense partisan debate. What cannot be denied, however, is that Reagan's actions and beliefs set the tone for the decade's political and economic life.

THE REAGAN REVOLUTION

THE MAKING OF A PRESIDENT Born in 1911, Ronald Reagan graduated from tiny Eureka College and then worked as a radio announcer and sportscaster before starting a movie career in Hollywood in 1937. As president of the Screen Actors Guild, Reagan was at first a liberal who supported Franklin Roosevelt's New Deal programs. But he bounced to the far right on the political spectrum during the 1950s. He campaigned for both Eisenhower (in 1952 and 1956) and Nixon (in 1960), switched his party affiliation to Republican in 1962, then achieved political stardom in 1964 when he delivered a rousing speech on national television on behalf of Barry Goldwater's presidential candidacy.

The Republican right found in Ronald Reagan a new idol, whose appeal survived the defeat of Goldwater. Those who discounted Reagan as a minor actor and a mental midget underrated his many virtues, including the importance of his years in front of the camera. Politics is a performing art, all the more so in an age of television, and few if any others in public life had Reagan's stage presence or extraordinary charm. Drawn by wealthy admirers into the campaign for governor of California in 1966, Reagan moderated his rawest rhetoric and won the governorship by a landslide.

Governor Reagan appealed especially to middle-class and lower-middle-class voters resentful of "high" taxes, welfare programs for the dependent, the "neurotic vulgarities" of university students running wild, crime in the streets, and challenges to traditional values in general. In the forefront of the counterculture, California was in the forefront of reaction to it as well. By the eve of the 1980 election, Reagan had become the beneficiary of a development that made his conservative vision of America more than a harmless flirtation with nostalgia. The 1980 census revealed that the elderly proportion of the nation's population was increasing and moving to the sunbelt states of the South and the West. This dual development—an increase in the number of senior citizens and the steady relocation of a significant portion of the population to conservative regions of the country, where hostility to "big government" was deeply rooted—meant that demographics were carrying the United States toward Reagan's conservative political philosophy.

The Great Communicator

Ronald Reagan in 1980, shortly before his election.

THE MORAL MAJORITY   Reagan's presidential aspirations also benefited from a major revival of evangelical religion. No longer a local or provincial phenomenon, Christian evangelicals now owned television and radio stations and operated schools and universities. A survey in 1977 revealed that more than 70 million Americans described themselves as born-again Christians.

The Reverend Jerry Falwell's Moral Majority (later renamed the Liberty Alliance) expressed the major goals of the religious right wing: the economy should operate without "interference" by the government, which should be reduced in size; the Supreme Court decision in *Roe v. Wade* (1973) legalizing abortion should be reversed; Darwinian evolution should be replaced in schoolbooks by the biblical story of creation; prayer should be allowed back in public schools; and Soviet communism should be opposed as a form of pagan totalitarianism. The moralistic zeal and financial resources of the religious right made its adherents formidable opponents of liberal political candidates and programs. By 1980 Falwell's Moral Majority claimed over 4 million members. Its base of support was in the South and was strongest among Baptists, but its appeal extended across the country.

A curiosity of the 1980 presidential campaign was that the religious right opposed Jimmy Carter, a self-professed born-again Christian, and supported Ronald Reagan, a man who was neither conspicuously pious nor even often in church. His divorce and remarriage, once an almost automatic disqualification for the presidency, raised little notice. Nor did the fact that as governor he had signed one of the most permissive abortion laws in the country. That Ronald Reagan became the messiah of the religious right was a tribute both to the force of social issues and the candidate's political skills. Although famous for his personal piety, Carter lost the support of religious conservatives because he failed to promote their key issues. He was not willing to support a ban on abortions or the restoration of daily prayers in public schools. His endorsement of the Equal Rights Amendment for women and civil rights protections for gays also lost him votes from the religious right.

FEMINIST BACKLASH   Another factor contributing to the conservative resurgence was a well-organized and well-financed backlash against the feminist movement. During the 1970s women who opposed the social goals of feminism formed counterorganizations with names such as Women Who Want to Be Women and Females Opposed to Equality. Spearheading such efforts was Phyllis Schlafly, a right-wing Republican activist from Illinois. She orchestrated the campaign to defeat the equal-rights amendment (ERA) and thereafter served as the galvanizing force behind a growing anti-feminist movement. Schlafly characterized feminists as a "bunch of bitter women seeking a constitutional cure for their personal problems," and she urged women to embrace their "God-given" roles as wives and mothers. Feminists, she charged, were "anti-family, anti-children, and pro-abortion."

Many of Schlafly's supporters in the anti-ERA campaign also participated in the mushrooming anti-abortion, or "pro-life," movement. By 1980 the National Right to Life Committee, supported by the National Conference of Catholic Bishops, boasted 11 million members representing all religious denominations. The intensity of its members' commitment made it a powerful political force in its own right, and the Reagan campaign was quick to highlight its own support for traditional "family values," gender roles, and the "rights" of the unborn. Such cultural issues helped persuade many northern Democrats—mostly working-class Catholics—to support Reagan. Whites alienated by the increasingly liberal social agenda of the Democratic party became a crucial element in Reagan's electoral strategy.

THE ELECTION OF 1980   By 1980 voters were applauding Reagan's cheery promises of a new era of less government, lower taxes, renewed prosperity, waning inflation, and revived military strength and national pride. His "supply-side" economic proposals, soon dubbed Reaganomics by supporters and voodoo economics by critics, suggested that the stagflation of the 1970s had resulted from excessive taxes that weakened incentives to work, save, and reinvest. The solution was to slash tax rates. For a long-suffering nation it was, in theory, an alluring economic panacea.

Reagan was a colorful campaigner who presented a consistent message to the voters: Carter and the Democrats, he insisted, believed that the United States had entered an era of permanent limits on economic growth and personal initiative. On the contrary, he asserted, the Republicans believed that America's greatest economic accomplishments were just around the corner. Reagan pledged that his recovery plans would restore prosperity and public confidence. He often used folksy maxims and jokes to punctuate his themes. At one campaign stop, for instance, he quipped: "A recession is when your neighbor loses his job. A depression is when you lose yours. A recovery is when Jimmy Carter loses his."

On election day, Reagan swept to a decisive victory, with 489 electoral votes to 49 for Carter, who carried only six states. The popular vote was 44 million (51 percent) for Reagan to Carter's 35 million (41 percent), with 7 percent going to John Anderson, a moderate Republican who had bolted the party after Reagan's nomination and run on an independent ticket.

More than a victory for the "new conservatism," the 1980 election reflected the triumph of what one political scientist called the "largest mass movement of our time"—nonvoting. Almost as striking as Reagan's one-sided victory was the fact that his total votes represented only 28 percent of the potential electorate. Only 53 percent of eligible voters cast ballots in the 1980 election; in western European countries such as France and Germany, voter participation hovered at 85 percent in national elections during the 1970s.

Where had all the voters gone? Analysts noted that most of the nonvoters were working-class Democrats in the major urban centers. Voter turnout was lowest in poor inner-city neighborhoods. Turnout was highest, by contrast, in the affluent suburbs of large cities, areas where the Republican party was experiencing a dramatic surge in popularity. Explanations for the high levels of voter apathy among working-class Americans vary. Some argue that they reflected the continuing sense of disillusionment with government

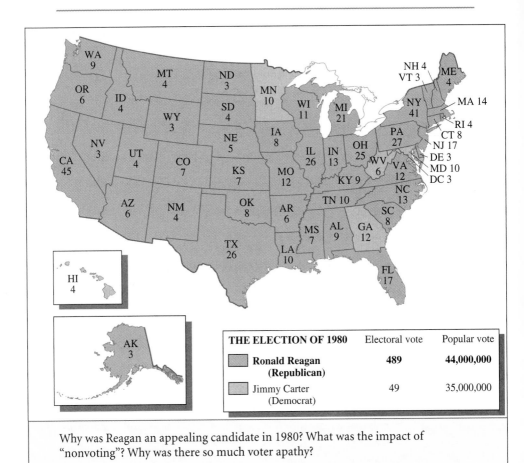

THE ELECTION OF 1980	Electoral vote	Popular vote
Ronald Reagan (Republican)	**489**	**44,000,000**
Jimmy Carter (Democrat)	49	35,000,000

Why was Reagan an appealing candidate in 1980? What was the impact of "nonvoting"? Why was there so much voter apathy?

itself, growing out of the Watergate affair. Others point to the widespread perception that the Democratic party had turned its back on its traditional blocs of support among common folk. Democratic leaders no longer spoke eloquently on behalf of those at the bottom of America's social scale. By embracing a fiscal conservatism indistinguishable from that of the Republicans, as Carter had done, Democrats lost their appeal among blue-collar workers and ghetto dwellers. And so the largest group of nonvoters in the 1980 election was made up of former Democrats who had decided that neither party served their interests. When viewed in this light, Ronald Reagan's victory represented both a resounding victory for conservative Republicans and a self-inflicted defeat by a fractured Democratic party. Flush with a sense of power and destiny, President-elect Reagan headed toward Washington with a blueprint for dismantling the welfare state.

REAGAN'S FIRST TERM

REAGANOMICS   Ronald Reagan brought to Washington a simple conservative philosophy. "Government is not the solution to our problem," he insisted; "government is the problem." He credited Calvin Coolidge and Coolidge's Treasury secretary, Andrew Mellon, with demonstrating that by reducing taxes and easing government regulation of business, free-market capitalism would revive the economy. By cutting taxes and domestic federal spending, he claimed, a surging economy would produce *more* government revenues, which in turn would help reduce the budget deficit.

Early on, Reagan increased defense spending, reduced social spending, and passed a sweeping tax-reform proposal. On August 1, 1981, the president signed the Economic Recovery Tax Act, which cut personal income taxes by 25 percent, lowered the maximum rate from 70 to 50 percent for 1982, cut the capital gains tax by one third, and offered a broad array of other tax concessions.

The new legislation embodied an idea that went back to Alexander Hamilton, George Washington's Treasury secretary: more money in the hands of the affluent would benefit society at large, since the wealthy would engage in productive investment. A closer parallel was Treasury Secretary Andrew Mellon's tax-reduction program of the 1920s. The difference was that the

Reaganomics

Demonstrators in Ohio rail against the effects of Reaganomics, protesting the Reagan economic package that sacrificed funding in areas such as Social Security.

Reagan tax cuts were accompanied by massive increases in defense spending, which generated ever-mounting federal deficits. Reagan's advisers insisted that the unbalanced budgets were only temporary; the new tax plan would eventually fuel economic growth and thereby boost tax revenues as personal income and corporate profits skyrocketed. But it did not work out that way. By the summer of 1983, a major economic recovery was under way, but the federal deficits had grown ever larger, so much so that the president, who in 1980 had pledged to balance the federal budget by 1983, had in fact run up debts larger than those of all his predecessors combined. Yet Congress was in part responsible for the deficits. Reagan failed in his efforts to bring about substantial reductions in federal spending. Legislators consistently approved budgets that were higher than the president requested.

BUDGET CUTS   David Stockman, Reagan's budget director, pushed through $35 billion in budget cuts in education and cultural programs, housing, food stamps, and school lunches. Reagan assured critics that despite these cuts he was committed to maintaining the "safety net" of government services for the "truly needy." This meant that aid would remain available only to those who could not work because of either disability or child-care responsibilities. Cuts in programs for the disadvantaged, when added to the sluggish economy, helped raise the percentage of persons living under the poverty level from 11.7 in 1979 to 15.3 in 1983.

David Stockman realized that the cuts in domestic spending had fallen far short of what would be needed to balance the budget in four years as Reagan had promised. The result was a soaring budget deficit and the worst economic recession since the 1930s. Aides finally convinced Reagan that to reassure the public about deficits and the threat of inflation, the government needed "revenue enhancements," a euphemism for tax increases. With Reagan's support, Congress passed a new tax bill in 1982 that would raise almost $100 billion. During the midterm elections of 1982, Reagan urged voters to "stay the course" and appealed for more time to let his economic program take effect. Meanwhile, the economic slump persisted through 1982, with unemployment standing at 10.4 percent, and the Republicans experienced moderate losses in the elections.

CONFLICTS OF INTEREST   The Reagan administration paralleled the Harding administration by finding itself embroiled in charges of conflict of interest, ethical misconduct, and actual criminal behavior. Public outcry forced the administrator of the Environmental Protection Agency to resign for granting favors to industrial polluters. Although some 200 Reagan appointees were accused of unethical or illegal activities, the president himself remained untouched by any hint of impropriety. His personal charisma and aloof managerial style helped shield him from the political fallout associated with the growing scandals and conflicts of interest involving his aides and cronies.

Organized labor suffered severe setbacks during the Reagan years. Presidential appointments to the National Labor Relations Board tended to favor management, and in 1981 Reagan fired members of the Professional Air Traffic Controllers Organization who had participated in an illegal strike. Even more important, Reagan's smashing electoral victories in 1980 and 1984 broke the political power of the AFL-CIO. His criticism of unions seemed to reflect a general trend in public opinion. Although record numbers of new jobs were created during the 1980s, union membership steadily dropped. By 1987 unions represented only 17 percent of the nation's full-time workers, down from 24 percent in 1979.

Reagan also went on the offensive against feminism. He opposed the ERA, abortion on demand, and the legal guarantee of equal pay for jobs of comparable worth. He did name Sandra Day O'Connor as the first woman justice to the Supreme Court, but critics labeled it a token gesture rather than a reflection of any genuine commitment to gender equality. Reagan also cut funds for civil rights enforcement and the Equal Employment Opportunity Commission, and he initially opposed renewal of the Voting Rights Act of 1965 but was overruled by Congress.

THE DEFENSE BUILDUP   Reagan's conduct of foreign policy reflected his belief that trouble in the world stemmed mainly from Moscow, the capital of what he called the Evil Empire. He charged that the Soviets were "prepared to commit any crime, to lie, to cheat" and do anything necessary to promote world communism. Reagan and Secretary of Defense Caspar Weinberger embarked on a major buildup of nuclear and conventional weapons. In 1983 Reagan escalated the nuclear arms race by authorizing the Defense Department to develop a Strategic Defense Initiative, which involved a complex anti-missile defense system in outer space. Despite skepticism among the media and many scientists that such a "Star Wars" defense system could be built, it forced the Soviets to launch an expensive research and development program of their own to keep pace.

Reagan borrowed the rhetoric of Harry Truman, John Foster Dulles, and John F. Kennedy's inaugural to express American resolve in the face of "Communist aggression anywhere in the world." Détente deteriorated even further when the Soviets imposed martial law in Poland during the winter of 1981. The crackdown came after Polish workers, united under the banner of an independent union called Solidarity, challenged the Communist monopoly of power. As with the Soviet interventions in Hungary in 1956 and Czechoslovakia in 1968, the United States could not force the Soviets to loosen their grip on eastern Europe. But Reagan did protest the crackdown and imposed economic sanctions against Poland's Communist government. He also worked behind the scenes to support the Solidarity movement.

THE AMERICAS Reagan's foremost international concern, however, was in Central America, where he detected the most serious Communist threat. The tiny nation of El Salvador, caught up since 1980 in a brutal struggle between Communist-supported revolutionaries and right-wing militants, received U.S. economic and military assistance. Reagan stopped short of sending American troops, but he did increase the number of military advisers and the amount of financial aid to the Salvadoran government. He also abandoned Jimmy Carter's strident criticism of right-wing Salvadoran militants whose "death squads" engaged in systematic terror and murder. Critics argued that U.S. involvement ensured that the revolutionary forces would emerge as the victorious representatives of Salvadoran nationalism by capitalizing on "anti-Yankee" sentiment. Supporters countered by warning that American failure to act would allow for a repeat of the Communist victories in Nicaragua and that Honduras, Guatemala, and then all of Central America would eventually enter the

"Shhhh. It's Top Secret."

A comment on the Reagan administration's covert operations in Nicaragua.

Communist camp. By 1984, however, the American-backed government of President José Napoleón Duarte brought a modicum of stability to El Salvador.

Even more troubling was the situation in Nicaragua. The State Department claimed that the Cuban-sponsored Sandinista government in Nicaragua, which had only recently taken control of the country after ousting a corrupt dictator, was funneling Soviet and Cuban arms to leftist Salvadoran rebels. In response the Reagan administration ordered the CIA to train and supply guerrilla bands of anti-Communist Nicaraguans, tagged Contras, who staged attacks on Sandinista bases and officials from sanctuaries in Honduras. In supporting these "freedom fighters," Reagan sought not only to impede the traffic in arms to Salvadoran rebels but also to replace the Sandinistas with a democratic government.

Critics of Reagan's anti-Sandinista policy accused the Contras of being mostly right-wing fanatics who indiscriminately killed civilians as well as Sandinista soldiers. They also feared that the United States might eventually commit its own combat forces, thus threatening another Vietnam-like intervention. Reagan warned that if the Communists prevailed in Central America, "our credibility would collapse, our alliances would crumble, and the safety of our homeland would be jeopardized."

THE MIDDLE EAST   The Middle East remained a tinderbox of conflict during the 1980s. No peaceable end seemed possible in the prolonged bloody Iran-Iraq War, entangled as it was with the passions of Islamic fundamentalism. In 1984 both sides began to attack tankers in the Persian Gulf, a major source of the world's oil. (The main international response was the sale of arms to both sides.) Nor was any settlement in sight for Afghanistan, where the Soviet occupation forces had bogged down as badly as the Americans had in Vietnam.

American governments continued to see Israel as the strongest and most reliable ally in the region, all the while seeking to encourage moderate Arab groups. But the forces of moderation were dealt a blow during the mid-1970s when Lebanon, long an enclave of peace despite its ethnic complexity, collapsed into an anarchy of warring groups. The capital, Beirut, became a battleground for Sunni and Shiite Muslims, the Druze, the Palestine Liberation Organization (PLO), Arab Christians, Syrian invaders cast as peacekeepers, and Israelis responding to PLO attacks across the border.

In 1982 Israeli forces pushed the PLO out of southern Lebanon all the way north to Beirut and then began shelling PLO strongholds in Beirut. The United States sent a special ambassador to negotiate a settlement. Israeli troops moved into Beirut and looked the other way when Christian militiamen slaughtered Muslim women and children in Palestinian refugee camps. French, Italian, and American forces then moved into Lebanon as "peace-keepers," but in such small numbers as to become only targets. Angry Muslims kept them constantly harassed. American warships and planes responded by shelling and bombing Muslim positions in the highlands behind Beirut, which only increased Muslim resentment. On October 23, 1983, an Islamic suicide bomber drove a truck laden with explosives into the U.S. Marine headquarters at the Beirut airport; the explosion left 241 Americans dead. In early 1984 Reagan announced that the marines would be "redeployed" to warships offshore. The Israeli forces pulled back to southern Lebanon, while the Syrians remained in eastern Lebanon. Bloody anarchy remained a way of life in a formerly peaceful country.

GRENADA   Fortune, as it happened, presented Reagan the chance for an easy triumph closer to home, a "rescue mission" that eclipsed news of the debacle in Lebanon. On the tiny Caribbean island of Grenada, the smallest independent country in the Western Hemisphere, a leftist government had admitted Cuban workers to build a new airfield and signed military agreements with Communist countries. In 1983 an even more radical military council seized power.

Appeals from the governments of neighboring islands led Reagan to order 1,900 marines to invade the island, depose the new government, and evacuate a small group of American students at Grenada's medical school. The UN General Assembly condemned the action, but it was popular among Grenadans and their neighbors and immensely popular in the United States. Although a lopsided affair, the action made Reagan look decisive, and it served as notice to Latin American revolutionaries that he might use military force elsewhere in the region.

REAGAN'S SECOND TERM

By 1983 prosperity had returned, and the Reagan economic program was at last working as touted. The gradual unraveling of the OPEC cartel and resultant decline in oil prices helped fuel economic growth.

THE ELECTION OF 1984   By 1984 Reagan had restored strength and vitality to the White House and the nation. The economy surged with new energy. The slogan at the Republican Convention was "America is back." By contrast, the nominee of the Democrats, former vice president Walter Mondale, never quite got his act together. Endorsed by the AFL-CIO, the National

Organization for Women, and many African Americans despite a serious challenge from Jesse Jackson, Mondale was viewed as the candidate of the special interests. He set a precedent by choosing as his running mate New York representative Geraldine Ferraro, who was quickly placed on the defensive by the need to explain her spouse's complicated finances.

A fit of frankness in his acceptance speech further complicated Mondale's campaign. "Mr. Reagan will raise taxes, and so will I," he told the convention. "He won't tell you. I just did." Reagan responded by vowing never to approve a tax increase and by chiding Mondale for his candid stand. Mondale never caught up. In the end, Reagan took 59 percent of the popular vote and lost only Minnesota and the District of Columbia. His coattails were not as strong, however. Republicans had a net gain of only fifteen seats in the House and lost two in the Senate.

DOMESTIC CHALLENGES   Buoyed by his overwhelming victory, Reagan called for "a Second American Revolution of hope and opportunity." He dared Congress to raise taxes. His veto pen was ready: "Go ahead and make my day," he said in echo of a popular line from a movie. Through much of 1985 the president drummed up support for a tax-simplification plan. After vigorous debate that ran nearly two years, Congress passed, and in 1986 the president signed, a comprehensive Tax Reform Act. The new measure reduced the number of federal tax brackets from fourteen to two and reduced rates from the maximum of 50 percent to 15 and 28 percent—the lowest since Calvin Coolidge was president. Tax shelters were also sharply limited.

THE IRAN-CONTRA AFFAIR   During the fall of 1986, the Reagan administration suffered a double blow. In the midterm elections, Democrats regained control of the Senate by fifty-five to forty-five. The Democrats picked up only six seats in the House, but they increased their already comfortable margin to 259 to 176. For his last two years as president, Reagan would face an opposition Congress.

What was worse, on election day reports surfaced that the United States had been secretly selling arms to Iran in the hope of securing the release of American hostages held in Lebanon by extremist groups sympathetic to Iran. Such action contradicted Reagan's repeated public insistence that his administration would never negotiate with terrorists. The disclosures angered America's allies as well as many Americans who vividly remembered the 1979 Iranian takeover of their country's embassy in Tehran.

There was even more to the sordid story. Over the next several months, revelations reminiscent of the Watergate affair disclosed a complicated series of covert activities carried out by administration officials. At the center of what came to be called the Iran-Contra affair was the much-decorated marine lieutenant colonel Oliver North. A swashbuckling aide to the National Security Council who specialized in counterterrorism, North had been running from the basement of the White House secret operations involving many government, private, and foreign individuals. His most far-fetched scheme sought to use the profits from the secret sale of military supplies to Iran to subsidize the Contra rebels fighting in Nicaragua at a time when Congress had voted to ban such aid.

Oliver North's activities, it turned out, had been approved by national security adviser Robert McFarlane; McFarlane's successor, Admiral John Poindexter; and CIA director William Casey. Both Secretary of State George Shultz and Secretary of Defense Caspar Weinberger criticized the arms sale to Iran, but their objections were ignored, and they were thereafter kept in the dark about what was going on. Later, on three occasions, Shultz threatened to resign over the continuing operation of the "pathetic" scheme. As information about the secret (and illegal) dealings surfaced in the press, McFarlane attempted suicide, Poindexter resigned, North was fired, and Casey, who denied any connection, left the CIA for health reasons. Casey died shortly thereafter from a brain tumor.

Under increasing criticism, Reagan appointed both an independent counsel and a three-man commission, led by former Republican senator John Tower, to investigate the scandal. The Tower Commission issued a devastating report early in 1987 that placed much of the responsibility for the bungled Iran-Contra affair on Reagan's loose management style. During the spring and summer of 1987, a joint House-Senate investigating committee began holding televised hearings into the Iran-Contra affair. The sessions revealed a tangled web of inept financial and diplomatic transactions, the shredding of incriminating government documents, crass profiteering, and misguided patriotism.

The investigations of the independent counsel led to six indictments in 1988. A Washington jury found Oliver North guilty of three relatively minor charges but innocent of nine more serious counts, apparently reflecting the jury's reasoning that he acted as an agent of higher-ups. His conviction was later overturned on appeal. Of those involved in the affair, only John Poindexter got a jail sentence—six months for his conviction on five felony counts of obstructing justice and lying to Congress.

TURMOIL IN CENTRAL AMERICA   The Iran-Contra affair showed the lengths to which members of the Reagan administration would go to support the rebels fighting the ruling Sandinistas in Nicaragua. Fearing heightened Soviet and U.S. involvement in Central America, neighboring countries pressed during the mid-1980s for a negotiated settlement to the unrest in Nicaragua. In 1988 Daniel Ortega, the Nicaraguan president, pledged to negotiate directly with the Contra rebels. In the spring of 1988, those negotiations produced a cease-fire agreement, ending nearly seven years of fighting in Nicaragua. Secretary of State George Shultz called the pact an "important step forward," but the settlement surprised and disappointed hard-liners within the Reagan administration, who saw in it a Contra surrender. The Contra leaders themselves, aware of the eroding support for their cause in the U.S. Congress, saw the truce as their only chance for tangible concessions such as amnesty for political prisoners, the return of the Contras from exile, and "unrestricted freedom of expression."

In neighboring El Salvador, meanwhile, the Reagan administration's attempt to shore up the centrist government of José Napoleón Duarte through economic and military aid suffered a setback when the far-right ARENA party scored an upset victory at the polls during the spring of 1988.

DEBT AND THE STOCK-MARKET PLUNGE   During the 1980s debt, all kinds of debt—personal, corporate, and government—increased dramatically. Whereas Americans in the 1960s saved on average 10 percent of their income, in 1987 the figure was less than 4 percent. The federal debt more than tripled, from $908 billion in 1980 to $2.9 trillion at the end of the 1989 fiscal year. Then, on October 19, 1987, the bill collector suddenly arrived at the

Black Monday

A frenzied trader calls for attention in the pit of the Chicago Board Options Exchange as the Dow Jones stock average loses over 500 points.

nation's doorstep. On that "Black Monday," the stock market experienced a tidal wave of selling reminiscent of the 1929 crash. The Dow Jones industrial average plummeted 508 points, or an astounding 22.6 percent. The market plunge nearly doubled the record 12.8 percent fall on October 28, 1929. Wall Street's selling frenzy reverberated throughout the capitalist world, sending stock prices plummeting in Tokyo, London, Paris, and Toronto.

In the aftermath of the calamitous selling spree on Black Monday, few observers actually feared a depression of the magnitude of the 1930s; there were too many safeguards built into the system to allow that. But there was real concern of an impending recession, and this led business leaders and economists to attack the president for glossing over such a profound warning signal. Within a few weeks, Reagan had agreed to work with Congress in developing a deficit-reduction package, and for the first time indicated that he was willing to include increased taxes in such a package. But the eventual compromise plan was so modest that it did little to restore investor confidence. As one Republican senator lamented, "There is a total lack of courage among those of us in the Congress to do what we all know has to be done."

THE POOR, THE HOMELESS, AND THE VICTIMS OF AIDS   The 1980s were years of vivid contrast. Despite unprecedented prosperity among the wealthiest Americans, there were beggars in the streets and homeless people sleeping in doorways, in cardboard boxes, and on ventilation grates. A variety of causes led to the shortage of low-cost housing: the government had given up on building public housing; urban-renewal programs had demolished blighted areas but provided no housing for those they displaced; and owners had abandoned unprofitable buildings in poor neighborhoods or converted them into expensive condominiums, a process called gentrification. After new medications allowed for the deinstitutionalization of the mentally ill, many individuals ended up on the streets because the promised community mental- health services failed to materialize. By the summer of 1988, the *New York Times* estimated, more than 45 percent of New York's adults constituted an underclass totally outside the labor force for lack of skills, lack of motivation, drug use, and other problems.

Still another group of outcasts were those suffering from the new malady that had come to be known as AIDS (acquired immunodeficiency syndrome). At the beginning of the 1980s, public health officials had begun to report that gay men and intravenous drug users were especially at risk for developing AIDS. Those infected with the virus that causes AIDS showed signs of fatigue, developed a strange combination of infections, and eventually died. People contracted the virus (HIV) by coming into contact with the blood or body fluids of an infected person. The Reagan administration showed little interest in AIDS in part because it initially was viewed as a "gay" disease. Patrick Buchanan, the conservative spokesman who served as White House director of communications, said that homosexuals had "declared war on nature, and now nature is extracting an awful retribution."

By 2000, however, AIDS had claimed almost 300,000 American lives and was spreading among a larger segment of the population. Nearly 1 million Americans were estimated to be carrying the deadly virus, and it had become the leading cause of death among men aged twenty-five to forty-four. The potential for the spread of HIV prompted the surgeon general to launch a controversial public-education program that included encouraging "safe sex" through the use of condoms. With no prospect for an early cure and with skyrocketing treatment costs, AIDS emerged as one of the nation's most intractable problems.

The AIDS Crisis

A quilt commemorating the deaths of many thousands of Americans from AIDS is displayed before the White House in October 1988 so that friends and family members can walk amid its panels and view them up close.

A HISTORIC TREATY   The main prospect for positive achievement before the end of Reagan's second term seemed to lie in an arms-reduction agreement with the Soviet government. Under Mikhail Gorbachev the Soviets pursued renewed détente in order to free their energies and financial resources to address pressing domestic problems. The logjam that had impeded arms negotiations suddenly broke in 1987, when Gorbachev announced that he was willing to deal separately on a medium-range missile treaty. After nine months of strenuous negotiations, Reagan and Gorbachev met amid much fanfare in Washington, D.C. on December 9, 1987, and signed a treaty to eliminate intermediate-range (300- to 3,000-mile) nuclear missiles.

Foreign Relations

A light moment at a meeting between U.S. president Ronald Reagan (left) and Soviet premier Mikhail Gorbachev (right).

It was an epochal event, not only because it marked the first time that the two nations had agreed to destroy a whole class of weapons systems but also because it represented a key first step toward the eventual end of the arms race altogether. Under the terms of the treaty, the United States would destroy 859 missiles, and the Soviets would eliminate 1,752. Still, the reductions would represent only 4 percent of the total nuclear-missile count on both sides. Arms-control advocates thus looked toward a second and more comprehensive treaty dealing with long-range strategic missiles.

Gorbachev's successful efforts to liberalize Soviet domestic life and improve East-West foreign relations cheered Americans. The Soviets suddenly began stressing cooperation with the West in dealing with hot spots around the world. They urged the PLO to recognize Israel's right to exist and advocated a greater role for the United Nations in the volatile Persian Gulf. Perhaps the most dramatic symbol of a thawing cold war was the phased withdrawal of 115,000 Soviet troops from Afghanistan, which began in 1988.

THE REAGAN LEGACY   Although Ronald Reagan had declared in 1981 his intention to "curb the size and influence of the federal establishment," the New Deal welfare state remained intact when he left office in early 1989. Neither the Social Security system nor Medicare was dismantled or overhauled, nor were any other major welfare programs. And the federal agencies that Reagan had threatened to abolish, such as the Department of Education, not only remained in place in 1989 but saw their budgets grow. The federal budget as a percentage of the gross domestic product was actually higher when Reagan left office than when he had entered. Moreover, he did not try to push through Congress the incendiary social issues championed by the religious right, such as school prayer and a ban on abortions.

What Ronald Reagan did accomplish was to redefine the national political agenda and accelerate the conservative insurgency that had been developing for over twenty years. Reagan's critics highlighted his lack of intellectual sophistication and his indifference to day-to-day administrative details. Yet he excelled as a leader because he was relentlessly optimistic about America's potential and unflinchingly committed to a philosophy of free enterprise, limited government, and strenuous anti-communism. His greatest successes were in renewing America's soaring sense of possibilities, bringing inflation under control, stimulating the longest sustained period of peacetime prosperity in history, negotiating the nuclear disarmament treaty, and helping to light the fuse of democratic freedom in Eastern Europe. In 1987 Reagan visited the Berlin Wall and in a key speech highlighted his efforts to convince the Soviet Union to allow greater freedom within the Warsaw Pact countries. "We hear much from Moscow about a new policy of reform and openness," he noted. But he chided the Soviets for not moving faster. "General Secretary Gorbachev, if you seek peace, if you seek prosperity for the Soviet Union and Eastern Europe, if you seek liberalization: Come here to this gate! Mr. Gorbachev, open this gate! Mr. Gorbachev, tear down this wall!" By redirecting the thrust of both domestic and foreign policy, Reagan put the fragmented Democratic party on the defensive and forced conventional New Deal "liberalism" into a panicked retreat. The fact that Reagan's tax policies widened the gap between the rich and poor and created huge budget deficits for future presidents to confront did not diminish the popularity of the Great Communicator.

THE ELECTION OF 1988   In 1988 eight Democratic presidential candidates entered a wild scramble for their party's nomination. As the primary season progressed, however, it soon became a two-man race, between Massachusetts governor Michael Dukakis and Jesse Jackson, the charismatic African-American civil rights activist who had been one of Martin Luther King Jr.'s chief lieutenants. Dukakis eventually won out and managed a difficult reconciliation with the Jackson forces that left the Democrats unified and confident as the fall campaign began.

The Republicans nominated Reagan's two-term vice president, George H. W. Bush, who after a bumpy start had easily cast aside his rivals in the primaries. As Reagan's handpicked heir, Bush claimed credit for the administration's successes, but like all dutiful vice presidents he also faced the challenge of asserting his own political identity. Although a veteran government official, having served as a Texas congressman, envoy to China, ambassador to the UN, and head of the CIA, Bush projected none of Reagan's charisma or rhetorical skills. One Democrat described him as a man born "with a silver foot in his mouth." Early polls showed Dukakis with a wide lead.

Yet Bush delivered a forceful convention address that sharply enhanced his stature. Although pledging to continue the Reagan agenda, he also recognized that "things aren't perfect" in America, an admission his boss rarely acknowledged. Bush promised to use the White House to fight bigotry, illiteracy, and homelessness. Humane sympathies, he insisted, would guide his conservatism. "I want a kinder, gentler nation," Bush said softly in his acceptance speech. But the most memorable line was a defiant statement on taxes: "The Congress will push me to raise taxes, and I'll say no, and they'll push, and I'll say no, and they'll push again, and I'll say to them, 'Read my lips: no new taxes.'"

The 1988 Election

George H. W. Bush (right) at the 1988 Republican National Convention with his newly chosen running mate, Dan Quayle, a senator from Indiana.

In a campaign given over to mudslinging, Bush and his aides attacked Dukakis as a camouflaged liberal in the mold of George McGovern, Jimmy Carter, and Walter Mondale. The Republican onslaught took its toll against the less organized, less focused Dukakis campaign. In the end, Dukakis took only ten states plus the District of Columbia, with clusters of support in the Northeast, Midwest, and Northwest. Bush carried the rest, with a margin of about 54 percent to 46 percent in the popular vote and 426 to 111 in the Electoral College.

Generally speaking, the more affluent and better-educated voters preferred the Republican ticket. While Dukakis won the inner-city vote, garnering

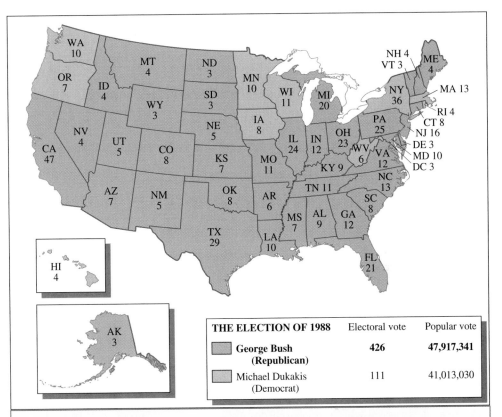

THE ELECTION OF 1988	Electoral vote	Popular vote
George Bush (Republican)	426	47,917,341
Michael Dukakis (Democrat)	111	41,013,030

How did George H. W. Bush overtake Dukakis's lead in the polls? What was the role of race and class in the election results? Who didn't vote in the election of 1988?

86 percent of the African-American vote, Bush scored big in the suburbs and in rural areas, especially in the once-Democratic South, where his margin of support by white voters ranged from a low of 63 percent in Florida to a high of 80 percent in Mississippi. More significant was Bush's success among blue-collar workers. He captured 46 percent of these typically Democratic voters.

Hidden among the election returns was a long-term trend that did not bode well for the American political system: voter turnout continued to decline. In the 1988 election, only 50 percent of the voting-age population cast ballots, the lowest in any presidential election since 1924. Voting was highest among affluent whites (52 percent), while 46 percent of eligible African Americans and only 23 percent of eligible Latinos turned out. But the most alarming statistic was that two fifths of all the nonvoters were under thirty years of age.

THE BUSH ADMINISTRATION

George Bush viewed himself as a guardian president rather than an activist. He lacked Reagan's visionary outlook. Bush was a pragmatist caretaker eager to avoid "stupid mistakes" and to find a way to get along with the Democratic majority in Congress. "We don't need to remake society," he announced. Bush sought to consolidate and nurture the initiatives that Reagan had put in place rather than launch his own array of programs and policies.

DOMESTIC INITIATIVES   The biggest problem facing the Bush administration was the national debt, which stood at $2.6 trillion in 1989, nearly three times its 1980 level. Bush's taboo on tax increases (meaning mainly income taxes) and his insistence upon lowering capital-gains taxes—on profits from the sales of stocks and other property—made it more difficult to reduce the annual deficit or trim the long-term debt. By 1990 the country faced "a fiscal mess." Eventually Bush decided "that both the size of the deficit problem and the need for a package that can be enacted" required a number of budget cuts and "tax revenue increases" which he had sworn to avoid.

Another domestic initiative was President Bush's war on illegal drugs. During the 1980s cocaine addiction spread through sizable segments of society, luring not only those with money to spend but also those with little money to spare, who used the drug in its smokable form, known as crack. Bush vowed to make drug abuse his number-one domestic priority and appointed William J. Bennett, former education secretary, as "drug czar," or head of a new Office of National Drug Control Policy, with cabinet status but no department. Yet federal spending on programs intended to curb drug abuse rose modestly. The message, on this and on education, housing, and other social problems, was that more of the burden should fall on state and local authorities.

THE DEMOCRACY MOVEMENT ABROAD   George Bush entered the White House with more foreign-policy experience than most presidents, and he found the spotlight of the world stage more congenial than wrestling with the intractable problems of the inner cities, drug abuse, and the deficit. Within two years of his inauguration, Bush would lead the United States into two wars. Throughout most of 1989, however, he merely had to sit back and observe the dissolution of one totalitarian or authoritarian regime after another. For the first time in years, democracy was suddenly on the march in a sequence of mostly bloodless revolutions that surprised the world.

Although a democracy movement in China came to a tragic end in 1989 when government forces mounted a deadly assault on demonstrators in Beijing's (Peking's) Tiananmen Square, Eastern Europe had an entirely different

Dissolution of the Soviet Empire

West Germans hacking away at the Berlin Wall on November 11, 1989, two days after all crossings between East Germany and West Germany were opened.

experience. With a rigid economic system failing to deliver the goods to the Soviet people, Mikhail Gorbachev responded with policies of perestroika (restructuring) and glasnost (openness), a loosening of central economic planning and censorship. His foreign policy sought rapprochement and trade with the West, and he aimed to relieve the Soviet economy of burdensome military costs.

Gorbachev also backed off from Soviet imperial ambitions. Early in 1989 Soviet troops left Afghanistan after spending nine years bogged down in civil war there. Gorbachev then repudiated the Brezhnev Doctrine, which asserted the right of the Soviet Union to intervene in the internal affairs of other Communist countries. The days when Soviet tanks rolled through Warsaw and Prague were over, and hard-line leaders in the Eastern-bloc countries found themselves beset by demands for reform from their own people. With opposition strength building, the old regimes fell with surprisingly little bloodshed. Communist party rule ended first in Poland and Hungary, then in Czechoslovakia and Bulgaria. In Romania the year of peaceful revolution ended in a bloodbath when the Romanian people joined the army in a bloody uprising against the brutal dictator Nicolae Ceaușescu. He and his wife were captured, tried, and then executed on Christmas Day.

The most spectacular event in the collapse of the Soviet Empire in Eastern Europe came on November 9, 1989, when the chief symbol of the cold war—the Berlin Wall—was torn down by Germans using small tools and even their hands. With the borders to the West now fully open, the Communist government of East Germany collapsed, a freely elected government came to power, and on October 3, 1990, the five states of East Germany were united with West Germany. The unified German nation remained in NATO, and the Communist Warsaw Pact alliance was dissolved.

The reform impulse that Gorbachev helped unleash in the Eastern-bloc countries careened out of control within the Soviet Union, however. Gorbachev proved unusually adept at political restructuring, yielding the Communist monopoly of government but building a new presidential system that gave him, if anything, increased powers. His skills in the Byzantine politics of the Kremlin, though, did not extend to an antiquated economy that resisted change. The revival of ethnic allegiances added to the instability. Although Russia proper included slightly over half the Soviet Union's population, it was only one of fifteen constituent republics, most of which began to seek autonomy, if not independence.

Action against Gorbachev

In August 1991, one day after Mikhail Gorbachev was placed under house arrest by Communists planning a coup, Russian Federation president Boris Yeltsin (holding papers) makes a speech criticizing the plotters.

Gorbachev's popularity shrank in the Soviet Union as it grew abroad. It especially eroded among the Communist hard-liners, who saw in his reforms the unraveling of their bureaucratic and political empire. Once the genie of freedom was released from the Communist lamp, however, it took on a momentum of its own. On August 18, 1991, a cabal of political and military leaders suddenly tried to seize the reins of power in Russia. They accosted Gorbachev at his vacation retreat in the Crimea and demanded that he sign a decree proclaiming a state of emergency and transferring his powers to them. He replied, "Go to hell," whereupon he was placed under house arrest.

The coup was doomed from the start, however. Poorly planned and clumsily implemented, it lacked effective coordination. The plotters failed to arrest popular leaders such as Boris Yeltsin, the president of the Russian republic, they neglected to close the airports or cut off telephone and television communications, and they were opposed by key elements of the military and KGB (the secret police). But most important, the plotters failed to recognize the strength of the democratic idealism unleashed by Gorbachev's reforms.

As the political drama unfolded in the Soviet Union, foreign leaders around the world spoke out against the coup. On August 20 President Bush, after a day of indecision, responded favorably to Yeltsin's request for support and convinced world leaders to join him in refusing to recognize the legitimacy of the new Soviet government. The next day, word began to seep out that the plotters had given up and were fleeing. Several committed suicide, and a newly released Gorbachev ordered the others arrested. Yet things did not go back to the way they had been. Although Gorbachev reclaimed the title of president, he was forced to resign as head of the Communist party and admit that he had made a grave mistake in appointing the men who had turned against him. Boris Yeltsin emerged as the most popular political figure in the country.

What began as a reactionary coup turned into a powerful accelerant for stunning new changes in the Soviet Union, or the Soviet Disunion, as one wag termed it. Most of the fifteen republics proclaimed their independence, with the Baltic republics of Latvia, Lithuania, and Estonia regaining the status of independent nations. The Communist party apparatus was dismantled, prompting celebrating crowds to topple statues of Lenin and other Communist heroes.

A chastened Gorbachev could only acquiesce in the breakup of the Soviet Empire, whereas the systemic problems burdening the Soviet Union before the coup remained intractable. The economy was stagnant, food and coal shortages loomed on the horizon, and consumer goods remained scarce. The reformers had won, but they had yet to establish deep roots in a country with no democratic tradition. Leaping into the unknown, they faced years of hardship and uncertainty.

The aborted coup also accelerated Soviet and American efforts to reduce the stockpiles of nuclear weapons. In late 1991 President Bush stunned the world by announcing that the United States would destroy all its tactical nuclear weapons on land and at sea in Europe and Asia, take its long-range bombers off twenty-four-hour-alert status, and initiate discussions with the Soviet Union for the purpose of instituting sharp cuts in ICBMs with multiple warheads. Bush explained that the prospect of a Soviet invasion of western Europe was "no longer a realistic threat," and this transformation provided an unprecedented opportunity for reducing the threat of nuclear holocaust. President Gorbachev responded by announcing reciprocal Soviet cutbacks.

PANAMA   The end of the cold war did not spell the end of international tensions and conflict, however. Indeed, before the end of 1989, U.S. troops were engaged in battle in Panama, where a petty tyrant provoked the first of America's military engagements under George Bush. In 1983 General Manuel Noriega had maneuvered himself into the position of leader of the Panamanian Defense Forces, which made him head of government in fact if not in title. Earlier, as chief of intelligence, Noriega had developed a profitable business of supplying information on the region to the CIA, a business that had operated during the period when Bush headed the agency. At the same time he was developing avenues in the region for drug smuggling and gunrunning, laundering the money from those activities through Panamanian banks. For a time American intelligence analysts looked the other way, regarding Noriega as a useful contact, but eventually he became an embarrassment. In 1987 a rejected associate published charges of Noriega's drug activities and accused him further of rigged elections and political assassination.

In 1988 federal grand juries in Miami and Tampa indicted Noriega and fifteen others on drug charges. The Panamanian president tried to fire Noriega, but the National Assembly ousted the president instead and named Noriega "maximum leader." It then proclaimed that Panama "is declared to be in a state of war" with the United States. The next day, December 16, 1989, an American marine in Panama was killed. President Bush thereupon ordered an invasion of Panama with the purpose of capturing Noriega for trial on the American indictments and installing a government headed by President Guillermo Endara.

The 12,000 American military personnel already in Panama were quickly joined by 12,000 more, and in the early morning of December 20 five military task forces struck at strategic targets in the country. Within hours, Noriega had surrendered to American forces. Twenty-three U.S. servicemen were killed in the action, and estimates of Panamanian casualties ranged up to 4,000, including many civilians. In April 1992 Noriega was convicted in the United States on eight counts of racketeering and drug distribution.

THE GULF WAR   Months after Panama had moved to the background of public attention, Saddam Hussein, dictator of Iraq, focused attention on the Middle East when his army suddenly invaded tiny Kuwait on August 2, 1990. Kuwait had raised its production of oil, contrary to agreements with OPEC. The resultant drop in oil prices offended the Iraqi regime, deep in debt and heavily dependent upon oil revenues.

Saddam Hussein was surprised by the backlash his invasion of Kuwait caused. The UN Security Council quickly voted fourteen to zero to condemn the invasion and demand withdrawal. U.S. Secretary of State James Baker and Soviet foreign minister Eduard Shevardnadze issued a joint statement of condemnation. On August 6 the Security Council endorsed Resolution 661, an embargo on trade with Iraq, by a vote of thirteen to zero, with Cuba and Yemen abstaining. Such unanimity, of course, would have been unlikely during the cold war era.

The Gulf War

U.S. soldiers adapt to desert conditions during Operation Desert Shield, December 1990.

Bush condemned Iraq's "naked aggression" and dispatched planes and troops to Saudi Arabia on a "wholly defensive" mission—to protect Saudi Arabia. British forces soon joined in, as did Arab units from Egypt, Morocco, Syria, Oman, the United Arab Emirates, and Qatar. On August 22 Bush ordered the mobilization of American reserve forces for the operation, now dubbed Desert Shield.

A flurry of peace efforts sent diplomats scurrying, but without result. Iraq refused to yield. On January 12 Congress passed a resolution authorizing the use of U.S. armed forces. By January 1991, over thirty nations were committed to Operation Desert Shield. Some nations sent only planes, ships, or support forces, but sixteen committed ground combat forces, ten of these Islamic countries. Desert Shield became Operation Desert Storm when the first allied cruise missiles began to hit Iraq on January 16.

Saddam Hussein concentrated his forces in Kuwait and expected a landing on the Kuwaiti coast and an allied attack northward into Kuwait. But the Iraqis were outflanked when 200,000 allied troops, largely American, British, and French, turned up on the undefended Iraqi border with Saudi Arabia 100 to 200 miles to the west. The allied ground assault began on February 24 and lasted only four days. Iraqi soldiers surrendered by the thousands.

On February 28, six weeks after the fighting began, President Bush called for a cease-fire, the Iraqis accepted, and the shooting ended. There were 137 American fatalities. The lowest estimates of Iraqi fatalities, civilian and military, were around 100,000. The coalition forces occupied about one fifth of Iraq. The consequences of the brief but intense Persian Gulf War, the "mother of all battles" in Saddam Hussein's words, would be played out far into the future.

MAKING CONNECTIONS

- Much of what characterized the 1980s, from economic and social policy to presidential leadership style, was reminiscent of the late nineteenth century as well as the 1920s and 1950s.

- Another parallel between the late nineteenth century and the 1980s was a rise in immigration and a change in immigration patterns. This is discussed in Chapter 37.

- Chapter 37 also shows how the economic and political conservatism of the 1980s became much more ideological in the early 1990s.

FURTHER READING

Two brief accounts of Reagan's presidency are David Mervin's *Ronald Reagan and the American Presidency* (1990) and Michael Schaller's *Reckoning with Reagan: America and Its President in the 1980s* (1992).

On Reaganomics, see David A. Stockman's *The Triumph of Politics: How the Reagan Revolution Failed* (1986) and Robert Lekachman's *Greed Is Not Enough: Reaganomics* (1982). On the issue of arms control, see Strobe Talbott's *Deadly Gambits: The Reagan Administration and the Stalemate in Nuclear Arms Control* (1984).

For Reagan's foreign policy in Central America, see James Chace's *Endless War: How We Got Involved in Central America and What Can Be Done* (1984) and Walter LaFeber's *Inevitable Revolutions: The United States in Central America,* 2nd ed. (1993). Insider views of Reagan's foreign policy are offered in Alexander M. Haig Jr.'s *Caveat: Realism, Reagan, and Foreign Policy* (1984) and Caspar W. Weinberger's *Fighting for Peace: Seven Critical Years in the Pentagon* (1990).

On Reagan's second term, see Jane Mayer and Doyle McManus's *Landslide: The Unmaking of the President, 1984–1988* (1988). For a masterful work on the Iran-Contra affair, see Theodore Draper's *A Very Thin Line: The Iran Contra Affairs* (1991). Several collections of essays include varying assessments of the Reagan years. Among these are *The Reagan Revolution?* (1988), edited by B. B. Kymlicka and Jean V. Matthews; *The Reagan Presidency: An Incomplete Revolution?* (1990), edited by Dilys M. Hill, Raymond A. Moore, and Phil Williams, and *Looking Back on the Reagan Presidency* (1990), edited by Larry Berman.

On the 1988 campaign, see Jack W. Germond and Jules Witcover's *Whose Broad Stripes and Bright Stars? The Trivial Pursuit of the Presidency, 1988* (1989) and Sidney Blumenthal's *Pledging Allegiance: The Last Campaign of the Cold War* (1990). For a social history of the decade, see John Ehrman's *The Eighties: America in the Age of Reagan* (2005).

37

TRIUMPH AND TRAGEDY: AMERICA AT THE TURN OF THE CENTURY

FOCUS QUESTIONS

- How did the demographic patterns in the United States change in the 1980s and 1990s?
- What led to the Democratic resurgence of the early 1990s and the subsequent Republican landslide of 1994?
- Why did the economy and the stock market surge during the 1990s?
- What were the consequences of the rise of global terrorism and the terrorist assaults on the United States?

To answer these questions and access additional review material, please visit www.wwnorton.com/studyspace.

The United States entered the final decade of the twentieth century triumphant. American vigilance in the cold war had led to the stunning collapse of the Soviet Union and the birth of democratic capitalism in eastern Europe. The United States was now the world's only superpower. Not since ancient Rome had one nation exercised such influence in world affairs. By the mid-1990s the American economy would become the marvel of the world as remarkable gains in productivity afforded by new technologies created the greatest period of prosperity in modern history. Yet no sooner did the century come to an end than America's comfortable sense of physical and material security was shattered by a horrifying terrorist assault that killed thousands, plummeted the economy into a steep recession, and called into question conventional notions of national security and personal safety. President George W. Bush observed in 2003, "America has gone from a sense of invulnerability to an awareness of peril, from bitter division in small matters to calm unity in great causes. And we go forward with confidence, because this call of history has come to the right country." But Bush claimed too much. There was less "calm unity" in the United States than he implied. It remained to be seen whether the nation was moving "with confidence" into the new century.

AMERICA'S CHANGING MOSAIC

DEMOGRAPHIC SHIFTS   During the 1980s and 1990s the nation's population grew by 20 percent, or some 50 million people, boosting the total to over 290 million in 2000. The much-discussed baby-boom generation—the 43 million people born between 1946 and 1964—entered middle age. This generation's maturation and its preoccupation with practical concerns such as raising families, paying for college, and buying houses helped explain the surge of political conservatism during the 1980s. Surveys revealed that baby boomers wanted stronger family and religious ties and a greater respect for authority than prevailed in the late 1960s. Yet having come to maturity during the turbulent sixties and early seventies, the baby boomers also displayed more tolerance of social and cultural diversity than their parents had.

During the last quarter of the twentieth century, the sunbelt states of the South and the West continued to lure residents from the Midwest and the Northeast. Fully 90 percent of the nation's total population growth during the 1980s occurred in southern or western states. These population shifts forced a massive redistricting of the House of Representatives, with Florida, California, and Texas gaining seats and northern states such as New York losing seats. The sunbelt states were attractive not only because of their mild climate; they also had the lowest tax rates in the nation, the highest rates of economic growth, and growing numbers of evangelical Christians. Such attributes also made the sunbelt states fertile ground for the Republican party.

Americans at the end of the twentieth century tended to settle in large communities. This continuing move to metropolitan areas largely reflected trends in the job market as the "postindustrial" economy continued to shift from manufacturing to professional-service industries, particularly those specializing in telecommunications and information processing. By 2000 fewer than 2 million people out of a total population of 290 million worked on farms.

Women continued to enter the workforce in large numbers. In 1970, 38 percent of the workforce was female; in 2000 the figure was almost 50 percent. Women made up over one third of the new doctors (up from 4 percent in 1970), 40 percent of the new lawyers (up from 8 percent in 1970), and 23 percent of the new dentists (up from less than 1 percent in 1970).

The decline of the traditional family unit continued. In 2005 less than 65 percent of children lived with two parents, down from 85 percent in 1970. And more people were living alone than ever before, largely as a result of high divorce rates or a growing practice of delaying marriage until well into the twenties. The number of single mothers increased 35 percent during the decade. The rate was much higher for African Americans: in 2000 fewer than 32 percent of black children lived with both parents, down from 67 percent in 1960.

Young African Americans in particular faced shrinking economic opportunities at the start of the twenty-first century. The urban poor more than others were victimized by high rates of crime and violence, with young black men suffering the most. In 2000 the leading cause of death among African-American men between the ages of fifteen and twenty-four was homicide. Over 25 percent of African-American men aged twenty to twenty-nine were in prison, on parole, or on probation, while only 4 percent were enrolled in college. And 40 percent of African-American adult men were functionally illiterate.

THE NEW IMMIGRANTS   The racial and ethnic composition of the country also changed rapidly at the turn of the century. During the 1990s the foreign-born population increased by 57 percent, to 31 million, the largest ever. By 2005 the United States had more foreign-born and first-generation residents than ever before, and each year 1 million more immigrants arrived. Over 30 percent of Americans claimed African, Asian, Latino, or American Indian ancestry. Latinos represented 14 percent of the total population, African Americans 11 percent, Asians about 4 percent, and American Indians almost 1 percent. The rate of increase among those four groups was twice as fast as it had been during the 1970s. In 2005 Latinos became the nation's largest minority group.

The primary cause of this dramatic change in the nation's ethnic mix was a surge of immigration. During the 1990s legal immigration to the United States totaled over 10 million people, 40 percent higher than in the previous decade and more than in any other decade. These figures do not include the hundreds of thousands of undocumented aliens, mostly Mexicans and Haitians. In 2000 the United States welcomed more than twice as many immigrants as all other countries in the world combined. For the first time in the nation's history, the majority of immigrants came not from Europe but from other parts of the

Illegal Immigration

Increasing numbers of Chinese risked their savings and their lives trying to gain entry to the United States. These illegal immigrants are trying to keep warm after being forced to swim ashore when the freighter carrying them to the United States ran aground near Rockaway Beach in New York City in June 1993.

world: Asia, Latin America, and Africa. Among the legal immigrants, Mexicans made up the largest share, averaging over 100,000 a year.

The wave of new immigrants, younger, poorer, and less well educated than the native population, heightened conflict between old and new ethnicities. Critics charged that the nation was being "overrun" with foreigners; they questioned whether Latinos and Asians could be "assimilated" into American culture. In 1994 a large majority of California voters approved Proposition 187, a controversial initiative that denied the state's estimated 4 million illegal immigrants access to public schools, nonemergency health care, and other social services. In 1998 California voters passed a referendum to end bilingual education.

The bitter irony of this new nativism was that it targeted recent immigrants for bringing with them to the United States virtues long prized by Americans: hope, energy, persistence, and an aggressive work ethic. Many new immigrants compiled an astonishing record of achievement, yet their very success contributed to the resentment they encountered from other groups.

THE COMPUTER REVOLUTION   Not only demographic shifts and immigration but also technological changes were transforming the nation. A dramatic revolution in information technology produced a surge in productivity and prosperity during the 1980s and 1990s. Cellular phones, laser printers, VCRs and then DVDs, fax machines, and personal computers became commonplace. The computer age had arrived.

The idea of a programmable machine that would rapidly perform mental tasks had been around since the eighteenth century, but it took the crisis of World War II to gather the intellectual and financial resources needed to create such a "computer." A team of engineers at the University of Pennsylvania created ENIAC (electronic numerical integrator and computer), the first all-purpose, all-electronic digital computer. Unveiled in 1946, it could perform 5,000 operations per second. ENIAC took up 3,000 cubic feet of space and housed 18,000 vacuum tubes (glass canisters designed to amplify electric current), 70,000 resistors, 10,000 capacitors, and 6,000 switches.

During the 1950s and 1960s corporations such as IBM and government agencies transformed computers from mathematical calculators into electronic data-processing machines. The key development in facilitating the

The Computer Age

Beginning with the cumbersome electronic numerical integrator and computer (ENIAC), pictured here in 1946, computer technology flourished, leading to the development of personal computers in the 1980s and the popularization of the Internet in the 1990s.

transformation occurred in 1947 when three physicists at Bell Laboratories in central New Jersey invented the transistor (so named because it *trans*fers electric current across a re*sistor*, which is a conductor used to control voltage in an electric circuit). Tiny transistors took the place of the bulky glass vacuum tubes. The availability of transistors led to the development of hearing aids and portable radios.

The next major breakthrough was the invention in 1971 of the microprocessor—a computer on a silicon chip. The functions that had once been performed by computers taking up an entire room could now be performed by a microchip circuit the size of a postage stamp. Engineers soon incorporated even smaller microchips into television sets, wristwatches, automobiles, kitchen appliances, and spacecraft.

The invention of the microchip made possible a personal computer. In 1975 an engineer named Ed Roberts developed the first prototype of the so-called personal computer. The Altair 8800 was imperfect and cumbersome, with no display, no keyboard, and not enough memory to do anything useful. But its potential excited a Harvard sophomore named Bill Gates. He improved the software of the Altair 8800, dropped out of college, and formed a company called Microsoft to sell the new system. By 1977, Gates and others had helped to transform the personal computer from a machine for hobbyists to a mass consumer product.

By the end of the 1980s, there were 60 million personal computers in the United States, and people began to talk about an "information superhighway," a worldwide network of linked computers and databases connected by fiber-optic lines that facilitated high-speed transmission. During the 1990s the development of the Internet and electronic mail meant that anyone with a personal computer and a modem could travel on the information superhighway. Such advances fostered instantaneous communication across the continents, thereby accelerating what came to be called the globalization of the economy and dramatically increasing productivity in the workplace. To the extent that computers had become essential tools for educational and economic success, however, they threatened to widen the gap between rich and poor. As always, it seems, technological progress has provided uneven and unequal benefits.

CULTURAL CONSERVATISM

Cultural conservatives helped elect Ronald Reagan and George Bush in the 1980s, but they were disappointed with the results. Once in office, neither president had, in the eyes of those conservatives, adequately addressed their moral agenda, including a complete ban on abortions and the restoration of prayer in public schools. By the 1990s a new generation of young conservative activists, mostly political independents or Republicans, largely from the sunbelt states, had emerged as a force to be reckoned with in national affairs. They were more ideological, more libertarian, more partisan, and more impatient than their predecessors. The new breed of cultural conservatives abhorred the excesses of social liberalism. They lamented the disappearance of basic forms of decency and propriety, and they attacked affirmative-action programs designed to redress historic injustices committed against women and minorities. During the 1990s powerful groups inside and outside the Republican party mobilized to roll back government programs giving preferences to specified social groups. Prominent African-American conservatives supported such efforts, arguing that recially based preferences were demeaning and condescending remedies for historical injustices.

THE RELIGIOUS RIGHT   Although quite diverse, cultural conservatives tended to be evangelical Christians or orthodox Catholics who joined together to exert increasing religious pressure on the political process. In 1989 the Virginia-based television evangelist Pat Robertson organized the Christian Coalition to replace Jerry Falwell's Moral Majority as the flagship organization of the resurgent religious right. The Christian Coalition encouraged religious conservatives to vote, run for public office, and support only those candidates who shared the organization's views.

The Christian Coalition chose the Republican party, with its well-organized grassroots movement in every state, as the best vehicle for transforming the religious right's pro-family campaign into public policies. The Christian Coalition encouraged its supporters to withhold political support from any candidate who did not provide an ironclad promise to support the coalition's school-prayer, anti-abortion, anti–gay rights positions. In addition to promoting "traditional family values," it urged politicians to "radically downsize and delimit government."

As a centrist professional politician, Republican George Bush initially tried to keep the cultural conservatives at arm's length, only to find himself the target—and victim—of their dogmatism. His successor, a Democrat also underestimated the growing strength of organized groups such as the Christian Coalition. In the 1994 congressional elections, religious conservatives went to the polls in record numbers, and 70 percent of them voted Republican. One third of the voters identified themselves as "white, evangelical, born-again Christians." In many respects they took control of the political and social agendas in the nineties. As one journalist acknowledged in 1995, "the religious right is moving toward center stage in American secular life."

BUSH TO CLINTON

For months after the Persian Gulf War in 1991, George H. W. Bush seemed unbeatable; his approval rating rose to 91 percent. But the aftermath of Desert Storm was mixed, with Saddam Hussein's despotic grip on Iraq still intact. Despite his image of strength abroad, Bush began to look weak even on foreign policy. The Soviet Union meanwhile stumbled on to its surprising end. On December 25, 1991, the Soviet flag over the Kremlin was replaced by the flag of the Russian Federation. The cold war had ended with the dismemberment of the Soviet Union and its fifteen constituent republics. As a result, the United States had become the world's only superpower.

"Containment" of the Soviet Union, the bedrock of U.S. foreign policy for more than four decades, had lost its reason for being. Bush, the ultimate cold war careerist—formerly ambassador to the UN, envoy to China, head of the CIA, vice president under Reagan—struggled to interpret the fluid new international scene. He spoke of a "new world order" but never defined it. By his own admission he had trouble with "the vision thing." The dynamic international situation, in fact, did not lend itself to a simple vision—unless the answer was for the nation to drift into isolation, a great temptation with foreign dangers seemingly on the decline. By the end of 1991, a listless Bush faced a challenge in the Republican primary from the feisty television commentator and former White House aide Patrick Buchanan, who adopted the slogan "America First" and called on Bush to "bring home the boys." As the euphoria of the Gulf War victory wore off, a popular bumper sticker reflected the growing public frustration with the Bush administration: "Saddam Hussein still has his job. What about you?"

RECESSION AND DOWNSIZING In November 1988, a few days after George Bush was elected president, a journalist observed that the most important issue to be addressed by the new administration was the nation's deepening financial debt: "It is the issue that probably will determine the fate of the President. Indeed, it could also be his ultimate undoing." It was an accurate prediction. For the Bush administration and for the nation, the most devastating development in the early nineties was a prolonged economic recession that began in 1990. The first major economic setback in more than eight years, it grew into the longest, if not the deepest, since the

Great Depression. During 1991, 25 million workers—about 20 percent of the labor force—were unemployed at some point.

What made this recession unusual was that its victims included a large number of white-collar workers. In the corporate world, terms such as *restructuring* and *downsizing* ruled the day as companies began to reduce personnel, switch employees to part-time status to reduce the cost of benefits, and find other ways to cut labor costs and improve productivity.

At the same time, the country was experiencing a continuing imbalance in foreign trade and soaring expenditures on defense and social-entitlement programs. During 1991 a $150-billion annual deficit had become a $450-billion shortfall. In addition, the country lacked a plan for the demobilization of the military-industrial complex, which had become antiquated in the post–cold war world. A Senate committee analysis of the the stagnant economy confirmed a chilling fact: under the Bush administration "the average standard of living has actually declined." The euphoria over the allied victory in the Gulf War quickly gave way to anxiety and resentment generated by the depressed economy. At the end of 1991, *Time* magazine declared that "no one, not even George Bush" could deny "that the economy was sputtering."

Whatever the reasons for the recession, the cure remained elusive. Although the Federal Reserve Board began cutting interest rates, the economy remained in the doldrums through 1992. The Democratic Congress and the Republican president squabbled over legislation to promote economic recovery but little was done to prod new growth or reduce the hemorrhaging deficits. With his domestic policies in disarray and his foreign policy abandoned, George Bush tried a clumsy balancing act in addressing the recession, on the one hand acknowledging that "people are hurting" while on the other urging Americans that "this is a good time to buy a car."

THE THOMAS HEARINGS AND THE WOMEN'S MOVEMENT

Other developments contributed to the erosion of the President Bush's popularity, among them the retirement in 1991 of the African-American Supreme Court justice, Thurgood Marshall, after twenty-four years on the bench. To succeed him Bush named Clarence Thomas, an African-American federal judge who had been raised in poverty in the segregated South. Thomas's views delighted conservative senators. He questioned the wisdom of the minimum wage, school busing for desegregation, and affirmative-action hiring programs, and he preached "black self-help," once declaring that all civil rights leaders ever did was "bitch, bitch, bitch, moan, and whine."

Such opinions promised trouble for Thomas's confirmation hearings in the Democratic Senate, but an explosion occurred when Anita Hill, a soft-spoken law professor at the University of Oklahoma, charged that Thomas had sexually harassed her when she worked for him in a federal agency during the 1980s. Pro-Thomas senators orchestrated an often-savage and sometimes absurd cross-examination of Hill. Some accused her of mental instability. An indignant Thomas denied her charges and called the hearings a "high-tech lynching for uppity blacks." He implied that Hill had fabricated the charges at the behest of civil rights groups determined to thwart his confirmation. The televised hearings revealed that either Hill or Thomas had lied, and the committee's tie vote reflected the doubt: seven to recommend confirmation and seven against. The full Senate then confirmed Thomas by the narrow margin of fifty-two to forty-eight.

The Thomas hearings sparked a resurgence of the women's movement. Many women grew incensed at the treatment of Anita Hill, and an unprecedented number of women ran for national and local offices in 1992. The Thomas confirmation struggle thus widened the gender gap for a Republican party already less popular with women than with men. As one political commentator put it, "The war with Anita Hill was not a war Bush needed."

REPUBLICAN TURMOIL   President Bush had already set a political trap for himself when he declared at the 1988 Republican Convention: "Read my lips: no new taxes." Fourteen months into his presidency, however, he had decided that the federal budget deficit was a greater risk than violating his no-tax pledge. After intense negotiations with congressional Democrats, Bush had announced that reducing the federal deficit required "tax revenue increases." Bush's backsliding set off a revolt among House Republicans, but a bipartisan majority (with most Republicans still opposed) finally approved a tax-increase measure, raising the top personal rate from 28 to 31 percent, disallowing certain deductions in the upper brackets, and raising various special taxes. Conservative Republicans would not let George Bush forget his abandoned pledge not to raise taxes.

Social issues had been one of the adhesives in the Reagan coalition, diverting the focus from divisive economic issues, but as hardships assaulted the attention of blue-collar workers, the economy became the primary concern. Moreover, social issues strengthened the force of the new "Christian Right." At the 1992 Republican Convention, Patrick Buchanan, who had won about one third of the votes in the party's primaries, used the occasion for a defense of "family values." Buchanan combined a sharp mind with a sharp tongue in promoting his campaign to restore traditional conservative values and "put America first." He lambasted Bush for breaking his pledge not to raise taxes and for becoming the "biggest spender in American history." Buchanan claimed to be a crusader "for a Middle American revolution" that would halt illegal immigration and liberal permissiveness. As the 1992 election unfolded, Bush's real problem was not Pat Buchanan and the conservative wing of the Republican party. What threatened his reelection was his own listless effort to jump-start the economy.

DEMOCRATIC RESURGENCE   In contrast to divisions among Republicans, the Democrats at their 1992 convention presented an image of centrist forces in control. For several years the Democratic Leadership Council, in which Arkansas governor William Jefferson Clinton figured prominently, had pushed the party from the liberal left to the center of the political spectrum. Clinton strove to move the Democrats closer to the mainstream of political opinion. A graduate of Georgetown University, he had won a Rhodes scholarship to Oxford and then earned a law degree from Yale, where he met and married Hillary Rodham. By 1979, at age thirty-two, he was back in his native Arkansas, serving as the youngest governor in the country. He served three more terms as governor and in the process emerged as a dynamic young leader committed to winning back the middle-class whites who had voted Republican during the 1980s. Democrats had grown so liberal, he argued, that they had alienated their key constituency, the "vital center."

A self-described moderate, Clinton promised to cut the defense budget, provide tax relief for the middle class, and create a massive economic aid package for the former republics of the Soviet Union to help them forge democratic societies. Handsome, witty, intelligent, and a compelling speaker, Clinton projected energy, youth, and optimism, reminding many political observers of John F. Kennedy.

But underneath the veneer of Clinton's charisma were several flaws. He often seemed so determined to become president that he was willing to sacrifice consistency and principle. He made extensive use of polls to shape his stance on issues, pandered to special-interest groups, and flip-flopped on controversial subjects, leading critics to label him Slick Willie. Said one former opponent in Arkansas: "He'll be what people want him to be. He'll do or say what it will take to get elected." Even more enticing to the media and more embarrassing to Clinton were charges that he was a chronic adulterer and that he had manipulated the ROTC program during the Vietnam War to avoid the draft. Clinton's evasive denials of both allegations could not dispel a lingering distrust of his personal character.

Yet after a series of bruising party primaries, Clinton emerged as the front-runner by the time of the nominating convention in the summer of 1992. Once nominated, Clinton chose Senator Albert Gore Jr. of Tennessee as his running mate. So the candidates were two Southern Baptists from adjoining states. Flushed with their convention victory and sporting a

The 1992 Presidential Campaign

Presidential candidate Bill Clinton and his running mate, Al Gore, brought youthful enthusiasm to the campaign trail.

ten-point lead in the polls, the Clinton-Gore team stressed economic issues to win over working-class white and black voters. Clinton won the election with 370 electoral votes and about 43 percent of the vote; Bush received 168 electoral votes and 39 percent of the vote; and off-and-on independent candidate H. Ross Perot of Texas garnered 18 percent of the popular vote but no electoral votes. A puckish billionaire, Perot found a big audience for his simplified explanations of public problems and his offers to just "get under the hood and fix them."

DOMESTIC POLICY IN CLINTON'S FIRST TERM

Bill Clinton had run a brilliant campaign, portraying himself as an outsider untainted by Washington politics and inertia. Yet his inexperience in international affairs and congressional maneuvering led to several missteps in his first year as president. Like George Bush before him, Clinton reneged on several campaign promises. He abandoned his proposed middle-class tax cut in order to keep down the federal deficit. When his attempt to allow professed homosexuals to serve in the armed forces aroused strong opposition among military commanders and in Congress, he backed down nine days into office and later announced an ambiguous new policy concerning gays in the military that came to be known as don't ask, don't tell. In Clinton's first two weeks in office, his approval rating dropped 20 percent.

THE ECONOMY   As a candidate, Clinton had pledged to reduce the federal deficit without damaging the economy. To this end, on February 17 he proposed higher taxes for corporations and for individuals in higher tax brackets and called for an economic stimulus package for "investment" in public works (transportation, utilities, and the like) and "human capital" (education, skills, health, and welfare). The Republicans in the Senate blocked the stimulus package, which they described as a "budget buster" that would fail to pep up the economy. In response to Clinton's deficit reduction package of spending cuts and tax hikes on upper incomes, both Republicans and conservative Democrats who favored even deeper spending cuts opposed the package. The hotly contested bill finally passed by 218 to 216 in the House and 51 to 50 in the Senate, with Vice President Gore breaking the tie.

Equally contested was the North American Free Trade Agreement (NAFTA), which the Bush administration had negotiated with Canada and Mexico. The debate over its congressional approval revived old arguments on the tariff. Clinton stuck with his party's tradition of low tariffs and urged approval of NAFTA, which would make North America the largest free-trade area in the world. He and his supporters argued that tariff reductions would open up foreign markets to American industries. Opponents of the bill, such as wealthy gadfly Ross Perot and organized labor, favored barriers that would discourage cheaper foreign products and believed that with NAFTA the country would hear a "giant sucking sound" of American jobs being drawn to Mexico. Yet Clinton prevailed with solid Republican support while losing a sizable minority of Democrats, mostly from the South, where people feared that textile mills would lose business to "cheap-labor" countries, as they did.

HEALTH-CARE REFORM   Clinton's major public policy initiative was a new federal health-care plan. Government-subsidized health insurance was not a new idea. Other industrial countries had long ago started national health-insurance programs, Germany as early as 1883, Britain in 1911. Off and on throughout the twentieth century the idea had been a subject of political discussion in the United States. Medicare, initiated in 1965, provided insurance for people sixty-five and older, and Medicaid supported state medical assistance for the indigent. Those programs had grown enormously, as had business spending on private health insurance.

Sentiment for health-care reform spread as annual medical costs skyrocketed and some 39 million Americans went without insurance either by choice or out of necessity. The Clinton administration argued that universal medical insurance would reduce the overall costs of health care. Medicare covered older people, the most vulnerable to medical expenses, and its costs were soaring. Many of the working poor could not afford insurance, and many younger, healthier people took a chance on doing without. When they got in trouble, they reported to emergency rooms, which were reluctant to reject desperate people. As a result, those who could pay covered the others' costs in higher medical fees.

Universal medical coverage as proposed by Clinton would entitle every citizen and legal immigrant to health insurance. Government would subsidize all or part of the payments for small businesses and the poor, the latter from funds that formerly went to Medicaid, and would collect a "sin tax" on tobacco and perhaps alcoholic beverages to pay for the program. Hillary Clinton, the president's wife, chaired the health-care-plan task force and became the administration's lead witness on the plan before congressional committees. Throughout 1994 a comprehensive health-insurance plan remained the centerpiece of the Clinton agenda. The bill aroused opposition from vested interests, however, especially the pharmaceutical and insurance industries. By the summer of 1994, Clinton's health-insurance plan was pretty well doomed. Republican senators began a filibuster to prevent a vote on the bill. Lacking the votes to stop the filibuster, the Democrats acknowledged defeat and gave up the fight for universal medical coverage.

MISTRUST OF GOVERNMENT AND THE MILITIA MOVEMENT

While Clinton sparred with Republicans in Washington, a "militia" or "patriot" movement spread in small pockets across the country in the 1990s, representing a paranoid and populist strain in cultural politics. Convinced that the federal government was conspiring against individual liberties (especially the right to bear arms), thousands of mostly working-class folk joined well-armed militia organizations. Some militias harked back to the origins of the Ku Klux Klan and fomented racial and ethnic hatred. Others aligned themselves with right-wing Christian groups, particularly the militant wing of the anti-abortion movement. In the Far West several of the militias challenged federal control of public lands, refused to pay taxes, and threatened to arrest and execute local government officials and judges.

In Waco, Texas, a confrontation between federal authorities and a cultlike militia group called the Branch Davidians sparked a tragedy. The Davidians, an apocalyptic religious sect headed by a charismatic leader named David Koresh, were found to be stockpiling weapons, engaging in child abuse, and violating immigration laws. On February 28, 1993, agents from the Treasury Department's Bureau of Alcohol, Tobacco, and Firearms (BATF) tried to serve a warrant on members of the sect, only to be met with gunfire. Four agents and two Branch Davidians were killed, and twenty people were injured. The next

Oklahoma City

The Alfred P. Murrah Federal Building in Oklahoma City after it was bombed on April 19, 1995, in what was then the deadliest terrorist act on U.S. soil.

day the FBI took over the siege of the compound, waging fruitless psychological warfare against the Branch Davidians. On April 19, the fifty-first day of the siege, FBI agents recklessly attacked the compound with armored vehicles and tear gas. Amid the commotion the compound caught fire and quickly burned to the ground. At least seventy-seven people died in the inferno.

On the second anniversary of the Waco incident, April 19, 1995, a massive truck bomb exploded in front of the federal office building in Oklahoma City, Oklahoma. The entire front portion of the nine-story building collapsed, killing 168 people, 19 of them children in a day-care center in the building. Six hundred others were injured. Within days the FBI had arrested Timothy McVeigh and Terry Nichols and charged them with the bombing. A third man pleaded guilty to separate charges of conspiring to produce explosives. All three men were militia members who hated the federal government and had been incensed by the way the BATF and FBI had dealt with the Branch Davidians at Waco. The Oklahoma City bombing shocked and saddened the nation. It brought to public attention the rise of right-wing militia groups and revealed the depth of anti-government sentiment among those fringe groups.

REPUBLICAN INSURGENCY

During 1994 Bill Clinton began to see his coveted presidency unravel. Unable to get either health-care reform or welfare-reform bills through the Democratic Congress and having failed to carry out his campaign pledge for middle-class tax relief, he and his party found themselves on the defensive. In the midterm elections of 1994, the Democrats suffered a humbling defeat. It was the first election since 1952 in which Republicans captured both houses of Congress at the same time. In both the majority was solid: 52 to 48 in the Senate, a majority that soon increased when two Democrats declared themselves Republicans, and 230 to 204 in the House. Not a single Republican

incumbent was defeated. Republicans also won a net gain of eleven governorships and fifteen state legislatures.

The election returns signaled a repudiation of Clinton and the Democratic Congress. Squabbling between the president and the congressional
Democrats did not help matters. Clinton's waffling on major issues convinced many in his own party that he was a politician rather than a leader,
someone who thrived as a campaigner but was bereft of genuine convictions. Said Democratic congressman David Obey, "I think most of us
learned some time ago that if you don't like the president's position on a
particular issue, you simply need to wait a few weeks." When Clinton
joined the chorus of conservatives calling for a scaling back of affirmative-
action plans designed to remedy historic patterns of racial discrimination
in hiring and the awarding of government contracts, liberal Democrats felt
betrayed.

THE CONTRACT WITH AMERICA A Georgian named Newton
Leroy Gingrich led the Republican insurgency in Congress during the
mid-1990s. Gingrich, a brilliant former history professor with an oversize
ego, had helped mobilize religious and social conservatives associated
with the Christian Coalition. In early 1995 he became the first Republican
Speaker of the House in forty-two years. Gingrich announced that "we are
at the end of an era." Liberalism was dead and the Democratic party was
dying. Gingrich pledged to start a new reign of congressional Republican
dominance that would dismantle the "corrupt liberal welfare state." He
was aided by the freshman Republicans who had come to Washington
filled with ardor for Gingrich. Now the majority in the House, they promoted what Gingrich called the Contract with America. The ten-point
contract outlined an anti-big-government program with less regulation,
less environmental conservation, term limits for members of Congress, a
line-item veto for the president, welfare reform, and a balanced-budget
amendment.

By April 13, exactly 100 days after taking office, the congressional Republicans had passed twenty-six bills stemming from the Contract with America
and had failed to pass only two: a proposal for an anti-missile ("Star Wars")
defense system and term limits for Congress. Nonetheless, twenty-two of
those bills did not become law. The only four successful bills were a law
mandating that all laws applicable to ordinary Americans should also apply
to members of Congress; a law by which Congress agreed to stop imposing
mandated programs on local and state governments without footing the
bill; a large defense-spending bill, which Clinton reluctantly accepted, lest

Republicans rebel on foreign policy; and a new crime bill providing for stiff penalties for child abuse and pornography.

Thereafter, the much-ballyhooed GOP revolution and the Contract with America fizzled out. The revolution that the imperious Gingrich touted was far too ambitious to carry out in so limited a time with so slim a majority and so little sense of crisis. What is more, many of the congressional Republican freshmen were scornful of compromise and were amateurs at legislative procedure, and they limited Gingrich's ability to maneuver. The Senate rejected many of the bills that had been passed in the House as senators were less under Gingrich's spell and not party to the Contract with America anyway. The "Republican revolution" of 1994 fizzled out, too, because Newt Gingrich became such an unpopular figure, both in Congress and among the electorate. He was too ambitious, too slick, too aggressive, too rambunctious. "No political figure in modern time," a journalist declared in 1996, "has done more to undermine the power of his message with the defects of his personality than the disastrously voluble Speaker of the House." And beyond all those factors, a presidential veto stood in the path of the Contract with America. President Clinton shrewdly moved to the political center and co-opted much of the Republican agenda. His distinctive strength—at least in the eyes of his supporters—resided in his agile responsiveness to changing public moods. To Clinton the Republican victory in the 1994 congressional elections and in the passage of the Contract with America initiatives bore a simple message: he must recapture the political center by radically changing his own agenda.

By the end of 1995, Clinton's fortunes were back on the rise as the Gingrich revolution petered out, leaving Gingrich with a bag of unfilled promises and low ratings in the polls. If the American people had voted a mandate for anything, it may have been a mandate for the status quo. Said one contrite freshman Republican congressman in 1996, "We scared too many people in the last year talking with such revolutionary fervor. I think we showed more guts than brains sometimes."

LEGISLATIVE BREAKTHROUGH   In the late summer of 1996, as lawmakers were preparing to adjourn and participate in the presidential nominating conventions, the 104th Congress broke through its partisan gridlock and passed a flurry of important legislation that President Clinton quickly signed, including bills increasing the minimum wage and broadening public access to health insurance. Even more significant was a comprehensive welfare-reform measure that ended the federal government's open-ended guarantee of aid to the poor, a guarantee that had been in place since

1935. The Personal Responsibility and Work Opportunity Act of 1996 turned over the major federal welfare programs to the states, which would receive federal grants to fund them. The bill also limited the amount of time during which a person could receive welfare benefits funded by federal money and required that at least half of a state's welfare recipients have jobs or be enrolled in job-training programs by 2002. States failing to meet the deadline would have their federal funds cut.

The Republican-sponsored welfare-reform legislation passed the Senate by a vote of seventy-four to twenty-four, and the president eagerly signed it into law. It had the effect of cutting $56 billion over six years from various welfare programs, several of which dated back to Franklin Roosevelt's New Deal. Liberals charged that Clinton was abdicating Democratic social principles in order to gain reelection amid the conservative climate of the times. Clinton and his centrist advisers, however, dismissed such criticism. With his reelection bid at stake, the president was determined to live up to his 1992 campaign pledge to "end welfare as we know it." Clinton also knew that most voters in both parties were eager to see major cuts in federal entitlement programs. "The era of big government is over," Clinton announced. Said one corporate executive, "Clinton is the most Republican Democrat in a long time."

THE 1996 CAMPAIGN   After clinching the Republican presidential nomination in 1996, Senate majority leader Bob Dole resigned his seat in order to devote his attention to defeating Bill Clinton. As the 1996 presidential campaign unfolded, however, Clinton maintained a large lead in the polls. With an improving economy and no major foreign-policy crises to confront, cultural and personal issues surged into prominence. Concern about Dole's age (seventy-three) and his acerbic manner, as well as rifts in the Republican party between economic and social conservatives over issues such as abortion and gun control, hampered Dole's efforts to generate widespread support.

On November 5, 1996, Clinton won again, with an electoral

Bob Dole

The Republican presidential candidate and former Senate majority leader on the campaign trail.

vote of 379 to 159 and 49 percent of the popular vote. Clinton was the first Democratic presidential candidate to win an election while the Republicans controlled Congress. And he was the first Democratic president to win a second term since Franklin Roosevelt in 1936. Voters viewed Clinton as bright and empathetic—but most of all he was an adept survivor. Throughout Clinton's career his relentless optimism and shrewd resilience enabled him to bounce back from repeated setbacks. As he once told a group of religious broadcasters, "My God is the god of second chances."

Dole received only 41 percent of the popular vote, and Ross Perot got 8 percent. The Republicans lost eight seats in the House but retained an edge, 227 to 207, over the Democrats in the House; in the Senate, Republicans gained two seats for a 55–45 majority. The resulting deadlock reflected the conservative mood of the times.

ECONOMIC AND SOCIAL TRENDS OF THE 1990s

After the 1996 election, Clinton reshuffled his cabinet and other posts. Madeleine Albright, ambassador to the United Nations, became the first woman to head the State Department, and Senator William Cohen, a Republican from Maine, took over the Defense Department. The overall direction of Clinton's changes was a move to the right that reflected profound economic and social developments during the 1990s.

THE "NEW ECONOMY"   As the twentieth century came to a close, the United States benefited from a prolonged period of unprecedented prosperity. Buoyed by low inflation, high employment, declining federal budget deficits, dramatic improvements in productivity, the rapid globalization of economic life, and the astute financial leadership of Federal Reserve Board chairman Alan Greenspan, business and industry witnessed record profits.

During the late 1990s the stock market soared. In 1993 the Dow Jones industrial average hit 3,500. By 1996 it had topped 6,000. During 1998 it reached 9,000, defying the predictions of experts that the economy could not sustain such performance. The "new economy" was centered on high-flying computer, software, telecommunications, and Internet firms, and on the whiz-kid techie entrepreneurs, venture capitalists, and stock-market promoters who capitalized on their overhyped potential. By early 2000 these dot-com enterprises had come to represent almost one third of stock-market values, even though many of them were hollow-shelled companies fueled by the speculative mania. The result was a financial bubble that would soon burst, but during the run-up in the 1990s investors gave little thought to a possible collapse, despite warnings from Alan Greenspan that an "irrational exuberance" had infected Wall Street trading. In 1998 unemployment was only 4.3 percent, the lowest since 1970. Inflation was a measly 1.7 percent. People began to claim that the new economy defied the boom-and-bust cycles of the previous hundred years. "It is possible," Greenspan suggested, "that we have moved 'beyond history.' "

One major factor producing the economic boom of the 1990s was the "peace dividend." The end of the cold war enabled the U.S. government to reduce the proportion of the annual budget devoted to defense spending. Another major factor was the Clinton administration's 1993 initiative cutting taxes and reducing overall federal spending. But perhaps the single most important reason for the surge in prosperity was dramatic growth in per-worker productivity. New technologies and new production processes enabled workers to be more efficient. Other favorable developments benefiting the economy of the 1990s included relatively low world oil prices, declining health-care costs, and changes in the way the consumer price index is calculated. Whatever the reasons, the robust economy set records in every area: low inflation, low unemployment, federal budget surpluses for the first time in modern history, and dizzying corporate profits. In the 1990s much of the surging economy resulted from efforts to promote free markets on a world scale—markets without tariffs and other barriers to free trade. More and more gigantic corporations such as IBM, Microsoft, and General Electric had become international in scope. This phenomenon encouraged free-trade agreements such as NAFTA as well as most-favored-nation treatment for China and other countries. With such agreements in place, American companies could easily outsource much of their production to plants in countries with lower labor costs. Increasingly, therefore, blue-collar labor lost ground to cheap foreign labor in assembly plants or "sweatshops" elsewhere in the world.

RACE INITIATIVES   After the triumphs of the civil rights movement in the 1960s, the momentum for minority advancement had run out—except for gains in college admissions and employment under the rubric of affirmative action. The conservative mood during the mid-1990s manifested itself in the Supreme Court. In 1995 the Court ruled against election districts redrawn to create African-American or Latino majorities and narrowed federal affirmative-action programs.

In one of the cases, *Adarand Constructors v. Peña* (1995), the Court assessed a program that gave some advantages to businesses owned by "disadvantaged" minorities. A Latino-owned firm had won a highway guardrail contract over a lower bid by a white-owned company. The white-owned company sued on the grounds of "reverse discrimination." Writing for the majority, Justice Sandra Day O'Connor said that such programs had to be "narrowly tailored" to serve a "compelling national interest." O'Connor did not define what the Court meant by a "compelling national interest," but the implication of her language was clear: the Court had come to embrace the growing public suspicion of the value and legality of such race-based programs.

In 1996 two major steps were taken against affirmative action in college admissions. In *Hopwood v. Texas*, the U.S. Court of Appeals for the Fifth Circuit ruled that considering race to achieve a diverse student body at the University of Texas was "not a compelling interest under the Fourteenth Amendment." Later that year the state of California passed Proposition 209, an initiative that ruled out race, sex, ethnicity, and national origin as criteria for preferring any group. These rulings eviscerated affirmative-action programs and drastically reduced African-American college enrollments, prompting second thoughts. In addition, the nation still had not addressed intractable problems that lay beyond civil rights—that is, problems of dependency: illiteracy, poverty, unemployment, urban decay, and slums.

THE SCANDAL MACHINE   During his first term, President Clinton was dogged by allegations of improper involvement in the Whitewater Development Corporation. In 1978, as governor of Arkansas, he had invested in a resort project on the White River in northern Arkansas. The project turned out to be a fraud and a failure, and the Clintons took a loss on their investment. In 1994 Kenneth Starr, a Republican, was appointed to serve as independent counsel in an investigation of the Whitewater case. Although Starr had a reputation for fairness, many observers believed that his unwillingness to end the expensive investigation and his former position in the Bush administration suggested the taint of partisanship. While revealing that Hillary Clinton had handled some legal work for the Whitewater Development Corporation, Starr's extensive investigation did not uncover evidence that the Clintons were directly involved in the fraud, although a number of their close associates had been caught in the web and convicted of various charges, some related to Whitewater and some not.

Separate from the Whitewater investigation, a salacious scandal erupted when it was revealed that Bill Clinton had engaged in a sexual affair with a White House intern, Monica Lewinsky, and the president had pressed her to lie about their relationship under oath. Headlines trumpeted the juicy story. Clinton initially denied the charges, but the tawdry scandal would not

The Whitewater Scandal

The ongoing Whitewater investigation threatened to derail important initiatives as it occupied the attention of the president and Congress.

disappear. In August 1998, President Clinton agreed to testify before a grand jury convened to investigate the sexual allegations. He was the first president in history to testify before a grand jury. On August 17, Clinton recanted his earlier denials and acknowledged having had "inappropriate intimate physical contact" with Monica Lewinsky. That evening, Clinton delivered a four-minute nationally televised address in which he admitted an improper relationship with Lewinsky. He admitted that it was "wrong" but insisted that he had done nothing illegal. "I know that my public comments and my silence about this matter gave a false impression. I misled people, including even my wife," Clinton said. "I deeply regret that."

Public reaction to Clinton's remarkable about-face was mixed. A majority expressed sympathy for the president because of his public humiliation and wanted the entire matter dropped. But Clinton's credibility had suffered a serious blow on account of his reckless lack of self-discipline and his efforts to deny and then cover up the scandal.

Meanwhile, Kenneth Starr continued his tenacious investigation. On September 9, 1998, he submitted to Congress a 445-page report and eighteen

Impeachment

Representative Edward Pease, a member of the House Judiciary Committee, covers his face during the vote on the third of four articles of impeachment charging President Clinton with "high crimes and misdemeanors," December 1998.

boxes of supporting material. The Starr Report found "substantial and creditable" evidence of presidential wrongdoing. On October 8 the House of Representatives voted 258 to 176 to begin a wide-ranging impeachment inquiry of President Clinton. Thirty-one Democrats joined the Republicans in supporting the investigation. On December 19, 1998, William Jefferson Clinton became the second president to be impeached by the House of Representatives. The House officially approved two articles of impeachment, charging Clinton with lying under oath to a federal grand jury and obstructing justice.

The Senate trial of President Clinton began on January 7, 1999, with the swearing in of Chief Justice William Rehnquist to preside and the senators as jurors. Five weeks later, on February 12, the Senate acquitted Clinton. Rejecting the first charge of perjury, ten Republicans and all fortyfive Democrats voted "not guilty." On the charge of obstruction of justice, the Senate split fifty-fifty (which meant acquittal, since sixtyseven votes were needed for conviction). In both instances, senators had a hard time interpreting Clinton's philandering as "high crimes and misdemeanors," the constitutional requirement for removal of a president from office. Clinton's supporters portrayed him as the victim of a puritanical special prosecutor and partisan conspiracy run amok. His critics lambasted him as a lecherous man without honor or integrity. Both characterizations were incomplete. Politically astute, charismatic, and well-informed, Clinton had as much ability and potential as any president. Yet he was also shamelessly self-indulgent. The result was a scandalous presidency punctuated by dramatic achievements in welfare reform, economic growth, and foreign policy.

FOREIGN-POLICY CHALLENGES

Like Woodrow Wilson, Lyndon Johnson, and Jimmy Carter before him, Bill Clinton was a Democratic president who came into office determined to focus on the nation's domestic problems only to find himself mired in foreign entanglements that had no easy resolution. Clinton continued the Bush administration's military intervention in Somalia, on the northeastern horn of Africa, where collapse of the government early in 1991 had left the country in anarchy, prey to tribal marauders. President Bush in 1992 had gained UN sanction for a military force led by American troops to relieve hunger and restore peace. The Somalian operation proved successful at its primary mission, but it never solved the political problems that lay at the root of the population's starvation.

HAITI   The most successful departure in foreign policy for the Clinton administration during its first term came in Haiti. The island nation had emerged suddenly from a cycle of coups with a democratic election in 1990, which brought to the presidency a popular priest, Jean-Bertrand Aristide. When a Haitian army general ousted Aristide, the United States immediately announced its intention to bring him back and welcomed the UN to the process.

With drawn-out negotiations leading nowhere, Clinton eventually moved in July 1994 to get a UN resolution authorizing force as a last resort. At that juncture, former president Jimmy Carter asked permission to negotiate. In Port-au-Prince he convinced the military leaders to quit by October 15. Aristide returned to Haiti and on March 31, 1995, the occupation was turned over to a UN force commanded by an American general.

THE MIDDLE EAST   Clinton also continued George Bush's policy of sponsoring patient negotiations between the Arabs and Israelis. A new development was the inclusion of the PLO in the negotiations. In 1993 secret talks between Israeli and Palestinian representatives in Oslo, Norway, resulted

Clinton and the Middle East

President Clinton presides as Israeli prime minister Yitzhak Rabin (left) and PLO leader Yasir Arafat (right), to a peace accord between Israel and the Palestinians, September 1993.

in a draft agreement between Israel and the PLO. This agreement provided for the restoration of Palestinian self-rule in the occupied Gaza Strip and in Jericho, on the West Bank, in an exchange of land for peace as provided in UN Security Council resolutions. A formal signing occurred at the White House on September 13, 1993. With President Clinton presiding, Israeli prime minister Yitzhak Rabin and PLO leader Yasir Arafat exchanged hand-shakes, and their foreign ministers signed the agreement.

In the aftermath of this dramatic agreement, additional negotiations continued by fits and starts, interrupted by violent incidents sparked by extremist Jewish settlers and Palestinian militants. The Middle East peace process suffered a terrible blow in early November 1995 when Prime Minister Rabin was assassinated at a peace rally in Tel Aviv by an Israeli Jewish zealot who resented Rabin's efforts to negotiate with the Palestinians.

Some observers feared that the assassin had killed the peace process as well when seven months later conservative hard-liner Benjamin Netanyahu narrowly defeated the U.S.-backed Shimon Peres in the Israeli national elections. Yet in October 1998 Clinton brought Arafat, Netanyahu, and King Hussein of Jordan together at a conference center in Wye Mills, Maryland, where they reached an agreement. Under the Wye River Accord, Israel agreed to surrender land in return for security guarantees by the Palestinians. As hard-liners attempted to derail the tenuous peace process, Netanyahu called elections early, and the Israeli public swept into power former general Ehud Barak, who promised to jump-start the peace process.

THE BALKANS   Bill Clinton's foreign policy also addressed the chaotic transition in eastern Europe from Soviet domination to independence. With the collapse of Communist power, old ethnic and religious hatreds resurfaced, often leading to violent clashes. When Yugoslavia imploded in 1991, fanatics and tyrants triggered ethnic conflict as four of its six republics seceded. Serb minorities, backed by the new republic of Serbia and Herzegovina, stirred up civil wars in Croatia and Bosnia. In Bosnia especially, the war involved "ethnic cleansing"—driving Muslims from their homes and towns. The United States faced sobering options: to ignore the butchery, to accept the refugees, to use airpower, or to risk introducing ground troops. Clinton settled for dropping food and medical supplies to besieged Bosnians and sending planes to retaliate for attacks on places designated "safe havens" by the United Nations.

In 1995 American negotiators finally persuaded the foreign ministers of Croatia, Bosnia, and the Federal Republic of Yugoslavia to agree to a comprehensive peace plan. Bosnia would remain a single nation but would be divided into two states: a Muslim-Croat federation controlling 51 percent of the territory and a Bosnian-Serb republic controlling the remaining 49 percent. Basic human rights would be restored and free elections held to appoint a parliament and joint presidency. To enforce the agreement, 60,000 NATO peacekeeping troops would be dispatched to Bosnia. A cease-fire went into effect in October 1995.

In 1998 the Balkan tinderbox flared up again, this time in the Yugoslav province of Kosovo. A rugged rural region the size of Connecticut, Kosovo has long been considered sacred ground by Christian Serbs. By 1989, however, over 90 percent of the 2 million Kosovars were ethnic Albanian Muslims. In that year, Yugoslav president Slobodan Milošević decided to reassert Serbian control over the province. He stripped Kosovo of its autonomy and established de facto martial law. When the Albanian Kosovars resisted and large numbers of Muslim men began to join the Kosovo Liberation Army, Serbian soldiers and state police ruthlessly suppressed them and launched another program of "ethnic cleansing," burning Albanian villages, murdering men, raping women, and displacing hundreds of thousands of Muslim Albanian Kosovars.

On March 24, 1999, NATO, relying heavily upon U.S. military resources and leadership, launched air strikes against Yugoslavia. "Ending this tragedy is a moral imperative," explained President Clinton. After seventy-two days of unrelenting bombardment, Milošević sued for peace on NATO's terms. An agreement was reached on June 3, 1999. It was an unprecedented victory for airpower and for NATO, which was celebrating its fiftieth birthday. Not a single allied pilot was killed in combat. As the Albanian Kosovars started to return to Kosovo, however, large numbers of Serbs, fearful of Muslim retribution, began to leave the province, and some of them were killed. Members of the Kosovo Liberation Army stepped into the vacuum left by the departing Serbs and began to take control of the province.

GLOBALIZATION   The deepening involvement of the United States in the complex affairs of eastern Europe symbolized the broadening scope of globalization. As the proliferation of global-spanning information and communications technologies shrank time and distance, a cornucopia of consumer goods was produced, distributed, marketed, and purchased by multinational companies all over the world, not just in the United States. Unlike the 1950s and 1960s, when the United States enjoyed a near monopoly on international commerce because of the devastation of European and Asian economies during World War II, the rest of the world was now aggressively competing with American businesses. Yet as more nations entered the world economy and experienced prosperity, they benefited corporations in the United States by buying more American goods and sending more and better goods to the United States. American exports rose dramatically in the last twenty years of the twentieth century. In 1970 exports totaled $43 billion; in 2000 they totaled $1.2 trillion. Globalization benefited American consumers by making available many more products—and at low prices.

By the end of the twentieth century, the U.S. economy had become global dependent; foreign trade had become central to American prosperity—and to American politics. "The global economy," said a leading bank executive, "is defined by capital, ideas, and energy, not by artificial, geographic or political boundaries." Foreign governments and foreign investors had become the primary purchasers of U.S. government bonds. Driven by a ferocious desire to cut production costs, large corporations moved more and more of their production overseas. Outsourcing work "offshore" to developing countries, where wages were low, became the rage. By 2000 over one third of the production of American multinational companies was occurring abroad, compared with only 9 percent in 1980. Likewise, executives in multinational countries became more multinational themselves. A growing number of chief executive officers were of a different nationality than that of the company they headed. By the end of the twentieth century, the U.S. economy had become internationalized to such a profound extent that global concerns exercised an overwhelming influence on domestic and foreign policies.

THE ELECTION OF 2000

The election of 2000 revealed that voters were split evenly along partisan lines. The two major-party candidates for president, Democratic vice president Al Gore and Texas Republican governor George W. Bush, son of the former president, presented sharply contrasting views on the role of the federal government, tax cuts, environmental policies, and the best way to preserve Social Security and Medicare. Gore, a Tennessee native and Harvard graduate whose father had been a senator, favored an active federal government that would preserve Social Security, subsidize prescription-medicine expenses for the elderly, and protect the environment.

Bush, on the other hand, sought to transfer power from the federal government to the states, particularly in regard to environmental and education policies. He promoted more exploration for oil on federal land, and he endorsed the use of vouchers (cash grants) to enable parents to send their children to private schools. In international affairs, Bush questioned the need to maintain U.S. peacekeeping forces in Bosnia and the continuing expense of other global military commitments. He urged a more "humble" foreign policy, one that would end efforts at "nation building" around the world.

Two independent candidates added zest to the 2000 presidential campaign: conservative columnist Patrick Buchanan and liberal activist Ralph Nader. Buchanan focused his campaign on criticism of NAFTA, while Nader concentrated on the corrupting effects of campaign finances and the need for more robust efforts to protect the environment.

In the end the election was the one of the closest—and most controversial—in history. The television networks initially reported that Gore had narrowly won the state of Florida and its decisive twenty-five electoral votes. Later in the evening, however, the networks reversed themselves and said that Florida was too close to call. In the chaotic early-morning hours, the networks declared Bush the overall winner. Gore called Bush to concede, only to issue a retraction a short time later when it appeared that Florida remained a toss-up. The final tally in Florida showed Bush with a razor-thin lead, but state law required a recount. For the first time in 125 years, the results of a presidential election remained in doubt for weeks after the voting.

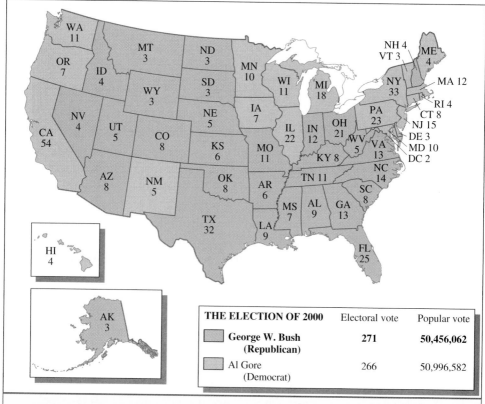

THE ELECTION OF 2000	Electoral vote	Popular vote
George W. Bush (Republican)	**271**	**50,456,062**
Al Gore (Democrat)	266	50,996,582

Why was the election so close? How was the conflict over the election results resolved? How were differences between urban and rural voters key to the outcome of the election?

As a painstaking hand count of presidential ballots proceeded in Florida, supporters of Bush and Gore pursued victory through legal maneuvers in the Florida courts and the U.S. Supreme Court; each side accused the other of trying to steal the election. The stalemated political drama continued for five weeks. At last, on December 12, 2000, a harshly divided Supreme Court halted the statewide manual recounts in Florida. In the case known as *Bush v. Gore,* a bare five-to-four majority ruled that any new recount would clash with existing Florida law.

Bush was deemed the winner in Florida by the slimmest of margins: 537 votes. Although Gore amassed a 540,000-vote lead nationwide, he lost in the Electoral College by two votes when he lost Florida. Although Al Gore "strongly disagreed" with the Supreme Court's decision, he asked voters to

The Florida Recount

A rally in Florida protesting the counting of ballots in the disputed 2000 presidential election.

rally around President-elect Bush and move forward: "Partisan rancor must be put aside."

The 2000 election revealed the remarkable balance that had emerged in American politics. Not since the 1880s had the two major parties been so evenly divided. Republicans retained a slim lead in the House, 49.2 percent to 47.9 percent. The number of senators was split down the middle, fifty-fifty. For all of the strident rhetoric in the campaign, both Bush and Gore represented the moderate center of their parties when compared with the more ideological candidacies of Buchanan and Nader. Bush talked frequently about his commitment to "compassionate conservatism." Gore ran on a platform dedicated to "fiscal responsibility." Analysts stressed that cultural issues such as abortion and gun control, as well as the Clinton scandals, had become more important to many voters than economic concerns over taxes or defense spending. Some 71 percent of city residents voted for Gore while only 26 percent chose Bush. Conversely, 59 percent of rural voters cast ballots for Bush while only 37 percent opted for Gore. Gore won fewer than one third of the votes in the South and his home state of Tennessee. Bush won the mountain West and the South while Gore dominated the Northeast, the West Coast, and the industrial Midwest. Women favored Gore over Bush by 11 percentage points, exactly the reverse of the male voters.

COMPASSIONATE CONSERVATISM

THE SECOND BUSH PRESIDENCY   During the 2000 election campaign, commentators criticized George Walker Bush's political inexperience and lack of knowledge about world affairs. As president-elect he addressed those concerns by naming to his cabinet seasoned public figures. His methodical vice president, Richard "Dick" Cheney, is a former congressman from Wyoming who served as secretary of defense under the senior George Bush. Colin Powell, former army general and chairman of the Joint Chiefs of Staff, became the first African-American secretary of state. Donald Rumsfeld, secretary of defense under Gerald Ford, returned to that position in the Bush administration. Bush named former Missouri senator John Ashcroft attorney general.

Bush not only arrived in the White House amid the controversy of a disputed election, but he also faced a sputtering economy and a falling stock market. By the spring of 2000, the high-tech companies that had led the dizzying run-up on Wall Street during the 1990s had collapsed. Many of the dazzling new dot-com businesses declared bankruptcy. Greed fed by record profits and speculative excesses had led businesses, investors, and consumers to take dangerous risks and engage in self-indulgent behavior. The high-tech bubble burst in 2001. Stock values collapsed, sucking over $2 trillion from household wealth. Consumer confidence and capital investment plummeted with the stock market. By March 2001 the economy was in recession for the first time in over a decade. "These are times of shattered illusions," said economist Robert Samuelson. "The mythology of the 'New Economy' is receding before the reality of declining jobs and profits." Some of the nation's largest corporations, it turned out, had been illegally cooking the books, reporting false financial results in order to keep investors happy. The senior officers of Enron Corporation, a huge international energy-trading company, and WorldCom, a telecommunications giant, were among the numerous corporate executives who would be convicted and imprisoned for accounting fraud.

Yet neither the plummeting stock market and floundering economy nor the close political balance in Congress prevented President Bush from launching an ambitious legislative agenda. Confident that he could win over Democrats, he promised to provide "an explosion of legislation" promoting his goal of "compassionate conservatism" within a few months of his inauguration. The top item on Bush's wish list was a $1.6-trillion tax cut intended to stimulate the sagging economy. The Senate eventually trimmed the cut to $1.35 trillion over eleven years, and Bush signed it into law on June 7,

2001. White House celebrations of the tax-cut victory were deflated by the defection of Vermont senator James Jeffords, who changed his party affiliation from Republican to independent—a major blow for the president since it resulted in the Democrats gaining narrow control of the Senate, 50–49.

NO CHILD LEFT BEHIND In addition to tax reduction, one of President Bush's top priorities was education reform. In late 2001 Congress passed a comprehensive education-improvement plan called No Child Left Behind, and the president signed the bill in early 2002. It required states to set new learning standards and ensure that all students were "proficient" at reading and math by 2014. It also mandated that all teachers be "highly qualified" in their subject area by 2005, allowed children in low-performing schools to transfer to other schools, and required states to submit annual reports of students' scores on standardized tests. Schools and school districts that fell short of the new standards were eligible for financial and technical assistance, but if progress did not occur the federal government would issue a series of sanctions culminating in the state's taking over deficient school districts. States soon criticized the program, claiming that it provided insufficient funds for remedial programs and that poor school districts, many of them in blighted inner cities or rural areas, would be especially hard pressed to meet the guidelines.

EXPLOITING THE ENVIRONMENT The Bush administration's environmental policies ignited a firestorm of controversy. The president refused to sign the Kyoto Protocol, an international agreement among dozens of nations setting limits on the emissions of carbon dioxide and other gases contributing to global climate change. Bush argued that the treaty would harm the economy. Administration officials also sought to roll back restrictions on economic development posed by long-standing environmental regulations. In addition, they wanted to allow more logging in national forests and open up more federal land, including wildlife sanctuaries, to exploration for energy sources in the face of dramatic increases in oil and gasoline prices.

Yet the Bush administration did take several steps to protect the environment. The EPA ordered General Electric Corporation to spend hundreds of millions of dollars to remove toxic chemicals it had deposited into the Hudson River. It also established the first limits on diesel-fuel emissions for trucks and off-road vehicles. And Bush appropriated funds to begin chipping away at a huge deferred-maintenance backlog at the national parks.

GLOBAL TERRORISM

With the collapse of the Soviet Union and the end of the cold war, world politics had grown more unstable during the 1990s. The basic premise of U.S. foreign policy was "unipolar": to maintain the nation's leadership role in global affairs. Yet the very preponderance of American military power and economic influence only added to the instability. A simmering mistrust of America's geopolitical dominance and economic globalization festered internationally. Where ideologies such as capitalism and communism had earlier been the cause of conflict and tension in foreign relations, issues of religion, ethnicity, and clashing cultural values now divided peoples. While many Americans, including President Bush, believed that the United States served as a shining example of pluralist democracy and free-market capitalism, people in other countries distrusted American motives and disliked the "invasion" of American capitalism. Islamic militants around the world especially resented what they viewed as the "imperial" globalization of American culture and power.

As the twenty-first century began to unfold, nations were no longer the sole actors on the stage of world politics. Instead, nebulous multinational groups inspired by religious fanaticism and anti-American rage were using high-tech terrorism to gain notoriety and exact vengeance. The very rootlessness of the zealots—their alienation from their native societies and their ability to infiltrate other countries and cultures—proved to be an ironic strength. Well-financed and well-armed terrorists flourished in the cracks of fractured nations such as Sudan, Somalia, Pakistan, Yemen, and Afghanistan. Throughout the 1990s the United States had fought a losing secret war against organized terrorism. The ineffectiveness of Western intelligence agencies in tracking the movements and intentions of militant extremists became tragically evident in the autumn of 2001.

SEPTEMBER 11, 2001: A DAY OF INFAMY   At 8:45 on the morning of September 11, 2001, a commercial airliner hijacked by Islamic terrorists slammed into the north tower of the World Trade Center in New York City. A second hijacked jumbo jet, traveling at 500 miles per hour, hit the south tower eighteen minutes later. The fuel-laden planes turned the majestic buildings into infernos. The twin towers, both 110 stories tall and filled with thousands of employees, collapsed from the intense heat. Surrounding buildings also collapsed. The entire southern end of Manhattan—ground zero—became a hellish scene of twisted steel, suffocating smoke, and wailing sirens.

September 11, 2001

Smoke pours out of the north tower of the World Trade Center as the south tower bursts into flames after being struck by a second hijacked airplane. Both towers collapsed about an hour later.

While the catastrophic drama in New York was unfolding, a third hijacked plane crashed into the Pentagon in Washington, D.C. A fourth airliner, probably headed for the White House, missed its mark when passengers—who had heard reports of the earlier hijackings via cell phones—assaulted the hijackers to prevent the plane from being used as a weapon. During the struggle in the cockpit, the plane went out of control and plummeted into the Pennsylvania countryside, killing all aboard.

The hijackings represented the costliest terrorist assault in the nation's history. There were 266 passengers and crew members aboard the crashed jets. More than 100 civilians and military personnel were killed at the Pentagon. The death toll at the World Trade Center was nearly 2,600, with many firefighters, police officers, and rescue workers among the dead. Hundreds of those killed were foreign nationals working in the financial district; some eighty nations lost citizens in the attacks. The terrorists also destroyed a powerful symbol of America: the World Trade Center towers were the central offices of global capitalism.

The terrorist attacks of September 11 created shock and chaos, grief and anger. They also prompted an unprecedented display of national unity and patriotism. People rushed to donate blood, food, and money. Volunteers clogged military-recruiting centers. American flags were in evidence everywhere. Citizens around the world held vigils at U.S. embassies. World leaders offered condolences and support. For the first time in its history, NATO invoked Article V of its charter, which states that an attack on any member will be considered an attack on all members.

Within hours of the hijackings, officials had identified the nineteen dead terrorists as members of al Qaeda (the Base), a well-financed worldwide network of Islamic extremists led by a wealthy Saudi renegade, Osama bin Laden. Years before, bin Laden had declared *jihad* (holy war) on the United States, Israel, and the Saudi monarchy. For several years he had been using remote bases in war-torn Afghanistan as terrorist training centers. Collaborating with bin Laden's terrorist agenda was Afghanistan's ruling Taliban, a coalition of ultraconservative Islamists that had emerged in the mid-1990s following the forced withdrawal of Soviet troops from Afghanistan. Taliban leaders provided bin Laden with a safe haven in exchange for his financial and military support against the Northern Alliance, a coalition of rebel groups opposed to Taliban rule. Bin Laden sought to mobilize Muslim militants energized by local causes into a global army aimed at the West. As many as 20,000 recruits from twenty different countries circulated through his training camps. Most of the terrorists received religious indoctrination and basic infantry training to prepare them to fight for the Taliban. A smaller group was selected by al Qaeda for elite training to organize secret cells around the world and engage in urban warfare, assassination, demolition, and sabotage.

WAR ON TERRORISM   The September 11 terrorist assault on the United States changed the course of the Bush presidency, the nation, and even the world. The economy, already in decline, went into free fall. With people worldwide hesitating to fly, airlines laid off tens of thousands of employees. Insurance companies struggled to pay off an estimated $30 billion in claims resulting from the attacks. On Wall Street, markets plummeted in anticipation of a deeper recession combined with a war against terrorism.

President Bush, who had never professed to know much about international relations or world affairs and had shown only disdain for Bill Clinton's "multilateralism," was thrust onto center stage as commander in chief of a wounded nation eager for vengeance. The new president, elected by the slimmest electoral margin since 1876, responded with unexpected poise, grit, and courage. He told the nation that the "deliberate and deadly attacks . . . were more than acts of terror. They were acts of war." The crisis gave the untested, happy-go-lucky Bush a profound sense of purpose. "I will not yield. I will not rest. I will not relent in waging this struggle for freedom and security."

The Bush administration immediately forged an international coalition to fight terrorism worldwide. The coalition demanded that Afghanistan's Taliban government surrender the terrorists or risk military attack. In a televised address on September 20, Bush warned Americans that the war against terrorism would be a lengthy campaign, involving covert action as well as conventional military forces, which would target not only terrorists but also the groups and governments that abet them. "Every nation in every region," he said, "now has a decision to make: either you are with us or you are with the terrorists."

On October 7, after the Taliban defiantly refused to turn over bin Laden, the United States and its allies launched a ferocious military campaign— Operation Enduring Freedom—to punish terrorists or "those harboring terrorists." American and British cruise missiles and bombers destroyed Afghan military installations and al Qaeda training camps. The coalition found key allies in neighboring Pakistan and in Afghanistan's Northern Alliance. U.S. military commanders used new high-tech weapons—precision-guided bombs, spy satellites, and laser-targeting devices—that enabled American forces to engage the enemy and occupy territory without risking soldiers' lives.

In the early hours of November 13, Northern Alliance troops captured the Afghan capital of Kabul. Many residents viewed the American and Northern Alliance forces as liberators. The Afghans took to the streets in celebration. They played music, the men shaved off their beards and women showed their faces in public actions that had been prohibited by the Taliban regime. On December 9, only two months after the U.S.-led military campaign in Afghanistan had begun, the Taliban regime collapsed entirely. With its collapse the war in Afghanistan devolved into a high-stakes manhunt for the elusive Osama bin Laden and an international network of terrorists operating in sixty countries.

In December 2001 Afghanistan's long-feuding factions, minus the Taliban, signed a UN-brokered peace agreement that created an interim government, led by Hamid Karzai, an exiled tribal leader who had reentered the country in October to rally opposition to the Taliban. While the American-led coalition forces continued to track down al Qaeda stragglers and search for bin Laden, the interim Afghan government faced the challenge of providing basic services and creating stability in a faction-ridden, war-torn country.

The Taliban

A young woman shows her face in public for the first time in five years after North-ern Alliance troops capture Kabul in November 2001. The strict sharia law enforced by the Taliban required that women be covered from head to foot.

TERRORISM AT HOME While the military campaign continued in Afghanistan, officials in Washington worried that terrorists might launch additional attacks in the United States with biological, chemical, or even nu-clear weapons. To address the threat and to help restore public confidence, President Bush created a new federal agency, the Office of Homeland Secu-rity, and another new federal agency, the Transportation Security Adminis-tration, assumed responsibility for the screening of airport passengers. At the same time, President Bush and a supportive Congress created new legis-lation, known as the USA Patriot Act, which gave government agencies the right to eavesdrop on confidential conversations between prison inmates and their lawyers and permitted terrorist suspects to be tried in military courts. Such tribunals would have less stringent standards regarding the burden of proof than civilian courts: they could be held in secret, they allowed for the admission of hearsay and illegally obtained information as evidence, and they required only a two-thirds majority for conviction. Civil liberties groups voiced grave concerns that the measures jeopardized consti-tutional rights and protections. But the crisis atmosphere after September 11 caused most people to support these extraordinary steps.

MIDDLE EAST TURMOIL The Middle East also exploded in violence in the new century. Seven years of relative calm ended when peace talks in

Oslo collapsed in 2000. Disputes over the fate of Jerusalem, a holy city to Jews, Christians, and Muslims, undermined any new accords between the Israelis and the Palestinians. After the collapse of negotiations, Palestinians again declared an intifada, or uprising. In October 2000 street demonstrations in the Israeli-controlled West Bank and Gaza Strip gave way to a series of suicide bombings against Israeli soldiers and civilians. Israeli troops retaliated. Hundreds of casualties resulted, many of them children.

In February 2001 Israeli voters, angry with the increasing violence, elected the party of Ariel Sharon, a militant conservative. As prime minister, Sharon vowed that there would be no negotiating with the Palestinians as long as their intifada continued. Sharon's government responded to attacks with air strikes and armored assaults on Palestinian-controlled areas. Israeli agents also assassinated leaders of Hamas and Islamic Jihad, two Palestinian terrorist organizations.

THE BUSH DOCTRINE   In the fall of 2002, President Bush unveiled a new national security doctrine that marked a distinct shift from that of previous administrations. Containment and deterrence had been the guiding strategic concepts of the cold war years. Beginning with Harry Truman in

Bush and the Middle East

President George W. Bush addresses soldiers in July 2002 as part of an appeal to Congress to speed approval of increased defense spending after the September 11 terrorist attacks.

1947, American presidents had helped organize multilateral international groups such as the United Nations and NATO to "contain" communism and keep it from spreading. Likewise, U.S. administrations had sought to "deter" the Soviets and Chinese Communists from overt military action by promising "massive retaliation." Thus the threat of nuclear war and mutual destruction kept the major nations in check during the cold war era. In the new unconventional war against terrorism, however, the cold war policies were outdated. Fanatics willing to act as suicide bombers would not be deterred. The growing menace posed by "shadowy networks" of terrorist groups and unstable rogue nations with "weapons of mass destruction," President Bush declared, required a new doctrine of preemptive military action. "If we wait for threats to fully materialize," he explained, "we will have waited too long. In the world we have entered, the only path to safety is the path of action. And this nation will act."

A SECOND GULF WAR   During 2002 and 2003 Iraq emerged as the focus of the Bush administration's decisive new policy of "preemptive" military action to prevent terrorism and destroy weapons of mass destruction. Following the Persian Gulf War of 1991, UN inspectors had gone to Iraq to search for such biological and chemical weapons. Iraqi tyrant Saddam Hussein never accepted the legitimacy of those efforts, and in the fall of 1998 he had ordered the UN inspectors to leave. Thereafter, U.S. officials grew increasingly concerned about Iraq's possession of biological and chemical weapons and its support of global terrorism. In September 2002 President Bush urged the UN to confront the "grave and gathering danger" posed by Hussein's dictatorial regime in Iraq. He warned that the United States would act alone if the UN did not respond. In October, Congress approved a resolution proposed by Bush authorizing him to use "all means that he determines to be appropriate, including force" to defend the United States against the threat posed by Iraq. On November 8, the UN Security Council passed Resolution 1441 ordering Iraq to disarm immediately or face "serious consequences." Hussein grudgingly allowed UN weapons inspectors to return to Iraq "without conditions."

As the UN inspectors resumed their efforts, however, the Iraqi government continued its partial cooperation and stalling tactics. President Bush gained the support of Great Britain and Spain in proposing a new UN resolution that would authorize military action to ensure that Iraq eliminated its weapons of mass destruction. "The United States," Bush insisted, "will not permit the world's most dangerous regimes to threaten us with the world's most destructive weapons."

During early 2003 U.S. and British military units began to assemble in the Persian Gulf. France, China, Germany, and Russia opposed the American-led effort to use force against Iraq, arguing that the UN inspectors should be given more time to complete their task. Secretary of State Colin Powell's efforts to marshal international support for the forceful American stance proved fruitless. On March 17, the United States, Great Britain, and Spain withdrew their proposed Security Council resolution, announcing that diplomatic efforts had failed. President Bush then issued an ultimatum to Saddam Hussein: he and his sons must leave Iraq within forty-eight hours or face a U.S.-led invasion. Hussein refused. Two days later, on March 19, American and British forces, supported by what George Bush called the "coalition of the willing," attacked Iraq.

Operation Iraqi Freedom involved a massive bombing campaign followed closely by a fast-moving invasion across the Iraqi desert from bases in Kuwait. Some 250,000 American soldiers, sailors, and marines were joined by 50,000 British troops as well as small contingents from other countries, including Australia and Poland. President Bush explained that the purpose

A Continued Presence in Iraq

U.S. military police patrol the market in Abu Ghraib, on the outskirts of Baghdad.

of the invasion was to "disarm Iraq, to free its people, and defend the world from grave danger." Critics at home and abroad, however, saw the allied assault as an imperialist effort to control Iraqi oil and impose a capitalist democracy on an Arab country.

On April 9, after only three weeks of intense fighting amid sweltering heat and blinding sandstorms, allied forces occupied Baghdad, the capital of Iraq. Iraqis cheered as American soldiers toppled an enormous statue of Saddam Hussein in the city center. Saddam's regime and his inept army collapsed and fled a week later. On May 1, 2003, an exuberant President Bush landed on the aircraft carrier U.S.S. *Abraham Lincoln* and proudly declared that the war was essentially over. "The battle of Iraq," he said, "is one victory in a war on terror that began on September 11, 2001, and still goes on."

The complicated Iraqi military campaign was a brilliantly orchestrated demonstration of intense firepower, daring maneuver, and complex logistical support. No one had predicted such a quick and decisive victory—or so few casualties among the allied forces. The six-week war came at a cost of fewer than 200 combat deaths among the 300,000 coalition troops. Over 2,000 Iraqi soldiers were killed; civilian casualties numbered in the tens of thousands.

REBUILDING IRAQ   Secretary of Defense Donald Rumsfeld saw the Iraq War as an opportunity to showcase America's new military strategy, with its focus on airpower, precision weaponry, sophisticated communications, and mobile ground forces trained in stealth and speed. Yet winning the peace proved far more difficult than winning the war. No sooner had Saddam Hussein's tyranny been destroyed than the allies faced the daunting task of restoring order and installing a democratic government in a chaotic Iraq torn by age-old religious feuds and ethnic tensions. Looting was rampant and basic services nonexistent. Hussein and many of his lieutenants evaded capture and organized insurgent attacks against the allied forces and the interim Iraqi government. Violence engulfed the war-torn country. Vengeful Islamic jihadists (holy warriors) from around the world streamed into Iraq to wage a merciless campaign of terror and sabotage against the coalition forces and their Iraqi allies.

Defense Department analysts had greatly underestimated the difficulty of pacifying and reconstructing postwar Iraq. By the fall of 2003, President Bush admitted that substantial numbers of American troops (around 150,000) would remain in Iraq much longer than originally anticipated and that the rebuilding of the fractured nation would take years. Victory on the battlefields of Iraq did not bring peace to the Middle East. Militant Islamic groups seething with hatred for the United States remained a constant global threat. In addition, the dispute over the war strained relations between the Anglo-American alliance and France, Germany, and Russia, all of which opposed the Iraq War.

After 2003, the Iraqi insurgency and its campaign of terror grew in scope and savagery. Near-daily suicide car bombings and roadside ambushes of U.S. military convoys wreaked havoc among Iraqi civilians and allied troops. Terrorists kidnapped foreign civilians and beheaded several of them in grisly rituals videotaped for the world to see. In the United States the euphoria of battlefield victory turned to dismay as the casualties and the expense of the Iraqi occupation soared. In the face of mounting criticism, President Bush urged Americans to "stay the course" in Iraq, insisting that a democratic Iraq would bring stability to the volatile Middle East and thereby blunt the momentum of Islamic terrorism.

But the president's credibility suffered a sharp blow in January 2004 when administration officials admitted that no weapons of mass destruction—the primary reason for launching the invasion—had been found in Iraq. The chief arms inspector told Congress that the intelligence reports about Saddam's supposed secret weapons were "almost all wrong." Shocking photographs that surfaced in April 2004 showing American soldiers torturing and abusing Iraqi prisoners further eroded public confidence in Bush's handling of the war and its aftermath.

By September 2004 American military deaths in Iraq had reached 1,000, and by the end of 2006 they were nearly 3,000. Although Saddam Hussein was captured in December 2003 and a new Iraqi government held its first democratic elections in January 2005, Iraq seemed less secure than ever to an anxious American public worried about the rising cost of an unending commitment in Iraq. The continuing guerrilla wars in Iraq and Afghanistan strained U.S. military resources and the federal budget. The Defense Department was forced to call up thousands of members of U.S. Army Reserve and National Guard units, and military recruiters found it increasingly difficult to meet their quotas.

THE ELECTION OF 2004   Growing public concern about the turmoil in Iraq complicated George Bush's campaign for a second term. Throughout 2004 his approval rating plummeted. And in the new century the electorate had become deeply polarized. A Gallup poll showed that Bush had the support of 91 percent of Republicans and only 17 percent of Democrats, the widest partisan gap in the poll's history. Volatile cultural issues such as abortion, school prayer, stem-cell research, and gay marriage continued to divide voters and inflame political discourse.

A ferocious partisanship dominated political discourse and media commentary in the early years of the century. Democrats still fumed over the contested election results of 2000. When asked about the intensity of his critics, a combative George Bush declared the furor "a compliment. It means I'm willing to take a stand." One of his advisers explained it more bluntly: "He likes being hated. It lets him know he's doing the right thing."

The 2004 presidential campaign was punctuated by negative attacks on each candidate as the two parties sought to galvanize their loyalists. Campaign rhetoric was especially caustic because both sides saw so much at stake. Democrats worried that the tide of Republican conservatism might sweep them into irrelevance. Republicans worried that the "jobless" economic recovery and deepening commitment in Iraq might derail their political momentum.

The Democratic nominee, Senator John Kerry of Massachusetts, was a decorated Vietnam War veteran who had helped organize the Vietnam Veterans against the War in the early 1970s. During the 2004 campaign, Kerry lambasted the Bush administration for misleading the nation on the issue of weapons of mass destruction in Iraq and for its inept handling of the Iraq

The 2004 Election

President George W. Bush (center) and Democratic candidate Senator John Kerry (left) participate in the second presidential debate, a town-hall style exchange held at Washington University in St. Louis, Missouri.

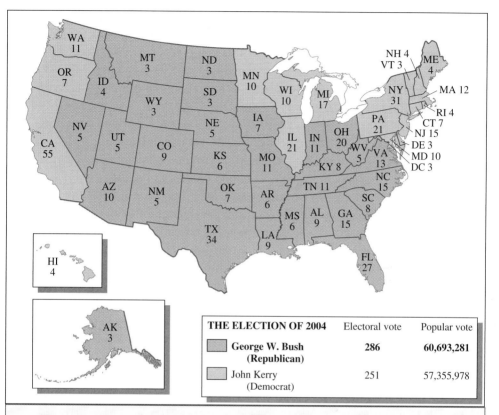

THE ELECTION OF 2004	Electoral vote	Popular vote
George W. Bush (Republican)	**286**	**60,693,281**
John Kerry (Democrat)	251	57,355,978

How did the war in Iraq polarize the electorate? In what ways did the election of 2004 give Republicans a mandate?

occupation, implying that the United States was foundering in another Vietnam-like quagmire. Kerry charged that the Iraq War was hurting rather than helping the war on global terror. He also highlighted the record budget deficits occurring under the Republican leadership. Bush countered that the tortuous efforts to create a democratic government in Iraq would enhance America's long-range security. The president also promised to continue his efforts to reform the Social Security pension program and the tax code and to reduce unemployment by restoring sustained economic growth.

On election day, November 2, 2004, the exit polls suggested a Kerry victory, but in the end the election hinged on the crucial swing state of Ohio. No Republican had ever lost Ohio and still won the presidency. After an anxious night viewing returns from Ohio, Kerry conceded the election. "The outcome," he stressed, "should be decided by voters, not a protracted legal battle." By narrowly winning Ohio, Bush garnered 286 electoral votes to Kerry's 251. The 2004 election was remarkable for its high voter turnout. Almost 120 million people voted, some 15 million more than in the disputed 2000 election.

Bush won the popular vote by 50.73 to 48.27 percent, the narrowest percentage margin of any incumbent president. Yet in some respects the close election was not so close. Bush received 3.5 million more votes nationwide than Kerry, and Republicans increased their control of both the House and the Senate. As was true in the election of 2000, Bush and the Republicans dominated in the South, the Midwest, and the Rocky Mountain states while the Democrats controlled the West Coast, Northeast, and the states bordering the Great Lakes. Trumpeting "the will of the people at my back," Bush pledged after his reelection to bring democracy and stability to Iraq, overhaul the tax code and eliminate the estate tax, revamp Social Security, trim the federal budget deficit, limit awards for medical malpractice lawsuits, pass a major energy bill, and create many more jobs. "I earned capital in the campaign, political capital, and now I intend to spend it," he told reporters.

SECOND-TERM BLUES Yet like many modern presidents, George Bush floundered in his second term. In 2005 he pushed through Congress an energy bill and a Central American Free Trade Act. But his effort to privatize Social Security retirement accounts, enabling individuals to invest their accumulated pension dollars themselves, went nowhere, and soaring budget deficits made many fiscal conservatives feel betrayed.

Developments within the Supreme Court commanded much of Bush's attention early in his second term. The retirement of Sandra Day O'Connor from the Court in July 2005 ignited a ferocious national debate over vexing cultural issues such as abortion, gay marriage, and affirmative action. Because O'Connor had been a moderate swing vote on the closely divided Court, the battle over her replacement was especially intense. Militants on the left and right pressured the White House to ensure that Bush's choice to succeed O'Connor fit their agenda's demands, but Bush's shrewd decision to nominate John G. Roberts Jr., a socially conservative circuit court judge, stalemated critics because Roberts's legal credentials were impeccable. The Senate overwhelmingly confirmed Roberts (seventy-eight to twenty-two) on September 29, 2005.

Yet the fractious debates over the future of the Court did not subside. In early September Chief Justice William Rehnquist died. Bush named Roberts the new chief justice and nominated Harriet E. Miers, a longtime friend and his former personal lawyer turned White House legal counsel, to replace O'Connor. Critics, many of them Republican conservatives, denounced Miers as a legal mediocrity and a presidential crony. The furor led Miers to withdraw her nomination in late October, a humiliating development for President Bush that further hobbled his stalled legislative efforts. To heal the ruptures within the Republican coalition, at the end of October Bush nominated Samuel Alito Jr., a federal judge and a favorite of conservatives, to fill O'Connor's seat on the Supreme Court. The Senate confirmed Alito on January 31, 2006.

HURRICANE KATRINA   In the summer of 2005, President Bush's eroding public support suffered another blow, this time when a natural disaster turned into a political crisis. In late August a killer hurricane named Katrina slammed into the Gulf coast, devastating large areas of Alabama, Mississippi, and Louisiana. Coastal towns such as Gulfport and Biloxi, Mississippi, were blown away. The sultry metropolis of New Orleans was virtually destroyed as levees and flood walls holding back the Mississippi River and Lake Pontchartrain burst, inundating three quarters of the city, most of which is below sea level and below the Mississippi River.

New Orleans had always been at war with its environment. Since its founding in the early eighteenth century, the sodden city surrounded by mosquito-infested swamps and regularly visited by floods had placed its faith in engineering to keep back the surrounding water. This time nature won. After Katrina roared through the city, whole neighborhoods were under water, often up to the roofline. Nearly 500,000 New Orleans residents were displaced, most of them poor and many of them African American. Looting was so widespread that officials declared martial law; the streets were awash with soldiers and police. Katrina's awful wake left over 1,000 people dead in three states, and millions were left homeless and hopeless. "The magnitude of the situation is untenable," Louisiana's governor lamented. "It's just heartbreaking."

Local political officials and the Federal Emergency Management Agency (FEMA) were caught unprepared as the catastrophe unfolded. Disaster plans were incomplete; communication and coordination were sorely lacking; confusion and incompetence abounded. Evacuation plans proved faulty, and government red tape compounded the misery. A wave of public outrage crashed against the Bush administration. Republican senator David Vitter of Louisiana gave the federal relief effort "a failing grade, across the board." Already-high gasoline prices skyrocketed as the hurricane shut down

Hurricane Katrina

Cars and buildings are partially submerged on Canal Street, a central thoroughfare in New Orleans, September 3, 2005.

refineries, oil platforms, and pipelines. In the face of blistering criticism, President Bush accepted responsibility for the balky federal response to the disaster and accepted the resignation of the FEMA director. Rebuilding the Gulf coast would take a long time and a lots of money.

Hurricane Katrina was one of the worst natural disasters in American history. Although thousands more people were killed in the hurricanes that destroyed Galveston, Texas, in 1900 and devastated the Lake Okeechobee area of Florida in 1928, the dollar cost of Katrina's fury was much greater. Experts predicted that it would take $200 billion to restore the Gulf coast. More worrisome were claims made by growing number of scientists that the increasing frequency and potency of hurricanes were a dreadful manifestation of global warming, a controversial phenomenon reputedly caused by carbon dioxide emissions from industrial smokestacks and automobile exhaust rising into the atmosphere and depleting the earth's protective ozone layer. Depleted ozone causes the temperature of the earth and the oceans to rise, thereby affecting climate and, according to some scientists, making weather more extreme.

The havoc wreaked by Katrina was only partly the result of natural forces run amok, however. Environmental calamities usually expose human failings. And in washing away property and lives, Katrina revealed all the elements of a disaster waiting to happen: poor planning, social inequalities, embedded corruption, and racial injustice. The destruction of New Orleans could have been mitigated or avoided altogether if, for example, warnings about the integrity of the aging levees had been heeded. The failure of the levees revealed scandalous breaches in public policy and political leadership. New Orleans had come to depend upon the Army Corps of Engineers for its lifeline of levees and pumps designed to keep the Mississippi River and Lake Pontchartrain at bay. Yet the city's flood-control funding had been reduced by 44 percent since 2001. At the same time, corruption and incompetence had been rife within the levee boards responsible for administering public funds. The weakening of wetlands protections to favor developers had also made the city far more vulnerable to the flood surge generated by hurricanes. Marshes absorb storm water, but much of the wetland surrounding New Orleans had disappeared as a result of strenuous efforts to reroute the Mississippi River in order to facilitate the passage of ships and, ironically, provide better flood control. Realigning the river had prevented silt from building up in the delta and nourishing the wetlands. So the natural calamity was made much worse by human action—and inaction.

A STALLED PRESIDENCY

George Bush bore the brunt of public indignation over the bungled federal response to the Katrina disaster. By the end of 2006, the White House was beset by political problems, a sputtering economy, and growing public dissatisfaction with the president's performance. Bush's job-approval rating fell well below 40 percent, an all-time low. Even his support among Republicans crumbled, and many social conservatives felt betrayed by his sporadic attention to their ideological concerns. The editors of *The Economist*, an influential conservative newsmagazine, declared in June 2005 that Bush had become "the least popular re-elected president since Richard Nixon became embroiled in the Watergate fiasco."

The soaring gasoline prices and the federal budget deficit fueled public frustration with the Bush administration. The president's efforts to reform the tax code, Social Security, and immigration laws languished during his second term, and the turmoil and violence in Iraq showed no signs of abating. Senator Chuck Hagel, a Nebraska Republican, declared in 2005 that "we're losing in Iraq." As 2005 came to an end, the embattled president visited the recovering Gulf coast. His purpose, explained an aide, was "to give people a sense of hope." George Bush might have done the same for his presidency. It, too, needed an infusion of hope and energy at the start of the new year.

FURTHER READING

On George H. W. Bush's presidency, see Mary E. Stuckey *Leadership and the Bush Presidency: Prudence or Drift in an Era of Change?* edited by Ryan J. Barilleaux (1992), and Charles Tiefer's *The Semi-Sovereign Presidency: The Bush Administration's Strategy for Governing without Congress* (1994). Among the journalistic accounts of the presidential election of 1992, the best narrative is Jack W. Germond and Jules Witcover's *Mad as Hell: Revolt at the Ballot Box, 1992* (1993). The best scholarly study is Theodore J. Lowi and Benjamin Ginsberg's *Democrats Return to Power: Politics and Policy in the Clinton Era* (1994).

Analysis of the Clinton years can be found in Joe Klein's *The Natural: The Misunderstood Presidency of Bill Clinton* (2002). Clinton's impeachment is assessed in Richard A. Posner's *An Affair of State: The Investigation, Impeachment, and Trial of President Clinton* (1999).

On changing demographic trends, see Sam Roberts's *Who We Are Now: The Changing Face of America in the Twenty-First Century* (2004). On social and cultural life in the 1990s, see Haynes Johnson's *The Best of Times: America in the Clinton Years* (2001). The onset and growth of the AIDS epidemic are traced in *And the Band Played On: Politics, People, and the AIDS Epidemic* (1987) by Randy Shilts.

Aspects of fundamentalist and apocalyptic movements are the subject of Paul Boyer's *When Time Shall Be No More: Prophecy Belief in Modern American Culture* (1992), George M. Marsden's *Understanding Fundamentalism and Evangelicalism* (1991), and Ralph E. Reed's *Politically Incorrect: The Emerging Faith Factor in American Politics* (1994).

On the invention of the computer and the Internet, see Paul E. Ceruzzi's *A History of Modern Computing* 2nd ed. (2003) and Janet Abbate's *Inventing the Internet* (1999). The booming economy of the 1990s is well analyzed in Joseph E. Stiglitz's *The Roaring Nineties: A New History of the World's Most Prosperous Decade* (2003). On the rising stress within the workplace, see Jill

Andresky Fraser's *White-Collar Sweatshop: The Deterioration of Work and Its Rewards in Corporate America* (2001). Aspects of corporate restructuring and downsizing are the subject of Bennett Harrison's *Lean and Mean: The Changing Landscape of Corporate Power in the Age of Flexibility* (1994).

For further treatment of the end of the cold war, see Michael R. Beschloss's *At the Highest Levels: The Inside Story of the End of the Cold War* (1993) and Richard Crockatt's *The Fifty Years War: The United States and the Soviet Union in World Politics, 1941–1991* (1995). On the Persian Gulf conflict, see Lester H. Brune's *America and the Iraqi Crisis, 1990–1992: Origins and Aftermath* (1993). On the transformation of American foreign policy, see James Mann's *Rise of the Vulcans: The History of Bush's War Cabinet* (2004); Claes G. Ryn's *America the Virtuous: Crisis of Democracy and the Quest for Empire* (2003), and Stephen M. Walt's *Taming American Power: The Global Response to U. S. Primacy* (2005).

The disputed 2000 presidential election is the focus of Jeffrey Toobin's *Too Close to Call: The Thirty-Six-Day Battle to Decide the 2000 Election* (2001). On the attacks of September 11, 2001, and their aftermath, see *The Age of Terror: America and the World after September 11,* edited by Strobe Talbott and Nayan Chanda (2001).

On the environmental history of New Orleans, see Craig E. Colten's *An Unnatural Metropolis: Wresting New Orleans from Nature* (2005).

GLOSSARY

Agricultural Adjustment Act (1933) New Deal legislation that established the Agricultural Adjustment Administration (AAA) to improve agricultural prices by limiting market supplies; declared unconstitutional in *United States v. Butler* (1936).

Alamo, Battle of the Siege in the Texas War for Independence, 1836, in which the San Antonio mission fell to the Mexicans, and Davy Crockett and Jim Bowie died.

***Alexander v. Holmes County Board of Education* (1969)** Case fifteen years after the *Brown* decision in which the U.S. Supreme Court ordered an immediate end to segregation in public schools.

Alien and Sedition Acts (1798) Four measures passed during the undeclared war with France that limited the freedoms of speech and press and restricted the liberty of noncitizens.

America First Committee Largely midwestern isolationist organization supported by many prominent citizens, 1940–41.

American Anti-Slavery Society National abolitionist organization founded in 1833 by New York philanthropists Arthur and Lewis Tappan, propagandist Theodore Dwight Weld, and others.

American Colonization Society Organized in 1816 to encourage colonization of free blacks to Africa; West African nation of Liberia founded in 1822 to serve as a homeland for them.

American Federation of Labor Founded in 1881 as a federation of trade unions, the AFL under president Samuel Gompers successfully pushed for the eight-hour workday.

American Protective Association Nativist, anti-Catholic secret society founded in Iowa in 1887 and active until the end of the century.

American System Program of internal improvements and protective tariffs promoted by Speaker of the House Henry Clay in his presidential campaign of 1824; his proposals formed the core of Whig ideology in the 1830s and 1840s.

Antietam, Battle of (Battle of Sharpsburg) One of the bloodiest battles of the Civil War, fought to a standoff on September 17, 1862, in western Maryland.

Anti-Federalists Forerunners of Thomas Jefferson's Democratic-Republican party; opposed the Constitution as a limitation on individual and states' rights, which led to the addition of a Bill of Rights to the document.

Appomattox Court House, Virginia Site of the surrender of Confederate general Robert E. Lee to Union general Ulysses S. Grant on April 9, 1865, marking the end of the Civil War.

Army-McCarthy hearings Televised U.S. Senate hearings in 1954 on Senator Joseph McCarthy's charges of disloyalty in the Army; his tactics contributed to his censure by the Senate.

Atlanta Compromise Speech to the Cotton States and International Exposition in 1895 by educator Booker T. Washington, the leading black spokesman of the day; black scholar W. E. B. Du Bois gave the speech its derisive name and criticized Washington for encouraging blacks to accommodate segregation and disenfranchisement.

Atlantic Charter Issued August 12, 1941, following meetings in Newfoundland between President Franklin D. Roosevelt and British prime minister Winston Churchill, the charter signaled the allies' cooperation and stated their war aims.

Atomic Energy Commission Created in 1946 to supervise peacetime uses of atomic energy.

Axis powers In World War II, the nations of Germany, Italy, and Japan.

Aztec Mesoamerican people who were conquered by the Spanish under Hernando Cortés, 1519–28.

baby boom Markedly higher birth rate in the years following World War II; led to the biggest demographic "bubble" in American history.

Bacon's Rebellion Unsuccessful 1676 revolt led by planter Nathaniel Bacon against Virginia governor William Berkeley's administration because it had failed to protect settlers from Indian raids.

***Bakke v. Board of Regents of California* (1978)** Case in which the U.S. Supreme Court ruled against the California university system's use of racial quotas in admissions.

balance of trade Ratio of imports to exports.

Bank of the United States Proposed by the first secretary of the treasury, Alexander Hamilton, the bank opened in 1791 and operated until 1811 to issue a uniform currency, make business loans, and collect tax monies. The Second Bank of the United States was chartered in 1816 but was not renewed by President Andrew Jackson twenty years later.

barbary pirates Plundering pirates off the Mediterranean coast of Africa; President Thomas Jefferson's refusal to pay them tribute to protect American ships sparked an undeclared naval war with North African nations, 1801–1805.

barbed wire First practical fencing material for the Great Plains was invented in 1873 and rapidly spelled the end of the open range.

Battle of the Currents Conflict in the late 1880s between inventors Thomas Edison and George Westinghouse over direct versus alternating electric current; Westinghouse's alternating current (AC), the winner, allowed electricity to travel over long distances.

Bay of Pigs Invasion Hoping to inspire a revolt against Fidel Castro, the CIA sent 1,500 Cuban exiles to invade their homeland on April 17, 1961, but the mission was a spectacular failure.

Bill of Rights First ten amendments to the U.S. Constitution, adopted in 1791 to guarantee individual rights and to help secure ratification of the Constitution by the states.

Black Codes (1865–66) Laws passed in southern states to restrict the rights of former slaves; to combat the codes, Congress passed the Civil Rights Act of 1866 and the Fourteenth Amendment and set up military governments in southern states that refused to ratify the amendment.

Black Power Post-1966 rallying cry of a more militant civil rights movement.

Bland-Allison Act (1878) Passed over President Rutherford B. Hayes's veto, the inflationary measure authorized the purchase each month of 2 to 4 million dollars' worth of silver for coinage.

"Bleeding" Kansas Violence between pro- and antislavery settlers in the Kansas Territory, 1856.

Bloody Shirt, Waving the Republican references to Reconstruction-era violence in the South, used effectively in northern political campaigns against Democrats.

Bonus Expeditionary Force Thousands of World War I veterans, who insisted on immediate payment of their bonus certificates, marched on Washington in 1932; violence ensued when President Herbert Hoover ordered their tent villages cleared.

Boston Massacre Clash between British soldiers and a Boston mob, March 5, 1770, in which five colonists were killed.

Boston Tea Party On December 16, 1773, the Sons of Liberty, dressed as Indians, dumped hundreds of chests of tea into Boston harbor to protest the Tea Act of 1773, under which the British exported to the colonies millions of pounds of cheap—but still taxed—tea, thereby undercutting the price of smuggled tea and forcing payment of the tea duty.

Boxer Rebellion Chinese nationalist protest against Western commercial domination and cultural influence, 1900; a coalition of American, European, and Japanese forces put down the rebellion and reclaimed captured embassies in Peking (Beijing) within the year.

brain trust Group of advisers—many of them academics—that Franklin D. Roosevelt assembled to recommend New Deal policies during the early months of his presidency.

Branch Davidians Religious cult that lived communally near Waco, Texas, and was involved in a fiery 1993 confrontation with federal authorities in which dozens of cult members died.

Brook Farm Transcendentalist commune in West Roxbury, Massachusetts, populated from 1841 to 1847 principally by writers (Nathaniel Hawthorne, for one) and other intellectuals.

***Brown v. Board of Education of Topeka* (1954)** U.S. Supreme Court decision that struck down racial segregation in public education and declared "separate but equal" unconstitutional.

Budget and Accounting Act of 1921 Created the Bureau of the Budget and the General Accounting Office.

Bull Run, Battles of (First and Second Manassas) First land engagement of the Civil War took place on July 21, 1861, at Manassas Junction, Virginia, at which surprised Union troops quickly retreated; one year later, on August 29–30, Confederates captured the federal supply depot and forced Union troops back to Washington.

Bunker Hill, Battle of First major battle of the Revolutionary War; it actually took place at nearby Breed's Hill, Massachusetts, on June 17, 1775.

"Burned-Over District" Area of western New York strongly influenced by the revivalist fervor of the Second Great Awakening; Disciples of Christ and Mormons are among the many sects that trace their roots to the phenomenon.

Burr conspiracy Scheme by Vice-President Aaron Burr to lead the secession of the Louisiana Territory from the United States; captured in 1807 and charged with treason, Burr was acquitted by the U.S. Supreme Court.

***Bush v. Gore* (2000)** U.S. Supreme Court case that determined the winner of the disputed 2000 presidential election.

Calhoun Resolutions In making the proslavery response to the Wilmot Proviso, Senator John C. Calhoun argued that barring slavery in Mexican acquisitions would violate the Fifth Amendment to the Constitution by depriving slaveholding settlers of their property.

Calvinism Doctrine of predestination expounded by Swiss theologian John Calvin in 1536; influenced the Puritan, Presbyterian, German and Dutch Reformed, and Huguenot churches in the colonies.

Camp David Accords Peace agreement between Israeli prime minister Menachem Begin and Egyptian president Anwar Sadat, brokered by President Jimmy Carter in 1978.

carpetbaggers Northern emigrants who participated in the Republican governments of the Reconstruction South.

Chancellorsville, Battle of Confederate general Robert E. Lee won his last major victory and General "Stonewall" Jackson died in this Civil War battle in northern Virginia on May 1–4, 1863.

Chattanooga, Battle of Union victory in eastern Tennessee on November 23–25, 1863; gave the North control of important rail lines and cleared the way for General William T. Sherman's march into Georgia.

Chinese Exclusion Act (1882) Halted Chinese immigration to the United States.

Civil Rights Act of 1866 Along with the Fourteenth Amendment, guaranteed the rights of citizenship to freedmen.

Civil Rights Act of 1957 First federal civil rights law since Reconstruction; established the Civil Rights Commission and the Civil Rights Division of the Department of Justice.

Civil Rights Act of 1964 Outlawed discrimination in public accommodations and employment.

clipper ships Superior oceangoing sailing ships of the 1840s to 1860s that cut travel time in half; the clipper ship route around Cape Horn was the fastest way to travel between the coasts of the United States.

closed shop Hiring requirement that all workers in a business must be union members.

Coercive Acts/Intolerable Acts (1774) Four parliamentary measures in reaction to the Boston Tea Party that forced payment for the tea, disallowed colonial trials of British soldiers, forced their quartering in private homes, and set up a military government.

cold war Term for tensions, 1945–89, between the Soviet Union and the United States, the two major world powers after World War II.

***Commonwealth v. Hunt* (1842)** Landmark ruling of the Massachusetts supreme court establishing the legality of labor unions.

Compromise of 1850 Complex compromise mediated by Senator Henry Clay that headed off southern secession over California statehood; to appease the South it included a stronger fugitive slave law and delayed determination of the slave status of the New Mexico and Utah territories.

Compromise of 1877 Deal made by a special congressional commission on March 2, 1877, to resolve the disputed presidential election of 1876; Republican Rutherford B. Hayes, who had lost the popular vote, was declared the winner in exchange for the withdrawal of federal troops from the South, marking the end of Reconstruction.

Congress of Industrial Organizations (CIO) Umbrella organization of semi-skilled industrial unions, formed in 1935 as the Committee for Industrial Organization and renamed in 1938.

Congress of Racial Equality (CORE) Civil rights organization started in 1944 and best known for its "freedom rides," bus journeys challenging racial segregation in the South in 1961.

conspicuous consumption Phrase referring to extravagant spending to raise social standing, coined by Thorstein Veblen in *The Theory of the Leisure Class* (1899).

Constitutional Convention Meeting in Philadelphia, May 25–September 17, 1787, of representatives from twelve colonies—excepting Rhode Island—to revise the existing Articles of Confederation; convention soon resolved to produce an entirely new constitution.

containment General U.S. strategy in the cold war that called for containing Soviet expansion; originally devised in 1947 by U.S. diplomat George F. Kennan.

Continental Army Army authorized by the Continental Congress, 1775–84, to fight the British; commanded by General George Washington.

Continental Congress Representatives of a loose confederation of colonies met first in Philadelphia in 1774 to formulate actions against British policies; the Second Continental Congress (1775–89) conducted the war and adopted the Declaration of Independence and the Articles of Confederation.

convict leasing System developed in the post–Civil War South that generated income for the states and satisfied planters' need for cheap labor by renting prisoners out; the convicts, however, were often treated poorly.

Copperheads Northerners opposed to the Civil War.

Coral Sea, Battle of the Fought on May 7–8, 1942, near the eastern coast of Australia, it was the first U.S. naval victory over Japan in World War II.

cotton gin Invented by Eli Whitney in 1793, the machine separated cotton seed from cotton fiber, speeding cotton processing and making profitable the cultivation of the more hardy, but difficult to clean, short-staple cotton; led directly to the dramatic nineteenth-century expansion of slavery in the South.

counterculture "Hippie" youth culture of the 1960s, which rejected the values of the dominant culture in favor of illicit drugs, communes, free sex, and rock music.

court-packing plan President Franklin D. Roosevelt's failed 1937 attempt to increase the number of U.S. Supreme Court justices from nine to fifteen in order to save his Second New Deal programs from constitutional challenges.

Credit Mobilier scandal Millions of dollars in overcharges for building the Union Pacific Railroad were exposed; high officials of the Ulysses S. Grant administration were implicated but never charged.

Cuban missile crisis Caused when the United States discovered Soviet offensive missile sites in Cuba in October 1962; the U.S.-Soviet confrontation was the cold war's closest brush with nuclear war.

crop-lien system Merchants extended credit to tenants based on their future crops, but high interest rates and the uncertainties of farming often led to inescapable debts (debt peonage).

D-Day June 6, 1944, when an Allied amphibious assault landed on the Normandy coast and established a foothold in Europe from which Hitler's defenses could not recover.

Dartmouth College v. Woodward (**1819**) U.S. Supreme Court upheld the original charter of the college against New Hampshire's attempt to alter the board of trustees; set precedent of support of contracts against state interference.

Declaration of Independence Document adopted on July 4, 1776, that made the break with Britain official; drafted by a committee of the Second Continental Congress including principal writer Thomas Jefferson.

Deism Enlightenment thought applied to religion; emphasized reason, morality, and natural law.

Department of Homeland Security Created to coordinate federal antiterrorist activity following the 2001 terrorist attacks on the World Trade Center and Pentagon.

Depression of 1893 Worst depression of the century, set off by a railroad failure, too much speculation on Wall Street, and low agricultural prices.

Dixiecrats Deep South delegates who walked out of the 1948 Democratic National Convention in protest of the party's support for civil rights legislation and later formed the States' Rights (Dixiecrat) party, which nominated Strom Thurmond of South Carolina for president.

Dominion of New England Consolidation into a single colony of the New England colonies—and later New York and New Jersey—by royal governor Edmund Andros in 1686; dominion reverted to individual colonial governments three years later.

Donner Party Forty-seven surviving members of a group of migrants to California were forced to resort to cannibalism to survive a brutal winter trapped in the Sierra Nevadas, 1846–47; highest death toll of any group traveling the Overland Trail.

***Dred Scott v. Sandford* (1857)** U.S. Supreme Court decision in which Chief Justice Roger B. Taney ruled that slaves could not sue for freedom and that Congress could not prohibit slavery in the territories, on the grounds that such a prohibition would violate the Fifth Amendment rights of slaveholders.

due-process clause Clause in the Fifth and the Fourteenth amendments to the U.S. Constitution guaranteeing that states could not "deprive any person of life, liberty, or property, without due process of law."

Dust Bowl Great Plains counties where millions of tons of topsoil were blown away from parched farmland in the 1930s; massive migration of farm families followed.

Eighteenth Amendment (1919) Prohibition amendment that made illegal the manufacture, sale, or transportation of alcoholic beverages.

Ellis Island Reception center in New York Harbor through which most European immigrants to America were processed from 1892 to 1954.

Emancipation Proclamation (1863) President Abraham Lincoln issued a preliminary proclamation on September 22, 1862, freeing the slaves in the Confederate states as of January 1, 1863, the date of the final proclamation.

Embargo Act of 1807 Attempt to exert economic pressure instead of waging war in reaction to continued British impressment of American sailors; smugglers easily circumvented the embargo, and it was repealed two years later.

Emergency Banking Relief Act (1933) First New Deal measure that provided for reopening the banks under strict conditions and took the United States off the gold standard.

Emergency Immigration Act of 1921 Limited U.S. immigration to 3 percent of each foreign-born nationality in the 1910 census; three years later Congress restricted immigration even further.

encomienda System under which officers of the Spanish conquistadores gained ownership of Indian land.

ENIAC Electronic Numerical Integrator and Computer, built in 1944, the early, cumbersome ancestor of the modern computer.

Enlightenment Revolution in thought begun in the seventeenth century that emphasized reason and science over the authority of traditional religion.

Enola Gay American B-29 bomber that dropped the atomic bomb on Hiroshima, Japan, on August 6, 1945.

Environmental Protection Agency (EPA) Created in 1970 during the first administration of President Richard M. Nixon to oversee federal pollution control efforts.

Equal Rights Amendment Amendment to guarantee equal rights for women, introduced in 1923 but not passed by Congress until 1972; it failed to be ratified by the states.

Era of Good Feelings Contemporary characterization of the administration of popular Democratic-Republican president James Monroe, 1817–25.

Erie Canal Most important and profitable of the barge canals of the 1820s and 1830s; stretched from Buffalo to Albany, New York, connecting the Great Lakes to the East Coast and making New York City the nation's largest port.

Espionage and Sedition Acts (1917–18) Limited criticism of government leaders and policies by imposing fines and prison terms on those who acted out in opposition to in the First World War; the most repressive measures passed up to that time.

Fair Deal Domestic reform proposals of the second Truman administration (1949–53); included civil rights legislation and repeal of the Taft-Hartley Act, but only extensions of some New Deal programs were enacted.

Fair Employment Practices Commission Created in 1941 by executive order, the FEPC sought to eliminate racial discrimination in jobs; it possessed little power but represented a step toward civil rights for African Americans.

Family and Medical Leave Act (1993) Allowed certain workers to take twelve weeks of unpaid leave each year for family health problems, including birth or adoption of a child.

Farmers' Alliance Two separate organizations (Northwestern and Southern) of the 1880s and 1890s that took the place of the Grange, worked for similar causes, and attracted landless, as well as landed, farmers to their membership.

Federal Trade Commission Act (1914) Established the Federal Trade Commission to enforce existing antitrust laws that prohibited business combinations in restraint of trade.

The Federalist Collection of eighty-five essays that appeared in the New York press in 1787–88 in support of the Constitution; written by Alexander Hamilton, James Madison, and John Jay but published under the pseudonym "Publius."

Federalist party One of the two first national political parties, it favored a strong central government.

Fence-Cutters' War Violent conflict in Texas, 1883–84, between large and small cattle ranchers over access to grazing land.

"Fifty-four forty or fight" Democratic campaign slogan in the presidential election of 1844, urging that the northern border of Oregon be fixed at 54°40′ north latitude.

***Fletcher v. Peck* (1810)** U.S. Supreme Court decision in which Chief Justice John Marshall upheld the initial fraudulent sale contracts in the Yazoo Fraud cases; Congress paid $4.2 million to the original speculators in 1814.

Fort Laramie Treaty (1851) Restricted the Plains Indians from using the Overland Trail and permitted the building of government forts.

Fort McHenry Fort in Baltimore Harbor unsuccessfully bombarded by the British in September 1814; Francis Scott Key, a witness to the battle, was moved to write the words to "The Star-Spangled Banner."

Fort Sumter First battle of the Civil War, in which the federal fort in Charleston (South Carolina) Harbor was captured by the Confederates on April 14, 1861, after two days of shelling.

"forty-niners" Speculators who went to northern California following the discovery of gold in 1848; the first of several years of large-scale migration was 1849.

Fourteen Points President Woodrow Wilson's 1918 plan for peace after World War I; at the Versailles peace conference, however, he failed to incorporate all of the points into the treaty.

Fourteenth Amendment (1868) Guaranteed rights of citizenship to former slaves, in words similar to those of the Civil Rights Act of 1866.

franchise The right to vote.

"free person of color" Negro or mulatto person not held in slavery; immediately before the Civil War, there were nearly a half million in the United States, split almost evenly between North and South.

Free Soil party Formed in 1848 to oppose slavery in the territory acquired in the Mexican War; nominated Martin Van Buren for president in 1848, but by 1854 most of the party's members had joined the Republican party.

Free Speech Movement Founded in 1964 at the University of California at Berkeley by student radicals protesting restrictions on their right to demonstrate.

Freedmen's Bureau Reconstruction agency established in 1865 to protect the legal rights of former slaves and to assist with their education, jobs, health care, and landowning.

French and Indian War Known in Europe as the Seven Years' War, the last (1755–63) of four colonial wars fought between England and France for control of North America east of the Mississippi River.

Fugitive Slave Act of 1850 Gave federal government authority in cases involving runaway slaves; so much more punitive and prejudiced in favor of slaveholders than the 1793 Fugitive Slave Act had been that Harriet Beecher Stowe was inspired to write *Uncle Tom's Cabin* in protest; the new law was part of the Compromise of 1850, included to appease the South over the admission of California as a free state.

Fundamentalism Anti-modernist Protestant movement started in the early twentieth century that proclaimed the literal truth of the Bible; the name came from *The Fundamentals*, published by conservative leaders.

Gadsden Purchase (1853) Thirty thousand square miles in present-day Arizona and New Mexico bought by Congress from Mexico primarily for the Southern Pacific Railroad's transcontinental route.

Gentlemen's Agreement (1907) United States would not exclude Japanese immigrants if Japan would voluntarily limit the number of immigrants coming to the United States.

Gettysburg, Battle of Fought in southern Pennsylvania, July 1–3, 1863; the Confederate defeat and the simultaneous loss at Vicksburg spelled the end of the South's chances in the Civil War.

***Gibbons v. Ogden* (1824)** U.S. Supreme Court decision reinforcing the "commerce clause" (the federal government's right to regulate interstate commerce) of the Constitution; Chief Justice John Marshall ruled against the State of New York's granting of steamboat monopolies.

***Gideon v. Wainwright* (1963)** U.S. Supreme Court decision guaranteeing legal counsel for indigent felony defendants.

The Gilded Age Mark Twain and Charles Dudley Warner's 1873 novel, the title of which became the popular name for the period from the end of the Civil War to the turn of the century.

Glass-Owen Federal Reserve Act (1913) Created a Federal Reserve System of regional banks and a Federal Reserve Board to stabilize the economy by regulating the supply of currency and controlling credit.

Glass-Steagall Act (Banking Act of 1933) Established the Federal Deposit Insurance Corporation and included banking reforms, some designed to control speculation. A banking act of the Hoover administration, passed in 1932 and also known as the Glass-Steagall Act, was designed to expand credit.

Good Neighbor Policy Proclaimed by President Franklin D. Roosevelt in his first inaugural address in 1933, it sought improved diplomatic relations between the United States and its Latin American neighbors.

grandfather clause Loophole created by southern disfranchising legislatures of the 1890s for illiterate white males whose grandfathers had been eligible to vote in 1867.

Granger movement Political movement that grew out of the Patrons of Husbandry, an educational and social organization for farmers founded in 1867; the Grange had its greatest success in the Midwest of the 1870s, lobbying for government control of railroad and grain elevator rates and establishing farmers' cooperatives.

Great Awakening Fervent religious revival movement in the 1720s through the 1740s that was spread throughout the colonies by ministers like New England Congregationalist Jonathan Edwards and English revivalist George Whitefield.

Great Compromise (Connecticut Compromise) Mediated the differences between the New Jersey and Virginia delegations to the Constitutional Convention by providing for a bicameral legislature, the upper house of which would have equal representation and the lower house of which would be apportioned by population.

Great Depression Worst economic depression in American history; it was spurred by the stock market crash of 1929 and lasted until World War II.

Great Migration Large-scale migration of southern blacks during and after World War I to the North, where jobs had become available during the labor shortage of the war years.

Great Society Term coined by President Lyndon B. Johnson in his 1965 State of the Union address, in which he proposed legislation to address problems of voting rights, poverty, diseases, education, immigration, and the environment.

Greenback party Formed in 1876 in reaction to economic depression, the party favored issuance of unsecured paper money to help farmers repay debts; the movement for free coinage of silver took the place of the greenback movement by the 1880s.

habeas corpus, writ of An essential component of English common law and of the U.S. Constitution that guarantees that citizens may not be imprisoned without due process of law; literally means, "you must have the body."

Half-Breeds During the presidency of Rutherford B. Hayes, 1877–81, a moderate Republican party faction led by Senator James G. Blaine that favored some reforms of the civil service system and a restrained policy toward the defeated South.

Harlem Renaissance African-American literary and artistic movement of the 1920s and 1930s centered in New York City's Harlem district; writers Langston Hughes, Jean Toomer, Zora Neale Hurston, and Countee Cullen were among those active in the movement.

Harpers Ferry, Virginia Site of abolitionist John Brown's failed raid on the federal arsenal, October 16–17, 1859; he intended to arm the slaves, but ten of his compatriots were killed, and Brown became a martyr to his cause after his capture and execution.

Hartford Convention Meeting of New England Federalists on December 15, 1814, to protest the War of 1812; proposed seven constitutional amendments (limiting embargoes and changing requirements for officeholding, declaration of war, and admission of new states), but the war ended before Congress could respond.

Hawley-Smoot Tariff Act (1930) Raised tariffs to an unprecedented level and worsened the depression by raising prices and discouraging foreign trade.

Haymarket Affair Riot during an anarchist protest at Haymarket Square in Chicago on May 4, 1886, over violence during the McCormick Harvester Company strike; the deaths of eleven, including seven policemen, helped hasten the demise of the Knights of Labor, even though they were not responsible for the riot.

Hessians German soldiers, most from Hesse-Cassel principality (hence the name), paid to fight for the British in the Revolutionary War.

holding company Investment company that holds controlling interest in the securities of other companies.

Homestead Act (1862) Authorized Congress to grant 160 acres of public land to a western settler, who had only to live on the land for five years to establish title.

Homestead Strike Violent strike at the Carnegie Steel Company near Pittsburgh in 1892 that culminated in the disintegration of the Amalgamated Association of Iron and Steel Workers, the first steelworkers' union.

House Un-American Activities Committee (HUAC) Formed in 1938 to investigate subversives in the government; best-known investigations were of Hollywood no tables and of former State Department official Alger Hiss, who was accused in 1948 of espionage and Communist party membership.

Hundred Days Extraordinarily productive first three months of President Franklin D. Roosevelt's administration in which a special session of Congress enacted fifteen of his New Deal proposals.

impeachment Bringing charges against a public official; for example, the House of Representatives can impeach a president for "treason, bribery, or other high crimes and misdemeanors" by majority vote, and after the trial the Senate can remove the president by a vote of two-thirds.

implied powers Federal powers beyond those specifically enumerated in the U.S. Constitution; the Federalists argued that the "elastic clause" of Article I, Section 8, of the Constitution implicitly gave the federal government broad powers, while the Antifederalists held that the federal government's powers were explicitly limited by the Constitution.

"In God We Trust" Phrase placed on all new U.S. currency as of 1954.

indentured servant Settler who signed on for a temporary period of servitude to a master in exchange for passage to the New World; Virginia and Pennsylvania were largely peopled in the seventeenth and eighteenth centuries by English indentured servants.

Independent Treasury Act (1840) Promoted by President Martin Van Buren, the measure sought to stabilize the economy by preventing state banks from printing unsecured paper currency and establishing an independent treasury based on specie.

Indian Peace Commission Established in 1867 to end the Indian wars in the West, the commission's solution was to contain the Indians in a system of reservations.

Indian Removal Act (1830) Signed by President Andrew Jackson, the law permitted the negotiation of treaties to obtain the Indians' lands in exchange for their relocation to what would become Oklahoma.

Industrial Workers of the World Radical union organized in Chicago in 1905 and nicknamed the Wobblies; its opposition to World War I led to its destruction by the federal government under the Espionage Act.

internal improvements In the early national period the phrase referred to road building and the development of water transportation.

Interstate Commerce Commission Reacting to the U.S. Supreme Court's ruling in *Wabash Railroad* v. *Illinois* (1886), Congress established the ICC to curb abuses in the railroad industry by regulating rates.

Iran-Contra affair Scandal of the second Reagan administration involving sale of arms to Iran in partial exchange for release of hostages in Lebanon and use of the arms money to aid the Contras in Nicaragua, which had been expressly forbidden by Congress.

Iron Curtain Term coined by Winston Churchill to describe the cold war divide between western Europe and the Soviet Union's eastern European satellites.

Irreconcilables Group of isolationist U.S. senators who fought ratification of the Treaty of Versailles, 1919–20, because of their opposition to American membership in the League of Nations.

Jamestown, Virginia Site in 1607 of the first permanent English settlement in the New World.

Jay's Treaty Treaty with Britain negotiated in 1794 by Chief Justice John Jay; Britain agreed to vacate forts in the Northwest Territories, and festering disagreements (border with Canada, prewar debts, shipping claims) would be settled by commission.

Jim Crow Minstrel show character whose name became synonymous with post-Reconstruction laws revoking civil rights for freedmen and with racial segregation generally.

Judiciary Act of 1801 Enacted by the lame duck Congress to allow the Federalists, the losing party in the presidential election, to reorganize the judiciary and fill the open judgeships with Federalists.

Kansas-Nebraska Act (1854) Law sponsored by Illinois senator Stephen A. Douglas to allow settlers in newly organized territories north of the Missouri border to decide the slavery issue for themselves; fury over the resulting nullification of the Missouri Compromise of 1820 led to violence in Kansas and to the formation of the Republican party.

Kellogg-Briand Pact Representatives of sixty-two nations in 1928 signed the pact (also called the Pact of Paris) to outlaw war.

Kentucky and Virginia Resolutions (1798–99) Passed in response to the Alien and Sedition Acts, the resolutions advanced the state-compact theory that held states could nullify an act of Congress if they deemed it unconstitutional.

King William's War (War of the League of Augsburg) First (1689–97) of four colonial wars between England and France.

King's Mountain, Battle of Upcountry South Carolina irregulars defeated British troops under Patrick Ferguson on October 7, 1780, in what proved to be the turning point of the Revolutionary War in the South.

Knights of Labor Founded in 1869, the first national union picked up many members after the disastrous 1877 railroad strike but lasted, under the leadership of Terence V. Powderly, only into the 1890s; supplanted by the American Federation of Labor.

Know-Nothing (American) party Nativist, anti-Catholic third party organized in 1854 in reaction to large-scale German and Irish immigration; the party's only presidential candidate was Millard Fillmore in 1856.

Korean War Conflict touched off in 1950 when Communist North Korea invaded South Korea, which had been under U.S. control since the end of World War II; fighting largely by U.S. forces continued until 1953.

Ku Klux Klan Organized in Pulaski, Tennessee, in 1866 to terrorize former slaves who voted and held political offices during Reconstruction; a revived organization in the 1910s and 1920s stressed white, Anglo-Saxon, fundamentalist Protestant supremacy; the Klan revived a third time to fight the civil rights movement of the 1950s and 1960s in the South.

Land Ordinance of 1785 Directed surveying of the Northwest Territory into townships of thirty-six sections (square miles) each, the sale of the sixteenth section of which was to be used to finance public education.

League of Nations Organization of nations to mediate disputes and avoid war established after World War I as part of the Treaty of Versailles; President Woodrow Wilson's "Fourteen Points" speech to Congress in 1918 proposed the formation of the league.

Lecompton Constitution Controversial constitution drawn up in 1857 by proslavery Kansas delegates seeking statehood; rejected in 1858 by an overwhelmingly antislavery electorate.

Legal Tender Act (1862) Helped the U.S. government pay for the Civil War by authorizing the printing of paper currency.

Lend-Lease Act (1941) Permitted the United States to lend or lease arms and other supplies to the Allies, signifying increasing likelihood of American involvement in World War II.

Levittown Low-cost, mass-produced development of suburban tract housing built by William Levitt on Long Island in 1947.

Lexington and Concord, Battle of The first shots fired in the Revolutionary War, on April 19, 1775, near Boston; approximately 100 minutemen and 250 British soldiers were killed.

Leyte Gulf, Battle of Largest sea battle in history, fought on October 25, 1944, and won by the United States off the Philippine island of Leyte; Japanese losses were so great that they could not rebound.

Liberty party Abolitionist political party that nominated James G. Birney for president in 1840 and 1844; merged with the Free Soil party in 1848.

Lincoln-Douglas debates Series of senatorial campaign debates in 1858 focusing on the issue of slavery in the territories; held in Illinois between Republican Abraham Lincoln, who made a national reputation for himself, and incumbent Democratic senator Stephen A. Douglas, who managed to hold onto his seat.

Little Bighorn, Battle of Most famous battle of the Great Sioux War took place in 1876 in the Montana Territory; combined Sioux and Cheyenne warriors massacred a vastly outnumbered U.S. Cavalry commanded by Lieutenant Colonel George Armstrong Custer.

Lost Colony English expedition of 117 settlers, including Virginia Dare, the first English child born in the New World; colony disappeared from Roanoke Island in the Outer Banks sometime between 1587 and 1590.

Louisiana Purchase President Thomas Jefferson's 1803 purchase from France of the important port of New Orleans and 828,000 square miles west of the Mississippi River to the Rocky Mountains; it more than doubled the territory of the United States at a cost of only $15 million.

Lusitania British passenger liner sunk by a German U-boat, May 7, 1915, creating a diplomatic crisis and public outrage at the loss of 128 Americans (roughly 10 percent of the total aboard); Germany agreed to pay reparations, and the United States waited two more years to enter World War I.

Lyceum movement Founded in 1826, the movement promoted adult public education through lectures and performances.

maize Indian corn, native to the New World.

Manhattan Project Secret American plan during World War II to develop an atomic bomb; J. Robert Oppenheimer led the team of physicists at Los Alamos, New Mexico.

Manifest Destiny Imperialist phrase first used in 1845 to urge annexation of Texas; used thereafter to encourage American settlement of European colonial and Indian lands in the Great Plains and Far West.

***Marbury v. Madison* (1803)** First U.S. Supreme Court decision to declare a federal law—the Judiciary Act of 1801—unconstitutional; President John Adams's "midnight appointment" of Federalist judges prompted the suit.

March on Washington Civil rights demonstration on August 28, 1963, where the Reverend Martin Luther King, Jr., gave his "I Have a Dream" speech on the steps of the Lincoln Memorial.

Marshall Plan U.S. program for the reconstruction of post–World War II Europe through massive aid to former enemy nations as well as allies; proposed by General George C. Marshall in 1947.

massive resistance In reaction to the *Brown* decision of 1954, U.S. senator Harry Byrd encouraged southern states to defy federally mandated school integration.

Maya Pre-Columbian society in Mesoamerica before about A.D. 900.

Mayflower Compact Signed in 1620 aboard the *Mayflower* before the Pilgrims landed at Plymouth, the document committed the group to majority-rule government; remained in effect until 1691.

Maysville Road Bill Federal funding for a Kentucky road, vetoed by President Andrew Jackson in 1830.

McCarran Internal Security Act (1950) Passed over President Harry S. Truman's veto, the law required registration of American Communist party members, denied them passports, and allowed them to be detained as suspected subversives.

McCulloch v. Maryland **(1819)** U.S. Supreme Court decision in which Chief Justice John Marshall, holding that Maryland could not tax the Second Bank of the United States, supported the authority of the federal government versus the states.

McNary-Haugen Bill Vetoed by President Calvin Coolidge in 1927 and 1928, the bill to aid farmers would have artificially raised agricultural prices by selling surpluses overseas for low prices and selling the reduced supply in the United States for higher prices.

Meat Inspection Act (1906) Passed largely in reaction to Upton Sinclair's *The Jungle,* the law set strict standards of cleanliness in the meatpacking industry.

mercantilism Limitation and exploitation of colonial trade by an imperial power.

Mestizo Person of mixed Native American and European ancestry.

Mexican War Controversial war with Mexico for control of California and New Mexico, 1846–48; the Treaty of Guadalupe Hidalgo fixed the border at the Rio Grande and extended the United States to the Pacific coast, annexing more than a half-million square miles of potential slave territory.

Midway, Battle of Decisive American victory near Midway Island in the South Pacific on June 4, 1942; the Japanese navy never recovered its superiority over the U.S. navy.

Military Reconstruction Act (1867) Established military governments in ten Confederate states—excepting Tennessee—and required that the states ratify the Fourteenth Amendment and permit freedmen to vote.

minstrel show Blackface vaudeville entertainment popular in the decades surrounding the Civil War.

Miranda v. Arizona **(1966)** U.S. Supreme Court decision required police to advise persons in custody of their rights to legal counsel and against self-incrimination.

Missouri Compromise Deal proposed by Kentucky senator Henry Clay to resolve the slave/free imbalance in Congress that would result from Missouri's admission as a slave state; in the compromise of March 20, 1820, Maine's admission as a free state offset Missouri, and slavery was prohibited in the remainder of the Louisiana Territory north of the southern border of Missouri.

Molly Maguires Secret organization of Irish coal miners that used violence to intimidate mine officials in the 1870s.

Monitor **and** *Merrimack,* **Battle of the** First engagement between ironclad ships; fought at Hampton Roads, Virginia, on March 9, 1862.

Monroe Doctrine President James Monroe's declaration to Congress on December 2, 1823, that the American continents would be thenceforth closed to colonization but that the United States would honor existing colonies of European nations.

Moral Majority Televangelist Jerry Falwell's political lobbying organization, the name of which became synonymous with the religious right—conservative evangelical Protestants who helped ensure President Ronald Reagan's 1980 victory.

Mormons Founded in 1830 by Joseph Smith, the sect (officially, the Church of Jesus Christ of Latter-Day Saints) was a product of the intense revivalism of the "Burned-Over District" of New York; Smith's successor Brigham Young led 15,000 followers to Utah in 1847 to escape persecution.

Montgomery bus boycott Sparked by Rosa Parks's arrest on December 1, 1955, a successful year-long boycott protesting segregation on city buses; led by the Reverend Martin Luther King.

Muckrakers Writers who exposed corruption and abuses in politics, business, meat-packing, child labor, and more, primarily in the first decade of the twentieth century; their popular books and magazine articles spurred public interest in progressive reform.

Mugwumps Reform wing of the Republican party which supported Democrat Grover Cleveland for president in 1884 over Republican James G. Blaine, whose influence peddling had been revealed in the Mulligan letters of 1876.

Munn v. Illinois **(1877)** U.S. Supreme Court ruling that upheld a Granger law allowing the state to regulate grain elevators.

NAFTA Approved in 1993, the North American Free Trade Agreement with Canada and Mexico allowed goods to travel across their borders free of tariffs; critics argued that American workers would lose their jobs to cheaper Mexican labor.

National Aeronautics and Space Administration (NASA) In response to the Soviet Union's launching of *Sputnik*, Congress created this federal agency in 1957 to coordinate research and administer the space program.

National Association for the Advancement of Colored People (NAACP) Founded in 1910, this civil rights organization brought lawsuits against discriminatory practices and published *The Crisis*, a journal edited by African-American scholar W. E. B. Du Bois.

National Defense Education Act (1958) Passed in reaction to America's perceived inferiority in the space race, the appropriation encouraged education in science and modern languages through student loans, university research grants, and aid to public schools.

National Industrial Recovery Act (1933) Passed on the last of the Hundred Days, it created public-works jobs through the Federal Emergency Relief Administration and established a system of self-regulation for industry through the National Recovery Administration, which was ruled unconstitutional in 1935.

National Organization for Women Founded in 1966 by writer Betty Friedan and other feminists, NOW pushed for abortion rights and nondiscrimination in the workplace, but within a decade it became radicalized and lost much of its constituency.

National Road First federal interstate road, built between 1811 and 1838 and stretching from Cumberland, Maryland, to Vandalia, Illinois.

National Security Act (1947) Authorized the reorganization of government to coordinate military branches and security agencies; created the

National Security Council, the Central Intelligence Agency, and the National Military Establishment (later renamed the Department of Defense).

National Youth Administration Created in 1935 as part of the Works Progress Administration, it employed millions of youths who had left school.

nativism Anti-immigrant and anti-Catholic feeling in the 1830s through the 1850s; the largest group was New York's Order of the Star-Spangled Banner, which expanded into the American, or Know-Nothing, party in 1854.

naval stores Tar, pitch, and turpentine made from pine resin and used in shipbuilding; an important industry in the southern colonies, especially North Carolina.

Navigation Acts Passed by the English Parliament to control colonial trade and bolster the mercantile system, 1650–1775; enforcement of the acts led to growing resentment by colonists.

Neutrality Acts Series of laws passed between 1935 and 1939 to keep the United States from becoming involved in war by prohibiting American trade and travel to warring nations.

New Deal Franklin D. Roosevelt's campaign promise, in his speech to the Democratic National Convention of 1932, to combat the Great Depression with a "new deal for the American people"; the phrase became a catchword for his ambitious plan of economic programs.

New England Anti-Slavery Society Abolitionist organization founded in 1832 by William Lloyd Garrison of Massachusetts, publisher of the *Liberator*.

New Freedom Democrat Woodrow Wilson's political slogan in the presidential campaign of 1912; Wilson wanted to improve the banking system, lower tariffs, and, by breaking up monopolies, give small businesses freedom to compete.

New Frontier John F. Kennedy's program, stymied by a Republican Congress and his abbreviated term; his successor Lyndon B. Johnson had greater success with many of the same concepts.

New Harmony Founded in Indiana by British industrialist Robert Owen in 1825, the short-lived New Harmony Community of Equality was one of the few nineteenth-century communal experiments not based on religious ideology.

New Left Radical youth protest movement of the 1960s, named by leader Tom Hayden to distinguish it from the Old (Marxist-Leninist) Left of the 1930s.

New Nationalism Platform of the Progressive party and slogan of former president Theodore Roosevelt in the presidential campaign of 1912; stressed government activism, including regulation of trusts, conservation, and recall of state court decisions that had nullified progressive programs.

New Orleans, Battle of Last battle of the War of 1812, fought on January 8, 1815, weeks after the peace treaty was signed but prior to its ratification; General Andrew Jackson led the victorious American troops.

New South *Atlanta Constitution* editor Henry W. Grady's 1886 term for the prosperous post–Civil War South he envisioned: democratic, industrial, urban, and free of nostalgia for the defeated plantation South.

Nineteenth Amendment (1920) Granted women the right to vote.

Nisei Japanese Americans; literally, "second generation."

normalcy Word coined by future president Warren G. Harding as part of a 1920 campaign speech—"not nostrums, but normalcy"—signifying his awareness that the public was tired of progressivism, war, and sacrifice.

North Atlantic Treaty Organization (NATO) Defensive alliance founded in 1949 by ten western European nations, the United States, and Canada to deter Soviet expansion in Europe.

Northwest Ordinance of 1787 Created the Northwest Territory (area north of the Ohio River and west of Pennsylvania), established conditions for self-government and statehood, included a Bill of Rights, and permanently prohibited slavery.

nullification Concept of invalidation of a federal law within the borders of a state; first expounded in the Kentucky and Virginia Resolutions (1798), cited by South Carolina in its Ordinance of Nullification (1832) of the Tariff of Abominations, used by southern states to explain their secession from the Union (1861), and cited again by southern states to oppose the *Brown* v. *Board of Education* decision (1954).

Nullification Proclamation President Andrew Jackson's strong criticism of South Carolina's Ordinance of Nullification (1832) as disunionist and potentially treasonous.

Office of Price Administration Created in 1941 to control wartime inflation and price fixing resulting from shortages of many consumer goods, the OPA imposed wage and price freezes and administered a rationing system.

Okies Displaced farm families from the Oklahoma dust bowl who migrated to California during the 1930s in search of jobs.

Old Southwest In the antebellum period, the states of Alabama, Mississippi, Louisiana, Texas, Arkansas, and parts of Tennessee, Kentucky, and Florida.

Oneida Community Utopian community founded in 1848; the Perfectionist religious group practiced universal marriage until leader John Humphrey Noyes, fearing prosecution, escaped to Canada in 1879.

OPEC Organization of Petroleum Exporting Countries.

Open Door Policy In hopes of protecting the Chinese market for U.S. exports, Secretary of State John Hay unilaterally announced in 1899 that Chinese trade would be open to all nations.

Operation Desert Storm Multinational allied force that defeated Iraq in the Gulf War of January 1991.

Operation Dixie CIO's largely ineffective post–World War II campaign to unionize southern workers.

Oregon fever Enthusiasm for emigration to the Oregon Country in the late 1830s and early 1840s.

Ostend Manifesto Memorandum written in 1854 from Ostend, Belgium, by the U.S. ministers to England, France, and Spain recommending purchase or seizure of Cuba in order to increase the United States' slaveholding territory.

Overland (Oregon) Trail Route of wagon trains bearing settlers from Independence, Missouri, to the Oregon Country in the 1840s through the 1860s.

overseer Manager of slave labor on a plantation.

Panic of 1819 Financial collapse brought on by sharply falling cotton prices, declining demand for American exports, and reckless western land speculation.

Panic of 1837 Major economic depression lasting about six years; touched off by a British financial crisis and made worse by falling cotton prices, credit and currency problems, and speculation in land, canals, and railroads.

Panic of 1857 Economic depression lasting about two years and brought on by falling grain prices and a weak financial system; the South was largely protected by international demand for its cotton.

Panic of 1873 Severe six-year depression marked by bank failures and railroad and insurance bankruptcies.

Peace of Paris Signed on September 3, 1783, the treaty ending the Revolutionary War and recognizing American independence from Britain also established the border between Canada and the United States, fixed the western border at the Mississippi River, and ceded Florida to Spain.

Pendleton Civil Service Act (1883) Established the Civil Service Commission and marked the end of the spoils system.

Pentagon Papers Informal name for the Defense Department's secret history of the Vietnam conflict; leaked to the press by former official Daniel Ellsberg and published in the *New York Times* in 1971.

Pequot War Massacre in 1637 and subsequent dissolution of the Pequot Nation by Puritan settlers, who seized the Indians' lands.

Personal Responsibility and Work Opportunity Act (1996) Welfare reform measure that mandated state administration of federal aid to the poor.

Philippine Sea, Battle of the Costly Japanese defeat of June 19–20, 1944; led to the resignation of Premier Tojo and his cabinet.

Pilgrims Puritan Separatists who broke completely with the Church of England and sailed to the New World aboard the *Mayflower*, founding Plymouth Colony on Cape Cod in 1620.

Pinckney's Treaty Treaty with Spain negotiated by Thomas Pinckney in 1795; established United States boundaries at the Mississippi River and the thirty-first parallel and allowed open transportation on the Mississippi.

planter In the antebellum South, the owner of a large farm worked by twenty or more slaves.

Platt Amendment (1901) Reserved the United States' right to intervene in Cuban affairs and forced newly independent Cuba to host American naval bases on the island.

Plessy v. Ferguson **(1896)** U.S. Supreme Court decision supporting the legality of Jim Crow laws that permitted or required "separate but equal" facilities for blacks and whites.

poll tax Tax that must be paid in order to be eligible to vote; used as an effective means of disenfranchising black citizens after Reconstruction, since they often could not afford even a modest fee.

popular sovereignty Allowed settlers in a disputed territory to decide the slavery issue for themselves.

Populist party Political success of Farmers' Alliance candidates encouraged the formation in 1892 of the National People's party (later renamed the Populist party); active until 1912, it advocated a variety of reform issues, including free coinage of silver, income tax, postal savings, regulation of railroads, and direct election of U.S. senators.

Pottawatomie Massacre Murder of five proslavery settlers in eastern Kansas led by abolitionist John Brown on May 24–25, 1856.

Potsdam Conference Last meeting of the major Allied powers, the conference took place outside Berlin from July 17 to August 2, 1945; United States president Harry Truman, Soviet dictator Joseph Stalin, and British prime minister Clement Atlee finalized plans begun at Yalta.

Proclamation of Amnesty and Reconstruction President Lincoln's plan for reconstruction, issued in 1863, allowed southern states to rejoin the Union if 10 percent of the 1860 electorate signed loyalty pledges, accepted emancipation, and had received presidential pardons.

Proclamation of 1763 Royal directive issued after the French and Indian War prohibiting settlement, surveys, and land grants west of the Appalachian Mountains; although it was soon overridden by treaties, colonists continued to harbor resentment.

Progressive party Created when former president Theodore Roosevelt broke away from the Republican party to run for president again in

1912; the party supported progressive reforms similar to the Democrats but stopped short of seeking to eliminate trusts.

Progressivism Broad-based reform movement, 1900–17, that sought governmental help in solving problems in many areas of American life, including education, public health, the economy, the environment, labor, transportation, and politics.

Protestant Reformation Reform movement that resulted in the establishment of Protestant denominations; begun by German monk Martin Luther when he posted his "Ninety-five Theses" (complaints of abuses in the Catholic church) in 1517.

Pullman Strike Strike against the Pullman Palace Car Company in the company town of Pullman, Illinois, on May 11, 1894, by the American Railway Union under Eugene V. Debs; the strike was crushed by court injunctions and federal troops two months later.

Pure Food and Drug Act (1906) First law to regulate manufacturing of food and medicines; prohibited dangerous additives and inaccurate labeling.

Puritans English religious group that sought to purify the Church of England; founded the Massachusetts Bay Colony under John Winthrop in 1630.

Quartering Act (1765) Parliamentary act requiring colonies to house and provision British troops.

Radical Republicans Senators and congressmen who, strictly identifying the Civil War with the abolitionist cause, sought swift emancipation of the slaves, punishment of the rebels, and tight controls over the former Confederate states after the war.

Railroad Strike of 1877 Violent but ultimately unsuccessful interstate strike, which resulted in extensive property damage and many deaths.

Reaganomics Popular name for President Ronald Reagan's philosophy of "supply side" economics, which combined tax cuts, less government spending, and a balanced budget with an unregulated marketplace.

Reconstruction Finance Corporation Federal program established in 1932 under President Herbert Hoover to loan money to banks and other institutions to help them avert bankruptcy.

Red Scare Fear among many Americans after World War I of Communists in particular and noncitizens in general, a reaction to the Russian Revolution, mail bombs, strikes, and riots.

Redcoats Nickname for British soldiers, after their red uniform jackets.

Redeemers/Bourbons Conservative white Democrats, many of whom had been planters or businessmen before the Civil War, who reclaimed control of the South following the end of Reconstruction.

Regulators Groups of backcountry Carolina settlers who protested colonial policies; North Carolina royal governor William Tryon retaliated at the Battle of Alamance on May 17, 1771.

Report on Manufactures First secretary of the treasury Alexander Hamilton's 1791 analysis that accurately foretold the future of American industry and proposed tariffs and subsidies to promote it.

Republican party Organized in 1854 by antislavery Whigs, Democrats, and Free Soilers in response to the passage of the Kansas-Nebraska Act; nominated John C. Frémont for president in 1856 and Abraham Lincoln in 1860.

Republicans Political faction that succeeded the Anti-Federalists after ratification of the Constitution; led by Thomas Jefferson and James Madison, it soon developed into the Democratic-Republican party.

Reservationists Group of U.S. senators led by Majority Leader Henry Cabot Lodge who would only agree to ratification of the Treaty of Versailles subject to certain reservations, most notably the removal of Article X of the League of Nations Covenant.

Revolution of 1800 First time that an American political party surrendered power to the opposition party; Jefferson, a Democratic-Republican, had defeated incumbent Adams, a Federalist, for president.

right-to-work State laws enacted to prevent imposition of the closed shop; any worker, whether or not a union member, could be hired.

Roe v. Wade (1973) U.S. Supreme Court decision requiring states to permit first-trimester abortions.

Roosevelt Corollary (1904) President Theodore Roosevelt announced in what was essentially a corollary to the Monroe Doctrine that the United States could intervene militarily to prevent interference from European powers in the Western Hemisphere.

Romanticism Philosophical, literary, and artistic movement of the nineteenth century that was largely a reaction to the rationalism of the previous century; romantics valued emotion, mysticism, and individualism.

Rough Riders The 1st U.S. Volunteer Cavalry, led in battle in the Spanish-American War by Theodore Roosevelt; they were victorious in their only battle near Santiago, Cuba, and Roosevelt used the notoriety to aid his political career.

Santa Fe Trail Beginning in the 1820s, a major trade route from St. Louis, Missouri, to Santa Fe, New Mexico Territory.

Saratoga, Battle of Major defeat of British general John Burgoyne and more than 5,000 British troops at Saratoga, New York, on October 17, 1777.

Scalawags Southern white Republicans—some former Unionists—who served in Reconstruction governments.

***Schenck v. U.S.* (1919)** U.S. Supreme Court decision upholding the wartime Espionage and Sedition Acts; in the opinion he wrote for the case, Justice Oliver Wendell Holmes set the now-familiar "clear and present danger" standard.

scientific management Analysis of worker efficiency using measurements like "time and motion" studies to achieve greater productivity; introduced by Frederick Winslow Taylor in 1911.

Scottsboro case (1931) In overturning verdicts against nine black youths accused of raping two white women, the U.S. Supreme Court established precedents in *Powell* v. *Alabama* (1932), that adequate counsel must be appointed in capital cases, and in *Norris* v. *Alabama* (1935), that African Americans cannot be excluded from juries.

Second Great Awakening Religious revival movement of the early decades of the nineteenth century, in reaction to the growth of secularism and rationalist religion; began the predominance of the Baptist and Methodist churches.

Second Red Scare Post–World War II Red Scare focused on the fear of Communists in U.S. government positions; peaked during the Korean War and declined soon thereafter, when the U.S. Senate censured Joseph McCarthy, who had been a major instigator of the hysteria.

Seneca Falls Convention First women's rights meeting and the genesis of the women's suffrage movement; held in July 1848 in a church in Seneca Falls, New York, by Elizabeth Cady Stanton and Lucretia Coffin Mott.

"separate but equal" Principle underlying legal racial segregation, which was upheld in *Plessy* v. *Ferguson* (1896) and struck down in *Brown* v. *Board of Education* (1954).

Servicemen's Readjustment Act (1944) The "GI Bill of Rights" provided money for education and other benefits to military personnel returning from World War II.

settlement houses Product of the late nineteenth-century movement to offer a broad array of social services in urban immigrant neighborhoods; Chicago's Hull House was one of hundreds of settlement houses that operated by the early twentieth century.

Seventeenth Amendment (1913) Progressive reform that required U.S. senators to be elected directly by voters; previously, senators were chosen by state legislatures.

Seward's Folly Secretary of State William H. Seward's negotiation of the purchase of Alaska from Russia in 1867.

Shakers Founded by Mother Ann Lee Stanley in England, the United Society of Believers in Christ's Second Appearing settled in Watervliet, New York, in 1774 and subsequently established eighteen additional communes in the Northeast, Indiana, and Kentucky.

sharecropping Type of farm tenancy that developed after the Civil War in which landless workers—often former slaves—farmed land in exchange for farm supplies and a share of the crop; differed from tenancy in that the terms were generally less favorable.

Shays's Rebellion Massachusetts farmer Daniel Shays and 1,200 compatriots, seeking debt relief through issuance of paper currency and lower taxes, stormed the federal arsenal at Springfield in the winter of 1787 but were quickly repulsed.

Sherman Anti-Trust Act (1890) First law to restrict monopolistic trusts and business combinations; extended by the Clayton Anti-Trust Act of 1914.

Sherman Silver Purchase Act (1890) In replacing and extending the provisions of the Bland-Allison Act of 1878, it increased the amount of silver periodically bought for coinage.

Shiloh, Battle of At the time it was fought (April 6–7, 1862), Shiloh, in western Tennessee, was the bloodiest battle in American history; afterward, General Ulysses S. Grant was temporarily removed from command.

single tax Concept of taxing only landowners as a remedy for poverty, promulgated by Henry George in *Progress and Poverty* (1879).

Sixteenth Amendment (1913) Legalized the federal income tax.

Smith-Connally War Labor Disputes Act (1943) Outlawed labor strikes in wartime and allowed the president to take over industries threatened by labor disputes.

***Smith v. Allwright* (1944)** U.S. Supreme Court decision that outlawed all-white Democratic party primaries in Texas.

Social Darwinism Application of Charles Darwin's theory of natural selection to society; used the concept of the "survival of the fittest" to justify class distinctions and to explain poverty.

social gospel Preached by liberal Protestant clergymen in the late nineteenth and early twentieth centuries; advocated the application of Christian principles to social problems generated by industrialization.

Social Security Act (1935) Created the Social Security system with provisions for a retirement pension, unemployment insurance, disability insurance, and public assistance (welfare).

Sons of Liberty Secret organizations formed by Samuel Adams, John Hancock, and other radicals in response to the Stamp Act; they impeded British officials and planned such harassments as the Boston Tea Party.

South Carolina Exposition and Protest Written in 1828 by Vice-President John C. Calhoun of South Carolina to protest the so-called Tariff of Abominations, which seemed to favor northern industry; introduced the concept of state interposition and became the basis for South Carolina's Nullification Doctrine of 1833.

Southeast Asia Treaty Organization (SEATO) Pact among mostly western nations signed in 1954; designed to deter Communist expansion and cited as a justification for U.S. involvement in Vietnam.

Southern Christian Leadership Conference (SCLC) Civil rights organization founded in 1957 by the Reverend Martin Luther King, Jr., and other civil rights leaders.

Southern renaissance Literary movement of the 1920s and 1930s that included such writers as William Faulkner, Thomas Wolfe, and Robert Penn Warren.

Spanish flu Unprecedentedly lethal influenza epidemic of 1918 that killed more than 22 million people worldwide.

spoils system The term—meaning the filling of federal government jobs with persons loyal to the party of the president—originated in Andrew Jackson's first term; the system was replaced in the Progressive Era by civil service.

Sputnik First artificial satellite to orbit the earth; launched October 4, 1957, by the Soviet Union.

Stalwarts Conservative Republican party faction during the presidency of Rutherford B. Hayes, 1877–81; led by Senator Roscoe B. Conkling of New York, Stalwarts opposed civil service reform and favored a third term for President Ulysses S. Grant.

Stamp Act (1765) Parliament required that revenue stamps be affixed to all colonial printed matter, documents, dice, and playing cards; the Stamp Act Congress met to formulate a response, and the act was repealed the following year.

Standard Oil Company Founded in 1870 by John D. Rockefeller in Cleveland, Ohio, it soon grew into the nation's first industry-dominating trust; the Sherman Anti-Trust Act (1890) was enacted in part to combat abuses by Standard Oil.

staple crop Important cash crop, for example, cotton or tobacco.

steamboats Paddlewheelers that could travel both up- and down-river in deep or shallow waters; they became commercially viable early in the nineteenth century and soon developed into America's first inland freight and passenger service network.

Stimson Doctrine In reaction to Japan's 1932 occupation of Manchuria, Secretary of State Henry Stimson declared that the United States would not recognize territories acquired by force.

Strategic Defense Initiative ("Star Wars") Defense Department's plan during the Reagan administration to build a system to destroy incoming missiles in space.

Student Non-violent Coordinating Committee Founded in 1960 to coordinate civil rights sit-ins and other forms of grassroots protest.

Students for a Democratic Society (SDS) Major organization of the New Left, founded at the University of Michigan in 1960 by Tom Hayden and A1 Haber.

Sugar Act (Revenue Act of 1764) Parliament's tax on refined sugar and many other colonial products; the first tax designed solely to raise revenue for Britain.

Taft-Hartley Act (1947) Passed over President Harry Truman's veto, the law contained a number of provisions to control labor unions, including the banning of closed shops.

tariff Federal tax on imported goods.

Tariff of Abominations (Tariff of 1828) Taxed imported goods at a very high rate; the South hated the tariff because it feared it would provoke Britain to reject American cotton.

Tariff of 1816 First true protective tariff, intended strictly to protect American goods against foreign competition.

Tax Reform Act (1986) Lowered federal income tax rates to 1920s levels and eliminated many loopholes.

Teapot Dome Harding administration scandal in which Secretary of the Interior Albert B. Fall profited from secret leasing to private oil companies of government oil reserves at Teapot Dome, Wyoming, and Elk Hills, California.

tenancy Renting of farmland by workers who owned their own equipment; tenant farmers kept a larger percentage of the crop than did sharecroppers.

Tennessee Valley Authority Created in 1933 to control flooding in the Tennessee River Valley, provide work for the region's unemployed, and produce inexpensive electric power for the region.

Tenure of Office Act (1867) Required the president to obtain Senate approval to remove any official whose appointment had also required Senate approval; President Andrew Johnson's violation of the law by firing Secretary of War Edwin Stanton led to the Radical Republicans retaliating with Johnson's impeachment.

Tertium Quid Literally, the "third something": states' rights and strict constructionist Republicans under John Randolph who broke with President Thomas Jefferson but never managed to form a third political party.

Tet Offensive Surprise attack by the Viet Cong and North Vietnamese during the Vietnamese New Year of 1968; turned American public opinion strongly against the war in Vietnam.

Tippecanoe, Battle of On November 7, 1811, Indiana governor William Henry Harrison (later president) defeated the Shawnee Indians at the Tippecanoe River in northern Indiana; victory fomented war fever against the British, who were believed to be aiding the Indians.

Title IX Part of the Educational Amendments Act of 1972 that required colleges to engage in "affirmative action" for women.

Tonkin Gulf Resolution (1964) Passed by Congress in reaction to supposedly unprovoked attacks on American warships off the coast of North Vietnam; it gave the president unlimited authority to defend U.S. forces and members of SEATO.

Tories Term used by Patriots to refer to Loyalists, or colonists who supported the Crown after the Declaration of Independence.

Townshend Acts (1767) Parliamentary measures (named for the chancellor of the exchequer) that punished the New York Assembly for failing to house British soldiers, taxed tea and other commodities, and established a Board of Customs Commissioners and colonial vice-admiralty courts.

Trail of Tears Cherokees' own term for their forced march, 1838–39, from the southern Appalachians to Indian lands (later Oklahoma); of 15,000 forced to march, 4,000 died on the way.

Transcendentalism Philosophy of a small group of mid-nineteenth-century New England writers and thinkers, including Ralph Waldo Emerson, Henry David Thoreau, and Margaret Fuller; they stressed "plain living and high thinking."

Transcontinental railroad First line across the continent from Omaha, Nebraska, to Sacramento, California, established in 1869 with the linkage of the Union Pacific and Central Pacific railroads at Promontory, Utah.

Truman Doctrine President Harry S. Truman's program of post–World War II aid to European countries—particularly Greece and Turkey—in danger of being undermined by communism.

trust Companies combined to control competition.

Twenty-first Amendment (1933) Repealed prohibition on the manufacture, sale, and transportation of alcoholic beverages, effectively nullifying the Eighteenth Amendment.

Twenty-second Amendment (1951) Limited presidents to two full terms of office or two terms plus two years of an assumed term; passed in reaction to President Franklin D. Roosevelt's unprecedented four elected terms.

Twenty-sixth Amendment (1971) Lowered the voting age from twenty-one to eighteen.

U.S.S. *Maine* Battleship that exploded in Havana Harbor on February 15, 1898, resulting in 266 deaths; the American public, assuming that the Spanish had mined the ship, clamored for war, and the Spanish-American War was declared two months later.

Uncle Tom's Cabin Harriet Beecher Stowe's 1852 antislavery novel popularized the abolitionist position.

Underground Railroad Operating in the decades before the Civil War, the "railroad" was a clandestine system of routes and safehouses through which slaves were led to freedom in the North.

Understanding clause Added to state constitutions in the late nineteenth century, it allowed illiterate whites to circumvent literacy tests for voting by demonstrating that they understood a passage in the Constitution; black citizens would be judged by white registrars to have failed.

Underwood-Simmons Tariff (1913) In addition to lowering and even eliminating some tariffs, it included provisions for the first federal income tax, made legal the same year by the ratification of the Sixteenth Amendment.

Unitarianism Late eighteenth-century liberal offshoot of the New England Congregationalist church; rejecting the Trinity, Unitarianism professed the oneness of God and the goodness of rational man.

United Farm Workers Union for the predominantly Mexican-American migrant laborers of the Southwest, organized by César Chavez in 1962.

United Nations Organization of nations to maintain world peace, established in 1945 and headquartered in New York.

Universal Negro Improvement Association Black nationalist movement active in the United States from 1916 to 1923, when its leader Marcus Garvey went to prison for mail fraud.

Universalism Similar to Unitarianism, but putting more stress on the importance of social action, Universalism also originated in Massachusetts in the late eighteenth century.

V-E Day May 8, 1945, the day World War II officially ended in Europe.

vertical integration Company's avoidance of middlemen by producing its own supplies and providing for distribution of its product.

veto President's constitutional power to reject legislation passed by Congress; a two-thirds vote in both houses of Congress can override a veto.

Vicksburg, Battle of The fall of Vicksburg, Mississippi, to General Ulysses S. Grant's army on July 4, 1863, after two months of siege was a turning point in the war because it gave the Union control of the Mississippi River.

Virginia and New Jersey Plans Differing opinions of delegations to the Constitutional Convention: New Jersey wanted one legislative body with equal representation for each state; Virginia's plan called for a strong central government and a two-house legislature apportioned by population.

Volstead Act (1919) Enforced the prohibition amendment, beginning January 1920.

Voting Rights Act of 1965 Passed in the wake of Martin Luther King's Selma to Montgomery March, it authorized federal protection of the right to vote and permitted federal enforcement of minority voting rights in individual counties, mostly in the South.

Wabash Railroad v. Illinois **(1886)** Reversing the U.S. Supreme Court's ruling in *Munn* v. *Illinois*, the decision disallowed state regulation of interstate commerce.

Wade-Davis Bill (1864) Radical Republicans' plan for reconstruction that required loyalty oaths, abolition of slavery, repudiation of war debts, and denial of political rights to high-ranking Confederate officials; President Lincoln refused to sign the bill.

Wagner Act (National Labor Relations Act of 1935) Established the National Labor Relations Board and facilitated unionization by regulating employment and bargaining practices.

War Industries Board Run by financier Bernard Baruch, the board planned production and allocation of war materiel, supervised purchasing, and fixed prices, 1917–19.

War of 1812 Fought with Britain, 1812–14, over lingering conflicts that included impressment of American sailors, interference with shipping, and collusion with Northwest Territory Indians; settled by the Treaty of Ghent in 1814.

War on Poverty Announced by President Lyndon B. Johnson in his 1964 State of the Union address; under the Economic Opportunity Bill signed later that year, Head Start, VISTA, and the Jobs Corps were created, and grants and loans were extended to students, farmers, and businesses in efforts to eliminate poverty.

War Production Board Created in 1942 to coordinate industrial efforts in World War II; similar to the War Industries Board in World War I.

War Relocation Camps Internment camps where Japanese Americans were held against their will from 1942 to 1945.

Warren Court The U.S. Supreme Court under Chief Justice Earl Warren, 1953–69, decided such landmark cases as *Brown v. Board of Education* (school desegregation), *Baker v. Carr* (legislative redistricting), and *Gideon v. Wainwright* and *Miranda v. Arizona* (rights of criminal defendants).

Washington Armaments Conference Leaders of nine world powers met in 1921–22 to discuss the naval race; resulting treaties limited to a specific ratio the carrier and battleship tonnage of each nation (Five-Power Naval Treaty), formally ratified the Open Door to China (Nine–Power Treaty), and agreed to respect each other's Pacific territories (Four-Power Treaty).

Watergate Washington office and apartment complex that lent its name to the 1972–74 scandal of the Nixon administration; when his knowledge of the break-in at the Watergate and subsequent coverup was revealed, Nixon resigned the presidency under threat of impeachment.

Webster-Ashburton Treaty Settlement in 1842 of U.S.-Canadian border disputes in Maine, New York, Vermont, and in the Wisconsin Territory (now northern Minnesota).

Webster-Hayne debate U.S. Senate debate of January 1830 between Daniel Webster of Massachusetts and Robert Hayne of South Carolina over nullification and states' rights.

Whig Party Founded in 1834 to unite factions opposed to President Andrew Jackson, the party favored federal responsibility for internal improvements; the party ceased to exist by the late 1850s, when party members divided over the slavery issue.

Whigs Another name for revolutionary Patriots.

Whiskey Rebellion Violent protest by western Pennsylvania farmers against the federal excise tax on corn whiskey, 1794.

Whitewater Development Corporation Failed Arkansas real estate investment that kept President Bill Clinton and his wife Hillary under investigation by Independent Counsel Kenneth Starr throughout the Clinton presidency; no charges were ever brought against either of the Clintons.

Wilderness, Battle of the Second battle fought in the thickly wooded Wilderness area near Chancellorsville, Virginia; in the battle of May 5–6, 1864, no clear victor emerged, but the battle served to deplete the Army of Northern Virginia.

Wilderness Road Originally an Indian path through the Cumberland Gap, it was used by over 300,000 settlers who migrated westward to Kentucky in the last quarter of the eighteenth century.

Wilmot Proviso Proposal to prohibit slavery in any land acquired in the Mexican War, but southern senators, led by John C. Calhoun of South Carolina, defeated the measure in 1846 and 1847.

Works Progress Administration (WPA) Part of the Second New Deal, it provided jobs for millions of the unemployed on construction and arts projects.

Wounded Knee, Battle of Last incident of the Indians Wars took place in 1890 in the Dakota Territory, where the U.S. Cavalry killed over 200 Sioux men, women, and children who were in the process of surrender.

writs of assistance One of the colonies' main complaints against Britain, the writs allowed unlimited search warrants without cause to look for evidence of smuggling.

XYZ Affair French foreign minister Tallyrand's three anonymous agents demanded payments to stop French plundering of American ships in 1797; refusal to pay the bribe led to two years of sea war with France (1798–1800).

Yalta Conference Meeting of Franklin D. Roosevelt, Winston Churchill, and Joseph Stalin at a Crimean resort to discuss the postwar world on February 4–11, 1945; Soviet leader Joseph Stalin claimed large areas in eastern Europe for Soviet domination.

Yazoo Fraud Illegal sale of the Yazoo lands (much of present-day Alabama and Mississippi) by Georgia legislators; by 1802 it had become a tangle of conflicting claims that the U.S. Supreme Court settled in *Fletcher* v. *Peck* (1810).

yellow journalism Sensationalism in newspaper publishing that reached a peak in the circulation war between Joseph Pulitzer's *New York World* and William Randolph Hearst's *New York Journal* in the 1890s; the papers' accounts of events in Havana Harbor in 1898 led directly to the Spanish-American War.

yeoman farmers Small landowners (the majority of white families in the South) who farmed their own land and usually did not own slaves.

Yorktown, Battle of Last battle of the Revolutionary War; General Lord Charles Cornwallis along with over 7,000 British troops surrendered at Yorktown, Virginia, on October 17, 1781.

Zimmermann telegram From the German foreign secretary to the German minister in Mexico, February 1917, instructing him to offer to recover Texas, New Mexico, and Arizona for Mexico if it would fight the United States to divert attention from Germany in case of war.

APPENDIX

THE DECLARATION
OF INDEPENDENCE

WHEN IN THE COURSE OF HUMAN EVENTS, it becomes necessary for one people to dissolve the political bands which have connected them with another, and to assume the Powers of the earth, the separate and equal station to which the Laws of Nature and of Nature's God entitle them, a decent respect to the opinions of mankind requires that they should declare the causes which impel them to the separation.

We hold these truths to be self-evident, that all men are created equal, that they are endowed by their Creator with certain unalienable rights, that among these are Life, Liberty, and the pursuit of Happiness. That to secure these rights, Governments are instituted among Men, deriving their just powers from the consent of the governed. That whenever any Form of Government becomes destructive of these ends, it is the Right of the People to alter or to abolish it, and to institute new Government, laying its foundation on such principles and organizing its powers in such form, as to them shall seem most likely to effect their Safety and Happiness. Prudence, indeed, will dictate that Governments long established should not be changed for light and transient causes; and accordingly all experience hath shown, that mankind are more disposed to suffer, while evils are sufferable, than to right themselves by abolishing the forms to which they are accustomed. But when a long train of abuses and usurpations, pursuing invariably the same Object evinces a design to reduce them under absolute Despotism, it is their right, it is their duty, to throw off such Government, and to provide new Guards for their future security.—Such has been the patient sufferance of these Colonies; and such is now the necessity which constrains them to alter their former Systems of Government. The history of the present King of Great Britain is a history of repeated injuries and usurpations, all having in direct object the establishment of an absolute Tyranny over these States. To prove this, let Facts be submitted to a candid world.

He has refused his Assent to Laws, the most wholesome and necessary for the public good.

He has forbidden his Governors to pass Laws of immediate and pressing importance, unless suspended in their operation till his Assent should be obtained; and when so suspended, he has utterly neglected to attend to them.

He has refused to pass other Laws for the accommodation of large districts of people, unless those people would relinquish the right of Representation in the Legislature, a right inestimable to them and formidable to tyrants only.

He has called together legislative bodies at places unusual, uncomfortable, and distant from the depository of their public Records, for the sole purpose of fatiguing them into compliance with his measures.

He has dissolved Representative Houses repeatedly, for opposing with manly firmness his invasions on the rights of the people.

He has refused for a long time, after such dissolutions, to cause others to be elected; whereby the Legislative powers, incapable of Annihilation, have returned to the People at large for their exercise; the State remaining in the mean time exposed to all dangers of invasion from without, and convulsions within.

He has endeavoured to prevent the population of these States; for that purpose obstructing the Laws of Naturalization of Foreigners; refusing to pass others to encourage their migrations hither, and raising the conditions of new Appropriations of Lands.

He has obstructed the Administration of Justice, by refusing his Assent to Laws for establishing Judiciary powers.

He has made Judges dependent on his Will alone, for the tenure of their offices, and the amount and payment of their salaries.

He has erected a multitude of New Offices, and sent hither swarms of Officers to harass our People, and eat out their substance.

He has kept among us, in times of peace, Standing Armies without the Consent of our legislatures.

He has affected to render the Military independent of and superior to the Civil Power.

He has combined with others to subject us to a jurisdiction foreign to our constitution, and unacknowledged by our laws; giving his Assent to their Acts of pretended Legislation:

For quartering large bodies of armed troops among us:

For protecting them, by a mock Trial, from Punishment for any Murders which they should commit on the Inhabitants of these States:

For cutting off our Trade with all parts of the world:

For imposing taxes on us without our Consent:

For depriving us of many cases, of the benefits of Trial by jury:

For transporting us beyond Seas to be tried for pretended offences:

For abolishing the free System of English Laws in a neighbouring Province, establishing therein an Arbitrary government, and enlarging its

Boundaries so as to render it at once an example and fit instrument for introducing the same absolute rule into these Colonies:

For taking away our Charters, abolishing our most valuable Laws, and altering fundamentally the Forms of our Governments:

For suspending our own Legislatures, and declaring themselves in vested with Power to legislate for us in all cases whatsoever.

He has abdicated Government here, by declaring us out of his Protection and waging War against us.

He has plundered our seas, ravaged our Coasts, burnt our towns, and destroyed the lives of our people.

He is at this time transporting large armies of foreign mercenaries to compleat the works of death, desolation, and tyranny, already begun with circumstances of Cruelty & perfidy scarcely paralleled in the most barbarous ages, and totally unworthy the Head of a civilized nation.

He has constrained our fellow Citizens taken Captive on the high Seas to bear Arms against their Country, to become the executioners of their friends and Brethren, or to fall themselves by their Hands.

He has excited domestic insurrections amongst us, and has endeavoured to bring on the inhabitants of our frontiers, the merciless Indian Savages, whose known rule of warfare, is an undistinguished destruction of all ages, sexes, and conditions.

In every stage of these Oppressions We have Petitioned for Redress in the most humble terms: Our repeated Petitions have been answered only by repeated injury. A Prince, whose character is thus marked by every act which may define a Tyrant, is unfit to be the ruler of a free people.

Nor have We been wanting in attention to our British brethren. We have warned them from time to time of attempts by their legislature to extend an unwarrantable jurisdiction over us. We have reminded them of the circumstances of our emigration and settlement here. We have appealed to their native justice and magnanimity, and we have conjured them by the ties of our common kindred to disavow these usurpations, which, would inevitably interrupt our connections and correspondence. They too must have been deaf to the voice of justice and of consanguinity. We must, therefore, acquiesce in the necessity, which denounces our Separation, and hold them, as we hold the rest of mankind, Enemies in War, in Peace Friends.

WE, THEREFORE, the Representatives of the UNITED STATES OF AMERICA, in General Congress, Assembled, appealing to the Supreme Judge of the world for the rectitude of our intentions, do, in the Name, and by Authority of the good People of these Colonies, solemnly publish and declare, That these United Colonies are, and of Right ought to be FREE AND INDEPENDENT STATES; that they are Absolved from all Allegiance to the

British Crown, and that all political connection between them and the State of Great Britain, is and ought to be totally dissolved; and that as Free and Independent States, they have full Power to levy War, conclude Peace, contract Alliances, establish Commerce, and to do all other Acts and Things which Independent States may of right do. And for the support of this Declaration, with a firm reliance on the Protection of Divine Providence, we mutually pledge to each other our Lives, our Fortunes, and our sacred Honor.

The foregoing Declaration was, by order of Congress, engrossed, and signed by the following members:

John Hancock

NEW HAMPSHIRE
Josiah Bartlett
William Whipple
Matthew Thornton

MASSACHUSETTS BAY
Samuel Adams
John Adams
Robert Treat Paine
Elbridge Gerry

RHODE ISLAND
Stephen Hopkins
William Ellery

CONNECTICUT
Roger Sherman
Samuel Huntington
William Williams
Oliver Wolcott

NEW YORK
William Floyd
Philip Livingston
Francis Lewis
Lewis Morris

NEW JERSEY
Richard Stockton
John Witherspoon
Francis Hopkinson
John Hart
Abraham Clark

PENNSYLVANIA
Robert Morris
Benjamin Rush
Benjamin Franklin
John Morton
George Clymer
James Smith
George Taylor
James Wilson
George Ross

DELAWARE
Caesar Rodney
George Read
Thomas M'Kean

MARYLAND
Samuel Chase
William Paca
Thomas Stone
Charles Carroll, of Carrollton

VIRGINIA
George Wythe
Richard Henry Lee
Thomas Jefferson
Benjamin Harrison
Thomas Nelson, Jr.
Francis Lightfoot Lee
Carter Braxton

NORTH CAROLINA
William Hooper
Joseph Hewes
John Penn

SOUTH CAROLINA
Edward Rutledge
Thomas Heyward, Jr.
Thomas Lynch, Jr.
Arthur Middleton

GEORGIA
Button Gwinnett
Lyman Hall
George Walton

Resolved, that copies of the declaration be sent to the several assemblies, conventions, and committees, or councils of safety, and to the several commanding officers of the continental troops; that it be proclaimed in each of the united states, at the head of the army.

ARTICLES OF
CONFEDERATION

To all to whom these Presents shall come, we the undersigned Delegates of the States affixed to our Names send greeting.

Whereas the Delegates of the United States of America in Congress assembled did on the fifteenth day of November in the Year of our Lord One Thousand Seven Hundred and Seventy-seven, and in the Second Year of the Independence of America agree to certain articles of Confederation and perpetual Union between the States of Newhampshire, Massachusetts-bay, Rhodeisland and Providence Plantations, Connecticut, New York, New Jersey, Pennsylvania, Delaware, Maryland, Virginia, North-Carolina, South-Carolina and Georgia in the Words following, viz.

Articles of Confederation and perpetual Union between the States of Newhampshire, Massachusetts-bay, Rhodeisland and Providence Plantations, Connecticut, New-York, New-Jersey, Pennsylvania, Delaware, Maryland, Virginia, North-Carolina, South-Carolina and Georgia.

Article I. The stile of this confederacy shall be "The United States of America."

Article II. Each State retains its sovereignty, freedom and independence, and every power, jurisdiction and right, which is not by this confederation expressly delegated to the United States, in Congress assembled.

Article III. The said States hereby severally enter into a firm league of friendship with each other, for their common defence, the security of their liberties, and their mutual and general welfare, binding themselves to assist each other, against all force offered to, or attacks made upon them, or any of them, on account of religion, sovereignty, trade or any other pretence whatever.

ARTICLE IV. The better to secure and perpetuate mutual friendship and intercourse among the people of the different States in this Union, the free inhabitants of each of these States, paupers, vagabonds and fugitives from justice excepted, shall be entitled to all privileges and immunities of free citizens in the several States; and the people of each State shall have free ingress and regress to and from any other State, and shall enjoy therein all the privileges of trade and commerce, subject to the same duties, impositions and restrictions as the inhabitants thereof respectively, provided that such restrictions shall not extend so far as to prevent the removal of property imported into any State, to any other State of which the owner is an inhabitant; provided also that no imposition, duties or restriction shall be laid by any State, on the property of the United States, or either of them.

If any person guilty of, or charged with treason, felony, or other high misdemeanor in any State, shall flee from justice, and be found in any of the United States, he shall upon demand of the Governor or Executive power, of the State from which he fled, be delivered up and removed to the State having jurisdiction of his offence.

Full faith and credit shall be given in each of these States to the records, acts and judicial proceedings of the courts and magistrates of every other State.

ARTICLE V. For the more convenient management of the general interests of the United States, delegates shall be annually appointed in such manner as the legislature of each State shall direct, to meet in Congress on the first Monday in November, in every year, with a power reserved to each State, to recall its delegates, or any of them, at any time within the year, and to send others in their stead, for the remainder of the year.

No State shall be represented in Congress by less than two, nor by more than seven members; and no person shall be capable of being a delegate for more than three years in any term of six years; nor shall any person, being a delegate, be capable of holding any office under the United States, for which he, or another for his benefit receives any salary, fees or emolument of any kind.

Each State shall maintain its own delegates in a meeting of the States, and while they act as members of the committee of the States.

In determining questions in the United States, in Congress assembled, each State shall have one vote.

Freedom of speech and debate in Congress shall not be impeached or questioned in any court, or place out of Congress, and the members of Congress shall be protected in their persons from arrests and imprisonments, during the time of their going to and from, and attendance on Congress, except for treason, felony, or breach of the peace.

ARTICLE VI. No State without the consent of the United States in Congress assembled, shall send any embassy to, or receive any embassy from, or enter into any conference, agreement, alliance or treaty with any king, prince or state; nor shall any person holding any office of profit or trust under the United States, or any of them, accept of any present, emolument, office or title of any kind whatever from any king, prince or foreign state; nor shall the United States in Congress assembled, or any of them, grant any title of nobility.

No two or more States shall enter into any treaty, confederation or alliance whatever between them, without the consent of the United States in Congress assembled, specifying accurately the purposes for which the same is to be entered into, and how long it shall continue.

No State shall lay any imposts or duties, which may interfere with any stipulations in treaties, entered into by the United States in Congress assembled, with any king, prince or state, in pursuance of any treaties already proposed by Congress, to the courts of France and Spain.

No vessels of war shall be kept up in time of peace by any State, except such number only, as shall be deemed necessary by the United States in Congress assembled, for the defence of such State, or its trade; nor shall any body of forces be kept up by any State, in time of peace, except such number only, as in the judgment of the United States, in Congress assembled, shall be deemed requisite to garrison the forts necessary for the defence of such State; but every State shall always keep up a well regulated and disciplined militia, sufficiently armed and accoutred, and shall provide and constantly have ready for use, in public stores, a due number of field pieces and tents, and a proper quantity of arms, ammunition and camp equipage.

No State shall engage in any war without the consent of the United States in Congress assembled, unless such State be actually invaded by enemies, or shall have received certain advice of a resolution being formed by some nation of Indians to invade such State, and the danger is so imminent as not to admit of a delay, till the United States in Congress assembled can be consulted: nor shall any State grant commissions to any ships or vessels of war, nor letters of marque or reprisal, except it be after a declaration of war by the United States in Congress assembled, and then only against the kingdom or state and the subjects thereof, against which war has been so declared, and under such regulations as shall be established by the United States in Congress assembled, unless such State be infested by pirates, in which case vessels of war may be fitted out for that occasion, and kept so long as the danger shall continue, or until the United States in Congress assembled shall determine otherwise.

Article VII. When land-forces are raised by any State of the common defence, all officers of or under the rank of colonel, shall be appointed by the Legislature of each State respectively by whom such forces shall be raised, or in such manner as such State shall direct, and all vacancies shall be filled up by the State which first made the appointment.

Article VIII. All charges of war, and all other expenses that shall be incurred for the common defence or general welfare, and allowed by the United States in Congress assembled, shall be defrayed out of a common treasury, which shall be supplied by the several States, in proportion to the value of all land within each State, granted to or surveyed for any person, as such land and the buildings and improvements thereon shall be estimated according to such mode as the United States in Congress assembled, shall from time to time direct and appoint.

The taxes for paying that proportion shall be laid and levied by the authority and direction of the Legislatures of the several States within the time agreed upon by the United States in Congress assembled.

Article IX. The United States in Congress assembled, shall have the sole and exclusive right and power of determining on peace and war, except in the cases mentioned in the sixth article—of sending and receiving ambassadors—entering into treaties and alliances, provided that no treaty of commerce shall be made whereby the legislative power of the respective States shall be restrained from imposing such imposts and duties on foreigners, as their own people are subjected to, or from prohibiting the exportation or importation of and species of goods or commodities whatsoever—of establishing rules for deciding in all cases, what captures on land or water shall be legal, and in what manner prizes taken by land or naval forces in the service of the United States shall be divided or appropriated—of granting letters of marque and reprisal in times of peace—appointing courts for the trial of piracies and felonies committed on the high seas and establishing courts for receiving and determining finally appeals in all cases of captures, provided that no member of Congress shall be appointed a judge of any of the said courts.

The United States in Congress assembled shall also be the last resort on appeal in all disputes and differences now subsisting or that hereafter may arise between two or more States concerning boundary, jurisdiction or any other cause whatever; which authority shall always be exercised in the manner following. Whenever the legislative or executive authority or lawful agent of any State in controversy with another shall present a petition to Congress, stating the matter in question and praying for a hearing, notice thereof shall be given by order of Congress to the legislative or executive authority of the other State in controversy, and a day assigned for the appearance of the parties by their lawful agents, who shall then be directed to appoint by joint consent, commissioners or judges to constitute a court for hearing and determining the matter in question: but if they cannot agree, Congress shall name three persons out of each of the United States, and from the list of such persons each party shall alternately strike out one, the petitioners beginning, until the number shall be reduced to thirteen; and from that number not less than seven, nor more than nine names as Congress shall direct, shall in the presence of Congress be drawn out by lot, and the persons whose names shall be so drawn or any five of them, shall be commissioners or judges, to hear and finally determine the controversy, so always as a major part of the judges who shall hear the cause shall agree in the determination: and if either party shall neglect to attend at the day appointed, without reasons, which Congress shall judge sufficient, or being present shall refuse to strike, the Congress shall proceed to nominate three persons out of each State, and the Secretary of Congress shall strike in behalf of such party absent or refusing; and the judgment and sentence of the court to be appointed, in the manner before prescribed, shall be final and conclusive; and if any of the parties shall refuse to submit to the authority of such court, or to appear or defend their claim or cause, the court shall nevertheless proceed to pronounce sentence, or judgment, which shall in like manner be final and decisive, the judgment or sentence and other proceedings being in either case transmitted to Congress, and lodged among the acts of Congress for the security of the parties concerned: provided that every commissioner, before he sits in judgment, shall take an oath to be administered by one of the judges of the supreme or superior court of the State where the case shall be tried, "well and truly to hear and determine the matter in question, according to the best of his judgment, without favour, affection or hope of reward:" provided also that no State shall be deprived of territory for the benefit of the United States.

All controversies concerning the private right of soil claimed under different grants of two or more States, whose jurisdiction as they may respect such lands, and the states which passed such grants are adjusted, the said grants or either of them being at the same time claimed to have originated antecedent to such settlement of jurisdiction, shall on the petition of either party to the Congress of the United States, be finally determined as near as may be in the same manner as is before prescribed for deciding disputes respecting territorial jurisdiction between different States.

The United States in Congress assembled shall also have the sole and exclusive right and power of regulating the alloy and value of coin struck by their own authority, or by that of the respective States—fixing the standard of weights and measures throughout the United States—regulating the trade and managing all affairs with the Indians, not members of any of the States, provided that the legislative right of any State within its own limits be not infringed or violated—establishing and regulating post-offices from one State to another, throughout all of the United States, and exacting such postage on the papers passing thro' the same as may be requisite to defray the expenses of the said office—appointing all officers of the land forces, in the service of the United States, excepting regimental officers—appointing all the officers of the naval forces, and commissioning all officers whatever in the service of the United States—making rules for the government and regulation of the said land and naval forces, and directing their operations.

The United States in Congress assembled shall have authority to appoint a committee, to sit in the recess of Congress, to be denominated "a Committee of the States," and to consist of one delegate from each State; and to appoint such other committees and civil officers as may be necessary for managing the general affairs of the United States under their direction—to appoint one of their number to preside, provided that no person be allowed to serve in the office of president more than one year in any term of three years; to ascertain the necessary sums of money to be raised for the service of the United States, and to appropriate and apply the same for defraying the public expenses—to borrow money, or emit bills on the credit of the United States, transmitting every half year to the respective States an account of the sums of money so borrowed or emitted,—to build and equip a navy—to agree upon the number of land forces, and to make requisitions from each State for its quota, in proportion to the number of white inhabitants in such State; which requisition shall be binding, and thereupon the Legislature of each State shall appoint the regimental officers, raise the men and cloath, arm and equip them in a soldier like manner, at the expense of the United States; and the officers and men so cloathed, armed and equipped shall march to the place appointed, and within the time agreed on by the United States in Congress assembled: but if the United States in Congress assembled shall, on consideration of circumstances judge proper that any State should not raise men, or should raise a smaller number of men than the quota thereof, such extra number shall be raised, officered, cloathed, armed and equipped in the same manner as the quota of such State, unless the legislature of such State shall judge that such extra number cannot be safely spared out of the same, in which case they shall raise officer, cloath, arm and equip as many of such extra number as they judge can be safely spared. And the officers and men so cloathed, armed and equipped, shall march to the place appointed, and within the time agreed on by the United States in Congress assembled.

The United States in Congress assembled shall never engage in a war, nor grant letters of marque and reprisal in time of peace, nor enter into any treaties or alliances, nor coin money, nor regulate the value thereof, nor ascertain the sums and expenses necessary for the defence and welfare of the United States, or any of them, nor emit bills, nor borrow money on the credit of the United States, nor appropriate money, nor agree upon the number of vessels to be built or purchased, or the number of land or sea forces to be raised, nor appoint a commander in chief of the army or navy, unless nine States assent to the same: nor shall a question on any other point, except for adjourning from day to day be determined, unless by the votes of a majority of the United States in Congress assembled.

The Congress of the United States shall have power to adjourn to any time within the year, and to any place within the United States, so that no period of adjournment be for a longer duration than the space of six months, and shall publish the journal of their proceedings monthly, except such parts thereof relating to treaties, alliances or military operations, as in their judgment require secresy; and the yeas and nays of the delegates of each State on any question shall be entered on the Journal, when it is desired by any delegate; and the delegates of a State, or any of them, at his or their request shall be furnished with a transcript of the said journal, except such parts as are above excepted, to lay before the Legislatures of the several States.

ARTICLE X. The committee of the States, or any nine of them, shall be authorized to execute, in the recess of Congress, such of the powers of Congress as the United States in Congress assembled, by the consent of nine States, shall from time to time think expedient to vest them with; provided that no power be delegated to the said committee, for the exercise of which, by the articles of confederation, the voice of nine States in the Congress of the United States assembled is requisite.

ARTICLE XI. Canada acceding to this confederation, and joining in the measures of the United States, shall be admitted into, and entitled to all the advantages of this Union: but no other colony shall be admitted into the same, unless such admission be agreed to by nine States.

ARTICLE XII. All bills of credit emitted, monies borrowed and debts contracted by, or under the authority of Congress, before the assembling of the United States, in pursuance of the present confederation, shall be deemed and considered as a charge against the United States, for payment and satisfaction whereof the said United States, and the public faith are hereby solemnly pledged.

ARTICLE XIII. Every State shall abide by the determinations of the United States in Congress assembled, on all questions which by this confederation are submitted to them. And the articles of this confederation shall be inviolably observed by every State, and the Union shall be perpetual; nor shall any alteration at any time hereafter be made in any of them; unless such alteration be agreed to in a Congress of the United States, and be afterwards confirmed by the Legislatures of every State.

And whereas it has pleased the Great Governor of the world to incline the hearts of the Legislatures we respectively represent in Congress, to approve of, and to authorize us to ratify the said articles of confederation and perpetual union. Know ye that we the undersigned delegates, by virtue of the power and authority to us given for that purpose, do by these presents, in the name and in behalf of our respective constituents, fully and entirely ratify and confirm each and every of the said articles of confederation and perpetual union, and all and singular the matters and things therein contained: and we do further solemnly plight and engage the faith of our respective constituents, that they shall abide by the determinations of the United States in Congress assembled, on all questions, which by the said confederation are submitted to them. And that the articles thereof shall be inviolably observed by the States we respectively represent, and that the Union shall be perpetual.

In witness thereof we have hereunto set our hands in Congress. Done at Philadelphia in the State of Pennsylvania the ninth day of July in the year of our Lord one thousand seven hundred and seventy-eight, and in the third year of the independence of America.

THE CONSTITUTION OF
THE UNITED STATES

WE THE PEOPLE OF THE UNITED STATES, in order to form a more perfect Union, establish Justice, insure domestic Tranquility, provide for the common defence, promote the general Welfare, and secure the Blessings of Liberty to ourselves and our Posterity, do ordain and establish this Constitution for the United States of America.

ARTICLE. I.

Section. 1. All legislative Powers herein granted shall be vested in a Congress of the United States, which shall consist of a Senate and House of Representatives.

Section. 2. The House of Representatives shall be composed of Members chosen every second Year by the People of the several States, and the Electors in each State shall have the Qualifications requisite for Electors of the most numerous Branch of the State Legislature.

No Person shall be a Representative who shall not have attained to the Age of twenty five Years, and been seven Years a Citizen of the United States, and who shall not, when elected, be an Inhabitant of that State in which he shall be chosen.

Representatives and direct Taxes shall be apportioned among the several States which may be included within this Union, according to their respective Numbers, which shall be determined by adding to the whole Number of free Persons, including those bound to Service for a Term of Years, and excluding Indians not taxed, three fifths of all other Persons. The actual Enumeration shall be made within three Years after the first Meeting of the Congress of the United States, and within every subsequent Term of ten Years, in

The Constitution of the United States · A59

such Manner as they shall by Law direct. The Number of Representatives shall not exceed one for every thirty Thousand, but each State shall have at Least one Representative; and until such enumeration shall be made, the State of New Hampshire shall be entitled to chuse three, Massachusetts eight, Rhode-Island and Providence Plantations one, Connecticut five, New-York six, New Jersey four, Pennsylvania eight, Delaware one, Maryland six, Virginia ten, North Carolina five, South Carolina five, and Georgia three.

When vacancies happen in the Representation from any state, the Executive Authority thereof shall issue Writs of Election to fill such Vacancies.

The House of Representatives shall chuse their Speaker and other Officers; and shall have the sole Power of Impeachment.

Section. 3. The Senate of the United States shall be composed of two Senators from each State, chosen by the legislature thereof, for six Years; and each Senator shall have one Vote.

Immediately after they shall be assembled in Consequence of the first Election, they shall be divided as equally as may be into three Classes. The Seats of the Senators of the first Class shall be vacated at the Expiration of the second Year, of the second Class at the Expiration of the fourth Year, and of the third Class at the Expiration of the sixth Year, so that one third maybe chosen every second Year; and if Vacancies happen by Resignation, or otherwise, during the Recess of the Legislature of any State, the Executive thereof may make temporary Appointments until the next Meeting of the Legislature, which shall then fill such Vacancies.

No Person shall be a Senator who shall not have attained to the Age of thirty Years, and been nine Years a Citizen of the United States, and who shall not, when elected, be an Inhabitant of that State for which he shall be chosen.

The Vice President of the United States shall be President of the Senate, but shall have no Vote, unless they be equally divided.

The Senate shall chuse their other Officers, and also a President pro tempore, in the Absence of the Vice President, or when he shall exercise the Office of President of the United States.

The Senate shall have the sole Power to try all Impeachments. When sitting for that Purpose, they shall be on Oath or Affirmation. When the President of the United States is tried, the Chief Justice shall preside: And no Person shall be convicted without the Concurrence of two thirds of the Members present.

Judgment in Cases of Impeachment shall not extend further than to removal from Office, and disqualification to hold and enjoy any Office of honor, Trust or Profit under the United States: but the Party convicted shall nevertheless be liable and subject to Indictment, Trial, Judgment and Punishment, according to Law.

Section. 4. The Times, Places and Manner of holding Elections for Senators and Representatives, shall be prescribed in each State by the Legislature thereof; but the Congress may at any time by Law make or alter such Regulations, except as to the Places of chusing Senators.

The Congress shall assemble at least once in every Year, and such Meeting shall be on the first Monday in December, unless they shall by Law appoint a different Day.

Section. 5. Each House shall be the Judge of the Elections, Returns and Qualifications of its own Members, and a Majority of each shall constitute a Quorum to do Business; but a smaller Number may adjourn from day to day, and may be authorized to compel the Attendance of absent Members, in such Manner, and under such Penalties as each House may provide.

Each House may determine the Rules of its Proceedings, punish its Members for disorderly Behaviour, and, with the Concurrence of two thirds, expel a Member.

Each House shall keep a Journal of its Proceedings, and from time to time publish the same, excepting such Parts as may in their Judgment require Secrecy; and the Yeas and Nays of the Members of either House on any question shall, at the Desire of one fifth of those Present, be entered on the Journal.

Neither House, during the Session of Congress, shall, without the Consent of the other, adjourn for more than three days, not to any other Place than that in which the two Houses shall be sitting.

Section. 6. The Senators and Representatives shall receive a Compensation for their Services, to be ascertained by Law, and paid out of the Treasury of the United States. They shall in all Cases, except Treason, Felony and Breach of the Peace, be privileged from Arrest during their Attendance at the Session of their respective Houses, and in going to and returning from the same; and for any Speech or Debate in either House, they shall not be questioned in any other Place.

No Senator or Representative shall, during the Time for which he was elected, be appointed to any civil Office under the Authority of the United States, which shall have been created, or the Emoluments whereof shall have been increased during such time; and no Person holding any Office under the United States, shall be a Member of either House during his Continuance in Office.

Section. 7. All Bills for raising Revenue shall originate in the House of Representatives; but the Senate may propose or concur with Amendments as on other Bills.

Every Bill which shall have passed the House of Representatives and the Senate shall, before it become a Law, be presented to the President of the United States; If he approve he shall sign it, but if not he shall return it, with his Objections to that House in which it shall have originated, who shall enter the Objections at large on their Journal, and proceed to reconsider it. If after such Reconsideration two thirds of that House shall agree to pass the Bill, it shall be sent, together with the Objections, to the other House, by which it shall likewise be reconsidered, and if approved by two thirds of that House, it shall become a Law. But in all such Cases the Votes of both Houses shall be determined by yeas and Nays, and the Names of the Persons voting for and against the Bill shall be entered on the Journal of each House respectively. If any Bill shall not be returned by the President within ten Days (Sundays excepted) after it shall have been presented to him, the Same shall be a Law, in like Manner as if he had signed it, unless the Congress by their Adjournment prevent its Return, in which Case it shall not be a Law.

Every Order, Resolution, or Vote to which the Concurrence of the Senate and House of Representatives may be necessary (except on a question of Adjournment) shall be presented to the President of the United States; and before the Same shall take Effect, shall be approved by him, or being disapproved by him, shall be repassed by two thirds of the Senate and House of Representatives, according to the Rules and Limitations prescribed in the Case of a Bill.

Section. 8. The Congress shall have Power To lay and collect Taxes, Duties, Imposts and Excises, to pay the Debts and provide for the common Defence and general Welfare of the United States; but all Duties, Imposts and Excises shall be uniform throughout the United States;

To borrow Money on the credit of the United States;

To regulate Commerce with foreign Nations, and among the several States, and with the Indian Tribes;

To establish an uniform Rule of Naturalization, and uniform Laws on the subject of Bankruptcies throughout the United States;

To coin Money, regulate the Value thereof, and of foreign Coin, and fix the Standard of Weights and Measures;

To provide for the Punishment of counterfeiting the Securities and current Coin of the United States;

To establish Post Offices and Post Roads;

To promote the Progress of Science and useful Arts, by securing for limited Times to Authors and Inventors the exclusive Right to their respective Writings and Discoveries;

To constitute Tribunals inferior to the supreme Court;

To define and punish Piracies and Felonies committed on the high Seas, and Offences against the Law of Nations;

To declare War, grant Letters of Marque and Reprisal, and make Rules concerning Captures on land and Water;

To raise and support Armies, but no Appropriation of Money to that Use shall be for a longer Term than two Years;

To provide and maintain a Navy;

To make Rules for the Government and Regulation of the land and naval Forces;

To provide for calling forth the Militia to execute the Laws of the Union, suppress Insurrections and repel Invasions;

To provide for organizing, arming, and disciplining, the Militia, and for governing such Part of them as may be employed in the Service of the United States, reserving to the States respectively, the Appointment of the Officers, and the Authority of training the Militia according to the discipline prescribed by Congress.

To exercise exclusive Legislation in all Cases whatsoever, over such District (not exceeding ten Miles square) as may, by Cession of Particular States, and the Acceptance of Congress, become the Seat of the Government of the United States, and to exercise like Authority over all Places purchased by the Consent of the Legislature of the State in which the Same shall be, for the Erection of Forts, Magazines, Arsenals, dock-Yards, and other needful Buildings;—And

To make all Laws which shall be necessary and proper for carrying into Execution the foregoing Powers, and all other Powers vested by this Constitution in the Government of the United States, or in any Department or Officer thereof.

Section. 9. The Migration or Importation of such Persons as any of the States now existing shall think proper to admit, shall not be prohibited by the Congress prior to the Year one thousand eight hundred and eight, but a Tax or duty may be imposed on such Importation, not exceeding ten dollars for each Person.

The Privilege of the Writ of Habeas Corpus shall not be suspended, unless when in Cases of Rebellion or Invasion the public Safety may require it.

No Bill of Attainder or ex post facto Law shall be passed.

No Capitation, or other direct, Tax shall be laid, unless in Proportion to the Census or Enumeration herein before directed to be taken.

No Tax or Duty shall be laid on Articles exported from any State.

No Preference shall be given by any Regulation of Commerce or Revenue to the Ports of one State over those of another: nor shall Vessels bound to, or from, one State, be obliged to enter, clear, or pay Duties in another.

No Money shall be drawn from the Treasury, but in Consequence of Appropriations made by Law; and a regular Statement and Account of the Receipts and Expenditures of all public Money shall be published from time to time.

No Title of Nobility shall be granted by the United States: And no Person holding any Office of Profit or trust under them, shall, without the Consent of the Congress, accept of any present, Emolument, Office, or Title, of any kind whatever, from any King, Prince, or foreign State.

Section 10. No State shall enter into any Treaty, Alliance, or Confederation; grant Letters of Marque and Reprisal; coin Money; emit Bills of Credit; make any Thing but gold and silver Coin a Tender in Payment of Debts; pass any Bill of Attainder, ex post facto Law, or Law impairing the Obligation of Contracts, or grant any Title of Nobility.

No State shall, without the Consent of the Congress, lay any Imposts or Duties on Imports or Exports, except what may be absolutely necessary for executing its inspection Laws: and the net Produce of all Duties and Imposts, laid by any State on Imports or Exports, shall be for the Use of the Treasury of the United States; and all such Laws shall be subject to the Revision and Controul of the Congress.

No State shall, without the Consent of Congress, lay any Duty of Tonnage, keep Troops, or Ships of War in time of Peace, enter into any Agreement or Compact with another State, or with a foreign Power, or engage in War, unless actually invaded, or in such imminent Danger as will not admit of delay.

ARTICLE. II.

Section. 1. The executive Power shall be vested in a President of the United States of America. He shall hold his Office during the term of four Years, and, together with the Vice President, chosen for the same Term, be elected, as follows:

Each State shall appoint, in such Manner as the Legislature thereof may direct, a Number of Electors, equal to the whole Number of Senators and Representatives to which the State may be entitled in the Congress: but no Senator or Representative, or Person holding an Office of Trust or Profit under the United States, shall be appointed an Elector.

The Electors shall meet in their respective States, and vote by Ballot for two Persons, of whom one at least shall not be an Inhabitant of the same State with themselves. And they shall make a List of all the Persons voted for, and of the Number of Votes for each; which List they shall sign and certify, and transmit sealed to the Seat of the Government of the United States, directed to the President of the Senate. The President of the Senate shall, in the Presence of the Senate and House of Representatives, open all the Certificates, and the Votes shall then be counted. The Person having the greatest Number of Votes shall be the President, if such Number be a Majority of the whole Number of Electors appointed; and if there be more than one who have such Majority, and have an equal Number of Votes, then the House of Representatives shall immediately chuse by Ballot one of them for President; and if no Person have a Majority, then from the five highest on the List the said House shall in like Manner chuse the President. But in chusing the President, the Votes shall be taken by States, the Representation from each State having one Vote; A quorum for this Purpose shall consist of a Member or Members from two thirds of the States, and a Majority of all the States shall be necessary to a Choice. In every Case, after the Choice of the President, the Person having the greatest Number of Votes of the Electors shall be the Vice President. But if there should remain two or more who have equal Votes, the Senate shall chuse from them by Ballot the Vice President.

The Congress may determine the Time of chusing the Electors, and the Day on which they shall give their Votes; which Day shall be the same throughout the United States.

No Person except a natural born Citizen, or a Citizen of the United States, at the time of the Adoption of this Constitution, shall be eligible to the Office of President; neither shall any Person be eligible to that Office who shall not have attained to the Age of thirty five Years, and been fourteen Years a Resident within the United States.

In Case of the Removal of the President from Office, or of his Death, Resignation, or Inability to discharge the Powers and Duties of the said Office, the Same shall devolve on the Vice President, and the Congress may by Law provide for the Case of Removal, Death, Resignation or Inability, both of the President and Vice President, declaring what Officer shall then act as

President, and such Officer shall act accordingly, until the Disability be removed, or a President shall be elected.

The President shall, at stated Times, receive for his Services, a Compensation, which shall neither be encreased or diminished during the Period for which he shall have been elected, and he shall not receive within that Period any other Emolument from the United States, or any of them.

Before he enters on the Execution of his Office, he shall take the following Oath or Affirmation:—"I do solemnly swear (or affirm) that I will faithfully execute the Office of President of the United States, and will to the best of my Ability, preserve, protect and defend the Constitution of the United States."

Section. 2. The President shall be Commander in Chief of the Army and Navy of the United States, and of the Militia of the several States, when called into the actual Service of the United States; he may require the Opinion, in writing, of the principal Officer in each of the executive Departments, upon any Subject relating to the Duties of their respective Offices, and he shall have Power to grant Reprieves and Pardons for Offences against the United States, except in Cases of Impeachment.

He shall have Power, by and with the Advice and Consent of the Senate, to make Treaties, provided two thirds of the Senators present concur; and he shall nominate, and by and with the Advice and Consent of the Senate, shall appoint Ambassadors, other public Ministers and Consuls, Judges of the supreme Court, and all other Officers of the United States, whose Appointments are not herein otherwise provided for, and which shall be established by Law; but the Congress may by Law vest the Appointment of such inferior Officers, as they think proper, in the President alone, in the Courts of Law, or in the Heads of Departments.

The President shall have Power to fill up all Vacancies that may happen during the Recess of the Senate, by granting Commissions which shall expire at the End of their next Session.

Section. 3. He shall from time to time give to the Congress Information of the State of the Union, and recommend to their Consideration such Measures as he shall judge necessary and expedient; he may, on extraordinary Occasions, convene both Houses, or either of them, and in Case of Disagreement between them, with Respect to the Time of Adjournment, he may adjourn them to such Time as he shall think proper; he shall receive Ambassadors and other public Ministers; he shall take Care that the Laws be faithfully executed, and shall Commission all the Officers of the United States.

Section. 4. The President, Vice President and all civil Officers of the United States, shall be removed from Office on Impeachment for, and Conviction of, Treason, Bribery, or other high Crimes and Misdemeanors.

ARTICLE. III.

Section. 1. The judicial Power of the United States, shall be vested in one supreme Court, and in such inferior Courts as the Congress may from time to time ordain and establish. The Judges, both of the supreme and inferior Courts, shall hold their Offices during good Behavior, and shall, at stated Times, receive for their Services, a Compensation, which shall not be diminished during their Continuance in Office.

Section. 2. The judicial Power shall extend to all Cases, in Law and Equity, arising under this Constitution, the Laws of the United States, and Treaties made, or which shall be made, under their Authority;—to all Cases affecting Ambassadors, other public Ministers and Consuls;—to all Cases of admiralty and maritime Jurisdiction;—the Controversies to which the United States shall be a Party;—to Controversies between two or more States;—between a State and Citizens of another State;—between Citizens of different States;—between Citizens of the same State claiming Lands under Grants of different States, and between a State, or the Citizens thereof, and foreign States, Citizens or Subjects.

In all cases affecting Ambassadors, other public Ministers and Consuls, and those in which a State shall be Party, the supreme Court shall have original Jurisdiction. In all the other Cases before mentioned, the supreme Court shall have appellate Jurisdiction, both as to Law and Fact, with such Exceptions, and under such Regulations as the Congress shall make.

The Trial of all Crimes, except in Cases of Impeachment, shall be by Jury; and such Trial shall be held in the State where the said Crimes shall have been committed; but when not committed within any State, the Trial shall be at such Place or Places as the Congress may by Law have directed.

Section. 3. Treason against the United States, shall consist only in levying War against them, or in adhering to their Enemies, giving them Aid and Comfort. No Person shall be convicted of Treason unless on the Testimony of two Witnesses to the same overt Act, or on Confession in open Court.

The Congress shall have Power to declare the Punishment of Treason, but no Attainder of Treason shall work Corruption of Blood, or Forfeiture except during the Life of the Person attainted.

ARTICLE. IV.

Section. 1. Full Faith and Credit shall be given in each State to the public Acts, Records, and judicial Proceedings of every other State. And the Congress may by general Laws prescribe the Manner in which such Acts, Records and Proceedings shall be proved, and the Effect thereof.

Section. 2. The Citizens of each State shall be entitled to all Privileges and Immunities of Citizens in the several States.

A Person charged in any State with Treason, Felony, or other Crime, who shall flee from Justice, and be found in another State, shall on Demand of the executive Authority of the State from which he fled, be delivered up, to be removed to the State having Jurisdiction of the Crime.

No Person held to Service or Labour in one State, under the Laws thereof, escaping into another, shall, in Consequence of any Law or Regulation therein, be discharged from such Service or Labour, but shall be delivered up on Claim of the Party to whom such Service or Labour may be due.

Section. 3. New States may be admitted by the Congress into this Union; but no new State shall be formed or erected within the Jurisdiction of any other State; nor any State be formed by the Junction of two or more States, or Parts of States, without the consent of the Legislatures of the States concerned as well as of the Congress.

The Congress shall have Power to dispose of and make all needful Rules and Regulations respecting the Territory or other Property belonging to the United States; and nothing in this Constitution shall be so construed as to Prejudice any Claims of the United States, or of any particular States.

Section. 4. The United States shall guarantee to every State in this Union a Republican Form of Government, and shall protect each of them against Invasion; and on Application of the Legislature, or of the Executive (when the Legislature cannot be convened) against domestic Violence.

ARTICLE. V.

The Congress, whenever two thirds of both Houses shall deem it necessary, shall propose Amendments to this Constitution, or, on the Application of the

Legislatures of two thirds of the several States, shall call a Convention for proposing Amendments, which, in either Case, shall be valid to all Intents and Purposes, as Part of this Constitution, when ratified by the Legislatures of three fourths of the several States, or by Conventions in three fourths thereof, as the one or the other Mode of Ratification may be proposed by the Congress; Provided that no Amendment which may be made prior to the Year One thousand eight hundred and eight shall in any Manner affect the first and fourth Clauses in the Ninth Section of the first Article; and that no State, without its Consent, shall be deprived of its equal Suffrage in the Senate.

ARTICLE. VI.

All Debts contracted and Engagements entered into, before the Adoption of this Constitution, shall be as valid against the United States under this Constitution, as under the Confederation.

This Constitution, and the Laws of the United States which shall be made in Pursuance thereof; and all Treaties made, or which shall be made, under the Authority of the United States, shall be the supreme Law of the Land; and the Judges in every State shall be bound thereby, any Thing in the Constitution or Laws of any State to the Contrary notwithstanding.

The Senators and Representatives before mentioned, and the Members of the several State Legislatures, and all executive and judicial Officers, both of the United States and of the several States, shall be bound by Oath or Affirmation, to support this Constitution; but no religious Test shall ever be required as a Qualification to any Office or public Trust under the United States.

ARTICLE. VII.

The Ratification of the Conventions of nine States, shall be sufficient for the Establishment of this Constitution between the States so ratifying the Same.

Done in Convention by the Unanimous Consent of the States present the Seventeenth Day of September in the Year of our Lord one thousand seven hundred and Eighty seven and of the Independence of the United States of America the Twelfth. In witness thereof We have hereunto subscribed our Names,

Go. WASHINGTON—Presdt.
and deputy from Virginia.

New Hampshire	John Langdon Nicholas Gilman		Delaware	Geo: Read Gunning Bedford jun John Dickinson Richard Bassett Jaco: Broom
Massachusetts	Nathaniel Gorham Rufus King			
Connecticut	Wm Saml Johnson Roger Sherman		Maryland	James McHenry Dan of St Thos Jenifer Danl Carroll
New York: . . .	Alexander Hamilton			
New Jersey	Wil: Livingston David A. Brearley. Wm Paterson. Jona: Dayton		Virginia	John Blair— James Madison Jr.
			North Carolina	Wm Blount Richd Dobbs Spaight. Hu Williamson
Pennsylvania	B Franklin Thomas Mifflin Robt Morris Geo. Clymer Thos FitzSimons Jared Ingersoll James Wilson Gouv Morris		South Carolina	J. Rutledge Charles Cotesworth Pinckney Charles Pinckney Pierce Butler.
			Georgia	William Few Abr Baldwin

AMENDMENTS TO THE CONSTITUTION

ARTICLES IN ADDITION TO, and Amendment of the Constitution of the United States of America, proposed by Congress, and ratified by the Legislatures of the several States, pursuant to the fifth Article of the original Constitution.

AMENDMENT I.

Congress shall make no law respecting an establishment of religion, or prohibiting the free exercise thereof; or abridging the freedom of speech, or of the press; or the right of the people peaceably to assemble, and to petition the Government for a redress of grievances.

AMENDMENT II.

A well regulated Militia, being necessary to the security of a free State, the right of the people to keep and bear Arms, shall not be infringed.

AMENDMENT III.

No Soldier shall, in time of peace be quartered in any house, without the consent of the Owner, nor in time of war, but in a manner to be prescribed by law.

AMENDMENT IV.

The right of the people to be secure in their persons, houses, papers, and effects, against unreasonable searches and seizures, shall not be violated, and no Warrants shall issue, but upon probable cause, supported by Oath or affirmation, and particularly describing the place to be searched, and the persons or things to be seized.

AMENDMENT V.

No person shall be held to answer for a capital, or otherwise infamous crime, unless on a presentment or indictment of a Grand Jury, except in cases arising in the land or naval forces, or in the Militia, when in actual service in time of War or public danger; nor shall any person be subject for the same offence to be twice put in jeopardy of life or limb; nor shall be compelled in any criminal case to be a witness against himself, nor be deprived of life, liberty, or property, without due process of law; nor shall private property be taken for public use, without just compensation.

AMENDMENT VI.

In all criminal prosecutions, the accused shall enjoy the right to a speedy and public trial, by an impartial jury of the State and district wherein the crime shall have been committed, which district shall have been previously ascertained by law, and to be informed of the nature and cause of the accusation;

to be confronted with the witnesses against him; to have compulsory process for obtaining witnesses in his favor, and to have the Assistance of Counsel for his defence.

Amendment VII.

In Suits at common law, where the value in controversy shall exceed twenty dollars, the right of trial by jury shall be preserved, and no fact tried by a jury, shall be otherwise re-examined in any Court of the United States, than according to the rules of the common law.

Amendment VIII.

Excessive bail shall not be required, nor excessive fines imposed, nor cruel and unusual punishments inflicted.

Amendment IX.

The enumeration in the Constitution, of certain rights, shall not be construed to deny or disparage others retained by the people.

Amendment X.

The powers not delegated to the United States by the Constitution, nor prohibited by it to the States, are reserved to the States respectively, or to the people. [The first ten amendments went into effect December 15, 1791.]

Amendment XI.

The Judicial power of the United States shall not be construed to extend to any suit in law or equity, commenced or prosecuted against one of the United States by Citizens of another State, or by Citizens or Subjects of any Foreign State. [January 8, 1798.]

AMENDMENT XII.

The Electors shall meet in their respective states, and vote by ballot for President and Vice-President, one of whom, at least, shall not be an inhabitant of the same state with themselves; they shall name in their ballots the person voted for as President, and in distinct ballots the person voted for as Vice-President, and they shall make distinct lists of all persons voted for as President, and of all persons voted for as Vice President, and of the number of votes for each, which lists they shall sign and certify, and transmit sealed to the seat of the government of the United States, directed to the President of the Senate;—The President of the Senate shall, in the presence of the Senate and House of Representatives, open all the certificates and the votes shall then be counted;—The person having the greatest number of votes for President, shall be the President, if such number be a majority of the whole number of Electors appointed; and if no person have such majority, then from the persons having the highest numbers not exceeding three on the list of those voted for as President, the House of Representatives shall choose immediately, by ballot, the President. But in choosing the President, the votes shall be taken by states, the representation from each state having one vote; a quorum for this purpose shall consist of a member or members from two-thirds of the states, and a majority of all the states shall be necessary to a choice. And if the House of Representatives shall not choose a President whenever the right of choice shall devolve upon them, before the fourth day of March next following, then the Vice-President shall act as President, as in the case of the death or other constitutional disability of the President.—The person having the greatest number of votes as Vice-President, shall be the Vice-President, if such number be a majority of the whole number of Electors appointed, and if no person have a majority, then from the two highest numbers on the list, the Senate shall choose the Vice-President; a quorum for the purpose shall consist of two-thirds of the whole number of Senators, and a majority of the whole number shall be necessary to a choice. But no person constitutionally ineligible to the office of President shall be eligible to that of Vice-President of the United States. [September 25, 1804.]

AMENDMENT XIII.

Section 1. Neither slavery nor involuntary servitude, except as a punishment for crime whereof the party shall have been duly convicted, shall exist within the United States, or any place subject to their jurisdiction.

Section 2. Congress shall have power to enforce this article by appropriate legislation. [December 18, 1865.]

AMENDMENT XIV.

Section 1. All persons born or naturalized in the United States, and subject to the jurisdiction thereof, are citizens of the United States and of the State wherein they reside. No State shall make or enforce any law which shall abridge the privileges or immunities of citizens of the United States; nor shall any State deprive any person of life, liberty, or property, without due process of law; nor deny to any person within its jurisdiction the equal protection of the laws.

Section 2. Representatives shall be apportioned among the several States according to their respective numbers, counting the whole number of persons in each State, excluding Indians not taxed. But when the right to vote at any election for the choice of electors for President and Vice President of the United States, Representatives in Congress, the Executive and Judicial officers of a State, or the members of the Legislature thereof, is denied to any of the male inhabitants of such State, being twenty-one years of age, and citizens of the United States, or in any way abridged, except for participation in rebellion, or other crime, the basis of representation therein shall be reduced in the proportion which the number of such male citizens shall bear to the whole number of male citizens twenty-one years of age in such State.

Section 3. No person shall be a Senator or Representative in Congress, or elector of President and Vice President, or hold any office, civil or military, under the United States, or under any State, who, having previously taken an oath, as a member of Congress, or as an officer of the United States, or as a member of any State legislature, or as an executive or judicial officer of any State, to support the Constitution of the United States, shall have engaged in insurrection or rebellion against the same, or given aid or comfort to the enemies thereof. But Congress may by a vote of two-thirds of each House, remove such disability.

Section 4. The validity of the public debt of the United States, authorized by law, including debts incurred for payment of pensions and bounties for services in suppressing insurrection or rebellion, shall not be questioned. But neither the United States nor any State shall assume or pay any debt or obligation incurred in aid of insurrection or rebellion against the United States, or any claim for the loss or emancipation of any slave; but all such debts, obligations and claims shall be held illegal and void.

Section 5. The Congress shall have power to enforce, by appropriate legislation, the provisions of this article. [July 28, 1868.]

AMENDMENT XV.

Section 1. The right of citizens of the United States to vote shall not be denied or abridged by the United States or by any State on account of race, color, or previous condition of servitude—

Section 2. The Congress shall have power to enforce this article by appropriate legislation.—[March 30, 1870.]

AMENDMENT XVI.

The Congress shall have power to lay and collect taxes on incomes, from whatever source derived, without apportionment among the several States, and without regard to any census or enumeration. [February 25, 1913.]

AMENDMENT XVII.

The Senate of the United States shall be composed of two senators from each State, elected by the people thereof, for six years; and each Senator shall have one vote. The electors in each State shall have the qualifications requisite for electors of the most numerous branch of the State legislature.

When vacancies happen in the representation of any State in the Senate, the executive authority of such State shall issue writs of election to fill such vacancies: *Provided,* That the legislature of any State may empower the executive thereof to make temporary appointments until the people fill the vacancies by election as the legislature may direct.

This amendment shall not be so construed as to affect the election or term of any senator chosen before it becomes valid as part of the Constitution. [May 31, 1913.]

Amendment XVIII.

After one year from the ratification of this article, the manufacture, sale, or transportation of intoxicating liquors within, the importation thereof into, or the exportation thereof from the United States and all territory subject to the jurisdiction thereof for beverage purposes is hereby prohibited.

The Congress and the several States shall have concurrent power to enforce this article by appropriate legislation.

This article shall be inoperative unless it shall have been ratified as an amendment to the Constitution by the legislatures of the several States, as provided in the Constitution, within seven years from the date of the submission thereof to the States by Congress. [January 29, 1919.]

Amendment XIX.

The right of citizens of the United States to vote shall not be denied or abridged by the United States or by any State on account of sex.

The Congress shall have power by appropriate legislation to enforce the provisions of this article. [August 26, 1920.]

Amendment XX.

Section 1. The terms of the President and Vice-President shall end at noon on the twentieth day of January, and the terms of Senators and Representatives at noon on the third day of January, of the years in which such terms would have ended if this article had not been ratified; and the terms of their successors shall then begin.

Section 2. The Congress shall assemble at least once in every year, and such meeting shall begin at noon on the third day of January, unless they shall by law appoint a different day.

Section 3. If, at the time fixed for the beginning of the term of the President, the President-elect shall have died, the Vice-President-elect shall become President. If a President shall not have been chosen before the time fixed for the beginning of his term, or if the President-elect shall have failed to qualify, then the Vice-President-elect shall act as President until a President shall have qualified; and the Congress may by law provide for the case wherein neither a President-elect nor a Vice-President-elect shall have qualified, declaring who shall then act as President, or the manner in which one who is to act shall be selected, and such person shall act accordingly until a President or Vice-President shall have qualified.

Section 4. The Congress may by law provide for the case of the death of any of the persons from whom the House of Representatives may choose a President whenever the right of choice shall have devolved upon them, and for the case of the death of any of the persons from whom the Senate may choose a Vice-President whenever the right of choice shall have devolved upon them.

Section 5. Sections 1 and 2 shall take effect on the 15th day of October following the ratification of this article.

Section 6. This article shall be inoperative unless it shall have been ratified as an amendment to the Constitution by the legislatures of three-fourths of the several States within seven years from the date of its submission. [February 6, 1933.]

AMENDMENT XXI.

Section 1. The eighteenth article of amendment to the Constitution of the United States is hereby repealed.

Section 2. The transportation or importation into any State, Territory or possession of the United States for delivery or use therein of intoxicating liquors, in violation of the laws thereof, is hereby prohibited.

Section 3. This article shall be inoperative unless it shall have been ratified as an amendment to the Constitution by convention in the several States, as provided in the Constitution, within seven years from the date of the submission thereof to the States by the Congress. [December 5, 1933.]

AMENDMENT XXII.

Section 1. No person shall be elected to the office of the President more than twice, and no person who has held the office of President, or acted as President, for more than two years of a term to which some other person was elected President shall be elected to the office of the President more than once. But this Article shall not apply to any person holding the office of President when this Article was proposed by the Congress, and shall not prevent any person who may be holding the office of President, or acting as President, during the term within which this Article becomes operative from holding the office of President or acting as President during the remainder of such term.

Section 2. This article shall be inoperative unless it shall have been ratified as an amendment to the Constitution by the legislatures of three-fourths of the several states within seven years from the date of its submission to the States by the Congress. [February 27, 1951.]

Amendment XXIII.

Section 1. The District constituting the seat of government of the United States shall appoint in such manner as the Congress may direct:

A number of electors of President and Vice-President equal to the whole number of Senators and Representatives in Congress to which the District would be entitled if it were a State, but in no event more than the least populous State; they shall be in addition to those appointed by the States, but they shall be considered, for the purposes of the election of President and Vice-President, to be electors appointed by a State; and they shall meet in the District and perform such duties as provided by the twelfth article of amendment.

Section 2. The Congress shall have the power to enforce this article by appropriate legislation. [March 29, 1961.]

Amendment XXIV.

Section 1. The right of citizens of the United States to vote in any primary or other election for President or Vice President, for electors for President or Vice President, or for Senator or Representative in Congress, shall not be denied or abridged by the United States or any State by reason of failure to pay any poll tax or other tax.

Section 2. The Congress shall have power to enforce this article by appropriate legislation. [January 23, 1964.]

Amendment XXV.

Section 1. In case of the removal of the President from office or of his death or resignation, the Vice President shall become President.

Section 2. Whenever there is a vacancy in the office of Vice President, the President shall nominate a Vice President who shall take office upon confirmation by a majority vote of both Houses of Congress.

Section 3. Whenever the President transmits to the President pro tempore of the Senate and the Speaker of the House of Representatives his written declaration that he is unable to discharge the powers and duties of his office, and until he transmits to them a written declaration to the contrary, such powers and duties shall be discharged by the Vice President as Acting President.

Section 4. Whenever the Vice President and a majority of either the principal officers of the executive departments or of such other body as Congress may by law provide, transmit to the President pro tempore of the Senate and the Speaker of the House of Representatives their written declaration that the President is unable to discharge the powers and duties of his office, the Vice President shall immediately assume the powers and duties of the office as Acting President.

Thereafter, when the President transmits to the President pro tempore of the Senate and the Speaker of the House of Representatives his written declaration that no inability exists, he shall resume the powers and duties of his office unless the Vice President and a majority of either the principal officers of the executive departments or of such other body as Congress may by law provide, transmit within four days to the President pro tempore of the Senate and the Speaker of the House of Representatives their written declaration that the President is unable to discharge the powers and duties of his office. Thereupon Congress shall decide the issue, assembling within forty-eight hours for that purpose if not in session. If the Congress, within twenty-one days after receipt of the latter written declaration, or, if Congress is not in session, within twenty-one days after Congress is required to assemble, determines by two-thirds vote of both Houses that the President is unable to discharge the powers and duties of his office, the Vice President shall continue to discharge the same as Acting President; otherwise, the President shall resume the powers and duties of his office. [February 10, 1967.]

Amendment XXVI.

Section 1. The right of citizens of the United States, who are eighteen years of age or older, to vote shall not be denied or abridged by the United States or by any State on account of age.

Section 2. The Congress shall have power to enforce this article by appropriate legislation [June 30, 1971.]

Amendment XXVII.

No law, varying the compensation for the services of the Senators and Representatives shall take effect, until an election of Representatives shall have intervened. [May 8, 1992.]

PRESIDENTIAL ELECTIONS

Year	Number of States	Candidates	Parties	Popular Vote	% of Popular Vote	Electoral Vote	% Voter Participation
1789	11	**GEORGE WASHINGTON**	No party designations			69	
		John Adams				34	
		Other candidates				35	
1792	15	**GEORGE WASHINGTON**	No party designations			132	
		John Adams				77	
		George Clinton				50	
		Other candidates				5	
1796	16	**JOHN ADAMS**	Federalist			71	
		Thomas Jefferson	Democratic-Republican			68	
		Thomas Pinckney	Federalist			59	
		Aaron Burr	Democratic-Republican			30	
		Other candidates				48	
1800	16	**THOMAS JEFFERSON**	Democratic-Republican			73	
		Aaron Burr	Democratic-Republican			73	
		John Adams	Federalist			65	
		Charles C. Pinckney	Federalist			64	
		John Jay	Federalist			1	
1804	17	**THOMAS JEFFERSON**	Democratic-Republican			162	
		Charles C. Pinckney	Federalist			14	

Presidential Elections · A81

Year	Number of States	Candidates	Parties	Popular Vote	% of Popular Vote	Electoral Vote	% Voter Participation
1808	17	**JAMES MADISON**	Democratic-Republican			122	
		Charles C. Pinckney	Federalist			47	
		George Clinton	Democratic-Republican			6	
1812	18	**JAMES MADISON**	Democratic-Republican			128	
		DeWitt Clinton	Federalist			89	
1816	19	**JAMES MONROE**	Democratic-Republican			183	
		Rufus King	Federalist			34	
1820	24	**JAMES MONROE**	Democratic-Republican			231	
		John Quincy Adams	Independent-Republican			1	
1824	24	**JOHN QUINCY ADAMS**	Democratic-Republican	108,740	30.5	84	26.9
		Andrew Jackson	Democratic-Republican	153,544	43.1	99	
		Henry Clay	Democratic-Republican	47,136	13.2	37	
		William H. Crawford	Democratic-Republican	46,618	13.1	41	
1828	24	**ANDREW JACKSON**	Democratic	647,286	56.0	178	57.6
		John Quincy Adams	National-Republican	508,064	44.0	83	

Year	Number of States	Candidates	Parties	Popular Vote	% of Popular Vote	Electoral Vote	% Voter Participation
1832	24	**ANDREW JACKSON**	Democratic	688,242	54.5	219	55.4
		Henry Clay	National-Republican	473,462	37.5	49	
		William Wirt	Anti-Masonic	101,051	8.0	7	
		John Floyd	Democratic			11	
1836	26	**MARTIN VAN BUREN**	Democratic	765,483	50.9	170	57.8
		William H. Harrison	Whig			73	
		Hugh L. White	Whig	739,795	49.1	26	
		Daniel Webster	Whig			14	
		W. P. Mangum	Whig			11	
1840	26	**WILLIAM H. HARRISON**	Whig	1,274,624	53.1	234	80.2
		Martin Van Buren	Democratic	1,127,781	46.9	60	
1844	26	**JAMES K. POLK**	Democratic	1,338,464	49.6	170	78.9
		Henry Clay	Whig	1,300,097	48.1	105	
		James G. Birney	Liberty	62,300	2.3		
1848	30	**ZACHARY TAYLOR**	Whig	1,360,967	47.4	163	72.7
		Lewis Cass	Democratic	1,222,342	42.5	127	
		Martin Van Buren	Free Soil	291,263	10.1		
1852	31	**FRANKLIN PIERCE**	Democratic	1,601,117	50.9	254	69.6
		Winfield Scott	Whig	1,385,453	44.1	42	
		John P. Hale	Free Soil	155,825	5.0		
1856	31	**JAMES BUCHANAN**	Democratic	1,832,955	45.3	174	78.9
		John C. Frémont	Republican	1,339,932	33.1	114	
		Millard Fillmore	American	871,731	21.6	8	

Year	Number of States	Candidates	Parties	Popular Vote	% of Popular Vote	Electoral Vote	% Voter Participation
1860	33	**ABRAHAM LINCOLN**	Republican	1,865,593	39.8	180	81.2
		Stephen A. Douglas	Democratic	1,382,713	29.5	12	
		John C. Breckinridge	Democratic	848,356	18.1	72	
		John Bell	Constitutional Union	592,906	12.6	39	
1864	36	**ABRAHAM LINCOLN**	Republican	2,206,938	55.0	212	73.8
		George B. McClellan	Democratic	1,803,787	45.0	21	
1868	37	**ULYSSES S. GRANT**	Republican	3,013,421	52.7	214	78.1
		Horatio Seymour	Democratic	2,706,829	47.3	80	
1872	37	**ULYSSES S. GRANT**	Republican	3,596,745	55.6	286	71.3
		Horace Greeley	Democratic	2,843,446	43.9	66	
1876	38	Rutherford B. Hayes	Republican	4,036,572	48.0	185	81.8
		Samuel J. Tilden	Democratic	4,284,020	51.0	184	
1880	38	**JAMES A. GARFIELD**	Republican	4,453,295	48.5	214	79.4
		Winfield S. Hancock	Democratic	4,414,082	48.1	155	
		James B. Weaver	Greenback-Labor	308,578	3.4		
1884	38	**GROVER CLEVELAND**	Democratic	4,879,507	48.5	219	77.5
		James G. Blaine	Republican	4,850,293	48.2	182	
		Benjamin F. Butler	Greenback-Labor	175,370	1.8		
		John P. St. John	Prohibition	150,369	1.5		
1888	38	**BENJAMIN HARRISON**	Republican	5,477,129	47.9	233	79.3
		Grover Cleveland	Democratic	5,537,857	48.6	168	
		Clinton B. Fisk	Prohibition	249,506	2.2		
		Anson J. Streeter	Union Labor	146,935	1.3		

Year	Number of States	Candidates	Parties	Popular Vote	% of Popular Vote	Electoral Vote	% Voter Participation
1892	44	**GROVER CLEVELAND**	Democratic	5,555,426	46.1	277	74.7
		Benjamin Harrison	Republican	5,182,690	43.0	145	
		James B. Weaver	People's	1,029,846	8.5	22	
		John Bidwell	Prohibition	264,133	2.2		
1896	45	**WILLIAM MCKINLEY**	Republican	7,102,246	51.1	271	79.3
		William J. Bryan	Democratic	6,492,559	47.7	176	
1900	45	**WILLIAM MCKINLEY**	Republican	7,218,491	51.7	292	73.2
		William J. Bryan	Democratic; Populist	6,356,734	45.5	155	
		John C. Wooley	Prohibition	208,914	1.5		
1904	45	**THEODORE ROOSEVELT**	Republican	7,628,461	57.4	336	65.2
		Alton B. Parker	Democratic	5,084,223	37.6	140	
		Eugene V. Debs	Socialist	402,283	3.0		
		Silas C. Swallow	Prohibition	258,536	1.9		
1908	46	**WILLIAM H. TAFT**	Republican	7,675,320	51.6	321	65.4
		William J. Bryan	Democratic	6,412,294	43.1	162	
		Eugene V. Debs	Socialist	420,793	2.8		
		Eugene W. Chafin	Prohibition	253,840	1.7		
1912	48	**WOODROW WILSON**	Democratic	6,296,547	41.9	435	58.8
		Theodore Roosevelt	Progressive	4,118,571	27.4	88	
		William H. Taft	Republican	3,486,720	23.2	8	
		Eugene V. Debs	Socialist	900,672	6.0		
		Eugene W. Chafin	Prohibition	206,275	1.4		

Year	Number of States	Candidates	Party	Popular Vote	% of Popular Vote	Electoral Vote	% Voter Participation
1916	48	**WOODROW WILSON**	Democratic	9,127,695	49.4	277	61.6
		Charles E. Hughes	Republican	8,533,507	46.2	254	
		A. L. Benson	Socialist	585,113	3.2		
		J. Frank Hanly	Prohibition	220,506	1.2		
1920	48	**WARREN G. HARDING**	Republican	16,143,407	60.4	404	49.2
		James M. Cox	Democratic	9,130,328	34.2	127	
		Eugene V. Debs	Socialist	919,799	3.4		
		P. P. Christensen	Farmer-Labor	265,411	1.0		
1924	48	**CALVIN COOLIDGE**	Republican	15,718,211	54.0	382	48.9
		John W. Davis	Democratic	8,385,283	28.8	136	
		Robert M. La Follette	Progressive	4,831,289	16.6	13	
1928	48	**HERBERT C. HOOVER**	Republican	21,391,993	58.2	444	56.9
		Alfred E. Smith	Democratic	15,016,169	40.9	87	
1932	48	**FRANKLIN D. ROOSEVELT**	Democratic	22,809,638	57.4	472	56.9
		Herbert C. Hoover	Republican	15,758,901	39.7	59	
		Norman Thomas	Socialist	881,951	2.2		
1936	48	**FRANKLIN D. ROOSEVELT**	Democratic	27,752,869	60.8	523	61.0
		Alfred M. Landon	Republican	16,674,665	36.5	8	
		William Lemke	Union	882,479	1.9		
1940	48	**FRANKLIN D. ROOSEVELT**	Democratic	27,307,819	54.8	449	62.5
		Wendell L. Willkie	Republican	22,321,018	44.8	82	
1944	48	**FRANKLIN D. ROOSEVELT**	Democratic	25,606,585	53.5	432	55.9
		Thomas E. Dewey	Republican	22,014,745	46.0	99	

Year	Number of States	Candidates	Parties	Popular Vote	% of Popular Vote	Electoral Vote	% Voter Participation
1948	48	HARRY S. TRUMAN	Democratic	24,179,345	49.6	303	53.0
		Thomas E. Dewey	Republican	21,991,291	45.1	189	
		J. Strom Thurmond	States' Rights	1,176,125	2.4	39	
		Henry A. Wallace	Progressive	1,157,326	2.4		
1952	48	DWIGHT D. EISENHOWER	Republican	33,936,234	55.1	442	63.3
		Adlai E. Stevenson	Democratic	27,314,992	44.4	89	
1956	48	DWIGHT D. EISENHOWER	Republican	35,590,472	57.6	457	60.6
		Adlai E. Stevenson	Democratic	26,022,752	42.1	73	
1960	50	JOHN F. KENNEDY	Democratic	34,226,731	49.7	303	62.8
		Richard M. Nixon	Republican	34,108,157	49.5	219	
1964	50	LYNDON B. JOHNSON	Democratic	43,129,566	61.1	486	61.9
		Barry M. Goldwater	Republican	27,178,188	38.5	52	
1968	50	RICHARD M. NIXON	Republican	31,785,480	43.4	301	60.9
		Hubert H. Humphrey	Democratic	31,275,166	42.7	191	
		George C. Wallace	American Independent	9,906,473	13.5	46	
1972	50	RICHARD M. NIXON	Republican	47,169,911	60.7	520	55.2
		George S. McGovern	Democratic	29,170,383	37.5	17	
		John G. Schmitz	American	1,099,482	1.4		

Year		Candidates	Party	Popular Vote	% Popular Vote	Electoral Vote	% Turnout
1976	50	**JIMMY CARTER** Gerald R. Ford	Democratic Republican	40,830,763 39,147,793	50.1 48.0	297 240	53.5
1980	50	**RONALD REAGAN** Jimmy Carter John B. Anderson Ed Clark	Republican Democratic Independent Libertarian	43,901,812 35,483,820 5,719,437 921,188	50.7 41.0 6.6 1.1	489 49	52.6
1984	50	**RONALD REAGAN** Walter F. Mondale	Republican Democratic	54,451,521 37,565,334	58.8 40.6	525 13	53.1
1988	50	**GEORGE H. W. BUSH** Michael Dukakis	Republican Democratic	47,917,341 41,013,030	53.4 45.6	426 111	50.1
1992	50	**BILL CLINTON** George H. W. Bush H. Ross Perot	Democratic Republican Independent	44,908,254 39,102,343 19,741,065	43.0 37.4 18.9	370 168	55.0
1996	50	**BILL CLINTON** Bob Dole H. Ross Perot	Democratic Republican Independent	47,401,185 39,197,469 8,085,295	49.0 41.0 8.0	379 159	49.0
2000	50	**GEORGE W. BUSH** Al Gore Ralph Nader	Republican Democrat Green	50,455,156 50,997,335 2,882,897	47.9 48.4 2.7	271 266	50.4
2004	50	**GEORGE W. BUSH** John F. Kerry	Republican Democrat	62,040,610 59,028,444	50.7 48.3	286 251	60.7

Candidates receiving less than 1 percent of the popular vote have been omitted. Thus the percentage of popular vote given for any election year may not total 100 percent.

Before the passage of the Twelfth Amendment in 1804, the electoral college voted for two presidential candidates; the runner-up became vice-president.

ADMISSION OF STATES

Order of Admission	State	Date of Admission	Order of Admission	State	Date of Admission
1	Delaware	December 7, 1787	26	Michigan	January 26, 1837
2	Pennsylvania	December 12, 1787	27	Florida	March 3, 1845
3	New Jersey	December 18, 1787	28	Texas	December 29, 1845
4	Georgia	January 2, 1788	29	Iowa	December 28, 1846
5	Connecticut	January 9, 1788	30	Wisconsin	May 29, 1848
6	Massachusetts	February 7, 1788	31	California	September 9, 1850
7	Maryland	April 28, 1788	32	Minnesota	May 11, 1858
8	South Carolina	May 23, 1788	33	Oregon	February 14, 1859
9	New Hampshire	June 21, 1788	34	Kansas	January 29, 1861
10	Virginia	June 25, 1788	35	West Virginia	June 30, 1863
11	New York	July 26, 1788	36	Nevada	October 31, 1864
12	North Carolina	November 21, 1789	37	Nebraska	March 1, 1867
13	Rhode Island	May 29, 1790	38	Colorado	August 1, 1876
14	Vermont	March 4, 1791	39	North Dakota	November 2, 1889
15	Kentucky	June 1, 1792	40	South Dakota	November 2, 1889
16	Tennessee	June 1, 1796	41	Montana	November 8, 1889
17	Ohio	March 1, 1803	42	Washington	November 11, 1889
18	Louisiana	April 30, 1812	43	Idaho	July 3, 1890
19	Indiana	December 11, 1816	44	Wyoming	July 10, 1890
20	Mississippi	December 10, 1817	45	Utah	January 4, 1896
21	Illinois	December 3, 1818	46	Oklahoma	November 16, 1907
22	Alabama	December 14, 1819	47	New Mexico	January 6, 1912
23	Maine	March 15, 1820	48	Arizona	February 14, 1912
24	Missouri	August 10, 1821	49	Alaska	January 3, 1959
25	Arkansas	June 15, 1836	50	Hawaii	August 21, 1959

POPULATION OF THE UNITED STATES

Year	Number of States	Population	% Increase	Population per Square Mile
1790	13	3,929,214		4.5
1800	16	5,308,483	35.1	6.1
1810	17	7,239,881	36.4	4.3
1820	23	9,638,453	33.1	5.5
1830	24	12,866,020	33.5	7.4
1840	26	17,069,453	32.7	9.8
1850	31	23,191,876	35.9	7.9
1860	33	31,443,321	35.6	10.6
1870	37	39,818,449	26.6	13.4
1880	38	50,155,783	26.0	16.9
1890	44	62,947,714	25.5	21.1
1900	45	75,994,575	20.7	25.6
1910	46	91,972,266	21.0	31.0
1920	48	105,710,620	14.9	35.6
1930	48	122,775,046	16.1	41.2
1940	48	131,669,275	7.2	44.2
1950	48	150,697,361	14.5	50.7
1960	50	179,323,175	19.0	50.6
1970	50	203,235,298	13.3	57.5
1980	50	226,504,825	11.4	64.0
1985	50	237,839,000	5.0	67.2
1990	50	250,122,000	5.2	70.6
1995	50	263,411,707	5.3	74.4
2000	50	281,421,906	6.8	77.0

IMMIGRATION TO THE UNITED STATES, FISCAL YEARS 1820–2005

Year	Number	Year	Number	Year	Number	Year	Number
1820–1989	55,457,531	1871–80	2,812,191	1921–30	4,107,209	1971–80	4,493,314
1820	8,385	1871	321,350	1921	805,228	1971	370,478
1821–30	143,439	1872	404,806	1922	309,556	1972	384,685
1821	9,127	1873	459,803	1923	522,919	1973	400,063
1822	6,911	1874	313,339	1924	706,896	1974	394,861
1823	6,354	1875	227,498	1925	294,314	1975	386,914
1824	7,912	1876	169,986	1926	304,488	1976	398,613
1825	10,199	1877	141,857	1927	335,175	1976	103,676
1826	10,837	1878	138,469	1928	307,255	1977	462,315
1827	18,875	1879	177,826	1929	279,678	1978	601,442
1828	27,382	1880	457,257	1930	241,700	1979	460,348
1829	22,520	1881–90	5,246,613	1931–40	528,431	1980	530,639
1830	23,322	1881	669,431	1931	97,139	1981–90	7,338,062
1831–40	599,125	1882	788,992	1932	35,576	1981	596,600
1831	22,633	1883	603,322	1933	23,068	1982	594,131
1832	60,482	1884	518,592	1934	29,470	1983	559,763
1833	58,640	1885	395,346	1935	34,956	1984	543,903
1834	65,365	1886	334,203	1936	36,329	1985	570,009
1835	45,374	1887	490,109	1937	50,244	1986	601,708
1836	76,242	1888	546,889	1938	67,895	1987	601,516
1837	79,340	1889	444,427	1939	82,998	1988	643,025
1838	38,914	1890	455,302	1940	70,756	1989	1,090,924
1839	68,069	1891–1900	3,687,564	1941–50	1,035,039	1990	1,536,483
1840	84,066	1891	560,319	1941	51,776	1991–2000	9,090,857
1841–50	1,713,251	1892	579,663	1942	28,781	1991	1,827,167
1841	80,289	1893	439,730	1943	23,725	1992	973,977
1842	104,565	1894	285,631	1944	28,551	1993	904,292
		1895	258,536	1945	38,119	1994	804,416
		1896	343,267	1946	108,721		

Year	Number	Year	Number	Year	Number	Year	Number
1843	52,496	1897	230,832	1947	147,292	1995	720,461
1844	78,615	1898	229,299	1948	170,570	1996	915,900
1845	114,371	1899	311,715	1949	188,317	1997	798,378
1846	154,416	1900	448,572	1950	249,187	1998	660,477
1847	234,968					1999	644,787
1848	226,527	**1901–10**	**8,795,386**	**1951–60**	**2,515,479**	2000	841,002
1849	297,024	1901	487,918	1951	205,717	**2001–5**	**4,904,341**
1850	369,980	1902	648,743	1952	265,520	2001	1,058,902
		1903	857,046	1953	170,434	2002	1,059,356
1851–60	**2,598,214**	1904	812,870	1954	208,177	2003	705,827
1851	379,466	1905	1,026,499	1955	237,790	2004	957,883
1852	371,603	1906	1,100,735	1956	321,625	2005	1,122,373
1853	368,645	1907	1,285,349	1957	326,867		
1854	427,833	1908	782,870	1958	253,265		
1855	200,877	1909	751,786	1959	260,686		
1856	200,436	1910	1,041,570	1960	265,398		
1857	251,306						
1858	123,126	**1911–20**	**5,735,811**	**1961–70**	**3,321,677**		
1859	121,282	1911	878,587	1961	271,344		
1860	153,640	1912	838,172	1962	283,763		
		1913	1,197,892	1963	306,260		
1861–70	**2,314,824**	1914	1,218,480	1964	292,248		
1861	91,918	1915	326,700	1965	296,697		
1862	91,985	1916	298,826	1966	323,040		
1863	176,282	1917	295,403	1967	361,972		
1864	193,418	1918	110,618	1968	454,448		
1865	248,120	1919	141,132	1969	358,579		
1866	318,568	1920	430,001	1970	373,326		
1867	315,722						
1868	138,840						
1869	352,768						
1870	387,203						

Source: U.S. Immigration and Naturalization Service, 2006.

IMMIGRATION BY REGION AND SELECTED COUNTRY OF LAST RESIDENCE, FISCAL YEARS 1820–2004

Region and Country of Last Residence[1]	1820	1821–30	1831–40	1841–50	1851–60	1861–70	1871–80	1881–90
All countries	8,385	143,439	599,125	1,713,251	2,598,214	2,314,824	2,812,191	5,246,613
Europe	7,690	98,797	495,681	1,597,442	2,452,577	2,065,141	2,271,925	4,735,484
Austria-Hungary	—[2]	—[2]	—[2]	—[2]	—[2]	7,800	72,969	353,719
Austria	—[2]	—[2]	—[2]	—[2]	—[2]	484[3]	63,009	226,038
Hungary	—[2]	—[2]	—[2]	—[2]	—[2]	7,124[3]	9,960	127,681
Belgium	1	27	22	5,074	4,738	6,734	7,221	20,177
Czechoslovakia	—[4]	—[4]	—[4]	—[4]	—[4]	—[4]	—[4]	—[4]
Denmark	20	169	1,063	539	3,749	17,094	31,771	88,132
France	371	8,497	45,575	77,262	76,358	35,986	72,206	50,464
Germany	968	6,761	152,454	434,626	951,667	787,468	718,182	1,452,970
Greece	—	20	49	16	31	72	210	2,308
Ireland[5]	3,614	50,724	207,381	780,719	914,119	435,778	436,871	655,482
Italy	30	409	2,253	1,870	9,231	11,725	55,759	307,309
Netherlands	49	1,078	1,412	8,251	10,789	9,102	16,541	53,701
Norway-Sweden	3	91	1,201	13,903	20,931	109,298	211,245	568,362
Norway	—[6]	—[6]	—[6]	—[6]	—[6]	—[6]	95,323	176,586
Sweden	—[6]	—[6]	—[6]	—[6]	—[6]	—[6]	115,922	391,776
Poland	5	16	369	105	1,164	2,027	12,970	51,806
Portugal	35	145	829	550	1,055	2,658	14,082	16,978
Romania	—[7]	—[7]	—[7]	—[7]	—[7]	—[7]	11	6,348
Soviet Union	14	75	277	551	457	2,512	39,284	213,282
Spain	139	2,477	2,125	2,209	9,298	6,697	5,266	4,419
Switzerland	31	3,226	4,821	4,644	25,011	23,286	28,293	81,988
United Kingdom[5,8]	2,410	25,079	75,810	267,044	423,974	606,896	548,043	807,357
Yugoslavia	—[9]	—[9]	—[9]	—[9]	—[9]	—[9]	—[9]	—[9]
Other Europe	—	3	40	79	5	8	1,001	682

Asia	69,942	124,160	64,759	41,538	141	55	30	6
China[10]	61,711	123,201	64,301	41,397	35	8	2	1
Hong Kong	—[11]	—[11]	—[11]	—[11]	—[11]	—[11]	—[11]	—[11]
India	269	163	69	43	36	39	8	1
Iran	—[12]	—[12]	—[12]	—[12]	—[12]	—[12]	—[12]	—[12]
Israel	—[13]	—[13]	—[13]	—[13]	—[13]	—[13]	—[13]	—[13]
Japan	2,270	149	186	—[14]	—[14]	—[14]	—[14]	—[14]
Korea	—[15]	—[15]	—[15]	—[15]	—[15]	—[15]	—[15]	—[15]
Philippines	—[16]	—[16]	—[16]	—[16]	—[16]	—[16]	—[16]	—[16]
Turkey	3,782	404	131	83	59	7	20	1
Vietnam	—[11]	—[11]	—[11]	—[11]	—[11]	—[11]	—[11]	—[11]
Other Asia	1,910	243	72	15	11	1	—	3
America	426,967	404,044	166,607	74,720	62,469	33,424	11,564	387
Canada & Newfoundland[17,18]	393,304	383,640	153,878	59,309	41,723	13,624	2,277	209
Mexico[18]	191,319	5,162	2,191	3,078	3,271	6,599	4,817	1
Caribbean	29,042	13,957	9,046	10,660	13,528	12,301	3,834	164
Cuba	—[12]	—[12]	—[12]	—[12]	—[12]	—[12]	—[12]	—[12]
Dominican Republic	—[20]	—[20]	—[20]	—[20]	—[20]	—[20]	—[20]	—[20]
Haiti	—[20]	—[20]	—[20]	—[20]	—[20]	—[20]	—[20]	—[20]
Jamaica	—[21]	—[21]	—[21]	—[21]	—[21]	—[21]	—[21]	—[21]
Other Caribbean	29,042	13,957	9,046	10,660	13,528	12,301	3,834	164
Central America	404	157	95	449	368	44	105	2
El Salvador	—[20]	—[20]	—[20]	—[20]	—[20]	—[20]	—[20]	—[20]
Other Central America	404	157	95	449	368	44	105	2
South America	2,304	1,128	1,397	1,224	3,579	856	531	11
Argentina	—[20]	—[20]	—[20]	—[20]	—[20]	—[20]	—[20]	—[20]
Colombia	—[20]	—[20]	—[20]	—[20]	—[20]	—[20]	—[20]	—[20]
Ecuador	—[20]	—[20]	—[20]	—[20]	—[20]	—[20]	—[20]	—[20]
Other South America	2,304	1,128	1,397	1,224	3,579	856	531	11
Other America	—[22]	—[22]	—[22]	—[22]	—[22]	—[22]	—[22]	—[22]
Africa	857	358	312	210	55	54	16	1
Oceania[22]	12,574	10,914	214	158	29	9	2	1
Not specified[22]	789	790	17,791	29,011	53,115	69,902	33,030	300

Region and Country of Last Residence[1]	1891–1900	1901–10	1911–20	1921–30	1931–40	1941–50	1951–60	1961–70
All countries	3,687,564	8,795,386	5,735,811	4,107,209	528,431	1,035,039	2,515,479	3,321,677
Europe	3,555,352	8,056,040	4,321,887	2,463,194	347,566	621,147	1,325,727	1,123,492
Austria-Hungary	592,707[23]	2,145,266[23]	896,342[23]	63,548	11,424	28,329	103,743	26,022
Austria	234,081[3]	668,209[3]	453,649	32,868	3,563[24]	24,860[24]	67,106	20,621
Hungary	181,288[3]	808,511[3]	442,693	30,680	7,861	3,469	36,637	5,401
Belgium	18,167	41,635	33,746	15,846	4,817	12,189	18,575	9,192
Czechoslovakia	—[4]	—[4]	3,426[4]	102,194	14,393	8,347	918	3,273
Denmark	50,231	65,285	41,983	32,430	2,559	5,393	10,984	9,201
France	30,770	73,379	61,897	49,610	12,623	38,809	51,121	45,237
Germany	505,152[23]	341,498[23]	143,945[23]	412,202	114,058[24]	226,578[24]	477,765	190,796
Greece	15,979	167,519	184,201	51,084	9,119	8,973	47,608	85,969
Ireland[5]	388,416	339,065	146,181	211,234	10,973	19,789	48,362	32,966
Italy	651,893	2,045,877	1,109,524	455,315	68,028	57,661	185,491	214,111
Netherlands	26,758	48,262	43,718	26,948	7,150	14,860	52,277	30,606
Norway-Sweden	321,281	440,039	161,469	165,780	8,700	20,765	44,632	32,600
Norway	95,015	190,505	66,395	68,531	4,740	10,100	22,935	15,484
Sweden	226,266	249,534	95,074	97,249	3,960	10,665	21,697	17,116
Poland	96,720[23]	—[23]	4,813[23]	227,734	17,026	7,571	9,985	53,539
Portugal	27,508	69,149	89,732	29,994	3,329	7,423	19,588	76,065
Romania	12,750	53,008	13,311	67,646	3,871	1,076	1,039	2,531
Soviet Union	505,290[23]	1,597,306[23]	921,201[23]	61,742	1,370	571	671	2,465
Spain	8,731	27,935	68,611	28,958	3,258	2,898	7,894	44,659
Switzerland	31,179	34,922	23,091	29,676	5,512	10,547	17,675	18,453
United Kingdom[5,8]	271,538	525,950	341,408	339,570	31,572	139,306	202,824	213,822
Yugoslavia	—[9]	—[9]	1,888[9]	49,064	5,835	1,576	8,225	20,381
Other Europe	282	39,945	31,400	42,619	11,949	8,486	16,350	11,604

Asia	427,642	153,249	37,028	16,595	112,059	247,236	323,543	74,862
China[10]	34,764	9,657	16,709	4,928	29,907	21,278	20,605	14,799
Hong Kong	75,007	15,541[11]	—[11]	—[11]	—[11]	—[11]	—[11]	—[11]
India	27,189	1,973	1,761	496	1,886	2,082	4,713	68
Iran	10,339	3,388	1,380	195	241[12]	—[12]	—[12]	—[12]
Israel	29,602	25,476	476[13]	—[13]	—[13]	—[13]	—[13]	—[13]
Japan	39,988	46,250	1,555	1,948	33,462	83,837	129,797	25,942
Korea	34,526	6,231	107[15]	—[15]	—[15]	—[15]	—[15]	—[15]
Philippines	98,376	19,307	4,691	528[16]	—[16]	—[16]	—[16]	—[16]
Turkey	10,142	3,519	798	1,065	33,824	134,066	157,369	30,425
Vietnam	4,340	335[11]	—[11]	—[11]	—[11]	—[11]	—[11]	—[11]
Other Asia	63,369	21,572	9,551	7,435	12,739	5,973	11,059	3,628
America	1,716,374	996,944	354,804	160,037	1,516,716	1,143,671	361,888	38,972
Canada & Newfoundland [17,18]	413,310	377,952	171,718	108,527	924,515	742,185	179,226	3,311
Mexico[18]	453,937	299,811	60,589	22,319	459,287	219,004	49,642	971[19]
Caribbean	470,213	123,091	49,725	15,502	74,899	123,424	107,548	33,066
Cuba	208,536	78,948	26,313	9,571	15,901[12]	—[12]	—[12]	—[12]
Dominican Republic	93,292	9,897	5,627	1,150[20]	—[20]	—[20]	—[20]	—[20]
Haiti	34,499	4,442	911	191[20]	—[20]	—[20]	—[20]	—[20]
Jamaica	74,906	8,869[21]	—[21]	—[21]	—[21]	—[21]	—[21]	—[21]
Other Caribbean	58,980	20,935[21]	16,874	4,590	58,998	123,424	107,548	33,066
Central America	101,330	44,751	21,665	5,861	15,769	17,159	8,192	549
El Salvador	14,992	5,895	5,132	673[20]	—[20]	—[20]	—[20]	—[20]
Other Central America	86,338	38,856	16,533	5,188	15,769	17,159	8,192	549
South America	257,954	91,628	21,831	7,803	42,215	41,899	17,280	1,075
Argentina	49,721	19,486	3,338	1,349[20]	—[20]	—[20]	—[20]	—[20]
Colombia	72,028	18,048	3,858	1,223[20]	—[20]	—[20]	—[20]	—[20]
Ecuador	36,780	9,841	2,417	337[20]	—[20]	—[20]	—[20]	—[20]
Other South America	99,425	44,253	12,218	4,894	42,215	41,899	17,280	1,075
Other America	19,630	59,711	29,276	25	31[22]	—[22]	—[22]	—[22]
Africa	28,954	14,092	7,367	1,750	6,286	8,443	7,368	350
Oceania	25,122	12,976	14,551	2,483	8,726	13,427	13,024	3,965
Not specified [22]	93	12,491	142	—	228	1,147	33,523[25]	14,063

Region and Country of Last Residence[1]	1971–80	1981–89	1990–99	1991–2000	2001	2002	2003	2004	Total 184 Years 1820–2004
All countries	4,493,314	5,801,579	9,781,496	9,095,417	1,064,318	1,063,732	705,827	946,142	69,869,450
Europe	800,368	637,524	1,291,299	1,359,737	177,833	177,652	102,843	130,151	39,049,276
Austria-Hungary	16,028	20,152	N/A	24,882	2,318	4,016	2,181	3,683	4,379,862
Austria	9,478	14,566	5,094	15,500	1,004	2,657	1,163	2,442	1,851,712
Hungary	6,550	5,586	11,003	9,382	1,314	1,359	1,018	1,241	1,682,074
Belgium	5,329	6,239	5,783	7,090	1,002	842	518	746	220,754
Czechoslovakia[27]	6,023	6,649	7,597	9,816	1,921	1,862	1,474	1,870	162,744
Czech Republic	N/A	N/A	723	N/A	N/A	N/A	N/A	N/A	N/A
Slovak Republic	N/A	N/A	3,010	N/A	N/A	N/A	N/A	N/A	N/A
Denmark	4,439	4,696	5,785	6,079	741	655	436	568	378,891
France	25,069	28,088	26,879	35,820	5,431	4,596	2,933	4,209	840,576
Germany	74,414	79,809	60,082	92,606	22,093	21,058	8,102	10,270	7,237,594
Germany, East	N/A	N/A	105	N/A	N/A	N/A	N/A	N/A	N/A
Germany, West	N/A	N/A	7,338	N/A	N/A	N/A	N/A	N/A	N/A
Greece	92,369	34,490	15,403	26,759	1,966	1,516	914	1,213	736,272
Ireland	11,490	22,229	67,975	56,950	1,550	1,419	1,010	1,518	4,787,580
Italy	129,368	51,008	23,365	62,722	3,377	2,837	1,904	2,495	5,446,443
Netherlands	10,492	10,723	12,334	13,308	1,895	2,305	1,329	1,713	394,782
Norway-Sweden	10,472	13,252	15,720	17,893	2,561	2,097	1,520	2,011	2,172,036
Norway	3,941	3,612	4,618	5,178	588	464	386	457	760,792
Sweden	6,531	9,640	11,102	12,715	1,973	1,633	1,134	1,554	1,265,817
Poland	37,234	64,888	180,035	163,747	12,355	13,304	11,016	13,972	820,730
Portugal	101,710	36,365	25,428	22,916	1,654	1,320	821	1,062	529,034
Romania	12,393	27,361	55,303	51,203	6,224	4,525	3,311	4,064	274,168
Russia	N/A	N/A	110,921						
Soviet Union[28]	38,961	42,898	126,115	462,874	55,099	55,464	33,563	36,646	4,087,352
Former Soviet Republics[29]	N/A	N/A	255,552						
Spain	39,141	17,689	14,310	17,157	1,889	1,603	1,107	1,453	308,357
Switzerland	8,235	7,561	8,840	11,841	1,796	1,503	867	1,193	376,639
United Kingdom	137,374	140,119	138,380	151,866	20,258	18,057	11,220	16,680	5,337,231
Yugoslavia[28]	30,540	15,984	25,923	66,557	21,937	28,100	8,296	13,211	274,372

Region/Country								
Former Yugoslavian States	N/A	N/A	61,389	57,651	11,766	10,573	10,321	283,859
Other Europe	9,287	7,324	822,161					10,029,817
Asia	1,588,178	2,416,278	2,965,360	2,795,672	337,566	326,871	236,039	
China, People's Republic	124,326	306,108	410,736	419,114	50,821	55,974	37,395	1,523,622
Hong Kong	113,467	83,848	78,016	109,779	10,307	7,952	5,020	440,709
India	164,134	221,977	371,925	363,060	65,916	66,864	47,157	1,064,185
Iran	45,136	101,267	129,055	68,556	8,063	7,730	4,709	271,807
Israel	37,713	38,367	33,814	39,397	4,925	4,938	3,719	195,725
Japan	49,775	40,654	60,112	67,942	10,464	9,150	6,724	565,176
Korea	267,638	302,782	187,794	164,166	19,933	20,114	12,177	878,079
Philippines	354,987	477,485	526,835	503,945	50,870	48,674	43,258	1,728,032
Taiwan	N/A	N/A	112,464	N/A	N/A	N/A	N/A	N/A
Turkey	13,399	20,028	26,178	38,212	3,477	3,934	3,332	465,771
Vietnam	172,820	266,027	443,173	286,145	34,648	32,425	21,270	862,829
Other Asia	244,783	557,735	769,425	735,356	78,142	69,116	51,278	2,033,882
Africa	80,779	144,096	374,149	354,939	50,209	56,135	45,640	903,578
Oceania	41,242	38,401	49,040	55,845	7,253	6,536	5,102	286,287
America	1,982,735	2,564,698	4,529,512	4,486,806	473,351	478,777	306,793	19,220,746
Canada	169,939	132,296	138,165	191,987	30,203	27,299	16,555	4,584,066
Mexico	640,294	975,657	2,756,513	2,249,421	204,844	217,318	114,984	6,848,960
Caribbean	741,126	759,416	1,023,237	978,787	96,958	94,240	67,660	4,022,715
Cuba	264,863	135,142	170,675	169,322	26,073	27,520	8,722	995,732
Dominican Republic	148,135	209,899	365,598	335,251	21,256	22,474	26,157	945,323
Haiti	56,335	118,510	179,725	179,644	22,535	19,189	11,942	481,569
Jamaica	137,577	184,481	182,552	169,227	15,099	14,567	13,082	655,040
Other Caribbean	134,216	111,384	124,687	125,343	11,995	10,490	7,757	945,051
Central America	134,640	321,845	611,597	526,915	73,063	66,520	53,435	1,599,860
El Salvador	34,436	133,938	274,989	215,798	31,054	30,539	27,915	609,258
Other Central America	100,204	187,907	336,608	311,117	42,009	35,981	25,520	990,602
South America	295,741	375,026	569,650	539,656	68,279	73,400	54,155	2,054,956
Argentina	29,897	21,374	27,431	26,644	3,459	3,811	3,217	172,921
Colombia	77,347	99,066	140,685	128,499	16,333	18,488	14,455	491,015
Ecuador	50,077	43,841	81,204	76,592	9,694	10,564	7,040	268,008
Other South America	138,420	210,745	320,330	307,921	38,793	40,537	29,443	1,123,012
Other America	995	458	595	40	4	3	4	110,189
Unknown or not reported	N/A	N/A	2,486	42,418	18,106	17,761	9,410	379,746

Source: U.S. Immigration and Naturalization Service, 2006.

[1]Data for years prior to 1906 relate to country whence alien came; data from 1906–79 and 1984–89 are for country of last permanent residence; and data for 1980–99 refer to country of birth. Because of changes in boundaries, changes in lists of countries, and lack of data for specified countries for various periods, data for certain countries, especially for the total period 1820–2004, are not comparable throughout. Data for specified countries are included with countries to which they belonged prior to World War I.

[2]Data for Austria and Hungary not reported until 1861.

[3]Data for Austria and Hungary not reported separately for all years during the period.

[4]No data available for Czechoslovakia until 1920.

[5]Prior to 1926, data for Northern Ireland included in Ireland.

[6]Data for Norway and Sweden not reported separately until 1871.

[7]No data available for Romania until 1880.

[8]Since 1925, data for United Kingdom refer to England, Scotland, Wales, and Northern Ireland.

[9]In 1920, a separate enumeration was made for the Kingdom of Serbs, Croats, and Slovenes. Since 1922, the Serb, Croat, and Slovene Kingdom recorded as Yugoslavia.

[10]Beginning in 1957, China includes Taiwan.

[11]Data not reported separately until 1952.

[12]Data not reported separately until 1925.

[13]Data not reported separately until 1949.

[14]No data available for Japan until 1861.

[15]Data not reported separately until 1948.

[16]Prior to 1934, Philippines recorded as insular travel.

[17]Prior to 1920, Canada and Newfoundland recorded as British North America. From 1820 to 1898, figures include all British North America possessions.

[18]Land arrivals not completely enumerated until 1908.

[19]No data available for Mexico from 1886 to 1893.

[20]Data not reported separately until 1932.

[21]Data for Jamaica not collected until 1953. In prior years, consolidated under British West Indies, which is included in "Other Caribbean."

[22]Included in countries "Not specified" until 1925.

[23]From 1899 to 1919, data for Poland included in Austria-Hungary, Germany, and the Soviet Union.

[24]From 1938 to 1945, data for Austria included in Germany.

[25]Includes 32,897 persons returning in 1906 to their homes in the United States.

[26]Data for fiscal year 1998 have been revised due to changes in the count for asylees and cancellation of removal. The previously reported total was 660,477.

[27]Prior to 1993, data include independent republics; beginning in 1993, data are for unknown republic only.

[28]Prior to 1992, data include independent republic; beginning in 1992, data are for Yugoslavia only.

[29]Prior to 1992, data include previously independent republics only; beginning in 1992, data are for all former republics except Russia.

— represents zero.

NOTE: From 1820 to 1867, figures represent alien passengers arrived at seaports; from 1868 to 1891 and 1895 to 1897, immigrant aliens arrived; from 1892 to 1894 and 1898 to 1989, immigrant aliens admitted for permanent residence. From 1892 to 1903, aliens entering by cabin class were not counted as immigrants. Land arrivals were not completely enumerated until 1908. For this table, fiscal year 1843 covers 9 months ending September 1843; fiscal years 1832 and 1850 cover 15 months ending December 31 of the respective years; and fiscal year 1868 covers 6 months ending June 30, 1868.

PRESIDENTS, VICE-PRESIDENTS, AND SECRETARIES OF STATE

	President	*Vice-President*	*Secretary of State*
1.	George Washington, Federalist 1789	John Adams, Federalist 1789	Thomas Jefferson 1789 Edmund Randolph 1794 Timothy Pickering 1795
2.	John Adams, Federalist 1797	Thomas Jefferson, Dem.-Rep. 1797	Timothy Pickering 1797 John Marshall 1800
3.	Thomas Jefferson, Dem.-Rep. 1801	Aaron Burr, Dem.-Rep. 1801 George Clinton, Dem.-Rep. 1805	James Madison 1801
4.	James Madison, Dem.-Rep. 1809	George Clinton, Dem.-Rep. 1809 Elbridge Gerry, Dem.-Rep. 1813	Robert Smith 1809 James Monroe 1811
5.	James Monroe, Dem.-Rep. 1817	Daniel D. Tompkins, Dem.-Rep. 1817	John Q. Adams 1817
6.	John Quincy Adams, Dem.-Rep. 1825	John C. Calhoun, Dem.-Rep. 1825	Henry Clay 1825
7.	Andrew Jackson, Democratic 1829	John C. Calhoun, Democratic 1829 Martin Van Buren, Democratic 1833	Martin Van Buren 1829 Edward Livingston 1831 Louis McLane 1833 John Forsyth 1834
8.	Martin Van Buren, Democratic 1837	Richard M. Johnson, Democratic 1837	John Forsyth 1837
9.	William H. Harrison, Whig 1841	John Tyler, Whig 1841	Daniel Webster 1841

President	Vice-President	Secretary of State
10. John Tyler, Whig and Democratic 1841	None	Daniel Webster 1841 Hugh S. Legaré 1843 Abel P. Upshur 1843 John C. Calhoun 1844
11. James K. Polk, Democratic 1845	George M. Dallas, Democratic 1845	James Buchanan 1845
12. Zachary Taylor, Whig 1849	Millard Fillmore, Whig 1848	John M. Clayton 1849
13. Millard Fillmore, Whig 1850	None	Daniel Webster 1850 Edward Everett 1852
14. Franklin Pierce, Democratic 1853	William R. King, Democratic 1853	William L. Marcy 1853
15. James Buchanan, Democratic 1857	John C. Breckinridge, Democratic 1857	Lewis Cass 1857 Jeremiah S. Black 1860
16. Abraham Lincoln, Republican 1861	Hannibal Hamlin, Republican 1861 Andrew Johnson, Unionist 1865	William H. Seward 1861
17. Andrew Johnson, Unionist 1865	None	William H. Seward 1865
18. Ulysses S. Grant, Republican 1869	Schuyler Colfax, Republican 1869 Henry Wilson, Republican 1873	Elihu B. Washburne 1869 Hamilton Fish 1869
19. Rutherford B. Hayes, Republican 1877	William A. Wheeler, Republican 1877	William M. Evarts 1877

	President	Vice-President	Secretary of State
20.	James A. Garfield, Republican 1881	Chester A. Arthur, Republican 1881	James G. Blaine 1881
21.	Chester A. Arthur, Republican 1881	None	Frederick T. Frelinghuysen 1881
22.	Grover Cleveland, Democratic 1885	Thomas A. Hendricks, Democratic 1885	Thomas F. Bayard 1885
23.	Benjamin Harrison, Republican 1889	Levi P. Morton, Republican 1889	James G. Blaine 1889 John W. Foster 1892
24.	Grover Cleveland, Democratic 1893	Adlai E. Stevenson, Democratic 1893	Walter Q. Gresham 1893 Richard Olney 1895
25.	William McKinley, Republican 1897	Garret A. Hobart, Republican 1897 Theodore Roosevelt, Republican 1901	John Sherman 1897 William R. Day 1898 John Hay 1898
26.	Theodore Roosevelt, Republican 1901	Charles Fairbanks, Republican 1905	John Hay 1901 Elihu Root 1905 Robert Bacon 1909
27.	William H. Taft, Republican 1909	James S. Sherman, Republican 1909	Philander C. Knox 1909
28.	Woodrow Wilson, Democratic 1913	Thomas R. Marshall, Democratic 1913	William J. Bryan 1913 Robert Lansing 1915 Bainbridge Colby 1920
29.	Warren G. Harding, Republican 1921	Calvin Coolidge, Republican 1921	Charles E. Hughes 1921
30.	Calvin Coolidge, Republican 1923	Charles G. Dawes, Republican 1925	Charles E. Hughes 1923 Frank B. Kellogg 1925

	President	Vice-President	Secretary of State
31.	Herbert Hoover, Republican 1929	Charles Curtis, Republican 1929	Henry L. Stimson 1929
32.	Franklin D. Roosevelt, Democratic 1933	John Nance Garner, Democratic 1933 Henry A. Wallace, Democratic 1941 Harry S. Truman, Democratic 1945	Cordell Hull 1933 Edward R. Stettinius, Jr. 1944
33.	Harry S. Truman, Democratic 1945	Alben W. Barkley, Democratic 1949	Edward R. Stettinius, Jr. 1945 James F. Byrnes 1945 George C. Marshall 1947 Dean G. Acheson 1949
34.	Dwight D. Eisenhower, Republican 1953	Richard M. Nixon, Republican 1953	John F. Dulles 1953 Christian A. Herter 1959
35.	John F. Kennedy, Democratic 1961	Lyndon B. Johnson, Democratic 1961	Dean Rusk 1961
36.	Lyndon B. Johnson, Democratic 1963	Hubert H. Humphrey, Democratic 1965	Dean Rusk 1963
37.	Richard M. Nixon, Republican 1969	Spiro T. Agnew, Republican 1969 Gerald R. Ford, Republican 1973	William P. Rogers 1969 Henry Kissinger 1973
38.	Gerald R. Ford, Republican 1974	Nelson Rockefeller, Republican 1974	Henry Kissinger 1974
39.	Jimmy Carter, Democratic 1977	Walter Mondale, Democratic 1977	Cyrus Vance 1977 Edmund Muskie 1980

	President	Vice-President	Secretary of State
40.	Ronald Reagan, Republican 1981	George H. W. Bush, Republican 1981	Alexander Haig 1981 George Schultz 1982
41.	George H. W. Bush, Republican 1989	J. Danforth Quayle, Republican 1989	James A. Baker 1989 Lawrence Eagleburger 1992
42.	William J. Clinton, Democrat 1993	Albert Gore, Jr., Democrat 1993	Warren Christopher 1993 Madeleine Albright 1997
43.	George W. Bush, Republican 2001	Richard B. Cheney, Republican 2001	Colin L. Powell 2001 Condoleezza Rice 2005

CREDITS

PART 1: p. 1, Giraudon/Art Resource, NY; **p. 3,** The Granger Collection.

CHAPTER 1: p. 5, Bettmann/Corbis; **p. 9,** Bettmann/Corbis; **p. 11** (*top*) Daniel S. Glover/University of Missouri Museum of Anthropology and (*bottom*) Bettmann/Corbis; **p. 16,** Bettmann/Corbis; **p. 19,** Bridgeman Art Library; **p. 20,** The Granger Collection; **p. 21,** The Granger Collection; **p. 25,** The Benson Latin American Collection, the University of Texas; **p. 32,** The Royal Library of Copenhagen; **p. 34,** Werner Forman/Art Resource, NY; **p. 37,** Bettmann/Corbis; **p. 41,** Bettmann/Corbis; **p. 42,** Bettmann/Corbis.

CHAPTER 2: p. 45, The Granger Collection; **p. 48,** (*left*) Bettmann/Corbis and (*right*) Bettmann/Corbis; **p. 51,** Bridgeman Art Library; **p. 54,** The Granger Collection; **p. 56,** Bettmann/Corbis; **p. 63,** The Granger Collection; **p. 65,** The Granger Collection; **p. 69,** The Granger Collection; **p. 75,** The Granger Collection; **p. 80,** Bettmann/Corbis; **p. 81,** South Caroliniana Library; **p. 82,** The Royal Library of Copenhagen; **p. 85,** Bettmann/Corbis; **p. 86,** Library of Congress; **p. 89,** Bettmann/Corbis; **p. 91,** The Granger Collection.

CHAPTER 3: p. 98, The Granger Collection; **p. 100,** The Granger Collection; **p. 103** (*left*) Worcester Art Museum, Worcester, MA, Sarah C. Garver Fund and (*right*) Bettmann/Corbis; **p. 106,** Connecticut Historical Society Museum; **p. 108,** The Granger Collection; **p. 110,** The Swem Library, the College of William & Mary; **p. 111,** The Granger Collection; **p. 114,** Abby Aldrich Rockefeller Folk Art Center, Colonial Williamsburg; **p. 116,** Courtesy of the Maryland Historical Society; **p. 117,** Library of Congress; **p. 119,** North Wind Picture Archive; **p. 120,** The Granger Collection; **p. 127,** Photograph Courtesy Peabody Essex Museum; **p. 129,** The Granger Collection; **p. 135,** Collection of the New-York Historical Society; **p. 137,** The Library Company of Philadelphia; **p. 139,** The Granger Collection; **p. 140,** The Granger Collection; **p. 142,** National Portrait Gallery, London.

CHAPTER 4: p. 147, The Granger Collection; **p. 150,** I.N. Phelps Stokes Collection, Miriam and Ira D. Wallach Division of Art, Prints and Photographs, New York Public

Library, Astor, Lenox and Tilden Foundations; **p. 151**, The Granger Collection; **p. 155**, The Granger Collection; **p. 158**, Snark/Art Resource, NY; **p. 161**, Emmet Collection, Miriam and Ira D. Wallach Division of Art, Prints and Photographs, New York Public Library, Astor, Lenox and Tilden Foundations; **p. 162**, Collection of the New-York Historical Society; **p. 165**, Library of Congress; **p. 169**, Library and Archives Canada.

CHAPTER 5: **p. 174**, Library of Congress; **p. 176**, The Granger Collection; **p. 178**, Library of Congress; **p. 182**, Library of Congress; **p. 183**, Library of Congress; **p. 186**, Library of Congress; **p. 187**, Library of Congress; **p. 190**, Library of Congress; **p. 192**, Library of Congress; **p. 197**, The Granger Collection; **p. 199**, Library of Congress; **p. 203**, American Antiquarian Society.

PART 2: **p. 209**, Art Resource, NY; **p. 210**, Library of Congress.

CHAPTER 6: **p. 213**, Giraudon/Art Resource, NY; **p. 217**, U.S. Senate Collection; **p. 220**, Anne S.K. Brown Military Collection, Brown University Library; **p. 223**, The Granger Collection; **p. 228**, The Granger Collection; **p. 234**, Library of Congress; **p. 235**, The Granger Collection; **p. 240**, Courtesy of the Maryland Historical Society; **p. 242**, The Granger Collection; **p. 244**, Library of Congress; **p. 245**, The Granger Collection.

CHAPTER 7: **p. 249**, Bettmann/Corbis; **p. 257**, The Library Company of Philadelphia; **p. 260**, The Historical Society of Pennsylvania; **p. 263**, Library of Congress; **p. 264**, Library of Congress; **p. 267**, Library of Congress; **p. 270**, Independence National Historical Park; **p. 276**, Library of Congress.

CHAPTER 8: **p. 279**, Art Resource, NY; **p. 280**, Library of Congress; **p. 283**, The Granger Collection; **p. 286**, Independence National Historical Park; **p. 289**, Courtesy of the Maryland Historical Society; **p. 292**, The Historical Society of Pennsylvania; **p. 294**, The Granger Collection; **p. 298**, Courtesy of the Burton Historical Collection; **p. 302**, The Granger Collection; **p. 305**, Art Resource, NY; **p. 306**, The Granger Collection; **p. 307**, The Metropolitan Museum of Art, Bequest of William Nelson, 1905 (05.35), Photograph ©1986 The Metropolitan Museum of Art; **p. 309**, The Granger Collection; **p. 310**, The Granger Collection; **p. 314**, Library of Congress.

CHAPTER 9: **p. 320**, Giraudon/Art Resource, NY; **p. 323**, Library of Congress; **p. 324**, Miriam and Ira D. Wallach Division of Art, Prints and Photographs, New York Public Library, Astor, Lenox and Tilden Foundations; **p. 327**, Cincinnati Museum Center – Cincinnati Historical Society Library; **p. 331**, Library of Congress; **p. 334**, From the Collections of the New Jersey Historical Society, Newark, NJ; **p. 336**, Library of Congress; **p. 337**, Collection of the New-York Historical Society; **p. 339**, Library of Congress; **p. 342**, Collection of the New-York Historical Society; **p. 347**, Library of Congress; **p. 350**, Collection of Davenport West, Jr.

p. 544, Bridgeman Art Library/The Atwater Kent Museum; **p. 545,** The Charleston Museum; **p. 548,** ©2006 Harvard University, Peabody Museum Photo 35-5-10/53044 T1874; **p. 549,** National Archives; **p. 553,** Library of Congress; **p. 557,** The Granger Collection; **p. 560,** (*left*) The Granger Collection and (*right*) Collection of the New-York Historical Society.

CHAPTER 16: **p. 565,** The Granger Collection; **p. 569,** The Long Island Museum of American Art, History & Carriages, Stony Brook, N.Y., Gift of Mr. and Mrs. Ward Melville, 1955; **p. 570,** The Granger Collection; **p. 575,** The Granger Collection; **p. 578,** Library of Congress; **p. 579,** The Granger Collection; **p. 581,** (*top*) Library of Congress and (*bottom*) The Granger Collection; **p. 586,** GLC 5116.19. Map: The Border Ruffian Code in Kansas, 1856. The Gilder Leherman Collection, courtesy of The Gilder Lehrman Institute of American History. Not to be reproduced without written permission; **p. 587,** Library of Congress; **p. 588,** The New York Public Library; **p. 592,** Library of Congress; **p. 597,** Library of Congress; **p. 600,** Library of Congress; **p. 601,** The Granger Collection; **p. 604,** The Granger Collection.

CHAPTER 17: **p. 607,** Library of Congress; **p. 612,** Bettmann/Corbis; **p. 613,** Bettmann/Corbis; **p. 617,** Bettmann/Corbis; **p. 623,** Bettmann/Corbis; **p. 627,** Bettmann/Corbis; **p. 629,** Library of Congress; **p. 631,** (*top*) Library of Congress and (*bottom*) Library of Congress; **p. 632,** Bettmann/Corbis; **p. 633,** Bettmann/Corbis; **p. 634,** Library of Congress; **p. 638,** Library of Congress; **p. 639,** National Archives; **p. 644,** Library of Congress; **p. 646,** Bettmann/Corbis; **p. 647,** Bettmann/Corbis; **p. 648,** Massachusetts Commandery Military Order of the Loyal Legion and the U.S. Army Military History Institute; **p. 650,** Bettmann/Corbis; **p. 651,** Library of Congress; **p. 655,** Library of Congress.

CHAPTER 18: **p. 659,** Library of Congress; **p. 661,** Library of Congress; **p. 663,** Library of Congress; **p. 664,** Library of Congress; **p. 667,** Bettmann/Corbis; **p. 668,** Library of Congress; **p. 670,** Library of Congress; **p. 671,** Library of Congress; **p. 672,** Library of Congress; **p. 677,** National Archives; **p. 680,** The Granger Collection; **p. 682,** Bettmann/Corbis; **p. 683,** Library of Congress; **p. 686,** Library of Congress; **p. 689,** Library of Congress; **p. 692,** Library of Congress.

PART 5: **p. 701,** The Granger Collection; **p. 702,** The Granger Collection.

CHAPTER 19: **p. 705,** Library of Congress; **p. 707,** Special Collections, Duke University; **p. 710,** The Granger Collection; **p. 713,** The Granger Collection; **p. 716,** Warder Collection; **p. 718,** Special Collections, University of Chicago Library; **p. 719,** Library of Congress; **p. 720,** Warder Collection; **p. 723,** Kansas State Historical Society; **p. 724,** Bettmann/Corbis; **p. 725,** Library of Congress; **p. 730,** Warder Collection; **p. 732,** Smithsonian Institution; **p. 735,** Bettmann/Corbis; **p. 736,** National Archives; **p. 740,** Western Historical Collections, University of Oklahoma Library.

CHAPTER 20: p. 743, Library of Congress; **p. 745,** Alfred Stieglitz, *The Hand of Man,* 1902, photogravure, P.1978.112, Amon Carter Museum; **p. 748,** Union Pacific Museum; **p. 750,** Collection of the New-York Historical Society; **p. 751,** National Archives; **p. 752,** The Granger Collection; **p. 753,** Warder Collection; **p. 754,** American Petroleum Institute Historical Photo Collection; **p. 756,** Carnegie Library of Pittsburgh; **p. 757,** Keystone-Mast Collection [WX13101], UCR/California Museum of Photography, University of California, Riverside; **p. 758,** Pierpont Morgan Library; **p. 759,** Carnegie Library of Pittsburgh; **p. 760,** The Granger Collection; **p. 762,** Bettmann/Corbis; **p. 766,** T.V. Powderly Photographic Collection, The American Catholic History Research Center and University Archives, The Catholic University of America, Washington, D.C.; **p. 768,** Bettmann/Corbis; **p. 769,** Bettmann/Corbis; **p. 771,** Library of Congress; **p. 773,** Bettmann/Corbis; **p. 774,** Walter P. Reuther Library, Wayne State University.

CHAPTER 21: p. 779, Library of Congress; **p. 783,** Culver Pictures; **p. 786,** Bettmann/Corbis; **p. 788,** The Byron Collection, Museum of the City of New York; **p. 789,** William Williams Papers, Manuscripts and Archives Division, The New York Public Library, Astor, Lenox and Tilden Foundations; **p. 791,** Library of Congress; **p. 792,** The Denver Public Library, Western History Collection; **p. 795,** The Granger Collection; **p. 797,** Brown Brothers; **p. 798,** Old York Library; **p. 800,** Library of Congress; **p. 802,** Bettmann/Corbis; **p. 803,** Special Collections, Vassar College Libraries; **p. 805,** American Museum of Natural History; **p. 806,** John Carter Brown Library; **p. 807,** National Library of Medicine; **p. 808,** Time Life Pictures; **p. 811,** The Salvation Army National Archives; **p. 812,** University of Illinois at Chicago; **p. 814,** The Granger Collection.

CHAPTER 22: p. 819, Library of Congress; **p. 823,** Library of Congress; **p. 827,** Bettmann/Corbis; **p. 829,** Warder Collection; **p. 830,** Warder Collection; **p. 833,** Bettmann/Corbis; **p. 835,** Warder Collection; **p. 839,** Library of Congress; **p. 843,** Wooten Studios; **p. 844,** Kansas State Historical Society; **p. 845,** Nebraska State Historical Society; **p. 850,** Library of Congress;

PART 6: p. 855, Library of Congress; **p. 857,** Library of Congress.

CHAPTER 23: p. 859, Bettmann/Corbis; **p. 863,** Bettmann/Corbis; **p. 864,** Hawaii State Archives; **p. 866,** Brown Brothers; **p. 867,** Library of Congress; **p. 874,** National Archives; **p. 876,** Library of Congress; **p. 880,** Bettmann/Corbis; **p. 882,** The New York Times; **p. 884,** Bettmann/Corbis; **p. 886,** Bettmann/Corbis.

CHAPTER 24: p. 890, Library of Congress; **p. 894,** Valdis Kupris; **p. 895,** Library of Congress; **p. 896,** Bettmann/Corbis; **p. 900** (*top*) Collection of the New-York Historical Society and (*bottom*) Library of Congress; **p. 902,** Bettmann/Corbis; **p. 904,** Library of Congress; **p. 906,** Bettmann/Corbis; **p. 907,** Bettmann/Corbis; **p. 911,** Library of Congress; **p. 915,** Library of Congress; **p. 917,** Warder Collection; **p. 923,** Warder Collection.

CHAPTER 25: p. 930, Library of Congress; p. 933, Bettmann/Corbis; p. 936, Warder Collection; p. 939, The New York Times; p. 940, Rollin Kirby; p. 942, Bettmann/Corbis; p. 945, Bettmann/Corbis; p. 947, Bettmann/Corbis; p. 950, National Archives; p. 951, Bettmann/Corbis; p. 953, National Archives; p. 955, Warder Collection; p. 957, Mary Evans Picture Library; p. 958, Courtesy of the "Ding" Darling Wildlife Society; p. 963, Bettmann/Corbis; p. 964, Chicago History Museum.

CHAPTER 26: p. 968, Bettmann/Corbis; p. 970, Digital Image © The Museum of Modern Art/Licensed by SCALA / Art Resource, NY; Art © Estate of Ben Shahn / Licensed by VAGA, New York, NY; p. 971, Bettmann/Corbis; p. 973, Bettmann/Corbis; p. 975, Bettmann/Corbis; p. 976, Ramsey Archive; p. 978, Bettmann/Corbis; p. 979, Bettmann/Corbis; p. 980, Bettmann/Corbis; p. 981, University of Chicago; p. 982, AP/Wide World Photos; p. 984, Warder Collection; p. 986, The Metropolitan Museum of Art, Bequest of Gertrude Stein, 1946 (47.106) Photograph © 1996 The Metropolitan Museum of Art; p. 987, Brown Brothers; p. 988, Brown Brothers.

CHAPTER 27: p. 991, Bettmann/Corbis; p. 996, © The Washington Post. Reprinted with permission; p. 998, Hulton Archive; p. 1000, Bettmann/Corbis; p. 1001, Bettmann/Corbis; p. 1002, Library of Congress; p. 1004, From the Collections of The Henry Ford Museum; p. 1006, Bettmann/Corbis; p. 1009, Bettmann/Corbis; p. 1012, Herbert Hoover Presidential Library; p. 1014, AP/Wide World Photos; p. 1017, Bettmann/Corbis; p. 1019, New York Daily News, DailyNewsPix.

CHAPTER 28: p. 1022, Bettmann/Corbis; p. 1025, AP/Wide World Photos; p. 1029, National Archives; p. 1030, Bettmann/Corbis; p. 1032, Bettmann/Corbis; p. 1035, Library of Congress; p. 1036, Bettmann/Corbis; p. 1040, National Archives; p. 1042, Bettmann/Corbis; p. 1045, Bettmann/Corbis; p. 1046, Hulton Archive; p. 1047, Bettmann/Corbis; p. 1050, Library of Congress; p. 1054, © 1936, The Washington Post. Reprinted with permission; p. 1056, Bettmann/Corbis.

CHAPTER 29: p. 1063, Bettmann/Corbis; p. 1066, AP/Wide World Photos; p. 1068, Bettmann/Corbis; p. 1070, The Granger Collection; p. 1072, National Archives; p. 1076, © 1938, The Washington Post. Reprinted with permission; p. 1077, Imperial War Museum, London; p. 1079, British Information Services; p. 1083, Bettmann/Corbis; p. 1088, Library of Congress.

CHAPTER 30: p. 1091, Bettmann/Corbis; p. 1092, Warder Collection; p. 1097, The Granger Collection; p. 1098, Library of Congress; p. 1099, AP/Wide World Photos; p. 1102, Russell Lee/Getty Images; p. 1108, AP/Wide World Photos; p. 1109, Copyright 1945 by Bill Mauldin. Reprinted courtesy of the William Mauldin Estate; p. 1111, Eisenhower Presidential Library; p. 1112, National Archives; p. 1115, National Archives; p. 1120, Hulton Archive; p. 1121, National Archives; p. 1124, National Archives; p. 1125, National Archives; p. 1128, Hulton Archive.

PART 7: **p. 1133,** Bill Eppridge/Getty Images; **p. 1135,** Bettmann/Corbis.

CHAPTER 31: **p. 1137,** Bettmann/Corbis; **p. 1139,** University of Louisville; **p. 1142,** Collections of the New York Public Library, Astor, Lenox and Tilden Foundations; **p. 1145,** Bettmann/Corbis; **p. 1147,** Herman Landshoff; **p. 1150,** Library of Congress; **p. 1152,** Hartford Courant; **p. 1154,** Hy Peskin/Getty Images; **p. 1155,** ©1948, The Washington Post. Reprinted with permission; **p. 1156,** Bettmann/Corbis; **p. 1157,** AP/Wide World Photos; **p. 1158,** Bettmann/Corbis; **p. 1164,** Bettmann/Corbis; **p. 1166,** Bettmann/Corbis; **p. 1167,** Yale Joel/Getty Images.

CHAPTER 32: **p. 1171,** Hulton Archive; **p. 1174,** AP/Wide World Photos; **p. 1176,** New York Public Library; **p. 1177,** Hulton Archive; **p. 1180,** The Metropolitan Museum of Art, George A. Hearn Fund, 1953 (53.183) Photograph ©1989 The Metropolitan Museum of Art; **p. 1181,** Fogg Art Museum, Harvard University; **p. 1183,** PNI/Archive Photos; **p. 1185,** Bettmann/Corbis; **p. 1187,** Culver Pictures; **p. 1188,** The New York Times; **p. 1189,** AP/Wide World Photos; **p. 1191,** Hulton Archive; **p. 1192,** AP/Wide World Photos.

CHAPTER 33: **p. 1195,** Bettmann/Corbis; **p. 1198,** Library of Congress; **p. 1201,** Bettmann/Corbis; **p. 1204,** "Don't Be Afraid—I Can Always Pull You Back," from *Herblock's Special for Today* (Simon & Schuster, 1958); **p. 1205,** Photoworld; **p. 1212,** Bettmann/Corbis; **p. 1214,** Detroit News; **p. 1216,** AP/Wide World Photos; **p. 1217,** AP/Wide World Photos; **p. 1219,** University of Louisville; **p. 1221,** Black Star/Stock Photo.

CHAPTER 34: **p. 1226,** Bettmann/Corbis; **p. 1229,** National Archives; **p. 1233,** National Archives; **p. 1235,** National Archives; **p. 1237,** Hulton Archive; **p. 1239,** Bettmann/Corbis; **p. 1240,** National Archives; **p. 1242,** Hulton Archive; **p. 1244,** National Archives; **p. 1245,** Time & Life Pictures; **p. 1248,** The New Statesman; **p. 1253,** National Archives; **p. 1254,** Newark Star-Ledger; **p. 1258,** Bettmann/Corbis; **p. 1259,** Jack Kightlinger, Lyndon Baines Johnson Library and Museum; **p. 1261,** Bettmann/Corbis.

CHAPTER 35: **p. 1266,** Bettmann/Corbis; **p. 1270,** AP/Wide World Photos; **p. 1271,** Magnum Photos; **p. 1273,** John Dominis/Getty Images; **p. 1274,** Warder Collection; **p. 1275,** Bettmann/Corbis; **p. 1277,** H. William Tetlow/Getty Images; **p. 1279,** AP/Wide World Photos; **p. 1281,** Bettmann/Corbis; **p. 1284,** National Archives; **p. 1286,** Valley News Dispatch; **p. 1288,** Bettmann/Corbis; **p. 1291,** Bettmann/Corbis; **p. 1294,** AP/Wide World Photos; **p. 1295,** NASA Kennedy Space Center; **p. 1297,** John Dominis/Getty Images; **p. 1302,** AP/Wide World Photos; **p. 1306,** White House; **p. 1308,** AP/Wide World Photos; **p. 1310,** Bettmann/Corbis.

CHAPTER 36: **p. 1313,** Bettmann/Corbis; **p. 1315,** Bettmann/Corbis; **p. 1319,** Bettmann/Corbis; **p. 1322,** Los Angeles Times Syndicate; **p. 1327,** Bettmann/Corbis; **p. 1329,** Black Star/Stock Photo; **p. 1330,** AP/Wide World Photos; **p. 1332,** Black

Star/Stock Photo; **p. 1335,** Woodfin Camp; **p. 1336,** AP/Wide World Photos; **p. 1339,** Bettmann/Corbis.

 CHAPTER 37: p. 1342, Bettmann/Corbis; **p. 1345,** AP/Wide World Photos; **p. 1346,** Library of Congress; **p. 1353,** Chris Wilkins/Getty Images; **p. 1356,** AP/Wide World Photos; **p. 1359,** AP/Wide World Photos; **p. 1363,** Hartford Courant; **p. 1364,** AP/Wide World Photos; **p. 1366,** AP/Wide World Photos; **p. 1371,** Bettmann/Corbis; **p. 1375,** Bettmann/Corbis; **p. 1378,** Bettmann/Corbis; **p. 1379,** Bettmann/Corbis; **p. 1381,** Bettmann/Corbis; **p. 1384,** Bettmann/Corbis; **p. 1388,** Bettmann/Corbis.

INDEX

Page numbers in *italics* refer to illustrations.

AAA, *see* Agricultural Adjustment Act
Abenakis, 73, 74, *93*
abolition movement, 487, 528–29, 556–62
  African Americans in, 559–60
  African colonization proposed in, 556
  free press and, 561
  Fugitive Slave Act and, 577–78, 585
  Polk on, 513
  radicalization of, 556–58
  reactions to, 560–62
  split in, 558–59
  women in, 483, 558–59
abortion issue, 978, 1275, 1276, 1315, 1316,
    1321, 1348, 1371, 1383
Abraham Lincoln, U.S.S., 1382
Abrams v. United States, 950
abstract expressionism, 1188, 1189
Abu Ghraib, *1381*
Acadia, 158, 166
  see also Nova Scotia
Acheson, Dean, 1165
Acomas, 494
acquired immune deficiency syndrome
    (AIDS), 1328–29, *1329*
Act for the Impartial Administration of
    Justice (1774), 191–92
Act of Settlement (1701), 50
Act of Union (1707), 50
Act to Prevent Frauds and Abuses (1696),
    153
ADA (Americans for Democratic Action),
    1154
Adams, Abigail, 243–44, 246, 313
  on Shays's Rebellion, 261–62
Adams, John, 236, 246, 247, 264, *309,* 320,
    336, 856
  Alien and Sedition Acts signed by, 313

  in Boston Massacre case, 187
  committee work of, 250
  and Declaration of Independence, 203,
    204
  description of, 308–9
  domestic discontent and, 312–14
  in election of 1789, 282
  in election of 1796, 308
  in election of 1800, 315–18, *317*
  foreign policy under, 309–12
  French conflict and, 309–10, 311
  Jefferson's split with, 312–13
  lame-duck appointments of, 316–17, 325
  on peace commission, 234, *235,* 283
  political philosophy of, 309
  Revolution and, 191, 221, 234, 236, 243–44
  as vice-president, 282, 283
  on women's rights, 244
Adams, John Quincy, 249, 332, 348, 363,
    366–67, *379,* 407, 513
  abolitionism and, 561
  as congressman, 394
  in election of 1824, 376, 377, 378, *378*
  in election of 1828, 380–84, *383,*
    446
  Indian lands and, 399
  on Mexican War, 517
  Monroe Doctrine and, 374–75
  named secretary of state, 363
  Oregon Country issue and, 374
  presidency of, 379–80
  Transcontinental Treaty and, 367, 374
  on Tyler, 490
Adams, Samuel, *186, 198*
  and Boston Tea Party, 191
  in Committee of Correspondence, 190
  in ratification debate, 273, 274

as revolutionary agitator, 185–86, *186*, 188, 190
warned by Paul Revere, 196
Adamson Act (1916), 927
Adarand Constructors v. Peña, 1361
Addams, Jane, 812–13, *812*, 876
Adena-Hopewell culture, 9–10
Adenauer, Konrad, 1151
Administrative Reorganization Act (1939), 1060
Admiralty courts, vice-admiralty courts, 153, 178–79, 180, 184, 188
Adventures of Huckleberry Finn, The (Twain), 808
Adventures of Tom Sawyer, The (Twain), 808
advertising, 1175, *1176*
affirmative action, 1275, 1348, 1350, 1357, 1361–62
Affluent Society, The (Galbraith), 1184–85
Afghanistan, 1135, 1309, 1323, 1330, 1335, 1374, 1376, 1377, *1378*, 1383
AFL (American Federation of Labor), 768–69, 775–76, 964, 999, 1008, 1055–56
AFL-CIO (American Federation of Labor-Congress of Industrial Organizations), 1175, 1299, 1321, 1324
Africa:
agriculture in, 112
European exploration of, 14, 15
imperialism in, 860
slaves in return to, 556
African Americans, *133,* 1344
in abolition movement, 559–60
accommodationist policy and, 720–21
African roots of, 111–12, 551–52
in agriculture, 680, 1041, 1178–79
in antebellum southern society, 112–16, *114,* 543–44
in baseball, 800
Black Code restrictions on, 669–70, 672
black power and, 1251–54, 1269
in Boston Massacre, 187
and B. T. Washington's vs. Du Bois's views, 720–21
in Carter administration, 1306
citizenship of, 268, 673
Civil War attacks on, 618
as Civil War soldiers, 632–33, *632, 633,* 679
in Congress, 684
as conservatives, 1348
constitutional rights lacked by, 266–67, 268, 284
as cowboys, 734
crime and, 1344
dance and, 552

in Democratic Party, 713, 1043, 1059
desegregation and, 1154, *1155,* 1218–23, 1232–37
disenfranchisement of, in South, 714–16, 820, 927, 1042
in early twentieth century, 981–83
in early U.S., 281
education of, 680–81, 685, 712, 714, 720, 1173
in election of 1948, *1156,* 1158
in election of 1960, 1229–30
in election of 1976, 1305
in election of 1984, 1325
in election of 1988, 1333
as entrepreneurs, 718
as "Exodusters," 722–23
first, 57
folklore of, 551–52
free blacks, 321, 544–45, *545*
gerrymandered districts and, 1361
Great Migration of, 946–47, 981–82, *981,* 1178–79
Hurricane Katrina and, 1387
as indentured servants, 110
Irish Americans' animosity toward, 445
as journalists, 719
labor movement and, 1009–10
land policy and, 662–64, 682
literature and, 808, 1188
lynchings of, 717, 719, 983, 995, 1153
marriage of, 115, 553–54, 669, 680
in military, 723–24, 1099
minstrel shows and, 442–43, *443*
mulattoes, 544–45
music and, 114, *114,* 552, 1191–92
Negro nationalism and, 982–83, *982*
in New Deal programs, 1041, 1042–43
population of, 113, 281
in post-Civil War South, 712–13
post-World War II economy and, 1175
pride and, 718
in Reconstruction, 662–64, 669–70, 679–84, *683*
as Reconstruction politicians, 678–79, 681–84, *683*
religion of, 114–15, 462, 533, 552–53, 679–80, 717–18
in Republican Party, 821, 1043
as Revolutionary War soldiers, 201, 239, 241–42, 321
segregation and, 716–21, 1041, 1099–1100, 1218–23, 1232–37
separatist, 1253
single mothers and, 1344
Underground Railroad and, 559

African Americans (*continued*)
  violence against, 717, 719, 723, 983, 995,
    1153
  voting rights for, 370, 669, 671, 674, 678,
    681, *682,* 684, 686, 690
  in West, 722–24
  women and, 718–19
  in World War I, 946–47
  in World War II, 1097, 1099–1100
  see also civil rights and liberties; civil
    rights movement; race riots;
    segregation, desegregation; slavery;
    slaves; slave trade; voting rights, for
    African Americans
Agnew, Spiro, *1261,* 1263, 1283, 1302
Agricultural Adjustment Act (AAA) (1933),
    1028, 1033–34, 1041
Agricultural Adjustment Act (AAA), Second
    (1938), 1034, 1058–59
Agricultural Marketing Act (1929), 1012
agriculture, 256, 258, 861, 1298
  in Africa, 112
  African Americans and, 680, 1041,
    1178–79
  agribusiness and, 909
  in Alabama, 386, 417, 535, 710
  biological exchange in, 19
  "bonanza" farms in, 838
  in California, 728, 739, 1279–80
  cattlemen in conflict with, 736–37
  in colonial period, 50, 52, 100–2, *100,*
    107–8, 119–20, 123–24, 131
  cooperatives and, 842–43
  crop lien system in, 710
  crop rotation and, 711
  currency and, 836–37
  diversity of interests in, 838–39
  dust bowl and, 1039
  in early nineteenth century, 358, 417–18,
    424
  in early U.S., 260, 280–81
  economic conditions and, 839–40
  electrification and, 1038
  environment and, 710–11
  Farmers' Alliances and, 841–45, *843*
  fertilizer use and, 711, 785
  in Georgia, 417, 533, 535
  Granger movement and, 840–41
  in Great Depression, 1018, 1024
  in Illinois, 535
  of Indians, 7, 10, 73, 101–2, 494
  in Kentucky, 306, 533, 534
  land policy and, 737–39
  in late nineteenth century, 744,
    838–46

  in Maryland, 533
  Mexican farm workers in, 1100
  in Mississippi, 386, 535
  in Missouri, 533, 534
  in New Deal, 1033–34, 1041, 1058–59
  in New England, 119–20
  in New West, 737–39
  "night soil" and, 785–86
  in 1920s, 1005–7, 1010, 1011–12
  in North Carolina, 533, 535
  in Pennsylvania, *305*
  plantations and, 539–40, 546–48
  in pre-Columbian cultures, 7, 10
  railroads and, 709, 840
  rural credit and, 926
  sharecropping and, 709–11, *709,* 710
  size of holdings in, 838–39
  in South, 533–37, 539–42, 554, 708–11
  in South Carolina, 533, 535, 536
  in South Carolina colony, 107
  steamboats' influence on, 424
  tariffs and, 837, 840, 1006–7
  technology of, 418, 419–20, 739, 751, 1006,
    1006, 1179
  in Texas, 535
  trust laws and, 924
  UFW and, 1279–80
  in Virginia, 533
  in Virginia colony, 52, *54*
  in West, 416, 418–20, 536–37
Agriculture Department, U.S., 905
Aguinaldo, Emilio, 869, 874–75, *874*
AIDS (acquired immune deficiency
    syndrome), 1328–29, *1329*
AIM (American Indian Movement),
    1281–82, *1281*
Air Commerce Act (1926), 1003
air conditioning, 1176
airplanes, 1002–3
  hijackings of, 1374
Alabama, 159, 329, 418, 1234–35
  agriculture in, 386, 417, 535, 710
  Hurricane Katrina and, 1387–89
  Indian conflicts in, 344–45
  migration to, 555
  secession of, 602
  segregation in, 1220, 1234–35, 1236,
    1251
  slave trade in, 546
  Union Loyalists in, 684
  voting rights in, 715, 716
  War of 1812 in, 344–45
Alabama, University of, 1236
Alamance, Battle of (1771), 189
Alamo, 508–10

Alaska:
gold rush in, 852
protected land in, 1306
purchase of, 862, *863*
Russian claim to, 374, 862
statehood for, 915
Albania, Albanians, 1073, 1148, 1367–68
Albany, N.Y., 694
Albany Congress (1754), 165–66
Albright, Madeleine, 1360
Alcatraz Island, Indian occupation of (1969), 1281
alcohol, consumption of, 301, 440
in colonial period, 136
in Old Southwest, 555–56
Puritans on, 125
temperance and, 479–80
Alcott, Bronson, 453, 468
Alden, John, 62
Aldrich, Nelson W., 837, 911–12
Alexander I, czar of Russia, 348, 381
Alexander VI, Pope, 17
Alexander v. Holmes County Board of Education, 1291
Algeciras, Act of (1906), 888
Algeria, 311
in World War II, 1103
Algiers, 327, 350, 1103
Algonquians, 57, 73, *80*, 86, 158
Alien Act (1798), 313, 315
Alien Enemy Act (1798), 313
Alito, Samuel, Jr., 1387
Allen, Ethan, 188, 198
Allende, Salvador, 1304
Alliance, Treaty of (1778), 224–25
Alliance for Progress, 1231
Allied Powers (Triple Entente), 934–35, 936, *937*, 955
All in the Family (television show), 1283
al Qaeda, 1376, 1377
Altair 8800, 1347
Altamont, Calif., music festival in (1969), 1273
AMA (American Medical Association), 1249
Amador, Manuel, 884
Amalgamated Association of Iron and Steel Workers, 770
Amalgamated Clothing Workers, 769, 1055
America First Committee, 1080
American and Foreign Anti-Slavery Society, 559
American Anti-Imperialist League, 875–76
American Anti-Slavery Society, 557, 558, 559, 561
American Association for the Advancement of Science, 431

American Civil Liberties Union, 972
American Colonization Society, 556
American Committee for the Outlawry of War, 1067
American Crisis, The (Paine), 215–17
American Federation of Labor (AFL), 768–69, 775–76, 964, 999, 1008, 1055–56
American Federation of Labor-Congress of Industrial Organizations (AFL-CIO), 1175, 1299, 1321, 1324
American Historical Association, 740
American Indian Movement (AIM), 1281–82, *1281*
American Indians, *see* Indians, American
American Individualism (Hoover), 1005
American (Know-Nothing) party, 448, *449*, 585, 589
American Liberty League, 1047
American Medical Association (AMA), 1249
American Missionary Association, 663
American Philosophical Society, 139
American Political Ideas (Fiske), 861–62
American Protective Association (APA), 791
American Railway Union, 771–72, 775
American Revolution, 196–235
African-American soldiers in, 201, 239, 241–42, 321
American society in, 218–21
backcountry in, 218–19, 225, 232
Boston Tea Party and, 190–91
British strategies in, 221–23, 225, 229–30
British surrender in, 233, 234
causes of, 204–6
as civil war, 218
and Committees of Correspondence, 190
coup attempt in, 251–52
events leading to, 177–96
finance and supply of, 220–21, 226, 250–51
first battles of, 196–98
France and, 202, 210, 221, 224–25, 226, 227–28, 233, 234–35
frontier in, 226–29, *227*
Hessians in, 201, 217, 219
independence issue in, 202–6, 214, 246
Indians in, 201, 224, 226, *227*, 228–29, 256
Loyalists in, 195–96, 200, 201, 218–19, 220, 223, 224, 225, 226, 228, 229, 230, 241, 242
mercenaries in, 201
militias in, 195–96, 198–99, 215–17, 219, *220*, 224, 230, 241
nationalism in, 175, 246–47
naval warfare in, 232–33
Patriot forces in, 195–202, 219–20, 224, 225–26

American Revolution (*continued*)
  peace efforts in, 200, 225, 234–35, *235*
  and Peace of Paris, 235
  political revolution and, 235–39
  slavery and, 201, 205, 219, 239, 240–43, 298, 299
  social revolution and, 239–46
  South in, 229–33, *231*
  Spain and, 202, 224, 225, 234–35
  spreading conflict in, 195–202
  summary of, 213–14
  support for, 210
  women in, 243–44
"American Scholar, The" (Emerson), 469
Americans for Democratic Action (ADA), 1154
American Society for the Promotion of Temperance, 479–80
American Sportsman, 906
"American System," 377
American Telephone and Telegraph, 752
American Temperance Union, 480
American Tobacco Company, 708, 902
American Unitarian Association, 460
American Woman's Home, The (C. Beecher), *482*
American Woman Suffrage Association, 813
Americas:
  Columbus's exploration of, 16–18
  early European visions of, 12–13
  European biological exchange with, 18–22
  name of, 18
  Norse discovery of, 12–13, *12*
  pre-Columbian, 7–12
  professional explorers of, 22–23
Amherst, Jeffrey, 168, 169–70
Amish, 36
Amity and Commerce, Treaty of (1778), 224
Anabaptists, 36
"Anaconda" strategy, 615–16
Anacostia Flats, shantytown at, 1019–20, *1019*
anarchism, 766–67
Anasazis, 11–12, *11*
Anderson, John, 1317
Anderson, Robert, 604, 609
Andersonville, Ga., Confederate prison at, 666
André, John, 232
Andros, Edmund, 150–51
Angel Island, 793
Anglican Church (Church of England), 36–38, 45, 49, 62, 99, *117*, 143
  Andros's support of, 151
  education and, 144

  Puritan views of, 65, 68–70, 125
  in South, 99, 117–18
  state support of, 244–45
  see also Episcopal Church
animals, domesticated, 7, 18–19, 25, 536
Annapolis Convention (1786), 262
Anne, queen of England, 50, 153
Anschluss, 1073
Anthony, Susan B., *483,* 484, 813, 814
anthropology, 985–86
anti-Americanism, 1374
Anti-Comintern Pact (1937), 1073
anti-communism:
  Eisenhower and, 1202
  McCarthyism and, 1166–68, 1179, 1201–2
  Nixon and, 1227
  Reagan and, 1321–22
  Truman and, 1160, 1166, 1168–69
  after World War II, 1142–43
  see also cold war
Anti-Debris Association, 728
Antietam (Sharpsburg), Battle of (1862), 625–28, 630
Antifederalists:
  and Bill of Rights, 273, 283–84
  in ratification debate, 271–72, 273
anti-feminism, 1316–17
Anti-Masonic party, 402, 407, 410
Anti-Saloon League, 795, 898, 974
anti-Semitism, 790
antislavery movement, *see* abolition movement
anti-trust laws:
  and American Tobacco Company, 708, 902
  and Bureau of Corporations, 902, 918, 923
  Clayton Anti-Trust Act, 923–24
  and Federal Trade Commission, 923, 924
  passage of, 836, 895
  and rebates, 902
  and regulation, 895, 899
  and Roosevelt (TR), 899
  Sherman Anti-Trust Act, 708, 755, 772, 836, 895, 899, 901
  and Standard Oil, 755, 902
  and Taft, 914
  and Wilson, 923–24
APA (American Protective Association), 791
Apaches, 12, 33, 494, 495, 731
Apalachees, *92*
Appalachian Forest Reserve Act (1911), 914
Appalachian Regional Development Act (1966), 1249
Appleby, Joyce, 321
Appomattox, Va., surrender at, 654–55
apprentices, 122, 322, 449–50

Arab countries, 1210–11, 1213, 1298,
    1365–67
  Camp David accords opposed by, 1308
Arabic, sinking of, 940
Arab-Israeli conflicts, 1152, 1211–13,
    1307–8, 1365–67, 1376, 1378–79
Arab League, 1211
Arafat, Yasir, 1366, *1366*
Arapahoes, 34, 494, 729
Arauntoff, Victor, *1032*
Arbella, 65–66
archaeology, 5–6
architecture:
  Georgian ("colonial"), 116
  Jefferson and, 294
  in New England, 118–19, *119*
  in pre-Columbian cultures, 10–11
  southern, 540
Area Redevelopment Act (1961), 1232
Arena, 892
ARENA party, 1327
Argentina, 932
Aristide, Jean-Bertrand, 1365
Arizona, 494, 619
  Gadsden Purchase and, 581
  in Spanish Empire, 495, 496
  statehood for, 725, 915
  voting rights in, 814
Arkansas, 501
  Civil War fighting in, 611
  cotton in, 417
  dust bowl in, 1039
  labor movement in, 1096
  military government of, 665
  secession of, 609
  segregation in, 1222–23
Arkansas Territory, 368–69
Armory Show (1913), 986–87
arms control negotiations, 1297, 1304, 1309,
    1329–30, 1338
Armstrong, Neil, 1295
Army, U.S., 311, 358
  in Constitution, 266
  after War of 1812, 350
  see also specific wars
Army Air Force, U.S., 1109
Army Appropriation Act (1916), 946
Army Corps of Engineers, U.S., 1389
Army-McCarthy hearings (1954), 1201–2, *1201*
Army Yellow Fever Commission, 877–78
Arnold, Benedict, 198, 200–201, 224, 232
Arrowrock Dam, 738
Arthur, Chester A., 792, 825, 826–28, *827*
Articles of Confederation (1781), 210,
    238–39, 249, 251, 258

  amendment process for, 262–77
  calls for revision of, 262–63
  debt under, 250–52
  finance under, 250–52
  unanimity required under, 271
arts:
  in Great Depression, 1031
  in mid-twentieth century, 1187–90
  modernist, 986–88, 989
  in New Deal, 1031, *1032*
  painting, 986–87, 1188
  performing, 441–43
  romanticism in, 466–70
  see also architecture; literature; movies;
      poetry
Asbury, Francis, 245, 462
Ashburton, Lord, 491
Ashcroft, John, 1372
Ashley-Cooper, Lord, 78
Asia:
  exploration and, 15, 22
  imperialism in, 860, 862
  trade with, 14, 862
  see also specific countries
Asian Americans, 1250, 1344, 1345
assembly, freedom of, 284
Astor, John Jacob, 455
astronomy, Mayan, 7
Aswan Dam, 1212
asylums, 481–82
Atchison, Topeka and Santa Fe Railroad,
    747
Atlanta, Ga., 1237
  capture of, 639, 648, 649, 650, *651*
Atlanta Confederacy, 599
Atlanta Constitution, 706
Atlantic, Battle of the, 1105, 1108
Atlantic Charter (1941), 1084, 1103, 1122
atomic bombs, *see* nuclear weapons
Atomic Energy Commission, 1141, 1142
Attucks, Crispus, 187
Auburn Penitentiary, 481
Audubon Society, 906
Auschwitz death camp, 1124
Austin, Stephen F., 507
Australia:
  in SEATO, 1207
  in second Gulf War, 1381
  in World War II, 1092
Austria, 28
  in colonial wars, 167
  French Revolution and, 296
  German annexation of, 1073
  in Napoleonic wars, 335
  U.S. peace with, 962

Austria-Hungary:
    Versailles treaty and, 959
    in World War I, 934–35, 950, 954, 955, 962
automobiles, 1003–4, 1293
    in Great Depression, 1056–57
    mass production and, 1004
    in 1950s, 1178, 1191
    suburban revolution and, 1178
    see also highways and roads
Ayala, Felipe Guamán Poma de, *32*
Aztecs, 9, *20*, 25–27, 29

"baby-boom" generation, 1140, 1173–74,
    1174, 1343
backcountry, 131, 134, 188–89
    in American Revolution, 218–19, 225, 232
    education in, 141
    and lack of organized government, 188–89
    popular culture in, 793
    ratification debate and, 274
    religion in, 141
    underrepresentation of, 240
    Whiskey Rebellion in, 300–302, *302*
    see also frontier
Bacon, Nathaniel, 59–60
Bacon's Rebellion, 58–60
Baffin Island (Helluland), 13
Baghdad, *1381,* 1382
Baghdad Pact, 1210
Bagot, Charles, 364
Baker, James, 1339
Bakke v. Board of Regents of California, 1292
Balboa, Vasco Nuñez de, 22, *30*
Baldwin, Hanson, 1127
Balfour, Arthur, *1066*
Balkans, 1367–68
Ballard, Martha, 106
Ballinger, Richard A., 912–13, 914
Baltimore, Benedict Calvert, fourth Lord,
    152
Baltimore, Cecilius Calvert, second Lord, 60,
    77
Baltimore, George Calvert, first Lord, 60
Baltimore, Md., 437, 438
    War of 1812 in, 346
Baltimore Carpenters' Society, 450
Baltimore Republican, 410
Bandung Conference (1955), 1205, 1209
Bankhead-Jones Farm Tenant Act (1937), 1058
Banking Act (1933), 1028, 1029
banking industry:
    1837 runs on, 405
    in Great Depression, 1025, 1027–29
    investment bankers in, 757–58
    regulation of, 816, 1028–29

state-chartered banks and, 368
    see also Federal Reserve System
Bank of North America, 250–51
Bank of the United States (national bank),
    289–91, *289,* 368, 377, 491
    Andrew Jackson and, 400–406, *402,* 413–14
    constitutionality of, 290–91, 359–60,
        400–401, *402*
    expiration of first charter of, 341
    Hamilton's recommendation for, 287,
        289–91
    Jefferson's acceptance of, 326
    McCulloch v. Maryland and, 372–73
    and Panic of 1819, 368
    removal of government deposits from, 403–4
    second charter of, 359–60, 362
    and speculative binge (1834), 404
    Tyler on, 490
Banks, Dennis, 1281
Bao Dai, Emperor of Vietnam, 1160–61,
    1206, 1207
Baptists, 36, 118, 128, 132, 143, 144, 679–80
    in revivals, 462
    in split over slavery, 561, 585
    in Whig party, 407
Barak, Ehud, 1367
Barbados, 78
Barbary pirates, 327–28, 350
    see also privateers
barbed wire, 736, 751
barley, 19, 131
"Barnburners," 568
Barnett, Ross, 1234
Barton, Clara, 634, *634*
Bartram, John, 139
Baruch, Bernard, 946, 1148
baseball, 800–801, *800,* 1153–54
basketball, 800
Bataan Peninsula, 1092
Bates, Edward, 608
BATF (Bureau of Alcohol, Tobacco, and
    Firearms), 1355, 1356
Batista, Fulgencio, 1217–18
Battle-Pieces (Melville), 473
Bayard, James, 348
Bay of Pigs invasion (1961), 1238
Bean, Roy, *736*
beans, 7, 19, 73, 101
Beard, Charles A., 272
Beats, 1188–90
Beauregard, Pierre G. T., 609, 614
Beecher, Catharine, 482, *482,* 558
Beecher, Henry Ward, 810
Beecher, Lyman, 448, 460, 461
beef trust, 901–2

Beer-Wine Revenue Act (1933), 1028
Beethoven, Ludwig van, 140
Begin, Menachem, 1307–8, *1308*
Beirut bombing (1983), 1324
Belgium, 1067
  as imperialist nation, 860
  in NATO, 1151
  in World War I, 935, 951, 952
  in World War II, 1079, 1113, 1118–19
Bell, Alexander Graham, 752, *752*
Bell, John, 601, 602, *603*
Bell Laboratories, 1347
Bellow, Saul, 1031, 1187, 1188–89
Bell Telephone Company, 752
Benedict, Ruth, 986
Bennett, William J., 1334
Benninghoff, John, *754*
Bennington, Battle of (1777), 224
Benton, Thomas Hart, 344, 359, 391, 394,
    400, 506, 511, 518, 567
  and Compromise of 1850, 572
Berger, Victor, 949
Bering Sea, 5
Berkeley, John, 87
Berkeley, William, 57, 59–60, 76, 117
Berlin, Irving, 789
Berlin Airlift (1948–1949), 1151
Berlin Conference (1889), 863
Berlin crises, 1150, 1215–16, 1238–39
Berlin Decree (1806), 335, 338
Berlin Wall, 1238–39, *1239, 1335,* 1336
Bermuda, 54, 55, 74
Bernard, Sir Francis, 180
Berry, Chuck, 1192
Bessemer, Henry, 756
Bethune, Mary Jane McLeod, 681
Beveridge, Albert J., 861, 876
Bhagavad Gita, 468
BIA (Bureau of Indian Affairs), 1041, 1281
Bibb, Henry, 559
Bible, 461, 804
bicycles, 796–97, *797*
Biddle, Nicholas, 368, 400–401, 404, 406
Bidlack Treaty (1848), 883
Bienville, Jean Baptiste le Moyne, sieur de,
    159
Bilbo, Theodore, 1019
Bill of Rights, English (1689), 50, 152
Bill of Rights, U.S., *242*
  debate on, 283–84
  in ratification of Constitution, 273, 275
  states subject to, 673
bills of attainder, 271
bills (declarations) of rights, state, 237–38
Bingham, George Caleb, *306, 403, 497*

bin Laden, Osama, 1376, 1377
biological exchange, 18–22
Birmingham, Ala.:
  church bombing in (1963), 1237, *1237*
  civil rights demonstrations in, (1963),
    1234–38, *1235*
  coal mining and, 708
Birney, James G., 561
birth control, 978–79, *979,* 1276–77, *1277*
Birth of a Nation, 1001
birthrates, 103–4, 1277
Bismarck Sea, Battle of the (1943), 1114
Black, Hugo, 1055
Black Ball Line, 426
Black Codes, 669–70, 672
Blackfoot Indians, 494, 730
Black Hawk, Sauk and Fox chief, 397
Black Hawk, Sioux chief, 495
Black Hawk War (1832), 397
Black Hills, 729
"Black Monday" (1987), 1327–28
Black Muslims, 1252
Black Panther party, 1252
black power, 1251–54, 1269
blacks, *see* African Americans
Blackwell, Elizabeth, 454–55
Blaine, James G., 694, 822, 824, 826, 828–31,
    829, 834, 835
Bland-Allison Act (1878), 825–26, 836, 847
Blithedale Romance, The (Hawthorne), 487
Blitzkrieg, 1078–79, 1081, 1083, 1093
blood sports, 440–41, *442*
Board of Customs Commissioners, 184,
    188
Board of Mediation, 1008
Board of Trade (Lords of Trade and
    Plantations), 149, 150, 154, 165
  functions of, 153
Bohemian Americans, 787
Bohemians, 132
Boleyn, Anne, 37
Bolshevik Revolution (1917), 944, 950, 953,
    964, 965–66
"bonanza" farms, 838
bonds, 636
Bonnie Prince Charlie (Charles Edward
    Stuart), 134
Bonus Expeditionary Force, 1019–20, *1019,*
    1023
Book of Common Prayer, 38
Boone, Daniel, 228, 304–6, 421
  background of, 305
Boone and Crockett Club, 906
Boonesborough, Ky., 306
  Revolutionary War fighting at, 228

Booth, John Wilkes, 653, 666
bootlegging, during Prohibition, 974–75, *975*
Borah, William E., 1080
Border Ruffian Code in Kansas (1856), *586*
Bork, Robert, 1301
"born-again" Christians, 1316, 1348–49
Bosnia, 1135, 1367, 1369
Boston, Mass.:
  antislavery demonstrations in, 585
  Boston Tea Party, 190–91
  class stratification in, 135
  in colonial period, 66, 134–35, *135*, *136*,
    150
  customs officials in, 150, 184
  disciplined by Parliament (1774), 191–92
  Great Awakening in, 143
  Irish Americans in, 445
  in nineteenth century, 437, 438
  police strike in (1919), 964
  poverty in, 136
  redcoats quartered in, 186
  school desegregation in, *1291*
  siege of (1775–1776), 200, 223
  subways in, 782
  tax protests in, 190–91
  Unitarianism in, 460
Boston English High School, 477
Boston Gazette, 194
Boston Manufacturing Company, 433
Boston Marathon, *1275*
Boston Massacre, 186–88, *187*
Boston Port Act (1774), *190*, 191, 193
Boston State House, *155*
Boston Tea Party, 190–91
Boudinot, Elias, *399*
Boulder (Hoover) Dam, 738
Bourbons (Redeemers), 711–14, *713*, 715
Bowie, Jim, 509
Boxer Rebellion (1900), 879–80, *880*
boxing, 440–41, *442*
boycotts, 193
  of grapes, 1279–80
bracero program, 1100, 1279
Braddock, Edward, 166–67
Bradford, William, 62, 68–69, 74
Bradley, Joseph P., 695
Bradley, Omar, 1119–20, 1165
Brady, Mathew, *655*
Bragg, Braxton, 645
Branch Davidians, 1355–56
Brandeis, Louis D., 919, 926, 950, 1049,
  1054–55
Brando, Marlon, 1190
Brandywine Creek, Battle of (1777), 223
Brant, Joseph (Thayendanegea), 228, *228*

Braun, Eva, 1123
Brazil, *21,* 111, 932
Breckinridge, John C., 600, 601, 602, *603,*
  652–53
Breed's Hill, Battle of (1775), 198–200,
  199
Brennan, William J., Jr., 1202
Brest-Litovsk, Treaty of (1918), 953
Brezhnev, Leonid, 1297, 1304
Brezhnev Doctrine, 1335
Briand, Aristide, *1066,* 1067
Bridger, Jim, 502
*Brief Relation of the Destruction of the Indies,
  A* (las Casas), 28
brinksmanship, 1204
British Empire, 29, 110, 111
  colonization in, 33, 41–42
  French Empire compared with, 73, 94–95,
    147, 157, 161–62
  maps of, *170, 171*
  Spanish Empire compared with, 28, 51,
    94–95, 147, 157
  trade in, 31
  see also American Revolution; colonial
    period; Great Britain
British military:
  American criticism of, 175
  and emancipation, 241
  quartering of, 180
  as standing army, 180, 186–87
  see also American Revolution; War of 1812
British navy, 232–33, 335–36
British Rule (1756), 335
Britton, Nan, 997
Brook Farm, 487
Brooklyn Dodgers, 1153, *1154*
Brooklyn Eagle, 943
Brooks, Preston S., *588,* 589
Brotherhood of Sleeping Car Porters,
  1099–1100
Brown, Frederick, 588
Brown, H. Rap, 1252, 1269
Brown, James, 1253
Brown, John, 589, 597–99, *597,* 601
  death of, 598–99
  Harper's Ferry raided by, 598
  Kansas violence led by, 587–88
Brown, Watson, 598
Brown, William Wells, 559
Brownson, Orestes, 468
Brown University (College of Rhode Island),
  144, 477–78
*Brown v. Board of Education of Topeka,
  Kansas,* 1219–20
Bruce, Blanche K., *683,* 684

Bry, Theodor de, *80*
Bryan, William Jennings, 874
　as fundamentalist, 972
　in presidential elections, 849–51, *850, 851,*
　　852, 881–82, 902, 910
　at Scopes trial, 973–74
　as secretary of state, 920, 931, 934, 936,
　　938, 939, *940*
　as silverite, 849
bubonic plague, 20
Buchanan, James, 515, 597
　Dred Scott decision and, 593
　in election of 1856, 592
　and election of 1860, 599
　in Kansas crisis, 594
　Lecompton constitution supported by,
　　594
　after Lincoln's election, 603–4
　and Panic of 1857, 595
　secession and, 603–5
Buchanan, Patrick, 1329, 1349, 1351–52,
　　1369, 1371
Buchanan v. Worley, 983
Buddha, 468
Budget and Accounting Act (1921), 994
Buena Vista, Battle of (1847), 520, 568
buffalo, 34–35, 438, *493, 494*
　demise of, 732–33
Buffalo soldiers, 723–24
Buford, deportation of radical aliens on
　　(1919), 965
Bulgaria, 955, 1148
　fall of communism in, 1335
　Soviet domination of, 1146
　in World War II, 1082, 1146
Bulge, Battle of the (1944), 1118–19
"Bull Moose" (Progressive) party, 915–16,
　　915, 918–20, 928, 942–43
Bull Run (Manassas), first Battle of (1861),
　　614–15, *615*
Bull Run (Manassas), second Battle of
　　(1861), 624
Bunau-Varilla, Philippe, 884
Bundy, McGeorge, 1231
Bunker Hill, Battle of (1775), 198–200, *199*
Bunting v. Oregon, 897
Bureau of Alcohol, Tobacco, and Firearms
　　(BATF), 1355, 1356
Bureau of Aviation, 1005
Bureau of Corporations, 902, 918, 923
Bureau of Foreign and Domestic Commerce,
　　1005
Bureau of Immigration, 788
Bureau of Indian Affairs (BIA), 1041, 1281
Bureau of Internal Revenue, 636, 1196

Bureau of Labor Statistics, 768
Bureau of Mines, 915
Bureau of Reclamation, 909
Bureau of Standards, 1005
Bureau of the Budget, 994
Burgoyne, John, 198, 223, 223–24, *223*
Burke, Edmund, 153
Burke Act (1906), 733
Burlingame Treaty (1868), 827
Burma (Myanmar), 1084–85, 1092, 1123, 1204
"Burned-Over District," 463–64
Burns, Anthony, 585
Burnside, Ambrose E., 628, 640
Burr, Aaron, 332, 333–34, *334*
　in election of 1796, 308
　in election of 1800, 316, *317*
　Hamilton's duel with, 332, 333, 543
Burr Conspiracy, 333–34
Burroughs, William, 1189
Bush, George H. W., 1334–40
　cultural conservatives and, 1347–48, 1348
　deficits and, 1334, 1349–50
　domestic initiatives of, 1334
　economy and, 1349–50, 1351–52
　in election of 1988, 1314, 1331–33, *1332,*
　　1333
　in election of 1992, 1351–52, 1353
　and fall of communism, 1334, 1337, 1338
　foreign policy of, 1349
　nuclear weapons and, 1338
　Panama invasion of, 1338–39
　Persian Gulf War and, 1339–40, 1349
　Somalia and, 1365
　tax policy of, 1332, 1334, 1351
　Thomas appointed by, 1350–51
Bush, George W., 1342
　economy and, 1372–73
　education reform and, 1373
　in election of 2000, 1369–71, *1370*
　in election of 2004, 1383–86, *1385, 1384*
　environment and, 1373
　foreign policy and, 1372, 1379–80
　Hurricane Katrina and, 1388, 1389, 1390
　job-approval rating of, 1389–90
　preemptive military action doctrine of,
　　1379–82
　as President, 1372–73
　and second Gulf War, 1380–83, 1390
　second term of, 1386–87, 1389–90
　September 11, 2001 attacks and, 1376–77,
　　1379
　social programs and, 1369, 1386, 1389
　Supreme Court appointments of, 1386–87
　taxes and, 1372–73, 1386, 1389
　terrorism and, 1376–78, 1380–83

Bush, Vannevar, 1094
Bush v. Gore, 1370–71
business:
  entrepreneurs, 753–60
  and Great Depression, 1101–15
  and growth in 1990s, 1360–61
  in late nineteenth century, 743–53
  mail order, 758–60
  regulation of, 895–96, 899
  and technological innovations, 751–53
  unethical practices in, 1372
  see also anti-trust laws; corporations,
    business; labor movement
busing, in school desegregation, *1291,* 1350
Butler, A. P., 589
Butler, Benjamin F., *677*
Byrd, Harry F., 1220, 1230, *1230*
Byrd, Lucy Parke, 105
Byrd, William, II, 105, 116
Byrnes, James F., 1096, 1146–47, 1149

Cabeza de Vaca, Núñez, 29, *30*
cabinet, British, 153, 177, 188
cabinet, U.S., 282–83, 293
Cable, George Washington, 716
cable cars, 782–83
Cabot, John, 22
Cadore, duc de, 338
Cairo Conference (1943), 1110
Cajuns, 166
calendar, Mayan, 7
Calhoun, Floride, 388
Calhoun, John C., 315, 341, 362, 363, 375,
    390, 409, 571, 585, 593
  Andrew Jackson's rift with, 393–94
  Calhoun Resolutions of, 566–67
  in Compromise of 1850, 572–74
  Eaton Affair and, 388
  on economic growth, 417
  in election of 1824, 376, 377, 378
  on Independent Treasury, 410
  Indian conflicts and, 366
  internal improvements and, 388–89
  on Mexican War, 565
  national bank issue and, 359–60, 400,
    403–4
  nullification issue and, 380, 389–95
  and slavery on frontier, 566–67
  tariff issue and, 380
  Texas annexation and, 510
  Van Buren's rivalry with, 387–88
  vice-presidency resigned by, 395
Calhoun Resolutions (1847), 566–67
California, 31, 40, 375, 498–501
  affirmative action in, 1362

agriculture in, 728, 739, 1279–80
annexation of, 507, 513, 518–19
anti-Asian sentiment in, 887
Chicanos in, 1278
Chinese in, 722, 792–93, *792*
and Compromise of 1850, 573–74, 576–77
gold rush in (1848), 427, 494, 502, 505,
  569–71, 724, 725, 728
in Great Depression, 1039–40
immigrants in, 1345
Indian conflicts in, 730
Indians in, 494
Mexican independence and, 499–500, 507
Mexican War and, 513, 518–19, 522, 523
migration to, 722
mining in, 724, 725, 728
missions in, 498–500
"Okies" in, 1039–40
Polk and, 513
population of, 1343
settlers in, 496, 501, 502, 504
slavery and, 507, 571–72, 573–74, 576–77
in Spanish Empire, 33, 498
statehood for, 507, 571–72, 573–74, 576–77
voting rights in, 814
workingmen's movement in, 764–65
California, University of, at Berkeley, 1268
California Trail, 501, *503*
Callender, James, 312
Calley, William, 1285
Call of the Wild, The (London), 809
Calvert, Leonard, 107
Calvin, John, 36
Calvinism, 36, 38, 68, 125–26, 132, 143,
  459–60, 461, 463
Cambodia, 1205, 1206, 1241
  Khmer Rouge in, 1305
  U.S. bombing of, 1285, 1286, 1288, 1300
Cambridge Agreement (1629), 126, 152
Camden, S.C., Revolutionary War fighting
  at, 229
Cameron, Simon, 608
campaign finance, 1369
  unions and, 1142
campaigns, *see* elections and campaigns
Camp David accords (1978), 1307–8
Camp of Israel, 465
Camp Winfield Scott, *623*
Canada:
  in American Revolution, 200–201, 223
  British acquisition of, 168, 169–72
  in colonial wars, 168, 169–72
  Indian conflicts and, 299–300, 340
  Maine border with, 410, 491
  migration to, 444, *444*

NAFTA and, 1354
in NATO, 1151
Quebec Act and, 192, 240
and War of 1812, 339, 342–44
in World War II, 1113
Canal Ring, 694
canals, *422–23, 424–26, 425,* 430, 431–32, 454
Cane (Toomer), 982
Canning, George, 375
Cannon, Joseph G., 913
Cape Verde, 15, 17
capitalism:
  communism vs., 1022
  Eastern Europe and, 1342
  Hamilton and, 285–86, 293, 294–95
  socialism vs., 1061
Capone, Al, 974–75
Caribs, 16
Carmichael, Stokely, 1252, 1269
Carnegie, Andrew, 636, 753, 755–57, *756,* 758, *759,* 770, 876
  philosophy of, 756–57
Carnegie Endowment for International Peace, 1166
carpetbaggers, 684, 691
Carranza, Venustiano, 932–33
Carrier, Martha, 129
Carrier, Willis Haviland, 1176
Carroll, John, 246
Carson, Christopher "Kit," 507
Carson, Rachel, 1294
Carter, Jimmy, 1306–11
  Camp David accords and, 1307–8, *1308*
  economy and, 1309
  in election of 1976, 1305
  in election of 1980, 1317–18, *1318*
  foreign policy of, 1307
  Haiti negotiations of, 1365
  inauguration of, 1306, *1306*
  Iran hostages and, 1309–10
  Latin American policy of, 1322
Carter, Landon, 205
Carter, Rosalynn, *1306*
Carteret, George, 87
Cartier, Jacques, 38
Cartwright, Peter, 462, 800
Casablanca Conference (1943), 1104–5
Casey, William, 1326
Cass, Lewis, 495, 567–68, 569
Castle Garden, 788
Castro, Fidel, 1238
  rise of, 1217–18, *1217*
Catawbas, 79, 82, *93*
Catherine of Aragon, 37
Catholicism, Catholic Church:

in Canada, 192
in Democratic party, 407, 821, 850–51
education and, 837–38
in England, 40, 45, 49, 50, 60
first U.S. bishop in, 246
in French colonies, 159
German Americans in, 446
Indians and, 27–28, 31–33, 157, 158, 495, 498–500
Irish Americans in, 445, 446
James II and, 151
Kennedy and, 1228
missionaries of, 31–33, 159, 161, 495, 498–500
prejudice against, 445, 446, 448, *449,* 790–91
pro-life movement and, 1316
Reformation attacks on, 35–36, 38
Religious Right and, 1348
in Spanish Empire, 27–28, 31–33, 157, 168, 495
Catlin, George, *493*
Catt, Carrie Chapman, 814, 979
cattle, 19, 101–2, 107, 120, 536, 640, 734–37
  drives of, 734–36
  farmers and, 736–37
  meat refrigeration and, 735–36, 744
  range wars and, 737
Cavaliers, 49
Cayugas, *93,* 228
CBS, 1002, 1048
CCC (Civilian Conservation Corps), 1028, 1029–30, *1030,* 1041, 1096
Ceausescu, Nicolae, 1335
Celia (slave), 549–50
Central American Free Trade Act (2005), 1386
Central Federated Union, 948
Central Intelligence Agency (CIA), 1143, 1169, 1207
  Central America and, 1323
  Chile and, 1304
  Cuba and, 1218, 1238
  Iran and, 1309
  Noriega and, 1338
Central Pacific Railroad, 746–47, 750
Central Park (New York City), 796
Central Powers (Triple Alliance), 934–35, 936, *937,* 950, 954
Century of Dishonor, A (Jackson), 733
Ceylon (Sri Lanka), 1204
Chamberlain, Joshua, 655
Chambers, Whittaker, 1166
Champlain, Samuel de, 38, 158, *158*
Chancellorsville, Battle of (1863), 640–41, 647
Chandler, Phoebe, 129
Chandler, Zachariah, 637

Channing, William Ellery, 460, 484
Chaplin, Charlie, *1000,* 1001
Charles, Ray, 1192
Charles I, king of England, *47, 48,* 49, 60, 65, 107, 149
    colonial administration under, 149
    execution of, 49, 76
Charles II, king of England, 49, 58, 76, 77, 83, 85, 147
    colonial administration under, 58, 149
    death of, 150
    France policy of, 162
Charles V, king of Spain, 28, 37
Charles VII, king of France, 14–15
Charleston, S.C.:
    in Civil War, 652, 661
    in colonial period, 78, 132, 134–35
    founding of, 78
    in Revolutionary War, 201, 229
    and secession of South, 602, 609
Charleston (dance), 977
Charlestown peninsula, Revolutionary War fighting at, 197
Chase, Salmon P., 608, 676
Chattanooga, Battle of (1863), 645
Chauncey, Charles, 143
Chavez, César, 1279–80, *1279*
checks and balances, 265
Cheever, John, 1031
Cheney, Richard "Dick," 1372
Cherokee Nation v. Georgia, 399
Cherokee Phoenix, 399
Cherokees, 79, *81,* 82, 83, *92,* 168, *227,* 229, 281, 302
    in Civil War, 620
    government of, 397, 398–99
    lands ceded by, 256
    post-Revolutionary War weakness of, 256
    removal of, 397, 397–400
    Tecumseh and, 340
Chesapeake, U.S.S., 336
Chesnut, Mary Boykin, 540, 541, 645
Cheves, Langdon, 368
Cheyennes, 34, 494, 505, 729
Chiang Kai-shek, 1110, 1160, 1209, 1296
Chibchas, 9
Chicago, Ill.:
    African Americans in, 1178
    Democratic Convention in (1968), 1260–61, 1270–71, *1271*
    growth of, 438
    Haymarket Affair in (1886), 767
    horse manure and, 785
    immigrants in, 787, 790
    labor radicalism and, 772
    Pullman Strike in (1894), 770–72
    race riot in (1919), 947, *964,* 965
    race riot in (1966), 1251
    saloons in, 794
Chicago Board Options Exchange, *1327*
Chicago Defender, 947
Chicago Tribune, 653
Chicanos, 1278
Chickamauga, Battle of (1863), 645
Chickasaws, 80, 83, *92,* 281, 302
    in Civil War, 620
    removal of, 397
    Tecumseh and, 340
child labor, 435, 452, 761–62, *762,* 773, 896–97, *896,* 925, 927, 993, 1034, 1036, 1059
    progressive campaign against, 896, 927
Children's Bureau, U.S., 813, 915, 1038
Chile, 27, 932, 1304
China, 83
    American plants in, 19
    Boxer Rebellion in, 879–80, *880*
    Communist takeover of, 1160–61, 1206
    foreign domination of, 878–80, 886–87
    Forty-niners from, 571
    immigration restrictions and, 792–93
    Japanese aggression in, 1065, 1069–71, *1070,* 1073, 1076–77, *1077,* 1084, 1085, 1087, 1160
    Open Door Policy and, 879–80, 886, 887, 1066–67, 1071
    Protestant missionaries to, 580
    in Sino-Japanese War, 878
    Soviet conflicts with, 1070
    trade with, 258, 406, 427, 580, 879, 1066–67
China, Nationalist:
    Communist defeat of, 1160–61, 1206
    United Nations and, 1144, 1162
    in World War II, 1092, 1114, 1123
    see also Taiwan (Nationalist China)
China, People's Republic of, 1212
    cold war and, 1134, 1380
    democracy movement in, 1334
    Indochina and, 1206–7
    Korean War and, 1163–65, 1200–1201
    "loss" of China to, 1160–61, 1206
    Nixon's visit to, 1296–97, *1297*
    and second Gulf War, 1381
    Taiwan and, 1209, 1215
    trade with, 1361
    United Nations and, 1162
    Vietnam War and, 1257
Chinese Americans, 447–48, 722, 764–65, 790, 887, *1345*
    railroads and, 747
    violence against, 764–65

Chinese Exclusion Act (1882), 792–93, *792*, 827
Chinooks, 494
Chippewas, 300, 1281
Chiricahua Apaches, 731
Chivington, J. M., 729
Choctaws, 83, *92*, 281, 302
  in Civil War, 620
  removal of, 397
  Tecumseh and, 340
cholera, 20, 785
Chou En-lai, 1209, 1296, *1297*
Christian Century, 1177
Christian Coalition, 1348
Christian evangelicals, 1343, 1348–49
Christianity and the Social Crisis (Rauschenbusch), 811
Christian missionaries and imperialism, 860
Christian right, 1315–16, 1331, 1348–49, 1351, 1355
Churchill, Winston, 1079, *1079*, 1080, 1083, 1119, 1216
  Atlantic Charter and, 1084
  at Cairo and Teheran, 1110
  at Casablanca, 1104–5
  cold war and, 1146
  D-Day and, 1113
  French occupation zone and, 1121
  nuclear weapons and, 1204
  Roosevelt's 1941 meeting with, 1084
  war aims and, 1103
  at Yalta, 1120–22, *1121*
Church of England, *see* Anglican Church
Church of Jesus Christ of Latter-Day Saints (Mormons), 464–66, *465*, 737
CIA, *see* Central Intelligence Agency
Cigarmakers Union, 768, *769*
Cincinnati, Ohio, *327*, 438
CIO (Congress of Industrial Organizations), 1056, *1056*, 1142, 1143
"circuit riders", Methodist, 462
cities and towns:
  allure and problems of, 783–84
  amenities in, 431, 785–86
  in colonial period, 134–38
  early factories in, 433–35, *433*
  in early twentieth century, *782*
  employment in, 135–36
  environment and, 785–86, *786*
  and growth of industry, 780
  immigrants in, 787, 790
  industrialization as impetus to, 437–39
  in late nineteenth century, 779, *781*
  in late twentieth century, 1343
  and mass transit, 781–83

  in nineteenth century, 437–39, *440*, *441*
  politics of, 784–85, 820
  poverty in, 135–36
  public water systems and, 785–86
  recreation in, 439–43
  reform movements in, 785–86, 812–17
  rise of, 13, 14–15
  rural migration to, 783–84
  segregation in, 780
  settlement house movement in, 812–13, 896
  technology and, 781, 784, 785–86
  transportation between, 136, 437–39
Citizen Genêt, 296–97
Citizens' Councils, 1220
citizenship and naturalization:
  of African Americans, 268, 673
  Constitutional Convention and, 268
  of Indians, 268, 733
  of Puerto Ricans, 877
city-manager plan, 894–95
"Civil Disobedience" (Thoreau), *470*
Civilian Conservation Corps (CCC), 1028, 1029–30, *1030*, 1041, 1096
civil liberties, *see* civil rights and liberties
Civil Rights Act (1866), 672–73
Civil Rights Act (1957), 1222
Civil Rights Act (1960), 1222
Civil Rights Act (1964), 1246, 1247, 1249
civil rights and liberties:
  in Civil War, 637–39
  in colonial period, 156, 180, 235–38
  in election of 1948, 1155, 1156
  Johnson and, 1245, 1250–51
  in the 1940s, 1152–59
  Reagan and, 1320–21
  Red Scare and (1919–1920), 965–66
  Truman and, 1153, 1154, 1155, *1155*
  in World War I, 949–50
Civil Rights Commission, 1222
civil rights movement:
  black power and, 1251–54, 1269
  Brown decision and, 1219–20
  colleges and, 1267
  early period of, 1218–23
  in election of 1960, 1228–30
  expansion of, 1232–37
  federal intervention in, 1234–37
  Little Rock crisis and, 1222–23
  massive resistance and, 1220, 1223
  Montgomery bus boycott and, 1220–21, 1233
Civil Service Commission, 828, 835, 1166

civil service reform, 691–93, 694, 823–26, 828
  Cleveland and, 831
  Harrison and, 835
  merit system and, 825
  Theodore Roosevelt and, 835, 881
Civil War, English (1642–1649), 76–77, 89, 148
Civil War, Spanish, 1073, 1075–76
Civil War, U.S., 484, 607–56
  African Americans attacked in, 618
  African-American soldiers in, 632–33, 632, 633, 679
  aftermath of, 659–64
  "Anaconda" strategy in, 615–16
  balance of force in, 612–13
  bond sales in, 636
  calls for peace in, 628, 637, 652–53
  casualties in, 529, 622, 633, 640, 656
  choosing sides in, 609–11
  civil liberties and, 637–39
  compromise attempted before, 605
  Confederate command structure in, 623–24, 641–42, 645
  Congress in, 605, 610, 629, 630, 633, 635–36, 660
  destruction of landscape in, 640
  diplomacy and, 618–19
  economic effects of, 744
  economy in, 612–13, 636–37
  emancipation in, 629–33
  environment and, 640
  financing of, 635–36
  government during, 635–40
  Indians in, 620
  Lincoln's appraisal of, 653–54
  Mexican War and generals of, 523
  military advantages in, 613
  naval warfare in, 616
  outbreak of fighting in, 609
  peninsular campaign in, 622–24, 625
  presidential transition and, 604–5, 607, 608–9
  press coverage of, 475
  recruitment and draft in, 616–18, 617, 632
  and secession of South, 602–3, 609–11, 610
  slavery and, 653
  southern blockade in, 613, 616
  strategies in, 614, 615–16, 646
  technology in, 656
  as total war, 646, 650–52, 655–56
  Union command changes in, 622, 624, 628, 640, 643, 645
  Union finances in, 635–36
  veterans of, 832, 835–36

West in, 619–20, 621
women in, 634–35
see also Confederate States of America; Reconstruction
Civil Works Administration (CWA), 1031
Clansman, The (Dixon), 1001
Clark, Bennett Champ, 917–18
Clark, George Rogers, 226–28
Clark, J. Ruben, 1069
Clark, William, 329–32, 330, 331
Clarke, James Freeman, 468
Clark Memorandum, 1069
Clay, Henry, 341, 348, 363, 370, 379–80, 388, 455
  African colonization and, 556
  "American System" of, 377
  in Compromise of 1850, 572–73, 575
  in duel, 543
  economic nationalism and, 407, 410, 490, 514
  in election of 1824, 376, 377–78, 378, 381
  in election of 1832, 402, 403
  in election of 1840, 410
  in election of 1844, 511, 512, 512
  and election of 1848, 568
  Missouri Compromise and, 370
  national bank debate and, 359–60, 401, 404, 405
  nullification and, 394–96
  tariff policy of, 405, 491
  Tyler administration and, 490, 490–91
Clayton, Henry D., 923
Clayton Anti-Trust Act (1914), 923–24
Clayton-Bulwer Treaty (1850), 883
Clean Air Act (1970), 1292
Cleaver, Eldridge, 1252
Clemenceau, Georges, 951, 956, 958, 959
Clemens, Samuel (Mark Twain), 807–8, 808, 819
Clermont, 423
Cleveland, Grover, 772, 792, 821, 830, 866
  and civil service reform, 831
  in election of 1884, 829–31
  in election of 1888, 834–35
  in election of 1892, 846
  first term of, 831–34
  Hawaii and, 864
  tariff issue and, 833–34, 833
Cleveland, Ohio, 438
  race riot in (1966), 1251
Clifford, Clark, 1259
Clinton, Bill:
  Balkans and, 1367–68
  deficits and, 1353, 1354, 1361
  draft issue and, 1352

economy and, 1360–61
in election of 1992, 1352–53, *1353*
and election of 1994, 1356–57, 1358
in election of 1996, 1359–60
foreign policy of, 1365–68, 1376
Haiti and, 1365
health care effort of, 1354–55
infidelity issue and, 1352
Lewinsky matter and, 1362–63
Middle East policy of, 1365–67, *1366*
Religious Right and, 1348
Republican Congress and, 1356–57
scandals under, 1362–65, 1371
second-term cabinet of, 1360
Theodore Roosevelt and, 871
Whitewater case and, 1362, *1363*
Clinton, De Witt, 425
Clinton, George:
in election of 1804, 332–33
in election of 1808, 338
in ratification debate, 273
Clinton, Henry, 198, 199, 201, 225, 226, 229
Clinton, Hillary Rodham, 1352, 1355, 1362
clipper ships, 427, *427*
closed shop, 769, 903, 1142
coal industry, 708, 762, 1141
Coast Guard, U.S., 286
Cobbett, William, 479
cocaine, 1334
"code talkers," 1101
Coercive (Intolerable) Acts (1774), 191–93
Coffin, Levi, 559
Cohen, William, 1360
Cohens v. Virginia, 371
Cohn, Roy, *1167*
Colbert, Jean Baptiste, 159
Cold Harbor, Battle of (1864), 647
cold war, 1143–52, 1160–69, 1172
brinksmanship and, 1204
China and, 1160–61, 1296–97
containment in, 1147–48, 1168–69, 1203, 1257, 1349, 1379–80
détente and, 1297–98
end of, 1135, 1361
Marshall Plan and, 1148–49, *1150*
origins of, 1134, 1137–38, 1144–47
segregation and, 1152–53
and spheres of influence, 1168–69
Truman Doctrine and, 1148–49, 1166, 1168–69, 1257
see also Korean War; Vietnam War
Cole, Thomas, *467*
Colfax, Schuyler, 689

colleges and universities, 477–79, 803–4
football at, 800
GI Bill of Rights and, 1173
graduate schools in, 804
land-grant, 635, 660
in late nineteenth century, 803–4
in 1920s, 977
in 1960s, 1267, 1267–70
religious movements and, 143–44, 460, 461
segregation at, 1173, 1219, 1234
women's, 478–79
see also education
Collier, John, 1041–42
Collier's, 904, 1190
Colombia, 27
Panama Canal and, 883–85, 1068
colonial governments:
assemblies' powers in, 66–68, 155–56, 193–95
charters in, 65–66, 68, 77, 126, 148, 150, 152, 153–54
in Connecticut, 150, 154
covenant theory in, 125–26
in Delaware, 154
and Dominion of New England, 150–51
in Dutch colonies, 84
English administration and, 148–53
in Georgia, 91, 94, 148, 152
governors' powers in, 154–55, 156
in Maryland, 60, 152, 154, 155
in Massachusetts, 65–68, 77, 150, 151, 152, 154, 155
in New Jersey, 150, 152
in New York, 150, 151–52
in North Carolina, 152
in Pennsylvania, 90, 152, 154
in Plymouth, 63–65
in Rhode Island, 77, 126, 150, 154
self-government developed in, 153–56
in South Carolina, 78, 152, 155
in Virginia, 55, 56–57, 57–58, 58–59, 155
colonial period:
agriculture in, 50, 52, 107–8, 119–20, 123–24, 131
alcoholic abuse in, 136
architecture in, 116, 118–19, *119*
assemblies' powers in, 155–56
backcountry in, 131, 134
birth and death rates in, 103–4
British folkways in, 99–100
cities in, 134–38
civil liberties in, 156, 180, 235–38
class stratification in, 135–36
colonial wars in, 162–72

colonial period (*continued*)
  currency shortage in, 123–24
  disease in, 54, 104
  education in, 140–41
  employment in, 135–36
  Enlightenment in, 138–41
  ethnic mix in, 131–34
  European settlement in, 50–73, *51*
  indentured servants in, 58, 59, 109–10,
    110
  Indian conflicts in, 57–60, 74–76, *75*,
    81–83, 87, 168, 177
  land policy in, 108–9, 131
  manufactures in, 432
  mercantile system in, 148–49
  newspapers in, 137–38
  population growth in, 102–5
  postal service in, 137
  prisons and punishment in, 481
  religion in, 124–28, 127–28, 132, 141–44
  science in, 138–40
  sex ratios in, 104–5
  slavery in, 78, 79, 108, 110–11, 112–16,
    114, 123
  social and political order in, 135–36
  society and economy in, 107–34, 322
  taverns in, 136–37, *137*
  taxation in, 66, 151, 156, 177–86
  trade and commerce in, 50, 52, 58, 60, 73,
    79–83, 91, 94, 107–9, 119–24, *124*,
    126–27, 148–49, 159, 175
  transportation in, 136
  triangular trade, 123, *124*
  ways of life in, 98–146
  westward expansion and, 177, 304–6
  witchcraft in, 128–31
colonial wars, 162–72
  French and Indian War, *see* French and
    Indian War
  with Indians, 57–60, 74–76, *75*, 76, 81–83,
    87, 168, 177
  King George's War, 162
  King William's War, 162
Colorado:
  dust bowl in, 1038
  Indian conflicts in, 730
  labor movement in, 773, 775
  statehood for, 724
  voting rights in, 814
Colorado Territory, 501, 619, 724
  Indian conflicts in, 729
Colored Farmers' Alliance, 842
Columbia, S.C., fall of, 652, 661
Columbia Broadcasting System (CBS), 1002,
  1048

Columbia University (King's College), 144,
  1269–70, *1270*
Columbus, Christopher, 2, 7, 13, *16*
  background of, 15
  voyages of, 15–18, *17*
Comanches, 34, 494, 495, 729
Command of the Army Act (1867), 674,
  676
commerce, *see* economy; trade and
  commerce
Commerce Court, 915
Commission on Civil Disorders, 1252
Committee of Correspondence, 190, 193
Committee of National Liberation, 1122
Committee of Safety (Boston), 196
Committee on Civil Rights, 1153
Committee on Public Information, 948
Committee to Defend America by Aiding the
  Allies, 1080
Committee to Re-elect the President
  (CREEP), 1299–1300
common law, 46–47
Common Sense (Paine), 202, 215
*Common Sense Book of Baby and Child Care,
  The* (Spock), 1186
Commonwealth v. Hunt, 450–51
communes, 1272
communications, 430–32
communism:
  capitalism vs., 1022
  in Cuba, 1218
  Eisenhower Doctrine and, 1215
  fall of, 1334–38, 1367
  Indochina and, 1204–9
  and Red Scare after World War I, 965–66,
    1007
  in Spain, 1075
  see also anti-communism; cold war; Soviet
    Union; Vietnam War
Communist Labor party (U.S.), 965
Communist party (China), 1160, 1206
Communist party (France), 1149
Communist party (Italy), 1149
Communist party (U.S.), 775, 965, 1167
  Gastonia Strike and, 1009
  in Great Depression, 1019, 1043, 1060
  in presidential elections, 1025
Community Action Program, 1247
Community Service Organization (CSO), 1279
compassionate conservatism, 11, 1371,
  1372–73
Compromise of 1850, 572–80, *576*
Compromise of 1877, 694–97
computer revolution, 1346–47
  ENIAC in, 1346

Internet and, 1347
transistor in, 1347
Comstock, H.T.P., 724
Comstock Lode, 724–25
Conciliatory Resolution (1775), 195
Concord, Battle of (1775), 196–98, *196*
Coney Island, 798, *798*, 799
Confederate States of America:
  command structure of, 623–24
  constitution of, 602
  devastation in, 661–62
  diplomacy of, 618–19
  finances of, 636–37
  formation of, 602–3, 609–11
  industry in, 612, 613
  navy of, 619
  politics in, 639–40
  recruitment in, 617
  states' rights in, 639
  Union Loyalists in, 611, 673, 684
  Union soldiers from, 611
  see also Civil War, U.S.
Confederation Congress, 238–39, 250–63
  accomplishments of, 250
  Articles of Confederation revision
    endorsed by, 263
  and development of the West, 252–56
  diplomacy and, 258–59
  end of, 275–76
  land policies of, 252–56
  Loyalist property and, 258–59
  paper currency issued by, 260
  powers of, 238–39, 250
  trade and commerce regulated by, 238–39,
    256–58
  weaknesses of, 259–61, 262, 285
Confiscation Act (1862), 630
Congregationalists, 65, 141, 143, 144, *245*, 460
  Presbyterians' union with, 461
  in Whig party, 407
Congress, Confederate, 636–37
Congress, U.S., 1295
  abolition and, 561
  African Americans in, 684
  Barbary pirates and, 350
  Carter and, 1306
  in Civil War, 605, 610, 629, 630, 633,
    635–36, 660
  Clinton impeachment and, 1364–65, *1364*
  commerce regulated by, 373–74
  in Constitution, 265–66, 267, 268–71
  currency policy of, 693–94
  education promoted by, 477
  Eisenhower and, 1198
  and election of 1876, 695–97

and election of 1948, 1155–59
and election of 1994, 1356–57
emancipation and, 629, 630
environmentalism and, 1294
Equal Rights Amendment and, 1275
executive departments established by,
  282–83
first meeting of, 282
Ford and, 1304
George H. W. Bush and, 1351
George W. Bush and, 1372, 1378
gerrymandering and, 1361
Grant's relations with, 687
in Great Depression, 1017–18
Great Society and, 1249–50
immigration investigated by, 788
immigration policy of, 448–49, 970
independent Treasury voted by, 410
Indian conflicts investigated by, 729
Indian policy and, 396
internal improvements and, 361–62, 363,
  430
Johnson's conflict with, 671–72
Johnson's impeachment and, 676
Kennedy and, 1231–32
in Korean War, 1162
land policy and, 304, 419, 491
McCarthyism and, 1168
Mexican War and, 516–17
Napoleonic Wars and, 338
national bank issue in, 289, 290, 359–60,
  372–73, 401–2
New Deal and, 1027, 1049–52
Nixon and, 1301–2, 1303
Persian Gulf War and, 1340
policy role of, 821–22
railroads and, 581
Reagan and, 1320, 1325, 1328
in Reconstruction, 663–64, 665–66,
  669–75, 678, 690, 693–94
religion promoted by, 1182–83
slavery issue and, 566–67, 568, 571–72,
  593, 594, 633
and suspension of habeas corpus, 637
Taiwan and, 1209
tariff policy of, 394–96
taxation power of, 266, 267
Texas annexation and, 510
trade policy of, 338, 365
Truman and, 1142, 1143
Tyler's conflicts with, 491
Vietnam War and, 1285
and War of 1812, 338, 339, 341
welfare reform and, 1358–59
West Virginia admitted to Union by, 610

Congress, U.S. (*continued*)
World War I and, 944, 982
see also House of Representatives, U.S.;
Senate, U.S.
Congressional Government (Wilson), 916, 921
Congress of Industrial Organizations (CIO),
1056, *1056*, 1142, 1143
Congress of Racial Equality (CORE), 1234
Conkling, Roscoe, 824, 825, 826, 827
Connecticut:
Constitution ratified by, *274*
at Hartford Convention, 349
Revolutionary War troops from, 198
slave trade halted by, 241
voting rights in, 382
Connecticut Anti-Slavery Society, 558
Connecticut colony:
charter of, 77, 154
in colonial taxation disputes, 188
European settlement of, 71–72
government of, 150, 154
Indian conflicts in, 74–76, *75*
in land disputes, 192
Connecticut (Great) Compromise, 266
Connor, Eugene "Bull," 1234–35, *1235*
conquistadores, 26
Conscience of a Conservative, The
(Goldwater), 1247, *1248*
conservation, 905–10, 912–13, 914–15
forest fire suppression and, 909–10
Indians and, 906, 907, 909
utilitarian, 907–10
Constellation, U.S.S., 311
Constitution, U.S., 249, 263–77, 279–80
Congress in, 265–66, 267, 268–71
foreign policy in, 269
habeas corpus in, 637
implied powers and, 290–91, 329, 360,
372–73
internal improvements and, 388–89, 748
judicial review principle and, 325
Louisiana Purchase and, 329
motivation of advocates of, 272
national bank issue and, 290–91, 359–60,
400–401, *402*
nullification issue and, 390–91, 396
presidency in, 268–71
ratification of, 271–77, *275*
Reconstruction and, 665–66, 668, 671–72
and separation of powers, 268–71
slavery in, 266, 267–68, 327
state-compact theory of, 315, 392
strict construction of, 329, 333, 334, 360,
376, 490
Theodore Roosevelt's view of, 898

treason in, 334
see also Constitutional Convention
Constitution, U.S.S.R., 311
constitutional amendments, U.S.:
First, 561
Fifth, 566–67, 593
Ninth, 284
Tenth, 271, 284, 290
Twelfth, 332–33
Thirteenth, 267, 633, 659, 669, 697
Fourteenth, 529, 673, 674, 675, 697, 716,
816, 983
Fifteenth, 529, 678, *682*, 697, 715, 813, 983,
110
Sixteenth, 915
Seventeenth, 893, 915
Eighteenth, 271, 974, 992, 1024
Nineteenth, 979, 992
Twentieth, 1025
Twenty-first, 1028
Twenty-second, 1196
Twenty-fifth, 1302
Twenty-sixth, 1292
proposed Equal Rights Amendment, 980,
1275–76, 1321
Constitutional Convention (1787), 210–11,
263–71, *263, 270,* 285
call for, 262–63
delegates to, 263–65
Madison at, 264–65, *264,* 269, 272
political philosophy of, 265
representation issue in, 266–67, 268–69
separation of powers issue in, 268–71
slavery issue in, 266–67, 268, 277
trade and commerce issue in, 266
women's rights ignored in, 267–68
Constitutional Union party, 601
constitutions:
British, 46, 48, 176
state, 237–38, 239, 242, 244, 268, 673, 684
see also Constitution, U.S.
containment, 1147–48, 1168–69, 1203, 1257,
1269, 1349, 1379–80
Continental army, 219–20
desertions from, 220, 226
recruitment to, 220, 221
supply problems of, 220–21, 226
winter quarters of, 221, 223, 225–26
see also American Revolution
Continental Association, 193–94
Continental Congress, First, 229
call for, 193–95
plan of union considered by, 193
Continental Congress, Second, 198, 214,
220–21, 226

extralegal nature of, 238
governmental functions taken by, 201
independence voted by, 202–3, *203*, 246
peace efforts and, 200, 225, 234, 235
supply problems and, 226, 250–51
Continental Divide, *503*
"Continental System," 335
contraception, 978–79, 1276–77, *1277*
Contract Labor Act (1864), 635, 765, 787
contract rights, 371–72
contract theory of government, 152, 204, 237
Contract with America, 1357–58
Contras, 1323, 1327
Iran-Contra affair and, 1325–26
Convention of 1800, 312
Convention of 1818, 363–64, 497
convict leasing, 712
Conwell, Russell, 811
Cooke, Jay, 636, 693
Coolidge, Calvin, 964, 983, 995, 997–99, *998*, 1002, 1007, 1010, 1319
in election of 1924, 999
Latin American policy of, 1069
Coolidge, John, 998
Copernicus, Nicolaus, 138
Copperheads, 637
Coral Sea, Battle of (1942), 1093, 1102, 1114
Corbin, Margaret, 243
CORE (Congress of Racial Equality), 1234
Corey, Giles, 130
corn (maize), 7, 19, 63, 73, 101–2, 306, 536
Cornell, Alonzo, 825
Cornwallis, Lord, 201, 223, 229, 230–32, 233, *234*
Coronado, Francisco Vásquez de, *30*, 31
corporations, business, *823*
abuses of, 822
downsizing in, 1350
in Europe, 14, 47
in Great Depression, 1017–18
growth of, 758
Harding and, 995
muckrakers and, 892–93
multinational, 1368–69
in New Deal, 1032, 1034–36, 1051–52
in 1920s, 995, 999, 1064
as "persons" in judicial reasoning, 673, 816
in post-World War II era, 1180–81
progressivism and regulation of, 891, 895–96, 903–5
see also industry; *specific corporations*; trusts
Corps of Discovery, 329–32, *330*, *331*
corruption, 822–24

Arthur's efforts against, 827
civil service reform and, 823–26, 828, 831, 835
Hayes's efforts against, 824–25
Corso, Gregory, 1189
Cortés, Hernando, 25–27, *25*, *30*
cotton, 281, 321, 358, 385–86, 417–18, 532, 533, 534–36, *534*, *535*, 1178–79
British trade in, 337, 389, 406, 528, 535, 539
in Civil War, 618, 661
French trade in, 389, 406, 535
in Great Depression, 1033
in Old Southwest, 555
in Panic of 1857, 595
see also textile industry
cotton gin, 417–18, *417*
Coubertin, Pierre de, 801
Coughlin, Charles E., 1048–49, 1052
Council for New England, 72
Council of Economic Advisers, 1141, 1245
Council of Foreign Ministers, 1146
Council of National Defense, 946
Council of the Indies, 28
counterculture, 1272–74
Country of the Pointed Firs, The (Freeman), 807
courts, *see* Admiralty courts, vice admiralty courts; legal system; Supreme Court, U.S.
covenant theory, 125–26
cowboys, 734–37, *735*
African Americans as, 723, 734
Cowpens, Battle of (1781), 230
Cox, Archibald, 1301
Cox, James, 993, 1024
Coxey, Jacob S., 848
"Coxey's Army," 848
crack cocaine, 1334
Crack in the Picture Window, The (Keats), 1185
Crane, Stephen, 808–9
Crawford, William, 363, 376, 377, 378, *378*, 408
Crédit Mobilier, 688–89, 750
Creeks, 80, 82, 83, *92*, 256, 281, 302, 365, 366
Andrew Jackson's campaign against, 344–45, 396
in Civil War, 620
removal of, 397, 399
Tecumseh and, 340
Creel, George, 948
CREEP (Committee to Re-elect the President), 1299–1300

Creole incident (1841), 491
crime:
Clinton and bills on, 1358
in colonial period, 135–36
immigration and, 109
juvenile delinquency and, 1190–91
in late twentieth century, 1344
prisons and, 712
Prohibition and, 974–75
Crisis, The, 983
Criterion, 987
Critique of Pure Reason (Kant), 467
Crittenden, John J., 605
Croatia, 1367
Croatian Americans, 787
Crockett, Davy, 508
Croly, Herbert, 918, 919
Cromwell, Oliver, 49, 76–77, 148
crop lien system, 710
croquet, 796
Crown Point, Battle of (1775), 198
Crows, 495, 730
cruel and unusual punishment, 50, 284
Cruikshank, Robert, *386*
CSO (Community Service Organization), 1279
C. Turner Joy, U.S.S., 1255
Cuba, 24, 26, 168, 169, 374, 375, 1069
Bay of Pigs invasion of, 1238
Castro's rise in, 1217–18
Columbus in, 16, 18
Grenada invasion and, 1324
missile crisis in (1962), 1239–41, *1240*
Ostend Manifesto and, 580
in Spanish-American War, 865–72, 873, 874
trade with, 1218
U.S. role in, 877–78
Cuban Americans, 971
Cudahy, Michael, 445
Cudahy Packing Company, 445
Cullen, Countée, 982
culture, U.S.:
emergence of, 246–47
in nineteenth century, 439–43
see also arts; popular culture
Cumberland (National) Road, 361–62, *361, 363,* 389, 421–22
Cumberland Road Bill, 363
currency:
agriculture and, 836–37
in American Revolution, 220, 252
after Civil War, 687–88, 744
in Civil War, 636–37
in colonial period, 123–24, 179, 189
Constitution and, 272

in early twentieth century, 903, 922
in early U.S., 259, 260–61, 289, 290
gold, 693–94, 847, 848–49, 852, 903, 1017, 1018, 1028, 1029, 1293–94
Great Depression and, 1015, 1017, 1028, 1029
greenbacks and, 636, 687–88, 691, 693–94, 847, 852
"In God We Trust" on, 1182–83
in late nineteenth century, 825–26, 828, 836–37, 847, 848–49
national bank issue and, 400, 401, 405
shortage of, 123–24, 259, 260–61
silver, 825–26, 836–37, 847, 848–49, 852
in War of 1812, 359
Currency Act (1764), 179, 188
Custer, George A., 729
customs, 179, 286
customs houses, 825
Cutler, Manasseh, 255
CWA (Civil Works Administration), 1031
Czech Americans, 787, 788
Czechoslovakia, 959
fall of communism in, 1335
German invasion of, 1073, 1078
Soviet domination of, 1149, 1321–22
Czolgosz, Leon, 882

Dakota Territory, 619, *724,* 729
Daley, Richard, 1260–61, 1271, 1299
dams, 738, 1212
dance, 977
African-American, 552
Dangling Man (Bellow), 1188
Daniel Boone Escorting Settlers through the Cumberland Gap (Bingham), *306*
Daniels, Jonathan, 989
Danish colonists, 132
Dare, Elinor, 43
Dare, Virginia, 43
Darrow, Clarence, 973
Dartmouth College, 144, 371–72
Dartmouth College v. Woodward, 371–72
Darwin, Charles, 804–6, *805,* 861, 972, 986
Darwinism:
banned from public schools, 972–74
natural selection in, 804, 805, 861
reform, 806
religious opposition to, 972–74
social, 805–6
Davenport, James, 143
Davis, David, 695
Davis, Henry Winter, 665
Davis, Jefferson, 581, 678

in Black Hawk War, 397
capture of, 654–55
Civil War strategy of, 616
and Compromise of 1850, 572, 573
as Confederate president, 602, 639–40
in duel, 543
enlistment efforts and, 617
and first Battle of Bull Run, 614
Fort Sumter and, 609
Lee's relationship with, 623, 624
in Mexican War, 520
stubbornness of, 639–40, 653
Davis, John W., 999, 1011, 1047
Dawes, Charles G., 1018
Dawes, Henry L., 733
Dawes, William, 196
Dawes Severalty (General Allotment) Act
(1887), 733, 1042
Day, Henry, 453
Day, William, 849
Dayan, Moshe, *1212*
Dean, James, 1190
Dean, John, 1299, 1300, 1301
Dearborn, Henry, 342, 344
Death of a Salesman (Miller), 1187, *1187*
death rates, in colonial period, 103–4
Debs, Eugene V., 771, 775, 776
and American Railway Union, 771–72
imprisonment of, 772, 949
pardon of, 997
in presidential elections, *774*, 775, 910,
918, 919, 949
and Pullman Strike, 771–72
as socialist, 774–75
in World War I, 949
debt:
agricultural, 738, 836, 840, 841, 1017–18
after American Revolution, 258, 260–61,
298–99
for Confederate cause, 668, 673
European, from World War I, 994–95,
1064–65
and issuance of paper currency, 259,
260–61
in 1980s, 1327, 1328
repudiated, post-Civil War, 712
Shays's Rebellion and, 261–62
state, federal assumption of, 286–87,
288–89, 292–93, 294
debt, national:
Andrew Jackson on, 404
after Civil War, 686, 687–88
Clinton and, 1353, 1354
in early U.S., 286–89, 292–93, 294, 304
George H. W. Bush and, 1334, 1349–50

gold vs. greenbacks in repayment of, 687
in Jefferson administration, 326
Reagan and, 1319–20, 1328, 1331
Truman and, 1143
under Articles of Confederation, 250–52
debtors, imprisonment of, 451, 481
Decatur, Stephen, 327, 350
Declaration of American Rights (1774), 193
Declaration of Cairo (1943), 1110
"Declaration of Causes" (Texas) (1836), 508
Declaration of Independence (1776), 202–6,
203, 210, 281, 458
Independence Day and, 246
sources of, 204
Declaration of London (1909), 938
Declaration of Rights, Virginia (1776), 204,
245, 264, 284
Declaration of Sentiments (1848), 483–84
Declaration of the Causes and Necessity of
Taking Up Arms (1775), 200
Declaration of the Causes of Secession
(South Carolina) (1860), 602
Declaration of the Rights and Grievances of
the Colonies (1765), 182
Declaration of the United Nations (1942),
1103
Declaratory Act (1766), 183
Deere, John, 419
defendants' rights, 1042–43, 1232
deficits, federal, *see* debt, national
deism, 138, 459–60
de Kooning, Willem, 1188
Delaware:
Constitution ratified by, 274, *274, 291*
in early interstate cooperation, 262
secession rejected by, 610
segregation in, 1219
voting rights in, 240, 382
Delaware, Thomas West De La Warr, Lord,
54–55
Delaware and Hudson Canal, 425
Delaware colony, 78, 91
European settlement of, 78, 99
government of, 154
Delawares, *93*, 131, 168, 177, 229
DeLeon, Daniel, 774, 775, 776
de Lôme, Depuy, 866–67
Democratic Leadership Council (DLC), 1352
Democratic National Committee, 1300
Democratic party, 295
African Americans in, 712, 1043, 1059
"Barnburners" in, 568
Bourbons (Redeemers) and, 712
budget deficits and, 1318
in Civil War, 628, 637, 638–39

Democratic party (*continued*)
  in Cleveland's presidency, 831
  cold war and, 1134
  and Congress in late nineteenth century,
    821–22
  corruption and, 823
  in election of 1832, 402–3
  in election of 1836, 407
  in election of 1840, 410–12, *412*
  in election of 1844, 511
  in election of 1848, 567–68
  in election of 1852, 579
  in election of 1856, 591
  in election of 1860, 599–600
  in election of 1864, 638–39
  in election of 1868, 686–87
  in election of 1874, 693
  in election of 1876, 694–97
  in election of 1880, 826
  in election of 1894, 848
  in election of 1896, 849–51, 852
  in election of 1900, 881–82
  in election of 1904, 902–3
  in election of 1908, 910
  in election of 1916, 942–43
  in election of 1918, 956
  in election of 1920, 993
  in election of 1924, 999
  in election of 1928, 1010–11
  in election of 1948, 1154, 1155, 1155–56
  in election of 1956, 1209–10
  in election of 1964, 1248
  in election of 1968, 1260–61, 1270–71,
    1271
  in election of 1972, 1298–99
  in election of 1980, 1317–18
  in election of 1988, 1331
  in election of 1992, 1352–53
  in election of 1994, 1356
  in election of 2000, 1371
  ethnic groups in, 820, 838
  Farmers' Alliances and, 843, 845
  in formation of Republican party, 585
  in formation of Whigs, 407
  Free Soil party and, 568–69
  George H. W. Bush and, 1334, 1351
  in Great Depression, 1016
  immigration issue and, 838
  Independent Treasury and, 409–10
  Irish Americans in, 407, 445–46
  in Kansas-Nebraska crisis, 585
  labor and, 451
  labor movement and, 1057
  late nineteenth-century components of, 821
  liberal social agenda of, 1317
    New Deal and, 1134–35
    new states resisted by, 725
    origins of, 379
    "real issues" and, 820
    in Reconstruction South, 690–91
    reshaped by F.D. Roosevelt, 1060
    slavery issue in, 513–14, 585, 599–600
    in South, 541, 1156–59
    Spanish-American War and, 873–74
    in Taft administration, 913
    tariff issue and, 822
    Vietnam War and, 1289
    voting rights and, 1042
    in Wilson's presidency, 919–20, 921
    World War II and, 1129
Democratic-Republicans, 379
  see also Democratic party
Democratic Review, 411
Denmark:
  in NATO, 1151
  in World War II, 1078–79
Dependent Pension Act (1890), 836
Dependent Pension Bill (1887), 832
Depression, Great, 857–58
  banking industry in, 1025, 1027–29
  children in, 1038
  congressional initiatives in, 1017–18
  culture in, 1043–46
  currency and, 1015, 1017, 1028, 1029
  dust bowl in, 1033, 1038–40, 1044
  farmers and, 1014, 1016, 1018, 1028–29,
    1033–34
  hardships of, 1015, 1016, 1018–19, 1025,
    1038, 1041–42
  Hoover's efforts at recovery, 1016–17
  human toll of, 1015, 1016, 1025, 1038–43
  isolationism in, 1071–72
  labor movement in, 1016, 1034–35, 1036,
    1037, 1049, 1053, 1055–57, 1059
  market crash and, 1013–15, *1014*
  unemployment in, 1014, 1015, 1019–20,
    1022, 1025, 1030–31, 1032, 1038
  World War I veterans in, 1019–20, *1019*
  see also New Deal
depression of 1893, 847–48
desegregation, *see* civil rights movement;
    segregation, desegregation
Deseret, 465, 572
Desert Shield, Operation, *1339*, 1340
Desert Storm, Operation, 1340, 1349
détente, 1297–98
Detroit, Mich., 438
  race riot in (1943), 1100
  race riot in (1967), 1251
  school desegregation in, 1291–92

Dewey, George, 869, 874
Dewey, John, 807
Dewey, Thomas E., 1081, 1118, 1155, 1157, *1158, 1159*
Dial, 468
Dias, Bartholomeu, 15
Díaz, Porfirio, 931
Dickinson, Emily, 471–72, *471,* 635
Dickinson, John, 185, 200, 238
Diem, Ngo Dinh, 1207–9, 1242, *1242,* 1243
Dien Bien Phu, Battle of (1954), 1206
Dies, Martin, 1060
Dillon, C. Douglas, 1231
Dingley Tariff (1897), 852
diphtheria, 20, 104
direct primaries, 893
disarmament and arms reduction:
    and détente, 1329–30
    SALT, 1297, 1304, 1309
    after World War I, 1065–67
discovery and exploration, 12–25
    of Africa, 14, 15
    biological exchange from, 18–22
    Dutch, *39*
    English, *39,* 41–42
    French, 38, *39,* 157–62
    Norse, 12–13, *12*
    Spanish, 15–18, 22–23, *23,* 28–33, *30*
    technology in, 13–14
    see also Columbus, Christopher
disease:
    AIDS, 1328–29, *1329*
    among poor southern whites, 542
    on Atlantic crossing, 444
    in Civil War, 640
    in colonial era, 54, 104
    Indian susceptibility to, 20–22, *20, 21,* 27, 74, 80, 86, 87
    influenza, 962–63, *963*
    Overland Trail and, 503
    in Southwest frontier, 555
    yellow fever, 877–78
disenfranchisement of blacks, in South, 714–16, 820, 927, 1042
distillation, 301
Distribution Act (1836), 405
District of Columbia, *see* Washington, D.C.
divine right of kings, 48–49, 152
divorce, 243, 1038
Dix, Dorothea Lynde, 481–82, 634
Dixie, Operation, 1143
Dixiecrats, 1156–58, *1157*
Dixon, Thomas, 1001
DLC (Democratic Leadership Council), 1352

Dodge, Richard, 732
Doeg Indians, 59
Dole, Bob, 1359–60, *1359*
dollar diplomacy, 933, 934
Dominica, 172
Dominican Republic, 16
    U.S. intervention in (1916–1925), 886, 934, 1068
Dominion of New England, 150–51
Donner, George, 505–6
Donner Party, 505–6
Doubleday, Abner, 800
Douglas, Stephen A., 430, *583,* 595, 596, 748
    and Compromise of 1850, 572, 576
    death of, 637
    in election of 1860, 599–600, 601–2, *603*
    Kansas-Nebraska issue and, 582–86
    Lecompton constitution and, 594
    Lincoln's debates with, 596–97
    popular sovereignty supported by, 567
Douglass, Frederick, 552, 559, *560,* 654, 662, *683*
downsizing, 1350
draft:
    in Civil War, 617–18
    in Vietnam War, 1268–69, 1284, 1306
    in World War I, 946, 949
    in World War II, 1094
Drake, Francis, 40
Dred Scott v. Sandford, 592–93, 595, 597, 601
Dreiser, Theodore, 809
drugs:
    from Americas, 20
    George H. W. Bush's policy on, 1334
    illegal, 1270–71, 1272, 1285, 1328, 1334, 1338, 1339
    patent medicines, 904, 905
Duarte, José Napoleón, 1322, 1327
Dubinsky, David, 1055
Du Bois, W. E. B., *242,* 719–21, *720,* 982, 983
duels, 312, 543
"due-process clause," 673, 816, 841
Dukakis, Michael, 1331–33, *1333*
Duke, James Buchanan "Buck," 708
Duke, Washington, 707–8
Dulles, John Foster, 1200, 1203–4, *1204,* 1206, 1207, 1209, 1210, 1212, 1213, 1321
Dunkers, 36
Durand, John, *135*
dust bowl, 1033, 1038–40, *1040,* 1044
Dutch Americans, 88, 90, 131, 132, *133,* 134, 140
Dutch East India Company, 83

Dutch East Indies, 1084, 1086, 1087, 1092, 1204–5
Dutch Empire, 38–40, 76, 83–84, 86
Dutch Reformed Church, 36, 131, 144
Dutch Republic, 38–40, 162
Dutch West India Company, 84
Dwight, Timothy, 461
Dylan, Bob, 1271
Dynamic Sociology (Ward), 806
dysentery, 104

Earhart, Amelia, 1003
Earth Day, *1294*
East India Company, 190–91
East St. Louis, Ill., race riot in (1917), 947
Eaton, John, 388
Eaton, Peggy, 388
Eaton Affair, 388
ecology, 908, 909–10, 1039
Economic Cooperation Administration (ECA), 1149
Economic Interpretation of the Constitution, An (Beard), 272
Economic Opportunity Bill (1964), 1246–47
Economic Recovery Tax Act (1981), 1319
economics, 809–10
    Keynesian, 1058
    Reaganomics, 1317, 1319–20, *1319*
    Veblen on, 809–10
Economist, The, 1389
economy:
    agriculture and, 839–40
    airplanes and automobiles in, 1002–4
    in antebellum South, 537–38
    Carter and, 1309
    in Civil War, 612–13, 636–37
    Civil War influence on, 744
    Clinton and, 1360–61
    in early nineteenth century, 349–50, 357–62, 385–86, 404, 406, 416–39
    in early twenty-first century, 1372–73
    in early U.S., 250–52, 259–61, 285–93
    entrepreneurs in, 753–60
    environmental regulations and, 1373
    exploitation, imperialism and, 860, 861
    Ford and, 1304
    George H. W. Bush and, 1349–50, 1351–52
    George W. Bush and, 1372–73
    globalization in, 1361, 1368–69
    Hamilton's views on, 285–93
    Hayes's views on, 825–26
    immigration as spur to, 443–46
    investment bankers in, 757–58
    in Jacksonian era, 385–86, 404, 406
    in laissez-faire policies, 413–14, 816–17

in late nineteenth century, 743–53
in late twentieth century, 1342–43
in 1920s, 994–95, 999, 1000–1010, 1011–13
Nixon and, 1292–94
of North vs. South, 528
and Panic of 1819, 367
"postindustrial," 1343
Reagan and, 1317, 1319–20, *1319*, 1324, 1328
rise of consumer goods in, 1000–1010
sea power in, 861
September 11, 2001 attacks and, 1376
social criticism and, 809–10
of South, 537–38, 707–8, 711–12
of Soviet Union, 1336, 1337
stock market and, 1012–15, 1327–28, *1327*, 1360–61
transportation improvements and, 421–30
trusts in, 755, 836, 899–902, 914, 919, 923–24, *980*
under Van Buren, 409–10
after War of 1812, 349–50, 357–62
of West, 489
after World War I, 963–64
in World War I, 946
after World War II, 1134, 1140–41, 1171–72
in World War II, 1094–96, 1096–97, 1129
see also agriculture, farmers; banking industry; corporations, business; currency; debt; Depression, Great; industry; manufactures; tariffs and duties; trade and commerce; *specific panics and depressions*
Economy Act (1933), 1028
Edison, Thomas, 752–53
Edison General Electric Company, 752
education:
    affirmative action in, 1275, 1362
    of African Americans, 680–81, 685, 712, 714, 720, 1173
    agricultural, 926
    of Asian Americans, 887
    in backcountry, 141
    bilingual, 1345
    busing and, *1291*, 1350
    in colonial period, 116–17, 140–41
    Dewey's views on, 807
    evolution in, 972
    Farmers' Alliances and, 842
    federal aid to, 254, 635, 660
    GI Bill of Rights and, 1173
    Great Society and, 1249, 1250
    higher, 477–79
    immigration and, 1345

learning standards and, 1373
in nineteenth century, 475–79, 680–81, 685, 780, 801–4
parochial, 822, 837–38
public schools, 451, 453, 801–2
in Reconstruction, *680–81*, 685
religion and, 143–44, 477
school prayer and, 1232, 1348, 1383
secondary schools, 801–2
segregation and desegregation in, 887, 1153, 1173, 1219–20, 1233, 1234, 1291, 1362
social reform and, 464, 475–79
in South, 712, 714
space program and, 1214
technical, 477–78
township support of, 254
2002 reform of, 1373
vocational training, 802, 926
vouchers and, 1369
women and, 454, 478–79, *478,* 482, 803–4, *803*
see also colleges and universities
Educational Amendments Act, Title IX of (1972), 1275
Education Department, U.S., 1306, 1331
Edwards, Jonathan, 141–43, 247, 461
EEOC (Equal Employment Opportunity Commission), 1321
Egypt, 1298, 1304
in Arab League, 1211
Camp David accords and, 1307–8
in Persian Gulf War, 1340
in Six-Day War, 1298
Suez War in, 1210, 1211–13
in World War II, 1082
Ehrlichman, John, 1290, 1299, 1300, 1301
Eighteenth Amendment, 271, 974, 992, 1024
eighteen-year-olds, voting rights for, 1292
eight-hour workday, 766, 767, 846, 927
Einstein, Albert, *984,* 985, 986, 1080
Eisenhower, Dwight D., 1172
assessment of, 1223–24
background of, 1198–99
Bonus Army and, 1020
brinksmanship under, 1204
civil rights movement and, 1218, 1220, 1222, 1223
Congress and, 1198
dynamic conservatism of, 1199–1200
economic policy of, 1199
in election of 1952, 1195–98, *1197,* 1227
in election of 1956, 1209–10
farewell address of, 1223–24
foreign alliances and, 1210–11
foreign policy of, 1203–4

Indochina and, 1206, 1207, 1242
internal security under, 1202–3
on John Kennedy, 1238
Khrushchev's summit with, 1216
Korean War and, 1165, 1200–1201
Little Rock crisis and, 1223
McCarthyism and, 1202
Middle East policy of, 1210–13
on military-industrial complex, 1193
New Deal and, 1210
political rise of, 1196
religion promoted by, 1182
Sputnik and, 1214
Suez War and, 1212
U-2 summit and, 1216–17
Vietnam and, 1206–9
in World War II, 1103, 1109, 1110–11, *1111,* 1113, 1119–20
Eisenhower Doctrine, 1215
Elaine, Ark., race riot in (1919), 965
elderly, aging population and, 1136
elections and campaigns:
of 1789, 282
of 1792, 295
of 1796, 308
of 1800, 211, 315–18, *317,* 324
of 1804, 324, 332–33
of 1808, 338
of 1816, 362
of 1820, 376
of 1824, 376–78, *401,* 407, 408
of 1828, 380–84, *382, 383,* 391, *405,* 408, 446
of 1832, 395, 401, 402–3
of 1836, 407–8
of 1840, 410–12, *411, 412,* 490, 561
of 1844, 510, 511–13, *512,* 561
of 1848, 567–68
of 1852, 579–80
of 1854, 448
of 1856, 589–91, *590*
of 1858, 596–97
of 1860, 528, 599–602, *600, 605*
of 1864, 638–39, 665, 667, 725
of 1868, 686–87
of 1872, 691–93
of 1874, 693
of 1876, 694–97, *696,* 824
of 1878, 841
of 1880, 826, 841
of 1884, 828–31, 841
of 1888, 834–35
of 1890, 837–38
of 1892, 845–46, 891
of 1894, 848, 849
of 1896, 848, 849–51, *851*

elections and campaigns (*continued*)
  of 1900, 775, 881–82, *882*
  of 1904, 775, 902–3
  of 1908, 910–11
  of 1910, 913, 917
  of 1912, 775, 914–16, 917–21, *920*, 949
  of 1916, 925–26, 941–43, *942*
  of 1918, 956
  of 1920, 949, 992–93
  of 1924, 999
  of 1928, 1010–11
  of 1930, 1016
  of 1932, 1023–25, *1025, 1026*
  of 1934, 1046
  of 1936, 1052–53
  of 1938, 1060
  of 1940, 1080–82
  of 1944, 1118, 1141
  of 1946, 1141, 1142
  of 1948, 1154–59, *1159*
  of 1952, 1195–98, *1197*, 1203, 1227
  of 1956, 1209–10
  of 1960, 1227–30, *1230*
  of 1964, 1247–48, 1255, 1314
  of 1966, 1314
  of 1968, 1259–63, *1261*, 1270–71, *1271*, 1283
  of 1972, 1287, 1289, 1298–99
  of 1976, 1305
  of 1980, 1315, 1317–18, *1318*, 1321
  of 1982, 1320
  of 1984, 1321, 1324–25
  of 1988, 1331–33, *1332, 1333*
  of 1992, 1135, 1351, 1351–53
  of 1994, 1356–57
  of 1996, 1359–60
  of 2000, 1369–71, *1370*
  of 2004, 820, 1383–86, *1384, 1385*
  congressional mechanisms for, 268–69
  direct primaries in, 893
  fraud and intimidation in, 690–91
  gerrymandering and, 1361
  nomination process in, 376–77
  partisanship of, in early 2000s, 1383–84
  platforms introduced into, 402–3
  precinct-level organization in, 411–12
  progressive reforms in, 893
  regional differences and, 1371
  saloons and, 794
  voter registration drives and, 1251
  voter turnout, 820, 928, 1305, 1317–18,
    1333
electoral college, in Constitution, 269–70
  see also elections and campaigns
Electoral Commission, 695, *696*
electrical motors, 431

electricity, 751–53
  industrial revolution and, 745–46
  TVA and, 1036–38
Electronic Numerical Integrator and
    Computer (ENIAC), 1346, *1346*
Elephant Butte Dam, 738
elevators, 781
Eliot, Charles W., 876
Eliot, T. S., 987
Elizabeth I, queen of England, 37–38, *37*, 40,
    41, 45, 48, 49, 50
Elkins Act (1903), 902, 903
Ellis Island, 788–89, *788, 789*
Ellison, Ralph, 1031, 1188, *1188*
Ellsberg, Daniel, 1287, 1300
El Salvador, 1290, 1322–23, 1327
emancipation, 629–33
  in Civil War, 629–33
  early proposals for, 556–57
  freedmen's plight after, 662–64, *663*
  in Revolutionary War, 241–42
  southern economy and, 661
Emancipation Proclamation (1863), 628,
    630, *631*, 632
Embargo Act (1807), 336–38, 432
embargoes:
  of Arab oil (1973), 1293, 1294
  against Iran, 1310
  against Iraq, 1339
  in World War II, 1075–76, 1085
Emergency Banking Relief Act (1933), 1027,
    1028
Emergency Farm Mortgage Act (1933), 1028,
    1029
Emergency Immigration Act (1921), 970
Emergency Relief Act (1932), 1018
Emergency Relief Appropriation Act (1935),
    1031
Emerson, Ralph Waldo, 354, 355, 468–69,
    468, 470, 484
  Brook Farm supported by, 487
  on Brooks's attack on Sumner, 589
  on Fugitive Slave Act, 578
  on John Brown, 599
  lectures of, 468–69
  on Mexican War, 565
employment, *see* labor, employment
Employment Act (1946), 1141
Empress of China, 258
enclosure movement, 47
encomenderos, 32
encomienda, 27
Endangered Species Act (1969), 1294
Endara, Guillermo, 1338
energy crisis, 1293, 1294, 1307, 1311

Energy Department, U.S., 1306
Enforcement Acts (1870–1871), 690
engineering, 454
England:
    background on, 45–50
    Catholics in, 40, 45, 49, 50, 60
    colonial administration of, 94–95, 147,
        148–53, 177–85, 186
    constitution of, 46, 48, 176
    explorations by, 22, *39*, 41–42
    government of, *see* Parliament, British
    landownership in, 47
    liberties in, 45–48
    monarchy of, 48–50, 147
    nobles in, 46, 47
    population explosion in, 47
    privateers from, 40, 77
    Reformation in, 36–38
    Scotland joined with, 50
    Spanish Armada defeated by, 40–41, *41*
    taxation in, 46, 49, 50, 178
    traders from, 31
    after Wars of the Roses, 15
    see also Anglican Church; Great Britain
English Civil War (1642–1649), 76–77, 89,
    148
English language:
    African influence in, 114
    Dutch influence in, 85
ENIAC (Electronic Numerical Integrator
    and Computer), 1346, *1346*
Enlightenment, 138–41, 459–60, 466–67
Enola Gay, 1127
Enron, 1372
entrepreneurs, 753–60
    see also specific entrepreneurs
environment, 1294–95, 1306
    cities and, 785–86, *786*
    Civil War and, 640
    conservation and, 905–10, 912–13, 914–15
    dust bowl and, 1038–39
    European attitude toward, 100–101
    George W. Bush and, 1373
    Great Plains and, 505
    Hurricane Katrina and, 1387–88
    industrialization and, 436–37, *438*
    introduced species and, 101–102
    mining and, 725, *725*, 728
    pollution and, 436, 786, 905, 1292
    tenancy, sharecropping and, 710–11
Environmental Protection Agency (EPA),
    1294, 1320, 1373
Episcopal Church, 245, 460
Equal Employment Opportunity
    Commission (EEOC), 1321

equality:
    American Revolution and, 239–40
    Jacksonian era and, 386–87, 455
    racial, 597
"equal protection" clause, 673
Equal Rights Amendment (ERA), 980,
    1275–76, 1316, 1321
Erie Canal, 424–26, *425*
Erie Railroad, 750, 751
Eries, 87, *92*
Eriksson, Leif, 13
Erik the Red, 13
Erskine, David, 338
Ervin, Samuel J., Jr., 1300, 1301
Escobedo v. Illinois, 1232
Essay on Calcareous Manures (Ruffin), 537
Essay on Human Understanding (Locke), 138
Essex Junto, 332
Estonia, 1337
Ethiopia, 1073, 1075
Ethiopian Regiment, 241
eugenics, 978
Europe:
    American biological exchange with, 18–22
    expansion of, 13–15
European Economic Community (Common
    Market), 1232
European Recovery Program (Marshall
    Plan), 1148–49, *1150,* 1160
evangelism, 462
Evers, Medgar, 1236
evolution, 804–5, *973*
    see also Darwinism
executive branch, 282–83
    see also presidency
"Exodusters," 722–23
exploration, *see* discovery and exploration
Export Control Act (1940), 1085
ex post facto laws, 271

factories:
    child labor and, 761–62, *762*
    conditions in, 760–62
    electrification and, 753
    Taylorism in, 894
    see also manufactures; working class
factory system, 321
Fair Deal, 817, 1154–55, 1158
Fair Employment Practices Commission
    (FEPC), 1100, 1139, 1153
Fair Labor Standards Act (1938), 1058, 1059
Fair Oaks (Seven Pines), Battle of (1862),
    623
Fall, Albert B., 996

Fallen Timbers, Battle of (1794), 300
Fall River (Rhode Island) system, 435
Falwell, Jerry, 1315–16, 1348
Familists, 36
family:
  in colonial period, 104–5
  in late twentieth century, 1344
  and life on trail, 503–4
  in 1940s and 1950s, 1186, 1190
  planning and, 978–79
  slave, 553–54, 553
  Spock and, 1186
  values, 1316, 1348, 1351
  see also marriage
Farewell to Arms, A (Hemingway), 988
Farm Credit Act (1933), 1028, 1029
Farm Credit Administration (FCA), 1029
farmers, see agriculture
Farmers' Alliances, 841–45, 843
Farmers' Holiday Association, 1018
Farm Security Administration (FSA), 1059
Farm Tenant Act (1937), 1058–59
Farouk, King of Egypt, 1211
Farragut, David, 616, 639
fascism, 1022, 1071
fashion, 977
Faubus, Orval, 1222–23
Faulkner, William, 988, 989
FBI (Federal Bureau of Investigation), 1236, 1300, 1356
FCA (Farm Credit Administration), 1029
FCC (Federal Communications Commission), 1002
FDA (Food and Drug Administration), 1276
FDIC (Federal Deposit Insurance Corporation), 1028, 1029
Federal Art Project, 1031, 1032
Federal Bureau of Investigation (FBI), 1236, 1300, 1356
Federal Communications Commission (FCC), 1002
Federal Deposit Insurance Corporation (FDIC), 1028, 1029
Federal Election Campaign Act (1972), 1292
Federal Emergency Management Agency (FEMA), 1387–88
Federal Emergency Relief Act (1933), 1028
Federal Emergency Relief Administration (FERA), 1030–31
Federal Farm Board, 1012, 1016
Federal Farm Loan Act (1916), 926
Federal Farm Loan Board, 926
Federal Highways Act (1916), 362, 926
Federal Home Loan Bank Act (1932), 1018

Federal Housing Administration (FHA), 1041, 1177–78
Federalist, The (Hamilton, Madison and Jay), 272–73, 283
Federalists, 211, 262, 311–12, 363
  Alien and Sedition Acts of, 313–14
  and army authorization of 1798, 311
  and Dartmouth College v. Woodward, 371–72
  decline of, 333–34
  in election of 1796, 308
  in election of 1800, 315–18
  in election of 1808, 338
  in election of 1816, 362
  in election of 1824, 376
  Essex Junto in, 332
  French Revolution and, 297
  land policy of, 304
  Louisiana Purchase as seen by, 329
  military spending of, 326–27
  Napoleonic wars and, 337, 338
  national bank and, 360
  officeholder conflicts and, 325
  in ratification debate, 271–72, 273–74
  Republican opposition to, 293–94
  Republicans' role reversal with, 350, 359
  and War of 1812, 349, 350
Federal Music Project, 1031
Federal Radio Commission, 1005
Federal Reserve Act (1913), 922
Federal Reserve System, 922–23, 924, 926, 995, 1013, 1029, 1199, 1350, 1360
  creation of, 922–23
  Glass-Steagall Banking Act, 1018
Federal Securities Act (1933), 1028, 1029
Federal Theater Project, 1031
Federal Trade Commission (FTC), 923, 924, 995, 1029, 1059
Federal Writers' Project, 1031, 1044
FEMA (Federal Emergency Management Agency), 1387–88
Feminine Mystique, The (Friedan), 1274–75, 1274
feminism, 980, 1274–76, 1316–17, 1321, 1351
Feminist Majority Foundation, 1277
Fence-Cutters' War, 737
FEPC (Fair Employment Practices Commission), 1100, 1139, 1153
FERA (Federal Emergency Relief Administration), 1030–31
Ferdinand II, king of Aragon, 15–16, 17
Ferguson, Miriam "Ma," 972
Ferguson, Patrick, 230
Fermi, Enrico, 1126
Ferraro, Geraldine, 1325

feudalism, 84
 English, 47
FHA (Federal Housing Administration), 1041, 1177–78
Field and Stream, 906
Fifteenth Amendment, 529, 678, *682,* 697, 715, 813, 983, 1100
Fifth Amendment, 566–67, 593
Fillmore, Millard, *575,* 580, *621*
 and Compromise of 1850, 575–77
 in election of 1856, 589
Finance Department, U.S., 250
Financier, The (Dreiser), 809
Finland, 1083, 1146
Finney, Charles Grandison, 463–64, 486
Finnish settlers, 88, 131
firearms, right to bear, 284
"First, Second, and Last Scene of Mortality, The" (Punderson), *106*
First African Church, *680*
First Amendment, 561
First Report on the Public Credit (Hamilton), 286–87
Fish, Hamilton, 687
fishing, in New England, 120, *120,* 123, 126–27, 436–37
Fisk, Jim, 688
Fiske, John, 861–62
Fisk University, 714
Fitzgerald, F. Scott, 976, 977, 987–88, *987,* 1043
Fitzgerald, Zelda, *987,* 988
Fitzhugh, George, 562
Five-Power Naval Treaty (1922), 1066, 1067, 1073
flax, 534
Fletcher, John, 205
Fletcher v. Peck, 371
Florida, 33, 91, 94, 256, 297, 333, 334
 acquisition of, 365–67
 after American Revolution, 235
 British colonies established in, 177
 Civil War in, 616
 in colonial wars, 168–69, 172
 in election of 1876, 695
 in election of 2000, 1369–71, *1370*
 exploration of, 29–30, 31
 Huguenots in, 31
 labor movement in, 1096
 Louisiana Purchase and, 328, 329
 population of, 1343
 real-estate boom in, 1012
 Reconstruction in, 683, 691
 secession of, 602
 Seminoles in, 397, 400
 Spanish exploration and colonization of, 29–30, 31, 81, 82, 495
 and War of 1812, 339, 340, 346
Flying Cloud, 427
Flynn, Elizabeth Gurley, 776–77
folklore, African-American, 552–53
Folkways (Sumner), 806
food:
 in colonial period, 119, 120
 reform movements and, 479
 safety of, 904–5
 of slaves, 548
 technology and, 431, 445, 751
Food, Drug and Cosmetic Act (1938), 1058, 1059
Food Administration, 946
Food and Drug Administration (FDA), 1276
food stamps, 1292
Foot, Samuel A., 391
football, 800
Foot Resolution, 391–93
Foraker Act (1900), 877
Foran Act (1885), 768
Force Bill (1833), 395–96, 404
Ford, Gerald, 1304–5
 appointed vice-president, 1302
 in election of 1976, 1305
 Nixon pardoned by, 1302–3
 presidency assumed by, 1302
 vetoes of, 1304
Ford, Henry, 1003–4
Ford Motor Company, 1003–4, *1004*
Fordney-McCumber Tariff (1922), 994
Foreign Affairs, 1147
Foreign Affairs Department, U.S., 250
foreign policy:
 brinksmanship, 1204
 containment, 1147–48, 1168–69, 1203, 1257, 1349, 1379–80
 cultural values and, 1374
 détente, 1297–98
 dollar diplomacy, 933, 934
 good neighbor policy, 1068–69
 human rights in, 1307
 isolationism, 1063–69, 1071–72, *1076*
 Marshall Plan, 1148–49, *1150,* 1160
 mutual defense treaties, 1207
 in the 1950s, 1203–9
 Open Door policy in, 879–80, 886, 887, 1066–67, 1071
 preemptive military action (Bush doctrine) and, 1379–80, 1380–82
 Progressive idealism in, 930–31, 954, 956
 reciprocal trade agreements, 1072

foreign policy (*continued*)
  shuttle diplomacy, 1298, 1304
  Truman Doctrine, 1148–49
  unipolar, 1374
  see also imperialism; *specific foreign powers, presidents, treaties, wars*
Forest and Stream, 906
Forest Reserve Act (1891), 908
Forest Service, 907
forfeited-rights theory, 671
Formosa, *see* Taiwan (Formosa)
Fort Detroit, *298*
Fort Donelson, 620
Fort Duquesne (Pittsburgh, Penn.), 164, 166, 170
Fort Henry, 620
Fort Jackson, Treaty of (1814), 344–45
Fort Laramie conference (1851), 728
Fort Laramie Treaty (1851), 495
Fort Le Boeuf, 163
Fort Louisbourg, attack on, 168
Fort McHenry, 346
Fort Necessity, 165
Fort Niagara, 168
Fort Pickens, 604
Fort Pitt, 170
Fort Sacramento, *501*
Fort Stanwix, Battle of (1777), 224
Fort Stanwix, Treaty of (1784), 256
Fort Sumter, 604–5
  fall of (1861), 609
Fort Ticonderoga, Battle of (1775), 198
Fort Ticonderoga, Battle of (1777), 224
Fortune, 1171
Fort Wagner, 633
Forty-niners (gold miners), 569–71, *570*
Foster, Stephen, 442–43
Foster, William Z., 964
Four-Minute Men, 948
Four-Power Treaty (1922), 1066
Fourteen Points, 954–55
Fourteenth Amendment, 529, 673, 674, 675, 697, 716, 983
  private property and, 816
Fox, George, 89
Foxes, *92,* 397
France, 122, 334
  American Revolution and, 202, 210, 221, 224–25, 226, 227–28, 233, 234–35, 286
  California and, 507
  in China, 878
  Citizen Genêt and, 296–97
  in colonial wars, 162–72, 174, 175
  communism in, 1149
  1823 Spanish incursion of, 375

  explorations of, 38, *39,* 157–62
  Germany occupied by, 1149, *1151*
  after Hundred Years' War, 14–15
  as imperialist nation, 860
  in Indochina, 1084, 1085, 1160–61, 1162, 1204–9
  in Kellogg-Briand Pact, 1067–68
  late eighteenth-century conflict with, 309–12, 313
  in League of Nations, 957
  in Lebanon, 1324
  Louisiana purchased from, 328–29, 368–69
  Marshall Plan and, 1149
  Monroe Doctrine and, 375
  Morocco crisis and (1905–1906), 888
  in Munich agreement, 1073
  in Napoleonic Wars, 335–38, *336,* 374, 495
  in NATO, 1151
  navy of, 233
  Normandy invasion in, 1110–13, *1112*
  Paris Peace Conference and, 956, 959
  in Persian Gulf War, 1340
  in post-World War I treaties, 1066–67, *1066*
  privateers from, 38, 298
  Revolution in, 295–97
  in SEATO, 1207
  in second Gulf War, 1381, 1383
  Spanish Civil War and, 1075
  in Suez War, 1210, 1212–13
  Texas Republic recognized by, 510
  traders from, 31
  in United Nations, 1144
  U.S. Civil War and, 616, 618, 630
  U.S. trade with, 285, 335–38, *336,* 338, 389, 406, 535
  Vichy government of, 1085, 1103
  in World War I, 934–35, 938, 945, 950–51, 952
  World War I debt of, 1064–65
  World War II and, 1073, 1074, 1078, 1079, 1081, 1103, 1109, 1110–13, 1118, 1172
  see also French Empire
Franciscans, 31, 32, 498–500
Franco, Francisco, 1073, 1075–76
Frankfurter, Felix, 789, 1049
Frank Leslie's Illustrated Newspaper, 475
Franklin, Battle of (1864), 650
Franklin, Benjamin, 108, 110, 127, 137, *139,* 142, *165,* 172, 202, 218, 313
  at Albany Congress, 166
  background of, 139–40
  Boston Tea Party condemned by, 191
  on British in Philadelphia, 223–24

on Constitution, 276
at Constitutional Convention, 264
and Declaration of Independence, 203, 204
as deist, 459
Paxton Boys and, 188–89
on peace commission, 234, *235*, 283
Plan of Union of, 166
on population growth, 103
as postmaster-general, 201
Franklin, William, 218
Franklin, William Temple, *235*
Franklin (Holston state), 256
Franklin Institute, 454
Franz Ferdinand, Archduke of Austria, 934
Freake, Elizabeth, *103*
Freake, John, *103*
Freake, Mary, *103*
Fredericksburg, Battle of (1862), 628, 640
Frederick Turnpike, 422
Freed, Alan, 1191–92
Freedmen's Aid Society, 663
Freedmen's Bureau, Mississippi, 681
Freedmen's Bureau, U.S., 663–64, *664*, 672, 680
freedom of assembly, 284
Freedom of Information Act (1966), 1303
freedom of petition, 50, 238
freedom of religion, *see* religious freedom
freedom of speech, 238, 284, 314
freedom of the press, 313–14
    abolitionism and, 561
    in Bill of Rights, 284
    in colonial period, 137–38
freedom riders, 1234
Freeman, Elizabeth, *242*
Freeport Doctrine, 597
Free Soil party, 568–69, 579, 585, 590
Free Speech Movement (FSM), 1268
Free State Hotel, *587*
free trade, 257, 286, 691, 833–34, 1072
    see also tariffs and duties
Frémont, John Charles, 506–7, *506*, 590
    in election of 1856, 591
    Mexican War and, 518, 519
French Americans, 132, *133*, 134, 313
    in Civil War, 617
French and Indian War (Seven Years' War) (1755–1763), 163–68, *169*
    American soldiers in, 175
    legacy of, 175–76
French Empire, 29, 76, 84, 111
    British Empire compared with, 73, 94–95, 147, 157, 161–62
    colonization in, 31, 38
    fur trade in, 73, 84, 159, 161

in Indian conflicts, 81, 83, 87, *158*
Indian relations with, 73, 157–59, 161–62
maps of, *160, 170, 171*
missionaries in, 159, 161
religious restrictions in, 159
trade in, 31, 159, 161
    see also France
French Revolution, 295–97
Freud, Sigmund, 977, 986
Frick, Henry C., 770, 903
Friedan, Betty, 1274–75, *1274*
From Here to Eternity (Jones), 1187
frontier, 489
    American Revolution and, 226–29
    in Civil War period, 619–20
    closing of, 740–41
    in colonial period, 134
    in early nineteenth century, 416
    in early U.S., 299–300
    Indian conflicts on, 728–32
    internal improvements and, 360–62
    in Jefferson administration, 326
    manifest destiny and, 354, 492–93, 512, 517
    mountain men and, 497
    Northwest Ordinance and, 254–56
    Overland Trail and, 502–5, *505*
    religious revivals on, 461–62
    slavery in, 566–71
    southern, 554–56
    statehood procedures for, 252
    transportation links to, 421–22
    Turner's thesis of, 740–41, 780
    and War of 1812, 339–40, 341
    westward expansion and, 177, 240, 252–56, 281, 303–6, 320–21, 326, 492–507, 705–6
    Wilderness Road and, 304–6
    see also backcountry; West
FSA (Farm Security Administration), 1059
FSM (Free Speech Movement), 1268
FTC (Federal Trade Commission), 923, 924, 995, 1029, 1059
Fuchs, Klaus, 1167
Fugitive Slave Act (1850), 577–78
    protests against, 585
fugitive slave laws, 572, 577–78, *578*, 585
Fulbright, J. William, 1257
Fuller, Margaret, 468
Fulton, Robert, 373, *373*, 423
Fundamental Constitutions of Carolina, 78
fundamentalism, 972–74, 1315–16, 1323

Fundamental Orders of Connecticut (1639), 72, 126, 152
fur trade, 107, 131, 258, 438
    Dutch, 73, 83, 84, 87
    French, 73, 84, 159, 161
    mountain men and, 496, 497
    rendezvous system in, 497
Fur Traders Descending the Missouri, 1845 (Bingham), *497*

Gadsden Purchase, 523, 581, *582*
Gage, Thomas, 192, 196, 223
Galbraith, John Kenneth, 1184–85
Gallatin, Albert, 324–25, 326, 341, 348
Galveston, Tex., 894, 1388
game hunting laws, 906, 907
Gandhi, Mahatma K., 470, 1221
Garfield, James A., *476*, 689, 695–96, 697, 824, 826–27, *827*
Garfield, Lucretia Randolph, *476*
Garrison, William Lloyd, 484, 557, *557*
Garvey, Marcus, 982–83, *982*
Gaspee, 189–90, 191
Gastonia Strike (1929), 1008–10, *1009*
Gates, Bill, 1347
Gates, Horatio, 201, 224, 229
Gates, Thomas, 54–55
Gauguin, Paul, 969
Gay Liberation Front (GLF), 1282
gays:
    AIDS and, 1328–29
    marriage and, 1383
    in military, 1353–54
    rights of, 1282
Gaza Strip, 1366, 1379
gender gap, 1321, 1351
General Accounting Office, 994
General Assembly of Virginia, 57
General Court, Connecticut, 72
General Court, Massachusetts, 66–68, 70, 71
General Electric Corporation, 1373
General Federation of Women's Clubs, 815
General Motors, 1140, 1199
General Theory of Employment, Interest and Money, The (Keynes), 1058
Genêt, Edmond Charles, 296–97
Geneva Accords (1954), 1206–9, 1241
Geneva Medical College, 454–55
"Gentlemen's Agreement" (1907), 887, 970
gentrification, 1328
gentry, in southern colonies, 116–17, *116*
geography, Renaissance, 13–14
George, Henry, 809
George I, king of England, 153

George II, king of England, 91, 153
    death of, 168
George III, king of England, 176, *176*, 177, 229
    accession of, 168, 174
    on Boston Tea Party, 191
    on colonial rebellion, 194–95
    mercenaries recruited by, 201
    ministerial changes of, 182, 186
    Paine on, 202
    peace efforts and, 200, 225
Georgia:
    African Americans in legislature of, 713
    African-American soldiers outlawed by, 241
    agriculture in, 417–18, 533, 535, 710
    Civil War fighting in, 616, 645, 648–52, *651*
    Confederacy and states' rights in, 639
    Constitution ratified by, 274, *274*
    Indian conflicts in, 256, 345
    Indians removed from, 397–99
    land claims of, *253*, 255
    paper currency in, 260
    Reconstruction in, 678, 691
    secession of, 602
    slave trade in, 241
    suffrage in, 240, 382
    Union Loyalists in, 684
    voting rights in, 240, 382, 715
Georgia colony:
    backcountry of, 134
    ethnic groups in, 94
    European settlement of, 91, 94
    government of, 91, 94, 148, 152
    Indians in, 81, 91
    slaves in, 113
German Americans, 90, 94, 109, 131–32, *133*, 134, 354, 443, 446–47, 455, 542, 787
    in Civil War, 617
    clubs of, 797
    in Democratic party, 407
    prejudice against, 448
    Prohibition and, 821, 974
    in Socialist Labor party, 774
    westward migration and, 722, 747
    in World War I, 936, 949, 959
    in World War II, 1101
German Reformed Church, 36
German states, Reformation in, 36
Germantown, Battle of (1777), 223
Germany:
    American scholarship influenced by, 804
    in China, 878, 879
    as imperialist nation, 860
    industrial revolution in, 745

in Morocco crisis, 887–88
occupied, 1149–50
Paris Peace Conference and, 956, 958–59
reparations from, 958–59, 1064–65
rise of Nazism in, 1071
in Samoa, 863, 873
and second Gulf War, 1381, 1383
Weimar Republic in, 1071
in World War I, 856–57, 934–35, 936, 938–40, 943–44, *950*, 951, 952–53, 955, 962
Germany, East, 1150, 1215–16, *1335*, 1336
Germany, Nazi:
  Anschluss and, 1073
  Blitzkrieg tactics of, 1078–79
  collapse of, 1123–24
  Czechoslovakia invaded by, 1073, 1078
  early aggression of, 1073–74
  Hitler's rise and, 1071
  Pearl Harbor and, 1089
  Poland invaded by, 1078
  Rhineland reoccupied by, 1073
  Spanish Civil War and, 1073, 1075–76
  in Tripartite Pact, 1085
  war criminals of, 1144
  see also World War II
Germany, West, 1149–50
  East Germany reunited with, *1335*, 1336
  in NATO, 1151
  wartime damage in, 1172
Geronimo, Chiricahua Apache chief, 731
Gerry, Elbridge:
  at Constitutional Convention, 264, 268
  in ratification debate, 273
  XYZ Affair and, 310
gerrymandering, 1361
Gettysburg, Battle of (1863), 641–45
Gettysburg Address (1863), 644–45
Ghent, Treaty of (1814), 347–48, 349, 350, 363
Ghost Dance, 731–32
Gibbons, Thomas, 373
Gibbons v. Ogden, 373–74
GI Bill of Rights (1944), 1140, 1173–74
Gideon v. Wainwright, 1232
Gilbert, Humphrey, 41–42
Gilbert Islands, 1092
Gilded Age, The (Twain and Warner), 819
Gingrich, Newt, 1357–58
Ginsberg, Allen, 1189–90, *1189*
Gladden, Washington, 811
glasnost, 1335
Glass-Steagall Act (1932), 1018
GLF (Gay Liberation Front), 1282
Glidden, Joseph, 736

globalization, 1347, 1361, 1368–69, 1374, 1376
global warming, 7, 1373, 1388–89
Glorious Revolution, 49–50, 148, 151–52, 156, 162, 176, 180
Godwin, Abraham, *292*
Goering, Hermann, *1145*
gold:
  currency and, 693–94, 847, 848–49, 852, 903, 1017, 1018, 1028, 1029, 1293–94
  in mercantile system, 148–49
  national debt repayments in, 686, 687–88
  paper currency redeemable in, 693–94
  Spanish Empire and, 16, 29, 31, 32, 157
gold miners (Forty-niners), 569–71, *570*
gold rushes, 619, 724–28, *724*
  California (1848), 427, 494, 502, 505, 569–71, 724, 725, 728
  Yukon, 780
Gold Standard Act (1900), 852
Goldwater, Barry, 1247–48, *1248*, 1314
Gompers, Samuel, 768–69, *768*, 776, 876, 964, 1008
Gomulka, Wladyslaw, 1213
Gone With the Wind, 531
Good, Sarah, 128
"good neighbor" policy, 1068–69
Goodnight, Charles, 705–6
Goodyear, Charles, 431
Gorbachev, Mikhail, *1329–30*, *1330*, 1335, 1336–37, *1336*, 1338
Gore, Albert, Jr., 1352–53, *1353*, 1369–71, *1370*
Gorges, Ferdinando, 72
Gosiutes, 494
"Gospel of Wealth, The" (Carnegie), 756–57
Gould, Jay, 688, 750, *750*
government:
  as "broker state," 1061
  of Cherokees, 397, 398–99
  in Civil War, 635–40, 664–65
  Cleveland's limited view of, 831
  contract theory of, 152, 204, 237
  divided, 821–22
  of early U.S., 282–84
  English, 45–47, 50, 147, 153, 175–76, 237
  federal vs. state, 1369, 1373
  implied constitutional powers of, 372–73
  in Iroquois League, 86–87
  Locke on, 152
  New Deal and role of, 1060–61
  new state constitutions and, 237–38
  planning failures in, 1387–89
  in post-Gulf War Iraq, 1382–83
  post-Revolutionary War debates on, 235–38

government (*continued*)
　progressive reforms in, 894–95
　Progressive view of, 891
　in Reconstruction South, 664–65, 674–75
　separation of powers in, 268–71
　social change and, 806
　Theodore Roosevelt's views on, 918–19
　transportation and, 427, 430
　World War II and, 1129
graduate schools, 804
Graduation Act (1854), 419
Grady, Henry W., 706, 708
graft, 784
Graham, Billy, *1183*
Grand Army of the Republic, 832, 835
Grand Canyon National Monument, 907
"grandfather clause," 715, 983
Grange (Patrons of Husbandry), 840–41
Grant, Ulysses S., 611, 620, 639, *646*, 678,
　　686, 821
　background of, 523
　at Chattanooga, 645
　early cabinet appointments of, 687
　economic policy of, 688, 693
　in election of 1868, 686–87
　in election of 1872, 691–93
　in election of 1880, 826
　Lee pursued by, 646–48
　Lee's surrender to, 655
　in post-Civil War army, 674, 676
　scandals under, 688–89, 824
　at Shiloh, 620–22
　at Vicksburg, 641
Grapes of Wrath, The (Steinbeck), 1033, 1044
　film version of, 1045
Grasse, Admiral de, 233
Gray, L. Patrick, 1300
Great Awakening, 141–44, 459
Great Awakening, Second, 460–66
Great Britain:
　Burr Conspiracy and, 334
　California and, 507
　Canadian border and, 363–64, 410
　in China, 878–79
　colonial administration of, 148–53
　colonial trade with, 108, 123, 175
　in colonial wars, 162–72, 174
　and Convention of 1818, 363–64
　cotton trade with, 337, 389, 406, 528, 535,
　　539
　creation of, 50
　early U.S. relations with, 258–59
　eighteenth-century politics of, 176–77
　French Revolution and, 296, 297
　Germany occupied by, 1149, *1151*

　and Greek civil war, 1148
　as imperialist nation, 860–61
　independence movements and, 1204
　Indian conflicts and, 281, *298*, 340
　Indochina and, 1206
　industry in, 432
　Israel and, 1152
　Jay's Treaty with, 298–99
　Jordan intervention of, 1215
　in League of Nations, 957
　Marshall Plan and, 1149
　in METO, 1210
　military of, 175, 180, 186–87
　Monroe Doctrine and, 375
　Morocco crisis and, 887–88
　in Munich agreement, 1073
　in Napoleonic wars, 296, 335–38, *336*, 338
　in NATO, 1151
　navy of, 232–33, 335–36
　nuclear weapons and, 1241
　Oregon Country and, 374, 497, 513,
　　514–15
　Panama Canal and, 883
　Paris Peace Conference and, 956
　in Persian Gulf War, 1340
　in post–World War I treaties, 1066–67,
　　1066
　in Samoa, 863
　in SEATO, 1207
　in second Gulf War, 1380–81
　slave trade and, 491
　Spanish Civil War and, 1075
　in Suez War, 1210, 1211–13
　Texas Republic relations with, 510
　tribute payments by, 327
　in United Nations, 1144
　U.S. Civil War and, 616, 618–19, 630
　U.S. missiles in, 1214, 1241
　U.S. trade with, 257, 259–60, 284–85, 297,
　　298–99, 309, 335–38, *336*, 338, 339, 348,
　　363, 365, 367, 389, 406, 408, 533
　in War of 1812, 344, 345–46, 365
　in World War I, 934–35, 938, 944, 945, 952
　World War I debt of, 1064–65
　in World War II, 1074, 1078, 1079,
　　1082–84, 1089, 1103, 1104, 1109–10,
　　1113, 1119, 1127, 1172
　see also American Revolution; British
　　Empire; England; Parliament, British;
　　War of 1812; *specific colonies*
Great (Connecticut) Compromise, 266
Great Depression, *see* Depression, Great;
　New Deal
Greater East Asia Co-Prosperity Sphere, 1085
Great Gatsby, The (Fitzgerald), 988

Great Migration of 1630s, 66
Great Migration of African Americans,
    946–47, 981–82, *981,* 1178–79
Great Northern Railroad, 748, 899
Great Plains:
    environment of, 505
    horses and, 33–35, 493–94
    seen as desert, 721–22
Great Railroad Strike of 1877, 763–64, 825
Great Society, 1244–51, 1262, 1283, 1292, 1293
Great White Fleet tour, 888
Greece:
    in NATO, 1151
    U.S. post-World War II aid to, 1148–49
    in World War II, 1082
Greek Americans, 788, 790
Greeley, Horace, 675, 692–93
Green, William, 1008
Greenback (Independent National) party,
    841, 846
greenbacks, 636, 687–88, 691, 693–94, 847,
    852
Greene, Catharine, 417–18
Greene, Nathanael, 220, 417
    description of, 230–32
Green Mountain Boys, 188, 198
Greensboro, N.C., sit-in in (1960), 1233,
    1233, 1234, 1267
Greenspan, Alan, 1360, 1361
Greenville, Treaty of (1795), 300, *300,* 304
Grenada invasion (1983), 1324
Grenville, George, 177–80, *178,* 179–80, 182,
    183, 184
Griffith, D. W., 1001
Grimké, Angelina, 558
Grimké, Sarah, 558
Grinnell, George Bird, 906
Griswald, Roger, *314*
Grovey v. Townsend, 1042
Gruening, Ernest, 1255
Grundy, Felix, 341
Guadalcanal, 1114
Guadalupe Hidalgo, Treaty of (1848), 522
Guam, 873, 1089, 1092
Guantánamo Bay, 878
Guatemala, 27, 933
guilds, 122, 449
Guinn v. United States, 983
Guiteau, Charles, 826, 828
Gulf of Tonkin incident (1964), 1287
Gullah, 551
Gutenberg, Johannes, 13

habeas corpus, 639, 690
    Lincoln's suspension of, 610–11, 637

Habeas Corpus Act (1863), 637
Haber, Al, 1267
hacienda, 28
Hagel, Chuck, 1390
Haig, Alexander, 1290
Haight-Ashbury, 1272
Haiti (Saint Domingue), 16, 933
    immigration from, 1344
    U.S. interventions in, 934, 1069, 1365
Halberstam, David, 1260
Haldeman, H. R., 1290, 1299, 1300, 1301
Hale, John P., 579
Half-Breeds, 824, 828
"Half-Way Covenant" (1662), 128
Halleck, Henry, 622, 624, 645
Hamas, 1379
Hamilton, Alexander, 211, 233, 251, 268, 301,
    312, 322
    Adams administration and, 310
    and army authorization of 1798, 311
    Burr's duel with, 332, 333, 543
    Constitutional Convention and, 262–63,
        264, 269, 285
    economic vision of, 285–93
    in election of 1796, 308
    and election of 1800, 315–16, 316
    Federalist and, 272–73, 283
    French Revolution and, 296–97
    Jefferson compared with, 293, 294–95
    Jefferson's continuation of programs of,
        326
    land policy of, 304
    national bank promoted by, 286, 287,
        289–91
    in ratification debate, 272–73
    as secretary of the treasury, 282, 285–93,
        286
    Washington's farewell and, 307
Hamilton, William, 226
Hammond, G. H., 735
Hammond, James H., 539
Hampton Institute, 802, *802*
Hancock, John, 196, 205
    in ratification debate, 274
Hancock, Winfield Scott, 826
handgun regulation, 1355, 1371
Hanna, Mark, 850, 882
Hanoverian succession, 176
Harding, Warren G., 885, 962, *998*
    accomplishments of, 997
    appointments and policy of, 993–95
    corruption under, 995–97
    death of, 997
    in election of 1920, 992
    Latin American policy of, 1068

Harding, Warren G. (*continued*)
  race question and, 995
  Washington Armaments Conference and, 1066, 1067
Harlem Renaissance, 982
Harlem Shadows (McKay), 982
Harper's Ferry, Va., 598, *612*
Harper's Illustrated Weekly, 475
Harper's Magazine, 475
Harper's Weekly, 615, 660, 801
Harriman, E. H., 899, 903
Harrington, Michael, 1246
Harris, Townsend, 581
Harrison, Benjamin, *835,* 837, 864, *909*
  civil service appointments of, 835
  in election of 1888, 834–35
  in election of 1892, 846
Harrison, William Henry, 340, 344, 834
  in election of 1836, 407–8
  in election of 1840, 410–12, *411,* 490
Hartford, Treaty of (1638), 74, 75
Hartford Convention (1814), 348–49, 391
Harvard Medical School, 454
Harvard University, 143–44, 804
Hathorne, John, 130
Haugen, Gilbert N., 1006
Hawaii, 863–65, 866, 873
  annexation by U.S. of, 863–65
  reciprocal trade agreement with U.S. of, 863
Hawkins, John, 40
Hawley-Smoot Tariff (1930), 1012, 1016
Hawthorne, Nathaniel, 458, 468, 471, 487
Hay, John, 879–80, 883–84, 1066
Hayden, Tom, 1267–68, 1269
Hayes, Lucy Ware, 824
Hayes, Rutherford B., 694–97, *696, 713,* 723, 733
  and civil service reform, 823–26
Hay-Herrán Treaty (1903), 883–84
Haymarket Affair, 767
Hayne, Robert Y., 391, 395, 536
Haynes, Lemuel, *245*
Hay-Pauncefote Treaty (1900), 883
Hays, Mary Ludwig (Molly Pitcher), 243
Hayward, James, 198
Haywood, William D. "Big Bill," 776
headright system, 109, 131
Head Start, 1247
health and medicine:
  AIDS, 1328–29, *1329*
  in Civil War, 634–35
  in colonial period, 104
  in late nineteenth century, 785–86
  in Old Southwest, 555
  patent medicines and, 904, 905

population density and, 783
  as profession, 453–54
  of slaves, 547
  yellow fever and, 877–78
  see also disease; drugs
health insurance, 1200
  health care reform and, 1354–55
  and Johnson, 1249
  Medicaid, 1249, 1354–55
  Medicare, 1249, 1250, 1330–31, 1354–55
  proposed by Truman, 1155
Hearst, William Randolph, 866, 1052
Heisenberg, Werner, 985
Hell's Angels, 1273
Helluland (Baffin Island), 13
Hemingway, Ernest, 808, 987, 988
hemp, 534, 661
Henderson, Clarence, *1233*
Henrico (Richmond), 55
Henrietta Maria, queen, 60
Henry, Joseph, 431
Henry, Patrick, 294
  Constitutional Convention avoided by, 263, 273
  at Continental Congress, 193, 195
  in ratification debate, 273, 274
  Virginia Resolves and, 181
Henry, prince of Portugal, 15
Henry VII, king of England, 15, 22, 40, 48
Henry VIII, king of England, 37
Henry Street Settlement, 812
Hepburn Act (1906), 903–4
Herbert, Victor, 445, 446
Herrán, Thomas, 883–84
Hess, Rudolf, *1145*
Hessians, 201, 217, 219
Hetch Hetchy Reservoir, 908–9
Hicks, Edward, *305*
Hidalgo y Costilla, Miguel, 495–96, *496*
Higher Education Act (1965), 1250
Highway Safety Act (1966), 1250
highways and roads, 136, 360–62, 388–89, *422–23*
  in colonial period, 134, 136, 306
  in early twentieth century, 926
  federal funding for, 358, 360–62, 427, 430
  to frontier regions, 134, 306, 421–22
  Maysville Road, 388–89
  National (Cumberland) Road, 361–62, *361,* 363, 389, 421–22
  safety on, 1250
  state funding for, 404, 430
  turnpike boom and (1820s), 421–22, 430
  Wilderness Road, 304–6, 421
  after World War II, 1178, 1200, 1250

Hill, Ambrose P., 624, 627
Hill, Anita, 1350–51
Hill, D. H., 624
Hill, James J., 899
Hill, Joe, 776–77
Hillman, Sidney, 1055
Hillsborough, earl of, 186
Hine, Lewis W., 896
Hirohito, emperor of Japan, 1087
Hiroshige Utagawa, *581*
Hiroshima, atomic bombing of (1945), 1126,
    1127, *1128*
Hispanics:
    definition of, 1278
    political power of, 1280
    rights of, 1278–80
    in Spanish America, 29
Hispaniola, 24
    Columbus in, 16
Hiss, Alger, 1166, *1166,* 1196
History of the Standard Oil Company
    (Tarbell), 892
*History of the U.S. Decision Making Process in
    Vietnam, The* (McNamara), 1287
Hitler, Adolf, 1071, *1072,* 1073, 1111
    assassination attempt on, 1113
    death of, 1123
    rise of, 1071
    see also Germany, Nazi
Hobbs, Abigail, 130
Hobson, J. A., 860
Ho Chi Minh, 1161, 1205–6, *1205,* 1207
Ho Chi Minh Trail, 1242, 1255
Hoe, Richard, 474
Hoe rotary press, 474
Hoffman, Abbie, 1270
HOLC (Home Owners' Loan Corporation),
    1028, 1029
Holmes, E. P., 679
Holmes, Oliver Wendell, Jr., 949–50, 1024
Holmes, Oliver Wendell, Sr., 471
Holocaust, 1123–24
Holy Roman Empire, 28
homelessness, 1328
Home Owners' Loan Act (1933), 1028, 1029
Home Owners' Loan Corporation (HOLC),
    1028, 1029
Homestead, Pa., *757*
Homestead Act (1862), 635, 660, 738
    steel strike in (1892), 770, 964
homesteading, 738–39
homosexuals, *see* gays
Honduras, 933
Hong Kong, 879
    in World War II, 1089, 1092

Hood, John B., 648–50
Hooker, Joseph E., 640–41
    at Chancellorsville, 640–41, 647
Hooker, Thomas, 71
Hoover, Herbert, 1010–20, *1012,* 1030
    in America First Committee, 1080
    in election of 1928, 1010–11
    in election of 1932, 1024–25, *1026*
    Latin American policy of, 1069
    Manchuria invasion and, 1070
    recovery efforts of, 1016–17
    reparations and, 1065
    as secretary of commerce, 993, 1004–5
    stock-market crash and, 1013
    in World War I, 946
Hoover, J. Edgar, 965, 1190, 1236
Hoover (Boulder) Dam, 738
Hope, Bob, 789
Hopewell, Treaty of (1785), 256
Hopewell culture, 10
Hopis, 11, 12, 494
Hopkins, Harry L., 1030, 1031, 1058
Hopper, Edward, *1180,* 1188
Hopwood v. Texas, 1362
horses, 101, 102, 536, 640
    Indians and, 33–35, 493–94, 732–33
    Spanish introduction of, 25, 26, 33–35, 734
    urban manure and, 785
Horseshoe Bend, Battle of (1814), 344–45
House, Edward M., 921, 936, 940, 954, 955
House of Commons, British, 46, 68
    American Revolution and, 225, 234
House of Lords, British, 46, 68
House of Representatives, U.S.:
    in Constitution, 268–69, 269
    election of 1800 decided by, 316, *317*
    Jay's Treaty opposed in, 299
    Johnson's impeachment in, 676, *677*
    see also Congress, U.S.
House of the Seven Gables, The (Hawthorne),
    471
House Un-American Activities Committee
    (HUAC), 1060, 1166, *1166*
housing:
    in antebellum South, 540, 541
    in colonial period, 118–19, *119*
    on frontier, 306
    gentrification and, 1328
    GI Bill of Rights and, 1173
    in Greaat Depression, 1047, 1058–59
    for immigrants, 790
    in late nineteenth century, 780
    in 1960s, 1232, 1249–50
    in 1980s, 1328
    public, 1179

housing (*continued*)
  segregation in, 1041, 1178
  of slaves, 547
  in suburbs, 1176–78, 1185–86
  technological advances in, 431
  after World War II, 1139, 1159, 1174,
    1176–78
Housing Act (1961), 1232
Housing and Urban Development Act
  (1965), 1249
Housing and Urban Development
  Department, U.S., 1249–50
Housing Authority, U.S. (USHA), 1058
Houston, Charles H., 1219
Houston, Sam, 509–10, *509,* 543
  and Compromise of 1850, 573
  Kansas-Nebraska Act denounced by,
    584
Howe, Elias, 431
Howe, Julia Ward, 814
Howe, Richard, Lord, 214
Howe, William, 198, 199, 200, 214–17, *216,*
    221, 223, 225
Howl (Ginsberg), 1189–90
How the Other Half Lives (Riis), 892
HUAC (House Un-American Activities
  Committee), 1060, 1166, *1166*
Hudson, Henry, 83
Huerta, Victoriano, 931–32
Hughes, Charles Evan, 942–43, 993, 1066,
    1066, 1069
Hughes, Langston, 982
Huguenots, 31, 36, 78, 132–34, *133,* 159
Hull, Cordell, 1072, 1085, 1086, 1087
Hull, William, 342–43
Hull House, 812
human rights, 1307
  see also civil rights and liberties
Humphrey, Hubert H., 1156, 1158, 1300
  in election of 1964, 1248
  in election of 1968, 1260–63, *1262,* 1270
Hundred Years' War (1338–1453), 14–15
Hungarian Americans, 617, 788, 790
Hungary:
  fall of communism in, 1335
  Soviet domination of, 1210, 1213–14,
    1321–22
  U.S. peace with, 962
  in World War II, 1082, 1146
Hunt, Harriet, 454
hunters and gatherers, 73
Hurons, 87, *93,* 158
Hurston, Zora Neale, 982
Hussein, King of Jordan, 1215, 1366
Hussein, Saddam, 1339–40, 1349, 1380–83

Hutchinson, Anne, 70–71, 72, 468
Hutchinson, Thomas, 181, 189, 192
hydrogen bomb, 1161, 1204

Iberville, Pierre le Moyne, sieur d,' 159
IBM, 1346
ICC (Interstate Commerce Commission),
    832–33, 903–4, 915, 924, 995
Iceland, in NATO, 1151
Ickes, Harold L., 1034, 1058
Idaho, 619, 730
  labor movement in, 775
  sheep in, 737
  statehood for, 725, 836
  voting rights in, 814
Illinois:
  agriculture in, 535
  German settlers in, 447
  Indian conflicts in, 397
  Revolutionary War fighting in, 227–28
  voting rights in, 814
Illinois Central Railroad, 430
immigration, 131–34, *133,* 969–71
  Alien Act and, 313
  attraction of U.S. for, 787–88
  from British regions, 99–100
  of Chinese, 447–48
  Constitutional Convention and, 268
  of convicts, 109
  Democratic Party and, 838
  in early twentieth century, 857, 965–66,
    969–71
  Eastern European wave of, 787–88
  education and, 1345
  Ellis Island and, 788–89, *788, 789*
  of Germans, 90, 94, 131–32, 134, 446–47
  Great Migration and, 66
  of Highland Scots, 94, 134
  illegal, 971, 1344–45, *1345*
  of Irish, 444–46
  in late nineteenth century, 786–93
  in late twentieth century, 1344–45
  nativism and, 448–49, 790–91, 821, 969–71
  in 1960s, 1220
  in nineteenth century, 443–49
  occupations of, 790
  Populist call for restriction on, 846
  rates of, 787–88
  restrictions on, 791–93, 965–66, 969–71
  of Scandinavians, 88, 131, 447
  of Scotch-Irish, 19, 131, 132, 134
  of Swiss, 500
  see also specific ethnic groups and countries
Immigration Act (1965), 1250
impeachment, 269, 271, 326

of Andrew Johnson, 675–78, *677*
of Clinton, 1364–65, *1364*
Nixon and, 1301–2
imperialism, 856, 860–65
American, 861
in East Asia, 878–80
European model of, 860–61
global, 860–61
independence movements and, 1204–9
motivating ideas of, 873–74
naval power in, 861, 888
Open Door policy and, 879–80, 886, 887, 1066–67, 1071
in Pacific, 863–65
as quest for markets, 860, 861, 872–73
as quest for raw materials, 859–60
theory of, 861–62
trade and, 861
see also Spanish-American War
implied powers, 329, 360, 372–73
impressment, 335–36, 348
Incas, 9, 27, 29
income tax, 636, 915, 941
indentured servants, 58, 59, 60, 106, 109–10, *110*
Africans as, 110
Independence Day, 246
independence movements, 1204–9
independent counsels, 1362
Independent National (Greenback) party, 841, 846
Independents (religious group), 49
Independent Treasury, 409–10, 513
Independent Treasury Act (1840), 409–10, 491
India, 168, 406, 1204, 1207
trade with, 363
Indiana, 300, 410
Indian conflicts:
Andrew Jackson in, 344–45, 366–67, *366,* 396, 508
Black Hawk War, 397
Canada and, 299–300, 340
in colonial period, 57–60, 74–76, *75,* 81–83, 86–87, 130, 168, 169–71, 177
in Connecticut colony, 74–76, *75,* 76–77
in early U.S., 258, 259, 281, 299–300
French in, 81, 83, 87, *158*
in Georgia, 256
Great Britain and, 281, *298,* 340
in Illinois, 397
Peace of Paris (1763) and, 169–71
in South, 168
Spain and, 256, 281, 302–3
Tecumseh and, 339–40, *339,* 344

in Virginia colony, 57–60
and War of 1812, 339–40, 343
in West, 728–32, *731*
Indian Peace Commission, 729, 733
Indian Removal Act (1830), 396–97
Indian Reorganization Act (1934), 1041–42
Indians, American, 320, 321
agriculture of, 7, 10, 73, 101–2, 494
Americanization of, 733
in American Revolution, 201, 224, 226, *227,* 228–29, 256
Americas settled by, 2, 5–6, *6*
Andrew Jackson's policy toward, 396–400
buffalo herds and, 34–35, 494, 728, 732–33
Catholicism and, 27–28, 31–33, 157, 158, 495, 498–500
Christian, 188
citizenship of, 268, 733
in Civil War, 620
colonial trade with, 50, 73, 79–83, 91, 159
constitutional rights lacked by, 284
and diseases contracted from Europeans, 20–22, *20, 21,* 24, 27, 74, 80, 86
Dutch relations with, 83
in early U.S., 281
education and, 144
English vs. French relations with, 73, 161–62
environment influenced by, 33–35, 100–102
forced labor of, 2, 26, *32*
in French and Indian War, 166–67
French relations with, 73, 157–59, 161–62
in fur trade, 73, 80, 87, 159, 496, 497
gold rush and, 571
Great Plains wars of, 728–32
horses and, 33–35, *34,* 493–94, 732–33
Kansas-Nebraska act and, 584–85
languages of, 19–20
in late twentieth century, 1344
Lewis and Clark expedition and, 329–31
massacres of, 18, 57, 74–76, 188, 729, 732
missionaries to, 31–33, 74–75, 81, 159, 161, 498–500
named by Columbus, 16
in Native American movement, 1280–82
in New Deal, 1041–42
in New England, 72–76, 130
in New York colony, 86–87, 131
Old Northwest land of, 252, 255, 256
in Pennsylvania colony, 131
Plymouth colony and, 63
poverty of, 1280–81
pre-Columbian civilizations of, 7–12, *8, 10*
Quakers' relations with, 90

Indians, American (*continued*)
  religious beliefs of, 28, 29, 32, 73
  removal of, 396–400, *398, 399,* 418
  reservation system and, 494
  rights of, 1280–82
  as slaves, 16, 74, 76, 80–83, 115
  technology of, 19, 33–35
  Virginia colony and, 52, 55–56, 57–60
  wagon trains and, 502, 505
  Western, 493–95
  westward migration and, 721, 728–29
  in World War II, 1101
  see also specific tribes
Indian Territory, 584–85
  see also Oklahoma
indigo, 107, 229, 533
individualism, 354–55, 466–67, 468–69
Indochina, 1241–43
  French in, 1084, 1085, 1160–61, 1162,
    1204–9
  Japanese aggression in (1940–1941), 1084,
    1085, 1087
  nationalist movement in, 1204–9
  see also Vietnam War
Indonesia, 1204–5, 1207
  in World War II, 1084, 1086, 1087, 1092,
    1118
Industrial Revolution, 432–39, 528, 702–3,
    743–45
  Second, 744–46
Industrial Workers of the World (IWW),
    775
industry:
  cities and, 437–39
  in Civil War, 613
  in early nineteenth century, 432–39, *437*
  environment and, 436–37, *438*
  family system in, 435
  German Americans in, 446–47
  innovations in business organizations and,
    744, 754–55, 757–58
  Irish Americans in, 445
  in late nineteenth century, 743–46
  Lowell System in, 433–35
  scientific research and, 746, 751–53
  technological innovations and, 430–32,
    744–46, 751–53
  see also corporations, business;
    manufactures; *specific industries*
inflation, 836, 847, 852, 1292–93
  control of, after World War II, 1140–41
  and discovery of gold, 852
  in the 1950s, 1199
  in the 1970s, 1292–93
  silver coinage and, 836, 847

Influence of Sea Power upon History,
    1660–1783, The (Mahan), 861
influenza, 962–63, *963*
initiative, right of, 893
Innocents Abroad (Twain), 808
In re Debs, 772
Institutes of the Christian Religion, The
    (Calvin), 36
instrumentalism, 807
"Insular Cases," 877
Interallied Conference (1917), 954
Interior Department, U.S., 379, 523, 907, 909
internal improvements, 360–62, 363, 377,
    427, 430
  Andrew Jackson on, 388–89, *389*
  Constitution and, 388–89, 748
  John Quincy Adams's promotion of, 379
  Polk on, 514
  Tyler on, 490
  Whigs on, 407
Internal Revenue Act (1862), 636
International Court, 1144
International Harvester, 767, 902
International Ladies' Garment Workers, 769,
    1055
International Workingmen's Association, 774
Internet, 1347
  economic "bubble" in, 1360–61, 1372
interposition, *see* nullification and
    interposition
Interstate Commerce Commission (ICC),
    832–33, 903–4, 915, 924, 995
intifada, 1379
Intolerable (Coercive) Acts (1774), 191–93
inventions, 751–53
investment bankers, 757–58
Invisible Man (Ellison), 1188, *1188*
Iran:
  in METO, 1210
  U.S. hostages in, 1309–11, *1310*
Iran-Contra affair, 1325–26
Iran-Iraq war, 1323
Iraq, 1135, 1215, 1349
  in METO, 1210–11
  in Persian Gulf War, 1339–40
  postwar, 1382–83, 1384–85
  in second Gulf War, 1380–83, *1381*
Ireland, 46, 50
Irish Americans, 109, 132, 134, 354, 542, 787
  African Americans' animosity toward, 445,
    446
  clubs of, 797
  in Democratic party, 407, 445–46
  and election of 1884, 831
  immigration by, 444–46, *444,* 747, 787

in labor force, 444
in nineteenth century, 444–46
prejudice against, 313, 445, 446, 448, *449*
prohibitionism and, 821
reasons for migration of, 444
westward migration of, 722
in World War I, 936, 959
iron industry, 537, 708
Iroquois League, 83, 86–87, *87*, *93*, 131, *162*, 166, 228, 238
Albany Congress and, 165–66
in American Revolution, 224
in Colonial wars, 168
French conflict with, 158–59, *158*
post-Revolutionary War weakness of, 256
Tuscaroras in, 82
Isabella I, queen of Castile, 15–16, 17
Ishii, Kikujiro, 1065
Islam, 1376, 1382–83
Islamic Jihad, 1379, 1382
isolationism:
in Great Depression, 1071–72, 1076
neutrality acts and (1930s), 1074–78
after World War I, 1063–69
Israel, 1293, 1298, 1304, 1323
Camp David accords and, 1307–8
founding of, 1152
Lebanon invaded by, 1323–24
Osama bin Laden and, 1376
Oslo accords and, 1365–67, 1379–80
in Six-Day War, 1298
in Suez War, 1210, *1212*, 1213
suicide bombings and, 1379
Wye accords and, 1366–67
Isthmian Canal Commission, 883, 884
Italian Americans, 132, 617, 787, 788, 790, 959
prohibitionism and, 821
in World War II, 1101
Italy:
Albania seized by, 1073
communism in, 1149
Ethiopia conquered by, 1073, 1075
Greece and Libya attacked by, 1082
as imperialist nation, 860
in League of Nations, 957
in Lebanon, 1324
Mussolini's rise to power in, 1071
in NATO, 1151
Paris Peace Conference and, 956, 959
in post-World War I treaties, 1066–67, *1066*
rise of fascism in, 1071
in Tripartite Pact, 1085
U.S. missiles in, 1214, 1241
in World War I, 934–35, 950

in World War II, 1082, 1089, 1104, 1108–9, 1123, 1146
Iwo Jima, 1125
IWW (Industrial Workers of the World), 775–77

Jack (Driver), *548*
Jackson, Andrew, *366*, *376*, *394*, 406–407, 430, 897
assessment of presidency of, 412–14
background of, 385–87
Calhoun's rift with, 393–94
California annexation and, 507
as commoner, 385–87
on debt, 404
in duel, 543
Eaton Affair and, 388
in election of 1824, 377, *378*
in election of 1828, 380–84, *381*, *382*, *383*, 391, 408, 446
in election of 1832, 402–3
and election of 1844, 510
in Florida campaign, 366–67
government appointments of, 387
Houston and, 510
inauguration of, *386*
in Indian conflicts, 344–45, 366–67, *366*, 396, 508
Indian policy of, 396–400
internal improvements and, 388–89, *389*
Irish-American support of, 445–46
land policy of, 405
national bank issue and, 400–406, *402*, 413–14
nullification issue and, 393, 394–96, 404, 406, 490
Polk compared with, 513
tariff issue and, 380, 395–96, 404
ten-hour workday and, 451
in War of 1812, 344–45, 346–47, *347*, 349
Jackson, "Drummer," *633*
Jackson, Frankie "Half Pint," *976*
Jackson, Helen Hunt, 733
Jackson, Henry, 1300
Jackson, Jesse, 1325, 1331
Jackson, Rachel, 381, 388
Jackson, Thomas "Stonewall," 623, 624
background of, 523
at Chancellorsville, 641
death of, 641
at first Bull Run, 614
nickname given to, 614
at second Bull Run, 624
Jackson State College, 1286
Jacobs, George, 129

Jamaica, 18, 77
James, William, 806–7, *807*, 876
James I, king of England, 45, 48, *48*, 50, 55, 153
James II, king of England, 49, *151*
    accession of, 150
    colonization and, 84, 150
    France policy of, 162
    overthrow of, 151, 176
Jamestown colony, 31, 33, 52, 55, 60, 110, 116
Japan:
    Asian expansion of, 1065, 1067, 1071, 1084–86, *1086*
    atomic bombing of, 1126–29
    in China, 878, 879, 886–87
    China invaded by, 1065, 1069–71, *1070*, 1073, 1076–77, *1077*, 1084, 1085, 1087, 1160
    early twentieth-century relations with, 886–87
    immigration from, 970
    Kamikaze units from, 1118
    in Korea, 1161
    in League of Nations, 957
    opening of, 878
    Pearl Harbor attack of, 1086–89, *1088*, 1092–93, 1103
    in post-World War I treaties, 1066–67, *1066*, 1073
    in Russo-Japanese War, 886–87, 1123
    in Sino-Japanese War, 878
    surrender of, 1128–29, 1139–40
    trade with, 580–81, *581*, 1087
    in Tripartite Pact, 1085
    U.S. occupation of, 1146
    war criminals of, 1144
    in World War I, 935, 953
    in World War II, 1092, 1102, 1105, 1114–18, 1120, 1121, 1123, 1125–26, 1204–5
Japanese Americans, 887
    in World War II, 1101–2, *1102*
Jaworski, Leon, 1301
Jay, John, *283*
    background of, 283
    Federalist and, 273, 283
    land policy of, 304
    on peace commission, 234, *235*, 283
    in ratification debate, 273
    treaty negotiated by, 298–99
Jayhawkers, 620
Jay's Treaty (1795), 298–99, *298*, 308, 309, 312, 335
Jazz Age, 976–77
Jefferson, Thomas, 210, 247, *294*, 312–13, 322–25, *324*, *337*, 357, 417, 562, 1205

and Alien and Sedition Acts, 315
background of, 294–95
Barbary pirates and, 327–28
Burr Conspiracy and, 334
on colonial protests, 193
on Constitutional Convention, *270*
debt issue and, 288–89
Declaration of Independence drafted by, 203–4, 458
as deist, 459
domestic reforms of, 326–27
as early Republican leader, 293–95
economic policies of, 295, 326, 432
education efforts of, 477
in election of 1796, 308
in election of 1800, 211, 316–18, *317*, 324
in election of 1804, 324
exploration of West promoted by, 329–32
French Revolution and, 296–97, *297*
Hamilton compared with, 293, 294–95
inauguration of, 322–24
internal improvements and, 361
land policy and, 252, 254–55, 304
Louisiana Purchase and, 328–29
on Missouri Compromise, 371
Monroe Doctrine and, 375
Napoleonic wars and, 335, 336, 337–38, 338
national bank and, 290, 291, 326
on religious freedom, 245
second Washington term urged by, 295
as secretary of state, 282
on Shays's Rebellion, 261–62
as slaveholder, 242, 318
on territories, 252
on Whiskey Rebellion, 301, 312
on women's rights, 244
Jeffords, James, 1373
Jeremiah, Thomas, 242
Jericho, 1366
Jerusalem, 1379
Jesuits, 31, 159
Jewett, Sarah Orne, 807
Jewish Americans, 78, 94, 132, *133*, 447, 790
Jews, 787–88, 997
    in Democratic Party, 821
    Holocaust and, 1123–24, *1125*
    immigration of, 787–88, 790
"Jim Crow" policies, 714, 717, *717*
    see also segregation, desegregation
Job Corps, 1246–47
Jodl, Alfred, 1123
Johns Hopkins University, 804
Johnson, Andrew, 637, *668*, *672*, 1244
    assassination plot against, 666

congressional conflicts with, 671–72
in election of 1864, 638–39, 667
impeachment and trial of, 675–78, *677*
Pacific policy and, 862
Radical Republicans' conflict with, 668, 673–74, 675–76
Reconstruction plans of, 667–69, 671–72
Johnson, Hugh S., 1034
Johnson, James Weldon, 964, 982, 983
Johnson, Lyndon B., 1222, *1245*
    antipoverty efforts of, 1136, 1245–47, 1249–50, 1261–62, 1280, 1293
    background of, 1031, 1244–45
    civil rights and, 1245, 1250–51
    elected to Senate, 1158
    in election of 1960, 1229
    in election of 1964, 1247–48
    and election of 1968, 1259–60, 1269
    Great Society and, 1243, 1244–51
    Kennedy assassination and, 1243, *1244*
    Vietnam War and, 1134, 1254–60, *1259,* 1289, 1293
    war on poverty of, 1245–47, 1249–50
Johnson, Richard M., 341
Johnson, William, 545
Johnson Debt Default Act (1934), 1065, 1082
Johnston, Albert Sidney, 620–22
Johnston, Joseph E., 614, 641–42, 646, 652, 654
    at Chattanooga, 645
    at Seven Pines, 623
    Sherman's march countered by, 648
    surrender of, 655
Joint Chiefs of Staff, 1203, 1238, 1242
Joint Committee on Reconstruction, 670, 671, 673
Joint Committee on the Economic Report, 1141
joint-stock companies, 47
Jolliet, Louis, 159, *160*
Jolson, Al, 789
Jones, James, 1187
Jones, Jehu, 544
Jones, John Paul, 232
Jones Act (1916), 877
Jordan:
    in Arab League, 1211
    in Six-Day War, 1298
Jordan, David Starr, 876
Joseph, Nez Percé chief, 730–31, *732*
journeymen, 122, 449–50
Joyce, James, 987
Jubilee Convention (1913), 898
judicial review, 271, 371
Judiciary Act (1789), 325

Judiciary Act (1801), 316–17, 325
Julian, George W., 637, 670
Jungle, The (Sinclair), 904
juries, 1043
Justice Department, U.S., Civil Rights Division of, 1222
juvenile delinquency, 1190–91

Kaaterskill Falls (Cole), *467*
Kadar, Janos, 1213
Kamikaze units, 1118
Kanagawa, Treaty of (1854), 580
Kansas:
    African Americans in, 722–23, *723*
    agriculture in, 841
    cattle industry in, 734, 735
    Civil War fighting in, 619–20
    dust bowl in, 1038, 1039
    Populists in, 843
    segregation in, 1219
    voting rights in, 814
Kansas-Nebraska Act (1854), 582–89, *584,* 591, 593
    proposed by Douglas, 582–86
    and violence in Kansas, 585–88
    and violence in Senate, 588–89
    Whig Party destroyed over, 585
Kansas Territory, 31
    Lecompton constitution in, 593–94
    settlement of, 585–88
    slavery issue and, 583, 585–88, 593–94
    statehood for, 587
    violence in (1856), 586–88
Kant, Immanuel, 467
Karzai, Hamid, 1377
Katrina, Hurricane, 1387–89, *1388*
Kearney, Denis, 764–65, 792
Kearny, Stephen, 519
Kearny, U.S.S., 1084
Keating-Owen Child Labor Act (1916), 927
Keats, John, 1185
Kelley, Florence, 897
Kelley, Oliver H., 840
Kellogg, Frank B., 1067
Kellogg-Briand Pact (Pact of Paris) (1928), 1067–68, 1070, 1071
Kelly Act (1925), 1003
Kennan, George F., 1147, *1147,* 1148, 1169, 1213, 1257
Kennedy, Jacqueline, *1244*
Kennedy, John F., 1218, 1267, *1295,* 1321, 1352
    assassination of, 1243, 1260
    background of, 1227–28
    cabinet of, 1230–31

Kennedy, John F. (*continued*)
  civil rights and, 1232–33, 1236
  Cuban missile crisis and, 1239–41
  in election of 1960, 1227–30, *1230*
  foreign policy of, 1238–43
  health of, 1227–28
  inauguration of, 1231
  New Frontier and, 1228, 1231
  Nixon's debate with, 1228, *1229*
  poverty and, 1246
  taxation and, 1231, 1245–46
Kennedy, Joseph, 1227
Kennedy, Robert, 1229
  assassination of, 1260
  as attorney general, 1231, 1232, 1234,
    1236, 1241
  Chavez and, *1279*
  in election of 1968, 1259, 1260
Kent State University, 1286, *1286*
Kentucky, 228, 256, 259, 281, 300, *300*, 421
  agriculture in, 306, 533, 534
  Civil War fighting in, 620
  debtors in, 481
  Indian lands ceded in, 256
  Indian removal and, 397
  religious revivals in, 462
  secession debate in, 610, 611
  settlement of, 304–6
  statehood for, 307
  tariff issue and, 380
  voting rights in, 382
Kentucky Resolutions (1798 and 1799), 315,
    391
Kerouac, Jack, 1189, 1190
Kerr, Clark, 1268
Kerry, John, in election of 2004, 1384–86,
    1384, 1385
Key, Francis Scott, 346
Keynes, John Maynard, 1058
Keynesian economics, 1058
Keystone Studios, 1001
KGB, 1337
Khmer Rouge, 1305
Khomeini, Ayatollah Ruhollah, 1309–10
Khrushchev, Nikita, 1213, 1215–16, *1216*,
    1218, 1238
  and crises in Berlin, 1215–16, 1238–39
  and Cuban missile crisis, 1239–41
  and U-2 summit, 1216–17
Kickapoos, *92*
King, Martin Luther, Jr., 470, *1221*, 1228–29,
    1251, 1253, 1331
  assassination of, 1260, 1269
  background of, 1220–21
  economic issues and, 1253–54

"Letter from Birmingham City Jail" of,
    1235–36
  in March on Washington, 1236–37
  in Montgomery bus boycott, 1220–22,
    1233
  and Southern Christian Leadership
    Conference (SCLC), 1222, 1232–33
King, Rufus, 333, 338, 362
King George's War (War of the Austrian
    Succession) (1744–1748), 162
King Philip's (Metacomet's) War
    (1675–1676), 74–76
King's College (Columbia University), 144,
    1269–70, *1270*
King's Mountain, Battle of (1780), 230
King William's War (War of the League of
    Augsburg) (1689–1697), 130, 162
Kiowas, 34, 494, 495, 729
Kissinger, Henry, 1290, 1295, 1296, 1298
  Vietnam and, 1285, 1287, 1288, 1304
KKK (Ku Klux Klan), 689–90, *689*, 925,
    971–72, *971*, 995, 997, 1153, 1220, 1355
Klamaths, 494
Kleindienst, Richard, 1301
Knight, Amelia, 503
Knights of Labor, 765–66, *766*, 767–68, 769,
    772–73, 844
Knights of the White Camellia, 690
Know-Nothing (American) party, 448, *449*,
    585, 589
Knox, Frank, 1080
Konoye, Fumimaro, 1085–87
Korea:
  division of, 1161
  independence of, 1110
  Japan in, 886–87, 1161
  Russo-Japanese rivalry over, 886–87
Korean Americans, 887
Korean War, 1161–66, *1163, 1164*, 1204,
    1206, 1223, 1269
  armistice in, 1200–1201
  casualties of, 1165–66
  and election of 1952, 1196, 1197
  Red Scare and, 1166
Koresh, David, 1355
Kosovo, 1367–68
Kosovo Liberation Army, 1367, 1368
Ku Klux Klan (KKK), 689–90, *689*, 925,
    971–72, *971*, 995, 997, 1153, 1220,
    1355
Ku Klux Klan Act (1871), 690
Kuomintang, *see* China, Nationalist
Kurile Islands, 1123
Kuwait, 1339–40, 1381
Kyoto Protocol, 1373

labor, employment:
apprentice-journeyman system of, 122,
322, 449–50
in California missions, 498–500
child, 435, 452, 761–62, *762*, 773, 896–97,
896, 925, 927, 993, 1034, 1036, 1059
in colonial cities, 135–36
diversification of, 291, *292*
in early nineteenth century, 434–35
immigrant, 444, 790
organized, 449–52
productivity and, 1347, 1361
rise of professions, 452–55
in southern colonies, 109–11, *110*
of women, 106–7, 434–35, *436*, 484,
634–35, 813, 897, 946, 947–48, *947*,
980–81, 1098–99, 1182, 1276, 1293, 1344
working conditions of, 433–35
in World War I, 946–48
after World War II, 1141
see also indentured servants; slavery;
slaves; working class
labor movement, 762–77
anarchism and, 766–67
and Clayton Anti-Trust Act, 924
closed shop in, 769, 903, 1142
disorganized protest and, 762–63
in early nineteenth century, 450–52
eight-hour workday and, 766, 767, 846,
927
Gastonia Strike and, 1008–10
in Great Depression, 1016, 1034–35, 1036,
1037, 1049, 1053, 1055–57, 1059
and Great Railroad Strike of 1877, 763–64
Hayes's policies toward, 825
Haymarket Affair, 767
Homestead strike and, 770
Knights of Labor in, 765–66, *766*, 767–68,
769, 844
minimum-wage laws and, 897, 993, 1059,
1139, 1159, 1350, 1358
NAFTA opposed by, 1354
in 1920s, 1007–8
in 1980s, 1321
open shop and, 1007
permanent unions and, 765
Pullman Strike and, 770–72, *771*
racism and, 1009–10
"right-to-work" laws and, 1096, 1143
"Sand Lot" incident in, 764–65
socialism and, 774–75
strikes and, 450, *450*, 451, 763–64, 766,
767, 770–72, *771*, 773, 776, 899–901,
1008–10, 1056–57, 1140–41, 1142,
1279–80

ten-hour workday and, 451, 897
trust laws and, 924
UFW and, 1279–80
violence and, 763–64, 767, 775, 1010
Wobblies in, 775–77
women in, 764, 772–73, 1008–10, *1009*
working conditions and, 760–62, 1008–9
after World War I, 963–64
in World War I, 948
after World War II, 1140–41, 1142–43
in World War II, 1096
see also working class; *specific unions*
Labrador (Markland), 13, 364
Ladies' Home Journal, 904
Lady's Magazine, 244
La Follette, Robert M., 895, *895*, 914, 999
La Follette Seamen's Act (1915), 925
Lagunas, 494
Lake Shore and Michigan Southern Railroad,
751
Lakota Sioux, 495, 732
Land Act (1796), 304
Land Act (1800), 304, 367–68
Land Act (1804), 304
Land Act (1820), 418
land grants:
for colleges, 635, 660
for railroads, 430, 660, 748–50
Landon, Alfred M., 1052–53
landownership:
and confiscation of Loyalist estates, 235,
240, 258–59, 371
in England, 47
European view of, 101–2
in late nineteenth century, 838–39, 840
in New England, 127
in Virginia colony, 56, 58–59
land policy, 491
African Americans and, 662–64, 684
agriculture and, 737–39
under Articles of Confederation, 252–56
in California, 500
under Cleveland, 831–32
in colonial period, 108–9, 131
Congress and, 304, 419, 491
in early nineteenth century, 418–19
in early U.S., 304
Foot Resolution on, 391–93
for freedmen, 662–64, 682
headright system and, 109, 131
Homestead Act and, 660
under Jackson, 405
Indians and, 733–34
Morrill Land Grant Act and, 635, 660
in New England, 118

land policy (*continued*)
  railroads and, 430, 738, 746–47, 832
  range wars and, 736–37
  Reconstruction and, 662–64, 682
  in southern colonies, 108–9
  in Southwest, 555
  for surveys and sales, 109, 304, 405,
    418–19, 555
  in Texas, 507–8
  under Van Buren, 410
land speculators, 304, 367–68, 404, 405
Lane Theological Seminary, 448
Langford, Nathaniel Pitt, *906*
Lansing, Robert, 936, 940, 1065
Lansing-Ishii Agreement (1917), 1065
Laos, 1205, 1206, 1241–42, 1255, 1288
Larkin, Thomas O., 500, 515–16
La Salle, Robert Cavalier, sieur de, 159,
  160
las Casas, Bartolomé de, 28
Latin America:
  Alliance for Progress, 1231
  Carter and, 1322
  Coolidge and, 1069
  dollar diplomacy in, 933, 934
  Franklin D. Roosevelt and, 1069
  "good neighbor" policy with, 1068–69
  Harding and, 1068
  Hoover and, 1069
  liberation of, 374–75
  Monroe Doctrine, 886
  Nixon and, 1215
  Reagan and, 1322–23
  Soviet Union and, 1323, 1326
  Wilson and, 1069
  see also specific countries
Latinos, 1250
  definition of, 1278
  gerrymandered districts and, 1361
  gold rush and, 571
  as largest minority group, 1344
  in late twentieth century, 1344, 1345
  in Spanish America, 495
  westward expansion and, 722
  in World War II, 1100–1101
Latrobe, Benjamin, *240*
Latvia, 1337
Laud, William, 49
Laurens, Henry, 205, *235*
Lawrence, Kans.:
  Civil War destruction of, 620
  proslavery violence in (1856), 587, *587*
law school, 453
League of Nations, 942, 954, 957–58, *958*,
  1063–64, 1070, 1071, 1120, 1152

Leary, Timothy, 1272
Lease, Mary Elizabeth, 844, *844*
Leaves of Grass (Whitman), 471, 473–74
Lebanon:
  in Arab League, 1211
  Iran-Contra affair and, 1325
  U.S. interventions in, 1215, 1323
Lecompton Constitution, 593–94
Le Duc Tho, 1287
Lee, Charles, 226
Lee, Henry, 301
Lee, Richard Henry:
  at Continental Congress, 202, 238
  in ratification debate, 273
Lee, Robert E., 623–24, 652, *655*
  at Antietam, 624
  background of, 523
  at Chancellorsville, 640–41
  Confederate side chosen by, 611
  at Fredericksburg, 628
  at Gettysburg, 642–44
  Grant's pursuit of, 646–48
  at Harper's Ferry, 598
  surrender of, 655, 656
legal system:
  Admiralty courts in, 153, 178–79, 180, 184,
    188
  in colonial period, 153–56
  in Constitution, 270–71
  English, 45–46
  judicial nationalism in, 371–74
  judicial review in, 271, 371–72
  and Judiciary Act of 1801, 316
  as profession, 453
  testimony of blacks in, 669
  U.S., establishment of, 283
  see also Supreme Court, U.S.
Legal Tender Act (1862), 636
legislatures, in colonial period, 154–55
Leisler, Jacob, 151–52
leisure, working women and, 798–99
LeMay, Curtis, 1263
Lemke, William, 1052
lend-lease program, 1082, *1083*
Lenin, V. I., 944, 953
Leopard incident, 336
Leslie, Frank, 475
Lesseps, Ferdinand de, 883
Lesser Antilles, 16, 18
"Letter from Birmingham City Jail" (King),
  1235–36
Letters of a Pennsylvania Farmer (Dickinson),
  185
Lever Food and Fuel Control Act (1917), 946
Levitt, William, 1177, 1178

Levittowns, 1177–78, *1177*, 1185–86
Lewinsky, Monica, 1362–63
Lewis, John L., 1055, 1057, 1096, 1141
Lewis, Meriwether, 329–32, *330*
Lewis, Sinclair, 975–76
Lexington, Battle of (1775), 196–98, *196, 197*
Lexington, U.S.S., 1093
Leyte Gulf, Battle of (1944), 1115, 1118
Liberator, 557
Liberia, 556
Liberty Loan Act (1917), 945, *945*
liberty of contract, 816
Liberty party, 512–13, 561
  Free Soil party and, 568
Libya, 1082, 1104
Liebowitz, Samuel, *1042*
Life, 1181–82
Liliuokalani, Queen of Hawaii, 864, *864*
Lincoln, Abraham:
  appraisal of Civil War by, 653–54
  assassination of, 666
  background of, 595–96
  and Battle of Petersburg, 648
  between election and inauguration, 604, 607
  in Black Hawk War, 397
  border states held by, 610–11
  cabinet appointments of, 608–9, 674
  on Chattanooga, 645
  civil liberties curtailed by, 637
  Douglas's debates with, 596–97
  in election of 1860, 528, 600–602, *600, 603*
  in election of 1864, 638–39, *638*
  emancipation and, 629–30, *631*
  and first Battle of Bull Run, 614
  first inauguration of, 608
  funeral procession for, *667*
  Gettysburg Address of, 644
  McClellan's antagonism with, 622, 624, 627–28, *627*
  Mexican War opposed by, 517
  military strategy of, 615, 619, 622, 645
  and outbreak of Civil War, 609
  railroads and, 746
  Reconstruction plans of, 654, 665, 665–66, 668, 669
  secession and, 604
  second inauguration of, 653–54
  in senatorial election of 1858, 596–97
  slavery issue and, 566, 596–97, 600, 605, 608, 629–30, 653
  Union command structure and, 622, 624, 628, 640, 645
  on use of African-American soldiers, 633
  western fighting and, 619
  on Wilmot Proviso, 566
Lincoln, Benjamin, 229
Lindbergh, Charles A., Jr., 1003, 1080
line-item veto, 1357
Lippmann, Walter, 1022
literacy tests, 715, 791–92, 1251
Literary Digest, 936
literature:
  antislavery, 578
  in Great Depression, 1043–44
  Harlem Renaissance and, 982
  local colorists in, 807
  in mid-twentieth century, 1187–90
  modernist, 986–88
  naturalism in, 808–9
  in nineteenth century, 466–74
  romanticism in, 470–74
  Southern Renaissance and, 988–89
  transcendentalism and, 467–70
  women and, 474
Lithuania, 1073, 1337
Little Bighorn, Battle of (1874), 729, *730*
Little Richard, 1192
Little Rock, Ark., desegregation in, 1222–23
Litvinov, Maxim, 1072–73
Livingston, Robert R., 203, 328, 373, *373*, 423
Lloyd, Henry Demarest, 892
Lloyd George, David, 956, 959
local colorists, 807
Lochner v. New York, 897
Locke, John, 78, 138, 152, 180, 204
Locofocos, 451
Lodge, Henry Cabot, 791, 803, 861, 868, 874, 958, 959–61, 995
Logan, George, 311
Logan Act (1799), 311
Log Cabin, 411
Log College, 142
London, Jack, 809
London, Treaty of (1915), 956
Lonely Crowd, The (Riesman), 1186
Long, Huey P., Jr., 1047–49, *1047*, 1052
Longfellow, Henry Wadsworth, 471
Long Island, Battle of (1776), 215
"Long Parliament", English, 49
Longstreet, James A., 624, 684
Longview, Tex., race riot in (1919), 964–65
Lon Nol, 1285
Look Homeward, Angel (Wolfe), 988–89
Lords of Trade and Plantations (Board of Trade), 149, 150, 153, 154, 165
Lords Proprietors, 78
Lorenz, Pare, 1045
Los Angeles, Calif., 780, 1097, 1100–1101
"Lost Colony" (Roanoke), 42–43
lost generation, 987–88

Louis XIV, king of France, 159, 162
Louis XVI, king of France, 296
Louisiana, 368–69
  agriculture in, 709, 710
  Civil War and, 630, 633
  cotton in, 417
  in election of 1876, 695, 696
  Hurricane Katrina and, 1387–89
  Reconstruction in, 665, 682, 683, 691, 697
  secession of, 602
  segregation in, 716
  slave trade in, 546
  voting rights in, 715, 716
Louisiana Purchase (1803), 328–32, 435, 582
  boundaries of, 328, 364, *364,* 366–67
  exploration of, 329–32, *330*
  slavery in, 369
Louisiana territory, 31, 166, 297, 368–69
  border of, 366–67
  Burr Conspiracy and, 334–35
  French settlement of, 159–62
  Jefferson's purchase of, 328–29
  name of, 159
  northern border of, 364, *364*
  in Peace of Paris, 168–69, 172
  and War of 1812, 346–47
Louisville, 438
Lovejoy, Elijah P., 561
Lowell, Francis Cabot, 433
Lowell, James Russell, 276, 471
Lowell System, 433–35
Loyalists (Tories), 190
  after American Revolution, 237
  in American Revolution, 195–96, 200, 201, 218–19, 220, 223, 224, 225, 226, 228, 229, 230, 241, 242
  confiscated estates of, 235, 240, 258–59, 371
Lublin Committee, 1122
Luce, Clare Boothe, 1277
Ludendorff, Erich, 953, 955
Ludlow Amendment (1938), 1077
Lusitania, 938–41, *939*
Luther, Martin, 35–36, 37
Lutheranism, 35–36, 132, 446
Luxembourg, 1118
  in NATO, 1151
Lynch, Charles, 218
lynchings, of African Americans, 717, 719, 983, 995, 1153
Lyon, Mary, 478
Lyon, Matthew, 314, *314*

MacArthur, Douglas:
  Bonus Army and, 1020
  firing of, 1165
  in Korean War, 1162–65
  in World War II, 1085, 1092, 1105, 1114, 1115, *1115,* 1118, 1128–29
McAuliffe, "Tony," 1119
McCain, Franklin, *1233*
McCarran Internal Security Act (1950), 1168
McCarthy, Eugene, 1259, 1260, 1270
McCarthy, Joseph R., 1167–68, *1167,* 1201–2, *1201,* 1223
McCarthyism, 1166–68, 1179, 1201–2
McClellan, George B.:
  at Antietam, 625–28
  background of, 523
  in election of 1864, 638–39
  in formation of West Virginia, 610
  Lincoln's antagonism with, 622, 624, 627–28, *627*
  peninsular campaign of, 622–24, *625*
  at second Bull Run, 624
McClure's, 892
McCord, James W., 1299–1300
McCormick, Cyrus Hall, 419–20, *419*
McCoy, Joseph G., 734
McCulloch v. Maryland, 372–73, 400
Macdonough, Thomas, 346
McDowell, Irvin, 622, 623
  at first Bull Run, 614
McFarlane, Robert, 1326
McGaffey, Ives W., 751
McGovern, George S., 1289, 1298–99
machine tools, 454
McKay, Claude, 982
McKinley, William, 837, 881, 883, 899, 972
  assassination of, 882
  Cuban government and, 877, 878
  in election of 1896, 849–51, *851*
  in election of 1900, 881–82, *882*
  Hawaii and, 864–65
  Philippines and, 873, 876
  Spanish-American War and, 866–69, *867,* 873
McKinley Tariff (1890), 836, 837, 864
McLane, Louis, 404
Macmillan, Harold, 1216
McNamara, Robert S., 1231, 1257, 1287
McNary, Charles L., 1006
McNary-Haugen Bill (1927), 1006–7, 1010
McNeil, Joseph, *1233*
Macon, Nathaniel, 338, 360
Macune, Charles W., 842
McVeigh, Timothy, 1356
Maddox, U.S.S., 1255
Madeira, 123
Madero, Francisco I., 931
Madison, James, 211, 262, 280, 313, 350, 388

African colonization and, 556
Alien and Sedition Acts opposed by, 315
Bill of Rights and, 283–84
at Constitutional Convention, 264–65,
  264, 269, 272
debt issue and, 288
as early Republican leader, 293–94, 295
in election of 1808, 338
Federalist and, 273
government strengthening recommended
  by, 269, 358
on Indians, 396
internal improvements and, 362
land policy and, 304
in *Marbury v. Madison,* 325
Monroe Doctrine and, 375
Napoleonic Wars and, 338
national bank and, 290, 358, 359
in ratification debate, 273
as secretary of state, 325
as slaveholder, 318
tariff policy and, 284
Virginia Plan, 265, 266
and War of 1812, 338, 340, 342, 348
magazines, proliferation of (1800–1850), 475
Magellan, Ferdinand, 22–23
Maggie: A Girl of the Streets (Crane), 808–9
Magna Carta (1215), 46
Mahan, Alfred Thayer, 861, 883
Mahicans, *93*
Maine:
  Canadian border with, 410, 491
  in colonial period, 72, 73
  Indians in, 73
  statehood for, 370
  voting rights in, 382
  in War of 1812, 349
Maine, U.S.S., explosion of (1898), 866–68,
  867
Main Street (Lewis), 975
maize (corn), 7, 19, 63, 73, 101–2, 306, 536
Makin, 1114–15
Malakoff Diggings, 728
malaria, 20, 104, 640
Malaya, 1084
Malay Peninsula, 1089, 1204
Malaysia, 1204
Malcolm X, 1252–53, *1253,* 1260
Mamout, Yarrow, *544*
Man and Nature (Marsh), 905
Manassas (Bull Run), first Battle of (1861),
  614–15, *615*
Manassas (Bull Run), second Battle of
  (1862), 624
Manchuria, Japanese in, 1069–71, *1070*

Mandan Sioux, 330–31
Manhattan Project, 1126
manifest destiny, 354, 512, 517, 859–60, 865
  origin of term, 492
Manila, 168
Manila Conference (1954), 1209
Mann, Horace, 476
Mann-Elkins Act (1910), 915
manufactures:
  cities and, 437–39
  in early nineteenth century, *358,* 360, 380,
    432–33
  in early U.S., 259–60, 284–85, 287, 291–92
  in handicraft stage, 432
  Jefferson's embargo and, 358
  in late nineteenth century, 751–53
  Lowell system and, 433–35
  in Oneida, 486
  of Shakers, 485
  in South, 537
  and War of 1812, 349
  see also factories; industry
Mao Tse-tung, 1160, 1296
Marbury, William, 325
Marbury v. Madison, 325–26, 371, 593
March on Washington (1963), 1236–37, *1237*
Marco Polo Bridge, 1073, 1076, *1077*
Mariana Islands, 1115
Marine Corps, U.S., 201
Marion, Francis, 230
Markland (Labrador), 13, 364
Marquette, Jacques, 159, *160*
marriage:
  African, 112
  of African Americans, 115, 553–54, 669,
    680
  of clergy, 38
  in colonial period, 103–4, 105
  and cult of domesticity, 482–83
  divorce and, 243, 1038
  gay, 1383
  in Great Depression, 1038
  of indentured servants, 109
  interracial, 669
  in Oneida Community, 486
  of slaves, 115, 553–54
  in West, 739
  women's rights and, 483
Marsh, George Perkins, 905
Marshall, George C., 1149, 1168
Marshall, John, 291, 323, *371,* 400
  African colonization and, 556
  Burr Conspiracy and, 334
  Indian lands and, 399
  judicial nationalism of, 371–74

Marshall, John (*continued*)
  in *Marbury v. Madison*, 325
  named as chief justice, 317
  XYZ Affair and, 310
Marshall, Thurgood, 1219
Marshall Islands, 1115
Marshall Plan, 1148–49, *1150,* 1160
Martí, José, *866*
Martin, Luther, 273
Martin v. Hunter's Lessee, 371
Marx, Karl, 986
Marx Brothers, 1045–46, *1045*
Marxism, 774
Mary, queen of Scots, 40, 48
Mary I, queen of England, 150
Mary II, queen of England, 49–50, 151, 152
Maryland:
  agriculture in, 533
  Civil War fighting in, 625–27, *626*
  Constitution ratified by, *274*
  free blacks in, 243
  Know-Nothing party in, 448
  labor laws in, 897
  land claims of, 238
  at navigation meeting of 1785, 262
  secession debate in, 610–11
  voting rights in, 382
  War of 1812 in, 346
Maryland colony, 59, *61, 62,* 77
  charter of, 60
  European settlement of, 60
  government of, 60, 152, 154, 155
  Indians in, 169
  slavery in, *111,* 113, *116*
  tobacco in, 107
Maryland Toleration Act (1649), 77
Mason, George, 204
  and Bill of Rights, 284
  at Constitutional Convention, 264, 267, 269
  in ratification debate, 273
Mason, James M., 574, 618–19
Mason, John, 72
Masonic order, 402
Massachusetts:
  asylums in, 481–82
  Civil War troops from, 632, 633, *648*
  constitution of, *242*
  Constitution ratified by, 274, *274*
  education in, 475, 476, 477
  at Hartford Convention, 349
  Know-Nothing party in, 448
  Revolutionary War fighting in, 196–200
  Revolutionary War troops from, 198, 241
  Shays's Rebellion in, 261–62

  slavery in, 241, 242, *242*
  taxation in, 66, 261
  temperance in, 480
  voting rights in, 382
  and War of 1812, 349
Massachusetts Bay Company, 65
Massachusetts colony, 2, 76, 107
  in border disputes, 72
  charter of, 65–66, 68, 77, 150, 154
  in colonial taxation disputes, 180, 181, 185–86, 195
  in colonial wars, 163
  education in, 140
  European settlement of, 65–68, 99
  government of, 65–68, 77, 150, 151, 152, 154, 155
  governors' salary in, 189
  heresy repressed in, 127–28
  Plymouth combined with, 151
  religious freedom in, 127–28
  shipbuilding in, 121
  taxation in, 66, 151
  trade and commerce in, 150
  see also Plymouth colony
Massachusetts Government Act (1774), 192, 225
Massachusetts Indians, 73, *93*
Massasoit, Wampanoag chief, 63, 75
massive resistance, 1220, 1223
massive retaliation, 1203
Mather, Cotton, 74, 128, *129*
Mather, Increase, 125
Matsu, 1209, 1215
Mauldin, Bill, *1109*
Mayaguez incident (1975), 1305
Mayas, 7–8, *9*
Mayflower, 62–63
Mayflower Compact (1620), 62–65, 126, 152
Mayhew, Jonathan, 143
Maysville Road Bill (1830), 388–89, 394
Mead, Margaret, 986
Meade, George, 646
  background of, 523
  at Gettysburg, 643–44
Meany, George, 1175
Meat Inspection Act (1906), 905
meat-packing industry, 786, *904*
  abuses in, 904–5
  anti-trust suit against, 901–2
  regulation of, 901–2, 904, 905
mechanics' lien laws, 451–52
media, *see* press
Medicaid, 1249, 1354–55
Medicare, 1249, 1250, 1330–31, 1354–55, 1369

medicine, *see* health and medicine
Medicine Creek Lodge conference (1867), 729
Mellon, Andrew W., 636, 993, 994, 1013, 1015, 1016, 1319
"melting pot," 99
Melville, Herman, 471, 472–73, *473*, 487
Memphis, Tenn., race riot in (1866), 673
Memphis Free Speech, 719
Mencken, H. L., 976, 998
Mennonites, 36, 132
mentally ill, 481–82
  deinstitutionalization of, 1328
  sterilization and, 978
mercantile system, 148–49, 256–57, 284–85
Mercer, Lucy, 1046
Meredith, James H., 1234
merit system, 825
Merrimack (*Virginia*), 616
Merrimack Mills and Boarding Houses, *435*
Metacomet (Philip), Wampanoag chief, 75–76
Metacomet's (King Philip's) War (1675–1676), 74–76
Methodists, 143, 245
  in revivals, 462
  split over slavery, 561, 585
METO (Middle East Treaty Organization), 1210–11
Mexican Americans, 495, 722, 970–71, 1344–45
  Chicanos and, 1278
  as cowboys, 734
  in New Deal, 1041
  northward migration of, 946
  as shepherds, 737
  UFW and, 1279–80
Mexican Revolution, 495–96
Mexican War (1845–1848), 514, 515–23, *521*, 567
  California annexation and, 515–16, 518–19
  casualties in, 523
  legacies of, 523
  opposition to, 517
  outbreak of, 515–17
  peace treaty in, 522
  Polk's intrigue with Santa Ana in, 520
  preparations for, 517–18
  slavery issue and, 470, 517
Mexico, 169
  European diseases in, *20*, 22
  exploration of, 31
  Gadsden Purchase from, 581
  as heart of Spanish Empire, 29

  immigration from, 970–71, 1041, 1100–1101, 1278–79
  independence of, 157, 495–96, *496*, 499–500, 507–8
  NAFTA and, 1354
  pre-Columbian, 7–9
  seasonal worker agreement with, 1100
  Texas independence from, 496, 508–10, 510
  and U.S. efforts to annex California, 507
  U.S. oil properties in, 1068–69
  U.S. trade with, 406, 501–2
  Wilson's intervention in, 931–33
  in World War I, 944
Mexico City (Tenochtitlán), 9, 26, 28
  U.S. capture of, 520–22
Miamis, *92*
microprocessors, 1347
Microsoft, 1347
middle class:
  in antebellum South, 541–42
  in Ku Klux Klan, 1220
  in late nineteenth century, 782, 793
  New Deal and, 1053, 1061
  in 1950s, 1181–82, 1192
  Nixon and, 1290
  performing arts and, 441–43
  progressivism and, 891, 928
  Reagan and, 1315
  reform movement and, 451, 811–12
  in South, 541–42
  women's rights in, 482
Middle Colonies, 131–34
  ethnic mix in, 131–34
Middle East Treaty Organization (METO), 1210–11
Midway Island, 1089, 1093, 1102, 1114
Miers, Harriet E., 1387
Milan Decree (1807), 335, 338
Milford, Conn., English settlers in, 73
military, U.S.:
  African Americans in, 723–24, 1099
  conscription into, 946, 1080
  in Constitution, 266, 269
  Eisenhower on, 1223–24
  gays in, 1353–54
  Hispanics in, 1278
  in Jefferson administration, 326–27
  massive retaliation strategy and, 1203, 1379–80
  in Mexican War, 517–18
  post-World War II budget of, 1172
  preemptive action and, 1379–82
  segregation in, 1099, 1153
  see also specific branches and wars

Military Academy, U.S. (West Point), 477
Military Assistance Advisory Group, 1162
Military Reconstruction Act (1867), 674, 675
militia movement, 1355–56
militias, 152, 343–44, 344, 452
   in American Revolution, 195–96, 198–99,
      215–17, 219, *220*, 224, 230, 241
   in War of 1812, 344, 346
Miller, Arthur, 1187, *1187*
Miller, Phineas, 418
Milliken v. Bradley, 1291
Mills, C. Wright, 1186–87
Milosevic, Slobodan, 1367
Milwaukee, 438
Milwaukee Leader, 949
Miners' National Association, 763
minimum-wage laws, 897, 993, 1059, 1139,
      1159, 1350, 1358
mining:
   of coal, 537, 708, 762, 1141
   environment and, 725, *725*, 728
   of gold, 570–71, *570*
   hydraulic, 725, 728
   of silver, 619, 724–25
   in West, 724–28
Minnesota, 447
   agriculture in, 739
   Populists in, 844
minstrel shows, 442–43, *443*
Mint Act (1792), 847
Minuit, Peter, 83
Miranda v. Arizona, 1232
missionaries:
   Catholic, 31–33, 159, 161, 495, 498–500
   to China, 580
   French, 159, 161
   to frontier, 461
   in Philippines, 873
   Puritan, 74–75
   Spanish, 31–33, 81, 495, 498–500
Mississippi, 329, 418
   agriculture in, 386, 535, 710
   Civil War fighting in, 641
   cotton in, 417
   Hurricane Katrina and, 1387–89
   migration to, 555
   Reconstruction in, 669–70, 678, 690
   secession of, 602
   segregation in, 716, 1234, 1291
   voting rights in, 715
   women's rights in, 484
Mississippi, University of, desegregation of,
      1234
Mississippian culture, 9–11, *11*
Mississippi Rifle Club, 691

Mississippi River, 159, 1387, 1389
   in Civil War, 616, 641
   navigation rights to, 259, 303, 328
   steamboats on, 423–24
   U.S. access to, 259, 303, 328
   in War of 1812, 345
Missouri:
   agriculture in, 533, 534
   Civil War fighting in, 611, 619–20
   dust bowl in, 1039
   emancipation in, 633
   German settlers in, 447
   secession debate in, 610, 611
Missouri, U.S.S., 1128–29
Missouri Compromise (1820), 368–71, *369*,
      390, 532, 567, 568, 574, 576, 582–83,
      590, 592–93
Missouri Territory, 368–69
Mitchell, George, 1281
Mitchell, John, 1290, 1301
Mobile, Ala., capture of, 639
Mobile and Ohio Railroad, 430
Moby-Dick (Melville), 471, 472, *473*
"Model of Christian Charity, A" (Winthrop),
      66
modernism, literature of, 986–88
Modocs, 730
Mohammed Reza Pahlavi, Shah of Iran, 1309
Mohawks, 83, 229
Molasses Act (1733), 179
Molly Maguires, 763
Molotov, Vyacheslav, 1146, 1149
monarchy:
   English, 48–50, 147
   Locke on, 152
Mondale, Walter F.:
   in election of 1976, 1305
   in election of 1984, 1324–25
"Mongrel Tariff" (1883), 828
Monitor, 616
Monmouth Court House, Battle of (1778),
      226
Monroe, James, 328, 335, 362–63, *362*, 388
   African colonization and, 556
   as ambassador to France, 309
   in American Revolution, 217
   description of, 363
   in election of 1816, 362–63
   in election of 1820, 363, 376
   Florida and, 366
   foreign policy under, 363–67, 374–76
   Missouri Compromise and, 370–71
   and relations with Britain, 363–65
   as slaveholder, 318
   and War of 1812, 348

Monroe Doctrine, 374–76
  Clark Memorandum and, 1069
  Kellogg-Briand Pact and, 1068
  Roosevelt Corollary to, 885–86
Montana, 619
  cattle industry in, 734
  Indian conflicts in, 729, 730
  labor movement in, 775
  statehood for, 725, 836
Montcalm, Louis Joseph de, 168
Montezuma II, Aztec Emperor, 9, 26
Montgomery, Bernard, 1104, 1113
Montgomery, Richard, 200
Montgomery bus boycott (1955–1956),
  1220–22, 1233
Montgomery Ward Company, 1096
Montreal, 38
Moore's Creek Bridge, Battle of (1776), 201
Moral Majority, 1315–16, 1348
Moravian Indians, 188
Moravians, 94, 132
Morgan, Daniel, 230
Morgan, J. Pierpont, 636, 752, 753, 757–58,
  758, 759, 899, 903, 910
Morgenthau, Henry, Jr., 1058
Mormons (Church of Jesus Christ of Latter-
  Day Saints), 464–66, *465,* 737
Mormon Trail, *503*
Morocco, 327
  in Persian Gulf War, 1340
  trade with, 258
  in World War II, 1073, 1103
Morocco crisis (1905), 887–88
Morrill Act (1890), 802
Morrill Land Grant Act (1862), 635, 660, 802
Morrill Tariff, 635, 660
Morris, Gouverneur, 264
Morris, Robert, 250–51, 287
Morristown, N.J., Washington's headquarters
  at (1776–1777), 221
Morse, Samuel F. B., 431
Morse, Wayne, 1255
Moscow Olympics (1980), 1309
Mossadegh, Mohammed, 1309
Mother Ann (Ann Lee Stanley), 484–85
Mother Jones, 772–73
Motherwell, Robert, 1188
Mott, Lucretia, 483, 484
Moultrie, William, 201
mountain men, 497, 506, 518
Mount Vernon, *307*
movable type, 13
movies, 1000–1001
  in Great Depression, 1044–46
  in 1920s, 1000–1001

Mozart, Wolfgang, 140
muckrakers, 892–93
Mugwumps, 829, 891
Muhammad, Elijah, 1252
Muir, John, 908–9
Mukden Incident (1931), 1070
mulattoes, 544–45
Muller v. Oregon, 897
Mulligan, James, 694
"Mulligan letters," 694, 829
multinational corporations, 1368–69
multinational terrorist groups, 1374
Munich Agreement (1938), 1073
Munn v. Illinois, 841
"Murchison letter," 834
Murray, John, 460
Murray, John (Lord Dunmore), 241
Murray, Judith Sargent, 243
Murray, William Vans, 311
music:
  African-American, 114, *114,* 552,
    1191–92
  Jazz Age and, 976–77
  rhythm and blues, 1191–92
  rock 'n' roll, 1191–92, 1272–73
Mussolini, Benito, 1071, *1072,* 1073, 1082,
    1108, 1123
  Spanish Civil War and, 1073
Myanmar (Burma), 1084–85, 1092, 1123,
    1204
My Lai massacre (1969), 1285, 1289

NAACP (National Association for the
    Advancement of Colored People), 983,
    1042, 1100, 1219, *1219,* 1236, 1253
Nader, Ralph, 1369, 1371
NAFTA (North American Free Trade
    Agreement), 1354, 1361, 1369
Nagasaki, atomic bombing of (1945), 1128
Nagy, Imre, 1213
Naismith, James, 800
Napoleon I, Emperor of France, 296, 311–12,
    328, 329, 335, 345, 349
Napoleon III, Emperor of France, 618
Narragansett Bay, 42
Narragansetts, 70, 73, *75, 93*
Narrative of the Life of Frederick Douglass
    (Douglass), 559
Narváez, Pánfilo de, 29, *30*
NASA (National Aeronautics and Space
    Administration), 1214
Nash, Beverly, 681
Nashville, Battle of (1864), 650
Nashville, U.S.S., 884
Nasser, Gamal Abdel, 1211–13, 1215

Nast, Thomas, *670*
Nation, 1078
National Aeronautics and Space
    Administration (NASA), 1214
National American Woman Suffrage
    Association, 813, 979
National Association for the Advancement of
    Colored People (NAACP), 719, 983,
    1042, 1100, 1219, *1219,* 1236, 1252
National Association of Colored Women,
    718
national bank, *see* Bank of the United States
National Banking Act (1863), 635, 660
National Broadcasting Company (NBC),
    1002, 1175
National Child Labor Committee, 896
National Conference of Catholic Bishops,
    1316
National Conservation Commission, 908
National Consumers League, 815, 897
national conventions, 402–3
National (Cumberland) Road, 361–62, *361,*
    363, 389, 421–22
National Defense Act (1916), 941
National Defense Education Act, 1214
National Defense Research Committee, 1080
National Environmental Policy Act (1970),
    1294
National Greenback party, 694
National Industrial Recovery Act (NIRA)
    (1933), 1028, 1034, 1049, 1055
nationalism, American, 389–90, 407
    Clay's "American System" and, 377
    development of, 175, 246–47
    in diplomacy, 374–76
    economic, in early nineteenth century,
        358, 363, 407, 410, 490, 514
    education and, 475
    of John Quincy Adams, 379
    judicial, 371–74
    Tyler and, 490
    after War of 1812, 341, 349, 350, *350*
    of Webster, 392
National Labor Relations Board (NLRB),
    1049, 1143, 1321
National Labor Relations (Wagner) Act
    (1935), 1049, 1053, 1055, 1055–56 1057,
    1274
National Labor Union (NLU), 765
National Liberation Front (Vietnam), 1209
National Military Establishment, 1143,
    1169
national mint, 287
National Oceanic and Atmospheric
    Administration, 1294

National Organization for Women (NOW),
    1275, 1324–25
National Park Service, 907
National Recovery Administration (NRA),
    1034–36, *1035*
National-Republicans, 379, 401, 402–3, 407
National Resources Planning Board, 1096
National Right to Life committee, 1316
National Security Act (1947), 1143
National Security Agency, 1169
National Security Council (NSC), 1143,
    1161, 1169, 1240
National Security League, 941
National Textile Workers Union (NTWU),
    1009–10
National Trades' Union, 451
National Typographical Union, 452
National Union for Social Justice, 1048
National War Labor Board, 1096
National Woman's Party, 980
National Woman Suffrage Association, 813,
    814, 979
National Youth Administration, 1031, 1096
Native American Association, 448
Native Americans, *see* Indians, American
Native Son (Wright), 1044
nativism, 448–49, 790–91, 821, 969–71
    anti-Catholic strain in, 790–91
    of Klan, 971–72
    in 1980s and 1990s, 1345
    after World War I, 965–66
NATO, *see* North Atlantic Treaty
    Organization
naturalism, 808–9
naturalization, *see* citizenship and
    naturalization
Naturalization Act (1798), 313
natural resource management, 906–10
Nausets, 73, *93*
Navajos, 12, 33, 494
Naval Academy, U.S., 477
Naval Construction Act (1916), 941
naval stores, 107, 229
Navigation Act (1651), 148, 149
Navigation Act (1660), 149
Navigation Act (1817), 365
navigation acts, enforcement of, 149–50,
    152–53
Navigation (Staple) Act (1663), 149
Navy, U.S., 232, 311, 326–27, 358, 364
    in Civil War, 613, 616
    in Constitution, 266
    formation of, 201
    Great White Fleet tour of, 888
    in late nineteenth century, 861

and Quemoy and Matsu, 1215
in Spanish-American War, 869
after War of 1812, 350
in War of 1812, 341–42, *342,* 344
after World War I, 1066–67
in World War I, 941, 945
in World War II, 1084
Navy Department, U.S., 311, 941
Nazism, 1071
see also Germany, Nazi
NBC (National Broadcasting Company),
1002, 1175
Nebraska:
cattle industry in, 734, 735
dust bowl in, 1038
Indian conflicts in, 729
migration to, 722
Populists in, 844, *845*
Nebraska Territory, 496
slavery issue and, 583, 585
"necessary and proper" clause, 372
Negro nationalism, 982–83, *982*
neo-orthodoxy, 1184
Ness, Eliot, 975
Netanyahu, Benjamin, 1366–67
Netherlands, 28, 40, 1067
American Revolution and, 225, 286
colonial trade with, 122
colonization by, 83–84, 131
Dutch Republic and, 38–40, 162
empire of, 38–40, 76, 77, 83–84
in fur trade, 73, 83, 84, 87
as imperialist nation, 860
independence movements and,
1204–5
in NATO, 1151
privateers from, 40
Puritans in, 62
in rebellion against Spain, 38–40
trade with, 258
in World War II, 1079
Neutrality Act (1935), 1075, 1076
Neutrality Act (1939), 1078, 1084
Nevada:
election reforms in, 893
gold rush in, 724–25
Indians in, 494
sheep in, 737
statehood for, 619, 725
New Amsterdam, 83, *85*
Newark, N.J., race riot in (1967), 1251
Newburgh Conspiracy, 251–52
New Deal, 817, 857–58, 927, 1022–61
agriculture in, 1033–34, 1041,
1058–59

banking industry and, 1025, 1027–29
business in, 1032, 1034–36, 1051–52
conservative criticism of, 1047–49, 1051,
1052
currency in, 1028, 1029
distribution of wealth in, 1052
Eisenhower and, 1200
electoral coalition of, 1052–53, 1155, 1195,
1198, 1305
industrial recovery program in, 1028,
1034–36
Keynesian theory and, 1058
labor unions and, 1055–57
late-1930s opposition to, 1059–61
leftwing ideas coopted into, 1048–49
legacy of, 1059–61, 1134–35
minorities and, 1041–42
Reagan and, 1330–31
and recession of 1937, 1057–58
regional planning in, 1036–38
regulation in, 1032–38, 1061
and role of government, 1060–61
Second, 1046–52
Social Security in, 1050–51
Supreme Court and, 1033, 1034, 1036,
1049, 1053–55
taxation in, 1050–52
three-pronged strategy of, 1026–27
Truman's support of, 1138–39
work relief in, 1029–32, 1034
in World War II, 1096, *1097*
see also Depression, Great; Roosevelt,
Franklin D.
"new economy," 1360–61, 1372
New England:
agriculture in, 119–20
architecture in, 118–19, *119*
child labor in, 762
colonial life in, 118–31
in colonial wars, 175
currency in, 179
education in, 140
European settlement of, 61–72, *64*
fishing in, 120, *120,* 123, 126–27
in French and Indian War, 175
Great Awakening in, 141–43
Hartford Convention and, 348–49
Indians in, 72–76
industry in, 121–22, *433*
Know-Nothing party in, 448
landownership in, 127
literature in (1800–1850), 468
Louisiana Purchase as seen in, 329
Mexican War as seen in, 517
post-Revolutionary War debt in, 288

New England (*continued*)
  religion in, 124–28, 127–28, 141–44; *see also* Puritans
  secession considered by, 332, 349
  sex ratios in, 105
  shipbuilding in, 121–22
  slaves in, 112–13
  social distinctions in, 455
  South compared with, 123
  and Tariff of 1816, 360
  temperance in, 479–80
  trade and commerce in, 119–24, 126–27, 280, 380, 433
  transcendentalist movement in, 467–70
  in War of 1812, 345
  water transportation in, 426
New England, Dominion of, 150–51
New England Anti-Slavery Society, 557
New England Confederation, 76
New England Free Trade League, 833
New England Primer, The, 140
New England Women's Club, 814–15
Newfoundland, 13, 29, 42, 123, 364
New France, 157–59
New Freedom, 918–19, 924
New Frontier, 1228, 1231
New Guinea, 1093, 1114, 1115
New Hampshire:
  in Constitutional Convention, 263
  Constitution ratified by, 274, *274,* 275
  Dartmouth's charter altered by, 371–72
  at Hartford Convention, 349
  Revolutionary War troops from, 198
  voting rights in, 382
New Hampshire colony, 72
  in land disputes, 188
New Harmony, 486
New Haven colony, 72
New Helvetia, 500–501
New Jersey:
  constitution of, 244
  Constitution ratified by, 274, *274*
  Gibbons v. Ogden and, 373
  paper currency in, 260
  Revolutionary War fighting in, 215–17, *216,* 221, 226
  voting rights in, 244, 382
  Wilson's governorship in, 917
New Jersey, College of (Princeton University), 144
New Jersey colony, 78
  ethnic mix in, 131
  European settlement of, 87–88, *88,* 99
  government of, 150, 152

New Jersey Plan, 265–66
Newlands, Francis G., 738
Newlands Reclamation Act (1901), 738
New Left, 1267–72
New Mexico, 31, 494, 496
  Chicanos in, 1278
  in Civil War, 619
  dust bowl in, 1038
  Gadsden Purchase and, 581
  Mexican War and, 520, 522
  slavery and, 571–72, 573, 574, 577
  in Spanish Empire, 31–33, 495
  statehood for, 571–72, 575, 725, 915
New Morality, 977–78
New Nationalism, 918–19
New Netherland colony, 83, 132, 140
New Orleans, La., 168, 172, 424, 437
  in Civil War, 616
  Hurricane Katrina and, 1387–89, *1388*
  race riot in (1866), 673
  segregation in, 716
  in War of 1812, 345, 346–47, 349
New Orleans, Battle of (1815), 346–47, *347,* 445
Newport, R.I., 132, 135
Newport News Shipbuilding and Drydock Company, 708
Newsom, Robert, 550
newspapers:
  in colonial period, 137–38
  proliferation of (1800–1850), 474–75
New Sweden, 84
Newsweek, 1175, 1259
Newton, Huey P., 1252, 1269
Newton, Isaac, 138, 459, 985
New View of Society, A (Owen), 486
New York:
  Adirondack Park of, 907
  canals in, 424–26
  Civil War troops from, 617
  at Constitutional Convention, 264
  Constitution ratified by, 274, *274, 276*
  and election of 1800, 316
  and election of 1844, 512–13
  Essex Junto and, 332
  in *Gibbons v. Ogden,* 373
  immigrants in, 787
  Indian lands ceded in, 256
  Jeffersonian Republicans in, 295
  Know-Nothing party in, 448
  land claims of, 238, *253*
  paper currency in, 260
  population of, 1343
  prisons in, 481
  Revolutionary Loyalists in, 218–19

Revolutionary War fighting in, 198,
214–17, *216,* 224, 226, 228, 233
school prayer and, 1232
slavery in, 242
spoils system in, 387
swing-vote role of, 821
temperance in, 480
voting rights in, 382, 446, 814
in War of 1812, 343–44
New York Central Railroad, 750–51, *751*
New York City, N.Y.:
Civil War draft riots in, 618
in colonial period, 132, 134–35, 135, *135*
demonstrations in, 1269–70
ethnic mix in, 132
housing in, 780, 784
immigrants in, 787, 788–90, *791*
Irish Americans in, 445
in nineteenth century, 437–38, *439*
Panic of 1837 in, 408–9
poverty in, 136
saloons in, 794
subways in, 782
Tammany Hall in, 829
Tweed Ring in, 694
Vietnam protests in, 1286
waste disposal and, 785, *786*
New York colony, 78, 137–38
in colonial taxation disputes, 182,
184
Dutch origins of, 83–84, 131, 132, 140
education in, 140
ethnic mix in, 131, 132
government of, 150, 151–52
Indians in, 86–87, 131
in land disputes, 188
Leisler government in, 151–52
quartering of British in, 180
New York Consumers League, 815
New York Customs House, 825
New York Herald, 691
New York Infirmary for Women and
Children, 455
New York Journal, 866
New York Mechanick Society, *292*
New York militia, 152, 343–44
New York Nation, 792
New York Sun, 829, 903, 956
New York Times, 934, 977–78, 1238, 1287,
1300, 1328
New York Tribune, 445, 446, *586,* 675, 692, 850
New York World, 866
New York World-Telegram, 1054
New Zealand, in SEATO, 1207
Nez Percés, 494, 730–31, *732*

Ngo Dinh Diem, 1207–9, 1242, *1242,* 1243
Nguyen Van Thieu, 1284
Niagara Movement, 983
Nicaragua, 933, 1290, 1326–27
Iran-Contra affair and, 1325–26
proposed canal in, 883
U.S. interventions in, 933–34, 1068–69,
1322–23, *1322*
Nichols, Terry, 1356
Niebuhr, Reinhold, 1184
Nietzsche, Friedrich, 809
Niles, Hezekiah, 475
Niles' Weekly Register, 475
Nimitz, Chester, 1093, 1105, 1114–15
Niña, 16
Nine-Power Treaty (1922), 1066–67, 1070
Nineteenth Amendment, 979, 992
"Ninety-five Theses" (Luther), 35
Ninth Amendment, 284
NIRA (National Industrial Recovery Act)
(1933), 1028, 1034, 1049, 1055
Nisquallys, 494
Nixon, Richard M., 1134, 1266, 1271
background of, 1031, 1227
China policy of, 1296–97, *1297*
domestic policy of, 1290–92
economy under, 1292–94
in election of 1952, 1196, 1227
in election of 1956, 1210
in election of 1960, 1227–30, *1230*
in election of 1968, 1261–63, *1261, 1262,*
1271
in election of 1972, 1298–99
Ford's pardon of, 1302–3
foreign policy of, 1295–98
Hiss affair and, 1167
Kennedy's debate with, 1228, *1229*
on Latin American tour (1958), 1215
resignation of, 1302, *1302,* 1311
segregation and, 1291
Vietnam War and, 1283–90, *1284*
wage freeze under, 1293–94
Watergate and, 1299–1303
Nixon Doctrine, 1296
NLRB (National Labor Relations Board),
1143, 1321
NLU (National Labor Union), 765
Nobel Peace Prize, 813, 888, 1236
nobles, English, 46, 47
No Child Left Behind (2002), 1373
Non-Aggression Pact (1939), 1073
Non-Intercourse Act (1809), 338
Noriega, Manuel, 1338–39
Norris, George W., 913, 995
Norris v. Alabama, 1043

Norse explorers, 12–13
North, Frederick, Lord, 186, 190–91, *190,* 195, 225, 234
North, Oliver, 1326
North American Free Trade Agreement (NAFTA), 1354, 1361, 1369
North American Review, 475
North American Telegraph Company, 431
North Atlantic Treaty Organization (NATO), 1160, 1336
  attacks on, 1376
  building of, 1150–52
  former Yugoslavia and, 1367–68
  missiles to, 1214
North Carolina:
  agriculture in, 533, 535
  Confederacy and states' rights in, 639
  Constitution ratified by, *274, 276*
  education in, 476
  free blacks in, 370
  Indian lands ceded in, 256
  Indians removed from, 256, 397–400
  labor unrest in, 1008–10, *1009*
  land claims of, 255
  migration from, 554–55
  newspapers in, 475
  paper currency in, 260
  Reconstruction in, 683, 691
  Revolutionary Loyalists in, 218–19
  Revolutionary War fighting in, 201, 229–32
  Revolutionary War troops from, 230
  secession of, 609
  segregation in, 1233, *1233,* 1234
  voting rights in, 240, 413, 715
North Carolina colony, 132
  backcountry of, 134, 188–89
  colonization of, 42–43, *42*
  European settlement of, 77–78, *79*
  government of, 152
  Indians in, 82
  naval stores in, 107
North Dakota:
  agriculture in, 739, 841
  migration to, 722
  statehood for, 725, 836
Northern Alliance, 1376, 1377, *1378*
Northern Pacific Railroad, 693, 748, 899
Northern Securities Company, 899
North Star, 559
Northwest Ordinance (1787), 254–56, 568, 574
Norway:
  in NATO, 1151
  in World War II, 1079
Norwegian settlers, 447
Notes on Virginia (Jefferson), 242, 562

Nova Scotia, 159, 166
NOW (National Organization for Women), 1275, 1324–25
Noyes, John Humphrey, 485–86
NRA (National Recovery Administration), 1034–36, *1035*
NSC (National Security Council), 1143, 1161, 1169, 1240
nuclear energy, 1142
nuclear weapons:
  hydrogen bomb and, 1161, 1204
  Korean War and, 1200–1201
  limited use of, 1203–4
  "missile gap" in, 1238
  Reagan and, 1321
  Soviet Union and, 1146–47, 1161, 1380
  treaties on, 1241, 1247, 1297, 1309, 1329–30, 1338
  in World War II, 1126–29
nullification and interposition, 315, 389–96
  Andrew Jackson and, 393, 394–96, 404, 406, 490
  Calhoun and, 380, 389–95
  South Carolina Ordinance and, 395
  theory of, 315
  Webster-Hayne debate on, 391–93
Nullification Proclamation (1832), 395
Nuremberg trials, 1144
Nurse, Rebecca, *119,* 129
nursing, 454
Nye, Gerald P., 1075

oats, 19, 120, 131, 536
Oberlin College, 464, 479
Obey, David, 1357
Observations Concerning the Increase of Mankind (Franklin), 103
Occupational Safety and Health Act (1970), 1292
ocean transportation, 426–27
O'Connor, Sandra Day, 1321, 1362, 1386, 1387
Odd Fellows, 718
Office of Economic Stabilization, 1096
Office of Homeland Security, 1378
Office of National Drug Control Policy, 1334
Office of Price Administration (OPA), 1095, 1141
Office of Scientific Research and Development, 1094
Ogden, Aaron, 373
Oglethorpe, James E., 94
Ohio, 300
  education in, 477
  in election of 2004, 1385–86

German settlers in, 447
Indian lands ceded in, 256
statehood for, 326, 361, 477
swing-vote role of, 821
Ohio Company, 163, 255
Ohio Life Insurance and Trust Company, 595
Ohio River, transportation on, 423–24
oil industry, 753–55, *754,* 1004, 1369,
1387–88
Okinawa, 1125–26, 1126
Oklahoma, 31
in Civil War, 619, 620
dust bowl in, 1038, 1039, 1044
Indians moved to, 729, 730, 733
socialism in, 775
statehood for, 725
voting rights in, 715, 983
see also Indian Territory
Oklahoma City bombing (1995), 1356, *1356*
older Americans, 1136
Old Northwest, 254–56, *254*
slavery banned from, 255, 566, 568, 574
Old Southwest, 554–56
Old Walton Road, 421
Olive Branch Petition (1775), 200
Oliver, James, 739
Oliver, John, 419
Olmsted, Frederick Law, 796
Olympic games, 801
of 1980, 1309
Oman, 1340
Omoo (Melville), 472
Oñate, Juan de, 31–32
Oneida Community, 485–86
Oneidas, *93*
Onondagas, *93*
"On the Equality of the Sexes" (Murray), 243
On the Origin of Species (Darwin), 804
On the Road (Kerouac), 1190
OPA (Office of Price Administration), 1095,
1141
OPEC (Organization of Petroleum
Exporting Countries), 1293, 1294, 1305,
1324, 1339
Opechancanough, Powhatan chief, 57
Open Door Policy, 879–80, 886, 887,
1066–67, 1071
open shops, 1007
opera houses, 441–42
Operation Desert Shield, *1339,* 1340
Operation Desert Storm, 1340, 1349
Operation Dixie, 1143
Operation Enduring Freedom, 1377
Operation Iraqi Freedom, 1381
Operation Rolling Thunder, 1255

opium, 406
Oppenheimer, J. Robert, 1126
Order of the Star Spangled Banner, 448
Orders in Council (Great Britain)
(1806–1807), 335, 338, 347–48
Ordinance of Secession (South Carolina)
(1860), 602
Ordinance of Secession (Virginia) (1861), 609
Oregon:
election reforms in, 893
voting rights in, 814
Oregon, U.S.S., 883
Oregon Country, 364, 496–97, 523
and election of 1844, 511
Great Britain and, 374, 497, 513, 514–15, *516*
Indian conflicts in, 730
Polk and, 513, 514–15, *515*
Russia and, 374, 497
slavery issue and, 567
U.S.-British border in, 514–15, *515, 516*
U.S. settlement of, 501, 502, 504
Oregon (Overland) Trail, 497, 502–5, *503,*
504, 505, 507
Organization of Petroleum Exporting
Countries (OPEC), 1293, 1294, 1305,
1324, 1339
Oriskany, Battle of (1777), 224
Orlando, Vittorio, 956
Ortega, Daniel, 1326–27
Osborne, Sarah, 128
Osceola, 397
Oslo accords (1993), 1365–67, 1378–79
Ostend Manifesto (1854), 580
O'Sullivan, John L., 492, 522
O'Sullivan, T. H., *644*
Oswald, Lee Harvey, 1243
Other America, The (Harrington), 1246
Otis, James, 176, 185–86
Otis Elevator Company, 781
Ottawas, 170, 300
Our Country: Its Possible Future and Its
Present Crisis (Strong), 862
Overland (Oregon) Trail, 502–5, *503, 504,*
505, 507
Owen, Robert, 486
Oxbow Route, *503*

Pacific Railroads Act (1862), 746
Page, Walter Hines, 936
Paine, Thomas:
in American Revolution, 215
background of, 202
painting:
romanticism and, *467*
in twentieth century, 986–87, 1188

Paiutes, 494, 731
Pakenham, Edward, 347
Pakistan, 1204
  in METO, 1210
  in SEATO, 1207, 1210
  terrorism and, 1374, 1377
Palestine, Palestinians, 1152, 1298, 1308,
  1365–67, 1379
Palestine Liberation Organization (PLO),
  1323, 1330, 1365–67
Palmer, A. Mitchell, 965, 966
Palmer, John M., 849
Palo Alto, Battle of (1846), 518
Panama, 22
  U.S. invasion of (1989), 1338–39
Panama Canal, 883–85, *884*, 1068, 1307
Pan-American Conference (1928), 1069
Pan-American Conference, Eighth (1936), 1069
Pan-American Conference, Seventh (1933),
  1069
Panay, 1077
Panic of 1819, 363, 367, 368, 380, 400, 418
Panic of 1837, 406, 408–9, *409,* 426, 427, 452,
  497, 536
Panic of 1857, 595
Panic of 1873, 693–94, 763
Paragon, 373
Paris, Pact of (Kellogg-Briand Pact) (1928),
  1067–68, 1070, 1071
Paris, Peace of (1763), 168–72, 174, 204
Paris, Peace of (1783), 235, 250, 258, 259, 283
Paris, Treaty of (1898), 872, 873
Paris Peace Conference (1919), 955–59, *957*
Parker, Alton B., 902–3
Parker, John, 197
Parker, Theodore, 468
Parkman, Francis, 161
Parks, Rosa, 1220
Parliament, British:
  American Revolution and, 225
  Charles I's conflict with, 49
  in colonial taxation disputes, 181–83, 184,
    185, 188, 191–92, 202
  colonies' undefined relationship with, 156
  on Continental Congress, 194–95
  Continental Congress on, 193
  currency policies of, 124, 179
  elections of, 186
  kings' conflict with, 49, 147, 154, 156
  Leisler government and, 152
  Restoration and, 49
  taxation and, 46, 156
  trade regulated by, 148
  see also House of Commons, British;
    House of Lords, British

Parris, Samuel, 128
party system:
  cultural-ethnic identity and, 407, 445–46
  establishment of, 294
  Jefferson's role in, 325
  patronage and, 784–85, 820, 822–23, *823*
  third parties and, 402, 448, 585
  Washington on, 307
patent medicines, 904, 905
Patent Office, U.S., 751
Paterson, N.J., silk strike in (1912), 776
Pathet Lao, 1242
patriot movement, 1355–56
Patrons of Husbandry (Grange), 840–41
Patterson, Heywood, *1042*
Patton, George S., Jr.:
  Bonus Army and, 1020
  in World War II, *1108,* 1113
Paul, Alice, 979, 980
Paxton Boys, 188–89
Paz, Octavio, 28
PCA (Progressive Citizens of America), 1154
Peabody, Elizabeth, 468
Peabody, Sophia, 468
Peace Corps, 1231–32, 1267
Peale, Charles Willson, *217, 264, 394, 544*
Peale, Norman Vincent, 1183–84
Pea Ridge, Battle of (1862), 611
Pearl Harbor attack (1941), 1086–89, *1088,*
  1092–93, 1103
Pease, Edward, *1364*
penal system, 480–82
Pendleton, George H., 687, 828
Pendleton Civil Service Act (1883), 828, 831
penitentiaries, 481
Penn, William, 87, 90, 132, 140, 188
Pennsylvania:
  canals in, 425
  Civil War fighting in, 641–45
  Constitution ratified by, *274*
  in early interstate cooperation, 262
  Indian lands ceded in, 256
  paper currency in, 260
  Revolutionary War fighting in, 215, *222,*
    223, 228
  slavery in, 241, 242
  spoils system in, 387
  voting rights in, 240, 382
  Whiskey Rebellion in, 300–302
Pennsylvania, University of (Philadelphia
  Academy), 139, 144
Pennsylvania Chronicle, 185
Pennsylvania colony, 78, 88–91, 152, 172
  backcountry of, 134
  discontent on frontier of, 188–89

education in, 140
ethnic groups in, 90, 132, 134
European settlement of, 88–91, 99
government of, 90, 154
Indians in, 131, 169
in land disputes, 188, 192
and protests against British, 185, 188–89
and Quakers, 88–90, 99
religion in, 88–90, 132
Pennsylvania Dutch, 132
Pennsylvania Gazette, 139
Pennsylvania Journal, 182
Pentagon, 1375
Pentagon Papers, 1287, 1300
People, The, 774
People's party, *see* Populist party
Pequots, 73, 74, *75, 93*
Pequot War (1637), 74
Peres, Shimon, 1366
perestroika, 1335
Perot, H. Ross, 1353, 1354, 1360
Perry, Matthew, 580, *581,* 878
Perry, Oliver H., 344
Pershing, John J., 933, 945–46, 951
Persian Gulf War, 1339–40, *1339,* 1349, 1350, 1380
Persian Gulf War (second), 1380–83
casualties in, 1382, 1383
personal computers, 1347
Personal Responsibility and Work
    Opportunity Act (1996), 1359
Peru, 157, 1215
Pescadores Islands, 878
Petersburg, Battle of (1864), 647–48
petition, freedom of, 50, 238
Philadelphia, 327–28
Philadelphia, Pa., 437
in colonial period, 132, 134–35, *135*
Declaration of Independence written in,
    203–4
and First Continental Congress, 193–95
founding of, 90
Irish Americans in, 445
labor in, 451
nativist clashes in (1844), 448
Second Continental Congress and, 198,
    202–6
subways in, 782
as U.S. capitol, 288
Whiskey Boys and, 301
Philadelphia, Battle of (1777), *222,* 223
Philadelphia Academy (University of
    Pennsylvania), 139, 144
Philadelphia-Lancaster Turnpike, 422
Philadelphia Navy Yard, 451

philanthropy, 755, 757
Philip II, king of Spain, 40
Philip (Metacomet), Wampanoag chief, 75–76
Philippine Government Act (1902), 877
Philippines, 23, 168
annexation debate about, 872–76
Japan and, 887
in SEATO, 1207
in Spanish-American War, 869, *870*
U.S. conquest of, 874–75, 882
in World War II, 1089, 1092, *1092,* 1115,
    1115, 1118, 1123, 1125
Philippine Sea, Battle of (1944), 1115
physics, 985
Picasso, Pablo, 987, *988*
Pickering, John, 326
Pickering, Thomas, 332
Pickering, Timothy, 310, 313
Pickett, George, 643–44
Pierce, Franklin:
in election of 1852, 579–80
in election of 1856, 591
foreign policy under, 580–81
Kansas-Nebraska Act and, 584, 585
pigs, 19, 25, 101–2, 120, 536, 640
Pike, Zebulon, *330,* 370
Pinchback, Pinckney B. S., 683
Pinchot, Gifford, 907–9, *907,* 910, 912–13, 914
Pinckney, Charles Cotesworth, 309, 310
in election of 1800, 316, *317*
in election of 1804, 333
in election of 1808, 338
Pinckney, Thomas, 309
in election of 1796, 308
and treaty with Britain, 302–3
Pinckney Treaty (1795), 302–3, *303,* 365
Pinochet, Augusto, 1304
Pinta, 16
pirates, Barbary, 327–28, 350
see also privateers
Pitcairn, John, 196–97
Pitcher, Molly (Mary Ludwig Hays), 243
Pitt, William, 167–68, 177, 183, 184
Pittsburgh, Pa. (Fort Duquesne), 164, 166,
    170, 438
Pizarro, Francisco, 27, *30*
Plains Indians, 33–35, *34,* 493–95, 505
railroads and, 747
Plains of Mesa, Battle of the, *519*
Planck, Max, 985
Planned Parenthood, 978, *1277*
Plan of Union (1801), 461
plantations, 321, 532, 539–41, 546–48
Platt Amendment (1901), 878, 1069
"Pledge of Allegiance," 1182

Plessy, Homer, 716
Plessy v. Ferguson, 716, 1219
PLO (Palestine Liberation Organization), 1323, 1330, 1365–67
Plow That Broke the Plains, The, 1045
Plunkett, James, 717
Plymouth colony, 31, 62–65, 75, 76, 77, 101
    government of, 63–65
    Indian relations with, 63
    Massachusetts combined with, 151
    as Virginia Company division, 50, *53,* 62
Pocahontas, 55–56, *56*
Poe, Edgar Allan, 472, *472*
poetry, 982, 986, 987, 1189–90
Poetry, 987
Poindexter, John, 1326
Point Four, 1160
Poland:
    fall of communism in, 1335
    in second Gulf War, 1381
    Soviet domination of, 1121–22, 1145, 1213, 1321–22
    in World War I, 954, 958–59
    in World War II, 1073–74, 1078, 1121–22
Poles, 132
Polish Americans, 617, 787, 788
Politics in an Oyster House (Woodville), *474*
Polk, James K., 511–15
    Andrew Jackson compared with, 513
    background of, 513
    in election of 1844, 511–13, *512*
    Mexican War and, 515–18, 520, 522, 523
    reelection bid eschewed by, 567
    slavery issue and, 566, 567
Pollock, Jackson, 1188
poll taxes, 715
pollution, 436, 786, 905, 1292, 1373
polygamy, 464
Ponce de León, Juan, 29, *30*
Pontiac, Ottawa chief, 170–71, 177, 188
Poor Richard's Almanac (Franklin), 139
Popé, 33
Pope, John, 624
popular culture:
    advertising in, 1175, *1176*
    in colonial period, 136–37, 439
    and community, 1182–84
    and conforming culture, 1179–84
    dueling and, 543
    in early nineteenth century, 439–43
    on the frontier, 306
    German immigrants and, 447, *447*
    in Great Depression, 1044–46
    Independence Day and, 246
    in late nineteenth century, 793–801
    and lonely crowd, 1184–87
    minstrel shows and, 442–43
    and movies, 1044–46
    and 1960s counterculture, 1272–74
    paradox of, 1193
    popular press and, 474–75
    and post-World War II consumer culture, 1174–76
    and radio, 1044
    and rock 'n' roll, 1191–92, 1272–73
    and saloons, 794–96
    slaves and, 114, *114,* 552–53
    southern planters and, 116–17
    and sports, 440–41, *442,* 796–98, 1153–54
    in suburbs, 1176–78
    taverns and, 136–37
    theater and, 441–43
    urban recreation and, 440–41
    vaudeville, 793–94
    and youth culture, 1190–92
Popular Science Monthly, 805
popular sovereignty, 567–68, 593
population:
    aging of, 1136
    "baby-boom" generation and, 1140, 1173–74, *1174,* 1343
    of cities, 437–38
    in colonial period, 102–5
    in early U.S., 280–82
    of Indians, 22, 27
    in late twentieth century, 1343–45
    Mayan, 8
    in nineteenth century, *420, 421*
    post-World War II growth in, 1140
    in South, *535*
    urban, density of, 783
    U.S., growth of, 385
Populist party (People's party), 843–44, 848
    agriculture and, 732
    in election of 1892, 845–46
    in election of 1896, 850, 852
    progressivism and, 817, 891
    Spanish-American War and, 873
Port Huron statement (1962), 1267–68
Portsmouth, Treaty of (1905), 886–87
Portugal, 1067
    colonial trade with, 122
    exploration and discovery by, 15, *23*
    Jews expelled from, 132
    in Napoleonic Wars, 337
    in NATO, 1151
    in slave trade, 115
Portuguese colonists, 132
Portuguese Empire, in Treaty of Tordesillas, 17

postal service, 137
  express, 430
Post Office Department, U.S., 201
potatoes, 19, 536, *536*
Potawatomis, 300
Potsdam Declaration (1945), 1127
Pottawatomie Massacre (1856), 587, 597
Pound, Ezra, 987
poverty:
  alcoholism and, 479
  among American Indians, 1280–81
  in antebellum South, 542
  in colonial period, 135–36
  education and, 476, 1373
  Hispanics and, 1278
  Hurricane Katrina and, 1387
  Internet and, 1347
  Johnson's efforts against, 1136, 1245–47,
    1249–50, 1261–62, 1280, 1293
  in late twentieth century, 1136
  in 1960s, 1245–47
  in 1990s, 1344
  in post–Civil War South, 661–62
  in post–World War II era, 1175, 1184, 1185
  Reagan and, 1320, 1331
  recreation and, 797–98
  "safety net" and, 1320
  urban, 780, 1344
  war on, 1245–47
  see also Depression, Great; welfare
Powderly, Terence V., 766, 768
Powell, Colin, 1372, 1381
Powell v. Alabama, 1042
Power of Positive Thinking, The (Peale), 1183
Powers, Gary, 1217
Powhatans, *93*
  colonists assisted by, *51,* 52
  Pocahontas and, 56
  settler conflicts with, 57
pragmatism, 806–7
*Pragmatism: A New Name for Some Old Ways
  of Thinking* (James), 806
predestination, 36
Preemption Act (1830), 419
Presbyterian Magazine, 968
Presbyterians, 36, 40, 48, 132, 142, 143, 144,
  245–46, 460
  in Civil War, 561
  Congregationalists' union with, 461
  in revivals, 461, 462
  in Whig party, 407
Prescott, Samuel, 196
presidency:
  in Constitution, 268–71
  electors for, 269–70, 382

  executive privilege of, 299, 334
  nominations for, 376–77, 402–3
  powers of, 268, 269–71
  war powers of, 1162, 1303
  see also executive branch
presidios, 31
Presley, Elvis, 1192, *1192*
press:
  antislavery and, 557, 561
  colonial newspapers, 137–38
  in election of 2000, 1369
  freedom of, 137–38, 284, 313–14, 561
  muckrakers in, 892–93
  popular, 474–75
  in Spanish-American War, 866
Preston, Levi, 205
Prevost, George, 346
Price, Birch & Co., *549*
primaries, direct, 893
primogeniture, 47
Princeton, Battle of (1777), 217
Princeton University (College of New
  Jersey), 144, 917
Principia (Newton), 138
Principles of Scientific Management, The
  (Taylor), 894
printing technology, 13, 474
prisons:
  convict leasing and, 712
  debtors in, 451, 481
  reform movements and, 480–82
privateers:
  American, 232
  Dutch, 40
  English, 40, 77
  French, 38, 298
Privy Council, British, 153
Proclamation Line, 177
Proclamation of 1763, 177, 240
Proclamation of Amnesty (1865), 668
Proclamation of Amnesty and
  Reconstruction (1863), 665
Professional Air Traffic Controllers, 1321
professions, rise of, 452–55
Profiles in Courage (Kennedy), 1238
Progress and Poverty (George), 809
Progressive ("Bull Moose") party, 915–16,
  915, 918–20, 928, 942–43
Progressive Citizens of America (PCA), 1154
Progressive National Committee, 942
Progressive party (1924), 999
Progressive party (1948), 1157, 1158
progressivism, 817, 852, 857, 890–9284, 991–92
  antecedents to, 891–92
  conservation and, 907–8

progressivism (*continued*)
  corporate regulation and, 891, 895–96, 903–5
  democratic reforms in, 893
  efficiency and, 894–95
  features of, 893–98
  income tax and, 941
  limits of, 927–28
  muckrakers and, 892–93
  NAACP and, 983
  populism compared with, 891
  resurgence of, 925–27
  social justice promoted in, 896–97
  Theodore Roosevelt and, 898–910
  utilitarian, 908
  Wilson and, 916–27
Prohibition movement, 271, 815–16, 822, 837, 897–98, 974–75
  bootlegging and, 974–75, *975*
  Eighteenth Amendment and, 974, 992, 1024
  World War I and, 974
Prohibition party, 898
Prohibitory Act (1775), 202, 225
Promise of American Life, The (Croly), 918
property:
  black ownership of, 669
  Fourteenth Amendment and, 816
  voting rights and, 155–56, 240, 382, 445–46, 451
  women's control of, 483
Proposition 187 (California), 1345
Proposition 209 (California), 1362
Protestantism, 45, 541
  anti-Catholicism and, 448
  rationalism in, 459–60
  Reformation and, 35–38
  see also specific denominations
Prussia:
  in colonial wars, 167
  French Revolution and, 296
  trade with, 258
Public Credit Act (1869), 688
public schools, 451, 801–2
Public Works Administration (PWA), 1034
Pueblo-Hohokam culture, 9
Pueblos, 29, 32–33, 494, 495
Puerto Ricans, 971
Puerto Rico, 24, 29, 374
  acquisition of, 871, 873, 877
Pulitzer, Joseph, 866
Pullman, George, 770–71
Pullman Strike (1894), 770–72, *771*
Punderson, Prudence, *106*
Pure Food and Drug Act (1906), 905, 1059

Puritans, 77, 118, 124–26
  Andros's conflict with, 151
  Anglican Church as viewed by, 65, 68–70, 125
  communitarian standards of, 126, 128
  in Connecticut, 72, *75*
  Cromwell and, 76, 148
  dissension among, 68–70, *69*, 143–44
  education and, 140
  in England, 36, 38, 48–49
  evolving doctrines of, 459–60
  Great Awakening and, 143–44
  Harvard founded by, 144
  lifestyle of, 125–26
  in Maine, 72
  in Massachusetts, 62, 65, 66, 68, 70, 99, 107
  missionaries of, 74–75
  in New Hampshire, 72
  Separatists, 38, 62, 65, 125
  transcendentalism and, 468
  in Virginia, 117
  witchcraft and, 128–31
"putting-out" system, 431, 432
PWA (Public Works Administration), 1034
Pythagoreans, 13

Qatar, 1340
quackery, 454
Quadruple Alliance, 375
Quakers (Society of Friends), 36, *89*, 118, 128, 131, 132, 188
  educational efforts of, 140
  and founding of Pennsylvania, 88–90, 99
  transcendentalism and, 468
  in Virginia, 117
Quantrill, William C., 620
Quarles, Benjamin, 632
Quartering Act (1765), 180, 184, 188
Quartering Act (1774), 192
quartering of military, 180, 188, 192, 284
Quayle, Dan, *1332*
Quebec, 38, 158, *161, 168, 169*
  as British colony, 177
  founding of, 158
  Revolutionary War attack on, 200–201
  in War of 1812, 342
Québec, battle of (1759), 168
Quebec Act (1774), 192, 240
Quechuas, *see* Incas
Queen's College (Rutgers University), 144
Quemoy, 1209, 1215
Quezon, Manuel, 877

Rabin, Yitzhak, 1366, *1366*
R & B (rhythm and blues), 1191–92

race riots:
in Chicago (1919), 947, *964*, 965
in Chicago (1966), 1251
in Cleveland (1966), 1251
in Detroit (1943), 1100
in Detroit (1967), 1251
in East St. Louis (1917), 947
in Elaine, Ark. (1919), 965
in Longview, Tex. (1919), 964–65
in Memphis (1866), 673
in Newark (1967), 1251
in New Orleans (1866), 673
in Washington, D.C. (1919), 965
in Watts (1965), 1251
racism, 717, 995
against Asians, 1101–2
Darwin and, 861
labor movement and, 1009–10
see also segregation, desegregation
Radical Republicans:
assessment of, 684–85
in Civil War, 628, 637, 638
corruption charges against, 685–86
Johnson's relations with, 668, 673–74,
675–76
presidential elections and, 376
in Reconstruction, 665–66, 668, 670–72,
684–86, 691, 712, 714
radio, 1001–2, *1001*
radioactivity, 985
RAF (Royal Air Force), 1109
railroads, 430, 431–32, 454, 581–82, 706, 927
agriculture and, 709, 840
building of, 744, 745
cattle drives and, 734–36
in Civil War, 613
in early nineteenth century, 426, 427, *428,*
429, 430
economic benefits of, 426
financing of, 748–51
Gadsden Purchase and, 581
in growth of cities, 780
ICC and, 832–33
immigration encouraged by, 787
Indian relocation and, 585
Kansas-Nebraska Act and, 583
labor disputes and, 766, 770–72, 1141
land grants to, 430, 660
land policy and, 738, 746–47, 832
Morgan and, 758
in Panic of 1873, 693
Populists and, 846
progressivism and, 896
regulation of, 816
segregation in, 716–17, 719

in South, 712
steam power introduced to, 426
Theodore Roosevelt's actions against, 899,
903–4
transcontinental, 581, 660, 746–48, *748,*
749
travel on, 426
Railway Labor Act (1926), 1008
Railway Labor Board, 1008
Rainbow, 427
Raker Act (1913), 909
Raleigh, Walter, 41–42
Ramsay, David, 194
Randolph, A. Philip, 1099–1100, *1156*
Randolph, Edmund, 275, 282
Randolph, Edward, 149–50
Randolph, John, 333, 341, 380
Randolph, Peyton, 193
Rankin, Jeanette, 1089
Rauschenbusch, Walter, 811–12
Ray, James Earl, 1260
RCA, 1002
Reagan, Ronald, 1135, 1307, 1310, *1315*
background of, 1313–14
budget cuts of, 1320
conflicts of interest under, 1320–21
cultural conservatives and, 1347–48
defense buildup under, 1321–22
deficits and, 1319–20, 1328, 1331
economy and, 1317, 1319–20, 1324, 1328
in election of 1976, 1305
in election of 1980, 1315, 1317–18, *1318*
in election of 1984, 1324–25
family values and, 1316
Iran-Contra affair and, 1325–26
legacy of, 1330–31
Middle East and, 1323–24
regulation under, 1320–21
scandals under, 1320–21
at summit meetings, 1329–30, *1330*
"Real Whigs," 180
recall elections, 893
recessions, 1057–58, 1292–94, 1304, 1309,
1320, 1328, 1343, 1349–50, 1372
Reclamation Act (1902), 909
Reclamation Bureau, U.S., 738
Reconstruction, 659–97
African Americans in, 662–64, 669–70,
679–84, *683*
Black Codes in, 669–70, 672
Bourbons (Redeemers) in, 711–14, *713,* 715
carpetbaggers in, 684, 691
Congress in, 663–64, 665–66, 669–75, 678,
690, 693–94
conservative resurgence in, 690–91

Reconstruction (*continued*)
  constitutional debates over, 665–66, 668,
    671–72
  corruption and abuses in, 685–86
  education in, 680–81, 685
  end of, 697
  Johnson's plans for, 667–69, 671–72
  land policy in, 662–64, 682
  Radical Republicans and, 665–66, 668,
    670–72, 684–86, 691, 712, 714
  scalawags in, 684, 690, 691
  southern intransigence over, 669–70
  Supreme Court in, 675, 697
  white terror in, 689–90
Reconstruction Act, Second (1867), 675
Reconstruction Act, Third (1867), 675
Reconstruction Finance Corporation,
    1017–18, 1199
Red Badge of Courage, The (Crane), 808–9
Redeemers (Bourbons), 711–14, *713*, 715
Red River War (1874–75), 729
Red Scare (1919), 965–66, 1007
Reed, Walter, 877–78
referenda, 893
Reformation, 35–38
  in England, 36–38
Reform Darwinism, 806, *806*
reform movements, 451–52, 479–87, 817
  antislavery, 556–60, 578–79
  churches in, 811–12
  for civil service, 691–93, 694, 823–26, 828,
    831, 835
  Cleveland and, 829
  dietary, 479
  education, 475–79
  elements of, 891–93
  municipal, 785–86
  for prisons and asylums, 480–82
  Prohibition movement, 479–80
  utopian, 484–87
  for women's rights, 482–84, 559–60,
    815–16
  see also progressivism
refrigeration, 751, 786
Refunding Act (1870), 688
regulation, governmental, 1061
  of agriculture, 1033–34, 1058–59
  of atomic energy, 1142
  of banking industry, 922–23, 1018,
    1028–29
  of child labor, 816, 896–97, 915, 927
  of communications, 915, 1002
  of corporations, 816–17, 891, 895–96, 899,
    901–2, 903–5, 923–24, 1034–36
  of drugs, 904, 1059

of electric power, 1036–38
of housing, 1058–59, 1139, 1159
of labor, 816–17, 896–97, 915, 1139,
    1141–43, 1159
of liquor, 837, 896, 897–98, 974–75
of meat packers, 901–2, 904, 905
pollution restricted by, 1292, 1294–95
progressivism and, 895–96
of railroads, 816, 832–33, 896, 903–4, 927,
    1096
of wages and prices, 1095–96, 1141,
    1293–94, 1304
of wartime industry, 946, 1094
of worker safety, 897
Regulators, 189, 201, 219
Rehnquist, William, 1386
relativity, 985
religion:
  African, 112
  African-American, 114–15, 462, 533,
    552–53, 679–80
  American Indian, 28, 29, 32, 73
  in backcountry, 141
  in colonial period, 124–28, 127–28, 132,
    141–44
  deism and, 459–60
  denominational splits in, 143–44
  education and, 143–44, 477
  Enlightenment and, 138
  freedom of, *see* religious freedom
  on frontier, 461–62
  fundamentalism and, 124–25, 972–74,
    1315–16, 1323
  Great Awakening and, 141–44, 459
  institutional churches in, 810–11
  in Massachusetts, 127–28
  missionaries, imperialism and, 860
  neo-orthodoxy and, 1184
  in New England, 124–28, 127–28,
    141–44
  in post-World War II era, 1182–84
  rational, 459–60
  Religious Right and, 1315–16
  revival meetings and, 461–62, *463*
  revivals in, *see* revivals, religious
  school prayer and, 1232, 1348
  Second Great Awakening and, 460–66
  segregation and, 717–18
  slavery justified through, 561
  in South, 117–18, 533
  temperance and, 479
  terrorism and, 1374, 1376
  transcendentalism and, 468
  unitarianism and, 460
  universalism and, 460

utopian communities and, 484–85
witchcraft and, 128–31, *129*
see also specific religions and denominations
religious freedom, 36, 49, 50, 89, 132
 after American Revolution, 244–46
 in Bill of Rights, 284
 French colonies and, 159
 in Maryland, 77
 in Massachusetts, 127–28
 in Pennsylvania, 90, 132
 Roger Williams and, 68–70, 70, 71
 and separation of church and state, 68–70
 in South Carolina, 78
 voting rights and, 155, 382
Religious Right, 1315–16, 1331, 1348–49, 1351
rendezvous system, 496
Rensselaer Polytechnic Institute, 454
Reparations Commission, 1065, 1121
"Report on Manufactures" (Hamilton), 286, 287, 291–92, 294
"Report on the Condition of the Indian Tribes," 729
Representative Men (Emerson), 470
Republican party:
 African Americans in, 1043
 in Civil War, 635
 cold war and, 1134
 and Congress in late nineteenth century, 821–22
 and Contract with America, 1357–58
 corruption and, 821, 823
 cultural conservatives and, 1347–49
 in election of 1856, 589–90
 in election of 1860, 600–602
 in election of 1868, 686–87
 in election of 1872, 691–93
 in election of 1876, 694–97
 in election of 1884, 828–29
 in election of 1888, 834–35
 in election of 1894, 848
 in election of 1896, 849–51
 in election of 1908, 910–11
 in election of 1912, 914, 919
 in election of 1916, 925–26, 941–43
 in election of 1918, 956
 in election of 1920, 992–93
 in election of 1928, 1010–11
 in election of 1932, 1023
 in election of 1936, 1052–53
 in election of 1940, 1081
 in election of 1948, 1155
 in election of 1952, 1196, 1203
 in election of 1956, 1210
 in election of 1964, 1247–48
 in election of 1968, 1261, 1271
 in election of 1972, 1298–99
 in election of 1976, 1305
 in election of 1980, 1317–18
 in election of 1982, 1320
 in election of 1992, 1351–52
 in election of 1994, 1356–57
 in election of 2000, 1371
 emergence of, 585
 KKK intimidation of, 690
 late nineteenth-century components of, 820–21
 Lincoln's early involvement with, 596
 Mugwumps in, 829
 nativism in, 821
 New Deal and, 1134–35
 new states approved by, 725
 in 1920s, 857, 921
 1960s conservatism of, 1247
 nineteenth-century dominance of, 836
 Reagan's rise in, 1314–15
 "real issues" and, 820
 in Reconstruction, 690–91
 scalawags in, 684, 690, 691
 slavery compromise sought by, 605
 in South, 712, 1198, *1198*, 1246, 1248
 Spanish-American War and, 873
 Stalwarts vs. Half-Breeds in, 824, 826–28
 sunbelt and, 1343, 1348
 in Taft administration, 911, 912, 913
 tariff issue and, 822, 833, 834, 837
 see also Radical Republicans
Republicans, Jeffersonian, 211, 312–13, 363
 Adams criticized by, 309
 Alien and Sedition Acts and, 313, 313–14
 and *Dartmouth College v. Woodward*, 371–72
 in election of 1796, 308
 in election of 1800, 315–18
 in election of 1816, 362
 in election of 1824, 376
 Federalists' role reversal with, 350, 357
 formation of, 293–95
 French conflict and, 311, 313
 French Revolution and, 297
 Hartford Convention and, 349
 Jay's Treaty and, 299
 Jefferson's role with, 324–25
 land policy of, 304
 Louisiana Purchase and, 328–29
 national bank and, 326, 359–60
 officeholder conflicts and, 325
 split among, 333
 and War of 1812, 350
 Whiskey Rebellion and, 301

Republic Steel, 1057
Resaca de la Palma, Battle of (1846), 518
reservation (Indian) system, 494, 733–34
Restoration, English, 49, 77
Resumption Act (1875), 693
retail, 758–60
Reuben James, U.S.S., 1084
Reuther, Walter, 1056, 1140
Revels, Hiram, *683,* 684
Revenue Act (1767), 184–85
Revenue Act (1916), 941
Revenue Act (1926), 994
Revenue Act (1935), 1051–52
Revenue Act (1942), 1095
Revenue Act (1964), 1246
revenue sharing, 1292
Revenue (Sugar) Act (1764), 179, 180, 181,
    184, 188
Revere, Paul, *187*
    warning ride of, 196
revivals, religious:
    and "burned over" district, 463–64
    on the frontier, 461–62
    Great Awakening, 141–44, 459
    Mormons and, 464
    Second Great Awakening, 460–66
Revolutionary War, *see* American Revolution
Rhett, Robert Barnwell, 577
Rhineland, 1073
Rhode Island:
    Civil War troops from, 632
    Constitutional Convention avoided by,
        263
    Constitution ratified by, *274, 276*
    at Hartford Convention, 349
    paper currency in, 260–61
    Revolutionary War troops from, 198,
        241
    slavery in, 241, 242
Rhode Island, College of (Brown University),
    144, 477–78
Rhode Island colony, 78
    charter of, 77, 126, 154
    European settlement of, 68–71
    in events before American Revolution,
        189–90
    government of, 77, 126, 150, 154
    as refuge, 132
Rhode Island (Fall River) system, 435
rhythm and blues (R & B), 1191–92
Ricard, Cyprien, 545
rice, 19, 107, 358, 533, 661, 709
rich, the:
    in colonial period, 135
    in early nineteenth century, 455

housing of, 431
    in late nineteenth century, 760, 793
    in late twentieth century, 1136
    in post–World War II era, 1175
    recreation of, 441–43
    social origins of, 455
    in South, 116–17, 538–41
    wartime profits of, 636
Richardson, Elliot, 1301
Richmond, Va., *661*
    bread riot in (1863), 639
    capture of (1865), 654
    as Confederate capital, 614, 615
    first settlements in, 55
    as military goal of Union army, 614, 615,
        622–23, 647, 654
    Tredegar Iron Works in, 537, *538*
Richmond Times, 717
Ridgway, Matthew B., 1164, 1165
Riesman, David, 1186
"right-to-work" laws, 1096, 1143
Riis, Jacob, 892
riots:
    in Memphis (1866), 673
    in New Orleans (1866), 673
    in New York (1863), 618
    in Richmond (1863), 639
    see also race riots
Ripley, George, 468, 487
Rittenhouse, David, 139
River, The, 1045
river transportation:
    federal funding for, 358, 360–62, 389
    to frontier regions, 423–26
    Gibbons v. Ogden, 373–74
    state funding for, 404, 425
    steamboats on, 373–74, 423–24, *424*
roads, *see* highways and roads
Roanoke Island, 42–43, *42*
Roaring Twenties, 975–83
Roberts, Ed, 1347
Roberts, John G., Jr., 1386–87
Robertson, Pat, 1348
Robinson, Jackie, 1153–54, *1154*
Rockefeller, John D., 636, 753–55, *753,* 758,
    805
Rockingham, marquis of, 182–83, 184
Rockne, Knute, 789
rock 'n' roll, 1191–92, 1272–73
Roebuck, Alvah, 753, 759
Roe v. Wade, 1275, 1315
Rogers, Will, 999
Rogers, William P., 1285, 1290
Rolfe, John, 55–56, 57
Rolfe, Rebecca (Pocahontas), 55–56, *56*

Rolfe, Thomas, 56
Rolling Stones, 1273
Rolling Thunder, Operation, 1255
Romania, 959
    fall of communism in, 1335
    Soviet domination of, 1145
    in World War II, 1082–83, 1146
Romanian Americans, 788
romanticism, 355, 466–74
    American literature and, 470–74
    in art and architecture, 466–70
    transcendentalism and, 467–70
Rommel, Erwin, 1082, 1104, 1113
Roosevelt, Eleanor, 1023, 1024, 1046–47, *1046*
Roosevelt, Franklin D., 857
    Atlantic Charter and, 1084
    atomic bombs and, 1126
    background of, 1023–24
    brain trust of, 1027
    at Cairo and Teheran, 1110
    at Casablanca, 1104–5
    China and, 1160
    Churchill's 1941 meeting with, 1084
    court-packing plan of, 1053–55, *1054*
    death of, 1123
    Democratic primary intervention of, 1060
    in election of 1920, 993
    in election of 1932, 1023–25, *1025, 1026*
    in election of 1936, 1052–53
    in election of 1940, 1080–82
    in election of 1944, 1118
    fireside chats of, 1002, 1044, 1082
    first inauguration of, 1025–26
    French occupation zone and, 1121
    growing war involvement and, 1079–80, 1082–84
    Japanese Americans relocated by, 1101
    Japanese assets frozen by, 1085
    Johnson's admiration of, 1245, 1249
    labor movement and, 1057
    Latin American policy of, 1069
    leftward movement of, 1049
    legacy of, 1134–35
    postwar world as seen by, 1143
    racial issues ignored by, 1043
    Truman compared with, 1138
    U.S. neutrality and, 1075–77, 1078
    war aims and, 1103
    war financing and, 1095
    in Yalta, 1120–22, *1121*
    see also Depression, Great; New Deal
Roosevelt, Theodore, 821, 835, 850, 861, 892, *900,* 916, 970
    assassination attempt on, 918

big stick diplomacy of, *886,* 887–88
    child labor and, 773
    coal strike and, 899–901
    conservation promoted by, 905–10
    Cuban insurrection and, 878
    in election of 1900, 881–82, *882*
    in election of 1904, 902–3
    in election of 1912, 914–16, *915,* 918–21, *920*
    in election of 1916, 941–43
    executive action favored by, 899
    food safety and, 904–5
    Japan relations and, 886, 887
    legacy of, 888
    Panama Canal and, 883–85, *884*
    progressivism of, 898–910, 1061
    rise of, 880–83
    second term of, 902–10
    Spanish-American War and, 867–68, 869, 871, 881, 882
    Taft's break with, 913–15
    Taft selected as successor by, 910–11
    trusts and, 899–902, *902*
    Versailles Treaty opposed by, 960
    World War I and, 939, *940*
Roosevelt Corollary, 885–86
Roosevelt Dam, 738
Root, Elihu, 887, 915
rope, 121–22
Rosecrans, William S., 645
Rosenberg, Ethel, 1167, 1202
Rosenberg, Julius, 1167, 1202
Rossiter, Thomas Pritchard, *270*
Rostow, Walt, 1242–43
Rothko, Mark, 1188
Rothman, David, 481
Roughing It (Twain), 808
Rough Riders, 871, 881
Roundheads, 49
Royal Air Force (RAF), 1080, 1109
Royal Navy, 1080
Royal Proclamation of 1763, 177, 240
Ruby, Jack, 1243
Ruckelshaus, William, 1301
Rudd, Mark, 1269, *1270*
Ruffin, Edmund, 537, 577
Rule of 1756, 298
Rump Parliament, 49
Rumsfeld, Donald, 1372, 1382
Rush, Benjamin, 479
Rush, Richard, 364
Rush-Bagot Agreement (1817), 363–64
Rusk, Dean, 1231, 1241, 1257
Russell, Jonathan, 348

Russia:
  Alaska and, 862
  Bolshevik Revolution in, 944, 950, 953, 964, 965–66
  California and, 498
  in China, 878, 879
  in colonial wars, 167
  in Napoleonic wars, 335
  Oregon Country and, 374, 497
  in Russo-Japanese War, 886–87, 1123
  seal traders from, 31, 498
  and second Gulf War, 1381, 1383
  after Soviet era, 1349, 1352
  in World War I, 934–35, 944, 950, 953
  see also Soviet Union
Russian Americans, 788
Russo-Japanese War, 886–87, 1123
Rutgers University (Queen's College), 144
Rutledge, John, 266
rye, 536

Saar Basin, 958, 1073
Sacagawea, 331
Sacco, Nicola, 969, *970*
Sackville-West, Sir Lionel, 834
Sadat, Anwar el-, 1298, 1307–8, *1308*
Saddam Hussein, 1339–40, 1349, 1380–83
Safire, William, 1292
St. Augustine, Fla., 31, 157
St. James Church, *117*
St. Lawrence Seaway, 1200
St. Leger, Barry, 224
St. Louis, Mo., 438, 845–46
St. Louis Post-Dispatch, 800–801
St. Mary's, Md., 101
St. Vincent, 172
Saipan, 1115
Salem, Mass., *119,* 121, 125, *127,* 128–31, *129*
saloons, 794–96, *795,* 821
SALT (Strategic Arms Limitation Talks), 1297, 1304, 1309
Salvation Army, 810, *811*
Samoa, 862–63, 873
Sampson, Deborah, 243
Samuelson, Robert, 1372
San Antonio, Tex., 157
Sand Creek massacre, 729
San Diego, Calif., 1097
Sandinistas, 1323, 1326
Sandino, César Augusto, 1068–69, *1068*
"Sand Lot" incident, 764–65
Sandys, Edwin, 56
San Francisco, Calif., 780, 782, 1097
  anti-Chinese violence in, 764–65

gold rush and, *569*
saloons in, 794
San Francisco *Alta Californian,* 808
San Francisco Conference (1945), 1143–44, 1146
Sanger, Margaret, 978–79, *979*
San Salvador, 16
Santa Anna, Antonio López de, 508–9, 510, 520
Santa Barbara, Mission of, *499*
Santa Fe, N.Mex., 33, 157, 501
Santa Fe Railroad, 747, 780
Santa Fe Trail, 501–2, *503,* 505
Santa María, 16
Santo Domingo, 22, 24, 374–75
Saratoga, Battle of (1777), *222,* 223–24, 225
Sargent, A. A., 814
Sartoris (Faulkner), 989
Sassacus, Pequot chief, 74
Sassamon, 75
Saudi Arabia:
  in Arab League, 1211
  Persian Gulf War and, 1340
  terrorism and, 1376, 1382–83
Sauks, *92,* 397
SAVAK, 1309
Savannah, Battle of (1778), 229
Savannah, Ga., *91*
  fall of (1864), 651
  founding of, 94
Savio, Mario, 1268
Sawyer, Lorenzo, 728
scalawags, 684, 690, *691*
Scandinavia, Reformation in, 36
Scandinavian Americans, 447, 722
  in Civil War, 616
Scarlet Letter, The (Hawthorne), 471
Schanzer, Carlo, *1066*
Schechter Poultry Corporation v. United States, 1049
Schenck v. United States, 949
Schlafly, Phyllis, 1316
Schmacher, Ferdinand, 446
school prayer, 1232, 1348, 1383
Schrank, John, 918
Schurz, Carl, 669, 692, 824
Schwenkfelders, 36
science:
  in colonial period, 138–40
  in early nineteenth century, 431–32
  in twentieth century, 984–86
Science, 963
SCLC (Southern Christian Leadership Conference), 1222, 1233–34

Scopes, John T., 972–74, *973*
Scotch-Irish Americans, 19, 90, 99, 131, 132, *133,* 134, 142, 306, 461, 542
Scotland, 36, 46, 48, 49
  English union with, 50
Scots, Highland, 94, 134
Scott, Dred, 592–93
Scott, Thomas, 756
Scott, Winfield, 341, 410
  in Civil War, 611, 615, 622
  in election of 1852, 579
  in Mexican War, 518, 520–22, 523
Scottish Americans, 88, 94, 131, 132, *133,* 134, 542
  in American Revolution, 201
  in Civil War, 616–17
Scottsboro case, 1042–43
Screen Actors Guild, 1314
SDI (Strategic Defense Initiative), 1321
SDS (Students for a Democratic Society), 1267, 1268–69, *1270,* 1271
Seamen's Union, 925
search and seizure, unreasonable, 284
search warrants, 175–76
Sears, Richard, 753, 759
Sears, Roebuck and Company, 758–60, *760*
SEATO (Southeast Asia Treaty Organization), 1207
Seattle, Wash., 1097
  strikes in, 963–64
Sea Wolf, The (London), 809
secession, considered by New England, 332, 349
secession of South, 602–3, *610*
  Buchanan's response to, 604–5
  choosing sides in, 609–11
  efforts at compromise in, 605
  forfeited-rights theory and, 671
  Lincoln's response to, 604, 608, 610–11
  movement for, 602–3
Second Great Awakening, 460–66
  "burned-over" district and, 463–64
  on frontier, 461–62
  Mormons and, 464–66
  New England colleges and, 461
  salvation and, 463
Second Report on Public Credit (Hamilton), 287
Securities and Exchange Commission (SEC), 1029
Sedition Act (1798), 313–14, *314,* 315
Sedition Act (1918), 949–50
segregation, desegregation:
  in armed forces, 1099, 1153
  of Asian Americans, 887

under Bourbons (Redeemers) in New South, 713, 716–18
  busing and, *1291,* 1350
  cold war and, 1152–53
  in early twentieth century, 983
  in education, 887, 1153, 1173, 1219–20, 1233, 1234, 1291, 1362
  Eleanor Roosevelt and, 1047
  and election of 1948, *1156*
  and election of 1968, 1261
  in housing, 1041, 1178
  "Jim Crow" laws, 717, 719
  Montgomery bus boycott and, 1220–22, 1233
  in New Deal programs, 1041
  in nineteenth century, 713, 714, 716–21
  in public accommodations, 716–17, 1246
  of schools, 1219–20, 1222–23, 1234, 1291
  "separate but equal" rubric of, 716, 1219–20, 1221–22
  suburbanization and, 1178
  in transportation, 716–17, 719, 1220–22, 1246
  Wilson's endorsement of, 925
  in World War II, 1099–1100
  see also African Americans; civil rights movement
Selective Service Act (1917), 946
self-incrimination, 238, 284
"Self-Reliance" (Emerson), 469
Seminoles, 281, 365–66, *365*
  in Civil War, 620
  removal of, 397
Senate, U.S.:
  Compromise of 1850 in, 572–77
  in Constitution, 269
  Convention of 1800 ratified by, 312
  Jay's Treaty approved by, 298, 299
  Johnson's trial in, 676–78
  Louisiana Purchase approved by, 329
  violence on floor of (1856), 588–89
  see also Congress, U.S.
Seneca Falls Convention (1848), 483–84
Senecas, *93,* 228
Sennett, Mack, 1001
"separate but equal," 716, 1219–20, 1221–22
separation of church and state, 69–70
separation of powers, 237, 268–71
Separatists, 38, 62, 65, 125
separatists, African-American, 1253
September 11, 2001 terrorist attacks, 1342–43, 1374–76, 1378, *1379*
  national unity and, 1376
Serb Americans, 788

Serbia, 1367–68
  in World War I, 934, 959
serfdom, 47
Serra, Junipero, 598
servants, *see* indentured servants
settlement house movement, 812–13, 896
Seven Pines (Fair Oaks), Battle of (1862),
  623
Seventeenth Amendment, 893, 915
Seven Years' War, *see* French and Indian War
Seward, William H., 630
  appointed secretary of state, 608
  assassination attempt on, 666
  and Compromise of 1850, 572, 574
  and election of 1856, 590
  in election of 1860, 600–601
  Pacific policy and, 862, *863*
sewer systems, 431, 785–86
sewing machines, 431
sex ratios, 104–5
sexual relations:
  AIDS and, 1328–29
  in 1920s, 977–78, *978*–79
  Puritans on, 125
  sexual revolution and, 1276–77
  slavery and, 540–41
Seymour, Horatio, 678, 687
Shahn, Ben, *970*
Shah of Iran (Mohammed Reza Pahlavi),
  1309
Shakers, 484–85, *485*
Shakespeare, William, 54
Shame of the Cities, The (Steffens), 892
sharecropping, 709–11, *709, 710*
  environment and, 710–11
Share Our Wealth program, 1048
Sharon, Ariel, 1379
Sharpsburg (Antietam), Battle of (1862),
  625–28, 630
Shaw, Anna Howard, 813–14
Shaw, Robert Gould, 632–33
Shawnees, 169, 177, 228–29, 300, 339–40,
  339, 410
Shays, Daniel, 261
Shays's Rebellion, 261–62
sheep, 19, 101, 120, 536
  in nineteenth-century West, 737
Shepard, Alan B., Jr., 1214
Sheridan, Philip Henry, *647*, 729
Sherman, John, 687–88, 821, 836
Sherman, Roger, 203, 264, 266
Sherman, William Tecumseh, 646, *650*
  Atlanta destroyed by, 639
  Johnston's surrender to, 655
  in march to sea, 648–52, *652*, 661

Sherman Anti-Trust Act (1890), 708, 755,
  772, 836, 895, 899, 901, 923
Sherman Silver Purchase Act (1890), 836,
  847, 848
Shevardnadze, Eduard, 1339
Shiloh, Battle of (1862), 620–22
shipbuilding, 121–22
Shitehara, Kijuro, *1066*
shoemakers' strike (1860), 452
Sholes, Christopher, 751
Shultz, George, 1326, 1327
Siberia, 5
Sierra Club, 909
"Significance of the Frontier in American
  History, The" (Turner), 740–41
Signing the Constitution (Rossiter), *270*
Sihanouk, Prince Norodom, 1285
"silent majority," 1283
Silent Spring (Carson), 1294
silver:
  currency and, 825–26, 836–37, 847,
    848–49, 852
  in mercantile system, 148–49
  mining of, 619, 724–25
  Spanish Empire and, 29, 32, 157
Simmons, William J., 971
Simpson, "Sockless Jerry," 844–45
Sims, William S., 945
Sinai, 1304
Sinclair, Upton, 904
Singer, Isaac Merritt, 431
Singleton, Benjamin "Pap," 722
"Sinners in the Hands of an Angry God"
  (Edwards), 142–43
Sino-Japanese War, 878
Sioux, 34, 330–31, 397, *493, 494*, 495
Sioux War (1860s-1870s), 729, 732, *788*
Sirhan, Sirhan, 1260
Sirica, John J., 1299–1300
Sister Carrie (Dreiser), 809
Six-Day War (1967), 1298
Sixteenth Amendment, 915
"slash-and-burn" techniques, 100
Slater, Samuel, 432, 447
slavery, 396, 483, 487, 523, 533, *533*
  American Revolution and, 205, 239,
    240–43, 320
  banned from Old Northwest, 255, 566,
    568, 574
  California and, 507, 571–72, 573–74,
    576–77
  Civil War and, 629–30, 653
  in colonial period, 78, 108, 110–11,
    112–16, *114*, 123
  and Compromise of 1850, 572–80, *576*

Congress and, 566–67, 568, 571–72, 593, 594, 633
in Constitution, 266–67, 268, 327
defense of, 561–62
in District of Columbia, 410
Dred Scott case and, 592–93, 595, 597, 601
economics of, 538
and election of 1844, 511
emancipation and, 629–33, 661
in Kansas-Nebraska crisis, 581–91
Lincoln-Douglas debates on, 596–97
Mexican War and, 517
Missouri Compromise and, 368–71, *369*, 390, 532, 567, 568, 574, 576–77, 582–83, 590, 592–93
New Mexico and, 571–72, 573, 574, 577
origins of, 110–11, 113–14
religious justification of, 561
southern defense of, 532–33, 561–62
in territories, 566–72
Texas annexation and, 510, 514
Thirteenth Amendment and, 267, 633, 659, 669, 697
Tyler and, 490
Wilmot Proviso and, 566, 574
see also abolition movement
Slavery is Dead? (Nast), *670*
slaves, 94, 98–99, 120, 134, 320
African roots of, 27, 111–12, *114*
after American Revolution, 256, 321
in American Revolution, 201, 219, 298, 299
baptism and status of, 114–15
black ownership of, 545
childhood among, 554
community of, 551–52
as "contraband," 629, *629, 632*
culture of, 112–16, *114*
escaped, 365, *365*, 548, 549
freed, 321, 544–45, *545*
fugitive slave laws and, 572, 577–78, *578*, 585
Indians as, 17, 74, 76, 80–83, 115
in industry, 537–38, *538*
infant mortality of, 547
insurrections of, 112, 390, 550–51, 557, 599
management of, 541–42
manumission of, 242–43
marriage of, 115, 553–54
middle-class southerners and, 541–42
in Old Southwest, 556
plantations and, 539–41, 546–48
population of, 540, *546, 547*
religion and, 552–53
sexual exploitation of, 540–41, 549–50, 556
as skilled workers, 450
in South, 110–11, 112–16, 281, 545–54
in southern mythology, 531–32
southern white culture and, 539–82
in West, 418
women, 548–50
slave trade, 3, 78, 79, 112, *113*, 123, *267*, 545–46
Constitutional provisions on, 266–67, 268
in District of Columbia, 410, 577
end of, 241, 327, 491, 545
foreign outlawing of, 327, 491, 545
within U.S., 545–46, 548, 572, 577
Slavs, 115, 787
Slidell, John, 516, 618–19
Sloat, John D., 519
Slovak Americans, 788
Slovene Americans, 788
smallpox, 20–22, *20*, 74, 87, 104, 170, 200–201, 221, 241
inoculation for, 221
Smeal, Eleanor, 1277
Smith, Adam, 257, 293
Smith, Alfred E., 1010–11, 1047, 1228
Smith, Billy, *1233*
Smith, "Cotton" Ed, 1059
Smith, Francis, 196
Smith, Hyrum, 464
Smith, John, *51*, 52–54, 56, 57
Smith, Joseph, Jr., 464–65
Smith Act (1940), 1167, 1168, 1203
Smith College, 800, 804
Smith-Connally War Labor Disputes Act (1943), 1096
Smith-Hughes Act (1917), 926
Smith-Lever Act (1914), 926
Smithson, James, 431
Smithsonian Institution, 431
Smith v. Allwright, 1100
smuggling, 122, 179, 184, 189, 205
SNCC (Student Nonviolent Coordinating Committee), 1233–34, 1252
Snyder, Gary, 1189
social change, theories of, 804–10
social criticism, 809–10
Social Darwinism, 805–6, 810
Social Democratic party, 775
Social Gospel, 810–12, 817
socialism:
labor movement and, 774–75
public utilities and, 895
vs. capitalism, 1061
Socialist Labor party, 774
Socialist party, 774–75, 892, 999
in presidential elections, 910, 918, 919, 1025

Socialist party (*continued*)
  after World War I, 965, 966
  in World War I, 949
Socialist Trade and Labor Alliance, 774
Social Security, 1057, 1060, 1159, 1200, 1232,
    1247, *1319*, 1330–31, 1369, 1386
  inflation and, 1292
  Supreme Court and, 1053
Social Security Act (1935), 1050–51, 1055
Society of Female Manufacturing Workers,
    1041
Soil Conservation and Domestic Allotment
    Act (1936), 1033–34
Solidarity, 1321, 322
Solomon Islands, 1114
Somalia, 1135, 1365, 1374
Somme, Battle of, 935
Sons of Liberty, 181, 185–86, *186*
Sons of Temperance, 479
Soto, Hernando de, 30, *30*
Soulé, Pierre, 580
Sound and the Fury, The (Faulkner), 989
South, 528–29, 531–64, 706–21
  African-American culture in, 112–16, *114*,
    543–44
  African Americans in politics of, 712–13
  agriculture in, 107–8, 533–37, 539–42,
    708–11
  in American Revolution, 229–33, *231*
  anti-union sentiment in, 1008
  architecture of, 540
  Bourbons (Redeemers) in, 711–14, *713*,
    715
  child labor in, 762
  Civil War devastation of, 650–52, 661–62
  in colonial period, 107–18
  cotton in, 417–18
  distinctiveness of, 532–38
  dueling in, 543
  economy of, 537–38, 707–8, 711–12
  education in, 140–41, 712, 714
  in French and Indian War, 168
  frontier of, 554–56
  gentry in, 116–17, *116*
  honor and violence in, 542–43
  Indian conflicts in, 168
  Irish Americans in, 444
  land policies in, 108–9
  literacy rates in, 475
  manufactures in, 537
  masculine culture in, 542–43, 555–56
  middle class in, 541–42
  Middle Colonies' trade with, 131
  and migration to Southwest, 554–55
  military tradition in, 613

  mythology of, 531–32, 533
  New Deal and, 1059
  New England compared with, 123
  plantations in, 539–41, 546–48
  poor whites in, 533, 542
  post–Civil War devastation in, 661–62
  railroads in, 712
  after Reconstruction, 706–21
  religion in, 533
  Republican Party in, 712, 1198, *1198*, 1246,
    1248
  secession of, 602–3, 609–11, *610*
  sex ratios in, 104–5
  slaves in, 110–11, 112–16, 281, 318, 545–54
  society and economy in, 107–18
  soil exhaustion in, 536–37
  and Tariff of 1816, 360
  urbanization in, 780
  War of 1812 in, 344–45, *345*
  Whigs in, 407–8
  white society in, 538–43
  under Wilson, 920–21
  see also Civil War, U.S.; Confederate States
    of America; Reconstruction
South Carolina, 321
  African Americans in legislature of, 713
  African-American soldiers outlawed by, 241
  agriculture in, 533, 535, 536, 709–10
  Civil War fighting in, 609, 616, 633, 652
  Constitution ratified by, *274*
  cotton in, 417, 418
  education in, 476, 712
  in election of 1800, 316
  in election of 1876, 695, 696
  government of, 78
  Indian lands ceded in, 256
  land claims of, *253*
  migration from, 554–55
  nullification and, 380, 389–91, 393, 394–96
  paper currency in, 260
  post-Revolutionary War debt in, 288
  primaries adopted in, 893
  Reconstruction in, 679, 683, 691, 697
  Revolutionary Loyalists in, 218–19
  Revolutionary War fighting in, 201,
    229–32
  Revolutionary War troops from, 229–30,
    230–32
  secession of, 602, *604*
  segregation in, 716, 1219
  slave trade in, 241, 327
  voting rights in, 382, 715
South Carolina colony:
  agriculture in, 107
  backcountry of, 134, 189

gentry of, 116
government of, 78, 152, 155
Huguenots in, 31
Indians in, 79–83
as refuge, 132, 134
Regulators in, 189
settlement of, 78, *79*
slaves in, 111, 113, *114*
trade and commerce in, 108
South Carolina Exposition and Protest
  (Calhoun), 380, 390, 391
South Carolina Ordinance, 395
South Carolina Red Shirts, 691
South Dakota:
  agriculture in, 739, 841
  election reforms in, 893
  Indian conflicts in, 729
  Populists in, 844
  statehood for, 725, 836
Southeast Asia Treaty Organization
  (SEATO), 1207
South End House, 812
Southern Christian Leadership Conference
  (SCLC), 1222, 1233–34
Southern Manifesto (1956), 1220
Southern Pacific Railroad, 747–48, 780
Southern Patriot, 246
Southern Renaissance, 988–89
Southwest, Old, 554–56
Soviet Union, 950, 1296
  Afghanistan invaded by, 1309, 1323, 1330,
    1335, 1376
  Berlin crises and, 1150, 1215–16,
    1238–39
  Chinese conflicts with, 1070
  containment and, 1147–48, 1168–69, 1203,
    1257, 1349, 1379–80
  Cuba and, 1218
  Cuban missile crisis and, 1239–41, *1240*
  détente with, 1297–98
  dissolution of, 1336–37, 1342, 1349, 1374
  Dulles's alliances and, 1210
  Eastern Europe dominated by, 1121–22,
    1144–46, 1203, 1213–14, 1334–36
  economy of, 1336, 1337
  Germany occupied by, 1149–50, *1151*
  Indochina and, 1206–7, 1242
  Korean War and, 1161–62, 1163, 1165
  Latin America and, 1323, 1326
  liberalization in, 1330, 1335
  Marshall Plan and, 1149
  Nasser and, 1215
  1991 coup attempt in, *1336*, 1337
  nuclear arms treaties with, 1241, 1247,
    1297, 1309, 1329–30, 1338

nuclear weapons of, 1161, 1204
  Reagan and, 1321–22
  SALT treaties with, 1297, 1304, 1309
  Spanish Civil War and, 1075
  Sputnik launched by, 1214
  Suez War and, 1210, 1213
  trade with, 1072–73, 1297–98
  in United Nations, 1144
  Vietnam War and, 1257
  in World War II, 1082–83, 1085, 1103,
    1110, 1119–20, 1121–23, 1127, 1128,
    1129–30, 1172
  see also cold war; Russia
space program, 1214, 1295–96, *1295*
Spain, 328, 329, 333, 365–67
  American Revolution and, 202, 224, 225,
    234–35, 286
  Civil War in, 1073, 1075–76
  colonial trade with, 122
  in colonial wars, 168, 169, 172
  decline of, 365
  early U.S. relations with, 258, 259, 296, 299
  explorations by, 15–18, 22–23, *23*, 28–34,
    30, 31
  as imperialist nation, 860
  Indian conflicts and, 256, 281, 302–3
  Mexican independence from, 157, 495–96,
    496, 499–500, 507–8
  Mississippi River access and, 259
  in Napoleonic wars, 335, 337, 374–75, 495
  in NATO, 1151
  Oregon Country claim of, 374, 497
  Pinckney Treaty with, 302–3
  in second Gulf War, 1380
  in slave trade, 115
  and War of 1812, 340, 346
  see also Spanish Empire
Spanish Americans, 132, 617
Spanish-American War, 852, 856, 865–78,
  872
  annexation debate after, 872–76
  casualties in, 871–72
  Cuba in, 865–72, 873, 874
  Maine incident and, 866–68
  Manila Bay taken, 869, *870*
  organizing acquisitions from, 876–78
  Philippines in, 871
  pressure for, 866–69
  Rough Riders in, 871
Spanish Armada, 40–41, *41*
Spanish Empire, 23–33, 81, 83
  Aztecs defeated by, 9
  British Empire compared with, 28, 51,
    94–95, 147, 157
  California as territory of, 33, 498

Spanish Empire (*continued*)
 Catholicism and, 27–28, 31–33, 157, 168,
  495
 challenges to, 38–43
 colonization in, 31
 conquests of, 25–27
 Cromwell's conflicts with, 77
 decline of, 157, 365
 decolonization of, 374–75
 European diseases spread in, 20–22
 Florida as territory of, 29, 31, 168–69, 328,
  340, 366–67, 495
 maps of, *160, 170, 171*
 Mexico as territory of, 29, 499
 missionaries in, 31–33, 81, 495, 498–500
 privateers' attacks against, 38–40
 in Treaty of Tordesillas, 17
Spanish flu, 962–63, *963*
Specie Circular, 405
speculators:
 in bonds, 286, 287
 in gold, 688
 in land, 304, 367–68
 in real estate, Florida, 1012
 in stocks (1929), 1012–15
speech, freedom of, 238, 284, 314
speedy trial, right to, 284
Spencer, Herbert, 805–6
Spindletop gusher (1901), 1004
Spock, Benjamin, 1186
spoils system, patronage, 387, 822–23, *823*
 Cleveland and, 831
 Harrison and, 835
 Hayes's efforts against, 824–25
Spokanes, 494
sports:
 baseball, 800–801, 1153–54
 basketball, 800
 bicycling, 796–97, *797*
 boxing, 797
 croquet, 796
 football, 800
 in nineteenth century, 440–41, *442,*
  796–98, 799–801
 segregation in, 1153–54
 spectator, 799–801
 tennis, 796
 women in, 796, 797
Spotsylvania Court House, Battle of (1864),
 647
Spotted Tail, Chief of Sioux, *730*
Sputnik, 1214
Squanto, 63
squatter sovereignty, 567–68, 593
Sri Lanka (Ceylon), 1204

Stabilization Act (1942), 1096
stagecoaches, 136
stagflation, 1293, 1294, 1304, 1311, 1317
Stalin, Joseph, 1043
 containment and, 1147
 death of, 1201
 denunciation of, 1213
 Korean War and, 1161–62
 in World War II, 1104–5, 1110, 1113,
  1120–22, 1123, 1145, 1160
Stalwarts, 824, 826–28
Stamp Act (1765), 179, 180, *182*, 205–6
 colonial protests against, 180–82
 repeal of, 182–84, *183*
Stamp Act Congress (1765), 181–82
Standard Oil Company, *753*, 754–55, 892,
 902
Standard Oil Trust, 755
Standish, Miles, 62
Stanford, Leland, 747
Stanley, Ann Lee (Mother Ann), 484–85
Stanton, Edwin M., 637, 674, 676, 677
Stanton, Elizabeth Cady, 483, *483*, 484, 813,
 814
Staple (Navigation) Act (1663), 149
Stark, John, 224
Starr, Ellen, 812
Starr, Kenneth, 1362, 1363–64
Star of the West, 604
Star Route Frauds, 827
"Star-Spangled Banner, The," 346
Star Wars, *see* Strategic Defense Initiative
state-compact theory, 315, 392
state and local power:
 civil rights movement and, 1218
 after Civil War, 820–21, 822
 in Constitution, 265–66
 Granger Laws and, 841
 interstate commerce and, 832–33
 vs. federal government, 1369
 and paper currency, 260–61
State Department, U.S., 282
 McCarthyism and, 1168
states' rights, 333, 376, 407, 490
 Confederacy and, 639
 at Constitutional Convention, 264, 270
 Webster-Hayne debate on, 391–93
 see also nullification and interposition
States' Rights Democratic (Dixiecrat) party,
 1156–58, *1157*
Statue of Liberty, 788
steamboats, 373–74, *373*, 423–24, *424*, 430,
 431–32, 745
 Gibbons v. Ogden and, 373–74
steam engine, 432, 454

steel industry, 755–57, 758, 770, 1140
Steel Workers Organizing Committee, 1057
Steffens, Lincoln, 892
Steicher, Edward, *758*
Stein, Gertrude, 968–69, 987, *988*
Stein, Leo, 987
Steinbeck, John, 1033, 1040, 1043–44
Steinway, Heinrich, 447
stem-cell research, 1383
Stephens, Alexander, 602, 639, 669
Stephens, Uriah S., 765
sterilization laws, 978
Steuben, Frederick William Augustus Henry
    Ferdinand, baron von, 226
Stevens, John, 218
Stevens, Thaddeus, 637, 670, *677*, 686
Stevens, William, 121
Stevenson, Adlai, 1199
    in election of 1952, 1196–98, *1197*
    in election of 1956, 1210
    at United Nations, 1230–31
Stewart, Alexander T., 444
Stieglitz, Alfred, *745*
Stimson, Henry L., 1070–71, 1080, 1087, 1126
Stimson Doctrine, 1071
Stockman, David, 1320
stock market:
    in early 2000s, 1360–61, 1372
    in late 1990s, 1360–61
    1929 crash of, 1012–15, *1014*
    1987 crash of, 1327–28, *1327*
    terrorism and, 1376
Stockton, Robert F., 519
Stonewall Inn, 1282
Stono uprising (1739), 112
Stowe, Harriet Beecher, 532, 578
Strategic Arms Limitation Talks (SALT),
    1297, 1304, 1309
Strategic Defense Initiative (SDI), 1321
Strauss, Levi, 447
Strong, Josiah, 862
Stuart, Charles Edward (Bonnie Prince
    Charlie), 134
Stuart, J.E.B., 624
    at Harper's Ferry, 598
Student Nonviolent Coordinating
    Committee (SNCC), 1233–34, 1252
Students for a Democratic Society (SDS),
    1267, 1268–69, *1270*, 1271
Stuyvesant, Peter, 84
Styron, William, 1187
submarines:
    in World War I, 938–40, 943, 944–45
    in World War II, 1080, 1084, 1093, 1102,
    1105, 1108

suburbs, 782–83, 1176–78, 1179–80
    criticisms of, 1185–86
    housing in, 1176–78, 1185–86
    streetcars in growth of, 781–83, *783*
subway systems, 782
Sudan, 1374
Suez War, 1210, 1211–13
Suffolk Resolves (1775), 193
suffrage, *see* voting rights
Sufis, 468
sugar, 533–34, 661, 709, 863, 864
    in Cuba, 1218
    and tariffs, 837, 864
    trust, 899
Sugar (Revenue) Act (1764), 179, 180, 181,
    184, 188
suicide bombings, 1379, 1380
Sullivan, John, 228
Sumner, Charles, 637, 671, *671*, 672, 673, 676
    Brooks's attack on, 588–89, *588*
Sumner, William Graham, 744, 805–6
Sumter, Thomas, 230
Sun Also Rises, The (Hemingway), 988
"superfund" sites, 1306
Supreme Court, U.S.:
    on abortions, 1275
    on affirmative action, 1361–62
    on anti-communism, 1167, 1202–3
    anti-trust cases and, 708
    appointments to, 283, 316–17, 993, 1350,
    1386–87
    in *Brown* case, 1219–20
    on busing, 1291–92
    in *Cherokee Nation v. Georgia,* 399
    civil rights decisions of, 697
    on Civil War, 609
    in Constitution, 270–71
    on defendants' rights, 1232
    in *Dred Scott* case, 592–93
    election of 2000 and, 1370–71
    on Espionage and Sedition Acts, 949–50
    establishment of, 283
    FDR's court-packing plan for, 1053–55, *1054*
    in *Gibbons v. Ogden,* 373–74
    on Granger Laws, 841
    implied powers broadened by, 291
    Indian lands and, 399
    in "Insular Cases," 877
    on interstate commerce, 832
    judicial nationalism and, 371–74
    judicial review by, 371–72
    on labor issues, 772, 897, 927, 993–94
    laissez-faire and, 816
    legislative power reduced by, 816
    in *McCulloch v. Maryland,* 372–73

Supreme Court (*continued*)
  in *Marbury v. Madison*, 325–26
  in New Deal, 1033, 1034, 1036, 1049,
    1053–55
  Pentagon Papers case and, 1287
  in Reconstruction, 675, 697
  Religious Right and, 1315
  school prayer and, 1232
  segregation and, 716, 1219–20, 1221–22,
    1291
  on sexual equality, 1275
  Thomas appointed to, 1350–51
  on trade associations, 1005
  on trusts, 899, 901–2
  on voting rights, 983, 1042, 1100
  Watergate and, 1301
Surrender of Lord Cornwallis (Trumball), *234*
Susquehannocks, 59, 188
Sussex, sinking of (1916), 940
Sutter, John A., 500
Sutter's Fort, 500–501, *501*
*Swann v. Charlotte-Mecklenburg Board of
    Education,* 1291
Sweatt v. Painter, 1219
Sweden, trade with, 258
Swedish Americans, 88, 90, 131, *133,* 134, 447
Swedish colonies, 83–84
Swift, Gustavus, 735–36
Swift and Company v. United States, 901–2
Swiss Americans, 94, 132
Switzer, Kathy, *1275*
Switzerland, Reformation in, 36
syndicalism, 775–76
Syria, 1215
  in Arab League, 1211
  in Lebanon, 1323, 1324
  in Persian Gulf War, 1340
  in Six-Day War, 1298
Taft, Helen "Nellie," 911–12
Taft, Martha, 1142
Taft, Robert A., 1081, 1142
Taft, William Howard, 792, 821, *911*
  and anti-trust action, 914
  Ballinger-Pinchot controversy and,
    912–13
  Cuba and, 878
  dollar diplomacy of, 933, 934
  in election of 1908, 910–11
  in election of 1912, 914–15, 918–20, *920*
  and federal income tax ratification, 915
  Japan and, 887
  Philippines and, 876–77, 887
  and regulation of communications, 915
  Roosevelt's break with, 913–15
  selected as Roosevelt's successor, 910–11

  as Supreme Court chief justice, 911,
    993–94
  tariff reform of, 911–12
Taft-Hartley Act (1947), 1142–43, *1142*
Taft-Katsura Agreement (1905), 887
Taiwan (Formosa), 878, 1087, 1114
Taiwan (Nationalist China), 1164, 1296
  Chinese threats against, 1209, 1215
  Nationalist flight to, 1160
  see also China, Nationalist
Taliban, 1376, 1377, *1378*
Talleyrand-Perigord, Charles-Maurice de,
  310, 328
Tallmadge, James, Jr., 369
Tammany Hall, 451, 829
Taney, Roger B., 404, 592–93, *592*
Taos Indians, 494
Tappan, Arthur, 557, 558
Tappan, Lewis, 557, 558
Tarawa, 1114, 1115
Tarbell, Ida M., 892
Tariff Commission, 828
Tariff of 1816, 360, 367
Tariff of 1824, 380
Tariff of 1828 (Tariff of Abominations),
  390–91, 395
Tariff of 1832, 394, 395
Tariff of 1857, 595
tariffs and duties, 179, 239, 377, 405, 491, 528
  Adams's view on, 380
  agriculture and, 837, 840, 1006–7
  Andrew Jackson on, 380, 394–96, 404
  in Civil War, 635, 636, 660
  under Cleveland, 833–34, *833*
  under Coolidge, 1006–7
  Constitution and, 390–91
  Dingley Tariff (1897), 852
  in early twentieth century, 911–12,
    921–22, 994–95, 1006–7
  in early U.S., 259, *260,* 284–85, 291–92
  economic nationalism and, 350, 358, 360
  Fordney-McCumber Tariff (1922), 994
  in Great Depression, 1012, 1016, 1024,
    1072
  in Hamiltonian program, 285, 291–92
  under Harding, 994–95
  Hawley-Smoot Tariff (1930), 1012
  under Jefferson, 326
  under Kennedy, 1232
  in late nineteenth century, 744, 822, 828,
    837, 840, 852, 864, 865
  McKinley Tariff (1890), 837, 864
  Mellon and, 994–95, 1015
  NAFTA and, 1354, 1361
  under Polk, 513, 514

with Puerto Rico, 877
in South Carolina nullification crisis,
    389–91
and Taft, 911–12
Tyler on, 490
after War of 1812, 360
see also specific tariffs and duties
Tarleton, Banastre, 230
taverns, 136–37, *137*, 440
taxation:
    under Articles of Confederation, 238, 250
    British, 46, 49, 50, 156, 178
    Carter and, 1309
    churches supported by, 245
    in Civil War, 635–36
    Clinton and, 1353, 1354
    in colonial period, 66, 150, 156, 177–86, 245
    congressional power of, 266, 267
    in Constitution, 266, 267
    in early U.S., 284–85, 286, 287–88, 294
    estate, 1051
    "external" vs. "internal," 183, 184
    George H. W. Bush and, 1332, 1334, 1351
    George W. Bush and, 1372–73
    gift, 1051
    Grenville's program of, 177–80
    in Hamiltonian program, 286, 287–88
    Harding and, 994
    income, 636, 915, 941
    Johnson and, 1245–46, 1293
    in Massachusetts, 66, 150, 261
    Mellon and, 994, 1013, 1015
    national bank and, 372–73
    in New Deal, 1050–52, 1057–58
    in 1950s, 1199
    Reagan and, 1315, 1317, 1319–20, 1325, 1331
    representation and, 180, 181, 186
    and revenue sharing with states, 1292
    "single-tax" idea and, 809
    state and local, 822
    Townshend's program of, 184–85
    Truman and, 1143
    voting rights and, 240, 382
    on whiskey, 294, 301, 326
    in World War II, 1095
Tax Reform Act (1986), 1325
Taylor, Frederick W., 894
Taylor, Maxwell, 1242–43
Taylor, Zachary:
    California statehood and, 571, 572
    and Compromise of 1850, 573, 575
    death of, 575
    in election of 1848, 568–69
    in Mexican War, 516, 518, 520, 523
    New Mexico statehood and, 571, 575

Taylorism, 894
tea, trade in, 427
Tea Act (1773), 191
teaching, 453, 454
Teapot Dome scandal, 996, *996*
technology:
    agricultural, 417–18, 419–20, 739, 751,
        1006, *1006*, 1179
    cities and, 781, 784, 785–86
    in early nineteenth century, 430–32
    education and, 477–78
    exploration aided by, 13–14
    failure of, 1389
    food and, 431, 445, 751
    and growth of industry, 430–39
    of Indians, 19, 24–25
    in late nineteenth century, 751–53
    in late twentieth century, 1342
    post-World War II automation and, 1172
    of printing, 13, 474
    of Spanish vs. Indians, 24–25
    transportation and, 421–22, 426, 427, 751
    weaponry and, 1377, 1382
    in World War I, 935
Tecumseh, Shawnee chief, 339–40, *339*, 344
Teheran Conference (1943), 1110
telegraph, 430, 431, 619, 745, 756
telephone, 752, *752*
television, 1174–75, 1228, 1243
Teller Amendment (1898), 868
temperance, 479–80, *480*
    women's suffrage and, 815–16
    see also Prohibition movement
Tempest, The (Shakespeare), 54
tenancy, 47, 709–11, *709*, *710*
    environment and, 710–11
tenements, 784
ten-hour workday, 451, 897
Tennent, William, 142
Tennessee, 259, 421
    Civil War fighting in, 620–22, 645, 650
    emancipation in, 630, 633
    free blacks in, 370
    Indian conflicts in, 302
    Indian lands ceded in, 256
    Indian removal and, 256, 397
    migration to, 555
    military government of, 665
    in Reconstruction, 673, 674, 691
    secession of, 609
    segregation in, 716, 719
    statehood for, 307
    and teaching of evolution, 972
    Union loyalists in, 673, 684
    voting rights in, 382

Tennessee Coal and Iron Company, 914
Tennessee militia, 344
Tennessee Valley Authority (TVA), 1036–38, *1036, 1037,* 1041, 1247
Tennessee Valley Authority Act (1933), 1028
Tennessee volunteers, 366
tennis, 796
Tenochtitlán (Mexico City), 9, 26, 28
Tenskwatawa, 339
Tenth Amendment, 271, 284, 290
Tenure of Office Act (1867), 674, 676, 677
Terrell, Mary Church, 718
terrorism, 1342–43, 1374–83
  domestic, 1378
  global, 1374, 1380, 1382–83, 1385
  international coalition against, 1377, 1380–82, 1383
  religious fanaticism and, 1374, 1376, 1382–83
  and second Gulf War, 1380–83
  September 11, 2001 attacks and, 1374–76, *1379*
  war on, 1376–77, 1380–83
Tesla, Nikola, 753
Tet offensive (1968), 1258–59, *1258*
Texas, 29, 31, 33, 367, 375, 495, 501, 507–10
  agriculture of, 535, 842, *843*
  annexation of, 510, 514, 523
  border of, 573, 575, 577
  Chicanos in, 1278
  in Civil War, 619
  and Compromise of 1850, 573, 575, 577
  dust bowl in, 1038, 1039
  in election of 1844, 511–12
  evolution teaching and, 972
  German settlers in, 447
  independence of, from Mexico, 496, 508–10
  Mexican War and, 515–16, 522, 523
  population of, 1343
  Reconstruction in, 678, 683
  secession of, 602
  segregation in, 1219
  slavery issue and, 507, 566, 573, 577
  U.S. settlers in, 507–8
  voting rights in, 1100
Texas, University of, 1362
Texas and New Mexico Act (1850), 577
Texas Seed Bill (1887), 831
Texas v. White, 675
textile industry, *358, 380,* 385–86, 432–37, *436,* 528, 618
  Lowell System in, 433–35
  mechanization of, 432–33
  in South, 707, 762, 1008–10, *1009*

water power and, 436–37
  see also cotton
Thailand, 1207
Thames, Battle of the, *339,* 344
Thayendanegea (Joseph Brant), 228, *228*
theater, 441–43
  in mid-twentieth century, 1187
Theory of the Leisure Class, The (Veblen), 810
Thieu, Nguyen Van, 1284
third parties:
  Anti-Masonic party, 402
  Dixiecrats, 1156–58, *1157*
  and emergence of Republican party, 585
  introduction of, 402
  Know-Nothing party, 448, 585
  Progressive ("Bull Moose") party, 915–16, 918–20, 928, 942–43
  Progressive party (1924), 999
  Progressive party (1948), 1157, 1158
Third World, independence movements and, 1204–9
Thirteenth Amendment, 267, 633, 659, 669, 697
Thirty Years' War (1618–1648), 84
This Side of Paradise (Fitzgerald), 977, 988
Thomas, Clarence, 1350–51
Thomas, George H., 645, 650
Thomas, Norman, 1025
Thomson, Charles, 193
Thoreau, Henry David, 355, 468, 469–71, *470,* 1221
Three Lives (Stein), 987
Thurmond, J. Strom, 1156, 1157–58, *1157, 1159*
Tiananmen Square massacre (1989), 1334
Tientsin, Treaty of (1858), 580
Tilden, Samuel J., 694–97, *696,* 824
Tillman, Benjamin, 717
timber industry, 101, 708
Time, 1259, 1350
Timucuas, *93*
Tippecanoe, Battle of (1811), 340, 410
Titan, The (Dreiser), 809
Title IX of the Educational Amendments Act (1972), 1275
Tito (Josip Broz), 1148
Tituba (slave), 128–29
Titusville, Pa., 753
Tlaxcala Lienzo, 25
tobacco, 20, 50, *108,* 229, 256, 358, 533, 537
  advertising and, *707*
  Civil War and, 661
  in early U.S., 281
  increase in, 707–8
  in Maryland colony, 60

Rolfe's experiments with, 55
soil depleted by, 109
in Virginia colony, 55, 57, 57–58, 107
Tocqueville, Alexis de, 461, 1130
Tojo, Hideki, 1087, 1115
Toleration Act (1689), 50, 152, 155
Toltecs, 8
Tonkin Gulf Resolution (1964), 1255
Tonnage Act (1789), 284–85
Toombs, Robert, 572
Toomer, Jean, 982
Tordesillas, Treaty of (1494), 17
Tories, *see* Loyalists (Tories)
Tower, John, 1326
Townsend, Francis E., 1048–49, 1052
Townshend, Charles, 184–85
Townshend Acts (1767):
    colonial protest against, 185
    modification and repeal of, 187–88, 225
townships, 252–54
Trade Agreements Act (1934), 1072
trade and commerce:
    agriculture and, 256, 258
    after American Revolution, 256–58, 257
    American Revolution and, 225, 256–58
    in California, 500–501
    with China, 258, 406, 427, 580, 879,
        1066–67
    in Civil War, 618–19
    in colonial period, 50, 52, 58, 60, 73, 91,
        94, 107–9, 119–24, 124, 126–27, 148–49,
        159, 175, 177–86, 190–95
    in Confederation period, 256–58, 259–61
    congressional power over, 238–39
    in Constitution, 266
    Continental Congress and, 193–94
    in cotton, 337, 389, 406, 418, 528, 535–36,
        537, 539, 539
    with Cuba, 865
    in early U.S., 259–61, 262
    with France, 285, 335–38, 336, 338, 389,
        406, 535
    in French colonies, 31, 157–59, 161
    globalization and, 1347, 1361, 1368–69
    with Great Britain, 257, 259–60, 284–85,
        297, 298–99, 309, 335–38, 336, 338, 339,
        348, 363, 365, 367, 389, 406, 408, 533
    imperialism and, 861
    with Indians, 50, 73, 91, 94, 159
    interstate, regulation of, 373–74
    interstate commerce and, 901–2
    with Iran, 1310
    in late nineteenth century, 745–46
    mercantile system in, 148–49, 256–57,
        284–85

with Mexico, 406, 501–2
NAFTA and, 1354, 1361
Napoleonic Wars and, 335–38
in New England, 119–24, 126–27
in pre-Columbian cultures, 10
in southern colonies, 107–9, 108
with Soviet Union, 1072–73, 1297–98
in Spanish Empire, 31, 157
in Virginia colony, 52
with West Indies, 94, 120, 122, 123, 131,
    175, 179, 256, 257–58, 297, 298, 299,
    335, 365
in World War I, 936, 938–40, 944
see also fur trade; tariffs and duties;
    taxation; transportation
trade associations, 449–50, 1005
Trade Expansion Act (1962), 1232
Traffic Safety Act (1966), 1250
Trail of Tears, 397–400
Tramp Abroad (Twain), 808
Transcendental Club, 468
transcendentalism, 355, 467–70
transcontinental railroads, 635, 746–48, 748,
    749
Transcontinental Treaty (1819), 367, 374
transistors, 1347
transportation, 416
    in colonial period, 136
    in early nineteenth century, 421–30,
        422–23
    government role in, 427, 430
    highways and roads, 136, 306, 360–62, 363,
        389, 421–22, 422–23, 427, 430
    internal improvements to, 360–62
    ocean, 426–27
    in post-Civil War era, 685
    railroads, 426
    technology of, 751
    urban growth and, 780, 781–83
    water, 262, 373–74, 426–27
    see also highways and roads; railroads
Transportation Security Administration,
    1378
Travis, William B., 508–9
treason, 334
Treasury Department, U.S., 282, 636, 687,
    688, 694
    Hamilton's program for, 292–93
    under Van Buren, 409–10
Treatise on Domestic Economy, A (Beecher),
    482
Tredegar Iron Works, 537, 538
Trent affair, 618–19
Trenton, Battle of (1776), 217
trial by jury, 180, 238, 284

Triangle Shirtwaist Company fire (1911), 897
"trickster tales," 553
Trinidad, 18
Triple Alliance (Central Powers), 934–35, 936, *937*, 950, 954
Triple Entente (Allied Powers), 934–35, 936, *937*, 955
Tripoli, 327–28, 350
Trist, Nicholas P., 522
Truman, Harry S, 1249
    anti-communism and, 1160, 1166, 1168–69, 1321, 1379–80
    atomic bomb and, 1126
    background of, 1138
    Berlin blockade and, 1150
    civil rights supported by, 1153, *1155*
    demobilization under, 1138–43
    in election of 1948, 1154–59, *1158, 1159*
    and election of 1952, 1196
    Fair Deal of, 1154–55, 1158
    foreign policy of, 1144, 1144–46, 1296
    and health insurance, 1155
    Indochina and, 1205, 1206, 1254
    Israel recognized by, 1152
    Korean War and, 1162, 1163–65
    labor movement and, 1141–43
    MacArthur fired by, 1165
    Roosevelt compared with, 1138
    social agenda of, 1158–59
    as vice-president, 1118
Truman Doctrine, 1148–49, 1166, 1168–69, 1257
Trumbull, John, *234*
trusts, 755, 836
    Taft and, 914
    Theodore Roosevelt and, 899–902, *902*
    Wilson and, 919, 923–24
    see also anti-trust laws
Truth, Sojourner, 559–60, *560*
Tryon, William, 189
Tubman, Harriet, 559
Tunis, 327, 350
Tunisia, 1103, 1104
Turkey, 1152
    in METO, 1210
    in NATO, 1151, 1210
    U.S. missiles in, 1214, 1239, 1241
    U.S. post-World War II aid to, 1148–49
    in World War I, 935, 955
turkeys, 7, 19
Turner, Frederick Jackson, 740–41, 780
Turner, Nat, 551, 557
turnpikes, 422, 430
Tuscaroras, 82, *93*

Tuscarora War (1711–1713), 82
Tuskegee Airmen, *1099*
TVA (Tennessee Valley Authority), 1028, 1036–38, *1036, 1037*, 1041, 1247
TV Guide, 1175
Twain, Mark (Samuel Clemens), 807–8, *808*, 819
Tweed Ring, 694
Twelfth Amendment, 332–33
Twentieth Amendment, 1025
Twenty-fifth Amendment, 1302
Twenty-first Amendment, 1028
Twenty-one Demands (1915), 1065
Twenty-second Amendment, 1196
Twenty-sixth Amendment, 1292
Twice-Told Tales (Hawthorne), 471
Twining, David, *305*
Two Treatises on Government (Locke), 152, 180
Tydings-McDuffie Act (1934), 877
Tyler, John, 410, 490–91, 514, 605
Typee (Melville), 472
typhoid fever, 785
typhus, 20, 21

U-2 incident (1960), 1216–17
U-2 spy planes, 1214, 1216–17
UAR (United Arab Republic), 1215
UAW (United Auto Workers), 1057, 1140
UFW (United Farm Workers), 1279–80
Ulysses (Joyce), 987
UMW (United Mine Workers), 769, 899–901, 1055, 1141
U.N., *see* United Nations
uncertainty principle, 985
Uncle Tom's Cabin (Stowe), 532, 578, *579*
Underground Railroad, 559
Underwood, Oscar, 917–18
Underwood-Simmons Tariff (1913), 922
unemployment:
    in Great Depression, 1014, 1015, 1019–20, 1022, 1025, 1030–31, 1032, 1038
    in 1970s, 1292, 1293, 1309
    in 1980s, 1320
    in 1990s, 1350
    in 2000s, 1372
unemployment insurance, 1050–51
UNIA (Universal Negro Improvement Association), 982–83, *982*
Union League, 678, 681, 690
Union Manufactories, *358*
Union of Russian Workers, 965
Union Pacific Railroad, 688–89, 746–47, *748*, 750, 899
Union party, 1052

Unitarians, 50, 460, 468
United Arab Emirates, 1340
United Arab Republic (UAR), 1215
United Auto Workers (UAW), 1057, 1140
United Farm Workers (UFW), 1279–80
United Mine Workers (UMW), 769, 773,
    899–901, 1055, 1141
United Nations (U.N.), 1149, 1152, 1160,
    1231, 1330
  Afghanistan and, 1377
  Balkans and, 1367
  China in, 1162
  Grenada invasion condemned by, 1324
  Haiti and, 1365
  Iran hostages and, 1310
  Israel and, 1366
  Korean War and, 1162–64, 1200
  origins of, 1120, 1121, 1143–44, 1146
  Persian Gulf War and, 1339, 1380
  and second Gulf War, 1380–81
  Somalia and, 1365
United States, U.S.S., 311
United States Sanitary Commission, 634
United States Steel Corporation, 758, 902,
    914, 1057
United States v. Butler, 1033
United States v. E. C. Knight and Company,
    899
United States v. Richard Nixon, 1301
United Steelworkers, 1140
United Textile Workers (UTW), 1008–9
Universal Asylum and Columbian Magazine,
    280
Universalists, 460
Universal Negro Improvement Association
    (UNIA), 982–83, *982*
universities, *see* colleges and universities
Upanishads, 468
Updike, John, 1187
USA Patriot Act, 1378
USHA (Housing Authority, U.S.), 1058
Utah:
  and Compromise of 1850, 577
  Indians in, 494
  Mormons in, 465–66, *466*
  statehood for, 725
  voting rights in, 814
Utah Act (1850), 577
Utes, 730
utopian communities, 484–87

Valens, Ritchie, 1192
Vallandigham, Clement L., 637–38
Valley Forge, winter quarters at (1777–1778),
    223, 225–26

Van Buren, Martin, 378, 380, 406–12, *408,
    409,* 510
  background of, 408
  Calhoun's rivalry with, 387–88
  Eaton Affair and, 388
  in election of 1832, 403
  in election of 1836, 407–8
  in election of 1840, 411–12, *411*
  in election of 1844, 511
  in election of 1848, 568–69, 579
  Great Britain post denied to, 393–94
  Independent Treasury under, 409–10
  national bank issue and, 401
  ten-hour workday and, 451
Vance, Cyrus, 1307, 1308, 1310
Vanderbilt, Cornelius, 750–51, *751*
Vanderbilt, William Henry, 751
van Honthorst, Gerrit, *48*
Van Rensselaer, Stephen, 342, 343
Vanzetti, Bartolomeo, 969, *970*
Vassar College, 478, 800, *803*, 804
vaudeville, 793–94
Veblen, Thorstein, 809–10
Venezuela, 1215
Verdict of the People (Bingham), *403*
Verdun, Battle of, 935
Vermont, 188
  constitution of, 242
  at Hartford Convention, 349
  Revolutionary War fighting in, 224
  Revolutionary War troops from, 198
  slavery in, 242
  statehood for, 307
  voting rights in, 382
Verrazano, Giovanni da, 38
Versailles Treaty (1919), 959, *960*, 962, 1071,
    1073
  ratification debate on, 959–62
vertical integration, 754–55
Vesey, Denmark, 390, 550–51
Vespucci, Amerigo, 18
Veterans Administration, 1173
Veterans Bureau, 995
veto, line-item, 1357
Vicksburg, Battle of (1863), 641, *642,*
    644
Victor Emmanuel III, king of Italy, 1108
Vienna Summit (1961), 1238
Viet Cong, 1209, 1242, 1254, 1255, 1257,
    1258–59, 1284, 1287
Viet Minh, 1205, 1206
Vietnam, 1160–61, 1162, 1205–9, *1242*
  gradual withdrawal from, 1283–84
  Kennedy and, 1241–43
  see also Indochina

Vietnam War, 1134, 1254–60, *1256*, 1293, 1303, 1304
  amnesty for draft evaders of, 1306
  bombing of North in, 1255, 1260
  Cambodian incursion in, 1285
  casualties in, 1289
  collapse of South Vietnam in, 1305, 1311
  conscientious objectors in, 1269
  context for policy in, 1256–58
  domestic opposition to, 1257, 1268–69, 1271–72, 1284, 1285–87
  draft in, 1268–69, 1284, 1306
  in election of 1964, 1247, 1248, 1255
  end of, 1287–90
  escalation of, 1255–56
  Geneva Accords and, 1206–9, 1241
  Hispanics in, 1278
  My Lai massacre in, 1285, 1289
  negotiations in, 1283–84, 1287–88
  Nixon and, 1283–90, *1284*
  Tet offensive in, 1258–59
  Tonkin Gulf Resolution and, 1255
  Vietnamization of, 1284
vigilantes, 189, 191, 261–62, 301, 419, 570–71
Villa, Pancho, 932–33, *933*
Vincennes, Ill., Revolutionary War fighting in, 227–28
Vindication of the Rights of Woman, A (Wollstonecraft), *244*
Vinland (Newfoundland), 13
Virginia:
  agriculture in, 533
  Civil War fighting in, 614–15, 616, 622–24, *626*, 628, 640–41, 646–48, *648, 649*
  Constitution ratified by, 274–75, *274*
  and Declaration of Independence, 204
  emancipation in, 242, 561, 630
  land claims of, 238, *253*, 255, 281
  Loyalist property in, 371
  migration from, 554–55
  at navigation meeting of 1785, 262
  post-Revolutionary War debt in, 288
  Reconstruction in, 678, 683, 691
  religious freedom in, 245
  Revolutionary War fighting in, 201, 229, 232–33
  Revolutionary War troops from, 232
  secession of, 609
  segregation in, 1219, 1223
  slave trade in, 267
  voting rights in, 715
Virginia, University of, 294, 477
Virginia colony, *61*, 62, 76, 77, 132
  agriculture in, 52, *54*
  Anglican Church in, 117
  Bacon's Rebellion in, 58–60
  charter of, 50, 52–54, 238
  in colonial taxation disputes, 186, 188
  Committees of Correspondence in, 190
  European settlement of, 51–60, *51, 53*, 99
  first permanent settlement in, 51–55
  gentry of, 116
  government of, 55, 56–57, 57–58, 58–59, 155
  Indians in, 52, 55–56, 57–60, 169
  John Smith's administration of, 52–54
  in land disputes, 192
  landownership in, 56, 58–59
  Loyalists in, 201
  population of, 102
  religion in, 117
  Roanoke colony, 42–43, *42, 61*
  as royal colony, 57
  Sandys's reforms in, 56
  sex ratios in, 104
  slavery in, 110, 113, 115, 241
  Stamp Act and, 181
  "starving time" in, 54–55
  tobacco in, 55, 57–58, 107
  voting rights in, 156
Virginia Company, 52–54, *54*, 62, 109
  origins of, 50, 51–52, *53*
Virginia Declaration of Rights (1776), 204, 245, 264, 284
Virginia (Merrimack), 616
Virginia Plan, 265–66, 270–71
Virginia Resolutions (1798), 315, 391
Virginia Resolves (1765), 181
Virginia Statue of Religious Freedom (1786), 245
VISTA (Volunteers in Service to America), 1247, 1267
Vitter, David, 1387
Vladivostok Summit (1974), 1304
vocational training, 802
Volstead Act (1919), 1011, 1028
Voltaire, 138
Volunteers in Service to America (VISTA), 1247, 1267
voter turnout:
  in election of 1840, 411–12
  in election of 1980, 1317–18
  in election of 1988, 1333
  in election of 2004, 1386
  in late nineteenth century, 820
voting rights:
  for African Americans, 370, 669, 671, 674, 678, 681, *682*, 684, 686, 690
  for eighteen-year-olds, 1292
  Eisenhower and, 1222

grandfather clauses and, 715, 983
literacy tests and, 715, 1251
poll taxes and, 715
property qualifications and, 155–56, 240, 382, 413, 445–46, 451
religion and, 155
southern disenfranchisement of African Americans and, 714–16, 820, 927
Supreme Court and, 983, 1042, 1100
taxation and, 240, 382
voter registration and, 1251
Wilson and, 925
women and, 244, 483
women's suffrage and, 813–16, *815*, 942, 948, *980*
Voting Rights Act (1965), 1251, 1291, 1321

Wabash Railroad v. Illinois, 832
WAC (Women's Army Corps), 1098
Waco, Tex., standoff at (1993), 1355–56
Wade, Benjamin F., 637, 665, 668, 670
Wade-Davis Bill, 665–66
Wagner, Robert G., 1018, 1049
Wagner National Labor Relations Act (1935), 1049, 1053, 1055, 1055–56, 1057, 1279
Wagner-Steagall National Housing Act (1937), 1058
Wake Island, 873, 1092
Wald, Lillian, 812–13
Walden (Thoreau), 470–71, *470*
Wales, 46
Walker, Robert J., 593–94
Walker Tariff (1846), 513
Wallace, George, 1236, 1261–63, *1262*, 1283, 1298
Wallace, Henry A., 1118, 1142, 1154
    in election of 1948, 1157
    in New Deal, 1033, 1055
Wallace, Henry C., 993
Walloons, 132
Wall Street Journal, 999
Walpole, Horace, 184
Walpole, Robert, 153
Wampanoags, 63, 73, 75–76, *93*
wampum, *86*
Wanghsia, Treaty of (1844), 580
Ward, Aaron Montgomery, 759
Ward, Lester Frank, 806, *806*
War Department, U.S., 250, 941
Warehouse Act (1916), 926
War Industries Board (WIB), 946
Warner, Charles Dudley, 819
War of 1812, 338–50, *342, 343, 350*, 358, 365, 430, 432

aftermath of, 349–50
Baltimore attacked in, 346
causes of, 338–41
in Chesapeake, 346
Hartford Convention and, 348–49
Indian troubles in, 339–40
militias in, 344, 346
naval warfare in, 341–42, *342*, 344
New Orleans battle of, 346–47, *347*, 445
northern front of, 342–44, *343*, 346
peace treaty in, 347–48
preparations for, 341–42
southern front of, 344–45, *345*
Washington, D.C. captured in, 346
War of the Austrian Succession (King George's War) (1744–1748), 162
War of Independence, *see* American Revolution
War of the League of Augsburg (War of the Palatinate) (King William's War), 162
War of the Spanish Succession (Queen Anne's War) (1701–1713), 162
War Powers Act (1941), 1094
War Powers Act (1973), 1303
War Production Board (WPB), 1094
War Refugee Board, 1124
Warren, Earl, 1202, 1219, 1232, 1243
Warren, Joseph, 198
wars, *see specific conflicts and wars*
Warsaw Treaty Organization, 1213, 1336
Washington, Booker T., 719–21, *719*, 802
Washington, D.C.:
    and Compromise of 1850, 572
    first inauguration in, 322–24
    march on (1963), 1236–37
    plan of 1792, *323*
    race riot in (1919), 965
    segregation in, 1219
    slaves in, 410, 561, 572, 577, 630
    voting rights in, 674
    in War of 1812, 346
Washington, George, 247, 261, 262, 279, 285, 309, 312, *337*, 430
    Algerian conflict and, 311
    in American Revolution, 198, 202, 205, 210, 214–18, *216, 217*, 221, 226, 228, 229, 232, 233, 241, 251–52
    called from retirement, 311
    chosen as commander-in-chief, 198
    on Constitution, 276
    at Constitutional Convention, *263*, 264, 265, *270*
    at Continental Congress, 193
    farewell address of, 307–8, 856, 1169
    on foreign alliances, 308

Washington, George (*continued*)
in French and Indian War, 163–65, 167
French Revolution and, 296, 297
Jay's Treaty and, 299
on national bank issue, 290–91
parties opposed by, 293
in presidential elections, 282, 295
as slaveholder, 241
Whiskey Rebellion and, 301, *318*
Washington Armaments Conference (1921),
1066–67, *1066*
Washington Federalist, 336
Washington (state):
statehood for, 725, 836
voting rights in, 814
Washington Territory, 496
"Waste Land, The" (Eliot), 987
water, as commodity, 436
water frame, 432
Watergate scandal, 1299–1303, 1311
water transportation, 262, 373–74, 426–27
canals, 424–26, 430
in early nineteenth century, 423–26, *425*
Watervliet Arsenal, *613*
Watson, Thomas E., 845, 850
Watt, James, 432
Watts riot (1965), 1251
Waud, Alfred R., *647*
WAVES (Women Accepted for Volunteer
Emergency Service), 1098, *1098,* 1101
Wayne, Anthony, 299–300
Wealth against Commonwealth (Lloyd),
892
Wealth of Nations, The (Smith), 257, 293
weapons of mass destruction, 1380, 1383,
1384
Weathermen, 1271
Weaver, James B., 846
Weaver, Robert C., 1250
Webb, James Watson, *543*
Webster, Daniel, 372, 380, 407, 513
African colonization and, 556
in Compromise of 1850, 572, 574,
575
in election of 1836, 407–8
Hayne's debate with, 391–93
national bank issue and, 359–60, 401
on nullification issue, 391–93, *392*
Texas annexation and, 514, 517
in Tyler administration, 490, 491
Webster-Ashburton Treaty (1842), 491,
492
Webster-Hayne debate, 390–93
Weimar Republic, 1071
Weinberger, Caspar, 1321, 1326

Welch, Joseph, *1201,* 1202
Weld, Theodore Dwight, 558, 561
welfare, 1250–51
Clinton and, 1358–59
Gingrich and, 1357
New Deal and, 1061
promotion of general, 816–17
Reagan and, 1320, 1331
see also specific programs
Welles, Orson, 1031
Wellesley College, 804
Wells, Ida B., 718–19, *718*
Welsh Americans, 94, 131, 132, *133,* 542
West, 501–7, 721–410
African Americans in, 722–24
agriculture in, 416, 418–20, 536–37
cattle and cowboys in, 734–37, *735*
in Civil War, 619–20, *621*
farmers in, 737–39
gold rushes and mining in, 427, 494, 502,
505, 569–71, 619, 724–28, *724,* 780
growth of, 721–22
Indian conflicts in, 728–32, *731*
Indian policy, 733–34
map of, *726–27*
migratory stream to, 722–24, 780
North and South in conflict over,
528–29
range wars in, 737
before statehood, 822
trails through, 501–7
urbanization in, 780
Whigs in, 407
women in, 739, *740*
in World War II, 1097
see also frontier
West, Benjamin, *235*
West Bank, 1366, 1379
Western Federation of Miners, 775, 776
Western Reserve Eclectic Institute, *476*
Western Union Company, 431, 752
West Indies, 24, 27, *67,* 111, 175
French-U.S. conflict in, 311
Napoleonic wars and, 335
trade with, 94, 120, 122, 123, 131, 175,
179, 256, 257–58, 297, 298, 299, 335,
365
Westinghouse, George, 751, 752–53
Westinghouse Company, 752, 1002
Westmoreland, William C., 1255, 1257,
1258–59
Westos, 80, *82*
West Virginia, 664–65
formation of, 610
labor unrest in, 773

Weyler, Valeriano, 865–66
whaling, 120, *473*
wheat, 19, 131, 536
Wheeler, Burton K., 1082
Wheelwright, John, 72
Whig party:
  "Conscience" vs. "Cotton" members of, 568
  Constitutional Union party and, 601
  destruction of, 585
  economic policies of, 409–12, 490–91
  in election of 1840, 410–12, *412*, 490
  in election of 1844, 512
  in election of 1848, 567, 568
  in election of 1852, 579
  in election of 1856, 589–90
  in election of 1860, 601
  formation of, 406–7
  in formation of Republican party, 585
  Free Soil party and, 568
  on Independent Treasury, 409–10
  Mexican War and, 517, 523
  scalawags and, 684
  slavery issue in, 567, 575, 585
  Taylor supported by, 571
Whigs, British, 176, 205
whiskey, tax on, 294, 301, 326
Whiskey Rebellion, 300–302, *302*, 312
Whiskey Ring, 689
White, Hugh Lawson, 407–8
White, John, *19*, 43, *80*
White, William Allen, 993
White Collar Society (Mills), 1186
Whitefield, George, 142, *142*, 143
White House Conference on Conservation (1908), 908
White League, *689*
Whitewater scandal, 1362, *1363*
Whitman, Walt, 471, 473–74, 484
Whitney, Eli, *417*, 418
Whittier, John Greenleaf, 471
WIB (War Industries Board), 946
Wicker, Tom, 1292
Wiggins, Ella May, 1010
Wilderness, Battle of the (1863), 641, 647
Wilderness Road, 304–6, 421
Wilhelm II, Kaiser of Germany, 887–88
Wilkinson, Eliza, 267–68
Wilkinson, James, 333–34
Willard, Emma, 478
William III, king of England, 49–50, 151, 152, 153, 162
William and Mary, College of, 144
Williams, Roger, 68–70, 70, 71, 74, 261
Willkie, Wendell L., 1081

Wills, Garry, 1269
Wilmot, David, 566, 567, 568
Wilmot Proviso, 566–67, 568, 574, 577
Wilson, Edith, 934, 939, 961
Wilson, Henry, *686*
Wilson, Jack (Wovoka), 731
Wilson, James, at Constitutional Convention, 264, 269–70
Wilson, Woodrow, 792, 857, 909, 992, 1024, 1075
  background of, 819, 916–17
  Debs and, 997
  in election of 1912, 917–21, *917, 920*
  in election of 1916, 925–26, 941–43, *942*
  Federal Reserve and, 922–23
  foreign policy of, 931–34
  Fourteen Points of, 954–55
  Latin American policy of, 1069
  League of Nations and, 954, 957–58, 960–62
  Mexican intervention of, 931–33
  at Paris Peace Conference, 955–59, *957*
  preparedness issue and, 941
  progressivism of, 916–27, 1061
  social justice and, 924–25
  stroke suffered by, 961, 962
  tariffs and, 921–22
  trusts and, 919, 923–24
  and U.S. entry into World War I, 944–50
  U.S. neutrality and, 936, 937, 938–40, *940, 942*
  Versailles Treaty promoted by, 959–62
  women's suffrage supported by, 979
  World War I and, 953
Wilson-Gorman Tariff (1894), 865
Winthrop, John, 65–68, *65*, 70, 71, 105, 126
Winthrop, John, IV, 139
Winthrop, John, Jr., 139
Wirt, William, 402, 403
Wirz, Henry, 666
Wisconsin:
  Civil War troops from, 616
  education in, 837–38
  immigration to, 447
  progressivism in, 895
Wisconsin Territory, Indian conflicts in, 397
witchcraft, 128–31, *119, 129*
Wobblies (Industrial Workers of the World), 775–77
Wolfe, James, 168
Wolfe, Thomas, 988–89

Wollstonecraft, Mary, *244*
women, 320
 in abolition movement, 483, 558–59
 African-American, 718–19
 in Alliance movement, 842
 American Revolution and, 243–44
 birth control and, 978–79, *979*, 1276–77
 in Carter administration, 1306
 in Civil War, 634–35
 in colonial period, 103–4, 105–7
 Constitutional Convention and, 267–68
 domestic role of, 106–7, 243, 482–83,
  540–41
 education and, 454, 478–79, *478*, 482,
  803–4, *803*
 in election of 2000, 1371
 employment of, 106–7, 434–35, *436*, 484,
  634–35, 813, 897, 946, 947–48, *947*,
  980–81, 1098–99, 1182, 1276, 1293,
  1344
 equal pay for, 766
 gender gap and, 1321, 1351
 in labor movement, 764, 772–73, 1008–10,
  1009
 legal status of, 105, 243–44, 483
 literature and, 474
 in Lowell System, 434–35
 marriage and child-bearing patterns of,
  103–4, *103*, 243–44
 in mining frontier (California), 571
 in 1920s, 977–78, *978*
 in 1950s, 1181–82
 occupations of in 1900s, 798–99
 in Old Southwest, 555, 556
 on Oregon Trail, 503–4, *504*
 as professionals, 454–55
 Quaker, 89, *89*
 in Reconstruction, 662
 in religious revivals, 462
 sexual exploitation of, 540–41, 549–50,
  556
 sexual revolution and, 1276–77
 slave, 115, 541, 548–50, 556
 southern honor and, 542
 on southern plantations, 540–41
 in sports, 796, 797
 theater and, 442
 voting rights and, 719, 813–16, *815*, 925,
  948
 in West, 739, *740*
 witchcraft and, 130
 working, and leisure, 798–99
 in World War I, 946, 947–48, *947*, 980
 in World War II, 1098–99, *1098*
 see also feminism
Women Accepted for Volunteer Emergency
  Service (WAVES), 1098, *1098*, 1101
Women's Army Corps (WAC), 1098
Women's Christian Temperance Union, 795,
  897, 974
women's clubs, 814–15
women's rights, 482–84, 813–16
 abolitionism and, 483, 558–59
 in Civil War, 634
 Sojourner Truth on, 559–60
 voting and, 244, 483
women's suffrage movement, 813–16, 844,
  925, 948, 979, *980*
Women's Trade Union League, 948
Wood, Jethro, 419
*Woodruff v. North Bloomfield Gravel Mining
  Company,* 728
Woods, Robert A., 812
Woodstock Music Festival (1969), 1272,
  1273
Woodville, Richard Caton, *474*
Woodward, C. Vann, 714
Worcester v. Georgia, 399
workers:
 American Revolution and, 239–40
 see also labor
working class:
 child labor and, 761–62, *762*
 conditions for, 760–62, *763*
 and distribution of wealth, 760–61
 in early nineteenth century, 434–35,
  436
 and election of 1896, 851
 housing of, 431
 Irish Americans in, 444
 legislative protection of, 816
 in Panic of 1837, 408–9
 recreation of, 797–98, *798*
 religion of, 460
 Taylorism and, 894
 at theater, 441–43
 women in, and leisure, 798–99
 see also labor, employment; labor
  movement
Workingmen's Party, 451, 475, 764, 792
Works Progress Administration (WPA),
  1031–32, 1096
WorldCom, 1372
World Court, 957
World Trade Center, 1374–76, *1375*
World War I, 856–57, 930–66
 airplanes in, 1003
 armistice in, 955, *955*
 casualties in, 935, 953
 conscription in, 946

decisive role of U.S. in, 950–55
disarmament efforts after, 1065–67
domestic unrest in, 955–56
firepower in, 935
labor movement in, 776
loans to Europe in, 936–37, 994–95, 1017, 1064–65
Paris Conference after, 955–59, *957*
Prohibition and, 974
propaganda in, 948
reparations after, 958–59, 1064–65
Socialist party and, 775
submarines and neutral rights in, 938–40, 943, 944–45
trench warfare and, 935
U.S. entry into, 944–50
U.S. isolationism after, 1063–69
U.S. mobilization in, 946
U.S. neutrality in, 934–44
U.S. preparedness in, 940–41
veterans of, 1019–20, *1019*
western front in, 951–53, *952*
women in, 946, 947–48, *947*, 980
World War II, 1091–1130, 1144–46
    African Americans in, 1097, 1099–1100
    air conflicts in, 1080, 1109
    atomic bombs in, 1126–29
    Battle of the Atlantic in, 1105, 1108
    Blitzkrieg in, 1078–79
    computers and, 1346
    conscription in, 1080
    D-Day in, 1109, 1110–13, *1112*
    debt in, 1095
    demobilization after, 1138–43
    domestic mobilization in, 1094–96
    drive toward Berlin in, 1102–13
    economy in, 1094–96, 1096–97, 1129
    ethnic minorities in, 1100–1102
    final ledger from, 1129–30
    financing of, 1095
    growing U.S. involvement in, 1079–80
    Holocaust in, 1123–24, *1125*
    Indonesia in, 1204–5
    Leyte Gulf in, 1115, 1118
    maps of, *1106–7, 1116–17*
    New Deal programs eliminated in, 1096, *1097*
    North Africa fighting in, 1103–5
    Pacific fighting in, 1092–93, 1102, 1105, 1114–18, 1125–26
    Pearl Harbor attack in, 1086–89, *1088*, 1092–93, 1103
    selective service in, 1094
    social effects of, 1096–1102
    strategic bombing in, 1109
    submarines in, 1080, 1084, 1093, 1102, 1105, 1108
    U.S. arms aid in, 1082–84, 1085
    U.S. neutrality in, 1074–78, 1084
    veterans of, 1140, 1173–74
    war aims and strategy in, 1102–3, 1114–15
    war criminals of, 1144
    women in, 1098–99, *1098*
Wormley House agreement (1877), 696–97
Worthington, Amanda, 662
Wounded Knee, S.Dak.:
    FBI-AIM standoff at (1973), 1281–82, *1281*
    massacre at (1890), 732
Wovoka (Jack Wilson), 731
WPA (Works Progress Administration), 1031–32, 1096
WPB (War Production Board), 1094
Wright, Orville, 1002, *1002*
Wright, Richard, 1043, 1044, 1179
Wright, Wilbur, 1002, *1002*
writs of assistance, 175–76
Wye accords (1998), 1366–67
Wyoming:
    cattle industry in, 734
    Indian conflicts in, 729
    statehood for, 725, 836
    voting rights in, 814

XYZ Affair, 310–11, *310*

Yakimas, 494
Yale College, 144, 461, 804
Yalta Conference (1945), 1120–23, *1121*, 1145, 1146
Yamamoto, Isoruku, 1093, 1114
Yamasees, *92*
Yamasee War (1715), 82–83
Yancey, William Lowndes, 577, 599
yellow fever, 20, 785, 877–78
yellow journalism, 866, *867*, 868
Yellowstone National Park, *906*, 907
Yeltsin, Boris, *1336*, 1337
Yemen, 1211, 1374
"ye old deluder Satan" Act (1647), 140
Yippies (Youth International Party), 1270–71
YMCA (Young Men's Christian Association), 810, 814
Yom Kippur War (1973), 1292, 1298
York, duke of, *see* James II, king of England
Yorktown, Battle of (1781), *231*, 233–34, *234*

Yosemite National Park, 908–9
Young, Brigham, 465–66
Young Chicanos for Community Action, 1278
Young Men's Christian Association (YMCA), 810, 814
young people, 1190–92
   juvenile delinquency and, 1190–91
   in 1960s, 1267
   voting rights for, 1292
Young Women's Christian Association, 814

Youth International Party (Yippies), 1270–71
Yugoslavia, 959, 1082, 1148, 1367–68
Yukon gold rush, 780
Yumas, 495

Zenger, John Peter, 137–38
Zias, 494
Zimmermann, Arthur, 944
Zionism, 1152
"zoot suit" riots (1943), 1100–1101
Zunis, 11, 494

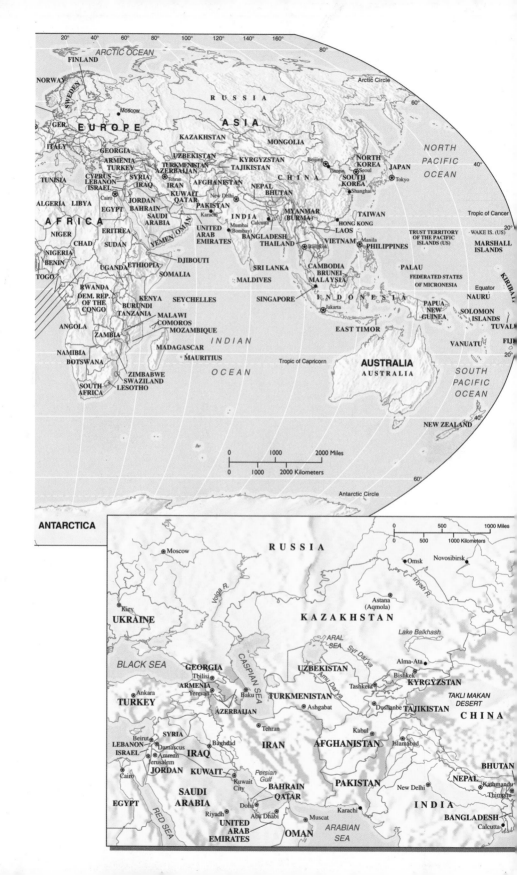